Social Media Websites Related to I-O Psychology

SIOP TWITTER ACCOUNT:
http://twitter.com/sioptweets

SIOP FACEBOOK PAGE:
http://www.facebook.com/siop.org

SIOP EXCHANGE/BLOG & GOOGLE NEWS FEED:
http://siopexchange.typepad.com

WORKPLACE PSYCHOLOGY BLOG BY STEVE NGUYEN:
http://workplacepsychology.net/

BLOG ON TECHNOLOGY, EDUCATION, & TRAINING BY DR. RICHARD LANDERS:
http://neoacademic.com/

I-O AT WORK: WEBSITE/BLOG ON SCIENCE BEHIND HR:
http://www.ioatwork.com/

Work in the 21st Century

Dedicated to the memory of Frank J. Landy and his many contributions to the science, practice, and teaching of industrial and organizational psychology

WORK IN THE 21ST CENTURY

AN INTRODUCTION TO INDUSTRIAL AND ORGANIZATIONAL PSYCHOLOGY

FOURTH EDITION

FRANK J. LANDY

Late Professor Emeritus, Penn State University

JEFFREY M. CONTE

San Diego State University

VICE PRESIDENT AND EXECUTIVE PUBLISHER	Jay O'Callaghan
SENIOR ACQUISITIONS EDITOR	Robert Johnston
ASSISTANT EDITOR	Brittany Cheetham
SENIOR MARKETING MANAGER	Margaret Barrett
SENIOR CONTENT MANAGER	Lucille Buonocore
SENIOR PRODUCTION EDITOR	Anna Melhorn
DESIGN DIRECTOR	Harry Nolan
COVER DESIGN	Tom Nery
PHOTO EDITOR	Sheena Goldstein
PRODUCTION SERVICES	Suzanne Ingrao/ Ingrao Associates
COVER AND PART OPENER PHOTO CREDIT	Echo/Getty Images, Inc
"COLOURED FILES IN A PILE"	© mark wragg/iStockphoto
"SOLAR PANELS IN A POWER PLANT"	© Shelley Dennis/iStockphoto

This book was set in 10/12 Minion by Aptara, Inc., and printed and bound by Quad Graphics/Versailles. This book is printed on acid-free paper. ∞

Founded in 1807, John Wiley & Sons, Inc. has been a valued source of knowledge and understanding for more than 200 years, helping people around the world meet their needs and fulfill their aspirations. Our company is built on a foundation of principles that include responsibility to the communities we serve and where we live and work. In 2008, we launched a Corporate Citizenship Initiative, a global effort to address the environmental, social, economic, and ethical challenges we face in our business. Among the issues we are addressing are carbon impact, paper specifications and procurement, ethical conduct within our business and among our vendors, and community and charitable support. For more information, please visit our website: *www.wiley.com/go/citizenship*.

978-1-118-29120-7

Printed in the United States of America

10 9 8 7 6 5 4 3 2 1

About the Authors

Frank J. Landy (1942–2010) was Professor Emeritus of Industrial Psychology at Penn State University, where he taught for 26 years. In addition to serving at Penn State, he was a visiting lecturer or researcher at Stanford University, the University of California at Berkeley, Stockholm University, Gothenburg University, Cluj-Napoca University (Romania), Griffeths University (Australia), and Ljubljana University (Slovenia). He received his PhD in Industrial and Organizational Psychology from Bowling Green State University. Throughout the course of his academic career, Frank published over 70 journal articles, more than 20 book chapters, and 15 books. He served as president of the Society for Industrial and Organizational Psychology and was involved in the development of the Civil Rights Act of 1991, the Age Discrimination in Employment Act, and the Americans with Disabilities Act. In addition to his academic work, Frank had a successful consulting career, working with organizations in the United States and abroad. He testified as an expert witness in numerous state and federal employment discrimination cases that had significant implications for the organizations involved. In his private life, Frank was a true 21st-century Renaissance man. He traveled widely and lived abroad when possible. He spoke foreign languages and was highly interested in global events. Frank was an avid runner, completing over 60 marathons. He loved to fly fish and ski. Frank played and collected guitars and was a great lover of music. And when the mood struck him, he acted in community theater. Of all of his pursuits, writing brought him the most enjoyment.

Jeffrey M. Conte is an Associate Professor in the Department of Psychology at San Diego State University. He received his BA in Psychology and Biology from the University of Virginia and his PhD in Industrial and Organizational Psychology from Penn State University. He teaches approximately 800 students each year in I-O psychology and personality psychology courses. He has conducted research on a variety of topics, including personnel selection, personality predictors of job performance, time management, polychronicity and multitasking, the measurement of emotional intelligence, and the factors associated with health and stress in the workplace. Jeff also has interests in cross-cultural research and has conducted research in organizations across the United States as well as in Canada and France. Jeff's research has been funded by the National Institute of Mental Health and the U.S. Army Research Institute for the Behavioral and Social Sciences. His research has been published in a variety of I-O psychology and management journals, including the *Journal of Applied Psychology, Academy of Management Review, Journal of Organizational Behavior, Human Performance, Journal of Business and Psychology, Personality and Individual Differences, Journal of Managerial Psychology,* and *Journal of Applied Social Psychology*. Jeff has worked with a variety of organizations, dealing with such issues as human resource selection, test construction/validation, work attitudes, performance appraisal, job-related stress, compensation systems, downsizing, and organizational factors related to safety. He has also performed job analyses, conducted statistical analyses, and contributed to written briefs and reports in a variety of employment discrimination court cases. His research and practice have included a wide variety of occupations, including lawyers, engineers, managers, firefighters, police officers, and public transportation drivers. In his spare time, Jeff enjoys running, soccer, tennis, and other outdoor sports. Jeff lives in San Diego with his wife, Michelle, and daughters, Caroline and Colleen.

Brief Contents

Contents

PART 2 INDUSTRIAL PSYCHOLOGY

PART 3 ORGANIZATIONAL PSYCHOLOGY

Preface

In the first three editions of this book, we pursued the premise that the world of work in the 21st century was very different from what it had been as recently as 15 years earlier. That premise is even more relevant today and worth repeating. Today's workplace is technological and multicultural. Work is often accomplished by teams rather than by single individuals. In any given company or department, there is greater diversity in terms of demographic characteristics, interests, and styles than in past decades. Although mental and physical abilities remain important attributes for predicting job success, other attributes such as personality, interpersonal skills, and emotional intelligence are receiving increased attention. A satisfying life is increasingly defined as striking a balance between work and non-work. In addition, the psychological stability of work may be at an all-time low. Mergers, acquisitions, downsizing, outsourcing, the challenges to financial and housing markets, and rapidly changing technologies have all made the idea of lifelong employment at one company, or even in one occupation, an elusive dream. This text ties together all of these themes in a way that explores the rich and intriguing nature of the modern workplace.

An important thing to keep in mind in studying I-O psychology is that work is complex and cannot be reduced to a set of equations or principles. In the real world, all of the components of work, the work environment, and, most importantly, the people who populate the workplace interact in complicated ways. For example, in considering organizational and individual effectiveness, we cannot think of hiring strategies in a vacuum. Hiring is preceded by recruiting and screening. It is followed by training and socialization. Once the individual joins the organization, there are issues of satisfaction, performance, rewards, and motivation. The way the organization is designed, both psychologically and physically, can limit or enhance productive efforts and worker emotions. This textbook necessarily treats these topics one at a time, but no topic covered in the text can really stand alone. In the real world, the topics are related, and we will show these relationships in the text.

Objectives for the Fourth Edition

The first three editions of this text were warmly received by both instructors and students, not only in the United States but internationally as well. The objectives for this fourth edition are to retain the accessibility of the first three editions, incorporate the latest research findings, and provide organizational applications of the principles of I-O psychology.

Accessibility

A continuing goal of this book is to package information in a way that makes it accessible to students and instructors. The fourth edition retains the 14-chapter format, which we believe provides a comfortable way to present the substance of I-O psychology. We have also retained the four-color design, which brings I-O psychology to life, especially with the use of color photographs. The art program also engages students with *New Yorker* and *Dilbert* cartoons, carefully chosen to emphasize the point at hand. Although recent I-O research provides a wealth of new material to explore, the book's length has been reduced in this fourth edition by omitting, or streamlining the discussion of, less current material.

Cutting Edge Topics and Research

As has been the custom in earlier editions, this edition provides the most important citations for topics rather than all relevant citations. When the first edition was published, it had the most current coverage of the field of I-O in any available text. That remained true of the second and third editions, and it is now true of the fourth edition as well. This edition presents many new topics, including social networking sites (e.g., Facebook) and the workplace, I-O psychologists' role in sustainable and environmentally conscious organizations, employee engagement, genetics and entrepreneurship, SIOP's new status as a consultative nongovernmental organization (NGO) to the United Nations, and evidence-based I-O psychology. There is expanded coverage of many topics, including international and cross-cultural issues, competency modeling, core self-evaluations, legal issues, entrepreneurial motivation, authentic leadership, personality-based job analysis, emotional intelligence, bullying, leader stereotypes, emotional labor, procedural justice in performance evaluations, and telecommuting.

Applying I-O Psychology Principles

Industrial-organizational psychology is a dynamic field with many applications to real-life experiences. Throughout the text, you will find applications of I-O principles ranging from popular television shows like *The Apprentice* to timely examples like the Wal-Mart gender discrimination lawsuit and the growing use of technology in training and in teams.

Structure of the Book: Parts, Chapters, and Modules

Because the field of industrial and organizational psychology is so broad, the text is broken into three parts. Part I, "Fundamentals," addresses the basics of the field by examining what I-O psychologists do and where they do it, as well as the methods we use to accomplish research and application. Part II, "Industrial Psychology," considers topics in personnel psychology such as individual differences, assessment, job performance, job analysis, performance evaluation, staffing, and training. Part III, "Organizational Psychology," examines organizational topics such as motivation, work attitudes, stress and workplace health, fairness, leadership, work teams, and organizational design.

Within each chapter, concepts and topics have been further divided into stand-alone modules, which offer a great deal of flexibility for learning and instruction. A module consists of material that is relatively homogeneous within a particular chapter. As examples, one module might deal with the historical development of a concept, the second with modern approaches, the third with applications of the concept, and the fourth with related concepts. Some chapters have as few as three modules, whereas others have four or five modules, depending on how much material is covered by the chapter. Each module ends with a summary of the main points and a list of glossary terms.

Every module can be considered valuable in one way or another. Nevertheless, covering every module may not be compatible with every course syllabus. Thus, each module has been designed as a stand-alone unit, permitting the instructor to cover or skip any particular module. As an example, an instructor might cover the first three modules in a chapter but choose to skip the final module on "Specialized Topics." This modular approach gives instructors maximum flexibility. In addition to covering or deleting a module within a chapter, or changing the order of modules within a chapter, an instructor can assign modules across chapters, in essence creating a new "chapter." For example, an instructor might assign a module on statistics from Chapter 2, a module on job analysis from Chapter 4, and a module on assessment from Chapter 3 to create a "validity" chapter. Although we believe that the modules within a chapter complement one another, instructors might prefer a different order of modules.

As you read through the book, you will notice that a given topic may appear in several different chapters. That is not a mistake or oversight. The fact is that some topics have relevance in many different chapters, and to mention them only once presents too simplistic a view of work dynamics. As an example, competencies are higher-order forms of ability, personality, interests, and attitudes. Competency modeling is an enhanced form of job analysis. Competencies can be learned, and there are both leader competencies and team competencies. This means that you will see the term "competency" in several chapters. Even though you will see the term often, it will be treated from a different perspective each time it appears. You will see similar treatments of issues related to work/family balance. This balance is important in the attitudes that an individual holds toward work and organizations. Balance is also important in addressing work stress and work design. So "balance" will appear in multiple chapters. We hope that this method of treatment provides a richer understanding of the effects of work on people and people on work.

Supplements for Students and Instructors

Work in the 21st Century offers several supplements to enhance learning processes and teaching activities. The supplements are available on the text's website: www.wiley.com/college/landy

Website for Instructors

The instructor side of the *Work in the 21st Century* website contains all the material instructors need for course design, and it is a convenient way to access the Instructor's Manual, Test Bank, PowerPoint slides, Internet resources for each chapter, and supplementary material.

Instructor's Manual

The Instructor's Manual includes learning objectives, chapter outlines, glossary terms, and suggestions for class discussions and activities.

PowerPoint Slides

This package of 30–50 slides per chapter includes lecture outlines in addition to figures and tables from the text. The slides can be used as is or customized to match your course design and goals.

Test Bank

This array of 30–50 multiple-choice items per chapter covers all the important concepts with factual and applied questions as well as questions of a more conceptual nature to facilitate critical thinking.

Website for Students

The student side of the *Work in the 21st Century* website at www.wiley.com/college/landy contains the Student Study Guide and Workbook as well as links to a variety of Internet resources for further exploration.

Student Study Guide and Workbook

Available on the student side of the website, this study guide is a valuable tool for maximizing students' understanding of material and preparation for exams. The guide was developed in close conjunction with the textbook and facilitates the instructor's course design by providing students with the same learning objectives, chapter outlines, and glossary terms as the Instructor's Manual. In addition, it includes practice exam questions and exercises for each chapter. The workbook exercises, based on organizational issues that I-O psychologists are often asked to study and resolve, promote active learning, critical thinking, and practical applications of the ideas and concepts discussed in class and in the textbook.

Acknowledgments

Throughout our work on all four editions of this book, many colleagues have been kind enough to send us their work in particular areas or to provide helpful suggestions for particular topics. These colleagues include Patti Ambrose, Bruce Avolio, Zeynep Aycan, Talya Bauer, Laura Borgogni, Wally Borman, André Büssing, Dan Cable, Paula Caligiuri, Gian Vittorio Caprara, Gary Carter, Wayne Cascio, Diane Catanzaro, Donna Chrobot-Mason, Jan Cleveland, Cary Cooper, Filip de Fruyt, Peter Dorfman, Fritz Drasgow, Dov Eden, Miriam Erez, Jim Farr, Harold Goldstein, Irv Goldstein, Randy Gordon, Mark Griffin, Art Gutman, Richard Hackman, Lee Hakel, Michael Harris, Dave Harrison, Chris Hartel, Beryl Hesketh, Scott Highhouse, David Hofmann, Geert Hofstede, Ann Howard, Susan Jackson, Dick Jeanneret, Ruth Kanfer, Jerry Kehoe, Rich Klimoski, Laura Koppes, Steve Kozlowski, Filip Lievens, David Lubinski, Dianne Maranto, John Mathieu, Jack Mayer, Terry Mitchell, Susan Mohammed, David Morris, Nigel Nicholson, Rupande Padaki, Sharon Parker, Elizabeth Poposki, Bob Pritchard, Anat Rafaeli, Doug Reynolds, Tracey Rizzuto, Ivan Roberston, Robert Roe, Paul Sackett, Wilmar Schaufeli, Gary Schmidt, Heinz Schuler, Graham Seager, Norbert Semmer, Peter Smith, Karen Smola, Dirk Steiner, Robert Tett, Paul Thayer, Kecia Thomas, Susan Vanhemmel, Peter Warr, Dieter Zapf, and Shelly Zedeck. In addition, several colleagues went well out of their way to help us by providing reviews of draft material, suggestions for additional research, and contacts with researchers whose excellent work might have gone unnoticed. These colleagues include Robert Baron, Dave Bartram, Stuart Carr, David Day, Michelle Dean, Michael Frese, Bob Guion, Rick Jacobs, Tim Judge, Kurt Kraiger, David Kravitz, Kevin Murphy, Neal Schmitt, Ben Schneider, Rolf van Dick, Bernie Weiner, Howard Weiss, and Bob Wood.

Several colleagues at Landy Litigation Support Group (LLSG) and San Diego State University (SDSU) provided substantive and logistic support throughout multiple editions of work on this book. At LLSG, these include Kylie Harper, Barb Nett, Erik Olson, and Angie Rosenbaum. At SDSU, many colleagues within and outside the psychology department helped to provide a supportive environment in which to work. In particular, Mark Ehrhart, Kate Hattrup, Lisa Kath, Jorg Matt, Scott Roesch, and Emilio Ulloa represent a wonderful group of applied psychologists at SDSU. Lauren Ostroski, Gina Sadler, and Jacob Seybert provided outstanding support in identifying relevant research updates.

Thanks are also due to those who accepted Wiley's invitation to review the previous edition of this book. These reviewers include Michele Baranczyk (Kutztown University), Tara Behrend (George Washington University), Margaret Beier (Rice University), Jeremy Beus (Texas A&M University), John Binning (Illinois State University), Greg Loviscky (Penn State University), Russell Matthews (Louisiana State University), and Mitchell Sherman (University of Wisconsin–Stout).

Our editorial team at Wiley was led by acquisitions editor Robert Johnston and assistant editor Brittany Cheetham, both of whom provided expert guidance through all of the critical steps in developing this fourth edition. We are also grateful for the assistance and support of our previous executive editor, Chris Cardone, who brought us to Blackwell Publishing before it merged with Wiley. We are very fortunate to have had the help and guidance of freelance development editor Elsa Peterson on multiple editions of this book. Elsa is a spectacular editor and a good friend who enhances everything she touches. Senior production editor Anna Melhorn oversaw the transformation of the manuscript into the book, and production editor Suzanne Ingrao did a fantastic job of seeing the book through the copyediting and proofing stages. Photo editor Sheena Goldstein was very helpful in identifying relevant photos that highlighted concepts in the text. Margaret Barrett and Patrick Flatley have taken charge of bringing the text to the attention of our target audience of instructors and students. We express our heartfelt thanks to these individuals and the many other members of our Wiley team.

A Note from Jeff Conte

Frank Landy's influence on me and on this book is immeasurable. He was my advisor, mentor, textbook co-author, advocate, and friend. I feel very fortunate to have worked so closely with Frank on this textbook for over a decade. During the course of our work on the book, we had many interesting discussions and debates about I-O psychology, work, life, and work/life balance. We worked very hard on this book, but we also had a lot of fun, including many belly laughs that were often brought on by an outrageous but accurate remark by Frank. I miss him greatly, and I know many others in the field do, too. Frank's knowledge and ideas about I-O psychology live on in this book and in his many other publications. In addition, I'd like to highlight two sources that show Frank's personality and zest for life. First, the April 2010 issue of *The Industrial-Organizational Psychologist* (http://www.siop.org/tip/april10/toc.aspx) is dedicated to Frank and includes several fond and funny stories about him. Second, Frank's autobiography (http://www.siop.org/Presidents/landy.aspx), written as part of his responsibilities after having served as president of SIOP, provides an engaging and entertaining view of a series of developmental episodes in Frank's career and life.

I would like to thank Kylie Harper, Frank's wife, for writing Frank's updated author bio. I also thank Rick Jacobs, a friend and mentor who has greatly influenced my thinking about I-O psychology and who has been very supportive throughout my career. I greatly appreciate the support and encouragement that I have received over the years from my parents (Anne and Tom) and siblings (T. J., Scott, and Deanna). I would also like to thank Paula Caligiuri and Kat Ringenbach for their support throughout the four editions of this book. I am very thankful to Kevin and Mary Dean, who have helped in so many ways with our home and family life over the past few years. Most importantly, I would like to thank my wife, Michelle Dean, and my daughters, Caroline and Colleen, for their support while I was working on this book and for the wonderful diversions they provided when I was taking breaks.

I welcome and appreciate comments and suggestions about the book from instructors and students alike. I look forward to receiving feedback about the book and improving future editions based on this feedback.

Jeff Conte
jeff.conte@mail.sdsu.edu

I Fundamentals

Echo/Getty Images, Inc.

1 What Is Industrial and Organizational Psychology?

MODULE 1.1

The Importance of I-O Psychology

The Importance of Work in People's Lives

Most adults devote the majority of their waking weekday (and often weekends as well!) to work. High school and college students, too, find themselves using a great deal of their discretionary hours in part-time jobs, particularly during the summer months. For many, this is a greater devotion of time and energy than to any other single waking human activity. For this reason alone, we can assume that work is important to people. Then there is the fact that most people need to earn money, and they do so by working. But the experience of work goes well beyond the simple exchange of time for money.

Work is easy to describe to others and, as a result, has been the subject of many good nonpsychological books about the experience of work. For example, a book called *Gig* (Bowe, Bowe, & Streeter, 2000) presented interviews with workers describing their jobs. It is easy to find the best and the worst work experiences in those interviews. Consider the two workers quoted in Box 1.1: a bus driver in Los Angeles who describes her work as a good experience and a flagger on state highways in Kentucky who describes it in less favorable terms. Although these interviews are at the lower rungs on the job ladder, they tell us as much about the meaning of work as interviews with CEOs, engineers, and midlevel managers.

In spite of ambivalent feelings about their jobs, most people would keep working even if they had the opportunity to stop. The National Research Council, in a book about the changing nature of work (NRC, 1999), adds support to this observation. When asked the question "If you were to get enough money to live as comfortably as you would like for the rest of your life, would you continue to work or would you stop working?" the percentage of people reporting that they would continue working has averaged approximately 70 percent since at least 1973. This is dramatic evidence of the centrality of work as a noneconomic experience. This is strong testimony to the meaning of work—not a particular job, but the experience of working—in defining who we are.

The importance of work is further confirmed by talking to people who are about to lose or who have lost their jobs. As we will see, work is a defining characteristic of the way people gauge their value to society, their family, and themselves.

BOX 1.1 INTERVIEWS FROM *GIG: AMERICANS TALK ABOUT THEIR JOBS AT THE TURN OF THE MILLENNIUM* (BOWE ET AL., 2000)

I'm a "bus operator." They don't like calling us bus drivers, they like to call us "bus operators." I have no idea what the difference is. "You're not bus drivers, you're bus operators." Okay, no problem. . . .

The route I prefer—everybody thinks I'm nuts—is the 81. . . . Let's face it, the 81, basically we pick up the poor people. The 81 is basically what they consider the low-class passengers. But for being low class, they pay. And they don't give me any hassles. And they always say, "Hi, how are you?" Or "Good afternoon," or "Good morning." . . .

Of course, the biggest thing is learning about how to deal with so many different types of people. You deal with different nationalities. Different kinds of everything. You gotta know the rules. In this part of town, they treat me good, maybe because they see me as the same nationality. But, like, when I go to South Central, umm, it's okay for them to treat me like garbage, but I can't go around and treat them like garbage. That's the way it is. And then like when I go into San Marino or Beverly Hills, I get treated different and I have to treat them different, because hey, I'm nothing compared to what they are. You learn to read and you have to adjust yourself to whatever area you're driving in. Because each area is different and people act different. And every day is something new. Fortunately, for me, I enjoy that aspect. Most of the time, I love these people. They make the job for me. (pp. 151–153)

******

Flagging's miserable. Your feet hurt, your back aches, and constantly all day long you're told what a piece of shit you are for holding people up. A town'll call in and want a pothole fixed, but they don't want to stop and wait while you actually do the work. So it's just really—it's aggravating that you're tryin' to do your job yet you're gettin' bitched at for doin' it. . . . [And] after you do let traffic go and you're standin' off to the side of the road letting 'em go by, they'll swerve over like they're goin' to hit you. Just to be mean, I guess.

But that's not the worst. The worst is to be the back flagger, the one who works behind all the equipment as they go up the road blacktopping. Because when they lay the blacktop, it's just incredibly hot, so you're standin' on this fresh laid blacktop that's, I think, three hundred degrees. . . .

But, you know, I kind of like it. Because it's a challenge. I feel like I've accomplished something just standing out there, just making it through each day. Because I guess when I first started working, I was the first girl that worked here. . . . I was actually the first girl to ever work on the road crew. (pp. 139–140)

SOURCE: Bowe, J., Bowe, M., & Streeter, S. (2000). *Gig: Americans talk about their jobs at the turn of the millennium.*

The Concept of "Good Work"

Gardner (2002) notes that psychology has often ignored how workers actually "conceptualize their daily experiences—the goals and concerns they bring to the workplace." He goes on to characterize what he calls "good work" (Gardner, Csikszentmihalyi, & Damon, 2001). Good work is work that "exhibits a high level of expertise, and it entails regular concern with the implications and applications of an individual's work for the wider world" (Gardner, 2002, p. B7). These concepts have been turned into an extensive endeavor, called the "GoodWork Project," which is directed toward identifying and, if possible, creating good work. As the project leaders point out, good work is tougher to do than it might seem. "Pressure to keep costs low and profits high, to do more in less time, and to fulfill numerous life roles, including that of a parent, a spouse, a friend,

© Photo courtesy of David Morris

American I-O psychologist David Morris screened applicants in Iraq for several years.

(a student!!), a worker, can all make cutting corners tempting" (www.goodworkproject.org). This "corner cutting" leads to what the researchers call "compromised" work: work that is not illegal or unethical, but that still undermines the core values of a trade or a profession—the lawyer who creates opportunities for billing extra hours, the plumber who uses inferior, cheaper materials for a repair.

Martin Luther King, Jr., captured the essence of good work eloquently: "If a man is called to be a street sweeper, he should sweep streets even as Michelangelo painted, Beethoven composed music, or Shakespeare wrote poetry. He should sweep streets so well that all heaven and earth will pause to say, 'Here lived a great street sweeper who did his job well'" (King, 1956).

Consider the role of an I-O psychologist who worked in Iraq to hire and train the new Iraqi police force. David Morris is an I-O psychologist who had been helping cities and states in the United States select police officers until September 2004. He decided to trade "his comfortable house in Alexandria, Virginia for a bunk bed in the converted office of Baghdad's former police training facility" (Dingfelder, 2005, p. 34). Every day, Morris and his staff of 15 administered various tests to up to 300 candidates for possible hire. He and his staff could have earned as much if not more screening applicants for the Philadelphia, or Atlanta, or Dallas police force. But instead, they did such screening in Baghdad to help with the restoration of civil order to Iraq. This is good work as well.

The interesting aspect of "good" and "bad" work is that the individual worker and the employer together have the power to define good work or to transform good work into bad and vice versa. A disreputable accounting firm can cheat and mislead clients and the public, thus engaging in bad work; that same firm and its employees could be doing good work if they are helping people to manage their money and protect their retirement plans. Good work is not simply the province of politicians or soldiers or relief workers.

Gardner describes the depressing consequences of settling for "bad" work:

> We resign ourselves to our fate. It is difficult to quit one's job, let alone one's whole profession, and few in midlife . . . have the fortitude to do so. As a result, . . . few feel in a position where they can perform good work. (Gardner, 2002, p. B7)

The study of work by I-O psychologists and students (you!) is potentially "good work" because it enables you to develop and use skills, and to use them for the benefit of someone other than simply yourself. I-O psychologists have also broadened their focus of study to consider the experience of work. Since the mid-1990s there has been a rapid and substantial increase in I-O research related to the feelings that workers bring to and take from the workplace. In addition, there has been a dramatic increase in research directed toward work–life balance issues. Thus, I-O psychology has recognized that the "experience" of work is more complex than simply tasks and productivity and accidents. You will see the results of this research in Chapter 9.

Authenticity: A Trend of Interest to I-O Psychologists

I-O psychology often incorporates cultural shifts and changes. In the past few years, "authenticity"—referring to that which is real, genuine, not artificial—has become a popular concept in America. You will see references to "authentic" coffee, music, clothing and furniture lines, foods, and so forth. The attraction of authenticity may also be reflected in some popular TV reality shows such as *American Idol, Ice Road Truckers*, and *The Deadliest Catch*, as well as some less dramatic shows dealing with changing families or embarking on a new diet to lose weight. A popular book (Gilmore & Pine, 2007) argues that, in a world where virtual reality is becoming increasingly prevalent, authenticity is "what consumers really want."

In I-O psychology, we might extend the definition of authenticity to a more philosophical level: "an emotionally appropriate, significant, purposive, and responsible mode of human life" (McKean, 2005, p. 106). Viewing authenticity in that way, we can see authenticity reflected in the search for "good work" and inspirational leadership. In fact, the term "authentic leadership," which had not appeared in the literature before 2002, has now appeared over 50 times since then. We will cover this form of leadership in Chapter 12. In various chapters, we will take note of what appears to be the search for authenticity in work and organizations.

How Does I-O Psychology Contribute to Society?

What Is I-O Psychology?

Throughout this book we will use the term **I-O psychology** as a synonym for **industrial and organizational psychology**. The simplest definition of industrial and organizational psychology is "the application of psychological principles, theory, and research to the work setting." In everday conversation, I-O psychologists are often referred to as work psychologists. Don't be fooled, however, by the phrase "work setting." The domain of I-O psychology stretches well beyond the physical boundaries of the workplace because many of the factors that influence work behavior are not always found in the work setting. These factors include things like family responsibilities, cultural influences, employment-related legislation, and non-work events (reflect, for example, on how the terrorist attacks of September 11, 2001, changed the working life of most people).

Industrial-organizational (I-O) psychology The application of psychological principles, theory, and research to the work setting.

Even more significant is the influence of personality on work behavior. Whereas an individual's personality may actually influence work behavior, his or her personality is often influenced by events that occurred before he or she began full-time employment. In addition, I-O psychologists are concerned about the effect of work on non-work behaviors. Spouses and children are well aware of the effect of a "bad day at work" on home life. I-O psychology concentrates on the reciprocal impact of work on life and life on work.

We can also think of I-O psychology as a combination of knowledge and skills that can be applied in a wide diversity of settings rather than just in the arena of traditional work. The example of David Morris helping to select the Iraqi police force is one of those examples. In a similar vein, I-O psychologists are helping to revise the test given to individuals seeking U.S. naturalization (Ulewicz, 2005).

I-O psychologists have become increasingly interested in building sustainable and environmentally conscious organizations (Huffman, Watrons-Rodriguez, Henning, & Berry, 2009). Several I-O psychologists have described efforts to lead the way in helping organizations to be more sustainable (e.g., DuBois & DuBois, 2010; Jackson & Seo, 2010). Some of these efforts

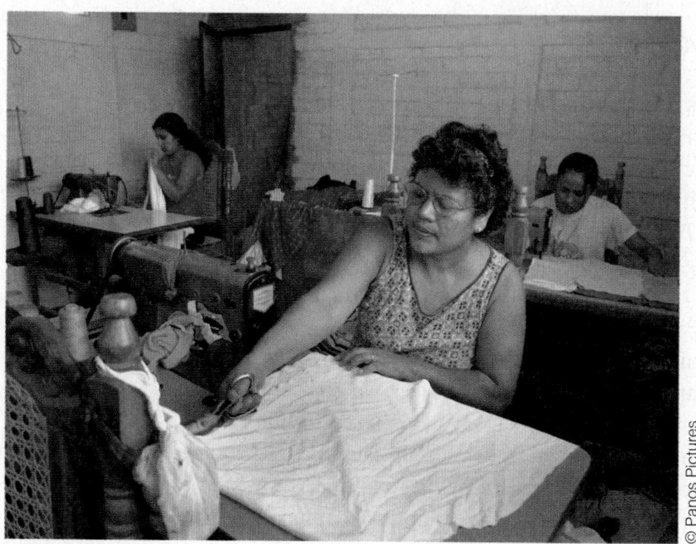

I-O psychologists have been instrumental in a micro-loan program to help women in Nicaragua start their own businesses.

include organizational initiatives that were implemented for traditional business purposes (e.g., cost savings, process efficiency) but can in turn yield environmental benefits, which are also known as eco-benefits (Klein, Sanders, & Huffman, 2011). For example, organizational policies involving online testing and assessment (Chapter 3), telecommuting (Chapter 9), and compressed workweeks (Chapter 9) have all been linked with environmental sustainability. Klein and colleagues (2011) note that I-O psychologists can guide organizations in identifying and measuring their eco-benefits and in promoting these benefits as another important outcome that can be considered along with more traditional outcomes such as individual, team, and organizational performance. The electronics company Panasonic (2011) has announced major new eco-sustainability goals (e.g., double the number of drop-off locations in its electronics recycling program from 800 to 1,600 sites, reduce greenhouse gas emissions at its headquarters by half) that are likely to be adopted by other organizations. I-O psychologists can help lead the way in documenting both intended and unintended eco-benefits in organizations.

In one of the broadest and most ambitious extensions of I-O psychology, Stuart Carr, a New Zealand I-O psychologist, has suggested ways in which I-O psychologists can bring their expertise to bear on humanitarian issues (Carr, 2007). Along with other I-O psychologists such as Lori Foster Thompson and Adrian Furnham, Carr has been working to promote prosocial applications of psychology called humanitarian work psychology: the application of I-O psychology to the humanitarian arena, especially poverty reduction and the promotion of decent work, aligned with local stakeholders' needs, and in partnership with global aid/development groups. Carr suggests that our expertise in areas such as team building and training, stereotypes, organizational justice, and mental models is exactly the type of knowledge and skill necessary for bringing together the essential coalition of governments, aid organizations, and private industry. Carr and colleagues have formed a global network of fellow I-O psychologists interested in addressing the I-O contributions to reducing world poverty (http://www.humworkpsy.org/). Carr also writes a column (e.g., Carr, 2012) related to I-O psychology and poverty reduction in the quarterly publication of the Society for Industrial and Organizational Psychology called *TIP (The Industrial-Organizational Psychologist)* (see below).

In a recent symposium, Carr and other I-O psychologists discussed projects as broad as a U.N. resolution addressing psychological issues in poverty and as narrow as a micro-credit project directed by an I-O psychologist for desperately poor women in rural Nicaragua (Schein, 2008). Interestingly, many in the audience for that symposium were psychology students who expressed great appreciation for examples of how I-O psychologists could make a difference in some of the major global problems of the 21st century. Carr's work, and the examples in the previous paragraphs, demonstrate how far-reaching I-O psychology can be.

Society for Industrial and Organizational Psychology (SIOP) An association to which many I-O psychologists, both practitioners and researchers, belong. Designated as Division 14 of the American Psychological Association (APA).

A more formal definition of I-O psychology, approached from the perspective of the I-O psychologist and what he or she does, has been adopted by the **Society for Industrial and Organizational Psychology** (an association to which many I-O psychologists, both practitioners and researchers, belong, and which we will refer to in this text by the acronym **SIOP**):

> Industrial-Organizational (called I-O) Psychologists recognize the interdependence of individuals, organizations, and society, and they recognize the impact of factors such as increasing government influences, growing consumer awareness, skill shortages, and the changing nature of the workforce. I-O psychologists facilitate responses to issues and problems involving people at work by serving as advisors and catalysts for business, industry, labor, public, academic, community, and health organizations.

They are:

> *Scientists* who derive principles of individual, group, and organizational behavior through research; *Consultants and staff psychologists* who develop scientific knowledge and apply it to the solution of problems at work; and *Teachers* who train in the research and application of Industrial-Organizational Psychology. (http://www.siop.org/history/crsppp. aspx. © 2012 Society for Industrial and Organizational Psychology, Inc. All Rights Reserved. Reprinted by permission of SIOP, www.siop.org.)

Refer to Tables 1.1 and 1.2 for lists of the common areas of concentration for I-O psychologists and the common job titles they hold. A new series on the SIOP website (http://www.siop.org/psychatwork.aspx) called "Psychology at Work: What do I-O psychologists

TABLE 1.1 **Common Areas of Concentration for I-O Psychologists**

Selection and placement
Developing tests
Validating tests
Analyzing job content
Identifying management potential
Defending tests against legal challenge
Training and development
Identifying training and development needs
Forming and implementing technical and managerial training programs
Evaluating training effectiveness
Career planning
Organizational development
Analyzing organizational structure
Maximizing satisfaction and effectiveness of employees
Facilitating organizational change
Performance measurement
Developing measures of performance
Measuring the economic benefit of performance
Introducing performance evaluation systems
Quality of work life
Identifying factors associated with job satisfaction
Reducing stress in the workplace
Redesigning jobs to make them more meaningful
Engineering psychology
Designing work environments
Optimizing person–machine effectiveness
Making workplaces safer

SOURCE: Adapted from http://www.siop.org/history/ crsppp.aspx. © 2012 Society for Industrial and Organizational Psychology, Inc. All Rights Reserved. Reprinted by permission of SIOP, www.siop.org.

TABLE 1.2 **Common Job Titles for I-O Psychologists**

Staff member, manager, director, vice president of:
Personnel
Human resources
Organizational planning
Personnel development
Organizational development
Management development
Personnel research
Employee relations
Training
Affirmative action
Assistant, associate, full professor of:
Psychology
Management
Organizational behavior
Industrial relations
Human resources
Corporate consultant
Private consultant
Research scientist: private sector
Research scientist: government
Research scientist: military
Research scientist: test publisher

Personnel psychology Field of psychology that addresses issues such as recruitment, selection, training, performance appraisal, promotion, transfer, and termination.

Human resources management (HRM) Practices such as recruitment, selection, retention, training, and development of people (human resources) in order to achieve individual and organizational goals.

Organizational psychology Field of psychology that combines research from social psychology and organizational behavior and addresses the emotional and motivational side of work.

Human engineering or **human factors psychology** The study of the capacities and limitations of humans with respect to a particular environment.

really do?" provides profiles of I-O psychologists that include how they became interested in I-O psychology, what a typical day is like, what aspects of the job are most challenging, why I-O psychology matters, and advice to future I-O psychologists.

Traditionally, I-O psychology has been divided into three major concentrations: personnel psychology, organizational psychology, and human engineering. We will briefly consider each of these concentrations. Even though we will talk about them separately, they often overlap considerably, as we will see.

Personnel psychology (often seen as part of **human resources management**, or **HRM**) addresses issues such as recruitment, selection, training, performance appraisal, promotion, transfer, and termination. The approach assumes that people are consistently different in their attributes and work behaviors and that information about these differences can be used to predict, maintain, and increase work performance and satisfaction.

Organizational psychology combines research and ideas from social psychology and organizational behavior. It addresses the emotional and motivational side of work. It includes topics such as attitudes, fairness, motivation, stress, leadership, teams, and the broader aspects of organizational and work design. In some senses, it concentrates on the reactions of people *to* work and the action plans that develop as a result of those reactions. Both work and people are variables of interest, and the issue is the extent to which characteristics of the people match the characteristics or demands of the work. Of course, organizational psychology has implications for performance, but they may not be as direct as is the case with personnel psychology.

Human engineering (also called **human factors psychology**) is the study of the capacities and limitations of humans with respect to a particular environment. The human engineering approach is almost the opposite of the personnel approach. Remember, in the personnel approach the goal is to find or fit the best person to the job. In the human engineering approach the task of the human engineer is to develop an environment that is compatible with the characteristics of the worker. The "environmental" aspects this may include are quite diverse; among them are tools, work spaces, information display, shift work, work pace, machine controls, and even the extent to which safety is valued in the organization or work group. Human engineering, more than personnel or organizational psychology, integrates many different disciplines. These disciplines include cognitive science, ergonomics, exercise physiology, and even anatomy. For that reason, we will touch only lightly on topics that form the core of human engineering—work design and safety in the workplace. Nevertheless, if human engineering interests you, there are many excellent texts in the area (e.g., Salvendy, 2006; Wickens & Hollands, 2000; Wickens, Lee, Gordon, & Liu, 2004).

In the past few pages, you have seen a number of examples of the capabilities of the I-O psychologist. The most striking characteristic of the profession is that research is actually *used* to address a concrete problem or issue. There is a clear connection between research conducted using the tools of science and the practice of I-O psychology. This emphasis on the application of scientific knowledge is known as the **scientist-practitioner model**. This does not mean that every practicing I-O psychologist must also be an active researcher or that every I-O psychologist who does research must be an active practitioner. It simply means that science and practice are both important parts of I-O psychology. As an example, real problems related to medical accidents and mistakes in operating rooms lead to research on safety culture in hospitals. Similarly, university-based research on team training is tested in hospital environments. An excellent popular version of the scientist-practitioner model can be seen in the TV show *CSI: Crime Scene Investigation*. A badly decomposed body is found and a team of forensic practitioners (i.e., the detectives) bring back samples of clothing, skin, teeth, and so forth to the laboratory for analysis (by the scientists). Sometimes they do their own analysis and sometimes they have more skilled colleagues do the analysis. But regardless of who actually does the analysis, it is done for one reason—to find the murderer. I-O psychology is a bit less exciting than detective work, but the underlying motivation is the same—to address a real issue or problem in the workplace.

Scientist-practitioner model A model that uses scientific tools and research in the practice of I-O psychology.

Evidence-Based I-O Psychology

I-O psychologists have become increasingly focused on making evidence-based decisions in their work in organizations. Cascio and Aguinis (2011) have updated their well-known *Applied Psychology in HRM* textbook with "Evidence-Based Implications for Practice" in every chapter. Many of these evidence-based implications are based on empirical research conducted by I-O psychologists. This trend can also be seen in the human resources (HR) field with Rousseau and Barends's (2011) discussion about how to become an evidence-based HR practitioner. They suggest that HR practitioners use a decision-making process that combines critical thinking with use of the best available scientific evidence. I-O psychologists are well positioned to develop and utilize evidence-based practices as they have adopted the scientist-practitioner model to guide the field as well as to guide the training of I-O Master's and PhD students. In a focal article in the journal *I-O Psychology: Perspectives on Science and Practice*, Briner and Rousseau (2011) point out that the medical field has done a better job of implementing evidence-based practice than has I-O psychology and that making I-O psychology research more accessible to HR practitioners will help with such implementation. In this direction, SIOP and the Society for Human Resource Management (SHRM) are taking steps to put evidence-based I-O psychology into the hands of HR practitioners by publishing collaborative articles. The first two articles in the series are on "Skill-Based Pay: HR's Role" and "Driving Customer Satisfaction through HR: Creating and Maintaining a Service Climate," and many more articles are planned for this series. This is a promising first step in the process of increasing evidence-based practice and decision making in I-O psychology and the related field of human resources management. Nevertheless, additional collaborative efforts will be needed to increase the use of evidence-based I-O psychology in organizations.

SIOP as a Resource

The Society for Industrial and Organizational Psychology is the single best resource for anyone interested in I-O psychology. The society accepts student members. SIOP's website (www.siop.org) is regularly updated and includes the following types of information:

- The history of I-O psychology and of SIOP
- Membership information
- An electronic version of the quarterly newsletter of SIOP, called ***TIP (The Industrial-Organizational Psychologist)***
- JobNet, a system that matches employers seeking I-O psychologists with applicants for I-O positions
- A listing of educational institutions that offer graduate training programs in I-O psychology
- A list of SIOP publications
- A list of upcoming conferences
- A social media page that includes information about SIOP's Facebook, Twitter, Exchange Blog, and Wiki sites
- High-interest topics to I-O psychologists

TIP (The Industrial-Organizational Psychologist) Quarterly newsletter published by the Society for Industrial and Organizational Psychology; provides I-O psychologists and those interested in I-O psychology with the latest relevant information about the field.

How This Course Can Help You

Working is a part of almost everyone's life. Outside of the classroom, you will likely do what most other people do: spend 50 percent or more of your waking weekday hours at work. This means that a course in I-O psychology should benefit you in several ways. First, it can help you understand what you are experiencing in the workplace. Most students have an exposure to work by the time they finish high school. Most continue to work in some capacity in college (during the summer and/or at part-time jobs during the school year). This textbook does not tell you what emotions to experience at work. Instead, we try to provide a broader context for you to understand various policies and practices that you are likely to experience in your work. For example, material in this text will provide a basis for knowing if the HR policies your organization follows are new or old, tested or untested, likely to be effective or ineffective. Second, chances are that you will eventually be placed in the position of managing the work of others and in that role either developing or at least implementing work-related policies. You may very well become a leader even without asking to be one. The material of this course and the text itself should provide you with a good foundation for developing and/or implementing effective policies. Third, in the course of your daily life you will almost certainly hear friends and family talk about their joys and frustrations with their organizations and work. Many of them will not have the understanding gained from a course like the one you are taking now. You will be able to act as a resource in helping them understand the policies that are affecting them.

You might wonder why a course in I-O might be preferred over a course in human resources, or labor relations, or general management. The answer can be found in the earlier discussion of the scientist-practitioner model. That is how I-O is different. It applies the results of scientific research to real-world problems. These other courses consider the same real-world problems, but they do not depend on research for drawing conclusions. Instead they depend on experience, or current practices, or suggested "best" practices. And this is a valuable approach *as well*, but an I-O course is built around the results of scientific research. Although most of the students who read this book for a course they are taking will be neither active researchers nor active practitioners of I-O psychology, there is a high probability that they will be *consumers* of I-O research in considering their own jobs or the jobs of subordinates. In addition, many will be exposed to concepts of I-O psychology through interactions with psychological consultants or other managers. This course will help those readers become knowledgeable consumers.

You will see another benefit from this course that goes beyond the relationship of you or your friends and relatives to a particular organization or job. There are national debates that relate to work. As a result of having taken this course, you will be better informed about many of the issues that form these debates than your colleagues or relatives. As examples of the debates that are currently on the table, consider the following:

1. Is employment discrimination old news or is it still occurring? If it is occurring, who are its most common victims? To the extent that it is occurring, what can be done to reduce it? What are the various steps in an employment discrimination lawsuit?
2. How serious is the issue of stress in the workplace? How can workplace stress affect the rest of your life? Is stress a legitimate "disease"? Can it be considered as an occupational hazard? How can stress be reduced at work?
3. Are today's workplaces adequately safe? How can work be made safer? What are the respective responsibilities of workers and employers for creating and maintaining safety at the workplace?
4. How can the jobless be brought back into the workforce? How effective are **welfare-to-work programs**, which require work in return for government subsidies? What can be done to increase the probability of today's welfare recipient becoming tomorrow's full-time employee? If the government proposes to pay welfare recipients less than the minimum wage in return for their work requirement, will this help or hinder the passage from welfare to work?
5. To what extent should work and non-work lives be kept separate? Should working parents expect their employing organizations to provide family-friendly workplaces? In households with two wage earners, how can both partners lead productive and satisfying work lives yet still maintain a productive and satisfying relationship with each other?
6. Do foreign-based companies actually have better methods of production, or are they more profitable simply because they pay their workers less? Is there any value to U.S. employers in adopting the work practices of other countries, or should we stick with what has made America great? Should everyone working for an American company, either in the United States or in another country, be expected to accept American culture as part of the work environment?

Welfare-to-work program Program that requires individuals to work in return for government subsidies.

These are just some of the debates that you will see in any newspaper or on any television news program over the course of several months. When you have finished this course, you will have a knowledge base to discuss these and similar issues responsibly. That does not mean that you can solve these problems, but it does mean that you will have something sensible and unique to add to the discussion.

You may also have discussions with others who have taken a course like this; perhaps your parents, co-workers, or managers. If they have not taken this course in the past 5 to

10 years, they may be working from an outdated experience and knowledge base. Just consider how the world has changed since, say, the 1980s:

Telecommuting Accomplishing work tasks from a distant location using electronic communication media.

Virtual team Team that has widely dispersed members working together toward a common goal and linked through computers and other technology.

- Personal computers now dominate the workplace.
- Many workers do their work from home (**telecommute**), and many work groups and work teams are located in many different offices and work as **virtual teams,** seldom if ever meeting physically as a group.
- Client meetings, organizational meetings, and training are conducted through videoconferencing.
- Work performance can be monitored electronically.
- Three out of every five jobs are now directly or indirectly providing a service rather than manufacturing "goods."
- Increasingly more work is done by teams as opposed to individuals.
- There is little stability in many business sectors. Downsizing, rightsizing, mergers, and acquisitions have radically altered the psychological contract between an organization and its employees so that few workers can expect to spend their careers with one organization.
- Workers are expecting greater recognition and support from their organizations with respect to creating and maintaining family-friendly workplaces.
- Workforces are becoming increasingly diverse, and not only in terms of age, gender, sexual orientation, race, and disability. Managing diversity today means embracing an increasingly broad spectrum of interests, values, attitudes, and cultures.
- The nature of work has become more fluid, where jobs may not be well defined, tasks may not be routine, and the groups assigned to tasks may vary in their type and number of people.
- Work is now international or global.

The information you derive from this course will be substantially different from what your parents' generation learned in a similar course.

The Importance of Understanding the Younger Worker

A great deal of the published research in I-O psychology deals with managerial, professional, and other white-collar full-time employees who are older than a category that might be labeled "young adults." In the 21st century, we need to question the appropriateness of this research focus. As Loughlin and Barling (2001) report, in Austria, Denmark, and Sweden combined, approximately 70 percent of young people between the ages of 15 and 24 are employed in some capacity. In the United States and Canada, 80 percent of high school students work for pay. By 12th grade, most of these students are employed for more than 20 hours per week.

Loughlin and Barling (2001) argue that it is a mistake to ignore the population of young workers for several reasons: (1) They represent a large portion of a population of part-time workers, and as part-time work becomes more common, we need to know all we can about the experience of part-time work; (2) one's first job is likely to have a substantial influence on the filters through which subsequent work experiences are viewed. As Loughlin and Barling (2001) suggest, "teenagers seem to be more influenced by their work environments than adults and . . . these attitudes and aspirations are stable once established during teenage years" (p. 548).

Mainstream literature tends to characterize the "first job" as the first full-time job after a decision is made to forgo further education. But your first job might be more correctly seen as your first paying job outside of the home environment, regardless of whether it occurs at age 14, age 19, or age 25. Surveys the authors of this text have done with college students suggest that jobs such as cashier, customer service rep, camp counselor, lifeguard/swim instructor, waitserver, and retail salesperson are the most common paid positions for younger adults. Experiences in these jobs are often memorable if for no other reason than motivating the job holder to aspire to work that will never repeat these experiences! Nevertheless, they help form early impressions of management and supervision, "good" work, and work/life balance. As such, these experiences are understudied.

© Jim West/Alamy Limited

By age 20, most young people have held some sort of a job.

The little I-O research that has been done on younger workers suggests the following:

1. For younger adults, jobs that provide an opportunity to use current skills or develop new skills are most satisfying (Green & Montgomery, 1998; Mortimer, Pimental, Ryu, Nash, & Lee, 1996).
2. For younger adults who do not have the opportunity to use current skills, or develop new skills, cynicism and lack of interest in the work can result (Stern, Stone, Hopkins, & McMillion, 1990).
3. Young workers represent a very valuable commodity or resource since their education levels tend to be higher than their parents', they are more sophisticated technologically, they tend to see the world globally rather than domestically, they have no problem being "connected" 24 hours a day, and multicultural school environments have given them an open-mindedness that was rare in earlier generations (Loughlin & Barling, 2001).

The paradox of younger workers goes beyond issues of research focus, too. Younger adults represent a valuable resource in terms of skills and experiences they have independent of paid work. Yet at the entry level, paid work often consists of menial activities that neither tap current skills nor develop new ones. This, in turn, leads to demotivation, cynicism, and a negative view of work in general. Zemke, Raines, and Filipczak (2000) cite management and supervision as the real culprit in the negative experiences of younger part-time workers.

Virtually everyone reading this text has had some experience as a paid worker, and we encourage you to consider this experience when reading the following chapters. Moreover, it will be useful for you to remember these experiences when you become a supervisor or leader, even in your part-time life. As a shift manager at Burger King, think twice on slow days before directing subordinates to wipe tables that are already clean. Instead, take the opportunity to ask them what they are good at that might contribute to the shift productivity or what they'd like to become good at that might contribute to future productivity.

Recently, Butler (2007) has examined the issue of work–school conflict for college-age students. Many students work part-time (and some even full-time) to fund their education. Not surprisingly, Butler found that students struggled to keep a balance between work and school and that work often had a negative effect on schoolwork. This was particularly true when the work consisted of long hours and difficult schedules, provided little real control to the student-worker, and did not permit opportunities to complete schoolwork. The research showed that when the nature of the student work was related to the student's major, both school satisfaction and school performance increased. In contrast, long hours and work that allowed no control on the part of the student actually decreased academic performance. As we will see in Chapter 10, these results are similar to what has been found when studying work–life balance outside of the school years.

Butler justifiably argues that school should come first and work should simply facilitate the educational experience. He suggests that universities and colleges become more proactive in creating or facilitating work programs that foster, rather than impede, education and in counseling students with respect to what jobs might create conflict versus those that will promote the educational experience. The lesson may be that mindless jobs with long hours can do more harm than good for the student.

MODULE 1.1 SUMMARY

- Work is important because it occupies much of our time, provides us with a livelihood, and defines how we feel about ourselves. "Good work" enables workers to develop and use skills to benefit others.
- I-O psychology applies psychological principles, theory, and research to the workplace and to all aspects of life that are touched by work. SIOP is the primary professional membership organization for I-O psychologists.
- In this course you will gain knowledge about the workplace, work-related issues, and the ways that work has changed over recent decades.

KEY TERMS

industrial-organizational (I-O) psychology
Society for Industrial and Organizational Psychology (SIOP)
personnel psychology
human resources management (HRM)
organizational psychology
human engineering or human factors psychology
scientist-practitioner model
TIP (The Industrial-Organizational Psychologist)
welfare-to-work program
telecommuting
virtual team

MODULE 1.2

The Past, Present, and Future of I-O Psychology

The Past: A Brief History of I-O Psychology

We will present the historical context of various I-O topics when we cover them in subsequent chapters; here we will sketch the evolution of I-O psychology in broad and simple terms. For the interested reader, Koppes (2007) has published a useful book tracing this development of I-O psychology in great detail. In particular, we will present a brief description of the development of American I-O psychology as it is valuable for you to see how the science evolved in the United States. Having said that, we also point out that there were parallel developments in other countries, such as Britain (Chmiel, 2000; Kwiatkowski, Duncan, & Shimmin, 2006), Australia, Germany, the Netherlands (van Drunen & van Strien, 1999), and eastern European countries such as Romania (Pitariu, 1992; Rosca & Voicu, 1982). For many foreign countries, unfortunately, there is no published English-language account of their development of I-O psychology. However, one of the first modern American I-O psychologists, Morris Viteles, did a wonderful job of describing the status of I-O psychology around the world during the period from 1922 to 1932 (Viteles, 1932). Arthur Kornhauser (1929) also provided a description of I-O psychology in England and Germany. One of the most comprehensive surveys of international applied psychology (particularly with respect to vocational counseling) as it was practiced in 1937 appears in a book by Keller and Viteles (1937). In addition, a more recent survey of early non-American I-O psychology, in particular the work of Otto Lipmann (German) and Charles Myers (British), has been provided by Vinchur (2005), and there is an entire chapter on the topic of non-American I-O by Warr (2006). As we present the various topics, note that we make use of a wide variety of contemporary research and theory produced by non-American scholars. Salgado (2001) has published a comprehensive review of the landmarks of scientific personnel selection internationally covering the period 1900–2001. For further reading on the development of I-O psychology as a science and a practice in America, we recommend several excellent and detailed reviews (Benjamin, 1997; Katzell & Austin, 1992; Landy, 1997).

You may ask why we need *any* historical treatment. The answer is that to know where we are now and where we are going as a field, it helps to know how we got here. As an example, much of the current effort being devoted to research on emotional intelligence is wasted because the researchers ignored 60 years of earlier research on social intelligence—a similar concept—and wandered down the same dead ends as their earlier counterparts

(Landy, 2005b, 2006). As the philosopher Santayana suggested (1905), those who cannot remember the past are condemned to repeat it (p. 284).

When we look at history from a broad perspective, it is possible to make some good guesses about the future. And knowing the discipline's history helps us understand the context in which research and application were conducted, which in turn helps us appreciate the value of that research today. Consider Table 1.3, which lists the titles of articles in the first year of publication of one of the major I-O journals, the *Journal of Applied Psychology (JAP)*. Now look at Table 1.4. This is a list of articles that appeared in 2008 in the same journal. Quite a contrast! There are two reasons for the difference between what was important in 1917 and what is important today. The first reason is the change in the world of work. The second reason is the accumulation of knowledge about work-related behavior in the past 90 years. Figure 1.1 presents a broad time line in the evolution of I-O psychology. Important dates and developments in I-O psychology that have occurred since 1982 are covered throughout the remainder of this book.

1876–1930

The roots of I-O psychology trace back nearly to the beginning of psychology as a science. Wilhelm Wundt founded one of the first psychological laboratories in 1876 in Leipzig, Germany. Within 10 years, he had established a thriving graduate training and research enterprise. He hoped to put scientific psychology on an even footing with the more established physical sciences of chemistry, physics, and biology. In the mid-1880s, he trained two psychologists who would have a major influence on the eventual emergence of I-O psychology: Hugo Munsterberg and James McKeen Cattell (Landy, 1997; Sokal, 1982). Munsterberg left Germany for America in 1892 and became the director of the psychological laboratories at

TABLE 1.3 Titles of Research Articles in the *Journal of Applied Psychology*, 1917

Estimates of the military value of certain personal qualities
The legibility of the telephone directory
The psychology of a prodigious child
A test for memory of names and faces
Practical relations between psychology and the war
The moron as a war problem
Mental tests of unemployed men
A trial of mental and pedagogical tests in a civil service examination for policemen and firemen
The attitude and reaction of the businessman to psychology
A note on the German recruiting system

TABLE 1.4 Titles of Research Articles in the *Journal of Applied Psychology*, 2008

A new archival approach to the study of values and value–behavior relations: Validation of a value lexicon
Early predictors of job burnout and engagement
Event justice perceptions and employee's reactions: Perceptions of social entity justice as a moderator
Harmful help: The costs of backing up behavior in teams
The productivity measurement and enhancement system: A meta-analysis
Subjective cognitive effort: A model of states, traits, and time
Safety in work vehicles: A multilevel study linking values and individual predictors to work-related driving crashes
"Did you have a nice evening?" A day-level study on recovery experiences, sleep, and affect
Ethnic and gender subgrouping differences in assessment center ratings: A meta-analysis
Personality and organizational culture as determinants of influence

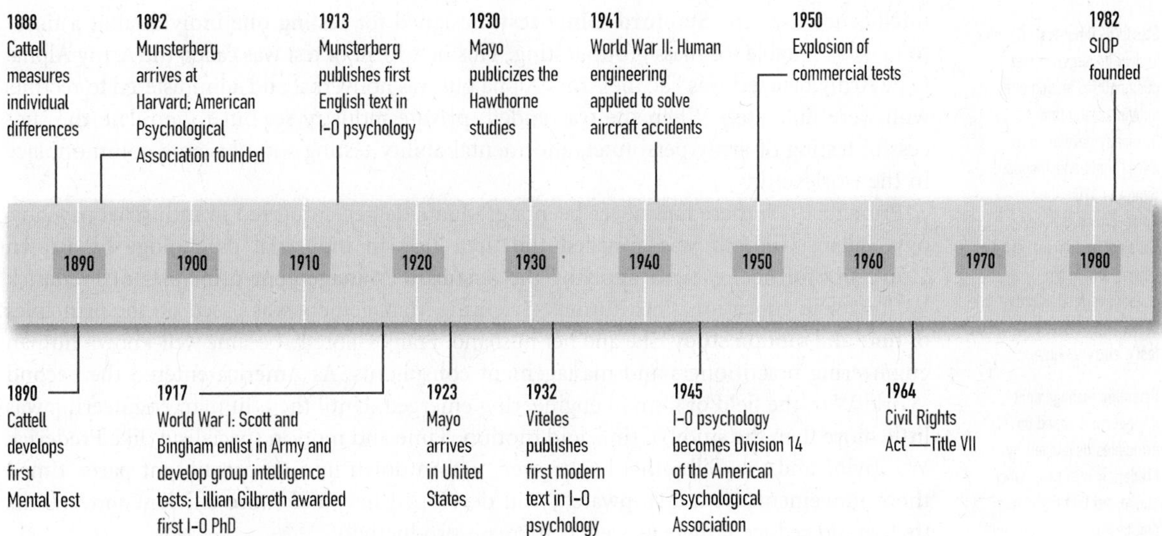

FIGURE 1.1 Important Dates in the Evolution of I-O Psychology

Harvard University. Initially, he was a devoted experimental psychologist who actually rejected any value for the application of psychology to the workplace (Benjamin, 2006). Soon, however, he saw the potential of psychology to address many practical problems of the early 20th century.

Munsterberg was also one of the first to measure abilities in workers and tie those abilities to performance—something that in hindsight may seem like an obvious path to follow but was innovative at the time. In another departure from the practice of his day, he applied rudimentary statistics to "analyze" the results of his studies. The world's first I-O psychology textbook, written in 1912 and translated from German to English in 1913, was another of Munsterberg's memorable contributions to the field. At the time of his death in 1916, Munsterberg was at the pinnacle of his career at Harvard. In conjunction with pursuing his research on industrial efficiency, he devoted considerable energy to persuading the leaders of American government and industry that I-O psychology was a key contributor to the nation's economic development. I-O psychology was really only "industrial" psychology in those days, devoted to the goal of increasing productivity. It was known by some as "economic" psychology.

Cattell was an American contemporary of Munsterberg and is recognized for being among the first to realize the importance of differences among individuals as a way of predicting their behavior. Wundt, under whose direction Cattell studied, was interested in general laws of behavior and less interested in the differences among participants in responding to his experimental stimuli. He and other experimental psychologists of the time considered those differences to be "errors" that served to complicate and muddy their results. Cattell observed instead that these differences were reliable properties of the participants and could be used to understand behavior more fully. After a brief stay in England, Cattell joined the faculty of the University of Pennsylvania in 1888, and then of Columbia University in 1893, where he remained until his retirement in 1917.

At around the same time as Munsterberg and Cattell were doing their work, two other leaders in I-O psychology, Walter Dill Scott and Walter Van Dyke Bingham, were working at the Carnegie Institute, developing methods for selecting and training sales personnel (Landy, 1997). When the United States entered the First World War in 1917, Scott and Bingham volunteered to help with the testing and placement of more than a million army recruits. Together with other prominent psychologists, they adapted a well-known

Stanford–Binet test A well-known intelligence test designed for testing one individual at a time. Originally developed by Alfred Binet and Theodore Simon in 1905, the Binet–Simon test was updated starting in 1916 by Lewis Terman and colleagues at Stanford University, which led to the test's current name.

Scientific Management A movement based on principles developed by Frederick W. Taylor, who suggested that there was one best and most efficient way to perform various jobs.

Time and motion studies Studies that broke every action down into its constituent parts, timed those movements with a stopwatch, and developed new and more efficient movements that would reduce fatigue and increase productivity.

intelligence test (the **Stanford–Binet test**, designed for testing one individual at a time) to make it suitable for mass group testing. This new form of test was called the Army Alpha. (The Army Beta test was like the Army Alpha but was nonverbal and administered to recruits who were illiterate.) When the war ended, private industry set out to emulate the successful testing of army personnel, and mental ability testing soon became commonplace in the work setting.

Prior to 1917, there had never been a graduate degree conferred in industrial psychology. Lillian Gilbreth was awarded the first PhD in industrial psychology by Brown University for her research applying the **Scientific Management** principles of Frederick W. Taylor to educational institutions. Scientific Management was based on the principles of **time and motion study**. She and her husband, Frank Gilbreth, became well-known human engineering practitioners and management consultants. As America entered the Second World War, the field of human engineering emerged. Until then, human engineering was little more than the study of time and motion. Time and motion specialists (like Frederick W. Taylor and the Gilbreths) broke every action down into its constituent parts, timed those movements with a stopwatch, and developed new and more efficient movements that would reduce fatigue as well as increase productivity.

It may surprise us to know that leaders of government and industry, not generally known for acceptance of new science, embraced industrial psychology in its infancy. In 1911, Harry Hollingworth, an early applied psychologist, was asked by Coca-Cola to help the company persuade the federal government that caffeine, which was an important part of the recipe for the drink, was not harmful to those who ingested it. The government contended that caffeine impaired motor performance and mental efficiency (Benjamin, 2003). Hollingworth conducted a series of laboratory studies and concluded that in normal amounts, caffeine enhanced performance rather than impairing it (Hollingworth & Poffenberger, 1923). Based in part on Hollingworth's research, Coca-Cola was successful in defending the use of caffeine in its recipe. The case resulted in substantial exposure for Hollingworth, and within a short period of time, he was besieged with requests for consulting help. Topics on which advice was requested included the following (Benjamin, 2003):

- How to interview farmers
- The effect of perfume on emotions
- The hours of the day when advertising was most effective
- The correct height for work benches
- The best color for a railroad to paint its boxcars
- The legibility of traffic signs
- The differences in buying habits of men and women
- The value of auditory versus visual channels for advertising
- The selection of clerks
- The legibility of typeface

Hollingworth was not unique in this respect. Most applied psychologists of the day (e.g., Walter Dill Scott, Walter Van Dyke Bingham, Hugo Munsterberg, James McKeen Cattell) were in demand for applications of the new science of human behavior.

1930–1964

Revery obsession Australian psychologist Elton Mayo proposed that this mental state resulted from the mind-numbing, repetitive, and difficult work that characterized U.S. factories in the early 20th century, causing factory workers to be unhappy, prone to resist management attempts to increase productivity, and sympathetic to labor unions.

Industrial psychology underwent a sea change when Elton Mayo, a psychologist from Australia, arrived in the United States in 1924 (Griffin, Landy, & Mayocchi, 2002) and immediately began studying not the efficiency of workers, but their emotions. He was particularly interested in the possibility that work "caused" workers to act in pathological ways. He proposed that there was a mental state known as **revery obsession** that resulted from the mind-numbing, repetitive, and difficult work that characterized the factories of the day. Mayo proposed that since workers were not required to use their intellect but only their physical effort, their minds would inevitably wander and, in this wandering, various paranoid thoughts would arise. As a result, they would be unhappy, prone to resist management attempts to increase productivity, and sympathetic to labor unions. Notably, such a reaction to boring work today would likely be considered normal rather than pathological.

When Mayo was given a faculty appointment at Harvard in 1926 (Trahair, 1984), research was being done at the Hawthorne, Illinois, plant of the Western Electric Corporation. These studies, now classics, are known collectively as the **Hawthorne studies**. The research had begun as simple attempts to increase productivity by manipulating lighting, rest breaks, and work hours (Roethlisberger & Dickson, 1939). But the results of the experiments were puzzling. Sometimes, when conditions were actually made worse (e.g., lighting was reduced), production improved; when conditions were made better (e.g., lighting was enhanced), production sometimes dropped! Mayo suggested the workers be interviewed to see what was going on. This led to the rather dramatic discovery (for the time) that workers' attitudes actually played a role in productivity. In the context of the Hawthorne experiments, the very fact that someone was finally paying attention to the workers seemed to have affected behavior. This has become known as the "Hawthorne effect"—the change in behavior that results from researchers paying attention to the workers. We will revisit this concept in the chapter on emotion in the workplace. Until the Hawthorne studies, it had been generally accepted that the only significant motivator of effort was money and that the environment, rather than the person, was of primary importance.

Hawthorne studies
Research done at the Hawthorne, Illinois, plant of the Western Electric Company that began as attempts to increase productivity by manipulating lighting, rest breaks, and work hours. This research showed the important role that workers' attitudes played in productivity.

The results of these studies ushered in a radically new movement known as the **Human Relations Movement**. Researchers in this movement were interested in more complicated theories of motivation, as well as in the newly discovered emotional world of the worker. Studies of job satisfaction became more common. After his successful use of interviews to examine the puzzling performance effects of the experiments, Mayo convinced management to embark on a much more extensive series of interviews with workers that lasted for almost a decade. Mayo was a frustrated clinician (as well as an avowed critic of labor unions) and believed that these interviews would result in a decrease in worker stress and unhappiness. There was some speculation that these interviews (called "counseling" at the Hawthorne facility) were really only intended to reduce the number of formal employee grievances (Highhouse, 1999; Mahoney & Baker, 2002). Many social observers over the years have been suspicious of the objectivity of industrial psychology when it comes to the needs and values of workers versus managers (Baritz, 1960; Carr, 2005). A notable exception to this general suspicion was Arthur Kornhauser, who from the 1920s to early 1950s was relentless in his application of applied psychology on behalf of the worker rather than on behalf of management (Zickar, 2003).

Human Relations Movement
The results of the Hawthorne studies ushered in this movement, which focused on work attitudes and the newly discovered emotional world of the worker.

The Second World War brought some interesting new problems, particularly in the Air Force. The aircraft that had been used in the First World War were primitive and differed little from one model to another. They were biplanes (i.e., structured with two wings, one on top of the other) with simple controls for the throttle, the flaps, and the rudder. Some also had crudely mounted machine guns. Bombs were dropped over the side by hand. But in the two decades between the wars, tremendous advances had been made in aircraft and other tools of battle. There were many different types of aircraft: fighters, bombers, and transport planes, to name a few. And even *within* a type of aircraft, controls (flaps, landing gear, throttle) and displays (gauges and dials that signaled airspeed or altitude) were located in different places. This meant that as pilots moved from one plane to another, they would encounter completely different cockpit configurations. This in turn led to an astounding number of crashes, many fatal, as pilots would mistakenly activate the landing gear instead of the flaps or the flaps instead of the throttle. Applied psychologists suggested that cockpits be standardized with respect to the placement of displays and controls and that controls be given unique shapes so that a pilot would know simply by grasping a control that it was the correct one. The landing gear control was to be shaped like a wheel or tire, the flap control to feel like a flap would feel, and so forth. When these innovations were implemented, the resulting immediate reduction in accidents assured human engineering its place as a subarea of industrial psychology.

In the more traditional areas of I-O psychology, the war brought renewed interest in ability testing (to accurately place recruits in these new technologically advanced military jobs) as well as the introduction of the assessment center, a technique we will examine in Chapter 3. The Office of Strategic Services (OSS) was the department of the government charged with gathering and analyzing military intelligence. Part of its responsibility was to run a spy network to anticipate enemy strategies. Candidates for these spy positions were sent to a secluded farm near Washington, DC—hence the term assessment "center" (Guion, 2011)—for extensive testing, which often took a week or longer. The testing consisted not only of interviews and paper-and-pencil tests but also of "exercises" intended to determine which candidates could withstand the stress and rigors (often very physical) of working behind enemy lines. As it has been described, "To this end, they were sent over obstacle courses, attacked in stress interviews, and observed when they were falsely told that they had flunked out—the week was calculated to reveal every strength and weakness they might have" (Bray, Campbell, & Grant, 1974, p. 17). A well-known personality theorist, Henry Murray, was in charge of the assessment center for the OSS; thus, it is not surprising that personality attributes were central to the assessment exercises (Guion, 2011).

In both the United States and allied countries (e.g., the United Kingdom), the morale of war industry workers was a central concern, as were the effects of fatigue on performance. In the United Kingdom, psychologists were particularly interested in munitions workers and conducted various studies to reduce fatigue and increase morale.

In contrast to the Depression of the early 1930s, when employers were laying off workers rather than hiring them and consequently had little interest in selection testing, the post–Second World War years were a boom time for industry, with many jobs to be filled and applicants to be tested. Interestingly, however, when the war ended and the soldiers came back to work, there was an increasing trend toward labor unrest. Increasing numbers of authorized and unauthorized (sometimes called "wildcat" strikes) work stoppages were staged by unions and workers, and management was very concerned about the effect of these strikes on productivity. This was also a period of unprecedented interest in worker attitude surveys. The results of these surveys were regularly published in business publications. There is no clear reason for this rapid increase in labor unrest. One might speculate that having faced death on the battlefields of Germany, France, Italy, and the islands of the Pacific, workers were less willing to passively accept the decisions of organizations or their leaders.

By 1950, as employers realized that interests and attitudes and personality might be contributors to desirable outcomes such as productivity and workforce stability, a glut of tests had entered the market. The influx of new tests for selection continued unabated until the passage of the **Civil Rights Act of 1964**. The Civil Rights Act was written in sections, called "titles," with each title addressing a specific area of possible discrimination, such as voting, education, or housing. The section dealing with employment discrimination was **Title VII**, and it required employers to justify the use of tests for selection. If the test could not be shown to be related to job performance, and if a protected group (demographic groups specifically identified in the legislation, e.g., African Americans, Hispanics, women) tended to score lower on that test, on average, than the nonprotected group, resulting in fewer offers of employment, the test might be considered illegal. This legislation revolutionized selection testing and led to the development of a broad base of technical knowledge about the characteristics of employment tests.

Title VII of the Civil Rights Act of 1964 Federal legislation that prohibits employment discrimination on the basis of race, color, religion, sex, or national origin, which define what are known as protected groups. Prohibits not only intentional discrimination but also practices that have the unintentional effect of discriminating against individuals because of their race, color, national origin, religion, or sex.

Defining a "historical" period is, to some extent, difficult and arbitrary. Nevertheless, the mid-1960s seems to mark a line of demarcation between "classic" and "modern" thinking. As an example, during this period, the field changed its name from industrial psychology to industrial and organizational psychology. The earlier periods addressed work behavior from the individual perspective, examining performance and attitudes of individual workers. Although this was a valuable approach, it became clear that there were other, broader influences not only on individual but also on group behavior in the workplace. Thus, in 1973, "organizational" was added to our name to emphasize the fact that when an individual joins "an organization" (e.g., the organization that hired him or her), he or she will be exposed to a common goal and a common set of operating procedures. In other words, the worker will be "organized" not only by his or her individual characteristics but also by a larger social system. This recognition provided the foundation for an approach to theory and data analysis, called multi-level analysis, that we will refer to throughout the text. We will address these larger organizing forces in the second part of the text.

Because we will pick up on the continuing evolution of theory and practice in the chapters that follow, we will conclude our formal "history" section in this period of the mid-1960s. But we leave you with some generalizations that can be drawn from the early history of I-O psychology that point out important themes.

1. Mental ability tests have always played an important part in the practice of industrial psychology.
2. Most industrial psychologists were focused on improving productivity and reducing counterproductive behavior such as absenteeism and turnover.
3. There was a tendency to see the three different branches of I-O psychology as unrelated to, and possibly in competition with, one another to explain industrial behavior.
4. It was taken for granted that the unit of analysis was the individual worker rather than the work group, organization, or even culture.

We make these generalizations to highlight the difference between the I-O psychology of 1964 and the I-O psychology of today. Consider how those generalizations above would change to be applicable today.

1. Mental ability is only one of a number of important attributes that play a role in the practice of I-O psychology. Personality characteristics are assuming an increasingly important role in understanding and predicting work behavior.
2. Although many I-O psychologists continue to address issues of productivity and efficiency, others explore issues of worker well-being, work–family balance, and the experience of work by workers. Some I-O psychologists are embracing large 21st-century issues such as an aging workforce and world poverty.
3. I-O psychologists see the three major branches of the discipline as complementary rather than independent or antagonistic. I-O psychologists take a systems view of work behavior and acknowledge that there are many individual, social, work environment, and organizational variables that interact to produce behavior at the workplace.
4. The worker is one level of analysis, but the work group, the organization, and even the culture represent additional and valuable levels of analysis.

In the chapters that follow, we will trace the evolution of I-O psychology from what it was in 1964 to what it is today. It is our hope that this will provide a foundation for understanding how the science of I-O psychology will continue to evolve over your lifetime.

The Present: The Demographics of I-O Psychologists

The major professional organization for psychologists of all kinds in the United States is the **American Psychological Association (APA)**, founded in 1892. Nearly a century later, the Association for Psychological Science (APS) was formed to serve the needs of

American Psychological Association (APA) The major professional organization for psychologists of all kinds in the United States.

the more experimental and theoretical areas of psychology. Clinical, counseling, and school psychologists make up over 50 percent of the more than 96,000 APA members, while the remaining members are active in a wide range of specialties ranging from I-O psychology to forensic psychology, sport psychology, and adult development and aging. The APA has more than 50 divisions that represent different types of psychologists; Division 14 of APA represents SIOP. In 2012, I-O psychologists represented approximately 4 percent of all members of the APA, and approximately 8,600 I-O psychologists (including approximately 4,000 students) were members of Division 14. As an indication of the vitality of I-O psychology, consider the following statistics:

- In 1986, there were 23 I-O master's degree programs in the United States; in 2008, there were at least 75; in 2012, there were over 100.
- In 1986, there were 44 I-O PhD degree programs in the United States; in 2008, there were at least 65; in 2012, there were over 70.

It is interesting to trace the changes in the demographic characteristics of I-O psychologists who were members of the APA between 1985 and 2003. The major shift was in gender. In 1985, 15 percent of I-O psychologists were women. By 2003, that percentage had doubled to 30 percent. The most recent salary survey conducted by SIOP estimated that 42 percent of the responding members were women (Khanna & Medsker, 2010). The ethnic minority membership since SIOP was founded in 1982 has also increased dramatically (Medsker, Katkowski, & Furr, 2005). According to recent salary and employment surveys conducted by SIOP (Khanna & Medsker, 2010), the median salary for a PhD in I-O psychology was $105,000; for a master's level I-O psychologist it was $74,500. The highest-paid PhD I-O psychologists in private industry were self-employed consultants and averaged approximately $180,000 per year; the median salary for those who worked in pharmaceuticals was $159,950; those employed in energy production followed closely behind, averaging approximately $149,500; the lowest earners were found in transportation positions, averaging approximately $85,000. I-O psychologists whose primary responsibility is teaching at private and public colleges and universities often earn additional income from consulting with government and industry (Medsker et al., 2005).

I-O psychologists work in a wide variety of employment settings. Figure 1.2 presents percentages for areas of primary employment (SIOP, 2011). A book by Hedge and Borman (2008) provides a detailed description of the life of an I-O consultant and how to prepare for such a role.

Pathways to a Career in I-O Psychology: A Curious Mixture

You may believe that the instructor of this course knew from an early age that he or she was destined to become an I-O psychologist—but you would most likely be wrong. The reasons for gravitating to a profession are as varied as the people in that profession, and I-O psychology is no exception. In a column called "What I Learned along the Way," which appeared regularly in *TIP* (the newsletter of SIOP) for several years, I-O psychologists described various serendipitous events that led them to their career or led to radical shifts in their interests. These accounts are very personal, often amusing and sometimes touching. They give very different views of I-O psychology. Some of the events that have led to a choice of I-O psychology as a career include the following:

- A casual discussion with a dishwasher (Vol. 42, no. 1, p. 42)
- The discovery that some men prefer their underwear ironed (Vol. 42, no. 2, p. 119)
- Working on a Ford assembly plant line (Vol. 41, no. 3, p. 64)
- Doing community service for underage drinking (Vol. 41, no. 3, p. 69)
- Chopping off the heads of hamsters (Vol. 42, no. 4, p. 73)
- Counseling students on academic probation (Vol. 42, no. 3, p. 39)

- Looking for "cruiser" courses at registration and seeing that the Psych line was shorter than the Poli Sci line (Vol. 41, no. 4, p. 101)
- Observing a spouse's dental problems (Vol. 43, no. 1, p. 94)
- Deciding the job of college professor seemed pretty cool (Vol. 44, no. 1, p. 119)
- Choosing psychology as a major because a friend was a psychology major and seemed to like psychology (Vol. 44, no. 1, p. 122)
- making a $999,999 mistake in the first day on the job as a bank teller (Vol. 44, no. 4, p. 67)

We are not making these up—go read them! They make it abundantly clear that a profession just as often finds you as you find a profession.

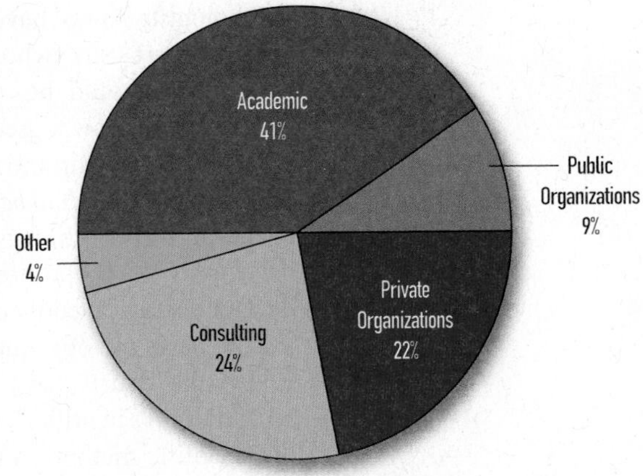

FIGURE 1.2 Where I-O Psychologists Are Employed

What We Call Ourselves

I-O psychologists in other countries use different labels from those we use in the United States. For example, our colleagues in the United Kingdom call themselves occupational psychologists, while our German and Dutch colleagues prefer the label work and organizational psychologist. Even among U.S. I-O psychologists, there is some variation in labeling. Some call themselves organizational psychologists, while others refer to themselves as work psychologists or applied psychologists. Throughout the text, we will use several terms interchangeably to describe what we do. These terms will include I-O, industrial and organizational, organizational, work and organizational, or simply work psychologist. Nevertheless, each of these terms describes a psychologist who studies work behavior.

The Future: The Challenges to I-O Psychology in the 21st Century

As we have seen, there are many opportunities for I-O psychology to contribute to employers, workers, and the broader society in which we live. To make these contributions, I-O psychology needs to meet four challenges.

- *I-O psychology needs to be relevant.* This means that we need to study the problems of today, not those of yesterday. In the early 21st century, relevance means addressing problems of globalization of the economy; increasing technological evolution of the workplace; team and group contributions rather than exclusively individual contributions; nontraditional employment conditions, including part-time, temporary, contract, and tele-work; and the balance of work with non-work. That is not to say that earlier research was misguided or "wrong," but rather that older research gives us a foundation for newer research and application.
- *I-O psychology needs to be useful.* I-O psychology, like counseling, school/educational, and clinical psychology, is an applied subdiscipline. The value the discipline adds is in putting our theories and research findings into action. I-O psychologists must always be thinking of ways to put our research into practice.
- *I-O psychology needs to think bigger.* In the past, I-O psychology concentrated on the behavior of single individuals and tended to shy away from larger issues such as poverty, unemployment, globalization, and workforce diversity. Certainly, I-O

psychologists do not have all the tools necessary to address these large global issues. But, as Stuart Carr (whose research on poverty we described earlier) explains, I-O psychology should be represented at the "table" where such issues are being debated. We know a great deal about work behavior, and work behavior is implicated in one way or another in virtually every pressing global challenge.

- *I-O psychology needs to be grounded in the scientific method.* The confidence that society has in I-O psychology depends on this. Careful and systematic observation, the development of hypotheses that can be tested, the public collection and analysis of data, and a logical connection between the data and the interpretations of these data are the bases for our "reputation" in research and practice. Beginning in the early 1990s, the courts have become more exacting about what testimony will be accepted as "scientific." This is further evidence of the importance of science and the scientific method in the larger world.

A notable step in terms of I-O psychology being relevant and useful is that SIOP was granted special consultative status as a nongovernmental organization (NGO) with the United Nations in 2011. This NGO consultative status provides opportunities for SIOP members to address a variety of humanitarian and societal issues. In applying for NGO consultative status, SIOP outlined some areas in which I-O psychologists' expertise can be useful in the UN's initiatives, including (1) talent selection and development, (2) corporate social responsibility research and initiatives, (3) entrepreneurship (enterprise development), and (4) occupational health and safety. In using this expertise, I-O psychologists can do "good work" with the UN in tackling important issues such as poverty and hunger, maternal and child mortality, disease, inadequate shelter, gender inequality, and environmental sustainability (Aguinis, 2011; Scott, 2011).

Anderson, Herriot, and Hodgkinson (2001) describe the research of I-O psychologists as falling into one of four categories. We have renamed these categories but kept the sense of each:

1. Junk science: fascinating topic with shoddy research
2. Pragmatic science: important topic with well-designed research
3. Irrelevant science: unimportant topic with meticulous research
4. Hopeless science: unimportant topic with shoddy research

Using this scheme for categorization, the goal for the I-O psychologist should be to conduct or apply pragmatic science. Throughout the book, we will consider it our job to help you navigate among these categories, because examples of all of them appear in either the popular or scientific arena. Realize, of course, that 100 percent pragmatic science is an ideal and that, as a field, we will never realize that ideal. But we can continue to look for important and relevant topics and study them in as rigorous a manner as conditions permit.

A Personal View of the Future: Preparing for a Career in I-O Psychology

We assume that most of the students who take this course are doing so to fulfill a requirement for their major or as an elective. We also assume that some will decide to go to graduate school for further training in HR or I-O psychology. The following section is written for those who are considering the merits of graduate school.

Education and Training

To call yourself an I-O psychologist, you will need either a master's degree or a PhD. If you expect to practice (as opposed to teach) I-O psychology, the issue of licensing quickly comes up, as virtually all states also require that you possess a license to practice under the heading of a professional psychologist. Fewer I-O psychologists are licensed than clinical or counseling psychologists, in part because what is being licensed is the use of the term "psychologist" rather than what is actually done. Thus, an individual doing HR consulting may not need a professional license. The licensing requirements vary by state, and all require some form of advanced degree. In addition, many require a period of supervised practice. The SIOP website provides a good general description of these licensing requirements, as well as contact information for each state's licensing body. It is clear that licensing is necessary to protect the public from untrained or poorly prepared therapists in clinical and counseling psychology. It is not so clear in the area of I-O because I-O psychologists are not health care providers. I-O psychologists are almost always retained by organizations rather than by single individuals, and most organizations have professionals within their ranks who can (or should be able to) distinguish between the trained and untrained I-O psychologist. Individual members of the public considering using the services of a therapist are less able to make such distinctions. Licensure continues to be a controversial topic among I-O psychologists, and you can follow this debate on the SIOP website.

Advanced training in I-O psychology is widely available, both in the United States and elsewhere. The SIOP website provides a list of those programs as well as links to many of them. Some programs offer only a PhD, some offer either a PhD or a master's degree, and some offer only a master's degree (often called a "terminal" master's degree). The SIOP website also provides an elaborate description of the type of curriculum you will encounter, as well as a list of the skills and competencies that would be expected of a master's or PhD candidate to qualify for graduation.

Getting into a Graduate Program

There is no "standard" process by which departments choose students, but it's generally the case that students are admitted only once a year, in the fall. All programs will examine both your overall grade point average (GPA) and the GPA you achieved in your major. Most programs will also examine your last two years independently of your overall GPA. They want to know how you did once you chose and became committed to a major. Most programs will place some emphasis on your Graduate Record Examination (GRE) scores (both general and advanced). They will also examine how many courses you took in I-O, statistics, tests and measurements, and possibly relevant courses in business, sociology, and labor studies. There is usually an emphasis on a background in statistics because you will need to be comfortable with a wide range of statistics to understand much of the published I-O research. At the very least, you will be expected to have done well in the basic descriptive and inferential statistics course offered at your school. Additional statistics and research methods courses will make you a more attractive candidate.

In many programs, there is no requirement that you be a psychology major. The emphasis is on what courses you have taken (and, of course, your grades in those courses) rather than the major you chose. All programs will expect letters of reference from knowledgeable faculty. You may also solicit letters from nonfaculty sources, but they should address skills that you will need in an I-O graduate program (e.g., communication skills, research skills, statistical experience, relevant work experience).

There are some additional "credentials" that you can accumulate to improve your chances of admission. If you have had experience as a research assistant to one of your professors as an undergraduate, that will be noticed and considered favorably. If that experience was in an I-O or testing area, or involved statistical analysis or data gathering, it will be viewed even more favorably. A second valuable credential is an internship at a local management or I-O consulting firm or in the HR department of a local business. You might assume that internships are available only to students already enrolled in a graduate program, but that is not always the case. Mueller-Hanson and Phillips (2005) describe internship opportunities for undergraduates interested in pursuing their interests in applied psychology. These internships often pay between $8 and $10 per hour, involve 10 to 25 hours of work per week, and include such activities as data collection/entry/analysis, library research, and project management activities. Successful applicants for these internships have one or more of the following attributes: interpersonal skills, statistical skills, project management skills, and teamwork skills. Because a critical ingredient for success in a graduate program is the "fit" between the program and the student, it is a good idea to make a personal visit to the universities you are considering, if possible. Although you may not be able to meet with all of the faculty members of the program, you can certainly meet some of their current students and get a feel for the program. If you are unable to visit, ask each program for the names and phone numbers of current students who can answer some of your questions. In addition, most graduate programs have websites (many listed on the SIOP website) that will allow you to make a "virtual" visit to the campus. Some I-O grad programs (e.g., George Mason University, Bowling Green State University, San Diego State University) also have newsletters that are available on the program's website. If you visit a campus, it is a good idea to read the research articles and review the books written by the I-O faculty of that program before you go. See what their interests are and, if you can, set up a meeting with one or more of the faculty. This will enable you to get a better idea of their areas of interest and give them a chance to get to know something about you.

MODULE 1.2 SUMMARY

- I-O psychology began with studies of industrial efficiency and individual differences. The latter led to mental ability tests. The Hawthorne studies prompted the study of workers' emotions. Human engineering came to prominence during the Second World War. Title VII of the Civil Rights Act of 1964 required employers to justify testing and other policies in terms of equal opportunity.
- I-O psychology in the 21st century needs to be relevant, useful, broadly focused, and grounded in the scientific method.
- To call yourself an I-O psychologist, you need to earn a graduate degree and, in many jurisdictions, obtain a license. SIOP provides information about licensing requirements.
- To be admitted to a graduate program, it is advantageous to do well in statistics and methods courses, obtain strong letters of recommendation, and gain experience as a research assistant or as an intern with a management or I-O consulting firm.

KEY TERMS

Stanford–Binet test
Scientific Management
time and motion studies
revery obsession
Hawthorne studies
Human Relations Movement
Title VII of the Civil Rights Act of 1964
American Psychological Association (APA)

MODULE 1.3

Multicultural and Cross-Cultural Issues in I-O Psychology

The Multicultural Nature of Life in the 21st Century

There are some pretty dramatic differences between the world you know and the world your parents experienced when they were your age. You might immediately think of technological differences, but equally dramatic are the "people" differences. In the course of a day, you probably encounter a wide range of nationalities—possibly East African, Israeli, Russian, Mexican, Pakistani, Japanese, Chinese, or Dutch, just to mention a few. A few decades ago, you would have expected to encounter this diversity in New York City or London. Now you are just as likely to see such diversity in almost any medium-sized to large city and even more so in educational settings.

Nationalities can be thought of as boxcars. In and of itself, a nationality is simply a geographic reality. You claim a nation as your country of birth—you were born in the United States, or Russia, or Thailand, or India. Your nationality, like a boxcar, has importance only because it carries important psychological material. Geographers, economists, and political scientists may be interested in nationality per se, but psychologists are concerned with the behavioral implications of nationality. Perhaps the most important material for a psychologist is **culture**. A culture can be defined as a "system in which individuals share meanings and common ways of viewing events and objects" (Ronen, 1997). It is culture that distinguishes people more than nationality. For example, you might sit next to someone on a plane going from Denver to Chicago and strike up a conversation. If you were to ask your seatmate where she was from and she said, "the United States," you wouldn't know much more than before you asked. But if she said New Orleans, Detroit, or Austin, you might very well follow up with a question or comment about the food, music, or politics of her home city or state. When you do that, you have begun to address cultural similarities and differences between yourself and your seatmate.

Culture A system in which individuals share meanings and common ways of viewing events and objects.

In I-O psychology, some of the most obvious cultural differences we need to address are related to nationalities. As you saw above, the definition of culture emphasizes the *sharing* of meanings and interpretations. This highlights the opportunity for people to bring *different* meanings and interpretations to an event or an object. This is why a recognition of culture's influence is so important for I-O psychology. As the world of work brings together people of many different nationalities (and, more important, cultures), the opportunities for misunderstandings and ineffective or counterproductive human resource applications grow as the number of different cultures grows. Consider the findings of some I-O research studies:

1. Asians have a very different understanding of time than Americans (Brislin & Kim, 2003).
2. In considering who gets a bonus and how much, Chinese managers make decisions based more on the personal needs of the individual, whereas in the United States, these decisions are based more on the performance of that individual (Zhou & Martocchio, 2001).
3. Compared to American managers, Japanese managers are much more likely to solve a strategic problem by being cooperative and making sure that individuals share equally in rewards (Wade-Benzoni et al., 2002).
4. Japanese managers are much more likely to seek compromise solutions than their American counterparts, who tend to follow win–lose strategies (Gelfand et al., 2001).
5. Shame as a result of a poor salesperson–customer interaction motivates salespersons from the Philippines but demotivates their Dutch counterparts (Bagozzi, Verbeke, & Gavino, 2003).
6. American software engineers provide assistance to a colleague only when they expect to need that colleague's help at some future time; Indian software engineers provide help to whoever needs it without any expectation of future reciprocation (Perlow & Weeks, 2002).
7. Teams of American financial advisors will be more cohesive and likely to work as a unit when a task is complex; teams of Hong Kong financial advisors are cohesive even when the task is not complex; American financial advisors value autonomy and independence of action more than their Hong Kong counterparts (Man & Lam, 2003).
8. Most countries have employment protections for "disadvantaged" groups, but these groups vary widely from country to country. In Canada, there are protections for French-speaking citizens; in Greece, there are protections for Albanians, Bulgarians, Georgians, and Romanians; in Israel, there are protections for Palestinian Arabs, Sephardic Jews, and Druze; New Zealand has protections for Maoris and Australia for indigenous Australians (Myors et al., 2008).
9. U.S. workers are less concerned about job insecurity than are Chinese workers (Probst & Lawler, 2006).

Notice that with the exception of points 5 and 8 above, all of these studies showed differences between Americans and their non-American counterparts. This is just the tip of the iceberg with respect to culture and organizational behavior. American workers and managers interact with dozens of different nationalities (and different sets of beliefs and values) over the course of a year. The same is true of Egyptian, Thai, South African, and Australian managers. As an example, at the Holden automobile assembly plant on the outskirts of Melbourne, Australia, no fewer than 57 first languages could be spoken on the production floor. The point is not about language, since all communication occurs in English. The point is that each of these languages is likely a surrogate for a different culture or sets of beliefs and expectations.

To make the situation even more complex, individuals often simultaneously embrace several cultures and subcultures. As an example, a middle-level manager in South Africa may very well embrace the competitive and individualistic culture of his colleagues yet take a place in the collective and process-oriented circle of elders when he returns to his native village in Zimbawe. Chao and Moon (2005) refer to this phenomenon as the "cultural mosaic" and suggest that each individual is really a composite of several interacting cultural influences (in keeping with the metaphor of a mosaic, Chao and Moon refer to each of these influences as a "tile"). Thus, person A might be an Italian American Generation X male from an urban environment who is employed as a manager, while person B might be a Japanese American female who is a Baby Boomer and also from an urban environment and also a manager. Although these two individuals share the fact that they are managers and work in an urban environment, they differ in gender and national origin; thus, they may hold different values regarding certain behaviors and might be expected to behave differently in certain situations.

Consider one rather dramatic example: Located in Foshan, China, Lee Der Industrial Co. Ltd. produced toys for Fisher-Price and Mattel. The toys they produced were found to contain high levels of lead (Barboza, 2007; Telegraph.co.uk, 2007). Soon after being alerted to the problem, the factory manager, Zhang Shuhong, hanged himself from the factory rafters—even though the culprit was actually a subcontractor who had supplied the paint. How many American managers would be likely to take such drastic action?

A less dramatic example of culture in the classroom, your "production floor," might help to make the issue of culture more concrete (Aguinis & Roth, 2002). Imagine that, instead of your current instructor, your instructor in this course was a well-known Taiwanese professor of I-O psychology. This psychologist had never taught in the United States before but spoke excellent English. Imagine that this instructor engaged in the following behaviors:

1. Changed the syllabus for the course frequently throughout the term without warning or explanation
2. Read lectures directly from notes
3. Would not accept any questions from students during the class period
4. Expected unquestioning deference and respect both in and out of the classroom

In most American classrooms, the Taiwanese scholar might not fare very well. He might be viewed as arbitrary, imperious, and poorly prepared. Yet in most traditional Taiwanese college classrooms, his behavior would be considered appropriate. Similarly, if you were an American student in a traditional Taiwanese college classroom, other students and the instructor might be horrified if you challenged the instructor on a point he or she had made or expressed any personal feelings or emotions on a topic. These would be examples of the clash between the American and Taiwanese cultures. Without an understanding of the differences in culture, you might interpret the same actions very differently.

Cross-National Issues in the Workplace

Consider the following facts:

- More than 100,000 U.S. companies are involved in worldwide ventures that are worth over $1 trillion; U.S. corporations have invested more than $400 billion abroad and employ more than 60 million overseas workers (Cascio, 2010).
- One in five American jobs is tied directly or indirectly to international trade; foreigners hold top management positions in one-third of large U.S. firms, and Americans hold similar positions in one-fourth of European-based firms (Cascio, 2010).
- The demise of the former Soviet Union and the development of the European Union has led to mass movements of people across borders.
- Economic blocs have formed, enabling easy movement of the goods and people of one nation to another. These blocs include the North American and Central American Free Trade Agreements (NAFTA and CAFTA), the Southern Cone Common Market (MERCOSUR), the European Union (EU), the Association of Southeast Asian Nations (ASEAN), and the Economic Community of West African States (ECOWAS) (Aguinis & Henle, 2002).

The facts above define what has come to be called the global economy. It is no longer possible for any country, regardless of size, to exist without economic connections with other countries. To be sure, there have always been "connections" between countries, but they usually shared a border or a culture. Now, connections are much wider, more complex, and more intense. Connectedness may be either a positive force or a negative force. Economic blocs such as those above are formed for the purpose of enhancing the future of all members. But corporations can make decisions about where to hire workers or locate facilities that can devastate local, and sometimes even national, economies. As an example, although in the late 1990s India became the IT and call-center outsourcing darling of Western nations, as the amount of work increased and the number of available Indian workers decreased, Western customers began a search for cheaper sources of labor (Scheiber, 2004). It now appears that this work can be done more cheaply in Kenya (Lacey, 2005). Cheap Chinese labor, an article of faith for much of the 20th century, may be a thing of the past as the salaries of Chinese skilled workers rise geometrically (Reuters, 2012). Western nations will soon need to begin looking elsewhere for cheaper manufacturing and assembly labor. There are two points to be made here. The first is that an American or Australian or British manager may be connected to two or three or five different cultures in the course of a year as labor sources and partnerships gravitate from one culture to another. (As an example, the Swedish retail company IKEA warns management recruits that in the first 10 years that they are with the company, they should expect to work in at least three different countries.) The second is that this sense of global connectedness makes jobs even less secure than they might have been last year—or even last month.

For the I-O psychologist, the importance of this connectedness is that it brings many different cultures into contact with one another at the workplace, particularly when that workplace is a virtual one. The challenge then becomes one of developing systems (e.g., training, motivation, or reward) that will be compatible with so many different ways of viewing objects or events, that is, compatible with so many different cultures. For example, American workers might expect individual rewards for outstanding performance, while Japanese or Swedish workers might consider them insulting. Conversely, group or team rewards would be compatible with Swedish or Japanese cultures yet considered inappropriate for American workers (Fulkerson & Tucker, 1999). Consider that almost *half* of McDonald's restaurants are located outside the United States (Cascio, 2010). Developing a uniform human resource system for such a diverse workforce is a challenge for the U.S.-based central management. The key to meeting this challenge is understanding culture.

Erez and Gati (2004) make the point that individual behavior is the result of many different forces, and culture is one of those forces. They further distinguish between layers or levels of culture. As is illustrated in Figure 1.3, the broadest level is the global culture. By that, they mean that because Western societies dominate the global economy, the global culture is largely a Western one characterized by freedom of choice, individual rights, and competition. This means that most global or multinational corporations will be distinctively Western in "personality." But this does not mean that national cultures do not also have an influence in the *manner* by which work gets done in individual

As more corporations employ workers in foreign countries, work in the 21st century is increasingly a global concept.

domestic locations. This is the second level or layer of culture in their model. The third layer is that of the organization, then the work group, and finally the core—the extent to which the individual identifies with these various cultures. Am I a citizen of the world (i.e., identified with the global culture) or a Swede, or an employee of IBM, or a software engineer? The center core or layer is the resolution of these questions. It represents how I see myself, and for most people that means a weighted combination of all of those influences. Nevertheless, each has an influence in some way. This is what makes organizational behavior so much harder to understand now, in the 21st century, than it was 50 years ago. Throughout the text, we will touch on all of these levels of cultural identification.

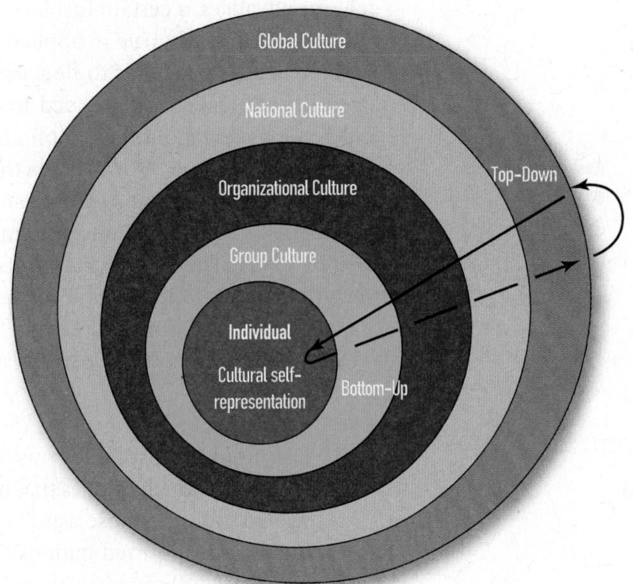

FIGURE 1.3 The Dynamic of Top-Down–Bottom-Up Processes across Levels of Culture

SOURCE: Adapted from Erez, M. A., & Gati, E. (2004). A dynamic, multi-level model of culture: From the micro level of the individual to the macro level of a global culture. *Applied Psychology: An International Review, 53*, 583–598. © 2004 by John Wiley & Sons. Used by permission.

Why Should Multiculturalism Be Important to You?

It seems clear that living and working in a multicultural environment is part of the definition of the 21st century. Not only are we exposed to multiple national cultures, but there are multiple domestic cultures to experience as well. As suggested by the mosaic theory of Chao and Moon described earlier, these domestic cultures (or subcultures) are defined by age, gender, race, disability, geographic region, education, or even leisure pursuits (Thomas, 1998). And many of these cultures and subcultures overlap and interact with each other, resulting in even greater complexity (Brett, Tinsely, Janssens, Barsness, & Lytle, 1997). Consider the overlapping cultures represented by a 52-year-old Pakistani chemical engineer who is also vegetarian, female, Christian, a New York City resident, and a marathon runner; or a 27-year-old African American male police officer who plays the cello in his spare time, is a Jehovah's Witness, and lives in Boise, Idaho.

In your working life, it is a virtual certainty that you will come into contact with co-workers, superiors, subordinates, clients, and vendors who have cultural values and beliefs different from your own. For that reason, you need to understand not only the fact that cultures *do* differ systematically but also *how* they may differ.

As a student in I-O courses, you will also find it useful to recognize how cultural differences influence what is examined in field and laboratory research. In many of the leading I-O psychology and human resource management (HRM) publications, the participants are most commonly American, the context of the research is American, and the outcomes or results of the research are interpreted for application to the American context. There is nothing necessarily wrong with limiting research investigations to uniquely American situations and problems. But it is important to remember that these results may not always generalize to non-American cultures, particularly since many of those cultures are considerably more homogeneous than is true of the United States. And many, if not most, of those cultures have existed considerably longer than their younger American counterpart.

Why Is Multiculturalism Important for I-O Psychology?

American scholars and researchers have dominated many areas of psychology since the discipline began almost 135 years ago. Although these psychologists have contributed many genuine advances, a certain insularity has characterized American psychology as well. This has been particularly true in applied areas such as I-O psychology. In applied psychology, research and theory tends to flow *from* "problem" areas rather than anticipating them. As a result, researchers have tended to develop theories that are relevant to U.S. situations, with less concern about their applicability in other countries. Hermans and Kempen (1998) have dubbed this the **"West versus the Rest" mentality**. Not surprisingly, attempts to apply American theories to non-American situations are not always successful. It appears that culture may actually determine (or "moderate") the effectiveness of an HRM initiative (Earley & Erez, 1997). This is important information because it provides a roadmap for modifying a theory developed in one culture for application to a different culture.

"West versus the Rest" mentality Tendency for researchers to develop theories relevant to U.S. situations, with less concern given to their applicability in other countries.

Consider the following reasons for valuing a multicultural psychology in general (Fowers & Richardson, 1996), and notice how they fit with the goals of I-O psychology in particular.

1. Definitions of psychology usually include the phrase "the scientific study of human behavior," which implies that human behavior in all parts of the world must be investigated, not just those aspects of behavior conveniently available to investigators in highly industrialized nations (Triandis & Brislin, 1984). Work psychologists should be just as interested in theories of work motivation or personnel selection as they apply to cultures other than the United States as they are in U.S. applications.
2. Psychology has tried hard to be color blind and, according to some critics, in the process it has "perpetuated racism in blinding us to the discrimination that is an everyday experience for members of minority groups. . . . This color blind approach . . . does not recognize authentic differences that are defining features of identity" (Fowers & Richardson, 1996). While striving for fairness, American employers (and other American institutions, such as universities) have tended to downplay or ignore cultural differences among men and women, whites, Hispanics, blacks, and other groups. Similarly, U.S.-based multinational corporations have often attempted to apply a "one-size-fits-all," American-oriented mentality to human resource practices in all of their locations throughout the world. A major challenge for work psychology today is to determine how policymakers can acknowledge and value multiple cultures while upholding standards of fairness and equality.

As we will see throughout this textbook, non-American scholars have proposed many excellent theories of work behavior based on research with non-American workers. These theories are valuable for application not only in the United States but also by U.S. multinational corporations in foreign countries.

Although both the I-O psychology and HRM fields are beginning to recognize the importance of a multicultural foundation for understanding work behavior, the recognition has come mostly in the form of applications devoid of theory. A case in point has been the problem of **expatriates:** American managers and professionals assigned to work in locations outside the United States. A great deal of expense and effort is involved in getting an expatriate settled in a new location. If the expatriate is not successful in that new location, the parent organization has wasted a considerable financial investment, in addition to losing productivity and goodwill in the new location. Some expatriates fail because they cannot or will not adapt to the culture of the new location (including colleagues and subordinates). As a result, expatriate selection and training has become a booming area for practice and has inspired many effective programs.

Expatriate Manager or professional assigned to work in a location outside of his or her home country.

It is only recently that the I-O literature has begun to include research of a theoretical nature concerning expatriate success. Some examples include applications of personality theory (Caligiuri, Tarique, & Jacobs, 2009; Ones & Viswesvaran, 1999), models of expatriate adjustment (Takeuchi, 2010), and studies of feelings of fairness held by the expatriate

(Garonzik, Brockner, & Siegel, 2000). Several of these studies have demonstrated the value of using personality factors, such as emotional stability and tolerance for novel experiences, for the selection of expatriates. Interestingly, many of these theoretical developments may also serve the purpose of understanding the broader issues of relocation, even relocation within the United States.

Some Theories of Cultural Influence

It does not necessarily take a behavioral scientist to realize that principles or strategies that apply in one culture might not apply in another. But it does take a behavioral scientist to understand *why* they may not apply. By understanding the "why," we are actually understanding the meaning and importance of that cultural variable. To return to our example, a manager may realize that individual rewards seem ineffective in Japan but effective in the United States. But that manager may not understand the underlying principle: The Japanese culture is a **collectivist culture** that values the group more than the individual. The U.S. culture is an **individualist culture** that values the individual more than the group. By understanding the underlying cultural principle, and gaining the ability to place other cultures on the collectivist–individualist continuum, the manager might be able to design effective reward schemes for operations elsewhere, for example, in Germany, Thailand, or Egypt. Consider the experiment with students from individualist and collectivist cultures that is presented in Box 1.2. This is a great example of the actual workings of culture in everyday life.

Collectivist culture A culture that values the group more than the individual.

Individualist culture A culture that values the individual more than the group.

Hofstede's Theory

As you might expect, culture is more complex than a single continuum like individualist–collectivist. As a result of some pioneering research by the Dutch researcher Geert Hofstede (1980a, 2001), we know a good deal about the defining characteristics of culture, particularly culture in the workplace. Hofstede distributed questionnaires to IBM employees worldwide between 1968 and 1972, and more than 116,000 employees from 72 countries returned them. In his continuing analysis of those data, he has developed a theory that proposes five basic elements on which cultures can be distinguished. Think of each of these elements as a continuum stretching from one pole to another. As an example, think of the individualist–collectivist continuum discussed in the previous paragraph. Indeed, the ***individualism–collectivism*** continuum was one of the primary aspects of culture that Hofstede uncovered. This characteristic also plays an important role in other theories of culture (e.g., Schwartz, 1999; Triandis, 1995b). The five elements are presented and defined in Table 1.5; in Figure 1.4 you can see how these elements are represented in the cultures of five different countries. These can almost be thought of as the "personality" of a nationality. This is the essence of what a culture is: a "collective psyche." The importance of Hofstede's theory for I-O psychology is substantial. In the past few decades, Hofstede has refined his theory to address specific aspects of the workplace. By examining each of the five dimensions of culture, he has been able to propose suggested characteristics of cultures that fall on one or the other end of his cultural continua and the relationship of these characteristics to work behavior. Table 1.6 presents Hofstede's characterizations. As you can see, each of the five dimensions has implications for the workplace.

Individualism/collectivism The degree to which individuals are expected to look after themselves versus remaining integrated into groups.

Noe, Hollenbeck, Gerhart, and Wright (2010) provide additional applications of Hofstede's findings in contrasting countries. They make the following observations:

- *Individualism/collectivism.* In countries such as the United States, the United Kingdom, and the Netherlands, individuals tend to show greater concern for

BOX 1.2 THE FACES OF CULTURE

In a clever experiment designed by a multicultural research team (Masuda et al., 2008), faces expressing happiness or unhappiness were presented to both Western (e.g., U.S., U.K., Canadian) and Japanese students.

The central figure in the two panels was drawn to be either Asian or Caucasian. Western students (from individualist cultures) assigned emotional meaning (happiness or unhappiness) based on the expression of the central figure and did not use the faces of the background group to interpret the emotion of the central figure. They identified the central figure in the top panel as happy and the one in the bottom panel as unhappy.

In contrast, the Japanese students' interpretation of the emotion experienced by the central figure was influenced by the expressions of the group members in the background. Further confirmation of the importance of the "group" was provided by eye-tracking measurements—the Japanese students spent more time looking at the surrounding people than did the Westerners.

The researchers concluded that the Japanese interpret emotions in a much broader collectivist social network, while more individualistic Westerners see emotions as individual feelings.

Consider a workplace application. An expatriate American manager in Japan might concentrate on only the emotional signals of one Japanese subordinate (e.g., a team leader or subordinate) to estimate satisfaction or happiness; but her Japanese counterpart would be more likely to include social information from the entire group rather than just the group leader.

Source: Masuda, T., Ellsworth, P. C., Mesquita, B., Leu, J., Tanida, S., & van de Veerdonk, E. (2008). Placing the face in context: Cultural differences in the perception of facial emotion. *Journal of Personality and Social Psychology, 94*(3), 365–381. © 2008 by the American Psychological Association. Reproduced with permission.

TABLE 1.5 The Five Dimensions of Hofstede's Theory of Culture

- **Individualism/collectivism**: The degree to which individuals are expected to look after themselves versus remaining integrated into groups (usually the family).
- **Power distance**: The degree to which less powerful members of an organization accept and expect an unequal distribution of power.
- **Uncertainty avoidance**: The extent to which members of a culture feel comfortable in unstructured situations.
- **Masculinity/femininity**: The distribution of emotional roles between the genders, with the masculine role being seen as "tough" and the feminine role seen as "tender." Masculine cultures tend to emphasize accomplishment and technical performance, while feminine cultures tend to emphasize interpersonal relationships and communication.
- **Long-term versus short-term orientation**: The extent to which members of a culture expect immediate versus delayed gratification of their material, social, and emotional needs.

Source: Adapted from Hofstede, G. (2001). *Culture's consequences: Comparing values, behaviors, institutions, and organizations across nations* (2nd ed.). Thousand Oaks, CA: Sage. And adapted from Hofstede, G., Hofstede, G. J., & Minkov, M. (2010). *Cultures and organizations: Software of the mind*, 3rd rev. ed. New York: McGraw-Hill. © 2001 Geert Hofstede; © 2010 Geert Hofstede BV. Adapted by permission.

themselves and their families than for the community; in Colombia, Pakistan, and Taiwan, greater concern is expressed for the community than for the individual.

- *Power distance.* Denmark and Israel seek to reduce inequalities in power, while India and the Philippines accept and maintain such power distances.
- *Uncertainty avoidance.* The cultures of Singapore and Jamaica accept uncertainty and take one day at a time, but Greek and Portuguese cultures seek certainty.
- *Masculinity/femininity.* In masculine cultures such as the United States, Japan, and Germany, performance, success, and accumulated wealth are important, but in feminine cultures such as Sweden, Norway, and the Netherlands, people, relationships, and the environment are more important than wealth and accomplishment.
- *Long-term versus short-term orientation.* Cultures with a short-term orientation, such as the United States and Russia, focus on the past and present and honor tradition. Conversely, countries like Japan and China tend to have a long-term orientation and are not nearly as concerned with immediate benefit as they are with thrift and persistence.

China
France
Indonesia
Japan
United States

Key:
PD = Power Distance
ID = Individualism versus Collectivism
MA = Masculinity versus Femininity
UA = Uncertainty Avoidance
LT = Long-Term versus Short-Term Orientation

FIGURE 1.4 Cultural Differences among Countries

Source: Hofstede, G. (1993). Cultural constraints in management theories. *Academy of Management Executive, 7,* 91. Republished with permission of The Academy of Management. Permission conveyed through Copyright Clearance Center, Inc.

Noe and colleagues (2010) also identified several reasons why managers ought to be sensitive to culture.

- Cultures differ strongly on how subordinates expect leaders to lead and what motivates individuals; therefore, the selection and training of managers should vary across cultures.
- Cultures influence human resource practices. For example, in the United States hiring decisions depend heavily on an applicant's technical skills, whereas in collectivist cultures such as Japan much more emphasis is placed on how well the individual will fit into a group.
- Compensation policies vary greatly across cultures. In the United States, the highest-paid individual in a company may earn 200 times more than the lowest-paid individual. In collectivist cultures, the highest-paid individual rarely earns more than 20 times the compensation of the lowest-paid individual.
- In collectivist cultures, group decision making is more highly valued, but in individualist cultures, individual

Within national cultures, there are subcultures that may differ greatly from the norms of the mainstream national culture. Here, Amish men help on a sandbag crew to control Mississippi River flooding.

TABLE 1.6 The Implications of Cultural Dimensions for Human Resource Management

DIMENSION	*HRM IMPLICATION*
High power distance	Centralized decision making Many supervisors per employee Autocratic leadership
Low power distance	Decentralized decision making Few supervisors per employee Participative leadership
High uncertainty avoidance	Accepting of technical solutions Strong loyalty to employer Innovators constrained by rules
Low uncertainty avoidance	Skeptical of technical solutions Weak loyalty to employer Innovators not constrained by rules
High individualism	Employees act in their individual interest Poor performance a legitimate reason for dismissal Training focused at individual level
Low individualism	Employees act in the interest of their in-group Poor performance a legitimate reason for reassignment of tasks Training focused at group level
High masculine	Fewer women in professional/technical jobs Pressure toward traditional gender roles Men describe themselves as more competitive than women do
Low masculine	More women in professional/technical jobs Nontraditional gender roles more common Women describe themselves as more competitive than men do
High long-term orientation	Building relationships and market position valued Ordinary human relations source of satisfaction Deferred gratification of needs accepted
Low long-term orientation	Short-term results and bottom line valued Daily human relations not a source of satisfaction Immediate gratification of needs expected

SOURCE: Adapted from Hofstede, G. (2001). *Culture's consequences: Comparing values, behaviors, institutions, and organizations across nations*, 2nd ed. Thousand Oaks, CA: Sage. And adapted from Hofstede, G., Hofstede, G. J., & Minkov, M. (2010). *Cultures and organizations: Software of the mind*, 3rd rev. ed. New York: McGraw-Hill. © 2001 Geert Hofstede; © 2010 Geert Hofstede BV. Adapted by permission.

decision making is more the norm. This type of cultural discrepancy will inevitably lead to problems in communication and decision making when an individual from one culture is placed into work groups or work settings with individuals from another culture.

If diversity is to produce the anticipated economic and intellectual rewards, managers must be aware of the various cultures operating in the workplace and be prepared to provide the training and support necessary to work with those cultures productively. We will consider the topic of workplace diversity in greater detail in Chapter 11. The point here is that diversity comes with a cost. It may very well bring about cultural clashes and conflict. Nevertheless, the benefits are likely to outweigh the costs.

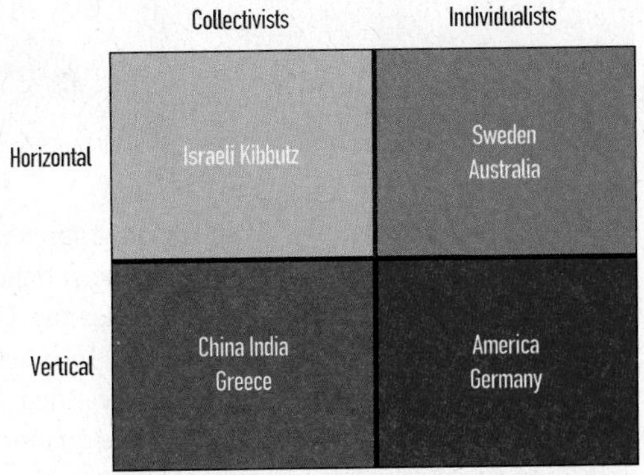

FIGURE 1.5 Triandis's View of Cultural Determinants in the Workplace

SOURCE: Adapted from Triandis, H. C., & Bhawuk, D. P. S. (1997). Culture theory and the meaning of relatedness. In P. C. Earley & M. Erez (Eds.), *New perspectives on international industrial/organizational psychology* (pp. 13–51). San Francisco: Jossey-Bass. Copyright © 1997. Reprinted by permission of John Wiley & Sons, Inc.

Some Thoughts on Theories of Cultural Influence

Hofstede's theory is not the only theory of cultural influence. Triandis (1995a,b; Triandis & Bhawuk, 1997) suggested a variation on Hofstede's dimension of individualism/collectivism—that is, a horizontal/vertical dimension interacts with individualism/collectivism, as shown in Figure 1.5. **Horizontal cultures** are those that minimize distances between individuals (much like Hofstede's power distance dimension), whereas **vertical cultures** accept and depend on those distances.

Horizontal culture A culture that minimizes distances between individuals.

Vertical culture A culture that accepts and depends upon distances between individuals.

Most theories of cultural influence have incorporated the individualism/collectivism dimension of Hofstede in one way or another (e.g., Trompenaars & Hampden-Turner, 1998), and it appears that this dimension will be the backbone of any future theories. But Hofstede's analysis was conducted by averaging the responses of all respondents from a given country and assigning that average as the country value on the dimension. Thus, we really have a theory of countries, not individuals. Some implications of the theory are seen in Box 1.3. However, it is vitally important to realize that, within a country, not all individuals share the same culture. As we will see in Chapter 14, the extent to which values are shared varies across work groups and has an effect on the behavior of each group. As an example, the Honda of America Corporation has four production plants in Ohio. Those plants have adopted a collectivist, high power distance, masculine, long-term orientation culture, much as one might expect to see in Japan. Here is a Japanese culture embedded in the heartland of America. The entire Honda organization, regardless of where a plant may be, applies this culture and trains all of its employees in it, with successful results.

Keep in mind that cultural variables represent only one of the many influences on work behavior. Other influences include individual skills and motivation, managerial skills, leadership behaviors, HRM practices, and other individual and group variables. Nevertheless, culture is a key factor in appreciating the complexity of the modern workplace. It is important to acknowledge that psychology is neither sociology nor anthropology. I-O psychology focuses on the *perception* of the culture by the individual worker, not necessarily any "objective" measure of culture. Although mainstream I-O psychology has only recently acknowledged the importance of culture in work behavior (Earley & Erez, 1997; Kraut & Korman, 1999), we can predict that its role in the new global definition of work will become more obvious in the next decade. We will remind you of the issue of culture as it applies in the chapters that follow.

BOX 1.3 *THE APPRENTICE*

In the United States, the TV show *The Apprentice* has been a great success. The show has also been franchised in more than a dozen other countries: the United Kingdom, Brazil, Norway, Russia, and Indonesia, to name a few. The show could easily be titled "Who Wants to Be an American?" because the qualities that lead to success for the contestants are very American. The U.S. mainstream culture is decidedly individualistic. It is exactly that characteristic "me-first" perspective that has made reality TV shows like *The Apprentice* and *Survivor* so popular. In the United States, the individualist perspective is taken as normal.

That is not the case in Japan, where the culture is strongly collectivistic. According to Fremantle Media, a company that attempted to produce a Japanese version of *The Apprentice*, several Japanese executives turned down the opportunity to star as Donald Trump's counterpart. As a *Los Angeles Times* article explained, "the Japanese concept of success differs markedly from that of the West. One must be more humble about success in Japan" (Ibison, 2006). Similarly, Japanese culture is long term in time orientation, whereas the American culture is short term; in Japan a company's success is seen as the result of many people working together over a period of many years. And the trademark *Apprentice* denunciation, "You're fired!" (which, in the Japanese version, was planned to be a Samurai phrase meaning "Off with your head!"), is almost never heard in Japan, where the custom is to quietly transfer a poorly performing worker to a remote position where he or she will have little effect on the organization.

Greece is another country where *The Apprentice* fared poorly. This failure might be due to the fact that, according to Hofstede's data, Greece is one of the nations highest on uncertainty avoidance. Greeks tend to be uncomfortable in any situations that are not predictable. One can imagine how painful it would have been to tune in each week not knowing who would be fired and why. The ancient Greek tradition of consulting oracles (such as the famous Oracle at Delphi) before making decisions may have been an early attempt to overcome this discomfort.

Personally, we hope to see the advent of an international version of *The Apprentice*, with contestants chosen from radically different cultures. Now that would be interesting!

SOURCE: Ibison (2006).

MODULE 1.3 SUMMARY

- Culture is a system of shared meanings and ways of viewing events and things.
- The global economy has made it important for all countries to foster economic connections with others.
- It is important for I-O psychologists to recognize and study the multiplicity of cultural factors that influence workplace behavior.
- Individualism/collectivism, power distance, uncertainty avoidance, masculinity/femininity, and long-term versus short-term orientation are some of the key considerations in describing and characterizing various cultures.

KEY TERMS

culture
"West versus the Rest" mentality
expatriates
collectivist culture
individualist culture
individualism/collectivism
horizontal culture
vertical culture

MODULE 1.4

The Organization of This Book

Themes

Several themes run through the chapters of this book. They will be more apparent in some chapters than others. The first theme is one of a unified science of industrial and organizational psychology. Unified means several things in this context. First, to truly understand work behavior, we must be willing to consider and acknowledge the interplay of many different approaches. For example, when we consider the issue of safety in the workplace, we could consider the individual strategies for creating a safe workplace embodied in the personnel, organizational, or human engineering approaches. The personnel approach would suggest selecting people who are likely to act in safe ways and then training them in those ways. The organizational approach might suggest rewarding people for safe behavior and reducing stress in the workplace. The engineering approach might endorse modifying the environment, equipment, and work procedures to eliminate the hazards associated with common accidents, as well as creating and maintaining a climate of safety in individual work groups. The unified approach means not preferring one or another of these approaches, but realizing that all approaches are useful and can be skillfully applied, either individually or in combination, depending on the situation at hand. We will apply the same theme of unity to the many other topics you will encounter in the book.

"Unified" has another meaning in our treatment of I-O psychology. It means that research and theories from non-American researchers are just as valuable to understanding work behavior as the work by American researchers. We are all in this together: Our fellow Croatian, Japanese, Swedish, and New Zealand I-O psychologists are just as intent on understanding the experience of work as we are, and they are just as skilled at forming theories and conducting research. For those reasons, we will freely discuss the work of our colleagues in other countries and combine it with what has been learned in the United States to develop a broader and deeper understanding of work behavior. As you read in Module 1.3, all workers and work have been globalized, whether or not they embraced the concept of globalization. As a result, in many instances the research of a single country will not be sufficient to understand the behavior of workers in that country or any other. So we will present you with the best thoughts of those who study work behavior, regardless of the country in which it is studied.

The second theme that will be apparent in our treatment is a holistic one. By this we mean that we cannot and should not try to understand any work behavior by considering variables in isolation. There is a natural temptation to look for quick and simple answers. In some senses, the scientific method yields to that temptation by having the goal of parsimony, that is, choosing simple explanations and theories over complex ones. But in the real world, unlike the laboratory, we cannot control multiple forces that act on an individual. Your behavior is not simply a result of your mental ability or of your personality. The behavior of your instructors is not just the result of their knowledge or attitudes or of the culture in which they were raised. These behaviors are influenced by all of those things, and to consider only one variable as *the* explanatory variable is an endeavor doomed to failure. We will remind you frequently that you must look at the person as a whole entity, not as a single variable. Human behavior in real-world situations is like a stew. We may know every ingredient that went into that stew, yet the actual experience of tasting the stew is much more than the single elements that made it up and is certainly not described by any one of those elements.

A third theme that will run through the chapters is the vast cultural diversity of virtually any workforce in any country. A key facet of cultural diversity is differing *values*. It is these differing values that present the greatest challenge for employee selection, motivation, leadership, teamwork, and organizational identification. The organization that can "solve" the diversity puzzle (i.e., how to effectively integrate diverse ways of thinking and acting) is likely the organization that will enjoy high productivity, low turnover, and high satisfaction. I-O psychology can play a major role in helping to accomplish this integration, and we will address these issues throughout the text.

Parts

The book is divided into three parts.

- The first part presents descriptive information about I-O psychology, some historical background and principles, and the basic methods of data collection and analysis.
- The second part deals with material that has often been labeled "industrial" (as opposed to "organizational"). This includes material on individual differences, assessment, training, performance and its evaluation, and job analysis.
- The third part covers material that is usually referred to as "organizational" and includes topics such as emotion, motivation, stress, leadership, groups and teams, fairness and justice, and organizational theory.

Resources

As a student of I-O psychology, you will want to consult resources beyond those offered by your instructor, this text, and its supplements. The most important of these resources are knowledge bases. This knowledge can come in two forms: paper and electronic. The electronic resources are websites and search engines that will identify useful information for you. Because website addresses change frequently, we will use this book's companion website to list the most useful websites for the material covered in each chapter. The paper

TABLE 1.7 **Scientific Journals in I-O Psychology**

Journal of Applied Psychology
Personnel Psychology
Human Performance
Human Factors
Academy of Management Journal
Academy of Management Review
Annual Review of Psychology
The Industrial-Organizational Psychologist (TIP)
Organizational Behavior and Human Decision Processes
International Review of I/O Psychology
International Review of Applied Psychology
Journal of Occupational and Organizational Psychology
Leadership Quarterly
Applied Psychology: An International Review
International Journal of Selection and Assessment
Work and Stress
Journal of Occupational Health Psychology
Journal of Organizational Behavior
Industrial and Organizational Psychology: Perspectives on Science and Practice
Australian Journal of Management
European Journal of Work and Organizational Psychology
Journal of Business and Psychology

resources are the various journals and books that provide information about the topics covered in the text. Table 1.7 presents a list of the most common scientific journals that carry articles relevant to the text material.

In the references at the end of the book, you will see these journals cited frequently. If you want to do additional reading on a topic or are preparing a course paper or project, you should go to these journals first. In addition to journals, SIOP publishes the most current thinking on various topics in two series: the Frontier Series for research and the Practice Series for practice. These volumes present the most recent work available from some of the world's best I-O psychologists. Table 1.8 provides the titles and publication year of recent books in these two series. These books represent another excellent information base for your further reading.

TABLE 1.8 Frontiers and Professional Practice Series Books

ORGANIZATIONAL FRONTIERS SERIES

Multilevel Theory, Research and Methods in Organizations: Klein & Kozlowski (2000)
Measuring and Analyzing Behavior in Organizations: Drasgow & Schmitt (2002)
Work Careers: Feldman (2002)
Measuring and Analyzing Behavior in Organizations: Drasgow & Schmitt (2002)
Emotions in the Workplace: Lord, Klimoski, & Kanfer (2002)
Personality and Work: Barrick & Ryan (2003)
Managing Knowledge for Sustained Competitive Advantage: Jackson, Hitt, & DeNisi (2003)
Health and Safety in Organizations: Hofmann & Tetrick (2003)
The Dark Side of Organizational Behavior: Griffin & O'Leary Kelly (2004)
Discrimination at Work: Dipboye & Collela (2004)
Situational Judgment Tests: Weekley & Ployhart (2006)
The Psychology of Entrepreneurship: Baum, Frese, & Baron (2007)
The Psychology of Conflict and Conflict Management in Organizations: De Dreu & Gelfand (2007)
Perspectives on Organizational Fit: Ostroff & Judge (2007)
Work Motivation: Kanfer, Chen, & Pritchard (2008)
Adverse Impact: Outtz (2009)
Commitment in Organizations: Klein, Becker, & Meyer (2009)
Nepotism in Organizations: Jones (2011)
Errors in Organizations: Hofmann & Frese (2011)
Politics in Organizations: Ferris & Treadway (2012)

PROFESSIONAL PRACTICE SERIES

Compensation in Organizations: Rynes & Gerhart (2000)
Creating, Implementing and Managing Effective Training: Kraiger (2001)
Organizational Development: Waclawski & Church (2001)
The 21st Century Executive: Silzer (2001)
The Nature of Organizational Leadership: Zaccaro & Klimoski (2001)
Organization Development: Waclawski & Church (2002)
Implementing Organizational Interventions: Hedge & Pulakos (2002)
Creating, Implementing, and Managing Effective Training and Development: Kraiger (2002)
Resizing the Organization: DeMeuse & Marks (2003)
Improving Learning Transfer in Organizations: Holton & Baldwin (2003)
The Brave New World of eHR: Guettal & Stone (2005)
Employment Discrimination Litigation: Landy (2005)
Getting Action from Organizational Surveys: Kraut (2006)
Customer Service Delivery: Fogli & Salas (2006)
Alternative Validation Strategies: McPhail (2007)
Performance Management: Smither & London (2009)
Handbook of Workplace Assessment: Scott & Reynolds (2010)
Technology Enhanced Assessment of Talent: Tippins & Adler (2011)

MODULE 1.4 SUMMARY

- This book treats I-O psychology in a unified and holistic manner.
- The three parts of this book discuss the basics of I-O psychology, industrial psychology topics, and organizational psychology topics.
- You can use this book's supplements, I-O journals, websites, and the SIOP Frontiers Series and Practice Series to find additional information for your coursework, papers, and projects.

CASE STUDY 1.1 POLICE OFFICER, MILFORD, USA

CASE STUDY EXERCISE

Below is a realistic case for you to read that includes topics from every chapter in the book. After each paragraph, you will find the number of the chapter that contains information relevant to the case. We don't expect you to be able to "solve" the case or address the issues presented. Instead, we present the case as a vivid example of the complexity of work behavior and environments. After you complete each chapter in class, you will find it useful to come back to this case, identify the paragraphs relevant to the chapter you have read, and determine how the chapter material applies to the case. What we want you to do now is simply read and appreciate the experience of work in the 21st century.

Welcome to Milford. We're a "rust belt" survivor: Unlike a lot of towns around here, we've actually grown in the past few decades. Our town, with a current population of 600,000, has a fairly good economic base, since we have an auto assembly plant and a glass factory, as well as a state university campus and a regional airport. About 50,000 of our residents are Hispanic, mostly descended from Mexicans and Central Americans who came to the area decades ago as migrant farmworkers and moved into town when agriculture declined. We have the kinds of problems with crime and drugs that you'd expect in any city of this size, but on the whole it's a pretty good place to live. *(Chapter 1)*

I'm 48 now and a captain of patrol with the Milford Police Department. I started working for the department when I was 26 years old, a little later than most of the other officers. Before that I spent five years in the Navy maintaining sonar units, then used my military education benefit to get a college degree in law enforcement. At age 33 I was promoted from patrol officer to patrol sergeant. Five years after that I became a lieutenant, and in four more years I made my present grade. Except for two years behind a desk during my stint as a lieutenant, I've spent my entire career on the street. *(Chapter 3)*

I've seen lots of different "systems" in my 22 years on the force—systems for hiring, systems for promotion, systems for discipline, systems for training. If you didn't like a particular system, all you had to do was wait a few years, and it would change because someone in power wanted a change. But now I'm a "person in power" and I have a say in these "systems." I remember reading once that the best performance evaluation system people ever saw was the one they had in their *last* job. Boy, is that on the money! You hear people's criticisms and you try to think of a way to make the system better, but no matter what you propose, they come back and complain that the old way was better. Sometimes it seems my work life was easier when I just had to *put up* with systems, not help *make* them up. *(Chapters 5, 6, and 11)*

I have four direct reports: patrol lieutenants, shift commanders. We work the evening watch, which is roughly from 3:00 p.m. to 11:00 p.m. I say "roughly" because some of the subordinates come in at 2:30 and others leave at 11:30 to cover shift changes. We tried a rotating shift schedule many years ago, but that was a disaster. Now we follow a fixed shift system in which officers work consistent hours weekdays and every third weekend. Shift assignment follows strict seniority rules: New hires and newly promoted officers work what we call "graveyard"—the night shift, from 11:00 p.m. to 7:00 a.m. They have to wait until someone else quits, is fired, or retires before they can move up to evening and day shifts. This is good and bad. It's good for the cops because building your seniority to move off the graveyard shift, and eventually making it to the day shift, is something to look forward to. But it's bad from a law enforcement standpoint because there's a natural tendency to have a lot more problems during graveyard hours than at other times. I mean, when John Q. Public decides to act stupid, it's usually between 11:00 p.m. and 7:00 a.m. And here we are with mostly green recruits right out of the police academy on that shift, being supervised by newly promoted officers. We don't even have any top-echelon officers working:

CONTINUED

Lieutenants cover the captain's duty on the night shift. If you ask me, the department would have far fewer problems with patrol officer performance if only you could put the most experienced officers and supervisors where they were needed the most, on night watch. *(Chapters 10 and 12)*

There's a new breed of officer that I've been seeing in the past 5 to 10 years and I can't say I like it. These young guys don't really seem as committed to being a cop as I was when I started. They treat it like a "job," not like a profession. They use all their sick time; they're always looking to join "better" departments where the pay scale is higher. They seem to "expect" that they'll be respected by civilians and fellow officers. They don't seem to understand that respect is earned, not bestowed. Something funny happens to them after the academy. When they arrive for their first shift after graduation, they're like kids starting first grade. Big eyes, lots of questions, asking for "feedback," asking for responsibility. They think they can do it all. But in less than a year, it's a different story. You have to stay on their case to get anything done. They take longer meal breaks, find more excuses for not being able to respond to a call, and saunter in two minutes before roll call. Just another job to them. *(Chapters 7, 8, and 9)*

Maybe this is because of the way recruits are tested. When I started, only the best were hired. The person who got the highest score on the civil service test, and was the fastest and the strongest on the physical ability test, was the person who got hired. You filled out a questionnaire to see if you had emotional problems; this was reviewed by the department shrink. You took a medical and they ran a background check on you. But now it's different. Now, in addition to the civil service test, recruits are interviewed about things like "interests" and "values" and "ethics." They also take a personality test, whatever that is. And they fill out a form about what they like and don't like in a job. I don't understand why they changed the system. Bad guys are still bad guys and they still do bad things. What's so complicated about that? You want a cop who is standup, not afraid to do what it takes. You want a cop who is honest. You want a cop who is in for the long haul and who understands the chain of command. Why, all of a sudden, does the cop have to have a "personality"? *(Chapter 3)*

Another thing is the job is getting much more technical. The city council just approved funds for giving every cop a personal digital assistant/handheld computer with WiFi capabilities. They thought the police officers would love coming into the 21st century. According to them, we can use the computers, GPS systems, listen to departmental podcasts, and use handheld PDAs to analyze various crime patterns in our sectors, run more sophisticated checks for wants and warrants, look at traffic patterns for selective enforcement of moving violations where they are most dangerous. They don't realize that we are being suffocated with equipment. It takes 10 minutes now just to load the stuff in the patrol car and get it up and running—and use simultaneously!! *(Chapter 3)*

Since I've been on the force I've seen various trends and fads come and go. The latest buzzwords seem to be statistical control, or "stat con," where crime is analyzed by an "operations researcher." Not surprisingly, the new cops seem to take to stat con better than the veterans, and this is causing a certain amount of friction. The veterans call the new cops who understand stat con "stat cops." The new cops joke that the veterans are "knuckle draggers" and "Neanderthals." It doesn't help that some of the new cops score better on the promotional exams and get promoted faster. That means that the younger "bosses" don't always have the respect of the older subordinates. And the beat cops who aren't promoted just get older and more cynical. *(Chapters 3, 6, and 14)*

The force has changed in other ways as well. When I started, I could count the number of female police officers in the department on one hand and have a finger or two left over. Now the department is almost 40 percent female. That makes it tougher for the supervisors, because even though the law says they have to treat females the same as males, in reality the women get treated with kid gloves because the bosses are afraid of being accused of bias. Given the Hispanic community in town, we've always had a small but steady percentage of Hispanic officers. In recent years more blacks have gotten on the force, and now black officers outnumber the Hispanics. This has led to rivalry and competition, particularly when it comes to promotion exams. Everybody counts to see how many white, black, and Hispanic officers are promoted. Since the Hispanics have more seniority, they expect to have more promotions, but the blacks figure since there are more of them there should be proportionately more black supervisors. To make matters worse, the female officers always seem to do better on the exams than the men.

As a result, I actually report to a female assistant chief. And she's been in the department for only 13 years! But she's a great test taker. And everybody knows that we had to have a woman somewhere up there in the chain of command, whether she could do the job or not. The problem is that you don't get respect for being a good test taker—you get it for being a good cop. Most of the officers don't pay much attention to her. Her decisions are always second-guessed and checked out with the other two male assistant chiefs. *(Chapter 11)*

The chief of police is a good guy. He has been in the department for just 16 years, but he's a college grad and went nights to get a master's in public administration. He's sharp and is always trying out new stuff. Last year he hired an outside consulting firm to run the promotion exams. Some of the consultants are psychologists, which was a little strange, since the department already has a shrink on retainer. For the last sergeant's exam, they had a bunch of the current sergeants complete some "job analysis" forms. That seemed like a pretty big waste of time. Why not just get the most experienced officers together for an hour's discussion and have the consultants take notes? This "job analysis" thing led to an unusual promotion examination. They did use a knowledge test that made sure the candidates knew the criminal code and department policies, but they also had the candidates play the role of a sergeant in front of a panel of judges. The judges were from other police departments, which didn't make sense. How could they know what would be the right way to behave in our department? But the good part was that everyone got a score for performance and this score was added to the written test score. It was objective. The time before that, the lieutenants and captains got together for a few hours and talked about all the candidates and just made up a list according to their experiences with the candidates, which everybody agreed was unfair. *(Chapters 1, 2, and 4)*

Over the past several years, there has been a new kind of tension in the department. It became really obvious after 9/11, but it was building up before that and has not gone away. In a nutshell, officers are more interested in having a life outside the department instead of making the department their whole life. I'm talking about the veterans, not just the young new guys. Their mind is not on their work the way it ought to be. It got a lot worse after 9/11 because we've been expected to do so much more but with the same number of officers. We've tripled our airport detachment and had to post officers at city court, the bus station, and the power plant. And we've been getting a lot more calls about suspicious people and activities, especially people from other countries. A lot of private citizens have gotten so distrustful of foreigners that they act as if they'd like nothing better than to have the police force arrest every illegal alien it could find. But when you talk to those same people at work, all of a sudden they'd just as soon we look the other way because they know their corporate profits depend on having a cheap labor pool of undocumented workers. You'd expect the immigration authorities to give us some guidelines about this, but when I think about them, I get just as annoyed as I do thinking about the other federal law enforcement agencies we're supposed to "interface" with now. We get overlapping or conflicting information from the different agencies, or else the information is so general or outdated that it doesn't really help us do our jobs. All of this extra responsibility has meant lots of overtime. Overtime used to be a big reward; now it's a punishment. And it looks like sick leave is off the charts. Some of the officers are snapping at each other and civilians. And a week does not go by when we don't have at least one police cruiser in a wreck. The officers seem really distracted. *(Chapter 10)*

Citizens are not doing so well either. The economy headed south and unemployment went way up. Ever notice that people act funny when they lose their jobs? Men are the worst. They feel worthless and angry. They do things that they would never do otherwise. A traffic stop turns into World War III. All of a sudden, we cops are the enemy—a complete about-face from the first few months after 9/11, when we were the heroes. We still remember that. People couldn't thank us enough for keeping them safe. It made us feel really good. It sure helped recruiting, too. All of a sudden we had a big surge in applicants to take the test. It was nice while it lasted. But when the conventions canceled, and the orders for cars dropped, and the state had to start cutting back on services, we were not the good guys anymore. I know life is tough. I know people take hits when the economy sours, but how can we help them? It's not our fault. We just end up dealing with the consequences. *(Chapters 9 and 10)*

One of the other captains just came back from a seminar on new techniques in law enforcement

CONTINUED

where they talked about "teams." I don't know what is so new about that. We've always had squads of officers assigned to a beat or sector. But he says that is not what they were talking about. They were talking about putting teams together based not on seniority but on abilities and interests. They were talking about "competencies," whatever that means. I didn't think the officers would go for this. But he showed us a half-dozen studies that were done by people from top law enforcement schools. When I looked at the results, I had to agree that this team approach might actually work. What they found, when they gave it a chance, was that the officers were more involved in their jobs, felt more in control, and took pride in showing that they were more effective on patrol. Response times went down, more problems were handled with summonses and bench warrants rather than arrests, and resisting arrest charges and claims of brutality went down. The studies showed that sick leave went down as well. Hard to understand, but the numbers don't lie. Maybe these experts are right—"team" policing would help us get out of this slump. *(Chapter 13)*

But the academics can have some pretty dumb ideas, too. One of the sergeants is taking a course at the community college on employee attitudes, so he asked some of us to fill out a form to determine our job satisfaction. It was pretty simple, just asking us to agree or disagree with some sentences. He took the forms away, analyzed them, and came back to tell us what we already knew. We like our work, we don't like our bosses, there are too many "rules" we have to follow in the department, our pay is OK, and we can get promoted if we are lucky and study hard. Why did we need to fill out a questionnaire to come to those conclusions? *(Chapter 9)*

The job satisfaction questionnaire did reveal one sore point that all of us can sense. We have a problem in the department with leadership. There are plenty of "bosses," but not many of them are leaders. Some of them play tough and threaten their officers with three-day suspensions for making mistakes. If the officer dares to speak back, it might go up to five days off without pay. Some of the other bosses try to be your friend, but that won't work either. What you want is someone to help you do your job, not somebody to have coffee with. I was lucky when I was a lieutenant. My captain was somebody I could look up to, and he showed me what it takes to be a good cop and a good leader at the same time. Not everybody gets that kind of training. It seems like there should be a training program for bosses, just like there's one for new officers—sort of an academy for supervisors. I mentioned that to one of the other captains, who said it would be money down the drain. You would take officers off the street and have nothing to show for it. I know there's an answer to his objection, but I can't think what it would be. *(Chapter 12)*

There is another problem that I see, but the questionnaire didn't ask any questions about it. We don't really trust anybody except other cops. The courts seem to bend over backward to give the perps a break. The lawyers are always picking away at details of the arrest. Are you sure you saw him on the corner *before* you heard the alarm? Did you ask for permission to search her purse? How could you see a license plate from 25 feet away when the sun was almost down? Even the DA, who is supposed to be on your side, is always telling you that you should have done something differently. The problem is that this makes the average cop just want to make up whatever details are necessary to get the perp off the street. On the one hand, I can't disagree with my officers that the system seems to be working against us and what we are trying to do. On the other hand, I don't think that this is the way a police department should think or behave. We should all be working together in the criminal justice system, not trying to "win." *(Chapter 14)*

But this is why the police force feels defensive against the rest of the city government. And it's why we were not pleased last week when the mayor announced that all city employees would have their performance evaluated once a year, and that includes the police department. It has something to do with "accountability in government." He has asked each city department to develop its own system, but it has to be numerical. He also said that there have to be consequences for poor performance. The chief is thinking about preventing anyone from taking a promotion exam if his or her performance is "unacceptable," but he hasn't told us how he plans to determine what is acceptable. I think this is a disaster waiting to happen. *(Chapter 5)*

I'm proud of being a cop and I feel a lot of satisfaction with what I've achieved in my career. But to tell you the truth, the way things are going around here, retirement is starting to look more and more attractive to me. *(Chapter 9)*

2 Methods and Statistics in I-O Psychology

© Shelley Dennis/iStockphoto

MODULE 2.1

Science

What Is Science?

Science Approach that involves the understanding, prediction, and control of some phenomenon of interest.

For many of us, the term "**science**" evokes mental images of laboratories, test tubes, and computers. We may imagine people wearing white lab coats, walking around making notes on clipboards. Certainly laboratories are the homes for some scientific activity and some scientists do wear white lab coats, but the essence of science is not where it is done or how scientists are dressed. Science is defined by its goals and its procedures.

All sciences share common goals: the understanding, prediction, and control of some phenomenon of interest. Physics addresses physical matter, chemistry addresses elements of matter, biology deals with living things, and psychology is concerned with behavior. The I-O psychologist is particularly interested in understanding, predicting, and influencing behavior related to the workplace. All sciences also share certain common methods by which they study the object of interest, whether that object is a chemical on the periodic table of elements or a human being employed in a corporation. These common methods include the following:

Hypothesis Prediction about relationship(s) among variables of interest.

1. Science is marked by a logical approach to investigation, usually based on a theory, a **hypothesis**, or simply a basic curiosity about an object of interest. In I-O psychology, this might be a theory about what motivates workers, a hypothesis that freedom to choose work methods will lead workers to be more involved with their work, or curiosity about whether people who work from their homes are more satisfied with their jobs than people who work in offices.
2. Science depends on data. These data can be gathered in a laboratory or in the real world (or, as it is sometimes referred to, the field). The data gathered are intended to be relevant to the theory, hypothesis, or curiosity that precipitated the investigation. For example, I-O psychologists gather data about job performance, abilities, job satisfaction, and attitudes toward safety.
3. Science must be communicable, open, and public. Scientific research is published in journals, reports, and books. Methods of data collection are described, data are reported, analyses are displayed for examination, and conclusions are presented. As a result, other scientists or nonscientists can draw their own conclusions about

the confidence they have in the findings of the research or even replicate the research themselves. In I-O psychology, there is often debate—sometimes heated argument—about theories and hypotheses. The debate goes on at conferences, in journals, and in books. Anyone can join the debate by simply reading the relevant reports or publications and expressing opinions on them or by conducting and publishing their own research.

4. Science does not set out to prove theories or hypotheses. It sets out to *disprove* them. The goal of the scientist is to design a research project that will eliminate all plausible explanations for a phenomenon except one. The explanation that cannot be disproved or eliminated is the ultimate explanation of the phenomenon. For example, in lawsuits involving layoffs brought by older employees who have lost their jobs, the charge will be that the layoffs were caused by age discrimination on the part of the employer. A scientific approach to the question would consider that possibility, as well as the possibility that the layoffs were the result of:
   - Differences in the past performance of the individuals who were laid off
   - Differences in the skills possessed by the individuals
   - Differences in projected work for the individuals
   - Differences in training, education, or credentials of the individuals
5. One other characteristic of science that is frequently mentioned (MacCoun, 1998; Merton, 1973) is that of **disinterestedness**—the expectation that scientists will be objective and not influenced by biases or prejudices. Although most researchers are, and should be, passionately interested in their research efforts, they are expected to be *dispassionate* about the results they expect that research to yield—or, at the very least, to make public any biases or prejudices they may harbor.

Disinterestedness
Characteristic of scientists, who should be objective and uninfluenced by biases or prejudices when conducting research.

It will become apparent as we move through the chapters of this book that I-O psychology is a science. I-O psychologists conduct research based on theories and hypotheses. They gather data, publish those data, and design their research in a way that eliminates alternative explanations for the research results. I-O psychologists (and scientists in general) are not very different from nonscientists in their curiosity or the way they form theories, hypotheses, or speculations. What sets them apart as scientists is the method they use.

The Role of Science in Society

We are often unaware of the impact that science has on our everyday lives. The water we drink, the air we breathe, even the levels of noise we experience have been influenced by decades of scientific research. Consider the challenge faced by a pharmaceutical company that wants to make a new drug available to the public. The Food and Drug Administration (FDA) requires the pharmaceutical company to conduct years of trials (experiments) in the laboratory and in the field. These trials must conform to the standards of acceptable science: They will be based on a theory; data will be gathered, compiled, and interpreted; and all alternative explanations for the effects of the drug will be considered. In addition, the data will be available for inspection by the FDA. Before the drug can be released to the public, the FDA must agree that the data show that the drug actually makes a contribution to medicine and that it has no dangerous side effects.

As you will see in a later section of this chapter that deals with ethics, the burden of trustworthy science must be shouldered by a trustworthy scientist. An example is provided by a 2008 congressional inquiry involving the pharmaceutical company Pfizer and its cholesterol drug Lipitor. A Lipitor advertising campaign was launched in 2006 featuring Robert Jarvik, the physician who was famous for developing an artificial heart valve. In one ad,

Jarvik was engaged in a vigorous rowing exercise on a lake immediately after endorsing the drug. When the public learned that a stunt double actually did the rowing, the drug and Jarvik were the objects of immediate criticism. Moreover, it was revealed that although Jarvik held a medical degree, he had never completed the certification necessary to practice medicine. Thus, he was not qualified to give medical advice, which he appeared to be doing in the ads. The inauthentic scientist brought the science into question.

The importance of the scientific method for the impact of human resource and I-O practices can also be seen in society, particularly in the courts. As we will see in several of the chapters that follow (most notably, Chapter 6), individuals often bring lawsuits against employers for particular practices, such as hiring, firing, pay increases, and harassment. In these lawsuits, I-O psychologists often testify as expert witnesses. An **expert witness**, unlike a fact witness, is permitted to voice opinions about practices. An I-O psychologist might be prepared to offer the opinion that an employer was justified in using a test, such as a test of mental ability, for hiring purposes. This opinion may be challenged by opposing lawyers as "junk science" that lacks foundation in legitimate scientific research. You will recall that we described "junk science" in Chapter 1 as a fascinating topic (un)supported by shoddy research. The scientific method is one of the most commonly accepted methods for protecting individuals from the consequences of uninformed speculation.

Expert witness Witness in a lawsuit who is permitted to voice opinions about organizational practices.

Why Do I-O Psychologists Engage in Research?

An old truism admonishes that those who do not study history are condemned to repeat it. In Chapter 1, we cautioned that researchers studying emotional intelligence but ignoring 60 years of research on social intelligence might have been condemned in just that way. A less elegant representation of the same thought was the movie *Groundhog Day*, in which Bill Murray gets to repeat the events of a particular day over and over again, learning from his mistakes only after a very long time. Without access to scientific research, the individuals who make human resource (HR) decisions in organizations would be in Murray's position, unable to learn from mistakes (and successes) that are already documented. Each HR director would reinvent the wheel, sometimes with good and sometimes with poor results. By conducting research, we are able to develop a model of a system—a theory—and predict the consequences of introducing that system or of modifying a system already in place. Remember that in Chapter 1 we described the importance of research in the scientist-practitioner model. Even though you may not actually *engage in* scientific research, you will certainly consume the results of that research.

Consider the example of hiring. Imagine that an organization has always used a first-come, first-served model for hiring. When a job opening occurs, the organization advertises, reviews an application blank, does a short unstructured interview, and hires the first applicant who has the minimum credentials. Research in I-O psychology has demonstrated that this method does not give the employer the best chance of hiring successful employees. An employer that conducts a structured job-related interview, and that also includes explicit assessments of general mental ability and personality, will tend to make better hiring decisions. We can predict this because of decades of published research that form the foundation for our theory of successful hiring. When organizational decision makers decide on a course of action, they are predicting (or anticipating) the outcome of that course of action. The better the research base that employers depend on for that prediction, the more confident they can be in the likely outcome. Both science and business strategy are based on the same principle: predictability. Business leaders prefer to avoid unpleasant surprises; theory and research help them to do so.

In most of your course texts, you will be exposed to "theory." Think of theories as either helpful or not helpful, rather than "right" or "wrong." Klein and Zedeck (2004) remind us that theories provide meaning and specify which variables are important and for what reasons. Theories also describe and explain relationships that link the variables. Klein and Zedeck suggest that *good* theories display the following characteristics:

- Offer novel insights
- Are interesting
- Are focused
- Are relevant to important topics
- Provide explanations
- Are practical

As you read the material that will follow in the subsequent chapters and, more importantly, if you dig further and read the original statements of the theories, keep these characteristics of *good* theory in mind in order to decide which ones are helpful and which ones are not.

MODULE 2.1 SUMMARY

- Like other scientists, I-O psychologists conduct research based on theories and hypotheses. They gather data, publish those data, and design their research to eliminate alternative explanations for the research results.
- The scientific method has important repercussions in society, particularly in the courts, where I-O psychologists often testify as expert witnesses.
- I-O research is important to organizations because every course of action that an organization decides on is, in effect, a prediction or anticipation of a given outcome. The better the research base that supports that prediction, the more confident the organization can be of the outcome.

KEY TERMS

science
hypothesis
disinterestedness
expert witness

MODULE 2.2

Research

Research Design

In the introductory module, we considered the scientific method and the role of research in I-O psychology. Now we will consider the operations that define research in greater detail. In carrying out research, a series of decisions need to be made before the research actually begins. These decisions include the following:

- Will the research be conducted in a laboratory under controlled conditions or in the field?
- Who will the participants be?
- If there are different conditions in the research (e.g., some participants exposed to a condition and other participants not exposed to the condition), how will participants be assigned to the various conditions?
- What will the variables of interest be?
- How will measurements on these variables be collected?

Research design Provides the overall structure or architecture for the research study; allows investigators to conduct scientific research on a phenomenon of interest.

Experimental design Participants are randomly assigned to different conditions.

Quasi-experimental design Participants are assigned to different conditions, but random assignment to conditions is not possible.

Nonexperimental design Does not include any "treatment" or assignment to different conditions.

Collectively, the answers to these questions will determine the **research design**, the architecture for the research.

Spector (2001) has reviewed research designs in I-O psychology and devised a system of classification for distinguishing among the typical designs. He breaks designs down into three basic types: **experimental**, **quasi-experimental**, and **nonexperimental**. Experimental designs, whether the experiment is conducted in a laboratory or in the field, involve the assignment of participants to conditions. As an example, some participants may receive a piece-rate payment for their work, whereas others receive an hourly rate. These two different rates of pay would be two separate conditions, and participants might be assigned randomly to one condition or the other. The random assignment of participants is one of the characteristics that distinguishes an experiment from a quasi-experiment or nonexperiment. If participants are randomly assigned to conditions, then any differences that appear after the experimental treatment are more likely to conform to cause–effect relationships. Random assignment to conditions allows researchers to be more confident that there were not pre-existing systematic differences between the groups that were assigned to different conditions.

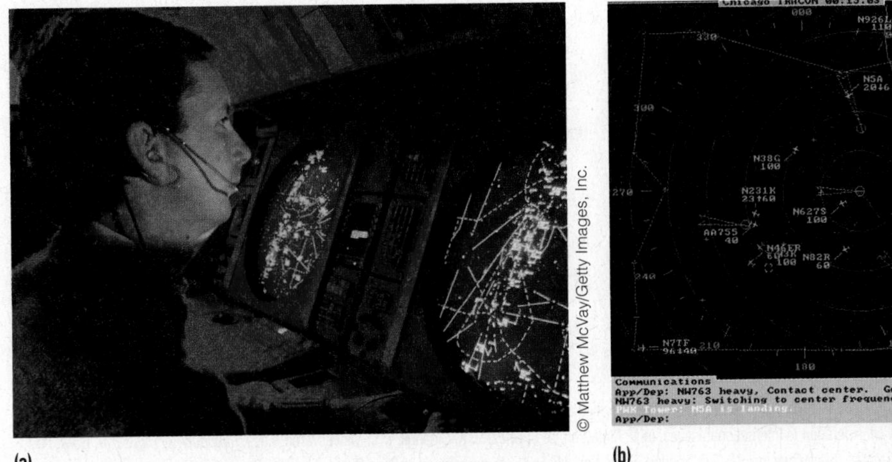

(a) (b)

One way to enhance validity is to make experimental conditions as similar as possible to actual work situations. (a) Actual radar being used by an air traffic controller; (b) a simulated radar screen designed for an experiment

It is not always possible to assign participants randomly to a condition. For example, an organization might institute a new pay plan at one plant location but not at another. Or the researcher would assess employee satisfaction with an existing pay plan, then the organization would change the pay plan, and the researcher would assess satisfaction again with the new plan. This would be called a quasi-experimental design.

In the experimental and quasi-experimental designs described above, the pay plan was a "treatment" or condition. Nonexperimental designs do not include any "treatment" or conditions. In a nonexperimental design, the researcher would simply gather information about the effects of a pay plan without introducing any condition or treatment. Researchers often use the term "independent variable" to describe the treatment or antecedent condition and the term "dependent variable" to describe the subsequent behavior of the research participant. Spector (2001) identifies two common nonexperimental designs as the **observational design** and the **survey design**. In the observational design, the researcher watches an employee's behavior and makes a record about what is observed. An observer might, for example, study communication patterns and worker efficiency by recording the number of times a worker communicates with a supervisor in a given time period. Alternatively, in the survey design, the worker is asked to complete a questionnaire describing typical interaction frequency with his or her supervisor. Table 2.1 presents an outline of the more common research designs in I-O psychology.

Observational design The researcher observes employee behavior and systematically records what is observed.

Survey design Research strategy in which participants are asked to complete a questionnaire or survey.

Because of the increasing use of the Internet for survey research, one might question whether online surveys and paper-and-pencil surveys produce equivalent results. Although differences in administration mode are not dramatic, it does appear that younger respondents prefer an online to a paper-and-pencil survey (Church, 2001). We will discuss the strengths and weaknesses of various research designs in greater detail in Chapter 7 when we consider the evaluation of training programs.

The various research designs we have described in this chapter are not used with equal frequency. Schaubroeck and Kuehn (1992) found that 67 percent of published studies conducted by I-O psychologists were done in the field and 33 percent in a laboratory. Laboratory-based studies were usually experimental in design and used students as participants. Most field studies were not experimental and typically used employees as participants. In a follow-up study, Spector (2001) found very similar results.

There are several reasons for the prevalence of nonexperimental field research in I-O psychology. The first is the limited extent to which a laboratory experiment can reasonably

TABLE 2.1 **Common Research Designs in I-O Psychology**

DESIGN	*DESCRIPTION*
Experimental Laboratory Field	Random assignment of participants to conditions
Quasi-experimental	Nonrandom assignment of participants to conditions
Nonexperimental Survey Observational	No unique conditions for participants

SOURCE: Adapted from Spector, P. E. (2001). Research methods in industrial and organizational psychology: Data collection and data analysis with special consideration to international issues. In N. Anderson, D. S. Ones, H. K. Sinangil, & C. Viswesvaran (Eds.), *Handbook of industrial, work, and organizational psychology* (pp. 10–26). London: Sage. Republished with permission of Sage Publications Inc Books; permission conveyed through Copyright Clearance Center, Inc.

simulate "work" as it is experienced by a worker. The essence of laboratory research is control over conditions. This means that the work environment tends to be artificial and sterile, and the research deals with narrow aspects of behavior. Another, related reason is that experiments are difficult to do in the field because workers can seldom be randomly assigned to conditions or treatments. The goal of a real-life business organization is an economic one, not a scientific one. Finally, laboratory experiments often involve "samples of convenience" (i.e., students), and there is considerable doubt that the behavior of student participants engaging in simulated work reasonably represents the behavior of actual workers. Laboratory studies provide excellent methods of control and are more likely to lead to causal explanations. Field studies permit researchers to study behaviors difficult to simulate in a laboratory, but cause–effect relationships are more difficult to examine in such field studies.

Recently, there has been spirited debate (Landy, 2008a,b; Rudolph & Baltes, 2008; Wessel & Ryan, 2008) about the concept of stereotyping and its possible role in making work-related decisions. Social psychologists have argued that research on stereotyping shows that women, or older employees, or ethnic minority employees are treated more harshly when it comes to distributing work rewards such as pay increases and promotions. But the lion's share of that research has been conducted with college students who are asked to make decisions about fictitious employees. Some organizational psychologists argue that operational decisions (those involving real managers making decisions about their respective subordinates) provide the best opportunity to study the possible effects of stereotyping, not "artificial" decisions. Unlike the decisions made by managers, those that student participants make have no effect on a real person, are not made public to anyone, do not need to be defended to an employee, are made with little or no training or experience, and do not have the benefit of a deep and broad interaction history with the "employee." Although it is easier and more convenient to do research with students, the conclusions drawn from such research may be too far removed from the real world of work to be of any enduring value.

Methods of Data Collection

Qualitative and Quantitative Research

Quantitative methods Rely on tests, rating scales, questionnaires, and physiological measures and yield numerical results.

Historically, I-O psychology, particularly the "I" part of I-O, has used **quantitative methods** for measuring important variables or behavior. Quantitative methods rely heavily on tests, rating scales, questionnaires, and physiological measures (Stone-Romero, 2002). They yield results in terms of numbers. They can be contrasted with more **qualitative methods** of investigation, which generally produce flow diagrams and narrative descriptions of events or processes, rather than "numbers" as measures. Qualitative methods include procedures like observations, interviews, case studies, and analysis of diaries or written documents. The preference for quantitative over qualitative research can be attributed, at least in part, to the apparent preference of journal editors for quantitative research (Hemingway, 2001), possibly because numbers and statistical analyses conform to a traditional view of science (Symon, Cassell, & Dickson, 2000). As an example, fewer than .3 percent of the articles published in the *Journal of Applied Psychology* since 1990 would be classified as qualitative (Marchel & Owens, 2007). You may be surprised to know that in the early days of psychology, the "experimental method" was **introspection**, in which the participant was also the experimenter, recording his or her experiences in completing an experimental task. This method would be considered hopelessly subjective by today's standards. Some (e.g., Marchel & Owens, 2007) have speculated that the founding fathers of psychology would be unable to find academic employment today!

Qualitative methods Rely on observations, interviews, case studies, and analysis of diaries or written documents and produce flow diagrams and narrative descriptions of events or processes.

Introspection Early scientific method in which the participant was also the experimenter, recording his or her experiences in completing an experimental task; considered very subjective by modern standards.

You will notice that we described the issue as qualitative *and* quantitative research, as opposed to qualitative *versus* quantitative research. The two are not mutually exclusive (Rogelberg, 2002). As an example of qualitative research, consider an extended observation of a worker, which might include videotaped episodes of performance. That qualitative video record could easily be used to develop a quantitative frequency count of a particular behavior.

Much of the resistance to qualitative research is the result of viewing it as excessively subjective. This concern is misplaced. All methods of research ultimately require interpretation, regardless of whether they are quantitative or qualitative. The researcher is an explorer, trying to develop an understanding of the phenomenon he or she has chosen to investigate, and, in so doing, should use all of the information available, regardless of its form. The key is in combining information from multiple sources to develop that theory. Rogelberg and Brooks-Laber (2002) refer to this as **triangulation**—looking for converging information from different sources. Detailed descriptions of qualitative research methods have been presented by Locke and Golden-Biddle (2002) and Bachiochi and Weiner (2002). Stone-Romero (2002) presents an excellent review of the variations of research designs in I-O psychology, as well as their strengths and weaknesses.

Triangulation Approach in which researchers seek converging information from different sources.

The Importance of Context in Interpreting Research

The added value of qualitative research is that it helps to identify the *context* for the behavior in question (Johns, 2001a). Most experiments control variables that might "complicate" the research and, in the process, eliminate "context." In doing so, this control can actually make the behavior in question *less*, not *more*, comprehensible. Consider the following examples:

1. A study of patient care teams directed by a nurse-manager found that there was a strong association among coaching, goal setting, team satisfaction, medical errors by the team, and the performance of the team as perceived by team members. Unfortunately, however, the association was positive: The higher the ratings of each of the first three elements, the greater the number of medical errors by that team! By collecting qualitative data through interviews and observations, the researchers were able to unravel this seeming mystery. It turned out that the most positive teams (more coaching, goal setting, satisfaction) were also those most willing to acknowledge errors and use them to learn, while the least positive teams (less coaching, fewer goals, lower satisfaction) covered up errors and did not learn from them (Hackman, 2003).

2. A study of convenience stores found that those stores with less friendly salespersons had higher sales than the stores with more friendly sales staff (Sutton & Rafaeli, 1988). Further investigation revealed that, because the less friendly stores were busier to start with, the staff had less time to be friendly. It was not that a nasty demeanor in a salesperson spurred sales.
3. You have already been introduced to the Hawthorne studies. They were largely completed by 1935. Nevertheless, controversy continues to surround their interpretation (Olson, Verley, Santos, & Salas, 2004). At the simplest level, it appeared that simply paying attention to workers improved productivity. But things are not that simple. The studies were carried out during the Great Depression, when simply having a job—any job—was considered lifesaving. Additionally, the psychologist who described these studies to the popular press was an avowed anti-unionist (Griffin, Landy, & Mayocchi, 2002) and inclined to highlight any practice that contradicted the position of the union movement. If there were consistent productivity increases—and it is not clear that there were—these changes could not be understood without a broader appreciation for the context in which they occurred and were reported.

In each of these examples, the critical variable was *context*. It was the situation in which the behavior was embedded that provided the explanation. Had the researchers not investigated the context, each of these studies might have resulted in exactly the wrong policy change (i.e., don't coach or set goals for medical teams, don't hire friendly sales clerks). Context enhances the comprehensibility and, ultimately, the value of research findings.

Generalizability and Control in Research

Generalize To apply the results from one study or sample to other participants or situations.

Generalizability

One of the most important issues in conducting research is how widely the results can be generalized. There is a relatively simple answer to that question. An investigator can **generalize** results to areas that have been sampled in the research study. Consider Figure 2.1, which is made up of concentric circles representing various factors or variables that might be sampled in a study. The first area for sampling might be participants or employees. If our research sample is representative of a larger population (e.g., all individuals who work for the organization and have a given job title), then we can feel more confident in generalizing to this larger population of participants who *might have been* in our study. The next circle represents job titles. If the job titles of the participants in our study are a representative sample of the population of job titles that exist in a particular company, then we can be more confident about generalizing to this larger population of jobs. The next circle represents time. If we have collected data at several different points in time, we can feel more confident in generalizing across time periods than we would if all the data came from one point in time. The final circle represents organizations. If we have collected our data from many different organizations, we can be more confident in extending our findings beyond a single organization.

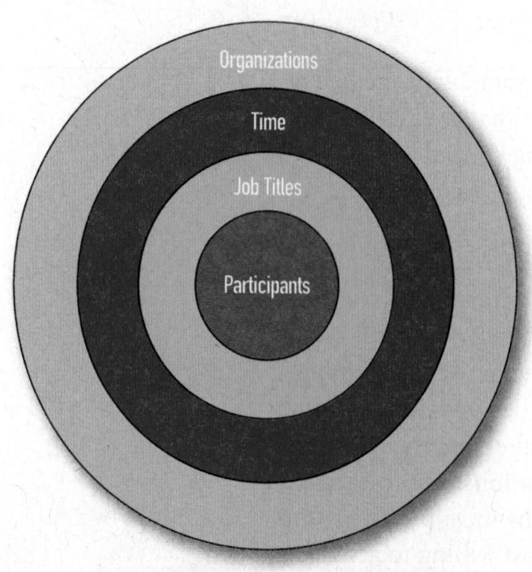

FIGURE 2.1 Sampling Domains for I-O Research

CASE STUDY 2.1 TRIANGULATION: THE FINANCIAL CONSULTANT

In Chapter 4, we will consider the topic of **job analysis**. Job analysis is a process used by I-O psychologists to gain understanding of a job. It includes an investigation of the tasks and duties that define the job, the human attributes necessary to perform the job, and the context in which that job is performed. Job analysis typically involves the combination of data from many different sources in coming to a complete understanding, or theory, of the job in question.

Job analysis Process that determines the important tasks of a job and the human attributes necessary to successfully perform those tasks.

Consider the job of a financial consultant or stockbroker who advises individual private investors on how to invest their money. Large financial investment firms employ thousands of these financial consultants to provide service to their high-end clients. Suppose you were hired as an I-O psychologist to study and "understand" the job of a financial consultant with an eye toward developing a recruiting, selection, and training program for such individuals.

How might you achieve this understanding? First, you might examine what the organization has to say about the job on its website and in its recruiting materials. Then you might talk with senior executives of the organization about the role the financial consultant plays in the success of the organization. Next you might tour the country interviewing and observing a sample of financial consultants as they do their work, in the office and outside the office. You might also ask them to show you their daily appointment calendars and answer questions about the entries in these calendars. As part of this experience, you might spend several days with a single financial consultant and observe the variety of tasks he or she performs. Next you might interview the immediate managers of financial consultants and explore their views of what strategies lead to success or failure for consultants.

You might also interview retired financial consultants, as well as financial consultants who left their consulting positions with the company to become managers. Finally, you might ask a sample of financial consultants and managers to complete a questionnaire in which they rate the relative importance and frequency of the tasks that consultants perform, as well as the abilities and personal characteristics necessary to perform those tasks successfully. By gathering and interpreting this wealth of information, you will gain an excellent understanding of the job. Each of the methods of investigation gave you additional information. No one method was more important than any other method, and no method alone would have been sufficient to achieve an understanding of the position. This is the type of triangulation that Rogelberg and Brooks-Laber (2002) advocate.

Let's take a concrete example. Suppose you conducted a research study to assess how well recent college graduates from the United States would adapt to working overseas. How would you maximize the generalizability of your conclusions? You might take the following steps:

1. Sample graduates from many different educational institutions.
2. Sample graduates from several different graduating classes.
3. Sample graduates with degrees in a wide variety of majors.
4. Sample graduates who work for many different companies.
5. Sample graduates who work in many different departments within those companies.
6. Sample graduates assigned to many different countries outside the United States.

If you were able to achieve this sampling, your results would be quite generalizable. But, of course, sampling as wide ranging as this is time consuming and expensive, so compromises are often made. Every time a compromise is made (e.g., data are gathered from graduates of only one institution, or from only one graduating class, or from only one major, or who were assigned to only one country), the generalizability of the results is reduced. Finally, do not confuse sample size with sample representativeness. A large but nonrepresentative sample is much less valuable for purposes of generalizability than a smaller but representative sample.

Control

When research is conducted in the field, events and variables can often obscure the results. The primary reason why psychologists do laboratory studies, or experiments, is to eliminate these distracting variables through **experimental control**. If you tried to study problem-solving behaviors among industrial workers in the workplace, you might find your study disrupted by telephone calls, machine breakdowns, missing team members, and urgent requests from a supervisor. But if you conducted the same study in a laboratory, none of those distractions would be present. By using this form of control, you eliminate possible confounding influences that might make your results less reliable or harder to interpret.

Experimental control Characteristic of research in which possible confounding influences that might make results less reliable or harder to interpret are eliminated; often easier to establish in laboratory studies than in field studies.

Unfortunately, the strength of experimental control is also its weakness. As we discussed earlier in the chapter, experimental control can make the task being studied sterile and reduce its practical value. Consider the physical trainer who employs exercise machines to isolate muscles versus the trainer who prefers to use free weights in training. The first trainer is exercising experimental control, whereas the second is not. The free-weight trainer knows that in everyday life you cannot use isolated muscle groups. When a heavy box you are carrying shifts, you have to compensate for that shift with abs and back muscles and leg muscles. Training without control (i.e., with free weights) prepares you for that real-life challenge; training with exercise machines may not. To return to our research situation, there are times when the lack of experimental control actually enhances what we learn about a behavior.

There is another form of control that can be equally powerful. It is known as **statistical control**. As an example, suppose you wanted to study the relationship between job satisfaction and leadership styles in a company and had at your disposal a representative sample of employees from many different departments, of both genders, of varying age, and of varying educational backgrounds. Suppose you were concerned that the relationship of interest (job satisfaction and leadership style) might be obscured by other influences, such as the employees' age, gender, educational level, or home department. You could use statistical techniques to control for the influence of these other variables, allowing you to concentrate exclusively on the relationship between satisfaction and leadership style. In I-O psychology, statistical control is much more common and more realistic than experimental control.

Statistical control Using statistical techniques to control for the influence of certain variables. Such control allows researchers to concentrate exclusively on the primary relationships of interest.

Ethical Behavior in I-O Psychology

Physicians swear to abide by the Hippocratic oath, whose first provision is to "do no harm." This is the keystone of their promise to behave ethically. Most professions have ethical standards that educate their members regarding appropriate and inappropriate behavior, and psychology is no exception. Every member of the American Psychological Association agrees to follow the ethical standards published by that governing body (APA, 2002). If a member violates a standard, he or she can be dropped from membership in the organization. Although I-O psychologists do not have a separate code of ethics, SIOP has endorsed a collection of 61 cases that illustrate ethical issues likely to arise in situations that an I-O psychologist might encounter (Lowman, 2006). In addition to the APA principles and the case book that SIOP provides, other societies (e.g., Academy of Management, 1990; Society for Human Resources Management, 1990) publish ethical standards that are relevant for I-O psychologists.

Formulating ethical guidelines for I-O psychologists can be very challenging because the work of an I-O psychologist is incredibly varied. Issues include personnel decisions, safety, organizational commitment, training, and motivation, to name but a few. The issues may be addressed as part of a consulting engagement, in-house job duties, or research. Because every situation is different, there is no simple formula for behaving ethically (although the "do no harm" standard never ceases to apply). The SIOP case book addresses topics as varied as testing, validity studies, result reporting, layoffs, sexual harassment, employee assistance programs, data collection, confidentiality, and billing practices. In addition, Joel Lefkowitz (2003) has published a text on the broad issues of values and ethics in I-O psychology. It covers psychological practice generally, as well as issues specific to I-O psychology. Table 2.2 describes some of the ways in which an I-O psychologist can contribute to ethical practice by organizations. More recently, Lefkowitz (2012) contributed a chapter on ethics in I-O psychology in the *APA Handbook of Ethics in Psychology*.

As more and more organizations expand their operations to include international and multinational business dealings, the ethical dilemmas for I-O psychologists will become much more complex. Suppose an I-O psychologist works for an organization that exploits inexpensive Third World labor in one of its divisions. How can the psychologist balance his or her duty to the employer and shareholder (i.e., enhance profitability) with the notion of doing no harm (Lefkowitz, 2004)? Suppose a psychologist is asked to design a leadership training program emphasizing the use of hierarchical and formal power for a culture that is low in power distance or a motivational program based on interpersonal competition for a culture that would be characterized as noncompetitive (i.e., in Hofstede's terms,

TABLE 2.2 **Potential Roles Available to the I-O Psychologist and Other Human Resource Managers with Respect to Ethical Problems**

ROLES	*DESCRIPTION*
Advisory	Advising organizational members on ethical standards and policies
Monitoring	Monitoring actions/behaviors for compliance with laws, policies, and ethical standards
Educator	Instructing or distributing information regarding ethical principles and organizational policies
Advocate	Acting on behalf of individual employees or other organizational stakeholders, and protecting employees from managerial reprisals
Investigative	Investigating apparent or alleged unethical situations or complaints
Questioning	Questioning or challenging the ethical aspects of managers' decisions
Organizational	Explaining or justifying the organization's actions when confronted by agents external to the organization
Model	Modeling ethical practices to contribute to an organizational norm and climate of ethical behavior

SOURCE: Lefkowitz, J. (2003). *Ethics and values in industrial-organizational psychology*. Mahwah, NJ: Lawrence Erlbaum Associates. © 2003 by Taylor & Francis Group LLC–Books. Reproduced with permission of Taylor & Francis LLC-Books. Permission conveyed through Copyright Clearance Center, Inc.

feminine). Is it ethical to impose the culture of one nation on another through HR practices? There are no clear answers to these questions, but as I-O psychologists expand their influence to global applications, issues such as these will become more salient.

Although it is not universally true, unethical or immoral behavior is generally accompanied by a clash between personal values and organizational goals in which the organizational goals prevail. Several business schools are now offering courses to MBA students that are intended to bring personal values and organizational behavior into closer alignment (Alboher, 2008). Lefkowitz (2008) makes a similar argument, pointing out that although I-O psychologists profess a strong commitment to understanding *human* behavior, they may forget the human part of the equation in favor of the corporate economic objectives. He proposes that to be a true profession, I-O psychology needs to adopt and reflect societal responsibilities. As an example, rather than simply assisting in a downsizing effort, the I-O psychologist should see downsizing in the larger context of unemployment and all of its consequences—both individual and societal. Seen from this perspective, the work by Stuart Carr and his colleagues in the arena of world poverty (mentioned in Chapter 1) represents the moral and ethical high ground for I-O psychologists. Not every I-O psychologist need address poverty or hunger or illiteracy or environmental sustainability, but they should at least be aware that their interventions often have consequences that are considerably broader than the specific task they have undertaken. Instead of simply asking if a selection system is effective or if a motivational program is likely to increase productivity, the I-O psychologist might ask the broader question: Is this the *right* thing to do (Lefkowitz, 2008)?

MODULE 2.2 SUMMARY

- Research designs may be experimental, quasi-experimental, or nonexperimental; two common nonexperimental designs are observation and survey. About two-thirds of I-O research uses nonexperimental designs.
- Quantitative research yields results in terms of numbers, whereas qualitative research tends to produce flow diagrams and descriptions. The two are not mutually exclusive, however; the process of triangulation involves combining results from different sources, which may include both kinds of research.
- The results of research can be generalized to areas included in the study; thus, the more areas a study includes, the greater its generalizability. Researchers eliminate distracting variables by using experimental and statistical controls.
- Ethical standards for I-O psychologists are set forth by the APA, SIOP, and other organizations such as the Society for Human Resource Management and the Academy of Management. The overriding ethical principle is "do no harm."

KEY TERMS

research design
experimental design
quasi-experimental design
nonexperimental design
observational design
survey design
quantitative methods
qualitative methods
introspection
triangulation
job analysis
generalize
experimental control
statistical control

MODULE 2.3

Data Analysis

Descriptive and Inferential Statistics

Descriptive Statistics

In our discussion of research, we have considered two issues thus far: how to design a study to collect data and how to collect those data. Assuming we have been successful at both of those tasks, we now need to analyze those data to determine what they may tell us about our initial theory, hypothesis, or speculation. We can analyze the data we have gathered for two purposes. The first is simply to describe the distribution of scores or numbers we have collected. A distribution of numbers simply means that the numbers are arrayed along two axes. The horizontal axis is the score or number axis running from low to high scores. The vertical axis is usually the frequency axis, which indicates how many individuals achieved each score on the horizontal axis. The statistical methods to accomplish such a description are referred to as **descriptive statistics**. You have probably encountered this type of statistical analysis in other courses, so we will simply summarize the more important characteristics for you. Consider the two distributions of test scores in Figure 2.2. Look at the overall shapes of those distributions. One distribution is high and narrow; the other is lower and wider. In the left graph, the distribution's center (48) is easy to determine; in the right graph, the distribution's center is not as clear unless we specify the central tendency measure of interest. One distribution is bell shaped or symmetric, while the other is lopsided. Three measures or characteristics can be used to describe any score distribution: **measures of central tendency**, **variability**, and **skew**. Positive skew means that the scores or observations are bunched at the bottom of the score range; negative skew means that scores or observations are bunched at the top of the score range. As examples, if the next test you take in this course is very easy, there will be a negative skew to score distribution; if the test is very hard, the scores are likely to be positively skewed.

Measures of central tendency include the **mean**, the **mode**, and the **median**. The mean is the arithmetic average of the scores, the mode is the most frequently occurring score, and the median is the middle score (the score that 50 percent of the remaining scores fall above and the other 50 percent of the remaining scores fall below). As you can see, the two distributions in Figure 2.2 have different means, modes, and medians. In addition, the two distributions vary on their lopsidedness, or skewness. The left distribution has no

Descriptive statistics Statistics that summarize, organize, and describe a sample of data.

Measure of central tendency Statistic that indicates where the center of a distribution is located. Mean, median, and mode are measures of central tendency.

Variability The extent to which scores in a distribution vary.

Skew The extent to which scores in a distribution are lopsided or tend to fall on the left or right side of the distribution.

Mean The arithmetic average of the scores in a distribution; obtained by summing all of the scores in a distribution and dividing by the sample size.

Mode The most common or frequently occurring score in a distribution.

Median The middle score in a distribution.

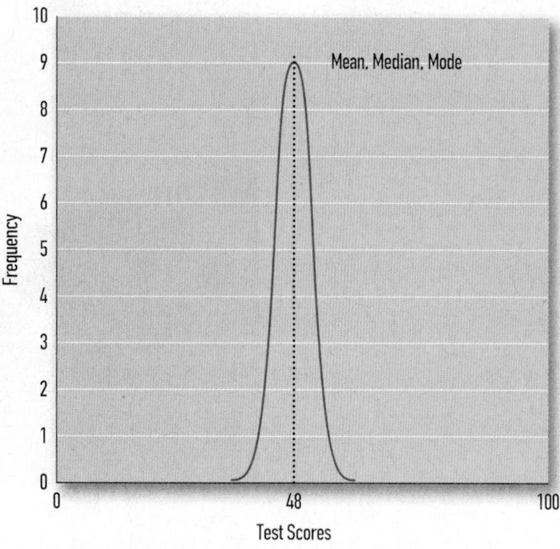

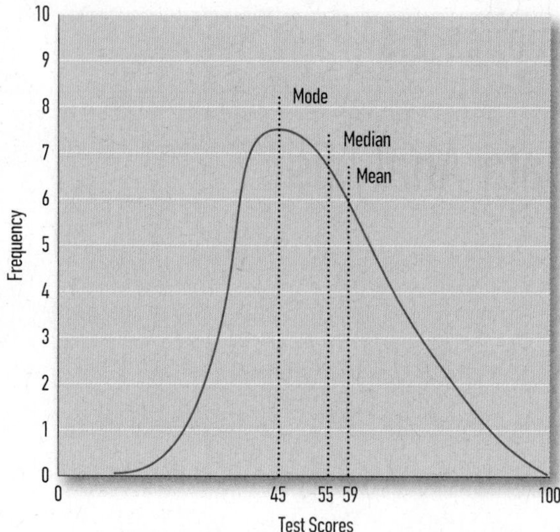

FIGURE 2.2 Two Score Distributions ($N = 30$)

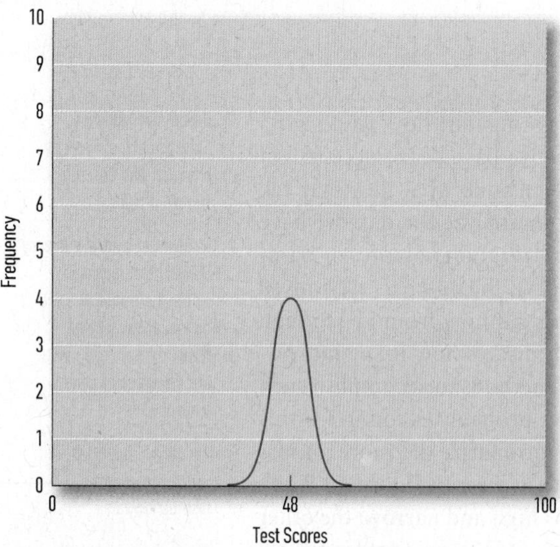

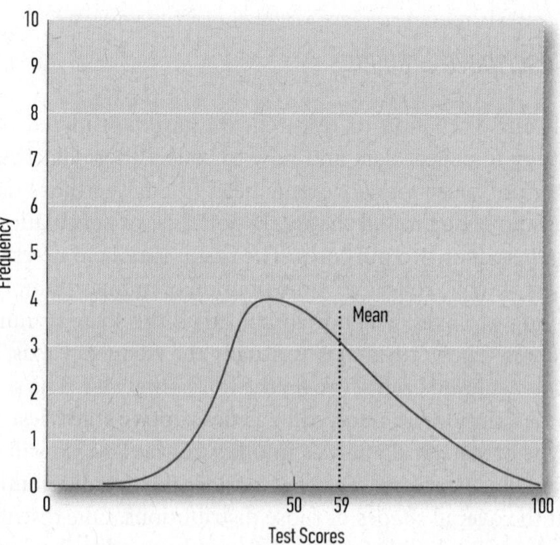

FIGURE 2.3 Two Score Distributions ($N = 10$)

skew; the right distribution is positively skewed, with some high scores pulling the mean to the positive (right) side.

Another common descriptive statistic is the standard deviation, or the variance of a distribution. In Figure 2.3, you can see that one distribution covers a larger score range and is wider than the other. We can characterize a distribution by looking at the extent to which the scores deviate from the mean score. The typical amount of deviation from a mean score is the standard deviation. Since distributions often vary from each other simply as a result of the units of measure (e.g., one distribution is a measure of inches, while another is a measure of loudness), sometimes it is desirable to standardize the distributions so that they all have means of .00 and standard (or average) deviations of 1.00. The variance of a distribution is simply the squared standard deviation.

Inferential Statistics

SOURCE: © The New Yorker Collection 1989 Mick Stevens from cartoonbank.com. All rights reserved.

In the studies that you will encounter in the rest of this text, the types of analyses used are not descriptive, but inferential. When we conduct a research study, we do it for a reason. We have a theory or hypothesis to examine. It may be a hypothesis that accidents are related to personality characteristics, or that people with higher scores on a test of mental ability perform their jobs better than those with lower scores, or that team members in small teams are happier with their work than team members in large teams. In each of these cases, we design a study and collect data in order to come to some conclusion, to draw an inference about a relationship. In research, we use findings from the sample we collected to make inferences to a larger population. Once again, in other courses, you have likely been introduced to some basic **inferential statistics**. Statistical tests such as the *t* test, analysis of variance or *F* test, or chi-square test can be used to see whether two or more groups of participants (e.g., an experimental and a control group) tend to differ on some variable of interest. For example, we can examine the means of the two groups of scores in Figure 2.3 to see if they are different beyond what we might expect as a result of chance. If I tell you that the group with the lower mean score represents high school graduates and the group with the higher mean score represents college graduates, and I further tell you that the means are statistically significantly different from what would be found with simple random or chance variation, you might draw the inference that education is associated with higher test scores. The statistical test used to support that conclusion (e.g., a *t* test of mean differences) would be considered an inferential test.

Inferential statistics Statistics used to aid the researcher in testing hypotheses and making inferences from sample data to a larger sample or population.

Statistical Significance

Two scores, derived from two different groups, might be different, even at the third decimal place. How can we be sure that the difference is a "real" one—that it exceeds a difference we might expect as a function of chance alone? If we examined the mean scores of many different test groups, such as the two displayed in Figure 2.3, we would almost never find that the means were *exactly* the same. A convention has been adopted to define when a difference or an inferential statistic is significant. **Statistical significance** is defined in terms of a probability statement. To say that a finding of difference between two groups is significant at the 5 percent level, or a probability of .05, is to say that a difference that large would be expected to occur only 5 times out of 100 as a result of chance alone. If the difference between the means was even larger, we might conclude that a difference this large might be expected to occur only 1 time out of 100 as a result of chance alone. This latter result would be reported as a difference at the 1 percent level, or a probability of .01. As the probability goes down (e.g., from .05 to .01), we become more confident that the difference is a real difference. It is important to keep in mind that the significance level addresses only the confidence that we can have that a result is not due to chance. It says nothing about the strength of an association or the practical importance of the result. The standard, or threshold, for significance has been set at .05 or lower as a rule of thumb. Thus, unless a result would occur only 5 or fewer times out of 100 as a result of chance alone, we do not label the difference as statistically significant.

Statistical significance Indicates that the probability of the observed statistic is less than the stated significance level adopted by the researcher (commonly $p < .05$). A statistically significant finding indicates that the results found are unlikely to have occurred by chance, and thus the null hypothesis (i.e., hypothesis of no effect) is rejected.

I-O psychologists have vigorously debated the value of significance testing (Bonett & Wright, 2007; Murphy, 1997; Schmidt, 1996). Critics argue that the .05 level is arbitrary and that even higher levels—up to .10, for example—can still have practical significance. This is a very complex statistical debate that we will not cover here, but it is important to remember that you are unlikely to encounter studies in scientific journals with probability values higher than .05. The critics argue that there are many interesting findings and theories that never see the scientific light of day because of this arbitrary criterion for statistical significance.

The Concept of Statistical Power

Many studies have a very small number of participants in them. This makes it very difficult to find statistical significance even when there is a "true" relationship among variables. In Figure 2.3 we have reduced our two samples in Figure 2.2 from 30 to 10 by randomly dropping 20 participants from each group. The differences are no longer statistically significant. But from our original study with 30 participants, we know that the differences between means are not due to chance. Nevertheless, the convention we have adopted for defining significance prevents us from considering the new difference to be significant, even though the mean values and the differences between those means are identical to what they were in Figure 2.2.

Statistical power The likelihood of finding a statistically significant difference when a true difference exists.

The concept of **statistical power** deals with the likelihood of finding a statistically significant difference when a true difference exists. The smaller the sample size, the lower the power to *detect* a true or real difference. In practice, this means that researchers may be drawing the wrong inferences (e.g., that there is no association) when sample sizes are too small. The issue of power is often used by the critics of significance testing to illustrate what is wrong with such conventions. Schmidt and Hunter (2002b) argued that the typical power of a psychological study is low enough that more than 50 percent of the studies in the literature do not detect a difference between groups or the effect of an independent variable on a dependent variable when one exists. Thus, adopting a convention that requires an effect to be "statistically significant" at the .05 level greatly distorts what we read in journals and how we interpret what we do read.

Power calculations can be done before a study is ever initiated, informing the researcher of the number of participants that should be included in the study in order to have a reasonable chance of detecting an association (Cohen, 1988, 1994; Murphy & Myors, 2004). Research studies can be time consuming and expensive. It would be silly to conduct a study that could not detect an association even if one were there. The power concept also provides a warning against casually dismissing studies that do not achieve "statistical significance" before looking at sample sizes. If the sample sizes are small, we may never know whether or not there is a real effect or difference between groups.

Correlation and Regression

As we saw in the discussion about research design, there are many situations in which experiments are not feasible. This is particularly true in I-O psychology. It would be unethical, for example, to manipulate a variable that would influence well-being at work, with some conditions expected to reduce well-being and others to enhance well-being. The most common form of research is to observe and measure natural variation in the variables of interest and look for associations among those variables. Through the process of **measurement**, we can assign numbers to individuals. These numbers represent the person's standing on a variable of interest. Examples of these numbers are a test score, an index of

Measurement Assigning numbers to characteristics of individuals or objects according to rules.

stress or job satisfaction, a performance rating, or a grade in a training program. We may wish to examine the relationship between two of these variables to predict one variable from the other. For example, if we are interested in the association between an individual's cognitive ability and training success, we can calculate the association between those two variables for a group of participants. If the association is statistically significant, then we can predict training success from cognitive ability. The stronger the association between the two variables, the better the prediction we are able to make from one variable to another. The statistic or measure of association most commonly used is the **correlation coefficient.**

Correlation coefficient Statistic assessing the bivariate, linear association between two variables. Provides information about both the magnitude (numerical value) and the direction (+ or −) of the relationship between two variables.

The Concept of Correlation

The best way to appreciate the concept of correlation is graphically. Examine the hypothetical data in Figure 2.4. The vertical axis of that figure represents training grades. The horizontal axis represents a score on a test of cognitive ability. For both axes, higher numbers represent higher scores. This graph is called a **scatterplot** because it plots the scatter of the scores. Each dot represents the two scores achieved by an individual. The 40 dots represent 40 people. Notice the association between test scores and training grades. As test scores increase, training grades tend to increase as well. In high school algebra, this association would have been noted as the slope, or "rise over run," meaning how much rise (increase on the vertical axis) is associated with one unit of run (increase on the horizontal axis). In statistics, the name for this form of association is correlation, and the index of correlation or association is called the correlation coefficient. You will also notice that there is a solid straight line that goes through the scatterplot. This line (technically known as the **regression line**) is the straight line that best "fits" the scatterplot. The line can also be presented as an equation that specifies where the line intersects the vertical axis and what the slope of the line is.

Scatterplot Graph used to plot the scatter of scores on two variables; used to display the correlational relationship between two variables.

Regression line Straight line that best "fits" the scatterplot and describes the relationship between the variables in the graph; can also be presented as an equation that specifies where the line intersects the vertical axis and what the angle or slope of the line is.

As you can see from Figure 2.4, the actual slope of the line that depicts the association is influenced by the units of measurement. If we plotted training grades against years of formal education, the slope of the line might look quite different, as is depicted in Figure 2.5, where the slope of the line is much less steep or severe. For practical purposes, the regression line can be quite useful. It can be used to predict what value on the Y variable (in Figure 2.4, training grades) might be expected for someone with a particular score on the X variable (here, cognitive test scores). Using the scatterplot that appears in Figure 2.4, we might predict that an individual who achieved a test score of 75 could be expected to also get a training grade of 75 percent. We might use that prediction to make decisions about whom to enroll in a training program. Since we would not want to enroll someone who might be expected to fail the training program (in our case, receive a training grade of less than 60 percent), we might limit enrollment to only those applicants who achieve a score of 54 or better on the cognitive ability test.

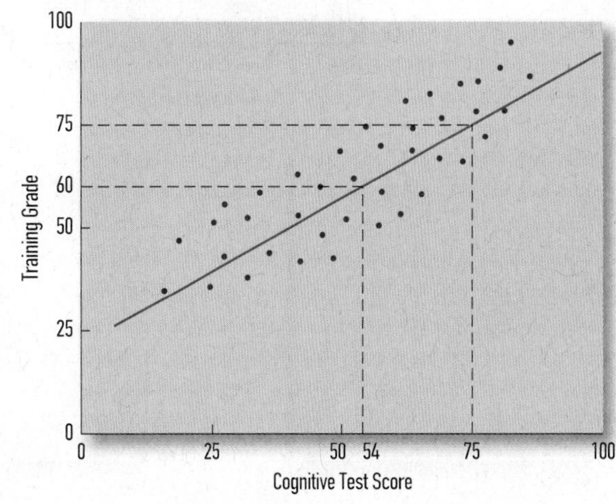

FIGURE 2.4 Correlation between Test Scores and Training Grades

The Correlation Coefficient

For ease of communication and for purposes of further analysis, the correlation coefficient is calculated in such a way that it always permits the same inference, regardless of the variables that are used. Its absolute value will always range between .00 and 1.00. A high value (e.g., .85) represents a strong association and a lower value (e.g., .15)

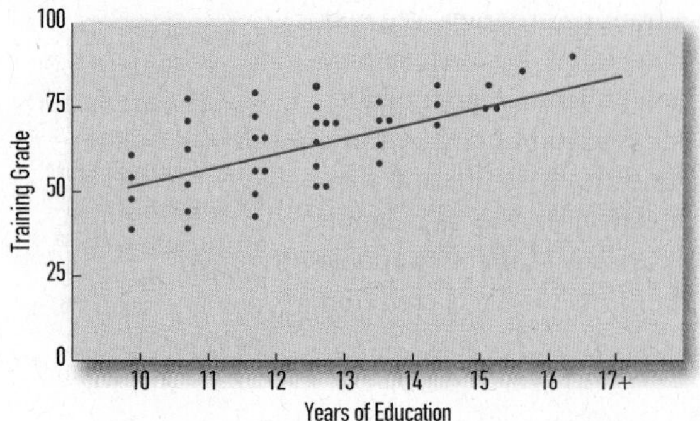

FIGURE 2.5 **Correlation between Years of Education and Training Grades**

represents a weaker association. A value of .00 means that there is no association between two variables. Generally speaking, in I-O psychology, correlations in the range of .10 are considered close to trivial, while correlations of .40 or above are considered substantial.

Correlation coefficients have two distinct parts. The first part is the actual value or magnitude of the correlation (ranging from .00 to 1.00). The second part is the *sign* (+ or −) that precedes the numerical value. A positive (+) correlation means that there is a positive association between the variables. In our examples, as test scores and years of education go up, so do training grades. A negative (−) correlation means that as one variable goes up, the other variable tends to go down. An example of a negative correlation would be the association between age and visual acuity. As people get older, their uncorrected vision tends to get worse. In I-O psychology, we often find negative correlations between measures of commitment and absence from work. As commitment goes up, absence tends to go down, and vice versa. Figure 2.6 presents examples of the scatterplots that represent various degrees of positive and negative correlation. You will notice that we have again drawn straight lines to indicate the best-fit straight line that represents the data points.

By examining the scatterplots and the corresponding regression lines, you will notice something else about correlation. As the data points more closely approach the straight line, the correlation coefficients get higher. If all of the data points fell exactly on the line, the correlation coefficient would be 1.00 and there would be a "perfect" correlation between the two variables. We would be able to perfectly predict one variable from

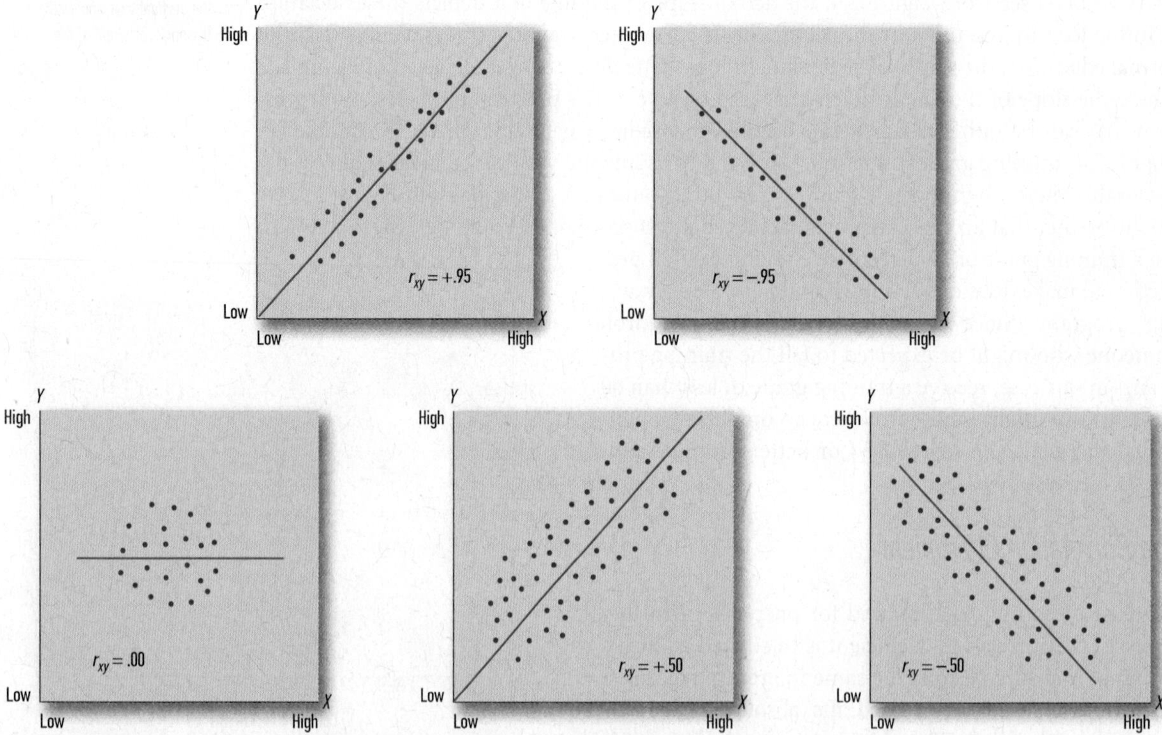

FIGURE 2.6 **Scatterplots Representing Various Degrees of Correlation**

another. As the data points depart more from the straight line, the correlation coefficient gets lower until it reaches .00, indicating no relationship at all between the two variables.

Up to this point, we have been assuming that the relationship between two variables is **linear** (i.e., it can be depicted by a straight line). But the relationship might be **nonlinear** (sometimes called "curvilinear"). Consider the scatterplot depicted in Figure 2.7. In this case, a straight line does not represent the shape of the scatterplot at all. But a curved line does an excellent job. In this case, although the correlation coefficient might be .00, one cannot conclude that there is *no* association between the variables. We can conclude only that there is no *linear* association.

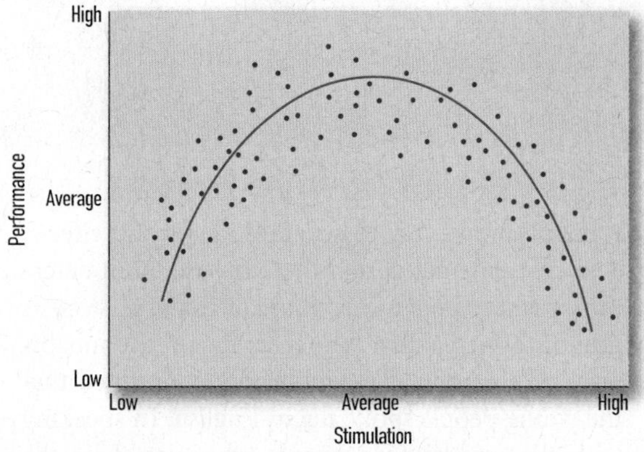

FIGURE 2.7 An Example of a Curvilinear Relationship

In this figure we have identified the two variables in question as "stimulation" and "performance." This scatterplot would tell us that stimulation and performance *are* related to each other, but in a unique way. Up to a point, stimulation aids in successful performance by keeping the employee alert, awake, and engaged. But beyond that point, stimulation makes performance more difficult by turning into information overload, which makes it difficult to keep track of relevant information and to choose appropriate actions. Most statistics texts that deal with correlation offer detailed descriptions of the methods for calculating the strength of a nonlinear correlation or association. But for the purposes of the present discussion, you merely need to know that one of the best ways to detect nonlinear relationships is to look at the scatterplots. As in Figure 2.7, this nonlinear trend will be very apparent if it is a strong one. In I-O psychology, many, if not most, of the associations that interest us are linear.

Linear Relationship between two variables that can be depicted by a straight line.

Nonlinear Relationship between two variables that cannot be depicted by a straight line; sometimes called "curvilinear" and most easily identified by examining a scatterplot.

Multiple Correlation

As we will see in later chapters, there are many situations in which more than one variable is associated with a particular aspect of behavior. For example, you will see that although cognitive ability is an important predictor of job performance, it is not the only predictor. Other variables that might play a role are personality, experience, and motivation. If we were trying to predict job performance, we would want to examine the correlation between performance and all of those variables simultaneously, allowing for the fact that each variable might make an independent contribution to understanding job performance. Statistically, we could accomplish this through an analysis known as multiple correlation. The **multiple correlation coefficient** would represent the overall linear association between several variables (e.g., cognitive ability, personality, experience, motivation) on the one hand and a single variable (e.g., job performance) on the other hand. As you can imagine, these calculations are so complex that their study is appropriate for an advanced course in prediction or statistics. For our purposes in this text, you will simply want to be aware that techniques are available for examining relationships involving multiple predictor variables.

Multiple correlation coefficient Statistic that represents the overall linear association between several variables (e.g., cognitive ability, personality, experience) on the one hand and a single variable (e.g., job performance) on the other hand.

Correlation and Causation

Correlation coefficients simply represent the extent to which two variables are associated. They do not signal any cause–effect relationship. Consider the example of height and weight. They are positively correlated. The taller you are, the heavier you tend to be. But you would

BOX 2.1 EXPERIMENTAL DESIGN AND CAUSATION

It is not always easy to separate causes and effects. The experimental design that you use often determines what conclusions you can draw. A story is told of the researcher who interviewed the inhabitants of a particular neighborhood. He noted that the young people spoke fluent English. In speaking with the middle-aged people who would be the parent generation of the younger people, he found that they spoke English with a slight Italian accent. Finally, he spoke with older people (who would represent the grandparent generation of the youngest group) and heard a heavy Italian accent. The researcher concluded that as you grow older, you develop an Italian accent. It is a safe bet that had the researcher studied a group of people as they aged, he would have come to a very different conclusion, perhaps even an opposite one.

SOURCE: Adapted from Charness, N. (Ed.). (1985). *Aging and human performance*, p. xvii. New York: John Wiley & Sons. Reproduced by permission of John Wiley & Sons.

hardly conclude that weight *causes* height. If that were the case, we could all be as tall as we wish simply by gaining weight.

In an earlier section of this chapter that dealt with the context of research results, we described the anomalous finding that better-functioning medical teams appeared to be associated with more medical errors. Would it make sense, then, to retain only poorer-functioning teams? Similarly, we gave the example of less friendly sales personnel in convenience stores being associated with higher sales. Would it make sense to fire pleasant sales reps? In both cases, it was eventually discovered that a third variable intervened to help us understand the surprising correlation. It became clear that the initial association uncovered was not a causal one.

The question of correlation and causality has an important bearing on many of the topics we will consider in this book. For example, there are many studies that show a positive correlation between the extent to which a leader acts in a considerate manner and the satisfaction of the subordinates of that leader. Because of this correlation, we might be tempted to conclude that consideration *causes* satisfaction. But we might be wrong. Consider two possible alternative explanations for the positive correlation:

A key characteristic of leaders is that they influence followers.

1. Do we know that considerate behavior on the part of a business leader causes worker satisfaction rather than the other way around? It is possible that satisfied subordinates actually elicit considerate behavior on the part of a leader (and conversely, that a leader might "crack down" on dissatisfied work group members).
2. Can we be sure that the positive correlation is not due to a third variable? What if work group productivity was high because of a particularly able and motivated group? High levels of productivity are likely to be associated with satisfaction in workers, and high levels of productivity are likely to allow a leader to concentrate on considerate behaviors instead of pressuring workers for higher production. Thus, a third variable might actually be responsible for the positive correlation between two other variables.

Meta-Analysis

Cancer researchers, clinicians, and patient advocates have engaged in a vigorous debate about whether women aged 40 to 70 can decrease their chances of dying from breast cancer by having an annual mammogram. One expert asserts that the earlier cancer can be detected, the greater the chance of a cure, and that an annual mammogram is the only reliable means of early detection. Another argues that this is not necessarily true and, furthermore, because mammograms deliver potentially harmful radiation, they should be used only every two or three years unless a patient has significant risk factors for the disease. Still another says that mammograms give a false sense of security and may discourage patients from monitoring their own health. Experts on all sides cite multiple studies to support their position. And women are left with an agonizing dilemma: Who is right? What is the "truth"?

Similar confusion exists over the interpretation of study results in psychology topics. You may find *hundreds* of studies on the same topic. Each study is done with a different sample, a different sample size, and a different observational or experimental environment. It is not uncommon for individual studies to come to different conclusions. For example, one study of the relationship between age and job satisfaction may have administered a locally developed satisfaction questionnaire to 96 engineers between the ages of 45 and 57 who were employed by Company X. The study might have found a very slight positive correlation (e.g., +.12) between age and satisfaction. Another study might have distributed a commercially available satisfaction questionnaire to 855 managerial-level employees between the ages of 27 and 64 who worked for Company Y. The second study might have concluded that there was a strong positive correlation (e.g., +.56) between age and satisfaction. A third study of 44 outside sales representatives for Company Z between the ages of 22 and 37 using the same commercially available satisfaction questionnaire might have found a slight negative correlation between age and satisfaction (e.g., −.15). Which study is "right"? How can we choose among them?

Meta-analysis is a statistical method for combining results from many studies to draw a general conclusion (Murphy, 2002b; Schmidt & Hunter, 2002a). Meta-analysis is based on the premise that observed values (like the three correlations shown above) are influenced by **statistical artifacts** (characteristics of the particular study that distort the results). The most influential of these artifacts is sample size. Others include the spread of scores and the reliability of the measures used ("reliability" is a technical term that refers to the consistency or repeatability of a measurement; we will discuss it in the next module of this chapter). Consider the three hypothetical studies we presented above. One had a sample size of 96, the second of 855, and the third of 44. Consider also the range of scores on age for the three studies. The first had an age range from 45 to 57 (12 years). The second study had participants who ranged in age from 27 to 64 (37 years). The participants in the third study ranged from 22 to 37 years of age (15 years, with no "older" employees). Finally, two of the studies used commercially available satisfaction questionnaires, which very likely had high reliability, and the third study used a "locally developed" questionnaire, which may have been less reliable. Using these three studies as examples, we would probably have greater confidence in the study with 855 participants, with an age range of 37 years, that used a more reliable questionnaire. Nevertheless, the other studies tell us something. We're just not sure what that something is because of the influences of the restricted age ranges, the sample sizes, and the reliabilities of the questionnaires.

Meta-analysis Statistical method for combining and analyzing the results from many studies to draw a general conclusion about relationships among variables.

Statistical artifacts Characteristics (e.g., small sample size, unreliable measures) of a particular study that distort the observed results. Researchers can correct for artifacts to arrive at a statistic that represents the "true" relationship between the variables of interest.

In its most basic form, meta-analysis is a complex statistical procedure that includes information about these statistical artifacts (sample size, reliability, and range restriction) and corrects for their influences, producing an estimate of what the actual relationship is across the studies available. The results of a meta-analysis can provide accurate estimates (i.e., population estimates) of the relationships among constructs (e.g., intelligence, job performance) in the meta-analysis, and these estimates do not rely on significance tests. In addition, it is possible to consider variables beyond these statistical artifacts that might also influence results. A good example of such a variable is the nature of the participants in the study. Some studies might conclude that racial or gender stereotypes influence performance ratings, while other studies conclude that there are no such effects. If we separate the studies into those done with student participants and those done with employees of companies, we might discover that stereotypes have a strong influence on student ratings of hypothetical subordinates but have no influence on the ratings of real subordinates by real supervisors.

Meta-analysis can be a very powerful research tool. It combines individual studies that have already been completed and, by virtue of the number and diversity of these studies, has the potential to "liberate" conclusions that were obscure or confusing at the level of the individual study. Meta-analyses are appearing with great regularity in I-O journals and represent a real step forward in I-O research. Between 1980 and 1990, approximately 60 research articles in I-O journals used meta-analytic techniques. Between 1991 and 2008, that number had grown to almost 400. The actual statistical issues involved in meta-analysis are incredibly complex, and they are well beyond what you need to know for this course. Nevertheless, because meta-analysis is becoming so common, you at least need to be familiar with the term. As an example, we will examine the application of meta-analysis to the relationship between tests and job performance in Chapter 3.

Micro-, Macro-, and Meso-Research

In the same spirit in which we introduced you to the term meta-analysis, we need to prepare you for several other terms you may encounter while reading the research literature, particularly the literature associated with organizational topics in the last few chapters of this book. Over the 100-plus years of the development of I-O psychology as a science and area of practice, there has been an evolution of areas of interest from individual differences characteristics to much broader issues related to teams, groups, and entire organizations. In later chapters, you will encounter topics such as team training, group cohesiveness, and organizational culture and climate. In our discussion of Hofstede (2001), Chao and Moon (2005), and others in Chapter 1, we have already introduced you to a very broad level of influence called national culture. As a way of characterizing the research focus of those who are more interested in individual behavior as opposed to those more interested in the behavior of collections of individuals (e.g., teams, departments, organizations), the terms **micro-research** and **macro-research** were introduced, with micro being applied to individual behavior and macro being applied to collective behavior (Smith, Schneider, & Dickson, 2005). But it is obvious that even individual behavior (e.g., job satisfaction) can be influenced by collective variables (e.g., group or team cohesion, reputation of the employer, an organizational culture of openness). As a result, a third term—**meso-research** (meso literally means "middle" or "between")—was introduced to both describe and encourage research intended to integrate micro- and macro-studies (Buckley, Riaz Hamdani, Klotz, & Valcea, 2011; Rousseau & House, 1994).

Micro-research The study of individual behavior.

Macro-research The study of collective behavior.

Meso-research The study of the interaction of individual and collective behavior.

In practice, meso-research is accomplished by including both individual differences data (e.g., cognitive ability test scores) and collective data (the technological emphasis of the company, the team culture, etc.) in the same analysis. This type of analysis, known as multilevel or cross-level analysis (Klein & Kozlowski, 2000), is too complex for a discussion in an introductory text such as this. Nevertheless, you need to be aware that meso-research is becoming much more common for many of the same reasons we described in the consideration of "context" earlier in the chapter. Behavior in organizations cannot be neatly compartmentalized into either micro or macro levels. There are many influences that cut across levels of analysis.

Many important questions about the experience of work require such a multi-level consideration (Drenth & Heller, 2004). Even though we don't expect you to master the analytic techniques of multi-level research, you should at least be able to recognize these terms and understand at a basic level what they are meant to convey. As we will see in the final chapter of this book, the value of multi-level considerations can be seen when studying safety in the workplace. Safe behavior results from an intricate combination of individual worker characteristics (e.g., knowledge of how to work safely and abilities to work safely), work team influences (the extent to which team members reinforce safe work behavior in one another), leader behavior (the extent to which the work group leader adopts and reinforces safe work behavior), and the extent to which senior leaders of the organization acknowledge the importance of safe work behavior (Wallace & Chen, 2006).

MODULE 2.3 SUMMARY

- Descriptive statistics are expressed in terms of absolute values without interpretation. Inferential statistics allow a researcher to identify a relationship between variables. The threshold for statistical significance is .05, or 5 occurrences out of 100. Statistical power comes from using a large enough sample to make results reliable.
- A statistical index that can be used to estimate the strength of a linear relationship between two variables is called a correlation coefficient. The relationship can also be described graphically, in which case a regression line can be drawn to illustrate the relationship. A multiple correlation coefficient indicates the strength of the relationship between one variable and the composite of several other variables.
- Correlation is a means of describing a relationship between two variables. When examining any observed relationship and before drawing any causal inferences, the researcher must consider whether the relationship is due to a third variable or whether the second variable is causing the first rather than vice versa.
- Meta-analysis, the statistical analysis of multiple studies, is a powerful means of estimating relationships in those studies. It is a complex statistical procedure that includes information about statistical artifacts and other variables, and corrects for their influences.

KEY TERMS

descriptive statistics
measure of central tendency
variability
skew
mean
mode
median
inferential statistics
statistical significance
statistical power
measurement
correlation coefficient
scatterplot
regression line
linear
nonlinear
multiple correlation coefficient
meta-analysis
statistical artifacts
micro-research
macro-research
meso-research

MODULE 2.4

Interpretation

So far, we have considered the scientific method, the design of research studies, the collection of data, and the statistical analyses of data. All of these procedures prepare us for the most important part of research and application: the interpretation of the data based on the statistical analyses. The job of the psychologist is to make sense out of what he or she sees. Data collection and analysis are certainly the foundations of making sense, but data do not make sense of themselves; instead, they require someone to interpret them.

Any measurement that we take is a sample of some behavioral domain. A test of reasoning ability, a questionnaire related to satisfaction or stress, and a training grade are all samples of some larger behavioral domain. We hope that these samples are consistent, accurate, and representative of the domains of interest. If they are, then we can make accurate inferences based on these measurements. If they are not, our inferences, and ultimately our decisions, will be flawed, regardless of whether the decision is to hire someone, institute a new motivation program, or initiate a stress reduction program. We use measurement to assist in decision making. Because a sample of behavior is just that—an example of a type of behavior but not a complete assessment—all samples, by definition, are incomplete or imperfect. So we are always in a position of having to draw inferences or make decisions based on incomplete or imperfect measurements. The challenge is to make sure that the measurements are "complete enough" or "perfect enough" for our purposes.

Reliability Consistency or stability of a measure.

Validity The accuracy of inferences made based on test or performance data; also addresses whether a measure accurately and completely represents what was intended to be measured.

The technical terms for these characteristics of measurement are **reliability** and **validity**. If a measure is unreliable, we would get different values each time we sampled the behavior. If a measure is not valid, we are gathering incomplete or inaccurate information. Although the terms "reliability" and "validity" are most often applied to test scores, they could be applied to any measure. We must expect reliability and validity from any measure that we will use to infer something about the behavior of an individual. This includes surveys or questionnaires, interview responses, performance evaluation ratings, and test scores.

Reliability

When we say that someone is "reliable," we mean that he or she is someone we can count on, someone predictable and consistent, and someone we can depend on for help if we ask for it. The same is true of measures. We need to feel confident that if we took the measure again, at a different time, or if someone else took the measurement, the value would remain the same. Suppose you went for a physical and before you saw the doctor, the nurse took your temperature and found it to be 98.6°. If the doctor came in five minutes later and retook your temperature and reported that it was 101.5°, you would be surprised. You would have expected those readings to agree, given the short time span between measurements. With a discrepancy this large, you would wonder about the skill of the nurse, the skill of the doctor, or the adequacy of the thermometer. In technical terms, you would wonder about the reliability of that measure.

Test–Retest Reliability

There are several different aspects to measurement reliability. One aspect is simply the temporal consistency—the consistency over time—of a measure. Would we have gotten the same value had we taken the measurement next week as opposed to this week, or next month rather than this month? If we set out to measure someone's memory skills and this week find that they are quite good, but upon retesting the same person next week we find that they are quite poor, what do we conclude? Does the participant have a good memory or not? Generally speaking, we want our measures to produce the same value over a reasonable time period. This type of reliability, known as **test–retest reliability**, is often calculated as a correlation coefficient between measurements taken at time 1 and measurements taken at time 2. Consider Figure 2.8. On the left, you see high agreement between measures of the same people taken at two different points in time. On the right, you find low levels of agreement between the two measurements. The measurements on the left would be considered to have high test–retest reliability, while those on the right would be considered to have low test–retest reliability.

Test–retest reliability
A type of reliability calculated by correlating measurements taken at time 1 with measurements taken at time 2.

Equivalent Forms Reliability

Remember when you took the SAT®? The SAT has been administered to millions of high school students over the decades since its introduction. But the *same* SAT items have not

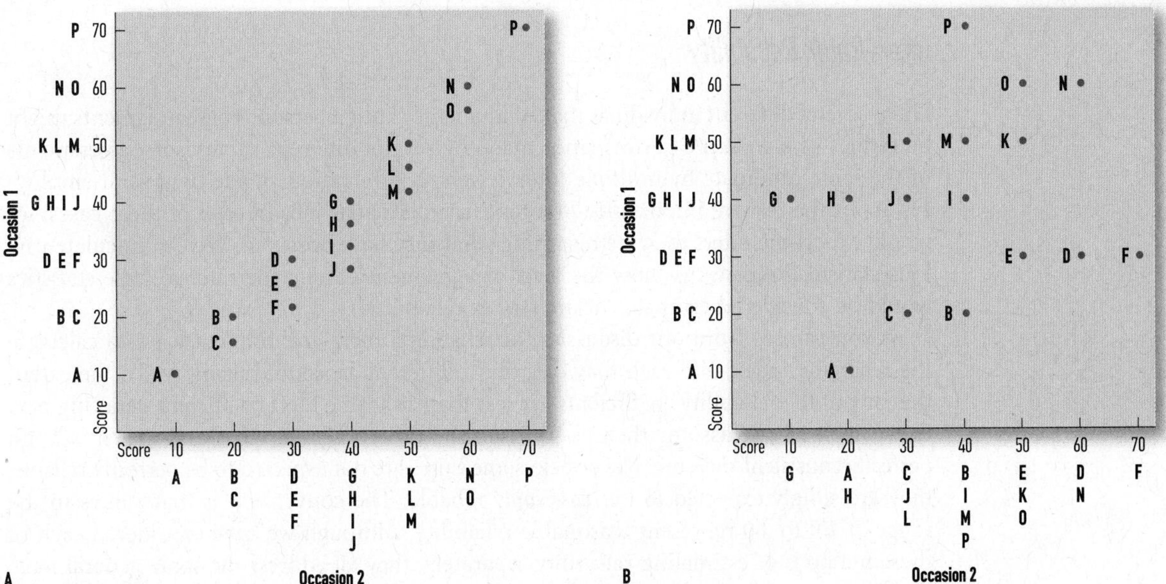

FIGURE 2.8 Examples of High and Low Test–Retest Reliability: Score Distributions of Individuals Tested on Two Different Occasions

been administered to those millions of students. If that were the case, the answers to those items would have long since been circulated among dishonest test takers. For many students, the test would simply be a test of the extent to which they could memorize the right answers. Instead, the test developers have devised many different *forms* of the examination that are assumed to cover the same general content, but with items unique to each form. Assume you take the test in Ames, Iowa, and another student takes a different form of the test in Philadelphia. How do we know that these two forms reliably measure your knowledge and abilities, that you would have gotten roughly the same score had you switched seats (and tests) with the other student? Just as is the case in test–retest reliability, you can have many people take two different forms of the test and see if they get the same score. By correlating the two test scores, you would be calculating the **equivalent forms reliability** of that test. Look at Figure 2.8 again. Simply substitute the term "Form A" for "Occasion 1" and "Form B" for "Occasion 2" and you will see that the left part of the figure would describe a test with high equivalent forms reliability, while the test on the right would demonstrate low equivalent forms reliability.

Equivalent forms reliability A type of reliability calculated by correlating measurements from a sample of individuals who complete two different forms of the same test.

Internal Consistency

As you can see from the examples above, to calculate either test–retest or equivalent forms reliability, you would need to have two separate testing sessions (with either the same form or different forms). Another way of estimating the reliability of a test is to pretend that instead of one test, you really have two or more. A simple example would be to take a 100-item test and break it into two 50-item tests by collecting all of the even-numbered items together and all of the odd-numbered items together. You could then correlate the total score for all even-numbered items that were answered correctly with the total score for all of the odd-numbered items answered correctly. If the subtest scores correlated highly, you would consider the test reliable from an **internal consistency** standpoint. If we are trying to measure a homogeneous attribute (e.g., extraversion, stress), all of the items on the test should give us an equally good measure of that attribute. There are more sophisticated ways of estimating internal consistency reliability based on the average correlation between every pair of test items. A common statistic used to estimate internal consistency reliability using such averages is known as *Cronbach's alpha.*

Internal consistency Form of reliability that assesses how consistently the items of a test measure a single construct; affected by the number of items in the test and the correlations among the test items.

Inter-Rater Reliability

Often several different individuals make judgments about a person. These judgments might be ratings of a worker's performance made by several different supervisors, assessments of the same candidate by multiple interviewers, or evaluations made by several employees about the relative importance of a task in a particular job. In each of these cases, we would expect the raters to agree regarding what they have observed. We can calculate various statistical indices to show the level of agreement among the raters. These statistics would be considered estimates of inter-rater reliability.

As you can see from our discussion of reliability, there are different ways to calculate the reliability index, and each may describe a different aspect of reliability. To the extent that any of the reliability coefficients are less than 1.00 (the ideal coefficient denoting perfect reliability), we assume there is some error in the observed score and that it is not a perfectly consistent measure. Nevertheless, measures are not expected to be perfectly reliable; they are simply expected to be *reasonably* reliable. The convention is that values in the range of .70 to .80 represent reasonable reliability. Although we have considered each of these methods of estimating reliability separately, they all address the same general issue that we covered earlier in the chapter: generalizability. The question is: To what extent can we generalize the meaning of a measure taken with one measurement device at one point in time? A more sophisticated approach to the question of reliability is based in **generalizability theory** (Guion, 2011), which considers all different types of error (e.g., test–retest, equivalent forms, and internal consistency) simultaneously, but a description of this technique is beyond the scope of this text. Putka and Sackett (2010) present an excellent conceptual and historical treatment of the evolution of modern reliability theory.

Generalizability theory A sophisticated approach to the question of reliability that simultaneously considers all types of error in reliability estimates (e.g., test–retest, equivalent forms, and internal consistency).

Validity

The second characteristic of good measurement is validity, which addresses the issue of whether the measurements we have taken accurately and completely represent what we had hoped to measure. For example, consider the job of a physician in general practice. Suppose we wanted to develop a measure of the performance of general practitioners and that we decided to use malpractice insurance rates over the years as a measure of performance. We note that these rates have gone up every year for a particular physician, and we conclude that the physician must not be very good. If he or she were good, we would have expected such malpractice premiums to have gone down.

In the physician example, the measure we have chosen to represent performance would be neither accurate nor complete. Malpractice rates have much less to do with a particular doctor than they do with claims in general and with amounts awarded by juries in malpractice lawsuits. Both the number of malpractice suits and the jury awards for those suits have climbed steadily over the past few decades. As a result, you would note that malpractice premiums (like car insurance premiums) have climbed steadily *every year for almost every physician*. Furthermore, a physician in general practice has a wide variety of duties, including diagnosis, treatment, follow-up, education, referral, record keeping, continuing education, and so forth. Even if malpractice premium rates were accurate representations of performance in certain areas such as diagnosis and treatment, many other areas of performance would have been ignored by this one measure.

For both reliability and validity, the question is whether what we have measured allows us to make predictions or decisions, or take actions, based on what we assume to be the content of those measures. In our physician example, if we were deciding whether to allow a physician to keep a medical license or to be added to the staff of a hospital, and we based that decision on our chosen "performance" measure (malpractice premiums), our decision (or inference that physicians with a history of increasing premiums are poor performers) would not be a valid decision or inference. Note that the reliability of a measure puts a ceiling, or limit, on the validity of that measure. That is, if the reliability of a measure is low, then it will be difficult to find a valid relationship or correlation between that measure and another measure.

You will remember that we concluded our discussion of reliability by introducing the concept of generalizability. What we said was that reliability was really a unitary phenomenon and that the various estimates of reliability (e.g., test–retest) were really just different ways to get at a single issue: consistency of measurement. The important concept to keep in mind was generalizability. The same is true of validity. Like reliability, there are several different ways to gather information about the accuracy and completeness of a measure. Also like reliability, validity is a unitary concept; you should not think that one type of validity tells you anything different about the completeness and accuracy of a measure than any other type of validity (Binning & Barrett, 1989; Guion, 2011; Landy, 1986, 2007). Like reliability, validity concerns the confidence with which you can make a prediction or draw an inference based on the measurements you have collected. There are three common ways of gathering validity evidence. We will describe each of these three ways below.

Although validity is relevant to discussions of any measurement, most validity studies address the issue of whether an assessment permits confident decisions about hiring or promotion. Although most validity studies revolve around tests (e.g., tests of personality or cognitive ability), other assessments (e.g., interviews, application blanks, or even tests of aerobic endurance) might form the basis of a validity study. For the purposes of this chapter, we will use hiring and promotion as the examples of the decisions that we have to make. For such purposes, we have a general hypothesis that people who score higher or better on a particular measure will be more productive and/or satisfied employees (Landy, 1986). Our validity investigation will be focused on gathering information that will make us more confident that this hypothesis can be supported. If we are able to gather such confirming information, we can make decisions about individual applicants with confidence—our inference about a person from a test score will be valid. Remember, validity is not about tests, it is about decisions or inferences.

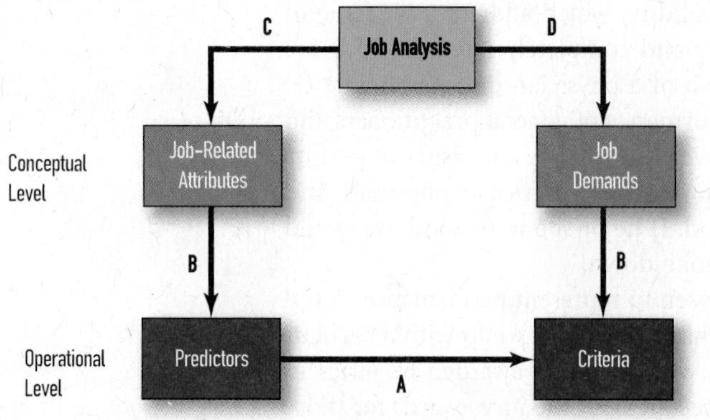

FIGURE 2.9 **Validation Process from Conceptual and Operational Levels**

I-O psychologists usually gather validity evidence using one of three common designs. We will consider each of these designs in turn. All three fit into the same general framework shown in Figure 2.9. The box on the top is labeled "Job Analysis." Job analysis is a complex and time-consuming process that we will describe in detail in Chapter 4. For the purposes of the current discussion, you simply need to think of job analysis as a way of identifying the important demands (e.g., tasks, duties) of a job and the human attributes necessary to carry out those demands successfully. Once the attributes (e.g., abilities) are identified, the test that is chosen or developed to assess those abilities is called a **predictor**, which is used to forecast another variable. Similarly, when the demands of the job are identified, the definition of an individual's performance in meeting those demands is called a **criterion**, which is the variable that we want to predict. In Figure 2.9, a line with an arrow connects predictors and criteria. This line represents the hypothesis we outlined above. It is hypothesized that people who do better on the predictor will also do better on the criterion—people who score higher will be better employees. We gather validity evidence to test that hypothesis.

Predictor The test chosen or developed to assess attributes (e.g., abilities) identified as important for successful job performance.

Criterion An outcome variable that describes important aspects or demands of the job; the variable that we predict when evaluating the validity of a predictor.

Criterion-related validity Validity approach that is demonstrated by correlating a test score with a performance measure; improves researcher's confidence in the inference that people with higher test scores have higher performance.

Validity coefficient Correlation coefficient between a test score (predictor) and a performance measure (criterion).

Criterion-Related Validity

The most direct way to support the hypothesis (i.e., to connect the predictor and criteria boxes) is to actually gather data and compute a correlation coefficient. In this design, technically referred to as a **criterion-related validity** design, you would correlate test scores with performance measures. If the correlation was positive and statistically significant, you would now have evidence improving your confidence in the inference that people with higher test scores have higher performance. By correlating these test scores with the performance data, you would be calculating what is known as a **validity coefficient.** The test might be a test of intelligence and the performance measure might be a supervisor's rating. Since we mentioned a "supervisor's rating," something becomes immediately obvious about this design: We are using the test scores of people who are employed by the organization. This can be done in two different ways.

Predictive Validity

The first method of conducting a criterion-related study is to administer a particular test to all applicants and then hire applicants without using scores from that particular test to make the hiring decision. You would then go back to the organization after some time period had passed (e.g., six or nine months) and collect performance data. This design, where there is a time lag between the collection of the test data and the criterion data, is known as a **predictive validity design** because it enables you to predict what would have happened had you actually used the test scores to make the hiring decisions. If the test scores were related to performance scores, you might conclude that you should not have hired some people. Their performance was poor, as were their test scores. From the point at which the employer knows that the validity coefficient is positive and significant, test scores can be used for making future hiring decisions. The validity coefficient does not, by itself, tell you *what* score to designate as a passing score. We will deal with this issue in Chapter 6, where we consider the actual staffing process. The predictive validity design we have described above is only one of many different predictive designs you might employ.

Predictive validity design Criterion-related validity design in which there is a time lag between collection of the test data and the criterion data.

Concurrent Validity

In research on many diseases, such as cancer and coronary heart disease, researchers carry out a process known as a clinical trial. The clinical trial design assigns some patients to a treatment group and others to a control group. The treatment group actually gets the treatment under study (e.g., a pill), whereas the control group does not. Instead, the control group gets a placebo (e.g., a pill with neutral ingredients). It is difficult to recruit patients for many clinical trials because they want to be in the treatment group and don't want to take the chance of being assigned to a control group (although they would not typically know to which group they had been assigned). If the treatment is actually effective, it will benefit the treatment group patients, but the control group patients will not experience the benefits. Many employers and I-O researchers are like the prospective patients for the control group—they don't want to wait months or even years to see if the "treatment" (e.g., an ability test) is effective. While they are waiting for the results, they may be hiring ineffective performers.

There is a criterion-related validity design that directly addresses that concern. It is called the **concurrent validity design**. This design has no time lag between gathering the test scores and the performance data because the test in question is administered to current employees rather than applicants, and performance measures can be collected on those employees simultaneously, or concurrently (thus the term "concurrent design"). Since the employees are actually working for the organization, the assumption is made that they must be at least minimally effective, alleviating any concern about adding new employees who are not minimally effective. As in the case of the predictive design, test scores are correlated with performance scores to yield a validity coefficient. If it is positive and significant, the test is then made part of the process by which new employees are hired.

Concurrent validity design Criterion-related validity design in which there is no time lag between gathering the test scores and the performance data.

There is a potential disadvantage in using the concurrent design, however. We have no information about those who are *not* employed by the organization. This has both technical and practical implications. The technical implication is that you have range restriction—only the scores of those who scored highly on the predictor—so the correlation coefficient may be artificially depressed and may not be statistically significant. There are statistical corrections that can offset that problem. The practical problem is that there might have been applicants who did less well than the employees did on the test yet might have been successful performers. Since they were never hired, the employer will never know. I-O psychologists have conducted a good deal of research comparing concurrent and predictive designs, and their general conclusion has been that, even though the concurrent design might underestimate validity coefficients, in practice this does not usually happen (Schmitt, Gooding, Noe, & Kirsch, 1984). One final problem with concurrent designs is that the test-taking motivation may not be as high for those who are already employed. It is also useful to remember that both concurrent and predictive designs are only two variations on many different ways to assemble validity data (Guion, 1998; Landy, 1986, 2007). We will now consider two additional methods for collecting validity data.

Content-Related Validity

Content-related validation design A design that demonstrates that the content of the selection procedure represents an adequate sample of important work behaviors and activities and/or worker KSAOs defined by the job analysis.

The SIOP Principles define a **content-related validation design** as "a study that demonstrates that the content of the selection procedure represents an adequate sample of important work behaviors and activities, and/or worker knowledge, skills, abilities or other characteristics (KSAOs) defined by the analysis of work" (SIOP, 2003). The job analysis in Figure 2.9 is an example of this strategy. As another example, assume you are the director of a temporary employment agency and want to hire applicants who can be assigned to word-processing tasks for companies. You know that these companies typically use either WordPerfect or Microsoft Word and use either a Macintosh or a PC system. So you ask the job applicants to demonstrate their proficiency with both of these word-processing packages on both PCs and Macs. Since not all employers have the latest hardware or software, you also ask the applicants to perform sample word-processing tasks on various versions of the software and different vintages of hardware. By doing this, you have taken the essence of the work for which you are hiring individuals—word processing on any of a number of hardware and software configurations—and turned it into a test.

There can be little argument that, at least conceptually, there is a clear link in our example between test scores and probable performance. Of course, you would also need to demonstrate that the test you had assembled fairly represented the types of word-processing projects that the temporary employees would encounter. If you were using only the word-processing test, you would also need to show that actual word-processing (e.g., as opposed to developing financial spreadsheets with Excel) is the most important part of the work for which these temps are hired. If, for example, the temps were hired to answer phones or manually file records, the test of word processing would be largely irrelevant. But assuming that the job the temps will be asked to do is word processing, you can infer that applicants who do better on your test will tend to do better at the actual word-processing tasks in the jobs to which they are assigned. The validity of the inference is based not on a correlation but on a logical comparison of the test and the work. To return to Figure 2.9, although the focus of the study is the association between a predictor and a criterion (in this case the speed and accuracy of word processing), no criterion information from the work setting is collected.

The example of the word-processing test was simple and straightforward. Many jobs are not quite as simple as that of a word processor. Consider the position of a manager of a cellular telephone store with 5 inside and 15 outside sales and technical representatives. Suppose the company opened a companion store in the next town and needed to hire a manager for that store. How could we employ a content-related design to gather data that would give us confidence in making the hiring decision? The job of manager is complex, involving many varied tasks, as well as a wide variety of knowledge, skills, abilities, and interpersonal attributes. Using Figure 2.9 as our model, we would analyze the job to determine the most important tasks or duties, as well as the abilities needed to perform those tasks. We would do this by asking experienced employees and supervisors in other cellular phone stores to give us the benefit of their observations and personal experience. We would ask them to complete one or more questionnaires that covered tasks and their importance and necessary abilities. Based on an analysis of their answers, we could then identify or develop possible predictors for testing manager candidates. We would then choose the set of predictors that measured abilities that had been judged to be most closely related to various performance demands for managers.

Through the use of knowledgeable employees and supervisors, we would have been able to make the logical connection between the predictors and anticipated performance.

Although content-related validation designs for jobs can become rather complex, we have described the "basic" model so you can get a feel for how the content-related strategy differs from the criterion-related strategy. But remember, both strategies are addressing the same basic hypothesis: People who do better on our tests will do better on the job.

Construct-Related Validity

Construct validity Validity approach in which investigators gather evidence to support decisions or inferences about psychological constructs; often begins with investigators demonstrating that a test designed to measure a particular construct correlates with other tests in the predicted manner.

Calling **construct validity** a "type" of validity is a historical accident and not really correct (Landy, 1986). In the 1950s, a task force outlined several ways to gather validity evidence and labeled three of them: criterion, content, and construct (Cronbach & Meehl, 1955). The labels have stuck. Modern I-O psychology, however, does not recognize that distinction—referred to sarcastically by Guion (1980) as the "holy trinity." Instead, as we have described above, validity is considered "unitarian." There are literally hundreds of ways of gathering evidence that will increase the confidence of our decisions or inferences. Criterion-related designs and content-related designs are two of the many available approaches (Guion, 2011; Landy, 1986). Every study could have a different design, even though some may be more popular than others. The same is true with validity designs. Every validity study could have a different design, but criterion- and content-related designs are among the most popular, for reasons we will describe below.

Construct Psychological concept or characteristic that a predictor is intended to measure; examples are intelligence, personality, and leadership.

Construct validity represents "the integration of evidence that bears on the interpretation or meaning of test scores—including content and criterion-related evidence—which are subsumed as part of construct validity" (Messick, 1995, p. 742). A **construct** can be defined as a "concept or characteristic that a predictor is intended to measure" (SIOP, 2003). A construct is a broad representation of a human characteristic. Intelligence, personality, and leadership are all examples of constructs. Memory, assertiveness, and supportive leader behavior are all examples of these broader entities.

Examine Figure 2.10. As you can see by comparing this with Figure 2.9, we have simply added the term "construct" to our generic validation model. The modified figure demonstrates that constructs are related to both attributes and job demands. Let's consider the job of a financial consultant for an investment banking firm. As a result of a job analysis, we were able to determine that memory and reasoning were important parts of the job of a financial consultant because the job required the consultant to remember data about various stocks and bonds and to use that information to develop an investment strategy for an individual client. What is one of the broad and essential attributes necessary both to do well on a test of reasoning and memory and to be effective in advising clients on how they should invest their money? It is intelligence, or cognitive ability. In this case, the construct is intelligence, and we see it as underlying both performance on the test and performance on the job. In other words, doing well on the job requires the same construct as doing well on the test.

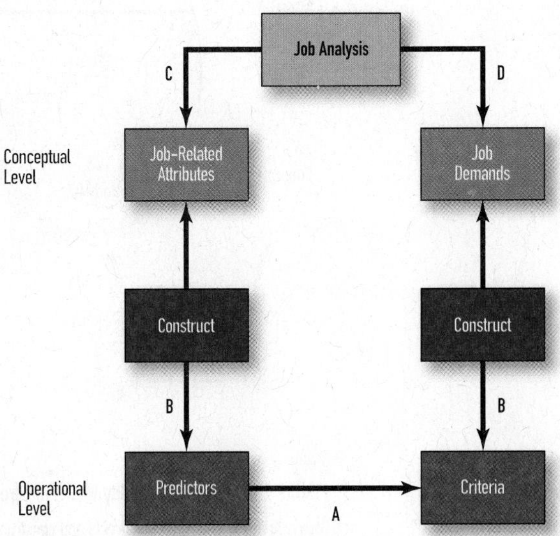

FIGURE 2.10 A Model for Construct Validity

The contribution of the concept of construct validation is that it encourages the investigator to cast a broad net in gathering evidence to support decisions or inferences. In a criterion-related study, there is a tight focus on a test score and a performance score. In content-related validation, there is a tight focus on a job analysis. In our example of the financial consultant, construct validation would allow for evidence from studies that have been done previously on the topics of intelligence, reasoning, and memory; job analysis information on the financial consultants in many different forms and industries; well-developed theories of decision making and memory; and even observations of how memory and reasoning are used in a broad range of occupational groups. It could also include evidence from criterion- or content-related studies of the job in the firm that is considering using the memory and reasoning test. Arvey (1992) presents another example of a construct validation design in the area of physical ability testing for police officers. That example is shown in Figure 2.11. In this case, the constructs are strength and endurance rather than intelligence. In the case of strength, the hypothesis is that strength underlies the ability to perform bench dips, climb walls, wrestle with a dummy, and drag a dummy in a test environment, as well as the ability to climb real walls and restrain real suspects. Similarly, the endurance hypothesis is that individuals who can do well on a mile run can also do well in pursuing suspects in a foot chase. Endurance is the construct that underlies doing well both on the test and on the job. Evidence that bears on these two hypotheses could come from a literature review on physical performance, laboratory studies, field studies, accepted theories of muscular strength and aerobic endurance, and observations or interviews of police officers (or even suspects). The key is in the integration of this evidence to strengthen our confidence that making hiring decisions based on strength or endurance measures will lead to more effective performance for police officers.

The more evidence we can gather, the more confident we can be in our decisions and inferences. As you will recall, we began this module by pointing out that we seldom have complete information on which to base decisions. We deal in samples of behavior. As a result, we must eventually make a decision that the information we have is sufficiently reliable, accurate, and comprehensive to make the necessary decisions or draw the necessary inferences. Sometimes the decisions are small and simple and don't require a great deal of evidence, as in the example of hiring the word-processing temps. In other situations, such as the development of a national recruiting and selection program for financial consultants, the decisions are big and complicated; for these we need a lot of evidence. The scope of the decisions and inferences will dictate how much evidence we need to be confident in those decisions. There is no clear bright line that says "collect this much evidence and no more." As a general principle, it is more effective to use several different designs

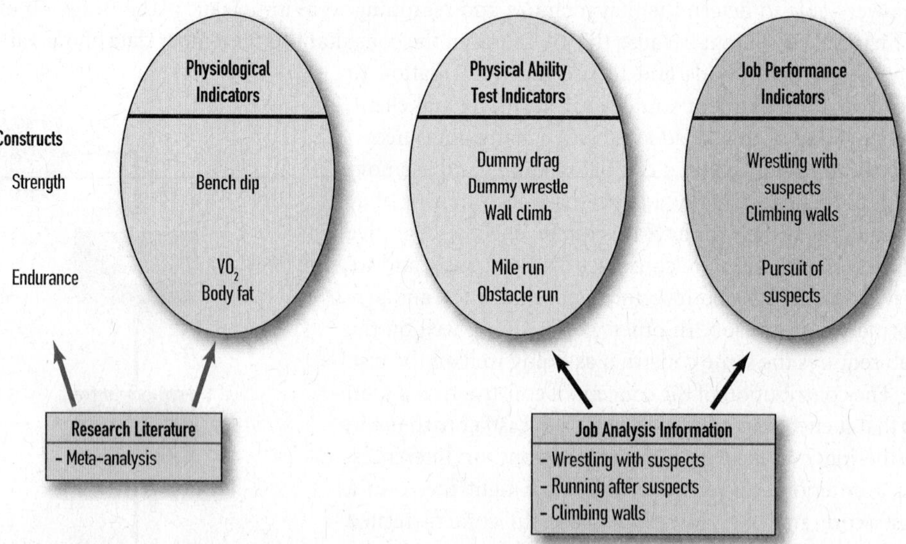

FIGURE 2.11 Construct Validity Model of Strength and Endurance Physical Factors

SOURCE: Arvey, R. D. (1992). Constructs and construct validation: Definitions and issues. *Human Performance, 5,* 59–69. Fig. 3, p. 65. Copyright © 1992. Reprinted by permission of Lawrence Erlbaum Associates, Inc. and Taylor & Francis Ltd, http://www.tandf.co.uk/journals. Permission conveyed through Copyright Clearance Center, Inc.

and gather substantial evidence, regardless of what we call the evidence, than to depend on a single design, such as a criterion-related or content-related design. The greater the accumulation of evidence, the greater our confidence (Landy, 2007). Here we might think of the combination of the lab and field study. The lab study provides rigorous cause–effect analyses, and the field study provides real-world relevance.

Validity and the Law: A Mixed Blessing

Until the 1960s, discussions about validity and the validation process were of interest only to a relatively small community of I-O psychologists and psychometricians. The Civil Rights Act of 1964 and the resulting development of the Equal Employment Opportunity Commission changed all that. By 1972, the government was requiring employers to present validity evidence as a defense against employment discrimination claims. If, for example, a minority or female applicant complained of failing to receive a job offer because of unfair discrimination, the employer was required to show that the test or hiring practice in question was fair and job-related (in I-O terms, "valid"). Furthermore, the employer was told that the only convincing evidence would be in the form of a criterion-related study. By 1978, the government had grudgingly broadened its view a bit to permit content-related and construct-related evidence, but it was clear that the "gold standard" would still be criterion-related evidence (Landy, 1986).

For the past 30 years, in the context of employment discrimination lawsuits, judges have issued opinions on the adequacy of validity models and validity evidence and, more importantly, on what they believe to be the necessary elements for those models. As a result, what had originally been three *examples* of designs for gathering evidence have become the *only* three acceptable models or designs, and the characteristics that constitute an "acceptable" study have become increasingly detailed. This is a good news–bad news situation. The good news is that the concept of validity is receiving the attention it deserves. The bad news is that the evolving view of validation is becoming more distant from the way it was originally conceived and from the way I-O psychologists think of the concept in the 21st century. Most judges are not particularly talented psychometricians (just as, we hasten to add, most psychometricians would not necessarily be talented judges). There is an increasing tension between I-O psychology and the courts on technical issues related to assessment and decision making (Landy, 2002a,b). The current federal guidelines, which are often relied upon in discrimination cases (Uniform Guidelines, 1978), are hopelessly out of date on issues such as validation strategies. As long as they remain an "authority" in discrimination cases, there will be a serious lack of agreement between I-O psychology and public (and employer) policy. We will revisit the issue of the interface of law and I-O psychology in Chapters 6 and 11. For those who find this topic interesting, SIOP has published a book in the Practice Series that covers virtually every aspect of employment discrimination litigation (Landy, 2005a).

MODULE 2.4 SUMMARY

- To interpret data, it is important to consider reliability, which is the extent to which the measures are consistent over time, in different equivalent forms, and from one rater to another.
- There are several traditional designs for demonstrating validity, including content-, criterion-, and construct-related. All designs are intended to answer the question of whether better performance on the test, or predictor, is associated with better performance on the job.
- The question of validity is significant in many court decisions affecting workplace issues, the advantage being that it gives recognition to the value of I-O research. The drawback is that the courts and legislatures have narrowed the range of research designs that are considered acceptable and have established guidelines that do not keep up with current work in the field.

KEY TERMS

reliability
validity
test–retest reliability
equivalent forms reliability
internal consistency
generalizability theory
predictor
criterion
criterion-related validity
validity coefficient
predictive validity design
concurrent validity design
content-related validation design
construct validity
construct

II Industrial Psychology

3 Individual Differences and Assessment

MODULE 3.1

An Introduction to Individual Differences

What do Justin Bieber, the Pope, Lady Gaga, Stephen King, Carmelo Anthony, Barack Obama, your grandmother, and your instructor have in common? Not much. They are different in abilities, interests, experiences, personality, age, gender, race, and backgrounds. Indeed, the only thing we can say with certainty about these individuals is that they are substantially different from one another. We would not expect your grandmother to try out for an NBA team, or Stephen King to officiate at a religious service, or your instructor to meet with foreign heads of state. Many psychologists, including I-O psychologists, believe that the differences among individuals can be used, at least in part, to understand and predict their behavior.

But it isn't good enough to say simply that people are different. You don't have to be a psychologist to recognize that. Some types of differences prove more useful than others in predicting and understanding behavior. The differences among people on various attributes like intelligence, personality, and knowledge are important in understanding a wide variety of socially important outcomes (Lubinski, 2000), including the following:

- Academic achievement
- Intellectual development
- Crime and delinquency
- Vocational choice
- Income and poverty
- Occupational performance

Individual differences Dissimilarities between or among two or more people.

This chapter will deal first with the concept of **individual differences** and then with how the assessment of these differences can help to predict occupational performance.

Some Background

Psychology began in a laboratory in Germany in 1876. The father of the discipline, Wilhelm Wundt, was anxious to show that psychology was different from philosophy and medicine. Since this was a new science and the existing physical sciences like chemistry, biology, and physics had discovered many general principles that enhanced their importance, Wundt set out to uncover general principles of human behavior as well. He developed techniques for studying the sensations and reactions of people, examining the dimmest light that individuals could see, the faintest sound they could hear, and how quickly they could react to a signal. But those who assisted in conducting his experiments quickly discovered that not everyone had the same reaction time, or could see the same dim light, or could hear the same soft tone. In other words, they discovered that there were *differences* among individuals.

These differences detracted from the precise results Wundt sought, but to one of his students they represented a fascinating discovery. James McKeen Cattell (1860–1944), an American who received a PhD in psychology under Wundt's direction, soon began measuring and charting the differences among people using "psychological" variables. In 1890 Cattell developed the concept of a **mental test** as a way of charting these differences. Because the subject matter of this research was differences, the study of differences became known as **differential psychology** (Landy, 1997).

After leaving Wundt's laboratory at the University of Leipzig, Cattell went to England and worked with another researcher very interested in individual differences, Francis Galton. Galton was gathering information that would support his cousin Charles Darwin's radical theory of evolution. In earlier years, Galton had measured inherited characteristics like height, weight, reach, and hair color. With his new mental test, Cattell was able to expand the number of inherited characteristics that he could examine. After working with Galton for several years in developing a comprehensive mental test, Cattell returned to America and used this test to measure the **intelligence** of incoming college students. He believed that he could use the resulting scores to help students choose curricula and to predict who would successfully complete college. Cattell had developed methods of measuring **mental ability**, placing it on a scale or **metric**. As a result, the actual measurement of abilities became known as **psychometrics**.

While Freud and other early psychologists began to focus on *pathological* aspects of mental function, the pioneers of differential psychology were primarily interested in the mental abilities of "normal" people. Several were aware of Cattell's work in measuring intelligence. In France, Alfred Binet was measuring mental abilities of French schoolchildren. Lewis Terman was conducting similar studies in California with a translation of Binet's test. Hugo Munsterberg was measuring the abilities of trolley drivers in order to predict the likelihood of accidents. When the United States entered the First World War in 1917, the leading industrial psychologists of the time persuaded the army to use an **intelligence test** to screen recruits and determine who should attend officers' candidate school. Two years after the war's end, Walter Dill Scott, one of the founding fathers of I-O psychology, proclaimed that "possibly the single greatest achievement of the American Psychological Association is the establishment of individual differences" (Lubinski, 2000).

In the postwar years, intelligence tests were adapted for use in selecting individuals for jobs with government and industry. By 1932, measuring the differences in intelligence among individuals in order to predict things like accidents and productivity was a well-established practice (Landy, 1997; Viteles, 1932). As we will see later in the chapter, intelligence is still one of the most generally assessed characteristics of job applicants. As we will also see, the hunt for new "abilities" continues even in the 21st century. We will consider two such abilities (emotional intelligence and situational judgment) in this chapter.

Mental test Instrument designed to measure a subject's ability to reason, plan, and solve problems; an intelligence test.

Differential psychology Scientific study of differences between or among two or more people.

Intelligence The ability to learn and adapt to an environment; often used to refer to general intellectual capacity, as opposed to cognitive ability or mental ability, which often refer to more specific abilities such as memory or reasoning.

Mental ability Capacity to reason, plan, and solve problems; cognitive ability.

Metric Standard of measurement; a scale.

Psychometrics Practice of measuring a characteristic such as mental ability, placing it on a scale or metric.

Intelligence test Instrument designed to measure the ability to reason, learn, and solve problems.

Differential Psychology, Psychometrics, and I-O Psychology

Nearly a century later, measuring the differences among individuals to predict later behavior ("psychometrics") remains one of the most common frameworks applied by I-O psychologists. It is different from the framework used by an experimental psychologist. The experimental psychologist usually designs an experiment that will show how all people are alike in their response to a stimulus and looks outside the individual to the stimulus as a way to explain behavior. In contrast, the differential psychologist is person-centered, looking for qualities or characteristics within the person that will help us understand that person's behavior. In the past, I-O psychology—particularly the applied aspect of it—depended on these differences to predict things like job success, job satisfaction, and counterproductive work behavior. I-O psychology still makes great use of the individual differences approach, but it also considers factors like organizational practices, team characteristics, physical work and work environment design, and even broad cultural influences.

Psychometrician Psychologist trained in measuring characteristics such as mental ability.

Cognitive ability Capacity to reason, plan, and solve problems; mental ability.

"g" Abbreviation for general mental ability.

General mental ability The nonspecific capacity to reason, learn, and solve problems in any of a wide variety of ways and circumstances.

The marriage of psychometrics and differential psychology was a good one. The differential psychologist identified what should be measured, and the **psychometrician** set about measuring it. As we saw from the work of Cattell and his contemporaries, the attribute most often measured—and considered most important—was some form of intelligence, or **cognitive ability**. People use cognitive abilities to acquire knowledge, solve problems, and apply reason to situations. Consequently, many studies were conducted to show that an individual's general intellectual capacity was closely associated with that individual's occupational and vocational success. The pioneers in theories of intelligence referred to this attribute as "**g**," an abbreviation for **general mental ability** (Hull, 1928; Spearman, 1927). Today's psychologists still use that term, and we will use it in this book. We have just introduced three terms—"intelligence," "cognitive ability," and "mental ability"—in rapid succession. These all refer to general mental ability, and for the present discussion, you may consider them interchangeable. Later in this chapter we will explore the distinction between these general abilities versus specific mental processes such as memory and perception.

Identifying Individual Differences

As we saw in the earlier section describing the history of individual differences, Francis Galton was one of the early advocates of studying such differences. In 1890 Galton wrote: "One of the most important objects of measurement is . . . to obtain a general knowledge . . . of capacities . . . by sinking shafts at a few critical points" (cited in Lubinski, 2000, p. 407). By this, Galton meant that we can use psychometric tests to explore individual abilities and other attributes the way miners use drilling to explore minerals in the earth. That is an excellent metaphor for the study of individual differences: sinking shafts to obtain more general knowledge about behavior at work. This concept also provides a good framework for explaining how I-O psychologists explore individual differences today as opposed to 25 years ago. In the past, we concentrated on only one shaft—intelligence. Today we are sinking many more shafts, as well as deeper ones (e.g., specific mental abilities such as memory, specific aspects of personality such as emotional stability, potentially new abilities such as emotional intelligence). Before, we were content to stop at a more superficial level ("intelligence" or "personality"). Today our explorations are broader and deeper, and we can reach more meaningful conclusions because the reliability and validity of our measuring devices are better.

We need to keep in mind that not all individual differences will tell us something important. As in drilling for oil, water, or gold, we don't always "strike it rich." This is one of the reasons we do research: to see which shafts provide encouragement. For example, there is considerable discussion about whether emotional intelligence is a new shaft producing results or merely a shaft that connects to shafts (e.g., personality and intelligence) that have already been drilled.

To continue the drilling metaphor, we can distinguish among the differential psychologist, the psychometrician, and the applied I-O psychologist. The differential psychologist examines the psychological landscape and identifies areas for drilling. The psychometrician actually sinks the shaft. The applied I-O psychologist uses what comes out of that shaft—in this case not oil, water, or gold, but valuable predictors of performance. Later in this chapter, we will examine the actual assessment methods for examining these individual differences.

However, you must remember (and we will remind you) that behavior is complex and people are whole. No single area of individual difference (e.g., intelligence) is likely to completely (or even substantially) explain any important aspect of work behavior. You cannot separate an individual's intelligence from his or her personality, knowledge, or experience. In fact, some environments (e.g., stressful ones) may actually cancel out the effect of individual variables such as intelligence. When you look at the behavior of any individual, you need to remember that he or she is a whole, intact entity. To acknowledge a person's individuality, we need to go beyond considering just one or another possible predictor of his or her behavior.

g-ocentric model Tendency to understand and predict the behavior of workers simply by examining "g."

Physical abilities Bodily powers such as muscular strength, flexibility, and stamina.

Personality An individual's behavioral and emotional characteristics, generally found to be stable over time and in a variety of circumstances; an individual's habitual way of responding.

Interests Preferences or likings for broad ranges of activities.

Knowledge A collection of specific and interrelated facts and information about a particular topical area.

Emotion An effect or feeling, often experienced and displayed in reaction to an event or thought and accompanied by physiological changes in various systems of the body.

Varieties of Individual Differences

In the past 20 years, there has been a substantial shift in thinking about individual differences. Instead of simply examining general mental ability ("g") to understand and predict the behavior of workers—a tendency that Sternberg and Wagner (1993) called the **g-ocentric model**—researchers are broadening the field of examination. In addition to cognitive ability, work psychologists now consider individual differences in **physical abilities**, **personality**, **interests**, **knowledge**, and **emotion**. This is the result of several forces. In the early years of testing, the only available tests were intelligence tests. Today there are many reliable methods for measuring personality, knowledge, interests, and emotional reactions to work. In addition, our understanding of the many facets of performance has become more sophisticated. Instead of simply assessing overall job performance, we now consider specific facets of performance such as technical task performance, organizational citizenship, counterproductive work behavior, and adaptability, topics we will address in Chapters 4 and 5. Murphy (1996) proposes that people have many different attributes that predict behavior in organizations (see Figure 3.1).

Let's apply that view to the job of firefighter, which requires driving the fire truck to the fire, applying water to the fire, providing medical assistance, rescuing trapped citizens, and learning new procedures and how to use new equipment. To accomplish these tasks, firefighters work in teams. To provide medical assistance and learn new procedures, the firefighter needs cognitive ability. To rescue trapped citizens and apply water to the fire, the firefighter needs physical ability, courage, and problem-solving skills that come from experience in fighting fires. To accomplish teamwork and to deal with victims, the firefighter needs communication skills. To drive the truck to the fire accurately and safely, the firefighter needs good vision, coordination, and the knowledge or memory of how to get to the location. If we only bothered to consider "g," we would only be able to understand and predict a limited portion of the firefighter's job performance. To understand the full range of performance, we need to consider attributes beyond "g."

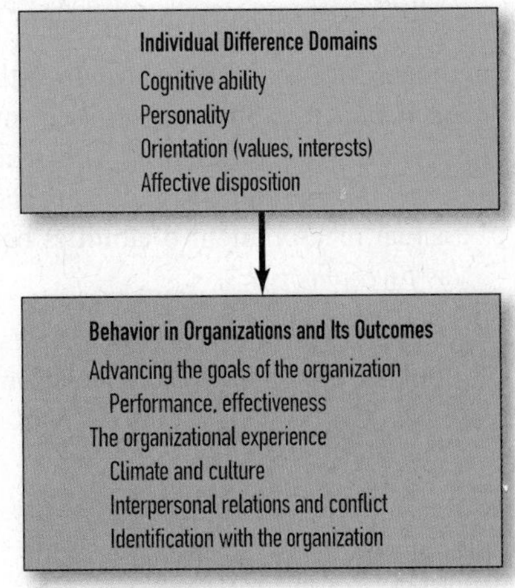

FIGURE 3.1 The Link between Attributes and Behavior in Organizations

SOURCE: Murphy, K. R. (1996). Individual differences and behavior: Much more than "g." In K. R. Murphy (Ed.), *Individual differences and behavior in organizations* (pp. 3–30). San Francisco: Jossey-Bass. Copyright © 1996. Reproduced with permission of John Wiley & Sons, Inc.

Before moving on to the next section, we need to consider the following fundamental assumptions that I-O psychologists make when they apply the individual differences model (adapted from Guion, 2011):

1. Adults have a variety of attributes (e.g., intelligence, personality, interests), and the levels of these attributes are relatively stable over a reasonable time period (several years).

© Michael Newman/PhotoEdit

The performance of most jobs requires multiple abilities. What are some of the abilities called for in the job of firefighter?

2. People differ with respect to these attributes (i.e., there are "individual differences"), and these differences are associated with job success.
3. The relative differences between people on these attributes remain even after training, job experience, or some other intervention. Thus, if individual A has less of an attribute than individual B before training or job experience, and if they both receive the same training or experience to increase that attribute, individual A will still have less of that attribute than individual B after the training or intervention, even though both may have higher levels of the attribute after training or experience.
4. Different jobs require different attributes.
5. These attributes can be measured.

With these assumptions in mind, we can now examine these attribute categories in the next modules.

MODULE 3.1 SUMMARY

- The *individual differences* among people on various attributes like intelligence, personality, and knowledge are important in understanding a wide variety of socially important outcomes.
- James McKeen Cattell developed the concept of a *mental test.* Since the subject matter of this research was differences, the study of differences became known as *differential psychology*. The actual measurement of abilities became known as *psychometrics*.
- The differential psychologist is person-centered, looking for characteristics within the person that will help explain that person's behavior. The differential psychologist identifies what should be measured, and the *psychometrician* measures it.
- Early differential psychologists most commonly measured *intelligence*, or *cognitive ability*. They referred to this attribute as "*g*," an abbreviation for *general mental ability*.
- In addition to cognitive ability, I-O psychologists consider individual differences in *physical abilities, personality, interests, knowledge,* and *emotion.*

KEY TERMS

individual differences	psychometrics	g-ocentric model
mental test	intelligence test	physical abilities
differential psychology	psychometrician	personality
intelligence	cognitive ability	interests
mental ability	"g"	knowledge
metric	general mental ability	emotion

MODULE 3.2

Human Attributes

Abilities

In the 1950s, Edwin Fleishman began a program of research to determine the most common mental and physical abilities associated with human performance, including work performance. The result was a comprehensive list, or **taxonomy**, of 52 abilities (Fleishman & Reilly, 1992), which can be divided into the broad categories of cognitive, physical, and **perceptual-motor abilities.** The full list of abilities is beyond the scope of this introductory textbook, but it is noteworthy that the abilities Fleishman identified cover quite an impressive variety—and they do not cover personality, **affect**, or interest!

Fleishman's taxonomy of abilities can be used for many different applied purposes. It is an effective way to analyze the most important abilities in various occupations (Landy, 1989). It can also be used to determine training needs, recruiting needs, and even work design. In Chapter 4, you will see how Fleishman's ability list contributed to the development of a comprehensive expert computer system called O*NET that connects human abilities with job demands.

Taxonomy An orderly, scientific system of classification.

Perceptual-motor abilities Physical attributes that combine the senses (e.g., seeing, hearing, smell) and motion (e.g., coordination, dexterity).

Affect The conscious, subjective aspect of emotion.

Cognitive Abilities

Intelligence as "g"

As we mentioned in Module 3.1, many people consider the terms "intelligence," "IQ," "cognitive ability," and "mental ability" to be synonyms for one another. In general, we agree—but it is important to understand how some psychologists distinguish among them. **IQ** is a historical term that stood for **intelligence quotient** and refers to the way early intelligence test scores were calculated. The term no longer has scientific meaning, although it is still often used by the general public. Intelligence can be defined as the ability to learn and adapt to an environment. One or another variation of this definition has been used since at least 1921 (Sternberg & Kaufmann, 1998). A group of leading I-O psychologists defined it as follows: "Intelligence is a very general mental capability that, among other things, involves the ability to reason, plan, solve problems, think abstractly, comprehend complex ideas, learn quickly, and learn from experience" (Arvey et al., 1995 p. 67).

IQ Abbreviation for intelligence quotient.

Intelligence quotient Measure of intelligence obtained by giving a subject a standardized IQ test. The score is obtained by multiplying by 100 the ratio of the subject's mental age to chronological age.

It might be easier to think of this very general ability the same way as we think of someone as "athletic." This doesn't mean that the person is an expert at every sport, just that the

Critical abilities for the job of emergency dispatcher include verbal comprehension, reaction time, and problem solving.

person is coordinated, picks up new sports easily, and is usually better at sports than someone who is "unathletic." There are specific subparts to doing well at a particular sport like golf or baseball or swimming, but being "athletic" seems to generally capture many of those subparts. Similarly, when we refer to someone as intelligent, we imply that he or she would be good at a range of activities that require learning and adaptation.

Sternberg and Kaufmann (1998) pointed out that no matter how enduring this definition may be for Western cultures, other cultures have different views of who is "an intelligent person." Speed of learning, for example, is not always emphasized in non-Western cultures. In fact, "other cultures may be suspicious of work done quickly" (Sternberg & Kaufmann, 1998), and in some cultures, the word "intelligence" means "prudence" and "caution." Nevertheless, for our purposes, we will accept the meaning generally assigned by Western psychologists. Intelligence is required whenever people must manipulate information of any type (Murphy, 1996). Measures of "g" assess reasoning ability, knowledge acquisition, and problem-solving ability (Lubinski, 2004).

Is "g" Important at Work?

Meta-analysis Statistical method for combining and analyzing the results from many studies to draw a general conclusion about relationships among variables.

Yes. Almost every job requires some active manipulation of information, and the greater the amount of information that needs to be manipulated, the more important "g" becomes. **Meta-analyses** of the relationship between "g" and job performance (Schmidt & Hunter, 2004) have demonstrated very clearly that as the complexity of the job increased, the predictive value (i.e., criterion validity) of tests of general intelligence also increased. This means that if the information-processing demands of a job are high, a person with lower "g" is less likely to be successful than a person with higher "g." That does not mean, however, that high "g" guarantees success on that job. If the job also requires interpersonal skills, communication skills, and certain personality traits, even a person with high "g" (but lower levels of those noncognitive traits) might fail.

In 1965 Tanner showed that he could accurately predict which Olympic athletes were competing in which sports by looking at their body builds. But *within* each Olympic event, the same individual differences were useless as predictors of who would get a medal (Lubinski, 2000). In this example, think of body build as "g" and all the other attributes of the athletes as specific abilities and attributes; "g" may help a candidate get into the police academy, but it will not ensure that the person will become a successful police officer.

Some, but far from all, of today's psychologists continue to believe that nothing more than measures of "g" are needed to predict training performance, academic performance, and job performance. An excellent review of the debate can be seen in an entire issue of the journal *Human Performance* devoted to the topic (Ones & Viswesvaran, 2002). One psychologist framed the issue as follows:

> General mental ability (g) is a substantively significant determinant of individual differences for any job that includes information-processing tasks. . . . The exact size of the relationship will be a function of . . . the degree to which the job requires information processing and verbal cognitive skills. (Campbell, 1990a)

From Campbell's statement we can infer that because "g" represents information-processing ability, then it should logically predict information-processing performance in the workplace. In addition, we can infer that jobs differ in terms of not only how much "information processing" they require but also how quickly that processing must be completed. A backhoe operator or a nutritionist certainly has to process some information, but not as much or as quickly as a software help-desk operator or an air traffic controller. The backhoe operator will depend much more heavily on visual/spatial ability than on problem-solving or reasoning ability. The nutritionist will depend more heavily on acquired knowledge of the composition of various foods and the nutritional needs of a client.

Is "g" as Important in Other Countries as It Is in the United States?

The simple answer seems to be "yes," at least as far as Europe is concerned. Several meta-analyses have been published demonstrating the predictive value of "g" in the European Union (EU) (Salgado, Anderson, Moscoso, Bertua, & DeFruyt, 2003) and specifically in the United Kingdom (Bertua, Anderson, & Salgado, 2005). Salgado and Anderson (2002) also report that the use of tests of mental ability is even more prevalent in the EU than in the United States.

Much less is known about non-European countries. As long as globalization is controlled by Western nations, it has been fairly safe to assume that "g" would remain important in non-European countries as well. But in the near future, as China emerges as a dominant global player, it will be interesting to see how important a role "g" continues to play in the global economy. It is possible that with such a massive potential employee population in China, success in the global arena may be defined determined by throwing a large number of people at a project rather than by hiring only the most intelligent applicants. We may see a different, and possibly diminished, role for "g" in both China and India over the next few decades. Conversely, it may be that, at least on the global stage, the United States will need to compete by working "smarter" rather than by employing massive numbers of cheap workers, making "g" even *more* important than it has been before.

Can Your Level of "g" Change?

Researchers have observed a fascinating phenomenon: Intelligence continues to rise over time. Individuals appear to be getting smarter and smarter through the life span, and new generations appear to be smarter than their parents. The phenomenon, labeled the **Flynn effect** after a political scientist who has done extensive research on the topic (Flynn, 1999), amounts to a gain of 15 points in average intelligence test scores per generation. This is a substantial increase, considering that the **mean** intelligence on most tests is pegged at 100 with a **standard deviation** of 15. There are many theories as to why this is occurring, including better health care, better nutrition, increased schooling, and better-educated parents (Sternberg & Kaufmann, 1998). Another factor may be the increasingly complex environment we live in both at work and at home (Neisser et al., 1996). This phenomenon exists in the United States and many other countries (Daley, Whaley, Sigman, Espinosa, & Neumann, 2003). So, at least at a generational level, the answer seems to be that on the average, your generation will be "smarter" than your parents' generation. Within generations, however, "g" appears to be more stable (Lubinski, Benbow, Webb, & Bleske-Recheck, 2006; Wai, Lubinski, & Benbow, 2005). And as we get older, the intelligence level we possessed when we were younger may become even more stable (Bouchard, 2004; Plomin & Spinath, 2004). So there is good news and bad news. The good news is that your generation is likely smarter than your parents' generation and that your level of "g" will possibly increase. The bad news is that as you age, the amount of change will get smaller—so start working on it now!

Flynn effect Phenomenon in which new generations appear to be smarter than their parents by a gain of 15 points in average intelligence test score per generation; named after the political scientist who did extensive research on the topic.

Mean The arithmetic average of the scores in a distribution; obtained by summing all of the scores in a distribution and dividing by the sample size.

Standard deviation Measure of the extent of spread in a set of scores.

Specific Cognitive Abilities Beyond "g"

The majority of today's psychologists agree that although "g" is important, more specific or refined cognitive abilities also play a role in performance, with some specific abilities important for some jobs and other specific abilities important for other jobs. To return to the example of an "athletic person," your roommate or partner may be incredibly (disgustingly?) athletic but is unlikely to go head-to-head with Phil Mickelson on the golf course. The pros must have something (e.g., coordination, visual acuity, endurance, joint flexibility) that your roommate does not have. These would be specific physical abilities. This holds true for cognitive abilities as well.

A question then arises: How many specific abilities are there? There is no conclusive answer to that question, but we can say with great confidence that there is more than one (i.e., more than just "g"). As we mentioned earlier, Fleishman and his colleagues posited 52 abilities, 21 of which are in the cognitive category, but "g" is not one of them. Fleishman was more concerned with identifying *specific* abilities than general mental ability. It is now generally accepted that cognitive ability is best conceptualized as having multiple layers of abilities.

Carroll (1993) proposed that there are three layers, or strata, to intelligence (see Figure 3.2). The highest layer is "g"; the next layer down consists of seven more specific abilities: fluid intelligence, crystallized intelligence, memory, visual perception, auditory perception, information retrieval, and cognitive speed (Murphy, 1996). The lowest and most specific level includes abilities that are tied to the seven broad abilities in the middle level. For example, information ordering (one of Fleishman's proposed abilities) would be connected to fluid intelligence, and spatial relations would be associated with visual perception.

There are many other theories of specific cognitive abilities (e.g., Ackerman, Beier, & Boyle, 2002, 2005), but all resemble Carroll's. The important thing to remember is that "g" will only get you so far in understanding work behavior. It is fair to say that a person with a high level of "g" will probably succeed at certain tasks of almost every job, particularly complex jobs (Schmidt & Hunter, 1998), but that depending on the job, other abilities such as personality, emotional reactions, and interests will also play a role in job success.

Recently, some researchers have begun to nominate and explore very specific cognitive abilities as predictors of work and vocational success. David Lubinski and his colleagues have been studying intellectually talented adolescents for many decades, following them from age 13 through adulthood. Although Lubinski agrees that general mental ability has a substantial impact on adult vocational accomplishments, he also finds that the difference between SAT math and verbal scores has implications for which careers are chosen. Adolescents who had higher scores in math were more likely to pursue careers in the sciences and technology and more likely to secure a patent (Park, Lubinski, & Benbow, 2007). In contrast, adolescents with higher verbal scores were drawn to the humanities rather than science and were more likely to publish a novel. Although these gifted adolescents,

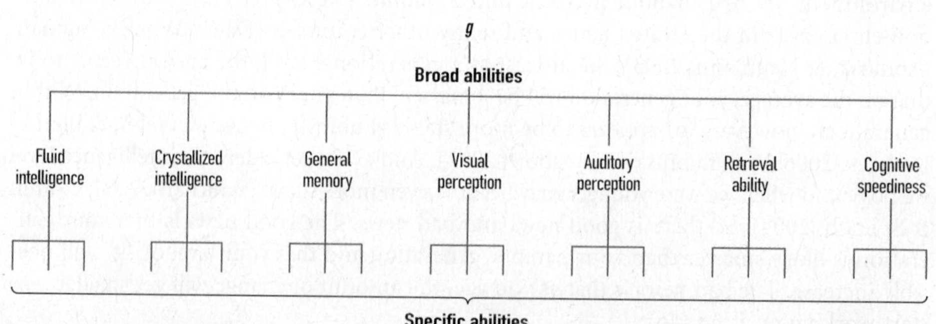

FIGURE 3.2 Carroll's Hierarchical Model

SOURCE: Carroll, J. B. (1993). *Human cognitive abilities: A survey of factoranalytic studies*. Cambridge, U.K.: Cambridge University Press.

BOX 3.1 DIFFERENT KINDS OF READING ABILITY?

© Nicole Bengiveno /The New York Times/Redux Pictures

Does reading materials on electronic devices (e.g., laptop, iPad, Kindle) involve different abilities than does reading traditional printed materials?

Have you ever thought about the fact that parents and children read differently? It is not so much that they read different material (although you would be surprised to see your parents reading Perez Hilton's blog on the web!) but that they read using different media. Many adults still spend a great deal of time reading print material (newspapers, books, magazines), while their children read web-based sources. This has prompted some educators and testing experts to suggest that some abilities may be peculiar to Internet reading and that the speed and accuracy of this reading ability is not captured by reading textual material. The result is a lively debate that involves organizations like the National Council of Teachers of English, the International Reading Association, and the Organization for Economic Cooperation and Development. Many European countries are beginning to assess electronic reading in addition to more traditional textual reading. Advocates of the assessment of electronic reading propose that this 21st-century mode of reading uses abilities such as searching for answers to questions in real time, navigating the web, evaluating information from multiple and occasionally conflicting sources, and communicating through web posts and blogs.

SOURCE: Based on material from Rich (2008).

generally, had high levels of creative accomplishment, the area of those accomplishments was influenced by the predominance of verbal or mathematical skills. Lubinski and his colleagues (Webb, Lubinski, & Benbow, 2007) also found that spatial ability (i.e., the ability to visualize what an object in three-dimensional space would look like if it were rotated) in combination with mathematical ability predicted career choice as well as educational success in math and science. Even though these studies tell us more about how careers evolve, they also seem to point to the importance of specific cognitive abilities in certain vocational domains.

One final specific dimension of cognitive ability—memory—has received attention from I-O psychologists. Each computer has a storage capacity, usually indexed as gigabytes. More gigs means more memory, and more memory means great power (both speed and capacity). König, Bühner, and Mürling (2005) proposed that humans are like computers with respect to working memory and that some individuals have more than others. They further proposed that people with more working memory are better at juggling multiple tasks simultaneously (known as multitasking). Multitasking is an important part of many working lives (e.g., completing a report while answering e-mail messages and phone calls and questions from the person at the desk next to you). The researchers measured working memory by a person's capacity to keep things (e.g., sentences, positions of objects) fresh in his or her mind. Not surprisingly, they discovered that the more working memory a person had, the better he or she was at multitasking. Thus, there is reason to propose including a measure of working memory in the assessment of applicants for jobs that require substantial amounts of multitasking. We simply do not know as much as we need to about the contribution of specific cognitive abilities to work performance, as general mental ability (or "g" or "intelligence") dominated the research and application scene for well over 80 years. Applied psychologists are only now beginning to reexamine the contribution of specific cognitive abilities to behavior. We expect that this reexamination will yield substantial insights over the next decade.

Physical, Sensory, and Psychomotor Abilities

Physical Abilities

Hogan (1991a,b) suggested that seven physical abilities are sufficient for analyzing most jobs. Guion compared Hogan's seven abilities with similar abilities identified by Fleishman and Reilly (1992) and found a close match. As you can see in Figure 3.3, several of Hogan's dimensions are combinations of the Fleishman and Reilly (1992) dimensions (e.g., she combines extent flexibility and dynamic flexibility into a single dimension called "flexibility"). In a manner reminiscent of Carroll's theory of intelligence, Hogan then combines her seven measures to form three higher-order physical abilities: muscular strength, cardiovascular

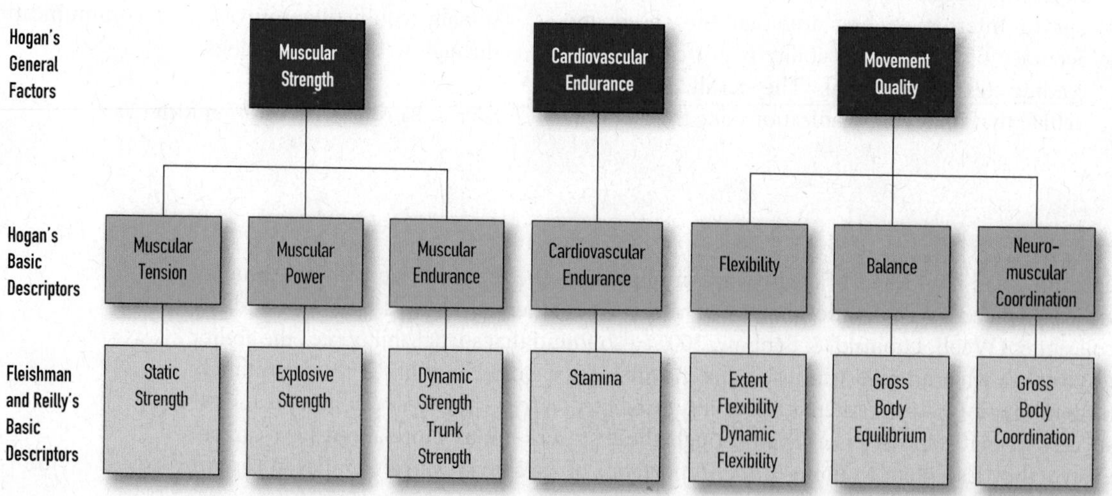

FIGURE 3.3 A Model of Physical Abilities

SOURCE: Guion, R. M. (1998). *Assessment, measurement and prediction for personnel decisions*. Mahwah, NJ: Lawrence Erlbaum Associates. © 1998 by Taylor & Francis Group LLC–Books. Used by permission. Permission conveyed through Copyright Clearance Center, Inc.

endurance, and movement quality. For most jobs, this three-ability taxonomy would likely be sufficient because most physically demanding jobs require **muscular tension, muscular power**, and **muscular endurance**, not just one of the three. Similarly, flexibility and balance usually go together in a physically demanding job.

Muscular tension Physical quality of muscular strength.

Muscular power Physical ability to lift, pull, push, or otherwise move an object; unlike endurance, this is a one-time maximum effort.

Muscular endurance Physical ability to continue to use a single muscle or muscle group repeatedly over a period of time.

Stamina Physical ability to supply muscles with oxygenated blood through the cardiovascular system; also known as cardiovascular strength or aerobic strength or endurance.

Fairness of Physical Ability Tests

Because employers often use physical ability tests to screen applicants for physically demanding jobs, it is important to determine whether such tests are fair to female applicants and older applicants. Because we lose muscle, **stamina**, and flexibility as we age, the older an applicant is, the less well he or she is likely to perform on physical ability tests. For women the situation has an additional consideration. On average, females have less muscle mass (which means diminished muscular strength) and lower levels of cardiovascular endurance (or stamina) than men (Hogan, 1991a). In contrast, on measures of flexibility (e.g., sit and reach tests), women tend to do better than men. However, most physically demanding jobs require—or are perceived by employers to require—more muscular strength and stamina than flexibility. This has meant that male candidates, who tend to excel on those physical tests, are predominantly hired for such jobs. As a result, women candidates for popular positions such as firefighter have filed employment discrimination suits (*Brunet* v. *City of Columbus*, 1995).

Women and men of all ages can increase their individual physical abilities with exercise and training. In addition, many jobs require a fixed level of strength and endurance, beyond which more is not always better. If your job requires you to lift 25-pound boxes, the fact that you are strong enough to move 100-pound boxes is irrelevant. In this case, more strength would not lead to higher performance. Thus, individuals do not always have to compete *against* each other on physical ability tests; they merely need to demonstrate sufficient strength and endurance to perform the job tasks. By training for several months prior to taking physical ability tests, female candidates can improve their performance significantly. Thus, one way of helping females to do better on these tests is for employers to encourage them to train ahead of time (McArdle, Katch, & Katch, 2001). We can predict that this same strategy may help older job seekers as well.

Employers are usually eager to contain the cost of medical and disability programs for workers—if possible, by predicting who is likely to experience an injury and rejecting those applicants. Physical ability tests have been used as the predictor for future injury. The problem is that while they may be good (but far from perfect) predictors of future injury, such tests may not be particularly relevant for present or future job performance. In a case against Armour Star meat-packing facility in Iowa, 52 women successfully sued the company for denying them jobs based on a strength test. A federal judge awarded $3.3 million to the women because the test was used to predict injuries, not performance on the job (Business and Legal Reports, 2005a).

Sensory abilities Physical functions of vision, hearing, touch, taste, smell, and kinesthetic feedback (e.g., noticing changes in body position).

Americans with Disabilities Act Federal legislation enacted in 1990 requiring employers to give applicants and employees with disabilities the same consideration as other applicants and employees, and to make certain adaptations in the work environment to accommodate disabilities.

Sensory Abilities

Sensory abilities are the physical functions of vision, hearing, touch, taste, smell, and kinesthetic feedback (e.g., noticing changes in body position). Hogan includes kinesthetic feedback in a dimension she calls "movement quality." The sensory abilities of vision and hearing are particularly interesting for applied I-O psychologists because employers often test these abilities in would-be employees.

To prevent employers from using a disability as an excuse to reject an applicant who is capable of performing a job, the **Americans with Disabilities Act** of 1990 forbids them to ask about or test areas such as sensory or physical abilities that may be considered "disabilities" until after they have made a job offer to the candidate.

Until recently, cognitive psychologists considered sensory abilities to be independent of cognitive abilities, but Carroll's (1993) model of intelligence calls that assumption into question—remember that two of his midlevel abilities are visual perception and auditory perception. In addition, Ackerman's research (e.g., Ackerman et al., 2002, 2005) shows the close association between perceptual speed and other measures of cognitive ability. But in most real-life settings, sensation and perception are inextricably bound together. We usually infer from some kind of report (verbal or behavioral) that a person has sensed something. Further research will shed light on the extent to which "noncognitive" abilities are really "noncognitive."

Psychomotor Abilities

Psychomotor abilities Physical functions of movement, associated with coordination, dexterity, and reaction time; also called motor or sensorimotor abilities.

Psychomotor abilities, sometimes called sensorimotor or just motor abilities, deal with issues of coordination, dexterity, and reaction time. Once again, Fleishman (Fleishman & Reilly, 1992) has done the most extensive work in identifying these abilities. We can easily name some jobs for which they may be important (e.g., crane operators, organists, watch repair technicians, surgeons, wait staff, and bartenders). From this discussion it should be clear that many psychomotor abilities (e.g., rate control and aiming) may very well be associated with visual and/or auditory perception or cognitive speed, facets of Carroll's theory of intelligence. See Box 3.2 for a discussion of reaction time in work situations.

The work of researchers like Carroll and Ackerman blurs the classical distinctions between cognitive and "noncognitive" abilities. In some senses, this is a good development, for it is clear in real life (and—more importantly for us—in work) that all of these abilities interact within a single person to produce a response or action.

BOX 3.2 REACTION TIME IN WORK SITUATIONS

It is interesting to note that some specific mental abilities show remarkable stability well into the life span. As an example, reaction times change very little between age 30 and age 65, "slowing" by perhaps 1/20 of a second from .45 second to .50 second. Technically, it is true that reaction time "diminishes" with age, but what are the practical consequences for most jobs of a decrease of .05 second? Neverthless, the belief that older workers are "slower" may influence staffing decisions. As an example, the Vermont State Police requires troopers to retire at age 55 because of the fear that this "decrease" in reaction time might lead to dangerous behaviors (e.g., drawing and firing a weapon "too slowly"). Not only is that nonsense from a physiological standpoint, but with the advent of the semiautomatic handheld weapons issued by most police departments, more problems have arisen because officers fire their weapons too rapidly, not because of lags in reaction times. Two famous examples occurred in New York City when civilians Amadou Diallo (Cooper, 1999) and Sean Bell (Buckley & Rashbaum, 2006) were each killed in a hail of bullets by police officers who reacted quickly. In retrospect, slower rather than faster reaction time might have been in order in each case.

SOURCES: Buckley & Rashbaum (2006); Cooper (1999).

Personality and Work Behavior

Personality is really a big deal in I-O psychology, probably the biggest deal since the consideration of the role of intelligence in work behavior a century ago. There is now a broad consensus that personality predicts not only general behavior and happiness (Steele, Schmidt, & Shultz, 2008) but also specifically work-related behavior. This work-related behavior includes performance, absenteeism, counterproductive work behavior, and team effectiveness. Barrick and Mount (2005) provide the following seven reasons why "personality matters in the workplace" and document those reasons using recent research:

1. Managers care about personality. In hiring decisions, they weigh personality characteristics as heavily as they do intelligence.
2. Many research studies show the importance of various personality measures in predicting both overall job performance and specific aspects of performance. Personality addresses the "will do" aspects of performance, while intelligence addresses the "can do" aspects of performance.
3. When we combine personality characteristics (rather than considering them one at a time), the relationship between personality and work performance becomes even stronger.
4. Personality measures improve the predictability of work performance over what would be found using only measures of intelligence or experience.
5. There are much smaller differences among age, gender, and ethnic minority subgroups on measures of personality than on measures of intelligence.
6. Personality measures predict not only near-term behavior (e.g., current job performance) but also distant outcomes such as career success, job and life satisfaction, and occupational status.
7. Personality measures predict a wide variety of outcomes that are important to managers, including counterproductive behavior, turnover, absenteeism, tardiness, group success, organizational citizenship behavior, job satisfaction, task performance, and leadership effectiveness.

In the last several years, three major journals (*Human Performance*, 2005; *International Journal of Selection and Assessment*, 2007; *Personnel Psychology*, 2007) have addressed the role of personality in understanding work behavior. The interested reader can use these sources to examine the issues and promise of personality in understanding work behavior. Although these treatments highlight some disagreements among researchers (e.g., Hogan, 2005; Morgeson et al., 2007a; Roberts, Chernyshenko, Stark, & Goldberg, 2005; Tett & Christiansen, 2007) regarding how many personality factors there are, how to assess them, and how predictive they are of work performance, the general conclusion confirms our position: Personality is a big deal in understanding work behavior.

The Big Five and Other Models of Personality

Historically, an increased interest in personality measurement (both in general human behavior and more specifically in work behavior) began with the development of a taxonomy of personality dimensions labeled the **Big Five** or the **Five-Factor Model (FFM)** (Digman, 1990; McCrae & Costa, 1985, 1987). According to this model, an individual's personality can be described by where that individual falls on five dimensions: openness to experience, conscientiousness, extraversion, agreeableness, and neuroticism (the opposite of emotional

Big Five A taxonomy of five personality factors; the Five-Factor Model (FFM).

Five-Factor Model (FFM) A taxonomy of five personality factors, composed of conscientiousness, extraversion, agreeableness, emotional stability, and openness to experience.

CASE STUDY 3.1 A LEVEL PLAYING FIELD

It is common to test for physical abilities before choosing candidates for recruit positions in fire training academies. Although physical abilities will be improved in the 16 weeks of the academy training program, recruits still require a minimum amount of ability to profit from the training. Most fire departments administer physical ability tests that simulate actual tasks performed by firefighters. As examples, candidates may be asked to carry heavy hose bundles up stairs, open fire hydrants with wrenches, or hang heavy exhaust fans in windows. Two tests, in particular, seem to be harder for female applicants than their male counterparts. The first is the "dummy drag" simulation. In this test, the candidate is asked to drag a 150-pound dummy through a 40-foot maze with several left and right turns in it. The second task is pulling 50 feet of a simulated fire hose through a 50-foot maze with two right turns. Since men tend to be larger and stronger, they simply pick up the dummy and carry it through the maze, while women are more likely to drag the dummy along the floor of the maze. Similarly, for the hose pull, men tend to simply loop the hose over their shoulder and pull it through the maze in one single movement. The test is not exactly the same as the actual task, however; in an actual fire situation the firefighter is usually pulling a person or a hose through a burning room and must stay close to the ground because the toxic fumes, smoke, and temperature (often as high as 2,000 degrees) are more deadly in the upper part of a room.

If you wanted to make these test components more realistic, how would you redesign the test course? If you did redesign it, do you think that the performance of women would improve? Why or why not?

stability); a useful acronym for the five scales is OCEAN. The FFM was the result of both statistical analyses of personality test information gathered over many decades and a careful conceptual analysis of what most personality tests were trying to assess. The FFM is a good way to gain a broad understanding of the structure of personality, but it may be a bit too general for dealing with specific aspects of work behavior. In fact, many work-related personality models have developed from the more generic FFM and seem to have more relevance for work behavior. These include the Five-Factor Model Questionnaire (FFMQ; Gill & Hodgkinson, 2007), the Hogan Personality Inventory (Hogan, Davies, & Hogan, 2007), and the Personal Characteristics Inventory (Mount & Barrick, 2002).

Virtually all modern personality models resemble the Five-Factor Model in that they propose that we can describe someone's "personality" by looking at some small number of relatively independent factors. Personality can be defined in simplest terms as the typical way that an individual has of responding. It is considered to be a collection of traits because it is fairly stable, even though situations and circumstances might lead a person to behave in a way that is out of character with his or her overall personality. Using the FFM as an example, the model identifies five different components that, when taken together, give a fair representation of how a person typically responds to events and people (see Table 3.1). Considerable evidence suggests that although the five factors might express themselves in slightly different ways in various cultures, the FFM seems applicable across cultures (Cheung, 2004).

Conscientiousness Quality of having positive intentions and carrying them out with care.

It is important to keep in mind that personality factors are intended to measure normal personality, not to identify any evidence of psychopathology. We will make that distinction clearer later in this chapter when we discuss how personality is measured. Of the five FFM factors, the first to attract attention from I-O psychologists was **conscientiousness**. More

TABLE 3.1 **The Five-Factor Model**

FACTOR	CHARACTERISTICS
1. Conscientiousness	Responsible, prudent, persistent, planful, achievement oriented
2. Extraversion	Sociable, assertive, talkative, ambitious, energetic
3. Agreeableness	Good-natured, cooperative, trusting, likable, friendly
4. Emotional stability	Secure, calm, poised, relaxed
5. Openness to experience	Curious, imaginative, independent, creative

SOURCE: Based on Digman (1990).

recently, extraversion, openness to experience, and agreeableness have also been attracting increased attention (Barrick & Mount, 2005). In some early research, Barrick and Mount (1991) proposed, on the basis of a meta-analysis, that conscientiousness was likely positively related to success in all aspects of work for all occupations. That was a strong statement, but it was supported by their analyses. Naturally, there were disagreements with the five-factor taxonomy and with the presumed overarching importance of conscientiousness. The first criticism was that five factors were too few to capture the full range of aspects of personality (Hough, 1992; Tellegen & Waller, 2000). The second criticism was that although conscientiousness might be correlated with a wide range of work behaviors, it was not *highly* correlated with them. In addition, extraversion often correlated as highly with behavior as did conscientiousness. A third criticism was that there were combinations of the five factors that led to greater predictive power than any one of the factors by itself (Ones, Viswesvaran, & Schmidt, 1993). The first and third criticisms present an interesting dilemma, since one argues for *more* factors, whereas the other seems to be arguing for *fewer* factors.

It does, however, appear that there are more than the originally proposed five factors. Roberts and colleagues (2005) argue that conscientiousness can be broken down further into three "subfactors" (industriousness, order, and self-control). Roberts and Mroczek (2008) suggest that extraversion can be further broken down into gregariousness and assertiveness. Lee, Ashton, and de Vries (2005) propose that a dimension of "honesty–humility" needs to be added to the FFM. Some evidence (Marcus, Lee, & Ashton, 2007) suggests that this new dimension might be useful in predicting counterproductive work behavior such as theft. We believe that there is still valuable work to be done in identifying "the" relevant parameters of the personality at work, and the FFM represents a useful starting point. No one seems to disagree that the FFM contains the *minimum* number of relevant personality characteristics; the debate seems to be about the *optimum* number.

What seems to be true is that, although each of the five broad personality factors does predict successful (in contrast to unsuccessful) performance of certain behaviors, some combinations of the factors may be stronger predictors than any single factor. This introduces the idea of a **functional personality at work** (Barrick, Mount, & Judge, 2001), meaning that not just one factor predicts success, but a combination of factors. For example, Ones and colleagues (1993) found that individuals who were high on conscientiousness, **agreeableness**, and **emotional stability** tended to have higher **integrity**. In this context, integrity means being honest, reliable, and ethical. Dunn (1993) found that managers believed

Functional personality at work The way that an individual behaves, handles emotions, and accomplishes tasks in a work setting; a combination of Big Five factors.

Agreeableness Likable, easy to get along with, friendly.

Emotional stability Displaying little emotion; showing the same emotional response in various situations.

Integrity Quality of being honest, reliable, and ethical.

that a combination of conscientiousness, agreeableness, and emotional stability made applicants more attractive to managers who had hiring responsibilities. In a review of meta-analyses, Barrick and colleagues (2001) confirmed the importance of conscientiousness across a variety of occupations and performance measures. Emotional stability also appeared to predict overall performance across occupations. Judge and Erez (2007) found that a combination of high emotional stability and high extraversion (which they labeled a "happy" or "buoyant" personality) led to higher performance for employees and supervisors at a health and fitness center. In another meta-analysis, Clarke and Robertson (2005) found that low agreeableness, high extraversion, and low conscientiousness were related to accidents, both in occupational and traffic situations. They suggested that individuals low on agreeableness have more difficulty managing interpersonal relations, including following group safety norms.

Other meta-analyses also reveal relationships between the FFM and job performance, both in the United States (Hurtz & Donovan, 2000) and in Europe (Salgado, 1997, 1998). The latter series of meta-analyses suggest that, at least for many European countries, culture may not be a moderator variable of the personality/performance relationship. More recent research suggests that personality is a critical predictor for work behavior in Germany (Moser & Galais, 2007), Australia (Carless et al., 2007), Thailand (Smithikrai, 2007), and the Netherlands (Klehe & Anderson, 2007a). Nevertheless, remember from Chapter 1 (Hofstede, 2001) that cultural influences can be substantial and that substantial differences exist between Western and Asian cultures. As examples, Tyler and Newcombe (2006) show that additional personality characteristics such as "face," "graciousness versus meanness," and "thrift versus extravagance" might be necessary to describe the Chinese work personality. The importance of face (as in "to avoid losing face") had been shown in earlier studies of Chinese students and managers by Cheung and colleagues (2001). It is tempting to recall the dramatic example from Chapter 1 of the Chinese manager who hanged himself, possibly because of a loss of face. Much more research on the nature of the non-Western work personality is in order. As suggested by the work of McCrae, Terracciano, and colleagues (2005), there is reason to expect that significant differences in work personality will be found in Asian societies as compared to Europe or the United States, if for no other reason than the emphasis on group outcomes over individual outcomes in the collectivist cultures of China and Japan.

Implications of Broad Personality Models

As the aspect of work behavior we are trying to predict gets broader (e.g., overall job performance), large factors (e.g., conscientiousness) seem to be as predictive of behavior as are smaller and more discrete factors. There is some debate about whether or not to use broad or narrow personality dimensions (Hogan & Roberts, 1996; Ones & Viswesvaran, 1996; Schneider, Hough, & Dunnette, 1996). It turns out that narrow traits seem useful for predicting very specific job behaviors (Dudley, Orvis, Lebeicki, & Cortina, 2006) and broader traits for predicting broader behaviors (Tett, Steele, & Beauregard, 2003). Each has its own use. In fact, there appears to be a movement to keep broad personality models from reducing research on other possible personality characteristics (Borman, 2004a; Murphy & Dzieweczynski, 2005). Schmitt (2004) has suggested three promising personality characteristics:

1. Core self-evaluation (Judge & Bono, 2001), a type of inner-directedness and sense of efficacy
2. Tolerance for contradiction (Chan, 2004), a way of thinking that prefers apparently contradictory information

3. Achievement motivation and aggression (Frost, Ko, & James, 2007; James, 1998), the tendency to aggressively seek out desired ends

We are not necessarily suggesting that these are "variables to watch"—we are simply echoing Schmitt's sentiment that it is too early to close the door on variables beyond those in broad personality models such as the FFM.

As we will see in Chapter 4, I-O psychology is becoming more specific in discussions of performance outcomes. Thirty years ago, most research and discussions would have addressed the issue of "overall performance." Now discussion of performance includes specific aspects of work behavior such as citizenship behavior (e.g., volunteering, persisting), technical task performance, adaptive performance (adjusting to technical or procedural unpredictability in the work context), and counterproductive work performance. As it becomes more common to break down work performance into more discrete categories, narrower personality characteristics may begin to show their value over broad dimensions such as those represented by the FFM.

There is a final aspect of the research on personality and work behavior that deserves discussion. Have you ever had a job in which you were closely supervised and required to follow very detailed work and organizational procedures? In that environment, you would have had little opportunity to show your "habitual way of responding" (i.e., your personality). Think of the opposite situation—a job where you had a good deal of control over your work habits. In the latter, you could really be "you," and whether you performed well or poorly probably depended on how well your personality was suited to the job's demands. That is exactly what Barrick and Mount (1993) found with their research on the FFM. In jobs where the employee had a great deal of control (i.e., autonomy), personality was much more predictive of performance than in jobs where the employee had little or no control. Thus, control moderated the relationship between personality and performance. In statistical terms, control would be called a "moderator variable"—a variable that changes the nature of the relationship between two other variables. It has been commonly found that if a situation does not allow the person much discretion (referred to as a "strong" situation), personality will play a minor role in his or her behavior.

To summarize what we know about the relationship between personality and work behavior, we believe the following conclusions can be drawn with confidence:

1. Personality differences play an important role in work behavior independent of the role played by cognitive ability (Mount & Barrick, 1995; Murphy, 1996).
2. Personality is more closely related to motivational aspects of work (e.g., effort expenditure) than to technical aspects of work (e.g., knowledge components). Personality is more likely to predict what a person will do, and ability measures are more likely to predict what a person can do (Campbell, 1990a; Mount & Barrick, 1995).
3. The FFM is a good general framework for thinking about important aspects of personality (Digman, 1990; Guion, 1998; Lubinski, 2000).
4. The more relevant and specific the work behavior we are trying to predict, the stronger the association between personality and behavior (Mount & Barrick, 1995).
5. Conscientiousness is best considered a combination of **achievement** and **dependability**. Achievement will predict some behaviors (e.g., effort) and dependability will predict other behaviors (e.g., attendance) (Hough, 1992; Moon, 2001; Mount & Barrick, 1995; Stewart, 1999).
6. Conscientiousness (along with its constituent factors achievement and dependability) has widespread applicability in work settings. It is possibly the most important personality variable in the workplace, and it may be the equivalent of "g" in the noncognitive domain (Schmidt & Hunter, 1992).

Achievement A facet of conscientiousness consisting of hard work, persistence, and the desire to do good work.

Dependability A facet of conscientiousness consisting of being disciplined, well organized, respectful of laws and regulations, honest, trustworthy, and accepting of authority.

ADDITIONAL ATTRIBUTES

The collection of cognitive abilities, physical and motor abilities, personality, and interests cover the major categories of proposed individual differences. The patterns formed by their combinations describe much of the variation among individuals. Nevertheless, some scientists propose additional aspects of individual differences.

NON SEQUITUR BY WILEY

Sometimes skill in reading a blueprint can be very important.

Skills

Skills Practiced acts, such as shooting a basketball, using a computer keyboard, or persuading someone to buy something.

Skills are practiced acts. Shooting a basketball, using a computer keyboard, and persuading someone to buy something are all examples of skills. They come with hours, days, and weeks of practice. Skills also depend on certain abilities (eye–hand coordination, or memory, or reasoning), personality characteristics (persistence or agreeableness), and knowledge (understanding the controls that activate a piece of equipment). Although skills depend on these other factors, the reason we call them skills is that they develop through practice. Technical and job-related skills are as varied as jobs and job tasks. There are other nontechnical skills that are more widespread than any technical skill. Examples include negotiating skills, communication skills, and conflict resolution skills. These three are often lumped together by nonpsychologists and called **people skills**. Since they come into play most commonly in situations involving leader–follower and team member interactions, we will discuss them in the chapters that deal with teams and leadership.

People skills A nontechnical term that includes negotiating skills, communication skills, and conflict resolution skills.

Knowledge

Knowledge can be defined as "a collection of discrete but related facts and information about a particular domain. It is acquired through formal education or training, or accumulated through specific experiences" (Peterson, Mamford, Borman, Jeanneret, & Fleishman, 1999, p. 71). Many cities known for tourism (e.g., London, New York City) require taxi drivers to complete map tests demonstrating intricate knowledge of streets and areas. Recently, Philadelphia considered an ordinance that would require licensing of tour guides with particular attention to knowledge of the city's history (Associated Press, 2007). Knowledge is closely connected to skill when we are considering job-related skills (as opposed to psychomotor skills like shooting a basketball). Knowledge supports skill development, and it comes in many varieties. It can be very basic (knowledge of mathematical operations or of vocabulary), or it can be sophisticated (knowledge of computer circuitry). Representative categories of knowledge as identified in the comprehensive **Occupational Information Network** that has

Occupational Information Network (O*NET) Collection of electronic databases, based on well-developed taxonomies, that has updated and replaced the *Dictionary of Occupational Titles (DOT)*.

come to be known as **O*NET** are too detailed to present here, but they can be found in Peterson, Mamford, and Colleagues (1999). The O*NET architecture, which is described further in Chapter 4, presents the name of the knowledge domain, the definition of the knowledge, and examples of what someone with a great deal or very little of the knowledge might be capable of doing. Perhaps the most immediate example of individual differences in knowledge is the distribution of test grades in your class. Although many variables may play a role in this grade distribution, one of those variables is certainly knowledge of the course material as presented in the text and lectures.

Another kind of knowledge that has been proposed is called **tacit knowledge**, studied by Sternberg and his colleagues (Sternberg, Wagner, & Okagaki, 1993). They distinguish between "academic" and "tacit" knowledge, the latter described as "action oriented knowledge, acquired without direct help from others, that allows individuals to achieve goals they personally value" (Sternberg, Wagner, Williams, & Horvath, 1995). They describe tacit knowledge as "knowing how" rather than "knowing that." Box 3.3 provides a practical example of tacit knowledge. A more formal way of distinguishing these two types of knowledge is **procedural knowledge** (knowing how) in contrast to **declarative knowledge** (knowing that). Interestingly, Rapp, Ahearne, Mathieu, and Schillewart (2006) find that pharmaceutical sales representatives work harder when they have high levels of declarative knowledge but lower levels of experience (which would eventually lead to procedural knowledge).

Tacit knowledge Action-oriented, goal-directed knowledge, acquired without direct help from others; colloquially called street smarts.

Procedural knowledge Familiarity with a procedure or process; knowing "how."

Declarative knowledge Understanding what is required to perform a task; knowing information about a job or job task.

These researchers give an example of how tacit knowledge about getting along with your boss might affect your behavior. If you need to deliver bad news, and you have reason to believe your boss is in a bad mood, tacit knowledge would tell you that it would be best to deliver the bad news later. A common nonscientific term for tacit knowledge might be "street smarts." One of the important distinctions researchers make between formal or academic knowledge on the one hand and tacit knowledge on the other is that tacit knowledge is always goal-directed and useful, while academic knowledge may not be. People develop tacit knowledge about environments and processes that are personally valuable to them. Research suggests that tacit knowledge is something above and beyond intelligence (Sternberg et al., 1995). Learning little tricks to perform better might be considered the light side of the tacit knowledge coin, and learning how to manipulate people might be the dark side. Knowledge, particularly tacit knowledge, is often thought to accumulate as a result of experience.

BOX 3.3 AN EXAMPLE OF TACIT KNOWLEDGE

A postal worker gets on an elevator in a 25-story building and pushes the button for the 18th floor. Just before exiting the elevator at that floor, she pushes the button for the 25th floor, puzzling those left on the elevator who are going no higher than the 21st floor. The postal worker drops off mail and picks up mail from a central location on the 18th floor in less than 60 seconds, returns to the elevator, pushes the down button, and reenters the elevator she just left making its way down from the 25th floor. She has learned that if she does not follow this routine, the elevator may not go to the 25th floor and she may have to wait several minutes for another elevator to travel up the 18 floors to retrieve her. This is tacit knowledge at its finest.

Competencies

Competencies Sets of behaviors, usually learned by experience, that are instrumental in the accomplishment of desired organizational results or outcomes.

I-O psychologists talk about combinations of knowledge, skills, abilities, and other personality characteristics (KSAOs) in terms of **competencies**. Kurz and Bartram (2002) have defined competencies as "sets of behaviors that are instrumental in the delivery of desired results or outcomes" (p. 229). Following from that definition, it is reasonable to assume that people differ in the extent to which they possess various competencies. But competencies are different from knowledge—or a skill, ability, or personality characteristic—in that a competency is really a collection of all of these specific individual difference characteristics. The essence of a competency is the *combination* of these characteristics and is not dominated by any one of them (Campion et al., 2011; Harris, 1998a). We will review a model of competencies called The "Great Eight," as proposed by Bartram (2005), in Chapter 4 when we discuss performance models.

Competencies are unique in another way as well. Abilities can be defined and measured in the abstract, as can personality characteristics. But competencies only have meaning in the context of organizational goals. For example, you could distinguish between two individuals based on their measured conscientiousness, their reasoning ability, or their skill with a word-processing program. But the competency of organizing and executing a business plan would require a combination of these three individual elements, in addition to various aspects of technical and procedural knowledge (Kurz & Bartram, 2002), and would have relevance only to that series of actions. Thus, competencies are really collections and patterns of the individual difference attributes we have already covered, rather than separate characteristics. We will return to competencies and how they are identified (competency modeling) in Chapter 4 as a new way of thinking about analyzing jobs—a process called **job analysis**.

Job analysis Process that determines the important tasks of a job and the human attributes necessary to successfully perform those tasks.

Emotional Intelligence

In the 1980s Howard Gardner (1983, 1993) proposed a novel theory of intelligence. Rather than a unitary approach to intelligence such as "g," he posited seven different types of intelligence, including logical-mathematical, bodily-kinesthetic, linguistic, musical, spatial, interpersonal, and intrapersonal. He described the latter two intelligences as follows:

> Interpersonal intelligence is the ability to understand other people: what motivates them, how they work, how to work cooperatively with them. . . . Intrapersonal intelligence, a seventh kind of intelligence, is a correlative ability turned inward. It is a capacity to form an accurate veridical model of oneself and to be able to use that model to operate effectively in life. (Gardner, 1983, p. 9)

Emotional intelligence (EI) A proposed kind of intelligence focused on people's awareness of their own and others' emotions.

Gardner's notion of inter- and intrapersonal intelligence was popularized by Goleman (1995) using the label **emotional intelligence (EI)**. Two important questions about EI have emerged. The first is whether this actually represents a kind of intelligence, a skill developed and honed with practice, or a personality characteristic (Barrett, 2001). Mayer, Roberts, and Barsade (2008) have recently defined EI as "the ability to carry out accurate reasoning about emotions and the ability to use emotions and emotional knowledge to enhance thought" (p. 507). The second question is how to measure EI; two different approaches have been proposed. One has been labeled the "mixed" approach and addresses EI as a personality characteristic. The other is called an ability approach and measures EI like any other measure of cognitive ability.

In many respects, this becomes more a semantic battle than a theoretical one. Nevertheless, many of the studies that have been done on the **construct** have been disappointing, failing to identify EI as something different from attributes with which we are already familiar (Davies, Stankov, & Roberts, 1998; Roberts, Zeidner, & Matthews, 2001). Van Rooy, Viswesvaran, and Pluta (2005) report considerable overlap between the mixed model and personality measures as well as similar overlap between the ability model and measures of cognitive ability. This type of overlap has led critics to question whether EI is really a new human attribute. A recent review of the two models (Mayer et al., 2008) finds little support for the mixed model as opposed to the ability model. In 2005, the *Journal of Organizational Behavior* devoted an entire section to the debate (Ashkanasy & Daus, 2005; Conte, 2005; Daus & Ashkanasy, 2005; Landy, 2005a; Locke, 2005; Spector, 2005). In addition, Murphy (2006) edited an important book on EI that includes vigorous advocates on both sides.

Construct Psychological concept or characteristic that a predictor is intended to measure; examples are intelligence, personality, and leadership.

A recent meta-analysis by O'Boyle and colleagues (2011) found that EI showed some evidence of incremental validity above cognitive ability and the Big Five in predicting job performance. In addition, an interesting focal article on EI (Cherniss, 2010) and several commentaries were recently published in the SIOP journal entitled *Industrial and Organizational Psychology: Perspectives on Science and Practice.* Emotional intelligence remains a popular topic, and the construct will continue to be the focus of both research and practice.

MODULE 3.2 SUMMARY

- Fleishman and his associates developed a taxonomy of 52 abilities, divided into the broad categories of cognitive, physical, and perceptual-motor abilities.
- Intelligence (or "g") is a very general mental capability that describes a person's ability to learn from experience.
- Meta-analyses of the relationship between "g" and job performance demonstrated that the more complex the job, the stronger the predictive value of general intelligence tests.
- Carroll proposed that intelligence had three layers, or strata. The highest layer is "g"; the next layer down consists of seven more specific abilities: fluid intelligence, crystallized intelligence, memory, visual perception, auditory perception, information retrieval, and cognitive speed.
- Physically demanding jobs require strength, flexibility, and stamina or aerobic endurance. Hogan proposed a seven-measure taxonomy of physical abilities and combined these seven measures to form three higher-order physical abilities: muscular strength, cardiovascular endurance, and movement quality.
- It is important to determine whether employers' physical ability tests are fair to female applicants and older applicants, since both of these groups tend to have less strength than young men do. One way of enhancing the performance of females and older applicants on these tests is to encourage applicants to train ahead of time. It is also important that these tests relate to job performance prediction rather than injury prediction.
- There are clear connections between aspects of personality and various work behaviors, both productive (e.g., job performance) and counterproductive (e.g., dishonesty, absenteeism). I-O psychologists studying personality use a taxonomy labeled the Big Five or the Five-Factor Model (FFM).
- Of these five factors, the one that has attracted the most attention from I-O psychologists is conscientiousness. Barrick and Mount concluded, on the

basis of a meta-analysis, that conscientiousness was positively related to success in all aspects of work for all occupations.

- Barrick and Mount found through FFM research that in jobs where the employee had a great deal of control or autonomy, personality was much more predictive of performance than in jobs where the employee had little or no control.
- Skills are practiced acts. Although skills depend on ability, personality, and knowledge factors, what makes us call them skills is that they develop through practice.
- Knowledge can be defined as "a collection of discrete but related facts and information about a particular domain. It is acquired through formal education or training, or accumulated through specific experiences." Another proposed kind of knowledge is tacit knowledge, described as "knowing how" rather than "knowing that." A more formal way of distinguishing these two types of knowledge is procedural knowledge (knowing how) compared with declarative knowledge (knowing that).
- Competencies are "sets of behaviors that are instrumental in the delivery of desired results or outcomes." Competencies are different from knowledge—or a skill, ability, or personality characteristic—in that they are really a collection of all of these specific individual difference characteristics.
- Those who invoke the concept of emotional intelligence suggest that there is a unique kind of intelligence that is focused on our awareness of our own and others' emotions.

KEY TERMS

taxonomy
perceptual-motor abilities
affect
IQ
intelligence quotient
meta-analysis
Flynn effect
mean
standard deviation
muscular tension
muscular power
muscular endurance
stamina
sensory abilities
Americans with Disabilities Act
psychomotor abilities
Big Five
Five-Factor Model (FFM)
conscientiousness
functional personality at work
agreeableness
emotional stability
integrity
achievement
dependability
skills
people skills
Occupational Information Network (O*NET)
tacit knowledge
procedural knowledge
declarative knowledge
competencies
job analysis
emotional intelligence (EI)
construct

MODULE 3.3

Foundations of Assessment

The Past and the Present of Testing

Yvonne felt as if she had been preparing for this day forever. There had been similar days, sure: the SAT exam to get into college and the civil service test she took to get her summer job in the State Personnel Department. But this was show time. A high GRE score would be the ticket she needed for getting into a good graduate program. And that was exactly the problem. Yvonne choked up on standardized tests—always had and probably always would. Even though her SAT score had been low, she would finish with a 3.26 overall GPA and a 3.5 in her major. But getting into graduate school was not going to be as easy as it had been to qualify for her undergraduate program. The thing that really annoyed her was that these tests measured such a narrow band of who she was and what her capabilities were that they were a joke. How would they know that Yvonne was funny, loyal, and friendly, and had learned to read music in a weekend? Did they even care that she took hard courses rather than "cruisers"? She understood that there had to be *some* standard way of selecting among applicants, but she just wished that it was not a standardized test.

Society seems to have a love–hate relationship with psychological testing, a practice almost as old as psychology itself. The term "**mental test**" was introduced by Cattell in 1890. As we described in Chapter 1, in the First World War over a million soldiers were tested for intelligence in order to determine which were best suited to be officers and which, infantry. Up to that point, intelligence testing had been done on an individual basis, and this first trial of group testing was considered a massive success for the testing enterprise.

Mental test Instrument designed to measure a subject's ability to reason, plan, and solve problems; an intelligence test.

But with this success came an embarrassment; soon after the war, psychological testing began to be used as the justification for limiting immigration. The army testing program discovered that immigrants and their offspring, who did not speak English as a first language, scored lower on these intelligence tests. Fearing that unchecked immigration would reduce the national intelligence level, Congress enacted immigration quotas. Although social critics were quick to point out the potential unfairness of intelligence testing, advocates saw it as a way to avoid the class system that had characterized industry and education in the 19th century. In their view, a test was "objective" and thus freed decisions (about jobs or education) from the grasp of favoritism and nepotism.

Private industry, like the government, was impressed by the success of the army testing programs and moved to implement testing as a way of selecting the most promising candidates from a pool of job applicants. Soon, however, the Great Depression of the 1930s arrived, drastically reducing the need to select from an applicant pool. There were no jobs to be had. When America entered the Second World War, the country returned to a full employment mode and virtually every able-bodied and motivated worker, male or female, either had a job or was serving in a branch of the armed forces. Ships and airplanes were being built in record numbers, requiring one of the first 24/7 industrial environments. Now there was no need for selection for the opposite reason: There were many more jobs than people.

On the military front, commanders quickly realized that war was now much more technologically advanced than it had been a generation earlier. Personnel needed to operate many different types of aircraft and ships with complex maintenance and repair demands. The task of the armed forces was no longer simply distinguishing between officers and infantry. The war effort needed pilots, bombardiers, artillery personnel, radar and sonar operators, and an enormous training and administrative staff. Psychological testing was once again pushed to the forefront as a tool in the war effort, this time with more sophisticated tests for the placement of recruits.

By the end of the Second World War, test developers had virtually glutted the market, offering ability, personality, interest, and knowledge tests. Neither the government nor the psychological profession exercised much control over the quality of the tests or the meaning of the test scores. A thriving and competitive testing industry operated without constraint until the early 1960s, when two societal forces converged to rein in testing. The first was a new wave of criticism about the value of testing from social observers (Gross, 1962; Whyte, 1956). These critics pointed out that employers were expecting job applicants to submit to a range of tests that had little apparent relationship to the job for which they were applying. Many of the tests, particularly the interest and personality tests, asked questions of a personal nature—topics like religion, sex, and politics. The second force was the passage of the Civil Rights Act of 1964, which prohibited discrimination in employment, including testing. If a test had the effect of reducing the employment opportunities of protected subgroups (e.g., African Americans, women), then the employer would need to provide evidence of the validity of that test. Since many of the tests available at that time had little validity evidence, employers saw this as a difficult hurdle to overcome.

As a result of the questions about the invasion of privacy and the possible discriminatory effects of tests, there was a marked reduction in test use for selection purposes, particularly intelligence and personality tests. The reticence lasted well into the 1970s, by which time more evidence of validity for tests had become available and the courts had clarified what was acceptable evidence for validity. At this time, research began to emerge showing that tests of cognitive ability were just as valid for minority test takers as for majority test takers. By the mid-1980s, testing was back in full swing, and both intelligence and personality testing began to appear with greater frequency.

As we will see in the modules that follow, the content and process of employment testing is varied and encouraging. I-O psychologists have identified many different attributes that appear to contribute to work performance. Furthermore, I-O psychologists have identified many different methods for assessing these attributes.

But concerns about the "fairness" of testing continue to arise in many different settings. To mention just a few, some universities have decided to abandon standardized testing for applicants and introduce nonstandardized techniques that will permit motivation, interests, and values to play a greater role in student admissions. In both teacher and student testing in K–12 environments, there is a vigorous debate—and occasional lawsuits (e.g., *Gulino et al.* v. *Board of Education of the New York City School District of the City of New York and the New York State Education Department*, 2002)—about the value of standardized tests for teacher certification and the awarding of high school diplomas. For example, many school districts require the successful completion of a series of content-specific tests (e.g., in mathematics or biology) as well as more general tests (e.g., knowledge of liberal arts) before granting teachers a permanent teaching certificate. In response to scandals such as the Enron and WorldCom accounting fraud cases, MBA programs began considering the use of new "tests" of ethics, morality, and integrity to determine whom to admit to their MBA programs (Jackson, 2002).

Underlying all of these debates, the issue of fairness remains: Are standardized tests both effective and fair instruments for selecting among individuals? For every standardized test, there will be critics suggesting that the standardization prevents an illumination of the "essence" of the person. For every nonstandardized suggestion, there will be critics who will argue that the lack of standardization permits favoritism. Psychological testing will always have a values component to it in addition to the issues related to content and process.

What Is a Test?

Test An objective and standardized procedure for measuring a psychological construct using a sample of behavior.

Robert Guion (1998) defined a **test** as "an objective and standardized procedure for measuring a psychological construct using a sample of behavior" (p. 485). Seventy years earlier, Clark Hull (1928) had proposed a virtually identical definition. Few definitions in psychology have remained so constant for such a long time. One of the appealing characteristics of this definition is that it is broad enough to cover a wide variety of tests and testing procedures. It encompasses paper-and-pencil tests, Internet testing, interviews, actual attempts to perform a piece of work (a work sample test), and even an application blank. The definition is also broad enough to cover many different types of content, including cognitive ability, personality, values, communication skills, interpersonal skills, and technical knowledge. In the modules that follow, we will review various content categories, as well as various techniques for assessing that content. As an example, if we were interested in the technical knowledge of an applicant for a word-processing position, we could give the applicant a paper-and-pencil test and an interview, check with previous employers, have the applicant complete an actual word-processing task at a workstation, or examine the applicant's formal education credits. Each of these techniques could be used to assess the same attribute: technical knowledge. Similarly, we might be interested in a number of different attributes of the applicant beyond technical knowledge, including communication skills, personality characteristics, interests, integrity, and career plans. We might use one or more interviews to assess each of these additional attributes. As you can see from Figure 3.4, in most practical testing situations, we are looking at the combination of attributes to be assessed (content) and ways to assess those attributes (process). Most employers look at several attributes using several techniques. Earlier in this chapter, we introduced the term KSAO (knowledge, skill, ability, other characteristics) to summarize the attributes of a worker. In one way or another, every test is an assessment of one or more of these content areas.

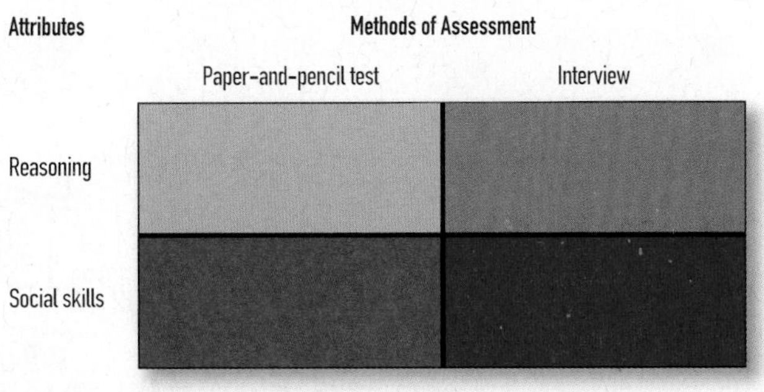

FIGURE 3.4 Two Attributes Measured Using Two Different Procedures

What Is the Meaning of a Test Score?

As Guion (1998) suggested, the term "objective" in his definition of a test implies quantification—some kind of score on the test. It may be a simple pass–fail score (e.g., you may pass or fail a driver's license examination) or a score on some graded continuum (such as an 88 percent or a B+). But the simple process of assigning a score is quite different from interpreting the meaning of that score. For example, if your instructor curves exam scores, and the exam was a tough one, an 88 might be in the A range. If, on the other hand, the test was an easy one and virtually everyone got a 94 or above (except you), your 88 might be in the B range or lower.

Norming Comparing a test score to other relevant test scores.

Meaning is usually assigned to test scores through a process known as **norming**. Norming simply means comparing a score to other relevant test scores. In many employment settings, we compare individuals to one another, so the rules we use for making these comparisons should be unambiguous and fair. Test scores are often interpreted relative to some set of norms. In the classroom example above, your score of 88 percent is given meaning, or interpreted, by comparing it to the grades of your fellow students (the **norm group**). Instead of being compared to others in your class who took the same test you did, the instructor could have compared your score (and the scores of your classmates) to those of earlier classes who took midterms in the same content area. Or the instructor might not have curved the test at all but held to some previously determined comparison scale (90 to 100 percent = A, 80 to 89 percent = B, etc.). The development of test norms is very technical; excellent discussions of the process are presented in Guion (1998) and Cohen and Swerdlik (2010). For our purposes, it is simply important to be aware that while a test produces a "score," there is a need to interpret or give meaning to that score. As you will recall from our earlier discussion of validity in Chapter 2, validity is about inference: What can we infer from a test score about future performance? The meaning of a test score is a question of validity (Messick, 1995).

Norm group Group whose test scores are used to compare and understand an individual's test score.

What Is a Test Battery?

Test battery Collection of tests that usually assess a variety of different attributes.

A **test battery** is a collection of tests, usually of different attributes. These attributes may be within a single area, such as a cognitive battery including subtests of reasoning, memory, and comprehension; or the attributes may be from conceptually different areas, such as a battery that includes a measure of cognitive ability, a personality test, a physical ability test, and a test of vocational interests. The term "battery" usually implies that all of the tests will be taken either in a single testing period or over a very short period of time. But whether the information being considered is from several different assessment devices administered at one time or over a lengthy period of time, the critical issue is how to combine that

information. Will it be combined to yield a single score with weights assigned to individual tests using a statistical equation of some type, or will the evaluator combine the individual test scores using a logical or nonstatistical process to yield a final recommendation? We will consider the issue of how test information can be combined in Chapter 6 when we address staffing decisions.

Where to Find Tests

At various points in the text, we mention some specific tests by name. There are literally thousands of psychological tests available on a broad range of topics. Textbooks on testing provide lists and examples of tests. For example, Anastasi and Urbina (1997) presented an extensive list of tests covering a range of topics, as well as a listing of test publishers. A more complete listing of tests, as well as reviews of those tests, can be found in two established sources. The first is the ***Mental Measurements Yearbook***. This was first published in 1938 and has been updated 16 times. The 17th edition (Geisinger, Spies, Carlson, & Plake) was published in 2007. The Buros Institute (named after the founder of the MMY, Oscar K. Buros) also publishes a companion volume without reviews called *Tests in Print*.

Mental Measurements Yearbook Widely used source that includes an extensive listing of tests as well as reviews of those tests.

Scott and Reynolds (2010) published an excellent handbook on workplace assessment. It focuses on evidence-based practices for selecting and developing organizational talent, and it includes assessment for entry-level jobs as well as supervisory and leadership positions.

Administrative Test Categories

In descriptions of tests and testing, you may encounter several terms that require a brief explanation.

Speed test A test with rigid and demanding time limits; most test takers will be unable to finish the test in the allotted time.

Power test A test with no rigid time limits; enough time is given for a majority of the test takers to complete all of the test items.

Speed versus Power Tests

Some tests have rigid and demanding time limits such that most test takers will be unable to finish the test in the allotted time. These are called **speed tests**. As Murphy and Davidshofer (2005) have pointed out, if someone scores poorly on a speed test, it is not clear whether the person actually knew the answers but could not respond quickly enough or would have been unable to answer correctly no matter how much time was allotted. **Power tests** have no rigid time limits. While some test takers may still not finish, enough time is given for a majority of the test takers to complete all of the test items. The items on power tests tend to be answered correctly by a smaller percentage of test takers than those on speed tests.

Assessment professionals find that speed tests yield greater variability among candidates, allowing for more effective prediction, but they carry some vulnerabilities. The most obvious of these is whether the job actually requires such speed for successful performance. Few jobs have such demands. The second potential pitfall is the possibility of introducing unfairness to the testing

The television show *Jeopardy* is an example of a speed test.

process by emphasizing speed. One of the documented effects of the aging process is a decline in information-processing speed. As we age, we take longer to complete cognitive operations. In many instances, this slowing process is irrelevant to the actual demands of a job; it won't matter that a worker took 10 or 20 seconds rather than 3 seconds to accomplish a task. As we saw in Box 3.2, in terms of simple reaction time, the difference between an "old" person and a "young" person is as little as 1/20th of a second! Nevertheless, there are some professions (e.g., airline pilot, police officer, firefighter, bus driver) where speed of information processing or time to completion of an action might be critical. Disabled individuals, particularly those with learning disabilities, may also find themselves at a disadvantage on a speed test. One of the most common requests for a testing accommodation made by individuals under the Americans with Disabilities Act (1990) is for additional time to complete a test. Thus, speed tests may increase the risk of legal challenge from many groups unless it can be shown that the type of speed required by the test is also required by the job.

Group versus Individual Tests

Most standardized written tests, even if administered to single individuals, could be administered in group format. A cognitive ability test could be given to 20,000 police academy candidates in a convention center or individually in a room on an army base where an officer candidate is stationed. **Group tests** are efficient because they allow for the testing of many candidates simultaneously, resulting in rapid screening compared to individually administered tests. Group testing is also often valuable in reducing the costs (in both time and money) of testing many applicants. As we will see shortly, Internet testing involves a virtual group rather than a physical group.

Group test A test that can be administered to large groups of individuals; often valuable in reducing the costs (both in time and money) of testing many applicants.

Certain tests, however, can be given only on an individual basis. Examples include an interview, a test of hand–eye coordination, or an elaborate assessment of candidates for a high-level executive position based on interviews, work samples, and individually administered personality tests. **Individual tests** are also often more appropriate when the employer wishes to assess a candidate's *style* of problem solving rather than the simple *products* of the problem-solving process. Individual testing formats are also appropriate when the examiner needs to establish an interpersonal rapport with the test taker.

Individual test A test given only on an individual basis.

Paper-and-Pencil versus Performance Tests

Paper-and-pencil tests are one of the most common forms of industrial testing. By extension, the modern version of the paper-and-pencil test might be the computer keyboard test where the keys and mouse are used only to choose the correct response or produce a narrative response to a question. Given the increasing popularity of computer- and Internet-administered tests, it might be better to adopt a term other than "paper-and-pencil testing"; a distinction such as nonmanipulative versus manipulative might be more appropriate. We will discuss computer and Internet testing later in this chapter.

Paper-and-pencil test One of the most common forms of industrial testing that requires no manipulation of any objects other than the instrument used to respond.

Performance tests require the individual to make a response by manipulating a particular physical object or piece of equipment. The score that the individual receives on the test is directly related to the quality or quantity of that manipulation. An example might be a test administered to a candidate for a dental hygienist position. The candidate might be asked to prepare a tray for cleaning or scaling teeth, to prepare a syringe of novocaine for administration by the dentist, or to prepare a mold for taking an impression of a row of teeth. In this case, the candidate's *skill* in performing these tasks may be as important as his or her knowledge of *how* to carry out the actions.

Performance test A test that requires the individual to make a response by manipulating a particular physical object or piece of equipment.

Testing and Culture

In the 1950s and 1960s, testing was largely lacking in controls, either legal or professional. As social critics pointed out, the quality of tests was therefore variable, and the potential for cultural influence and bias was substantial. An example would be a test that used a very high level of vocabulary to assess a relatively simple and straightforward skill. Instead of asking "How much is two plus two?" the item might have read, "If one were asked to calculate the arithmetic sum of the two integers that have been reproduced below, what would the resultant number be?" The second item would surely be more difficult for someone with a limited vocabulary or low reading comprehension to answer, even though both items are ostensibly assessing the same basic math skill. Modern tests have eliminated most if not all of these reading-level problems. What they may not have done, however, is to eliminate cultural influences.

Murphy and Davidshofer (2005) distinguished among three terms in discussing tests and testing: **bias**, **fairness**, and **culture**. They correctly pointed out that bias is a technical and statistical term that deals exclusively with the situation in which a given test results in errors of prediction for a subgroup. Thus, if a test underpredicts the job performance of women (i.e., predicts that they will score lower on job performance than they actually do) and overpredicts the job performance of men (i.e., predicts that they will score higher on job performance than they actually do), then the test would be said to be biased. You will remember that earlier in this chapter, we described a case involving a strength test for female applicants in a meat-packing plant. In essence, the judge in that case ruled that the strength test was *biased* because it predicted that a substantial percentage of women would perform poorly and almost all men would perform well at meat-packing tasks. In fact, the test might have predicted injuries but was not effective in predicting actual performance on the job.

Bias Technical and statistical term that deals exclusively with a situation where a given test results in errors of prediction for a subgroup.

Fairness Value judgment about actions or decisions based on test scores.

Culture A system in which individuals share meanings and common ways of viewing events and objects.

In contrast, fairness is a value judgment about actions or decisions based on test scores. Many employers base hiring decisions on tests of general mental ability. Many applicants believe that in addition to (or instead of) the cognitive ability test, dependability and motivation should play a role. This was the view of Yvonne in the example at the beginning of this module. In the view of many applicants, the test and the method of hiring are unfair even though there may be no statistical bias in predictions of success.

Murphy and Davidshofer (2005) considered fairness to be a philosophical or political term, not a scientific one. They gave an example to make their point. A test of physical strength might predict job success equally for male and female firefighter applicants, and yet it might eliminate most of the female applicants because they have less upper body strength than males. Many individuals would consider such a test unfair even though it was unbiased, because it prevents women from becoming firefighters. In contrast, a biased test might be used to increase the number of minorities in a particular job or company but still be considered fair because it corrects for a past underrepresentation of those minority group members.

Culture is a third concept, separate in many respects from either fairness or bias. Culture addresses the extent to which the test taker has had an opportunity to become familiar with the subject matter or processes required by a test item (Murphy & Davidshofer, 2005). In many tests for teacher certification, there is a component that addresses the general cultural literacy of the candidate—for example, how well he or she knows works of art and music, variations of modern dance, and the deeper meaning of literary passages (National Evaluation Systems, 2002). Consider the following hypothetical test items:

A crackberry is
a) a late summer wild fruit that thrives in northern Sweden
b) a hybrid of a raspberry and blackberry

c) a personal digital assistant
d) a person addicted to crack cocaine

Phishing is
a) fishing while drunk
b) criminally acquiring sensitive information
c) a method of advancing electrical wire through a conduit
d) a lip noise intended to make another be quiet

The answers to these questions (c and b respectively) are generationally "biased." Your grandmother, or maybe even your father, might not know the answers to these questions, but chances are good that your roommate will. Would items like these be considered generationally "fair"? Probably not.

Greenfield (1997) presented examples of difficulties in "transporting" North American cognitive ability tests to other cultures. Sternberg (2004) has argued vigorously that intelligence cannot be understood without taking into account the culture in which it is measured. He cites the example of the Taoist culture, in which intelligence includes the importance of humility, freedom from conventional standards of judgment, and full knowledge of oneself; in contrast, the Confucian perspective emphasizes the importance and persistence of lifelong learning with enthusiasm.

As Americans from different ethnic groups increasingly mingle in public schools, universities, other public institutions, and work settings, they are becoming more familiar with one anothers' subcultures today than was the case 30 years ago. As a result, the concept of the cultural content in current tests is becoming less of an issue in explaining differences among ethnic groups. At the same time, cultural content is becoming an increasingly important issue in the workplace because of the increasingly multicultural nature of work and the growing cultural diversity of applicant populations.

International Assessment Practices

Earlier in the chapter, we reported research that found that tests of mental ability were used more commonly in Europe than in the United States. This is just one example of the differences that can be found worldwide in assessment practices. Variations in global assessment practice will become increasingly important in the next decade for both multinational employers and applicants to multinational organizations. Several reviews of assessment in other countries help to illustrate the differences between assessment in the United States and assessment elsewhere (Oakland, 2004; Roe & van den Berg, 2003). Highlights from these reviews include the following:

- European psychologists would like to have a more structured role for professional institutions in developing and monitoring good testing practices. In response to that expressed need, the International Test Commission developed the *International Guidelines for Test Use* (International Test Commission, 2000).
- In industrial settings, the countries in which tests were most frequently administered by psychologists were Croatia, Bulgaria, Finland, Slovakia, Denmark, Japan, and Slovenia. The countries in which tests were most frequently administered by nonpsychologists included Canada, Sweden, Cyprus, Norway, Switzerland, the United Kingdom, and Germany.
- The greatest amount of information about test quality could be found in the United States, the Netherlands, Japan, the United Kingdom, Canada, Spain, Finland, Belgium, and Slovakia; the least amount of information was available in China, Denmark, Ukraine, and South Africa.

- In India and China, testing is largely unregulated; many countries are moving toward the certification and training of nonpsychologists who use tests (Bartram, 2005).

In general, it would appear that the various guidelines available for test evaluation, test use, and test users in the United States (American Educational Research Association et al. Standards, 1999; SIOP, 2003; Turner et al., 2001; Uniform Guidelines, 1978) are ideals to which many other countries aspire.

MODULE 3.3 SUMMARY

- Employment testing was first widely used after the First World War and has been heavily influenced by the Civil Rights Act of 1964. I-O psychologists are interested in determining how effective various tests are in predicting work performance. They have identified many different attributes that appear to contribute to work performance and many different methods for assessing these attributes.
- The definition of a test encompasses paper-and-pencil tests, interviews, actual attempts to perform a piece of work (a work sample test), and even an application blank. The definition is also broad enough to cover many different types of content, including cognitive ability, personality, values, communication skills, interpersonal skills, and technical knowledge.
- In Module 3.2 we introduced the term KSAO (knowledge, skill, ability, other characteristics) to summarize the attributes of a worker. In one way or another, every test is an assessment of one or more of these content areas.
- Tests can be described or differentiated according to categories that include speed versus power tests, individual versus group tests, and paper-and-pencil versus performance tests.
- In discussing tests and testing, it is important to consider three factors: bias, or errors of prediction; fairness, a value judgment about decisions based on test scores; and culture, the extent to which a test taker has the opportunity to become familiar with the subject matter.

KEY TERMS

mental test
test
norming
norm group
test battery
Mental Measurements Yearbook
speed test
power test
group test
individual test
paper-and-pencil test
performance test
bias
fairness
culture

MODULE 3.4

Assessment Procedures

Assessment Content versus Process

Employers and applicants often confuse the content of testing with the process of testing. As we suggested earlier in this chapter, there is a difference between *what* attribute is being assessed and *how* it is being assessed. For example, after applying for a job with a local company, an applicant might describe the process as including a personality test, a cognitive test, an interview, and a background check. The terms "personality" and "cognitive" describe the content of the assessment and the terms "interview" and "background check" describe the process of the assessment. The reason why this content–process distinction is important is that you will often see claims for the "validity" of the interview or work sample. But the validity depends not so much on the process by which the information was gathered as on the content of that information. In the sections that follow, we will consider information gathered in various formats, ranging from a paper-and-pencil test to an interview. But as we discussed earlier, many of these methods can be used to gather many different kinds of information. For example, an interview could assess communication skills, knowledge, ability, or personality—or, as is most often the case, a combination of those "content" categories. First, we will consider the content of assessment, and then the process for gathering this content.

Assessment Procedures: Content

Cognitive Ability Tests

Cognitive ability test A test that allows individuals to demonstrate what they know, perceive, remember, understand, or can work with mentally; includes problem identification, problem-solving tasks, perceptual skills, the development or evaluation of ideas, and remembering what one has learned through general experience or specific training.

Guion (1998) defined **cognitive ability tests** as those that:

> allow a person to show what he or she knows, perceives, remembers, understands, or can work with mentally. They include problem identification, problem-solving tasks, perceptual (not sensory) skills, the development or evaluation of ideas, and remembering what one has learned through general experience or specific training. (p. 486)

Wonderlic WPT-R Sample Questions 

1. Which of the following is the earliest date?

   A) Jan. 16, 1898 B) Feb. 21, 1889 C) Feb. 2, 1898 D) Jan. 7, 1898 E) Jan. 30, 1889

2. **LOW** is to **HIGH** as **EASY** is to __?__.

   J) **SUCCESSFUL** K) **PURE** L) **TALL** M) **INTERESTING** N) **DIFFICULT**

3. A featured product from an Internet retailer generated 27, 99, 80, 115 and 213 orders over a 5-hour period. Which graph below best represents this trend?

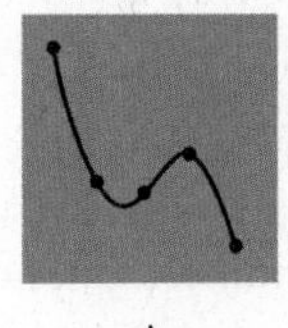
A

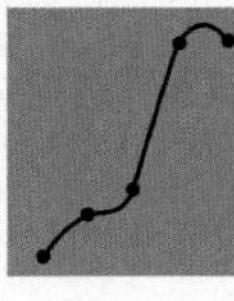
B

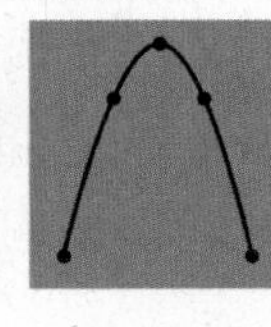
C

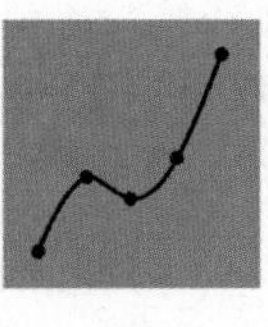
D

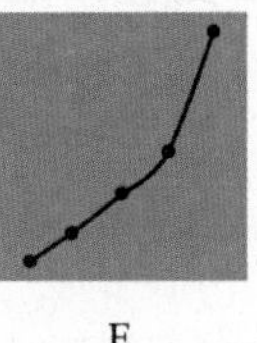
E

4. What is the next number in the series? 29 41 53 65 77 __?__

   J) 75 K) 88 L) 89 M) 98 N) 99

5. *One word below appears in color. What is the OPPOSITE of that word?*
   She gave a complex answer to the question and we all agreed with her.

   A) long B) better C) simple D) wrong E) kind

6. Jose's monthly parking fee for April was $150; for May it was $10 more than April; and for June $40 more than May. His average monthly parking fee was __?__ for these 3 months.

   J) $66 K) $160 L) $166 M) $170 N) $200

7. *If the first two statements are true, is the final statement true?*
   Sandra is responsible for ordering all office supplies.
   Notebooks are office supplies.

   Sandra is responsible for ordering notebooks.

   A) yes B) no C) uncertain

8. Which THREE choices are needed to create the figure on the left? Only pieces of the same color may overlap.

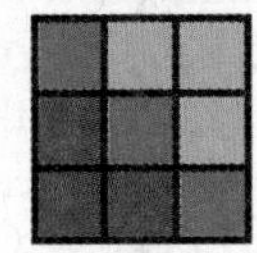

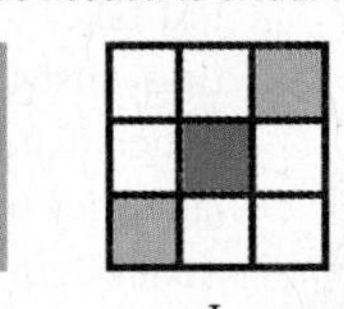
J

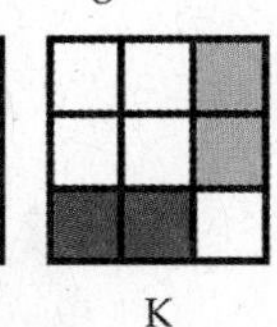
K

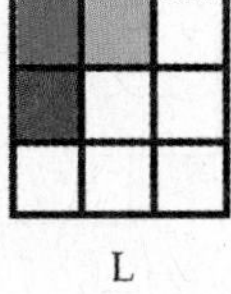
L

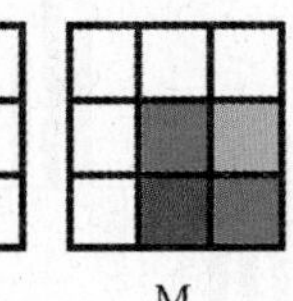
M

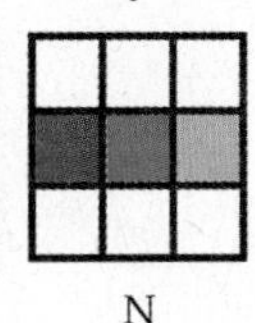
N

9. Which THREE of the following words have similar meanings?

   A) observable B) manifest C) hypothetical D) indefinite E) theoretical

10. Last year, 12 out of 600 employees at a service organization were rewarded for their excellence in customer service, which was __?__ of the employees.

    J) 1% K) 2% L) 3% M) 4% N) 6%

Answers: 1. E, 2. N, 3. D, 4. L, 5. C, 6. M, 7. A, 8. KLM, 9. CDE, 10. K

FIGURE 3.5 Wonderlic Personnel Test—Revised Sample Items

SOURCE: Wonderlic Personnel Test–Revised © 2007 Wonderlic, Inc., 1795 N. Butterfield Road, Suite 200, Libertyville, IL 60048, 800.323.3742, www.wonderlic.com. Used by permission.

Which would be the better shears for cutting metal?

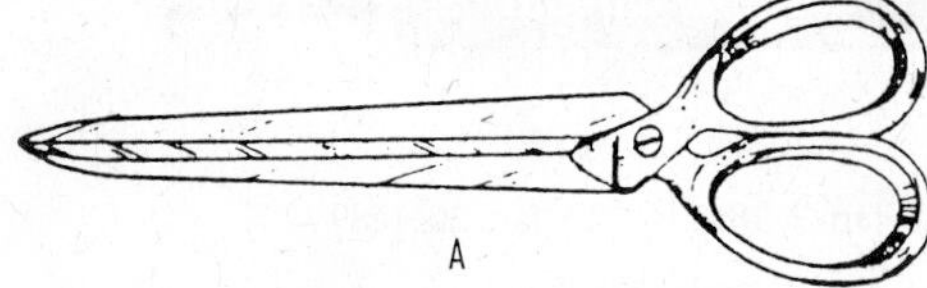

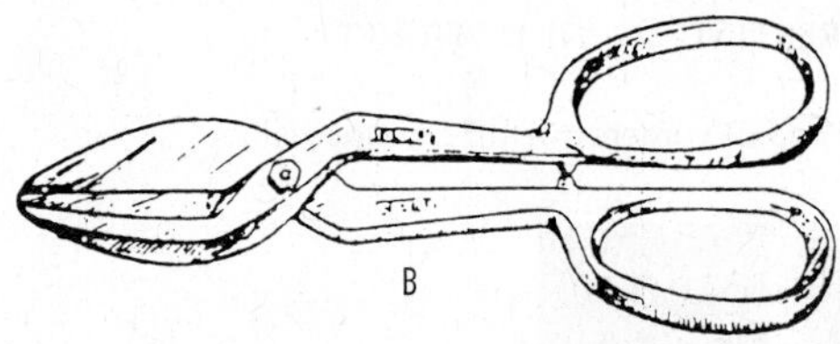

FIGURE 3.6 Sample Item from Bennett Mechanical Comprehension Test

SOURCE: Bennett Mechanical Comprehension Test, Form BB, Item Y.

Even though Guion identified what seem to be a variety of cognitive abilities (e.g., remembering, problem identification), as we saw earlier in this chapter, there is still a vigorous debate regarding whether there is only one overarching cognitive ability—"g" or general mental ability—or several distinct facets or abilities (Ackerman et al., 2002, 2005; Ree, Earles, & Teachout, 1994).

In more than a century of cognitive ability testing, there have been tests that produce a single number intended to represent cognitive ability, tests of specific abilities, and test batteries that purport to measure several different facets of cognitive ability.

Tests That Produce a Single Score

An example of a test intended to produce a single score representing general mental ability is the Wonderlic Personnel Test. It includes 50 items that assess verbal, numerical, and spatial abilities. Because its administration time is 12 minutes and most applicants cannot finish the test in the allotted time, the Wonderlic is considered a speed test. There are elaborate norms for the Wonderlic, making its interpretation relatively simple. Its ease of administration and scoring make it a popular device for many organizations. Murphy and Davidshofer (2005) endorsed the use of the Wonderlic, pointing to its high reliability and strong correlations with other, more elaborate, tests of intelligence. Figure 3.5 presents sample items from the Wonderlic Personnel Test—Revised.

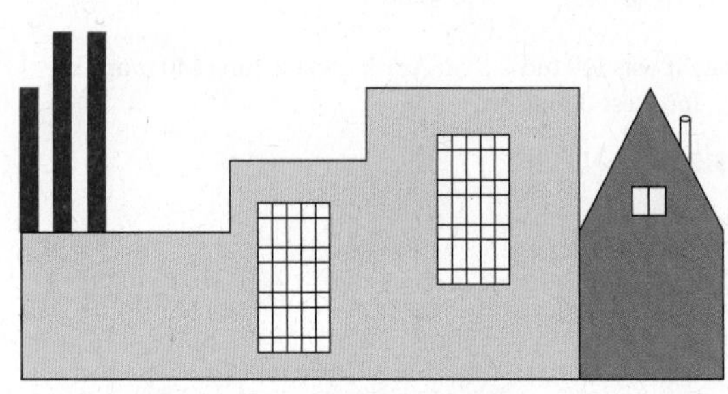

Above is a picture of a factory shown from the front.
From the back, it would look like:

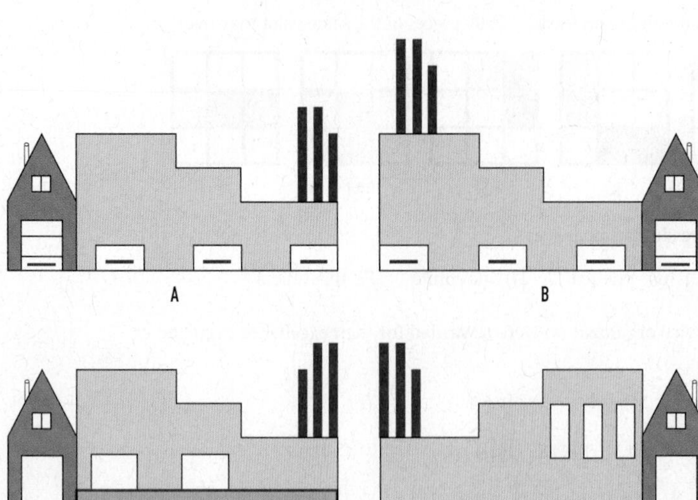

FIGURE 3.7 Spatial Relations Item from a Test for Firefighters

Tests of Specific Abilities

As implied by Guion's definition, many tests concentrate on only one aspect of cognitive ability. One such test is the Bennett Mechanical Comprehension Test. The sample item from this test (see Figure 3.6) asks the test taker to examine the two different cutting instruments and to deduce, from either experience or logic, that the shears labeled B would be more effective at cutting metal than those labeled A. One can imagine that such a test item might be well suited for choosing applicants for the trade position of sheet metal worker or plumber.

Another example of a specific mental ability is spatial relations. Consider the item in Figure 3.7. It requires the test taker to do some actual mental manipulation of the factory shown from the front by "turning" the factory in his or her mind and then choosing the response that would most closely resemble how the factory would look from the back. This ability to manipulate objects in one's mind is particularly useful for many hardware repair or "troubleshooting" professions, such as an auto mechanic or computer repair technician, where it is necessary to visualize a component buried deep under the hood of a car or in a hard drive. There are many other examples of specific cognitive abilities, such as clerical and perceptual accuracy, memory, and reasoning. Most testing texts (Cohen & Swerdlik, 2010; Murphy & Davidshofer, 2005) provide detailed descriptions of these tests. Mumford, Baughman, Supinski, and Anderson (1998) presented a sophisticated treatment of how to measure complex cognitive abilities such as reasoning and creative problem solving.

Cognitive Test Batteries

Multiple-aptitude test batteries have a long history in psychological testing in industry. Thurstone (1938) introduced a test of Primary Mental Abilities (PMA) that assessed numerical ability, verbal ability, reasoning, spatial relations, perceptual speed, and memory. More recent examples of multiple-aptitude test batteries include the Armed Services Vocational Aptitude Battery or ASVAB (Murphy & Davidshofer, 2005) and the General Aptitude Test Battery or GATB (Hartigan & Wigdor, 1989). The ASVAB, as implied by its name, is used exclusively by the armed services. The GATB is used exclusively by the federal government. Students are more likely to be familiar with the Scholastic Aptitude Test (SAT) or Graduate Record Examination (GRE), both examples of cognitive test batteries. In one way or another, these batteries all measure verbal, numerical, spatial, and reasoning abilities. Although **cognitive test batteries** take longer to administer than a "single score" test like the Wonderlic or any test of an individual facet of cognitive ability, they do have the advantage of providing more detailed information about particular manifestations of cognitive ability that may be more important in one job than another.

Cognitive test battery Collection of tests that assess a variety of cognitive aptitudes or abilities; often called multiple-aptitude test batteries.

Knowledge Tests

Tests you will take in this and other courses are **knowledge tests**. They assess the extent to which you know course material. These types of tests are typically tailored to course or training material. Knowledge tests are also administered for licensing and certification purposes, including teacher certification, nuclear power plant operator licensing, and licenses to practice law or medicine or to sell investments. Knowledge tests are like any other type of test and require the same care in development, norming, and administration. We will discuss non-paper-and-pencil forms of knowledge tests later in this chapter.

Knowledge test A test that assesses the extent to which individuals understand course or training materials; also administered for licensing and certification purposes.

Tests of Physical Abilities

As we saw earlier in the chapter, there are seven basic physical ability attributes (Hogan, 1991a). These include static strength, explosive strength, coordination, and stamina or aerobic endurance. While it is possible to measure each of these physical abilities in isolation, most physically demanding jobs actually require combinations of these abilities. As a result, many physical ability testing procedures tend to use simulated pieces of work to assess the combined abilities. For example, a test frequently used to assess the physical abilities of firefighter candidates (see Table 3.2) is composed of several events, each of which requires multiple abilities. An excellent review of physical abilities and their measurement appears in a study of age and physical abilities conducted for the Equal Employment Opportunity Commission (EEOC) and the Department of Labor (Landy et al., 1992). There is substantial evidence that measures of physical abilities can improve the prediction of job success for many physically demanding jobs (e.g., Hoffmann, 1999). Arvey, Landon, Nutting, and Maxwell (1992) provide a good

TABLE 3.2 **Physical Ability Tests for Firefighters**

Stairway climb: Candidate wears fire-protective clothing and air tank and carries seven pieces of equipment up three flights of stairs, one piece at a time. Each piece of equipment weighs between 25 and 55 pounds.
Hose pull: Candidate wears air tank, stands in one spot, and pulls 50 feet of fire hose filled with water using a hand-over-hand technique.
Ladder pull: Candidate wears air tank and pulls a 16-foot ladder from the ladder bed of a fire truck, places it on the ground, picks it back up, and replaces it in the ladder bed.
Dummy drag: Candidate drags a 125-pound sandbag around a serpentine course of 40 feet. The candidate must keep one knee in contact with the ground and may not lift or carry the sandbag but must drag it.
Blind crawl: Candidate wears fire-protective clothing and an air tank. After putting on a blackened face mask, the candidate must crawl through a plywood maze that has several turns in it. In addition, there are sandbags located strategically throughout the maze. The maze is approximately 40 feet in length.
Pike pole: Candidate wears an air tank and alternately pulls and pushes a 75-pound weight attached to a pole hanging from a frame. The candidate must complete as many repetitions as possible in a 4-minute period. A repetition is defined as one push and two pulls.
Fan hang: Candidate wears fire-protective clothing and an air tank and lifts a 50-pound fan from ground level, hanging it on a standard door frame.

description of the development and validation of an entry-level physical ability examination for police officers. The caution, as we saw earlier, is that the physical ability tests are most defensible when used to predict *performance* rather than *risk of injury*.

Psychomotor abilities Physical functions of movement, associated with coordination, dexterity, and reaction time; also called motor or sensorimotor abilities.

Psychomotor Abilities

Tests of **psychomotor abilities** involve the coordinated movement of the limbs in response to situational factors. It may be a complex task in which the individual is required to move arms and legs in coordination, as in flying an airplane, driving a vehicle, or playing an organ; or it may be a simple or discrete action such as firing a weapon, pulling a lever, or administering an injection to a patient. For some jobs, psychomotor abilities represent characteristics of the individual that have some potential for contributing to successful job performance above and beyond cognitive abilities, physical abilities, or personality characteristics. Psychomotor abilities are usually assessed using a task or test that requires dexterity, such as is depicted in Figure 3.8. Ackerman and his colleagues have developed some sophisticated computer-based psychomotor tests for the selection of applicants for jobs such as air traffic controllers (Ackerman & Cianciolo, 2002).

FIGURE 3.8 **The Perdue Pegboard Dexterity Test**
This test is commonly used as a pre-employment screening test.

Personality

As we saw earlier in the chapter, personality attributes are now widely recognized as contributors to job success. There are many commercially available instruments for measuring personality characteristics, many based on the Big Five model described earlier. The history of personality testing can be described in two general phases. The early foundation of personality testing was focused on the identification of the abnormal personality and evidence of possible psychopathology (i.e., mental illness). Using personality testing for that purpose might be thought of as an attempt to screen *out* potentially problematic employees. With the advent of instruments intended to provide quantitative descriptions of normal (rather than abnormal) personality, personality testing in employment shifted to a process intended to screen *in* candidates; that is, employers sought to identify applicants with positive personality characteristics (e.g., conscientiousness, emotional stability, or agreeableness) that would contribute to effective performance.

TABLE 3.3 **Some Commonly Used Personality Instruments**

Instruments
Minnesota Multiphasic Personality Inventory II (MMPI-II)
California Psychological Inventory (CPI)
Personality Research Form (PRF)
Edwards Personal Preference Schedule
Jackson Personality Inventory–Revised (JPI-R)
16 PF Select
NEO-PI
Hogan Personality Inventory
Saville Consulting Wave

Table 3.3 lists some of the more commonly used personality instruments. As you can see, this table is separated into two sections. The upper section includes tests that have been frequently used for purposes of identifying signs of psychopathology—**screen-out tests.** The tests listed in the lower section have been more frequently used to identify variations of normal personality—**screen-in tests.** There is an important distinction between these two different categories of tests. Tests developed or intended to identify psychopathology, or used commonly for that purpose, are considered "medical tests" under the Americans with Disabilities Act (1990), particularly if the test is administered by a clinical or counseling psychologist or a psychiatrist. As such, they may not be administered until *after* an offer of employment has been made, as is the case with physical examinations, because emotional disorders are considered covered disabilities under the ADA. Applicants might be placed at a disadvantage in the selection process if their condition was revealed through pre-employment testing. If an employer administers a test such as the MMPI-II in order to choose among applicants prior to an offer of employment, that practice can be challenged in court and the applicant will likely win that challenge. On the other hand, tests developed or intended to assess normal personality may be administered as pre-employment tests and used for purposes of choosing among applicants prior to an offer of employment.

Screen-out test A test used to eliminate candidates who are clearly unsuitable for employment; tests of psychopathology are examples of screen-out tests in the employment setting.

Screen-in test A test used to add information about the positive attributes of a candidate that might predict outstanding performance; tests of normal personality are examples of screen-in tests in the employment setting.

There are many positions of public trust (e.g., public safety officers, nuclear power plant operators, air traffic controllers, commercial airline pilots) that warrant testing for possible psychopathology to guard against dangerous actions by the incumbent. But most job titles in industry do not directly involve the health and welfare of the public, and testing for personality abnormalities would be questionable in such jobs. Figure 3.9 presents some sample items from the Saville Consulting Wave test, which is frequently used to assess normal personality in job applicants.

Practical Issues Associated with Personality Measures

Up to this point, we have been dealing with the "science" of personality. But there are also practical questions that arise about using measurements of personality to make employment decisions. Hogan, Hogan, and Roberts (1996) addressed those larger practical questions, as summarized in Box 3.4.

You will see a range of responses varying from very strongly agree to very strongly disagree. Choose the response alternative that best describes how you feel. Some statements are about being good at something and others are about what you prefer, need, or are interested in. Read each statement carefully because there may be differences between what you are good at and what you may need. Try to answer the questions from a work perspective as much as possible.

	Very Strongly Disagree	Strongly Disagree	Disagree	Slightly Disagree	Unsure	Slightly Agree	Agree	Strongly Agree	Very Strongly Agree
a) I need to have a clear set of priorities			✓						
b) I am great at encouraging others								✓	

FIGURE 3.9 Sample Items from the Saville Consulting Wave

SOURCE: Adapted from Saville Consulting WAVE. Used by permission of Saville Consulting UK Ltd.

BOX 3.4 PERSONALITY TESTING FAQS

Q: There are many personality tests and scales available. How do you choose among them?

A: Use valid and reliable tests that cover at least the Five-Factor Model dimensions.

Q: Why should you use a test that measures more than one aspect of personality when you are interested in only one?

A: Because behavior is usually a function of many different influences, not just one.

Q: What do personality tests measure?

A: A person's typical "style."

Q: Why use personality tests to make employment decisions?

A: Because most workers and managers say that such attributes as "being a team player," "remaining calm under pressure," "being persistent," and "taking initiative" are critical for success in almost any job.

Q: Do personality tests predict job performance?

A: Yes.

Q: Do personality tests predict performance in all jobs?

A: Probably, but they are less predictive for jobs with little autonomy.

Q: Weren't personality tests developed to measure psychopathology and for use in clinical settings?

A: Many years ago, that was true. The tests available today are designed to assess normal personality.

Q: People's behavior changes constantly. Doesn't this invalidate personality tests?

A: By definition, personality is relatively stable over time and from one set of circumstances to another and continues to affect our lives in important ways. Even though behavior changes occasionally, stable aspects of personality are still effective predictors.

Q: Do personality measures discriminate against ethnic minorities, women, older individuals, and the disabled?

A: There is no evidence of discrimination against these groups in well-developed personality tests. People over 40 tend to receive more positive scores than those under 40. There are some differences between males and females (men have higher scores on emotional stability and women have higher scores on conscientiousness), but these are not significant enough to result in different hiring decisions.

Q: Do personality tests invade privacy?

A: Some appear to. Choose tests with the highest validity and reliability and the fewest number of offensive-appearing questions.

Q: What is the best way to use personality measures for pre-employment screening?

A: In combination with measures of technical skills, experience, and the ability to learn.

SOURCE: Based on Hogan et al. (1996).

Faking

There is one final and controversial point about personality tests that is not addressed directly in Box 3.4. Some tests, particularly some commercially available integrity tests, are very transparent. It is obvious how one should answer the test questions in order to appear to have high integrity. This is a bit different from a cognitive ability test, where a candidate cannot pretend to be "smarter" than he or she actually is. A candidate might bear the following "script" in mind when answering integrity test questions:

> I have never stolen anything since I was a young child, and even then, I don't think I ever stole anything. I do not have any friends who steal or would even *think* of stealing anything. If they did, they could not be my friends anymore, and I would tell the appropriate authorities that they had stolen something. I think that showing up for work late, not doing a complete job, leaving work early, and taking sick days when you are not sick is also stealing, and I would not do any of those things or be friends with anyone who would. I would inform management if I ever found out that a co-worker was engaging in any of these behaviors.

Although this "script" is amusing in its extremity, it makes the point that it is possible to answer questions on a personality-like device in a way that gets the best result—that is, an offer of employment. But what about tests that are not so transparent? From a practical standpoint, there are actually three questions to answer: (1) How difficult is it to fake personality tests? (2) How many people do it? (3) How much does it matter whether people do or do not fake? Let's take these one at a time.

How difficult is it to fake personality tests? Not difficult. As Hogan and colleagues (1996) pointed out, some are easier to fake than others. But you can answer items on any personality test in a way that makes you look "good." The real question is whether doing that truly qualifies as "faking." From some perspectives, personality is all about **self-presentation**; it is your public face, your "game face." So to the extent that a personality test is a paper-and-pencil form of self-presentation, it is not faking, nor is it distortion (Hogan et al., 1996; Mount & Barrick, 1995). Interestingly, and surprisingly, De Fruyt, Aluja, Garcia, Rolland, and Jung (2006) found little relationship between intelligence and the tendency to fake.

Self-presentation
A person's public face or "game face."

Some researchers (e.g., Young, White, & Heggestad, 2001) suggest that the way to neutralize faking is to develop forced-choice tests that require an individual to rank or order him- or herself by considering a number of alternative positive-appearing items. The logic is that by requiring a forced choice among items that all appear positive, an individual cannot "fake good." Although this technique appears to reduce unintentional distortion of responses to personality test items, it appears to have little effect on an individual who intentionally fakes a response (Heggestad, Morrison, Reeve, & McCloy, 2006). Ellingston, Sackett, and Connelly (2007) argue that there may be no need for any elaborate techniques, such as forced-choice items, to reduce unintentional distortion. They compared results on a personality test given to the same employee, once for selection purposes within an organization (e.g., promotion) and at a different point in time (sometimes before and sometimes after) for purposes of employee development (for training, not selection). The differences were minimal, suggesting little distortion. The authors hasten to point out, however, that all of the participants had jobs and may have felt less motivated to distort than would a person applying for a job with a new employer.

Some have suggested that the real issue is whether the test taker has the correct frame of reference (FOR) for taking the test (Lievens, De Corte, & Schollaert, 2008). As an example, consider being asked to take a personality test and told to use one of three perspectives: at school, at work, or in general (Schmit, Ryan, Stierwalt, & Powell, 1995). Chances are that your personality at work differs from your personality in non-work social settings. As a sales representative, for example, you could be outgoing, but in non-work settings, you might be more reserved because there are fewer demands for extraversion. In a study with customer service reps for an airline, Hunthausen, Truxillo, Bauer, and Hammer (2003) found that specifically instructing employees to adopt an "at work" FOR increased validity of personality test scores. If these findings are replicated in other studies, it may have an effect on both research and practice. In the research context, it may mean that many of the reported validities of personality tests for predicting performance may substantially underestimate those values because a FOR other than "at work" may have been adopted by the test takers. In practice, this finding suggests that when personality tests are administered in a selection context, the respondent should explicitly be told to adopt an "at work" FOR.

How many people fake personality measures? It is hard to know (Mount & Barrick, 1995) because the prevalence depends, as we have seen in the preceding paragraph, on how you define faking. Some studies suggest the rate of faking is substantial, whereas others suggest it is minimal. The main evidence to suggest that faking may be occurring is that applicant groups often have significantly more positive scores on given personality measures than employed groups (Weekley, Ployhart, & Harold, 2004), and, not surprisingly, the tendency seems to be greater among American than non-American applicants (Sandal & Endresen, 2002). In addition, sophisticated statistical analyses of responses to personality questionnaires (Schmit & Ryan, 1993) show that there are different patterns of responses from applicants than from employees or students. Birkeland, Manson, Kisamore, Brannick, and Smith (2006) found that the pattern of faking corresponds to what an applicant might guess are the most important characteristics of the job in question. Generally, applicants received substantially high scores on emotional stability and conscientiousness than nonapplicants; the positive differences for extraversion and openness to experience were smaller.

This brings us to a third question: How much does it matter? The answer is that it does not appear to matter much. In studies where participants were instructed to distort their responses to make themselves look good, the predictive validity of the personality measures remained the same (Hough, Eaton, Dunnette, Kamp, & McCloy, 1990). If we return to the self-presentation view of personality, "distortion" could either increase or decrease the validity of the personality measures. If the job in question is a sales position, some have suggested that a desire to look "good" in the eyes of another might actually be a job-related attribute (Hogan et al., 1996). A meta-analysis (Viswesvaran, Ones, & Hough, 2001) seems to effectively rebut that hypothesis, at least for managers. There was essentially a zero correlation between a test taker's desire to look "good" and his or her supervisory ratings on interpersonal skills. On the other hand, if an individual is having a performance counseling discussion with a supervisor, a more realistic presentation of strengths and weaknesses by the individual would be more effective than trying to look good. The issue of faking is not "settled" yet (Mueller-Hanson, Heggestad, & Thornton, 2003), but there does seem to be some agreement that it is not a fatal flaw in personality testing (Hough & Ones, 2001; Salgado, Viswesvaran, & Ones, 2001; Weekley et al., 2004).

There is one additional cautionary note of some practical significance for test takers inclined to intentionally distort their responses. Most personality tests have a "lie" scale, which indicates whether a person is trying to make himself or herself look "ideal" in some way. The test report for an individual will usually include a cautionary note indicating a lack of confidence in the resulting scores if the applicant scored too high on the lie scale. In addition, there is some research (Dwight & Donovan, 2003) indicating that if an individual test taker is warned that (1) faking can be identified and (2) faking will have negative consequences in terms of being selected for a position, the test taker will be less likely to fake.

Integrity Testing

Until recently, integrity testing meant honesty testing. Employers have always been concerned with dishonest employees. We will consider counterproductive employee behavior in depth in Chapter 4, but for now, note that employee theft can make the difference between profitability and failure for an organization. Employers are often vigorous in investigating incidents of employee dishonesty after the fact. Money or product is disappearing—who is taking it? But honesty and integrity tests were developed to *predict* who might act dishonestly in the future rather than who is actually responsible for a counterproductive act.

Although honesty and integrity tests have been around for more than 50 years (Ash, 1976), there has been more enthusiasm for them in the past 15 to 20 years for several reasons. The first reason is economic: More and more employers are concerned about the high cost of dishonest employees, and integrity tests are relatively inexpensive. In addition, from the I-O perspective, various meta-analyses have demonstrated the predictive power of such tests. Finally, legislation passed in 1988 radically reduced the use of the polygraph for pre-employment honesty screening, making paper-and-pencil tests more attractive, particularly those shown to be valid for predicting important work behaviors such as theft and absence. In jobs where polygraphs tests are permitted, integrity tests are considerably cheaper than extensive background checks or polygraph tests.

Overt integrity test A test asks questions directly about past honesty behavior (stealing, etc.) as well as attitudes toward various behaviors such as employee theft.

Personality-based integrity test A test that infers honesty and integrity from questions dealing with broad constructs such as conscientiousness, reliability, and social responsibility and awareness.

There are two different types of integrity tests: overt and personality based. The **overt integrity test** asks questions directly about past honesty behavior (stealing, etc.) as well as attitudes toward various behaviors such as employee theft. The **personality-based integrity test** measures honesty and integrity with less direct questions dealing with broader constructs such as conscientiousness, reliability, and social responsibility and awareness. Examples of both types of items are presented in Table 3.4.

TABLE 3.4 **Examples of Overt and Covert Integrity Test Items**

Overt Items

There is nothing wrong with telling a lie if no one suffers any harm (True or False?)

How often have you arrived at work under the influence of alcohol?

Do your friends ever steal from their employers?

Covert or Personality-Based Items

Do you like taking risks?

Would your friends describe you as impulsive?

Would you consider challenging an authority figure?

SOURCE: Spector, P. E. (2000). *Industrial and organizational psychology: Research and practice* (2nd ed.). New York: John Wiley & Sons. Copyright © 2000. Reprinted with permission of John Wiley & Sons, Inc.

There have been many extensive and high-quality reviews of integrity test research, and these reviews have concluded that those who score poorly will be poorer employees for any number of different reasons. They may be more likely to lie or steal, be absent, or engage in other counterproductive behaviors (Ones et al., 1993; Sackett & Wanek, 1996). In the abstract, this sounds promising, but in the concrete, there are some problems with integrity tests. Murphy and Davidshofer (2005) summarized these concerns as follows:

1. It is difficult to know exactly what any given test of integrity measures. For example, taking a long lunch hour may be considered "theft" (of time) on one test and not even mentioned in another. A study by Wanek, Sackett, and Ones (2003) suggests that there are four basic components to "integrity tests" in general, but all four do not appear in any one test. These components are antisocial behavior (e.g., driving violations, theft admissions), socialization (e.g., emotional stability, extraversion), positive outlook (e.g., safe behavior, acceptance of honesty norms), and orderliness/diligence.
2. Unlike ability or even personality tests, applicants are seldom informed of their scores or the results of an integrity test. This is particularly disturbing to a candidate who has been rejected for a position and can't find out why.
3. Often, integrity test scores are reported in a pass–fail or, more commonly, a recommended–not recommended format. As we will see in Chapter 6, the setting of pass–fail scores is very technical, and it is not clear that the test publishers take these

technical issues into account. That raises the possibility of false negatives—the possibility that an individual would be erroneously rejected as a "risk."

Cascio (2010) made an additional point about integrity as a concept. Many employers and test publishers treat honesty as a trait, much like intelligence. But it is much easier for a person to "go straight," by behaving more honestly and morally, than it is for a person with lower general mental ability to "go smart." Yet organizations treat an honesty or integrity score like a cognitive ability score: A person who gives honest answers to overt questions about past indiscretions may be rejected even though he or she may have reformed. Ironically, the only way for the reformed individual to pass the test might be to lie!

You will recall that we discussed the concept of integrity in the section on the FFM of personality earlier in this chapter. Some argue for a "narrow bandwidth" (e.g., separate scores for separate dimensions such as conscientiousness or emotional stability), and others argue for a wider bandwidth, which would involve developing a complex test to assess a complex trait. Integrity is a perfect example of this debate. One might approach the measurement of integrity by using a "broad bandwidth instrument" such as an integrity test or by inferring integrity from the combination of scores on conscientiousness, agreeableness, and emotional stability. Although this debate is largely theoretical, it also has practical implications. If an employer wants to assess the integrity of an applicant, what is the best way to do so? On the one hand, there is the ease of administering an instrument to get right at integrity—the dedicated integrity test—rather than combining scores from three different dimensions of a broader personality test, such as the NEO-PI. On the other hand, much more is known about the meaning of any of the FFM dimensions than the typical score on an integrity test. In addition, the information gathered using a traditional FFM instrument can be used for predicting many behaviors beyond honesty.

What, then, is the employer to do? A meta-analysis by Ones and Viswesvaran (2001) compared personality tests with integrity tests for predicting various work outcomes and behaviors. The results were compelling. Integrity tests did much better ($r = +.41$) than FFM personality tests at predicting overall job performance ($r = +.23$), but FFM-based tests did much better ($r = +.51$) than integrity tests ($r = +.32$) at predicting counterproductive work behaviors (e.g., theft, violence). In a more recent meta-analysis, Ones, Viswesvaran, and Schmidt (2003) found a strong relationship between personality-based measures of integrity and absenteeism. To the extent that absenteeism can be considered to be a counterproductive work behavior (as we suggest in the next chapter), then FFM personality tests might be more useful than individual integrity tests. On the other hand, if overall work performance is most important for an organization, then an integrity test might be a better choice. Optimally, the employer might cover all bases and use *both* types of tests.

Emotional Intelligence

Emotional intelligence (EI) A proposed kind of intelligence focused on people's awareness of their own and others' emotions.

Emotional intelligence quotient (EQ) Parallels the notion of intelligence quotient (IQ); a score on a test of emotional intelligence.

As we saw earlier in the chapter, the concept of **emotional intelligence (EI)** has achieved some notoriety with the public as well as arousing a great deal of interest among psychologists. As there is no general agreement on the definition of EI, there can be no agreement on how to measure it. Recall also that Davies and colleagues (1998) found little evidence for the reliability or validity of existing EI tests. A score on a test of EI is often called an **emotional intelligence quotient**, or EQ, to parallel the notion of IQ. As an example, Multi-Health Systems, Inc. (MHS) is marketing an array of products related to EI and EQ, including the Mayer-Salovey-Caruso Emotional Intelligence Test (MSCEIT™), a scale for measuring organizational emotional intelligence, a 360-degree measure of emotional intelligence, an emotional intelligence interview protocol, a youth version of the emotional intelligence test to be used with children between the ages of 7 and 18, and a series of books and videotapes

TABLE 3.5 **A Sample Item from the MSCEIT™**

SECTION H				
1. Ken and Andy have been good friends for over 10 years. Recently, however, Andy was promoted and became Ken's manager. Ken felt that the new promotion had changed Andy in that Andy had become very bossy to him. How effective would Ken be in maintaining a good relationship, if he chose to respond in each of the following ways?				
Response 1: Ken tried to understand Andy's new role and tried to adjust to the changes in their interactions.				
a. Very ineffective	b. Somewhat ineffective	c. Neutral	d. Somewhat effective	e. Very effective
Response 2: Ken approached Andy and confronted him regarding the change in his behavior.				
a. Very ineffective	b. Somewhat ineffective	c. Neutral	d. Somewhat effective	e. Very effective

Source: Adapted from MSCEIT™

intended to help people more fully develop their emotional intelligence. Table 3.5 presents a sample item from a popular test of EI. Conte (2005) reviewed the available measures as well as their strengths and weaknesses. Unfortunately, he found more weaknesses than strengths. The best that might be said at this stage is that the advocates of EI have yet to make a convincing case for either the construct or its measurement (Murphy, 2006). Additionally, EI researchers seem to be ignoring a substantial body of historical research on social intelligence that is also discouraging (Landy, 2006).

The scientific debate about the meaning or value of emotional intelligence has not slowed the pace of research by applied psychologists. It appears that as the criterion of interest becomes more narrow, the effectiveness of EI predictors increases. As an example, Rode and colleagues (2007) examined public speaking and group effectiveness among undergraduates and found that a combination of EI and a motivational measure predicted speaking and group effectiveness. The EI measure was an ability rather than a personality characteristic.

In 1966 Marvin Dunnette wrote "Fads, Fashions, and Folderol," a sobering piece about research, theory, and practice in I-O. Fads were defined as "practices and concepts characterized by capriciousness and intense but short-lived interest" (p. 343). As data accumulate, emotional intelligence may very well prove to be a useful addition to the testing toolbox, but to avoid the graveyard of the "fads," more concerted efforts to assess emotional intelligence will be required. The previously mentioned focal article on EI (Cherniss, 2010) and numerous commentaries about EI in the same journal issue indicate that I-O psychologists remain actively interested in understanding the meaning, measurement, and predictive validity of EI.

Individual Assessment

By their design, most paper-and-pencil tests are intended to be administered to large groups. In an **individual assessment**, however, only one candidate (or a very few) will be assessed on many different attributes. To select a CEO for a Fortune 500 company, for example, an executive recruiting firm may be retained to create a short list of three to five candidates who will then undergo intensive assessment. This assessment often includes paper-and-pencil tests, but they are administered and scored individually and may be used for creating a profile of a candidate rather than comparing one candidate with another. Because

Individual assessment Situation in which only one candidate (or a very few) is assessed on many different attributes.

the target populations are usually upper-level executives in an organization, individual assessment is sometimes referred to as executive or senior leader assessment (Howard, 2001). Although frequently used for selection, individual assessment can also be used to identify training needs or to provide career counseling or performance feedback to key organizational members. Because it is time-intensive and requires skilled assessors, it is expensive and unlikely to be used for any other than key positions in the company.

Individual assessment is complex, involving a wide variety of content areas as well as a wide variety of assessment processes. The tools most frequently used include various interactive assessment tools rather than paper-and-pencil tests. A primary reason for this is that the nature of the position is usually so complex that no paper-and-pencil test would, by itself, provide sufficient information. Although more than one candidate may be undergoing assessment, each candidate is usually assessed in isolation from the others. This allows the organization to keep the identity of candidates a closely held secret for the protection of the reputation of both the company (should a chosen candidate reject an offer) and the candidate (should the organization ultimately reject a candidate).

The "typical" individual assessment is likely to include ability tests, personality tests, a personal history statement, and interviews. It may also include simulation exercises or work samples and, less frequently, a clinically based personality test such as the Rorschach Inkblot Test or the Thematic Apperception Test (TAT). There is not much scientific support for the use of these clinically oriented tests, but they are still occasionally used.

Although we will not cover individual assessment beyond this description, Silzer and Jeanneret (1998) have provided rich detail on the typical process and content of individual assessment for the interested reader, and Highhouse (2002) has presented a history of individual assessment that incorporates a more critical evaluation of the role of individual assessment in I-O psychology.

Interviews

In one form or another, an interview plays a role in virtually every selection or promotion decision. This has been true for many decades; one of the first texts dealing with employment interviewing was written by Bingham and Moore in 1931. Over the years, there have been many fine texts (e.g., Webster, 1982) and reviews of the research on the interview (e.g., Guion, 2011; Landy, 1989; Posthuma, Morgeson, & Campion, 2002).

Interview Content

Interview content is often dictated by the amount of structure in the interview. A **structured interview** consists of very specific questions asked of each candidate, often anchored in asking the interviewee to describe in specific and behavioral detail how he or she would respond to a hypothetical situation. This has been labeled the **situational interview**, a subcategory of the structured interview. In addition, structured interviews typically have tightly crafted scoring schemes with detailed outlines for the interviewer with respect to assigning ratings or scores based on interview performance. The situational interview can be contrasted with another form of structured interview known as the behavior description interview. The basic difference between them is a time orientation. The situational interview asks the applicant what he or she *would* do, whereas the behavior description interview asks the applicant what he or she *did* do in the past. Recent research seems to favor the behavior description format (Taylor & Small, 2002), particularly when the interviews are being used to fill very high-level executive positions (Huffcutt, Weekley, Wiesner, DeGroot, & Jones, 2001; Krajewski, Goffin, McCarthy,

Structured interview Assessment procedure that consists of very specific questions asked of each candidate; includes tightly crafted scoring schemes with detailed outlines for the interviewer with respect to assigning ratings or scores based on interview performance.

Situational interview An assessment procedure in which the interviewee is asked to describe in specific and behavioral detail how he or she would respond to a hypothetical situation.

Rothstein, & Johnston, 2006). Huffcutt and colleagues speculate that the prevalence of the behavior description format at higher levels may be because the behavior description interview allows for a greater influence from verbal/presentation skills than the situational interview. Day and Carroll (2003) suggest another possible explanation: The behavior description interview assesses experience to a greater degree than abilities or personal characteristics. It is also likely that as one moves up the organizational (and complexity) ladder, experience trumps ability or personality.

An **unstructured interview** includes much broader questions that may vary by candidate and allows the candidate to answer in any form he or she prefers. In addition, unstructured interviews usually have less detailed scoring formats, allowing the interviewer greater discretion in scoring. An example of structured interview questions is presented in Table 3.6. The questions were developed to elicit behavioral skills from candidates for 911 emergency dispatcher positions.

Unstructured interview An interview format that includes questions that may vary by candidate and that allows the candidate to answer in any form he or she prefers.

For the most part, interviews cover one or more of the following content areas: job knowledge, abilities, skills, personality, and person–organization fit (Huffcutt, Conway, Roth, & Stone, 2001). Huffcutt and colleagues found that the most frequently assessed constructs in interviews were personality and applied social skills, followed by cognitive ability, job knowledge, and skills. Salgado and Moscoso (2002) provided more detail on content. In a meta-analysis of the employment interview, they found interesting content differences between conventional interviews and tightly structured behavioral interviews. They discovered that the less structured or conventional interview seems to be more closely associated with personality and social/communication skills. On the other hand, the tightly structured behavioral interview is more closely associated with job knowledge and technical attributes, and, to a much lesser extent, personality characteristics. Similar results have been reported by Huffcutt and colleagues (2001).

TABLE 3.6 **Examples of Structured Interview Questions and the Real-Life Incidents That Are the Foundation for These Questions**

These questions were used to interview applicants for emergency telephone operator positions.

INTERVIEW QUESTION	*CRITICAL INCIDENT*
1. Imagine that you tried to help a stranger, for example, with traffic directions or to get up after a fall and that person blamed you for their misfortune or yelled at you. How would you respond?	1. Telephone operator tries to verify address information for an ambulance call. The caller yells at them for being stupid and slow. The operator quietly assures the caller an ambulance is on the way and that she is merely reaffirming the address.
2. Suppose a friend calls you and is extremely upset. Apparently, her child has been injured. She begins to tell you, in a hysterical manner, all about her difficulty in getting babysitters, what the child is wearing, what words the child can speak, and so on. What would you do?	2. A caller is hysterical because her infant is dead. She yells incoherently about the incident. The operator talks in a clear calm voice and manages to secure the woman's address, dispatches the call, and then tries to secure more information about the child's status.
3. How would you react if you were a salesclerk, waitress, or gas station attendant, and one of your customers talked back to you, indicated you should have known something you did not, or told you that you were not waiting on them fast enough?	3. A clearly angry caller calls for the third time in an hour complaining about the 911 service because no one has arrived to investigate a busted water pipe. The operator tells the caller to go to _____ and hangs up.

SOURCE: Schneider, B., & Schmitt, N. (1986). *Staffing organizations* (2nd ed.). Glenview, IL: Scott Foresman. Original copyright © 1986, 1976 by Scott, Foresman, and Company. Copyright © 1991 by Benjamin Schneider and Neal Schmitt. Reprinted by permission of the authors.

These results take on more meaning when considered in the context of reviews of the validity of the interview. It has been generally found (McDaniel, Whetgel, Schmidt, & Maurer, 1994) that the highest validity coefficients are associated with structured and behavioral interviews (often in the range of +.60) compared to the more personality-based interviews, which have validity coefficients more often in the range of +.30. These results would seem to be a strong recommendation for tightly structured interviews based on task-based job demands over interviews intended to assess personality characteristics or personal style. But a note of caution should be sounded here. Many of the studies on which these meta-analyses were based were conducted in an earlier time, before the emergence of team environments and client-centered work. As a result, many of the criteria used in the validation studies were task based. It is not surprising, then, that lower validity coefficients would be observed for interviews centered on personality characteristics. These "personality-based" interviews were also done in a time when few sound personality tests were available. Schmidt and Zimmerman (2004) present some intriguing findings that seem to demonstrate that when three or four independent unstructured interviews are combined, the validity for that unstructured combination is as high as the validity for a structured interview conducted by a single individual. This is good news and bad news. The good news is that certain administrative steps can be taken to increase the validity of unstructured interviews. The bad news is that it might be necessary to conduct three or four independent interviews to accomplish that increase, thus increasing the time and money the interview process requires.

In the context of the current state of the field, it might be reasonable to use psychometric devices (e.g., the NEO-PI, the Hogan Personality Inventory, or the Saville Consulting Wave) to assess personality attributes and the structured behavioral interview to assess knowledge and skills. Guion (1998) concluded that the structured interview is a valuable tool in the assessment toolbag. We agree.

Paradoxically, however, it appears as if managers may not agree. They tend to prefer unstructured to structured interviews (van der Zee, Bakker, & Bakker, 2002). Lievens and De Paepe (2004) have shed some light on this paradox. It appears that managers avoid structure because they feel that it makes the process too impersonal; they want more control over the interview questions and process. Chapman and Zwieg (2005) found that applicants agree, preferring less to more structure, seeing structured interviews as more "difficult." Lievens and De Paepe also found that those managers with formal training in interviewing (e.g., through workshops) were much more likely to impose more structure on the format.

TABLE 3.7 **Potential Influences on Employment Interviews**

Potential Influences on Employment Interviews
Nature of the information: negative versus positive
Placement of information: early or late in the interview
Presence of interviewer stereotypes (e.g., ideal candidate)
Interviewer knowledge of the job in question
Method used by interviewer to combine information
Nonverbal behavior of candidate: posture, gestures
Attitudinal or racial similarity of candidate and interviewer
Gender similarity of candidate and interviewer
Quality of competing candidates
Interviewer experience
Applicant physical appearance
Attention to factual detail by interviewer
Extent to which interview is structured
Note taking by interviewer
Use of same interviewer(s) for all candidates

SOURCE: Huffcutt, A. I., & Woehr, D. J. (1999). Further analysis of the employment interview validity: A quantitative evaluation of interviewer-related structuring methods. *Journal of Organizational Behavior, 20*, 549–560.

Interview Process

Independent of the actual content of the interview, there are many relevant process issues. How should interviews be conducted? How should interviewers be trained? What are some potential sources of bias in interviews? Table 3.7 presents information on many of these practical issues. Studies (e.g., Huffcutt & Roth, 1998; Sacco, Scheu, Ryan, & Schmitt, 2003) appear to confirm, at least on a preliminary basis, that little adverse impact is associated with the structured interview, particularly when compared with more traditional paper-and-pencil tests of cognitive ability. Nevertheless, these studies have examined traditional domestic demographic characteristics such as race and gender. As applicant populations become increasing multicultural, the issues of bias in the interview may reemerge due to the more dramatic cultural differences that may appear in applicant responses. For example, many Asian cultures value modesty in self-presentation. Thus, Asian applicants may be less comfortable than American applicants in extolling their virtues when asked by an interviewer to describe strengths and weaknesses (a common question in unstructured interviews).

Interviewees may have a completely different set of anxieties and priorities when it comes to the interview. McCarthy and Goffin (2004) have identified five aspects of the interview that may be associated with the "weak knees and sweaty palms" of the applicant. These anxieties revolve around communication, appearance, social skills, interview performance, and behavioral control (i.e., observable tension in the applicant). Anyone who has been an applicant has experienced one or more of these "anxieties." Maurer and Solamon (2006) presented a treasure trove of recommendations for interview preparation and performance in the form of a coaching program to help prepare candidates for Atlanta fire department and police department promotions. Many of their recommendations apply to preparation for *any* interview.

Assessment Centers

Even though the word "center" evokes an image of a physical place, **assessment centers** are collections of procedures for evaluation, no matter where these procedures are carried out. Assessment centers are very much like the individual assessment procedure we described earlier, except they are administered to groups of individuals rather than single individuals, and the assessments are typically done by multiple assessors rather than a single assessor. Assessment centers have a long and successful history, and there are many good books and articles describing variations on the technique (Bray, Campbell, & Grant, 1974; Guion, 1998). A recent book illustrates the global value of the assessment center methodology, showing applications in settings outside of the United States (Krause & Thornton, 2008). In earlier years, there were as many variations of assessment centers as there were users. For this reason, a task force published *Guidelines and Ethical Considerations for Assessment Center Operations* (Task Force on Assessment Center Guidelines, 1989). These guidelines have done much to standardize the assessment center process and protect the rights of those being assessed.

Assessment center
Collection of procedures for evaluation that is administered to groups of individuals; assessments are typically performed by multiple assessors.

Most assessment centers share the following characteristics (Finkle, 1976):

1. Assessment is done in groups. A typical group size is 12, although smaller subgroups may be formed for specific exercises. The group format provides opportunity for peer evaluation.
2. Assessment is done by groups. Unlike the usual evaluators in individual assessment, assessment center evaluators are usually managers chosen from the organization but unfamiliar with the candidates.
3. Multiple methods of assessment are employed. As with individual assessment, these might include paper-and-pencil tests, group exercises, interviews, and clinical testing. A typical group exercise might be a leaderless group discussion that is observed and rated by the assessors. An individual exercise might be an in-basket exercise in which a candidate is presented with the contents of a typical in-basket and asked to deal with each element in the basket by making a phone call, sending an e-mail, writing a memo, or starting a file for information.
4. Assessment centers invariably have a "feel" of relevance to them, both for assessors and for those being assessed. They are seen as much more "real" than interviews, paper-and-pencil tests, or even isolated work simulations.

TABLE 3.8 **Portion of a Report Based on Assessment Center Evaluation**

There were several indications from his behavior that his strong desire to make a favorable impression promoted above-average tenseness in the assessment situation. On several occasions, his behavior was characterized by nervousness and controlled quietness, as though he were reluctant to enter into a situation until he felt absolutely sure of himself.
The picture he created was that of a young man eager to cooperate, comply, and do his best in order to fulfill the expectations others had for him.
In most respects, the trainee's general abilities compare favorably with the total sample of men in the Management Progress study.
Most members of the staff anticipated a very successful career in the Bell System for the trainee. . . . There was a mild amount of disagreement concerning the speed with which he is likely to reach the district level of management. Everyone agreed that he presently displays the abilities and potential to perform effectively at the district level.

SOURCE: Bray, D. W., Campbell, R. J., & Grant, D. L. (1974). *Formative years in business: A long-term AT&T study of managerial lives*. New York: John Wiley & Sons.

As in the individual assessment procedure, the results of the assessment center may include a report, recommendation, and feedback to the participants. An excerpt from a typical report appears in Table 3.8. On the basis of assessment center results, the organization may make one or more of the following decisions (Finkle, 1976):

1. An assessee may or may not qualify for a given job or job level.
2. Assessees may be ranked on a series of attributes and placed into different categories representing anticipated speed of promotion (e.g., fast track versus normal progression groups).
3. Predictions of long-range potential may be made for one or more of the assessees.
4. Development and learning experiences for aiding the assessee in personal or professional growth might be recommended.

There is general agreement that assessment centers can be valuable procedures for selection, promotion, and training needs analysis (Arthur, Day, Mcnelly, & Edens, 2003; Bartram, 2002; Hermelin, Lievens, & Robertson, 2007). There is less agreement with respect to *why* they work (Lance, 2008; Sackett & Tuzinski, 2001). Although the "why" question may be an interesting one for scientific and research purposes (e.g., Bowler & Woehr, 2006), it is less important and more mind-numbing from a practical perspective. Assessment centers include many different types of exercises and assess many different attributes. The information is eventually combined to yield a decision or recommendation that will be as good or as poor as the information that went into it.

Decomposing the assessment center into its constituent elements is difficult to do. Nevertheless, I-O researchers cannot resist the temptation to decompose. And the temptation seems to be yielding informative results. The rationale of the assessment center is to provide opportunities for candidates to display effective performance in some tightly constructed simulated environments. But it is appearing more likely that it is not the performance that strikes the assessors, but underlying abilities and personality characteristics illuminated by those simulated environments. Overall assessment ratings appear to be closely associated with assessee cognitive ability and, to a substantial but lesser extent, to assessee personality characteristics, particularly extraversion and emotional stability (Collins et al., 2003; Hoeft & Schuler, 2001; Lievens, De Fruyt, & van Dam, 2001). These results would

BOX 3.5 *THE APPRENTICE*

Perhaps the most vivid popular version of the assessment center is the reality television show *The Apprentice*, which we discussed from another angle in Chapter 1. This show pits a number of candidates against one another to see who will become an "apprentice" for a year with real estate tycoon Donald Trump. The candidates are assigned to teams, whose composition changes as one candidate is fired each week. Within the candidate pool, the situation is largely leaderless at the outset, although, as tends to happen in more traditional assessment centers, a leader eventually emerges from the pack. In *The Apprentice*, the implicit leader of the assessor pack is easy to pick out by simply noting hair style (although efforts are made to identify multiple assessors). The candidates are asked to work in teams with (and often expected to work *against*) each other on practical tasks including design, manufacturing, marketing, distribution, and sales. Then there is the "board room" confrontation between and among assessors and assessees. This crucible often produces memorable moments. For example, in season two, one candidate who offered to give up his "immunity" from being fired is fired by "The Donald" for being "stupid, impulsive, and life threatening" (Stanley, 2004). The feel of relevance of the situation, at least to candidates and the viewing public, is apparent (thus, the term "reality" show). As the number of candidates dwindles, it is clear that some assessees do not "qualify" (they can be identified as the ones getting into the taxi with luggage at the end of each episode), that the eventual "apprentice" has been identified as having long-term potential, and that many of the unsuccessful candidates view the experience as developmentally valuable.

© Photofest

Donald Trump presides over a group of would-be apprentices.

seem to indicate that the combination of a good cognitive ability test and personality test might do as well as, if not better than (and at considerably lesser expense), a full-blown assessment center. Box 3.5 provides a familiar example of an assessment center.

Assessment centers can be expensive and time consuming. They are likely to be of greatest value to large organizations that favor internal movement and promotions and invest heavily in the learning and development of their members. In addition, candidates who are evaluated through assessment centers are often very enthusiastic about the process, and this enthusiasm likely translates into acceptance of feedback. This can be particularly important when the goal is employee development rather than employee selection. Nevertheless, many organizations can accomplish assessment more effectively with more traditional assessment procedures.

On a less optimistic note, however, African Americans and Hispanics appear to do less well in assessment centers than whites, although women tend to receive higher scores than men (Dean, Roth, & Bobko, 2008). This finding warrants more extensive replication since assessment centers have often been adopted by employers to *reduce* adverse impact against ethnic minority applicants. Researchers (e.g., Cascio & Aguinis, 2011) often express the expectation that assessment centers are likely to have less or no adverse impact against ethnic minority applicants. It may be that the connection between assessment center ratings and cognitive ability that we noted above is responsible for this effect, but we need to more seriously examine the possible adverse impact of assessment centers not only with respect to ethnic subgroups, but also with respect to age subgroups.

Work Samples and Situational Tests

Work Sample Tests

Work sample test Assessment procedure that measures job skills by taking samples of behavior under realistic job-like conditions.

As the name implies, **work sample tests** measure job skills by taking samples of behavior under realistic job-like conditions. One of the earliest applications of this technique was in the selection of trolley car operators in Boston in 1910. Trolley cars frequently came into contact with people, horses, bicycles, and the newly introduced automobile. In 1913, Munsterberg set up a "work station" to simulate the controls of the trolley car and projected events onto a screen to see how potential operators would respond. Since this study was carried out a decade before the correlation coefficient became a common index of validity, Munsterberg's assertion that his work station predicted operator success is anecdotal.

In today's work sample tests, the performance may or may not be assessed at an actual workstation, but the task assigned and the equipment used to complete the task are designed to be realistic simulations of the actual job. Consider the example of an individual applying for a position as a call-center representative (i.e., answers customer service line calls). The applicant sits at a computer screen and responds to a customer call. The applicant has to enter account information, look up order information, and even deal with an angry customer who is disputing a charge. The applicant's score is a combination of hard skills (e.g., amount of time on the call, efficiency of screen navigation) and soft skills (e.g., anger management). As another example, an applicant for the job of accounts payable clerk might be given a checkbook in which to make entries, a work report from which to generate an invoice, a petty cash ledger to balance, and a payroll task. The results would then be compared against some standard and a score assigned representing the level of test performance. Table 3.9 illustrates some work sample tests.

Work sample tests work well for customer service and call center positions.

Like assessment centers, work samples have a "real" feeling to them and usually elicit good reactions from candidates. Further, various studies have affirmed that work samples can be valid assessment devices (e.g., Roth, Bobko, & McFarland, 2005). This is not surprising because work samples usually come directly from the tasks of the job in question, and it is easier to document their job relatedness. But like other formats, work samples are not intrinsically valid. Their job relatedness depends heavily on the attributes being assessed by the format. Using the example of the call-center applicant, good performance may be the result of specific knowledge (the candidate is familiar with the software), general knowledge (the candidate is familiar with computer operations), or cognitive ability (the candidate is able to solve the problem presented by the task through trial and error). When work sample tests make unique contributions to test performance (e.g., above and beyond what might be predicted by a simple test of cognitive ability), it is likely due to general or specific knowledge. As Guion (1998) pointed out, the value of a work sample

TABLE 3.9 **Some Examples of Work Sample Tests**

MOTOR WORK SAMPLES	*VERBAL WORK SAMPLES*
Carving dexterity test for dental students	A test of common facts of law for law students
Blueprint reading test	Group discussion test for supervisor
Shorthand and stenography test	Judgment and decision-making test for administrators
Rudder control test for pilots	Speech interview for foreign student
Programming test for computer programmers	Test of basic information in chemistry
Map reading test for traffic control officers	Test of ability to follow oral directions

can be evaluated just as one would evaluate any assessment device: job relatedness, perceived fairness, and cost effectiveness. In Chapter 5, we will describe various techniques used to elicit knowledge from nuclear power plant operators, such as the "walk-through" method. This might also be considered an example of a work sample.

Situational Judgment Tests

Situational judgment test Commonly a paper-and-pencil test that presents the candidate with a written scenario and asks the candidate to choose the best response from a series of alternatives.

Recently, the notion of the work sample test has been expanded to cover white-collar positions by creating what Motowidlo and Tippins (1993) have referred to as low-fidelity simulations and others have referred to as **situational judgment tests** (SJT) (McDaniel, Morgeson, Finnegan, Campion, & Braverman, 2001). A situational judgment test presents the candidate with a written scenario and then asks the candidate to choose the best response

FIGURE 3.10 An Example of a Situational Judgment Exercise

A man on a very urgent mission during a battle finds he must cross a stream about 40 feet wide. A blizzard has been blowing and the stream has frozen over. However, because of the snow, he does not know how thick the ice is. He sees two planks about 10 feet long near the point where he wishes to cross. He also knows where there is a bridge about 2 miles downstream. Under the circumstances he should:

A. Walk to the bridge and cross it.

B. Run rapidly across on the ice.

C. Break a hole in the ice near the edge of the stream to see how deep the stream is.

D. Cross with the aid of the planks, pushing one ahead of the other and walking on them.

E. Creep slowly across the ice.

Source: Northrup, L. C. (1989). *The psychometric history of selected ability constructs*. Washington, DC: Office of Personnel Management.

from a series of alternatives (see Figure 3.10). A text in the SIOP Frontiers Series does an excellent job of reviewing the theory, research, and applications related to situation judgment tests (Weekley & Ployhart, 2006).

McDaniel and colleagues (2001) have reviewed the research on situational judgment tests and noted that in one form or another, such tests have been part of the assessment practice of I-O psychologists since the 1920s. In a meta-analysis of 102 validity coefficients, they concluded that there is substantial evidence of validity or job relatedness in these types of tests. They found that the single strongest component of these tests was general mental ability. Nevertheless, there appears to be more to SJTs than just "g." In a recent meta-analysis, McDaniel, Hartman, Whetzel, and Grubb (2007) demonstrated that SJT scores have incremental validity above and beyond the prediction afforded by personality tests and intelligence tests.

Clevenger, Pereira, Weichmann, Schmitt, and Harvey (2001) evaluated the use of SJTs in hiring decisions for a government agency and a private-sector transportation company. In addition to SJTs, they collected data on personality, cognitive ability, technical job knowledge, and job experience of the candidates. They found that SJTs were able to improve the prediction of performance even after the contributions of all these other variables had been controlled and even though the SJT scores were substantially correlated with the measure of cognitive ability. They suggested that SJTs are best used to measure procedural knowledge (what we referred to as tacit knowledge earlier in this chapter). In a more recent review, Chan and Schmitt (2005) have added adaptability (which we will cover in detail in Chapter 4) to their hypothesis about what is measured by SJTs. As you can see from Figure 3.11, it appears that various KSAOs produce competencies related to tacit knowledge and adaptability (which could also be labeled practical intelligence) and that these, in turn, produce positive and prevent negative job behavior. Weekley and Ployhart (2005) suggest that SJTs assess general rather than job-specific forms of knowledge. The relationship between KSAOs and practical intelligence helps explain why there are positive correlations between SJT scores, "g," and personality test scores. It also helps explain why SJTs predict performance beyond any one or combination of those attributes—namely, because the attributes support the development of tacit knowledge and adaptability but are different from any of those supporting KSAOs. This model is supported by the research of McDaniel and Nguyen (2001), which shows an increase in SJT scores with increasing years of experience. It is plausible that tacit knowledge and adaptability increase with experience.

Another advantage of SJTs discovered in the study by Clevenger and colleagues was that the differences in scores between whites and both African Americans and Hispanics were considerably less than typically found in standard tests of cognitive ability. This may be a

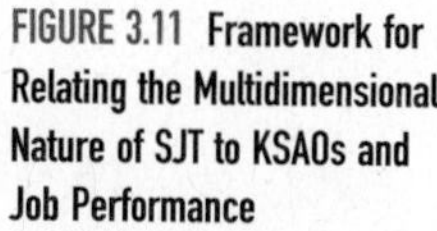

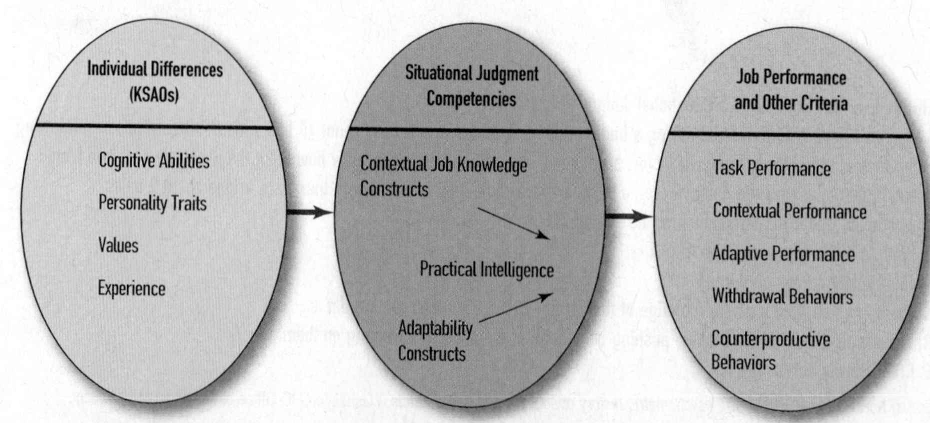

FIGURE 3.11 Framework for Relating the Multidimensional Nature of SJT to KSAOs and Job Performance

SOURCE: Chan, D., & Schmitt, N. (2005). Situational judgment tests. In N. Anderson, A. Evers, & O. Voskuijil (Eds.), *Blackwell handbook of personnel selection*. Oxford, U.K.: Blackwell Publishing, p. 47. © 2005 by Blackwell Publishing Ltd. Reprinted by permission.

case of having your cake and eating it, too. Not only did the SJT give a good assessment of general mental ability with lower adverse impact, it also measured something in addition to "g" that was job related. This "something" was most likely practical intelligence as described above. In a follow-up study, Chan and Schmitt (2002) found once again that SJT scores contributed to the prediction of job performance for 160 civil service employees, beyond what could be predicted from cognitive ability, personality, and job experience. This study is particularly interesting because it was done in Singapore, suggesting that at least the format of the SJT can travel internationally.

SJTs have also been adapted for video presentation by using video vignettes, rather than a written description, to present the scenario. The results are encouraging. In two similar studies, Weekley and Jones (1997) and Chan and Schmitt (1997) found that black–white differences in SJT scores were smaller with a video than with a paper-and-pencil presentation, and that SJTs produced more favorable attitudes toward the assessment process, particularly among African American test takers. Further, Lievens and Sackett (2006) found that the video version of an SJT had higher validities than a written version for predicting interpersonal behavior in medical students.

The results of research on SJTs are very positive. They seem to possess three important characteristics for modern and practical assessment: They are job related, they are well accepted by test takers, and they have reduced adverse impact compared to other traditional assessment devices. The research on video presentations suggests that further advances are likely to occur in this area, particularly in terms of increasing the fidelity of the simulation from low to high and in further increasing the acceptance of the format by test takers. If there is any caution in the wholesale adoption of SJTs, it is that they may be susceptible to faking (McDaniel et al., 2007; Peeters & Lievens, 2005), particularly when the instructions ask for "what would you tend to do?" versus "what is the best answer?" Much more needs to be known about the extent to which the SJT is susceptible to faking.

MODULE 3.4 SUMMARY

- A vigorous debate continues over whether there is only one overarching cognitive ability—"g" or general mental ability—or several distinct facets or abilities. Psychologists have developed tests that produce a single number intended to represent cognitive ability, tests of specific abilities, and test batteries designed to measure several different facets of cognitive ability.
- Because most physically demanding jobs require combinations of physical abilities, many physical ability assessment procedures use simulated pieces of work (e.g., carrying a load up a ladder) rather than individual physical tests (e.g., sit-ups or bench presses). There is substantial evidence that measures of physical abilities can improve the prediction of job success for many physically demanding jobs.
- Personality testing in employment has shifted from a screen-*out* process to a screen-*in* process whereby employers seek to identify applicants with positive personality characteristics (e.g., conscientiousness, emotional stability, or agreeableness). There are many commercially available instruments for measuring personality characteristics, many based on the Big Five model.
- Hogan, Hogan, and Roberts addressed practical questions about using the measurement of personality for making employment decisions.
- Practical considerations in personality testing include the use of integrity tests on which "faking" is sometimes an issue; emotional intelligence tests; and tests of interests and values.
- It is important for employers and applicants to distinguish between the content of testing (*what* attribute is being assessed) and the process of testing (*how* it is being assessed). For example, the terms "personality" and "cognitive" describe

the content of the assessment, and the terms "interview" and "background check" describe the process of the assessment.

- Individual assessment is complex, involving a wide variety of content areas and assessment processes. The tools used most frequently include various interactive assessment tools rather than paper-and-pencil tests, as the nature of the position is usually so complex that no paper-and-pencil test would, by itself, provide sufficient information.
- An interview plays a role in virtually every selection or promotion decision. Interviews vary in their structure and content. They can range on a continuum from very unstructured to very structured and can cover one or more of the following content areas: job knowledge, abilities, skills, personality, and person–organization fit.
- Assessment centers have a long and successful history. They are administered to groups of individuals rather than single individuals, and the assessments are typically performed by multiple assessors. There is general agreement that an assessment center can be a valuable procedure for selection, promotion, and training needs analysis.
- Other common assessment devices include work samples and situational judgment tests.

KEY TERMS

cognitive ability test
cognitive test battery
knowledge test
psychomotor abilities
screen-out test
screen-in test
self-presentation
overt integrity test
personality-based integrity test
emotional intelligence (EI)
emotional intelligence quotient (EQ)
individual assessment
structured interview
situational interview
unstructured interview
assessment center
work sample test
situational judgment test

MODULE 3.5

Special Topics in Assessment

Incremental Validity

In the preceding modules, we have described quite a few tools that might go into the assessment toolbag. Until recently, assessment research often took on the flavor of a competition: Which tool was better, a paper-and-pencil test of "g" or an interview? One study reported that "the validity" of a test of general mental ability was +.35, whereas another study reported that "the validity" of an interview was +.46, suggesting somehow that an interview is a more valid assessment device. Similarly, one might explore the differences in validity between a personality test and an interest test or a work sample and a paper-and-pencil test. These are misleading questions for a number of reasons. First, we cannot answer these questions without answering another question: Better for what? Predicting satisfaction, or performance, or tenure, or management potential? Another reason why the questions are misleading is their implication that one is forced to choose a single instrument rather than developing a battery of assessment devices. Finally, the questions were misleading because they mixed test content with test process (e.g., test of "g" versus interview) (Sackett & Lievens, 2008).

In the past few years, dozens of studies have purported to demonstrate the value of one or another device or test. Many of these studies compared the device of interest to another device. In addition, studies examined the predictive validity of particular combinations to demonstrate the added, or incremental, value of combining two devices. Thus, a study might show that the validity of a paper-and-pencil test of general mental ability was found to be +.35, but when it was combined with an interview, the validity of the two measures combined was +.51. Thus, one might conclude that the value of the interview is incremental; that is, it added to the validity of the paper-and-pencil test. Examples of **incremental validity** studies include the following:

Incremental validity The value in terms of increased validity of adding a particular predictor to an existing selection system.

- Personality measures and biographical data (McManus & Kelly, 1999)
- Biodata and general mental ability (Mount, Witt, & Barrick, 2000)
- Personality measures and assessment centers (Goffin, Rothstein, & Johnston, 1996)
- Cognitive ability, interviews, and biodata (Bobko, Roth, & Potosky, 1999)
- Personality measures and mental ability (Bing, Whanger, Davison, & VanHook, 2004; Kanfer & Kantrowitz, 2002)
- Situational judgment and cognitive ability/personality/job experience (Chan & Schmitt, 2002; Weekley & Ployhart, 2005)
- Situational judgment and cognitive measures (Lievens, Boyse, & Sackett, 2005a)

These studies point to an important principle: In assessment the issue is not *which* tool to use, but what *combination* of tools to use for the greatest predictive ability at the lowest cost.

As we saw earlier in the chapter when we discussed individual differences, and as we will see in greater detail in the chapters covering performance theory and prediction, behavior at work is very complicated. It involves technical tasks as well as social ones. Successful performance in virtually any job depends on many different KSAOs. As a result, it makes little sense to limit the toolbag to one and only one tool. As Maslow said many years ago (1971), when the only tool in your bag is a hammer, you tend to treat everything as if it were a nail. As we continue to gather information about the incremental validity of various combinations of assessment tools, we will be better able to make practical recommendations about the most fair and effective assessment programs, as well as what tests and procedures might act as substitutes for other tests and procedures.

Biographical Data

Biodata Information collected on an application blank or in a standardized test that includes questions about previous jobs, education, specialized training, and personal history; also known as biographical data.

Ecology model Underlying model for life history biodata instruments. Proposes that the events that make up a person's history represent choices made by the individual to interact with his or her environment. These choices can signal abilities, interests, and personality characteristics.

It is common for organizations to gather personal information from applicants for positions. The best example is the type of information collected on an application blank: information about previous jobs, education, and specialized training. This type of information can also be used to predict job performance; collecting it can be thought of as a "test" if the collection method is standardized, the scoring is objective, and the sample of behavior examined is reasonable. This type of information has been variously labeled personal history, life history, biographical information, or—the simplest label—**biodata**.

In the 1950s and 1960s, biodata predictors were based less on theory than on statistics. If a particular piece of information (e.g., educational accomplishment) could be shown to predict success, it was included in an application blank. If no relationship could be found, it was not included. William Owens pioneered what has been called the rational approach to the use of life history data for the prediction of success (Mumford & Owens, 1982; Mumford, Snell, & Reiter-Palmon, 1994; Mumford & Stokes, 1991). Instead of simply looking at statistical relationships between individual history information items and success, Owens identified broader life history factors as a way of arranging all of the hundreds of pieces of information that could be gathered about someone. The underlying model for this type of biodata instrument is the **ecology model** (Mumford, Uhlman, & Kilcullen, 1992). In its simplest form, this model proposes that the events that make up a person's history are neither accidental nor random. They represent choices made by the individual to interact with his or her environment. As a result, these choices can signal abilities, interests, and personality characteristics. Thus, personal history data can be used as a surrogate or as an addition to other assessment information. As Figure 3.12 shows, there are many potential influences on the situations and actions that individuals choose from all available situations and actions. These precursors of situational choice and actions are the focus of biodata instruments. One implication of the ecology model is that as individuals mature (i.e., enter different life stages such as college, first job, parenthood, career), the predictability of biodata items might change (Dean & Russell, 2005).

Like other assessment instruments we have discussed, biodata instruments derive their job relatedness and value from the constructs they try to assess (e.g., cognitive ability, personality, experience, knowledge), not from any magical properties of the format itself. Several studies have demonstrated that biodata items can improve prediction of success when added to other discrete assessment techniques such as the interview (Dalessio & Silverhart, 1994), personality tests (McManus & Kelly, 1999), and even general

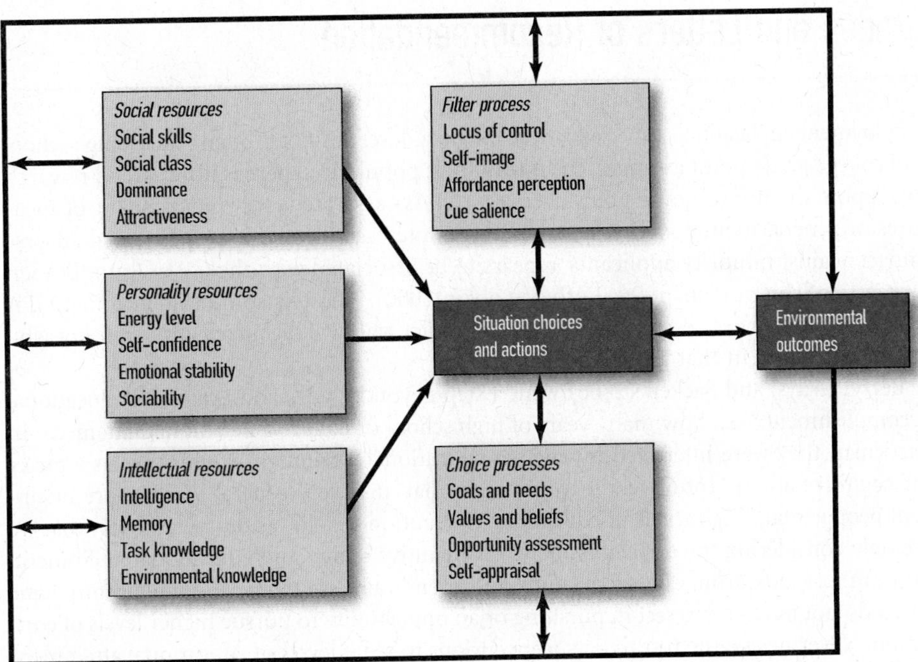

FIGURE 3.12 Construct Categories Drawn from an Ecology Model

SOURCE: Mumford, M. D., & Stokes, G. S. (1991). Developmental determinants of individual action: Theory and practice in applying background measures. In M. D. Dunnette & L. M. Hough (Eds.), *Handbook of industrial and organizational psychology* (2nd ed., Vol. 3, pp. 61–138). Palo Alto, CA: Consulting Psychologists Press. Copyright permission by Leaetta Hough.

mental ability (Mount et al., 2000). But if one were to develop a comprehensive battery of devices including cognitive ability, personality, interest inventories, and job knowledge, it is not yet clear how biodata information would add to what is assessed by those other techniques. There are also some lingering concerns about the fairness of certain types of biodata items. For example, Whitney and Schmitt (1997) found that compared with whites, blacks were more likely to describe past experiences that emphasized "the maintenance or restoration of long-standing traditions" and activities that were group rather than individually oriented. Even though the research was performed with college students, it certainly suggests that more research needs to be done in the area of ethnic and cultural influences on biodata instruments. There has been also some concern about whether biodata items are susceptible to faking, or at least **social desirability** influences in responding (Schmitt & Kunce, 2002). Schmitt and colleagues (2003) demonstrated that when the candidate was required to elaborate on various biodata responses, biodata scores did go down. But even though the scores changed, they seemed to change for everyone, since there was no reduction in the criterion-related validity of the biodata scores. Either people did not want to take the energy to elaborate, or everyone appears to claim experiences that they may not have had. Harold, McFarland, and Weekley (2006) suggest that there is less faking on biodata than on personality inventories because questions about the presence or absence of experiences (i.e., a biodata question) are less likely to lead to self-deception (I *was* a neurosurgeon for several years before going to work for Lowe's) than questions about tendencies (I *am* very careful in my work). The researchers suggest that maximum validity can be obtained from biodata tests when the answers to the question appear to be verifiable to the candidate (i.e., the employer *could* check on the accuracy of the answer). The good news is that current research on biodata is considerably more theory-based than it has been in the past (Mitchell, 1994). Once biodata instruments become more standardized and there is some agreement regarding what they measure most effectively, biodata instruments are likely to represent an attractive alternative to other available assessment devices.

Social desirability Desire to be appealing to others.

Grades and Letters of Recommendation

Employment applications, especially those for entry-level positions, often request high school and college grade point averages. In spite of their popularity, there is little careful research to support the use of grade point averages (GPAs) as a predictor, independent of measures of general mental ability, personality, or interests. In addition, substantial adverse impact against minority applicants appears to be associated with the GPA (Roth, BeVier, Switzer, & Schippmann, 1996; Roth & Bobko, 2000). There is some evidence that GPA and positive letters of recommendation can predict who will be *offered* a job, but not who will be successful in that job (Marshall, 1985).

Berry, Gruys, and Sackett (2006) went a step beyond grades and examined educational accomplishment (i.e., how many years of high school or college a person had attained). In particular, they were interested in whether educational attainment could serve as a proxy for cognitive ability. Intuitively it would seem that, in a very general sense, more intelligent people attain high levels of education. We caution to add (as do the authors) that we are only considering the *correlation* between cognitive ability and educational attainment. You can just look around at your family and friends and see that many intelligent people either do not have an interest in pursuing or an opportunity to pursue higher levels of education. Nevertheless, the researchers were curious to see if levels of educational attainment might substitute for a test that measures cognitive ability. This would be useful for employers, since gathering and verifying educational information is often much easier and cheaper than administering, scoring, and interpreting a test. The analysis showed that, even though the most *accurate* measure of cognitive ability was a test, setting the successful completion of at least one year of college as an educational requirement could act as a reasonable proxy for a cognitive ability test score. The researchers recommended that employers might want to set one year of college as a screen for those who would be permitted to take a test of cognitive ability (i.e., make it a minimum qualification for application), thus assuring that those who took the test would already be in the upper ranges of cognitive ability. They also found that if the "one year of college" hurdle was used *instead of* the test of cognitive ability, adverse impact against ethnic minority applicants would be reduced. Many employers would see the tradeoff between lessened adverse impact at the risk of less complete information regarding "g" as a good one. Not all jobs require high levels of "g," and for some openings, a surrogate for "g" might work just fine.

Similarly, even though employers almost always ask job applicants for references or letters of recommendation, there has been little serious research on the validity or fairness of these devices (Loher, Hazer, Tsai, Tilton, & James, 1997). Since the threat of litigation from disgruntled rejected applicants looms large in the minds of many recommenders and reference sources, they are unlikely to provide negative information. In addition, without a great deal of imposed structure and a clear understanding of the information base of the reference source, the information provided is often irrelevant, uninterpretable, or both.

Minimum Qualifications

Above, we indicated that the GPA is of largely unknown value as a predictor of job success. But that does not mean that education as a construct is of no value in a selection program. As we saw above (Berry et al., 2006), in certain circumstances, educational accomplishment can function as a surrogate for cognitive ability. In public-sector employment, there is a widely applied concept known as minimum qualifications (MQs). MQs usually involve a combination of education and experience, and they are used to make sure that individuals who wish to be considered as legitimate applicants have the prerequisite formal training and/or

TABLE 3.10 **Typical MQ Statements**

Communications Technician II
High school diploma/GED equivalency and 4 years of experience in the repair of two-way radios
Graduation from an accredited technical/trade school in electronics or a closely related field and 2 years of experience in the repair of two-way radios
Civil Engineer—Construction Area
High school diploma/GED and 5 years of civil engineering experience in the construction area performing one or more of the following duties: project inspection; designing, drafting, or reviewing plans, contracts, and specifications; material calculations; and record keeping (checking contractor payrolls) and related duties
High school diploma/GED and 8 years of civil engineering experience, 4 years of which must be in the construction area performing one or more of the following duties: project inspection; designing, drafting, or reviewing plans, contracts, and specifications; material calculations; and record keeping (checking contractor payrolls) and related duties
High school diploma/GED and 8 years of experience as an engineering assistant in any work area
Bachelor's degree in civil engineering or civil engineering technology
Senior Real Property Valuation Analyst
High school diploma/GED; completion of Appraisal Institute courses 110, 120, 310, and 510; and 7 years right of way specialist/real property valuation analyst experience with at least 3 of those years in real estate appraising
Four-year degree; completion of Appraisal Institute courses 110, 120, 310, and 510; and 3 years in real estate appraising

experience to assume a position without further training or experience. That is why they are called "minimum." That does not mean that the candidates will not be asked to complete additional assessment exercises such as tests or interviews. What it does mean is that applicants who lack the stated MQs will not be considered for subsequent assessment for the position.

Typical MQ statements appear in Table 3.10. As you can see, MQs vary widely depending on the position in question. As you can also see, some MQs can be satisfied in several ways, which makes them less restrictive. Since MQs are selection devices in every sense of the word, they must be developed and validated just like any other selection device. The research on MQs is sparse (Levine, Maye, Ulm, & Gordon, 2006), but a recent demonstration of how MQs might be developed and validated provides the historical context, the methods that can be used, and the legal defensibility of MQs (Buster, Roth, & Bobko, 2005). Buster and colleagues suggest some principles for the development, use, and defense of MQs. These include the following:

1. Base them on a job analysis.
2. Direct them with a newly appointed job incumbent in mind.
3. Think about alternatives to formal course requirements that permit multiple avenues for meeting the MQ requirement.

Because MQs are used so frequently by public-sector employers, particularly for promotional positions, they will continue to be challenged legally. As a result, particular care must be taken in their development.

Controversial Assessment Practices: Graphology and the Polygraph

This section will be quite brief. Research indicates that two selection practices, which are still used by too many employers, are not very useful. We could devote several pages to demonstrating why this is so, but we would rather devote those pages to practices that have some value. The two practices we are referring to are polygraphs (electronic lie detection) and graphology (handwriting analysis). The polygraph is permitted only in certain job sectors but is generally not very useful even in the job sectors for which it *is* permitted (e.g., screening for national security). The research showing the lack of validity of these practices is substantial and compelling (e.g., Ben-Shakhar, Bar-Hillel, Bilu, Ben-Abba, & Flug, 1986; Iacono & Lykken, 1997). So let's move on.

Drug and Alcohol Testing

There are several issues to address with respect to drug and alcohol testing in the workplace. The first is how acceptable the practice is to employees and prospective employees. As we will see in Chapter 11 when we consider fairness issues related to assessment, this type of screening is considered more acceptable by the public at large, as well as by employees, when the job in question involves the possible risk to the public (Paronto, Truxillo, Bauer, & Leo, 2002).

The second issue relates to the legality of this type of screening. The courts have not yet finished deciding which practices impinge too greatly on an individual's right to privacy. Courts have upheld the right of railroads to test for the presence of drugs following an accident. In addition, it has been judged acceptable to test for drugs when screening applicants for drug enforcement posts with the federal government (Cascio, 2010). In many areas of the private sector, drug screening is common for new hires. Harris (2000) reported that as many as two-thirds of large and medium companies screen new hires and as many as one-third of these companies screen current employees for drugs. With respect to alcohol use, current laws permit the random testing of individuals who work for commercial trucking companies, the aviation and rail industries, and mass transit, as well as nonrandom testing after an accident. Cascio (1998b) suggested several steps that an employer might take to enhance the defensibility and acceptability of a drug-testing program (see Table 3.11). In addition to the courts, employees and the public in general are very concerned about maintaining procedural justice when implementing a drug-testing program. In 1988 the federal government passed the Drug-Free Workplace Act (DFWA) as a more affirmative approach to the problem of drugs in the workplace. As a result of DFWA, all federal contractors with contracts worth more than $25,000 are required to establish a drug-free policy. For non-government contractors, the DWFA allows for reduced worker compensation insurance

TABLE 3.11 **Ways to Enhance the Defensibility of a Drug-Testing Program**

To avoid legal challenge, companies should consider instituting the following commonsense procedures:

1. Inform all employees and job applicants, in writing, of the company's policy regarding drug use.
2. Include the policy, and the possibility of testing, in all employment contracts.
3. Present the program in a medical and safety context—that is, state that drug screening will help improve the health of employees and will also help ensure a safer workplace.
4. Check the testing laboratory's experience, its analytical methods, and the way it protects the security and identity of each sample.
5. If drug testing will be used with employees as well as job applicants, tell employees in advance that it will be a routine part of their employment.
6. If drug testing is done, it should be uniform—that is, it should apply to managers as well as nonmanagers.

SOURCE: Adapted from Cascio, W. F. (1998b). *Managing human resources* (5th ed.). New York: McGraw-Hill. © 1998 by McGraw-Hill. Reprinted by permission of The McGraw-Hill Companies, Inc.

premiums for employers, as well as access to an information network regarding drug testing (Gutman, Koppes, & Vadonovich, 2010).

Extensive literature exists on the effects of alcohol and drugs on various aspects of physical and mental performance. As examples, it is well known that alcohol will slow reaction time, impair reasoning ability, induce drowsiness and clumsiness, and have a generally dulling effect on various senses. The same is true for various other drugs, both illegally obtained and prescribed. Thus, from the performance perspective it seems clear that such substances will lead to lowered performance in a wide range of physical and mental tasks. But that is a "here and now" issue. Few would disagree that if an individual can be classified as intoxicated due to alcohol or drugs, he or she should not be permitted to engage in any work activity that might bring harm to the person, a co-worker, or the public. But the more intriguing question is whether a past history of use predicts future behavior. In fact, there is some evidence that drug use affects absenteeism and involuntary turnover. Normand, Salyards, and Mahoney (1990) reported that 5,500 applicants for postal positions were given drug tests. After 15 months, the new employees who had tested positive for drugs at the time of hire had an absenteeism rate almost 60 percent higher than those who had tested negative. In addition, almost 50 percent more of employees who had tested positive were fired during the 15 months than those who had tested negative (many for excessive absenteeism). But some have raised the issue of cause and effect. Galaif, Newcomb, and Carmona (2001) present evidence suggesting not only that drug problems lead to job instability but also that job instability predicts later drug use. The problem of drugs or alcohol at the workplace must be kept in perspective. Most estimates suggest that fewer than 4 percent of applicants, and only 2 percent of incumbents, will test positive for drugs. But this may be an instance in which a mean or average does not tell the entire story. In a recent survey study (Frone, 2006), it appeared that two specific occupational groups were more likely than others to experience high levels of illicit drug use: (1) arts, entertainment, sports, and media; and (2) food preparation and serving occupations. In these groups, the impairment level varied from 7 percent to 28 percent! But even "low-risk" occupational groups cause concern. At 10:30 a.m. on July 1, 2002, both the pilot and the co-pilot of an America West flight were stopped before they were able to take off in a jet bound for Phoenix from Miami with 124 passengers on board. Each had a blood alcohol level that indicated impairment.

Given these concerns, why not simply test all employees all the time? Isn't that the safest policy? Perhaps it would be, if we could have perfect confidence in the accuracy of those tests. But large numbers of false-positive indications (a person who fails a drug screen urinalysis and then tests negative using a different and more sophisticated protocol) have undermined confidence in the results of most mass-administered drug-screening programs. These false positives come from sloppy procedures, inaccurate tests, or both. There are alternative types of drug tests, particularly those called immunoassay tests, that are considerably more reliable (Harris, 2000), but they are often prohibitively expensive for the employer. However, the tests and testing procedures are outside the expertise of the I-O psychologist. What I-O psychologists can do is identify the performance areas most likely to be affected by the use of drugs or alcohol and suggest occupations or jobs where such testing makes most sense.

Computer-Based and Internet Assessment

Virtually every commercial test available in paper form is also available on the computer. Many are also available on the Internet, allowing for direct transmission and scoring of the tests. This is a win–win situation for the employer and the applicant. It reduces time and effort for the applicant, and it permits the employer to process large amounts of data in very sophisticated ways in order to make selection decisions. It also cuts down on the time it takes to inform applicants of their status in the hiring sequence. Via the Internet, an employer can administer a test worldwide in a matter of minutes; a candidate can receive a test score and an interpretive report within *seconds* of completing a test; a test can be revised in minutes at little cost; and scoring errors can be almost completely eliminated from the testing process (Naglieri et al., 2004).

The variety of tests that can be presented on a computer platform is almost without limits (Reynolds & Rupp, 2010). One might test for cognitive ability, personality, interests, and even psychomotor abilities. In addition, it is possible to present work samples, situational judgment tests, and very sophisticated and complex interactive cognitive tasks. The use of web cameras also permits some limited interpersonal testing, although there are still some elements of one-on-one interaction that are impossible to simulate by means of the computer. Aguinis, Henle, and Beaty (2001) provide fascinating examples of virtual reality technologies for assessment.

The topic of computer and web-based interaction brings up a frequently asked question regarding computer-based test presentation: Are we measuring the same thing as we are with a paper-and-pencil test or interview? The answer is yes and no. For personality tests, Salgado and Moscoso (2003) present data showing not only that the psychometric properties of the tests in the two modalities are equivalent but also that test takers actually prefer the Internet medium to the paper-and-pencil format. Ployhart, Weekley, Holtz, and Kemp (2003) present evidence suggesting that for some attributes (e.g., situational judgment, biodata, personality), web-based assessment produces *superior* psychometric results (e.g., reliability). For most measures of general mental ability and specific cognitive abilities, the answer is also yes, unless the tests are speed tests rather than power tests (Potosky & Bobko, 2004). Because it requires the test taker to be dexterous with the mouse or keyboard, speed adds a different dimension to the assessment (Mead & Drasgow, 1993). In addition, because web-based assessment has some built-in system time, applicants often worry that they are being penalized on speed tests for this "load time." Even though the system adds time to the testing period for this load time, and even though applicants are told this, they often forget that this is the case and fret over time "lost" (Potosky & Bobko, 2004). Finally, web-based testing often puts limits on test-taking "style." Many test takers prefer to go back and forth in a written test booklet, completing items in different sequences, and the display screen seldom provides the amount of information that a test booklet page might. The screen might have room for one or a few items, whereas a test booklet might display a dozen or more items simultaneously (Potosky & Bobko, 2004).

In addition, the computer can be used to assess attributes that could never have been assessed by paper-and-pencil tests, such as reaction time and spatial and perceptual abilities (Murphy & Davidshofer, 2005). The following are some examples:

- Schmitt, Gilliland, Landis, and Devine (1993) described a computer-based system for assessing applicants for secretarial positions.
- We saw earlier that Ackerman and Cianciolo (1999, 2002) developed computer-based exercises for air traffic control positions.
- Olson-Buchanan and colleagues (1998) developed a video-interactive test for assessing conflict resolution skills.
- Baron and Chaudry (1997) developed a computer-based interactive device for assessing customer relations skills.

There are many excellent reviews of the promise of computer-based testing, as well as its potential problems (Naglieri et al., 2004; Olson-Buchanan, 2001). At this point in development, the elegance and excitement of this medium is tempered by its costs. Well-developed and engaging computer (and particularly video) assessment exercises are expensive, putting them out of the reach of the small to middle-sized organization. Virtual reality testing environments, for example, can easily exceed $300,000 in cost (Aguinis et al., 2001). For large organizations that screen many applicants (e.g., federal and state agencies, large municipal and state police and fire departments, large manufacturing organizations), such a web-based or computerized testing format can be extremely powerful and cost-effective because, among other advantages, it does not require applicants to actually come to a central location for assessment. This is an exciting area for psychological assessment, and substantially more data should be available in the next few years.

Unproctored Internet Testing

One final issue related to Internet testing is proctoring. Many organizations prefer that candidates be able to take tests based on their own schedule and at their convenience. This means that there is no proctor available to ensure that the candidate is really the one providing the answers and that the employer is actually screening the candidate, not the candidate's roommate or relative. For ease of discussion, we will refer to this as UIT (unproctored Internet testing). This is more of an issue for ability testing (e.g., cognitive ability) than for testing constructs such as personality or motivation, since the latter constructs are less likely to have a "correct" answer and are more likely to depend on the behavioral tendencies of the test taker. There is mixed reaction to the challenges presented by UIT (Tippins et al., 2006). One position is that assessment for high-level jobs (high-stakes assessment) simply cannot be conducted using UIT but that screening for low-level jobs (low-stakes assessment) may be not as vulnerable to cheating. One way to deal with the potential for cheating is to require follow-up proctored testing for those candidates who look particularly promising after UIT. Another issue has to do with the ethics of UIT. A clear case can be made that UIT directly contradicts the ethical principles of both the APA and SIOP with regard to ethical assessment practices, regardless of whether the assessment is high stakes or low stakes. One thing that is in little dispute is the fact that UIT will increase in popularity as employers seek to reduce costs and applicant assessment time. These preliminary discussions of UIT (Tippins et al., 2006) have yielded the following conclusions:

1. Cognitive tests are less suitable for UIT than noncognitive tests.
2. UIT alone is inappropriate for high-stakes assessment.
3. If UIT is used in high-stakes assessment, follow-up proctored testing is required.
4. It is not clear if unproctored tests demonstrate the same validity as proctored versions of the same tests.
5. Some cheating is likely in high-stakes assessment, but neither the extent nor the effects of that cheating are known.
6. One can never be certain of the identity of the actual test taker in UIT.
7. UIT may be limited by an applicant's access to and comfort with a computer.
8. UIT may provide greater exposure to test items, compromising their security.

Who Is a Candidate?

Until recently, there was some confusion and concern among employers regarding who was and was not an official "candidate" when Internet recruiting and job posting systems were used. The problem was that, depending on the definition, the employer might be charged with unfair discrimination based on the proportion of majority and minority applicants who were hired when recruitment relied on Internet-based search engines to advertise openings. The Office of Federal Contract Compliance (OFCCP) clarified that issue in 2005. In order for an individual to be considered an applicant, four conditions must be met:

1. The individual submits an expression of interest in employment through Internet or related electronic data technologies.
2. The employer considers the individual for employment in a particular position.
3. The individual's expression of interest indicates that the individual possesses the basic objective qualifications for the position.
4. The individual at no point in the employer's selection process (prior to receiving an offer of employment from the employer) removes himself or herself from further consideration or otherwise indicates that he or she is no longer interested in the position (Business and Legal Reports, 2005b).

SIOP (Reynolds, 2004) considered these issues in some detail and generally approved the OFCCP's proposed definition. At this point, it is not clear that the OFCCP definition will be universally accepted by various federal agencies. The EEOC has a competing, and less precise, definition in draft stage, and it is not clear at this point whether the agencies will agree on a common definition. If they do not, employers are likely to be confused.

Computer adaptive testing (CAT) A type of testing that presents a test taker with a few items that cover the range of difficulty of the test, identifies a test taker's approximate level of ability, and then asks only questions to further refine the test taker's position within that ability level.

Routing test Preliminary test used in computer adaptive testing that identifies a test taker's approximate level of ability before providing additional questions to refine the test taker's position within that ability level.

Computer Adaptive Testing

An interesting innovation in computer testing is a "tailored" procedure known as **computer adaptive testing (CAT)** (Murphy & Davidshofer, 2005). In this procedure, a candidate does not need to answer every item on a test for adequate assessment. By presenting a candidate with a few items (e.g., 10) that cover the range of difficulty of the test, it is possible to identify a candidate's approximate level of ability and then ask only questions that will further refine the applicant's position within that ability level. The preliminary test, which every candidate takes, is called a **routing test**. The subsequent tests are the actual measurement tests (see Figure 3.13).

The potential advantages of CAT are obvious. Naglieri and colleagues (2004) describe CAT systems for the assessment of musical aptitude, dermatology expertise, and conflict resolution skill. In addition, Drasgow (2004) provides illustrations of CAT for CPAs and architects. Borman and his colleagues (Borman, Houston, Schneider, & Ferstl, 2008) have recently described the development of a CAT of personality for predicting performance in U.S. Navy jobs. In addition to the power of stimulus presentation and manipulation, CAT can be done more quickly because each candidate answers fewer items than would appear on a paper-and-pencil test. There are some additional, less obvious, advantages. This type of test produces scores with equal or higher validity and reliability than conventional tests. In addition, CAT provides much finer discrimination among applicants

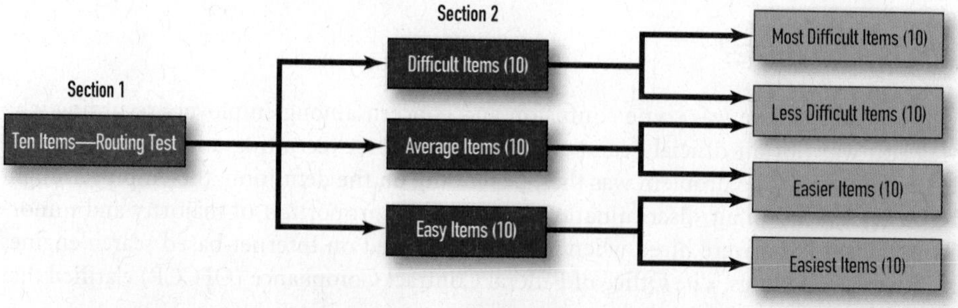

FIGURE 3.13 The Routing Test in Computer Adaptive Testing. In computer adaptive testing, test items are arranged in terms of their difficulty. Every candidate takes the same routing test, then one test from Section 2 and one from Section 3, based on his or her performance on the earlier section test.

SOURCE: Murphy, K. R., & Davidshofer, C. O. (2005). *Psychological testing: Principles and applications* (6th ed.), Fig. 12.2, p. 254. © 2005. Reproduced by permission of Pearson Education, Inc., Upper Saddle River, NJ.

at the high and low ends of the ability scale. The American Council on Education has published an informative set of guidelines related to the use of CAT in educational settings (Green et al., 1995), and these guidelines are also useful for industrial application. Because of the technical and empirical challenges of CAT, it is still out of the reach of most employers, but the armed services are currently using and refining such systems for recruit screening on the ASVAB (Murphy & Davidshofer, 2005). A CAT-based examination you may take if you consider pursuing a graduate career in I-O psychology is the Graduate Record Examination (GRE). The CAT promise is that reliable and accurate assessment can be accomplished more quickly through the power of the computer to narrow the range of the tested attribute quickly. In theory, it should not matter if that attribute is knowledge, a personality dimension, or cognitive ability. We expect that there will be substantial advances in the application of CAT technology to assessment in the next five to ten years.

MODULE 3.5 SUMMARY

- An important issue in assessment is not *which* tool to use but what *combination* of tools to use for the greatest predictive ability at the lowest cost. I-O psychologists have examined the predictive validity of particular combinations to demonstrate the added value of combining two or more assessment devices.
- Virtually every commercial test available in paper form is also available on the computer. The variety of tests that can be presented on a computer platform is almost without limits. At this point, however, the elegance and excitement of the computer-based medium is tempered by its costs: Well-developed and engaging computer (and particularly video) assessment exercises are extremely expensive.

KEY TERMS

incremental validity
biodata
ecology model
social desirability
computer adaptive testing (CAT)
routing test

cost of theft at small businesses (Zipkin, 2004) places that value at almost $130,000 per year, often perpetrated by bookkeepers and those with access to the company's assets. This may be a conservative estimate, as recorded theft is generally assumed to underestimate actual theft figures. **Dishonesty** involves more than employee theft of goods. It can also involve theft of time (arriving late, leaving early, taking unnecessary sick days) or dishonest communications with customers, co-workers, or management. Each of these behaviors lowers productivity by raising the cost of production, lowering output, or both. There is some research suggesting that theft, at least in part, may be precipitated by feelings of inequity and perceived violations of principles of justice (Baron, 2004; Neuman & Baron, 2005). Organizations typically attempt to control dishonesty through the modification of attitudes toward the organization, as we will discuss in Chapter 9; they also seek to screen it out by using selection batteries that include integrity and/or conscientiousness assessments (Chapter 3).

Dishonesty Employee theft of goods and theft of time (arriving late, leaving early, taking unnecessary sick days) or dishonest communications with customers, co-workers, or management.

Absenteeism

Employers lose money with every employee absence, for an absent employee cannot be a productive employee. Although absence for reasons of illness or injury is, of course, recognized as legitimate, many employers strive to minimize these kinds of absences through stress reduction (Chapter 10) or increases in workplace safety (Chapters 10 and 14). The type of **absenteeism** that most attracts the interest of I-O psychologists, however, is "avoidable" absence: those occasions when an employee decides to stay away from work for reasons other than illness or injury. Nicholson and his colleagues (Chadwick-Jones, Nicholson, & Brown, 1982; Nicholson, Brown, & Chadwick-Jones, 1976) suggested that absenteeism is really a function of an informal agreement between a worker and a supervisor or a worker's estimate of what is permitted by the organization. In Chapter 9, we will address the issue of absenteeism through the concepts of commitment and job dissatisfaction.

Absenteeism Type of counterproductive behavior that involves failure of an employee to report for or remain at work as scheduled.

Sabotage

Employee **sabotage** can be defined as "the intention to damage, disrupt, or subvert the organization's operations for personal purposes of the saboteur by creating unfavorable publicity, damage to property, destruction of working relationships, or harming of employees or customers" (Crino, 1994, p. 312). In the early 1970s, at the height of the microassembly movement in automobile production, employers began to require line workers to complete their operations on a moving auto body in 30 seconds or less—a difficult, if not impossible, task. As stress and frustration among the workers grew, acts of sabotage increased. Workers intentionally dropped nuts and bolts into the engine or neglected to anchor parts to the car body appropriately. This became known as the **Lordstown syndrome**, named after one General Motors plant particularly plagued with these acts of sabotage. Although Chen and Spector (1992) found that high levels of sabotage were associated with low levels of satisfaction, this type of acting out clearly includes other dynamics as well. There are many dissatisfied workers in some work environments, yet few of them resort to sabotage, which is likely to result from some combination of personality factors (e.g., very low levels of conscientiousness and emotional stability bordering on the pathological) and extremely high levels of dissatisfaction and alienation.

Sabotage Acts that damage, disrupt, or subvert the organization's operations for personal purposes of the saboteur by creating unfavorable publicity, damage to property, destruction of working relationships, or harming of employees or customers.

Lordstown syndrome Act of sabotage named after a General Motors plant plagued with acts of sabotage.

Causes of and Treatments for CWB

Current research seems to identify personality factors as most closely associated with CWB. However, proportionally speaking, CWBs are dwarfed by productive behaviors, so you should not jump to the conclusion that anyone with an implicated personality characteristic is likely to be involved in CWB. Factors such as situational constraints (e.g., opportunity to steal), feelings of injustice, and even individual need will also play a role. Detert and colleagues (2007) seem to confirm the obvious by reporting that closer supervision reduces CWB and that punitive supervisory styles *increase* CWB. Beyond these findings, there are some intriguing studies that hint at the possible foundations for CWB. Marcus and Schuler (2004) apply some general theories of criminal behavior to CWB and propose that the key is the lack of self-control on the part of an individual. Roberts, Harms, Caspi, and Moffit (2007) conducted a longitudinal study of New Zealand children as they progressed through adolescence and into young adulthood. They found that children and adolescents who were abusive and threatening to other children were more likely to engage in CWB as young adult workers. Colbert, Mount, Harter, Witt, and Barrick (2004) found that employees high on conscientiousness and agreeableness, particularly if they like their work situation, are least likely to engage in CWB. Berry, Ones, and Sackett (2007) caution that individual deviance is predicted by different personality factors than is organizational deviance. Other suggested culprits in the CWB scenario include narcissism (Penney & Spector, 2002), openness to experience (Salgado, 2002), negative emotion and anger (Spector & Fox, 2002), and low humility (Lee, Ashton, & Shin, 2005). Although this research is preliminary, there is a strong surge toward examining personality characteristics.

One of the most intriguing and ambitious measurement projects for identifying individuals prone to aggression and CWB has been conducted by Larry James and colleagues (Bing et al., 2007; Frost, Ko, & James, 2007; James, Ko, & McIntyre, 2008; LeBreton, Barksdale, Robin, & James, 2007). James proposes that aggression in the workplace actually stems from a flawed rationalization on the part of the aggressor that his or her behavior is justified. James has created a "test" that appears to assess reasoning but in fact is a hidden or implicit test of aggressive tendencies. Consider a sample item from his Test of Conditional Reasoning (James et al., 2008):

> The old saying "an eye for an eye" means that if someone hurts you, then you should hurt that person back. If you are hit, then you should hit back. If someone burns your house, then you should burn that person's house.
>
> Which of the following is the biggest problem with the "eye for an eye" plan?
>
> a) It tells people to turn the other cheek
> b) It offers no way to settle a conflict in a friendly manner
> c) It can only be used at certain times of the year
> d) People have to wait until they are attacked before they can strike
>
> (James, L. R., Ko, C. E., & McIntyre, M. D. (2008, April). Dealing with arbitrary metrics in conditional reasoning. Paper presented at the Annual SIOP Conference, San Francisco. Reprinted by permission of the authors.)

The hidden aggressive response is "d." It appeals to aggressive individuals who see this as a problem since they cannot engage in a preemptive strike. Answer "b" is attractive to nonaggressive individuals because it implicitly accepts the notion that compromise and cooperation are more reasonable than conflict. Answers "a" and "c" are clearly illogical and hardly ever chosen by respondents, but they give the test the appearance of assessing reasoning rather than aggression.

Preliminary results from both laboratory and field settings are very promising using this technique. As an example, intramural basketball players who scored high on this hidden aggression test committed more egregious fouls, and were more inclined to get into fights and to verbally harass other players or officials. This is a fascinating new development, both from a conceptual and measurement perspective. It also appears to be immune from faking (LeBreton et al., 2007), probably because it is seen as a "reasoning" test rather than a personality or aggression test.

In part because the study of CWB is so new, we don't know much about what actually prevents these behaviors. Certainly, the material presented in the previous paragraphs suggests that part of the answer to prevention is in selection—and there certainly seems to be some merit in that suggestion. Baron (2004) has reviewed basic social psychological literature and suggests several techniques unrelated to selection that might be used with incumbents. These include the following:

- Punishment that is prompt, certain, strong, and justified.
- Quick and genuine apologies to individuals who are unjustly treated.
- Exposure to models (co-workers and supervisors) who do not engage in CWB even when provoked.
- Training in social and communication skills for individuals who might otherwise tend to interact in a provocative manner.
- Putting angry people in a better mood by using humor or expressing empathy.

At this stage, these tactics simply represent suggestions, but, again, they are at least a good start.

OCB and CWB: Two Ends of the Same Continuum?

If you stop to consider our earlier discussion of OCB, you might wonder whether OCB is simply the opposite of CWB. You would not be alone in that speculation. Many researchers and theorists are now proposing just that possibility, both in the more general literature dealing with prosocial behavior (Caprara, Steca, Zelli, & Capanna, 2005) and in the more specific context of the work setting (Miles, Borman, Spector, & Fox, 2002). Miles and colleagues (2002) suggest that emotions play a critical role: Positive emotions at work lead to OCB, whereas negative emotions at work lead to CWB. Some researchers argue that since we can find co-occurrences of OCB and CWB in the same person, these must be distinct concepts (Kelloway, Loughlin, Barling, & Nault, 2002; Sackett, 2002). Recent research (Sackett et al., 2006) and a meta-analysis (Dalal, 2005) seem to support the view that CWB and OCB are two distinct behavior patterns, not just opposite ends of the same continuum. Practically, this means that it is necessary to use different assessment schemes for increasing OCBs or decreasing CWBs.

Adaptive Performance

Adaptive performance Performance component that includes flexibility and the ability to adapt to changing circumstances.

Another performance component to consider is an area known as **adaptive performance** (Pulakos, Arad, Donovan, & Plamondon, 2000). A changing work environment puts increased importance on workers who are flexible and able to adapt to changing circumstances. Pulakos and colleagues cited the following circumstances of today's workplace that favor this adaptability:

- Changing technologies alter work tasks.
- Mergers, downsizing, and corporate restructuring require employees to learn new skills.
- Globalization requires individuals to work in different cultures.

For better or for worse, it is often emergencies that bring out the importance of adaptive behavior. An example of this was Hurricane Katrina, which devastated the Mississippi and Louisiana coastline and all but destroyed New Orleans in 2005. As we will describe in Chapter 14 when we discuss the importance of organization of effort, the lack of organization in the government response to the disaster made it all the more important that some individuals and nongovernmental groups were capable of adaptive performance. Consider the adaptability of the New Orleans–based Acadian Ambulance Company as described in Box 4.1.

Globalization emphasizes the importance of adaptive performance because it requires individuals to work in different cultures.

Pulakos and colleagues (2000) proposed adaptive performance as a valid performance component that can be further divided into eight types of adaptive behavior. As Table 4.3 shows, each aspect of adaptability requires flexibility, but in a different way. "Cultural adaptability" involves an appreciation of differences in values, customs, and cultures, while "emergency or crisis situation" adaptability requires quick response, analysis, decision making, and action. Applying Table 4.3 to Box 4.1, we see that the Acadian Ambulance Company displayed the following characteristics of adaptive performance: handling crises, handling stress, solving problems creatively, dealing with uncertainty, and physically oriented adaptability. Pulakos and colleagues (2000) have tested this taxonomy on a wide variety of jobs, and the results provided support for their propositions.

Although this research is very new, it appears promising. Pulakos, Dorsey, and Mueller-Hanson (2005) have confirmed the eight-factor description of adaptability and identified some attributes that may predict adaptive performance, including cognitive ability, personality, and past experience. We conclude from the accumulating research that

BOX 4.1 ACADIAN AMBULANCE COMPANY AND ADAPTIVE PERFORMANCE

The city's communication system was wiped out, but Acadian dispatchers kept working thanks to a backup power system and a portable antenna rushed here the day after the hurricane. As stranded patients wondered what happened to the city's medics and ambulances, Acadian medics filled in at the Superdome and evacuated thousands from six hospitals. While Louisiana officials debated how to accept outside help, Acadian was directing rescues by helicopters from the military and other states. . . . No government planners expected the only working radio network in New Orleans to be run by a private company, but Acadian had the flexibility to take on the job. . . . When the phone system failed, . . . medics were ready with satellite phones. When the hurricane winds knocked over both the company's antennas in the New Orleans area, Acadian quickly located a mobile antenna and communications trailer owned by Iberia, a rural parish, west of New Orleans. The sheriff, fortunately, didn't ask FEMA for permission to move it to Acadian's command post across the river from the city.

Source: Excerpted from *The New York Times*, September 17, 2005

TABLE 4.3 **Eight Adaptive Performance Areas and Definitions**

Handling emergencies or crisis situations: Reacting with appropriate urgency in life-threatening, dangerous, or emergency situations; quick analysis and decision making in emergency situations; maintaining emotional control and objectivity.
Handling work stress: Remaining calm in spite of demanding workload or schedule; managing frustration with constructive solutions instead of blaming others; acting as a calming and settling influence on others.
Solving problems creatively: Uses unique types of problem analysis; generates new and innovative ideas in complex areas; considers a wide range of possibilities; thinks outside of the box.
Dealing with uncertain and unpredictable work situations: Taking effective action without having all the facts or information; easily changes gears; adjusts plans, goals, and schedules to match a changing situation; provides focus for self and others when situation is changing rapidly.
Learning work tasks, technologies, and procedures: Enthusiastic about learning new approaches and technologies; keeps knowledge and skill up to date; seeks out and participates in training that will prepare for changes in work demands.
Demonstrating interpersonal adaptability: Flexible and open-minded in dealing with others; considers others' viewpoints and opinions and alters own opinion when appropriate; works well with a wide diversity of people; accepts negative feedback without defensiveness.
Demonstrating cultural adaptability: Seeks to understand the culture of others; adapts easily to other cultures and behavior patterns; shows respect for others' values and customs; understands the implications of own behavior for maintaining positive relationships with other groups, organizations, or cultures.
Demonstrating physically oriented adaptability: Adjusts to challenging physical environments and extremes of temperature, noise, dirt, etc.; pushes self to complete physically demanding tasks; improves physical condition to meet job demands.

SOURCE: Adapted from Pulakos, E. D., Arad, S., Donovan, M. A., & Plamondon, K. E. (2000). Adaptability in the workplace: Development of a taxonomy of adaptive performance. *Journal of Applied Psychology, 85*, 612–624. © 2000 by the American Psychological Association. Adapted with permission.

occupations will vary not only in the *extent* to which adaptability is required but also in terms of the *type* of adaptive performance that is most critical.

A Brief Recap

From 1900 until 1980, I-O psychology dealt with work performance as a large homogeneous construct. Researchers seldom broke down performance into more discrete categories (e.g., technical or task performance, OCB, CWB). This was in contrast to a growing appreciation for the value of breaking down predictors of performance (e.g., intelligence, personality, skill, knowledge) into discrete categories. With the introduction of the concept of OCB by Organ and his colleagues, that monolithic view of performance began to change. Today, we have a wide variety of criteria from which to choose. The criterion categories include technical or task performance, OCB, CWB, and adaptive performance. This is a good place to be in. By breaking down performance more finely, we can discover much more about the nature of work as well as considerably improve our prediction of worker success.

A Comprehensive Framework for Considering Performance: The "Great Eight"

Bartram (2005) has tried to combine some of the performance categories we have outlined above into a broader model of performance that he calls the "Great Eight" model of competencies. These competencies, which cover Campbell's dimensions, OCB, and the adaptability concept of Pulakos, are presented in Table 4.4.

The Great Eight model has been validated in 29 different studies, including nine different countries and over 4,800 study participants. As you can see from the right-hand column of Table 4.4, Bartram (2005) has also hypothesized which traits and abilities are likely to predict each of these competencies. He presents preliminary data suggesting that

TABLE 4.4 **The Great Eight Competencies**

FACTOR	COMPETENCY DOMAIN TITLE	COMPETENCY DOMAIN DEFINITION	HYPOTHESIZED BIG FIVE, MOTIVATION, AND ABILITY RELATIONSHIPS
1	Leading and deciding	Takes control and exercises leadership. Initiates action, gives direction and takes responsibility.	Need for power and control, extraversion
2	Supporting and cooperating	Supports others and shows respect and positive regard for them in social situations. Puts people first, working effectively with individuals and teams, clients and staff. Behaves consistently with clear personal values that complement those of the organization.	Agreeableness
3	Interacting and presenting	Communicates and networks effectively. Successfully persuades and influences others. Relates to others in a confident and relaxed manner.	Extraversion, general mental ability
4	Analyzing and interpreting	Shows evidence of clear analytical thinking. Gets to the heart of complex problems and issues. Applies own expertise effectively. Communicates well in writing.	General mental ability, openness to experience
5	Creating and conceptualizing	Works well in situations requiring openness to new ideas and experiences. Seeks out learning opportunities. Handles situations and problems with innovation and creativity. Thinks broadly and strategically. Supports and drives organizational change.	Openness to experience, general mental ability
6	Organizing and executing	Plans ahead and works in a systematic and organized way. Follows directions and procedures. Focuses on customer satisfaction and delivers a quality service or product to the agreed standards.	Conscientiousness, general mental ability
7	Adapting and coping	Adapts and responds well to change. Manages pressure effectively and copes well with setbacks.	Emotional stability
8	Enterprising and performing	Focuses on results and achieving personal work objectives. Works best when work is related closely to results and the impact of personal effects is obvious. Shows an understanding of business, commerce, and finance. Seeks opportunities for self-development and career advancement.	Need for achievement, negative agreeableness

SOURCE: Bartram, D. (2005). The Great Eight competencies: A criterion-centric approach to validation. *Journal of Applied Psychology, 90*, 1185–1203. Table 1, p. 1187.

these guesses about the important attributes supporting these competencies may be fairly accurate.

More of these "super" models of performance are likely to appear in the next few years, but it is likely that they will build on the Great Eight model, just as the Great Eight model was a combination of earlier unconnected theories of performance. This represents a great stride forward in coming to some agreement about how we will choose to break down performance. Rather than seeing disconnected facets of performance, we have an integrated understanding of what underlies success at work and how we might select those individuals likely to be good performers in a wide range of settings and circumstances.

The Case of Expert Performance

Expert performance Performance exhibited by those who have been practicing for at least 10 years and have spent an average of four hours per day in deliberate practice.

Most of us admire the performance of experts in various settings. We marvel at the intricacy of a world-class pianist or violinist, or the speed and ruthlessness of a master chess player. In our daily lives, we also appreciate **expert performance** when we encounter a software engineer who solves our computer problem in minutes after we have struggled fruitlessly for hours, or a garage mechanic who listens to our car for 30 seconds and is able to diagnose a problem deep in the bowels of the engine.

We tend to assume that such expertise is a result of an innate ability, a talent bestowed on few mortals but, unfortunately, not on us (Ericsson & Charness, 1994). This common assumption appears to be wrong. It is not that the experts are more intelligent or have faster reaction times. What separates the experts from you and me is depressingly simple: They practice. Of course, you may practice, too, and still not attain the level of the expert you admire. But the difference is in the *type* of practice and the *duration* of that practice. In virtually any area, including sports, music, chess, science, and work, people have become experts by following a demanding regimen. They have been practicing for at least 10 years, they spend an average of four hours a day in practice, and their practice is deliberate (Ericsson & Charness, 1994).

Types of Performance Measures

Objective performance measure Usually a quantitative count of the results of work, such as sales volume, complaint letters, and output.

Judgmental measure Evaluation made of the effectiveness of an individual's work behavior; judgment most often made by supervisors in the context of a performance evaluation.

Personnel measure Measure typically kept in a personnel file, including absences, accidents, tardiness, rate of advancement, disciplinary actions, and commendations of meritorious behavior.

Most I-O literature distinguishes among different types of performance indicators; these indicators are concerned with how performance is indexed, not the nature of that performance (e.g., OCB, CWB, task performance). Three different categories have been suggested: objective measures, judgmental measures, and personnel measures (Guion, 1965).

Objective performance measures are usually a "count of the results of work" (Guion, 1965). This might mean the number of strokes it took a golfer to complete a round in a tournament. It could also mean the number of cases heard by a municipal judge or the number of claims processed by an insurance adjuster.

Judgmental measures are evaluations of the effectiveness of an individual's work behavior. The judgments are usually made by supervisors in the context of a yearly performance evaluation. The supervisor is asked to consider the subordinate's performance on a number of discrete aspects of performance and to assign a rating that represents the supervisor's assessment of that subordinate on each performance aspect. We will consider the process and elements of performance evaluation in greater detail in Chapter 5.

Employers typically keep a record of **personnel measures** in a personnel folder; these include such data as absences, accidents, tardiness, rate of advancement (in salary or job title), disciplinary actions, and commendations. These measures usually record an event rather than an outcome (e.g., production measure) or an evaluation (e.g., a performance rating).

In light of Campbell's model, we have reason to be concerned with most objective measures, as well as many of the personnel measures. Many would fail as indicators of performance because they are not under the complete control of the individual (e.g., total dollars in sales) or are not actual behaviors (e.g., promotional history). As I-O psychologists, we should focus on individually controlled behavior when we examine performance (Campbell et al., 1993). In Campbell's view, the type of measure most likely to yield a reasonable estimate of individual behavior is the judgmental measure (e.g., performance rating), which permits the evaluator to account for influences outside the control of the individual worker. For example, if a sales representative is assigned to a difficult sales territory, the manager is aware of that handicap and can adjust the judgment accordingly. If the manager was required to use an "objective" measure of sales success, the employee would be at a considerable disadvantage. It is not so much that objective measures are to be avoided or that ratings are to be preferred. They each have their advantages and disadvantages, as we will see in the next chapter.

MODULE 4.2 SUMMARY

- I-O psychologists are increasingly interested in organizational citizenship behavior (OCB)—behavior that goes beyond what is expected on the job. This concept has been further developed to include extra-role behaviors, which are contrasted with traditional views, called *task* performance. Research indicates that measures of cognitive ability are most closely associated with task performance, whereas measures of personality do a better job of predicting OCB performance.
- I-O psychologists also study counterproductive work behaviors, including deviance directed toward the organization and toward other individuals. Three common counterproductive behaviors are dishonesty, absenteeism, and sabotage.
- Adaptive performance is a new component that can be added to Campbell's performance model. Research suggests that occupations vary not only in the *extent* to which adaptability is required but also in the *type* of adaptive performance that is most critical.
- I-O psychologists commonly distinguish among different types of performance indicators. Three categories commonly discussed are objective measures, judgmental measures, and personnel measures.

KEY TERMS

organizational citizenship behavior (OCB)
altruism
generalized compliance
task performance
counterproductive work behavior (CWB)
dishonesty
absenteeism
sabotage
Lordstown syndrome
adaptive performance
expert performance
objective performance measure
judgmental measure
personnel measure

MODULE 4.3

Job Analysis: Fundamental Properties and Practices

Job analysis Process that determines the important tasks of a job and the human attributes necessary to successfully perform those tasks.

In earlier chapters, we have used the term **job analysis** in a general sense to mean a process that determines the essence of a collection of tasks falling within the scope of a particular job title. We will now consider that process in much greater detail.

The purpose of a job analysis is simple. The analyst wants to understand what the important tasks of the job are, how they are carried out, and what human attributes are necessary to carry them out successfully. In short, job analysis is an attempt to develop a theory of human behavior about the job in question. This theory will include performance expectations (properties of the job in the context of the organization's expectations) as well as the required abilities, knowledge, experience, skill, and personal characteristics necessary to meet those expectations.

The Uses of Job Analysis Information

The results of a job analysis can be used for many different purposes, including those addressed below.

Job Description

This is a list of the type of tasks that are carried out, the required worker attributes, and training and experience requirements. Job descriptions are very useful for recruiting.

Recruiting

If we know what the job requires and which human attributes are necessary to fulfill those requirements, we can target our recruiting efforts to specific groups of potential candidates. For technical jobs, these groups might be defined by credentials (a bachelor's degree in engineering) or experience (five years of programming in C++).

Selection

Once we know the attributes most likely to predict success in a job, we can identify and choose (or develop) the actual assessment tools. Based on the job analysis, we may choose a personality test that measures the Big Five, a commercially available test of general mental ability, or an interview format intended to get at some subtle aspects of technical knowledge or experience.

Training

A job analysis helps us to identify the areas of performance that create the greatest challenge for incumbents; based on this, we can provide preassignment or postassignment training opportunities. We may discover that in automobile manufacturing subassembly, one of the most troublesome tasks is installing the dashboard console without pinching the bundled wiring that powers the displays on that dash. Newly hired assembly-line workers who will be assigned to that subassembly task can receive specific training modules designed to help them perform this task better. Modules can also be prepared for the line supervisors who direct that subassembly operation so that they can follow up the initial training with online coaching.

Compensation

Because a job analysis identifies the major performance components and expectations for each job, management can place a monetary value to the organizational mission on each of those components. Management can also determine the level of performance expected on each of those components for each job in the organization as a way of identifying the comparative value of each job. These components and levels of performance can then help set the budget for the organization's human resources. An organization may decide, for example, that rapidly changing technology makes its market so unstable that it will place higher value on demonstrated individual adaptability (as defined above by Pulakos et al., 2000) and non-job-specific task proficiency (as defined above in Campbell's model) and less value on written and oral task communication proficiency or the maintenance of personal discipline (from Campbell's model). This means that jobs that depend heavily on the first two performance components will pay better than jobs with heavy concentrations of the latter components.

Promotion/Job Assignment

The concept of a **job ladder** or **job family** is based on the observation that a particular job may have closer connections to a subset of other jobs than to a job chosen at random. Accounting jobs are closer to budgeting and invoicing positions than they are to engineering or production positions. Job analysis permits the identification of clusters of positions that are similar, either in terms of the human attributes needed to be successful at them or in terms of the tasks carried out in those jobs. This in turn allows the organization to identify logical career paths and the possibility of transfer from one career ladder to another.

Job ladder or job family Cluster of positions that are similar in terms of the human attributes needed to be successful in those positions or in terms of the tasks that are carried out.

Job Design

A comprehensive job analysis can assist in design changes for eliminating or automating tasks in a job. Examples include tasks that are particularly dangerous (e.g., welding an auto body in the assembly process) or are associated with high performance failures (e.g., preparing neonatal feeding solutions in which minute differences in ingredients could harm, or even kill, a newborn baby). It may also be advisable to automate tasks associated with inefficient use of workers' time; consider the examples in Box 4.2.

Workforce Reduction/Restructuring

Mergers, acquisitions, downsizing, and rightsizing are all terms that imply job changes—often involuntary ones on the part of the employees. Mergers and acquisitions call for identifying duplicate positions and centralizing functions. The challenge is to identify which positions are

BOX 4.2 JOB ANALYSIS AND JOB DESIGN

The interface between work design and performance demands can present interesting situations. Generally, the question is when to have a work design characteristic override an individual behavior. Consider the following two examples.

Left-hand turns are one of life's built-in inconveniences. We seem to sit endlessly, waiting for oncoming traffic to break in order to make the turn. We wait whether there is a protected left turn arrow or not. It is a waste of time and fuel. But is there any alternative? United Parcel Service found one by instituting a computer-driven mapping system known as DIAD (Delivery Information Acquisition Device) that uses right-hand turns wherever possible (Lovell, 2007). Using DIAD, during 2006, UPS eliminated 28.5 million (yes, million!) miles from its delivery routes, resulting in a reduction of fuel by 3 million gallons and a reduction in CO_2 emissions of 31,000 metric tons. The next time you are in a left-hand turn lane and see no Big Brown trucks in line with you, consider that UPS has taken a possibly faulty driver decision out of the performance mix.

Another one of life's seemingly inevitable inconveniences is e-mail overload. One consulting firm estimated that a typical information worker in a high-tech firm accesses e-mail 50 times per day and instant messaging 75 times (Richtel, 2008). This nonstop communicating has contributed to cutting the "thinking and reflecting" time so crucial for product development down to 12 percent of the workday. The major issue is not the seconds it takes to review an e-mail; it is the interruption of thought and the reordering of tasks that creates the greatest productivity loss—it has even led to a physical habit that one writer refers to as e-mail apnea (holding one's breath upon seeing the sheer volume of e-mails in the inbox). Recognizing the problem, several high-tech firms (Google, IBM, Intel, Microsoft) created a nonprofit group dedicated to helping employees stop the flood and reclaim lost creative time. Google introduced a software support called E-Mail Addict that can disconnect e-mail so that the user does not see or hear newly arrived messages. When E-Mail Addict's "take a break" feature is activated, the e-mail screen turns gray and reads "Take a walk, get some real work done, or have a snack. We'll be back in 15 minutes." As another strategy, one Intel location encouraged face-to-face communication by declaring "zero e-mail Fridays." While employees liked the idea in theory, they continued to send e-mail messages, finding them essential.

SOURCE: Lovell (2007); Richtel (2008).

A winning job design initiative: Using DIAD (Delivery Information Acquisition Device), UPS drivers saved 3 million gallons of fuel and reduced CO_2 emissions by 31,000 metric tons during 2006.

truly redundant and which provide a unique added value. In downsizing interventions, positions with somewhat related tasks are often consolidated into a single position. The job descriptions of those who stay with the organization are enlarged, with the result that fewer people assume more responsibilities. In both the merger/acquisition and the downsizing/rightsizing scenarios, management's key role is deciding which tasks to fold into which positions; detailed job analyses provide a template for making these decisions rationally.

Criterion Development

As you will recall from our discussion of validity in Chapter 2, the criterion is the behavior that constitutes or defines successful performance of a given task. It is the outcome variable in criterion-related validity studies. Predictor variables such as scores on a test of mental ability are correlated with criterion measures to demonstrate that those scores are valid predictors of probable job success. In content-related validity studies, as we saw in Chapter 2, the I-O psychologist establishes logical links between important task-based characteristics of the job and the assessment used to choose among candidates. It is the job analysis that provides the raw material for criterion development. For example, in a criterion-related validity study of a problem-solving test for software engineers, a job analysis might tell us that one of the engineer's most common and important tasks is to identify a flaw in a software program. As a result, we might then develop a measure of the extent to which the engineer does consistently identify the flaw without asking for assistance. This measure might be in the form of a rating scale of "troubleshooting" to be completed by the engineer's supervisor. We would then have both the predictor score and a criterion score for calculating a validity coefficient.

Performance Evaluation

An extension of the use of job analysis for criterion development is the development of performance evaluation systems. Once the job analyst identifies critical performance components of a job, it is possible to develop a system for evaluating the extent to which an individual worker has fallen short of, met, or exceeded the standards set by the organization for performance on those components. We will deal with the issue of performance evaluation in detail in Chapter 5.

Litigation

When tests or other assessment practices are challenged in court, the employer must provide evidence that the test or assessment practice is valid or job related, regardless of what validity model (e.g., criterion/content/construct) is used. The first step in such a defense is demonstrating that the employer truly knows which critical tasks define the job in question, as well as the attributes necessary to perform those tasks. Job analysis information is the easiest way to demonstrate that knowledge base. In addition, as we will see later in this chapter, job analysis can be used to distinguish between those workers entitled to overtime pay (i.e., nonexempt) and those who are not (exempt). This is an important distinction because exempt status is the crux of many lawsuits involving the right to overtime pay. The various applications of job analysis are covered in great detail in a book by Brannick, Levine, and Morgeson (2007) as well as reviews by Levine and Sanchez (2007) and Pearlman and Sanchez (2010).

Types of Job Analysis

The purpose of a job analysis is to combine the task demands of a job with our knowledge of human attributes and produce a theory of behavior for the job in question. There are two ways to approach building that theory. One is called the work- or

Task-oriented job analysis Approach that begins with a statement of the actual tasks as well as what is accomplished by those tasks.

Worker-oriented job analysis Approach that focuses on the attributes of the worker necessary to accomplish the tasks.

task-oriented job analysis; this approach begins with a statement of the tasks the worker actually performs, the tools and machines used, and the work context. A second method is called the **worker-oriented job analysis**; this approach begins by focusing on the attributes and characteristics of the worker necessary to accomplish the tasks that define the job (Brannick et al., 2007). The following example might help to clarify the distinction. For the job of a snowcat operator at a ski slope, a work- or task-oriented job analysis might include the statement:

> Operates Bombardier Snowcat, usually at night, to smooth out snow rutted by skiers and snowboard riders, and new snow that has fallen.

In contrast, a worker-oriented job analysis statement might be:

> Evaluates terrain, snow depth, and snow condition and chooses the correct setting for the depth of the snow cut, as well as the number of passes necessary on a given ski slope.

KSAOs Individual attributes of knowledge, skills, abilities, and other characteristics that are required to successfully perform job tasks.

Regardless of which approach is taken, the next step in the job analysis is to identify the attributes—the **KSAOs** we covered in Chapter 3 on individual differences—that an incumbent needs for either performing the tasks or executing the human behaviors described by the job analysis. KSAOs can be defined as follows:

- Knowledge: "a collection of discrete but related facts and information about a particular domain . . . acquired through formal education or training, or accumulated through specific experiences" (Peterson, Mumford, Borman, Jeanneret, & Fleishman, 1999, p. 71)
- Skill: a practiced act, or the capacity to perform a specific task or job duty (Gatewood, Feild, & Barrick, 2011; Harvey, 1991)
- Ability: the stable capacity to engage in a specific behavior
- Other characteristics: personality variables, interests, training, and experience

Finally, when the appropriate KSAOs are identified, tests and other assessment techniques can be chosen to measure those KSAOs (see Figure 4.6).

Job analysis methods have evolved using both work- or task-oriented and worker-oriented systems (e.g., Fine, 1988; McCormick, Jeanneret, & Mecham, 1972). Since both approaches end up in the same place—a statement of KSAOs—neither can be considered the "right" way to conduct a job analysis. For practical purposes, since worker-oriented job analyses tend to provide more generalized descriptions of human behavior and behavior patterns, and are less tied to the technological aspects of a particular job, they produce data more useful for structuring training programs and giving feedback to employees in the form of performance appraisal information. In addition, as we have seen, the volatility that exists in today's typical workplace can make specific task statements less valuable in isolation. Tasks move from job to job, are made obsolete by technology changes, or are assumed by teams rather than individuals. For all of these reasons, employers are significantly more likely to use worker-oriented approaches to job analysis today than they were in the past.

Drivers lacking the required skills and abilities are likely to have accidents.

FIGURE 4.6 **The Role of Job Analysis in Assessment**

How Job Analysis Is Done

Regardless of the approach the job analyst decides to use, information about the job is the backbone of the analysis, and there are many ways to get it. The more information and the more ways the analyst can collect that information, the better the understanding of the job.

A term frequently used in job analysis is **subject matter expert (SME)**. An SME is usually an incumbent worker or that worker's supervisor. The person will have accumulated the "expertise" in the "subject matter" of the job by actually performing the job tasks under investigation.

Subject matter expert (SME) Employee (incumbent) who provides information about a job in a job analysis interview or survey.

Some common methods of job analysis include the following:

1. *Observation.* This was perhaps the first method of job analysis I-O psychologists used. They simply watched incumbents (SMEs) perform their jobs and took notes. Sometimes they asked questions while watching, and sometimes they even performed job tasks themselves. Near the end of the Second World War, Morris Viteles studied the job of navigator on a submarine. He attempted to steer the submarine toward the island of Bermuda. After five not-so-near-misses of 100 miles in one direction or another, one frustrated officer suggested that Viteles raise the periscope, look for clouds, and steer toward them (since clouds tend to form above or near landmasses). The vessel "found" Bermuda shortly thereafter. Your authors have observed or participated in jobs as diverse as police patrol, iron ore mining 4 miles beneath the surface north of the Arctic Circle, cookie packing, airport runway repair, packing baggage into the cargo hold of a Boeing 727 and 747, nuclear control room operation, overhead crane operation, and piloting a 100,000-ton container ship into the Seattle harbor. The more jobs one seriously observes, the better one's understanding becomes not only of the jobs in question but also of work in general.
2. *Interviews.* It is important to supplement observation by talking with incumbents, either at the worksite or in a separate location. These interviews are most effective when structured with a specific set of questions based on observations, other analyses of the types of jobs in questions, or prior discussions with HR reps, trainers, or managers knowledgeable about the jobs.
3. *Critical incidents and work diaries.* I-O psychologists have used other techniques to capture important information about jobs. The **critical incident technique** asks SMEs to identify critical aspects of behavior or performance in a particular job that led to success or failure. The supervisor of an electric utility repair person might report that in a very time-urgent project, the repair person failed to check a blueprint and as a result cut a line, causing a massive power loss. In fact, this is exactly what happened in Los Angeles in September 2005 when half the city lost power for over 12 hours (*New York Times*, 2005c). The second method—a **work diary**—asks workers and/or supervisors to keep a log of their activities over a prescribed period of time. They may be asked to simply jot down what they were doing at 15 minutes after the hour for each hour of their workday. Or they may list everything that they have done up to a lunch break. (Our guess is that if the utility repair person above had been keeping a diary, the entry for the day of the error would have read "Oh, my God!")

Critical incident technique Approach in which subject matter experts are asked to identify critical aspects of behavior or performance in a particular job that led to success or failure.

Work diary Job analysis approach that requires workers and/or supervisors to keep a log of their activities over a prescribed period of time.

4. *Questionnaires/surveys*. Expert incumbents or supervisors (SMEs) often respond to questionnaires or surveys as part of a job analysis. These questionnaires include task statements in the form of worker behaviors. Based on their experience, SMEs are asked to rate each statement on a number of dimensions such as frequency of performance, importance to overall job success, and whether the task or behavior must be performed on the first day of work or can be learned gradually on the job. Questionnaires also ask SMEs to rate the importance of various KSAOs for performing tasks or task groups. Unlike the results of observations or interviews, the questionnaire responses can be statistically analyzed to provide a more objective record of the components of the job. To a greater and greater extent, these questionnaires and surveys are being administered online to SMEs.

Over the years, several commercially available job analysis surveys have been popular. Perhaps the best known and most widely used of these instruments is the Position Analysis Questionnaire (PAQ) developed by McCormick and colleagues (1972). Jeanneret (1992) has expanded and revised the PAQ system and maintained a substantial database of job analysis information for many occupations over the 40 years of its use. Other survey-based systems include the Fleishman Job Analysis System (based on the Fleishman taxonomy that we referred to in Chapter 3); the Occupational Analysis Inventory (Cunningham, Boese, Neeb, & Pass, 1983), best suited for occupational education and guidance work; and the Common Metric Questionnaire (CMQ) developed by Harvey (1993). A book published by the National Research Council (1999) provides an excellent description of several of these commercially available systems. Most commercial consulting companies have web-based expert job analysis systems that match the essential functions of jobs with the human attributes required to complete those essential functions.

MODULE 4.3 SUMMARY

- Job analysis attempts to develop a theory of human behavior about the job in question. This theory includes performance expectations as well as the experience and KSAOs necessary to meet those expectations.
- The results of a job analysis can be used for many different purposes, including job description, recruiting, selection, training, compensation, job design, criterion development, and performance assessment.
- Job analysis methods are often broken down into two different but related approaches: a task-oriented approach and a worker-oriented approach. Whichever approach is initially selected, the next step in a job analysis is to identify the KSAOs that an incumbent needs for performing the tasks or executing the human behaviors described in the job analysis.
- There are many ways to obtain job analysis information, including observation, interviews, critical incidents, work diaries, and questionnaires or surveys. The more ways the analyst can collect information, the better the understanding of the job.

KEY TERMS

job analysis
job ladder or job family
task-oriented job analysis
worker-oriented job analysis
KSAOs
subject matter expert (SME)
critical incident technique
work diary

MODULE 4.4

Job Analysis: Newer Developments

Electronic Performance Monitoring as Part of a Job Analysis

In the 1980s and 1990s, the introduction of computers and other technology-based information networks into the workplace clearly revolutionized planning, production, and distribution. But this technology has introduced another, less obvious, opportunity: the opportunity to monitor work processes, both actively and passively. When a commercial airplane crashes, investigators scramble to find the two "black boxes" containing the voice recorder and the flight data recorder. The voice recorder may reveal certain information about the accident—what the cabin crew heard and saw—and the flight data recorder may reveal independent information—altitude, position of flaps and throttle, and so on. The flight can be "monitored" after the fact.

In many jobs, similar monitoring can occur during work as well as after the fact. Consider the phone call you make to ask a question about your telephone bill. A recorded message will tell you that your "call may be monitored for quality control purposes." That means that the performance of the agent or representative with whom you are talking is being monitored and "critical incidents" in success and failure can be identified. Similarly, the new and powerful planning and monitoring system that tells UPS drivers how to drive their route by eliminating left-hand turns can also provide information about how *fast* they make their deliveries. That software can provide information about the actual delivery behavior of the driver, alerting him or her (and a supervisor) when they are running "behind" schedule. Unfortunately, that software cannot recognize when a driver is required to wait for a loading dock to open up or when a driver is making 15 deliveries to a single address that is an apartment building in New York City. As you might expect, drivers in congested city environments are not amused when told they are "running behind" a schedule monitored by a computer and a GPS.

The good news for employers about **electronic performance monitoring** is that many jobs lend themselves to producing job analysis information without any input at all from SMEs. Since the system records the actions of workers, it is a simple step to develop a frequency count of those actions, telling the analyst how often the action occurs in a day or week. Frequency is often highly correlated with the importance of a task. Electronic performance monitoring can be very cost effective and has the potential for providing detailed and accurate work logs.

Electronic performance monitoring Monitoring work processes with electronic devices; can be very cost effective and has the potential for providing detailed and accurate work logs.

Indeed, the practice of monitoring without SME input is not unique to the digital age. One of the jobs discussed in Barbara Garson's (1994) book on boring work was that of a Blue Shield insurance claims adjuster. The adjuster's performance output was monitored regularly—and that was in 1970. In a more recent example, Sanchez and Levine (1999) described truck-leasing companies that monitor driver performance by hooking an onboard computer to the truck engine and tracking speed, idle time, and other characteristics of driving behavior. The dark side, of course, is related to employee privacy rights and perceptions of fairness. Workers generally dislike the fact that their performance can be "tracked" electronically because the tracking is most often used to identify errors in performance or violations of work rules rather than instances of outstanding performance. If the new technology of the workplace is to provide raw material for job analysis, there will need to be checks and balances to ease workers' concerns regarding punitive actions by the employer. In Chapter 5, we will cover electronic monitoring in more detail from the employee's perspective.

Cognitive Task Analysis

Cognitive task analysis
A process that consists of methods for decomposing job and task performance into discrete, measurable units, with special emphasis on eliciting mental processes and knowledge content.

Think-aloud protocol
Approach used by cognitive psychologists to investigate the thought processes of experts who achieve high levels of performance; an expert performer describes in words the thought process that he or she uses to accomplish a task.

In line with the movement toward worker-oriented job analysis, experts have suggested that **cognitive task analysis** is a needed extension of traditional job analysis procedures (Sanchez & Levine, 2012). Most job analyses concentrate on observable behavior—either task completion or action patterns. But cognitive behavior is not directly observable, so a new technique must be used. DuBois, Shalin, Levi, and Borman (1998) describe cognitive task analysis as a method of decomposing job and task performance into concrete units, with an emphasis on identifying mental processes and knowledge required for task completion.

A precursor of cognitive task analysis is a technique known as a **think-aloud protocol** (Ericsson & Simon, 1993), which cognitive psychologists have been using for many years to investigate the manner in which experts think in order to achieve high levels of performance (Goldstein & Ford, 2002). In a think-aloud protocol, an expert performer actually describes in words the thought process that he or she uses to accomplish a task. An observer/interviewer takes notes and may ask some follow-up questions based on what the performer says. In this way, the unobservable becomes observable.

In cognitive task analysis, the focus is not on the KSAOs that the expert calls upon but on the cognitive operations employed. Put another way, cognitive task analysis concentrates on *how* behavior occurs rather than on *what* is accomplished. It is not that the old methods are replaced with cognitive task analysis. Instead, cognitive task analysis is added to the job analysis toolbag. Goldstein and Ford (2002) made the following distinction:

> Rather than looking at tasks and KSAOs as separate entities, a cognitive task analysis approach attempts to link tasks and KSAOs based on the flow from the goals of the people completing a task to the various actions a person might take in performing the task. An examination of the differences between experts and novices in terms of goals and actions can help identify areas for training and development to transform novices toward expertise. (p. 96)

As the workplace becomes more technologically complex and volatile, it is clear that the old methods of task-based observation and interview will be ineffective in describing many of the more critical cognitive operations that lead to success. Much of the work done involves diagnosis, problem solving, and planning—activities that are not easy to observe.

TABLE 4.5 **Cognitive Task Analysis versus Work-Oriented Task Analysis**

WORK-ORIENTED TASK ANALYSIS	COGNITIVE TASK ANALYSIS
Emphasizes behavior	Emphasizes cognitive processes
Analyzes target performance	Analyzes expertise and learning
Evaluates knowledge for each task	Evaluates the interrelations among knowledge elements
Segments tasks according to behaviors required	Segments tasks according to cognitive skills required
Representational skills are not addressed	Representational skills are addressed
Describes only one way to perform	Accounts for individual differences

SOURCE: Brannick, M. T., Levine, E. L., & Morgeson, F. P. (2007). *Job and work analysis: Methods, research and applications for human resource management* (2nd ed.), Table 3.8, p. 84. Thousand Oaks, CA: Sage. Copyright 2007 Reproduced with permission of SAGE PUBLICATIONS INC BOOKS in the format Textbook via Copyright Clearance Center.

Cognitive task analysis is time consuming and requires a good deal of expertise to do well. As a result, it may be a luxury for low-level jobs or jobs in which the cost of a mistake is small. But for critical positions where the consequence of an error is extremely high, cognitive task analysis may be a useful addition to the job analysis arsenal. DuBois (1999) suggested that employers consider the following indicators to determine whether a cognitive task analysis may be worthwhile:

- There are persistent performance problems.
- There are costly errors or accidents.
- Training is difficult to transfer to job behavior.
- Achieving high levels of performance takes a long time.

Cognitive task analysis clearly falls into the worker-oriented approach to job analysis rather than the task- or work-oriented approach. Table 4.5 contrasts cognitive task analysis with work-oriented task analysis.

Cognitive task analysis can be accomplished using a number of methods, all quite new and relatively untested. Nevertheless, because cognitive task analysis is a genuine advance in the understanding of work, I-O psychologists are confident that this area will grow quickly.

Personality-Based Job Analysis

As you read in Chapter 3, personality measures have become very popular in selection systems. But historically, job analysis instruments ignored personality attributes and concentrated on abilities, skills, and, less frequently, knowledge. Guion and his colleagues (Guion, 1998; Raymark, Schmit, & Guion, 1997) developed a commercially available job analysis instrument, the **Personality-Related Position Requirements Form (PPRF)**, devoted to identifying personality predictors of job performance. This instrument is intended not to replace other job analysis devices that identify knowledge, skills, or abilities, but to supplement job analysis by examining important personality attributes in jobs. Guion enlisted 145

Personality-Related Position Requirements Form (PPRF) Job analysis instrument devoted to identifying personality predictors of job performance.

experienced I-O psychologists to nominate and evaluate the relevance of 44 different aspects of personality for work performance. A subsequent statistical analysis revealed 12 basic work-related personality dimensions, each of which relates to one or more of the Big Five personality dimensions described in Chapter 3. An example of a page from the actual PPRF job analysis booklet appears in Figure 4.7.

Raymark and colleagues (1997) found that because the PPRF correlated different personality requirements with different jobs, it could be used to distinguish among 260 different job titles. A "friendly disposition," for example, was judged most valuable for sales clerk and cashier positions, and least valuable for janitorial occupations. For "thoroughness and attention to details," personnel administration, management, and accounting occupations had the highest scores. "General trustworthiness" scores were considered most valuable for cashier and teller occupations. Researchers are increasingly emphasizing the importance of personality-oriented job analysis, arguing that job demands favor certain personality characteristics and disfavor others (Goffin et al., 2011; Tett & Burnett, 2003).

Effective Performance in this Position Requires the Person to:	Not Required	Helpful	Essential
Set 1			
1) lead group activities through exercise of power or authority.	☐	☐	☐
2) take control in group situations.	☐	☐	☐
3) initiate change within the person's work group or area to enhance productivity or performance.	☐	☐	☐
4) motivate people to accept change.	☐	☐	☐
5) motivate others to perform effectively.	☐	☐	☐
6) persuade co-workers or subordinates to take actions (that at first they may not want to take) to maintain work effectiveness.	☐	☐	☐
7) take charge in unusual or emergency situations.	☐	☐	☐
8) delegate to others the authority to get something done.	☐	☐	☐
9) make decisions when needed.	☐	☐	☐
Set 2			
10) negotiate on behalf of the work unit for a fair share of organizational resources.	☐	☐	☐
11) work with dissatisfied customers or clients to achieve a mutually agreeable solution.	☐	☐	☐
12) help people in work groups settle interpersonal conflicts that interface with group functioning.	☐	☐	☐
13) help settle work-related problems, complaints, or disputes among employees or organizational units.	☐	☐	☐
14) negotiate with people outside the organization to gain something of value to the organization.	☐	☐	☐
15) mediate and resolve disputes at individual, group, or organizational levels.	☐	☐	☐
16) negotiate with people within the organization to achieve a consensus on a proposed action.	☐	☐	☐
17) mediate conflict situations without taking sides.	☐	☐	☐

FFIGURE 4.7 A Sample Page from the PPRF

SOURCE: Guion, R. M. (1998). *Assessment, measurement and prediction for personnel decisions.* Mahwah, NJ: Lawrence Erlbaum Associates.

A Summary of the Job Analysis Process

It should be apparent from the preceding discussion that there is no one best way to perform a job analysis, but we can draw some general conclusions about the process:

1. The more information one can gather from the greatest number of sources, the better one's understanding of the job is likely to be.
2. Task-based analyses tend to be less useful for many purposes than worker- or behavior-based analyses.
3. Most job analyses should include considerations of personality demands and work context; some job analyses should also include considerations of purely cognitive tasks.

Computer-Based Job Analysis

As we mentioned earlier, many consulting companies and larger employers are using computer-based job analysis systems. Such systems provide a number of advantages. The first is time and convenience to the employer. SMEs need not be assembled in one spot at one time, as is often the case with traditional job analysis; instead, they can work from their desks at their own pace and submit their responses electronically. A second advantage is the efficiency with which the expert system can create reports. The reports can serve a wide range of purposes, from individual goal setting and performance feedback to elaborate person–job matches to support selection and placement strategies. Finally, because systems like this use the same taxonomies and processes across jobs, they make it easier to understand job similarities and career paths, thus facilitating vocational counseling and long-term strategic HR planning in the form of replacement charts for key positions. Possible shortcomings of such systems, of course, are the same shortcomings that would be apparent with more traditional paper-and-pencil-based systems. If the data being collected are poor, or the task or human attribute taxonomies are flawed or irrelevant, then the results, reports, and decisions made on the basis of that system will also be flawed or irrelevant.

O*NET

In the early 1930s, the federal government introduced a program to match applicants with job openings (Dunnette, 1999). It was up to each local office to develop its own occupational information base; because these bases were local, there could be little collaboration among the network of offices. Accordingly, in 1934 efforts were begun to standardize these services and develop a national database. The cornerstone of this effort was a program of job analysis; by 1939, 54,000 job analyses had been completed and the first ***Dictionary of Occupational Titles (DOT)*** was published. One of the major purposes of the *DOT* was, and still is, for use in occupational counseling.

Dictionary of Occupational Titles (DOT) Document that includes job analysis and occupational information used to match applicants with job openings; a major purpose of the *DOT* was, and still is, for use in occupational counseling.

In 1991, the last year of its publication, the *DOT*'s fifth edition contained information on more than 13,000 occupations. By this time the *DOT*, at least in the form of its fifth edition, had become less useful. The primary reason for this was its heavy dependence on task-based information, with no direct link to human abilities or attributes. As we have seen, task-based descriptions of occupations provide limited value in work environments with shifting job boundaries. Further, each revision of the *DOT* was expensive and time consuming. A decision was made to change both the format and the content of the *DOT* (Dunnette, 1999).

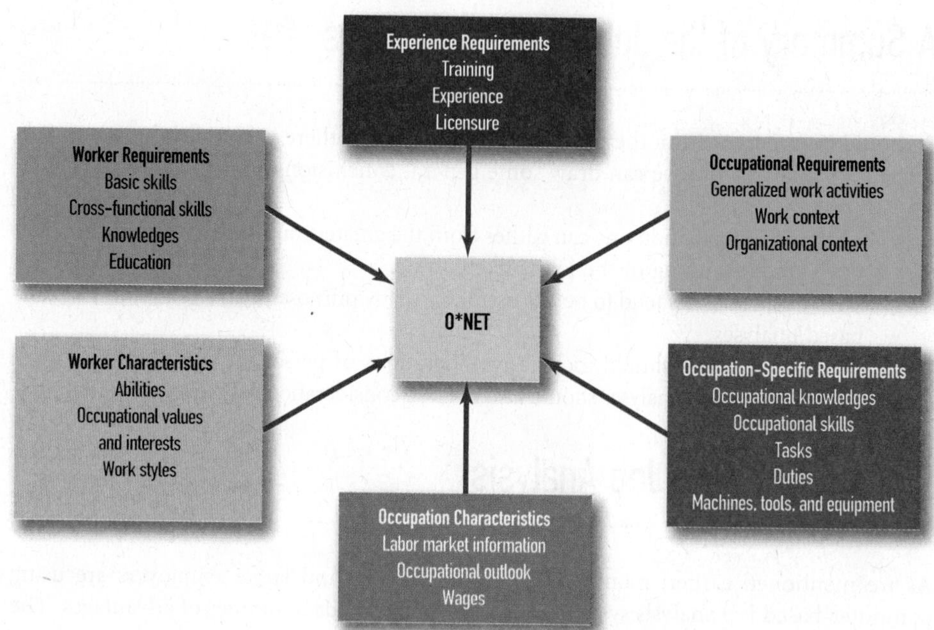

FIGURE 4.8 Databases Forming the Foundation for O*NET

SOURCE: Mumford, M. D., & Peterson, N. G. (1999). The O*NET content model: Structural considerations in describing jobs. In N. G. Peterson, M. D. Mumford, W. C. Borman, P. R. Jeanneret, & E. A. Fleishman (Eds.), *An occupational information system for the 21st century* (pp. 21–30). Fig. 3.2, p. 25. Washington, DC: American Psychological Association, © 1999 by the American Psychological Association. Reproduced with permission.

Occupational Information Network (O*NET) Collection of electronic databases, based on well-developed taxonomies, that has updated and replaced the *Dictionary of Occupational Titles* (*DOT*).

In 1995 the federal government introduced the concept of an electronic database to replace the *DOT*. The database was called the **Occupational Information Network** or **O*NET** (Dye & Silver, 1999; Peterson et al., 2001). O*NET is actually a collection of databases. Figure 4.8 presents the six major databases that form the foundation for O*NET. All of O*NET's six major databases are still being developed and completed. When O*NET is completed, information describing each job in the system will be available for each of the six databases. In addition, expert computer systems allow the databases to be combined in ways that will facilitate person–job matches, the same goal set for the original *DOT* in 1939. Thus, if you were interested in pursuing a career as a jet engine mechanic you could search O*NET for jet engine mechanic and get information on variables such as experience requirements, work context, typical tasks and duties, wage expectations, requisite abilities, and basic skills. And you could get all of this information in seconds while sitting at your own computer. Furthermore, unlike the old printed *DOT*, O*NET can be updated instantaneously as changes occur in the labor market, technology, or training and experience requirements.

In addition to the transformation from a print medium (*DOT*) to an electronic medium (O*NET), an even greater change occurred in content. Each of the O*NET databases is now based on well-developed taxonomies, such as the Fleishman taxonomy for abilities we described in Chapter 3. O*NET was not designed as a job analysis system, but it will have the capability to compare a new job to its current job base and identify jobs most similar to that new job. This matching process will, in turn, permit instantaneous access to a description of the new job's probable required KSAOs. It would also make it possible to fit the job into other labor market databases, including estimates of the probable worth or initial wage estimate for that job.

Not all jobs and job families have yet been entered into the O*NET databases, but when the system is complete, it is expected to meet at least the following needs:

- Identifying occupational skill standards common to clusters of occupations, or job families

- Facilitating school-to-work transitions by linking educational programs to occupational standards
- Assisting laid-off workers in finding reemployment through job search assistance, labor market information, and training
- Assisting employers in building high-performance workplaces by providing information about the business practices associated with existing high-performance workplaces (adapted from Peterson, Borman, Hansen, & Kubisiak, 1999)

As you can see, O*NET can serve multiple users, including workers looking for jobs or occupations, employers looking for workers, or I-O psychologists serving as consultants to organizations—or even students in I-O psychology courses interested in examining job descriptions for various occupations.

Since the development of the O*NET architecture, several novel applications have been described:

- Carter, Dorsey, and Niehaus (2004) demonstrate how O*NET can be connected to online job search transactions to trigger updates in job requirements and other factors, based on the most common jobs being sought, and provide applicants with up-to-date information regarding those requirements.
- LaPolice, Carter, and Johnson (2005) demonstrate how O*NET can be used to derive estimates of the literacy requirements for various jobs.
- Jeanneret and Strong (2003) show how O*NET can be used to assist in the identification of relevant selection instruments for consultants and HR professionals.
- Johnson, Carter, and Dorsey (2003) demonstrate how O*NET can be applied to derive occupational ability requirements.

O*NET is a broad public policy initiative that embodies all of the best characteristics of defining performance in the modern workplace (National Research Council, 2010). It is accessible to many different user groups, including both employees and applicants. In addition, this electronic system lends itself to quick updating of changes in existing jobs as well as the appearance of new jobs.

One need not have a license or certificate to access O*NET, and it is surprisingly user-friendly. We suggest that you simply click on the web address (www.onetonline.org/) and give it a whirl. Enter a particular job title (e.g., Customer Greeter or University Professor or Prison Guard) and click on the first occupational title listed. This lets you through the front door of O*NET; once inside, you are free to explore aspects of the job as diverse as tasks, wages, and related occupations.

Competency Modeling

We introduced the concept of competencies in the discussion of individual differences and assessment (see Chapter 3). In this section we will deal with competencies from a different perspective: the process of **competency modeling.** You will recall that we defined competencies as "sets of behavior that are instrumental in the delivery of desired results or outcomes" (Kurz & Bartram, 2002). We further described competencies as being rooted in a context of organizational goals rather than in an abstract taxonomy of human attributes.

Just as job analysis seeks to define jobs and work in terms of the match between required tasks and human attributes, competency modeling seeks to define organizational units (larger entities than simply jobs or even job families) in terms of the match between the goals

Competency modeling
Process that identifies the characteristics desired across all individuals and jobs within an organization; these characteristics should predict behavior across a wide variety of tasks and settings, and provide the organization with a set of core characteristics that distinguish it from other organizations.

and missions of those units and the competencies required to meet those goals and accomplish those missions. Thus, competency modeling is a natural extension of the job analysis logic rather than a replacement for job analysis. It is competency modeling that has the power to connect individual behavior with organizational viability and profitability. The competency modeling approach "emphasizes the characteristics desired across all individuals and jobs within an organization . . . these more global competencies are expected to not only predict behavior across a wide variety of tasks and settings but also provide the organization with a set of core characteristics that distinguish the company from others in terms of how it operates its business and treats its employees" (Goldstein & Ford, 2002, p. 272).

Like cognitive task analysis and the Personality-Related Position Requirements Form, competency modeling goes beyond traditional job analysis by recognizing that work and the workplace are in a state of rapid evolution. Sanchez and Levine (1999) provided an example. In considering the job title "quality auditor," a traditional job analysis might suggest that the "ability to perform accurate numerical calculations involving unit transformations" and "knowledge of relevant standard operating procedures" would be important KSAOs. Competency modeling, in contrast, might identify the need for "constructive communication involving nontechnical aspects of the job like the management of trust and the effective delivery of potentially threatening information" (Sanchez & Levine, 1999, p. 58).

Goldstein and Ford (2002) presented examples of two different approaches to competency modeling. One approach is to identify outstanding performers and analyze their performance and competencies. The employer could then take that home-grown taxonomy of performance components and competencies and use it as a model for the match between individuals and organizationally relevant work. This might be accomplished through a combination of traditional job analysis techniques, such as observation and critical incident interviews, with the addition of newer techniques such as cognitive task analysis and think-aloud protocols.

In contrast to this process, a second approach is that of using mission statements and corporate goals as the foundation for competency modeling. This approach was in fact adopted by Intel Corporation, which tied it to identifying employee competencies compatible with the corporation's core values. These values were: (1) taking risks and challenging the status quo; (2) emphasizing quality by setting high goals; (3) demonstrating discipline in project planning, meeting commitments, and conducting business with a high level of integrity; (4) serving customers by delivering innovative and competitive products as well as communicating expectations in a clear and timely fashion; (5) being results oriented; and (6) working as a team that has mutual respect for its members (Goldstein & Ford, 2002; Meister, 1994).

Competency modeling is not without its critics (e.g., Sanchez & Levine, 2001). Much if not most of the criticism is about the definitions of competencies, although recent work (Bartram, 2005; Campion et al., 2011) addresses those issues. In addition, some have criticized the apparent lack of agreement between the results of traditional job analyses and those of competency modeling. Lievens, Sanchez, and De Corte (2004) argue that rather than asking which method—job analysis or competency modeling—is *better*, it is more useful to *combine* the job analysis and competency modeling processes. We agree.

Competency modeling represents the evolution of work analysis along the lines suggested by Campbell's (1990a) study of performance components; it addresses the issue of what organizations pay people to do. In the past, traditional task-oriented job analysis often stopped short of considering the strategic goals of the organization. There was a link missing between human behavior and organizational goals, and competency modeling provides that link. In some senses, motivation theories attempted to fill that gap, as we will see in Chapter 8. But as we suggested in Chapter 1, I-O practice and theory need to be unified rather than fragmented. It is not enough to place the burden for the link between behavior and organizational success on the shoulders of one process (e.g., motivation of employees or methods of selection or job analysis). Instead, the link should be apparent in many different approaches, including job, work, and competency analysis. By directly addressing the needs and the goals of the organization, competency modeling helps to reinforce that link. Recent publications (e.g., Pearlman & Sanchez, 2010) have adopted new terms for what has been called competency modeling—strategic work analysis or strategic job analysis. This is a good replacement since it both identifies what is new (i.e., strategic) and avoids the debate about what is and what is not a competency. It is likely that these new terms will catch on rapidly.

MODULE 4.4 SUMMARY

- Electronic performance monitoring facilitates the gathering of job analysis information independent of what might be collected from subject matter experts (SMEs). Although electronic performance monitoring can be very cost effective and has the potential for providing detailed and accurate work logs, it is often unpopular with workers.
- Cognitive task analysis can provide a valuable addition to traditional job analysis procedures. Most job analyses concentrate on observable behavior, but special data collection techniques must be used for cognitive behavior because it is not directly observable. Because cognitive task analysis concentrates on *how* behavior occurs rather than on *what* is accomplished, it is a useful addition to the job analysis toolbag.
- Historically, job analysis instruments ignored personality attributes, concentrating on abilities, skills, and, less frequently, knowledge. A recently developed job analysis instrument (the Personality-Related Position Requirements Form) identifies personality predictors of job performance.
- The *Dictionary of Occupational Titles* (*DOT*) was developed to provide a national database of jobs and job analysis information. In 1995 the federal government supplanted the *DOT* with the Occupational Information Network, or O*NET, which is a collection of databases that contains information on experience requirements, work context, typical tasks and duties, wage expectations, requisite abilities, and basic skills.
- Just as job analysis seeks to define jobs and work in terms of the match between required tasks and human attributes, competency modeling seeks to define organizational units in terms of the match between the goals and missions of those units and the competencies required to meet those goals and accomplish those missions. Thus, competency modeling is a natural extension of the job analysis logic rather than a replacement for job analysis.

KEY TERMS

electronic performance monitoring
cognitive task analysis
think-aloud protocol
Personality-Related Position Requirements Form (PPRF)
Dictionary of Occupational Titles (DOT)
Occupational Information Network (O*NET)
competency modeling

that the more they were monitored, the more likely they were to feel that their privacy had been invaded, their role in the workplace was uncertain, their self-esteem was lowered, and workplace communication suffered. However, a recent meta-analysis by Carroll (2008) presented preliminary evidence that electronic performance monitoring was positively associated with performance at work. On the other hand, a good deal of laboratory research has been done, and the results seem to support both the advocates and the critics of electronic performance monitoring (Alge, 2001; Douthitt & Aiello, 2001). These studies usually involve monitoring the performance of students who are assigned computer-based tasks, in general concluding that employees are more likely to be positive toward performance monitoring if the following conditions apply:

- They believe the activities monitored are job relevant.
- They are able to participate in the design or implementation of the monitoring system (in Chapter 11, where we deal with fairness, we will see that participation is seen as "voice," an opportunity to be heard). In addition, the possibility of exerting an influence can reduce stress.
- They are able to delay or prevent monitoring at particular times.
- They have advance warning that the monitoring will occur (Hovorka-Mead, Ross, Whipple, & Renchin, 2002). This study, done with summer workers at a water park, found that those employees who had been warned in advance of monitoring (videotaping by private detectives), compared to those who had not been warned, were more likely to reapply for work with the company for the following summer.

These studies also indicated that improved performance resulted under these circumstances:

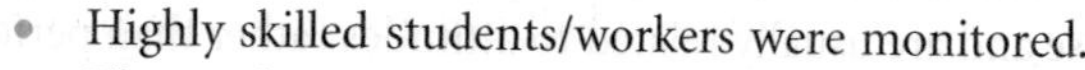

- Highly skilled students/workers were monitored.
- The student/worker was able to delay or prevent monitoring at particular times.
- Lower-skilled students/workers were not monitored.

© AIMSTOCK/iStockphoto

Electronic performance monitoring is often used in customer service call centers and other telephone-based work situations.

Certainly, there is a difference between actual workers and students playing the role of workers. It is unfortunate that more field research has not been conducted to date, but as monitoring continues to increase, more such research is likely to emerge.

It appears that electronic performance monitoring must be used carefully to avoid reducing motivation and satisfaction while improving performance. Hedge and Borman (1995) suggested that the most effective use might be for employee development, as a way of providing feedback concerning effective and ineffective work behaviors. Similar recommendations came from an interviewing study (Laabs, 1992) conducted with managers and employees at companies like Duke Power, AT&T, Toyota, Avis, and Charles Schwab. In a sample of nonmanagerial employees, Spitzmüller and Stanton (2006) found substantial resistance to electronic monitoring; many respondents reported that they would try to avoid or escape monitoring if it were instituted or, alternatively, alter or manipulate the monitoring system to their advantage.

In an interesting twist on the question of electronic performance monitoring, Alge, Ballinger, and Green (2004) focused on managers' concerns rather than on the reactions of subordinates. In both a laboratory study and subsequent interviews with managers, it was clear that the decision to monitor was closely related to managers' fears of poor future performance, particularly when the manager had to depend heavily on subordinate performance for unit success. Since this research question is very new, these results simply reach the "intriguing" level. But it is an interesting avenue for further research.

Performance Management

Twenty years ago, I-O and HR texts had extensive sections on "performance appraisal" or "performance evaluation." Now you are just as likely to encounter the term "performance management" along with the other two because most people who have been evaluated are unhappy with their evaluation—unless, of course, they receive the highest marks available. The cynic might suggest that by choosing the term "performance management" we have simply put old wine in new bottles and that there is really no difference. The cynic would be wrong.

As we saw in Chapter 4, the term "performance" derives its meaning from the organizational context in which it occurs. As Campbell, McCloy, Oppler, and Sager (1993) observed, performance is determined by what is valuable to the organization. It is the behavior for which the employee is compensated. Prior to the 1990s, performance appraisal and evaluation systems were usually based exclusively on task-oriented job analysis systems and were only accidentally related to organizational goals or profitability. **Performance management** systems emphasize the link between individual behavior and organizational strategies and goals by defining performance in the context of those goals (Aguinis, 2009; Smither & London, 2009). They combine traditional task analysis with strategic job analysis, thus including goals and organizational strategies in the process.

Performance management System that emphasizes the link between individual behavior and organizational strategies and goals by defining performance in the context of those goals; jointly developed by managers and the people who report to them.

Performance management also differs from performance appraisal in several other important ways. Banks and May (1999) have noted the following differences:

- Performance appraisal occurs once a year and is initiated by a request from HR; performance management occurs at much more frequent intervals and can be initiated by a supervisor or by a subordinate.
- Performance appraisal systems are developed by HR and handed to managers to use in the evaluation of subordinates; performance management systems are jointly developed by managers and the employees who report to them.
- Performance appraisal feedback occurs once each year and follows the appraisal process; performance management feedback occurs whenever a supervisor or subordinate feels the need for a discussion about expectations and performance.
- In performance appraisal, the appraiser's role is to reach agreement with the employee appraised about the level of effectiveness displayed and to identify areas for improvement; in performance management, the appraiser's role is to understand the performance criteria and help the employee understand how his or her behavior fits with those criteria, as well as to look for areas of potential improvement. Thus, in performance management, the supervisor and the employee are attempting to come to some shared meaning about expectations and the strategic value of those expectations, rather than simply clarifying the meaning of a nonstrategic performance area and definitions of effectiveness in that area.
- In performance appraisal, the appraisee's role is to accept or reject the evaluation and acknowledge areas that need improvement, whereas in performance management, the role of the appraisee is identical to the role of the appraiser: to understand the performance criteria and understand how his or her behavior fits with those criteria.

Performance management has three distinct components. The first component consists of the definition of performance, which includes organizational objectives and strategies. The second component is the actual measurement process itself. The third component is the communication between supervisor and subordinate about the extent to which individual behavior fits with organizational expectations (Banks & May, 1999). When seen in this light, it becomes clear that performance *appraisal* is most closely related to the second component of the performance management system, the measurement component. But because it lacks the additional components entailed in performance *management* (i.e., active involvement of the appraisee in developing and understanding the measurement system, and follow-up and ongoing communication regarding expectations and accomplishments of the organization and individual), performance appraisal is a one-dimensional process in a multidimensional world.

Many of the components of performance management have been recommended for years as valuable to performance assessment. The importance of performance management is that the process combines most of these suggestions and adds the overlay of the strategic importance of various performance areas, a concept seldom adopted in more traditional performance assessment initiatives.

MODULE 5.1 SUMMARY

- In many work settings, performance measurement goes beyond the annual review and is used for many purposes, such as employee development, motivation, rewards, transfer, promotion, and layoffs.
- Hands-on performance measures are simulations of critical pieces of work that involve single workers. Hands-on performance measurement also permits the assessment of infrequent but important work activities.
- Since the 1980s, many organizations have replaced the terms "performance appraisal" and "performance evaluation" with the term "performance management." Performance management systems emphasize the link between individual behavior and organizational strategies and goals by defining performance in the context of those goals.
- Electronic performance monitoring can be a cost-effective way to gather performance information. The research data on electronic performance monitoring from actual work situations are sparse and are usually related to attitudes rather than performance. However, it appears that organizations must use electronic performance monitoring carefully to avoid impairing worker motivation and satisfaction while improving performance.

KEY TERMS

objective performance measure
judgmental performance measure
hands-on performance measurement
walk-through testing
electronic performance monitoring
performance management

MODULE 5.2

Performance Rating—Substance

Close-Up on a Rating System

In many of the courses you take, you will be asked to rate the instructor's effectiveness at the end of the term. An example of a typical rating form appears in Table 5.1. As you can see, there are seven rating questions and one open-ended question. This rating form has four distinct parts. The first part consists of instructions (i.e., how to enter the responses). The second part consists of the actual areas of instruction to be rated. For example, question 4 deals with how well organized the instructor is, question 5 deals with testing techniques, and question 6 deals with interpersonal factors. The third part of the form contains the actual numbers or ratings that will be assigned (1–6), and the fourth part deals with the definition of those numbers (e.g., 1 = very poor, 3 = satisfactory, 5 = outstanding). If you were the instructor, how would you feel about being evaluated on this form? Suppose that your evaluation determined whether or not you would get a salary increase for the coming year. Suppose further that your evaluation was poor. Would you feel "fairly" treated in this evaluation process? You might not, and you might single out the rating form and process as the source of your feelings of unfairness. You might raise the following objections:

1. You have high standards and gave few As; students punished you for those standards.
2. The form ignores many classroom behaviors that add to the value of your teaching, such as your creative ability to devise easy-to-understand examples or your habit of arriving early and staying after class to chat with students.
3. There are no definitions of what is meant by "poor" or "satisfactory" or "outstanding"; the standard of each student is used in deciding what rating correctly conveys his or her evaluation.
4. Students in your course are mostly nonmajors who lack a firm base in the major area and struggled with the material because it was unfamiliar. The nonmajors would probably not take another course in this area because this course simply filled an elective slot.
5. Many of the written comments indicated that the students wanted more humor in the lectures, but you are simply not a humorous lecturer.

TABLE 5.1 **Hypothetical Instructor Evaluation Form**

Preliminary questions

1. What grade do you expect to receive in this course? _______________
   For the remaining questions, use the following response scale:
   1 = Very poor
   2 = Poor
   3 = Satisfactory
   4 = Good
   5 = Outstanding
   6 = Irrelevant to this course
2. The degree to which your knowledge and understanding of subject matter was enhanced by this course
3. Your overall summary evaluation of this course

Instructor-related questions

4. Degree to which the instructor is clear and well organized
5. Degree to which exams and assignments contribute to learning
6. Degree to which instructor is helpful to students in and out of class
7. Degree to which this instructor has made you want to take additional courses in this area
8. Your overall summary evaluation of the instructor
9. Any additional comments you would like to make:

____

____

____

6. You have been assigned the most popular class time, 11:00 a.m.; as a result, your section had three times more students than any other section.

Many psychologists have studied student ratings of instructors (Centra, 1993; Greenwald & Gillmore, 1997; Marsh & Roche, 1997). Their general conclusions are that the departments that create these rating forms are unsophisticated with respect to the theory of rating and to the best practices in the development of performance rating forms (McKeachie, 1997). Like any performance rating forms, instructor rating forms can be valuable adjuncts to the instructional process if they are well developed.

Students are often asked to rate their instructors.

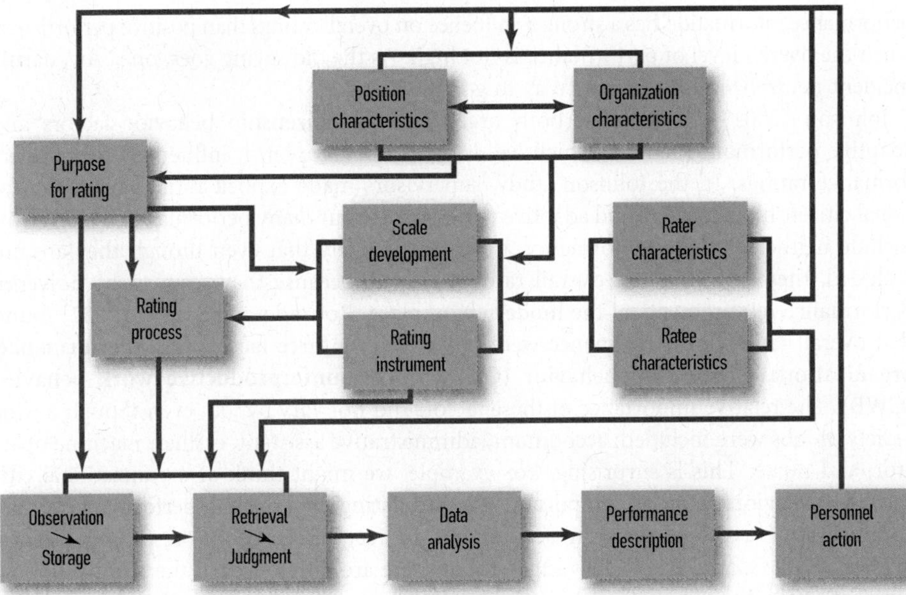

FIGURE 5.1 A Process Model of Performance Rating

SOURCE: Landy, F. J., & Farr, J. L. (1980). Performance rating. *Psychological Bulletin, 87*, 72–107. Copyright © 1980 by the American Psychological Association. Reprinted with permission.

Theories of Performance Rating

Since performance rating is one of the most common techniques for performance measurement, it has received a great deal of attention (Landy & Farr, 1980, 1983; Landy, Zedeck, & Cleveland, 1983; Murphy & Cleveland, 1995). This attention has led to increasingly sophisticated models of the performance rating process. One of the early theories was presented by Landy and Farr (1980), who addressed the various factors in the process of rating. These are described in Figure 5.1. This dizzying array of possible influences points out the complexity of the performance rating process. In the years since that model was proposed, other researchers have presented additional models. These models have often emphasized cognitive factors (e.g., memory, reasoning, and information processing) rather than situational ones (Feldman, 1981; Woehr & Feldman, 1993).

Focus on Performance Ratings

Overall Performance Ratings

Performance rating forms often have different levels of magnification. Some are very broad and culminate with overall ratings of performance, such as you saw in questions 3 and 8 of Table 5.1. This high-level focus is usually driven by a desire for simplicity, usually for administrative purposes. For example, monetary rewards may be distributed to people who have been rated above some predetermined level. But, for all practical purposes, overall performance has no "real" or conceptual meaning. It is like a grade point average. It is a simple administrative index. Studies have demonstrated that these overall ratings are differentially affected by various factors, including some that have not been explicitly presented to raters for consideration. For example, Ganzach (1995) demonstrated that negative performance information has a stronger influence on overall ratings than positive performance when the overall level of performance is not high. As the old saying goes, one "Aw, darn!" incident neutralizes a thousand "Way to go!" incidents.

Johnson (2001) showed that both organizational citizenship behavior factors and adaptive performance factors, which we described in Chapter 4, influenced overall performance ratings. In the Johnson study, supervisors made explicit ratings on organizational citizenship behaviors and adaptive performance, but many performance rating forms include neither of these performance aspects. It is likely that even though they are not included, they still influence overall ratings, in part because they seem to be universal performance requirements of the modern workplace. Rotundo and Sackett (2002) found that overall ratings of performance were influenced by three factors: **task performance**, **organizational citizenship behavior (OCB)**, and **counterproductive work behavior (CWB)**. The relative importance of these factors did not vary by job, even though a wide variety of jobs were included: accountant, administrative assistant, cashier, machine operator, and nurse. This is surprising. For example, we might think of organizational citizenship behaviors as more important for evaluating the overall performance of an administrative assistant than an accountant. In fact, more recent research (Lievens, Conway, & De Corte, 2008) does suggest that there are differences in the relative importance of OCB. Team-based work settings place higher value on OCB than on task performance, as do peers. What we can conclude from this research on the value of "overall performance ratings" is that they are complicated, at least from the psychological perspective. This overall rating is like a boxcar carrying a mix of "freight." Campbell (1990a) suggests that there is substantial value in looking at what is inside the boxcar rather than at the boxcar itself.

Task performance Proficiency with which job incumbents perform activities that are formally recognized as a part of their job.

Organizational citizenship behavior (OCB) Behavior that goes beyond what is expected.

Counterproductive work behavior (CWB) Voluntary behavior that violates significant organizational norms and threatens the well-being of the organization, its members, or both.

A "New" Perspective on Overall Performance

Viswesvaran, Schmidt, and Ones (2005) have presented some data suggesting that overall performance may, in fact, represent something real—a general performance factor. They completed a meta-analysis of over 300 studies of performance rating scales published between 1974 and 1999. After statistically controlling for what might be labeled rating error (often called halo error, a source of error we will consider shortly), they found a general performance factor that seemed to tie together the individual factors such as those that appear in many performance rating scales. They explain this result by suggesting that OCB influences virtually all aspects of performance—including technical task performance—thus representing a general underlying factor that may appear as "overall" performance. Note that we had a hint of this possibility above in the studies by Johnson (2001) and Rotundo and Sackett (2002) that showed how OCB factors influence supervisory ratings. This is a very new finding and will certainly generate a good deal of research that will either strengthen or weaken the argument. For now, we consider it an interesting possibility. This means that there may be some value in examining *either* overall performance *or* individual performance factors, depending on the purpose of the examination.

Trait Ratings

The only reason we discuss trait ratings is to warn you against them. Performance ratings were introduced by Paterson in 1923 and, at that time, it was common to have supervisors evaluate subordinates on traits such as persistence, concentration, or alertness. The modern view of performance evaluation is that the rater should be describing actions or behaviors (Campbell, 1990a) rather than broad and amorphous "traits" that may or may not be of value in a job. Well-defined traits, such as the Big Five personality characteristics, may very well support effective performance, but they are not actions or behaviors. Traits are habits or tendencies that can be used as predictors of performance but not as measures of performance. In addition, as we will see in Module 5.4, performance measurement systems based on behaviors are much more legally defensible than those based on traits.

Task-Based Ratings

Task-based performance rating systems are usually a direct extension of job analysis (Harvey, 1991). The rater is asked to indicate the effectiveness of an employee on individual critical tasks or on groups of similar tasks, often called **duties**, to distinguish task groups from individual tasks. Table 5.2 presents examples of duty areas for the position of patrol officer. As you can see from those examples, the tasks actually help raters to better understand what they are rating in that duty (group) area. These types of ratings tend to be the most easily defended in court, and most easily accepted by incumbents, because of the clear and direct relationship between the duties rated and the job in question.

TABLE 5.2 **Duty Areas for a Patrol Officer**

1. Apprehension/intervention
2. Providing information to citizens
3. Traffic control
4. Report writing
5. Testifying
6. First aid
7. Research
8. Training

Critical Incidents Methods

Critical incidents (Flanagan, 1954) are examples of behavior that appear to be "critical" in determining whether performance would be good, average, or poor in specific performance areas (Landy, 1989). As an example, consider the duty area of "written communication" for a middle-level managerial position as it appears in Table 5.3. As you can see, the examples (i.e., critical incidents) are arranged along a scale from effective to ineffective. By using these incidents, it is possible to develop rating scales that can serve as defining points or benchmarks along the length of that scale. In practice, one identifies a duty area through job analysis, interview, or workshop, and then asks incumbents or supervisors to describe particularly effective and ineffective instances of behavior in this duty area. In examining the rating scale, the rater gets a sense of both what is being rated and the levels of performance.

Duties Groups of similar tasks; each duty involves a segment of work directed at one of the general goals of a job.

Critical incidents Examples of behavior that appear "critical" in determining whether performance would be good, average, or poor in specific performance areas.

TABLE 5.3 **Effective and Ineffective Behaviors in the Duty Area of Written Communication**

	WRITTEN COMMUNICATION
Effective	It is concise and well written; includes relevant exhibits and references to earlier communication on same topic. It communicates all basic information without complete reference to earlier communications.
Average	All of the basic information is there, but it is necessary to wade through excessive verbiage to get to it. Important pieces of information, needed to achieve full understanding, are missing.
Ineffective	It borders on the incomprehensible. Facts are confused with each other, sequences are out of order, and frequent references are made to events or documents with which the reader would be unfamiliar.

OCB and Adaptive Performance Ratings

Although the rating of OCB is still relatively new by psychological standards, it has accumulated an impressive research base. The research on the identification of OCB dimensions suggests that these are valuable additions to task-based performance rating (van Scotter, Motowidlo, & Cross, 2000). As we described above, it seems like a natural evolution, since at least some OCB factors appear to play a role in virtually all jobs and all aspects of performance—including task performance. The same appears to be true of adaptive performance dimensions (Pulakos, Anad, Donovan, & Plamondon, 2000). Some jobs simply require more adaptability than others, regardless of the person who occupies the particular position. And there are times when virtually every job requires one or more adaptability behaviors. From a defensibility perspective, however, it would be prudent to include questions about the value of these dimensions in a job analysis to show that they are important for the performance of a particular job. Judges and juries tend to be very literal and are reluctant to simply take a psychologist's word that these are important "for every job." They would prefer that this association be confirmed by subject matter experts (SMEs) (incumbents or supervisors).

Structural Characteristics of a Performance Rating Scale

Regardless of which technique you use to gather performance information, the characteristics of the scale you use can also affect the validity of the resulting ratings. Consider Figure 5.2, which presents an array of rating scales that differ in certain respects. There are actually three fundamental characteristics of rating scales, and they are displayed in that figure. The first characteristic is the extent to which the duty or characteristic being rated is behaviorally defined. The second characteristic is the extent to which the meaning of the response categories is defined (what does a rating of "satisfactory" or "4" mean?). The benchmarks on the scale that define the scale points are called "anchors." The final characteristic is the degree to which a person interpreting or reviewing the ratings can understand what response the rater intended. Table 5.4 evaluates the scales that appear in Figure 5.2 on each of these three characteristics. A checkmark means that the characteristic is adequate in the scale being evaluated. Only scale (f) has all three of the structural characteristics. To the extent that any of these three characteristics is missing, there is an opportunity for error in either assigning or interpreting ratings.

TABLE 5.4 Evaluating the Rating Formats in Figure 5.2

FORMAT	BEHAVIORAL DEFINITION	RESPONSE CATEGORY DEFINED	RESPONSE UNAMBIGUOUS
(a)			
(b)			
(c)	×	×	
(d)	×	×	
(e)			×
(f)	×	×	×
(g)			×
(h)	×	×	

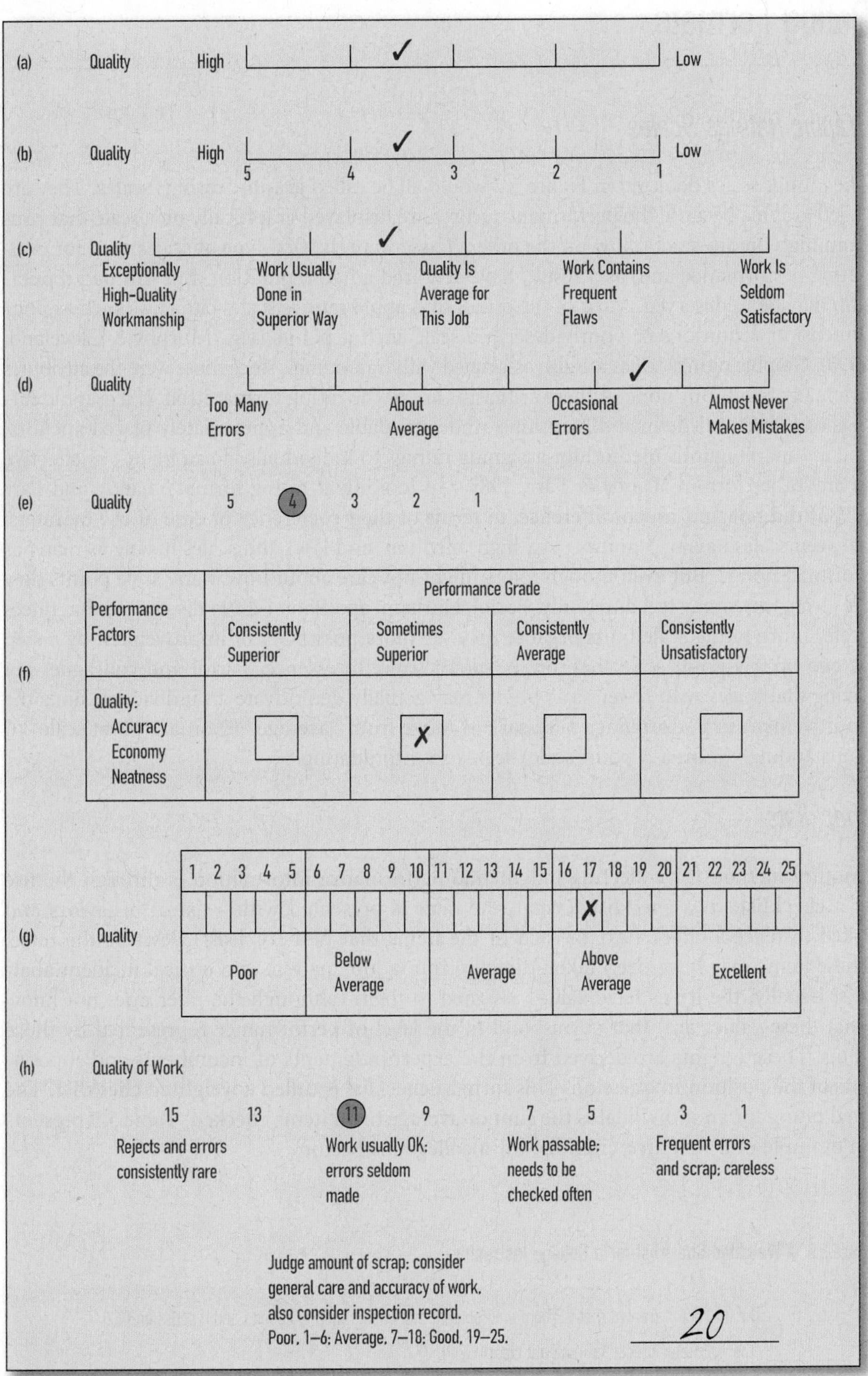

FIGURE 5.2 A Variety of Graphic Ratings Scales

Source: Guion (1965).

Rating Formats

Graphic Ratings Scales

Graphic ratings scale Graphic display of performance scores that runs from high on one end to low on the other end.

The ratings scales depicted in Figure 5.2 would all be called **graphic ratings scales**. They are called graphic because the performance scores are displayed graphically on a scale that runs from high on one end to low on the other. These were the first type of scales used for evaluating performance and, as a result, have acquired a bad reputation. But this bad reputation may be undeserved. Most of the critics of graphic ratings scales cite flaws such as poor dimension definitions or poorly described scale anchor points (e.g., Murphy & Cleveland, 1995). Graphic ratings scales are also associated with trait ratings, since those were the attributes originally rated. But none of these criticisms are of the rating format itself. If a graphic ratings scale has well-defined dimensions, understandable and appropriately placed anchors, and an unambiguous method for assigning ratings to individuals, it can be just as effective as any other format (Landy & Farr, 1983). In looking at rating formats, Landy and Farr (1983) did not find much difference, in terms of their preference or ease of use by raters, between scales having 3 points (e.g., high, medium, and low) and scales having as many as 8 distinct points. But even though raters might not care about how many scale points they are given, *ratees* may feel differently. Bartol, Durham, and Poon (2001) discovered that ratees prefer more rating scale units because they see more possibility of improvement by a step or two on a 9-point scale than on a 3-point scale. In essence, Bartol and colleagues are saying that scales with fewer scale points may actually demotivate an individual, since the improvement in performance necessary to move from "average" (2 on a 3-point scale) to "outstanding" (3 on a 3-point scale) seems so intimidating.

Checklists

Checklist List of behaviors presented to a rater, who places a check next to each of the items that best (or least) describe the ratee.

Weighted checklist A checklist that includes items that have values or weights assigned to them that are derived from the expert judgments of incumbents and supervisors of the position in question.

Another method for collecting judgmental performance information is through the use of a **checklist**. In a checklist format, the rater is presented with a list of behaviors and asked to place a check next to each of the items that best (or least) describe the ratee. These items may have been taken directly from a job analysis or a critical incident analysis. Usually, the items have values assigned to them (although the rater does not know what these values are) that correspond to the level of performance represented by those items. These weights are derived from the expert judgments of incumbents and supervisors of the position in question. This form of checklist is called a **weighted checklist**. The final rating for an individual is the sum or average of all items checked. Table 5.5 presents an example of a weighted checklist for a college instructor.

TABLE 5.5 **A Weighted Checklist for a College Instructor**

________	The instructor created a classroom environment that encouraged questions and discussion (4.2).
________	The instructor presented material clearly (2.2).
________	Lectures were adequately organized (1.7).
________	The instructor was enthusiastic and friendly (2.7).
________	The instructor used examples from his/her experience or research (3.8).

NOTE: Effectiveness values range from 1.00 (minor contribution to effectiveness) to 5.00 (major contribution to effectiveness). The instructor's score is the average of the items checked.

TABLE 5.6 **An Example of a Forced-Choice Format**

Choose the two items that best describe your instructor:

_________ (a) Will only answer questions after class or during office hours but not during lecture.

_________ (b) Is friendly toward students when he/she meets them outside of class.

_________ (c) Creates a classroom environment that is conducive to discussion and questioning.

_________ (d) Often comes to class wearing wrinkled clothing.

One variation of the checklist is known as the forced-choice format. In the generic checklist approach, the number of statements checked is left to the rater. One rater might check eight statements and another rater only four. One rater might check only positive statements, whereas another might choose positive and negative. The rater who checked only positive items might be said to be influenced by social desirability, the desire to say nice things rather than true things about a ratee. The **forced-choice format** requires the rater to pick two statements out of four that could describe the ratee. These statements have been chosen based on their social desirability values, as well as their value in distinguishing between effective and ineffective performance. As an example, let's consider the college instructor again. Look at the four statements in Table 5.6. Statements (a) and (c) have been shown to be associated with effective (c) and ineffective (a) instructor classroom behavior. Statements (b) and (d) are unrelated to classroom effectiveness but do represent desirable (b) and undesirable (d) things to say about classroom behavior. If raters are required to choose two statements, it is unlikely that they will choose both a desirable and an undesirable statement, for example, both (b) and (d). Nevertheless, raters are permitted to choose a desirable statement *and* a statement associated with effective classroom behavior. Managers do not like forced-choice methods because it is difficult for them to see exactly what will yield a high or low performance score for the person they are rating. Of course, that was exactly why I-O psychologists developed this type of measurement method in the first place!

Forced-choice format Format that requires the rater to choose two statements out of four that could describe the ratee.

Both checklists and forced-choice formats represent easy ways to generate a performance score for an individual, but they are not particularly conducive to providing feedback to the employee. In that sense, they represent the "old" view of performance *assessment* rather than the newer view of performance *management* (Aguinis, 2009). Nevertheless, Bartram (2007) conducted a meta-analysis and discovered that the forced-choice format produced validity coefficients that were 50 percent higher than ratings of the more traditional form. This is a big deal and may suggest that when validating a test, forced-choice formats be employed for generating criterion scores. More traditional rating formats may be used as an additional procedure to foster feedback.

Behavioral Rating

In the above discussion of critical incidents, we introduced you to **behaviorally anchored rating scales (BARS)**. These ratings are only one of a class of rating formats that include behavioral anchors. The anchors describe what a worker has done, or might be expected to do, in a particular duty area. Although they all include behavioral anchors, they vary somewhat in the way that the behavior is considered.

Behaviorally anchored rating scale (BARS) Rating format that includes behavioral anchors describing what a worker has done, or might be expected to do, in a particular duty area.

Behaviorally Anchored Rating Scales

These rating scales are sometimes called behavioral expectation scales because they occasionally ask the rater to describe what a worker might be expected to do (i.e., behave) in a

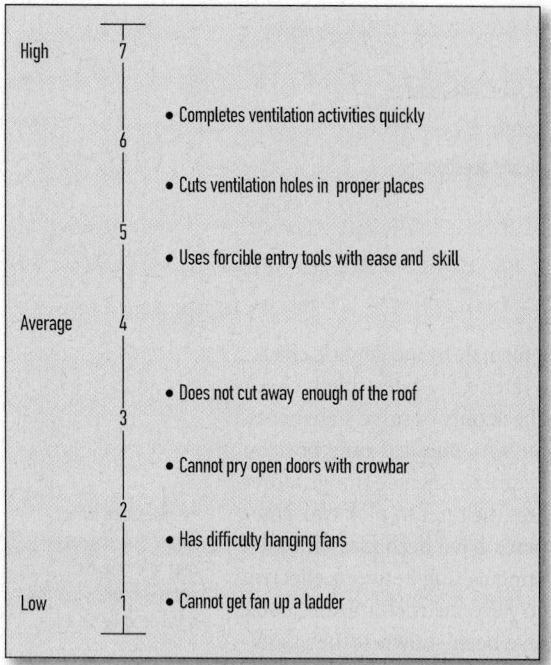

FIGURE 5.3 Behaviorally Anchored Rating Scale for Firefighters

hypothetical situation. An example of a BARS format appears in Figure 5.3. The traditional method for constructing BARS is very time consuming and involves a great deal of SME interaction (Guion, 2011; Landy & Farr, 1983). This is good news and bad news. The good news is that this interaction enhances perceptions of fairness and tends to promote a more strategic focus on performance improvement. The bad news is that it might take months to develop an effective set of scales. But if we accept performance improvement as a worthwhile goal, this time is well invested because it is spent getting a more refined understanding of performance and a tool that will help communicate that understanding to workers.

Behavioral Observation Scales

In BARS evaluation, the rater picks a point on the rating scale that describes either how the individual has behaved in the past or, absent any direct observation of relevant behavior by the rater, how the individual *might be expected* to behave. The **behavioral observation scale** (BOS) method grew out of the idea that it would be more accurate to have raters evaluate what someone actually *did* rather than what he or she *might* do.

Unlike the BARS method, the BOS asks the rater to consider how *frequently* an employee has been seen to act in a particular way (Guion, 2011). Consider the example of a dimension called "overcoming resistance to change," which is depicted in Table 5.7. As you can see, the rater

Behavioral observation scale (BOS) Format that asks the rater to consider how frequently an employee has been seen to act in a particular way.

TABLE 5.7 An Example of a Behavioral Observation Scale

*Overcoming Resistance to Change**

1. Describes the details of the change to subordinates
   Almost Never 1 2 3 4 5 Almost Always
2. Explains why the change is necessary
   Almost Never 1 2 3 4 5 Almost Always
3. Discusses how the change will affect the employee
   Almost Never 1 2 3 4 5 Almost Always
4. Listens to the employee's concerns
   Almost Never 1 2 3 4 5 Almost Always
5. Asks the employee for help in making the change work
   Almost Never 1 2 3 4 5 Almost Always
6. If necessary, specifies the date for a follow-up meeting to respond to the employee's concerns
   Almost Never 1 2 3 4 5 Almost Always

Total =

Below Adequate	Adequate	Full	Excellent
6–10	11–15	16–20	21–25

*Scores are set by management.

SOURCE: Latham, G. P., & Wexley, K. N. (1981). *Increasing productivity through performance appraisal*. Fig. 3.8, p. 56. © 1981. Reprinted by permission of Pearson Education, Inc., Upper Saddle River, NJ.

assigns ratings that range from "almost never" to "almost always." The score for an individual is calculated by the number of times each anchor is chosen. The BOS method does support feedback and is considerably easier to develop than the BARS format. Because it is often developed directly from a job analysis, it is also somewhat easier to defend than some other techniques (Guion, 2011). Finally, recent studies examining the preference of the users of rating scales seem to indicate that the BOS format is favored by raters because of its clarity and tendency to focus raters and ratees on the frequency of particular aspects of performance (Tziner & Kopelman, 2002).

Employee Comparison Methods

In rating methods, an individual employee is evaluated with respect to a standard of some sort. These standards are embodied in the anchors of the rating scale and the definition of the dimension to be considered. There are other forms of evaluation that involve the direct comparison of one person to another; these are called **employee comparison methods**. The most obvious of these methods is a **simple ranking** of employees on some dimension, duty area, or standard. Employees are ranked from top to bottom according to their assessed proficiency. If multiple dimensions are considered, the individual can be assigned a score equal to the sum of his or her ranks or the average of those ranks. Recalling our earlier discussion of overall performance, it would be better to get individual ranks on independent aspects of performance and average or sum them than to ask for an overall rank of an individual.

Employee comparison methods Form of evaluation that involves the direct comparison of one person with another.

Simple ranking Ranking of employees from top to bottom according to their assessed proficiency on some dimension, duty area, or standard.

Paired comparison Technique in which each employee in a work group or a collection of individuals with the same job title is compared with every other individual in the group on the various dimensions being considered.

A variation of ranking is the **paired comparison** method, in which each employee (typically in a work group or a collection of individuals with the same job title) is compared with every other individual in the group on the various dimensions being considered. If there are three individuals in the group, person A is compared with persons B and C on one dimension; then person B is compared with person C on that dimension. The individual's "score" is the number of times he or she was chosen over the other members. The same comparison is then made on a second and a third dimension until each individual is compared with every other individual on each of the relevant dimensions. Paired comparison ranking can become extremely time consuming as the number of people to be compared increases. In a group with 10 members (a common work group size), the evaluator would have to make 45 comparisons for each dimension considered. If the group has 20 individuals, the number of comparisons grows to 190, so if each individual is considered on 10 dimensions, that becomes 1,900 comparisons! The formula for calculating the number of paired comparisons is

$$n(n-1)/2$$

where n is the number of individuals to be compared.

Employee comparisons can be useful in certain situations. One common problem that confronts organizations is whom to lay off when downsizing is required. The context is usually a decreased volume of available work. In the defense industry, for example, the end of the Cold War in the early 1990s and the subsequent closure of a number of military bases resulted in the cancellation of many defense-related contracts to build submarines, tanks, planes, and weapon systems. This meant that in a department where 50 design or software engineers might have been needed to satisfy the military contracts in 1980, only 10 were needed in 2000. The challenge would be in deciding which 10 would stay. The issue is not performance management or feedback. It is a simple issue of deselection. In these situations, organizations typically rank individuals on dimensions including technical performance, new or anticipated work to be completed, knowledge and skills necessary for new or anticipated work, and so forth. Overall rankings are then calculated based on the rankings achieved in the individual dimensions, the employees are ordered from the most to least valuable, and the least valuable employees are laid off. Such downsizing is a harsh reality, but it can be a fair one and can be accomplished relatively quickly.

A clear disadvantage of employee comparison methods for purposes other than layoffs is the absence of any clear standard of performance, other than an employee's rank among colleagues. This makes feedback difficult. The obvious goal for an employee is to get a better rank, but little guidance is provided on how to do that.

There is also the difficulty of comparing individuals in different groups. This difficulty becomes even more obvious when we return to considering the situation when layoffs are required. Assume that a defense contractor had to lay off 40 software engineers from a group of 50, but they were spread across seven departments and three plant locations. There would be no way to compare the 50 engineers directly to one another. Instead, the comparisons might have to be done within a department, within a location, or even within departments in each separate location. Then, in order to end up with one layoff list, it would be necessary to assume that the ranks in each group were comparable; that is, 1 in department A was equal to 1 in department B. As the number of groups grows, this assumption becomes increasingly difficult to accept.

A New Variation on the Paired Comparison Method: CARS

As we have just seen, the paired comparison method has two major drawbacks: It is time consuming, and it does not provide any clear standard for judging performance, instead simply indicating that one individual is better or worse than another on some particular dimension. Borman and his colleagues (Borman, Buck, et al., 2001; Schneider, Goff, Anderson, & Borman, 2003) have introduced a computer-based technology called computer adaptive rating scales (CARS) that eliminates both of those drawbacks. Instead of pairing two employees in a better than/worse than format, CARS presents two statements that might characterize a given ratee, and the rater is asked to choose the statement that is more descriptive of the individual. So this technique is actually a variation on the behavioral checklist/forced-choice format described above. Along with behavioral statements that have scale values attached to them, Borman and colleagues have used the logic of computer adaptive testing (CAT) that we described in Chapter 3. You will remember that CAT zeroes in on the probable ability level of a candidate and then presents a smaller number of test questions that all fall close to the probable ability range of the candidate. Borman and his colleagues do the same thing—except with performance levels instead of ability levels. The computer helps to identify the probable performance range of the employee, then presents pairs of performance statements that further help to narrow that range. The value of CARS, like the value of CAT, depends on the speed of the computer to narrow the range of probable performance, thus dramatically reducing the number of comparisons that need to be made. Table 5.8 presents some examples of the anchored statements that might be presented to a rater. This is a very promising technological development since more and more organizations are going online to accomplish performance evaluation.

Concluding Thoughts on Performance Rating Formats

There are many performance rating formats from which to choose, each with its own advantages and disadvantages. One distinction among them seems to be that some are better

TABLE 5.8 **Sample Behavioral Statements and Their Corresponding Effectiveness Levels for Each Management Performance Model Dimension**

DIMENSION	SAMPLE BEHAVIORAL STATEMENT	EFFECTIVENESS LEVEL
Focus on the customer	Proactively identifies and rectifies potential customer concerns before they surface as complaints.	3.81
Understand the business	Makes decisions for his or her work group that are not consistent with the company's strategic priorities.	1.20
Take action	Achieves closure or significant progress on most key issues in meetings that he or she conducts.	3.00
Value diversity and respect others	Evaluates direct reports based on performance without regard to their differences.	3.25
Teach and learn	Supports direct reports' self-development but does not become actively engaged in the process.	2.07
Take responsibility	Offers to assume the responsibility for addressing difficult problems and issues that others seek to avoid.	3.77
Demonstrate integrity	Does not engage in actions that undermine co-workers for personal gain.	2.89
Foster safe and healthy environment	Makes decisions about work process or product design that demonstrate a lack of awareness or concern about safety issues.	1.05
Recognize individual and team contributions	Encourages team members to draw on each others' knowledge, skills, and experience to improve team performance.	3.27
Communicate	Leads the way in creating a climate in which candid dialogue is valued and encouraged.	3.89

SOURCE: Schneider, R. J., Goff, M., Anderson, S., & Borman, W. C. (2003). Computerized adaptive rating scales for measuring managerial performance. *International Journal of Selection and Assessment, 11*, 237–246. © 2003. Reprinted by permission of Blackwell Publishing Ltd.

suited to providing feedback, goal setting, and supervisor/subordinate communication than others. This is a major issue in performance management, and the research we have cited indicates that those methods that make communication difficult are less attractive. In addition, some methods seem to be more defensible than others, which is another important consideration in today's increasingly litigious workplace. Beyond those distinctions, however, any of the methods can work as long as the dimensions to be considered are well defined and job related; the anchors are behavioral, appropriate, and accurately placed; and the method used to assign ratings or rankings and interpret them is unequivocal. Added to those characteristics, of course, are the motivation and training of the rater, topics we will cover shortly.

MODULE 5.2 SUMMARY

- Because performance rating is one of the most common techniques for performance measurement, it has received a great deal of attention, which has led to increasingly sophisticated models of the performance rating process. Research suggests that it is better to obtain ratings of specific aspects of performance than of overall performance.
- Although the rating of organizational citizenship behavior is still relatively new, it has accumulated an impressive research base. Research on OCB dimensions suggests that these are valuable additions to task-based performance rating.
- Rating formats for performance evaluation instruments include graphic rating scales, checklists, behaviorally anchored rating scales (BARS), and behavioral observation scales (BOS).
- Regardless of which rating format is used, the characteristics of the performance scale can affect the validity of the resulting ratings. Three fundamental characteristics of rating scales are (1) the extent to which the rated dimension is behaviorally defined, (2) the extent to which the meaning of the response categories is defined, and (3) the extent to which a person interpreting the ratings can understand what response the rater intended.
- Performance evaluation methods that involve direct comparison of one person to another are called employee comparison methods. These methods include simple ranking and the paired comparison method.

KEY TERMS

task performance
organizational citizenship behavior (OCB)
counterproductive work behavior (CWB)
duties
critical incidents
graphic rating scale
checklist
weighted checklist
forced-choice format
behaviorally anchored rating scale (BARS)
behavioral observation scale (BOS)
employee comparison methods
simple ranking
paired comparison

MODULE 5.3

Performance Rating—Process

Rating Sources

Up to this point, we have been using the generic term "the rater" or specifying supervisory ratings in our discussion of performance evaluation. But there are many different sources of rating information. These include not only the supervisor but also peers, the incumbent, subordinates of the incumbent, clients, suppliers, and others. A relatively new and increasingly popular development in performance measurement is called the 360-degree assessment, which includes many and sometimes all of these sources. We will discuss **360-degree feedback** systems in the section on performance feedback. For now, we will consider each of these sources independently.

360-degree feedback Process of collecting and providing a manager or executive with feedback from many sources, including supervisors, peers, subordinates, customers, and suppliers.

Supervisors

First- and second-level managers and supervisors are by far the most common source of performance information. Supervisors can closely observe the behavior of the incumbent, and they are in a good position to evaluate the extent to which that behavior contributes to department and organizational success. It is also the supervisor who is expected to provide feedback to the individual worker, both informally on a frequent basis and formally in periodic structured performance evaluations.

In spite of the supervisor being the logical choice for at least one important perspective on employee performance, many supervisors actively avoid evaluation and feedback. Why? Fried, Tiegs, and Bellamy (1992) found a number of factors that explained why supervisors avoided evaluating subordinates. The most important of these was the length of time that the subordinate had reported to the superior (less time led to more reluctance), the amount of experience the subordinate had (less experience, resulting in more corrective feedback, led to more reluctance), and the amount of trust between the supervisor and subordinate (lower levels of trust on the part of the subordinate led to more challenges of the evaluations and more reluctance on the part of the supervisor to evaluate). The study also suggested that the subordinate's confidence in the operation of the performance evaluation system (i.e., perceptions of procedural, distributive, and interpersonal justice) might influence the behavior of the subordinate and, in turn, the level of reluctance on the part of the supervisor. In other words, the less confident the subordinate is in the system, the more likely he or she is to feel unfairly evaluated and to challenge the evaluation.

BOX 5.2 A SAMPLING OF THOUGHTS ON PERFORMANCE MEASUREMENT AND PERFORMANCE EVALUATION

- "Honest criticism is hard to take, particularly from a friend, relative, an acquaintance, or a stranger."—Franklin P. Jones (1908–1980), Philadelphia reporter, public relations executive, and humorist
- "Appraisals are where you get together with your team leader and agree what an outstanding member of the team you are, how much your contribution has been valued, what massive potential you have and, in recognition of all this, would you mind having your salary halved."—Guy Browning (1964–), Humorist and film director
- "It is much more difficult to measure nonperformance than performance."—Harold S. Geneen (1910–1997), CEO of International Telegraph and Telephone (ITT)
- "In business, words are words, explanations are explanations, promises are promises, but only performance is reality."—Harold S. Geneen (1910–1997), CEO of International Telegraph and Telephone (ITT)
- "How you measure the performance of your managers directly affects the way they act."—Gustave Flaubert (1821–1880), French writer and novelist
- "Don't rate potential over performance."—Jim Fassel (1949–), American football coach and executive
- "I have yet to find the man, however exalted his station, who did not do better work and put forth greater effort under a spirit of approval than under a spirit of criticism."—Charles Schwab (1862–1939), president of Bethlehem Steel
- "Performance appraisal is that occasion when once a year you find out who claims sovereignty over you."—Peter Block (1940–), American author and business speaker
- "Evaluate what you want—because what gets measured, gets produced."—James Belasco, business author and speaker
- "You get what you measure. Measure the wrong thing and you get the wrong behaviors."—John H. Lingle, Business Author
- "What gets measured gets done, what gets measured and fed back gets done well, what gets rewarded gets repeated."—John E. Jones

There are logistical and procedural reasons why supervisors might avoid evaluating subordinates (Fried et al., 1992). The most obvious reason is that it takes time—time the manager would prefer to be spending on other work-related tasks. When you consider the supervisor's responsibility in an idealized performance management system, there would seem to be little time left for doing anything but "managing" the performance of subordinates. But when a supervisor complains that it takes too much time to provide performance goals and feedback to subordinates, the supervisor may be misconstruing his or her job. In the performance management arena, defining and communicating about subordinate performance with the subordinate is seen as one of *the* major duties of a supervisor, not as a distraction from more important tasks. It is important to help supervisors understand that the more effective their performance evaluation and feedback, the easier their job becomes and the more effective their work groups and departments become.

The more subtle reasons for supervisors' avoidance of the evaluation process include the desire to avoid giving negative feedback for fear of creating hostility in the workplace, fear of experiencing the dissatisfaction the process can cause incumbents, fear that they may be challenged on their evaluations, and even fear that they may become a party to a lawsuit brought by an incumbent charging unfairness. This is how some supervisors see performance evaluation: a recipe for trouble.

As the nature of work changes, the emphasis on supervisory ratings will also change. An increasing number of workers will have fewer opportunities for regular face-to-face communication with supervisors. Downsizing has resulted in more direct reports to fewer managers. Team and group work has recast the supervisor/manager as a resource to the team rather than a director of activity. The virtual nature of work may mean that a supervisor and a subordinate are in physically different locations. All of these influences suggest that supervisors may be less central to the performance evaluation process than was previously the case. It is not that supervisors will have no information to add, but that collecting information from a supervisor may not be sufficient for a complete assessment of a worker's performance.

Peers

Peers are more likely than supervisors to interact with a worker on a daily basis; thus, peers may be more likely to know more about typical performance. In contrast, supervisors are more likely to be familiar with maximum performance. Thus, in theory, peers should be a good source for performance information. Latham (1986) suggested that peers are an excellent source not only because of their immediate interactions but also because the peer sees how the worker interacts with others, including supervisors, subordinates, and (in a service-oriented business) customers. Hedge and Borman (1995) noted some downsides to peer evaluation. One obvious obstacle is the same one facing supervisors in the case of telecommuting: Many "peers" may be geographically separated from one another, particularly in situations where an individual may work from home. Problems are likely to arise when the peer ratings are used for administrative purposes (e.g., promotions, pay increases) because a conflict of interest is likely when peers are competing for fixed resources. Nevertheless, peers as a source of performance information may be valuable for nonadministrative purposes such as performance improvement or new skills development, as well as in the context of work group or team performance. Additionally, as we saw earlier, it appears that peers may be much more in tune with the presence or absence of OCB. The possible value of peer ratings needs to be tempered, however, with some research that indicates that when the peer is similar in personality to the person being rated, the peer ratings will tend to be higher (Antonioni & Park, 2001; Strauss, Barrick, & Connerly, 2001).

Self-Ratings

Self-ratings have often been part of the traditional performance appraisal system. An individual is told to complete a rating form on himself or herself and bring it to a meeting with the supervisor, who has filled out the identical form on the subordinate. The supervisor and subordinate then discuss agreements and disagreements in the ratings they have assigned. As a result of the discussion, the "final" rating form that the supervisor places in the employee's personnel file is a consensus form, one that evolves from the discussion. The supervisor may change a rating after the discussion, or the employee may agree that the supervisor's rating was more accurate than his or her own rating. The very act of soliciting information from the worker is likely to increase perceptions of procedural justice on the part of that worker (Greenberg, 1986a,b). The potential for distortion and inaccuracy in self-ratings obviously exists because it is common for individuals to have higher opinions of their own work than their supervisors do (Atwater, 1998). This distortion is minimized, however, when the employee knows that the self-ratings will be discussed with the supervisor. Further, if ratings are to be used for administrative purposes (e.g., salary increases, promotions), there is a conflict of interest, much as there is for peer ratings. Once again, however, for nonadministrative purposes and in the context of a performance management system, self-ratings may play an important role in understanding performance.

Subordinate Ratings

Increasing numbers of organizations are looking at the value of a subordinate's evaluation of a boss. Bernardin, Dahmus, and Redmon (1993) found that supervisors were supportive of this source of information, as long as it was not used for administrative decisions. This parallels our cautions above about peer and self-ratings. It appears that there is a valuable role for information from a wide variety of sources, as long as it is used for feedback and employee development. As you will see when we cover leadership in Chapter 12, subordinates may be in the best position to evaluate leadership behaviors (or the lack thereof) and the effect of those behaviors on subordinates. Hedge and Borman (1995) suggested another positive outcome from the use of subordinate performance evaluations: They encourage the subordinate to consider the challenges and performance demands of that supervisor, thus gaining a better appreciation of the duties of a supervisor. This in turn might act as a modest form of realistic job preview for those subordinates who seek to advance up the management ladder. Hedge and Borman (1995) also cautioned that it is critical for subordinate feedback to be kept anonymous to prevent retaliation from a less-than-enthusiastic supervisor.

Customer and Supplier Ratings

Many job titles require interaction with individuals outside the organization. The most obvious of these is the customer, but employees may also have important interactions with suppliers and vendors who provide materials and services to the organization. The perspective of these outside parties is likely to be unique and provides the opportunity to fill out the employee's performance profile. You will remember that Campbell (1990a) anchored performance in business goals and strategies. Very few managers and executives would say that they have *not* adopted a customer-driven focus. Thus, in our new view of how performance should be defined, we should pay particular attention to customer-oriented behavior. We must be cautious, however, to limit our inquiries to those areas of performance that a customer sees. This will represent a subset of all of the duties of the employee and may be limited to interpersonal, communication, and motivational issues. Although the ratings of suppliers might be less salient than those of customers to the issue of customer service, suppliers also have an opportunity to see the interpersonal and communication aspects of an employee's performance. In addition, suppliers may provide valuable information about some of the more technical aspects of performance, since they are likely to be involved in discussions about product specifications, costs, and delivery schedules.

360-Degree Systems

The collection of information sources we have reviewed represents a wide variety of perspectives. It seems clear that by using these sources, we can examine the behavior of an employee from many possible angles (Oh & Berry, 2009). Thus, the use of the varied sources has become known as the 360-degree evaluation. Because of the sensitivity of information from some of these sources and because of the potential conflicts that arise when administrative issues are involved, 360-degree systems are often used for feedback and employee development. Figure 5.4 shows the many different potential sources of 360-degree feedback.

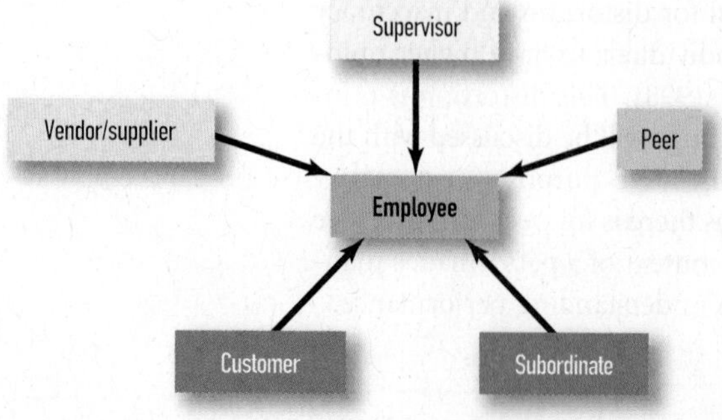

FIGURE 5.4 Potential Sources for 360-Degree Feedback

Rating Distortions

Even though the intent of a rating system is to collect accurate estimations of an individual's performance, and we build in structural characteristics to assist in the gathering of those accurate estimations, raters don't always provide accurate estimates. In Module 5.4, we will explore the motivational reasons for this inaccuracy, but here we will identify some of the most common inaccuracies that creep into ratings. These have traditionally been labeled **rating errors**, but they may not really be "errors" as much as intentional or systematic distortions. Although many different types of errors have been proposed, we will consider only the most common of them.

Rating errors Inaccuracies in ratings that may be actual errors or intentional or systematic distortions.

Central Tendency Error

It is often the case that raters choose a middle point on the scale as a way of describing performance, even though a more extreme point might better describe the employee. They are being "safe" by not picking a more extreme score and thus are committing a **central tendency error**. Some rating systems may encourage a central tendency bias by requiring any rater who chooses an extreme score to provide a written justification for that choice, thus making it more difficult to choose any rating other than an average one.

Central tendency error Error in which raters choose a middle point on the scale to describe performance, even though a more extreme point might better describe the employee.

Leniency/Severity Error

This type of distortion is the result of raters who are unusually easy (**leniency error**) or unusually harsh (**severity error**) in their assignment of ratings. The easy rater gives ratings higher than employees deserve, while the harsh rater gives ratings lower than employees deserve. In part, these errors are usually the result of anchors that permit the rater to impose idiosyncratic meanings on words like "average," "outstanding," and "below average." The problem is that the rater can feel free to use a *personal* average rather than one that would be shared with other raters. Many supervisors are well known for being "demanding" and requiring extraordinary accomplishment for any rating other than "average." Other supervisors give everyone good marks, either to avoid friction or to be seen favorably by their subordinates. One safeguard against this type of distortion is to use well-defined behavioral anchors for the rating scales. Yun, Donahue, Dudley, and McFarland (2005) found that raters high on the personality factor of agreeableness give higher ratings than those lower on that factor, particularly when the feedback to the ratee will be face-to-face. Nevertheless, these researchers found that the use of behavioral anchors reduced this lenient tendency in agreeable raters, once again showing the value of well-constructed rating scales.

Leniency error Error that occurs with raters who are unusually easy in their ratings.

Severity error Error that occurs with raters who are unusually harsh in their ratings.

Halo Error

Often, when a rater has a series of dimensions to rate, he or she assigns the same rating to the employee on each of those dimensions. In other words, there is a *halo* or aura that surrounds all of the ratings, causing them to be similar. This might be the result of simple laziness on the part of the rater or because the rater believes that one particular dimension is key and all the other dimensions or performance areas flow from that one important area. The rater might also subscribe to a "unitary view" of performance (Campbell, 1990a). In this view, raters assume that there is really one general performance factor and that people are either good or poor performers; they further assume that this level of performance appears in every aspect of the job. It might also be that the rater considers a performance area not included in the rating form (e.g., adaptability or OCB) as the key to successful performance and therefore allows that "invisible" area to influence all of the other ratings. One other downside to **halo error** is that it can have the effect of not identifying the employee's strengths and weaknesses, thus defeating one of the purposes of feedback.

Halo error Error that occurs when a rater assigns the same rating to an employee on a series of dimensions, creating a halo or aura that surrounds all of the ratings, causing them to be similar.

Rater Training

It has generally been assumed that rater distortions are unintentional, that raters are unaware of influences that distort their ratings. As we will see in the next module, that assumption may not be correct. Raters may know exactly what they are doing and why they are doing it. In other words, the distinct possibility exists that these distortions are *motivated*. Nevertheless, some distortions may be corrected through training. We will consider three types of training: administrative, traditional psychometric, and frame-of-reference training.

Administrative Training

Most evaluation systems are straightforward and easy to understand, such as the traditional graphic rating systems. Experienced managers have been doing performance ratings for their entire managerial careers. They themselves have also been evaluated in management and nonmanagement positions. So for simple, straightforward, and well-designed graphic rating systems, little administrative training is required. On the other hand, if the system is an uncommon one (e.g., BARS or BOS), the raters will need some training, if for no other reason than to understand how this system differs from others they may have seen in the past. If one or more of the structural characteristics (e.g., dimension definition, anchors, method for assigning or interpreting a rating) is deficient, administrative training becomes more important. The training would be directed toward developing a consensus among raters about the meaning of dimension headings or anchor meanings. Of course, the more direct solution would be to make the scale better, not to "train away" its deficiency.

Psychometric Training

Psychometric training Training that makes raters aware of common rating errors (central tendency, leniency/severity, and halo) in the hope that this will reduce the likelihood of errors.

Psychometric training involves making the raters aware of the common rating distortions described earlier (central tendency, leniency/severity, and halo) in the hope that making these distortions more salient will reduce the likelihood of distortions. While that makes some sense, assuming that the distortions are not motivated, the actual effect of this type of training is questionable. In a classic study, Bernardin and Pence (1980) demonstrated that when raters are instructed to avoid leniency and halo distortions, they do, but the resulting performance ratings are less accurate than if they had not received this training. Bernardin and Pence suggested that the reason for this surprising result was that the trained raters were concentrating on producing a distribution of ratings that had no leniency/severity or halo, which they were able to do. But the raters were less concerned about accurately describing performance than about avoiding "distortions." The battle was won, but the war was lost. These findings have been replicated by Woehr and Huffcutt (1994).

Frame-of-reference (FOR) training Training based on the assumption that a rater needs a context or "frame" for providing a rating; includes (1) providing information on the multidimensional nature of performance, (2) ensuring that raters understand the meaning of anchors on the scale, (3) engaging in practice rating exercises, and (4) providing feedback on practice exercises.

Frame-of-Reference Training

As you saw in the description of process models of performance rating (Landy & Farr, 1980; Woehr & Feldman, 1993), there has been an increasing interest in the cognitive aspects of performance rating. Researchers have concentrated on factors like the observational skills of the rater and the dynamics of memory. **Frame-of-reference (FOR) training** (Gorman & Rentsch, 2009; Melchers, Lienhardt, Aarburg, & Kleinmann, 2011) is based on the assumption that a rater needs a context for providing his or her rating—a "frame." This type of training includes the following steps: (1) providing information about the multidimensional nature of performance, (2) making sure that the raters understand the meaning of the anchors on the scale, (3) engaging in practice rating exercises of a standard performance presented by means of videotape, and (4) providing feedback on that practice exercise. This technique has been shown to be more effective than the traditional psychometric approach (Guion, 2011; Hauenstein, 1998). It has been suggested that as a result of the practice exercise and feedback, the information storage and retrieval in memory is more effective.

The Reliability and Validity of Ratings

Reliability

I-O psychologists have had lively debates about the reliability of performance ratings (Murphy & DeShon, 2000a,b; Schmidt, Viswesvaran, & Ones, 2000). Some researchers (e.g., Rothstein, 1990) have demonstrated that the inter-rater reliability of performance ratings (i.e., degree of agreement between two raters of the same person) may be in the range of +.50 to +.60, values usually considered to represent "poor" reliability. Those values should not be surprising, however. When we examined sources of performance information, we saw that each of these sources (e.g., supervisors, subordinates, peers, self) brought a *different* perspective to the process. That being the case, why should we expect high agreement among them? If agreement were high among these many sources, it would most likely mean that we were getting redundant information and wasting the time of at least some of the raters. Even when we compare ratings from the same level of the organization (e.g., two supervisors of an employee), these raters still probably see or concentrate on different behaviors. Supervisors are not, nor are they intended to be, redundant. Usually, the inter-rater reliabilities are calculated between a first- and a second-level supervisor. It is the first-level supervisor who has the most frequent interaction with the ratee and the most awareness of day-to-day *behavior*. The second-level supervisor is more likely aware of the *results* of behavior or of *extreme* behavior (either good or bad) on the part of the employee. It is likely that each information source is describing behavior reliably, but each is describing different behavior. The challenge is to combine those sources to get the full performance picture. The more information gathered, the more comprehensive and accurate the complete performance estimate will be.

Validity

The validity of performance ratings depends foremost on the manner by which the rating scales were conceived and developed. The first step in developing effective scales is a consideration of the meaning of performance in the organization; this can be based on a job or work analysis or competency modeling. The scales should represent important aspects of work behavior. If these aspects of work behavior are truly important, and if these rating scales fairly represent these aspects, they support valid inferences about performance level. Another step in supporting valid inferences is to make sure that the scales have appropriate structural characteristics (i.e., dimension definitions, anchors, and scoring schemes). Finally, because valid inferences are further supported by knowledgeable raters, rater training is a recommended way of assuring this knowledge base.

MODULE 5.3 SUMMARY

- Sources of performance rating information include supervisors, peers, the incumbent being rated, subordinates of the incumbent, clients, and suppliers. A relatively new development in performance measurement called 360-degree assessment includes many and sometimes all of these sources.
- I-O psychologists have identified some common inaccuracies or errors that affect performance ratings, including central tendency error, leniency error, severity error, and halo error.
- Some performance rating distortions may be corrected through rater training, which can include administrative training, traditional psychometric approaches, and frame-of-reference training.
- I-O psychologists continue to be concerned about the reliability and validity of performance ratings. The relatively low inter-rater reliability of performance ratings likely results from the different behavior described by each information source. The challenge is to combine those sources to get the full performance picture. The more information gathered, the more comprehensive and accurate the complete performance estimate will be.

KEY TERMS

360-degree feedback
rating errors
central tendency error
leniency error
severity error
halo error
psychometric training
frame-of-reference (FOR) training

MODULE 5.4

The Social and Legal Context of Performance Evaluation

The Motivation to Rate

As we discussed above, most attempts to improve performance evaluation systems make the assumption that raters desire to provide accurate ratings, but for various reasons (e.g., the rating format, training, unintentional tendencies to distort), they find it difficult to do. Some researchers take a very different view of the performance evaluation process. They suggest that many raters have no intention of being accurate. Instead, they use the process as a means toward an end of some kind, either personal or organizational (Banks & Murphy, 1985; Cleveland & Murphy, 1992; Kozlowski, Chao, & Morrison, 1998; Longnecker, Sims, & Gioia, 1987; Murphy, 2008; Murphy & Cleveland, 1995).

Longnecker and colleagues (1987) interviewed 60 managers from seven large organizations who, collectively, had performance appraisal experience in 197 organizations. Consider some quotes from those managers as presented in Box 5.4. They provide vivid examples of managers who are less concerned about the accuracy of ratings than they are about the effect of ratings on themselves, their subordinates, and the organization. These quotes ring true to anyone who has had an in-depth discussion with a manager about performance evaluations. One of your authors (FL) was once gathering performance ratings in a police department as part of a test validation project. Just as the rating session was to begin, one of the raters (a police sergeant) announced that he would be happy to help the city with the test validation project but that the researcher should be aware that he had no intention of telling the truth about his subordinates. He further explained that there was a bond of faith, trust, and interdependence between him and his subordinates and that he was not about to weaken that bond by possibly saying something negative about one of his reports.

Longnecker and colleagues (1987) described the theme of their interviews as the "politics of performance appraisal"; politics meant "the deliberate attempts by individuals to enhance or protect their self-interests when conflicting courses of action are possible" (p. 184). Cleveland and Murphy (1992) described the same phenomenon from a more psychological perspective. They recast performance appraisal as a goal-directed activity and identified three different stakeholders in the process, each with different goals. The first stakeholder was the rater, the second was the ratee, and the third was the organization. They delineated the goals of each stakeholder as follows.

Rater Goals

- Task performance: using appraisal to maintain or enhance the ratee's performance goals or levels
- Interpersonal: using appraisal to maintain or improve interpersonal relations with the ratee
- Strategic: using appraisal to enhance the standing of the supervisor or work group in the organization
- Internalized: using appraisal to confirm the rater's view of himself or herself as a person of high standards

Ratee Goals

- Information gathering: to determine the ratee's relative standing in the work group; to determine future performance directions; to determine organizational performance standards or expectations
- Information dissemination: to convey information to the rater regarding constraints on performance; to convey to the rater a willingness to improve performance

Organizational Goals

- Between-person uses: salary administration, promotion, retention/termination, layoffs, identification of poor performers
- Within-person uses: identification of training needs, performance feedback, transfers/assignments, identification of individual strengths and weaknesses
- Systems-maintenance uses: manpower planning, organizational development, evaluation of the personnel system, identification of organizational training needs

Cleveland and Murphy gathered data that support their propositions. It appears that raters who have positive attitudes about the value of performance appraisal, and about the appraisal process itself, give ratings that are more accurate, that distinguish among different aspects of performance, and that are not overly lenient (Tziner, Murphy, & Cleveland, 2001, 2002). They also discovered that disagreements between the ratings assigned by two different raters are related to the rater's purpose in rating (Murphy, Cleveland, Skattebo, & Kinney, 2004). This casts the notion of "unreliability" in ratings in a very different light.

BOX 5.3 DO "NICE GUYS" FINISH LAST?

In terms of who "wins" in the performance evaluation arena, we might observe anecdotally that there have traditionally been three schools of thought: (1) The winners are the best performers; (2) the winners are the "kiss-ups" who try to please everyone, particularly the boss; and (3) the winners are those who take no prisoners and undermine coworkers for personal gain at every turn. There seems to be some evidence suggesting that the "take no prisoners" explanation might be the correct one. Nyhus and Pons (2004) examined the relationship between personality characteristics and salary increases for 3,000 Dutch workers. They found a negative correlation between agreeableness and wages; the association was particularly strong for female workers. The authors suggest two explanations. The first is what they call Machiavellian intelligence—the ability to manipulate others *and* one's compensation level. Their second explanation is simply that agreeable people may be less pushy in seeking salary increases.

BOX 5.4 QUOTES BY MANAGERS ABOUT THE PERFORMANCE APPRAISAL PROCESS

I have used it to get my people better raises in lean years.

I have used it to give a guy a kick in the butt if he needed it.

I have used it to pick a guy up when he was down.

I have used it to tell a guy he was no longer welcome here.

I have used it to send a strong message to a nonperformer that low ratings will hit him in the wallet.

If you know a "5" will piss him off and a "6" will make him happy, which would you choose?

Some managers inflate ratings of people they can't stand to get rid of them (to make that employee more attractive to other managers).

SOURCE: Based on Longnecker et al. (1987).

Goal Conflict

The problem with having multiple stakeholders with differing goals is that they often conflict when a single system is used for performance evaluation. Consider some typical conflicts:

- A rater wants to make his or her group look good, a ratee wants to learn what the organizational performance standards are, and an organization wants to make salary decisions.
- A rater wants to motivate a ratee to perform at a higher level, a ratee wants to explain why his or her performance was constrained by work conditions, and an organization wants to make layoff decisions.

When a single system is used to satisfy multiple goals from different stakeholders, the rater must choose which goal to satisfy before assigning a rating. The rater may wish, for example, to "send a message" to the employee by giving an inappropriately low rating but at the same time does not want the individual to be laid off. The rater must choose between these conflicting goals.

There are no easy solutions to these problems. One solution is to have multiple performance evaluation systems, each used for a different purpose. For example, one system might be used for performance planning and feedback (a within-person use), and another, completely different, system might be used to make salary or promotion decisions (a between-person use). Another solution might be to obtain heavy involvement of the stakeholders (raters, ratees, and human resource reps) in the development of the system (Cleveland & Murphy, 1992). Finally, Cleveland and Murphy suggested rewarding supervisors for accurate ratings. The problem, of course, is that it is virtually impossible to determine which ratings (or raters) are accurate and which are not.

This line of theory and research is sobering. It calls into question the assumption that rating distortions are unintentional rather than intentional. Banks and Murphy (1985) found that, even though raters may be *capable* of producing accurate performance evaluations, they may be *unwilling* to do so.

MODULE 6.1

Conceptual Issues in Staffing

An Introduction to the Staffing Process

The day had started out fine for the vice president of HR. He met the CEO for breakfast to talk about the new performance management system that was being considered. At 9:30 he would interview a candidate for the HR compensation specialist position in the Seattle plant. But at 9:15, the administrative assistant rushed in and said, "Look out the window." On the spacious lawn outside, several dozen people were carrying signs protesting the underrepresentation of people of color in the company's management ranks. The signs also announced a boycott of the company until its staffing policies became "more responsible and sensitive to the makeup of the community." Seconds later, the phone rang and the receptionist said that reporters from two newspapers and a local TV station wanted interviews about the $30 million lawsuit that had just been announced by a national employment law firm, charging systemic discrimination against people of color. The VP felt as if he might faint. The thought that kept going through his mind was, "I've been so careful to comply with all the regulations, to make sure our policies are fair!"

In other chapters of this book, we have discussed the value of a diverse workforce, individual attributes and their value in job success, and assessment devices such as tests. For the organization, these are tools used to make decisions about whom to hire, whom to promote, or even whom to lay off. These decisions are called staffing decisions because they determine and define the staff or workforce of the organization. For the purposes of this chapter, we will define **staffing decisions** as those associated with recruiting, selecting, promoting, and separating employees. It is important to note that from practical, scientific, and legal perspectives, the decision to separate an individual from an organization (layoff or termination, sometimes called "deselection") involves many if not all of the same issues that are in play in hiring or promoting an individual.

Staffing decisions Decisions associated with recruiting, selecting, promoting, and separating employees.

Guion (1998) presented a sequential view of the staffing process (see Figure 6.1). As Guion's model shows, organizations use a job or need analysis to identify the characteristics of individuals they would like to hire (or, in the layoff situation, those they would like to retain). This information guides the selection process. In subsequent steps, the candidate pool is gradually narrowed through rejection decisions until a selection is made and an individual is placed in a position. Several recently published books present detailed

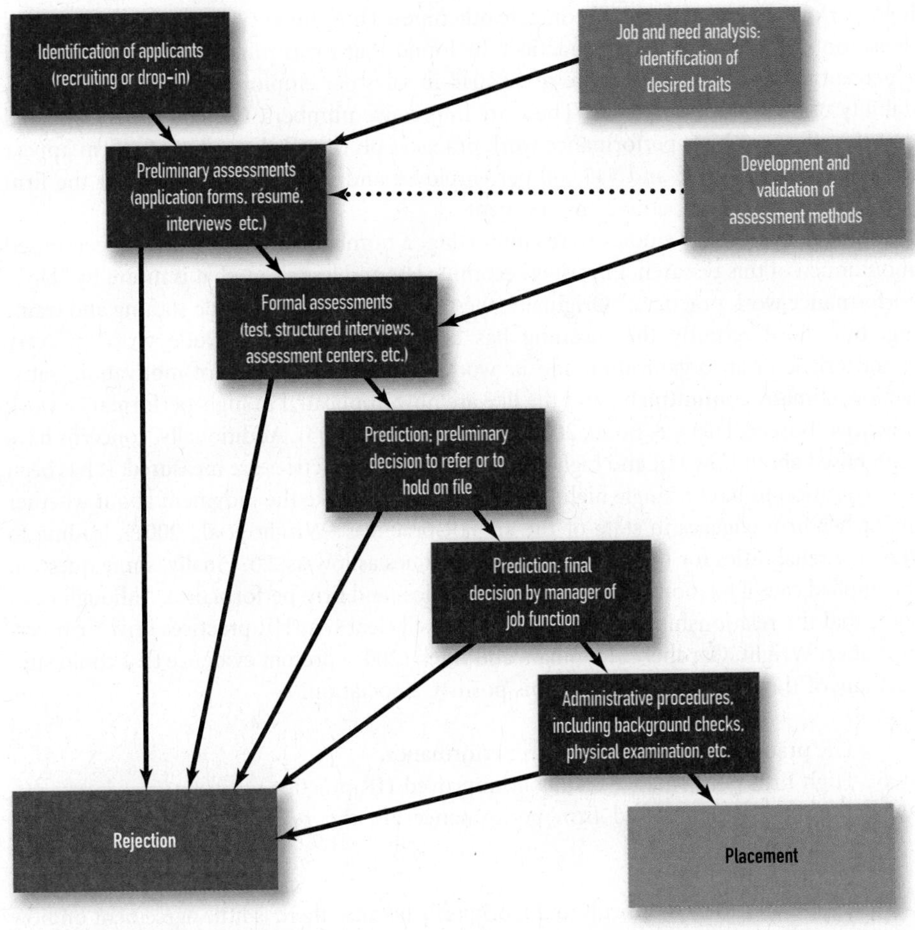

FIGURE 6.1 Sequential View of the Staffing Process

SOURCE: Guion, R. M. (1998). *Assessment, measurement and prediction for personnel decisions*. Mahwah, NJ: Lawrence Erlbaum Associates, p. 6. © 1998 by Taylor & Francis Group LLC–Books. Used by permission. Permission conveyed through Copyright Clearance Center, Inc.

considerations of staffing issues both from the domestic and international perspective (Guion, 2011; Harris, 2008; Schuler & Jackson, 2007).

The Impact of Staffing Practices on Firm Performance

In some respects, we have made an assumption in discussing staffing practices. We have simply asked you to assume that staffing practices will have a positive bottom-line effect, that firms that follow certain staffing practices will be better performers than firms that don't. This assumption has been the subject of research, and the conclusion is that staffing practices (and HR practices more generally as well) do have a positive association with firm performance. Huselid (1995) identified a number of "high-performance work practices" based on theory and research and then examined the relationship between those practices and outcomes such as turnover, firm productivity, and corporate financial performance (i.e., share value and percentage return on investment). **High-performance work practices** include the use of formal job analyses, selection from within for key positions, the amount of training received by employees, merit-based promotions, and the use of formal assessment devices for selection.

High-performance work practices Practices that include the use of formal job analyses, selection from within for key positions, merit-based promotions, and the use of formal assessment devices for selection.

By arranging almost 1,000 companies according to the extent to which each followed high-performance practices, Huselid was able to calculate the association between high-performance practices and concrete outcomes. Thus, for every increase of 1 standard deviation in high-performance practices, he found that firms might expect a decrease of 7 percent in turnover, an increase of $27,044 in sales per employee, and increased profitability of $3,814 per employee. These are impressive numbers. Cascio (2010) estimated that the effects of high-performance work practices on the market value of a firm appear to fall between $15,000 and $45,000 per employee and will also affect whether the firm even survives in a competitive environment.

Although these early studies were comforting, a number of questions have been raised about much of this research. First, it is becoming less and less clear what is meant by "high-performance work practices." Originally, these were thought to include staffing and training, but more recently the meaning has been broadened to include virtually every characteristic of an organization and its workforce. Thus, concepts of motivation, satisfaction, climate, commitment, and the like are now implicated in high-performance work practices (Boselie, Dietz, & Boon, 2005; Gelade & Ivery, 2003). Additionally, concerns have been raised about how HR and high-performance work practices are measured. It has been very common to have a single high-level HR executive make the judgment about whether his or her firm engages in state-of-the-art HR practices (Wright et al., 2001), leading to very low reliabilities for these measures—sometimes as low as .20. Finally, some question the implied causal relationship between HR practices and firm performance. Although most agree that the relationship is positive, it is not at all clear that HR practices *drive* firm performance. Wright, Gardner, Moynihan, and Allen (2005) present evidence that could support any of three interpretations of this positive association:

1. HR practices result in high firm performance.
2. High firm performance results in improved HR practice.
3. Both HR practice and firm performance are the result of leadership or CEO performance.

This type of research is difficult to do, primarily because there is little agreement on how "firm performance" should be measured. Nevertheless, it represents the "holy grail" for HR departments, which are often challenged to demonstrate the value of their practices. Gibson, Porath, Benson, and Lawler (2007) argue that various work practices will differentially affect various aspects of firm performance. So, for example, they showed that the financial success of an organization was positively influenced by the sharing of critical pieces of information (such as financial results, business unit outcomes, and new technology)—but the financial improvement does not show up until the following year. Furthermore, they found that boundary setting within the firm (e.g., strategic objectives, priorities, a clear mission statement) was related to customer service. Finally, they found that team building was associated with product quality. Combs, Liu, Hall, and Ketchen (2007) also found that the relationship between high-performance work practices and firm success became stronger as the definition of work practices became more specific and as the firm setting (e.g., manufacturing versus service organizations) became more finely defined. This type of research may represent a new path to studying the relationship between high-performance work practices and "firm performance." It suggests that like "overall individual performance," there is no such thing as "overall firm performance."

A recent study by Takeuchi, Lepak, Wang, and Takeuchi (2007) also suggests that there may be a cultural issue associated with the relationship between firm performance and high-performance work practices. They studied 56 Japanese companies and concluded that the social network within the organization may mediate the effect of work practices on firm performance. As we saw in Chapter 1, Asian cultures can be characterized as collectivist rather than individualist. Thus, it may be that variables such as collectivism, femininity, or even power distance play a role in the way in which HR practices translate into firm success.

It is tempting to view staffing as a logistical problem, with cost/benefit ratios, job demands, and applicant attributes. But there is another view that must be added for a complete consideration of the staffing process—a consideration of the various stakeholders in staffing.

Stakeholders in the Staffing Process

In making staffing decisions, the usual focus is on the organization itself. Does the decision enhance the position of the organization by increasing productivity, maintaining quality, increasing a customer base, or other benefits? That is the key question addressed by research linking firm performance to HR practice. But the organization as a whole is not the only customer or stakeholder in the staffing decision. Other stakeholders include the line managers, co-workers, and, as we will see in Chapter 11, the candidate (Gilliland & Cherry, 2000). Klehe (2004) presents a sobering view of the various forces that shape staffing decisions, including local and national government and shareholders. The point is that, as much as we would like to believe the contrary, I-O psychologists represent only one voice in the decision about what type of staffing model to use—and not always the loudest voice. For example, Muchinsky (2004) presents a case study of how various organizational forces played a role in job analysis, assessment development, and even the validity model chosen to demonstrate job relatedness. Below, we will briefly consider the three most obvious stakeholders.

Line Managers

In many, if not most, organizations, line managers are actively involved in the selection decision, in terms of both gathering information from applicants, usually in the form of one or more interviews, and sharing in the ultimate decision regarding whom to hire, promote, or lay off. As a result, the line manager seeks an accurate, easy-to-administer, and easy-to-defend staffing process (Gilliland & Cherry, 2000). Once a decision is made, it is the line manager who will be expected to supervise the new addition (whether a hire or promotion) to the work group. Or, if a department or work group is being downsized, it will be the manager's responsibility to maintain group effectiveness with a reconfigured work group. For all these reasons, it is in the best interest of the manager to see that the staffing decision is an effective one.

Co-Workers

Like the manager, the co-worker has a stake in the staffing decision. If the decision is a hiring or promotion decision, the co-worker will be either a peer or a subordinate. In a layoff, the decision may have both practical and emotional consequences. In many instances, after a layoff occurs, fewer people are expected to complete a broader range of tasks. In addition, the perceived fairness of the layoff decision may have direct effects on how committed to the organization the remaining co-workers feel. It is not uncommon for surviving co-workers to experience guilt. In addition to its direct effects on coworkers, the quality of the staffing decision may also affect the reputation of the work group or department (Gilliland & Cherry, 2000). Thus, co-workers may have a greater stake in the organizational citizenship behavior (OCB) performance of a new hire (Lievens, Conway, & De Corte, 2008). In contrast, the supervisor is more focused on technical task performance. Workers often have a stake in the hiring of effective supervisors, although they may not realize it. In 2007, two track workers on a New York City subway line were killed because of ineffective supervision. An investigation of the incident concluded that "[the supervisor's] ability to effectively supervise personnel performing duties on the right of way was extremely lacking" (Neuman, 2007a). Workers take it for granted that the individuals hired or promoted into supervisory positions will be effective. This assumes an effective staffing system. In fact, when catastrophic work accidents occur, there is almost always a concern expressed for hiring or promotional practices.

Applicants

Applicants can have very strong feelings about the staffing process, including communications about the staffing process (e.g., schedule for a hiring decision), the actual assessment devices themselves, and the process by which the decisions are made. Naturally, when applicants are rejected by the staffing system, they are more likely to think poorly of the organization and view the staffing process as biased or impersonal. Even if they are selected, the manner by which the staffing decision is carried out will have an influence on how they perceive the culture and climate of the organization.

Table 6.1 summarizes the goals of the various stakeholders beyond the formal organization or the HR department. Gilliland and Cherry (2000) suggested that the staffing practice of an organization will have direct consequences on outcomes as diverse as legal challenges (e.g., charges of discrimination in selection), likelihood of desirable applicants accepting offers, satisfaction of individuals hired or promoted, quality of the relationship between the line manager and the selected individual, and even the possibility of keeping unsuccessful candidates as customers of the organization.

There are additional potential stakeholders in the staffing process. These might include society at large in the example of high-reliability (e.g., nuclear power industry) and public safety (e.g., police, fire, and corrections) environments. It would also include the family of the newly hired or newly rejected applicant; the emotional investment at a family level can be substantial. In organizations whose workers are represented by collective bargaining agreements, unions may have (or seek) a voice in decisions such as promotions and layoffs. Finally, minority groups have a stake in staffing practices, particularly with respect to the potential impact of affirmative action programs (AAPs), which we will consider in detail in Chapter 11 when we discuss perceptions of fairness and justice in the workplace.

TABLE 6.1 Stakeholder Goals in the Staffing Process

CUSTOMER	NEEDS, DESIRES, AND GOALS FOR SELECTION
Line managers	Accurate and informative indicators of applicant potential Quick and easy-to-use selection process Flexibility and accommodation of selection procedures Perceived validity of selection process
Co-workers	Accurate and informative indicators of applicant potential Input into the selection decision-making process Perceived validity of selection process
Applicants	Appropriate hiring decision Unbiased, job-related selection process that gives them a chance to demonstrate their potential Honest and sensitive interpersonal treatment Timely and informative feedback

SOURCE: Gilliland, S. W., & Cherry, B. (2000). Managing "customers" of selection processes. In J. Kehoe (Ed.), *Managing selection in changing organizations* (pp. 158–195). San Francisco: Jossey-Bass. Copyright © 2000. Reprinted with permission of John Wiley & Sons, Inc.

Staffing from the International Perspective

Most of what we will discuss in this chapter is directed toward staffing in U.S. companies within the context of Equal Employment Opportunity laws and assessment systems commonly found in the United States. A related issue has to do with the responsibilities of international employers to follow U.S. law; however, that topic is far too complex for our present discussion. Interested readers may review an article on the issue by Posthuma, Roehling, and Campion (2006). But what about other countries? Are staffing decisions there made differently? For example, what are the laws and policies regarding fairness to minority candidates? As we saw in Chapter 1, different countries have diverse definitions of exactly *which* minority applicants deserve protection (Myors et al., 2008). Nyfield and Baron (2000) surveyed employers in 14 different countries around the world. Their analysis revealed the following:

- Job descriptions are used universally.
- Educational qualifications and application forms are also widely used for initial screening.
- The most common post-screening techniques include interviews and references.
- Unlike the common practice in the United States, cognitive ability tests are used less frequently and personality tests more frequently.
- Only 50 percent of the countries sampled used statistical/actuarial approaches to decision making.

Stakeholders in corporate performance may include customers, area residents, and others outside the structure of the organization.

Nyfield and Baron (2000) suggested that differences in staffing techniques and strategies flow from cultural differences among nations such as those suggested by Hofstede (1980a). They hypothesized that collectivist cultures prefer objective methods and are more likely to try to verify all candidate information, whereas individualist cultures prefer to take a more personal approach, examining the unique characteristics of the applicant, including such things as economic need and personal ties to the applicant. They concluded by pointing out the substantial differences that organizations may encounter when attempting to apply a staffing strategy from one country to another. As one example, they pointed to the different meanings of a high school diploma. In many countries, a student must take a demanding examination to complete high school, whereas this is less common in the United States. Another example of cultural differences is a cognitive test that includes numerical reasoning questions based on a table of life expectancies; such a test would be unremarkable in the United States, Germany, or the United Kingdom, but it would evoke a very negative reaction in Italy because the example deals with the taboo topic of death. With respect to governmental regulations that address staffing decisions, the strongest are found in the United States and South Africa. Increasing regulations are appearing in Italy, the United Kingdom, and Australia. In contrast, Switzerland has virtually no regulations regarding how assessment is to be done or who is to do it.

Multinational staffing Procedures that involve staffing for organizations in more than one country.

Love, Bishop, Heinisch, and Montei (1994) presented a case study in the challenges to **multinational staffing**. They studied a motor assembly plant that was predominantly Japanese owned and directed but located in the United States and staffed with American workers. Thus, there was the potential for a clash between Japanese management principles (based in part on cultural variables such as collectivism) and American staffing principles. Just such a clash did occur. The Japanese executives were opposed to traditional job analysis techniques for several reasons. The primary reason was that—contrary to the principles of Japanese management systems, in which the individual is less important than the group—job analysis tended to isolate the subject matter experts (SMEs) from the work group. Another objection was that, even though Japanese incumbent assemblers in a plant in Japan might have been used as SMEs, they would have resisted questionnaires and individual discussions without being able to discuss their responses with their fellow workers. Finally, since the collectivist culture in Japanese companies rejects individual performance measures, there were no performance measures to correlate with test scores in a criterion-related design that the American lawyers recommended for the company. This case study is an interesting example of the practical problems of multinational staffing. But in addition to the particular differences in applying a staffing method common in country A to an organization dominated by managers from country B, an equally interesting question is the broader dimensions on which countries may differ.

MODULE 6.1 SUMMARY

- In the staffing process, managers may use a job or needs analysis to identify the characteristics of individuals they would like to hire. Often the candidate pool is narrowed through sequential rejection decisions until a selection is made.
- Research indicates that staffing practices (and HR practices more generally) have a positive association with organizational performance. Several studies have indicated that high-performance work practices have a positive impact on the organization's productivity, share value, and percentage return on investment. However, some researchers question the definition of high-performance work practices.
- In making staffing decisions, the usual focus is on the organization itself. However, several other important stakeholders participate in the staffing decisions, including line managers, co-workers, and the candidate.
- Studies indicate that international differences in staffing techniques and strategies are associated with cultural differences among nations. Collectivist cultures prefer objective staffing methods and are more likely to try to verify all candidate information, whereas individualist cultures prefer to take a more personal approach to staffing by examining the unique characteristics of the applicant, including such things as economic need and personal ties to the applicant.

KEY TERMS

staffing decisions
high-performance work practices
multinational staffing

MODULE 6.2

Evaluation of Staffing Outcomes

Staffing outcomes might be evaluated in a number of different ways. The three major aspects of evaluation are validity, utility, and fairness. We will consider each of these separately.

Validity

Staffing decisions are intended to serve a business-related purpose. The outcomes of staffing decisions are expected to populate an organization with workers who possess the knowledge, skills, abilities, and personality characteristics that will enable the organization to succeed. Staffing decisions involve inferences about the match between a person and a job; the decision maker would like to infer or predict something about the probable success of various candidates and to choose those candidates with the highest probability of success. Thus, staffing decisions are, or ought to be, valid decisions.

As we saw in Chapter 2, there are many different methods for assessing the **validity** of a selection device or test, and the more sources of evidence there are, the more confident a manager can be that the right staffing decision is being made (Landy, 2007). The most common are the criterion-related, content-related, and construct-related designs. The **criterion-related validity** design provides perhaps the easiest way to illustrate the role of validity in staffing decisions. Consider the three scatterplots in Figure 6.2. These scatterplots depict various levels of association between a test or test battery being used for selection and some criterion of interest (e.g., level of performance). Consider part (c), where the validity coefficient =.00. No matter what predictor (test) score a candidate obtains, there is no useful predictive information in that test score. Regardless of whether the candidate obtains a test score of 10 or of 70, there is no way to predict what that candidate's performance will be. We only know it will be somewhere between 60 and 100.

Validity The accurateness of inferences made based on test or performance data; also addresses whether a measure accurately and completely represents what was intended to be measured.

Criterion-related validity Validity approach that is demonstrated by correlating a test score with a performance measure; improves researcher's confidence in the inference that people with higher test scores have higher performance.

Now look at part (b), where the validity coefficient = +.50. While prediction is not perfect, an individual's test score at least narrows the range of probable performance or criterion scores. For example, if the candidate receives a test score of 50, we can predict that the performance score will fall somewhere between 75 and 90.

Finally, consider the case of perfect prediction, as illustrated in part (a). Here, the validity coefficient = +1.00. This means that each and every test score has one and only one

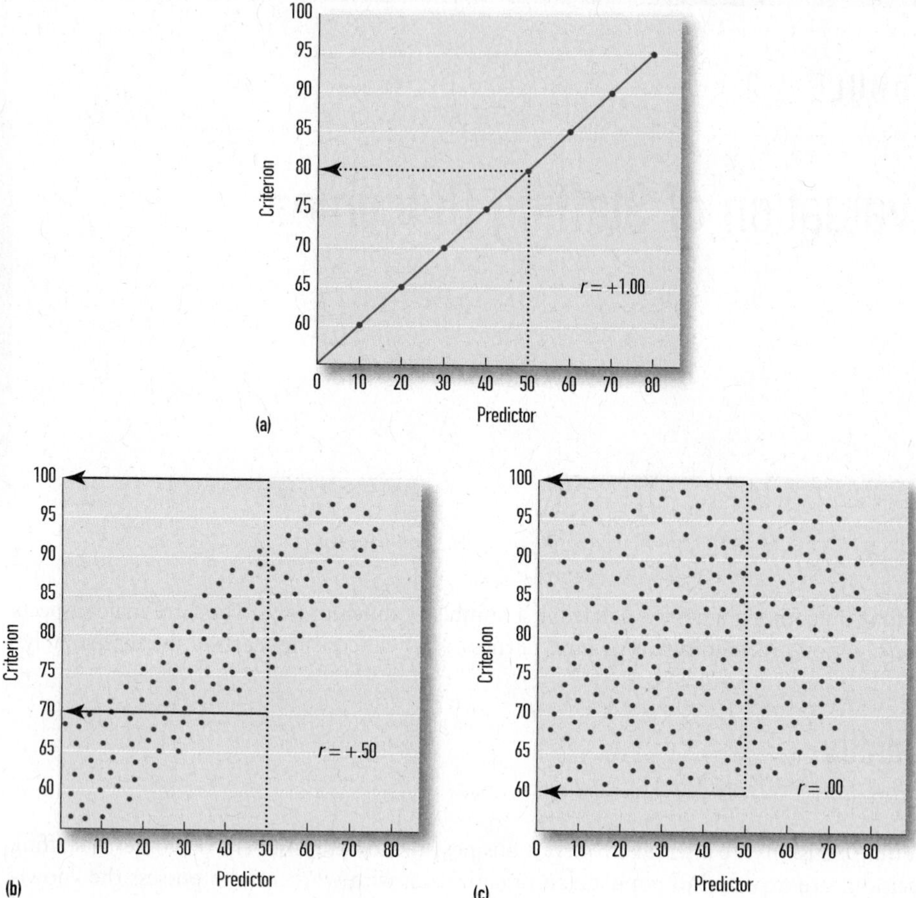

FIGURE 6.2 Scatterplots Depicting Various Levels of Relationship between a Test and a Criterion

performance score associated with it. If a candidate scores a 50 on the test, we can predict with great precision that the candidate will achieve a performance score of 80. Although such precision is never achieved with typical assessment devices, it gives us a graphic idea of the power of accurate staffing decisions.

Selection Ratios

Selection ratio (SR) Index ranging from 0 to 1 that reflects the ratio of positions to applicants; calculated by dividing the number of positions available by the number of applicants.

The relationship between the number of individuals assessed and the number actually hired is called the **selection ratio (SR)**. Although this may seem counterintuitive, low selection ratios are actually better than high selection ratios because the more people we assess, the greater the likelihood that we will find individuals who score high on the test. If the test is a valid one, this translates into a higher likelihood that we will be able to hire a good performer. The formula for calculating the selection ratio is $SR = n/N$, where n represents the number of jobs available (the number of hires to be made) and N represents the number of people assessed. For example, if we have 100 applicants for 10 positions, the SR would be .10(10/100). If there are 200 applicants instead of 100, the selection ratio would be .05(10/200). By assessing 200 applicants instead of 100, we are much more likely to find high scorers (and better performers). Of course, this comes with a cost—the cost of assessing 100 more applicants. We will discuss the issue of cost/benefit, or utility, later in this chapter.

Prediction Errors and Cut Scores

As you can see from the three cases illustrated above, the level of validity is associated with prediction errors. If the validity coefficient =.00, we are virtually assured of making a prediction error. Our best "prediction" about the eventual performance level of *any* applicant, regardless of his or her test score, would be average performance. In contrast, if the validity coefficient = 1.00, there will be no error in our prediction of eventual performance. When validity coefficients are less than 1.00, there will be some error in our predictions (and staffing decisions).

In making a staffing decision, we might commit two types of errors. We might predict that a person will be a successful performer, but the individual turns out to be unsuccessful. This is an error called a **false positive**: We falsely predicted that a positive outcome would occur and it did not—the person failed. The second type of error occurs when someone we predicted would be a poor performer actually turns out to be successful. This error is called a **false negative**: We falsely predicted a negative outcome would occur and it did not—the person succeeded.

Both of these types of errors can be costly for an organization. If we make a false negative error, we will decide not to hire an individual who might have contributed substantially to the organization—we might have failed to hire the engineer responsible for the iPod Nano or Blu-ray DVD design. If we make a false positive error, we will hire someone who will perform poorly on the job—a salesperson who is not able to sell anything. A **true negative** is an accurate prediction that someone will be a poor performer—your boss's ne'er-do-well son who is brought in to take over the company (for example, Chris Farley's character in the 1995 movie *Tommy Boy*). To complete the picture, a **true positive** is an accurate prediction that someone will be a good performer—the first-round NFL draft pick who leads his team to a Super Bowl win.

In Figure 6.3 we have graphically presented the two types of true and false decisions. But consider the effect of *moving* the score we use to hire individuals, known as the **cut score**, up or down, as we have shown in Figure 6.3. Instead of hiring all individuals with scores equal to or greater than 50, suppose we only hired individuals who had scores equal to or greater than 75. The consequence of increasing our cut score will be that we will make fewer false positive errors—almost everyone we hire will be an above-average performer. But we will make many more false negative errors. Many of the applicants we rejected would have been above-average performers. If we want to hire large numbers of individuals, this also means that we will have to assess many more candidates to get the small percentage who will score above 75.

What would happen if we were to lower our cut score instead of raising it? It would change the type of prediction errors that would occur. By lowering the cut score from 50 to 25, we would reduce the number of candidates that we incorrectly reject (i.e., false negatives), but we would also substantially increase the percentage of poor performers among the candidates that we hire (i.e., false positives).

As you can see from Figure 6.3, having a valid selection device is only one of the factors in determining whether or not our staffing decisions will be effective. Even with a valid selection device, the decision about where to set the cut score in conjunction with a given selection ratio can affect the predictive value of that device. In many situations,

False positive Decision in which an applicant was accepted but performed poorly; decision is false because of the incorrect prediction that the applicant would perform successfully and positive because the applicant was hired.

False negative Decision in which an applicant was rejected but would have performed adequately or successfully; decision is false because of the incorrect prediction that the applicant would not perform successfully and negative because the applicant was not hired.

True negative Decision in which an applicant was rejected and would have performed poorly if he or she were hired; decision is true because of the correct prediction that the applicant would not be a good performer and negative because the applicant was not hired.

True positive Decision in which an applicant was accepted and performed successfully; decision is true because of the correct prediction that the applicant would be a good performer and positive because the applicant was hired.

Cut score Specified point in a distribution of scores below which candidates are rejected; also known as a cutoff score.

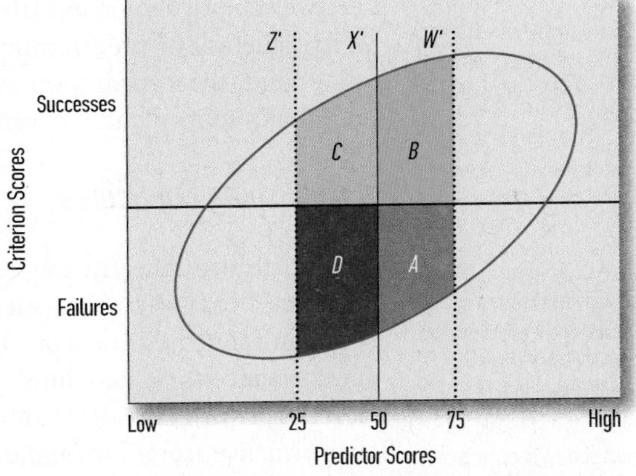

FIGURE 6.3 The Effect on Selection Errors of Moving the Cutoff Score The cutoff, *X'*, equates false positive (lower right) and false negative (upper left) errors, resulting in a minimum of decision errors. Raising the cutoff to *W'* results in a decrease of false positives (*A*) but also an increase in false negatives (*C*). Similarly, lowering the cutoff to *Z'* yields a decrease in false negatives (*C*) but also an increase in false positives (*A*).

the best staffing strategy is to choose a cut score that minimizes both types of errors. In some situations, however, where the cost of a performance mistake can be catastrophic (e.g., hiring workers at a nuclear power plant), a better strategy might be to be very selective and accept a higher false negative error rate to reduce the frequency of false positive errors. The technology of actually setting the "best" cut score is complex and beyond the scope of this discussion. Kehoe and Olson (2005) have written a comprehensive chapter detailing the practical, statistical, and legal issues related to cut scores. We will discuss various types of cut scores later in this chapter.

Using a criterion-related design, it is relatively easy to grasp the issue of false-positive and false negative prediction errors because we have a criterion score distribution on which we can designate the differentiating line between success and failure. By doing that, we can then designate a cut score on the test or predictor and actually see the extent to which errors are occurring. The same types of errors will occur regardless of which validity design we use, but in content- and construct-related designs they cannot be as easily quantified. Nevertheless, it remains true that the greater the number of unwanted errors (false positives or false negatives), the poorer will be the staffing decisions.

The concept of true negative and false negative errors may seem a bit too hypothetical because we can never *know* for sure that an individual we rejected would have been a poor performer (with the exception of your boss's son): We never had a chance to see him or her work. To some extent, that is true. But we can collect data on another group of individuals who are similar to the applicants—current employees. This is the concurrent validity design we studied in Chapter 2. Granted, most of the workers currently employed will be at least satisfactory. However, unless prediction is perfect (which it never is), some small percentage of workers will be less than satisfactory, perhaps 10 to 15 percent. These are the false positive errors made in selection. In addition, a company might use a true predictive validity design, collect assessment data for a period of years on a new assessment battery, put those data away and not use them to make actual decisions, then return to those data several years later and create a scatterplot showing the relationship between the assessment data and performance. This would tell the company how many errors and correct decisions it would have made with any cut score. In this case, a true negative occurs if the organization used this true predictive validity design and later found that someone who would have been rejected (based on a hypothetical or predetermined cut score) had below-average performance. A false negative occurs if the organization used this true predictive validity design and later found that someone would have been rejected (based on a hypothetical or predetermined cut score) who had an above-average performance. At that point, the organization would choose a cut score to minimize prediction errors and reject any subsequent applicants with predictor scores below that cut point.

Establishing Cut Scores

Criterion-referenced cut score Score established by considering the desired level of performance for a new hire and finding the test score that corresponds to the desired level of performance; sometimes called domain-referenced cut score.

There are two different ways of establishing cut scores: the criterion-referenced method and the norm-referenced method. **Criterion-referenced cut scores** (sometimes called domain-referenced cut scores) are established by actually considering the desired level of performance for a new hire and finding the test score that corresponds to that desired level of performance. Remember that in Figure 6.2 we presented the scatterplot of test and performance scores for candidates. In that case, we were discussing how one might determine the expected performance level from a test score. A cut score could be set by just reversing that process. We could have a sample of employees take the test, measure their job performance (e.g., through supervisory ratings), and then see what test score corresponds to acceptable performance as rated by the supervisor.

An alternative method of setting criterion-referenced cut scores would be to ask a group of SMEs to examine the test in question, consider the performance demands of the job, then pick a test score that they think a candidate would need to attain to be a successful performer. One well-known variation is called the Angoff method, named after the psychologist who developed the technique (Guion, 1998). These techniques tend to be complex for SMEs to accomplish and have been the subject of a great deal of debate with respect to their accuracy (Kehoe & Olson, 2005; Siskin & Trippi, 2005).

Norm-referenced cut scores are not tied to any expected level of performance on the job. The term "norm" is a shortened version of the word "normal," or average. Thus, norm-referenced cut scores are based on the average of the test takers' scores rather than any notion of job performance. In educational settings, passing scores are typically pegged at 60. Any score below 60 is assigned a letter grade of F (for "failing") and a student gets no accumulated credit for work in that course. Many civil service commissions use a similar method for determining who "passes" a test for a city or state government job. There is no connection between that score and any aspect of anticipated performance (other than the simple notion that people with scores below the cut score are likely to do less well on the job than people with scores higher than the cut score). Frequently, when there are many candidates for a few openings, a cut score will be chosen that will reduce the applicant population by a specific percentage (e.g., the test will "pass" the candidates who are in the top 25 percent of the score distribution). Naturally, if the applicant population turned out to be very talented, then the staffing strategy would yield many false negative errors because many who were rejected might have been good performers. On the other hand, the utility of the staffing strategy might be high because the expense of processing those additional candidates in later assessment steps might have been substantial.

Norm-referenced cut score Score based on some index of the test takers' scores rather than any notion of job performance.

When a test ends up in court and there are discussions of how cut scores were set, norm-referenced cut scores fare poorly compared with criterion-referenced scores (*Lanning* v. *SEPTA*, 1998, 1999, 2000a) because the **Uniform Guidelines on Employee Selection Procedures** (Uniform Guidelines, 1978), the official government administrative guidelines, instruct that cut scores should be set to be compatible with expected levels of job performance. Lacking this clear tie to expected job performance, norm-referenced cut scores are vulnerable to charges of unfairness.

Uniform Guidelines on Employee Selection Procedures Official government guidelines designed to assist employers, labor organizations, employment agencies, and licensing and certification boards to comply with federal requirements.

Utility

In the previous section on validity, we introduced two variables that interact with validity to determine the effectiveness of a staffing strategy. These variables were the number of people we would need to test to identify a sufficient number of high-quality candidates and the cost of hiring a candidate who turned out to be unsuccessful. Validity is one, but not the only, statistical indicator of a successful staffing strategy.

In general, a **utility analysis** addresses the cost/benefit ratio of one staffing strategy versus another. For that reason, the term "utility gain" is synonymous with utility. Consider the following possibilities:

Utility analysis Technique that assesses the economic return on investment of human resource interventions such as staffing and training.

1. The cost of testing a candidate for an entry-level job would be $10,000 per candidate.
2. There are 15 candidates for 10 jobs.
3. The cost of ineffective performance for the job in question is negligible.
4. The previous staffing strategy had identified large numbers of candidates who turned out to be successful on the job in question.

In each of those circumstances, we might be considering a demonstrably valid staffing strategy yet reject it. In the first scenario above, the cost of testing exceeds the outcome of testing.

In the second scenario, there is little selection to be done. As long as the 15 candidates meet minimal requirements, then elaborate testing is unnecessary. This is related to the selection ratio (SR) that we discussed earlier. In this example, the SR would be very high (10/15 = .67). In the case of the third scenario, there is little downside to a false positive error, so there is little to protect against. In the fourth scenario, unless the cost of testing for the new strategy is less than the cost for the old strategy, and/or unless the validity of the new strategy is considerably better than the validity of the old system, there is little advantage to changing systems. This last scenario introduces the concept of the **base rate**, or the percentage of the current workforce that is performing successfully. If performance is very high (i.e., the base rate of success is high), then any new system is likely to add very little to the productivity of the organization.

Base rate Percentage of the current workforce that is performing successfully.

The concept of economic utility, or utility gain, is a good one to keep in mind when evaluating the effectiveness of a staffing strategy. Often the calculations become so arcane that the point of the exercise is lost. In addition, some of the estimations of productivity gain and cost reduction can be staggering and result in arousing considerable skepticism on the part of managers about the procedures used to calculate them. Nevertheless, when evaluating a staffing strategy, the I-O psychologist needs to consider the anticipated costs and benefits to the organization.

Fairness

There are many different ways of defining a "fair" staffing strategy. Feelings of unfairness often lead to some negative action on the part of an employee or applicant. These actions include the initiation of lawsuits, filing of formal grievances with company representatives, and counterproductive behavior. As we saw above, there are also stakeholders beyond the applicant (e.g., line managers, co-workers, or union representatives) in whom feelings of unfairness might arise. When acted upon, these feelings of unfairness almost always cost the organization time and money and detract from the overall value of the staffing strategy. In Chapter 11, we will consider fairness from the perspectives of applicants and the law in much greater detail.

MODULE 6.2 SUMMARY

- Staffing outcomes can be evaluated in terms of various considerations, including validity, utility, and fairness.
- In making a staffing decision, false positive and false negative errors may be committed. Both of these types of errors can be costly for an organization. Alternatively, correct decisions in a staffing context are called true positives and true negatives.
- The concept of economic utility, or utility gain, is a good one to keep in mind when evaluating the effectiveness of a staffing strategy. I-O psychologists need to consider both the anticipated costs and benefits to the organization of the staffing strategy.
- Feelings of unfairness about a staffing strategy often lead to negative actions on the part of an employee or applicant. These actions include the initiation of lawsuits, filing of formal grievances with company representatives, and counterproductive behavior. Feelings of unfairness, when acted upon, almost always cost the organization time and money and detract from the overall value of the staffing strategy.

KEY TERMS

validity
criterion-related validity
selection ratio (SR)
false positive
false negative
true negative
true positive
cut score
criterion-referenced cut score
norm-referenced cut score
Uniform Guidelines on Employee Selection Procedures
utility analysis
base rate

MODULE 6.3

Practical Issues in Staffing

A Staffing Model

TABLE 6.2 **The Challenge of Matching Applicant Attributes and Job Demands**

APPLICANT ATTRIBUTES	*JOB DEMANDS*
Physical ability	Checking invoices
General mental ability	Processing customer orders
Problem solving	Reducing shipping costs
Oral communication	Attending staff meetings
Written communication	Developing price structure
Personality	Supervising assistants
Interests	Developing spreadsheets
Interpersonal skills	
Knowledge	

Modern jobs are complex. They consist of personal, interpersonal, and technical demands. In earlier chapters, we have reviewed the importance of task performance, OCB, CWB, and adaptive performance, which are the worker's attempts to meet those demands. To succeed in 21st-century jobs, individuals must have attributes like conscientiousness, general mental ability, communication skills, and specialized knowledge. Consider Table 6.2. On the left side of the table is a list of the attributes necessary to meet the job demands on the right side. High-quality staffing decisions are made based on a number of different pieces of information, not just one. This means that information about candidates must be combined in order to make a good staffing decision. Before we examine ways to combine information, we want to introduce two concepts. These concepts are ways that staffing strategies vary.

Comprehensive Selection Systems

Comprehensive staffing model Model that gathers enough high-quality information about candidates to predict the likelihood of their success on the varied demands of the job.

A staffing model needs to be comprehensive. A **comprehensive staffing model** should gather enough high-quality information about candidates to predict the likelihood of their success on the varied demands of the job. This does not mean we need to predict *every* aspect of job performance accurately, but it does mean that we should at least be trying to predict the important aspects of performance. Broadly, this might mean that we should be able to predict both technical performance and OCB performance. Within each of those domains, we should be trying to predict more specific important behaviors as well. These behaviors are usually identified through a job analysis.

Compensatory Selection Systems

Given that we have decided that we need to have multiple pieces of information in order to make good staffing decisions, we now need to decide how to combine the information.

© Richard Lord/PhotoEdit

An example of compensatory skills: A physically small woman uses social skills to succeed in the job of police officer.

Generally speaking, most knowledge, skills, abilities, and other characteristics (KSAOs) interact to yield successful performance. This means that we can average them together, much as we would average individual course grades to get an overall GPA. By averaging your grades, you see that one good grade can compensate for a poorer grade. Your A in industrial psychology will offset the B− you got in organic chemistry. The same is true with staffing decisions. A good score in an interview or work sample test might compensate for a slightly lower score on a cognitive ability test. If one attribute (e.g., communication skill) turns out to be much more important than another (e.g., stamina), there are ways to weight the individual scores to give one score greater influence on the final total score. We will review some of those methods below. The point here is that, in most instances, humans are able to compensate for a relative weakness in one attribute through a strength in another one, assuming both attributes are required by the job. Most exceptions to this rule relate to physical (e.g., muscular strength) or sensory (e.g., vision) abilities. A legally blind applicant for the position of bus driver would be an example of such an exception. This example reflects a noncompensatory or multiple hurdle model, which will be discussed shortly.

In our discussions to this point, we have alluded to multiple pieces of information about a candidate, each of which may help to predict eventual job performance. In the following section, we will discuss how such multiple pieces of information might be combined.

Combining Information

Statistical versus Clinical Decision Making

There are two basic ways to combine information in making a staffing decision: clinical and statistical. In **clinical decision making**, or the intuitive method, the decision maker examines multiple pieces of information, weights them in his or her head, and makes a decision about the relative value of one candidate over another—or simply makes a select/reject decision about an individual candidate. Clinical decisions tend to be unreliable and idiosyncratic (Meehl, 1954). In addition, there is some evidence that clinical decision making might lead to biased decisions. Powell and Butterfield (2002) analyzed the decisions made by federal managers regarding promotions to high-level government positions. Some of these decisions did seem to be related to race and gender, both of the applicants and of the decision makers. Surprisingly, African American male decision makers were more *negative* toward African American applicants than were their non–African American and female colleagues.

Clinical decision making Method uses judgment to combine information and to make a decision about the relative value of different candidates or applicants.

In **statistical decision making** (or, as it is often called, actuarial decision making), information is combined according to a mathematical formula. In Table 6.3, we present the test scores for five candidates for the job of customer service representative for a telephone

Statistical decision making Method combines information according to a mathematical formula.

TABLE 6.3 **Using Multiple Predictors to Choose a Candidate***

CANDIDATE	ORAL COMMUNICATION	WRITTEN COMMUNICATION	COGNITIVE ABILITY	EXPERIENCE	CONSCIENTIOUSNESS	TOTAL SCORE
A	5	7	8	4	5	29
B	9	8	6	5	9	37
C	9	9	4	3	6	31
D	6	6	9	7	5	33
E	5	5	7	6	7	30

*All attribute scores were transformed such that the highest possible score on any single attribute is 10 and the lowest score is 0.

company. As you can see, candidate B had the highest total score even though her score was not the highest on cognitive ability. In Chapter 3 we discussed online assessment and scoring provided by consulting companies. These systems typically employ statistical combinations of assessment data for making hiring recommendations.

The Hurdle System of Combining Scores

In the example from Table 6.3, we considered each of the five candidates, regardless of how low a score he or she obtained on any of the assessment dimensions. But sometimes a score on an attribute can be so low as to suggest there is little hope of compensation. For example, a firefighter must have a minimum amount of aerobic endurance or stamina to fight a fire using a self-contained breathing apparatus (Sothmann et al., 1990). If a candidate for a firefighter position lacks the necessary minimum of stamina, no amount of cognitive ability or motivation can make up for that. As a result, the fire department might want to set a minimum or cut score on the stamina measure and disqualify a candidate from further consideration unless he or she achieves that minimum. If the candidate does exceed that minimum, then all the scores, including the stamina score, can be combined in a **compensatory system**. In this case, the test of stamina would be called a "hurdle" because the candidate could not continue unless the hurdle was cleared. The **hurdle system** is a noncompensatory strategy because an individual knocked out of the assessment process has no opportunity to compensate at a later assessment stage for the low score that knocked him or her out of the process. In essence, the hurdle system establishes a series of cut scores rather than a single one.

Compensatory system Model in which a good score on one test can compensate for a lower score on another test.

Hurdle system Noncompensatory strategy in which an individual has no opportunity to compensate at a later assessment stage for a low score in an earlier stage of the assessment process.

Multiple hurdle system Strategy constructed from multiple hurdles so that candidates who do not exceed each of the minimum dimension scores are excluded from further consideration.

If there are several dimensions that warrant such minimum scores, a **multiple hurdle system** might be constructed that would exclude from further consideration all candidates who did not exceed each of the minimum dimension scores. No compensation from high scores on other dimensions would be permitted. It would also be possible to set relatively high hurdles on each dimension and only consider candidates who successfully passed every hurdle. If there were more successful candidates than positions, however, it would still be necessary to somehow order the candidates, possibly by a sum of their actual scores.

Often an employer will set up the hurdles so that they are sequential. For example, the first hurdle might be a test of cognitive ability. If the individual exceeds the minimum score, the next hurdle might be a work sample test. If the individual exceeds the cut score for the work sample test, he or she is scheduled for an interview. Generally, the more expensive and time consuming the step or hurdle, the later it is placed in the sequence. That way the costs are reduced because smaller and smaller numbers of candidates move on to the later hurdles. For individuals who pass all the hurdles, scores can then be combined in a compensatory system to allow for relative strengths and weaknesses to offset each other.

Hurdle systems are often employed when there are large numbers of candidates and few openings. This is a way to cut down on cost and processing time, as well as to make sure that only the best candidates are being considered. In years past, when the New York City Police Department tested for new police officers, it was not unusual to have 60,000 applications for 5,000 openings. The written cognitive ability test was used as a first hurdle to bring that number down to fewer than 20,000 for further consideration. In various years, the written examination was administered in Madison Square Garden (an arena that holds 20,000 spectators for a sports event) or in more than 300 different high schools in the five boroughs of New York City. To get a more personal feel for the size of this undertaking, imagine taking a test with 20,000 other individuals in any large football stadium where you have watched a game.

Although multiple hurdle systems can be effective in reducing large applicant pools to a more manageable size, there should be a rationale for how the hurdles are arranged and how the cut scores are chosen. A good rationale will not only help in defending the system if it is legally challenged but will also be more likely to lead to perceptions of fairness by those who fail to clear a hurdle.

Combining Scores by Regression (the Compensatory Approach)

In Chapter 2 we presented the concept of multiple correlation as a way of examining the association between a number of test scores (predictors) and a single performance score (criterion). A complementary analysis, known as **multiple regression analysis**, develops an equation for combining test scores into a composite based on the individual correlations of each test score dimension with the performance score and the intercorrelations between the test scores. The regression analysis uses a compensatory model where scoring higher on one predictor can make up for scoring low on another predictor.

Multiple regression analysis Method of analysis that results in an equation for combining test scores into a composite based on the correlations among the test scores and the correlations of each test score with the performance score.

Consider the three diagrams presented in Figure 6.4. In part (a), you can see that there is little overlap or correlation between the two predictor variables, but both are correlated with the criterion. In part (b), although there is some overlap or correlation between the two predictor variables, each still captures some unique variance in the criterion variable. In part (c), there is substantial overlap and correlation between the predictor variables; you predict about the same amount of criterion variance no matter which predictor you use. These figures graphically illustrate the concept of multiple regression. In the situation depicted in part (a), each variable contributes moderately to predicting a unique aspect of the criterion. As an example, predictor 1 might be a personality test and predictor 2 a test of cognitive

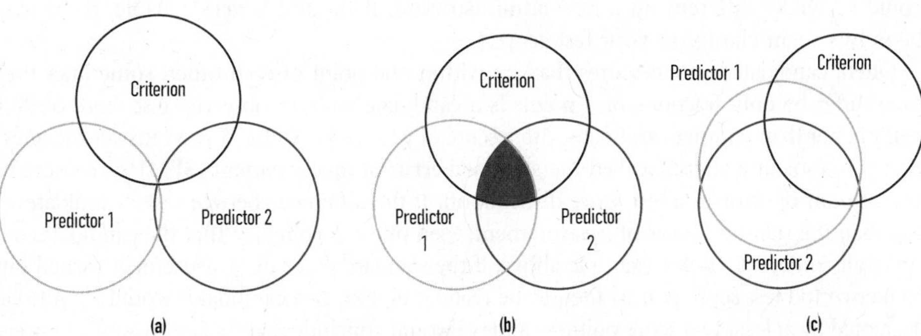

FIGURE 6.4 The Relationship between Predictor Overlap and Criterion Prediction

ability. If the job considered was a sales representative for a medical company, predictor 1 might predict customer interaction satisfaction and predictor 2 might predict troubleshooting the piece of equipment that is being sold. Thus, it makes intuitive sense that each predictor would add some unique value to the prediction situation.

In contrast, consider part (b). Assume that the two predictors are variations of a cognitive test with predictor 1 a test of general mental ability and predictor 2 a test of technical knowledge. Predictor 1 might correlate with the capacity of the sales representative to learn about new products, and predictor 2 might correlate with troubleshooting success. But as you can see, the two predictors themselves are correlated with each other, so we already cover some of the predictive value of predictor 2 when we use data on predictor 1. This means that we get some added or incremental value from the second predictor, but not as much as we would if the predictors were uncorrelated.

Finally, as in part (c), assume that predictor 1 is a test of general mental ability marketed by consulting company ABC, and predictor 2 is a test of general mental ability marketed by company XYZ. Both essentially measure the same attribute, and there is little value in using both tests because they are so highly correlated.

Combining scores using the multiple regression technique is a complex mathematical process that weights the individual predictor scores in terms of their individual correlations with the criterion and their correlation with each other. The multiple regression technique requires both predictor data and criterion data, so it can be used only if some measures of performance are available. This method takes advantage of the characteristics of the sample of people actually used for the calculation of the prediction equation (e.g., current employees). Consequently, while the equation may perfectly fit this sample, it may provide a less-than-perfect fit for another sample (e.g., the applicants). As a result, when using multiple regression techniques, it is common to try out the resulting equation on a second sample to see if it still fits well. This process is known as **cross-validation**. Cross-validation is usually carried out with an incumbent sample. The results are then used to weight the predictor scores of an applicant sample.

Cross-validation Process used with multiple regression techniques in which a regression equation developed on a first sample is tested on a second sample to determine if it still fits well; usually carried out with an incumbent sample, and the cross-validated results are used to weight the predictor scores of an applicant sample.

Score Banding

A method known as **score banding** is increasingly being used in selection procedures. Unlike the situation where there is a discrete pass–fail or cut score, score banding creates categories of scores, with the categories arranged from high to low. As a student, you are familiar with score bands as they relate to letter grades. For example, the "A band" might range from 100 to 90, the "B band" from 89 to 80, and so on. Psychometricians and statisticians universally accept that every observed score (whether a test score or a performance score) has a certain amount of error in it; the amount of error is associated with the reliability of the test. The less reliable the test, the greater the error. In practical terms, this means that when you take a test, the score you obtain might have been different had you taken the test yesterday or tomorrow or next week. If the test is very unreliable, then your score could be wildly different on a new administration. If the test is very reliable, there may be only a slight change in your test score.

Score banding Approach in which individuals with similar test scores are grouped together in a category or score band, and selection within the band is then made based on other considerations.

Standard error of measurement (SEM) Statistic that provides a measure of the amount of error in a test score distribution; function of the reliability of the test and the variability in test scores.

Often, candidates obtain scores that are within one point of each other; sometimes they even differ by only fractions of a point. Is a candidate with an observed test score of 92.1 *really* better than another candidate with a score of 92.0 or 91.6? One way to answer the question is to look at a statistic called the **standard error of measurement (SEM)**, a measure of the amount of error in a test score distribution. If the difference between two candidates is less than the standard error of measurement, then one can conclude that the candidates are not really different. In our example above, if the standard error of measurement turned out to be two full test score points, then to be really different, two candidates would need to be separated by at least two score points—and we would conclude that 92.1, 92.0, and 91.6 were not substantially different from one another. Because score banding has often been used as a way of reducing the gap between white and black test takers, the debate about its value takes on sociopolitical overtones. There are many different ways to implement a score banding system, but like utility analysis, they can become quite complex.

Subgroup Norming

As we saw in Chapter 3, African Americans typically score lower than whites on cognitive ability tests and, as a result, often get fewer job offers than their white counterparts. In any given instance, this difference may or may not eventually be found to represent unfair discrimination. If the test is job related, then the result may be unfortunate, but it is not necessarily illegal. Some organizations, however, have adopted affirmative action plans whereby they agree to work toward a goal of greater representation of minority workers in the organization. These goals can be difficult to meet if the employer uses a cognitive ability test and ranks candidates based on their scores. Many African Americans are likely to be out of selection range because of their relatively lower test scores on cognitive ability tests. One solution might be simply to develop separate score lists for whites and African Americans and select from each list using some predetermined proportion. The technical name for this is **subgroup norming** (i.e., developing separate appointment lists for white and African American candidates). As appealing as this may sound, it is illegal under the Civil Rights Act of 1991.

Subgroup norming Approach that develops separate lists for individuals within different demographic groups, then ranks the candidates within their respective demographic group.

Deselection

There are two typical situations in which an individual is selected to leave rather than join an organization. The first is termination for cause, and the second is a layoff or downsizing situation. In a **termination for cause**, the individual has usually been warned one or more times about a problem and either cannot or will not correct it. The individual is usually well aware that his or her behavior has fallen below some standard and that the consequences of failing to correct the deficiency may be termination. The worker may or may not believe the decision to terminate is fair, but it does not come unexpectedly.

Termination for cause Job loss that occurs when an individual is fired from an organization for a particular reason; the individual has usually been warned one or more times about a problem and either cannot or will not correct it.

Layoffs are different. They often come without warning or with a generic warning that the workforce is going to be reduced. But a given individual is often unaware that he or she may be the one losing a job. As a result, there is a great deal of emotion surrounding the layoff. Many employees become angry and feel that an implicit agreement has been violated. They agreed to do good work, and the employer agreed to maintain their employment. But in downsizing situations, it is often a matter of distinguishing between the outstanding employee and the adequate employee, not between the adequate and the inadequate employee. Thus, adequate employees often believe that they have been unfairly chosen for layoff because their work was "fine."

Layoff Job loss due to employer downsizing or reductions in force; often comes without warning or with a generic warning that the workforce will be reduced.

In layoff situations, the staffing strategy must be very clear (since the employer may very well end up defending it in a lawsuit). It is much better to have an actuarial or statistical decision rule than a clinical or intuitive one. The statistical rule makes it more difficult to argue that the decision was biased or inaccurate. It is also better to make the decision by combining multiple criteria rather than relying on a single dimension. Just as applicants seeking to be hired for a position sometimes question the fairness of both the procedure and the outcome, employees chosen for deselection may have feelings of perceived unfairness. But the feelings are likely to be more intense and lead to more dramatic actions. For that reason, the deselection staffing strategy needs to be coherent, consistent, and balanced. The best way to achieve consistency is to use a statistical approach for combining information rather than a clinical approach.

Number of Decisions to Be Made

Large Staffing Projects

Although we have been discussing staffing in relatively large and complex organizations in this chapter, the actual number of decisions that needed to be made might have been small (e.g., to choose three new hires from a group of 30 applicants). There are, however, occasions when the applicant pool is massive and the number of selection hires equally massive. Earlier we gave an example of the New York City Police Department. In 1984 the NYPD had 65,000 applicants for appointment to the police academy. The eventual eligibility list from which recruits would be chosen was to last for three years, at which time a new open application period would begin. During that three-year period, as many as four recruit classes would graduate each year. Each recruit class had 500 officers in it. Thus, the number of academy appointments would be 6,000 over the life of the list. Research by the NYPD had shown that it was necessary to test four candidates to get one who would pass all of the screens—psychological, background, and medical. Thus, to appoint 6,000 recruits, the NYPD would need to have at least 24,000 on the eligibility list. Making matters worse, it knew that as time passed, some individuals would lose interest and take other jobs; others would move out of state; and some would become ineligible because of felony convictions, emerging medical conditions, or other circumstances. Thus, the NYPD actually needed an initial list of about 30,000 candidates.

In staffing projects this large, concessions must be made. Clearly, labor-intensive assessment procedures such as interviews, assessment centers, or work samples are not feasible. In the NYPD staffing scheme, physical ability testing was also ruled out because there would be a rigorous fitness training program in the 16-week academy course. Although the only test used at the time was a cognitive ability test, the selection ratio of 50 percent (i.e., the NYPD would place one of every two applicants on the eligibility list) eliminated what would have been lower hiring rates for minority applicants had the selection ratio been smaller. In all likelihood, this would have led to a lawsuit. If the same project were undertaken today, there would be good reason to add personality tests and possibly a biodata form to the assessment battery. These three devices could be used in a hurdle or complete compensatory decision scheme.

The sheer size of the decision process requires an actuarial rather than a clinical decision strategy. But some compromise is necessary because it would be economically and logically difficult to get measures in any medium other than the paper-and-pencil one. This means that the post-hire training program would need to emphasize the KSAOs that were important parts of the job but were not initially assessed. Because the missing attribute information also represents potential inaccuracy in predictions, and the obtained paper-and-pencil scores might not fairly represent the complete set of skills brought to the job by the candidate, it might be wise to use a banding approach to appointment as well. If banding is used, it is important to make sure that race or gender is not used as a method for selecting from within a band. Although there may be some special circumstances in which race or gender might be considered a relevant factor in hiring, the use of these variables for selecting from within a band might be interpreted as subgroup norming (Sackett & Wilk, 1994).

In large-scale projects, utility can be a big issue. The cost of testing large numbers of candidates can be high. But if the validity of the proposed procedure is higher than the validity of the current procedure, these increased costs will be offset by the productivity gains realized from this increased validity. And this assumes that there even *is* a current procedure. Consider the task of hiring federal Transportation Security Administration (TSA) screeners in one year (Kolmstetter, 2003). TSA screeners represent a fascinating case of a large-scale staffing project completed over a short period of time. The only effort in U.S. history that came close to it was the testing of recruits for the armed forces in the First World War, which we reviewed in the history section of Chapter 1. In the case of the TSA screeners, during the period from February to December 2002, 1.7 million applicants were assessed for 55,000 positions. Although the two testing phases seem to have gone well (phase I, various abilities and personality characteristics; phase II, interview, physical abilities test, and medical evaluation), the third phase, including background checks, may not have gone so well. An internal investigation by the Department of Homeland Security uncovered flaws in the background check system that resulted in a substantial number of screeners being hired in spite of criminal histories. Over 1,900 were fired as a result (Shenon, 2004). It is not surprising that the weakest link in the assessment was the background check. These checks are very time consuming and expensive. It appears that although there was enough time to test 1.7 million applicants, there was not sufficient time to complete adequate background checks. This is the challenge of large-scale staffing projects—to do everything right within the time and budget available. It is a daunting challenge when the numbers get as large as they were for the TSA screener hiring process.

© J A Giordano/CORBIS SABA/©Corbis

Large staffing projects entail careful planning to make good selection decisions from a large pool of applicants.

In addition to utility, fairness is also a critical issue. If a device is used to make decisions that will cut down on the size of the applicant pool, but this device has adverse impact against protected subgroups, then the likelihood of a lawsuit increases, which also increases the eventual cost of the strategy and reduces utility. Even if the device is eventually shown to have high validity, the economic benefit of using the test will have been reduced by the cost of defending it.

In summary, large-scale projects such as hiring NYPD officers or TSA screeners would seem to suggest the need for standard, well-established, and feasible selection strategies. A good core strategy in these examples would be cognitive ability and personality testing. In addition, the size of the applicant pool and the availability of SMEs and incumbents to actually complete assessment devices suggest a place for scored biodata questionnaires.

Small Staffing Projects

Suppose that in contrast to the large-scale staffing challenges we have been discussing, we want to help our local coffeehouse choose a new shift manager. Instead of 60,000 applicants, there are five. Would the decision process be different? Yes and no. Yes, the decision maker would have the luxury of using a wider range of assessment tools. For example, the candidates might be asked to take part in a structured interview that would provide information about knowledge (e.g., of retail sales), skills (e.g., communication), abilities (e.g., personnel problem solving), and personality (e.g., conscientiousness and integrity). In addition, each candidate might be asked to complete a personality inventory and a test of math and reading skills.

The actual assessment devices and procedures, then, might be different when the project is a small one. But the decision-making process might not change. Even with a small number of candidates and decisions, it would still be wise to use an actuarial rather than clinical decision scheme. Adverse impact would be much less of an issue, though perceptions of psychological fairness would be just as important. Sackett and Arvey (1993) considered many of the issues related to selection in small settings and made the following recommendations:

- Develop a job-relatedness justification based on judgment and rationality rather than on numbers and data analysis.
- Consider the utility gain of the proposed staffing strategy; because of the small number of applicants and selections, there may be only a slight payoff in using expensive assessment programs.
- Make sure that every candidate is exposed to the same assessment procedures; because the number of candidates is small, it might be tempting to "wing it," but this would expose the organization to charges of adverse treatment despite the difficulty of demonstrating adverse impact.

Sackett and Arvey (1993) observed that many managers feel that if they can't do it by the book, they shouldn't do it at all. But the alternative to doing it by the (staffing) book is not random—the alternative is simply choosing a selection and decision-making strategy that is rational, job related, and feasible, given the constraints of the situation. Sackett and Arvey concluded: "We believe that I-O psychology can contribute to better selection in any setting, regardless of the size" (p. 445). We agree.

21st-Century Staffing

As we have pointed out in earlier chapters, work in the 21st century is radically different from earlier work. This difference is only now beginning to affect staffing practices. Cascio and Aguinis (2008) identify Internet technologies as the drivers of the need for redesigned staffing systems:

> The Net gives everyone in the organization, at any level, and in every functional area, the ability to access a mind-boggling array of information—instantaneously from anywhere. Instead of seeping out over months and years, ideas can be zapped around the globe in a heartbeat. By 2009, one quarter of the world's workforce, or 850 million people, will use remote access and mobile technology, to work on the go or at home, according to research firm IDC (Schweyer, 2006). That means that the 21st-century organization must adapt itself to management via the web. It must be predicated on constant change, not stability; organized around networks, not rigid hierarchies, built on shifting partnerships and alliances, not self-sufficiency; and constructed on technological advantages, not bricks and mortar. (Cascio, W. F., & Aguinis, H. (2008). Staffing 21st-century organizations. In J. P. Walsh & A. P. Brief (Eds.), *Academy of Management Annals* Vol. 2, 134-135. Reprinted by permission of the publisher, Taylor & Francis Ltd., http://www.tandf.co.uk/journals and http://www.informaworld.com. Permission conveyed through Copyright Clearance Center, Inc.)

Cascio and Aguinis argue for a core set of elements in the 21st-century staffing model, including adaptability (as we described it in Chapter 4), a global mindset (sensitivity to multiple cultures), cultural agility (a curiosity about how other people live and work), and relationship management ("knowing who" in addition to "knowing how"). Cascio and Aguinis think that we have gone as far as we can go in predicting work success using tests of intelligence and that the changing nature of work makes it imperative to move beyond "g." In particular, they argue that our now-outdated view of job performance is tied to a model of individual worker contribution rather than a consideration of the larger context of work. This larger context includes strategic, cultural, and situational elements. You will recall from Chapters 1 and 2 that we introduced the concept of multilevel analysis. Cascio and Aguinis are making the same point: One can better understand the nature of job performance by considering it in this broader context rather than taking a narrow view of a worker at a desk or machine. They use the term "*in situ* performance" to describe this new view. They suggest that the 21st-century staffing model should include the following departures from earlier staffing approaches:

1. Assessment of predictors over a longer period of time—weeks or months—rather than a single episode of testing such as a test of general mental ability or personality
2. Assessment of predictors in a more realistic environment (such as an assessment center) rather than in a decontextualized testing situation
3. Greater use of accumulated candidate performance information in predicting future success rather than tests and other traditional assessment procedures

As examples of the tools of the new staffing model, they suggest things such as internships, greater use of a contingent workforce (contract workers, part-time workers, temporary workers) as a way of gathering information about possible full-time employees, and assessment using a virtual reality platform that permits a more realistic presentation of the work environment.

As you can see, this new staffing model may not be particularly efficient or inexpensive, and it may be more reasonable to use for managerial staffing than for lower-level employees. Nevertheless, Cascio and Aguinis argue that fast and cheap has taken us as far as it can—we need a new model of staffing for gaining incremental value. Time will tell if the HR community adopts this new model, but we agree that it is more compatible with 21st-century work than the more traditional models.

MODULE 6.3 SUMMARY

- High-quality staffing decisions are based on combining a number of different pieces of information about candidates. Staffing strategies vary in their comprehensiveness and in whether they are compensatory or noncompensatory.
- There are two basic ways to combine information in making a staffing decision: clinical and statistical. Clinical decisions tend to be more variable and reflect the strategies of the decision maker, whereas statistical decisions tend to be more reliable and consistent across decision makers.
- Score banding is a staffing strategy that has been used to identify successful candidates. However, banding is controversial, and in organizations where tension exists between demographic subgroups, staffing strategies such as banding may exacerbate that tension.
- Prior to 1991, one way of dealing with racial subgroup differences on selection tests was to develop separate lists for these subgroups and then to rank the candidates within their respective demographic group. However, the 1991 Civil Rights Act made race norming illegal. Notably, one form of special-group norming for which there is no explicit prohibition is age norming.
- Two typical situations in which an individual is selected to leave rather than join an organization are termination for cause and layoffs. In layoff situations, the staffing strategy must be very

clear because the employer may end up defending it in a lawsuit.

- Large-scale staffing projects will often require standard and well-established selection strategies. In small staffing projects, managers are encouraged to choose a selection and decision-making strategy that is rational, job related, and feasible, given the constraints of the situation.
- Newer research suggests that selection in the 21st century should center less on the individual and more on work performance in context.

KEY TERMS

comprehensive staffing model
clinical decision making
statistical decision making
compensatory system
hurdle system
multiple hurdle system
multiple regression analysis
cross-validation
score banding
standard error of measurement (SEM)
subgroup norming
termination for cause
layoff

MODULE 6.4

Legal Issues in Staffing Decisions

Charges of Employment Discrimination

Although discussions of employment litigation often revolve around a practice (e.g., performance appraisal) or an assessment device (e.g., a test or an interview), employment discrimination charges result not from practices or devices but from decisions about whom to hire, whom to promote, or whom to lay off. Although it is common to think of applicants who were denied a job as bringing lawsuits, it is seven times more likely that a company will be sued by an employee or a former employee than by an applicant (Sharf & Jones, 2000).

There are many bases for bringing charges against an employer, including not only employment discrimination but also the Equal Pay Act, the Fourteenth Amendment of the Constitution promising "due process," or the Family and Medical Leave Act of 1993. Cases can be filed in state as well as federal courts. A fuller explanation of all relevant federal laws and a description of important or defining cases can be found in Landy (2005a), which covers all aspects of employment discrimination litigation. For our discussion, however, we will concentrate on employment discrimination cases filed in federal courts, usually by groups of individuals, claiming violations of Title VII of the Civil Rights Act of 1964, the Americans with Disabilities Act, or the Age Discrimination in Employment Act. These are the types of cases in which I-O psychologists are most commonly involved as **expert witnesses.**

Expert witness Witness in a lawsuit who is permitted to voice opinions about organizational practices.

Regardless of who sues a company, the consequences can be substantial. Consider the settlements of employment discrimination suits brought by the Equal Employment Opportunity Commission (EEOC) in the past 20 or 25 years (Sharf & Jones, 2000). The *lowest* settlement in a discrimination case was in an age discrimination suit brought against Maytag—that settlement was $16 million and covered hundreds of individual plaintiffs. These figures only cover suits in which the EEOC was involved. Most suits are filed by single individuals without any involvement of the EEOC. The largest was a race discrimination case brought against Texaco, a case that settled for almost $180 million, covering several thousand individual plaintiffs. If we look at jury verdicts, we see the same expensive picture. The average winning plaintiff in a gender discrimination case was awarded $264,000; in race cases, plaintiffs were awarded, on average, $242,000 each. In age cases the average award jumped to $300,000 (Sharf & Jones, 2000). Since lawyers for plaintiffs typically receive anywhere from 25 to 40 percent of the award, it is easy to see why employment discrimination cases are brought against employers. For a large corporation, the costs of defending

The employee took the letter to a local lawyer, who proceeded with the case. In the meantime, the EEOC regional office also entered the suit on behalf of not only the single African American employee but also other African American employees who worked in other MCA offices and had filed similar individual charges. After further information requests and analyses, the EEOC concluded that evidence of adverse impact against African Americans in hiring had occurred in 16 of the 37 offices of MCA.

The EEOC had initiated mediation discussions between the plaintiffs and the company, but not much progress had been made. Then MCA was informed by a large employment law firm that it would ask the court to certify a class of African American applicants and employees who would charge the company with systematically discriminating against African Americans in virtually all aspects of employment—recruiting, hiring, pay, training, performance evaluation, promotions, and discipline. The class was expected to include not only the 43 black employees but also 26 black former employees and 322 black applicants for positions with the company over the past three years. Company lawyers estimated that if the company lost at trial, the award might be in excess of $10 million. Since the plaintiffs were now represented by an experienced and effective private law firm, the EEOC dropped out of the suit for budgetary reasons. The private law firm filed suit in federal district court and asked for the certification of a class.

This was the first time that Mortgage Company of America had faced such a threat. As a result, the in-house company lawyer suggested that they retain an outside law firm to handle the case. The outside law firm recommended that the I-O psychologist who had developed the screening system be retained as an expert in the case. She was contacted and agreed to serve in that role.

Over the course of **discovery**, the company produced papers that filled approximately 17 cardboard boxes. These included personnel records, applicant flow data, details of company policy, and various administrative memos. In addition, the CEO, vice presidents of human resources and operations, two regional managers, and six office managers were deposed by lawyers for the plaintiffs. Lawyers for the company deposed 16 plaintiffs. In a hearing following this phase of discovery, the judge considered **class certification** and ultimately granted the designation of two classes: one class that included applicants and a second class that included past and present employees. Class certification is a process that allows the different plaintiffs to present a common complaint. The judge also set a date for trial and a schedule for additional discovery, including reports from and sworn testimony (called **depositions**) of expert witnesses. The plaintiffs also retained a statistician and an I-O psychologist, as well as an economist who would testify about monetary issues such as lost wages.

Discovery Process in which lawyers are given access to potential witnesses who will be called by the other side, as well as any documents relevant to the complaints.

Class certification Judge's decision based on several criteria that determine whether individual plaintiffs can file together under a class action suit.

Deposition Interview under oath taken by an opposing attorney in a lawsuit.

Although the I-O psychologist had been involved in the development of the screening system, she had not been consulted on issues related to compensation, training, performance evaluation, discipline, or promotion. She discovered that the policies regarding these practices had not yet been fully established and that each office had developed its own methods for making these decisions. In contrast, the screening system she had developed was being used consistently in each office, and hiring decisions were ultimately made by the vice president of HR using an equation she had developed when creating the screening system.

The plaintiffs' expert reports were filed, and 30 days later the defendant's expert replied with a rebuttal report. The I-O psychologist for the plaintiffs had made a number of criticisms of the hiring policies of the defendant company. His major points were that there had been no formal job analysis, that the structured interview was subjective and influenced by stereotypes, that the interviewers were not adequately trained, that the work sample was inappropriately influenced by speed factors, and that no criterion-related validity study had been performed to justify the use of the personality test.

In the rebuttal report submitted in response to these criticisms, the company I-O psychologist answered that even though she had not administered and scored questionnaires, a job analysis had been done. She further contended that since she had developed the interview questions along with the scoring scheme for answers to those questions, the interview was not subjective. She pointed out that speed *was* a factor in the job and that brokers needed to get preliminary information to a potential client about the availability of loans within hours. Finally, she identified several meta-analyses that concluded that conscientiousness and agreeableness were valuable predictors in sales positions, and the broker job was a type of sales position. In the midst of the expert discovery process, the original African American employee was fired for refusing to accept an assignment, and the lawsuit was amended to include charges of retaliation for having filed the original suit.

As the trial date approached, the judge required the company to have **settlement discussions** with the plaintiffs. Settlement discussions are attempts to reach a mutually acceptable resolution rather than have a trial. The company offered to settle the case for $1 million without any admission of wrongdoing. The plaintiffs' lawyers countered with a request for $13 million and agreements to replace the current hiring system and to provide opportunities for training and development for current African American employees. The company I-O psychologist argued strongly that the current hiring system was defensible and effective. It had identified successful brokers, was fast and efficient, and had never been the source of complaints prior to this recent charge.

Settlement discussions Discussions conducted by the parties in a lawsuit in an attempt to reach a mutually satisfying resolution of the complaint before proceeding with all of the other steps that lead to a trial.

Three days before trial, the company lawyers and the plaintiffs' lawyers reached a settlement agreement. The plaintiff class would be given a total of $4 million, of which $1.3 million would go to the plaintiffs' law firm. In addition, the HR department would modify the screening program as follows:

- The work sample test time limit would be increased from 30 minutes to one hour.
- A criterion-related validity study of the personality test would be initiated (although the current test and cut scores would continue to be used until that study had been completed).
- Interviewers would be brought to corporate HR for training.
- The I-O psychologist for the plaintiffs would collaborate with the I-O psychologist for the company in developing the validity study and the interviewer training.
- The company would establish a budget of $100,000 for this work and would pay the fees of the plaintiffs' psychologist as well as the fees of their own expert from this fund.

The agreement was presented to the judge, who approved it without comment. The litigation process from initial complaint to approved settlement lasted 27 months. The cost to the company for outside counsel, expert witnesses, and administrative expenses was approximately $1.7 million. This figure did not include the salaries of company staff members who worked in various phases of the defense. Although the company had been considering going public at the time the initial complaint was filed with the EEOC, it postponed the public offering until after the settlement was approved. The initial public offering was well received by the investment community, and the company continues to grow. The cost of the settlement as well as the direct costs for defense (excluding salary costs) were paid by an insurance policy held by the company. The company recognized its vulnerability in areas related to promotional systems, compensation, training, and discipline. With the help of the I-O expert, the company recruited and hired a full-time I-O psychologist to assist in the development of the additional HR systems stipulated in the settlement agreement.

MODULE 6.4 SUMMARY

- Although discussions of employment litigation often revolve around a practice (e.g., performance appraisal) or an assessment device (e.g., a test or an interview), employment discrimination charges result not from practices or devices but from decisions about whom to hire, promote, or lay off.
- I-O psychologists commonly serve as expert witnesses in employment discrimination cases filed in federal courts. These cases are most often filed by groups of individuals claiming violations of Title VII of the Civil Rights Act of 1964, the Americans with Disabilities Act, or the Age Discrimination in Employment Act.
- The law and the courts recognize two different theories of discrimination. The adverse treatment theory charges an employer with intentional discrimination. The adverse impact theory acknowledges that the employer may not have *intended* to discriminate against a plaintiff, but a practice implemented by the employer had the *effect* of disadvantaging the group to which the plaintiff belongs.
- In an adverse impact case, the burden is on the plaintiff to show that (1) he or she belongs to a protected group and (2) members of the protected group were statistically disadvantaged compared to majority employees or applicants. The Uniform Guidelines suggest using an 80 percent, or 4/5ths, rule to demonstrate evidence of adverse impact.

KEY TERMS

expert witness
adverse (or disparate) treatment
adverse impact
80 percent or 4/5ths rule
adverse impact ratio
discovery
class certification
deposition
settlement discussions

7 Training and Development

MODULE 7.1

Foundations of Training and Learning

Jackie slid into the driver's seat and checked the map one more time before backing out of the garage. It was Monday, and for the duration of the week she would be commuting not to her office but to an off-site center where she and other new managers from various departments and locations in her company would receive training to develop their supervisory skills. As she drove, Jackie realized that she was more nervous than she had anticipated. She didn't know what to expect from the training program, in terms of either what would be required of her or what she would be learning. She also wondered how her fellow engineers, who had become her subordinates when she was promoted, would react when she returned to work. Would they be on the lookout for her to "act like a manager" instead of like a colleague? She wasn't even sure how supportive her own boss was of this training program or of any changes in her supervisory style that might result from it. As we will describe in this chapter, Jackie's apprehension about the purpose and effects of the training program is legitimate. I-O psychologists have done a great deal of research on training relevant to Jackie's concerns and questions. Research on training has also provided guidelines for training practitioners about the best ways to identify training needs, design and implement training programs, and evaluate the effectiveness of training.

Training is big business, particularly in the United States, Japan, and western Europe. A survey by researchers at the American Society for Training and Development (2010) indicated that training expenditures as a percentage of payroll averaged about 3 percent in European companies, 2 percent in U.S. organizations, and 1 percent in Japanese companies. Organizations in the United States spend approximately $126 billion annually on training and development (ASTD, 2010). Evidence indicates that training is effective and that these training expenditures are paying off in terms of higher net sales and gross profitability per employee (Arthur, Bennett, Edens, & Bell, 2003). Training can be beneficial for the organization and for employees in terms of increasing their value to their organization as well as their employability in the broader marketplace. Many organizations are using training and development as a way to attract and retain their most successful employees. In addition, web-based and computer-based training are increasingly being used to expand employees' access to training (Welsh, Wanberg, Brown, & Simmering, 2003).

Given how expensive and important training is, it is important for I-O psychologists to use a systematic approach to training that includes an assessment of training needs, incorporation of principles of learning, consideration of transfer of the training, and evaluation of training programs. In this chapter, we will discuss this systematic approach, which has resulted in great strides in our understanding of training and development.

In an assessment of training research over the preceding decade, Salas and Cannon-Bowers (2001) expressed optimism about the fact that there are more theories, models, empirical studies, and meta-analyses on training than ever before. They concluded that "there has been nothing less than an explosion in training-related research in the past 10 years" (p. 472). Two other reviews offer a similarly optimistic view of the state of training research and practice (Aguinis & Kraiger, 2009; Kraiger & Ford, 2006). Although the science of training has progressed greatly in recent years, many challenges lie ahead. We will describe these encouraging advances as well as the hurdles facing today's training researchers and practitioners.

In Chapter 3 we discussed individual differences and how they relate to a variety of work outcomes. For selection purposes, I-O psychologists assume that individual difference characteristics on which hiring decisions are based are relatively stable over time. This assumption is supported by research evidence for certain individual difference characteristics (e.g., general mental ability, personality) that are used in selection (Costa & McCrae, 1997; Murphy & Davidshofer, 2005). In contrast, researchers and practitioners in the training field assume that knowledge and skills can be changed and enhanced. For example, effective training programs can enhance knowledge about sexual harassment and safety procedures. Training can also develop employees' interpersonal and computer skills, which in turn can be applied back on the job. Skills and knowledge, then, are generally more "trainable" than abilities or personality characteristics. In sum, although training cannot change or enhance all individual difference characteristics, it can be used in combination with selection and other human resource systems to assemble a strong workforce.

Training, Learning, and Performance

Training is the systematic acquisition of skills, concepts, or attitudes that result in improved performance in another environment (Goldstein & Ford, 2002). The basic foundation for training programs is **learning**, a relatively permanent change in behavior and human capabilities that is produced by experience and practice. Learning outcomes can be organized into three broad categories: cognitive, skill-based, and affective outcomes (Kraiger, Ford, & Salas, 1993). An example of a **cognitive outcome** is declarative knowledge: knowledge of rules, facts, and principles. In training programs, for example, police officers acquire declarative knowledge about laws and court procedures. Declarative knowledge is an important component of Campbell, McCloy, Oppler, and Sager's (1993) theory of performance, which we discussed in Chapter 4. **Skill-based outcomes**, which are similar to procedural knowledge as defined by Campbell and colleagues, concern the development of motor or technical skills. For example, motor skills might involve the coordination of physical movements such as using a specialized tool or flying a certain aircraft, whereas technical skills might include understanding a certain software program or exhibiting effective customer relations behaviors. **Affective outcomes** include attitudes or beliefs that predispose a person to behave in a certain way. Attitudes may be developed or changed through training programs, which can be powerful sources of socialization (discussed further in Chapter 14) for new and existing employees (Klein & Weaver, 2000). Examples of attitudes that can be acquired or modified through training are organizational commitment and appreciation of diversity.

It is important to note that training, learning, and performance are distinct concepts. First, training is a planned experience intended to lead to learning, which may occur through informal experiences as well. How much is learned in training, however, is influenced by several factors (characteristics of trainees and training design) that we will describe in greater

Training Systematic acquisition of skills, concepts, or attitudes that result in improved performance in another environment.

Learning A relatively permanent change in behavior and human capabilities produced by experience and practice.

Cognitive outcome Type of learning outcome that includes declarative knowledge, or knowledge of rules, facts, and principles.

Skill-based outcome Type of learning outcome that concerns the development of motor or technical skills.

Affective outcome Type of learning outcome that includes attitudes or beliefs that predispose a person to behave in a certain way.

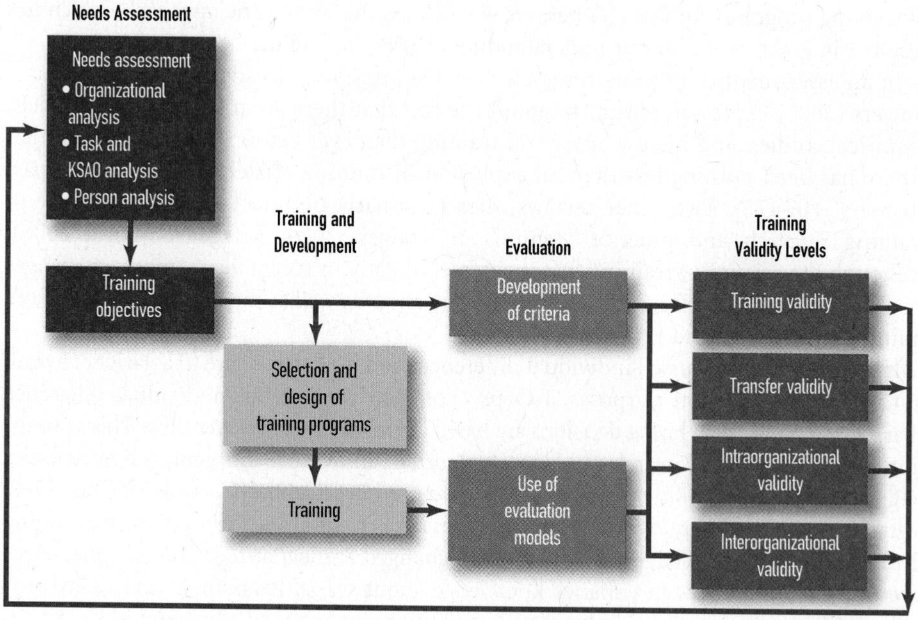

FIGURE 7.1 Goldstein and Ford's Training Model

SOURCE: Adapted from Goldstein, I. L. (1989). Critical training issues: Past, present, and future. In Irwin L. Goldstein and associates (Eds.), *Training and development in organizations* (pp. 1-21). San Francisco: Jossey-Bass. Reprinted in Goldstein, I. L., & Ford, J. K. (2002). *Training in organizations: Needs assessment, development, and evaluation* (4th ed.). Belmont, CA: Wadsworth. Used by permission of John Wiley & Sons, Inc.

Performance Actions or behaviors relevant to the organization's goals; measured in terms of each individual's proficiency.

detail below. Second, learning is expected to improve performance on the job. As we discussed in Chapter 4, **performance** is something that people actually do and, in many cases, performance can be directly observed. In contrast, learning cannot be observed, so we often assume that learning has taken place when we observe performance, such as in a test following a class or a training session. Thus, learning often results in better performance, both in training and back on the job. However, this desirable situation is not necessarily the case, particularly if the work environment is not supportive of employees demonstrating newly learned knowledge and skills. Although all learning does not result in improved performance, careful attention to training design, principles of learning, and work environment characteristics can greatly increase its likelihood of doing so. The point is that training increases the probability of learning, and learning increases the probability of better job performance (Landy, 1989). By understanding the factors that affect learning, training researchers and practitioners can enhance the performance of individuals, teams, and organizations.

Organizations offer many types of training programs, including—among many others—new employee orientation, team training, sexual harassment awareness, and the development of cross-cultural, management, and leadership skills. Although the specific requirements of these training programs vary greatly, training researchers and practitioners benefit from using a consistent framework or model when designing, implementing, and evaluating all training programs. In this chapter we follow Goldstein and Ford's (2002) training model, which is shown in Figure 7.1. This model begins with needs assessment and then moves to training and development, followed by training evaluation, and finally to a consideration of training validity levels. Following that, we consider special issues in training and development, including leadership and management development, sexual harassment awareness training, and cross-cultural training.

Training Needs Analysis

Before training design issues are considered, a careful needs analysis is required to develop a systematic understanding of where training is needed, what needs to be taught or trained,

TABLE 7.1 **Training Needs Analysis**

A. Organizational analysis	Examines company-wide goals and problems to determine where training is needed
B. Task analysis	Examines tasks performed and KSAOs required to determine what employees must do to perform successfully
C. Person analysis	Examines knowledge, skills, and current performance to determine who needs training

and who will be trained (Goldstein & Ford, 2002). **Training needs analysis** (Table 7.1) typically involves a three-step process that includes organizational, task, and person analysis (Dierdorff & Surface, 2008).

Training needs analysis A three-step process of organizational, task, and person analysis; required to develop a systematic understanding of where training is needed, what needs to be taught or trained, and who will be trained.

Organizational analysis examines organizational goals, available resources, and the organizational environment to determine where training should be directed. This analysis identifies the training needs of different departments or subunits. Organizational analysis also involves systematically assessing manager, peer, and technological support for the transfer of training, a topic that is discussed in more detail later in the chapter. Similarly, organizational analysis takes into account the climate of the organization and its subunits. For example, if a climate for safety is emphasized throughout the organization or in particular parts of the organization (e.g., production), then training needs will likely reflect this emphasis (Zohar, 2002a). Organizational analysis also can help ensure that training follows the wider human resources strategy, which in turn needs to follow the overall business strategy. Otherwise, training managers may design a training program that would be appropriate only for a different organization.

Organizational analysis Component of training needs analysis that examines organizational goals, available resources, and the organizational environment; helps to determine where training should be directed.

Research also indicates that several organizational characteristics can affect how much impact training has back on the job. For example, supervisor and peer support for training helps to motivate employees entering training and increases the likelihood that they will transfer newly acquired knowledge, skills, abilities, and other characteristics (KSAOs) to the job (Colquitt, LePine, & Noe, 2000). Consider an employee who is welcomed back after a training program by a manager who says, "Now that you've got that out of your system, I hope you're ready to get back to work"; the employee is not likely to be highly motivated to apply the newly learned skills back on the job. Thus, it is critical to conduct an organizational analysis before developing a training program so that appropriate support for training exists.

Task analysis examines what employees must do to perform the job properly. As we discussed in Chapter 4, a job analysis identifies and describes the tasks performed by employees and the KSAOs needed for successful job performance. If available, the results of a job analysis are very helpful in determining training needs. Task analysis, which examines what the content of training should be, can consist of (1) developing task statements, (2) determining homogeneous task clusters (which are more usable and manageable than individual task statements), and (3) identifying KSAOs required for the job. The links between task clusters and KSAOs can be used to develop training programs that are directed toward enhancing critical KSAOs. Table 7.2 shows task clusters derived from a task analysis performed on the job of a train operator. The results of the task analysis would be used to design training to ensure that train operators would, for example, know the steps they must take in an emergency.

Task analysis Component of training needs analysis that examines what employees must do to perform the job properly.

Task analysis can also include an assessment of competencies, which are broader than knowledge, skills, or abilities. As we discussed in Chapter 4, **competencies** are "sets of behaviors that are instrumental in the delivery of desired results or outcomes" (Kurz & Bartram, 2002). Organizations are increasingly trying to identify "core competencies" that are required for all jobs (Shippmann et al., 2000), and training needs analysis is an important part of the

Competencies Sets of behaviors, usually learned through experience, that are instrumental in the accomplishment of desired organizational results or outcomes.

TABLE 7.2 Task Clusters for Train Operators

1.	Preoperation responsibilities	Preparing for operating the train for a given shift. This includes reporting for duty in a state of preparedness with proper equipment and getting information from the bulletin board and/or dispatcher.
2.	Preoperation equipment inspection	Checking the train for defects and safety, including checking brake system, gauges, and track under the train.
3.	Train operations	The actual operation of the train in a safe and timely manner. This includes controlling the train in the yard or on the road; consideration of conditions such as weather, curves, and grades; speed restrictions; and interpretation of warnings/signals.
4.	Maintaining schedule	Activities associated with timely operations, including adhering to the timetable and communicating with personnel to prevent disruption of service.
5.	Emergency situation activities	Identifying and reacting to emergency situations, keeping customers safe, communicating with the control center, and troubleshooting mechanical difficulties.

process of identifying and developing such competencies. For example, if a training needs analysis indicates that innovation is important to the success of a particular company, a training program may be designed to help employees become more innovative and creative. Given the increased emphasis on competencies in organizations, competency training might be included as a supplement to existing training on more specific technical skills (Kraiger, 2003).

Person analysis Component of training needs analysis that identifies which individuals in an organization should receive training and what kind of instruction they need.

Person analysis identifies which individuals in an organization should receive training and what kind of instruction they need. Employee needs can be assessed using a variety of methods that identify weaknesses that training and development can address. Many of the issues we discussed in Chapter 3 on assessment and Chapter 5 on performance evaluation are relevant when training specialists are conducting a person analysis. For example, KSAOs can be assessed through the performance evaluation system or through a 360-degree feedback system that provides input for training and development activities. Objective data on accidents and job performance are often examined as part of the needs analysis, and written tests are used to assess employees' current job knowledge. Organizations are increasingly using person analysis to determine how prepared employees are for a particular training program. Specifically, assessments of trainee personality, ability, and experience are increasingly being used as part of the needs assessment process. We will further discuss trainee characteristics below.

To summarize, assessing training needs is a three-part process that includes: (1) organizational analysis, which identifies company-wide goals and problems; (2) task analysis, which identifies the tasks to be performed, how work should be done, and the KSAOs needed to complete those tasks; and (3) person analysis, which focuses on identifying individuals who need training. Careful needs assessment sets the stage for specifying the objectives of the training program. Training objectives are needed to design the training program, to use as goals to motivate trainees to learn, and to evaluate the effectiveness of the training program. The needs analysis makes it possible to identify the training program's objectives, which are important for several reasons. First, they represent information for both the trainer and the trainee about what is to be learned. Second, training objectives help to motivate trainees by providing clear goals for them. Third, training objectives are necessary to evaluate a training program properly. We will discuss training evaluation in more detail later in the chapter.

The Learning Process in Training

After training needs have been determined and used to develop training objectives, training design begins with an understanding of how learning occurs. As shown in Figure 7.2, several trainee characteristics (e.g., readiness to learn, motivation to learn) and training design characteristics (e.g., principles of learning, objectives) affect the learning process and learning outcomes.

Trainee Characteristics

Trainee readiness Refers to whether employees have the personal characteristics necessary to acquire knowledge from a training program and apply it to the job.

Trainee readiness refers to whether employees have the personal characteristics necessary to acquire knowledge from a training program and apply it to the job (Noe, 2010). These characteristics include general mental ability, goal orientation, and experience level. Several studies involving a variety of occupations (e.g., pilots, technicians, enlisted army and air force recruits, and computer programmers) indicate that general mental ability ("g") is predictive of performance in training (Brown, Le, & Schmidt, 2006; Ree & Carretta, 2002). In a meta-analysis spanning 85 years, Schmidt and Hunter (1998) found that "g" had a validity of +.56 in predicting training outcomes. A recent meta-analysis of 90 German studies indicated that the validity of "g" in predicting training performance was slightly lower in German samples but was nevertheless comparable to results found in U.S. samples (Hülsheger, Maier, & Stumpp, 2007). Although there are few empirical studies of training in China or India, it would be interesting to examine these relationships in those countries. As mentioned in Chapter 3, one could hypothesize that training is less important in China and India because these countries have such a large labor pool, but this has yet to be examined. Overall, research indicates that "g" is important for predicting performance in training, which in turn is related to performance on the job. Assessing cognitive ability before training can be useful in grouping individuals based on their readiness to learn the material. For example, with a group of trainees of widely varying cognitive ability, high-ability trainees will be bored, whereas low-ability trainees will have trouble keeping pace with their peers. With a group of trainees of similar ability, training facilitators can proceed through material at a pace appropriate to the backgrounds of the participants (Fleishman & Mumford, 1989).

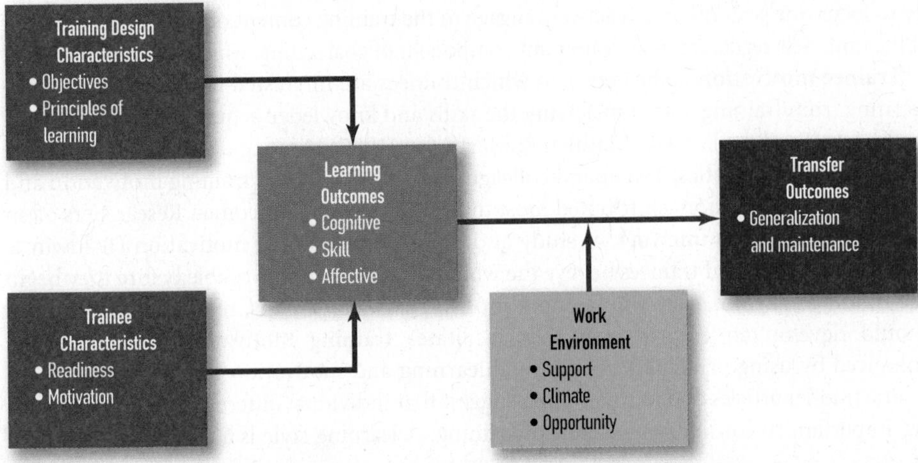

FIGURE 7.2 Characteristics Affecting Learning and Transfer Outcomes

SOURCE: Adapted from Baldwin, T. T., & Ford, J. K. (1988). Transfer of training: A review and directions for future research. *Personnel Psychology, 41,* 63–105. Copyright © 1988 by Personnel Psychology. Reprinted by permission of John Wiley & Sons Ltd.

Performance orientation Orientation in which individuals are concerned about doing well in training and being evaluated positively.

Mastery orientation Orientation in which individuals are concerned with increasing their competence for the task at hand; they view errors and mistakes as part of the learning process.

Another indicator of trainee readiness is goal orientation. Individuals with a **performance orientation** are concerned about doing well in training and being evaluated positively. They perceive their abilities as somewhat fixed, and they are generally not open to learning environments in which errors and mistakes are encouraged. They direct their energy toward performing well on tasks, often at the expense of learning. Performance-oriented learners are often sensitive to feedback, which can lead them to reduce their efforts and goals in challenging situations (Farr, Hofmann, & Ringenbach, 1993; Tziner, Fisher, Senior, & Weisberg, 2007). In contrast, individuals with a **mastery orientation** are concerned with increasing their competence for the task at hand, and they view errors and mistakes as part of the learning process. Mastery-oriented individuals are flexible and adaptable in learning situations, which is particularly critical for learning dynamic tasks and complex decision making (Phillips & Gully, 1997).

An additional indicator of readiness is the trainee's experience level. Inexperienced trainees with lower ability generally benefit more from longer and more structured training programs (Gully, Payne, Koles, & Whiteman, 2002). In contrast, experienced trainees with high ability thrive in shorter, less structured training programs. Even prior negative experiences and failures can be useful in heightening motivation to learn before training begins. For example, pilots often receive assertiveness training because some air accidents have been caused by a lack of communication and hesitancy to express concerns in the cockpit. As an example, during a snowstorm in January 1982, an Air Florida jet taking off from Reagan National Airport in Washington, DC, crashed into the 14th Street bridge over the Potomac River, killing 74 of the 79 people on board the plane as well as four motorists on the bridge. Among the elements responsible for this accident was the unwillingness of a co-pilot to disagree with the pilot and abort the take-off to return for additional deicing (Wilber, 2007). Smith-Jentsch, Jentsch, Payne, and Salas (1996) found that pilots who had experienced accidents or near-accidents benefited more from assertiveness training and subsequently performed better after training than those who had no negative experiences. The authors suggested that the negative experiences motivated the pilots to learn how to avoid aviation mishaps and that an opportune time to provide training is after a negative experience such as an accident, injury, or production problem. The negative experience provides a window of opportunity for the organization to offer immediate training rather than merely make a note of the incident for a later training effort. Meta-analytic research also indicates that integrating errors into the training process can improve subsequent performance (Keith & Frese, 2008). Such error management training is being used in military, aviation, and medical settings as well as in driving simulators. For example, Ellis and Davidi (2005) found that the performance of Israeli soldiers doing successive navigation exercises improved significantly when they were debriefed on their failures and successes after each training day. This emphasis on learning from errors highlights the increasing focus in the training field on self-regulatory processes, which involve the ability to focus one's attention and actively engage in the training content or other tasks required at the time. Self-regulation is an important component of goal setting, which is discussed below.

Trainee motivation Extent to which trainees are interested in attending training, learning from training, and transferring the skills and knowledge acquired in training back to the job.

Expectancy framework Approach in which employees' expectations about the relationship between how much effort they expend and how well they perform are important to their motivation and learning.

Trainee motivation is the extent to which trainees are interested in attending training, learning from training, and transferring the skills and knowledge acquired in training back to the job (Ford et al., 1998; Mathieu & Martineau, 1997). Among a variety of individual difference characteristics, Tziner and colleagues (2007) found that training motivation and learning goal orientation contributed most to positive training outcomes. Researchers often use an **expectancy framework** to study and understand training motivation (Baldwin & Ford, 1988). That is, if trainees believe the work environment is favorable before they begin the training program, they will be more motivated to learn. Thus, managers and trainers should develop an environment that facilitates training motivation, which can be enhanced by using principles from several learning and motivation theories.

Practitioner articles and journals often suggest that individual differences in *learning styles* are important to consider in advance of training. A learning style is a preferred method of learning that can focus on sensory modalities (auditory, visual, kinesthetic) or on preferences for concrete experiences versus reflective observations. Several different learning style inventories have been developed (e.g., Kolb, 2005), and the results of these inventories are being used to customize training to match trainee learning preferences. For example, if an online learning tool that includes a preassessment identifies trainees as visual learners, then the bulk of training content might be offered with interesting visual displays; alternatively, if trainees are found to be more comfortable with auditory formats, online training content might have a narrator speaking throughout the training program (Hartley & West, 2007). Though learning style inventories are increasingly being used as part of training programs, little research has investigated the usefulness, reliability, and validity of learning styles in improving training and its transfer to the job (Noe, 2010). Quite a bit of research has been conducted on learning styles in educational settings and in the educational psychology literature (Kolb & Kolb, 2005); however, given that these inventories are being used widely in work settings, it is also important for I-O psychologists to rigorously examine their usefulness.

Learning and Motivational Theories Applied to Training

Reinforcement Theory

B. F. Skinner's (1954) work on reinforcement was important in early theories of motivation, which we discuss further in Chapter 8. Skinner also applied principles of reinforcement theory to the educational and learning process. He proposed that learning results from the association between behaviors and rewards. **Positive reinforcement** occurs when behavior is followed by a reward, which increases the probability that the behavior will be repeated. As a learning mechanism, positive reinforcement is useful in pointing out when a trainee or job incumbent demonstrates the correct behaviors and skills. Reinforcement is generally most effective when it occurs immediately after a task has been completed or performed. Rewards that positively reinforce desired behaviors can range from praise from a supervisor, peer, or trainer to gifts, cash bonuses, attention, recognition, and career opportunities. For example, a trainer can praise trainees who effectively demonstrate the skill they were just taught. Employers can provide positive reinforcement by offering career opportunities to employees who engage in training and development programs. Reinforcement theory suggests that trainers and supervisors can best enhance learning and transfer of knowledge and skills by identifying what rewards or outcomes the learner finds most positive (Goldstein & Ford, 2002; Noe, 2010).

Positive reinforcement
Occurs when desired behavior is followed by a reward, which increases the probability that the behavior will be repeated.

Cognitive and Social Learning Theories

Cognitive theories focus on how individuals process and interpret information, while acknowledging that humans do not always learn by performing a task themselves and receiving direct reinforcement. Instead, humans can use memory, judgment, and reasoning to make connections between what they observe and how they should behave or perform in work and non-work situations. **Social learning theory** is a cognitive theory that proposes that there are many ways to learn. For example, humans can learn indirectly by observing others (Bandura, 1997). Observational learning occurs when people watch someone (in person or via a videotape) perform a task and then rehearse those activities mentally until they have an opportunity to try them out. Social learning theory is at work when trainees are being mentored and when they are "learning the ropes" by watching more experienced colleagues perform certain tasks. Trainees can also learn by asking more experienced employees questions and by listening to them describe the critical behaviors that lead to successful performance.

Social learning theory
Cognitive theory that proposes that there are many ways to learn, including observational learning, which occurs when people watch someone perform a task and then rehearse those activities mentally until they have an opportunity to try them out.

Given the increasing number of jobs in the service industry and the use of teams in organizations, interpersonal skills training has become ever more important. A technique

Behavioral modeling Learning approach that consists of observing actual job incumbents (or videos of job incumbents) who demonstrate positive modeling behaviors, rehearsing the behavior using a role-playing technique, receiving feedback on the rehearsal, and trying out the behavior on the job.

called **behavioral modeling** is often used to apply principles of social learning theory to the development of interpersonal skills in managers and supervisors. Behavioral modeling consists of observing actual job incumbents or videos of job incumbents that demonstrate positive modeling behaviors, rehearsing the behavior using a role-playing technique, receiving feedback on the rehearsal, and finally trying out the behavior on the job. For example, behavioral modeling occurs when telemarketing trainees listen in while an experienced telemarketer talks with a customer. May and Kahnwieler (2000) used behavioral modeling to improve interpersonal skills using role-play practice exercises. They found that practice sessions that broke down tasks into manageable parts led to high retention rates and high scores on a simulated interpersonal skills case study. In a meta-analysis, Taylor, Russ-Eft, and Chan (2005) found that the largest effects of behavioral modeling were on declarative and procedural knowledge.

Applications of behavioral modeling are also being utilized in technical and computer skills training programs. In a field experiment examining different approaches to computer training for novice computer users in the Navy, Simon and Werner (1996) compared the behavioral modeling approach to a self-study course and a traditional classroom approach. Behavioral modeling included observing the trainer, practicing the tasks, receiving feedback, and experimenting with new ways to carry out the tasks. Results indicated that behavioral modeling was superior to the other approaches at time 1 (immediately after training) and time 2 (one month later) across evaluation measures that included attitudes about the training, knowledge gained from the training, and demonstration of skills learned. Another study found that managerial trainees performed better when exposed to behavioral modeling for computer training than to computer-assisted instruction (Gist, Schwoerer, & Rosen, 1989). These studies indicate that both managerial and nonmanagerial employees can benefit from behavioral modeling in terms of computer skill development and demonstration.

Self-efficacy Belief in one's capability to perform a specific task or reach a specific goal.

Social learning theory is a broad-based approach that includes self-efficacy, goal setting, and feedback, which are important aspects of the learning process that occur in training. As we will discuss further in Chapter 8, these three concepts are also important parts of motivational theory and practice. **Self-efficacy**, the belief in one's capability to perform a specific task or reach a specific goal, enhances trainees' motivation, learning, and subsequent performance on the job (Bandura, 1997; Colquitt et al., 2000). Trainees high in self-efficacy are likely to attempt difficult tasks both in training and back on the job. Researchers have found that self-efficacy plays an important role in a variety of training programs, including negotiation skills training, computer software training, and training in innovative problem solving. Training specialists can increase trainees' self-efficacy by using behavioral modeling and by providing words of encouragement. Machin (2002) and Noe (2010) noted that trainees' self-efficacy levels can also be increased in the following ways:

1. Before training begins, providing as much information as possible about the training program and the purpose of training
2. Reducing perceived threats to trainees by initially emphasizing learning outcomes and de-emphasizing performance outcomes, which become more important after training
3. Showing employees the training success of peers in similar jobs
4. Helping trainees develop better learning strategies to use during training, such as summarizing main points and using memory aids to help retention

Goal setting Motivational approach in which specific, difficult goals direct attention and improve performance in training and on the job.

Goal setting can strengthen trainee motivation and self-efficacy, which in turn are helpful in enhancing learning and skill acquisition in training. A great deal of research indicates that specific, difficult goals improve performance in training and on the job (Austin & Vancouver, 1996). For example, a recent meta-analysis (Mesmer-Magnus & Viswesvaran, 2007) indicated that setting pre-training goals resulted in higher post-training performance than when no goals were set. Thus, trainers should encourage trainees to set specific, difficult goals, which help to direct and focus their attention on the most important tasks. Machin (2002) emphasized the importance of goal setting and suggested that trainers ensure that all trainees have the following:

1. Clear short-term goals for the training program (e.g., "I will complete all of the required modules in the allocated time")
2. Short-term goals for the immediate transfer of their training (e.g., "I will begin to use my new knowledge and skills at the first opportunity I have")
3. Long-term goals that focus on continued mastery and use of training content (e.g., "I will seek feedback from my supervisor and peers after one month and continue to review my progress each month")

Feedback is also important in enhancing learning and performance in training and on the job. Feedback enhances motivation and keeps goal-directed behavior on target. Feedback about performance in training and on the job is most effective when it is accurate, timely, and constructive (Goldstein & Ford, 2002). Managers should use a clear and nonthreatening manner when they deliver feedback, which should deal specifically with job-relevant behaviors (Kluger & DeNisi, 1996).

Feedback Knowledge of the results of one's actions; enhances learning and performance in training and on the job.

Principles of Learning

Practice and Overlearning

The old saying "practice makes perfect" is applicable to training, particularly because practice is critical to retaining newly learned skills. The Greek philosopher Aristotle stated that "what we have to do we learn by doing," which indicates that **active practice** has been emphasized for many centuries. The principle of active practice is still used today in many training programs. For example, military recruits actively practice assembling and disassembling guns, which promotes learning far more effectively than having them passively watch someone else, such as a drill sergeant, perform the task. Recent research indicates that active practice emphasizing learning and exploration during computer training tasks has positive effects on transfer of training back to the job (Bell & Kozlowski, 2008).

Active practice Approach that involves actively participating in a training or work task rather than passively observing someone else performing the task.

Training researchers and practitioners often ask, "How much practice is enough?" Some suggest that it is sufficient to practice until the task can be performed once without errors. However, as many concert musicians can attest, this approach is unlikely to lead to adequate, long-term task performance. If you have ever taken piano lessons, you have probably observed that playing a piece without errors in one practice session does not in any way guarantee that you will be able to play it flawlessly a week later or even the next day. Instead, you need to continue practicing it to the point of overlearning. Similarly, training programs should emphasize overlearning by presenting trainees with several extra learning opportunities even after they have demonstrated mastery of a task. Overlearning results in **automaticity**, which enables the person to perform the task with limited attention. An example of automaticity is when experienced drivers pay little attention to steering while driving. People often refer to automaticity by saying they can do the task "on autopilot" or "in my sleep."

Automaticity Result that occurs when tasks can be performed with limited attention; likely to develop when learners are given extra learning opportunities after they have demonstrated mastery of a task.

Overlearning is critical in jobs in which the task is not likely to be performed on the job very often, where performance on the first attempt is critical, and where there is little to no room for error; examples include the avoidance of accidents while driving, emergency routines performed by pilots, and military operations performed by soldiers (Rohrer & Pashler, 2007). In a meta-analysis of over 50 studies on overlearning, Driskell, Willis, and Copper (1992) found that overlearning had a significant and positive effect

© Larry Kolvoord/The Image Works

In an example of overlearning, military trainees continue to practice assembling and disassembling their weapons even after they have demonstrated initial mastery of this task.

on long-term retention for both physical and cognitive tasks. In sum, overlearning increases the length of time training material is retained; thus, if training involves learning a skill, then employees should be asked to demonstrate the skill even after they have reached some initial mastery level.

The extent to which the task trained is similar to the task required on the job is referred to as **fidelity**. It is important that training tasks have fidelity so that the extra time and expense of overlearning in training can directly benefit performance on the job. To best develop the three types of learning outcomes (cognitive, skill-based, and affective) described by Kraiger and colleagues (1993), training tasks should have both physical and psychological fidelity. **Physical fidelity** refers to the extent to which the training task mirrors the physical features of the actual task. For example, airplane simulator tasks possess physical fidelity when they accurately represent the layout of the cockpit as well as the motion that occurs in actual aircraft (Goldstein & Ford, 2002). **Psychological fidelity** refers to the extent to which the training task helps trainees to develop the KSAOs that are necessary to perform the job. A training program that emphasizes the development of critical KSAOs identified in a task analysis would possess high psychological fidelity. For example, if lieutenant candidates in a fire department are trained (and tested) in a simulated setting where they have to respond to a fire by actually speaking the directions and orders they would give, this setting would elicit their communication and decision-making skills and would possess psychological fidelity (Goldstein, Zedeck, & Schneider, 1993).

Fidelity Extent to which the task trained is similar to the task required on the job.

Physical fidelity Extent to which the training task mirrors the physical features of the task performed on the job.

Psychological fidelity Extent to which the training task helps trainees to develop the knowledge, skills, abilities, and other characteristics (KSAOs) necessary to perform the job.

High-fidelity simulators are often very expensive. Research has investigated whether low-fidelity simulators are effective in training required KSAOs. For example, Jentsch and Bowers (1998) found that flight simulators with low physical fidelity do elicit behaviors that are important for on-the-job performance. Nevertheless, pilots often prefer to receive training on the more expensive, high-fidelity simulators. Overall, training specialists must consider the tradeoffs among fidelity, cost, trainee preferences, and transfer of training to the job.

Whole versus Part Learning

Whole learning Training approach in which the entire task is practiced at once.

Part learning Training approach in which subtasks are practiced separately and later combined.

Another important consideration in training is the size of the tasks practiced. **Whole learning** occurs when the entire task is practiced at once. **Part learning** occurs when subtasks are practiced separately and later combined. Trainers and training designers should consider the task's difficulty level (task complexity) and the extent to which the subtasks are interrelated (task organization) in determining the usefulness of whole and part learning. Whole learning is more effective when a complex task has relatively high organization. When a complex task has low organization, part learning is more efficient. For example, developing skills to land airplanes involves complex tasks that can be decomposed; thus, it is often beneficial to use a part learning approach, which is less intimidating and frustrating to novice pilot trainees than a whole learning approach. Once some of the difficult parts of the task have been automatized, trainees can gradually be moved to performing the whole task (Rogers, Maurer, Salas, & Fisk, 1997). Another example of part learning is the way that actors rehearse various parts of a play (e.g., dance steps, fight scenes, pieces of dialogue) without the other actors. Gradually, the pieces are brought together until the actors are ready for a run-through of the entire play, which they then do intact for the rest of rehearsals. When using part learning approaches, it is important for trainers to determine the correct sequence for learning the subtasks and how they should be combined so that trainees can eventually perform the overall task effectively and efficiently (Goldstein & Ford, 2002).

© Michael Dunning /Getty Images, Inc.

Trainee pilots use simulators with high physical and psychological fidelity.

Massed versus Distributed Practice

Trainers and training researchers have also considered how to set up practice sessions. **Massed practice** conditions are those in which individuals practice a task continuously and without rest. **Distributed practice** gives individuals rest intervals between practice sessions, which are spaced over a longer period of time. In general, distributed practice results in more efficient learning and retention than massed practice because the rest periods reduce fatigue and allow time for strengthening of learned associations (Cascio & Aguinis, 2011). For simple motor tasks (e.g., computer keyboard skills), brief rest periods between practice sessions are helpful. For tasks of high complexity (e.g., air traffic control simulation, airplane flight simulation), longer rest periods between practice sessions are more beneficial for learning and skill acquisition. In terms of implications for training design, these findings suggest that we can expect a significant increase in learning from training programs that present distributed as opposed to massed material (Donovan & Radosevich, 1999).

Massed practice Conditions in which individuals practice a task continuously and without rest.

Distributed practice Condition that provides individuals with rest intervals between practice sessions, which are spaced over a longer period of time.

College students preparing for a test often wonder whether weeks of inattention to a course can be remedied by pulling an all-nighter, which involves cramming information into their memory just before an exam (Landy, 1987). Cramming is the equivalent of massed practice and, in general, is an ineffective learning strategy. Although cramming may improve performance marginally if the exam comes within hours of the massed practice, the material will not be retained as part of the body of knowledge students accumulate in school. The research described above suggests that students can benefit from studying that is distributed over time, which will lead to better exam performance and higher retention of the material. This research also suggests that although foreign-language immersion classes are a popular way to learn a new language, their lack of rest periods and breaks is likely to produce high levels of initial learning but not long-term retention (Rohrer & Pashler, 2007). Even students who have taken semester-long foreign-language classes are often disappointed at how few foreign words they can remember a few months later unless they continue using the language regularly. This is even more likely to be the case if the student crammed for the language exams.

Learning Organizations

Learning organization Company that emphasizes continuous learning, knowledge sharing, and personal mastery.

Peter Senge's (1990) book *The Fifth Discipline: The Art and Practice of Learning Organizations* popularized the concept of the learning organization, which is a useful extension of the principles of learning described above. **Learning organizations** are companies that emphasize continuous learning, knowledge sharing, and personal mastery (Jeppensen, 2002). Several additional features include the following:

1. Emphasizing problem solving and innovation
2. Developing systems that enhance knowledge generation and sharing
3. Encouraging flexibility and experimentation
4. Valuing the well-being and development of all employees
5. Encouraging employees to find or make opportunities to learn from whatever situation is presented (Confessore & Kops, 1998; London & Mone, 1999)

Organizations with such features are more likely to have the knowledge and skills essential for innovation and new product development (Kim & Wilemon, 2007). Successful organizations encourage learning at the individual, team, and organizational levels by emphasizing and rewarding knowledge sharing in their training and performance management systems (Noe, 2010).

Executives and managers interested in fostering a learning organization have increasingly developed corporate universities, which promote learning throughout the organization. Corporate universities provide relevant learning opportunities for different job families in the organization for new hires as well as for the development of workers throughout their careers (Morrison & Meister, 2000).

Well-known corporate universities include Motorola University, General Motors University, Xerox's Document University, Caterpillar University, Capital One University, and McDonald's Hamburger University, which has granted more than 65,000 "bachelors of hamburgerology" degrees since the program began in 1961 in the basement of a McDonald's restaurant. At Hamburger University, McDonald's managers learn about supervisory skills, employee motivation, and company values such as quality, service, cleanliness, and pride (Wexley & Latham, 2002). Training and learning are taken seriously at Hamburger University, which has university housing where students stay during their training, often lasting five full days. The university recently shifted training styles to incorporate more small-group activities and interactive learning. The training center includes a simulated kitchen and drive-through window that are exact replicas of what trainees will find at the restaurants where they will eventually work. Trainees practice taking orders, preparing food in the kitchen, and working at the drive-through window. Finally, McDonald's has created alliances to ensure that some of the coursework (e.g., business management, adult education courses) at Hamburger University can be counted as course credit at more traditional universities and colleges (Weinstein, 2008). With the use of electronic and computer-based technology, training courses are provided in 22 languages at Hamburger University, which currently operates in Japan, Germany, Britain, and Australia.

Tolbert, McLean, and Myers (2002) emphasized that global changes and challenges facing corporations require an emphasis on global learning organizations. They argued that many organizations are ethnocentric but that successful organizations will instead need to be globally inclusive. Figure 7.3 shows how an ethnocentric organization might become a globally inclusive one. Organizations aiming to become truly global will need to plan and structure management development that includes international and cross-cultural experiences. They will also need to train their employees to work in cross-cultural teams. To help employees be prepared to think and work with a global perspective, organizations can use features of learning organizations (e.g., continuous learning and improvement) in combination with recruitment and selection procedures. Successful multinational organizations place a heavy emphasis on knowledge sharing among team members and across teams so that information is transferred across different parts of the organization. (Gibson, Waller, Carpenter, & Conte, 2007). Overall, training researchers and practitioners are

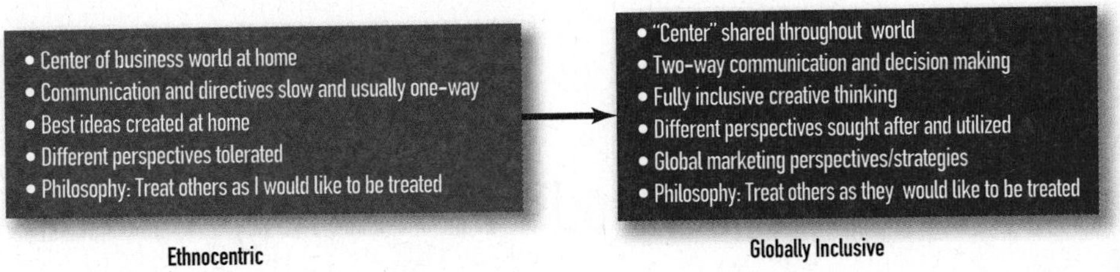

Ethnocentric		Globally Inclusive
• Center of business world at home • Communication and directives slow and usually one-way • Best ideas created at home • Different perspectives tolerated • Philosophy: Treat others as I would like to be treated	→	• "Center" shared throughout world • Two-way communication and decision making • Fully inclusive creative thinking • Different perspectives sought after and utilized • Global marketing perspectives/strategies • Philosophy: Treat others as they would like to be treated

FIGURE 7.3 Global Learning Organizations

Source: Tolbert, A. S., McLean, G. N., & Myers, R. C. (2002). Creating the global learning organization. *International Journal of Intercultural Relations, 26*, 463–472. Copyright © 2002. Reprinted with permission from Elsevier.

optimistic about these systematic, integrated approaches to learning. Additional research is needed that evaluates the conditions under which learning organizations thrive and the barriers to changing an organization's culture in this way.

MODULE 7.1 SUMMARY

- Training is a major expenditure for many companies, and evidence suggests that it pays off in higher sales and profitability. Many organizations also use training to attract and retain their most successful employees.
- Work psychologists often use a training model that begins with needs assessment, then training and development, followed by training evaluation, and finally a consideration of training validity levels.
- Needs analysis is a systematic means of understanding where training is needed, what needs to be taught or trained, and who will be trained. Training needs analysis typically involves organizational, task, and person analysis.
- After determining training needs and training objectives, training design begins with an understanding of how learning occurs. Trainee characteristics (readiness to learn, motivation to learn) and training design characteristics (principles of learning, objectives) affect the learning process and learning outcomes.
- Principles from reinforcement theory and social learning theory are useful in designing training programs and enhancing learning processes during training.
- Emerging trends in training and learning include the learning organization and the globally inclusive organization.

KEY TERMS

training
learning
cognitive outcome
skill-based outcome
affective outcome
performance
training needs analysis
organizational analysis
task analysis
competencies
person analysis
trainee readiness
performance orientation
mastery orientation
trainee motivation
expectancy framework
positive reinforcement
social learning theory
behavioral modeling
self-efficacy
goal setting
feedback
active practice
automaticity
fidelity
physical fidelity
psychological fidelity
whole learning
part learning
massed practice
distributed practice
learning organization

MODULE 7.2

Content and Methods of Training

Training Methods

Training methods are generally categorized into on-site and off-site programs, and each of these categories can be divided into several types. The following discussion is meant to be a representative description of commonly used methods. Later in the chapter, we will discuss additional types of training (e.g., cross-cultural, management development, and sexual harassment awareness training). Although these methods differ in their specific applications, all have in common the learning principles discussed in Module 7.1. Salas and Cannon-Bowers (2001) echoed this idea by noting that most effective training methods are created around four basic principles:

1. They present relevant information and content to be learned.
2. They demonstrate KSAOs to be learned.
3. They create opportunities for trainees to practice the required skills.
4. They provide feedback to trainees during and after practice.

On-Site Training Methods

On-the-job training Approach that involves assigning trainees to jobs and encouraging them to observe and learn from more experienced employees.

On-the-job training involves assigning trainees to jobs and encouraging them to observe and learn from more experienced employees. Nearly all employees receive some on-the-job training following initial formal training. Although on-the-job training is necessary and can be very beneficial, its effectiveness is often reduced when it is done in an unsystematic way that is at odds with many of the ideas discussed in Module 7.1. Alternatively, if on-the-job training includes training objectives, behavioral modeling, and regular feedback, then it is likely to be an effective training method (Goldstein & Ford, 2002).

Apprenticeship

Apprenticeship Formal program used to teach a skilled trade.

A particular form of on-the-job training is an **apprenticeship**, which is a formal program used to teach a skilled trade (Goldstein & Ford, 2002). The apprenticeship approach is used for many jobs such as bricklayer, electrician, plumber, carpenter, sheet metal worker, roofer, cement mason, and pipefitter. Approximately 61 percent of organizations employing individuals in such jobs have apprenticeship training programs that last from two to five years (McMurrer, van Buren, & Woodwell, 2000). Apprenticeship programs combine on-the-job instruction with a minimum of 144 hours a year of classroom instruction. An apprentice becomes a journeyman after a specified training period. With further experience, the journeyman goes on to become a certified skill tradesperson.

A successful apprenticeship program includes modeling, practice, feedback, and evaluation. Apprentices should begin their training by gaining the prerequisite knowledge, generally in trade schools or technical colleges. Next, behavioral modeling is used as apprentices observe journeymen and certified tradespersons performing the correct behaviors on the job. The apprentice then has an opportunity to perform and practice job tasks. Finally, the apprentice receives feedback and additional practice opportunities until each task is performed satisfactorily and safely (Noe, 2010).

Apprenticeship programs are a more important part of education and training in several European countries, such as Germany and Denmark, than in the United States. The German apprenticeship program is often highlighted as a model for providing young workforce entrants with the skills and credentials needed for an occupation (Noe, 2010). Many Germans who do not go on to college (approximately two-thirds) participate in apprenticeship programs, which are supported by leaders from government, labor, business, and education. One concern about apprenticeship systems, however, is that they provide workers with very specific skills that are not always adaptable to other jobs. The changing nature of work in the United States and abroad may create difficulties for apprentices whose skills are very narrowly focused. Although apprenticeship systems in Germany, the United States, and other countries successfully train individuals in developing specialized skills, retraining may be needed to enable employees to move to related jobs when economic conditions change. Personal characteristics such as adaptability, flexibility, and openness will allow all employees, including apprentices, to remain valuable assets in changing times (Ilgen & Pulakos, 1999).

Job Rotation

Another common training method is **job rotation**, which involves moving employees to various departments or areas of a company or to various jobs in a single department (Noe, 2010). Employees who participate in job rotation develop a wider range of skills than they would by remaining in a single job, area, or level of the organization. For example, an entry-level employee in a large human resources (HR) department might be rotated through the staffing, compensation, benefits, and training areas in order to learn about these different HR functions. This rotation might involve three to six months in each specialty area. Job rotation can also be used to prepare high-potential employees for future management responsibilities. New college graduates and MBAs may participate in job rotation as a way to determine where they would be most effective in the organization (Wexley & Latham, 2002). For example, a newly hired executive or manager might be rotated through the HR, operations, accounting, and finance departments in order to develop firsthand knowledge of the departments and functions within the organization. On the interpersonal level, employees who have been rotated through a series of jobs often develop an important network of contacts across the organization. Job rotation also promotes the development of decision-making and problem-solving skills and provides employees with experiences that will help them qualify for future promotions. Research indicates a positive association between job rotation and both job promotions and salary increases (Campion, Cheraskin, & Stevens, 1994). As with other training techniques, job rotation is most successful if it is part of an overall career development system that offers employees a variety of job-relevant experiences and opportunities.

Job rotation Approach that involves moving employees to various departments or areas of a company or to various jobs within a single department.

The PricewaterhouseCoopers (PwC) consulting company provides an example of a successful job rotation program. Its "Tours of Duty" program typically lasts one to two years and allows consultants to rotate among different PwC consulting teams from around the world. Consultants who are "on tour" share their knowledge and skills with members of the host team, thereby increasing that team's business efficacy. In the process, consultants develop language skills, experience a foreign culture, and enhance their technical and interpersonal skill sets (Barbian, 2002).

Off-Site Training Methods

Classroom lecture Training method in which the trainer communicates through spoken words and audiovisual materials what trainees are supposed to learn; also commonly used to efficiently present a large amount of information to a large number of trainees.

Classroom lectures are one of the most common training methods. Lectures are an efficient way to present a large amount of information to a large number of trainees. They are often supplemented with class discussion, case studies, and audiovisual materials. The lecture method is relatively inexpensive compared to other training methods, and it works well when the goal is for trainees to obtain knowledge. In a meta-analysis, Arthur, Bennett, and colleagues (2003) found that lectures were quite effective as a training delivery method. However, because lectures can foster a passive environment that does not require trainees to become involved in learning the material, the lecture method does not work well in situations where skill acquisition is critical (Goldstein & Ford, 2002). In those situations, hands-on training may be preferable. If the lecture method is used, the trainer should encourage active participation from trainees by including job-related examples and exercises that promote learning and transfer to the job (Noe, 2010).

Programmed instruction Approach in which trainees are given instructional materials in written or computer-based forms that positively reinforce them as they move through the material at their own pace.

Linear programming Type of programmed instruction in which all trainees proceed through the same material.

Branching programming Type of programmed instruction that provides a customized approach, enabling each learner to practice material he or she had difficulty with when it was first presented.

Simulator Teaching tool designed to reproduce the critical characteristics of the real world in a training setting that produces learning and transfer to the job.

Programmed instruction presents information to learners using principles of reinforcement (Goldstein & Ford, 2002). In this approach, trainees are given instructional materials in written or computer-based forms that reinforce them positively as they move through the material. This self-paced approach works most effectively if it provides immediate feedback and reinforcement regarding correct and incorrect responses. It can be structured as **linear programming**, in which all trainees proceed through the same material, or **branching programming**, a customized approach that gives each learner extra practice on material he or she had difficulty with when it was first presented. Reviews of programmed instruction, lecture, and discussion training methods found no significant differences in immediate learning and retention across the three methods, but trainees using programmed instruction learned material in approximately 30 percent less time (Goldstein & Ford, 2002).

With recent advances in computer and multimedia technology, a great deal of programmed instruction is moving from written formats to computer-assisted instruction. Multimedia technology that can simultaneously present text, graphics, animation, and videos is making computer-assisted programmed instruction more interesting and appealing, but researchers have yet to examine the effects of these advances empirically. Nevertheless, computer-based training holds vast potential as a way to improve the delivery and cost effectiveness of programmed instruction.

Simulators are designed to reproduce the critical characteristics of the real world in a training setting that produces learning and transfer to the job. If you have taken a course in CPR (cardiopulmonary resuscitation), you have probably used a simulator: a dummy designed to resemble a stroke or heart attack victim. The drive-through windows at Hamburger University that were mentioned earlier are examples of training simulators. In addition, simulators are virtually the only safe way to train pilots to fly airplanes and to prepare nuclear power plant operators to work in and respond to crises in their facilities. Simulators are very useful for developing motor skills. They are also useful in developing management and decision-making skills, as they allow trainees to see the impact of their decisions in a risk-free environment (Noe, 2010). Goldstein and Ford (2002) provided four reasons for using simulators:

1. *Controlled reproducibility*. Simulators effectively reproduce the real-world environment in the training setting.
2. *Safety considerations*. Required real-world behavior is often too complex to be handled safely by the trainee.
3. *Learning considerations*. Most simulators effectively utilize learning principles such as active practice and feedback, and they are designed to support transfer of training.
4. *Cost*. Simulators provide a low-cost method for trainees to practice and acquire skills. Although simulators are expensive, they are a better use of organization money than the cost of trainee mistakes on the job when high-priced equipment and even human lives are at stake.

The concept of fidelity, which we discussed in Module 7.1, is particularly important in simulators, which must be as similar to the actual task as possible in terms of physical layout (physical fidelity) and in mirroring the KSAOs required for performing the task on the job (psychological fidelity). Flight schools use high-fidelity flight simulators to train and evaluate pilots and their coordination with co-pilots. Flight simulators provide physical fidelity by replicating the cockpit as well as the motion that a pilot would feel in a real aircraft (Goldstein & Ford, 2002). For example, helicopter simulators have a screen on which images are projected, as well as a tilt platform that is used to simulate balance in the ear. Such simulators can induce motion sickness in seconds! Flight simulators provide psychological fidelity by requiring trainees to use relevant KSAOs while performing all technical aspects of flight, including altitude control, navigation, and the use of safety checklists (Smith-Jentsch, Salas, & Brannick, 2001). Greater fidelity in the simulator task leads to higher job-relevant learning and subsequent transfer to the job. One exciting development that is increasingly being used to enhance fidelity is the use of virtual environments as training simulators in military, aviation, and medical settings. Given the many benefits simulators provide, they will continue to be used in a variety of industries, and I-O psychologists will continue to explore ways to maximize the transfer of skills learned while using simulators.

Distance learning has become an efficient and popular method of training workers.

Distance Learning and Computer-Based Training

Distance learning allows trainees to interact and communicate with an instructor by using audio and video (television, computer, or radio) links that allow for learning from a distant location (Goldstein & Ford, 2002). Distance learning can occur across multiple sites at one time, and it provides a more affordable, learning-tailored alternative to live instruction (Hannafin & Hannafin, 1995). Although distance learning by radio and television has long been used for elementary schooling, especially in sparsely populated areas such as rural Alaska and the Australian outback, advances in technology since the 1980s have expanded the available media to videoconferencing and online collaboration. The added benefits of these interactive media have made computer-based distance learning increasingly popular in the workplace. Many U.S. businesses (including General Electric and IBM), as well as colleges and universities, offer extensive distance learning programs. In addition, many countries including the United Kingdom, the Netherlands, Germany, and Spain have widely recognized open universities that use distance learning (Hawkridge, 1999).

Distance learning Approach that allows trainees to interact and communicate with an instructor by using audio and video (television, computer, or radio) links that allow for learning from a distant location.

Distance learning has great promise, but I-O research in this area is just beginning. Threlkeld and Brozoska (1994) studied achievement levels in distance and traditional learners, and they found no significant differences between the two groups. Two subsequent studies indicated that higher levels of interaction and feedback enhance attitudes about distance learning (Webster & Hackley, 1997; Zhang & Fulford, 1994). Not surprisingly, distance learning works best when it is free of technical problems. Specifically, audio and video transmissions should be fast, clear, and consistent so that equipment concerns do not detract from the advantages of this new learning platform (Goldstein & Ford, 2002).

Blended learning An instructional approach that uses distance learning in combination with face-to-face learning.

A relatively new training approach involves **blended learning**, which refers to the use of distance learning in combination with face-to-face learning. Klein, Noe, and Wang (2006) compared blended learning and traditional classroom instruction. They found that blended learning increases learning motivation more than classroom instruction. We look forward to additional comparisons of blended and traditional learning in future research.

Like distance learning, computer-based training has expanded greatly in recent years. Many organizations are moving a growing proportion of their training from traditional classroom settings to computer-based training because of its reduced costs and increased flexibility. In a recent industry report, approximately 89 percent of companies reported using the Internet for delivering some of their training (Dolezalek, 2004). For example, Merrill Lynch uses computer-based training with its financial planners and consultants, who have responded positively to the increased individualization and accessibility that this form of training provides (Guernsey, 2000). **Computer-based training** is defined as "text, graphics, and/or animation presented via computer for the express purpose of teaching job-relevant knowledge and skills" (Brown & Ford, 2002, p. 194). This definition includes web-based training, corporate intranets, multimedia environments, and e-learning; thus, computer-based training may involve distance learning or the participants may be physically in one location. From a learning perspective, the differences among these specific types of computer-based training are often negligible. What is important is that they all allow trainees to have more control over their instruction and to individualize their learning experience (Welsh et al., 2003). Successful computer-based training will need to incorporate learning principles derived from the more general training literature, such as specific learning objectives, active practice, and feedback. Computers and other technological developments will continue to drive training applications. There is an increasing emphasis on multiple delivery methods for training programs, including the use of laptops, iPads, and other tablets for audio/video training content. Computers and smartphones are also being increasingly used to provide embedded on-the-job training using instant messaging (Noe, 2010).

Computer-based training An instructional approach that includes text, graphics, and/or animation presented via computer for the express purpose of teaching job-relevant knowledge and skills.

Because trainees do not naturally make good use of the increased control they are given in computer- and web-based training programs (Brown, 2001; Kraiger & Jerden, 2007), studies have examined the effects of providing trainees with adaptive guidance. **Adaptive guidance** provides trainees with information that helps them interpret their past performance and also determine what they should be studying and practicing to improve their future performance. Bell and Kozlowski (2002b) found that such adaptive guidance had positive effects on trainees' practice habits, knowledge acquired, and performance. Although there is much promise to computer-based training, many unanswered questions also remain regarding how effective this approach will be in terms of learning and transfer back to the job.

Adaptive guidance An instructional approach that provides trainees with information that helps them interpret their past performance and also determine what they should be studying and practicing to improve their future performance.

Training "Critical Thinking"

Above we described different modes or types of training. In this section we will focus on training in a specific content area, critical thinking, that is receiving increased attention in colleges and universities as well as in some organizations. What distinguishes critical thinking from ordinary thought is that it requires active involvement in applying the principles under discussion rather than simple memorization of facts or principles. Critical thinking skills will continue to be important in preparing for tests, making decisions, and adapting to challenges in the changing workplace. Training approaches and teaching philosophies that encourage students to develop transferable critical thinking skills will better prepare them for the unknown challenges in their future endeavors (Halpern, 1998).

Advances in technology and changes in necessary skills have made the ability to think critically in the workplace more important than ever before. Whenever workers grapple with complex issues, difficult decisions, and ill-defined problems, they will benefit from using **critical thinking skills** (Halpern, 1998). The importance of critical thinking can be seen in the U.S. Navy's Tactical Decision Making Under Stress (TADMUS) program. This program focuses on the development of naval officers' critical thinking skills in novel or unexpected situations. Critical thinking skills training in the TADMUS program uses instruction, demonstration, and practice to teach naval officers methods for identifying and handling different kinds of uncertainty. The training program provides practice with realistic problems and exercises that naval officers are likely to encounter on the job. For example, one exercise involves a time-pressured situation in which a navy ship needs to be defended against an approaching aircraft whose intent is unclear. Officers are asked to think through the situation and make a decision about how they would respond. Next, they receive feedback about the likely result of their decisions and information regarding the correct way to approach and resolve the situation, which helps to further develop their critical thinking skills. Independent tests of the critical thinking skills training with naval officers indicated positive effects on decision-making processes, accuracy of situation assessment, and appropriateness of actions suggested (Cohen, Freeman, & Thompson, 1998).

Critical thinking skills
Skills that require active involvement in applying the principles under discussion.

One of the goals of this book is to show how many of the broad principles of I-O psychology can be applied in situations encountered in the workplace. We believe the best way to achieve this is to encourage you to use critical thinking. We are confident you will be able to retain and apply these I-O principles beyond this course if you think critically about how they might apply to practical problems and follow up by discussing alternative solutions and applications with your instructor and peers.

Transfer of Training

Throughout this chapter, we have emphasized how important it is that material learned in training transfer back to the job. **Transfer of training** is the degree to which trainees apply the knowledge, skills, and attitudes gained in training to their jobs (Machin, 2002; Wexley & Latham, 2002). An organization's **transfer of training climate** refers to workplace characteristics that either inhibit or facilitate the transfer to the job of what has been learned in training. A positive transfer climate is one that provides adequate resources, opportunities for using skills learned in training, and positive reinforcement for using training content (Colquitt et al., 2000). Table 7.3 provides a summary of characteristics of a positive transfer of training climate. A positive transfer climate is particularly important because new employees learn about the way training is viewed in the organization early in the socialization process and continue gathering information with each training course they attend (Klein & Weaver, 2000). For example, new employees whose co-workers grin sarcastically and ask "when do you go for training?" are likely to conclude that the less time spent in training, the better impression they will make on peers. Thus, organizations should pay careful attention to messages employees hear about training within and across departments.

Transfer of training
Degree to which trainees apply the knowledge, skills, and attitudes gained in training to their jobs.

Transfer of training climate
Workplace characteristics that either inhibit or facilitate the transfer to the job of what has been learned in training.

TABLE 7.3 Characteristics of a Positive Transfer of Training Climate

Early socialization indicating that training is important
Continuous learning culture
Adequate peer and supervisor support
Opportunities to use learned capabilities
Access to equipment or resources that are essential for transfer of training
Adequate working conditions
Regular feedback and positive reinforcement for improved performance

Kozlowski, Brown, Weissbein, Salas, and Cannon-Bowers, and colleagues (2000) noted that both horizontal and vertical transfer are important. **Horizontal transfer** refers to transfer across different settings or contexts at the same level of the organization. **Vertical transfer** refers to transfer across different levels of the organization and is concerned with the link between individual training outcomes and outcomes at higher levels, such as teams and departments.

Several studies indicate that a positive transfer of training climate has a significant impact on the extent to which course material is applied back on the job. For example, Tracey and colleagues (1995) investigated the effects of the work environment on the transfer of newly trained supervisory skills in a sample of 505 supermarket managers from 52 different stores. They found that supermarket managers who received social support from their peers and bosses were more effective in utilizing the skills learned in training. A meta-analysis by Colquitt and colleagues (2000) indicated that the transfer of training climate also influences reactions to training, motivation to learn, and skill acquisition. Finally, a study by Saks and Belcourt (2006) highlighted the importance of what is done before and after training occurs. They found that activities before training (e.g., supervisor involvement, training attendance policy) and after training (supervisor support, organization support) were more strongly related to transfer of training than activities during training (e.g., training rewards, training feedback).

Horizontal transfer Transfer across different settings or contexts at the same level of the organization.

Vertical transfer Transfer across different levels of the organization; concerned with the link between individual training outcomes and outcomes at higher levels of the organization, such as teams.

A work environment that supports what is learned in training and co-workers/supervisors who reinforce those new skills, abilities, and attitudes are necessary supplements to training programs (Lim & Morris, 2006). In particular, off-site training programs will be effective only if management supports and reinforces the efforts of training facilitators. Off-site training programs sometimes use elaborate and expensive methods like paintball wars, fighter-pilot simulations, and a course at the BMW Performance Center that features driving a car while blindfolded. Ellin (2000) noted that although it may be fun to pelt one's boss with paint or to drive a BMW blindfolded with the help of a colleague, most of these off-site programs create an artificial, almost vacation-like atmosphere that does not easily transfer back to the workplace. Some employees report that such off-site training programs increase morale for a day or so, and then everyone returns to their heavy workload and forgets about such team-building exercises (Ellin, 2000). Thus, it is important for managers to consider transfer issues when adopting training programs and to take steps to ensure the supportiveness of the post-training work environment. For example, managers might carefully consider what knowledge and skills were learned in training and then ensure that trainees are given opportunities to use the new skills and knowledge soon after they return to the job.

In what ways might an off-site training program featuring paintball wars provide learning that will transfer well to the workplace?

MODULE 7.2 SUMMARY

- Most effective training methods are created on four basic principles: presenting relevant information and content to be learned; demonstrating KSAOs to be learned; creating opportunities for trainees to practice the required skills; and providing feedback to trainees during and after practice.
- Training methods are generally categorized into on-site and off-site programs. On-site training methods include on-the-job training, apprenticeships, and job rotation. Off-site programs include classroom lectures, programmed instruction, and simulators.
- Distance learning and computer-based training have both expanded greatly in recent years. They provide opportunities for reduced costs and for increased flexibility for both trainers and trainees.
- An important consideration for I-O psychologists, trainers, and trainees is the extent to which material learned in training transfers back to the job. A positive transfer of training climate has a significant impact on the extent to which course material is applied back on the job.

KEY TERMS

on-the-job training
apprenticeship
job rotation
classroom lecture
programmed instruction
linear programming
branching programming
simulator
distance learning
blended learning
computer-based training
adaptive guidance
critical thinking skills
transfer of training
transfer of training climate
horizontal transfer
vertical transfer

MODULE 7.3

Evaluating Training Programs

Training Evaluation

Training evaluation
The systematic collection of descriptive and judgmental information that can be used to make effective training decisions.

Training evaluation involves the systematic collection of descriptive and judgmental information that can be used to make effective training decisions. Such decisions include the selection, adoption, modification, and financial evaluation of various training activities (Goldstein & Ford, 2002). Implicit in this definition are several purposes of training evaluation (Sackett & Mullen, 1993):

1. To determine whether trainees have achieved the objectives of the training program.
2. To provide feedback that can improve training programs for future participants, ultimately increasing their job performance and productivity.
3. To justify the costs of training programs, which can be expensive. Evaluation can demonstrate the worth of training to top management by indicating whether the accomplishment of key business objectives improved after training.

As you can see, the goal of training evaluation is not simply to label a training program as good or bad. This is important to keep in mind; some trainers avoid evaluations that might identify minor problems or errors for fear that top management may try to "pull the plug" on such a program. Instead, the focus should be on how making minor modifications based on training evaluation can make a training program more effective in meeting its objectives (Brown & Gerhardt, 2002). Training objectives are critical in identifying the criteria by which the training program is judged. For training evaluation to be done well, it has to be planned in advance based on the overall training objectives, rather than simply being considered at the end of the program. Often, multiple criteria or outcomes are used to assess the success of a training program. The approaches discussed below provide various frameworks with which to think about criteria in the context of training evaluation.

Training Criteria

Kirkpatrick's (1959, 1998) four-level model is the most common and well-known framework with which to categorize training criteria. **Reaction criteria** (level 1) are measures of trainee impressions of the training program. Measures of reaction criteria are sometimes called "smile sheets" because they simply assess trainees' enjoyment of and satisfaction with the training program (Sitzmann, Brown, & Casper, 2008). **Learning criteria** (level 2) assess how much trainees learned in the training program. Learning criteria are often assessed with a written test, which might evaluate knowledge acquired in a training program. **Behavioral criteria** (level 3) measure how well the behaviors learned in training transfer to the job. Behavioral criteria might include ratings of on-the-job performance of behaviors taught in the training program. **Results criteria** (level 4) provide measures of how well the training can be related to organizational outcomes. For example, results criteria might assess the extent to which a training program resulted in productivity gains, cost savings, error reductions, or increased customer satisfaction. Results criteria are often considered most important to organizational decision makers because they have direct implications for organizational objectives and outcomes.

Reaction criteria Measures of trainee impressions of the training program.

Learning criteria Measures that assess how much was learned in the training program.

Behavioral criteria Measures of how well the behaviors learned in training transfer to the job.

Results criteria Measures of how well training can be related to organizational outcomes such as productivity gains, cost savings, error reductions, or increased customer satisfaction.

Internal criteria Measures that assess trainee reactions to and learning in the training program; generally assessed before trainees leave the training program.

External criteria Measures that assess whether changes as a result of training occur when trainees are back on the job.

Reaction and learning criteria are considered **internal criteria** because they focus on what occurred within the training program. Behavioral and results criteria are considered **external criteria** because they assess changes that occur back on the job. Surveys of companies' evaluation practices indicate that organizations frequently use reaction criteria, but they use learning, behavioral, and results criteria much less frequently. Specifically, a 2005 survey by the American Society for Training and Development indicated that organizations were using the four evaluation levels at the following percentages: reaction, 91 percent; learning, 54 percent; behavior, 23 percent; and results, 8 percent (Sugrue & Rivera, 2005).

For many years, Kirkpatrick's framework was considered to be a hierarchical approach to evaluation that included reaction criteria at the lowest level and results criteria at the highest level. This approach assumed that lower-level measures were correlated with higher measures and that positive trainee reactions were critical in achieving favorable outcomes for learning, behavioral, and results criteria. Because reaction criteria are the easiest to collect, researchers have investigated whether they are truly correlated with the other levels of training criteria. If so, then there would be little need to collect the other criteria because one could make the inference that positive trainee reactions would have beneficial effects on learning, transfer, and results criteria.

A meta-analysis by Alliger, Tannenbaum, Bennett, Traver, and Shotland (1997) found only modest correlations among the various levels of training criteria. Their results suggested that Kirkpatrick's taxonomy should be augmented to include multiple criteria at levels 1 and 2 (see Table 7.4). Specifically, their framework divided level 1 criteria into affective reactions ("I found this training program to be enjoyable") and utility reactions ("This training program had practical value" or "This training program was job relevant"). They concluded that affective reactions can be important, particularly when unfavorable reactions to training have negative effects on perceptions of the training department and future training efforts. However, utility reactions were more closely linked with learning and behavioral criteria than were affective reactions. Accordingly, if the purpose of collecting reaction criteria is to predict transfer of training, then evaluators should ask utility-oriented questions.

Alliger and colleagues (1997) suggested that learning outcomes should be divided into immediate knowledge, knowledge retention, and

TABLE 7.4 **Training Criteria Taxonomies**

KIRKPATRICK'S TAXONOMY	*AUGMENTED FRAMEWORK*
Reaction	Reaction Affective reactions Utility judgments
Learning	Learning Immediate knowledge Knowledge retention Behavior/skill demonstration
Behavior	Transfer
Results	Results

SOURCE: Alliger, G. M., Tannenbaum, S. I., Bennett, W., Traver, H., & Shotland, A. (1997). A meta-analysis of the relations among training criteria. *Personnel Psychology, 50*, 341–358.

behavior/skill demonstration. This is consistent with Kraiger and colleagues' (1993) expanded framework of learning outcomes that we discussed in Module 7.1. Recall that Kraiger and colleagues described learning as a multidimensional process that includes three types of outcomes (cognitive, skill-based, and affective). Alliger and colleagues did not revise Kirkpatrick's level 3 criteria except to use the term "transfer" instead of "behavioral" to emphasize that these measures assessed on-the-job performance. Consistent with other studies and organizational reports, Alliger and colleagues found that assessors rarely examined level 4 results criteria.

Utility Analysis

Utility analysis Technique that assesses the economic return on investment of human resource interventions such as staffing and training.

Although organizations do not often collect results criteria, training evaluators and specialists continue to be interested in ways to assess the financial return for training investments. **Utility analysis**, which we mentioned briefly as it related to staffing in Chapter 6, is a technique that assesses the return on investment of training and other human resource interventions. Utility analysis uses accounting procedures to measure the costs and benefits of training programs. Costs generally include the equipment, facilities, materials, and personnel expenditures across different stages of the training process. The benefits of the training program are based on several factors, including the following:

1. The number of individuals trained
2. Estimates of the difference in job performance between trained and untrained employees
3. The length of time a training program is expected to influence performance
4. The variability in job performance in the untrained group of employees (Noe, 2010)

A utility analysis can provide training evaluators and organizational decision makers with an overall dollar value of the training program. For example, Mathieu and Leonard (1987) examined the effects of a training program on supervisory skills for bank supervisors. After taking into account the costs of the program, they found that the utility of training a group of 15 bank supervisors was more than $13,000 for the first year after training. Although a utility of less than $1,000 per trainee might not seem like a lot, the net utility of the training program in the third year was estimated to be more than $100,000 owing to the increased effectiveness of the supervisors. Utility analysis can also compare the return on investment of different training programs. In their examination of the utility of managerial, sales, and technical training programs, Morrow, Jarrett, and Rupinski (1997) found that sales and technical training programs had greater effects on job performance and greater returns on investment than did managerial training programs. To perform utility analysis, training evaluators use complex formulas that are beyond the scope of this book but are covered in detail in other sources (Cascio, 2000a; Wexley & Latham, 2002).

Training Evaluation Designs

The purpose of training is to bring about systematic changes in knowledge, skills, and attitudes. Evaluation designs are used to determine whether training objectives have been met and whether post-training improvements in knowledge, skills, and attitudes are a result of training. Training evaluators attempt to infer whether such improvements are a result of the training program. However, a variety of factors can make these inferences difficult. Developing a good evaluation design can help to reduce concerns about such factors, which are called threats to validity.

The characteristics of strong experimental designs that we discussed in Chapter 2 are the same as those required for strong training evaluation designs. Why? Because these designs assess whether training or other organizational interventions caused changes in job performance or other outcomes. Since training is so expensive, particularly when one considers the time trainees spend away from work, it is important for training managers to provide evidence that training brought about desired changes in knowledge, skills, or attitudes.

The strongest training evaluation designs include random assignment of participants to conditions, a control group, and measures that are obtained both before and after training has occurred. An example of a design that includes these characteristics is the **pretest–posttest control group design** (shown in Table 7.5). In this design, participants are randomly assigned to either the experimental group (training) or the control group, which does not receive training. Both groups are measured prior to training on knowledge or skills to be trained (e.g., computer skills). The experimental group receives training, whereas the control group does not. After the training, the trained and control groups are assessed on the knowledge or skills trained. After controlling for any preexisting differences—which may occur, but are unlikely with the use of random assignment—a statistical test is conducted to determine if the trained group changed significantly more than the control group.

Pretest–posttest control group design Design that generally includes random assignment of participants to conditions, a control group, and measures obtained both before and after training has occurred.

In a training program that we discussed earlier, Simon and Werner (1996) used a variation of the pretest–posttest control group design that included random assignment to conditions, three experimental groups, and a control group. Their design, which is shown in Table 7.6, included three types of computer skills training: lecture, self-paced, and behavior modeling. Each of the three training groups received pretests and posttests, as did the control group. This design allowed the researchers to compare the training programs to each other and to a control group. The results indicated that participants in all experimental conditions

TABLE 7.5 **Pretest–Posttest Control Group Design**

GROUP	*PRETEST*	*TRAINING*	*POSTTEST*
Trained (experimental)	Yes	Yes	Yes
Not trained (control)	Yes	No	Yes

SOURCE: Simon, S. J., & Werner, J. M. (1996). Computer training through behavior modeling, self-paced, and instructional approaches: A field experiment. *Journal of Applied Psychology, 81*, 648–659. © 1996 by the American Psychological Association. Reprinted by permission of the publisher.

TABLE 7.6 **Pretest–Posttest Control Group Design Used by Simon and Werner**

GROUP	*PRETEST*	*TRAINING*	*POSTTEST*
Lecture	Yes	Yes	Yes
Self-paced	Yes	Yes	Yes
Behavior modeling	Yes	Yes	Yes
Control group	Yes	No	Yes

SOURCE: Simon, S. J., & Werner, J. M. (1996). Computer training through behavior modeling, self-paced, and instructional approaches: A field experiment. *Journal of Applied Psychology, 81*, 648–659. © 1996 by the American Psychological Association. Reprinted by permission of the publisher.

performed significantly better than participants in the control group. Among the experimental groups, the behavioral modeling program resulted in the highest learning, retention, and demonstration of computer skills.

Rigorous training evaluation designs are often difficult to implement in organizations. For example, evaluation is difficult when a training program that has already begun gets shortened or interrupted because of events in the organization or the economy. Another difficulty in evaluation occurs when changes in training materials are made during the course of the training program. From a training design perspective, rigorous training evaluation will be difficult when managers insist on sending all employees from a particular department to training at the same time; thus, random assignment of trainees to conditions would not be possible. In other cases, a control group may not be possible. In such situations, modified versions of the training evaluation designs described above may be used to lessen concerns that arise when either random assignment or the use of a control group is not possible (e.g., Haccoun & Hamtiaux, 1994). Thus, it is critical for training specialists to be aware of a variety of training evaluation designs and to understand the strengths and weaknesses of each. Discussions of more complex training evaluation designs can be found in several sources (Goldstein & Ford, 2002; Wexley & Latham, 2002).

Equal Employment Opportunity Issues in Training

Training programs can also be evaluated in terms of whether decisions associated with training opportunities unfairly discriminate against members of protected groups (e.g., women, minorities, disabled individuals). First, applicants cannot be eliminated from consideration for hiring if they lack a skill or knowledge that can be learned in a brief training session (Uniform Guidelines, 1978). Second, protected group members who are current employees should have the same access to training experiences and challenging work assignments that majority group members have. Organizations should also be concerned if protected group members fail training programs at higher rates than majority group members. To defend against charges of unfair discrimination in training, organizations should document their training practices and programs thoroughly. This should include monitoring each employee's progress in training and development programs (Jackson & Schuler, 2006).

A recent concern about unfair discrimination in training concerns age discrimination. Given the aging population and workforce, organizations are employing an increasing number of individuals 40 years of age and over (Noe, 2010). The Age Discrimination in Employment Act (ADEA) prohibits discrimination on the basis of age in human resource decisions such as hiring, firing, and pay, as well as employer-provided training and development. If older workers are not given equal access to training and development, the Equal Employment Opportunity Commission (EEOC) may take on the case on their behalf. For example, four employees from the University of Wisconsin Press, who were aged 46 through 54 and who were the oldest employees at the time, were discharged and replaced by four younger employees. The employer's rationale for this decision was that the older employees lacked updated computer skills. The EEOC

© Michael Newman/PhotoEdit

The ADEA mandates that older workers must be given equal access to training and development of new job skills.

successfully argued that the older workers were ready, willing, and able to receive training for these computer skills and were illegally denied the opportunity. The jury returned a verdict of intentional age discrimination and awarded $430,427 in pay and damages to be shared by the four plaintiffs (Gutman, 2001).

Maurer and Rafuse (2001) noted that "although most employees are very sensitive to sexism and racism, somehow the ageist idea that you can't teach an old dog new tricks does not seem to carry the same taboo in society and the workplace" (p. 117). They provided suggestions for managing employee development and avoiding claims of age discrimination, including the following:

1. Developmental opportunities such as training classes, job assignments, job rotations, and tuition assistance should be allocated on an age-neutral basis.
2. All employees, regardless of age, should be encouraged to participate in training, development, and learning opportunities.
3. Personnel decisions should be monitored to ensure that older employees have access to training.
4. Workshops or training interventions should be offered to teach managers about age-related stereotypes and the potential effects they can have on decisions and behavior. Managers should also be trained specifically on the ADEA.
5. As with other HR procedures, job-relevant criteria should be used for all decisions about training and development opportunities.

Overall, organizational efforts to avoid age and other types of discrimination in training and development opportunities will result in a reduced likelihood of lawsuits, an increased skill base, and an increased return on investment in their employees (Walker, 1999).

MODULE 7.3 SUMMARY

- Training evaluation involves the systematic collection of descriptive and judgmental information that can be used to make effective training decisions such as the selection, adoption, modification, and financial evaluation of various training activities.
- Kirkpatrick's four-level model is the most common and well-known framework with which to categorize training criteria. This model includes reaction, learning, behavioral, and results criteria.
- Training evaluation can include a utility analysis that employs accounting procedures to measure the costs and benefits and assess the return on investment of training.
- Training evaluation designs determine whether training objectives have been met and whether post-training changes in knowledge, skills, and attitudes are a result of training. I-O psychologists use a variety of different training evaluation designs, including the pretest–posttest control group design.

KEY TERMS

training evaluation
reaction criteria
learning criteria
behavioral criteria
results criteria
internal criteria
external criteria
utility analysis
pretest–posttest control group design

MODULE 7.4

Specialized Training Programs

Training and development are lifelong processes for workers at all levels, from executives and managers to entry-level employees, all of whom are increasingly finding that learning is necessary for job security and career opportunities. Whereas training is most often focused on the employee's current job, development involves learning that prepares the employee for future challenges, opportunities, and jobs. **Development** generally refers to formal education, job experiences, relationships, and assessments of personality and abilities that help employees prepare for the future (Noe, 2010). In this module, we focus on management and leadership development as well as specific training applications, including sexual harassment awareness training, ethics training, and cross-cultural training.

Development Formal education, job experiences, mentoring relationships, and assessments of personality and abilities that help employees prepare for the future.

Management and Leadership Development

As we will describe further in Chapter 12, effective leaders and managers are critical to organizational success. Leaders provide structure to work activities and help a diverse workforce be productive in increasingly complex and unpredictable times. The increased use of teams and the globalization of the economy require leaders to have broad skills that help to enhance individual, team, and organizational effectiveness. Trainers have met these challenges with an increased focus on management and leadership development that includes both formal and informal experiences (Goldstein & Ford, 2002). Such development strives to develop critical competencies in leaders, such as the capacity to solve business problems and to transmit the organization's strategy and values (Hollenbeck & McCall, 1999). A meta-analysis of managerial leadership development programs found that such programs have positive results on the development of leadership skills (Collins & Holton, 2004).

In this module we will focus on several training methods that are increasingly being used in the field of management and leadership development, including assessment centers, 360-degree feedback, coaching, and informal training experiences (McCauley, 2001).

Assessment center Collection of procedures for evaluation that is administered to groups of individuals; assessments are typically performed by multiple assessors.

Assessment Centers

As we saw in Chapter 3, **assessment centers** are being used in corporations in the United States and abroad. An assessment center is not a physical place or location. Instead, it is a method that has traditionally been used as a selection procedure to assess "managerial potential" (Bray, Campbell, & Grant, 1974). More specifically, assessment centers evaluate organizational, leadership, and communication skills by having candidates participate in numerous exercises (e.g., role play, leaderless group discussion, in-basket) and complete many paper-and-pencil tests. An increasing number of organizations are using assessment centers as a part of leadership and management development programs. In the late 1990s, approximately 69 percent of companies using assessment centers were using them for developmental purposes (Kudish et al., 1998). In these companies, managers deemed to have high potential are invited to participate in an assessment center that evaluates their strengths and weaknesses. Feedback obtained from the assessment center is used to create a developmental plan based on the skills and competencies required for successful performance as a manager or executive.

Jones and Whitmore (1995) conducted a 10-year follow-up evaluation of a developmental assessment center in a large insurance company. They found no differences in terms of career advancement between a group of 113 participants who went through the assessment center and a control group of 167 who did not. Nevertheless, among those who participated in the assessment center, those who followed the developmental recommendations they received based on the assessment center were more likely to be promoted than those who did not. Because the results indicated that assessment center ratings of career motivation were the best predictors of participation in development and subsequent promotions, the authors concluded that the overall effectiveness of the developmental assessment center was limited. In contrast, Englebrecht and Fischer (1995) found that participation in a developmental assessment center led to superior performance among supervisors compared to participants in a control group. This study also showed that the positive effects of the developmental assessment center did not diminish over a three-month period, indicating that assessment centers can have lasting effects as developmental experiences (Gist & McDonald-Mann, 2000). Researchers and practitioners in I-O psychology will continue to examine the short- and long-term outcomes associated with developmental assessment centers.

360-Degree Feedback

Feedback is critical in motivating change and providing direction for development (Hollenbeck & McCall, 1999). As we discussed in Chapter 5, the term **360-degree feedback** (also called multisource feedback) describes the process of collecting and providing a manager or executive with feedback that comes from many sources, including supervisors, peers, subordinates, customers, and suppliers. To help with development, such feedback should be timely, anonymous, and confidential (only to the recipient for his or her use). Raters who provide feedback anonymously are likely to be more open and honest. Recipients who know that the feedback is confidential are likely to be more open to receiving it. Computers and technology make it easier to collect multisource feedback and provide it to the executive or manager in a timely manner. Such feedback provides a rich source of information that can be used to generate a specific developmental plan and increase managerial learning (Morgeson, Mumford, & Campion, 2005).

360 degree feedback
Process of collecting and providing a manager or executive with feedback from many sources, including supervisors, peers, subordinates, customers, and suppliers.

As we discussed in Chapter 1, in cultures in which power distance is high, workers expect supervisors to have and exercise considerable power over them. Upward feedback may be seen as offensive in cultures with high power distance, as it might threaten both the subordinate and the supervisor. Not only would managers be offended in getting the feedback from subordinates, but subordinates would be offended by being asked to give it. Alternatively, 360-degree feedback might actually be better accepted in low power distance and collectivist cultures, where any feedback that helps the team succeed is likely to be received positively. Indeed, in the United States and abroad, 360-degree feedback for teams is increasingly being used for team development, a topic that we will discuss in Chapter 13.

Coaching

Coaching A practical, goal-focused form of personal, one-on-one learning for busy employees that may be used to improve performance, enhance a career, or work through organizational issues or change initiatives.

Like 360-degree feedback, **coaching** has become an important part of leadership and management development. Coaching is a practical, goal-focused form of personal, one-on-one learning for busy employees that may be used to improve performance, enhance a career, or work through organizational issues or change initiatives (Hall, Otazo, & Hollenbeck, 1999; London, 2002). A coach works individually with an employee to help develop his or her skills and to provide reinforcement and feedback. Coaching provides a flexible and targeted form of individualized learning for managers and executives. Coaching has grown rapidly because it meets the need for a leadership development tool that responds to changes in the business environment (Hollenbeck, 2001). Before 1990, coaching was considered to be a remedial technique that was used for managers with flaws or weaknesses. Peterson (2002) noted that by the late 1990s coaching had taken on a positive, proactive tone. He described the old and new assumptions about coaching, which are summarized in Table 7.7.

Although coaches may come from within the organization, external consultants are increasingly used as coaches. Feldman and Lankau (2005) reviewed the coaching literature and

TABLE 7.7 **Old and New Assumptions about Coaching**

ASSUMPTIONS IN REMEDIAL APPROACHES TO COACHING	*ASSUMPTIONS FOR POSITIVE PROACTIVE COACHING*
People resist change and the coach's task is to motivate them to develop.	People are motivated to learn and grow; the coach's task is to tap into motivation to develop.
Coaching needs to start with a thorough assessment or needs analysis so people have an accurate picture of themselves and their development needs.	Insight is a never-ending discovery process that is nurtured throughout the entire coaching process; all that is necessary to begin is a good starting point.
Coaches need to provide feedback to the people they coach.	Although feedback from the coach may be helpful, the coach's primary role is to help people improve their ability to nurture deeper insights by gathering their own feedback.
Coaches have a more objective understanding than the participant.	Both coaches and participants have important insights and information. By working together, they can put together a more useful picture of what is happening.
Coaches need to be experts in a given topic in order to teach it to people.	Coaches need to be experts in how people learn so they can help people actually change behaviors and become more effective. One of the most valuable things a coach can do is help people learn how to learn for themselves.
Coaching takes a great deal of time and effort.	Coaching is about finding leverage so that people focus on the one or two things that will have the greatest payoff.
Coaching is about fixing problem behaviors. This assumption often leads to a focus on the past.	Coaching is about improving future performance; it works best when the focus is on understanding what works for the person, what does not work, and what the person will do the next time he or she is in that situation.

SOURCE: Peterson, D. B. (2002). Management development: Coaching and mentoring programs. In K. Kraiger (Ed.), *Creating, implementing, and managing effective training and development* (pp. 160–191). San Francisco: Jossey-Bass.

identified four major activities that commonly occur in coaching relationships: (1) data gathering, (2) feedback, (3) intervention (coaching), and (4) evaluation. They also summarized research on the backgrounds of executive coaches, who typically have a PhD or a master's in business or the social sciences. Hollenbeck (2001) reported that coaches are generally chosen based on their credibility, trustworthiness, and expertise in coaching and business. A survey of 87 executive coaching clients indicated that the most important credentials for executive coaches were graduate training in psychology, experience in and understanding of business, listening skills, professionalism, and reputation as a coach established through years of experience (Wasylyshyn, 2003).

A special issue of the *Australian Psychologist* in 2007 focused on coaching and received contributions from experts from around the world. There was consensus that (1) research and practice related to coaching is still in the early stages of development and (2) there is a strong need for an evidence-based approach to coaching that is informed by research rather than by fads (Grant & Cavanagh, 2007; Latham, 2007).

Initial studies indicate that executive coaches tend to achieve significant results (Hall et al., 1999; Smither, London, Flautt, Vargas, & Kucine, 2003). Finn, Mason, and Bradley (2007) explored the effects of executive coaching on leaders' psychological states and on transformational leadership behavior, a quality of inspirational leaders that we will discuss in more detail in Chapter 12. Participants were undergoing a year-long leadership training program that included executive coaching and other components. Participants were randomly assigned to training and control groups to separate the effects of executive coaching from those of the other training components. The results indicated that leaders who received executive coaching reported higher self-efficacy, openness to new behaviors, and developmental planning than leaders who had not received such coaching. In addition, team members gave higher ratings of transformational leadership behavior to leaders who had received executive coaching than to leaders who did not receive coaching. Nevertheless, given the high cost of coaching, additional research is needed to evaluate its impact on learning and on-the-job behaviors as well as its overall cost effectiveness.

Informal Training

Informal training, which can include specific job assignments, experiences, and activities outside work, has received increased attention as an important part of leadership and management development. The notion is that challenges in the job itself can stimulate learning. McCall, Lombardo, and Morrison (1988) described the "lessons of experience" that help propel some managers to the top of their organizations. They noted that learning from experience is a continuous process that often entails dealing with hardship or failure. For example, executives who learn from business mistakes often recognize the importance of being persistent and correcting or compensating for weaknesses. This work suggested that employees must be adaptable and resilient in the face of change and career barriers (London & Mone, 1999).

Informal training Training experiences that occur outside of formal training programs. Can include specific job assignments, experiences, and activities outside of work.

Liu and Batt (2007) examined the relationship between informal training and job performance among over 2,800 telephone operators in a large unionized U.S. telecommunications company. They analyzed data over a five-month period from the company's electronic monitoring system and found that informal training was associated with higher productivity over time. On-the-job experiences and informal training can be an important part of the learning and development of managers as well. For example, work transitions (e.g., taking on a new assignment), task-related job demands (e.g., implementing changes), and job demands from obstacles (e.g., lack of adequate resources) are three important types of work experiences that provide the challenge that promotes learning and development (McCauley, Ruderman, Ohlott, & Morrow, 1994). Job assignments that require high levels of responsibility and critical decision making help managers develop the knowledge, skills, and insights that are critical to effective performance (Tesluk & Jacobs, 1998). In sum, relevant experiences on the job provide informal training that can lead to both short-term (KSAO development) and long-term (job performance, career development) outcomes. Although much training occurs in formal organizational settings, informal training and development can also be a critical component of individual and organizational success.

Sexual Harassment Awareness Training

Sexual harassment Unwelcome sexual advances, requests for sexual favors, and other conduct of a sexual nature constitute sexual harassment when submission to or rejection of this conduct explicitly or implicitly affects an individual's employment, unreasonably interferes with an individual's work performance, or creates a hostile work environment.

Quid pro quo sexual harassment Situation that involves direct requests for sexual favors, for example, when sexual compliance is mandatory for promotions or retaining one's job.

Hostile working environment sexual harassment Situation that occurs when a pattern of conduct, which is perceived as offensive and is related to sex or gender, unreasonably interferes with work performance.

Prohibition against sex discrimination in Title VII of the Civil Rights Act of 1964 includes coverage for **sexual harassment**, which includes direct requests for sexual favors (**quid pro quo sexual harassment**) and workplace conditions that constitute a **hostile working environment**. Sexual harassment claims in the United States more than tripled in the period from 1991 to 2007, from 7,906 to over 27,000, respectively. Sexual harassment has negative consequences for employee health, job satisfaction, organizational commitment, attendance, productivity, and turnover (Bowling & Beehr, 2006; Willness, Steel, & Lee, 2007). Research indicates that simply observing hostility toward women and perceiving the organization as lenient in enforcing policies against sexual harassment can have negative effects, including lower reported levels of psychological well-being and higher organizational withdrawal for both women and men (Miner-Rubino & Cortina, 2007). In addition, sexual harassment lawsuits against companies can be extremely costly. Mitsubishi's $34 million settlement in 1998 is one of the largest on record for a sexual harassment claim. As another example, Ford Motor Company settled a $7.75 million sexual harassment lawsuit that involved as many as 900 women in Ford plants across the nation (Robinson, 1999).

The Equal Employment Opportunity Commission (EEOC) encourages employers to take steps to prevent sexual harassment, including the following:

- Clearly communicate to employees that the organization has a zero tolerance policy toward sexual harassment.
- Establish an effective complaint or grievance process.
- Take immediate and appropriate action when an employee complains.

In two important cases in 1998, the Supreme Court ruled that an employer's liability can be reduced if it has training programs and other procedures in place to reduce sexual harassment (*Faragher v. City of Boca Raton*, 1998; *Burlington Industries v. Ellerth*, 1998).

Sexual harassment awareness training programs attempt to reduce the incidence of sexual harassment by increasing employee knowledge about the law and about inappropriate behaviors and situations. For example, employees may evaluate various hypothetical scenarios, determining whether they represent a hostile environment and/or quid pro quo. Employees also learn how to access the company's procedure for reporting sexual harassment.

Sexual harassment awareness training for supervisors and employees should have similar content, but supervisors should be given additional training because of their specific duties under the law and because of the formal power inherent in their position (Johnson, 1999). Supervisors and human resource representatives need to know how to implement a response to a sexual harassment charge, from communicating the initial complaint to managing sexual harassment investigations, resolving ongoing harassment situations, executing corrective actions against the perpetrator, and supporting the victim's healing process. The first consideration in educating managers and their employees is to communicate an unequivocal "no tolerance" message about sexual harassment (O'Leary-Kelly, Tiedt, & Bowes-Sperry, 2004).

BOX 7.1 A QUESTION OF SEXUAL HARASSMENT

Brenda works in a school office and reports to the principal, Ms. White. Ms. White's husband is a teacher in the school, and Brenda has frequently observed Ms. White criticizing him or being rude to him in front of others. Brenda's impression is that their marriage is unhappy. On several occasions, Mr. White has tried to engage Brenda in conversation and suggested that they have lunch together sometime. Brenda, who is married, did not want to be impolite, so she gave him noncommittal responses. Then one day he came up from behind and kissed Brenda, who pushed him away. Mr. White quickly apologized and asked Brenda not to tell anyone, especially his wife, about the incident.

Would Mr. White's behaviors fit the sexual harassment definition of hostile working environment, quid pro quo, or both? Why?

Several studies indicate that sexual harassment awareness training is effective in increasing knowledge about sexual harassment and the ability to identify inappropriate behaviors (Blakely, Blakely, & Moorman, 1998; Moyer & Nath, 1998). Wilkerson (1999) found that frontline supervisors, managers, and executives who had attended awareness training were able to identify harassment more effectively than a similar sample that had not attended training. Unfortunately, this study did not examine whether participants in sexual harassment awareness training were actually less likely to engage in sexual harassment or were more likely to intervene when they saw it happening. Perry, Kulik, and Schmidtke (1998) found that sexual harassment awareness training using videos showing appropriate and inappropriate behaviors increased knowledge acquisition and reduced the inappropriate behavior of those who had a high propensity to harass. However, this training program did not influence participants' long-term attitudes about sexual harassment. Goldberg (2007) found that, compared to a control group, individuals who received sexual harassment awareness training had significantly lower intentions of confronting their perpetrators, partly because they had a realistic view of likely consequences associated with reporting harassment. This finding was an unintended consequence of the training program and seems to create a dilemma for those involved with sexual harassment awareness training. Given this situation, Goldberg suggested that additional research be conducted on how organizations and trainers can manage employees' concerns while still accurately describing what they might expect after filing a sexual harassment complaint. Overall, more research is needed on the short- and long-term effects of sexual harassment awareness training, which will remain an important component of training for executives, managers, and their employees.

Ethics Training

An increasingly important consideration for educators and training specialists is whether training can improve ethics or integrity. The highly publicized Enron, Arthur Andersen LLP, and WorldCom accounting scandals of the late 1990s and early 2000s prompted calls for ethics training in business schools and organizations, with the presumption that such courses would improve participants' ethical decision making in the short and long term. Although many companies have ethics training programs, they typically last for only a few hours; moreover, in some cases the behaviors of upper management do not support the principles taught in these programs. An ironic example of this point was the flurry of activity on the Internet auction site eBay by people eagerly attempting to buy items from an ethics training program that Enron once offered for its employees (Hubbard, 2002).

Lefkowitz (2003) published a comprehensive book addressing ethics and values in I-O psychology. He has also contributed to a regular column called "The I-O Ethicist" in *The Industrial-Organizational Psychologist* that provides advice and ethical perspectives on various I-O topics and practices (e.g., Lefkowitz, 2004). In addition, two books have addressed social and behavioral research into business ethics (Darley, Messick, & Tyler, 2001; Messick & Tenbrussel, 1996). It appears that nearly everyone agrees that people should behave ethically in organizations, but individuals often do not believe that what they themselves just did (or are about to do) is unethical. The key point in training is to give people clear, concrete examples of what is unethical so that they can avoid unethical behaviors and the subsequent troubles that accompany them.

Research by Valentine and Fleischman (2004) indicates that the presence of an ethics training program has a positive effect on employees' perceptions of their company's ethical context. A survey from the Ethics Resource Center (2005) indicated that an increasing number of organizations have formal ethics and compliance training. Lefkowitz (2006) noted that in addition to ethics training, moral and ethical leadership from senior executives is critical in creating strong ethical climates and cultures. In Chapter 12, we will address ethical leadership and in Chapter 14 we will cover climate and culture in detail.

Given how important integrity and ethics are for organizational decision making, an appropriate approach would be to use both selection and training to increase the likelihood that employees will perform their jobs ethically. For example, organizations could select individuals who are high on integrity and conscientiousness and then provide ethics training and other learning opportunities that supplement an overall human resource system that supports ethical behaviors (Wells & Schminke, 2001). As we have discussed throughout this chapter, all types of training benefit from a work environment that supports and further develops the knowledge, skills, and attitudes learned in training.

Cross-Cultural Training

Expatriate Manager or professional assigned to work in a location outside of his or her home country.

Culture shock Condition typically experienced four to six months after expatriates arrive in a foreign country; symptoms include homesickness, irritability, hostility toward host nationals, and inability to work effectively.

Cross-cultural training Training designed to prepare individuals from one culture to interact more effectively with individuals from different cultures; the goal is to develop understanding of basic differences in values and communication styles.

We tend to assume that other cultures exist in other countries, but not here at home. In fact, we all interact daily with people from a variety of cultures, including corporate or work cultures, gender cultures, sports-fan cultures, and politically based cultures. Nevertheless, many employers encounter the greatest cross-cultural challenge when they send employees to work abroad. Such employers are increasingly finding that training is critical in helping **expatriates**—managers and employees who are working abroad—to adapt to the new environment (Stahl & Caligiuri, 2005). Serious and expensive problems occur when expatriates return from their assignments early because of poor performance or, more commonly, lack of adjustment to the new culture. Expatriate turnover is often attributed to the **culture shock** that typically occurs four to six months after arrival in the foreign country. Symptoms of culture shock include homesickness, irritability, hostility toward host nationals, and loss of ability to work effectively (Cascio, 2006).

To facilitate adjustment to the host country, companies often offer language training programs for expatriates. Many organizations offer additional forms of **cross-cultural training** designed to prepare persons of one culture to interact more effectively with persons from different cultures (Bhawuk & Brislin, 2000; Lievens, Harris, Van Keer, & Bisqueret, 2003). The goal of cross-cultural training is to develop trainees' understanding of basic differences in values and communication styles. Because cultural values are usually subconscious, cross-cultural training strives to enhance awareness of these values by using written scenarios as well as behavioral and experiential components that involve active participation by the trainees. Cross-cultural training also attempts to reduce the potential for misunderstandings in cross-cultural interactions. An example of a common misunderstanding that can result from cross-cultural interactions is as follows. A German couple bought an inn in rural Nova Scotia and hired local carpenters to make improvements. The husband then left for a two-week business trip, and the wife found that the carpenters failed to arrive for work. When she made phone calls to find out why they were absent, she learned that, in the local culture, it is unacceptable for a woman to have men working in her house when she is there alone.

A variety of different cross-cultural training approaches have been developed, including videos, brief orientation sessions led by consultants, and fully developed cross-cultural training programs. One of the most valid methods of cross-cultural training is the **cultural assimilator**, a written or computer-based tool for individual use that presents a collection of scenarios describing challenging cross-cultural critical incidents (Triandis, 1995a). In this programmed instruction technique, trainees are asked to review the critical incidents and select one of several behavioral alternatives. Next they receive feedback on the cultural implications of their choice and the desired response. Box 7.2 provides an example incident and alternative responses from a cultural assimilator developed by Harrison (1992).

Cultural assimilator Written or computer-based tool for individual use that presents a collection of scenarios describing challenging cross-cultural critical incidents.

BOX 7.2 EXAMPLE INCIDENT FROM A CULTURAL ASSIMILATOR

A professor was 20 minutes late for an appointment that he had made with two of his graduate students. The students were looking at their watches when the professor finally came into the room. The professor said, "I am terribly sorry I am late."

Which one of the following is most likely in East Asia?

1. The students might jokingly say, "Better late than never."
2. The students might be very aggressive toward the professor in the subsequent discussion.
3. The students would say, "That's OK. We don't mind."
4. The students would be very surprised at the professor's saying that he is sorry.

Alternative Responses

1. The students might jokingly say, "Better late than never." This is not the correct answer. It is not very likely that Asian students would joke with a professor in the classroom.
2. The students might be very aggressive toward the professor in the subsequent discussion. This is very unlikely. It is unlikely for an East Asian student to be aggressive toward a professor. In general, a person in a subordinate position rarely becomes aggressive toward a person in a superordinate position.
3. The students would say, "That's OK. We don't mind." This is the correct answer. Even when students are angry at a professor, they usually do not express their feelings. However, if the students were late for their appointment, then the professor would be angry and would express his impatience.
4. The students would be very surprised at the professor's saying that he is sorry. This is a wrong answer. Being late is certainly thought of negatively in East Asia, and even the professor would apologize to students for his delay.

SOURCE: Harrison, J. K. (1992). Individual and combined effects of behavior modeling and the cultural assimilator in cross-cultural management training. *Journal of Applied Psychology*, *77*, 952–962.

When trainees use a cultural assimilator, they learn about behaviors that are appropriate in their own culture but not appropriate in another culture, and they learn to make attributions that are similar to those made by people in the new culture (Kraiger, 2003). An assimilator developed for a particular culture is called a **culture-specific assimilator**. Researchers and cross-cultural trainers have developed such assimilators for several countries, including Venezuela, China, Greece, Thailand, and Honduras (e.g., Tolbert & McLean, 1995).

Culture-specific assimilator Assimilator developed for a particular culture.

Culture-specific assimilators have been criticized for focusing narrowly on one culture. This criticism is becoming increasingly relevant given that the global workplace often involves interactions with individuals from several cultures. In response to this criticism, a **culture-general assimilator** has been developed that is used to sensitize people to cross-cultural differences that they might encounter across a wide variety of cultures (Cushner & Brislin, 1996). This assimilator consists of 100 critical incidents based on a model of competencies that are valuable in cultural and business interactions in any culture. Bhawuk (1998) extended this work by incorporating Hofstede's (1980a) individualism–collectivism construct to develop a theory-based culture assimilator that prepares people for successful interactions in a number of different countries. Bhawuk found that individuals trained using the theory-based assimilator compared favorably to a control group; they also compared favorably to those trained using a culture-specific assimilator for Japan in terms of satisfaction with the training program, intercultural sensitivity, and the appropriateness of attributions made in difficult critical incidents. Future work will likely continue developing theory-based, cross-cultural training approaches that prepare expatriates for interactions in any culture.

Culture-general assimilator Assimilator used to sensitize people to cross-cultural differences they might encounter across a wide variety of cultures.

Three reviews have summarized and evaluated the benefits of cross-cultural training across the wide variety of methods that have been developed. Littrell, Salas, Hess, Paley, and Riedel (2006) reviewed 25 years (1980–2005) of research examining the effectiveness of cross-cultural training. They found that cross-cultural training is indeed effective at improving expatriates' success on overseas assignments. Two other meta-analyses found positive effects of cross-cultural training on adjustment to the host country and the job performance of expatriate managers (Deshpande & Viswesvaran, 1992; Morris & Robie, 2001). All three studies found, however, that evaluation studies of cross-cultural training rarely included an assessment of actual turnover rates and cultural competence, which indicates that future research in this area should focus on examining these important outcomes. Nevertheless, the existing data indicate that cross-cultural training methods are effective in increasing job performance and cross-cultural adjustment.

Research has indicated that the cross-cultural adjustment of expatriates is also influenced by how well their family adjusts to the new culture (Caligiuri, Hyland, Bross, & Joshi, 1998; Shaffer & Harrison, 2001). If the expatriate's spouse and children are able to establish themselves and fit into the new culture, the expatriate is more likely to perform well in the new job and remain in the international assignment. These studies suggest that organizations that take steps to ensure that spouses and other family members receive cross-cultural training are likely to increase the odds of expatriate success.

MODULE 7.4 SUMMARY

- Specialized training programs that are receiving increased attention in organizations include management and leadership development programs, sexual harassment awareness training, and cross-cultural training.
- The increased use of teams and the globalization of the economy require leaders to have broad skills that enhance individual, team, and organizational effectiveness. Trainers have met these challenges with an increased focus on management and leadership development programs that include approaches such as developmental assessment centers, 360-degree feedback, and coaching.
- Sexual harassment awareness training programs attempt to reduce the incidence of sexual harassment by having employees evaluate various hypothetical scenarios to determine if they represent sexual harassment and by explaining how to access the company's procedure for reporting sexual harassment.
- Cross-cultural training is designed to prepare individuals from one culture to interact more effectively with individuals from different cultures. Employers are increasingly finding cross-cultural training critical in helping expatriate employees adapt to the new environment.

KEY TERMS

development
assessment center
360-degree feedback
coaching
informal training
sexual harassment
quid pro quo sexual harassment
hostile working environment sexual harassment
expatriate
culture shock
cross-cultural training
cultural assimilator
culture-specific assimilator
culture-general assimilator

III Organizational Psychology

8 The Motivation to Work

MODULE 8.1

An Introduction to Motivation

The Central Position of Motivation in Psychology

It was a Friday afternoon in November, and Ted was tired. A cold wind was blowing, the sun was going down, and he felt as if the semester had been dragging on forever. As he walked across campus, posters reminded him that the football team had an important game on Saturday and that one of his favorite groups would be giving a free concert on Sunday. He had promised his parents he'd come home for dinner tonight, and his friends were planning a party after tomorrow's football game. It could be a really fun weekend—but he had two midterms on Monday. Thinking about how great it would be to unwind for a couple of days, Ted considered how well prepared he was for the exams. He knew he didn't stand a chance to ace either one of them without some serious studying over the weekend, but he didn't feel motivated in that direction. He was doing pretty well so far in those classes, one of which was an elective. Maybe he could spend a few hours cramming on Sunday night after the concert. Or he could simply enjoy himself all weekend and go to the exams refreshed and revitalized on Monday. Then again, if he did poorly on the exams, his grades could suffer, which in turn could jeopardize his financial aid package. Ted's dilemma centers on motivation. Motivation is, among other things, about choices. It is about prioritizing goals, choosing where to expend your energy. By the end of this chapter, you will have a better idea of how Ted might find the motivation to study this weekend.

Motivation (M) Concerns the conditions responsible for variations in intensity, persistence, quality, and direction of ongoing behavior.

Motivation concerns the conditions responsible for variations in intensity, persistence, quality, and direction of ongoing behavior (Vinacke, 1962). The motivation of workers has been a key interest for I-O psychologists for a hundred years (Munsterberg, 1913). Latham and his colleagues (Latham & Budworth, 2007; Latham & Pinder, 2005) have reviewed the 100-year history of motivation research in I-O psychology. In the early 20th century, the pioneering I-O psychologist Hugo Munsterberg defined a motivation problem among employees of knitting mills. The employees, who worked 12-hour shifts, six days per week, needed to be constantly alert for spools of yarn that were about to run out so that they could immediately replace them with full spools. To help the employees stay alert, Munsterberg suggested a low-tech form of amusement: allowing kittens to play with balls of wool and yarn on the factory floor. This modification did in fact result in greater worker satisfaction and alertness.

Historically, factory and mill work has been a popular target for the application of motivational theories. Consider the auto plant of the 1970s described by Barbara Garson (1972):

> The underlying assumption in an auto plant is that no worker wants to work. The plant is arranged so that employees can be controlled, checked and supervised at every point. The efficiency of an assembly line is not only in its speed but in the fact that the workers are easily replaced. This allows the employer to cope with high turnover. But it's a vicious cycle. The job is so unpleasantly subdivided that men are constantly quitting and absenteeism is common. Even an accident is a welcome diversion. Because of the high turnover, management further simplifies the job and more men quit. But the company has learned to cope with high turnover. So they don't have to worry if men quit or go crazy before they're forty. (Garson, B. (1972). Luddites in Lordstown. *Harper's* Magazine, June, pp. 67–73 (quotation from p. 73). Copyright © 1972 by Harper's Magazine. All rights reserved. Reproduced from the June issue by special permission.)

Today's auto plants and textile mills are very different, with substantial automation and liberal use of robots to free the human operator from much of the boredom and danger of factory work. A great deal of the work of both managerial and nonmanagerial employees is done by computers with dynamic displays, multiple tabs, touch screens, and elaborate menus. No need for kittens here. In addition, our understanding of motivation has progressed from kittens on the factory floor to elaborate models involving worker expectancies, goals, feelings of competence, and vastly more interesting tasks for the worker to perform. In this chapter, we will consider many of the modern models of work motivation, as well as earlier research and theories that brought us to this point.

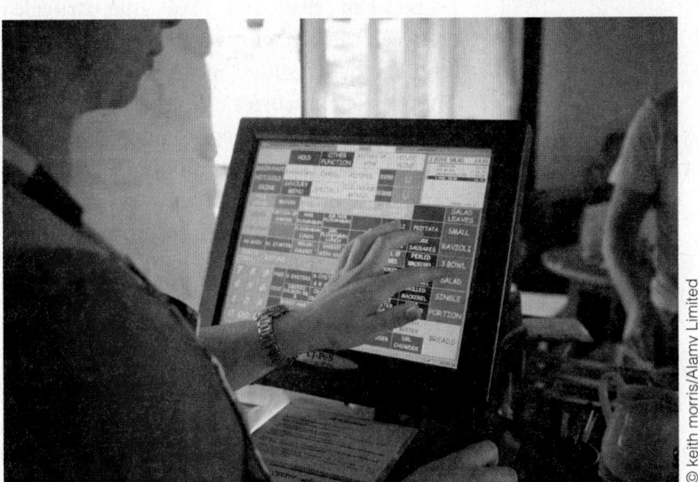

A 21st-century version of kittens: Dynamic computer screens help to prevent boredom and keep workers engaged and motivated.

A Brief History of Motivation Theory in I-O Psychology

The earliest I-O theories of motivation were anchored in the notions of **instincts**, principally driven by psychodynamic theories of personality, most notably Freud's approach. Instincts were thought to be inborn tendencies that directed behavior. An individual was said to engage in some activity (e.g., work) because of an economic "instinct," but the existence of that "instinct" was inferred from the fact that the individual engaged in work. This approach eventually proved useless because of its circular nature. In addition to the problem of circularity, since instinct theory emphasized internal "causes" of behavior, it largely ignored the interaction between an individual and an environment.

Instinct Inborn tendency that is thought to direct behavior.

The term "instinct" was gradually replaced with terms such as "need," "motive," and "drive" (Viteles, 1953). In 1943, Maslow proposed a need theory that replaced an infinite number of "instincts" with a specific set of needs. Like instincts, **needs** were thought to be inborn and universally present in humans. Because a great deal of motivational research was being conducted on animals (studying hunger and thirst), **drives** were the nonhuman equivalent of motives and needs. Maslow's need theory allowed for the environment to play a role in motivated behavior by suggesting that when one set of needs was satisfied by environmental forces, the next higher set of needs became activated. While Maslow's theory is an important part of the history of motivation, it receives little research attention these days. We will provide a brief sketch of the theory in the next module.

Need Internal motivation that is thought to be inborn and universally present in humans.

Drive Nonhuman equivalent of "motives" and "needs."

Behaviorist approach Approach developed by B. F. Skinner that placed the emphasis for behavior and directed activity directly on the environment rather than on any internal needs or instincts.

Field theory Approach developed by Kurt Lewin, who proposed that various forces in the psychological environment interacted and combined to yield a final course of action.

Group dynamics Field that grew out of the application of Kurt Lewin's field theory to industry.

At about the time that Maslow's need theory was becoming widely known, the behaviorism of B. F. Skinner (1938) was also becoming a powerful force. The **behaviorist approach** placed the emphasis for behavior directly on the environment rather than on any internal needs or instincts. The disagreements between the behaviorists and nonbehaviorists became known as the nature-versus-nurture controversy. Other, broader approaches also allowed for the influence of the environment, but in a much less mechanical way than suggested by the behaviorists. An example of this broader approach was Lewin's **field theory**, which proposed that various forces in the psychological environment interacted and combined to yield a final course of action (Lewin, 1935, 1938). Each force was thought to have a "valence" (much like the valences of chemical elements) that attracted or repelled the individual. The application of Lewin's approach in industry became known as **group dynamics**.

Between 1940 and 1960, the struggle for preeminence in motivation theory was between the behaviorists and the need theorists. By 1960, the emergence of cognitive psychology had resulted in a radical shift in the battle for "motivational superiority." New motivational theories emerged that emphasized the thought and decision processes of the individual. Today's theories of motivation are largely cognitive and emotional at their foundation. The differences among them are more a matter of *what* people think about and *how* they think about choosing courses of action rather than any dispute regarding *whether* thought enters into motivation.

Metaphors for Motivation

Given the number of citations for the term "motivation" in the literature, it should not surprise you to learn that hundreds of motivational theories have been proposed in the past hundred years. These theories can be collected into groups such as behaviorist theories or need theories or cognitive theories, and we will discuss representative theories in later sections of the chapter. Numerous theories have appeared as research has clarified various motivational dynamics. To show how motivational thinking has changed over time, we will consider the theories in the order in which they appeared.

Weiner (1991, 1992) suggested that the best way to gain an understanding of the wide variation in motivational theories, as well as of the evolution of motivational thinking, is through the use of metaphors. A metaphor is intended to illuminate an obscure or difficult concept by example. When we say that a supervisor has a "steel-trap mind," we don't expect to open his or her skull and find a steel trap. Instead, we are trying to convey some sense of the supervisor through the use of the metaphor. We may mean that the supervisor has an excellent memory, or is relentlessly logical, or very goal directed—once a topic or event is on the supervisor's radar screen (another metaphor!), it will not disappear by accident.

Weiner suggests that all motivational theories can be described by one of two metaphors: the person as machine and the person as scientist. (Actually, Weiner used the term "person as godlike," but this may be a bit misleading; Weiner implied no religious connotation, but instead proposed a cognitively more capable human being than what either behaviorism or need theory assumed. We prefer the term "person as scientist.") Weiner suggests that within these two metaphors, certain submetaphors have emerged as motivational theory has matured. We will examine these metaphors in some detail in the following section, but it might help to have a roadmap (see Table 8.1) before beginning this consideration.

Person as Machine

Machines have the following properties: They have parts that interact, they have a function, their behaviors/actions are reflexive and involuntary and performed without conscious

TABLE 8.1 **Motivational Metaphors**

METAPHOR	*CHARACTERISTIC*
Person as machine	Automatic response by individual
Pushed by internal needs	Responds to needs and drives
Pulled by environmental stimuli	Responds to external stimuli and reinforcement
Person as scientist	Voluntary response by individual; analyzes internal and external information
Person as judge	Hypothesizes about the foundation for events and actions of others
Person as intentional	Develops goals and action plans

awareness; instead, their actions and reactions are controlled by activating stimuli. Freudian psychoanalytic theory, drive theory proposed by animal learning theorists, behaviorism, and some versions of the field theory of Lewin all support the metaphor of **person as machine**, as do most motivational theories developed between 1930 and 1960. In the 1950s, learning theorists were forced to incorporate higher-order mental processes into their theories (Weiner, 1991), thus making the machine metaphor less applicable. Learning experiments demonstrated that participants developed expectancies about the connections between actions and rewards and set or accepted goals related to performance.

Person as machine
Metaphor that suggests that people's behaviors/actions are reflexive and involuntary and are performed without conscious awareness.

Person as Scientist

In contrast to machines, scientists are thought to be reflective rather than reflexive, intentional rather than automatic, and perfectly rational. As one cognitive psychologist wrote, "they are aware of all possible alternative goal-related actions, they know the likelihood that each action will result in goal attainment, and the value of each goal has been determined. Then, all of the available choices are compared regarding their expectancies of resulting in goal attainment and the value of the goals" (Weiner, 1991, p. 925). All modern motivational theories incorporate the notion of expectancies in one form or another and the role of those expectancies in directing behavior. Thus, we can see that a dramatic shift occurred in motivational thinking in the late 1950s and early 1960s.

The past several decades have also seen a shift in the manifestation of the person-as-scientist metaphor. As we will see, this metaphor captured the emphasis of most of the work motivation theories proposed between 1960 and 1990. The metaphor of the **person as scientist** suggested that people sought knowledge and understanding as a way of mastering their environment (Kelley, 1967), indeed, that the "ultimate aim of the individual is the accurate prediction of his or her environment" (Weiner, 1991, p. 926). The assumption is that people "want to know." *What* they want to know varies from theory to theory, but not the desire to know. And they want to know for a reason, which is to develop goals and action plans. That is, they intend to do something with the information, not just collect it in their mental junk drawer. This gives rise to the submetaphor of person as intentional, as listed in Table 8.1.

Person as scientist
Metaphor that suggests that people are active information gatherers and analysts who seek knowledge and understanding as a way of mastering their environment.

There is one problem with the person-as-scientist metaphor, which assumes that individuals are perfectly rational: They aren't. As Dawes (1988) has noted:

> Psychologists and behavioral economists studying the decision making of individuals tend to reach the conclusion that individuals do not make decisions based on rational and normative principles. Not only do [they] tend to violate the principle of maximizing expected utility, they are often patently irrational. (p. 13)

Limited rationality The inability of humans to reason and make decisions in perfectly rational ways.

This inability to reason in perfectly rational ways was recognized by two Nobel Prize winners, the psychologist and economist Herbert Simon (1960) and, more recently, the psychologist Daniel Kahneman. Simon described this phenomenon as the **limited rationality** (also known as bounded rationality) of the human decision maker. Kahneman and colleagues have demonstrated the limits of that rationality through both laboratory and field research (Kahneman, Slovic, & Tversky, 1982). One need only look around to see the effects of limited rationality. Consider a driver carefully obeying traffic laws while smoking and not wearing a seat belt—rationality can't get much more limited than that.

Person as judge Metaphor in which an individual seeks information about the extent to which the person and others are perceived as responsible for positive and negative events. The person looks for evidence of intention in the actions of others and considers those intentions in choosing a personal course of action.

Because of the growing recognition that individuals are not perfectly rational, newer theories of motivation have been emerging, theories that allow for the influence of emotionality on decision making. This in turn has led to a greater emphasis on the social world—the world outside the individual—as opposed to a focus on a completely internal process by which an individual calculates probabilities. Weiner has labeled this new submetaphor the **person as judge**. Within the context of this metaphor, an individual seeks information about the extent to which the self and others are responsible (or, more accurately, perceived as responsible) for positive and negative events. The person looks for evidence of intention in the actions of others and considers those intentions in choosing a personal course of action. Recently, several researchers have suggested that humans may have some universal motives. Cropanzano, Goldman, and Folger (2005) propose that we all have a basic self-interest motive, although that self-interest may be devoted to social goals as well as (or instead of) economic goals. Greenberg (2008) suggests that we all have self-esteem motives (i.e., the desire to feel worthy, valued, and skilled) and that these motives are driven largely by fear of our own mortality. In a sense, if we are valued by others, we somehow seem less vulnerable. Thus, the I-O view of motivation has become much more socially and emotionally oriented, and the evaluation of the actions of others has become more central to explaining motivated behavior.

In summary, modern motivational theory tends to view the individual as an active information gatherer (the scientist metaphor) rather than a passive respondent to either internal or external stimuli (the machine metaphor). Furthermore, it is increasingly obvious that the individual is not perfectly rational in gathering and using information. Instead, the individual is influenced by social information in the form of attributions involving the intentions of others (the person-as-judge metaphor). This evolution of motivational theory has not been accidental or capricious. It has resulted from decades of careful research and theorizing both in the laboratory and in the field. We will use these metaphors to provide a more detailed consideration of motivational theories in Modules 8.2 and 8.3. But first we need to deal with some other basic issues in work motivation.

The Meaning and Importance of Motivation in the Workplace

Motivation and Performance

In Viteles's (1953) pioneering book on motivation in the workplace, it was clear that he equated motivation with productivity. He saw motivation as the method by which an employer "aroused the cooperation of individual workers" (p. ix). He titled the first section of his book "Mobilizing the Will-to-Work." He noted that in a survey of employers conducted in 1946, 73 percent identified the "general indifference in workers" as the major reason for a decline in postwar productivity. In the time since Viteles's book appeared, I-O psychologists have not appreciably changed their general acceptance of the connections among the constructs of motivation, performance, and productivity. Indeed, Pritchard (1995) has developed an intricate performance and productivity measurement system called ProMES (Productivity Measurement and Enhancement System) based on the premise that increasing the amount of time and effort that an individual devotes to a task (i.e., increasing the task motivation for a person) will result in high levels of personal performance and increased productivity for the organization. We will examine the ProMES system in the last module of this chapter.

A very basic model for considering the role of motivation in performance is the following:

$$\text{Performance} = (\text{Motivation} \times \text{Ability}) - \text{Situational Constraints}$$

It is important to note the multiplication sign in this formula. This sign means that if motivation is equal to zero, then ability will not matter since anything times zero equals zero. Similarly, it means that even modest increases in ability can be magnified by motivation. In other chapters in the book, we consider ability (e.g., intelligence), performance (e.g., performance on demanding technical tasks), and situational (e.g., stress or difficult working conditions) constraints. Although performance can require very complex behavior, you can be certain that motivation plays a role in both successful and unsuccessful performance. It is important to recognize that motivation is not simply about productivity—sabotage and absence are motivated behaviors as well.

Motivation and Work–Life Balance

All of us probably know at least one person we would consider a workaholic: an individual who is addicted to work and pays the cost for that addiction in reduced physical health and mental well-being. In some senses, the workaholic might be described as being *too* motivated. This is because the overemphasis on work has led to an underemphasis on other aspects of life; the workaholic lacks **work–life balance**. We might think of motivation as a resource, with only so much to spread around. If too much is "spent" in one area, there is little left for other areas. Recall from Chapter 1 that research (Butler, 2007) has similarly identified the school–work balance as a critical consideration for student success. Too many hours of work diminish both the time for study and the long-term value of that study.

Work–life balance Area of research that investigates whether the satisfaction that one experiences at work is in part affected by the satisfaction that one experiences in non-work and vice versa, particularly to the extent that one environment has demands that conflict with the other.

In the early days of motivation theorizing, a great deal of attention was devoted to the concept of "energizing" an individual. It was assumed that unless incentives were available, an individual would remain passive. There is not much support for that view of motivation. Current motivational discussions revolve around the concept of direction more than that of simple energy enhancement. All people, unless ill or impaired, will expend energy in one way or another. The same principles that apply to work motivation will apply to the motivation to do things other than work. In some senses, the employer is always competing with other forces for the time and attention of the employee. Some employers might consider a workaholic to be a "win" because the person devotes inordinate energy to work.

© dusko matic/iStockphoto

Motivating workers is a greater challenge in a machine-controlled work environment.

The nonworkaholic employee feels tension between competing forces: work on the one hand, and family, leisure, school, and

"What do you think . . . should we get started on that motivation research or not?"

healthy activities on the other. A consideration of work motivation in a vacuum is a meaningless exercise. Work motivation can only have meaning within the context of a rich and complex life in which there are forces competing with the workplace for time and effort. We will consider the challenge of this work–life balance in detail in both the next chapter and Chapter 10 when we consider stress.

Motivation and Personality

As we saw in Chapter 3, I-O psychologists generally agree that personality can be divided into dimensions such as agreeableness, conscientiousness, and so forth. We also saw that personality can be a predictor of work performance and possibly even occupational choice. Since we know that motivation can also affect work performance, it is reasonable to consider what, if any, connections may exist between personality and work motivation. Judge and Ilies (2002) completed a meta-analysis on exactly that topic. They examined the relationship between measures of the Big Five personality traits and various indicators of motivation from several current motivational theories. These indicators included the number and difficulty of goals set by an individual, belief on the part of the individual that hard work would lead to rewards, and belief on the part of the individual in his or her ability to perform a task or job. Judge and Ilies found 65 studies and 105 correlation coefficients that could be included in the meta-analysis.

The results showed that strong and consistent relationships do exist between personality characteristics and performance motivation. Neuroticism was consistently negatively related to performance motivation (recall that the positive end of the neuroticism scale is emotional stability). In contrast, conscientiousness was positively related to all indicators of performance motivation. Put another way, conscientious and emotionally stable individuals set more challenging goals, were more likely to believe that hard work would lead to rewards, and were more confident in their ability to accomplish a task or job.

Locus of control The extent to which an individual views events as resulting from his or her own actions (an internal LOC) or from outside causes (an external LOC).

Research evidence continues to accumulate linking personality to motivation. Ng, Sorenson, and Eby (2006) conducted a meta-analysis of the relationships between locus of control and motivation. **Locus of control** (LOC) refers to the extent to which an individual views events as resulting from his or her own actions (an internal LOC) or from outside causes (an external LOC). People with an internal LOC believe that they can control their environments; people with an external LOC believe that they are at the mercy of external environments with little ability to influence outcomes. The researchers' meta-analysis showed a clear and positive connection between an internal LOC and work motivation. The point here is not that people with an internal LOC are in better objective circumstances for affecting outcomes, just that they *believe* they can control their fates. Xenikou (2005) also found a positive relationship between an optimistic view of life (called a positive attributional style) and work motivation among Greek managerial and nonmanagerial employees. Further, she discovered that this optimism seemed to diminish with organizational tenure such that after four years with an organization, employees tended to grow more pessimistic in outlook.

The personality–motivation connection is an important one. Past theories of work motivation gave little emphasis to individual difference measures such as personality traits. They tended to take a one-size-fits-all approach. Nor have work motivation theories paid much attention to individual differences in cognitive ability, assuming instead that everyone is smart enough to set and remember goals and to calculate expectancies. Perhaps one of the reasons why the person-as-scientist theories have lost ground to the person-as-judge theories is because not everyone is as intelligent or emotion-free as the "scientist" assumed by the theory. As motivation theory evolves into the person-as-judge metaphor, it should be increasingly valuable to look at personality traits in our attempts to understand work motivation. Equally interesting is the proposition of Kanfer and Ackerman (2004) that motivation and performance will actually change over time as both cognitive abilities and personality change in middle and later adulthood.

MODULE 8.1 SUMMARY

- Worker motivation has been a key interest for I-O psychologists for almost a hundred years. The earliest I-O theories of motivation were anchored in the notions of instincts. The term "instinct" was gradually replaced with terms such as "need," "motive," and "drive."
- Weiner suggested that the best way to understand the wide variation in motivational theories, as well as of the evolution of motivational thinking, is through one of two metaphors: the person as machine and the person as scientist. Within these two metaphors, certain submetaphors have emerged as motivational theory has matured.
- Modern motivational theory views the individual as an active information gatherer (the scientist metaphor) rather than as a passive respondent to either internal or external stimuli (the person-as-machine metaphor). Further, it is increasingly obvious that the individual is not perfectly rational in gathering and using information. Instead, the individual is influenced by social information in the form of attributions involving the intentions of others (the person-as-judge metaphor).
- Early and modern approaches to motivation are based on the premise that increasing the amount of time and effort that an individual devotes to a task (i.e., task motivation) will result in higher levels of individual performance and increased productivity for the organization. A basic model for considering the role of motivation in performance is: Performance = (Motivation × Ability) − Situational Constraints.
- In recent decades, personality characteristics have become more important in the study of work motivation.

KEY TERMS

motivation
instinct
need
drive
behaviorist approach
field theory
group dynamics
person as machine
person as scientist
limited rationality
person as judge
work–life balance
locus of control

MODULE 8.2

Motivational Theories—Classic Approaches

Person-as-Machine Theories

The preceding overview of motivational theories included two primary metaphors: person as machine and person as scientist. We will use these metaphors as organizing devices to consider some representative theories of work motivation.

As you will recall, the machine metaphor is based on the premise that motivation is a largely unconscious process, in which the individual responds to internal conditions (e.g., needs or drives) or external stimuli (e.g., rewards) in a reflexive or automatic way. We will consider two classic examples of these two mechanical approaches, an internal theory and an external theory.

An Internal Mechanical Theory: Maslow's Need Theory

Maslow's need theory
Theory that proposed that all humans have a basic set of needs and that these needs express themselves over the life span of the individual as internal "pushes" or drives. Identified five basic needs sets: physiological, security, love or social, esteem, and self-actualization.

Abraham Maslow (1943) proposed that all humans have a basic set of needs and that these needs express themselves over the life span of the individual as internal "pushes" or drives. As such, **Maslow's need theory** was more a theory of human development than one of work motivation. Generally, the theory proposed that when we are young, we are more concerned with our physical well-being. As we become more secure in our physical world, we then begin to emphasize social needs. Finally, when our social foundation seems secure, we then concentrate on developing our abilities and capacities to their fullest. Thus, Maslow proposed five different sets of needs and arranged them hierarchically. In his model, the lower needs take precedence over the higher needs. Physiological needs were the lowest and self-actualization needs the highest among the five categories.

1. *Physiological needs.* These are what learning theories generally refer to as basic needs or drives and are satisfied by such things as food, water, and sleep.
2. *Security needs.* This category refers to the need an individual has to produce a secure environment—one free of threats to continued existence.
3. *Love or social needs.* These needs are associated with interpersonal factors. They refer to an individual's desire to be accepted by others.
4. *Esteem needs.* These needs are associated with being respected for accomplishments or capabilities.

5. *Self-actualization needs.* These needs refer to the desire on the part of an individual to develop his or her capacities to the fullest. In Maslow's theory, few people ever completely satisfy this need. Instead, the individual would always be seeking to grow and develop. Some examples of fully self-actualized individuals might be Martin Luther King, Jr., Gandhi, or Mother Theresa (although even they might have claimed that they were not finished "growing").

In Maslow's theory, individuals would be motivated to fulfill the most basic set of unfulfilled needs. Thus, if an individual's physiological and security needs were fulfilled, then the individual would expend energy attempting to fulfill the love needs. When the love needs were met, the individual would be motivated by circumstances that would satisfy the esteem needs, and so on. Should a lower-level need that had once been satisfied reemerge (e.g., a life-threatening illness occurs to a formerly healthy person), the person would immediately revert to actions that might satisfy that now-unsatisfied lower-level need.

Maslow's model fits the person-as-machine metaphor quite well. The behavior of the individual is unconscious and automatic. The individual will respond to whatever satisfies the lowest unfulfilled need. In addition, as Maslow proposes that all individuals operate in the same manner, the theory is universal. Even though Maslow's theory is seldom explicitly invoked by organizations today, the adoption of a benefits/rewards menu or "cafeteria" plan (in which employees can choose a subset of benefits from a larger "menu") in many organizations indicates that Maslow's theory has had some influence on modern organizational practices. In these plans, workers are allowed to choose among alternative rewards and benefits packages, which can address multiple needs.

Although Scott Adams's cartoon character Dilbert is hardly a scientific reference, it may interest you to know that even Dilbert seems to acknowledge Maslow's hierarchy, as can be seen in Box 8.1.

Variations on Maslow's Theory

Since Maslow's five-factor need theory was introduced, psychologists have suggested a number of modifications. The most enduring and well known was proposed by

BOX 8.1 EMPLOYEE HIERARCHY OF NEEDS

As you can see in the pyramid, Dilbert identifies six need levels rather than the five proposed by Maslow. As Adams explains:

Before you can hope to motivate employees you must understand their hierarchy of needs. Employees will not develop a need for things at the higher levels of the pyramid until they have totally satisfied their needs at lower levels. Make sure they get plenty of the stuff on the lower levels, but not so much that they develop a need for more money.

SOURCE: Employee Hierarchy of Needs from Adams, S. (1996). *Dogbert's top secret management handbook.* New York: HarperCollins.

Two-factor theory Theory proposed by Herzberg that suggested that there were really two basic needs, not five as suggested by Maslow, and that they were not so much hierarchically arranged as independent of each other.

Hygiene needs Lower-level needs described in Herzberg's two-factor theory. Herzberg proposed that meeting these needs would eliminate dissatisfaction but would not result in motivated behavior or a state of positive satisfaction.

Motivator needs Higher-level needs described in Herzberg's two-factor theory. Herzberg proposed that meeting such needs resulted in the expenditure of effort as well as satisfaction.

Reinforcement theory Theory that proposes that behavior depends on three simple elements: stimulus, response, and reward. Proposed that if a response in the presence of a particular stimulus is rewarded (i.e., reinforced), that response is likely to occur again in the presence of that stimulus.

Contingent reward A reward that depends on or is contingent on a particular response.

Intermittent reward A reward that is given for only some correct responses.

Continuous reward A reward that is presented every time a correct response occurs.

Herzberg and was called the **two-factor theory**. Herzberg (1966) suggested that there were really two basic needs, not five, and that they were not so much hierarchically arranged as independent of each other. These two needs were called **hygiene needs** (Maslow's physical and security needs) and **motivator needs** (Maslow's social, esteem, and actualization needs). Herzberg believed that meeting hygiene needs would eliminate dissatisfaction but would not result in motivated behavior or a state of positive satisfaction. In contrast, meeting motivator needs would result in the expenditure of effort as well as positive satisfaction. Although Herzberg's theory generated considerably more research than the "parent" theory of Maslow, the support for his theory was as disappointing as it had been for Maslow's. As with Maslow's theory, it was also difficult to determine exactly what Herzberg's theory might predict (King, 1970). We mention these two theories—Maslow's and Herzberg's—only as historical markers of the person-as-machine era. Neither theory has received much research or practical attention in several decades. Today's theorists and practitioners have little enthusiasm for approaches that do not allow for the concepts of expectancy, evaluation, or judgment on the part of the individual.

An External Mechanical Theory: Reinforcement Theory

Approximately 60 years ago, a young psychologist working on problems of animal learning discovered that the manner by which rewards were connected to behavior could have a dramatic effect on animal performance. The psychologist was B. F. Skinner, now considered the father of modern behaviorism. In its simplest form, behaviorism (or **reinforcement theory**) proposes that behavior depends on three simple elements: stimulus, response, and reward. It does not matter whether the behavior being observed is that of a white rat in an experimental cage, a child learning how to use a knife and fork, or a worker faced with a production challenge. The mechanical proposition of behaviorism is that if a response in the presence of a particular stimulus is rewarded (i.e., reinforced), that response is likely to occur again in the presence of that stimulus. Consider, for example, a monetary bonus as a reward in a work setting. If a worker produces at a particular level and receives a bonus for that performance, reinforcement theory predicts that the worker is more likely to achieve that level of performance again in the future.

When a reward depends on a response, it is called a **contingent reward** (i.e., the reward is contingent on the response). Contingent reward or reinforcement is a central proposition of the behaviorist approach. A second important proposition has to do with the schedule of reward or reinforcement. Rewards can be given continuously (every time a correct response occurs, a reward is presented) or intermittently (only a portion of correct responses are rewarded). Ferster and Skinner (1957) discovered that **intermittent rewards** actually produced higher levels of performance than **continuous rewards.**

These two principles—contingent reinforcement and differing schedules of reinforcement—have been applied frequently in work settings; examples include piecework payment in manufacturing, year-end performance bonuses, sales commissions, and the like. We will present an example of this application in the last module of this chapter.

Although the results of experiments using contingent reinforcement—whether in the classroom, the nuclear family, or the workplace—can be impressive, there are many problems associated with such an approach to the concept of motivation. First, the approach is impractical. There are few jobs or tasks that can be neatly enough compartmentalized to make it clear exactly how much reinforcement should be given and how often. Single-contributor jobs are rapidly giving way to team and group work. In addition, we cannot observe some of the most important behaviors that occur in the workplace because they are not simple physical actions but complex cognitive processes. If we observed a technician

BOX 8.2

The popular book *Freakonomics* (Levitt & Dubner, 2005) provides a cautionary tale about an ill-advised use of behaviorism. A day-care center in Haifa, Israel, was experiencing a common and annoying parent behavior: Parents came late to pick up their children. Even though the policy stated that children were to be picked up by 4:00 p.m., they often were not. The day-care center imposed a fine of $3 for each late pickup by a parent. The number of late pickups promptly doubled. The fine was considerably cheaper than a babysitter would have been. Moreover, parents no longer felt guilty about showing up late since they were now paying for the additional service. After 17 weeks, the day-care center eliminated the $3 late fee, but the damage had been done. The parents no longer felt guilty, and the new, higher level of lateness continued!

troubleshooting a piece of electronic equipment, the behavior we observed would be looking at the equipment, referring to a manual, and occasionally activating the equipment, but when the equipment was finally fixed, we would recognize that it was fixed as a result of some behavior we could *not* observe: gathering information, thinking, and hypothesis testing. Finally, the principle of contingent reinforcement requires careful observation of the behavior of the worker, an additional and time-consuming task for a supervisor. More importantly, however, the approach has no role for any cognitive activity. As we indicated in Module 8.1, behaviorism, like other person-as-machine theories, cannot account for expectancies, the effects of goals, or even the simplest of intentions on the part of the worker. Locke (1980) presented an excellent critical review of the strengths and shortcomings of behaviorism as a theory of motivation. We are not arguing that reinforcement theory is "wrong" or ineffective. Nevertheless, as a complete theory of work motivation, behaviorism falls short, as do other person-as-machine approaches that fail to acknowledge higher mental activities such as reasoning and judgment.

© Bonnie Kamin/PhotoEdit

Pulling a lever is not an intrinsically interesting task, but people will do it repeatedly if they believe it yields generous rewards on an unpredictable timetable.

Person-as-Scientist Theories

By 1970, most areas of psychology were caught up in the so-called cognitive revolution. Motivation theory in general and work motivation theory in particular were no exception. The key ingredient in this approach was the capacity of an individual to both learn from the past and anticipate the future. This allowed for the possibility of intentional behavior, planning, goal acceptance, and, most importantly, choice. The mechanical theories did not include the concept of choice in any formal way. To use Weiner's person-as-scientist metaphor, workers were now seen as rational beings capable of gathering and analyzing information and of making decisions based on that information.

Vroom's VIE Theory

Path–goal theory of motivation First formal work motivation theory to suggest that people weighed options before choosing among them. Reasoned that if a worker saw high productivity as a path to the goal of desired rewards or personal goals (e.g., a pay increase or promotion, or increased power, prestige, or responsibility), he or she would likely be a high producer.

VIE theory Motivation theory that assumed that individuals rationally estimate the relative attractiveness and unattractiveness of different rewards or outcomes (valence), the probability that performance will lead to particular outcomes or rewards (instrumentality), and the probability that effort will lead to performance (expectancy).

Valence The strength of a person's preference for a particular outcome.

Instrumentality The perceived relationship between performance and the attainment of a certain outcome.

Expectancy An individual's belief that a particular behavior (e.g., effort, hard work) will lead to higher performance.

The first formal work motivation theory to suggest that people weighed options before choosing among them was the **path–goal theory** of Georgopoulos, Mahoney, and Jones (1957). They reasoned that if a worker saw high productivity as a path to the goal of desired rewards or personal goals (e.g., a pay increase or promotion, or increased power, prestige, or responsibility), that worker would likely be a high producer. Conversely, if low productivity was seen as a path to desired rewards (e.g., less stress, more time with family, approval of co-workers), that worker would likely be a low producer.

This theory was a simple one in conception, but it marked a dramatic shift in thinking about motivation: a shift from the person as machine to the person as scientist. The new approach was presented in a more elegant way by Vroom (1964) in a theory that has come to be known as **VIE (valence, instrumentality, expectancy) theory**. If you have studied chemistry, you will recall that valence refers to the attracting or repelling force of an element. Vroom reasoned that psychological objects in an environment also have attracting and repelling forces. For most people, money would be attracting, and uninteresting work would be repelling. For the most part, this element of Vroom's theory was not much different from the earlier person-as-machine approaches. It was a simple recognition that people have needs or desires.

The second element in Vroom's theory, instrumentality, represented the answer to the question, "If I am able to perform as expected, am I likely to receive expected outcomes or rewards?" Instrumentality deals with the relationship between performance and the attainment of a certain outcome. Consider a promotion. A promotion usually means a higher salary as well as increased prestige. But it may also include increased responsibility, longer hours, and even lower total annual compensation (since most managers and supervisors are not eligible for overtime pay). So you can see that there may be many instrumentalities in a given situation, each one related to the valued or nonvalued circumstances of a particular outcome, such as the promotion. This is where the person as scientist comes in. Vroom proposed that once an individual became aware of these various instrumentalities, he or she could combine that information in such a way as to decide whether, on balance, the outcome would be more positive than negative (i.e., there were more positive valences than negative valences associated with the outcome). This analysis would then lead to some choice of action.

The third element of the theory, expectancy, had to do with an individual's belief that increased effort would lead to successful performance. When we put the three elements (V, I, E) together, we can see the complete theory.

As you can see, the theory assumed that the individual was a "calculator." He or she was expected to estimate the probabilities associated with valence, instrumentality, and expectancy. This is where the person as scientist comes in as individuals attempt to combine information using V, I, and E to help them make a decision about a choice of action. If a manager wanted to apply Vroom's theory, he or she would concentrate on three things:

1. Motivate employees by offering outcomes that have high valence.
2. Clarify instrumentalities by letting employees know that high performance is associated with positive outcomes.
3. Clarify expectancies by making it clear to employees that hard work will lead to higher performance.

As was true of the need theories described earlier, there have been many variations of Vroom's VIE theory (Graen, 1969; Lawler, 1973; Porter & Lawler, 1968). Research on the model did seem to support the notion that effort was related to cognitions (i.e., perceived expectancies and instrumentalities). However, research also indicated that in making behavioral choices, individuals considered things other than instrumentalities and expectancies. The VIE model was elegant and uplifting. It elevated the status of the individual to that of a rational being. Nevertheless, it may have pushed the notion of rationality beyond reasonable limits by assuming that people could and would go through the somewhat tortured calculations the VIE model requires for all but the simplest of decisions. Not surprisingly, humans have been found to fall short of the cognitive capabilities of godlike entities.

In addition, VIE theory ignored many noncognitive elements in choice, such as personality and emotion. Erez and Isen (2002) have demonstrated that individuals in a positive emotional state had higher expectancy and instrumentality values than individuals in a neutral emotional state. A meta-analysis (van Eerde & Thierry, 1996) has raised an additional point. The original theory, as proposed by Vroom, was a within-individuals theory (i.e., which of Y choices would be most attractive to a single individual) rather than a between-individuals theory (i.e., which of X people would be more motivated). However, van Eerde and Thierry (1996) found that most of the research was done on the *between*-individuals version of the theory. In many respects, the job of a manager is to motivate each individual. Thus, the between-persons results are largely irrelevant to the challenge of increasing motivation within a single individual.

Production charts are used to motivate workers on a production floor.

Equity Theory

Another popular person-as-scientist theory was proposed by Adams (1965). As in Vroom's VIE theory, Adams proposed that people are calculators, but in a somewhat different way than proposed by Vroom. In 1957, Festinger proposed **dissonance theory**. This theory suggested that tension exists when individuals hold "dissonant cognitions" (incompatible thoughts). As an example, consider an individual who purchases a new sport-utility vehicle and later discovers that this SUV is prone to rollover accidents. The individual now has two incompatible thoughts: "I am a smart person who made a wise purchase of a neat car" versus "I am not a very smart person; I just bought an expensive new car that may result in my death or injury." This individual will then expend energy to reduce the tension caused by these dissonant cognitions. The energy may be directed toward the manufacturer of the car, and the new owner may try to return the SUV for a refund. Alternatively, the new owner may convince himself or herself that the rollover tests were inaccurate or that it is really driver behavior rather than vehicle characteristics that are responsible for rollovers. One way or another, energy will be expended to reduce the tension resulting from dissonant cognitions. This approach assumes that individuals always seek some sense of "balance" (i.e., absence of tension) and will direct their behavior toward seeking and maintaining that balance.

Adams (1965) transplanted Festinger's ideas to the workplace and developed a theory that has come to be known as **equity theory**. He suggested that individuals look at their world in terms of comparative **inputs** and **outcomes**. They calculate what they are investing in their work (e.g., training, effort, abilities) and what they get out of it (e.g., compensation, co-workers, interest level of the work itself). They then compare their inputs

Dissonance theory Theory suggested by Festinger that observed that tension exists when individuals hold "dissonant cognitions" (incompatible thoughts). This approach assumes that individuals always seek some sense of "balance" (i.e., absence of tension) and that they will direct their behavior toward reducing the tension resulting from dissonant cognitions.

Equity theory Motivational theory developed by Adams (1965) that suggested that individuals look at their world in terms of comparative inputs and outcomes. Individuals compare their inputs and outcomes with others (e.g., peers, co-workers) by developing an input/outcome ratio.

Inputs The training, effort, skills, and abilities that employees bring to or invest in their work.

Outcomes The compensation, satisfaction, and other benefits employees derive from their work.

Comparison other A co-worker or idealized other person to which the individual compares himself or herself in determining perceived equity.

Outcome/input ratio Ratio that results when employees compare their inputs and outcomes to those of others (e.g., peers, co-workers) to determine if they are being treated equitably.

and outcomes to those of **comparison others** (e.g., peers, co-workers) by developing a ratio. If their own **outcome/input ratio** is identical to the outcome/input ratio of their comparison other, then there would be no tension and no subsequent action to relieve that tension. Consider the example of a sales representative for a medical company who discovers that even though he or she is receiving a 5 percent commission on gross sales, a representative for the same company in a neighboring state is receiving a 7 percent commission. According to equity theory (and common sense!), something will happen. This "something" might be a call to the sales manager requesting an increase in commission rate, a call to a recruiter to look for a new job, an attempt to sabotage the efforts of the fellow sales representative, or a reduction in post-sales contacts with customers (activities that, while expected, generate no direct income in the short term).

The mathematical description of equity theory appears as Figure 8.1. In this formulation, *O* stands for outcomes and *I* stands for inputs. The subscripts *p* and *o* stand for "person" and "other" (i.e., comparison person or comparison other). As you can see, when the ratio of outcome to input is the same for "person" and "other," a condition of equity exists. However, if the *O/I* ratio for "person" is either higher or lower than the ratio for "other," then inequity exists, creating a state of tension.

The early laboratory studies of equity theory used method of payment as a way of manipulating outcomes. Participants were assigned to either an hourly payment or piece-rate payment, and they were intentionally either overpaid or underpaid. Overpaid participants were told that more money was available than had been originally anticipated, and, as a result, they would get $2.25 per hour instead of the agreed-upon $1.50 per hour (remember, these studies were done in the 1960s) or 10 cents per piece instead of 7 cents per piece. Conversely, in the underpayment condition, participants were told that less money was available than originally anticipated, and, as a result, they would be paid $1.50 per hour (or 4 cents per piece) instead of the $1.75 per hour (or 7 cents per piece) originally promised. Table 8.2 presents the predicted reactions of the participants. Generally, results supported the underpayment predictions but not the overpayment ones. Evidently, being paid more than you expected is not painful or tension-producing for most people.

$$\frac{O_p}{I_p} = \frac{O_o}{I_o}$$

Equity

$$\frac{O_p}{I_p} > \frac{O_o}{I_o} \quad \frac{O_p}{I_p} < \frac{O_o}{I_o}$$

Inequity

FIGURE 8.1 **Mathematical Description of Equity Theory**

Most of the research on equity theory was definitional. What was an "outcome"? What was an "input"? Who was a "comparison other"? Can outcomes (e.g., access to a training program) become inputs (i.e., increased ability level)? Do outcomes (e.g., salary or praise) diminish in value over time? Are individuals able (or willing) to conduct the often intricate calculations implied by the theory (Landy, 1989)? Is a moral maturity dimension involved in equity considerations (Vecchio, 1981)? As was the case with VIE theory, many

TABLE 8.2 **Equity Theory Predictions of Employee Reactions to Inequitable Payment**

	UNDERPAYMENT	*OVERPAYMENT*
Hourly payment	Subjects underpaid by the hour produce less or poorer-quality output than equitably paid subjects.	Subjects overpaid by the hour produce more or higher-quality output than equitably paid subjects.
Piece-rate payment	Subjects underpaid by piece rate will produce a large number of low-quality units in comparison with equitably paid subjects.	Subjects overpaid by piece rate will produce fewer units of higher quality than equitably paid subjects.

SOURCE: Steers, R. M., Porter, L. W., & Bigley, G. A. (1996). *Motivation and leadership at work*. New York: McGraw-Hill. © 1996 by McGraw-Hill. Reprinted by permission of The McGraw-Hill Companies, Inc.

researchers and practitioners questioned whether workers were as "rational" as the theory suggested. The only difference between them is that equity theory proposes a socially based rationality, and VIE theory makes no explicit mention of any comparison other.

Latham and Pinder (2005) suggest that the general thrust of equity theory has now been subsumed in the larger issue of justice and fairness perceptions. Individuals are concerned about being treated fairly in a wide range of situations—rewards represent only one class of situation. We will cover theories of fairness and justice in Chapter 11. Another issue that has emerged in social comparison theories in the 21st century is the definition of a comparison other when work is completed in a virtual environment rather than a "real" one (Conner, 2003). Finally, Bolino and Turnley (2008) suggest that equity theory may have less relevance for cultures outside of the United States. For example, they find that equity theory works better in individualistic (what the authors refer to as "doing-oriented" cultures) rather than in collectivist cultures. They give as an example Korean workplaces, where inputs are more likely to be defined by education and seniority rather than by actual accomplishments. With respect to outcomes, they suggest that collectivist cultures will be more likely to place a value on enhanced social relationships as a valuable outcome (as opposed to money or promotional opportunities). We will return to the issue of culture and motivation in Module 8.4.

MODULE 8.2 SUMMARY

- Maslow proposed a universal set of needs, expressed as internal drives. He further proposed a hierarchical arrangement of these needs: One need set must be fulfilled before the next-higher need set is activated. Maslow's theory has been a popular way to think about work motivation, even though there has been relatively little research supporting it.
- Two principles from behaviorist reinforcement theory—contingent reinforcement and differing schedules of reinforcement—are often applied in the work context. Nevertheless, as a complete theory of work motivation, behaviorism falls short because it fails to acknowledge higher mental activities such as reasoning and judgment.
- Person-as-scientist theories include Vroom's VIE theory and equity theory, both of which assume that individuals are intentional and rational in their behavior. The primary difference between them is that equity theory proposes a socially based rationality, whereas VIE theory makes no explicit mention of any comparison other.

KEY TERMS

Maslow's need theory
two-factor theory
hygiene needs
motivator needs
reinforcement theory
contingent reward
intermittent reward
continuous reward
path–goal theory of motivation
VIE theory
valence
instrumentality
expectancy
dissonance theory
equity theory
inputs
outcomes
comparison other
outcome/input ratio

MODULE 8.3

Modern Approaches to Work Motivation

Person-as-Intentional Approaches

VIE theory and equity theory may seem cumbersome because of their heavy reliance on the person-as-scientist model and, in particular, the concept of perfect rationality. But they share another characteristic as well. Both assume that individuals are intentional in their behavior. Other motivation theories arose at the same time as equity theory and VIE theory that placed less emphasis on the person as scientist and more emphasis on the notion of intentional behavior.

Goal-Setting Theory

Person-as-intentional approach Motivational approach that assumes that individuals are intentional in their behavior.

Goal-setting theory Theory proposed by Locke and colleagues in which the general concept of a goal is adapted to work motivation. In this approach, a goal is seen as a motivational force, and individuals who set specific, difficult goals perform better than individuals who simply adopt a "do your best" goal or no goal at all.

The most representative of the **person-as-intentional approach** is **goal-setting theory** as proposed by Locke and his colleagues (Locke & Latham, 2002). Unlike need, equity, and VIE theories, goal-setting theory has endured and evolved into a mature and comprehensive approach to work motivation. Thus, even though it arose in the "classic" period for motivational theories, it has become a distinctly modern theory.

The notion of a goal as a motivational force has been well established (Locke, Shaw, Saari, & Latham, 1981; Ryan, 1970). Austin and Vancouver (1996) present a detailed history of the concept as well as a framework that suggests that, one way or another, any coherent description of motivated behavior must include goals. It has become a very popular motivational construct. Between 1950 and 1999, "goal setting" appeared in the title or abstract of approximately 1,800 psychological articles. Since 2000, it has appeared almost 1,500 times. Locke (1968) was one of the first to adapt the general concept of goals to work motivation, and one of the most comprehensive descriptions of the theory appears in a book by Locke and Latham (1990). In a subsequent paper, Locke and Latham (1996) pointed out that it does not require much investigation to establish the centrality of goals in everyday life. Without prodding, people will readily express their actions in terms of a "purpose": You take a course in order to prepare for a career; you take a job in order to explore an occupation; you go to the gym in order to improve your general fitness or a specific muscle group. These purposes can also be thought of as intentions or goals. It is this notion of purposefulness and intentionality that is unique to goal-setting theory.

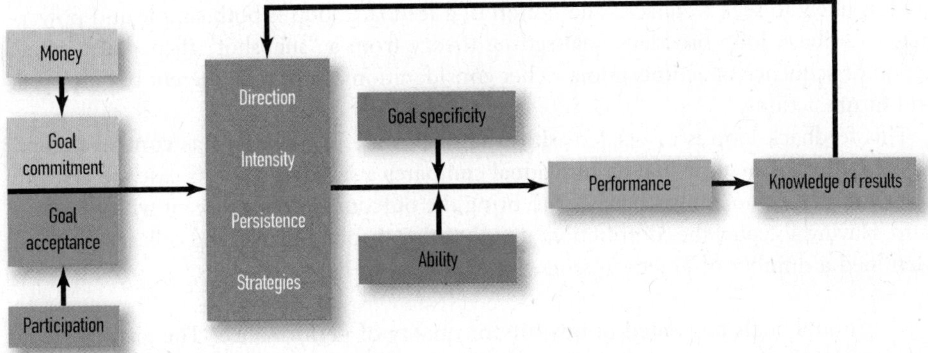

FIGURE 8.2 A Diagram of Goal Theory

A representation of goal-setting theory appears in Figure 8.2. Research on this basic theory has been supportive. Most studies show that specific, difficult goals lead to higher levels of performance, assuming that the individual has accepted the goals. For a student with a cumulative GPA of 3.0, a goal of achieving a GPA of 3.3 in the next semester would likely be a specific, difficult goal. This is true both within subjects (i.e., you will perform better if you set a more difficult goal than an easier one) and between subjects (individuals who set difficult goals perform better than individuals who set easy goals). There is also strong support for the notion that individuals who set specific, difficult goals perform better than individuals who simply adopt a "do your best" goal or no goal at all (Locke & Latham, 1990). Recent research (Wiese & Freund, 2005) demonstrates that goal difficulty is a critical ingredient to both performance and satisfaction. If a goal is not difficult, one will achieve lower levels of performance and be less satisfied with the fact of meeting that goal.

This model makes a distinction between goal acceptance and goal commitment. Goal acceptance implies that a goal has been assigned. Goal commitment is broader and can include not only assigned goals but self-set goals as well. In fact, as we will see shortly, when the individual is free to revise assigned and accepted goals, they can become self-set goals, thereby transforming what was acceptance into commitment. Most recent versions of goal-setting theory have concentrated on the concept of commitment (Mitchell, Thompson, & George-Falvy, 2000).

Goal-setting theory identifies the mechanisms, or intermediate states, by which goals affect performance. Locke and colleagues (1981) proposed that goals have the effect of "directing attention and action (direction), mobilizing energy expenditure or effort (effort), prolonging effort over time (persistence) and motivating the individual to develop relevant strategies for goal attainment (strategy)" (p. 145). Another important factor is the **feedback loop** between knowledge of results and the intermediate states between goal commitment and performance. This feedback connection makes the theory much more dynamic by showing that as the individual evaluates his or her performance, intermediate states may be changed. For example, if an individual falls short of a specific, difficult goal (e.g., to get an A on a term paper), he or she may concentrate harder on library research to the exclusion of other leisure activities (direction), increase the number of hours spent reading course material each week (effort), start the term paper sooner next time (persistence), or take advantage of the instructor's office hours for guidance on the paper (strategy). If the individual does one or all of these things, then he or she is eventually more likely to meet the difficult goal of completing the term paper in time to polish it and make sure it qualifies for a high grade. Tuckey, Brewer, and Williamson (2002) presented evidence suggesting that not all people seek feedback equally. They found that individuals who might be classified as "defensive" and interested in projecting a positive self-image

Feedback loop Connection between knowledge of results and the intermediate states that occur between goal commitment and performance.

are less likely to seek feedback. The notion of a feedback loop is both simple and powerful: A feedback loop broadens goal-setting theory from a "snapshot" theory of a single action or sequence of actions into a richer consideration of not only present but also past and future actions.

Control theory Theory based on the principle of a feedback loop that assumes that an individual compares a standard to actual outcome and adjusts behavior to bring the outcome into agreement with the standard.

This feedback loop is associated with what has come to be known as **control theory**. Control theories assume that an individual compares a standard (in this case the goal) to actual outcome and adjusts behavior to bring the outcome into agreement with the standard. Having accepted the contribution of goal-setting theory, Mitchell and colleagues (2000) identified a number of practical issues that still need to be addressed:

- Should goals be related to quantity or quality of performance? The answer seems to be that quantity and quality are related such that when high quantity goals are set, the quality of performance declines. In order to prevent such slippage, it seems best to set both quality and quantity goals rather than one or the other.
- Should goals be related to process or outcomes? Process goals refer to *how* work is done. Outcome goals are related to the actual level of production. The conclusion seems to be that process goals may be more appropriate for complex tasks, as these may require a great deal of learning. If the task is relatively simple, outcome goals will lead more quickly to higher performance.
- How should goals be set? The three major methods for setting goals are to assign them, to ask individuals who will receive the goals to participate in setting them, and to ask individuals to set their own goals. The emerging consensus seems to be that participative goal setting is most effective, although assigned goals can also be effective if they are "sold" rather than simply dictated. In Module 8.4, however, we will see that cultural issues may come into play as well.
- How many goals should be set? The answer to this question seems to be that multiple goals are acceptable but that they should be examined closely to make sure they are compatible (e.g., a goal of increasing production by 10 percent would be incompatible with a goal of decreasing overtime by 10 percent). It may also be wise to assign weights or priorities to multiple goals, since some are likely to be more important than others. Pritchard (1995) has developed a method for increasing motivation and performance (ProMES) that incorporates such a weighting scheme. We will examine ProMES in greater depth in the last module of this chapter.
- How difficult is a difficult goal? There is no good answer to this question. Difficulty can be determined by comparison to an individual's typical performance or by comparison to the performance of others. Generally, a difficult goal would be one that could be achieved by no more than 10 to 20 percent of the people attempting it or by an individual only 10 to 20 percent of the time that he or she attempts it. The critical issue here is that the individual needs to view a goal as possible; otherwise, he or she will not accept it.
- Should rewards be contingent on goal accomplishment? The conclusion seems to be that when goals are of medium difficulty, rewards are appropriate for goal accomplishment. If the goals are very difficult, the individual should be rewarded for partial goal attainment; otherwise, the goals themselves may become unattractive over time. It might also be appropriate to increase the bonus or reward as the individual gets closer to the difficult goal. It appears that if rewards are given on an all-or-nothing basis (i.e., no rewards unless complete goal accomplishment occurs), easy goals result in underperformance and difficult goals result in quitting. The best result seems to come from incremental rewards linked to increments of achievement (much like piece-rate systems).
- When should individual goals be used and when should group goals be used? Mitchell and colleagues (2000) suggest that the answer depends on the nature of the

task. If the task requires interdependence and cooperation, then group goals might be appropriate, whereas if the work is independent and workers are sole contributors, then individual goals may be more appropriate. Once again, however, we need to introduce the concept of culture. In collectivist cultures, it may be difficult to work within an individual goal-setting program; to do so may even be viewed as offensive.

Challenges for Goal-Setting Theory

The changing nature of work will present new challenges for the continuing development and relevance of goal-setting theory. Locke and Latham (2002) have depended heavily on laboratory and field research for the development of their theory. Historically, a great deal of that research involved single contributors working on relatively simple tasks, but because today's workplace is increasingly complex and team-based, in order to adapt the theory to the new work environment, the research design needs to include more complex cognitive work. In addition, Locke (2001) acknowledges that research efforts should be directed toward integrating variables such as knowledge and skill into the model.

Some researchers have begun an ambitious program of looking at the effect of goal setting on complex cognitive tasks (Atkins, Wood, & Rutgers, 2002; Wood, George-Falvy, & Debowsky, 2001). These research designs include some very relevant cognitive tasks, such as conducting automated literature searches on the Internet and examining the effect of the form of feedback on decision making. This is exactly the type of research that can help goal-setting theory remain relevant.

Levels of Explanation in Goal Setting

When Locke introduced goal-setting theory, it was presented as a relatively simple way to increase performance by recognizing a very human characteristic that seemed to be missing in other theories: intention. But Locke and Latham (1996) wisely make the point that simply identifying a goal to which a person may be committed does not fully explain the individual's behavior. They suggest that goal-setting theory is just a first-level explanation of behavior. Goals are seen as the most immediate antecedents to behavior. But the question of where goals come from remains. Locke and Latham hypothesize that goals may very well derive from higher-order concepts such as values or motives. These would be second-level explanations of goal-setting theory. They give the example of a person who has a goal to become CEO within 15 years of joining the company, a goal deriving from a motive of ambition. They also invoke the notion of the Type A personality. (We will see in Chapter 10 that a Type A personality, among other characteristics, seeks to accomplish more and more.) The Type A person is likely to set multiple and difficult goals, particularly when competing with others. Still a higher order, or third level, of explanation would investigate where motives or values originate. As you will recall, Maslow suggested that motives were inborn. All three of these levels describe an influence on action or behavior, but at increasingly higher levels. As you can see in Figure 8.3, needs influence motives, motives influence goals, and goals influence performance. As Locke and Latham (1996) point out, the closer the level of explanation is to the behavior in question, the stronger the connections. A recent meta-analysis (Payne, Youngcourt, & Beaubien, 2007) made

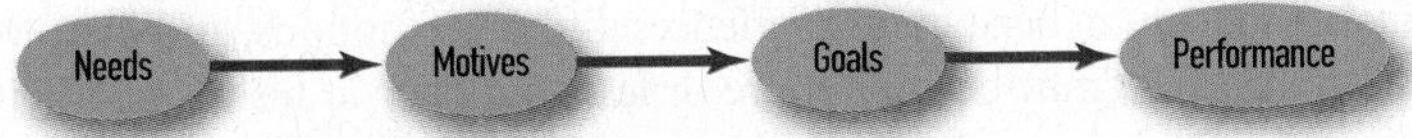

FIGURE 8.3 The Relationships among Needs, Motives, Goals, and Performance

SOURCE: Locke, E. A., & Latham, G. P. (1996). Goal setting theory: An introduction. In R. M. Steers, L. W. Porter, & G. A. Bigley (Eds.), *Motivation and leadership at work* (pp. 95–122). New York: McGraw-Hill. © 1996 by McGraw-Hill. Reprinted by permission of The McGraw-Hill Companies, Inc.

an interesting discovery: Goal orientation predicted that a person would achieve work performance above and beyond what could be predicted from knowing the cognitive ability or personality profile of the person.

The notion of levels of explanation leads us to examine other current theories of work motivation. As you will see, goals and goal setting play an important role in these theories. In some senses, the theories we will now consider are actually second-level explanations of behavior in the context of goals and goal setting. One way or another, they all include goals.

Control Theories and the Concept of Self-Regulation

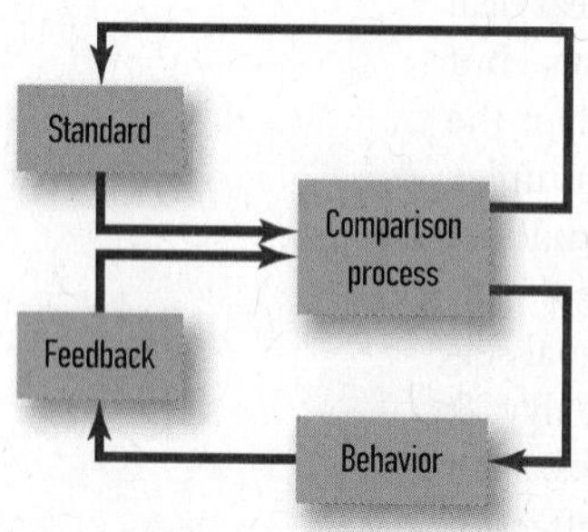

FIGURE 8.4 Simple Control Systems Model

SOURCE: Taylor, M. S., Fisher, C. D., & Ilgen, D. R. (1984). Individuals' reactions to performance feedback in organizations: A control theory perspective. In K. M. Rowland & G. R. Ferris (Eds.), *Research in personnel and human resources management* (Vol. 2, pp. 161–187) Fig. 1. Greenwich, CT: JAI Press. Copyright © 1984. Reprinted with permission from Emerald Group Publishing Limited. Permission conveyed through Copyright Clearance Center.

In the goal-setting model presented above, we pointed out the feedback loop between the actual results of behavior (i.e., performance and goal achievement) and the intermediate states. Control theory is based on the principle of a feedback loop. A simple example of a feedback loop is the thermostat in your home. When the temperature increases, the thermometer reading rises, and when it reaches a set point, it signals the thermostat to turn the heating system off. When the temperature drops below a certain level, the thermostat once again signals the heating system to bring the heat back on until the set temperature is achieved. The essence of a thermostat, or any control system, is the feedback loop. The system revolves around discrepancies; in the case of the room temperature, the discrepancy is between the actual temperature of the room and the thermostat setting. Figure 8.4 presents a simplified view of a control model.

The feedback loop in goal-setting theory deals with the discrepancy between actual goal accomplishment and the goal to which the individual is committed. Locke and Latham (1996) suggest that if the individual falls short of the goal, intermediate states will be influenced. It is also possible that an individual might replace the goal with an easier one (or negotiate with a supervisor or manager to make the goal easier). But this is just the tip of the iceberg with respect to work behavior in its richest form. Individuals have multiple goals, some assigned and some not assigned. In addition, the relative importance of these goals can change overnight based on shifting organizational priorities. Individuals can make more progress on some goals than others, and they feel more or less confident about the likelihood of achieving some goals rather than others. All of these complications introduce another concept into the motivational mix: the concept of **self-regulation**. Vancouver (2005) has written an excellent historical review and critical analysis of control theories for the interested reader. Cervone, Shadel, Smith, and Fiori (2006) presented a detailed review of the relationship between personality and self-regulation.

Self-regulation Process by which individuals take in information about behavior and make adjustments or changes based on that information. These changes, in turn, affect subsequent behavior (e.g., strategies, goal commitment).

Self-regulation is compatible with control theory. In its simplest form, self-regulation means that individuals take in information about behavior and make adjustments based on that information, just as the thermostat takes in information and makes adjustments. The only difference is that the thermostat doesn't feel discouraged or depressed when the temperature in the room drops. It never asks: "Is the temperature perhaps set too high? Should I adjust the setting?" It simply responds to whatever the setting is. But humans have bad days when they lose confidence in themselves and question the goals they have accepted or set for themselves. The complexity of the workplace suggests that, rather than a simple feedback loop, there are actually many feedback loops that are arranged in hierarchies. The person receives information about performance, abilities, and organizational expectations and, as a result, makes changes in behavior, experiences differing emotions, and may even change his or her self-image (i.e., may become more or less confident in his or her abilities or the likelihood of accomplishing a goal). These changes, in turn, affect subsequent behavior (e.g., strategies, goal commitment). Porath and Bateman (2006) suggest several specific self-regulatory tactics that one can use to improve performance. These include seeking feedback as a way of developing skills and task mastery as well as proactive behavior that seeks constructive change rather than accepting the status quo. Thus, according to self-regulatory theory, one can increase both work motivation and work performance by engaging in strategies such as seeking feedback and engaging in constructive change. It is an active and dynamic process, not a passive or stoic one.

The Concept of Self-Efficacy in Modern Motivation Theory

You can probably recall occasions when you were not feeling very confident of accomplishing a goal (e.g., getting a good grade on a midterm exam). This feeling of confidence (or lack thereof) has been labeled **self-efficacy** by Bandura (1986), and it is playing an increasingly important role in most modern theories of work motivation. Self-efficacy is defined as the belief in one's capacity to perform a specific task or reach a specific goal (Bandura, 1997). This is different from the broader notion of self-esteem, which is the pride (or lack thereof) in who one is as a human being, often boosted by the satisfaction of having accomplished a difficult task. Self-esteem has a social aspect to it to the extent that we experience increased self-esteem when we gain the respect of others. Like motivation generally, and goal setting more specifically, the construct of efficacy and self-efficacy has been extremely popular with psychological researchers.

Self-efficacy The belief in one's capability to perform a specific task or reach a specific goal.

Recently, there has been a spirited debate in both the scientific and popular press about whether the pursuit of self-esteem is good or bad. Some see it as natural and essential for emotional well-being (DuBois & Flay, 2004; Pyszczynski, Greenberg, Solomon, Arndt, & Schimel, 2004), while others (Crocker & Park, 2004; Sheldon, 2004) see it as a potentially destructive force, particularly when it is sought directly rather than enjoyed as a consequence of effective performance. As an example, seeking to enhance one's self-esteem through the failure of others (see our discussion of poker players [Harper, 2005] in a win–lose situation in the next module) might be effective in the short run, but ultimately may lead to depression because the individual may have so much of himself or herself invested in winning that the results of losing can be emotionally catastrophic (Crocker & Park, 2004).

Jamie Squire/Getty Images, Inc.

According to efficacy theory, coming close to winning will motivate some people to try harder next time.

Self-efficacy relates more specifically to our confidence in our ability or in the likelihood that we will be able to successfully complete a difficult task. In a comparison of the effects of self-esteem versus self-efficacy, Chen, Gully, and Eden (2004) found that self-efficacy beliefs were more closely related to motivation and behavior, while self-esteem was more closely related to emotions.

Because self-efficacy is so central to goal-directed behavior and performance, it is reasonable to ask how it is developed and increased. Wood and Bandura (1989) suggest four separate avenues:

- *Mastery experiences.* Successful performance of challenging tasks strengthens beliefs in one's capabilities, whereas failures decrease those beliefs.

- *Modeling.* People have a tendency to compare their capabilities with those of others. When individuals see someone similar to themselves (in terms of abilities, knowledge, etc.) succeed at a difficult task, their own efficacy beliefs can be strengthened. If, on the other hand, this comparison person fails, then their efficacy beliefs will be reduced.
- *Social persuasion.* Individuals can be encouraged by others who express confidence in their ability to accomplish a difficult task.
- *Physiological states.* When people experience the symptoms of stress or fatigue, they tend to interpret this as an indication that the task exceeds their capabilities, thus reducing their feelings of efficacy. Techniques that reduce the experience of stress or fatigue will increase one's feelings of self-efficacy when completing a difficult task.

How can we put these approaches to work in increasing our own self-efficacy or the self-efficacy of a friend or co-worker? Consider the following possibilities:

1. Provide guidance or technical or logistic support to the individual, increasing the likelihood that he or she will experience success on a challenging task (i.e., a mastery experience).
2. Provide successful role models, perhaps by pairing an individual with a fellow worker of similar experience who has mastered a difficult task.
3. Be a targeted "cheerleader," emphasizing the individual's knowledge and ability (as opposed to simply expressing confidence that he or she will succeed).
4. Take steps to reduce stress in the individual's environment that is unrelated to the challenging task.

Action Theory

Action theory (Rubicon theory) Theory that includes broad consideration of the role of intention in motivated behavior as well as the connection between intention and action.

Perhaps the broadest consideration of the role of intention in motivated behavior appears in the form of what has come to be known as **action theory**. This approach is most popular among German applied psychologists (Frese & Zapf, 1994; Gollwitzer, 1999; Gollwitzer, Heckhausen, & Ratajczak, 1990) and is also known as the **Rubicon theory**, based on a famous incident involving Julius Caesar's civil war on Rome and the Roman Senate. Prior to crossing the river Rubicon on his way to Rome, Caesar asked his advisors if this was a wise plan. Having concluded that it was a reasonable course of action, Caesar and his army did cross the river. One of his advisors then revisited the wisdom of the decision to wage war in Rome. Caesar is reported to have said that, since the army had already crossed the Rubicon, he would not talk about *whether* to wage war but only about how to win it (Heckhausen, Gollwitzer, & Weinert, 1987). Caesar had moved on from the decision to wage war to developing a plan to win the war. His advisors had not yet made that transition. Their minds were still on the other side of the Rubicon. An even more dire version of the Rubicon theory is set in China several thousand years earlier than the Rubicon crossing. After landing on a shore to prepare for an attack on an enemy, the commander ordered all of the boats *burned* so that there could be no turning back!

Gollwitzer (1993) has written extensively on the connection between intention and action, distinguishing between goal intentions ("I intend to achieve X") and implementation intentions ("I intend to initiate the goal-directed behavior X when I encounter situation Y"). He is particularly interested in how people turn intention into action. He identifies four consecutive action phases in active goal pursuit:

1. *Predecisional.* Examining one's desires in order to determine which desire is the strongest and most feasible to attain
2. *Postdecisional.* Planning and developing strategies for successful action

3. *Actional.* Actually expending effort to achieve the desired outcome
4. *Evaluative.* Comparing what was achieved with what was desired

Gollwitzer believes that intentions are particularly important for overcoming any obstacles that may arise in phases 1 or 2. He also believes that people are far more likely to accomplish goals when both goal intention and implementation intention are present.

When we have competing wishes and desires, we can remind ourselves of our intentions, and it is the intentions that help us establish priorities so that we can eliminate conflicts among our wishes and desires. Raabe, Frese, and Beehr (2007) demonstrate that even with activities as broad as career self-management, intentional behavior regarding career building can lead to increased career satisfaction. This is closely related to Locke and Latham's concept of commitment: Once an intention is formed as a result of establishing priorities, there is no longer any need to deliberate contrasting alternatives. Once Caesar crossed the Rubicon, it was no longer necessary or appropriate to debate the wisdom of that course of action. In addition, implementation intentions help us to articulate when, where, and how we intend to achieve our goals (Gollwitzer, 1993). You decide that you will complete your term paper by the middle of the semester. You buy some new software for your computer, set up a schedule for a period of research each week and post that schedule on your door, apply for a study carrel in the library, cancel plans for a trip with friends, and ask a professor if you can sit in on some lectures in another class that relate to your term paper. Because you have both a goal intention and an implementation intention, the chances are greatly enhanced that you will have your term paper done by the middle of the semester.

Action process Process that starts with a goal, proceeds to a consideration of events that may occur in the future, and then progresses to the development of several alternative plans, the selection of a plan, the execution and monitoring of the chosen plan, and the processing of information resulting from the execution of the plan. The last step, feedback, then influences goal development once again.

Action structure Structure that includes the notion that (1) observable action is the result of a number of prior events and plans, hierarchically arranged, and (2) the feedback and resulting regulation of actions occur at different levels.

Frese and Zapf (1994) have published the most accessible description of action theory. An action (e.g., performing a work task) has two elements: the **action process** and the **action structure**. The action process is displayed in Figure 8.5. An action starts with a goal (or choice among goals), proceeds to a consideration of events that may occur in the future, and then progresses to the development of several alternative plans, the selection of one of those alternative plans, the execution and monitoring of the chosen plan, and, finally, the processing of information resulting from the execution of the plan. The last step, feedback, then influences the goal development process once again.

The action structure includes two aspects. The first is the notion that no observable action occurs in a vacuum. It is the result of a number of prior events and plans, hierarchically arranged. The second is that the feedback and resulting regulation of actions occur at different levels. Some are at the conscious level (e.g., was my performance up to the standard I expected?) and others are at an unconscious or automatic level (e.g., adjusting the swing of a hammer to hit a nail more solidly).

In some senses, action theory is proposed as an alternative to motivation theory. Hacker (1992) notes that often the highest performers in a job are those with the best understanding of the job rather than those who are most motivated. Action theorists are, by definition, more concerned with action than motivation. Nevertheless, this may ultimately be a semantic exercise. The goal-setting advocates would claim that there is little difference between the various hierarchical levels of the action structure and the notion of goal specificity. Further, they would claim that the action process is virtually identical to the goal-setting and feedback model.

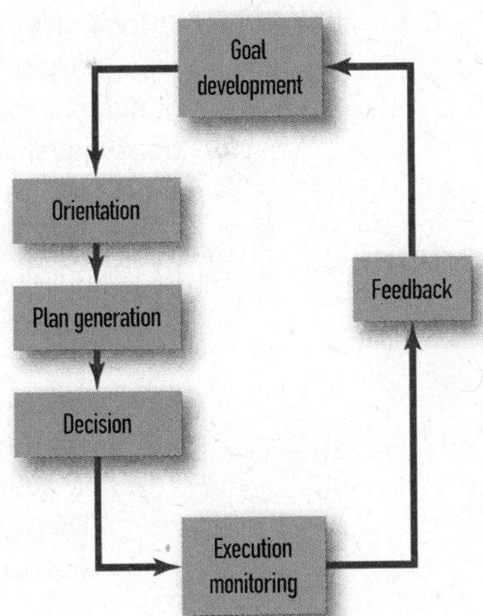

FIGURE 8.5 The Action Process

SOURCE: Frese, M., & Zapf, D. (1994). Action as core of work psychology: A German approach. In M. Dunnette, L. Hough, & H. C. Triandis (Eds.), *Handbook of industrial and organizational psychology* (2nd ed., Vol. 4, pp. 271–340). Palo Alto, CA: Consulting Psychologists Press. Copyright permission by Leaetta Hough.

Common Themes in Modern Approaches

After examining the modern approaches to motivation theory, can we find any common themes? Yes, there are several. First, intention plays a key role in motivated behavior. The most common form of that intention is a goal. Any viable theory of motivated behavior will need to have a goal-like element. These goals will be associated with anticipated happiness or unhappiness. Second, the concept of feedback is critical if we are to consider any but the simplest act at one point in time. Third, the theory needs to include some element of the person as scientist. The person need not be a completely rational or accurate scientist but must be considered an information gatherer and analyst. Fourth, the theory should include some concept of self-assessment. It is clear that individuals commonly take stock of where they are compared to where they want to be. Finally, there will be some noncognitive element in the "ultimate" motivation theory. This element may be personality, or values, or even the feeling that arises from the self-efficacy belief. What is becoming clearer from motivational research is that individuals are not just primitive scientists, they are critical scientists as well. They do not merely use information, they evaluate and judge it. As a result, the person-as-scientist metaphor is giving way to that of the person as judge.

From a practical standpoint, then, I-O psychologists know quite a lot about motivation, even without a complete and comprehensive theory. The challenge to motivation theory now is more theoretical and research based than practical. We have many of the pieces to the puzzle, and we just need to figure out how to assemble them. But another problem may emerge while we are assembling the puzzle. The nature of work will not stand still. It has changed radically and will continue to change. The real challenge will be to craft a theory that can deal with work as it exists in the 21st century: work that is team based, technological, multicultural, rapidly changing, and performed for organizations with limited loyalty to their members.

A New Motivational Topic: The Entrepreneur

Entrepreneurial yearnings can appear very early in life. It is not clear if the successful lemonade stand owner will become a Steve Jobs or Bill Gates, but it is clear that successful entrepreneurs are a different breed. As an example, after successfully taking the Virgin group (e.g., Virgin Records, Virgin Atlantic Airways) public in 1986, Sir Richard Branson bought all the shares back and took it private again because he disagreed with the directions that shareholders wanted him to pursue, believing that the investors were much too short term in their thinking (Glaister, 2005).

Baron (2002) makes a strong case for introducing entrepreneurial activity as a topic in I-O psychology with the following points:

- In the 1990s, even though large corporations cut over 6 million jobs, unemployment was at a record low because entrepreneurs were starting new companies.
- In 1998, more than 900,000 new start-up companies appeared in the United States.
- In 1998, more than 10 million U.S. workers were self-employed.
- The number of new businesses started by women and minorities has risen more dramatically than the number of those started by white males.

Baron argues convincingly that entrepreneurship is now a stable part of the U.S. economy. Even closer to home, Baron (2003) observes that in the pre-21st-century environment, many if not most students planned to work for a large corporation and progress through management ranks. In contrast, over 50 percent of the students he now encounters expect to start their own business either right after graduation or shortly thereafter. This phenomenon is not peculiar to the United States. Frese and his colleagues documented the rise of entrepreneurial activities in former socialist and Warsaw Pact countries following the end of the Cold War (Utsch, Rauch, Rothfuss, & Frese, 1999). Entrepreneurial activity in the Far East, particularly China, experienced remarkable growth in the early years of the 21st century.

The research data on the precursors and correlates of entrepreneurial activity are relatively new and thus are still tentative at this point. Some models have been proposed and a great deal of speculative writing has appeared. As a result, no firm conclusions are possible—except that this line of research is likely to increase geometrically in the next decade as more and more workers move away from traditional work settings. Nevertheless, since the topic is intriguing, it is worth reviewing these preliminary findings and hypotheses.

Compared to their less entrepreneurial colleagues, entrepreneurs:

- Recognize patterns of opportunity more easily and more quickly, both because of a deeper and broader knowledge of certain industries or markets (Baron, 2004) and because of well-developed cognitive abilities (Baron & Ensley, 2006)
- Regret business decisions that failed but not a career or occupational choice (Baron, 2000a)
- Are more socially skilled (Baron, 2000b; Baron & Markman, 2000), a finding that has recently been extended to include Chinese entrepreneurs (Baron & Tang, 2009)
- Are higher on self-efficacy and perseverance/persistence (Markman, Baron, & Balkin, 2005)
- Are more likely to set goals related to starting a new business (Baum & Locke, 2004)
- Are higher on achievement motivation (Collins, Hanges, & Locke, 2004)
- Are higher on conscientiousness, emotional stability, extraversion, and openness to experience (Zhao, Seibert, Lumpkin, 2010)
- Are more passionate and tenacious in seeking entrepreneurial success (Baum & Locke, 2004)
- Are willing to tolerate greater risk, particularly when their goal is venture growth rather than production of family income (Stewart & Roth, 2001)
- Are more likely to be prone to downward biases in evaluating risk (Hayward, Shepherd, & Griffin, 2006)
- Were often raised in the context of a family business and have higher levels of testosterone than nonentrepreneurs (White, Thornhil, & Hampson, 2007).

Hmieleski and Baron (2008) suggest an interesting finding with regard to the heightened self-efficacy noted in the above list. This self-efficacy, coupled with high levels of optimism, might just as easily lead to a business failure as a business success, particularly in unstable business environments. Entrepreneurs are more willing to bet the farm than they should be.

Frese and his colleagues have been looking at entrepreneurial activity in small businesses in several different cultures, including southern Africa (Frese et al., 2007; Krause, Frese, Friedrich, & Unger, 2005) and Vietnam (Hiemstra, van der Kooy, & Frese, 2006). These initiatives are particularly salient for the concept of world poverty that was introduced in Chapter 1. The Vietnamese study was with street food vendors; the southern African small businesses included scrap metal merchants, grocery stalls, and tailors. Frese and his colleagues suggest that teaching and reinforcing entrepreneurial behavior among small business owners may be one of the many steps that can be taken to reduce world poverty. It is fascinating (and unusual) to see the application of theories of work motivation in such extremely small business settings. Frese and his colleagues (Krause et al., 2005; Rauch & Frese, 2007b) have proposed that a central personality characteristic underlying entrepreneurial behavior is entrepreneurial orientation (EO). Frese and Fay (2001) see EO as a combination of achievement orientation, risk-taking orientation, and personal initiative (PI). They define personal initiative as a work behavior characterized by its self-starting nature and its persistent approach that helps in overcoming difficulties that arise in pursuit of a goal. It appears that EO is a higher-order construct and possibly even what we have referred to earlier as a competency, particularly if there are cognitive overtones to the construct, as Frese and colleagues suggest (Fay & Frese, 2001). Rauch and Frese (2007a) make a strong case for considering personality traits as the building blocks for entrepreneurial activity and success. In particular, they identify need for achievement, self-efficacy, stress tolerance, proactive style, and need for autonomy as key traits.

Shane, Nicolaou, Cherkas, and Spector (2010) examined two samples of twins from the United Kingdom and the United States to determine whether genetic factors account for part of the relationship between the tendency to become an entrepreneur and the Big Five personality dimensions. They found that common genes influenced the correlations between the tendency to be an entrepreneur and both extraversion and openness to experience. Although the correlations between the tendency to be an entrepreneur and the personality characteristics were not large, the authors found evidence that genetic factors accounted for most of these correlations. Their findings are intriguing and suggest that genetic factors should be considered in discussions about why individuals become entrepreneurs.

As we indicated above, all of these ideas are relatively new, and the research is barely off the ground. As a result, it is much too early to demand an exact definition of this new

BOX 8.4 ENTREPRENEURIAL ATTRIBUTES

Real-life entrepreneurs confirm many of the characteristics identified by the research we have reviewed. Consider four such entrepreneurs: Caitlin Adler, who started a small bakery and café; Jeff Takle, who founded an online property management company; Nicholas Khoo, who began an IT outsourcing company; and Bart Knaggs, principal of an athlete and artist management firm. Each of these entrepreneurs' stories reveals similar elements.

© Jodi Hilton/The New York Times/Redux

As predicted by research findings, real-life entrepreneurs like to be in control rather than being controlled: As café owner Caitlin Adler says, "I could never work for somebody else."

- They are all strongly achievement oriented. Nicholas Khoo puts it best: "It feels good to . . . go against the big boys and win."
- They like to be in control rather than being controlled: As Caitlin Adler says, "I could never work for somebody else."
- They all experienced failure early in the entrepreneurial effort yet persevered in spite of the lack of success. Bart Knaggs says, "Rejection . . . motivates me. I'm really offended when I get rejected, and I feel compelled to show whomever it is that he is wrong."
- Even in the face of negative information about the success of their enterprises, they remain optimistic. For example, even though Jeff Takle's property management company is close to going under, he says, "We're still on track for building a self-sustaining, profitable company."

In sum, entrepreneurs look at the world through very different lenses than do nonentrepreneurs.

SOURCE: Bowers (2008); EnterpriseOne (2006–7); Gunasegaran & Losefsky (2008).

construct. The simple fact is that some people exhibit entrepreneurial behavior (and not only in Western cultures) while others do not, and of those who do, some are more successful than others. It is clear that there is a strong motivational flavor to the behavior—words like "initiative," "tenacious," "achievement-oriented," and "energetic" predominate in discussions of entrepreneurs. It is also clear that more and more people will move into entrepreneurial environments from more traditional work environments. We will be watching this emerging research domain carefully in the next few years.

MODULE 8.3 SUMMARY

- The most representative of the person-as-intentional approach is goal-setting theory, which has evolved into a mature and comprehensive approach to work motivation. The notion of a goal as a motivational force is well established. Most studies indicate that specific, difficult goals lead to higher performance, assuming that the individual has accepted the goals.
- Additional motivational theories use the concept of goals and goal setting. Control theory is based on the principle of a feedback loop, which deals with the discrepancy between the set goal and the actual goal. Control theory suggests that people are active self-regulators who depend on feedback for adjusting to changes in their environment.
- Self-efficacy, which is playing an increasingly important role in most modern theories of work motivation, can be developed through mastery experiences, modeling, social persuasion, or physiological states.

KEY TERMS

person-as-intentional approach
goal-setting theory
feedback loop
control theory
self-regulation
self-efficacy
action theory (Rubicon theory)
action process
action structure

MODULE 8.4

Practical Issues in Motivation

Can Motivation Be Measured?

The short answer is yes. As we saw above, there are motivational indicators like the number and difficulty of goals accepted by an individual or the strength of a person's belief that hard work will yield rewards. Thus, we can estimate the motivation of a person in a particular context. But what about the broader issue of whether some people are simply more motivated, generally, than others? As we saw in Module 8.1, Judge and Ilies (2002) seem to suggest that conscientiousness and emotional stability may be surrogates for a general level of motivation. Erez and Judge (2001) have suggested that a broader construct, which they call "core self-evaluations," is related to both the motivation to complete a task and goal setting. Core self-evaluation is a combination of self-esteem, internal locus of control, generalized self-efficacy, and emotional stability. In their simplest form, the studies by both Judge and Ilies (2002) and Erez and Judge (2001) can be interpreted to mean that there may be certain trait requirements in order for motivational interventions to work, rather than that we can simply assume that certain personality types are "naturally" motivated. In their more dramatic form, these results may very well suggest that there is a trait (or better yet, a competency) that is at the heart of motivated behavior, at least with respect to tasks in the workplace. We will return to the concept of core self-evaluations in Chapter 9 when we consider attitudes and emotions.

Motivational Trait Questionnaire (MTQ) A 48-item questionnaire that provides a standardized method of assessing six distinct aspects of general performance motivation.

Kanfer and her colleagues (Heggestad & Kanfer, 2001; Kanfer & Ackerman, 2000) have developed an instrument known as the **Motivational Trait Questionnaire (MTQ)**. The MTQ measures six distinct aspects of what might be called "general" motivation. These aspects are assessed by a 48-item questionnaire. The six aspect areas and some sample items assessing them appear in Table 8.3. Some of the aspects (e.g., emotionality) are quite close to other well-known Big Five personality dimensions, such as emotional stability. But Kanfer and Ackerman have focused more directly on personality in the performance context. The MTQ has been carefully constructed and is the basis for a good deal of ongoing research. It appears that the MTQ is one standardized method for measuring general performance motivation. It also appears that there are some commonalities between the concept of core self-evaluations (particularly emotional stability and self-esteem) and the elements of the MTQ, but there seems to be a stronger emphasis on achievement striving in the MTQ than in the concept of core self-evaluations.

TABLE 8.3 **Sample Items from the Motivational Trait Questionnaire**

Desire to learn—the need to achieve by learning new skills or acquiring knowledge ("I prefer activities that provide me with an opportunity to learn something new")
Mastery—personal goal setting and continued task improvement even when not required ("I set high standards for myself and work toward achieving them")
Other referenced goals—tendency to compare performance to the performance of others ("Whether I feel good or not about my performance depends on how it compares to the performance of others")
Competitiveness—a focus on competition and wanting to do better than co-workers or peers ("I would rather compete than cooperate")
Worry—concerns about having one's performance evaluated ("Before beginning an important project, I think of the consequences of failing")
Emotionality—focus on the emotions of being evaluated in a performance context ("I am able to remain calm and relaxed before I take a test")

SOURCE: Kanfer, R., & Ackerman, P. L. (2000). Individual differences in work motivation: Further explorations of a trait framework. *Applied Psychology: An International Review, 49*, 470–482. Copyright © 2000 by John Wiley & Sons. Used by permission.

Cross-Cultural Issues in Motivation

As we have seen in many other sections of the book, the changing nature of work has made the issue of culture a critical one in many areas of I-O psychology. Motivation is no exception. Kanfer's model of motivation, presented above, can be used to highlight some of these cultural issues. For the purposes of this discussion, recall the cultural theory of Hofstede (2001). He proposed that cultures differed on the basis of five dimensions: (1) individualism–collectivism, (2) uncertainty avoidance, (3) masculinity–femininity, (4) power distance, and (5) long-term versus short-term orientation. Consider the theory and the MTQ questionnaire broadly. The first thing you notice is that it is directed toward the individual. Each sample question revolves around "I." It would appear, then, that the questionnaire is more suitable for an individualist culture than a collectivist one.

The MTQ dimensions themselves raise a similar question. In a collectivist culture, would an individual who is not interested in competition, or mastery, or comparing his or her performance to that of a peer or co-worker be considered unmotivated? As another example, recall Hofstede's view of masculinity and femininity as a cultural continuum. Masculine cultures tend to value success, whereas feminine cultures tend to value interpersonal relations. Hofstede's masculinity–femininity dimension predicts that women in low-masculine cultures will describe themselves as more competitive than men, while the opposite would be true in high-masculine cultures. Would a woman from a high-masculine culture (such as Japan) be considered less motivated when compared to her male counterparts? What about the woman from the high-masculine culture being compared to her female counterpart from a low-masculine culture (e.g., Sweden)? Would the woman from the high-masculine culture be considered less motivated? Finally, the Hofstede dimension of uncertainty avoidance suggests cultural interpretations of the MTQ. Hofstede (2001) speculates that in cultures low in uncertainty avoidance, "achievement" can be recast as "hope for success," whereas in cultures high in uncertainty avoidance, "achievement" is more appropriately thought of as "fear of failure."

We are not criticizing the work of Kanfer and her colleagues in these examples. On the contrary, we commend them for exploring individual differences in performance motivation and developing an instrument to assist in that exploration. Their research is quite new, and it is reasonable to pursue the theory and questionnaire within one culture before looking at its applicability across cultures. There is reason, however, to suspect that cultural differences will appear. Kanfer and Ackerman (2000) have already uncovered differences in response patterns to the MTQ as functions of age and gender. There is every reason to suspect that similar differences will emerge when the instrument and theory are examined from the cross-cultural perspective.

Erez (1997) notes that across all cultures, managers tend to employ four types of motivational practices:

1. Differential distribution of rewards—rewarding high performers
2. Participation in goal setting and decision making—allowing subordinates to help make decisions
3. Design and redesign of jobs and organizations—modifying task assignments and reporting relationships
4. Quality improvement interventions such as total quality management (TQM) or quality circles—focusing subordinates on strategic objectives

She then demonstrates how these motivational interventions need to be modified to fit the culture in which they are applied. As an example, in an individualist culture with low power distance (e.g., the United States), profit- and gain-sharing programs might work well as a way to distribute rewards. In contrast, in a collectivist culture with high power distance (e.g., Japan), it might be more suitable to distribute rewards unequally to organizational units or divisions, but equally within those units. A Japanese materials scientist shocked his fellow countrymen by suing a company for which he previously worked for a portion of the profits realized from an invention perfected by a team he directed (Onishi, 2005). He was given a $200 bonus for his efforts in 1993. The company realized profits of almost $1 billion from his efforts. The lawsuit was settled with a payment of $8 million to the scientist. His former colleagues and team members felt that he had betrayed them with his lawsuit and that it was inappropriate for any individual to place personal interests ahead of company interests.

© Chloe Johnson/Alamy Limited

Men substantially outnumber women at poker tables. Is this due to a gender difference in attitudes about competition?

If we consider the broader implications of Hofstede's dimensions, we can see some interesting implications within a domestic culture for the dimension of masculinity–femininity. Some laboratory research by Niederle and her colleagues (Gneezy, Niederle, & Rustichini, 2003; Niederle & Vesterlund, 2005) discovered that men and women differed sharply on their comfort with win–lose types of competitive environments. Men preferred head-to-head competition to a much greater extent than women, and as the competitiveness of the situation increased, men proportionally outperformed women as well. In noncompetitive environments, men and women performed equally. At this point these results are simply intriguing, since they were somewhat contrived because of the laboratory environment. But the implications for reward systems in organizations (e.g., contests for sales reps with one winner) are important—not just for women but for all workers, regardless of gender, who would be closer to the feminine end of Hofstede's dimension than the masculine end. Harper (2005) has speculated that the same phenomenon accounts for the disproportionate number of men seated around poker tables.

The practical implications of culture for work motivation are substantial. As Erez and Eden (2001) note, in the past it might have been unusual for workers from one culture to work alongside those from another culture (i.e., to work with "foreigners"). They point out that the practice is so common now that the word "foreigner" is rarely used, and it is generally considered insulting rather than descriptive. Not only do new workers come from different cultures with different expectations, but it is also increasingly likely that a supervisor or manager may bring a new culture into the workplace.

Bandura (2002) reinforces the point that the globalization of work requires some careful consideration of the way in which concepts such as self-efficacy express themselves in varying national cultures, particularly when one is considering efficacy associated with group beliefs (i.e., collective efficacy) and individual feelings of efficacy. The example provided by the Japanese materials scientist above is a perfect example of the occasional clash of beliefs. In that case, the work group felt a collective efficacy but was less enthusiastic about the individual efficacy implied by the lawsuit filed by their colleague.

In sum, while I-O psychologists within a given culture may have the research and theory to support a particular motivational intervention within that culture, the value of that intervention will decrease in direct proportion to the multicultural nature of the company and workforce.

Generational Differences and Work Motivation

In most families, the behaviors and interests of children—in music, dress, food, and attitudes toward work—differ substantially from the behaviors and interests of their parents. Given that culture is defined as a circumstance of shared values, generational differences could be construed as differences between cultures, much like the differences between nationalities as discussed by Hofstede (2001). In much the same way, there often seem to be differences in work values between workers (and managers) who are from one generation and those from a different generation. A generation (sometimes called a cohort) is defined by group members who were born at roughly the same time and share significant life events (Kupperschmidt, 2000). The implication of this definition is that the accident of birth years places individuals in the same "life experience" pool and, as a result, is likely to have an influence on the values of the members.

Generation X is defined as those born between 1961 and 1980, while Generation Y is generally defined as the cohort of those born between 1980 and 1995. There has been a continuing debate about the extent to which Gen Xers and Yers are motivated by similar values and processes as those from earlier generations, who were already in the workplace when earlier studies were conducted. An associated question might be whether Gen Xers and Yers (many of whom are now working as junior and middle managers) subscribe to similar motivational techniques and theories as those managers who were born in an earlier generation.

The terms "Generation X" and "Generation Y" have often been used in a stereotypic way, ascribing various characteristics to the "younger" generation in a universal fashion, assuming all of those born between 1961 and 1995 share similar behaviors and values. Consider the following debate between a critic of the "new" values and a member of the "new" generation:

> THE CRITIC: [They] grow up painfully, commercialized even in their school days, they cannot spell, flimsy, shallow, amusement-seeking creatures, their English is slipshod and commonplace, veteran teachers are saying that never in their experience were young people so thirstily avid of pleasure as now—selfish, and so hard!

> THE 25-YEAR-OLD RESPONDENT: [Our behaviors] are a logical reaction to the "helplessness" of parents and other adults. The modern child from the age of ten is almost his/her own boss. The complexity of the world we face makes only more necessary our bracing up for the fray, we have to work out this problem all alone. I doubt if any generation was ever thrown quite so completely on its own resources as ours is. We have a very real feeling of coming straight up against a wall of diminishing opportunity. I do not see how it can be denied that practical opportunity is less for this generation than it has been for those preceding it.

Consider how accurate this exchange is, or how well it reflects today's prevailing attitudes. Then consider that it was written in 1911 (Cited in Waclawski, 1999), and you will realize that the generation gap is nothing new.

Although there has been a great deal of speculation and opinion regarding the motivation of the Generation X and Y worker, there has been relatively little formal research. One study, however, provides some interesting data to add to the debate. Smola and Sutton (2002) contrasted the work values of the Baby Boom generation (those workers born between 1946 and 1964) with the Gen X workers. They chose these groups because together they represented the majority of the current workforce at the time of the study. Increasingly, those born between 1980 and 1995 (Generation Y) are entering the workforce and will present new challenges for the study of cohort interactions.

The question of the values and motivation of members of younger generations is an important one for many reasons. The most obvious of these is demographic reality. With the passage of time, members of a new generation will predictably continue to increase in representation in the workforce. Thus, it is important to understand what motivates them. In addition, they are the cohort that will be most influenced, in the long term, by the "new" workplace (teams, technology, globalization, multicultural environments, downsizing). As such, they represent the trial cohort for new methods of work organization (including motivational frameworks).

Smola and Sutton (2002) analyzed 362 responses to a work values questionnaire from employed individuals in a wide variety of occupations and organizational levels. Although the respondents represented a wide variety of ages and generations, they compared the responses of those who fell into the Boomer generation with those who were members of Gen X. They were also able to compare their questionnaire results with those collected in a similar study done in 1974 (Cherrington, 1980). The analyses were intended to answer three questions:

1. *Are there generational differences between Boomers and Gen Xers?* The data seemed to indicate that the answer to this question is yes. The younger employees appeared to be less loyal to the company and more "me" oriented, wanted to be promoted more quickly, and were less likely to consider work as the centerpiece of their lives. Surprisingly, the Gen Xers also appeared to feel more strongly than the Boomers that working hard made one a better person and that one should work hard even if a supervisor is not around.
2. *Are the work values of today's workers different from those of 1974?* Again, the data suggested that the answer is yes. Today's workers, regardless of age, valued "pride in work" less than the workers of 1974. Today's workers were also less likely to believe that work success should be equated to life success, that work should be a central part of life, and that hard work makes one a better person. In general, it appeared that work was simply less important than it was 25 years ago.
3. *Do work values change as workers grow older?* Values do appear to change with age. In general, work becomes less idealized. As workers age, they appear to be less convinced that work is a central part of life, that hard work makes you a better person, or that workers need to feel a sense of pride in their work.

The authors conclude that the work experience of the Gen Xers has influenced their work values and, to a lesser extent, the values of their Boomer co-workers. Although the researchers did not examine Generation Y workers, there is no reason to believe that the results would not also hold for them. Since the 1980s, downsizing initiatives have become a way of life. Downsizing sends the message that workers are disposable and that loyalty to an organization (and possibly to an occupation) is futile. As world events such as 9/11 remind individuals of their vulnerability, we may predict that the ties between individuals and work will become even weaker. There are several motivational implications of these results. The first, and most obvious, is that the employer of the 21st century needs to be concerned with the values and motivation of *all* employees, not just those born in a particular era. In addition, these results suggest that many traditional approaches to motivation—those that ignore issues such as a work–life balance or consider work to be in *competition* with non-work activities—are doomed to fail. Finally, if organizations expect commitment and loyalty *from* employees, they will need to demonstrate their commitment and loyalty *to* employees. Layoffs, downsizing, and temporary workers run contrary to any meaningful psychological contract between employers and employees. We realize, of course, that global competition is a reality and that cutting and controlling costs, including payroll costs, may be central to an organization's survival. Nevertheless, if that is to be the "new" work environment, then radically different models of motivation may be called for.

Motivational Interventions

Although we have considered the application of motivation theory at various points in the chapter, it might be helpful to describe some specific techniques that have been popular in applied settings. We will present examples of three specific types of interventions: contingent rewards (behaviorism), job enrichment, and a feedback program.

Contingent Rewards

Luthans, Paul, and Baker (1981) provide an example of the application of behaviorism in work behavior. They focused on the behavior of sales personnel in a department store. They were concerned with three specific behaviors (i.e., responses) of the sales personnel: responding quickly to potential buyers (defined as within five seconds of the customer's arrival), keeping merchandise shelves stocked to within 70 percent of capacity, and remaining within 3 yards of the assigned sales position in the store. Rewards for these behaviors included time off and cash bonuses. A total of 16 departments from a large store were chosen for the study. Eight of the departments were control departments where no rewards were given (although they were informed of the new performance expectations). Sales personnel in the other eight departments received contingent rewards for the target behaviors. The contingent reinforcement had immediate and dramatic results. On every target behavior, the experimental (reward) department exceeded the performance level of the control departments.

In a meta-analysis, Stajkovic and Luthans (2003) concluded that a combination of money, feedback, and social reinforcement had a very strong effect on a variety of task-related behaviors. Markham, Scott, and McKee (2002) showed similar effects for public recognition as a reward for reduced absenteeism. It seems clear that, as a technology for changing behavior, reinforcement theory can be helpful. Nevertheless, the ultimate explanation of why long-term change might have occurred will require a more complex model than stimulus–response–reinforcement. In addition, even as a technology, behaviorism is most likely to be effective in developing simple individual behaviors (e.g., improving attendance, increasing individual sales) rather than complex group behaviors (e.g., team-based marketing plan development for a new product).

Job Enrichment

Based in part on Maslow's theory, researchers have proposed that jobs that satisfy higher-order needs (love, esteem, and self-actualization) are capable of motivating individuals. Such jobs are considered more "enriched" and interesting than jobs that are tedious and simply represent a way to make money. The concept of **job enrichment** can be broadened to include the notion of making any job more interesting. The implication is that a job that has been enriched (i.e., given an increased capacity to satisfy higher-level needs) will be more motivating after it has been enriched than it was before. The application, then, is to enrich a job as a way of increasing motivation.

Job enrichment A motivational approach that involves increasing the responsibility and interest level of jobs in order to increase the motivation and job satisfaction of employees performing those jobs.

Hackman and Oldham (1976) developed a way of actually scoring jobs on their potential to motivate an individual. This motivation potential (assessed by a questionnaire) is tied to five job characteristics:

- *Skill variety*. The number of skills required to perform a task or job successfully
- *Task identity*. The extent to which a task or job is self-contained, with a clear beginning, middle, and end; the extent to which a task can be meaningfully understood in relation to other tasks
- *Task significance*. The perceived importance of the job for the organization or society as a whole
- *Autonomy*. The extent to which the individual worker can control schedules, procedures, and the like
- *Task feedback*. The extent to which the individual gets direct information from the task itself (as opposed to a supervisor) about his or her level of performance

A job high in motivating potential would be one that is high on each of these five characteristics. Hackman and Oldham (1976) also propose that the individual worker must be focused on higher-order needs in order for these job characteristics to have any effect. For the purposes of this example of application, we will assume that our hypothetical workers have this property.

Using the example from the application of reinforcement theory, we can see the differences in applied approaches. Consider the task of the sales personnel in that example. The job enrichment approach would not depend on cash bonuses and days off to motivate the employees. Instead, the manager might engage in the following actions for the sales position:

1. Provide sales personnel with computers to track customer patterns; involve them in planning promotions and special sales. (Skill variety)
2. Clarify exactly what the tasks and subtasks of retail selling are in the organization, identifying sales cycles (weekly, monthly, quarterly, annual) and distinctions between sales and marketing. (Task identity)
3. Show the effect of the retail sales of one person on department and store profitability and on organizational stability; point out the importance of the job to customers (e.g., pointing out how the community might change for the worse if the job did not exist). (Task significance)
4. Provide sales personnel the opportunity to have a say in scheduling and particularly which of several alternative procedures (or sales techniques) might be used to make a sale. (Autonomy)

5. Provide computer-based feedback on a daily and weekly schedule regarding individual "profitability," sales volume, and so on; provide simple "satisfaction with service" forms for customers to complete, or encourage sales personnel to ask the customer at the end of the transaction if he or she was satisfied with the transaction. (Feedback)

In practice, most applications of this job enrichment approach have also involved changing pay schedules, methods of supervision, planning and decision-making strategies, and work group interaction patterns. Nevertheless, a job enrichment approach might act as a vehicle for facilitating these changes and have a "value-added" effect beyond the enriching of the task and job.

ProMES

As we mentioned briefly earlier in this chapter, Pritchard and his colleagues (Pritchard, Paquin, De Cuir, McCormick, & Bly, 2001; Pritchard, Weaver, & Ashwood, 2011) have been developing a productivity improvement plan called **ProMES**, which stands for Productivity Measurement and Enhancement System.

ProMES The Productivity Measurement and Enhancement System: a motivational approach that utilizes goal setting, rewards, and feedback to increase motivation and performance.

Pritchard (1992) defines productivity as "how well a system uses its resources to achieve its goals." ProMES is intended to maximize motivation primarily through cognitive means. ProMES assumes that the real issue in productivity is knowing how to allocate time and energy across possible actions or tasks. Like the German action theorists, Pritchard concentrates on the "act" of producing a good or service, which he defines as the "doing of something, like writing, running, talking or repairing a machine" (Pritchard et al., 2001, p. 5). Every act has associated with it amplitude, direction, and persistence. The theory attempts to explain why certain acts are chosen over others (direction) and how much energy is devoted to the task once it has been chosen (amplitude and persistence).

The ProMES system involves workers and managers in making detailed plans for productivity improvement. In other words, it focuses them on a productivity "act" which will have a high likelihood of increasing overall unit performance. This includes forming a task team and having the task team identify detailed productivity objectives and equally detailed **indicators** of success at meeting those objectives. The ProMES system has been used by many organizations in many different countries. The cumulative evidence shows very significant gains in productivity following the introduction of ProMES. Based on a recent meta-analysis of 83 field studies of ProMES (Pritchard, Harrell, DiazGranados, & Guzman, 2008), the following conclusions were drawn:

Indicators Quantitative measures of how well each objective is being met in the ProMES approach.

1. ProMES results in large improvements in productivity.
2. These effects last for years.
3. The effects can be seen in a wide range of organizations and countries.

There do, however, seem to be some possible cultural implications for the success of ProMES. Paquin, Roch, and Sanchez-Ku (2007) studied the impact of ProMES in seven different countries and found that if the country could be described as high in power distance, then ProMES was effective. As an example, ProMES was actually less effective in the United States than in many European countries. The researchers suggest that this is due to the relatively low power distance in the United States. They also discovered that if collectivism was high in a country, this could offset low power distance. But even in the United States, which would be characterized as individualistic and low in power distance, ProMES had a positive influence on motivation and productivity.

The primary element of the ProMES system is information, particularly as it is fed back to workers. This is most clearly a person-as-scientist approach. But worker participation in the design and development of the system gives it a less sterile and calculating feel. It also assumes that individual workers will accept and commit to the system. It seems clear that when productivity increases, other good things are likely to happen as well (e.g., increased job security, compensation, and feelings of efficacy). Like the action theorists, Pritchard has some ideas about why ProMES works so well, but he is less interested in breaking down the process than in simply improving productivity. Like the action theorists, he believes that the key to productivity is not in "motivating" workers with traditional approaches but in helping them gain a better understanding of the job.

As you can see, each of these three motivational interventions is unique, and each has been shown to produce good results. This reinforces the point that even though we may not yet have a complete and accurate theory of work motivation, managers can nevertheless influence subordinate motivation through the various mechanisms we have covered in this chapter.

MODULE 8.4 SUMMARY

- Motivation can be measured by indicators such as the difficulty of goals accepted by an individual or the strength of a person's belief that hard work will yield rewards. Recent research suggests that conscientiousness and emotional stability may be surrogate measures for general motivation levels. An instrument called the Motivational Trait Questionnaire provides a standardized method for measuring general performance motivation.
- Culture has significant practical implications for work motivation. Although I-O psychologists in a given culture may have the research and theory to support a particular motivational intervention within that culture, the value of that intervention will decrease in direct proportion to the multicultural nature of the company and workforce.
- Debate continues on the extent to which Gen Xers and Yers are motivated by similar values and processes as earlier generations. There has been a great deal of speculation and opinion, but relatively little formal research, regarding the motivation of Gen X and Y workers. However, recent research has identified some differences in values and preferences between generations.
- Specific motivational interventions that have been popular in applied settings include contingent rewards, job enrichment, and feedback programs such as the ProMES system.

KEY TERMS

Motivational Trait Questionnaire (MTQ)
job enrichment
ProMES
indicators

9 Attitudes, Emotions, and Work

MODULE 9.1

Work Attitudes

The Experience of Emotion at Work

Imagine that you are a manager with a Fortune 500 company and you have just been promoted to a new position in a new location. Your emotions probably include happiness, pride, excitement, and enthusiasm—and perhaps some nervousness as you face the challenges of getting to know your new responsibilities and your new co-workers. In accordance with company policy, on your first day in the new location, you report to the security office to have your photo taken for an identification badge and turn your laptop over to the IT department for a routine security check and any needed software updates. Now imagine that, the following morning, your new boss calls you into her office and, with a cold stare, informs you that the IT department has discovered evidence in your laptop that you have been mishandling company funds! The previous day's positive emotions are instantly overcome by a wave of shock, dismay, embarrassment, and anger at what you are sure is a false accusation. You remain in an intense emotional state over the next few days as you investigate the details of the accusation and gather evidence to disprove it. Eventually, as you succeed in clearing your name, your fact finding reveals that an employee in the IT security department "cooked" your laptop financial records as an act of revenge because, months earlier, you fired his sister, who had been one of your subordinates in your previous job. The guilty IT employee is a total stranger to you, but he obviously harbored very strong emotions about you based on what his sister must have told him. How would you describe your emotional reaction to this discovery?

"Look, it's silly for you to come home from work miserable every day. Why don't you just stay there?"

Life is full of strong emotions. Consider the elation you experienced when you received an A on a term paper and the anger you experienced when you took a test that you felt was grossly unfair. Similar emotions occur in the workplace. In the course of a day at work, you may be angry with a co-worker, stressed by your boss, amused by another colleague, and proud from the praise given by a manager. You may have come to work in a foul mood because of an encounter with another driver on the commute. This foul mood might have put a damper on the first few hours at work. You might leave work in such a great mood that you decide to take your children and spouse out to dinner and a movie. The school experience is not much different; roommates are all too often aware of the effects on each other of good and bad days in class and in social activities.

Emotions experienced at work affect both work and non-work behavior. Similarly, non-work-related emotions affect both work and non-work behavior. Understanding emotions at work is no simple task. Not only do we experience both work and non-work stimuli but we also have a range of different reactions, ranging from attitudes to emotions to moods. In this chapter we will deal with the complex relationships of work and non-work emotions and attitudes as well as their effects on behavior.

Job Satisfaction: Some History

The Early Period of Job Satisfaction Research

In the mid-1920s, Elton Mayo, an Australian psychologist, introduced the concept of emotions into mainstream American I-O psychology. He argued that factory work resulted in various negative emotions such as anger, fear, suspicion, lowered performance, and increased illness (Mayo, 1923a,b,c). This in turn led to the development of labor unions and worker unrest. (It was no accident that Mayo identified labor unions as the pathological result of job dissatisfaction. He had been actively opposing labor unions in his native Australia long before he arrived in the United States [Griffin, Landy, & Mayocchi, 2002].) This was a novel suggestion. Until this point, there had been little interest among psychologists or managers in the happiness of workers. It was assumed that workers cared only about wages and that as long as they were paid adequately, they would be happy. There were occasional surveys of worker satisfaction, but the surveys asked managers about the happiness of the workers rather than asking the workers themselves (Houser, 1927).

In the early 1930s, two very different research projects breathed life into the concept of **job satisfaction**. The first was a survey of all the working adults in a small town in Pennsylvania. Robert Hoppock (1935) was interested in the answer to two questions: How happy were workers, and were workers in some occupations happier than workers in other occupations? He discovered that only 12 percent of workers could be classified as dissatisfied. He also found wide variations among individuals within occupational groupings; nevertheless, workers in some occupational groups (e.g., professionals and managers) were, on the whole, happier than those in other categories (e.g., unskilled manual laborers). These findings suggested that *both* job-related *and* individual differences variables might influence job satisfaction.

Job satisfaction Positive attitude or emotional state resulting from the appraisal of one's job or job experience.

The second research project was begun at the Hawthorne plant of the Western Electric Company in Cicero, Illinois, in the late 1920s (Roethlisberger & Dickson, 1939). As you may recall from our discussion in Chapter 1, the purpose of the Hawthorne studies was to examine the relationship between various physical aspects of work and the work environment, such as lighting, workday length, the timing of rest breaks, and their influence on productivity. The findings suggested that the *perceptions* of workers had a greater effect on productivity than the actual physical working conditions. More surprisingly, they also suggested that with almost all of the experimental conditions the researchers introduced,

Job satisfaction is a positive emotional state that can result from positive interactions with one's coworkers.

production improved. When illumination was reduced virtually to the level of candlelight, production improved. When the length of the workday was increased, production improved. When rest pauses were eliminated, production improved. These results were so unexpected that the researchers followed up the experiments with extensive interviews and an examination of workers' diaries in an attempt to determine why the reduced illumination and longer work periods did not have the hypothesized effect of reducing productivity. The researchers discovered that because of the experiment, the workers received considerably more attention from their supervisors and managers than they had previously. This increased attention was viewed positively by the workers and may explain why attitudes toward supervision improved. The improved attitudes of workers toward supervisors as a result of the increased attention appeared, in turn, to be responsible for the increase in productivity. This led to the introduction of a new term into the literature of social psychology: the **Hawthorne effect**, meaning a change in behavior or attitudes that was the simple result of increased attention.

Hawthorne effect A change in behavior or attitudes that was the simple result of increased attention.

Attitudes Relatively stable feelings or beliefs that are directed toward specific persons, groups, ideas, jobs, or other objects.

At the time this research was reported, the general conclusion drawn by I-O psychologists was that morale and production seemed to be closely linked. As we will see later in the chapter, this conclusion was wrong. Nevertheless, both researchers and managers were quick to embrace this conclusion, and it has been hard to dispel. The Hawthorne study results have been analyzed and reanalyzed, interpreted and reinterpreted, and many different theories have been proposed to account for the surprising results (Landsberger, 1958). But one thing is beyond dispute: Following closely on the heels of Mayo's early research on the effect of factory work on emotions and the discovery of individual differences in satisfaction by Hoppock, the Hawthorne studies galvanized social scientists and gave impetus to the study of worker **attitudes** and the new construct of job satisfaction.

The years between 1935 and 1955 were very active for job satisfaction research, largely because satisfaction was thought to be closely linked to two outcomes very important to industry: the prevention of labor unrest in the form of strikes, and productivity. The idea was that if an employer could keep worker morale high, the company would be strike-free and profitable. Most attempts to measure satisfaction asked workers about their most important needs and the extent to which those needs were being met. It was believed that the greater the extent to which important needs were met, the greater would be worker satisfaction (Schaffer, 1953). In addition, social psychology was emerging during this period as a specialty within psychology. Social psychologists became very interested in attitudes of all sorts, and attitudes toward work represented a good integration of the theories of social psychologists with the interests of industrial psychologists.

In the late 1950s, two reviews of the research conducted to that point came to very different conclusions. Brayfield and Crockett (1955) concluded that there was little evidence of any substantial connection between satisfaction and performance. In contrast, Herzberg, Mausner, Peterson, and Capwell (1957) concluded that there was a connection between satisfaction and at least some work behaviors, particularly absenteeism and turnover. This led to the introduction of one of the first modern theories of job satisfaction, the two-factor theory (Herzberg, Mausner, & Snyderman, 1959). Recall from Chapter 8 that, according to

Herzberg, job satisfaction was the result of intrinsic job characteristics (e.g., interesting work, challenge), whereas job dissatisfaction was the result of extrinsic characteristics (e.g., pay, working conditions). Herzberg proposed that extrinsic factors satisfied "hygiene" needs and intrinsic factors satisfied "motivator" needs. This theory resulted in a flurry of activity, but eventually the theory was rejected on both logical (King, 1970) and empirical grounds (Ewen, Smith, Hulin, & Locke, 1966).

Antecedents and Consequences of Job Satisfaction

Job satisfaction research between 1935 and 1990 has been characterized as atheoretical (Brief & Weiss, 2002). This criticism has been leveled in part because researchers depended on statistical analyses as a replacement for theory. They looked for correlations between reports of job satisfaction and observable aspects of work. The best example is pay. Studies would examine the relationships among desired levels of pay, observed levels of pay, and reported job satisfaction (Sweeney & McFarlin, 2005; Williams, McDaniel, & Nguyen, 2006). Similar analyses were made for virtually every aspect of work imaginable—work challenge, quality of supervision, company policies, and various aspects of the physical work environment, even including the use of stereo headsets by workers (Oldham, Cummings, Mischel, Schmidtke, & Jhou, 1995).

Locke (1976; Locke & Henne, 1986) presented an exhaustive review of many of the precursors of job satisfaction that have been examined. Table 9.1, which provides a summary of a sample of these investigations, is interesting for two reasons. First, it provides

TABLE 9.1 A Sample of the Effects of Events and Agents on Job Satisfaction

SOURCE	*EFFECT*
Events or conditions	
Work itself: challenge	Mentally challenging work that the individual can successfully accomplish is satisfying.
Work itself: physical demand	Tiring work is dissatisfying.
Work itself: personal interest	Personally interesting work is satisfying.
Reward structure	Just and informative rewards for performance are satisfying.
Working conditions: physical	Satisfaction depends on the match between working conditions and physical needs.
Working conditions: goal attainment	Working conditions that facilitate goal attainment are satisfying.
Agents	
Self	High self-esteem is conducive to job satisfaction.
Supervisors, co-workers, subordinates	Individuals will be satisfied with colleagues who help them attain rewards.
	Individuals will be satisfied with colleagues who see things the same way they do.
Company and management	Individuals will be satisfied with companies that have policies and procedures designed to help the individual attain rewards. Individuals will be dissatisfied with conflicting roles or ambiguous roles imposed by company, management, or both.
Fringe benefits	Benefits do not have a strong influence on job satisfaction for most workers.

NOTE: The interested reader is directed to Locke's (1976) review for a more detailed presentation of these conclusions.

a good summary of some general factors that appear to lead to satisfaction or dissatisfaction. Second, it is equally interesting for what it does *not* identify as an antecedent to job satisfaction, but remember, this is a table created from elements of the 20th century. In the 21st century, we would probably add a number of additional variables, including the following:

- Concern for job security (Probst, 2003)
- The extent to which an organization appears to be time-urgent (Francis-Smythe & Robertson, 2003)
- Satisfaction with the rate of job changes in an organization (van Dam, 2005)
- Effects of perceived discrimination on job satisfaction (Ensher, Grant-Vallone, & Donaldson, 2001)
- Attitudes toward a multicultural workplace
- Satisfaction with production models such as Six Sigma, which is discussed in Chapter 14

Issues such as these would not have been contemplated in 1920, or 1950, or even 1980. But they are part of the work landscape today.

In addition to looking at aspects of workers as precursors of satisfaction, investigators have also examined demographic variables such as age (Farr & Ringseis, 2002), gender (Konrad, Ritchie, Lieb, & Corrigal, 2000), and even inherited genetic disposition (Arvey, Bouchard, Segal, & Abraham, 1989; Lykken, McGue, Tellegen, & Bouchard, 1992). We will examine some data on inherited disposition in Module 9.2. Unfortunately, without a comprehensive and cohesive theory of job satisfaction to explain the findings of individual studies, this type of data-driven research is not particularly helpful.

Just as there has been wide variation in the investigation of the precursors of job satisfaction, there has also been wide variation in the variables examined as possible consequences of job satisfaction. It is generally assumed that job satisfaction is associated with work behavior (Fisher, 2003). There seems to be some support for this assumption. Consider the following:

- Barling, Kelloway, and Iverson (2003) reported that satisfying jobs are linked to fewer occupational injuries.

BOX 9.1 THE WORST JOBS IN SPORTS

There are good jobs and bad jobs. Lists of the "best" and "worst" jobs are frequently published in the popular press. A few years ago, *USA Today* published a list of the 10 worst jobs in sports (Pedulla, 2005). That list included a rodeo bullfighter, a urine specimen collector, and a boxing sparring partner. But the worst job of all was that of a horse-racing groom—an individual who tends to the needs of horses. The duties included feeding and bathing the horse, removing dirt from the hooves of the horse, and, of course, shoveling the manure deposited by the 1,100-pound animal. There is also the constant threat of being kicked or bitten. These tasks are performed for the princely sum of $400 per week. The pluses for the job include the fact that it involves few interruptions from e-mails or cell phones. An excellent TV show depicts some of the worst jobs imaginable. It is called *Dirty Jobs* and appears on the Discovery Channel.

- In a meta-analysis of 7,933 business units in 36 companies, Harter, Schmidt, and Hayes (2002) found positive relations between employee satisfaction and customer satisfaction, productivity, profit, safety, and employee retention.
- Several studies (LePine, Erez, & Johnson, 2002; Tang & Ibrahim, 1998) reported that increased satisfaction is associated with increased organizational citizenship behavior.
- A meta-analysis by Williams and colleagues (2006) found that satisfaction with pay is moderately associated with turnover intentions (−.31) and actual turnover (−.17).
- Judge, Thoreson, Bono, and Patton (2001) found a positive correlation of a substantial magnitude (+.30) between job satisfaction and task performance.
- Satisfied employees are less likely to be absent from work (Johns, 1997).
- Satisfied employees are less likely to be late for work (Kozlowsky, Sagie, Krausz, & Singer, 1997).
- Conte, Dean, Ringenbach, Moran, and Landy (2005) found that job satisfaction is associated with job analysis ratings: More satisfied employees give high ratings for the frequency and importance of various tasks.
- Several researchers have found a positive association between job satisfaction and general life satisfaction and feelings of well-being (Warr, 1999; Wright & Cropanzano, 2000).

With this wide array of desirable outcomes associated with job satisfaction, it is not surprising that employers would like to maintain or improve the satisfaction of their employees. There have been some estimates that the actual "cost" of dissatisfaction can rise to 1.5 times the salary of an unhappy and productive individual who leaves an organization (Koeppel, 2004). But Schneider and his colleagues (Schneider, Hanges, Smith, & Salvaggio, 2003) question the causal direction of this assumption. They were able to complete an analysis that examined which was the cart and which the horse: Did employee satisfaction *cause* profitability or did company success *cause* satisfaction? Interestingly, it appears that company success *results in* increased overall job satisfaction (a surprise) and increased satisfaction with job security (not as much of a surprise). Based on their results, they present a model that explains how and why job satisfaction *follows* company profitability rather than *drives* it. That model is shown in Figure 9.1. Thus, it appears that if companies wish to maintain or increase employee morale, money might be best invested in high-performance work practices, such as pay for performance, pay for skill acquisition, training, and performance management (Huselid, 1995; Morrison, Cordery, Girardi, & Payne, 2005), rather than simply in increased pay or improved working conditions. What is clear from these results is that we can no longer take for granted the direction of the satisfaction–performance relationship.

Taking into consideration all of the possible precursors of job satisfaction with all of the possible consequences—and all of the enthusiastic researchers—you can understand why 10,000 studies of job satisfaction have been produced. Figure 9.2 provides a graphic illustration of the range of possible studies. Although we have half a century of research on this topic, there are as yet no compelling theories or conclusions. We will return to the issues of antecedents and consequences in subsequent modules.

The Measurement of Job Satisfaction

There are two different measurement issues that we will discuss concerning job satisfaction. The first is the distinction between satisfaction with specific aspects of work (often called facet satisfaction) versus a measure of overall satisfaction. The second is the use of questionnaires to measure satisfaction.

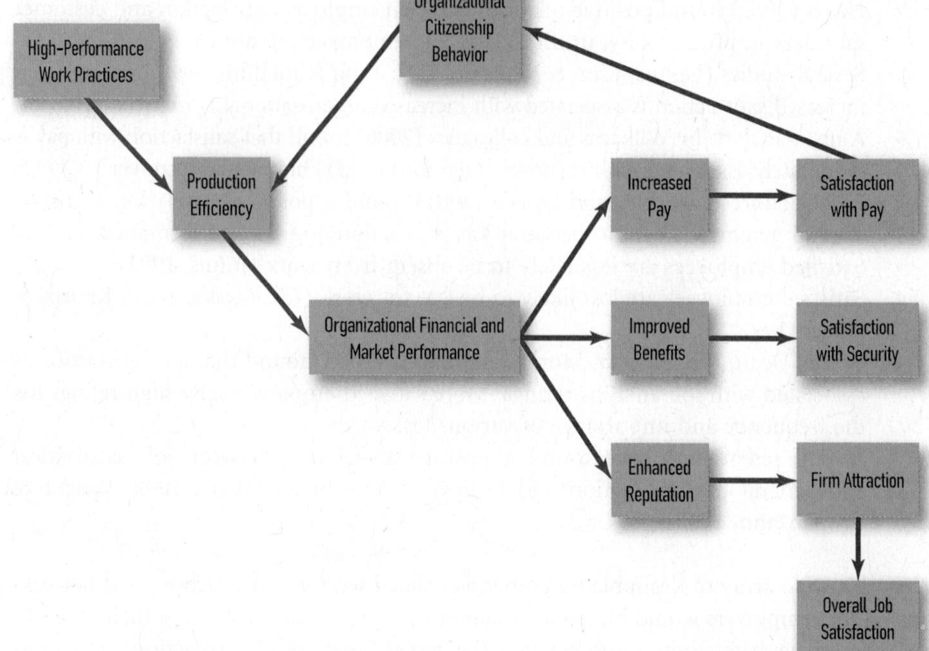

FIGURE 9.1 Relationship between High-Performance Work Practices and Job Satisfaction

SOURCE: Schneider, B., Hanges, P. J., Smith, D. B., & Salvaggio, A. N. (2003). Which comes first: Employee attitudes or organizational financial and market performance? *Journal of Applied Psychology, 88*, 836–851, p. 847. © 2003 by the American Psychological Association. Reprinted by permission of the publisher.

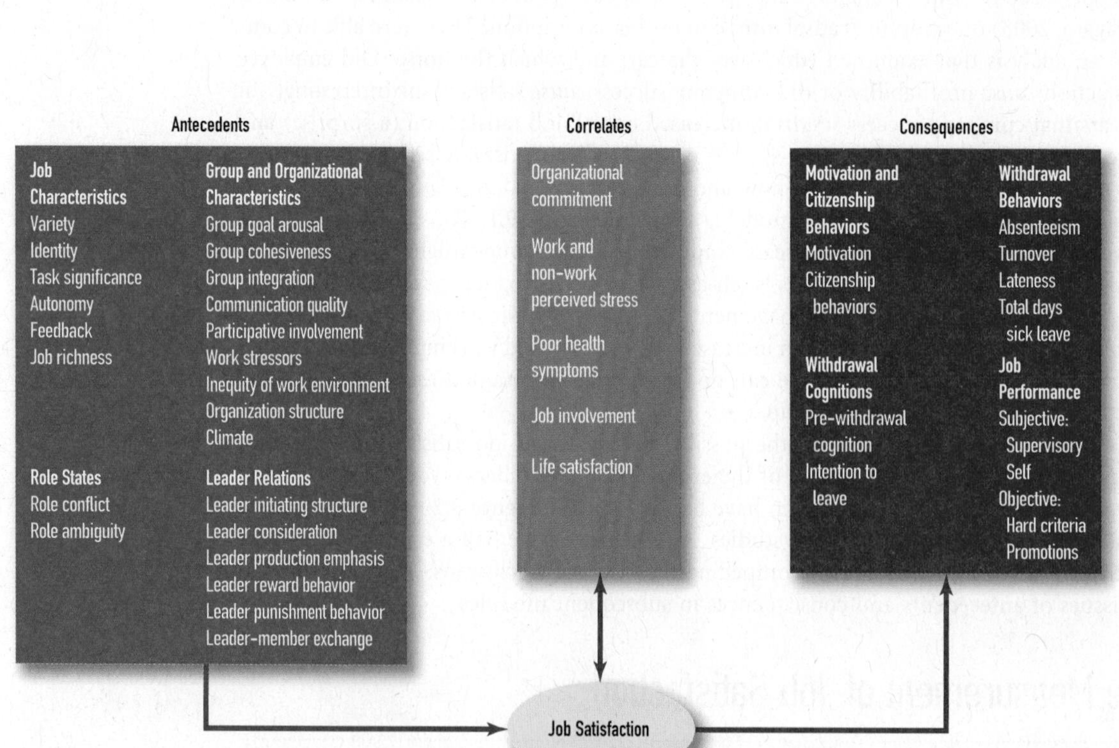

FIGURE 9.2 Classification of Presumed Antecedents, Correlates, and Consequences of Job Satisfaction

SOURCE: Kinicki, A. J., McKee-Ryan, F. M., Schriesheim, C. A., & Carson, K. P. (2002). Assessing the construct validity of the Job Descriptive Index: A review and meta-analysis. *Journal of Applied Psychology, 87*, 14–32, p. 20. © 2002 by the American Psychological Association. Reprinted by permission of the publisher.

Overall versus Facet Satisfaction

Various researchers and practitioners have taken different positions on both the value of **overall satisfaction** and how it might be calculated (Rice, Gentile, & McFarlin, 1991). As we saw above, many researchers took the position that overall satisfaction is the result of combining satisfaction with specific important aspects of work. Thus, they would advocate using a mathematical formula for weighting and combining satisfaction with specific aspects. Others pointed out the frequent high correlations between measures of satisfaction and various facets of work, so it seems useless to bother computing individual facet scores (Judge & Hulin, 1993). Indeed, there are some instances in which an overall score will work just fine (e.g., comparing one plant or division of an organization to another) and other instances in which facet information might be more useful (e.g., trying to identify which aspects of the work environment might play a central role in recruiting new employees). Wanous, Reichers, and Hundy (1997) demonstrated that even single-item measures of job satisfaction (e.g., "Overall, how satisfied are you with your current job?") may work well in many situations. As an example of this type of measure, consider the now-famous "faces" scale (see Figure 9.3), which was developed almost 60 years ago as a single-item measure of job satisfaction (Kunin, 1998). This format has been used to elicit overall satisfaction ratings from workers with their jobs, to determine the satisfaction of customers with food or service, and even to help patients describe their current level of experienced pain or discomfort. It appears to be both a simple and an elegant way to get right to the core of an emotional reaction.

Overall satisfaction Overall assessment of job satisfaction that results either from mathematically combining scores based on satisfaction with specific important aspects of work or a single overall evaluative rating of the job.

Judge, Thoreson, and colleagues (2001) described a simple five-item scale that appears to work well as a measure of overall satisfaction:

- I feel fairly satisfied with my present job.
- Most days I am enthusiastic about my work.
- Each day at work seems like it will never end.
- I find real enjoyment in my work.
- I consider my job to be rather unpleasant.

Respondents use an agree–disagree format to reflect their attitude. As we will see in the next module, the greatest concern in recent discussions of job satisfaction is not whether overall or **facet satisfaction** should be measured, but whether there is any value in measuring satisfaction (at least as an attitude) at all (Judge, Thoreson, et al., 2001; Weiss, 2002a).

Facet satisfaction Information related to specific facets or elements of job satisfaction.

Job Descriptive Index (JDI) One of the most extensively researched and documented job satisfaction instruments; assesses satisfaction with five distinct areas: the work itself, supervision, people, pay, and promotion.

Satisfaction Questionnaires

Table 9.2 displays some of the items from a questionnaire called the **Job Descriptive Index (JDI)** (Smith, Kendall, & Hulin, 1969). It is one of the most extensively researched and documented instruments used to measure job satisfaction (Kinicki et al., 2002). The JDI assesses satisfaction with five distinct areas of work: the work itself, supervision, people, pay, and promotion. The JDI also includes a separate overall satisfaction measure called the Job in General (JIG) scale, which contains 18 items (Balzer et al., 1990). A review and meta-analysis (Kinicki et al., 2002) confirmed the construct validity and reliability of the JDI.

FIGURE 9.3 Faces 1, 4, 6, 8, and 10 of the Circular Face Series

Source: Kunin, T. (1955). The construction of a new type of attitude measure. *Personnel Psychology, 8*, 70–71.

TABLE 9.2 **Sample Items from the JDI**

Think of the work you do at present. How well does each of the following words or phrases describe your job? In the blank beside each word or phrase below, write:

Y	for "Yes" if it describes your work
N	for "No" if it does NOT describe it
?	for "?" if you cannot decide

WORK ON PRESENT JOB	SUPERVISION
______ Fascinating	______ Doesn't supervise enough
______ Pleasant	______ Around when needed
______ Can see results	______ Knows job well
PRESENT PAY	CO-WORKERS
______ Barely live on income	______ Stimulating
______ Bad	______ Unpleasant
______ Well paid	______ Smart
OPPORTUNITIES FOR PROMOTION	JOB IN GENERAL
______ Opportunities somewhat limited	______ Pleasant
______ Promotion on ability	______ Worse than most
______ Regular promotions	______ Worthwhile

SOURCE: Brodke, M., Sliter, M., Balzer, W., Gillespie, J., Gillespie, M., Gopalkrishnan, P., Lake, C., Oyer, C., Withrow, S., & Yankelvich, M. (2009). *The Job Descriptive Index and Job in General: 2009 Revision Quick Reference Guide*. http://www.bgsu.edu/departments/psych/io/jdi/index.html. Reprinted by permission of Bowling Green State University.

Minnesota Satisfaction Questionnaire (MSQ) A commonly used job satisfaction instrument that assesses particular aspects of work (e.g., achievement, ability utilization) as well as scores for extrinsic satisfaction and intrinsic satisfaction.

The disadvantages of the JDI are that the questionnaire is lengthy (it has 72 items) and that the broad category of "work" does not provide much information about issues such as creativity, independence, variety, or other aspects of the work itself.

Similar to the research of Wanous and colleagues (1997) cited above with respect to overall satisfaction, Nagy (2002) has demonstrated that single-item measures of each of the JDI facets may work as well as, and possibly even better than, the multiple-item format. The downside to single-item measures, however, is the absence of any information about what might be *causing* the dissatisfaction, thus limiting any intervention. Other research has found support for shorter versions of the JDI (25 items) and the JIG (8 items) scales (Russell et al., 2004). If further research supports these findings, this would be a substantial practical step forward since it would reduce the expense—in both time and money—of administering a lengthy satisfaction survey.

Work that is well done provides intrinsic satisfaction, even if—as in the case of a Buddhist sand painting—the tangible result may not last long.

An alternative to the JDI is the **Minnesota Satisfaction Questionnaire (MSQ)** (Weiss, Dawis, England, & Lofquist, 1967). Whereas the JDI uses 72 items to assess five areas of satisfaction, the MSQ assesses more refined aspects of work (e.g., achievement, ability utilization) with only five items per area. The MSQ also allows one to calculate an extrinsic and an intrinsic satisfaction score. **Intrinsic satisfaction** is related to the work that individuals do—aspects that are central or intrinsic to their job. **Extrinsic satisfaction** concerns whether employees are satisfied with aspects that are extrinsic, or external, to job tasks, such as pay or benefits. There is as much research data available for the MSQ as for the JDI, so either one might be suitable for the assessment of specific areas of satisfaction. As Kinicki and colleagues (2002) pointed out, both are acceptable.

Intrinsic satisfaction Satisfaction that derives from aspects central, or intrinsic, to the job itself, such as responsibility.

Extrinsic satisfaction Satisfaction that derives from aspects extrinsic, or external, to job tasks, such as pay or benefits.

Up to this point, we have been considering the traditional method of collecting attitude data—the completion of a paper-and-pencil attitude survey—but researchers and, to an even greater extent, organizations are turning with increased frequency to the Internet to collect such data. Some preliminary findings are encouraging. It does not appear to matter whether attitude surveys are administered in paper-and-pencil format or over the Internet. Donovan, Drasgow, and Probst (2000) studied the JDI specifically and found that computerized administration worked well. Mueller, Liebig, and Hattrup (2007) conducted two field studies to evaluate the equivalence of computerized and paper-and-pencil job satisfaction measures. The results of both studies provide additional evidence that paper-and-pencil job satisfaction measures can be transformed into computerized versions without compromising the meaning of the test scores. The efficiency of computer and Internet administration means that these findings are of considerable practical significance. In addition, compared with paper-and-pencil respondents, Internet respondents appear to be more diverse with respect to demographic characteristics such as age, gender, and socioeconomic status (Gosling, Vazire, Srivastava, & John, 2004) and to express positive feelings toward the web-based administration mode (Thompson, Surface, Martin, & Sanders, 2003).

We have been considering the issue of job satisfaction from the scientific perspective, but it is important to remember that a job is embedded in the larger context of life. A major life event, such as a serious illness, the unexpected death of a co-worker with whom one has formed a friendship, or the catastrophic events of September 11, 2001, can tend to make us reevaluate our priorities. After an event of this nature, you may find yourself asking if the level of physical and emotional effort devoted to work is worthwhile: Am I getting as much out of work as I am putting in, and are the rewards of work equal to the rewards I might get from some other form of work or from non-work activities? We will return to these questions in the other modules of this chapter.

The Concept of Commitment

The concept of **commitment** is often associated with both attitudes and emotions. Commitment to a relationship, an organization, a goal, or even an occupation involves emotional attachment, as well as evaluations of whether current circumstances are what one expected or might expect in the future. Porter, Steers, Mowday, and Boulian (1974) proposed that organizational commitment includes three elements: (1) acceptance and belief in an organization's values, (2) a willingness to exert effort on behalf of the organization to help meet its goals, and (3) a strong desire to remain in the organization. We will address the issue of the match between the values of an individual and the values of the organization in Chapter 14. We have already touched on effort expenditure in the discussions of job performance in Chapters 4 and 5 and motivation in Chapter 8. In this chapter, we will address the third aspect of commitment: the desire to remain in an organization. In addition, we will concentrate on the related issue of voluntary organizational withdrawal in the form of lateness, absenteeism, and turnover.

Commitment Psychological and emotional attachment an individual feels to a relationship, an organization, a goal, or an occupation.

Forms of Commitment

Meyer and Allen (1997) suggested that organizational commitment could be based on any one of three elements: (1) an emotional attachment to an organization, or **affective commitment**;

Affective commitment An emotional attachment to an organization.

Continuance commitment Perceived cost of leaving an organization.

Normative commitment An obligation to remain in an organization.

(2) an element representing the perceived cost of leaving the organization, or **continuance commitment**; and (3) an element representing an obligation to remain in the organization, or **normative commitment**. Thus, some people stay with an organization because they want to (attachment), others because they need to (continuance), and others because they feel they ought to (normative). These three different foundations for commitment have differential relationships with various work-related behaviors. Thus, Meyer and Allen expected affective commitment and normative commitment, but not continuance commitment, to be related to job performance. Some research also suggests that affective commitment is a better predictor of absenteeism and turnover than either continuance or normative commitment (Luchak & Gellatly, 2007). Several studies have suggested that both normative and affective commitment are affected by tenure. This has been called the "honeymoon" effect: After a relatively short period of employment with a single organization, the worker experiences a growing disaffection, eventually leading to a decision to quit (Bentein, Vandenberg, Vandenberghe, & Stinglhamber, 2005; Wright & Bonett, 2002).

Several different scales have been used to assess organizational commitment. The most commonly used scale is Meyer, Allen, and Smith's (1993) Organizational Commitment Questionnaire (OCQ), which contains six items for each of the three commitment dimensions. The OCQ is a self-report scale that typically asks respondents to rate each statement from 1 (strongly disagree) to 5 (strongly agree). Example items from the OCQ include: (a) I would be very happy to spend the rest of my career with this organization (affective commitment); (b) it would be very hard for me to leave my organization right now, even if I wanted to (continuance commitment); and (c) this organization deserves my loyalty (normative commitment). In an extension of this three-component model of commitment, Meyer and colleagues (1993) suggested that one can be committed to entities or objects other than an organization. Traditionally, commitment had been associated with organizations and was studied in relation to turnover (Porter et al., 1974). It was assumed that an individual committed to an organization was less likely to leave than someone not so committed. Meyer and colleagues introduced the concept of commitment to an *occupation*. They found that the three foundations for organizational commitment could also be applied to the notion of **occupational commitment.** They further discovered, as with organizational commitment, that various types of commitment led to different predictions about behaviors, such as performance and turnover intention. They also found that these two forms of commitment—organizational and occupational—had independent influences on performance and turnover intention. Supporting research by Lee, Carswell, and Allen (2000) confirmed the importance of considering both organizational and occupational commitment when studying work-related behavior.

Occupational commitment Commitment to a particular occupational field; includes affective, continuance, and normative commitment.

Blau (2003) suggests that there are two underlying dimensions to occupational commitment: the practical and emotional costs of changing occupation and the extent to which current opportunities in the current occupation are available. Thus, if the costs of changing one's occupation are high and the availabilities in the current occupation are low, occupational commitment will be stronger than if the cost of changing one's occupation is low and the opportunities in the current occupation are high.

Ellemers, de Gilder, and van den Heuvel (1998) have suggested that one may also develop commitment to a work team. Presumably, this form of commitment would also influence decisions regarding absence and turnover. As you will see in Chapter 14 when we examine organization theory, interventions such as total quality management, lean manufacturing methods, and just-in-time production methods depend very heavily on the concept of team commitment. The study by Ellemers and colleagues is particularly encouraging because it was done with Dutch and Belgian workers, suggesting that the construct of commitment may also apply to non-U.S. cultures. But both of these cultures, like the mainstream U.S. culture, are strongly individualistic.

In contrast, Wasti (2003b) found some difficulties in applying the concept of normative commitment in collectivist cultures such as Turkey. Markovits, Davis, and van Dick

(2007) investigated organizational commitment in Greece, which tends to be higher in collectivism than the United States. They found that organizational commitment was higher in Greek employees in the public sector as compared to the private sector. These findings are in contrast to a U.S. study in which commitment was higher in private-sector employees (Goulet & Frank, 2002), but they make sense in terms of the cultural differences between the United States and Greece. We look forward to further investigations of cross-cultural similarities and differences in organizational commitment.

In a meta-analysis of commitment research, Cooper-Hakim and Viswesvaran (2005) identified no fewer than 24 commitment definitions, including, for example, union commitment and Protestant work ethic commitment. Neubert and Cady (2001) have nominated an additional type of commitment—program commitment, which is defined as a commitment to a particular initiative taken by a company (e.g., a new HR program such as 360-degree feedback or a new training program for managers). In addition, there has been increasing interest in the role of the supervisor, both as a critical mediator in work and organizational commitment and as a focus of commitment (Becker & Kernan, 2003; Bentein, Stinglhamber, & Vandenberghe, 2002; Stinglhamber & Vandenberghe, 2003). Mitchell, Holtom, Lee, Sablynski, and Erez (2001) introduced the term **job embeddedness** to represent the many and varied types of commitment between individuals and co-workers, teams, organizations, and careers.

Job embeddedness The many and varied types of commitment that individuals feel toward co-workers, teams, organizations, and careers.

We are still at an early stage in understanding the breadth and depth of the commitment construct. A good deal of the research is definitional (how many types there are, how they are best measured, etc.), so it is too early to bestow sainthood on one particular conceptualization. Nevertheless, the construct remains an interesting and potentially valuable one for understanding worker behavior, particularly the decisions that workers make to stay with or leave an occupation or organization.

Organizational Identification

Even though the concept of commitment has an affective component, its general thrust is more cognitive than emotional. The commitment concept profits from a cognitive orientation because it is commonly used to explain why people remain with or leave an organization or occupation. To be sure, these decisions can be emotional (or worse, irrational), but because they are usually life-altering, there is often a cognitive basis to those decisions.

The concept of **organizational identification (OID)** has been proposed as a way of dealing with the much more basic and emotional aspects of organizational membership. OID has its roots in social identity theory (Haslam, 2004; Tajfel & Turner, 1986). Social identity theory consists of three propositions: (1) People value and seek self-esteem, (2) group memberships play a role in a person's self-concept, and (3) individuals seek to maintain a positive social identity by making favorable distinctions between their social in-group and other out-groups (van Dick, 2004).

Organizational identification (OID) The process whereby individuals derive a feeling of pride and esteem from their association with an organization. Individuals may also take pains to distance themselves from the organization for which they work—this would be called organizational disidentification.

In its simplest form, OID proposes that people will seek to identify with an organization in order to bolster their self-esteem. The simplest example of this is sports fans who proclaim "We're number one!" after a victory by their team. Who is the "we" they are talking about? They didn't play the game or take part in the preparation. But they identify with that team, and their self-esteem waxes and wanes with the team's success. In the occupational realm, one can identify with a career ("I work in law enforcement"), a work group ("I am a detective"), an organization ("I work for the New York Police Department"), or an occupation ("I am a police officer") (van Dick, 2004). As you can see, one can identify with any or all of these entities. If the NYPD has just come out of a serious scandal,

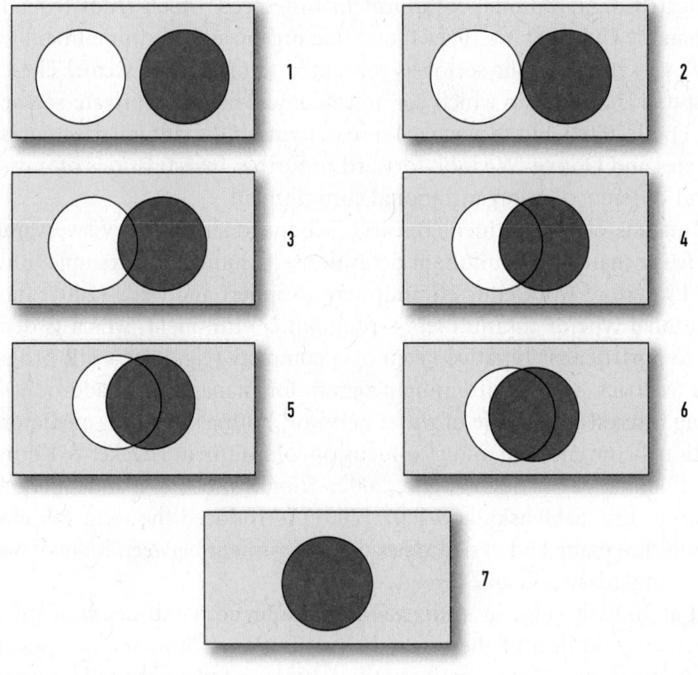

FIGURE 9.4 A Graphic Scale of Organizational Identification
The chart is intended to assess your relationship with the organization (or unit, company, branch, department, team) you belong to. Opposite you will find seven rectangles. In each rectangle there are two circles. One represents you and the other one the unit you belong to. In each rectangle the circles are overlapping differently. In the first rectangle (number 1), they are totally separate and represent a situation in which you do not identify at all with your unit. In the last rectangle (number 7), the circles are totally overlapping and represent a situation in which you totally identify with the unit. Choose out of the seven rectangles the one that most highly represents the extent to which you identify with your unit.

SOURCE: Shamir, B., & Kark, R. (2004). A single-item graphic scale of organizational commitment. *Journal of Occupational and Organizational Psychology, 17*, 115–123, Fig. 1, p. 118. © 2004 by The British Psychological Society. Reproduced with permission of John Wiley & Sons Ltd.

a detective might omit mention of her employer when traveling and simply tell people, "I'm a detective." On the other hand, after an event such as 9/11, that same person might announce that she works for the NYPD without mentioning her role as a detective. As you can see in this example, we are really dealing with emotions like pride or embarrassment, not with decisions about whether to stay or leave. As van Dick (2004) suggests, the purpose of organizational identification is to signal a "oneness" with an organization. In fact, Shamir and Kark (2004) have suggested a graphic way of measuring OID that emphasizes the extent of this "oneness." Figure 9.4 illustrates that measurement approach. It helps to answer the larger existential question of "Who am I?" In some senses, it also explains why job loss can be so devastating, because when one loses a job, one loses an in-group that helps in maintaining self-identity and self-esteem. Just as one can take pride in being a member of an organization ("I work for Google"), one can also take pains to distance oneself from the organization for which one works ("I work for Philip Morris tobacco company, but I am in their philanthropic giving division"). Kreiner and Ashforth (2004) have suggested four variations of identification:

1. *Identification*. Individuals define themselves in terms of the attributes of the organization.
2. *Disidentification*. Individuals define themselves as *not* having the attributes of the organization.
3. *Ambivalent identification*. Individuals identify with some attributes of the organization but reject other aspects.
4. *Neutral identification*. Individuals remain aggressively neutral, neither identifying nor disidentifying with the attributes of an organization (e.g., "I don't take sides, I just do my job").

Four facets of OID are presented in Figure 9.5. At this point, these types of identification are speculative, but they immediately raise the interesting question of the extent

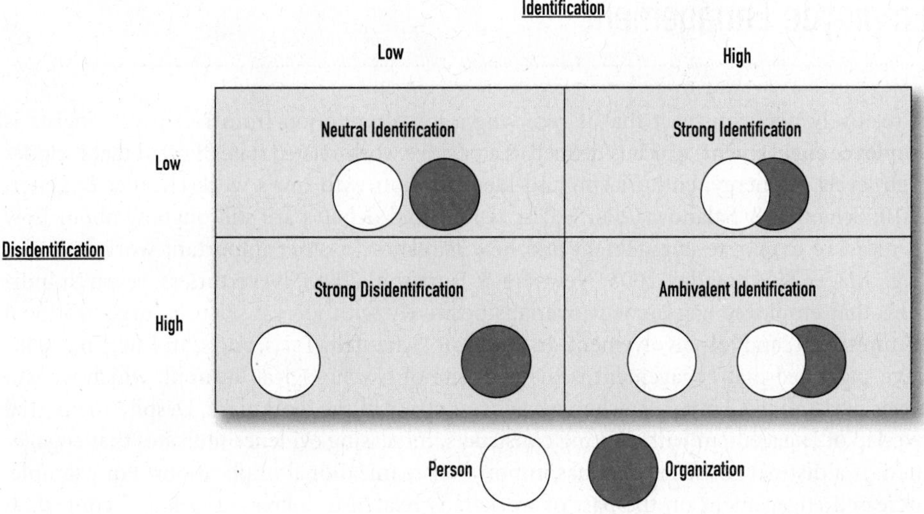

FIGURE 9.5 The Expanded Model of Identification

SOURCE: Kreiner, G. E., & Ashforth, B. E. (2004). Evidence toward an expanded model of organizational identification. *Journal of Organizational Behavior, 25*, 1–27, Fig. 1, p. 6. Copyright © 2004 by Journal of Organizational Behavior. Reprinted by permission of John Wiley & Sons.

to which they are represented within and between organizations. Imagine an organization in which 90 percent of the employees are identifiers, and compare that to an organization in which 90 percent are disidentifiers. In an example of possible disidentification, a warehouse worker for a Budweiser beer distributor was seen drinking a Coors beer and wearing a Coors hat during his off hours and was fired (Associated Press, 2005). As you might guess, he sued the distributor; the case was settled before trial. Nevertheless, one can't help but wonder if a worker who identified with Budweiser or the distributor would have been wearing a Coors hat and drinking a Coors beer. In contrast, an example of the benefits of organizational identification is the recent trend of companies supporting green initiatives in the workplace and in the community. Initial reports suggest that these green initiatives are helping in the attraction and retention of young workers, in part because such initiatives are consistent with young workers' values, thus increasing their identification (Aratani, 2008).

Although research on OID is quite new, it is intriguing. Given its social nature, OID has been associated with a variety of team and organizationally relevant outcomes, including higher cooperation, effort, participation, information sharing, and organizational citizenship behaviors (Ashforth, Harrison, & Corley, 2008; Riketta & van Dick, 2005). Furthermore, in three German samples, van Dick, Hirst, Grojean, and Wieseke (2007) found that a leader's OID is related to higher OID in subordinates and a greater willingness by subordinates to exert effort on the job. Thus, there are many positive correlates and consequences of OID. However, researchers are also finding evidence that there may be some negative consequences to overidentification; these include behaving unethically on behalf of the organization, continuing to be commited to a failing project, and suppressing dissent in group decision making (Ashforth et al., 2008). Research in this area is still fairly new, but investigations into the positive and negative correlates of OID are important, interesting, and of continued significance.

It does appear that OID is distinct from the construct of commitment (van Knippenberg & Sleebos, 2006). OID has a stronger emotional base and appears much more volatile than commitment. It would also appear to be much more susceptible to influence by the external environment than commitment. Think of the changes in identification that the innocent employees of Enron must have experienced after the scandal became public, especially when the documentary film *Enron: The Smartest Guys in the Room* was released in 2005. Like so many other constructs we have seen (e.g., intelligence and personality, OCB and CWB), there is room for and value in both OID and commitment. They will both be useful in describing different aspects of the experience of work.

Employee Engagement

Employee engagement A positive work-related state of mind that includes high levels of energy, enthusiasm, and identification with one's work.

A relatively new construct that is receiving a lot of attention from I-O psychologists is **employee engagement**, which is defined as a positive work-related state of mind that includes high levels of energy, enthusiasm, and identification with one's work (Bakker & Leiter, 2010; Schaufeli & Salanova, 2007). Discussions and debates are still ongoing about how to measure employee engagement and how it relates to other important work attitudes (e.g., Macey & Schneider, 2008; Newman & Harrison, 2008). Nevertheless, research indicates that employee engagement overlaps positively with job satisfaction, organizational commitment, and job involvement. In addition, Schaufeli, Taris, and Van Rhenen (2008) have suggested that engagement is the opposite of psychological burnout, which we will cover in detail in Chapter 10 when we address stress in the workplace. Despite the partial overlap of engagement with existing constructs, increasing evidence indicates that engagement is a distinct construct that has important organizational implications. For example, increased engagement on the part of workers is related to increased task and contextual performance (Christian, Garza, & Slaughter, 2011). In addition, Schaufeli and colleagues (2008) found that some employees who might be considered workaholics are actually very engaged in their work and thus do not have the negative health outcomes that often accompany workaholism. At this time, research is inconclusive regarding whether engagement is a stable "trait" or a fluctuating "state" that can change on a daily or weekly basis (Christian et al., 2011). Nevertheless, many companies are seeking the assistance of I-O psychologists to help them increase the engagement of their employees. We look forward to future research on engagement, which is being investigated widely in the United States, the Netherlands, and several other countries (Bakker & Leiter, 2010).

MODULE 9.1 SUMMARY

- The emotions we experience, whether at work or elsewhere, affect both our work and non-work behavior. To understand emotions at work, psychologists consider the complexity of work and non-work stimuli as well as the range of people's reactions, from attitudes to emotions to moods.
- Research at Western Electric's Hawthorne plant showed that the perceptions of workers had as great an effect on productivity as the physical working conditions. The Hawthorne studies gave impetus for the study of worker attitudes and the new construct of job satisfaction.
- Herzberg and colleagues found a connection between satisfaction and other work behaviors, which led them to introduce one of the first modern theories of job satisfaction, the two-factor theory. They proposed that extrinsic factors satisfied hygiene needs and intrinsic factors satisfied motivator needs.
- Two reliable, valid, and commonly used job satisfaction instruments are the Job Descriptive Index and the Minnesota Satisfaction Questionnaire. Research indicates that job satisfaction instruments have similar meaning and validity whether they are administered in paper-and-pencil format or over the Internet.
- Commitment to a relationship, an organization, a goal, or an occupation involves emotional attachments. Some people stay with an organization because they want to (affective commitment), others because they need to (continuance commitment), and others because they feel they ought to (normative commitment).
- Some research has focused on organizational identification (OID), which is found to be more emotional and volatile than commitment.

KEY TERMS

- job satisfaction
- Hawthorne effect
- attitudes
- overall satisfaction
- facet satisfaction
- Job Descriptive Index (JDI)
- Minnesota Satisfaction Questionnaire (MSQ)
- intrinsic satisfaction
- extrinsic satisfaction
- commitment
- affective commitment
- continuance commitment
- normative commitment
- occupational commitment
- job embeddedness
- organizational identification (OID)
- employee engagement

MODULE 9.2

Moods, Emotions, Attitudes, and Behavior

Is Everybody Happy? Does It Matter If They Are?

Comedian Drew Carey has an interesting recommendation for those who have low job satisfaction: "Oh, you hate your job? Why didn't you say so? There's a support group for that. It's called EVERYBODY, and they meet at the bar." Nevertheless, comedians are rarely considered definitive sources on work issues. In fact, job satisfaction researchers have been somewhat puzzled to find that very few people report dissatisfaction with their jobs. Hoppock (1935) estimated the number of dissatisfied workers at about 12 percent. This percentage has not changed appreciably in over 70 years. In addition, the percentage seems to be about the same in most countries (Büssing, 1992). A second puzzling finding has been the relatively low level of correlation between overall satisfaction and almost every work behavior, including performance and withdrawal. This is particularly noteworthy with respect to the low level of correlation between satisfaction and performance. Managers continue to believe that this relationship is stronger than the data show. This highlights one of the important differences between science and commonsense beliefs: Science is characterized not by assumption but by data collection. These two findings—the robust reports of high satisfaction and the low correlation between satisfaction and performance—have led to an increased effort to develop both theories of satisfaction and ways of thinking about it. These theoretical efforts have taken two very different directions, as we will discuss next.

The Concept of "Resigned" Work Satisfaction

Bruggemann and her colleagues (Bruggemann, Groskurth, & Ulich, 1975) proposed a theory of work satisfaction that addressed both of the puzzling phenomena described above. They suggested that there were multiple forms of work satisfaction and dissatisfaction. Only certain forms would be expected to correlate with particular work behaviors. As a result, simply measuring aggregate satisfaction (whether by a single overall measure or by a faceted questionnaire), without any consideration of its type, would yield low positive correlations. Further, with multiple types of satisfaction, there are many opportunities to report the experience of satisfaction, which accounts for the high levels of reported satisfaction

TABLE 9.3 **Different Forms of Work Satisfaction**

Progressive work satisfaction. A person feels satisfied with the work. By increasing the level of aspiration, a person tries to achieve an even higher level of satisfaction. Therefore, "creative dissatisfaction" with respect to some aspects of the work situation can be an integral part of this form.
Stabilized work satisfaction. A person feels satisfied with the job but is motivated to maintain the level of aspiration and the pleasurable state of satisfaction. An increase of the level of aspiration is concentrated on other areas of life because of few work incentives.
Resigned work satisfaction. A person feels indistinct work satisfaction and decreases the level of aspiration in order to adapt to negative aspects of the work situation on a lower level. By decreasing the level of aspiration, a person is able to achieve a positive state of satisfaction again.
Constructive work dissatisfaction. A person feels dissatisfied with the job. While maintaining the level of aspiration, a person tries to master the situation by problem-solving attempts on the basis of sufficient frustration tolerance. Moreover, available action concepts supply goal orientation and motivation for altering the work situation.
Fixated work dissatisfaction. A person feels dissatisfied with the job. Maintaining the level of aspiration, a person does not try to master the situation by problem-solving attempts. Frustration tolerance makes defense mechanisms necessary; efforts at problem solving seem beyond any possibility. Therefore, the individual gets stuck with his or her problems, and pathological developments cannot be excluded.
Pseudo–work satisfaction. A person feels dissatisfied with the job. Facing unsolvable problems or frustrating conditions at work but maintaining a level of aspiration—for example, because of a specific achievement motivation or because of strong social norms—the person develops a distorted perception or denies the negative work situation, which may result in pseudo–work satisfaction.

SOURCE: Büssing, A. (2002). Motivation and satisfaction. In A. Sorge (Ed.), *Organization* (pp. 371–387), p. 380. London: Thomson Learning..

typically found. Unfortunately, Bruggemann abandoned this research area in 1981 before her work was translated into English. André Büssing has taken up Bruggemann's model, completed its conceptual development, and begun gathering data that appear to support her theory.

Based on Bruggemann's initial theory, Büssing and his colleagues (Büssing, 2002; Büssing & Bissels, 1998) have proposed four different forms of work satisfaction and two forms of work dissatisfaction (see Table 9.3). These six forms are the result of the interaction of three basic variables: (1) the discrepancy between what a person desires from work and what he or she actually gets, (2) changes in goal or aspiration levels as a result of work experience, and (3) the extent to which a person engages in coping or problem-solving behavior.

This theory is of considerable practical significance. Büssing identified the forms of **resigned work satisfaction** and **constructive work dissatisfaction** as most salient for organizations. Individuals characterized as constructively dissatisfied are identified as aroused or energized; they are the most appropriate audience for joining in any attempts at organizational change. By harnessing this dissatisfaction and its associated energy and problem-solving character, the organization can be improved while the individual develops personally. On the other hand, resigned work satisfaction is associated with reduced effort and willingness to change or adapt, both of which create serious problems for organizations faced with the challenge of doing more work with fewer people while adapting to external pressures from customers and competitors to innovate. Resigned work satisfaction will make change more difficult. Büssing suggested that the most effective way to address resigned

Resigned work satisfaction A type of satisfaction associated with reduced work effort and a reduced willingness to change or adapt.

Constructive work dissatisfaction A type of dissatisfaction that energizes individuals and is beneficial for motivating them to join attempts at organizational change.

satisfaction is to prevent it. This might be accomplished by asking a "complainer" to join a group appointed to study the issue associated with the complaint—in other words, intervene before constructive dissatisfaction turns into resigned satisfaction. He reasoned that since resigned work satisfaction develops over long periods of time, once developed it is resistant to change. For the constructively dissatisfied employee, on the other hand, increasing opportunities for input in problem solving as well as increasing extrinsic rewards (e.g., flexible working hours, increased pay, and enhanced promotional opportunities) can be effective.

Büssing proposed that rather than treating dissatisfaction and satisfaction as simply two ends of a single continuum, we think of various forms of each. And each form requires a different approach. Because there are four different ways of being satisfied, it is not surprising that 80 percent of all employees report being "satisfied," but that does not necessarily mean the organization is healthy. Indeed, in the case of constructive dissatisfaction, a little bit of unhappiness of the right variety is good.

Others have pursued satisfaction research that builds on Büssing's theories. Norbert Semmer, a psychologist at the University of Bern, has been working extensively on the testing and validation of the Bruggemann/Büssing model (Semmer, 2002). He has been able to confirm four satisfaction types: true satisfaction, resigned satisfaction, resigned dissatisfaction, and constructive dissatisfaction. In preliminary work with sales personnel, he has found that the experience of true satisfaction is associated with the fewest number of health complaints, whereas both forms of dissatisfaction are associated with more health complaints and a stronger intention to quit. It is worth pursuing the difference between true satisfaction and resigned satisfaction.

Satisfaction versus Mood versus Emotion

Using Bruggemann's model, Büssing (2002) suggested that the problem with satisfaction research is that there are many different forms of satisfaction. Others, however, have taken a very different approach to solving the riddle of job satisfaction. Weiss argues that the problem is that satisfaction is conceptualized as a feeling or an emotion but measured as a cognition. Virtually all devices that measure job satisfaction deal with it as an attitude, as a cognitive evaluation of the discrepancy between "what I want" and "what I get" from a job. But the example that we used to introduce this chapter (the false accusation of mishandling company funds) was not a description of how someone calculated discrepancies. It described how a person might feel.

Weiss and his colleagues believe that most of the research on job satisfaction between 1930 and the present has missed the point by not explicitly recognizing the distinctions among moods, emotions, and attitudes (Brief & Weiss, 2002; Weiss, 2002b). Even though attitudes are thought to be composed of cognitions, affect, and behavioral intentions, most satisfaction researchers have tended to acknowledge only the cognitive aspects of attitudes. So when Weiss and his colleagues argue that one should study emotions rather than attitudes, they are really suggesting that research needs to be redirected to look at moods and emotions at work rather than focusing exclusively on cognitions. Weiss and his colleagues further suggest that we should focus on things like stressful events, interactions with supervisors and co-workers, and the effect of physical settings for evidence of the influence of moods and emotions on behavior.

An interesting study unintentionally illustrates this point. A large multinational company was in the midst of completing its annual employee survey on September 11, 2001. The company suspended the survey when the terrorist attacks occurred and then restarted it on October 1. Researchers were able to compare responses received between September 1 and 10, 2001, with responses received between October 1 and 17, 2001 (Ryan, West, & Carr, 2003). They found no differences in reported stress, job satisfaction, or perceptions of supervisory effectiveness. Other researchers reported similar findings (Macey, 2002). These results are in stark contrast with observations that employees went through a radical reevaluation of the importance of work and of their satisfaction with work-mediated versus family—and socially—mediated rewards. Nor do the results pass the commonsense test. It is plausible to interpret these results from the perspective of Weiss and his colleagues: The researchers in this case were measuring cognitions (the company had been using the same basic and traditional employee survey for many years) and, as a result, missed the emotional earthquake that followed 9/11.

Mood Generalized state of feeling not identified with a particular stimulus and not sufficiently intense to interrupt ongoing thought processes.

Emotion An effect or feeling, often experienced and displayed in reaction to an event or thought and accompanied by physiological changes in various systems of the body.

Affect circumplex Figure in which opposite emotions appear directly across from each other in the circle.

Substantial evidence is accumulating that moods and emotions are associated with work behaviors, including organizational citizenship behavior, performance judgments, creative problem solving, and withdrawal behaviors such as absenteeism and turnover (Barsade & Gibson, 2007). Lord, Klimoski, and Kanfer (2002) edited a book that provides detailed evidence confirming the importance of moods and emotions on work behavior. The journal *Human Performance* published a special issue on this topic as well (Ashkanasy, 2004).

Brief and Weiss (2002) defined **moods** as "generalized feeling states not . . . identified with a particular stimulus and not sufficiently intense to interrupt ongoing thought processes"; alternatively, **emotions** "are normally associated with specific events or occurrences and are intense enough to disrupt thought processes" (p. 282). Moods are usually described as positive or negative, whereas emotions are described more specifically (e.g., anger, fear, or joy). We may come to work feeling generally "down" but still get our work done. This would be a negative mood. We tell co-workers, "It's not my day." On the other hand, we may have a disagreement with a co-worker that ends in a shouting match. For the next few hours, our work is disrupted, we can't concentrate, and we go over the argument in our head. This is an emotion—a strong one.

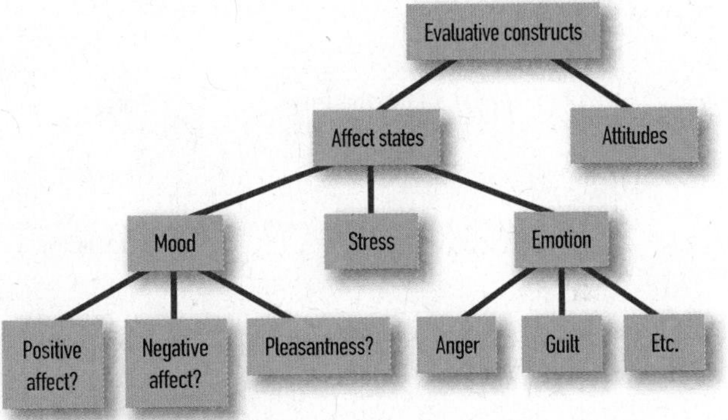

FIGURE 9.6 Distinctions among Emotions and Related Constructs

Source: Adapted from Weiss, H. M. (2002a). Conceptual and empirical foundations for the study of affect at work. In R. G. Lord, R. L. Klimoski, & R. Kanfer (Eds.), *Emotions in the workplace: Understanding the structure and role of emotions in organizational behavior* (pp. 20–63), p. 23. San Francisco: Jossey-Bass. Copyright © 2002. Reprinted with permission of John Wiley & Sons, Inc.

In general psychology, a great deal of work has been done on the identification of specific emotions. Weiss (2002a) presented a useful scheme for distinguishing emotions from other related constructs (see Figure 9.6). In this scheme, specific emotions are affective states, but they are conceptually different from moods and stress. It is generally accepted that discrete emotions can be positioned around a circle. The technical term for this arrangement is the **affect circumplex** (Weiss, 2002a). As shown in Figure 9.7, opposite emotions appear directly across from each other in the circle. Bored is the opposite of excited; unhappy is the opposite of delighted. In addition, there are two more basic dimensions on which emotions differ: degree of activation and degree of pleasantness.

Process emotion Reaction that results from consideration of the tasks one is currently doing.

Prospective emotion Reaction that results from a consideration of the tasks one anticipates doing.

Retrospective emotion Reaction that results from a consideration of the tasks one has already completed.

The emotional labels in Figure 9.7 are general and could be used to describe either work or non-work feelings. Pekrun and Frese (1992) suggested a structure for considering emotions specific to work. They proposed that emotional reactions can result from consideration of the tasks you are doing right now, which they labeled **process emotions** (e.g., you might experience boredom from reading a technical manual at work); from consideration of the tasks you anticipate doing, labeled **prospective emotions** (e.g., you are eagerly anticipating seeing a movie this evening); or from consideration of the tasks you have already completed, labeled **retrospective emotions** (e.g., you feel pride in receiving positive feedback from your boss). Furthermore, they proposed that emotions arising from social interactions are independent of those arising from task-related

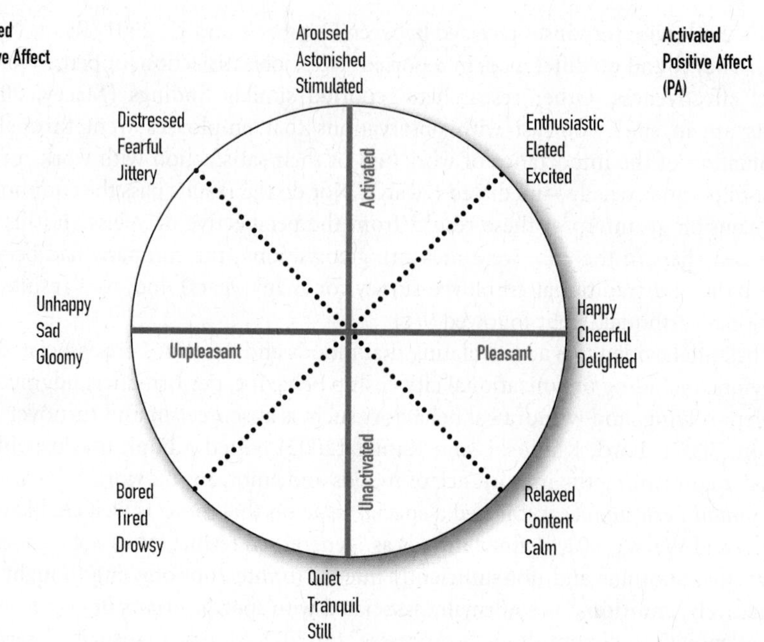

FIGURE 9.7 Affect Circumplex

SOURCE: Adapted from Weiss, H. M. (2002a). Conceptual and empirical foundations for the study of affect at work. In R. G. Lord, R. L. Klimoski, & R. Kanfer (Eds.), *Emotions in the workplace: Understanding the structure and role of emotions in organizational behavior* (pp. 20–63), p. 32. San Francisco: Jossey-Bass. Copyright © 2002. Reprinted with permission of John Wiley & Sons, Inc.

TABLE 9.4 Taxonomy of Work-Related Emotions

		POSITIVE	*NEGATIVE*
Task-related	Process	Enjoyment	Boredom/satiation Anxiety
	Prospective	Hope Anticipatory joy	Hopelessness (Resignation/despair)
	Retrospective	Relief Outcome-related joy	Sadness
Social		Pride	Disappointment Shame/guilt
		Gratitude Empathy Admiration Sympathy/love	Anger Jealousy/envy Contempt Antipathy/hate

SOURCE: Pekrun, R., & Frese, M. (1992). Emotions in work and achievement. *International Review of Industrial and Organizational Psychology, 7*, 153–200, p. 185. Copyright © 1992 by International Review of Industrial and Organizational Psychology. Reprinted by permission of John Wiley & Sons, Inc.

Negative affectivity (NA) Disposition wherein individuals are prone to experience a diverse array of negative mood states (e.g., anxiety, depression, hostility, and guilt).

Positive affectivity (PA) Disposition in which individuals are prone to describe themselves as cheerful, enthusiastic, confident, active, and energetic.

activities. Table 9.4, which presents the view of Pekrun and Frese, is not intended to be a definitive listing of all possible work-related emotions. Instead, it is an attempt to apply the construct of emotion more specifically to the work setting. These researchers also suggested that emotions can only result when barriers of some sort are present. We will return to this idea at the end of the chapter.

Dispositions and Affectivity

Brief and Weiss (2002) were enthusiastic about research on the role of dispositions on job satisfaction. Two dispositions that have received a great deal of attention are **negative affectivity** (NA) and **positive affectivity** (PA). Individuals high in NA are prone to experience a diverse array of negative mood states (e.g., anxiety, depression, hostility, and guilt), whereas individuals high in PA are prone to describe themselves as cheerful, enthusiastic, confident, active, and energetic (Brief & Weiss, 2002, p. 284).

Job satisfaction and affectivity have reciprocal influences on each other to the extent that positive people tend to be more satisfied with their jobs, and this satisfaction in turn helps individuals maintain a positive level of general life satisfaction, further enhancing their positive affectivity (Lyubomirsky, King, & Diener, 2005). It is also likely that disposition makes negative information about work more salient to the high-NA person and positive information more salient to the high-PA person—the proverbial difference between the person who sees the glass as half full and the person who sees it as half empty.

A recent meta-analysis by Bowling, Hendricks, and Wagner (2008) found that PA and NA had moderate relationships with some facets of job satisfaction. Positive affectivity and negative affectivity had the strongest relationships with the "satisfaction with work itself" facet (.31 and −.28, respectively). These results provide additional evidence of a dispositional basis to job satisfaction. However, despite findings of such stable relationships between dispositions and job satisfaction, organizational attempts to improve job satisfaction can still be successful (Gerhart, 2005). For example, a common approach to improving job satisfaction, based on job characteristics theory, includes increasing the variety of tasks worked on and completed on the job.

But the dispositional explanation of moods and emotions is only one of many alternative explanations. A range of external events might also exert influence on mood and emotion. Moreover, the things that happen outside work can influence emotions and moods that are brought to the workplace, and vice versa. Most of us can remember the effect of a failed romantic relationship on studying or working. Similarly, the threat of a layoff can spill over into non-work settings, leading to generalized anxiety and depression that make it difficult to enjoy previously pleasurable activities and relationships with friends and family.

There seems to be an emerging consensus that dispositions are likely to influence moods, but not necessarily discrete emotions. But moods might very well create circumstances that lead to discrete emotions. A person who is habitually "down" is not much fun to be with. As a result, co-workers may avoid interactions with the person, leading him or her to experience discrete emotions of anger or unworthiness. In contrast, a person who is habitually "up" might be sought out by co-workers and supervisors, leading that person to experience emotions of happiness and acceptance. It seems unlikely that this trait–situation debate will end anytime soon, since some of the advocates of the different positions seem intent on showing that the opposite position is "wrong" rather than developing models that show how both dispositions *and* situations might explain some of the variation in constructs such as job satisfaction (Davis-Blake & Pfeffer, 1989). In essence, this debate is an I-O version of the nature–nurture debate that has been going on in psychology for more than a hundred years. And, just as the nature–nurture dichotomy has evolved into an interactionist perspective, I-O psychologists have begun to identify roles for both situational and trait factors (Gerhart, 2005; Staw & Cohen-Charash, 2005). We believe that there is value in exploring the joint and individual contributions of disposition and environment on emotional experience. In the next section, we will consider a new method for examining situational influences.

The Time Course of Emotional Experience

In contrast with cognitive ability or personality, which are relatively stable, emotional experience can be a roller coaster. We can be excited when we arrive at work, angry by 10:00 a.m., disengaged by lunch, pleased by 2:00 a.m., and annoyed when we leave at the end of the day. Not only does one emotion replace another, but the strength of a single emotion can grow and diminish regardless of any competing emotions. Weak positive emotions (e.g., the pleasure from getting an unexpected small gift) may disappear in less than 20 minutes (Isen, Clark, & Schwartz, 1976). The variability of emotional experience has recently emerged as an important issue in understanding the effects of moods and emotions on both work and non-work behavior.

In the past, the relationship between satisfaction and work behavior was examined by looking at the correlation between satisfaction and a behavior (e.g., task performance, OCB, absenteeism) at one point in time and across a number of individuals. There are two problems with that approach. The first is that the satisfaction variable was defined as your satisfaction relative to some other person's satisfaction: You were low, medium, or high on satisfaction when compared to someone else. This is what we have called a between-persons design. But a different value would be produced if we looked at your satisfaction or mood at time 1 (e.g., 10:00 a.m.) and compared it to your satisfaction or mood at time 2 (e.g., 3:00 p.m. of the same day or 11:00 a.m. two days later). This is known as a within-person design. The second problem with the traditional approach is that, by assigning values to behavior and emotions measured at one point in time (e.g., the correlation between a satisfaction questionnaire score and an annual absence rate or performance rating), we assume that these values are stable and that the individual possesses the same level of an emotion at every moment for every day of the time period covered; we further assume that the behavior of the individual (e.g., effort expenditure, work attendance) is also stable over time. Most of us can look at our own behavior over the course of days or weeks and know that neither of these assumptions (i.e., constant emotion or constant behavior) is reasonable. You might be described as friendly in general terms, but that friendliness cannot account for the fact that you insulted a co-worker in a team meeting.

The notion that emotions change quickly in response to events in an environment is not a new one. Over 70 years ago, psychologist Rexford Hersey (1932, 1955) studied the day-to-day change in emotions, physiology, and behavior of industrial workers not only at work but also after work in their homes. More recently, Weiss and Cropanzano (1996) developed a framework called affective events theory to refocus attention on the effect of specific daily events on mood and emotion. This has led to a reawakening of interest in research that examines within-person changes in emotion and behavior across shorter time periods (Beal, Weiss, Barros, & MacDermid, 2005). This approach is known variously as experience sampling (Fisher & Noble, 2004) or event sampling (Tschan, Rochat, & Zapf, 2005). It most often involves the use of diaries in which the worker makes entries either at various times during the day or at the end of the workday. This research is still fairly new; nevertheless, preliminary results are intriguing and novel. These include the following:

- The effect of negative environmental events on mood is five times stronger than the effect of positive events, even though positive events are reported more frequently than negative events (Miner, Glomb, & Hulin, 2005).
- Positive experiences at work reduce end-of-day feelings of fatigue (Zohar, Tzischinski, & Epstein, 2003) and increase general feelings of well-being (Harris, Daniels, & Briner, 2003).
- Counterproductive work behavior is much more likely to result from momentary (state) hostility or experiences of injustice than from stable personality characteristics; the effects of these momentary experiences are then exaggerated if the individual is also chronically (trait) hostile (Judge, Scott, & Ilies, 2006).
- In samples of German and Swiss public service employees who had high stress levels after work, opportunities to recuperate and unwind were particularly important. Specifically, researchers found that activities involving relaxation, mastery experiences (e.g., engaging in sports and exercise), and high sleep quality were related to positive affect in the morning before the employees returned to work (Sonnentag, Binnewies, & Mojza, 2008).

- Insomnia at night contributes to negative emotions (hostility and fatigue) at work on subsequent days. These negative emotions subsequently relate to reports of lower job satisfaction (Scott & Judge, 2006).
- Employees experience more positive emotions when interacting with co-workers and customers than when interacting with their supervisors (Bono, Foldes, Vinson, & Muros, 2007).

We believe, and hope you will agree, that this sampling research is an exciting development in understanding how emotions relate to behavior. It has led to more progress in understanding the role of emotions at work in the past 10 years than the traditional approach yielded in 60 years of research, and we predict that researchers will continue to use this approach.

Research that uses experience sampling tracks emotional ups and downs for individuals, such as the return of happy feelings upon unwinding after a stressful day.

Genetics and Job Satisfaction

Another intriguing research hypothesis regarding job satisfaction and work-related emotional experiences is that emotional experience may be influenced by genetics. Staw, Bell, and Clausen (1986) reported that positive affectivity (e.g., individuals described as cheerful) or negative affectivity (e.g., individuals described as irritable or depressed) as measured in adolescence predicted job satisfaction as much as 50 years later. Thus, dispositions might be considerably more stable than implied by the term "mood." Irritable adolescents were dissatisfied workers in adulthood, and happy adolescents were happy workers in adulthood. Although this prediction was far from perfect (i.e., the correlation coefficient was of the magnitude of +.30), it was intriguing to find such stability over a 50-year period. In a more recent study, Ilies and Judge (2003) estimated that up to 45 percent of genetic influences on job satisfaction are expressed through stable personality traits. Another area that has found support for the notion that job satisfaction is influenced by stable personality characteristics is the literature on subjective well-being, which refers to how people evaluate their lives and includes job satisfaction, life satisfaction, and positive moods and emotions (Diener, 2000; Diener & Biswas-Diener, 2008). Specifically, a meta-analysis provided evidence that personality characteristics play a much stronger role in people's subjective well-being than previously thought (Steele, Schmidt, & Shultz, 2008).

For our present purposes, we will simply conclude that there is good reason to suspect that at least dispositions (if not more specific job attitudes) have a genetic element to them, but considerably more research will be required before anyone can speak with confidence on the possible connection. In addition, the emerging research on the momentary causes and effects of emotions on a daily basis (i.e., event or experience sampling) shows that stable constructs such as genetic makeup and personality traits are likely to have a smaller influence on emotions and behavior at any one time than do actual events occurring in the environment.

The Concept of Core Self-Evaluations

A number of I-O researchers have proposed that individuals make **core self-evaluations** of their circumstances and that these core self-evaluations affect both job and life satisfaction

Core self-evaluations Assessments that individuals make of their circumstances; elements of core evaluations include self-esteem, self-efficacy, locus of control, and the absence of neuroticism.

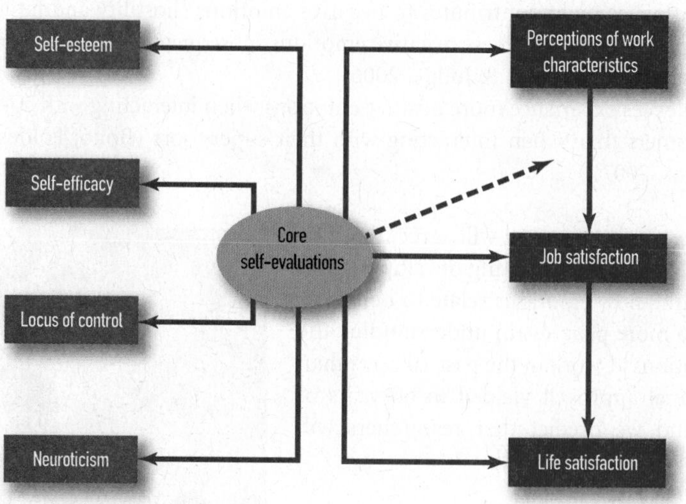

FIGURE 9.8 Elements of Core Self-Evaluations Hypothesized model relating dispositional characteristics to perceptions of intrinsic work characteristics, job satisfaction, and life satisfaction. The dashed line depicts a moderating effect of core self-evaluations on the relationship between perceived work characteristics and job satisfaction.

SOURCE: Judge, T. A., Locke, E. A., Durham, C. C., & Kluger, A. N. (1998). Dispositional effects on job and life satisfaction: The role of core evaluations. *Journal of Applied Psychology, 83*, 17–34, p. 18. © 1998 by the American Psychological Association. Reprinted by permission of the publisher.

(Judge & Bono, 2001; Judge, Bono, & Locke, 2000; Wu & Griffin, 2011). The elements of core self-evaluations include self-esteem, self-efficacy, locus of control, and the absence of neuroticism (see Figure 9.8). This combination of attributes can also be thought of as positive self-regard (Judge, Bono, Erez, & Locke, 2005).

Judge and colleagues (2000) found that core self-evaluations have effects on both job and life satisfaction, independent of the actual attributes of the job itself. They have also demonstrated that core self-evaluation measures taken in childhood and young adulthood predict an individual's job satisfaction as measured in middle adulthood. In a longitudinal study that first surveyed participants in 1979, Judge and Hurst (2007) found that core self-evaluations, family socioeconomic status, and academic achievement predicted subsequent income. They concluded that individuals with positive core self-evaluations are particularly adept at translating early advantages into later economic success.

These results are important for at least two reasons. First, they confirm once again that objective reality (i.e., actual job characteristics) may be a great deal less important than subjective reality (i.e., perceptions) in understanding how individuals adjust to work. Second, the longitudinal aspect of this research shows that these characteristics (i.e., core self-evaluation dimensions) are stable over time and predictably influence how a given individual perceives a circumstance (work or non-work).

Until recently, it was necessary to assess core self-evaluations using multiple measures, since there are four distinct components. Judge, Erez, Bono, and Thoreson (2003), however, have constructed and validated a simple 12-item scale that produces a core self-evaluation score (see Table 9.5). This should make it much easier to conduct research examining the effects of high and low core self-evaluation. Research has also begun on cross-cultural validation, showing that the scale is useful in other countries as well (Judge, van Vianen, & De Pater, 2004; Stumpp, Muck, Hulshegar, Judge, & Maier, 2010).

A caveat, however, is that these countries (Spain, Germany, and the Netherlands) all have individualistic cultures, as is the case in the United States. A recent study assessed the validity of core self-evaluations, positive affectivity, and negative affectivity in predicting job satisfaction in medical sales professionals in Japan, a non-Western and collectivist culture (Piccolo, Judge, Takahashi, Watanabe, & Locke, 2005). Core self-evaluations were significantly correlated with job satisfaction and explained incremental variance in job satisfaction beyond positive affectivity and negative affectivity. Taken together, these studies provide

TABLE 9.5 **The Core Self-Evaluations Scale (CSES)**

Instructions: Below are several statements about you with which you may agree or disagree. Using the response scale below, indicate your agreement or disagreement with each item by placing the appropriate number on the line preceding that item.

1	2	3	4	5
Strongly disagree	Disagree	Neutral	Agree	Strongly agree

1. _____ I am confident I get the success I deserve in life.
2. _____ Sometimes I feel depressed. (*r*)
3. _____ When I try, I generally succeed.
4. _____ Sometimes when I fail I feel worthless. (*r*)
5. _____ I complete tasks successfully.
6. _____ Sometimes I do not feel in control of my work. (*r*)
7. _____ Overall, I am satisfied with my life.
8. _____ I am filled with doubts about my competence. (*r*)
9. _____ I determine what will happen in my life.
10. _____ I do not feel in control of my success in my career. (*r*)
11. _____ I am capable of coping with most of my problems.
12. _____ There are times when things look pretty bleak and hopeless to me. (*r*)

NOTE: r = reverse-scored. This measure is nonproprietary (free) and may be used without permission.
SOURCE: Judge, T. A., Erez, A., Bono, J. E., & Thoreson, C. J. (2003). The core self-evaluations scale: Deve-lopment of a measure. *Personnel Psychology, 56*, 303–331.

initial support for the generalizability of core self-evaluations across cultures. Additional tests of the cross-cultural value of this scale should be undertaken in other countries that are collectivist, such as China, Indonesia, or Central and South American countries. The name of the construct (core *self*-evaluation) and the constituent elements (e.g., *self*-esteem, *self*-efficacy, *internal* locus of control) suggest that the scale and concept may be less useful in some cultures than in others.

Viewing job satisfaction through the lens of emotions and moods is very promising, but there is an enormous amount of research to do in this area. We do not yet know what the relative contributions are of discrete emotions, compared with more general moods, to work behavior. Moods may contribute to some behaviors (e.g., turnover) and emotions to other behaviors (e.g., problem solving). Nor do we know how long moods or emotions last and exert an influence. An hour? A day? A week? Do emotions that arise at work have a greater effect on work or non-work behavior? What about emotions that arise outside of work?

Grandey (2000) emphasized another concept in emotions: For many jobs, the *regulation* of emotional expression may be critical. This has been labeled **emotional labor** (Hochschild, 1983; Morris & Feldman, 1996), which we will discuss further in Chapter 10 when we consider stressors in the workplace. Employers (and customers) expect workers in customer service positions to display positive emotions and suppress negative ones. For emergency medical services (EMS) professionals, for example, it is critical to display a calm and confident demeanor, regardless of how dire the circumstances are. Research into the role of emotions at work is exciting and promising, and it has the potential to contribute greatly to the understanding of job satisfaction.

Emotional labor Regulation of one's emotions to meet job or organizational demands; can be achieved through surface acting and deep acting.

Withdrawal Behaviors

One of the earliest and most enduring research questions related to job satisfaction is the hypothesis that dissatisfaction leads to withdrawal from the workplace. In earlier years, behaviors such as absenteeism, turnover, and lateness were treated as separate variables. Hundreds of studies searched for statistically significant predictors of absence (Nicholson & Johns, 1985), turnover (Hom & Griffeth, 1995), or lateness (Blau, 1994). More recently, however, there has been a growing tendency to see each of these behaviors as simply a different manifestation of a larger construct called withdrawal (Johns, 2001a). Hulin (1991) has suggested that these various behaviors are all attempts to adapt to unfavorable job conditions and attitudes. He has added retirement to this list as well (Hanisch & Hulin, 1990). The need to understand employees' withdrawal behavior is not a trivial one. Sagie, Birati, and Tziner (2002) estimated that the cost of withdrawal behaviors for one year in a medium-sized Israeli high-tech company was $2.8 million dollars, or 16.5 percent of the company's pre-tax profit.

Withdrawal behaviors Absenteeism, turnover, tardiness, and retirement may be different manifestations of a larger construct called withdrawal.

Work withdrawal Action that represents an attempt by the individual to withdraw from work but maintain ties to the organization and the work role; includes lateness and absenteeism.

Job withdrawal Action that represents an individual's willingness to sever ties to an organization and the work role; includes intentions to quit or retire.

Progression hypothesis A progression of withdrawal behaviors that start with tardiness, increase to absenteeism, and eventually result in a decision to quit or retire.

Hanisch and Hulin (1990) further suggest that there are really two different types of **withdrawal behaviors**: work withdrawal and job withdrawal. **Work withdrawal** includes lateness and absenteeism and represents an attempt by the individual to withdraw from work but still maintain ties to the organization and the work role. **Job withdrawal**, on the other hand, includes intentions to quit or retire and represents an individual's willingness to sever ties to the organization and the work role. Viewed from that perspective, although turnover, absenteeism, and tardiness all represent withdrawal in one form or another, each represents a substantially different course of action. Subsequent research provides some support for the view that work withdrawal and job withdrawal are separate concepts (Fields, Dingman, Roman, & Blum, 2005). It is tempting to see these behaviors arranged as a progression (Johns, 2001a), with a gradual escalation of withdrawal behaviors, starting with tardiness, increasing to absenteeism, and eventually resulting in a decision to quit or retire. Some studies have found evidence of this proposed progression. In a study of hospital workers, Rosse (1988) found a progression from lateness to absence and from multiple absences to quitting. Kozlowsky and colleagues (1997) conducted meta-analyses of studies examining withdrawal behaviors and found some support for the lateness-to-absence progression. The **progression hypothesis** is an intriguing one and deserves additional consideration as it may provide employers with an early warning system for turnover and absence.

MODULE 9.2 SUMMARY

- Büssing and his colleagues updated the work of Bruggemann and her colleagues and identified resigned work satisfaction and constructive work dissatisfaction as most salient for organizations.
- Substantial evidence indicates that moods and emotions are associated with work behaviors, including organizational citizenship behavior, performance, creative problem solving, and withdrawal behavior.
- Researchers have considered the intriguing hypothesis that genetics may influence emotional experience.
- The elements of core evaluations include self-esteem, self-efficacy, locus of control, and the absence of neuroticism. Individuals make core evaluations of their circumstances, and these evaluations affect both job and life satisfaction.
- There has been a growing tendency to view lateness, absence, and turnover as different manifestations of a larger construct called withdrawal.

KEY TERMS

resigned work satisfaction
constructive work dissatisfaction
mood
emotion
affect circumplex
process emotion
prospective emotion
retrospective emotion
negative affectivity (NA)
positive affectivity (PA)
core self-evaluations
emotional labor
withdrawal behaviors
work withdrawal
job withdrawal
progression hypothesis

MODULE 9.3

Special Topics Related to Attitudes and Emotions

With a research base of over 10,000 studies to choose from, dozens of special and interesting topics related to attitudes and emotions might be covered in greater detail. We have chosen five topics that parallel a major theme of this book: the changing nature of work. Work is becoming less stable, there is a greater tendency toward working in a virtual workplace, work is more multicultural, and work–life balance is becoming more important to workers. We will consider the issues of involuntary job loss (typically through layoff), the special challenges that the virtual workplace and telecommuting bring to the experience of work, work–family balance, psychological contracts, and cross-cultural issues in attitudes and emotions.

Job Loss

The true and most basic meaning of work becomes apparent when someone loses a job. In many, if not most, instances, the worker who just lost his or her job may have strong affective, continuance, or normative commitments to the organization. This may be exactly why job loss, like an unwanted divorce or romantic breakup, can be so devastating. It represents an involuntary separation from an entity (job, organization, or work group) to which the individual remains committed. Although it appears that people can and do recover emotionally from a job loss, it also appears that they never recover completely or return to the level of satisfaction they enjoyed before that job loss (Lucas, Clark, Georgellis, & Diener, 2004).

Warr (2007) has systematically studied the effect of job loss on the well-being of individuals. He argued that "paid employment is central to the functioning of societies and to the mental health of individuals" (1999, p. 392). Warr has reached certain conclusions about the effects of unemployment:

1. The psychological health of unemployed workers is poorer than that of employed workers.
2. This poorer health is the result of (not the *cause* of) unemployment, since a return to paid employment is usually followed by an improvement in psychological well-being.

3. Losing one's job often results in depression, insomnia, irritability, lack of confidence, inability to concentrate, and general anxiety.

Warr concluded that the reasons for these effects are complex. First, the loss of work reduces income and daily variety. There is a suspension of the typical goal setting that guides day-to-day activity. There are fewer decisions to make because there is little to decide about. The decisions that are made border on the trivial: when to get up, when to shop, when to look for a job. New skills are not developed and current skills begin to atrophy. And social relations are changed radically. Jahoda (1981) concisely described the effects of employment on well-being:

> First, employment imposes a time structure on the waking day; second, employment implies regularly shared experiences and contacts with people outside the nuclear family; third, employment links individuals to goals and purposes that transcend their own; fourth, employment defines aspects of personal status and identity; and finally, employment enforces activity. (p. 188)

Meta-analyses have confirmed the positive effects of employment on these facets of life, as well as documenting negative effects of unemployment on mental health and well-being (McKee-Ryan, Song, Wanberg, & Kinicki, 2005).

Unemployment comes in many different forms. Chronologically, the first opportunity for unemployment comes when an individual finishes school and seeks paid employment for the first time. Interestingly, the experience of unemployment appears to be different for individuals who have never had full-time employment and those who have lost a full-time paid job. In a longitudinal study of students making the transition from school to paid employment, Winefield and Tiggemann (1990; Winefield, Winefield, Tiggemann, & Godney, 1991) discovered that the employed were higher on measures of self-esteem, optimism, and internal locus of control than the unemployed. But an unexpected finding involving those who did find employment, only to lose it, was that the newly unemployed did not really *deteriorate* on these measures as unemployment stretched out for several years. Although the experience of employment enhanced these measures, unemployment had little effect.

Winefield and Tiggemann also suggested that the effect of unemployment may not be as devastating to younger workers as it is to older workers. This makes sense from many perspectives. First, many younger individuals can continue to depend on parents and the extended family to provide moral and economic support until a new job arrives. In addition, their commitment foundations (i.e., affective, continuance, and normative) are considerably weaker. The practical and scientific lesson from this research is that the experience of unemployment is likely to be qualitatively different for younger workers than for older workers, just as it is likely to be different for men and women. Thus, any research that studies the effects of unemployment but does not distinguish among respondents by age, work experience, and gender is likely to produce confusing or misleading results. Similarly, there appear to be some traits that are directly related to responses to unemployment. Wanberg, Glomb, Song, and Sorenson (2005) found that individuals who were higher on core self-evaluation, as we described the concept in Module 9.2, engaged in a job search with greater intensity and thus were more likely to find new employment.

A relevant issue concerning the concept of job loss is the experience of psychological insecurity, in addition to the more obvious and associated economic insecurity. Are all individuals equally plagued with insecure feelings as a result of the increasing phenomena of downsizing, mergers, and acquisitions? The answer—at least according to research conducted prior to the financial crisis that began in 2008—seems to be no. Warr (2007) noted that good health, social support, and an absence of financial pressure all reduce the distress of unemployment to some degree. Probst (2000) found that the individuals most likely to be negatively affected by feelings of insecurity are those most invested and involved in their jobs and organizations. It is ironic that in many instances, those who have the least to fear, because of their high levels of performance and motivation, are those who are most fearful. This may be the result of having more at stake than those uninvolved with their work or organization. By extension, the effects of insecurity may actually diminish performance and motivation over time, resulting in a self-fulfilling prophecy: The most motivated and effective employees end up performing more poorly, thus confirming their fears by increasing the possibility that they might be laid off as a result of diminished performance.

Parker, Chmiel, and Wall (1997) studied the employees of a chemical plant in the United Kingdom that was embarking on a strategic downsizing initiative. It appears that downsizing may have a greater effect on survivor productivity than either the voluntary or involuntary departure of a co-worker (McElroy, Morrow, & Rude, 2001). Parker and colleagues found that the debilitating effects of insecurity in organizations undergoing downsizing can be counteracted by establishing clear roles and responsibilities for those workers who are not laid off, as well as increasing their participation in work-related decision making. Both of these measures reduce uncertainty and enhance feelings of control. In Chapter 10, we will see that uncertainty and lack of control are major determinants of stress.

Finally, Probst and Lawler (2006) found that employees with more collectivistic values (e.g., Chinese employees) reacted more negatively to job insecurity than those with more individualistic values (e.g., U.S. employees). They noted that job insecurity had a negative impact on all employees but that cultural values provided additional insight into employee reactions to job insecurity. We can speculate that the more collectivistic Chinese employees reacted more negatively than their American counterparts because they felt that they were letting down the "collectives" to which they belonged—family, work group, or organization.

Work in the 21st century is a great deal less secure, both actually and psychologically, than was the case in previous generations. For moral as well as pragmatic reasons, we need to know more about the experience and the threat of unemployment. It is likely that research and theory building in this area will grow substantially in the next decade.

Telecommuting

Nearly all the research on job satisfaction and work-related emotion has been done with participants who have traditional jobs in a particular workplace to which they are expected to report on a regular basis, usually 40 hours a week. But, as we have seen, the nature of work is changing. In 1990, roughly 4 million workers were engaged in **telecommuting**, which is defined as accomplishing work tasks from a distant location using electronic communication media. By 2010, that number had risen to over 26 million. There is every indication that the number of telecommuters will continue to increase in the foreseeable future. Even though the phenomenon of telecommuting is with us to stay, I-O psychologists have only begun to examine the emotional and attitudinal experiences associated with the practice.

Telecommuting Accomplishing work tasks from a distant location using electronic communication media.

Cascio (1998c) suggested a number of advantages to telecommuting, including psychological and economic ones. While acknowledging that some circumstances do not lend themselves to telecommuting (e.g., poor-quality electronic communications connections, lack of office space in the home or on the road, supervisors uncommitted to the concept), Cascio suggested that for many telecommuting workers, strategic planning skills and self-reported productivity went up. Furthermore, telecommuters reported higher satisfaction than in their former traditional work arrangements, as well as higher levels of life and family satisfaction.

Holland and Hogan (1998) took strong exception to Cascio's implied endorsement of telecommuting. They contended that telecommuting, like most other management initiatives, is a strategy intended to cut organizational costs by reducing the cost of office space, support personnel, and so forth. They argued that the possible negative effects of telecommuting are daunting. These include the following:

1. Worker alienation will increase due to lack of face-to-face social interaction.
2. Nonparticipation at the actual worksite will rob individuals of the important sense of identity that is derived from the work experience.
3. Telecommuters will be less likely to be promoted because, since they are out of sight, they will also be out of mind.
4. Telecommuting will require a particular type of person, individuals who are ambitious and conscientious. But the very characteristic that makes them good at telecommuting—ambition—will also lead to rapid disillusionment with the lack of promotional opportunities.

Fortunately, recent studies are providing some hard evidence from which conclusions about the effects of telecommuting can be drawn. A meta-analysis of 46 studies on telecommuters found that telecommuting has "a clear upside: small but favorable effects on perceived autonomy, work–family conflict, job satisfaction, performance, turnover intent, and stress" (Gajendran & Harrison, 2007, p. 1538). However, there is a downside to higher-intensity telecommuting (more than 2.5 days a week): It seems to harm relationships with co-workers (but not with supervisors). A recent study by Golden (2006) supports these findings. In a sample of 294 telecommuters in a large telecommunications company, Golden found that a moderate level of telecommuting increases job satisfaction, but extensive telecommuting leads to lower job satisfaction. His findings suggest that to maximize job satisfaction, telecommuting should be limited to about 2 days per week. This will help to maximize the benefits of flexibility and freedom but will still allow employees to be in the office a few days a week to develop relationships at work.

Hartig, Kylin, and Johansonn (2007) investigated telecommuting among full-time Swedish government employees whose workplace was relocated. Understanding that some employees could not relocate, management allowed them to telecommute, which provided the opportunity to reduce stress caused by commuting long distances and work–family demands. Telecommuting was found to be more beneficial for men than women and for those who had a separate room in the home in which to work. These findings suggest that telecommuting can have differing effects depending on one's home and family life. In particular, the authors speculated that women's typically greater domestic responsibilities may be a distraction when working from home, particularly when they do not have a separate room in which to work.

It is clear that telecommuting is here to stay and that it will become increasingly common. Notably, many telecommuters have had the experience of not being perceived as working by friends and acquaintances when they are working from home. This has both emotional (e.g., "My work is being devalued by my friends") and practical consequences (e.g., "People expect to be able to call me up to 'play hooky' whenever they feel like it"). It appears that the courts are also a bit behind the curve. In a case involving unemployment benefits, a court decided that for purposes of determining which state should pay benefits to a virtual employee (she lived in Florida but the company for which she worked electronically was in New York), it was physical presence that defined where one worked (Caher, 2003). We will learn much more about both practical and psychological aspects of telecommuting as additional research evidence accumulates.

Work–Family Balance

People obviously have both work and non-work lives. For many individuals, particularly those in the 30–50 age range, non-work life is dominated by the family. Data (and common sense) suggest that both physical and psychological well-being are affected whenever an individual's life is out of balance, when too much time and energy are invested in one sphere (Zedeck, 1992). A criticism commonly leveled at someone who seems overly obsessed with an activity or cause is "Get a life!" What this really means is, in effect, get more *balance* in your life. Many elite athletes look back on periods of their life with sadness, recognizing that their devotion to their training program brought them fame and fortune but regretting having lost out on other important experiences. Many working adults have the same experience, but without the fame and fortune. Few tombstones display the epitaph, "I wish I had spent more time at the office."

Work–family balance Area of research that investigates whether the satisfaction that one experiences at work is in part affected by the satisfaction that one experiences in non-work, and vice versa.

Most research and theory related to **work–family balance** actually concentrates on the effects of a *lack* of balance. These effects are often discussed in terms of the stress created by conflicting demands between work and non-work activities. Another way to say this is that the satisfaction that one experiences at work is in part affected by the satisfaction that one experiences in non-work, and vice versa, particularly to the extent that one environment has demands that conflict with the other. We will discuss these stresses and their consequences in Chapter 10. In the remainder of this chapter, we will deal more broadly with the concept of balance and some of the factors that play a role in achieving balance.

One of the most substantial influences on achieving a work–family balance is an organizational culture that specifically supports family values. As May (1998) pointed out, "many traditional (workplace) cultures still value 'face time' and reinforce the message that working in nontraditional arrangements (such as telecommuting) means that you are not serious about work" (p. 81). You will recall from our discussion of the definition of "success" in Chapter 4 (Cleveland, 2005) that there is some debate about the extent to which employers are truly committed to work–life balance. Wentworth (2002) noted the irony between the employer provision of various on-site services (e.g., child care, dry cleaning, auto maintenance) that appear to elevate family issues to equal status with work issues and the steady increase in the number of working hours. Interestingly, Goff, Mount, and Jamison (1990) found that supportive supervision was closely related to work–life balance. Workers cared less about whether the company provided on-site child-care services than they did about the organization's realization that child care was an important value for its workers. Bluestone and Rose (1997) estimated that by the end of the 1980s, "the typical dual earner couple . . . was spending an additional day and a half on the job every week" than they had in the 1970s (p. 12). American workers worked 36 hours more per year in 2000 than they did in 1990 (Wentworth, 2002). Although it is tempting to simply identify the number of hours worked as the culprit (Lewis & Cooper, 1999), Friedman

and Greenhaus (2000) suggested that the real problem is not hours but the interference and distraction that work poses for non-work enjoyment.

Greenhaus and Powell (2006) developed a model in which work and family can be allies rather than enemies (as they have typically been conceptualized in work–family conflict). They defined work–family enrichment as "the extent to which experiences in one role improve the quality of life in the other role." They suggested that experiences in one role can lead to positive outcomes in another role. For example, parents who learn about patience and development as they watch their kids grow can successfully apply this knowledge in managing new employees at work (Ruderman, Ohlott, Panzer, & King, 2002). Thus, behaviors and interpersonal skills (e.g., time management behaviors, empathy) required and developed in one's family life may lead to behaviors that are helpful at work. Conversely, experiences at work may have positive spillover to family life (e.g., having a successful day at work puts you in a good mood when playing with your children). This encouraging perspective is likely to be fruitful as I-O psychology researchers and practitioners increasingly consider the overlap between work and family.

Wentworth (2002) pointed to the electronically enhanced communications environment in which most people work, which includes e-mail, laptops, and smartphones. One is never out of touch, which may be a boon to sales representatives eager to strike while the client is hot, and to medical professionals whose timely advice may save a life, but a burden to many other workers who find no opportunity to "turn off" their thoughts about the job. As Wentworth noted, the idea that a job is 24/7 does not even raise an eyebrow today; on the contrary, it is seen as a positive value indicating commitment to a job, organization, and career. It suggests that a worker who needs to be constantly reachable must be important to the organization. But it also suggests that work is more important than non-work. A recent dispute at ABC News raised the question about when checking e-mail on one's smartphone after work should constitute working overtime (Shelter, 2008). ABC's news division had presented three writers with a waiver to sign stating that they would not be compensated for checking their company-issued smartphones after work. The writers agreed that they should not be paid for a late-night check of their e-mail, but they felt that if they were writing material or scheduling guest appearances from home, they should be paid for that work. This is an interesting offshoot of the work–life balance argument and the challenges of working with technology in a 24/7 digital world.

In assessing work–life imbalance, it has also been popular to point to multiple roles—particularly for employed women, who are traditionally caregivers in the home environment—as the culprit (Williams, Suls, Alliger, Learner, & Wan, 1991). The theory was that more roles meant more responsibility, a lesser degree of freedom and flexibility, and greater stress.

The challenges of work–family balance are being felt across many different nations and cultures. For example, despite having a woman as the head of its government at the time of this writing, Germany has one of the widest gender wage gaps in Europe (Plass, 2008). In Germany and the United States, wage gaps between men and women are at least partially driven by the decisions women (more so than men) often make to leave the workforce to raise a family. Nevertheless, an article entitled "Why Dad's Résumé Lists

© Michael Newman/PhotoEdit

The pervasiveness of electronic communications in today's careers can contribute to work–family conflict.

Car Pool" discusses the fact that, like women before them, men are now increasingly having to explain gaps in their résumés because it is more common for them to take time off to raise their children (Belkin, 2008). This is an example of work–family balance issues that were not common for men until recently and that are challenging in the 21st-century workplace.

The point we are making in this section is that one can only really understand the emotional experience of work by considering it in the larger context of life and non-work roles. One can imagine a continuum with an exclusive non-work focus on one end, an exclusive work focus on the other end, and a balance between work and non-work in the middle. The challenge for any individual is to design both work and non-work environments in a way that will increase the likelihood of a balance. And this balance will be disturbed at various times on both sides of the equation (Judge & Ilies, 2004). The birth of a child, an illness or death, or even the purchase of a new home will alter the non-work side; a promotion, a layoff, or even a major work-related project or deadline will alter the work side. Catastrophic events like the terrorist attacks of 9/11 will create seismic imbalances for both sides. The challenge, for organizations and individuals, is to restore balance.

The design of work is jointly shared by a worker and an organization. The design of non-work is jointly shared by a worker and others with whom the worker interacts in the non-work environment. Balance will be jointly determined by those two forces. Perhaps the most important element in achieving that balance, however, is for all parties—in both work and non-work environments—to acknowledge the legitimacy and importance of the other parties.

Psychological Contracts

Psychological contracts Beliefs that people hold regarding terms of an exchange agreement between themselves and the organization.

Psychological contracts are beliefs that people hold regarding terms of an exchange agreement between themselves and the organization (Conway & Briner, 2005; Rousseau, 1995). A key feature of psychological contracts is that individuals voluntarily agree to accept certain commitments; they then make plans and goals according to their understanding of those commitments. The psychological contract is an implicit understanding between an individual and an employer, and this understanding is likely to come from explicit or implicit agreements made during the recruitment process. For example, Rousseau (1995) noted that a marketing manager hired with the understanding that he will turn the department around and make it more successful is more likely to commit to a suitable course of action than someone who has not made such a commitment.

Psychological contracts have been receiving much more attention in the 21st-century workplace because long-term employment with one organization is increasingly rare. Employees' increased willingness to move from job to job has been called the "protean career" by Hall (2002), who noted that individuals have become much more focused on growth and mobility in their career rather than growth within a particular organization. Because today's typical job situation does not include a long-term commitment on the part of the employer, employees are more likely to examine their relationship with the organization and are willing to leave more quickly if they feel any short-term promises or commitments have not been upheld. Psychological contract breach, then, refers to an employee's perception of the extent to which the employer has failed to fulfill promises made to the employee, such as promotions and advancement, pay based on performance, long-term job security, sufficient power and responsibility, training opportunities, and career development (Montes & Zweig, 2009; Robinson, 2006). When psychological contracts are broken or breached, several negative outcomes commonly occur. Using a sample of customer service employees, Deery, Iverson, and Walsh (2006) found that psychological contract breach was related to lower organizational trust, which, in turn, was associated with lower perceptions of employment relations and higher levels of absenteeism. A meta-analysis by Zhao, Wayne, and Glibkowski (2007) examined the influence of psychological contract breach on eight work outcomes that were broken into three categories:

1. Affect (contract violation and mistrust)
2. Attitudes (job satisfaction, organizational commitment, and turnover intentions)
3. Performance (actual turnover, organizational citizenship behavior, and in-role performance)

They found that psychological contract breach was related to all outcomes except actual turnover. Research on psychological contracts in non-U.S. cultures is just beginning. Restubog, Bordia, and Tang (2007) examined contract breach among sales and marketing executives in the Philippines. They found that psychological contract breach had consistently negative consequences, including deviant behaviors against the organization and its members. We should expect more dramatic responses to contract breach in countries with a long-term orientation, where lifelong employment by a single employer had been both assumed by the employee and honored by the employer. In the next section, we will cover additional cross-cultural issues related to attitudes and emotions.

Work-Related Attitudes and Emotions from a Cross-Cultural Perspective

For most of its history, research on job satisfaction has been carried out by American researchers with U.S. participants (Judge, Parker, et al., 2001). Further, the studies conducted in other countries have tended to be unique, often yielding results not replicated in subsequent studies. Thus, the powerful research tool of meta-analysis is difficult to apply to these non-U.S. studies.

In contrast, recent work with a multicultural focus seems to be producing some interesting and logical results. You will recall that Hofstede's model of culture and its consequences identified the individualism–collectivism dimension as an important aspect of culture. Preliminary research findings indicate that individualism and job satisfaction are positively correlated in some countries, whereas collectivism and job satisfaction are correlated in other countries (Judge, Parker, et al., 2001). Hui and Yee (1999) found that in environments where work groups are "warm" and co-workers are enthusiastic about helping one another, the correlation between collectivism and satisfaction is more positive than that found in environments where the work group atmosphere is "cold" (i.e., mutual support is the exception rather than the rule). This in turn suggests that in individualist countries such as the United States, there would be a positive correlation between individualist values and job satisfaction, whereas in collectivist countries such as Japan, South Korea, or China, there would be a stronger positive correlation between satisfaction and collectivist values. Several studies have supported this hypothesis (Bordia & Blau, 2003; Cheng, Jiang, & Riley, 2003; Wasti, 2003a). At present, cross-cultural examinations of job satisfaction and work-related emotions tend to concentrate on differences between individualist and collectivist cultures. It would be useful for researchers to expand their interest to include additional cultural variables such as masculinity, power distance, uncertainty avoidance, and time orientation.

As we will see in Chapter 14, a key concept in organizational psychology is "fit." The degree of fit seems to be related to both emotional reactions to work and subsequent work behaviors. In another example of the concept of fit, Robert, Probst, Martocchio, Drasgow, and Lawler (2000) found that whereas worker empowerment was associated with higher levels of satisfaction in the United States, Mexico, and Poland, it was associated with dissatisfaction in India. In part, they explained this finding in terms of the desire for greater hierarchical structure in India, a country that values high power distance between levels of the organization. Here, we are talking about the fit between the design of work and cultural values as a possible determinant of job satisfaction. The practical implication is that multinational organizations must be sensitive to this fit between values and work if they are concerned about the satisfaction of their employees in differing cultural environments. This is particularly true in the case of expatriates transplanted into a new culture (Caliguri, Tarique, & Jacobs, 2009).

It is also clear that the instruments most commonly used to assess satisfaction (e.g., the Job Descriptive Index and the Minnesota Satisfaction Questionnaire) may not travel well across national borders. Hulin and Meyer (1986) found that approximately one-third of the JDI items did not appear to have the same meaning in non-U.S. samples as in U.S. samples. Other studies have also questioned the value of using U.S.-developed instruments for assessing satisfaction (Ryan, Chan, Ployhart, & Slade, 1999). However, two recent studies (Lievens, Anseel, Harris, & Eisenberg, 2007; Wang & Russell, 2005) found that satisfaction scales do provide meaningfully equivalent ratings across cultures. Regarding organizational commitment, Ko, Price, and Mueller (1997) were unable to reproduce the Meyer and Allen three-component commitment model in South Korea. In contrast, Hattrup, Mueller, and Aguirre (2008) examined two multinational samples and found that differences in commitment across national boundaries were both small and generally unrelated to individualism/collectivism. Although there is even less research on the issue of emotion and affectivity, the evidence that does exist suggests substantial differences in the emotional architecture of various cultures (Russell, 1991). In practical terms, this means that the greater the distance between a particular location and the United States with respect to basic cultural values such as individualism, masculinity, or power distance, the less relevant are the results of American studies of satisfaction and emotion. Like many other areas we cover in this text, we conclude that as the nature of work becomes more multicultural and global, it will be increasingly important to include cultural variables in our research designs.

MODULE 9.3 SUMMARY

- A major theme of this book is the changing nature of work. Four topics related to job satisfaction parallel this theme: (1) Work is becoming less stable, (2) there is a greater tendency toward working in a virtual workplace, (3) work is more multicultural, and (4) work–life balance is becoming more important to workers.
- Job loss can be devastating because it represents an involuntary separation from an organization to which the individual remains committed. Recent meta-analyses confirm that unemployment has negative effects on mental health and the experience of well-being. The experience of unemployment is likely to be qualitatively different for younger workers than for older workers, just as it is likely to be different for men and for women.
- Telecommuting is a relatively new work arrangement that is becoming increasingly common. The advantages and disadvantages of telecommuting are hotly debated, but too few data exist to form any firm conclusions about the emotional, attitudinal, and behavioral correlates of telecommuting.
- Both physical and psychological well-being are affected by the extent to which an individual's life is in balance. Most research and theory related to work–family balance concentrates on the effects of a *lack* of balance. One can only really understand the emotional experience of work by considering work in the larger context of life and non-work roles.
- Psychological contracts are beliefs that people hold regarding the terms of an exchange agreement between themselves and the organization. When psychological contracts are broken or breached, several negative outcomes commonly occur, including lower employee work attitudes and lower job performance.
- Multinational organizations must be sensitive to the preferences and values of employees from different cultural environments. This is particularly true for expatriates who are transplanted into a new culture. As the nature of work becomes more multicultural and global, it will be increasingly important to include cultural variables when examining attitudes and emotions at work.

KEY TERMS

telecommuting
work–family balance
psychological contracts

10 Stress and Worker Well-Being

MODULE 10.1

The Problem of Stress

At age 60, John Herbert (not his real name) was a successful executive with a Texas paper company, looking forward to several more years of work before moving on to a comfortable retirement. Imagine his distress when he was informed that his services in the executive offices were no longer needed and that he was being transferred to a warehouse position. In the warehouse, Herbert found himself reporting to a supervisor more than 30 years his junior. Assigned to a variety of low-level janitorial tasks, Herbert suffered abuse related to his age. Meanwhile, he observed that the company was moving younger workers into executive positions like the one he had vacated.

Herbert sued for both emotional distress and age discrimination; he was awarded $800,000 for emotional distress and $2,250,000 in punitive damages, as well as a lesser sum for age discrimination (DeFrank & Ivancevich, 1998). Herbert is not alone; since the early 1990s, an increasing number of employees have sued their employers for damages resulting from job-related stress (Keita & Hurrell, 1994; Moran, Wolff, & Green, 1995).

Lawsuits are just one among many major costs associated with work stress. American employers spend more than $700 million annually to replace the 200,000 individuals aged 45 to 65 who die from, or are incapacitated by, heart disease, a major cause of which is stress. In 2010 Americans paid over $440 billion for medical and disability-related costs of heart disease (Centers for Disease Control, 2011). Stress is also a known contributor to colds and flu, digestive difficulties, headaches, insomnia, stroke, and other physiological problems, as well as to impaired psychological well-being (e.g., anxiety, depression, burnout) and counterproductive behaviors such as absenteeism and drug abuse (Cooper, Dewe, & O'Driscoll, 2001; Krantz & McCeney, 2002).

It is no wonder, then, that I-O psychologists devote a great deal of effort to identifying the causes of work stress, to understanding how it relates to health, and to developing strategies for reducing or managing it. In this chapter we will describe these approaches, with a focus on understanding the variables that contribute to and reduce stress at work and in other domains.

Studying Workplace Stress

A comprehensive framework for studying work stress was developed by Kahn and Byosiere (1992). Their model presents several important factors in the stress process, including (1) work stressors (task and role stressors), (2) moderators of the stress process (individual

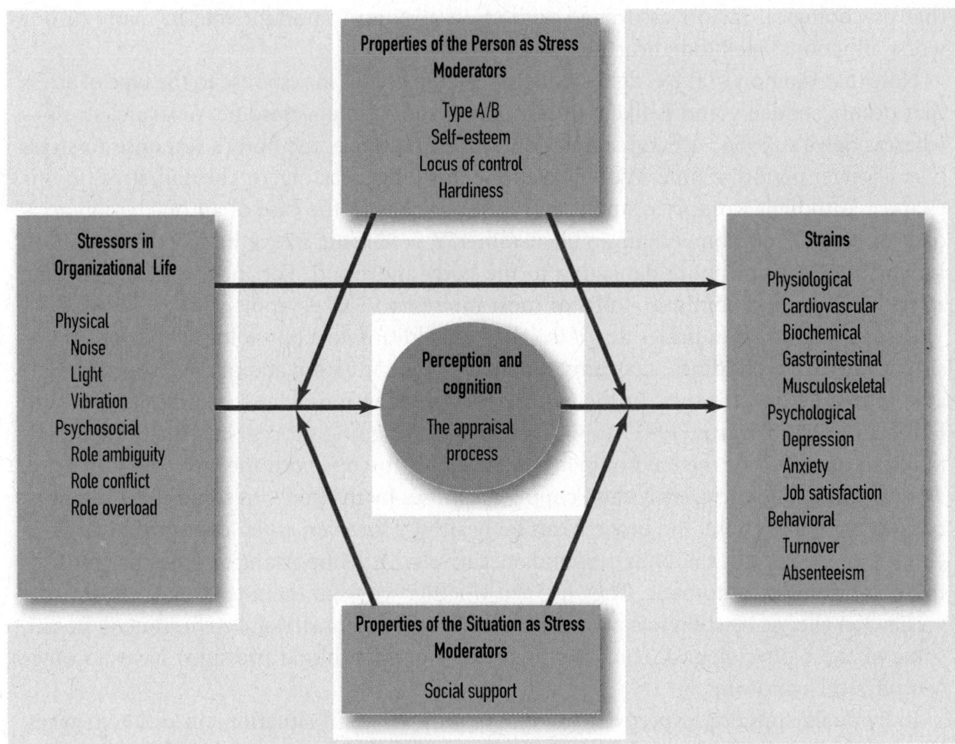

FIGURE 10.1 Theoretical Framework for the Study of Stress in Organizations

SOURCE: Adapted from Kahn, R. L., & Byosiere, P. (1992). Theoretical framework for the study of stress in organizations. In M. D. Dunnette & L. M. Hough (Eds.), *Handbook of industrial and organizational psychology* (2nd ed., Vol. 3, pp. 571–650). Fig. 9, p. 592. Palo Alto, CA: Consulting Psychologists Press. Copyright permission by Leaetta Hough.

differences, social support), and (3) strains, or the consequences of stress (burnout, heart disease) (see Figure 10.1).

Two of the first stress pioneers were Walter Cannon and Hans Selye. Cannon was a physiologist who studied animal and human reactions to dangerous situations. He noted that animals and humans have an adaptive response to stressful situations in which they choose to either fight or attempt to escape. Cannon (1929) called this response the **fight-or-flight reaction**, and he is often credited with being the first to use the term "stress."

Often referred to as the "father of stress," Hans Selye (1956, 1976) defined stress as the non-specific response of the human body to any demand made on it. He was the first to distinguish between good stress (**eustress**) and bad stress (**distress**). Selye noted that eustress provides challenges that motivate individuals to work hard and meet their goals. Alternatively, distress results from stressful situations that persist over time and produces negative health outcomes.

Selye observed that the response sequences to almost any disease or trauma (e.g., poisoning, injury, psychological stress) are nearly identical. He named the progression the **general adaptation syndrome (GAS)** and divided it into three stages. First, in the **alarm reaction** stage, the body mobilizes resources to cope with added stress. In this stage, the heart rate increases and **stress hormones,** such as adrenaline, noradrenaline, epinephrine, and cortisol, are released. Second, in the **resistance** stage, the body copes with the original source of stress, but resistance to other stressors is lowered. Third, in the **exhaustion** stage, overall resistance drops and adverse consequences, including burnout, severe illness, and even death, can result unless stress is reduced. The general adaptation syndrome suggests

Fight-or-flight reaction Adaptive response to stressful situations exhibited by animals and humans in which they choose to either fight or attempt to escape.

Eustress Type of stress that provides challenges that motivate individuals to work hard and meet their goals.

Distress Type of stress resulting from chronically demanding situations that produces negative health outcomes.

General adaptation syndrome (GAS) A nearly identical response sequence to almost any disease or trauma (poisoning, injury, psychological stress); identified by Hans Selye.

Alarm reaction Stage of the general adaptation syndrome in which the body mobilizes resources to cope with added stress.

Stress hormone Chemical (e.g., adrenaline, noradrenaline, epinephrine, or cortisol) released in the body when a person encounters stressful or demanding situations.

Resistance Stage of the general adaptation syndrome in which the body copes with the original source of stress, but resistance to other stressors is lowered.

Exhaustion Stage of the general adaptation syndrome in which overall resistance drops and adverse consequences (e.g., burnout, severe illness, and even death) can result unless stress is reduced.

that psychological factors associated with stress play an important role in many of our worst afflictions, including heart disease.

Note that Cannon's (1929) fight-or-flight reaction comes in response to the type of stress that occurs suddenly and is likely to last only a short time—episodic, or acute, stress—whereas Selye's (1956) general adaptation syndrome tracks the body's response to stress over a longer period of time. We will examine this longer-lasting, or chronic, stress in this chapter. Although workplace stress can be episodic, as in the case of an on-the-job accident or a confrontation with an irate customer, it is chronic stress that is more common in work settings and more damaging to the body and mind. For these reasons, chronic stress has been and continues to be of most interest to I-O psychologists.

Problem-focused coping Type of coping directed at managing or altering a problem causing the stress.

Emotion-focused coping Type of coping directed at reducing the emotional response to a problem by avoiding, minimizing, or distancing oneself from the problem.

Stressors Physical or psychological demands to which an individual responds.

Strains Reaction or response to stressors.

Research on stress indicates that it involves, in addition to a physiological response consistent with Selye's findings, a cognitive appraisal of the situation and of the resources available to handle the stressors. In their theory of stress, appraisal, and coping, Lazarus and Folkman (1984; Lazarus, 1991) viewed stress as an ongoing process in which individuals make an appraisal of the environment and attempt to cope with the stressors that arise. This appraisal often triggers a set of coping responses by the body. In some circumstances, such as during exercise, the process can be healthy. However, when exposure to stress is chronic or persistent, the body responds negatively. It is important to note that most of these reactions are automatic. They happen whether we want them to or not, almost as if we have an allergic reaction to a psychologically threatening or stressful environment. In fact, some of these physiological reactions to stress (e.g., high blood pressure) have no obvious physical symptoms.

Individuals appraise, experience, and cope with stressful situations in different ways, which we will consider in detail later in the chapter. At this point, it is helpful to note that coping styles are typically divided into problem-focused and emotion-focused coping. **Problem-focused coping** is directed at managing or altering the problem that is causing the stress. Such coping may include defining the problem, generating different solutions and weighing their costs and benefits, and acting to solve the problem (Lazarus, 2000). For example, problem-focused coping might involve developing and utilizing time management skills and designing a specific plan of action for handling a job with many demands. **Emotion-focused coping** involves reducing the emotional response to the problem, which can mean avoiding, minimizing, and distancing oneself from the problem. For example, emotion-focused coping might involve obtaining social support from one's family and friends to help minimize the effects of a stressful job. We will discuss social support in more detail in Module 10.3.

TABLE 10.1 **Common Stressors in the Workplace**

Heat, cold, noise
Role stressors
Workload
Work pace, time pressure
Work schedule (e.g., shift work)
Interpersonal demands and conflict
Situational constraints
Perceived control
Emotional labor
Traumatic job stressors (e.g., workplace violence)

What Is a Stressor?

Although we often talk about stress and the experience of stress, when it comes to research studies, it is often easier to get actual measurements of **stressors**, which are physical or psychological demands to which an individual responds (see Table 10.1). Examples of physical stressors include excessive heat, noise, and light. Examples of psychological stressors are role ambiguity, interpersonal conflict, lack of control, and even the incessantly ringing phone or the "ding" from your computer or smartphone telling you that you've got yet another incoming e-mail. Reactions or responses to these stressors are commonly called

strains (Cooper et al., 2001; Quick, Quick, Nelson, & Hurrell, 1997). Examples of strains that can result from chronic or persistent stress are burnout, anxiety, and physiological consequences such as high blood pressure and heart disease. These stressors and strains will be described in more detail in the next section.

Common Stressors at Work

Work stressors fall into two major categories: physical/task stressors, such as noise, light, heat, and cold, and psychological stressors, which involve a multitude of subtle and not-so-subtle factors that an individual may find demanding.

Physical/Task Stressors

In their early studies of work stress, I-O psychologists focused on physical stressors and their effects on the experience of stress and subsequent strains. According to many experimental and field studies, uncontrollable noise is particularly stressful and leads to lower task performance and diminished motivation (Szalma & Hancock, 2011; Wickens & Hollands, 2000). Although we may associate noise with factories where loud machinery is in operation, the effects of noise are not limited to manufacturing environments. Evans and Johnson (2000) found that exposure to low-level noise in an open office setting is associated with elevated levels of stress hormones and lower task performance. The importance of the increased hormone levels is that stressors may exist even when the worker is not aware of the stressor. For example, work psychologists often interview workers about their work on noisy factory floors. When asked, the workers typically report that their work environments are not noisy, despite the fact that the response—"No, it's not noisy"—has to be shouted. Interestingly, the same is true of workers in gambling casinos.

Employees in physically stressful workplaces are often not consciously aware of the stressful effects of noise, poor ventilation, or other adverse conditions.

The demands of a given job (e.g., pace of work, workload, the number of hours worked) can also contribute to the experience of stress and to subsequent strains (Ilies, Dimotakis, & De Pater, 2010). For example, a study of 936 British employees from 22 call centers investigated relationships between workload demands and back disorders (Sprigg, Stride, Wall, Holman, & Smith, 2007). Call-center employees were asked if their workload was heavy, demanding, and time pressured. The authors found that call-center employees who had a heavier workload were more likely to subsequently report upper body and lower back disorders than those with lower workloads. Although it may be clear that physical and task stressors have negative effects on employee health, more recent research in work stress has focused on psychological stressors that may not be as intuitively linked to health outcomes. As we will see in the following section, such psychological stressors play an equally important role in employee health and well-being. Keep in mind, however, that one type of stressor (e.g., physical or task) is not made less important by the presence of another stressor; thus, the effects of multiple stressors can be cumulative.

Psychological Stressors

Lack of Control/Predictability

Control is a major theme in the literature on stress (Ganster & Murphy, 2000). Varying levels of personal control and predictability have clear effects on job performance and work stress (Logan & Ganster, 2005; Rastegary & Landy, 1993). As with any stressor, the individual's *perception* of control or predictability determines his or her response to the situation, and such perceptions are affected by characteristics of the job and work environment. The scheduling and pace of work can influence feelings of control. For example, flexible time schedules enhance feelings of control over one's schedule, even though the average arrival and departure times may differ only by minutes after a flexible time schedule has been introduced (Baltes, Briggs, Huff, Wright, & Neuman, 1999; Totterdell, 2005). Flextime also increases perceptions of control by helping employees to balance work and family commitments (Golden, Veiga, & Simsek, 2006). Perceptions of control in the workplace are also related to **autonomy**, the extent to which employees can control how and when they perform the tasks of their job (Hackman & Oldham, 1980). Overall, interventions that enhance perceptions of control on the job, such as participative decision making or flexible time schedules, are likely to reduce stress and subsequent strains. In Module 10.2, we further discuss the importance of control, which is a major component of the demand–control model of stress developed by Karasek (1979).

Autonomy Extent to which employees can control how and when they perform the tasks of their job.

Interpersonal Conflict

Negative interactions with co-workers, supervisors, or clients—or **interpersonal conflict**—can range from heated arguments to subtle incidents of unfriendly behavior (Bruk-Lee & Spector, 2006; Jex, 1998). Interpersonal conflict can occur when resources at work are scarce (e.g., who gets to use the color copy machine first), when employees have incompatible interests (e.g., one member of a team is a stickler for detail, whereas another likes to complete the project as quickly as possible), or when employees feel they are not being treated fairly (e.g., bosses get big bonuses, but workers are told no funds are available for salary increases for the rest of the workforce). Interpersonal conflict can distract workers from important job tasks, and it can have physical health consequences. In a longitudinal study of more than 15,000 Finnish employees, the link between interpersonal conflict at work and subsequent health problems was significant—even when social class, marital status, conflict with spouse, and high alcohol consumption were taken into account (Romanov, Appelberg, Honkasalo, & Koskenvuo, 1996). Other negative work outcomes of interpersonal conflict range from depression and job dissatisfaction to aggression, theft, and sabotage (Frone, 2000a). Interpersonal conflict may also play a part in workplace violence, which we discuss in Module 10.4.

Interpersonal conflict Negative interactions with co-workers, supervisors, or clients, which can range from heated arguments to subtle incidents of unfriendly behavior.

Role Stressors

Role ambiguity, role conflict, and role overload are collectively referred to as **role stressors**. The concept of role stressors is based on the idea that most jobs have multiple task requirements and responsibilities, or **roles** (Rizzo, House, & Lirtzman, 1970), and that a job is likely to be particularly stressful if these roles conflict with one another or are unclear. **Role ambiguity** occurs when employees lack clear knowledge of what behavior is expected in their job. In such cases, individuals experience uncertainty about which actions they should take to perform their job most effectively. **Role conflict** occurs when demands from different sources are incompatible. Students are well aware of this form of conflict, particularly toward the end of the term when they complain, "I have four papers due and all my professors act like I'm not taking any courses but theirs!" In addition to conflict between different tasks or projects,

Role stressors Collective term for stressors resulting from the multiple task requirements or roles of employees.

Role The expectations regarding the responsibilities and requirements of a particular job.

Role ambiguity Stressor that occurs when employees lack clear knowledge of what behavior is expected in their job.

Role conflict Stressor that occurs when demands from different sources are incompatible.

role conflict may also involve conflict between organizational demands and one's own values or conflict among obligations to several different co-workers. As we will see in Chapter 14, the modern organization is best thought of as an open system in which part of the organization (e.g., worker, work group, department, division) interacts with its environment. That means that there is ample opportunity for role conflict and ambiguity, because every time an entity interacts with an environment, opportunity for confusion exists.

A more specific form of conflict is **role overload**, a stressor that occurs when an individual is expected to fulfill too many roles at the same time, another consequence of interacting with the environment (e.g., customers, supervisors). Role overload can cause people to work very long hours, increasing stress and subsequent strains. Some workers complain that they are stressed from working 24 hours a day, seven days a week. On the television show *Saturday Night Live*, cast members joked that some people have a different 24/7 plan for avoiding stress: a work schedule of 24 hours a week, seven months a year. Most of us would agree that such a schedule (with full-time pay) would be a great way to reduce stress! Indeed, research shows a positive correlation between role stressors and a variety of work and health problems, including tension, anxiety, and a propensity to leave the organization (Day & Livingstone, 2001). In addition, research indicates that role stressors have consistent effects on commitment and turnover intentions in samples of nurses in Hungary, Italy, the United Kingdom, and the United States, providing support for the importance of role stressors across cultures (Glazer & Beehr, 2005).

Role overload Stressor that occurs when an individual is expected to fulfill too many roles at the same time.

Work–Family Conflict

A different type of role stressor is **work–family conflict**, which occurs when workers experience conflict between the roles they fulfill at work and the roles they fulfill in their personal lives (Bellavia & Frone, 2005; Grzywacz & Butler, 2008). As dual-career families have become the norm rather than the exception, work–family conflict has become a widespread source of work stress. Given that working women continue to take on most of the responsibilities within the home, women often fill more roles than men (Cleveland, Stockdale, & Murphy, 2000). In a study of men and women working in high-ranking positions, women were more stressed by their greater responsibility for household and family duties. In addition, women with children at home had significantly higher levels of stress hormones after work than women without children at home or any of the men in the study (Lundberg & Frankenhauser, 1999). However, these findings do not necessarily mean that the effect of work on women is exclusively negative. In fact, there is little evidence to indicate that a woman's employment harms her marriage or her children (Cleveland et al., 2000). One study concluded that, compared to men, women appear to have better coping strategies to handle stress (Korabik & McDonald, 1991). In particular, women are more likely than men to have access to social support, which we discuss in Module 10.3 as a critical factor in reducing stress and its harmful effects.

Work–family conflict Situation that occurs when workers experience conflict between the roles they fulfill at work and in their personal lives.

Nevertheless, several studies have demonstrated the serious consequences that work–-family conflict has on the health and well-being of both men and women (e.g., Allen & Armstrong, 2006; Grant-Vallone & Donaldson, 2001). Thus, this type of conflict seems to be an "equal-opportunity stressor" (Allen, Herst, Bruck, & Sutton, 2000). A study of 2,700 employed adults found that individuals who reported experiencing work–family conflict were as much as 30 times more likely to experience a significant mental health problem, such as depression or anxiety, than employees who reported no work–family conflict (Frone, 2000b). As we mentioned in Chapter 1, research is also beginning to investigate work–school conflict for college-age students, and balancing school and work appears to be equally challenging (Butler, 2007).

Grzywacz and colleagues (2007) noted that work–family conflict research has focused almost exclusively on professional, white adults. They examined work–family conflict in an immigrant

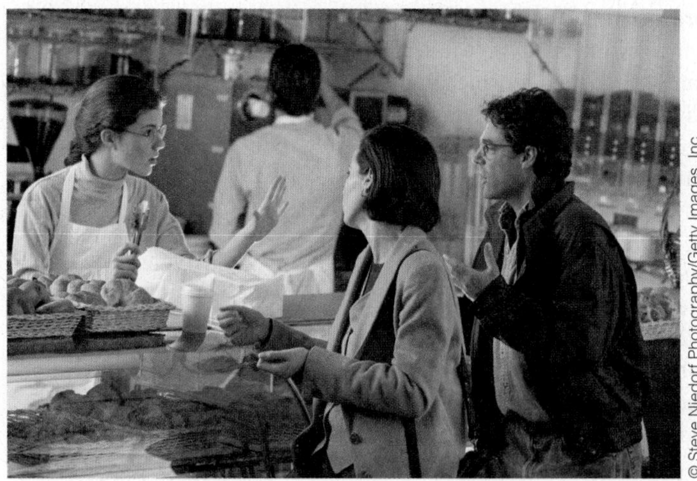
© Steve Niedorf Photography/Getty Images, Inc.

Service occupations often involve masking one's emotions to keep customers happy.

Latino sample employed in the poultry-processing industry. Results indicated that immigrant Latinos experienced infrequent work–family conflict, and there was little evidence that work–family conflict was associated with health in this sample. They noted that the results "demonstrate how traditional models of work–family conflict need to be modified to reflect the needs and circumstances of diverse workers in the new global economy" (p. 1119).

Flexible time schedules and child care are becoming increasingly important to working men and women in many different careers. For example, although one might not think that child care would be important to professional athletes, it is provided to members of several sports organizations, including professional race car drivers (NASCAR) and the men's and women's professional golf associations. Players in the Ladies' Professional Golf Association reported that the child-care program reduces their concerns about balancing work and family, thereby letting them concentrate on their work (Stewart, 2002). Unfortunately, the average working parent is more likely than these athletes to experience work–family stress related to the lack of good child care. A 2001 study by the human resources firm Hewitt Associates found that only 10 percent of U.S. companies offered on-site or off-site child care and another 10 percent arranged for employee discounts at local child-care providers (Finnigan, 2001). Thus, 80 percent of the workers polled were on their own in terms of child care. It is reasonable to assume that a majority of them experienced work–family conflict at some time. The precipitating event is often an unexpected one, such as an illness or injury that prevents a child from attending school or day care. When that happens in a dual-income family, husband and wife are prone to experience a good deal of tension at the breakfast table as they decide who will stay home that day and assume the caregiver role. Notably, the policies of some organizations include illness of a child as an acceptable reason for a parent to take a sick day, whereas others do not.

Emotional Labor

Emotional labor Regulation of one's emotions to meet job or organizational demands; can be achieved through surface acting and deep acting.

Surface acting Emotional labor that consists of managing or faking one's expressions or emotions.

Deep acting Emotional labor that consists of managing one's feelings, including emotions required by the job.

Interest in the role of emotions in the workplace has increased rapidly over the past decade (Fisher & Ashkanasy, 2000). Emotions are important to consider because stress is, first and foremost, an emotional reaction. As we mentioned in Chapter 9, **emotional labor** is the regulation of one's emotions to meet job or organizational demands. Emotional labor has been studied in many different occupations, including police officers, waiters and waitresses, bill collectors, salesclerks, bank tellers, and flight attendants (Hochschild, 1983). The study of emotional labor addresses the stress of managing emotions when jobs require that workers display only certain expressions to clients or customers (Adelmann, 1995). Workers can regulate their emotions through surface acting and deep acting (Morris & Feldman, 1996). **Surface acting** consists of managing or faking one's expressions or emotions. For example, waiters in fine restaurants report that they commonly display pleasant emotions while simultaneously hiding feelings of anger and frustration toward rude customers. Similarly, bill collectors are encouraged to ignore their feelings of irritation and hostility toward uncooperative debtors and instead to display neutrality or calmness—the emotions that their employers have found lead to a greater likelihood that debtors will pay their bills (Sutton, 1991). **Deep acting** consists of managing one's feelings, including trying to actually change one's emotional state to match the emotions required by the job. For example, a waitress might try to imagine herself in a difficult customer's situation to try to feel empathy for the customer and better understand the customer's point of view. Because deep acting involves modifying one's emotions and feelings, it results in expressions that are more authentic, more effective, and more associated with positive health outcomes than surface acting does (Chi, Grandey, Diamond, & Krimmel, 2011). This finding supports the notion that authenticity is important in the workplace. Chi and colleagues (2011) also found that surface acting can be a successful strategy for extraverts but not for introverts. They concluded by giving "a tip for service providers: Only extraverts should fake their surface-level expressions, but introverts can do as well as extraverts if they regulate their deeper feelings" (p. 1344).

Grandey, Kern, and Frone (2007) found that workers in jobs requiring emotional labor often encounter verbal abuse from customers, which can include insults, swearing, and yelling. In one study, U.S. call-center employees reported an average of seven hostile calls a day (Grandey, Dickter, & Sin, 2004); in another study, 75 percent of U.K. airline and railway employees reported that they were verbally abused at least once a month (Boyd, 2002). We can speculate that some of these abusive customers come to the situation already emotionally primed for a confrontation, either because they are frustrated with the employee's organization (e.g., they tried unsuccessfully to book tickets from a website) or because of unrelated stress (e.g., a romantic breakup).

Stress and discomfort are likely to occur when the required emotions differ from employees' actual emotions. Suppressing emotions or showing false emotions requires cognitive and physiological effort, which is likely to be stressful over the long term. Research indicates that the stress of emotional labor can lead to job dissatisfaction, burnout, and turnover intentions (Grandey, 2003; Pugh, Groth, & Hennig-Thurau, 2011). To reduce the stress of emotional labor, I-O psychologists recommend that employees use humor, obtain social support from co-workers, and depersonalize the encounter with customers or clients. Rupp and Spencer (2006) suggested that organizations might train employees to regulate their emotions (i.e., engage in deep acting) when dealing with difficult customers. In addition, a study that included samples from the United States and France found that when employees believed that they had control over their jobs, emotional labor that would otherwise be exhausting was not exhausting at all (Grandey, Fisk, & Steiner, 2005). The results suggested that if "managers in the U.S. and France were to enhance employees' perceptions of job autonomy, the reduction in burnout would be notable" (p. 902). Additional consideration of emotional labor as a stressor is needed, particularly as the service sector continues to grow and more employees are required to provide "service with a smile" (Pugh, 2001).

Recent research has begun to differentiate between challenge-related and hindrance-related stressors. **Challenge-related stressors** are defined as work demands or circumstances that, although potentially stressful, offer potential gains (Boswell, Olson-Buchanan, & LePine, 2004). Examples of challenge-related stressors are the number of projects assigned, time spent at work, volume of work in a given time, and the amount and scope of responsibilities. **Hindrance-related stressors** are defined as job demands or circumstances that tend to limit or interfere with work achievement. Examples of hindrance-related stressors include the degree to which politics rather than performance affects organizational decisions, administrative red tape, lack of job security, stalled career progression, and even malfunctioning office equipment (such as the infamous printer that everyone hated in the movie *Office Space*). A meta-analysis of 183 samples showed negative relationships between hindrance-related stressors and both job satisfaction and organizational commitment; it showed positive relationships between hindrance-related stressors and turnover and other withdrawal behaviors. Relationships with challenge-related stressors were generally the opposite: They showed positive relationships with job satisfaction and organizational commitment and negative relationships with turnover (Podsakoff, LePine, & LePine, 2007).

Challenge-related stressors Work demands or circumstances that, although potentially stressful, have potential gains for individuals.

Hindrance-related stressors Job demands or circumstances that tend to limit or interfere with an individual's work achievement.

TABLE 10.2 **Consequences of Stress**

Physical/Medical/Physiological
Heart disease and stroke
Digestive problems
Back pain and arthritis
Headaches
Increased blood pressure and heart rate
Production of Stress Hormones (adrenaline, noradrenaline, cortisol)
Psychological
Burnout
Depression
Anxiety
Family problems
Sleep problems
Job dissatisfaction
Behavioral
Absence
Lateness
Drug, alcohol, and tobacco abuse
Accidents
Sabotage/violence
Poor decision making/information processing
Job performance
Turnover

SOURCE: Quick, J. C., Quick, J. D., Nelson, D. L., & Hurrell, J. J. (1997). *Preventative stress management in organizations*. Washington, DC: American Psychological Association.

Consequences of Stress

The link between occupational stress and negative health outcomes among employees is clear (Cooper et al., 2001; De Jonge & Dormann, 2006). The negative consequences of chronic stress can be divided into three categories: behavioral, psychological, and physiological (see Table 10.2).

Behavioral Consequences of Stress

Among the behavioral consequences of stress are absenteeism, accidents, alcohol and drug abuse, poor job performance, and counterproductive behaviors including workplace violence (Kahn & Boysiere, 1992). We will focus on the effects of stressors on three particularly important behavioral outcomes: (1) information processing, which affects a variety of other critical work outcomes; (2) job performance, which can include information processing but often involves a global measure of effectiveness; and (3) counterproductive work behaviors.

Information Processing

The influence of stress on information processing has been widely investigated. Chronic stress has detrimental effects on memory, reaction times, accuracy, and performance of a variety of tasks (Smith, 1990). In addition, individuals under stress often have difficulty focusing their attention. Stress leads to premature reactions to stimuli, restricted use of relevant cues, and increased errors on cognitive tasks (Svenson & Maule, 1993).

Because each of us has limited cognitive resources, stressful situations that restrict such resources will impair our ability to cope with the task at hand. Stress is also associated with lower creativity and poorer decision making, particularly under time pressure (Rastegary & Landy, 1993). For example, fast-food delivery drivers commonly have accidents during the rush period for deliveries (usually Friday nights between 5:00 p.m. and 9:00 p.m.). They often report never seeing the object (e.g., car, truck, jogger, motorcycle) whose path they turned across. They simply did not "process" that information when they turned left across traffic because they were looking for a street sign or a street number during the hectic evening hours. This is just one example of how the effects of high levels of stress on information processing can lead to a variety of negative work outcomes.

Performance

For more than a century, psychologists have investigated the hypothesis that arousal and performance have an inverted-U relationship, as shown in Figure 10.2 (Yerkes & Dodson, 1908). The inverted-U graph indicates that as arousal (or stress) increases, performance increases, but only up to a certain point; when arousal becomes too high, performance begins to decline. Thus, compared to situations with moderate arousal, both low levels of arousal (boredom) and high levels of arousal (extreme stress) result in lower performance. Alternatively, moderate arousal can lead to high motivation, energy, and attentiveness; this outcome is consistent with Selye's concept of eustress, the "good stress" that we discussed earlier in this chapter. Research on task performance in the laboratory generally supports predictions from the inverted-U hypothesis (Jex, 1998).

Research in organizational settings indicates that work stress at any level, including moderate levels, has a direct, negative relationship with job performance. For example, in a sample of nurses, Motowidlo, Packard, and Manning (1986) found that stress was negatively correlated with several interpersonal aspects of job performance dimensions. Specifically, nurses under stress showed lower sensitivity, warmth, and tolerance toward patients. Meta-analyses indicate that a widespread stressor, role ambiguity, has consistent, negative relationships with job performance (Gilboa, Shirom, Fried, & Cooper, 2008; Tubre & Collins, 2000). The best explanation of these results has to do with the nature of the task. For the simple tasks performed in laboratory experiments, moderate arousal results in the highest performance. However, for complex tasks performed on the job, moderate to high levels of stress are detrimental to performance. When the complexity of the task is considered, the overall results seem to fit the inverted-U hypothesis.

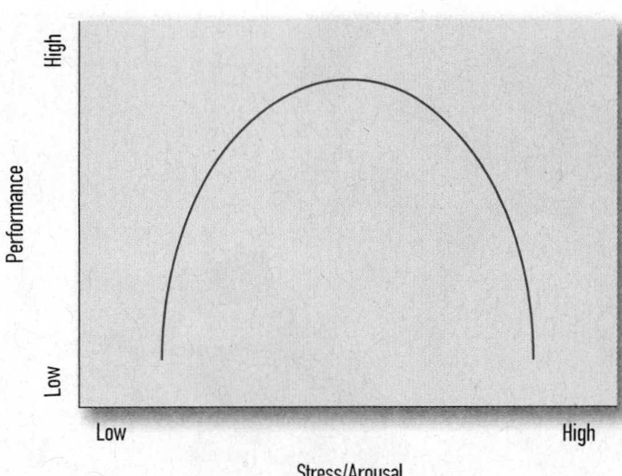

FIGURE 10.2 Stress and Performance: Inverted-U Relationship

SOURCE: Jex, S. M. (1998). *Stress and job performance: Theory, research, and implications for managerial practice*. Thousand Oaks, CA: Sage. © 1998 by Sage Publications Inc. Reproduced with permission of Sage Publications Inc Books.

It is important to note that stress represents only one of many factors that may affect job performance (Jex, 1998). This is consistent with one of the themes of this book: Multiple influences affect behavior at work. The effects of stress on performance depend on several factors, including the complexity of the task performed and the personality characteristics of the individual performing the task. Nevertheless, it is clear that chronic stress commonly has negative effects on work performance.

Counterproductive Work Behavior

Spector and Fox (2005) developed a stressor–emotion model that linked stressors with counterproductive work behaviors. They proposed that stressors from the work environment increase perceptions of stress, which can then lead to negative emotions and, subsequently, counterproductive work behaviors. This model shows how many of the topics we address in this course are related; we identified various types of stressors earlier in this chapter, discussed emotions in Chapter 9, and considered different types of counterproductive behaviors in Chapter 4. Penney and Spector (2005) found support for many of the relationships in this model; in particular, they found that stressors, including workplace conflict, predicted counterproductive work behaviors.

Psychological Consequences of Stress

The psychological consequences of stress include anxiety, depression, burnout, fatigue, job tension, and dissatisfaction with one's job and life (Kahn & Byosiere, 1992). **Burnout** is a particularly important and well-researched consequence of stress. It is an extreme state of psychological strain that results from a prolonged response to chronic job stressors that exceed an individual's coping resources (Maslach, Schaufeli, & Leiter, 2001). Burnout was first observed in the caring professions: nursing, social work, and teaching. For example, nurses in intensive care units (ICUs) are responsible day in and day out for patients on the cusp between life and death. A small mistake on a nurse's part could have fatal consequences. Thanks to ICU nurses, many patients recover from life-threatening conditions, yet no matter how good a nurse's work is, some patients will die in the ICU. It is easy to understand how these nurses'

Burnout Extreme state of psychological strain resulting from a prolonged response to chronic job stressors that exceed an individual's resources to cope with them.

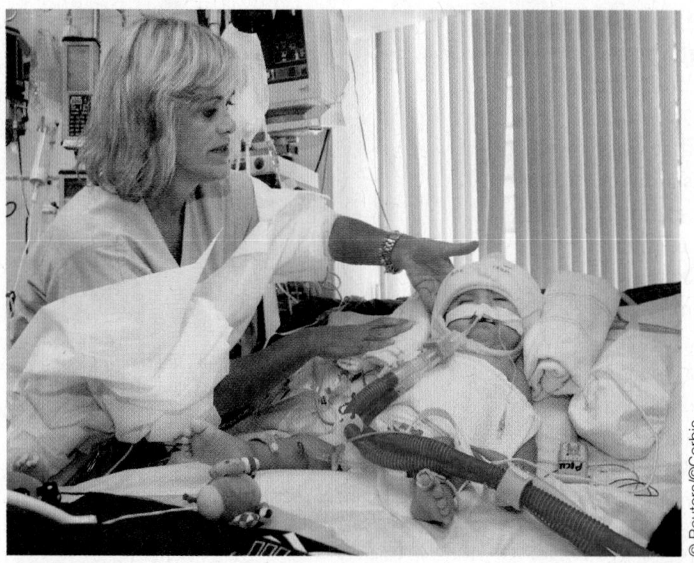
© Reuters/©Corbis

Working in a high-stakes job, where a mistake can be a matter of life or death, can lead to emotional burnout.

heavy workloads and demanding caregiving responsibilities can often lead to burnout. Researchers have identified three components of burnout in these health care and human services settings: emotional exhaustion, feelings of depersonalization, and feelings of low personal accomplishment.

Emotional exhaustion occurs when individuals feel emotionally drained by work. Individuals who suffer from feelings of **depersonalization** have become hardened by their job and tend to treat clients or patients like objects. For example, a stock character in many movies about teenagers is a "hard-boiled" school administrator who seems to have completely forgotten what it is like to be a student. Individuals who have feelings of **low personal accomplishment** cannot deal with problems effectively and cannot understand or identify with the problems of others. They feel powerless to have any actual impact on problems and thus are unlikely to implement effective solutions.

Emotional exhaustion Burnout that occurs when individuals feel emotionally drained by work.

Depersonalization Burnout that occurs when individuals become hardened by their job and tend to treat clients or patients like objects.

Low personal accomplishment Burnout in which individuals feel they cannot deal with problems effectively and understand or identify with others' problems.

Burnout is typically measured with the Maslach Burnout Inventory (MBI) (Maslach, Jackson, & Leiter, 1996), a self-report measure that includes scales for the three burnout dimensions. Table 10.3 shows examples of burnout items from this instrument. Extensive research indicates that chronic stressors (e.g., role ambiguity and role conflict) often lead to burnout (Jackson & Schuler, 1985; Lee & Ashforth, 1996). Research on burnout has expanded to occupations beyond the caring professions, including managers, air traffic controllers, insurance agents, and military professionals (e.g., Schaufeli & Bakker, 2004). As a result, researchers have broadened the three burnout dimensions so that they are relevant beyond the human services and health care professions. Work on burnout now refers to the dimensions as (1) exhaustion, (2) depersonalization and cynicism on the job, and (3) a sense of ineffectiveness and lack of accomplishment on the job (Maslach et al., 2001). The MBI-General Survey assesses these three dimensions with items parallel to those in the original MBI, with the modification that they do not explicitly refer to working with people.

Using samples from both the United States and the Netherlands, Schaufeli and Enzmann (1998) examined burnout across a variety of different occupations. This work indicated that police officers and security guards in both countries had relatively high levels of cynicism and feelings of ineffectiveness but low levels of exhaustion. In contrast, teachers had the highest levels of exhaustion in both countries but average levels of cynicism and feelings of ineffectiveness. Employees in the medical field had high levels of personal inefficacy but lower cynicism and exhaustion in both countries. Considering these findings, we might ask whether individuals exhibiting only one or two of the three burnout characteristics should be considered to have burnout. Indeed, there is a thriving research debate over that question, as well as whether one dimension of burnout precedes the others. Overall, however, research indicates that the basic patterns of burnout seem to be fairly similar across different occupations and countries (Maslach et al., 2001).

TABLE 10.3 **Examples of Burnout Items**

1. I doubt the significance of my work.
2. I feel I am making an effective contribution to what this organization does.
3. I feel used up at the end of the workday.

Source: Schaufeli, W. B., Leiter, M. P., Maslach, C., & Jackson, S. E. (1996). *Maslach Burnout Inventory: General survey.* Palo Alto, CA: Consulting Psychologists Press. Modified and reproduced by special permission of the Publisher, Mind Garden, Inc., Menlo Park, CA.

In a longitudinal investigation of staff members in a university setting, Maslach and Leiter (2008) found that early warning signs of burnout (e.g., initially high levels of exhaustion or cynicism) led to later and more serious burnout, but only in certain situations. The tipping point that determined whether people became burned out was their perception of fairness in the workplace, which we will discuss further in Chapter 11. If employees experienced problems with fairness (e.g., favoritism, unjustified inequities), their early warning pattern was likely to develop into burnout over time. In contrast, for those people who were not experiencing problems with fairness, the early warning signs of burnout were likely to diminish over time. In another study with promising findings, LeBlanc, Hox, Schaufeli, Taris, and Peeters (2007) developed a team-based burnout intervention program for burnout among oncology care providers in the Netherlands. The intervention was called Take Care! and included support group meetings in which care providers shared their feelings and discussed work problems and ways of solving them. The results indicated that care providers in the experimental group felt significantly less emotional exhaustion than care providers in the control group, both immediately after the program ended and six months later. In a sense, this is the same dynamic that drives group therapy in clinical and counseling settings: Simply knowing that others are having the same experiences seems to make things a bit more bearable, and listening to how others cope can often provide people with strategies for coping that they have not tried before.

In sum, work settings with chronic, overwhelming demands and time pressures put workers at high risk for burnout. As such, interventions intended to reduce burnout should be focused on both the individual and the job. A combination of stress management, skills training, and job design seems to be the most promising avenue to prevent or reduce the development of burnout (van Dierendonck, Schaufeli, & Buunk, 2001).

Physiological Consequences of Stress

Physiological changes in the body occur when stressful situations cause overactivation of the sympathetic nervous system, which produces several different kinds of stress hormones. These stress hormones cause an increase in heart rate and cardiac output in preparation for increased physical and cognitive activity. Initially, these effects of stress can be beneficial in terms of improved decision making, judgment, and physical performance. However, chronic activation of the sympathetic nervous system leads to excess amounts of stress hormones circulating in the blood supply and the brain.

Stress also causes the blood vessels to shrink in the peripheral areas of the body (Eliot & Buell, 1983). The combination of shrinking blood vessels and more blood moving through them causes wear and tear on the coronary arteries and the heart. This leads to thickening of plaque in the arteries (atherosclerosis) and heart disease. In addition, because the heart has to work harder to pump under these conditions, it requires more oxygen, which in turn often leads to elevated blood pressure. Greater oxygen consumption by the heart under these aroused conditions explains the increase in heart attacks among persons who are under stress (Krantz & McCeney, 2002).

Although many of the physiological outcomes of stress are interrelated—that is, one outcome can affect another to start a vicious circle or snowball effect—they are often categorized according to three types. Cardiovascular outcomes of stress include changes in blood pressure, heart rate, and cholesterol. Gastrointestinal outcomes include digestive problems of various kinds. Biochemical outcomes include increases in cortisol and catecholamines (stress hormones). Stressful work situations are linked to increased levels of cortisol, norepinephrine, and adrenaline in the bloodstream (Fox, Dwyer, & Ganster, 1993). Long-lasting, elevated stress hormone levels contribute to decreased functioning of the immune system and the development of coronary heart disease (Cohen & Hebert, 1996; Krantz & McCeney, 2002). In the United States, coronary heart disease is the leading cause of death among both men and women (American Heart Association, 2006). In sum, there is clear evidence of the negative physiological consequences that result from chronic exposure to stressors.

Work Schedules

As we saw in Chapter 9, work schedules are playing an increasingly important role in managing work–life balance in two ways: Individuals desire the freedom to pursue leisure activities outside of work, and they often have obligations to fulfill multiple roles as spouse, caregiver, and parent. This suggests that the scheduling of work can have substantial effects on stress and worker well-being. There are three different scheduling formats that bear discussion: shift work, flextime, and compressed workweeks.

Shift Work

The scheduling of work according to a particular time period is called **shift work**. The study of shift work and its effects on workers has a long and rich research history, which is well presented in a number of sources (e.g., Landy, 1989; Tepas, Paley, & Popkin, 1997). Much of this work has centered on the 24-hour or **circadian cycle** of humans, whose physiology tends to make them active during hours of light and inactive (e.g., sleeping or resting) during hours of darkness. Thus, workers assigned to shifts during daylight hours are following the circadian cycle, while those whose shift includes hours of darkness are working against the cycle. Psychologists have found that, in general, disturbance of the circadian cycle has adverse consequences for health, performance, and general satisfaction. Shift work is categorized into two different types: fixed shifts and rotating shifts. If workers are permanently assigned to a particular shift, the shift is called a **fixed shift**. Typical shifts include the day shift (e.g., 7:00 a.m. to 3:30 p.m.); the afternoon or evening shift, often called the "swing" shift (e.g., 3:00 p.m. to 11:30 p.m.); and the night shift, often called the "midnight" or "graveyard" shift (e.g., 11:30 p.m. to 7:00 a.m.). Workers who move from shift to shift are said to be working a **rotating shift**. Shifts can rotate rapidly (e.g., movement to a different shift every week) or slowly (e.g., a change of shift every three months). Union workers can often bid on shifts based on seniority, resulting in more frequent shift changes for workers with less seniority.

© George Hall/©Corbis

Shift work is a necessity in essential services that need to be fully functional 24 hours a day, seven days a week.

Shift work Scheduling of work into temporal shifts; common in particular occupational groups such as nurses, blue-collar workers, and public safety personnel.

Circadian cycle The 24-hour physiological cycle in which humans tend to be active during hours of light and inactive during hours of darkness.

Fixed shift A particular shift that is permanently assigned to a worker.

Rotating shift A shift that changes over a certain period of time.

Generally speaking, rotating shifts are more likely to be associated with problems than fixed shifts (Parkes, 1999). This is particularly true if the direction of the rotation is from day to night to evening (as opposed to day to evening to night). Rotating shifts lead to sleep disturbances, which in turn are associated with medical (e.g., gastrointestinal) and psychological (e.g., anxiety and depression) difficulties. Rotating shifts also seem to be particularly hard on older workers (Landy, 1989).

Moreover, the biological clock is not the only potential challenge to adjusting to shift work. Monk, Folkard, and Wedderburn (1996) found that daytime social obligations such as family, community, or church activities can throw off circadian rhythms for night-shift workers. In addition, Monk and Wagner (1989) found that even when night-shift workers have begun to adjust their circadian clocks with careful attention to guidelines for sleeping during hours off, these types of daytime activities can have negative effects that far outweigh improvements resulting from gradually adjusting the biological clock.

Shift work is more common in some occupational groups than others. Nurses, blue-collar workers, and public safety personnel have higher concentrations of shift workers than professional, managerial, or white-collar groups (Smith et al., 1999). The most frequently studied of those occupations is the nursing profession. Barton (1994) examined the differences between nurses who chose to work the night shift on a permanent basis and nurses who were assigned to rotating night shifts. Permanent night-shift nurses reported significantly fewer problems with health, sleep, and social or domestic activities. This was particularly true for individual nurses who chose to work on the permanent night shift compared with nurses who chose to work on a rotating-shift schedule. The most important reasons the nurses in this study gave for choosing the permanent night shift were that night-shift work permitted them to more easily fulfill domestic responsibilities and that it paid better. Thus, for those who chose permanent night work, doing so actually improved control and scheduling of work–non-work roles. But the nurses on a rotating-shift schedule felt that their lives were disrupted every time they had to work afternoon or night shifts. It appears that permanent night-shift work provides a significant opportunity for establishing a work–life balance that is not possible with rotating shifts or, in some circumstances, day or afternoon shifts. This seems to be particularly true of dual-wage-earning families with young children. In another study of nurses, Bohle and Tilley (1998) found that the level of work–non-work conflict was one of the strongest predictors of satisfaction with shift work.

Flexible and Compressed Workweek Schedules

Shift work, regardless of whether it is fixed or rotating, defines the work schedule rigidly. In general, shift workers are expected to work eight hours per day, five days per week. But there are other scheduling variations that are not so rigid.

Flextime

Individual workers who are given discretion over the time they report to work and the time they leave work on a given day are working a **flextime** schedule. Such schedules are uncommon in manufacturing organizations because the interdependence among workers in assembly-line and continuous-process operations makes the absence of a particular worker problematic (Baltes et al., 1999). A survey of organizations in 2009 revealed that 44 percent of them permitted some form of a flexible workday (Society for Human Resources Management, 2009). In a typical flexible work schedule, every worker is expected to be at work during a "core" period (e.g., 10:00 a.m. to 3:00 p.m.) but is permitted to arrive as early as 7:00 a.m. or leave as late as 9:00 p.m. (Baltes et al., 1999). Regardless of when they arrive and leave, they are expected to be at the workplace for 40 hours a week. In some organizations, the individual is also required to be at work 8 hours each day, whereas in other organizations, the individual is still expected to be at work for 40 hours a week but is permitted to balance those hours across days. For example, the employee may be at the workplace from 7:00 a.m. to 5:00 p.m. on Monday and Tuesday, from 9:00 a.m. to 3:00 p.m. on Wednesday and Thursday, and from 10:00 a.m. to 6:00 p.m. on Friday. Even though workers have the *option* of varying the time at which they arrive and depart, some research has suggested that the reality is less dramatic than the possibilities. Ronen (1981) found that after the introduction of flextime, the average arrival time for workers was 8 minutes later than it had been before and the average departure time was 22 minutes later.

Flextime Schedule in which individual workers are given discretion over the time they report to work and the time they leave work on a given day.

The benefits of flextime to the individual worker are obvious. In addition to the psychological advantages of perceiving some control over the work schedule (e.g., not having to worry if one is stuck in traffic en route to work), there is the practical advantage of achieving a better balance between work and non-work (e.g., being able to take a child to a special school event). Most workers express satisfaction with flextime schedules.

Compressed Workweek

Compressed workweek Schedule that permits an employee to work for longer than eight hours a day and fewer than five days a week.

Another nontraditional work schedule is the **compressed workweek**, which permits an employee to work for longer than eight hours a day and fewer than five days a week. A common plan is the 4/10 plan, which permits a worker to accumulate the 40 hours of the workweek in four days. For some workers, this affords the opportunity to enjoy an ongoing series of three-day weekends. For others, it permits them to take second jobs or pursue further education on a more regular basis while still working. A 2008 national sample of companies found that 35 percent offered workers the possibility of a compressed workweek (Tang & MacDermid-Wadsworth, 2008). This type of schedule is found most commonly in manufacturing organizations (Baltes et al., 1999).

Consequences of Flextime and Compressed Workweek Schedules

Worker satisfaction with flextime and compressed workweek schedules is well documented (Landy, 1989). But are these work schedules associated with organizational outcomes such as productivity, performance, and absenteeism? The process of creating and maintaining nontraditional work schedules inevitably incurs some administrative costs, so organizations may well ask, "What's in it for us?" Baltes and colleagues (1999) conducted a meta-analysis of 39 studies on the effects of flextime (27 studies) and compressed workweeks (12 studies). The results of the analysis are useful and encouraging for both of these scheduling variations. They found that flextime was associated with higher productivity and lower absenteeism, although the impact on absenteeism was considerably greater than the effect on productivity. For the compressed workweek, they found that while absenteeism was unaffected, supervisors' ratings of performance were higher (though productivity was not).

Baltes and colleagues (1999) did some further analyses of their data and found that flextime had little effect on productivity, performance ratings, or absenteeism for professionals and managers such as accountants or sales managers. In addition, they found that, for nonprofessional and nonsales managerial workers, programs with extremely flexible hours were less effective than more conservative programs. They concluded that this was probably the result of the inability of employees in the workplace to communicate with absent employees. This would, of course, be particularly troublesome in organizations that depend heavily on teams and groups as opposed to single contributors. They also found that the effects of flextime tended to diminish after the initial period of adjustment (typically a few months); as workers became accustomed to the new scheduling, it became the norm. Remember also that one study demonstrated that *actual* arrival and departure schedules remained very much the same (Ronen, 1981).

In general, the research suggests that both compressed workweeks and flextime offer advantages, particularly in terms of worker satisfaction, without any systematic disadvantages. But the results also demonstrate that these two schedules are not the same in their organizational effects. Flextime is associated with reduced absenteeism but compressed workweeks are not. This makes sense. With a flextime schedule, the definition of being late for work changes dramatically, so a worker can show up two hours late and still be counted present. In a compressed work schedule, late is still late. Many individuals in manufacturing environments will choose to be absent (perhaps take a sick day) rather than show up late. As a result, absences are unlikely to change in this environment. In addition, flextime is associated with increased productivity, but a compressed schedule is not.

Flextime and compressed workweeks are also consistent with green trends toward reducing energy consumption and carbon emissions. During the gasoline crisis of the mid-1970s, a number of companies allowed their employees to elect a 10-hour/4-day schedule, which reduced commuting miles by 20 percent per week and made it easier to avoid commuting in the midst of rush hour. The practice continued to gain in popularity; by 2002, a survey by the Families and Work Institute (Galinsky, Bond, & Hill, 2004) found that 42 percent of U.S. employees had access to compressed workweek arrangements at least some of the time. More recently, as oil prices rose dramatically, this measure found even more favor. For example, in 2008, Utah became the first state to shift most of its workers to a mandatory four-day workweek that included closing most state offices on Fridays, thereby saving not only commuting miles but also a day's worth of costs involved with heating, air conditioning, lighting, and running office machines. Around the same time, automaker Chrysler announced plans to negotiate with union employees represented by the United Auto Workers to shift some Chrysler assembly plants to a 10/4 schedule. Other local and state governments from Fairfax, Virginia, to Detroit, Michigan—as well as many private employers—have announced similar plans. In sum, flextime and compressed workweeks are on the rise as environmentally conscious employers endeavor to save energy, reduce traffic, and increase worker satisfaction (Aratani, 2008).

Further research is needed to investigate whether these work schedules are effective across different cultures. Encouraging evidence comes from a study by Kauffeld, Jonas, and Frey (2004), who found that flexible work schedules increased adherence to company goals, lowered absence, and increased the work quality of German service workers. Along with the research cited above, this finding suggests that flextime, which is directed toward individual personal schedules, can work well in individualistic cultures. Notably, a recent study by Wickramasinghe and Jayabandu (2007) investigated flextime among software development professionals in the information technology (IT) sector in Sri Lanka, a developing country in Asia. The new flexible schedules enhanced perceptions of work–life balance and increased employee commitment and loyalty. Although the researchers did not examine links to actual job performance or other external variables, this was one of the first studies to investigate flextime in a collectivistic culture, and the authors noted that the IT sector is the only sector known to be using flextime in Sri Lanka. We look forward to additional investigations of alternative work schedules across cultures.

MODULE 10.1 SUMMARY

- Although workplace stress can be episodic, chronic stress is more common in work settings and more damaging to the body. For this reason, chronic stress is of most interest to I-O psychologists.
- Stress involves a cognitive appraisal of the situation and the resources available to handle the stressors. This appraisal often triggers a set of coping responses by the body.
- Stressors are physical or psychological demands to which an individual responds. Examples of physical stressors include excessive heat, noise, and light. Examples of psychological stressors are role ambiguity, interpersonal conflict, and lack of control.
- Reactions to stressors are called strains, which are often divided into three categories: behavioral, psychological, and physiological. Specific examples of strains that can result from chronic stress include burnout, anxiety, and physiological ailments such as high blood pressure and heart disease.
- Shift work, which can be either fixed or rotating, has an important influence on worker satisfaction and performance. The same is true for flextime and compressed workweek schedules.

KEY TERMS

fight-or-flight reaction
eustress
distress
General Adaptation Syndrome (GAS)
alarm reaction
stress hormone
resistance
exhaustion
problem-focused coping
emotion-focused coping
stressors
strains
autonomy
interpersonal conflict
role stressors
role
role ambiguity
role conflict
role overload
work–family conflict
emotional labor
surface acting
deep acting
challenge-related stressors
hindrance-related stressors
burnout
emotional exhaustion
depersonalization
low personal accomplishment
shift work
circadian cycle
fixed shift
rotating shift
flextime
compressed workweek

MODULE 10.2

Theories of Stress

Several theories of stress have been developed to organize the relationships among stressors, strains, and potential moderators of those relationships. Two theories that have received a great deal of attention are Karasek's demand–control model and French's person–environment fit model. In addition, stress models have considered individual difference variables that influence the relationship between stressors and strains. We discuss several of these characteristics and then focus on one of the most intensively studied individual difference characteristics, the Type A behavior pattern, which is included in many models of the stress process.

Demand–Control Model

Demand–control model A model suggesting that two factors are prominent in producing job stress: job demands and individual control; developed by Karasek.

Job demand Component of demand–control model that refers to the workload or intellectual requirements of the job.

Job control Component of demand–control model that refers to a combination of autonomy in the job and discretion for using different skills.

Karasek's (1979) **demand–control model** suggests that two factors are prominent in producing job stress: job demands and job control (also known as decision latitude). In this model, **job demands** are defined according to two different criteria: workload and intellectual requirements of the job. **Job control** is defined as a combination of autonomy in the job and discretion for using different skills. Karasek proposed that the combination of high work demands and low control results in high-strain jobs that result in a variety of health problems. Food service worker, waitperson, nurse's aide, assembly-line worker, and computer help-desk operator are considered high-strain jobs. Machine-paced jobs, in particular, are highlighted as having high demands and low control. In contrast, jobs characterized by high demands that also provide sufficient control create an "active" job situation that is stimulating and health promoting. Active jobs include lawyer, engineer, manager, and physician. Jobs with low control and low demands (e.g., janitor, night watchman) are labeled as "passive" jobs. Finally, jobs with high control and low demands (e.g., architect, dentist) are considered to be low-strain jobs (see Figure 10.3). In a series of surveys involving U.S. and Swedish male workers, Karasek (1979) found that the combination of low control and heavy job demands correlated positively with mental strain (i.e., depression and exhaustion) and job dissatisfaction.

More recently, Karasek and Theorell (1990) found an increased risk of illness (two to four times more likely) for individuals whose lives or jobs make high demands on them but allow little control. Thus, an individual who has a demanding work schedule or environment and does

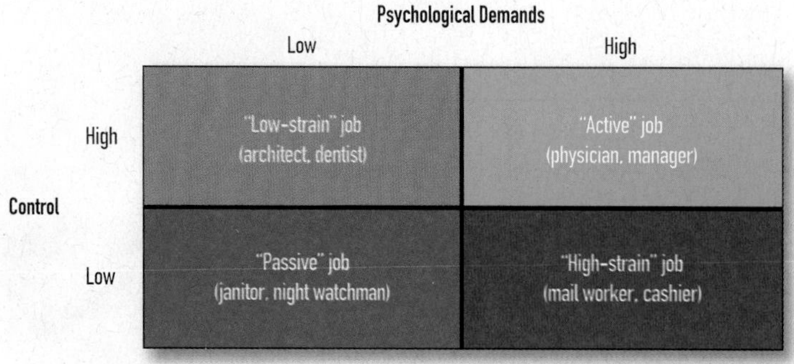

FIGURE 10.3 Demand–Control Model

SOURCE: Adapted from Karasek, R. A. (1979). Job demands, job decision latitude, and mental strain: Implications for job redesign. *Administrative Science Quarterly, 24*, 285–308. © 1979 by Johnson Graduate School of Management, Cornell University. Reprinted by permission of The Administrative Science Quarterly.

not have much decision latitude or control will have an increased risk for stress-related illnesses, both physiological and psychological. In contrast, individuals in active jobs that have high demands but high control maintain good health and have high job satisfaction. Karasek and Theorell (1990) noted that individuals in active jobs appear to participate actively in a variety of leisure activities as well, despite their high work demands. This finding is another example of the benefits of developing or designing jobs that allow workers to have control over decisions, resources, or the skills that they can use.

Ganster, Fox, and Dwyer (2001) tested the demand–control model in a sample of 105 full-time nurses. They found that nurses with the lowest perceptions of personal control and highest workload demands were ill more often and incurred the highest cumulative health care costs over the ensuing five-year period. Thus, jobs that have high demands and low control are costly to both individuals and the organizations for which they work. In a study of 800 Swedish workers, Grönlund (2007) found that women in jobs with high demands and high control do not experience more work–family conflict than men. Thus, the key seems to be whether or not there are sufficient resources to address demands, not the absolute level of demands. The demand–control model was also tested in a sample in China (Xie, 1996). The results of this study were consistent with findings obtained in Western cultures, suggesting that this model may apply in non-Western cultures as well.

Person–Environment Fit Model

The person–environment (P–E) fit model (French, Caplan, & Harrison, 1982) hypothesizes that the fit between a person and the environment determines the amount of stress that person perceives. This is compatible with the open-systems view of the organization that we mentioned earlier in the chapter. The environment makes demands and the person responds. A good person–environment fit occurs when a person's skills and abilities match the requirements of the job and work environment. For example, an introvert with a PhD in literature would be likely to have a good P–E fit with the job of university librarian, while an extraverted MBA might have a good P–E fit with the job of sales manager. The amount of stress a worker feels is influenced by perceptions of the demands made by the environment and by perceptions of his or her capability to deal with those demands. Using this model, French and colleagues (1982) found that a poor fit between a person and the environment was frequently associated with increased strains. Alternatively, employees whose skills and abilities fit well with the work environment reported less stress and fewer strains (Edwards, 1996). Shaw and Gupta (2004) found that the harmful effects of misfit are particularly severe for poorly performing employees, who suffer greater depression and physical health problems than high-performing employees.

Karasek (1979) did not formally emphasize perception in the demand–control model. In contrast, the P–E fit approach focuses explicitly on the perceptions of individuals concerning their skills and abilities relative to the demands of the work environment. In addition, unlike the demand–control model, the P–E fit approach considers external influences such as social support from family and work sources. For example, Edwards and Rothbard (1999) found that the well-being of employees varied according to their perceptions of work and family experiences. The results of this study indicate that interventions to manage stress should consider the fit between employees and both their work and family environments, which is consistent with the research we discussed above on work–family conflict. In particular, if fit is bad in both the family and the work environment, the cumulative stress is likely to lead to low job performance and high risk of health problems.

Early research did not always specify what "environment" was referred to in the P–E fit model. More recently, research has more clearly differentiated between person–job fit and person–organization fit (Lauver & Kristof-Brown, 2001). **Person–job (P–J) fit** refers to the extent to which the skills, abilities, and interests of an individual are compatible with the demands of the particular job. Alternatively, **person–organization (P–O) fit** refers to whether the values of an employee are consistent with the values held by most others in the organization. Researchers have found that perceptions of poor person–organization fit were associated with greater levels of stress, job dissatisfaction, and intentions to quit one's job (Lovelace & Rosen, 1996). Similarly, Saks and Ashforth (1997) found that favorable employee perceptions of person–organization fit correlated positively with intentions to remain with the organization and actual turnover. In addition, favorable employee perceptions of person–job fit correlated positively with job satisfaction and organizational commitment but negatively with stress.

Person–job (P–J) fit Extent to which the skills, abilities, and interests of an individual are compatible with the demands of the job.

Person–organization (P–O) fit Extent to which the values of an employee are consistent with the values held by most others in the organization.

Given that different types of fit have an influence on a variety of work outcomes, organizations should strive to ensure that employees fit well in their jobs and have the skills necessary to complete their job tasks. In fact, fit is often increased through recruitment and selection processes that help applicants and those doing the hiring assess the likelihood that candidates will fit well in the job and in the organization (Schneider, 1987).

The P–E fit model suggests mechanisms by which individuals can protect themselves from the stress that accompanies a mismatch between the person and the environment. One of these protective mechanisms is social support. For example, employees who have seemingly impossible deadlines might seek informational and emotional support from co-workers. By reducing their experience of stress in this way, employees might be able to focus better and come closer to meeting their deadlines than if they were overwhelmed and suffering from strains. Overall, the P–E fit model allows us to examine work stress by looking at the interaction between the person and stressors in the work environment. This approach specifically acknowledges that stress can influence individuals differently depending on their preferences, values, and abilities (Edwards, 1996).

Individual Differences in Resistance to Stress

As you have probably observed when you have been part of a group in a stressful situation, not everyone responds to stress in the same way. I-O psychologists have studied several individual characteristics as potential moderators of stressor–strain relationships. A moderator is a variable that affects the direction or strength of the association between two other variables. For example, if stressors lead to strains for individuals with low self-esteem but not for those with high self-esteem, then self-esteem would be a moderator of the stressor–strain relationship (see Figure 10.4). If moderators reduce strains for only certain types of individuals, they are said to have an indirect effect on the reduction of strains. Individual difference characteristics that have received the most attention as moderators of the stressor–strain relationship are locus of control, hardiness, self-esteem, and the Type A behavior pattern.

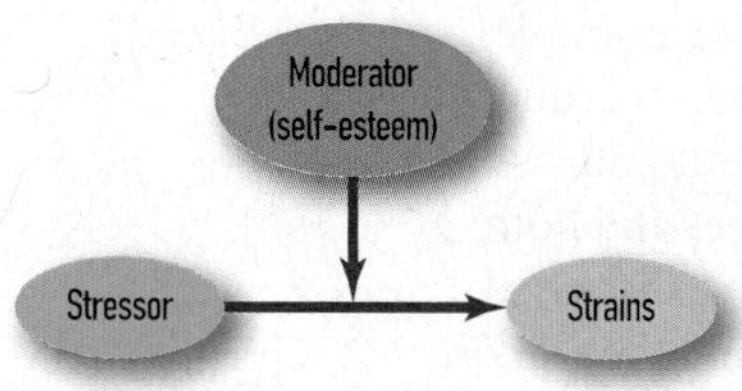

FIGURE 10.4 Example of a Moderator of the Stressor–Strain Relationship

Locus of control (LOC) Construct that refers to the belief of individuals that what happens to them is under their control (internal LOC) or beyond their control (external LOC).

Hardiness A set of personality characteristics that provide resistance to stress; hardy individuals feel in control of their lives, have a sense of commitment to their family and their work goals and values, and see unexpected change as a challenge.

Locus of control (LOC), as we saw in Chapters 8 and 9, is a construct that refers to whether individuals believe that what happens to them is under their control or beyond it (Rotter, 1966). Individuals with an internal locus of control believe that outcomes are a result of their own personal effort and ability, whereas persons with an external locus of control believe that outcomes are determined largely by other people, luck, or fate. Many elite professional athletes are confident—sometimes overconfident—that success lies completely in their hands (i.e., they are "internals"). In team sports, they like to be thought of as the "go-to" person. Several studies have indicated that internals experience lower strains than do externals exposed to the same stressors. Researchers have proposed that this is because internals believe they can control a stressful situation to achieve their goals. Overall, evidence indicates that having an internal LOC moderates the relationship between stressors and strains (Horner, 1996; Kahn & Byosiere, 1992).

Hardiness is a set of personality characteristics that provide resistance to stress (Kobasa, 1979; Maddi, 2005). Specifically, individuals described as having a "hardy personality" possess three characteristics:

1. They feel they are in *control* of their lives.
2. They feel a sense of *commitment* to their family and their work goals and values.
3. They see unexpected change as a *challenge* rather than as an obstacle.

Cohen and Edwards (1989) observed that hardy individuals actively adopt problem-focused and support-seeking strategies. Kobasa, Maddi, and Kahn (1982) found that hardy individuals had fewer physiological reactions to stressors, reported fewer illnesses, and had higher levels of general well-being than those who were not hardy. Among executives and lawyers who were under a great deal of stress, those with hardy personalities were found to have significantly fewer strains than those who were not characterized as hardy (Maddi & Kobasa, 1984). In a study of over 1,100 U.S. Army Special Forces candidates, Bartone, Roland, Picano, and Williams (2008) found that course graduates were significantly higher in hardiness than candidates who did not pass the course. The researchers concluded that hardiness is an important characteristic associated with stress resistance and successful performance in demanding occupations such as military Special Forces. A key component of hardiness is transformational coping, which involves actively changing perceptions of a stressful event by viewing it as a challenge that can be overcome. For example, hardy students facing an important and stressful exam might cope by interpreting their exam as an opportunity to show their knowledge, thereby exerting control through preparation and good study habits (Quick et al., 1997).

Self-esteem A sense of positive self-worth that is considered to be an important resource for coping.

Type A behavior pattern (TABP) Set of characteristics exhibited by individuals who are engaged in a chronic struggle to obtain an unlimited number of poorly defined things from their environment in the shortest period of time; subcomponents include hostility, achievement strivings, impatience/irritability, and time urgency.

Self-esteem, or a positive sense of self-worth, is considered an important resource for coping. Individuals with high self-esteem are more likely to adopt more effective coping strategies in the face of stress than individuals with low self-esteem (Ganster & Schaubroeck, 1995). Thus, when faced with the same environmental stressors, individuals with low self-esteem will experience more strains compared to those with high self-esteem. Overall, research generally indicates that self-esteem is a moderator of the stress–strain relationship (Cooper et al., 2001).

The Type A Behavior Pattern

A potential moderator of the stress–strain relationship that has been intensively studied is the **Type A behavior pattern (TABP)**, which was first identified in the late 1950s by two cardiologists, Meyer Friedman and Ray Rosenman (1959). Fifteen years later, Friedman and Rosenman wrote *Type A Behavior and Your Heart* (1974), in which they described the Type A behavior pattern as a set of characteristics exhibited by "individuals who are engaged in a relatively chronic struggle to obtain an unlimited number of poorly defined things from their environment in the shortest period of time and, if necessary, against the opposing effects of other things or persons in this same environment" (p. 67).

The Type A behavior pattern is also known as the **coronary-prone personality** because of its proposed links to coronary heart disease and heart attacks. Individuals who exhibit this behavior pattern (known as Type As) are characterized by ambitiousness, impatience, easily aroused hostility, and time urgency. A core characteristic of TABP is an incessant struggle to achieve more and more in less and less time (Friedman & Rosenman, 1974). In fact, descriptions of Type As who are overly obsessed with saving time are common. For example, Type A men have been known to use two electric razors simultaneously (one for each side of the face) in order to shave as quickly as possible (Bluedorn, 2002). Generally, Type As seem to thrive on "life in the fast lane" because they focus on quickly doing things that result in occupational and material success. In contrast, Type Bs are often described as relaxed, patient, and easygoing.

Coronary-prone personality Alternative name given to Type A behavior pattern (TABP) because of its links to coronary heart disease and heart attacks.

Sapolsky (1998) described how Friedman and Rosenman missed an opportunity to identify some of the typical characteristics of Type As in the early 1950s. In the waiting room outside Friedman and Rosenman's cardiology office, the lining of the chairs was worn down so much that the upholstery needed to be replaced frequently. The upholsterer noticed this first and asked, "What is wrong with your patients? People don't wear chairs out this way!" Only years later did Friedman and Rosenman begin their formal work on the Type A behavior pattern and thus realize that their heart patients had a consistent pattern of behavior, including nervous energy and fidgeting, that was related to heart disease.

Although the Type A behavior pattern was initially studied because of its association with health problems, it also appears to be associated with positive outcomes such as high work performance and career success. An important question is whether there is evidence that these positive outcomes come at the cost of higher strains and subsequent health problems. Specifically, researchers were interested in whether Type As respond to stressful situations with greater physiological arousal and thus suffer greater strains than Type Bs. Accordingly, many studies attempted to link the TABP to increased physiological arousal and to the development of coronary heart disease. However, these efforts were slowed by the use of imprecise, global TABP measures that attempted to assess several different TABP subcomponents (Edwards, Baglioni, & Cooper, 1990). This led researchers to focus on identifying specific subcomponents of the TABP that were most predictive of coronary heart disease. Subsequent studies indicated that **hostility** is the primary TABP subcomponent associated with increased secretion of stress hormones as well as increased risk of coronary heart disease and other long-term, harmful health outcomes (Krantz & McCeney, 2002). Thus, Type As who exhibit hostility pay a price for their accomplishments in terms of increasing their likelihood of suffering from a variety of long-term health problems.

Hostility Type A behavior pattern subcomponent associated with increased secretion of stress hormones and increased risk of coronary heart disease and other long-term, harmful health outcomes.

Achievement Striving and Impatience/Irritability

Although researchers had identified hostility as the TABP subcomponent that is related to long-term health outcomes, investigators continued to examine other TABP subcomponents in their attempts to predict work and short-term health outcomes in Type As. Two TABP subcomponents that have received attention are achievement striving

Achievement striving (AS) Subcomponent of the Type A behavior pattern that involves the tendency to be active and to work hard in achieving one's goals.

Impatience/irritability (II) Subcomponent of the Type A behavior pattern that reflects intolerance and frustration resulting from being slowed down.

and impatience/irritability (Spence, Helmreich, & Pred, 1987). **Achievement striving (AS)** is the tendency to be active and to work hard in achieving one's goals, whereas **impatience/irritability (II)** reflects the intolerance and frustration that result from being slowed down.

The AS dimension, which overlaps with the Big Five dimension of conscientiousness, is positively correlated with academic performance, sales performance, and job satisfaction (Bluen, Barling, & Burns, 1990). The II dimension is associated with health problems such as insomnia, headaches, poor digestion, and respiratory difficulties (Barling & Boswell, 1995). These studies indicate that AS and II are independent from each other and that these TABP subcomponents can be used to differentially predict performance and health outcomes.

Time Urgency

Time urgency Subcomponent of the Type A behavior pattern that refers to the feeling of being pressured by inadequate time.

An additional TABP subcomponent that appears to be related to important work and health problems is **time urgency**, which refers to the feeling of being pressured by inadequate time. Time-urgent individuals check their watches repeatedly, even when they are not under the pressure of deadlines, and they are concerned with saving relatively small amounts of time (often measured in minutes or seconds). Time-urgent individuals always seem to know what time it is, even when they are not wearing a watch, and they often try to do too many things in the available time. Research suggests that time urgency has multiple dimensions, including time awareness, eating behavior, nervous energy, list making, scheduling, speech patterns, and deadline control. These time-urgency dimensions are relatively independent, which means that individuals can be high on some dimensions but relatively lower on others (Conte, Landy, & Mathieu, 1995; Conte, Mathieu, & Landy, 1998). For example, workers may eat very quickly during a brief lunch break, but they may not focus much on making lists or closely following schedules. Alternatively, some task-oriented individuals may work quickly and focus closely on schedules and deadlines, but they may not speak quickly or exhibit nervous energy. Research also indicates that certain time-urgency dimensions (e.g., list making, scheduling) are related to work outcomes, whereas other time-urgency dimensions (e.g., eating behavior, nervous energy, speech patterns) are related to health outcomes.

In a sample of employees working in a multinational company in Malaysia and Pakistan, Jamal (2007) found that global Type A, time pressure, and competitiveness were significantly related to job satisfaction and health problems in both countries. Given that Malaysians and Pakistanis differ greatly in culture from the U.S. and European samples in which the majority of Type A research has been conducted, these findings are promising in showing similar relationships across such different samples. On the other hand, these findings may simply point to the Westernization of Asian cultures. Future research will need to address the issue of the true "transportability" of findings across cultures as opposed to cultures becoming more Western.

Conte, Schwenneker, Dew, and Romano (2001) found that the time-urgency dimension of deadline control was significantly related to work pace—that is, individuals who were focused on deadlines worked faster than those who were not focused on them. This finding is likely to be useful in organizations and industries in which a fast work pace is crucial. For example, in the computer industry there are immense pressures for efficient and timely development of new products. Time-urgent individuals who have experience working under time constraints may be able to withstand a higher level of time pressure when the work situation requires it (Freedman & Edwards, 1988).

Overall, specific TABP subcomponents do a better job of predicting particular criteria than a global Type A measure that combines a variety of different subcomponents. Thus, researchers and practitioners concerned about health and performance will have more success using TABP subcomponents to predict health and performance outcomes.

BOX 10.1 THE INCREASINGLY TIME-URGENT NATURE OF WORK AND LIFE

The importance of using time efficiently is certainly not a new idea. In 1757 Benjamin Franklin wrote that "time is money." In 1877 the English journalist W. R. Greg echoed the sentiment: "Beyond doubt, the most salient characteristic of life in this latter half of the 19th century is its speed." Arthur Schopenhauer, a 19th-century German philosopher, noted that "buying books would be a good thing if one could also buy the time to read them in." His quote suggests that people, when they buy a book, may be attempting to create an island of tranquility and control in a sea of stress. A more contemporary view of how many people think of time is given by comedian Stephen Wright, who boasts, "I have a microwave fireplace. You can lie in front of it all night in only eight minutes."

At the beginning of the 21st century, life revolves increasingly around the clock, particularly in Western cultures. In our culture, businesses cater to the time-conscious cravings of individuals. We have instant burgers, instant breakfasts, instant coffee, instant photos, and instant replays, to name a few (Gleick, 1999). Time-saving devices such as computers and smartphones are increasingly becoming indispensable parts of our work and personal lives. Most of us probably know people who would love a microwave fireplace—people who are so obsessed with saving time that they rush through leisure activities that are supposed to be enjoyed at a relaxed pace. The popularity of instant products and time-saving devices indicates that people today, like Ben Franklin, view their time as a scarce and valuable commodity.

Researchers have attempted to determine how people became so obsessed with time. For example, Wright (1988) identified critical experiences that were related to the obsession with time in his Type A heart patients. These early experiences involved (1) a high need to achieve, (2) success and therefore reinforcement for such efforts, and (3) exposure to timed activities that provided a personal blueprint for achieving by the more efficient use of time and by being constantly active. According to Wright, these critical experiences result in people developing a "shotgun-like" effort to achieve as much as possible in as little time as possible. Many individuals use this approach in their jobs because they consider speed and efficiency to be signs of success. This approach is often carried over to personal activities as well.

Questions

1. In which jobs or occupations is the rapid completion of work a particularly high priority?
2. Can you identify jobs in which there are no time pressures? Is identifying such jobs more or less difficult than it was 10 years ago? Why?

The desire for instant communication has resulted in cell phone use in even the most remote locations on the planet.

MODULE 10.2 SUMMARY

- Two theories of stress that have received a great deal of attention are Karasek's demand–control model and French's person–environment fit model.
- Karasek's demand–control model proposes two factors in job stress: job demands and job control (also known as decision latitude). High work demands coupled with low control results in high-strain jobs that result in a variety of health problems.
- French's person–environment (P–E) fit model proposes that the fit between a person and the environment determines the amount of stress that a person perceives.
- Several individual difference characteristics that are potential moderators of stressor–strain relationships include locus of control, hardiness, self-esteem, and the Type A behavior pattern.

KEY TERMS

demand–control model
job demand
job control
person–job (P–J) fit
person–organization (P–O) fit
locus of control (LOC)
hardiness
self-esteem
Type A behavior pattern (TABP)
coronary-prone personality
hostility
achievement striving (AS)
impatience/irritability (II)
time urgency

MODULE 10.3

Reducing and Managing Stress

In 1990, stress was listed for the first time as one of the top 10 occupational health risks in the United States. As a result, concerns about stress at work became much more prominent in public and government discussions of health (Sauter, Murphy, & Hurrell, 1990). These concerns led to the development of the field of **occupational health psychology**, which involves the application of psychology to improving the quality of work life and to protecting and promoting the safety, health, and well-being of workers. The *Handbook of Occupational Health Psychology* provides a comprehensive source for a variety of occupational health psychology issues, including work–family balance, work design, and stress management interventions (Quick & Tetrick, 2010).

Occupational health psychology Area of psychology that involves the application of psychology to improving the quality of work life and to protecting and promoting the safety, health, and well-being of workers.

Occupational health psychologists often divide their approaches to stress reduction and management into three major categories: primary, secondary, and tertiary interventions (Quick et al., 1997). Table 10.4 provides a framework for stress management interventions. We will discuss these three types of strategies as well as recent reviews of their effectiveness.

BOX 10.2 QUOTES ON STRESS AND HEALTH

- "The greatest mistake is trying to be more agreeable than you can be."—Walter Bagehot, British economist and writer (1826–1877)
- "If you are distressed by anything external, the pain is not due to the thing itself, but to your estimate of it; and this you have the power to revoke at any moment."—Marcus Aurelius Antoninus, Roman emperor (A.D. 121–180)
- "Adopting the right attitude can convert a negative stress into a positive one."—Dr. Hans Selye (1907–1982), known as the "father of stress"
- "The best thinking is done in solitude. The worst is done in turmoil."—Thomas Edison, U.S. inventor (1847–1931)

TABLE 10.4 **A Framework for Stress Management Interventions**

Primary Prevention: Stressor-Directed

Scope: Preventative—reduce the number and/or intensity of stressors.

Target: Alter work environments, technologies, or organizational structures.

Underlying assumption: Most effective approach to stress management is to remove stressors.

Examples: Job redesign, cognitive restructuring.

Secondary Interventions: Response-Directed

Scope: Preventative/reactive—modify individuals' responses to stressors.

Target: Individual.

Underlying assumption: May not be able to remove or reduce stressors, so best to focus on individuals' reactions to these stressors.

Examples: Relaxation training, biofeedback, stress management training, physical fitness, nutrition.

Tertiary Interventions: Symptom-Directed

Scope: Treatment—minimize the damaging consequences of stressors by helping individuals cope more effectively with these consequences.

Target: Individual.

Underlying assumption: Focus is on treatment of problems once they have occurred.

Examples: Employee assistance programs, medical care.

SOURCE: Adapted from Cooper, C. L., Dewe, P. J., & O'Driscoll, M. P. (2001). *Organizational stress: A review and critique of theory, research, and applications*. Thousand Oaks, CA: Sage. © 2001. Reproduced with permission of Sage Publications Inc Books.

Primary Prevention Strategies

Primary prevention strategy Stress prevention strategy concerned with modifying or eliminating stressors in the work environment.

Primary prevention strategies are concerned with modifying or eliminating stressors in the work environment and therefore said to be stressor-directed (Cartwright & Cooper, 2005). Primary interventions are the most proactive approaches to stress management (Cooper et al., 2001). Many primary prevention strategies give workers increased control over their job and work environment, which directly lowers stressors and increases employee satisfaction and well-being.

Primary prevention approaches include redesigning the task or work environment, encouraging participative management, developing clearer role descriptions, and changing negative thoughts through cognitive restructuring. Another primary prevention strategy involves providing flexible work schedules, which can be seen in recent trends toward flextime, shorter workweeks, and job sharing. In Module 10.1, we discussed different coping styles or strategies. Primary prevention approaches are aligned with problem-focused coping strategies, which are directed at managing or altering the source of stress (Lazarus, 2000). We next discuss examples of primary prevention approaches commonly used in organizations.

Work and Job Design

Work and jobs can be designed or redesigned to reduce such stressors as noise, interruptions, time pressure, role ambiguity, and the number of hours worked (Sparks, Cooper, Fried, & Shirom, 1997). In addition, jobs can be redesigned to increase autonomy on the job and worker participation in decision making. Decades ago, restaurant owners decided to reduce the stress on short-order cooks by requiring waitpersons to clip their orders to a small, circular, revolving order stand. The cooks could then spin the stand around, see what orders were pending, and decide which ones to pull off first. This principle was extended to auto manufacturing by Saab and Volvo. Automobile bodies circled work teams on an oval track, and the teams decided when to pull a body off the track into a workstation for assembly and paint operations. Another example of redesigning work is the common queuing process that is found at many banks, ticket counters, and other service centers. Customers stand in one line and are not permitted to approach a service window until their number is flashed or an available agent is identified by an electronic screen. This process increases the customer service agent's control over how quickly customers are served and thereby reduces the agent's stress. Such changes can help workers feel that their work is more meaningful and that they have control over work outcomes. This in turn leads to higher motivation and satisfaction as well as lower stress at work (Hackman & Oldham, 1980).

Cognitive Restructuring

Several of the approaches that we have discussed, including the person–environment fit model and the Type A behavior pattern, highlight the role of perceptions in the stress process. **Cognitive restructuring** interventions focus on changing perceptions and thought processes that lead to stress. These approaches reduce stress by changing an individual's perception of the work environment or his or her capacities to meet the demands of the environment. Cognitive restructuring approaches encourage individuals to change negative thoughts to more positive ones (Quick et al., 1997). For example, a worker who thinks "I can't handle this heavy workload" might be encouraged to think instead: "This workload is a challenge that I can handle if I break it down into manageable parts" or "I won't be considered a complete failure if I don't push very hard to finish this task today."

Cognitive restructuring Type of stress intervention that focuses on changing perceptions and thought processes that lead to stress; reduces stress by changing the individual's perception of, or capacity to meet the demands of, the work environment.

Secondary Prevention Strategies

Secondary prevention strategies involve modifying responses to inevitable demands or stressors; thus, they are said to be response-directed. Because secondary prevention addresses the experience of stress rather than the stress or stressors, its role is often one of damage control. Thus, this type of intervention is often described as the "Band-Aid" approach (Cooper & Cartwright, 2001). Secondary prevention approaches are aligned with emotion-focused coping strategies, which seek to reduce the emotional response to the stressor and can involve avoiding, minimizing, and distancing oneself from the stressor (Lazarus, 2000). For example, emotion-focused coping might be used to reduce the stress experienced in a job that requires emotional labor.

Secondary prevention strategy Stress prevention strategy that involves modifying responses to inevitable demands or stressors.

Secondary prevention strategies that require no special training (but might be formally encouraged through an employer-sponsored program) include lifestyle choices such as physical fitness, healthy eating, and weight control, along with reductions in smoking and caffeine consumption. Skills training programs in such areas as negotiation and conflict resolution are another form of secondary intervention. In addition, secondary stress management methods include relaxation techniques, biofeedback, and providing or encouraging social support at work. Many approaches use combinations of the above methods.

Secondary prevention can be proactive or reactive. For example, Cooper and colleagues (2001) noted that training in conflict resolution skills can be used to reduce interpersonal conflict and its effects after it has occurred. Alternatively, such training can be used proactively to prevent interpersonal conflict from developing. Similarly, individuals can be proactive in exercising and maintaining a healthy diet, which can reduce or moderate future stress.

© Chris Machian/The New York Times/Redux Pictures

Do "walkstations" reduce stress by allowing office workers to stay physically fit while working long hours?

Stress Management Training

Programs involving stress management training are very popular with both employers and employees. Cooper and Cartwright (2001) noted that the continued demand for stress management programs and the increasing stress levels reported in the literature are indicative of the acceptance by organizations that stress is an inherent and enduring feature of the work environment. Programs in **stress management training** are useful for helping employees deal with those stressors that are difficult to remove or change. They often include a variety of secondary prevention techniques and may even include some primary techniques. For example, many stress management programs are described as cognitive-behavioral skills training programs.

Stress management training A program useful for helping employees deal with workplace stressors that are difficult to remove or change.

Stress inoculation Common type of stress management training that usually combines primary prevention and secondary prevention strategies.

Cognitive-Behavioral Skills Training

A variety of techniques are designed to help workers modify the appraisal processes that determine how stressful they perceive a situation to be and to develop behavioral skills for managing stressors. The most common type of cognitive-behavioral skills training is **stress inoculation,** which usually consists of (1) an educational component (learning about how a person has responded to past stressful experiences); (2) rehearsal (learning various coping skills such as problem solving, time management, relaxation, and cognitive coping); and (3) application (practicing those skills under simulated conditions) (L. R. Murphy, 1996). Thus, in many cases, these approaches are a combination of primary (i.e., to reduce stressors by means of cognitive restructuring) and secondary (i.e., to manage or cope with symptoms of stress through behavioral skills training) prevention strategies.

Jones and colleagues (1988) developed an organization-wide stress management program that was used with employees of several hospitals. The program included video modules that enhanced the understanding of stress and provided information about how to develop and improve coping skills, health behaviors, and relaxation routines. In a longitudinal investigation that evaluated the impact of this stress management program, these researchers found that one result was a significant drop in the average number of monthly medication errors by doctors and nurses. In an additional two-year longitudinal investigation, they found that 22 hospitals that implemented the same organization-wide stress management program had significantly fewer medical malpractice claims compared with a matched sample of 22 hospitals that did not participate. This study showed that well-conducted psychological research efforts can decrease malpractice claims through stress management interventions.

Relaxation and Biofeedback Techniques

Progressive muscle relaxation Stress management technique to relax the muscles, thereby helping to progressively relax the entire body.

Relaxation techniques include progressive muscle relaxation and deep-breathing exercises. **Progressive muscle relaxation** involves starting at the top or bottom of one's body, tightening one set of muscles at a time for five to seven seconds, and then letting those muscles relax. Individuals can work through each major muscle group and thus progressively relax the entire body. These relaxation techniques are effective in reducing arousal and anxiety (L. R. Murphy, 1996).

Biofeedback is a stress management technique that involves teaching individuals to control certain body functions, such as heart rate, blood pressure, and even skin temperature, by responding to feedback about their body from an electronic instrument (Quick et al., 1997). One simple and inexpensive biofeedback device is a skin-sensitive "biodot" that monitors stress levels and physiological changes according to color changes. The dot darkens after individuals discuss a stressful event and lightens when they feel more relaxed (Ulmer & Schwartzburd, 1996). Thus, this device shows individuals that stress—and relaxation, for that matter—leads to measurable changes in the body and that careful monitoring of the body can reduce anxiety and arousal.

Biofeedback Stress management technique that teaches individuals to control certain body functions, such as heart rate, blood pressure, and even skin temperature, by responding to feedback from an electronic instrument.

Social Support

Social support is the comfort, assistance, or information an individual receives through formal or informal contacts with individuals or groups. Social support has been widely investigated as a way to reduce stress and strain at work. House (1981) identified four different kinds of social support:

Social support The comfort, assistance, or information an individual receives through formal or informal contacts with individuals or groups.

1. *Instrumental support.* Direct help, often of a practical nature; for example, a friend encourages a co-worker to slow down by suggesting joint walks during the lunch hour.
2. *Emotional support.* Interest in, understanding of, caring for, and sympathy with a person's difficulties; this type of support is often provided by a therapist or a family member.
3. *Informational support.* Information to help a person solve a problem; this type of support is often supplied by a health care professional. In addition, an increasing number of websites offer useful information.
4. *Appraisal support.* Feedback about a person's functioning that enhances his or her self-esteem; this often comes from a close friend, a therapist, family members, or other members of a support group.

Researchers have given considerable attention to the possibility that social support moderates or reduces health problems by protecting individuals from the negative effects of work stressors. The **buffer** or **moderator hypothesis** proposes that the negative effects of work stressors can be buffered or moderated by social support (Cohen & Wills, 1985). Evidence is mixed on the buffering hypothesis, which could be due to the failure of researchers to emphasize the match between stressors and support. That is, buffering should work when there is a reasonable match between the stressors and the available social support. A longitudinal study of 90 blue-collar metalworkers found evidence for the buffering hypothesis in reducing anxiety and other strains when social support was matched directly to a social stressor such as conflict with one's supervisor (Frese, 1999). Social support at work may be particularly important as a moderator of the stress–strain relationship today because traditional societal structures such as the extended family are less prevalent than they once were (Quick et al., 1997). For example, in 21st-century America, many adult children live hundreds of miles away from their parents or siblings. They may see family members infrequently, usually over holiday periods that carry their own stress and strain.

Buffer or moderator hypothesis Hypothesis that social support moderates or reduces health problems by protecting individuals from the negative effects of work stressors.

Employers can help build effective social support systems at work. For example, formal mentoring programs, reward and recognition systems, and newcomer socialization programs can make work environments more supportive. Allen, McManus, and Russell (1999) found evidence for the important role that more experienced peers can play in mentoring newcomers and in enhancing socialization. In turn, they found a negative correlation between socialization and work stress, indicating that formal peer relationships can be critical in reducing stress and subsequent strains. Finally, the supportive relationships formed in team building have been shown to improve performance and reduce stress (Klein, Diaz-Granados, et al., 2009).

Tertiary Prevention Strategies

Tertiary prevention strategy Stress prevention strategy focused on healing the negative effects of stressors.

Employee assistance program (EAP) Counseling provided by an organization to deal with workplace stress, alcohol or drug difficulties, and problems stemming from outside the job.

Tertiary prevention strategies are symptom-directed, that is, focused on healing the negative effects of stressors. Tertiary interventions include employee assistance programs and the use of medical care, individual psychotherapy, and career counseling (Quick et al., 1997).

Employee assistance programs (EAPs), originally developed by organizations to address alcohol and drug problems, were subsequently broadened to include stress management interventions. In most organizations, EAPs involve some form of counseling to deal with work stress, alcohol or drug difficulties, and problems outside the job (e.g., family problems, behavioral and emotional difficulties). Employee assistance programs can be provided by the human resources department within an organization, or they can be provided by external consultants or vendors. If an organization is to have a successful EAP, its management must express support for the program, make the program accessible to employees, and educate and train employees on its use (Milne, Blum, & Roman, 1994). Organizations must ensure that confidentiality is maintained and that use of an EAP does not harm job security or advancement. These suggestions are particularly important because unhealthy work climates and distrust of EAPs often prevent employees from seeking help for alcohol or drug abuse problems. For example, police officers often avoid in-house EAPs because they are uncertain of the confidentiality assurances and fear that they will be stigmatized by commanding officers and colleagues. Even to be seen talking with an EAP coordinator is "dangerous." Integrating positive messages about the EAP into different types of training programs may be effective in improving the use of EAPs by skeptical employees (Bennett & Lehman, 2001).

Although EAPs are not often systematically evaluated by the organizations using them, the few evaluations that have been done indicate that EAPs are successful. Cooper and Sadri (1991) found improvements in the mental health and self-esteem of employees participating in EAPs. In addition, Cooper and Cartwright (1994) found that EAPs can be very cost effective for organizations in terms of reducing absences, accidents, and health care costs. Nevertheless, even though focusing on the treatment of strains may be an effective short-term strategy, the approach is essentially reactive and recuperative rather than proactive and preventative (Cooper et al., 2001). Because EAPs focus on dealing with the long-term outcomes of stress, they should certainly not be the only approach that organizations utilize in the stress prevention and management process.

Summary of Stress Intervention Strategies

Several studies have evaluated a variety of stress management interventions. L. R. Murphy (1996) conducted a comprehensive review of the effects of worksite stress management interventions on a variety of health and work outcomes (e.g., blood pressure, anxiety, headaches, and job satisfaction). The stress management programs included in this review were progressive muscle relaxation, meditation, biofeedback, cognitive-behavioral skills, and combinations of these techniques. Meditation produced the most consistent results across outcome measures, but it was infrequently used in organizations. Relaxation and cognitive-behavioral techniques were found to be quite successful. Overall, the study indicated that using a combination of techniques (e.g., muscle relaxation and cognitive-behavioral skills) was more effective across outcome measures than using any single technique. Two meta-analyses found general support for the benefits of interventions for work-related stress (Richardson & Rothstein, 2008; van der Klink, Blonk, Schene, & van Dijk, 2001). They both found that cognitive-behavioral approaches worked best in reducing stress, but relaxation techniques were also successful, though less effective than cognitive-behavioral approaches. Richardson and Rothstein (2008) concluded that "cognitive-behavioral interventions encourage individuals to take charge of their negative thoughts, feelings, and resulting behaviors . . . and thus promote the development of proactive responses to stress" (p. 88). More generally, cognitive-behavioral approaches to work and non-work seem to be most effective if the behavior can be well described, whereas relaxation techniques do not address specific events or stimuli, so they might be more suited to broader experiences of stress that may be less tied to a specific cause. Overall, these studies show reason for optimism about stress management interventions, particularly when a combination of techniques is used. In addition, successful stress management interventions must accurately identify the stressors causing strains and then actively determine ways to reduce those stressors (Briner & Reynolds, 1999). Employees should also participate in the process of identifying stressors and implementing the various interventions designed to reduce stress and strains.

Primary and secondary stress prevention strategies are generally preferred because they take a more active approach to removing and reducing stressors (Quick et al., 1997). Tertiary interventions can play a useful role in stress management, but their effectiveness is limited because they fail to address the sources of stress itself. Thus, identifying and recognizing stressors and taking steps to remove or reduce them through job redesign, flexible work schedules, or other primary prevention strategies should receive the greatest attention in organizations. Indeed, the limited research that has examined primary-level interventions has shown that they yield consistently positive and beneficial long-term effects (Cooper & Cartwright, 2001). Similarly, the National Institute for Occupational Safety and Health (NIOSH) urges occupational health psychology professionals to give special attention to the primary prevention of organizational risk factors for stress, illness, and injury at work.

Future Work Trends and Challenges to Stress and Stress Management

The workforce of tomorrow will be more culturally and ethnically diverse, and will also include larger numbers of older workers and women, than the workforce of previous decades. For this reason, it is important for I-O psychologists to determine whether the stressors that predict coronary heart disease in male Caucasians (by far the most commonly studied group) are the same as those in other populations (Keita & Hurrell, 1994; Quick et al., 1997). For example, coronary heart disease is the leading killer of African Americans and Mexican Americans as well as Caucasians, and there is evidence that genetics and nutrition play a role in the development of coronary heart disease for these ethnic groups (American Heart Association, 2002). However, the large body of research indicating that work stress also plays a role in coronary heart disease has largely ignored the potential influence of ethnicity on the relationship between stressors and strains (Ford, 1985; Kahn & Byosiere, 1992). Gutierres, Saenz, and Green (1994) suggested that one underlying assumption in stress research is that employees of different ethnic backgrounds and genders respond similarly to work stressors. However, little data are available to support this assumption, and few researchers have investigated the moderators (e.g., individual differences, social support) of the stress–strain relationship in minority populations.

Similarly, the globalization of the economy presents new challenges in understanding and preventing stress in the workplace. Liu, Spector, and Shi (2007) investigated stress–strain relationships in American and Chinese workers. They found some culture-specific job stressors, such as the fact that mistakes at work were more stressful for Chinese than for American workers, a finding that may be consistent with the importance of saving face in Chinese culture. American workers, on the other hand, reported more interpersonal conflict than Chinese workers. Peterson and colleagues (1995) found that Western countries had significantly higher role ambiguity than non-Western countries. This raises the possibility that individuals from higher-stress Western countries working in non-Western cultures may "inject" stress into their organizations at great cost to both individual employees and the organization itself.

Modifications intended to reduce stress, such as increases in flexible employment (e.g., flex-time, part-time work), as well as changing organizational structures and work processes, are likely to lead to new stressors that are not yet well understood. The increasing role of technology in the workplace can create stress for employees in a variety of ways. As we discussed in Chapter 5, electronic performance monitoring is increasingly being used in a wide array of jobs. Such monitoring can be stressful to employees (e.g., customer service representatives, call-center operators), who often feel that they have little downtime when they are not actually being evaluated (Coovert, Thompson, & Craiger, 2005). Technology can also increase physical stressors such as work pace, noise, and workload, which were discussed in Module 10.1. Furthermore, the pace of technological change often means that workers find themselves in jobs and organizations that are rapidly changing, which can lead to additional stressors (Rafferty & Griffin, 2006). We discuss the many challenges of organizational change in Chapter 14.

Several additional influences are predicted to be stressful in future years, including global competition, downsizing, elder and child care, and increased teamwork (DeFrank & Ivancevich, 1998). There is little doubt that opportunities to experience stress at work are increasing rapidly. It is important to study and understand how these changes in the nature of work will influence the health and well-being of workers and their families. These new influences will clearly present challenges to I-O psychologists and occupational health psychologists in the years to come.

MODULE 10.3 SUMMARY

- Occupational health psychologists often divide their approaches to stress prevention into three major categories: primary, secondary, and tertiary interventions.
- Primary prevention strategies aim to modify or eliminate stressors at work, and they are generally preferred over other interventions because they take an active approach. Primary prevention strategies include redesigning the work environment, modifying Type A thought patterns, and providing flexible work schedules.
- Secondary prevention strategies involve modifying responses to inevitable stressors. They include physical fitness, healthy eating, weight control, smoking and caffeine reduction, skills training programs, relaxation techniques, biofeedback, and social support at work.
- Tertiary prevention strategies focus on healing the negative effects of stressors. They include employee assistance programs (EAPs) and the use of medical care, individual psychotherapy, and career counseling.

KEY TERMS

occupational health psychology
primary prevention strategy
cognitive restructuring
secondary prevention strategy
stress management training
stress inoculation
progressive muscle relaxation
biofeedback
social support
buffer or moderator hypothesis
tertiary prevention strategy
employee assistance program (EAP)

MODULE 10.4

Violence at Work

A man shot four co-workers to death at an aircraft parts plant Friday, then fired at police from a stolen company van during a high-speed chase that ended with him killing himself. . . . The gunman opened fire during a meeting, targeting particular co-workers. "He used to get in little squabbles with them because he didn't get his merchandise in time to ship it out. He was kind of rigid, a lone wolf. He was afraid of losing his job."

(Coyne, T. (2002). Employee kills four colleagues in Indiana. *Rocky Mountain News*, March 23, p. 11A. Copyright © 2002 The Associated Press. Reprinted by permission.)

In the past, the workplace was seen as a protected environment, one in which workers could feel safe. That is no longer the case (Barling, 1996). Violence is becoming more common in the workplace and therefore more important than ever to I-O psychologists (Bulatao & Vandenbos, 1996). Work-related violence falls into two different categories. The first deals with violent actions carried out by a nonemployee against an employee. Examples include armed robberies of convenience stores or gas stations in which a clerk is threatened, and often assaulted, by a robber. Similarly, workers in certain occupations, such as corrections and police officers, deal with violence as an essential function of their jobs. The second category of violence is perpetrated by employees and directed toward fellow employees. It is the second form of violence that we will consider. Several excellent reviews cover both types of violence (Kinney, 1995a,b; Vandenbos & Bulatao, 1996).

There have been many hypotheses about why we have seen the workplace become more violent since the early 1990s (Elliott & Jarrett, 1994; Mack, Shannon, Quick, & Quick, 1998), including the following:

- The surge of layoffs, mergers, and acquisitions has radically increased stress at the workplace.
- As a result of the large number of Baby Boomers in the workforce, fewer jobs are available as people strive to move up in the organization.
- Increasingly multicultural workplaces make it more likely that prejudices and biases will enter into worker interactions.
- There is a greater tendency for workers to abuse drugs and alcohol, thus lowering inhibitions that prevent violent behavior.
- In attempts to become leaner, organizations have eliminated layers of management, resulting in reduced opportunities for communication with employees about frustrating situations.

Stress is often associated with violent actions by individuals. To the extent that work is stressful, then, it should not come as a total shock to see violent behavior at work, such as the incident at the aircraft parts plant described above. Although to date there has been little careful and systematic research on workplace violence, a great deal of descriptive, anecdotal, and theoretical work exists on the topic.

Stress and Workplace Violence

© Liaison/Getty Images, Inc.

An on-the-job confrontation or stressful event is often a precursor of workplace violence.

Understanding why certain individuals engage in workplace violence requires consideration of both their personal characteristics and stressful aspects of their work environment. Kinney (1995a, b) noted that stressful factors correlated with workplace violence include being passed over for an expected promotion, financial problems, estranged or strained relationships with co-workers, and a perception of being targeted by management.

Contrary to the common perception that low self-esteem correlates with workplace violence, Baumeister, Smart, and Boden (1996) found that workplace violence is most commonly a result of a *high* self-esteem that is disputed by some person or circumstance (e.g., negative feedback or derogatory remarks). Stressors such as interpersonal conflict can lead to workplace violence when they result in wounded pride or "ego threats" to those with high self-esteem. Thus, managers and supervisors should be particularly careful to avoid disrespect or verbal abuse during stressful times (e.g., downsizing, performance reviews) that might interact with subordinates' high self-esteem and lead to workplace violence. Many perpetrators of workplace violence have just been passed over for a promotion, have received a negative evaluation, or have been fired. In fact, the last words spoken to three employees of an insurance company in Florida by a disgruntled former co-worker before he killed them were, "This is what you get for firing me" (Duncan, 1995).

Feldman and Johnson (1994) analyzed data from 60 incidents of workplace violence. They found that 68 percent of the perpetrators of violent acts had received some type of psychiatric diagnosis before the incident. About one-third were diagnosed with depression, and about half were diagnosed with either a personality disorder or substance abuse disorder. Overall, they concluded that most perpetrators of workplace violence had (1) personality disorders that made them respond poorly to stress, (2) conflicted relationships at work, or (3) inappropriate and angry reactions to perceived threats to their self-esteem.

Stress is clearly considered to be one of the causes of workplace violence. To compound the problem, recent work also suggests that workplace violence is a cause of stress. In particular, individuals who are victims of or witnesses to workplace violence report lower organizational commitment as well as high job stress and subsequent strains (Mack et al., 1998; van Emmerick, Euwema, & Bakker, 2007). For all of the above reasons, it is advisable that every organization have policies and plans in place to reduce work stress and workplace violence.

Levels of Violence

Shootings, such as the incident described at the beginning of this module, tend to grab the headlines. But most violent acts in the workplace are far less dramatic. They include such acts as verbal threats, insults, and bullying. Table 10.5 presents a three-level description of the most common forms of workplace violence. Kinney (1995a,b) suggested that managerial and supervisory responses such as counseling, discipline, and referral to EAPs are often the most appropriate reactions to level 1 behaviors. More formal responses, often including psychological assessment and law enforcement involvement, might be required for level 2, and certainly for level 3, behaviors.

TABLE 10.5 **Incidents or Behaviors Associated with Levels 1, 2, and 3 Violence and Responses**

Level 1 Violence
• Refuses to cooperate with immediate supervisor
• Spreads rumors and gossip to harm others
• Consistently argues with co-workers
• Displays belligerence toward customers or clients
• Constantly swears at others
• Makes inappropriate sexual comments
Available Responses
• Discipline or referral to EAP
Level 2 Violence
• Argues increasingly with customers, vendors, co-workers, and management
• Refuses to obey company policies and procedures
• Sabotages or destroys equipment or property of employer or co-worker
• Verbalizes wishes to hurt co-workers or management
• Sends sexual or violent notes to co-workers or management
• Sees self as victimized by management ("me versus them")
Level 3 Violence
Frequent displays of intense anger resulting in:
• Recurrent physical fights
• Destruction of property
• Recurrent suicide threats
• Use of weapons to harm others
• Murder, rape, or arson
Available Responses
• Psychological assessment, discipline, or law enforcement intervention

SOURCE: Kinney (1995a,b); National Safe Workplace Institute (1989).

The Experiential Sequence of Violence

1. Individual suffers trauma, which creates extreme tension or anxiety; may be a single major event (e.g., job loss or divorce) or cumulative minor events.
2. Individual thinks that problems are unsolvable.
3. Individual projects all responsibility onto the situation.
4. Individual's frame of reference becomes increasingly egocentric.
5. Self-preservation and self-protection gradually become sole objectives.
6. Violent act is perceived as only way out.
7. Violent act is attempted or committed.

FIGURE 10.5 Routine Experiential Sequence of Violence Perpetrators
SOURCE: Based on Kinney (1995a,b).

Kinney (1995a,b) outlined a common thought process that precedes the commission of a violent act in the workplace. The sequence is presented in Figure 10.5. The key steps in the sequence include an "event" in the individual's life (e.g., a poor performance appraisal), a belief that a "problem" cannot be resolved, and a perceived threat to the individual's self-esteem or well-being. We will consider the issue of self-esteem in greater detail shortly.

The "Typical" Violent Worker

With the exception of the worker who is suffering from a serious mental disorder (e.g., one who hears voices telling him to kill his supervisor), most cases of workplace violence involve some feeling of being treated unfairly; the perpetrator has some real or imagined grievance against the organization or a person in the organization. In addition, experts in workplace violence have assembled a laundry list of possible characteristics of a perpetrator. Any given perpetrator is not likely to have *all* of the characteristics listed below but will certainly have some of them (Douglas & Martinko, 2001; Paul & Townsend, 1998). Similarly, just because an individual has many, or even all, of these characteristics, it does not necessarily mean that he or she will engage in violence.

- Does not participate in organizational events
- Has few outside interests
- Has worked for the company for some time
- Has a history of violence
- Is a white male between 25 and 50 years of age
- Has lost or is worried about losing his or her job
- Has a history of conflicts with co-workers, supervisors, or both
- Has previous exposure to aggressive cultures
- Has difficulty accepting authority
- Commonly violates company policies and rules
- Works in a company or work group with an authoritarian management style
- Abuses alcohol

This list emphasizes the characteristics of the individual violent employee, but several of these individual factors (e.g., job loss, authoritarian management style) indicate that organizational characteristics may also be associated with workplace violence. These characteristics would include high levels of job-related stress (e.g., role conflict and role ambiguity); a continuing threat of layoff; few opportunities for communication between management and employees; and lack of a formal or informal appeal process for questioning such management actions as performance appraisals, compensation decisions, and transfers (Martinko & Zellars, 1998; Paul & Townsend, 1998). It would also seem logical to include the absence of group work or teamwork, since environments without them usually provide less opportunity for communication among workers. Poor communication between a worker and a supervisor or between co-workers seems to be central to many instances of workplace violence.

Theories of Workplace Violence

I-O psychologists commonly examine workplace violence using one of two theoretical approaches. The first is a variation on a traditional approach to all aggressive behavior, regardless of where it occurs. Its premise is that the individual worker has been frustrated—prevented from achieving some important goal or outcome—and this frustration results in aggression directed toward a co-worker or supervisor. The second approach is more specific to work situations and invokes the concept of justice (see Chapter 11). We will briefly consider these two approaches.

Frustration–Aggression Hypothesis

Over seventy years ago, Dollard, Doob, Miller, Mowrer, and Sears (1939) proposed a simple hypothesis: Frustration leads to aggression. They cited laboratory and field data to support that proposition. The initial **frustration–aggression hypothesis** proved to be far too broad. It became clear that aggression was only one possible response to frustration and that not everyone responded to frustration with aggression. Furthermore, it became clear that aggression has many different roots, only one of which is represented by frustration. To put it simply, not all frustrated individuals act aggressively, and not all aggressive acts are a result of frustration.

Frustration–aggression hypothesis Hypothesis that frustration leads to aggression; ultimately found to be too broad—aggression is only one possible response to frustration and not everyone responds to frustration with aggression.

Fox and Spector (1999) discussed the frustration–aggression hypothesis as it related to work behavior, particularly counterproductive behavior, which we discussed in Chapter 4. They defined frustrating events as "situational constraints in the immediate work situation that block individuals from achieving valued work goals or attaining effective performance" (p. 917). The modern view of the frustration–aggression connection is that frustration leads to a stress reaction and that the individual expends energy to relieve this stress, often in the form of destructive or counterproductive behavior.

The key to whether or not an individual engages in destructive behavior is thought to be the extent to which he or she believes that the obstacle to goal attainment—and thus the frustration—can be eliminated through constructive behavior. If the individual does not believe that constructive behavior will eliminate the frustration, then aggressive action may be taken instead (Spector & Fox, 2005). And this belief, of course, depends to some extent on the prior history of the individual. If constructive behavior has not worked before, the individual is less likely to try it again. Spector's (2000) model of this process is presented in Figure 10.6.

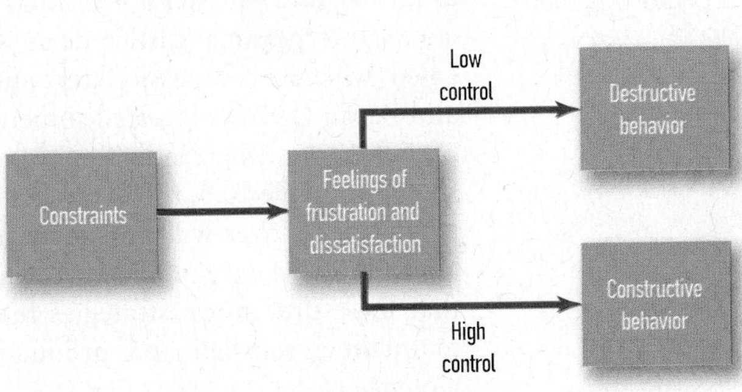

FIGURE 10.6 Constructive and Destructive Employee Behavior as a Result of Frustration and Employee Control

SOURCE: Spector, P. E. (2000). *Industrial and organizational psychology: Research and practice* (2nd ed.), p. 242. New York: John Wiley. Copyright © 2000. Reprinted with permission of John Wiley & Sons, Inc.

Fox and Spector (1999) identified several personality variables and beliefs that seem to intervene in the process by which frustration becomes aggression. The first of these variables is locus of control. As you will recall from Module 10.2, individuals with an external locus of control believe that events are controlled by forces outside of themselves, while internals believe that they are in control of their fate. Fox and Spector (1999) found that when confronted with obstacles, externals were more likely than internals to report unpleasant emotions and to engage in aggressive action. They also found that levels of anger and anxiety affected the likelihood that a worker would engage in counterproductive behaviors. Anger is a commonly observed emotion that appears to accompany violence—domestic or workplace. But anger is very often the by-product of anxiety or fear. This is particularly true in the workplace. When violence breaks out, fear of something (e.g., loss of a job, losing face in front of fellow workers) is often at the root of the violence.

As mentioned above, Baumeister and colleagues (1996) found that high self-esteem was positively associated with violence. Individuals and groups who believe in their own superiority are those most likely to engage in aggressive and violent actions. This positive self-image is often unrealistically positive, and this is where the problem arises. When individuals receive information that challenges this positive self-appraisal, they reject it and react against the source of this conflicting information, often violently. Thus, a realistic performance evaluation with some negative information can trigger a violent response in an individual with an unrealistically high opinion of his or her work. Similarly, an individual who believes that he or she is central to the success of an organization will find it hard to accept or understand a layoff notice. Two of the most common events that occur in advance of workplace violence are the loss of a job and a negative performance review, both of which challenge the individual's self-image as an effective and valuable employee.

Finally, assessment techniques are being developed and refined to predict aggressive behaviors (Berry, Sackett, & Tobares, 2010; Bing et al., 2007). Recall that in Chapter 4 we described a conditional reasoning test to assess unconscious biases in reasoning that are used to justify aggressive acts, accompanied by an example from a study of conditional reasoning among basketball players. Those players with the most aggressive tendencies were also those most likely to argue with officials and commit "hard" fouls on opponents. The workplace provides ample opportunities to commit "hard fouls" against co-workers or subordinates.

The Justice Hypothesis

Justice hypothesis of workplace violence Hypothesis that some violent acts can be understood as reactions by an employee to perceived injustice.

Several researchers have argued compellingly that at least some violent acts can be understood as reactions against perceived injustice by an employee (Bies & Tripp, 2005; Folger & Baron, 1996). This is the conceptual basis for the **justice hypothesis of workplace violence**. You will see in Chapter 11 that workers generally evaluate events in the workplace according to three types of justice. Procedural justice relates to issues of due process and whether all individuals are treated equally. Distributive justice relates to actual outcomes, such as layoffs, and whether a particular individual believes that he or she deserved the outcome. Interpersonal justice deals with the manner by which decisions are communicated, whether compassionately and respectfully or callously and demeaningly. Folger and Baron (1996) suggested some ways that an organization can reduce the likelihood of violent acts when individuals are laid off or given negative performance reviews. As shown in Table 10.6, the issues associated with each aspect of justice are different. The prudent employer will pursue ways to create justice perceptions in each of the three areas. Even when workplace violence is not the issue, organizations should be aware that these prevention strategies represent best practices; the same initiatives that can maintain a satisfied and productive workforce can also reduce the possibility of violence.

Greenberg and Barling (1999) examined the role of procedural justice in employee aggression among nonfaculty employees of a Canadian university. Their results not only confirm the hypotheses of Folger and Baron regarding the role of justice perceptions but also extend them in interesting ways. They found that perceptions of procedural injustice were associated with aggression against supervisors. They also found that alcohol consumption

TABLE 10.6 Distributive, Procedural, and Interpersonal Justice Actions to Prevent Workplace Aggression

DISTRIBUTIVE JUSTICE
Layoffs and firings
Do not raise chief executive officer's pay when downsizing
Try other financial alternatives to layoffs
If firing by performance ratings, check their validity
Performance appraisal
Use job-related, relevant criteria
Develop criteria based on job analysis
PROCEDURAL JUSTICE
Layoffs and firings
Use employee voice or input where possible
Provide details on severance
Follow suggestions on avoiding bias
Apply guidelines consistently
Provide timely feedback
Provide adequate explanations
Performance appraisal
Clarify standards and expectations in advance
Solicit employee's own opinion about performance (e.g., self-appraisal)
Explain and discuss ratings (explore discrepancies)
INTERPERSONAL JUSTICE
Layoffs and firings
Notify in a timely manner
Explain with sincere concern
Express sincere remorse
Avoid distancing and aloofness
Treat with dignity and respect
Performance appraisal
Same as for layoffs and firings

SOURCE: Folger, R., & Baron, R. A. (1996). Violence and hostility at work: A model of reactions to perceived injustice. In G. R. Vandenbos & E. Q. Bulatao (Eds.), *Violence on the job: Identifying risks and developing solutions* (pp. 51–86). Washington, DC: American Psychological Association. © 1996 by the American Psychological Association. Reprinted by permission of the publisher.

interacted with these feelings of injustice. If procedures were considered fair, then alcohol consumption was unrelated to aggression. On the other hand, if procedures were considered unfair, then alcohol consumption increased the likelihood of aggression toward a supervisor. (Virtually every examination of workplace violence has identified alcohol consumption as a substantial risk factor.) Greenberg and Barling (1999) also found that increased workplace surveillance was associated with a greater likelihood of aggressive acts directed toward supervisors. This last finding, however, is hard to interpret. In some organizations, increased surveillance may be the result of a history of counterproductive behavior. Thus, it is difficult to tell if surveillance is a cause of aggressive behavior or part of a vicious circle in which it is as much an effect as a cause.

Although job loss seems to be involved in many acts of workplace violence and aggression, Catalano, Novaco, and McConnell (1997) reported some intriguing findings about the effects of widespread job loss. They designed a study to examine the relationship between the reported number of layoffs on a weekly basis in San Francisco for a one-year period and civil commitments for posing a danger to others during the same period. This type of civil commitment is a court order that permits an individual whom mental health professionals deem likely to commit an act of violence against another to be held in custody for up to 72 hours. If, after 72 hours, the detainee is still perceived as a threat to another person, he or she may be held for a longer period after a hearing.

Catalano and colleagues discovered that as layoffs increased, so did violent and threatening behavior (as defined by increases in civil commitments) but *only up to a point.* As layoffs continued to increase, violent and threatening behavior began to diminish. The researchers explained this phenomenon as one of protecting one's job. As jobs became more scarce, workers were more likely to inhibit aggressive acts that might jeopardize those jobs. This suggests a dilemma for employers. In an attempt to reduce the potential for violence by laying off as few workers as possible, an organization may very well be *increasing* the potential. Thus, it might be more harmful for an organization to implement a series of small layoffs rather than one large layoff.

A way out of this dilemma may be in the manner by which layoffs are handled. Both Folger and Baron (1996) and Greenberg and Barling (1999) suggested that justice perceptions are crucial to preventing violent employee responses. With appropriate justice mechanisms in place, it is possible that studies such as those by Catalano and colleagues would find little or no relationship between layoffs and the threat of violence. Some of these mechanisms might include applying layoff policies consistently (Hemingway & Conte, 2003), treating those to be laid off with dignity and respect—for example, informing them in person rather than by e-mail or written memo (Greenberg, 1994)—and providing clear explanations of the criteria used to make layoff decisions.

A Special Type of Violence: Bullying

The topic of bullying, particularly as experienced by children and teenagers in school, has achieved some prominence in recent years. Sadly, the prominence has come from violent outbursts such as the killings at Columbine High School in Littleton, Colorado, in the spring of 1999. Two students who had been bullied by fellow students brought weapons to school and killed 12 fellow students and a teacher before committing suicide. But bullying is not confined to schools; it is just as likely to occur at the workplace. In light of what appears to be an increase in workplace violence in the United States, an understanding of the phenomenon of bullying should prove very useful in reducing such violence.

Strangely, the topic of bullying at work has received very little attention from American I-O psychologists (Rayner & Keashly, 2005). Most research on bullying has been carried out by European scholars. The *European Journal of Work and Organizational Psychology* published a special issue on the topic in December 2001, summarizing what is known about the phenomenon of bullying. In addition, a text by Einarson, Hoel, Zapf, and Cooper (2002) covered much of the same ground, but in somewhat greater detail. Furthermore, a recent book by two Australian researchers (Caponecchia & Wyatt, 2011) focused on evidence-based approaches to preventing workplace bullying. Since many who have worked in the United States have experienced at least one encounter with a workplace bully, the likely reason for the lack of interest among American scholars is cultural. In other cultures, power and its use often have negative connotations, particularly in countries characterized as collectivist. The United States, in contrast, is an individualist country where each worker might be expected to fend for him- or herself, without recourse to group support for protection from an abusive co-worker or supervisor.

Despite the relative lack of U.S. data on this topic, the increasing body of knowledge from non-U.S. workplaces provides us with some foundation for introducing the topic. We feel that this is an important area of research for I-O psychologists and, as a result, we will use the European experience as a way of introducing the topic.

Bullying has been defined as subjecting a victim to

Bullying Harassing, offending, socially excluding, or assigning humiliating tasks to a person of subordinate status repeatedly and over a long period of time.

> being harassed, offended, socially excluded, [having] to carry out humiliating tasks; [the victim] is in an inferior position. To call something bullying, it must occur repeatedly (e.g., at least once per week) and over a long time (e.g., at least six months). It is not bullying if it is a single event. Also, it is not bullying if two equally strong parties are in conflict. (Zapf, D., & Gross, C. (2001). Conflict escalation and coping with workplace bullying: A replication and extension. *European Journal of Work and Organizational Psychology, 10*(4), 497–522. Published by permission of Taylor & Francis Ltd., http://www.informaworld.com. Permission conveyed through Copyright Clearance Center, Inc.)

Most surveys that have examined the prevalence of bullying have concluded that it is widespread. Mikkelsen and Einarson (2001) reported rates as high as 25 percent in the workforce. Hoel, Cooper, and Faragher (2001) reported that when the period of time covered is five years, the rate rises to almost 50 percent in Great Britain. Zapf and Gross (2001) noted that bullying has seriously affected the health of between 1 and 4 percent of the victims. Even though the definition above cites a minimum period of 6 months before a situation can be called bullying, Leymann (1996) found that in Sweden the more common duration is 15 months; in Germany, Zapf (1999) found episodes lasting as long as 46 months. Note that the definition adopted by the European researchers for bullying requires weekly encounters over 6 months or more. If the definition were less stringent (e.g., one incident in the last 3 months, or three times in the last year), it is safe to say that the majority of workers would report either having observed bullying or been the victim of a bully.

In many European countries, the legal system makes it more difficult to terminate an employee than it is in the United States; at the same time, it provides less protection for the rights of individual workers. Because U.S. workers can more easily be terminated for bullying, and may very well sue the company if they are the victim of a bully, the duration, though not the severity, of bullying is likely to be less in the United States than in Europe. Hubert and Veldhoven (2001) and Salin (2001) reported that the prevalence of bullying is just as great in professional and white-collar positions as it is among blue-collar workers.

From an organizational point of view, bullying can be seen as the escalation of conflict (Leymann, 1996; Zapf & Gross, 2001). The steps in this escalation are as follows:

1. *A critical incident.* There is a work-related dispute between two individuals.
2. *Bullying and stigmatizing.* The person in the inferior position is stigmatized and subjected to increasingly aggressive acts by the bully. The intent of the bully is to damage the victim in some way.
3. *Organizational intervention.* The organization steps in and makes the dispute "official."
4. *Expulsion.* The victim (not the bully!), by now stigmatized and possibly acting in ineffective and traumatized ways, is separated from the organization.

In most instances, the victim of bullying is rendered powerless by the stigmatization. Once the bully has developed a head of steam, the victim can take very few actions that might be considered effective. In a large sample of Norwegian nurses, Eriksen and Einarsen (2004) found that male nurses, who represent a small gender minority in their profession, are exposed to bullying at work at twice the rate of their female colleagues. Their findings support the notion that being "different" in the workplace (in this case, being part of the gender minority) is a risk factor for bullying at work. Since males tend to engage in bullying more than females, it appears that the most likely bullying victim will be a male who works in a stereotypically female occupation and reports to a male boss.

The actual bullying behavior has also been broken down into three phases (Einarsen, 2000). First, the bully may spread rumors about the victim or engage in subtle acts of sabotage to make the victim look less effective. Next, the victim is singled out for public humiliation and ridicule. Finally, the victim may be directly threatened or characterized as emotionally unstable. Even though the victim might attempt to behave rationally at an early stage in the process by discussing the conflict or defusing it with humor or a concession, the bully will have none of it and increases his or her aggressive behavior. The victim eventually sees that the single goal of the bully is to drive him or her out of the organization (Zapf, 1999).

In a study of victims who successfully coped with bullying, Knorz and Zapf (1996) found that successful coping was invariably the result of a third-party intervention, rather than any behavior pattern of the victim; in most cases the intervention was some form of physical separation of the bully and the victim (e.g., the transfer of the bully or the victim to a different department or work unit). By far the single most common piece of advice given by victims to those experiencing bullying is to leave the organization (Zapf & Gross, 2001). If the third party confronts the bully in an attempt to restore order without taking administrative action such as transfer or termination, the most likely effect is simply an increase in the bullying behavior. The bully now sees the victim as having "declared war" and feels justified in increasing his or her aggression.

The critical finding in bullying research is that victims are often in a position of noncontrol. There is little they can do to improve their position other than to leave the work unit. Bullying scenarios require strong and immediate action by an organization. First, managers and supervisors need to be sensitive to the presence of bullying. Then they need to take steps to separate the victim and the bully from each other, by either terminating the bully or physically separating the bully and victim through internal transfer. Allowing the parties to work it out themselves is likely to end in failure, and possibly even tragedy. As noted by Hoel and colleagues (2001), the irony is that the first level of intervention is usually a manager who, at least in Great Britain, is more often than not the bully!

One cannot ignore the parallels between the phenomenon of bullying as described above and the phenomenon of sexual harassment as considered in Chapter 7. Not all sexual harassment can be thought of as a special case of bullying; harassment is a more complex phenomenon. Nevertheless, the tactics of the bully are often the tactics of the harasser. Similarly, the worker who is the target of a harasser often experiences the same sense of powerlessness as the more generic victim of a bully. Finally, the harasser is often a manager, as is the bully (Zellars, Tepper, & Duffy, 2002).

There is some indication that American researchers are indeed becoming interested in bullying. Lutgen-Sandvik, Tracy, and Alberts (2007) investigated the prevalence of bullying in a sample of American workers. They found that approximately 25 percent of respondents had been bullied at work. They also found that witnesses to bullying reported elevated stress and lower job satisfaction. Fox and Stallworth (2005) examined general bullying behavior as well as racial/ethnic bullying of minority group members. They sampled full-time U.S. employees from the following associations: the National Association of African-American Human Resources Professionals, the Hispanic MBA Association, the Loyola University Chicago Alumni Association (MBA graduates), and the National Black MBA Association in Illinois. The minority groups reported higher levels of racial/ethnic bullying than Caucasian employees did, but only Hispanics reported higher levels of general bullying than Caucasians. In addition, across the entire sample, bullied employees reported negative emotions (e.g., frequent worrying) resulting from bullying and counterproductive behaviors (e.g., arriving late, leaving early) in response to bullying. Zellars and colleagues (2002) examined the effect of bullying behavior by the military supervisors of an Air National Guard unit and found that supervisor bullying reduced the willingness of subordinates to engage in organizational citizenship behaviors.

Bullying at work is also being increasingly discussed in the American media (Parker-Pope, 2008), as evidenced by a popular book on bullying at work (Sutton, 2007) and polls indicating the severity of bullying (Zogby International, 2007). The Zogby poll, conducted in conjunction with the Workplace Bullying Institute, included over 7,000 online interviews and came to some stark conclusions: (1) Workplace bullying is an epidemic that involves 49 percent of workers when witnesses are included; (2) when made aware of bullying, 62 percent of employers ignored it; and (3) the majority of victims (77 percent) have to leave their jobs in order to stop the bullying.

American I-O psychology has a tradition of concentrating on the "bottom line." As we saw in Chapter 9, new work on emotions by I-O researchers is a departure from that tradition. European I-O psychologists study the phenomenon of bullying because it is morally wrong and has dreadful consequences on the well-being of the worker. European researchers (e.g., Leymann, 1990; Zapf & Einarsen, 2005) have also taken the lead on a related topic called **mobbing**, which is similar to bullying but is a group phenomenon that involves multiple bullies and a single victim. We hope that American researchers will follow that lead and increase their study of abusive work environments because they are wrong, not simply because they are negatively correlated with organizational efficiency.

Mobbing Situation in which a target is selected and bullied by a group of people rather than an individual.

What Can We Conclude about Workplace Violence?

Several themes emerge from the study of workplace violence. The first is that employees need avenues for communicating concerns about the fairness of organizational decisions that affect them. Second, managers need to be sensitive to signs of potential trouble in the form of individual worker behaviors. Perceived justice—distributive, procedural, and interpersonal—seems to be central to many, if not most, instances of workplace violence. Violent acts are often precipitated by an organizational action such as a layoff, termination, or negative performance review. Whenever an action of this kind is contemplated, it would be wise to analyze the action from the point of view of the person or persons likely to be affected by that action, with a particular emphasis on justice issues. At this point, there are no data that directly connect bullying in the workplace with worker violence. Nevertheless, the anecdotal and logical connections seem apparent. In extreme situations in a school environment, students who are bullied by fellow students appear to resort to violence to achieve some sense of control. One explanation of the tragic killings at Columbine is that the two protagonists had been the target of relentless bullying by fellow students. To be sure, it takes a unique and pathological personality to react in such a destructive manner to bullying, but given the increasing interest in violence at the workplace, it would be valuable to examine the role of bullying.

MODULE 10.4 SUMMARY

- Stress is recognized as a cause of workplace violence and, conversely, workplace violence can be a cause of stress. It is advisable for every organization to have policies and plans in place to reduce work stress and workplace violence.
- Most violent acts in the workplace stop well short of life-threatening acts, but violence in the workplace does seem to be on the increase.
- Problems in the workplace, accompanied by a belief that the problem cannot be resolved and that it threatens the self-esteem of an individual, often lead to an act of violence by that individual.
- One theory of workplace violence is the frustration–aggression hypothesis, which proposes that work-related events lead to stress, which in turn leads to aggressive and counterproductive acts. An alternative theory suggests that violent workplace behavior results from perceived injustice by a worker.
- Bullying is a special type of workplace violence, one that is widespread. The bully is often in a position of superiority to the victim. One of the few effective resolutions to bullying is to transfer either the victim or the bully to another work group or department.

KEY TERMS

frustration–aggression hypothesis

justice hypothesis of workplace violence

bullying

mobbing

11 Fairness and Diversity in the Workplace

© Shelley Dennis/iStockphoto

MODULE 11.1

Fairness

The Concept of Justice

Russell Cropanzano is an I-O psychologist who has done a great deal of research on the topic of fairness in the workplace. He begins one book with a true story about a small town in southern Colorado (Cropanzano, 2001). It is worth summarizing because it vividly captures the concept we will be discussing in this chapter. It makes the point that justice and the perception of fairness arouse such strong emotions that people are willing to die for them.

Ludlow, Colorado, is a ghost town today, with a small cemetery and plaque commemorating an event that took place nearly a century ago, in 1915. The Colorado Fuel and Iron Company was a major employer in that part of the state. It was owned by John D. Rockefeller and was typical of companies in the mining industry of the time. Colorado Fuel and Iron dominated the lives of the 9,000 miners and their families. In the decade preceding the event, miners had protested against mine owners in many parts of the country. The Irish miners in the anthracite region of Pennsylvania banded together to form a group called the Molly McGuires. This group was responsible for the destruction of mines and the death and injury of mine owners and foremen. In Idaho, miners were accused of killing the former governor of the state, Frank Steunenberg, for siding with mine owners. He died when he opened a booby-trapped mailbox as his daughter watched. An interesting sidelight of the trial of those accused of his murder was the attendance of Hugo Munsterberg, one of the first I-O psychologists, who was asked by a magazine to use his new lie detection technique to determine which side was telling the truth (Landy, 1992). He concluded that a prosecution witness was telling the truth and the defendant was not.

But back to Ludlow. The miners moved their families out of the company-owned housing and set up a tent city on the outskirts of town. This was the opening act that would signal a strike against the mining company. The working conditions and pay of a miner at that time were terrible. Cropanzano (2001) described the issues that led to the strike:

> [This was] an era when being a miner was little better than a paid death sentence . . . workers wanted better pay and working conditions. The Ludlow demands included a 10 percent pay increase, an eight-hour workday, and enforcement of state mining laws. But there were also concerns with personal dignity. The miners wanted to choose where they lived, select their own doctors, and spend their money in stores of their choosing. And perhaps, most fundamentally, they wanted the recognition of their union, the United Mine Workers, as a

> vehicle for ensuring that miners had a place at the decision-making table. (Cropanzano, R. (2001). *Justice in the workplace: From theory to practice (Vol. 2)*. Mahwah, NJ: Lawrence Erlbaum Associates.

The strike had stretched out for 15 months and the Colorado National Guard was brought in to restore "order." As the soldiers faced off against the miners, an inadvertent shot was fired, setting off a battle that lasted an entire day. The soldiers killed miners, women, and children, then looted and burned the tents. It became known as the Ludlow massacre.

As the Ludlow massacre demonstrated, people are often willing to place themselves in harm's way for the sake of justice.

Cropanzano believes that the miners were motivated to endure hardships, and even the possibility of death, by a desire for justice. Not money, not power—simply justice. The miners were denied three types of justice. First, they were denied a fair outcome. The mine owners got rich while the miners starved. Second, they were denied the opportunity to influence any important outcomes through joint decision making. The owners decided everything. Finally, the miners were treated as if they were beneath contempt, not even worth thinking about. These three types of justice have been labeled, respectively, *distributive, procedural,* and *interactional* justice (Colquitt, Conlon, Wesson, Porter, & Ng, 2001). These three types of justice play as significant a role in the workplace today as they did at Ludlow in 1915.

Consider the circumstances surrounding a layoff (Shaw, Wild, & Colquitt, 2003). Certain employees were instructed to appear at a local hotel at a specific time. When they arrived, they were greeted by managers who were complete strangers.

> The bosses stuck to their script. The economy was bad. We can't afford to keep you. ... There were no individual explanations for why these workers—out of a force of 40,000—had been picked. The members of the firing squad never introduced themselves. It was over in eight minutes. (Cohen & Thomas, 2001, p. 38)

Imagine yourself in that room. Then imagine how your stomach and head would feel as you walked out.

An individual's view of the extent to which he or she is being treated fairly will influence that individual's emotional and behavioral reactions to the work environment. Perceptions of justice have been found to affect organizational citizenship, trust in the organization, respect for leaders, thoughts of quitting, and job performance (Johnson & O'Leary-Kelly, 2003). In its most extreme form and for a small number of people, a perception of injustice can lead to violence in the workplace (Sackett & DeVore, 2001). Kabanoff (1991) suggested that justice is a framework for looking at an organization. It is "an ever present, deep, and slowly moving current that shapes people's relations with other organizational members and the nature and strength of people's attachments to organizations in general" (p. 436). Miller (2001) went further and suggested that justice is a central concept because it affects the way people think of themselves. People have certain beliefs about what they are "worth" as individuals. When a situation arises that challenges those beliefs (e.g., they do not receive the expected reward, they are told they are dispensable by being laid off), they are forced to change their belief about themselves ("I am not worth what I thought I was") or their belief about their organization ("My company is not honorable because it will not reward me as promised).

Interestingly, when workers consider an act of injustice, they see a violation of a contract—either a formal or a psychological contract, which we discussed in Chapter 9. The employer, in contrast, sees the event not as a contract violation but as something out of the employer's control that led to the event (Lester, Turnley, Bloodgood, & Bolino, 2002). Although most discussions of justice and psychological contracts have to do with the violation of that contract, it is important to realize that when an organization honors its promises to its employees, *good* things happen. Both sides become more committed to their agreement, and each is more likely to honor that agreement, including increased employee productivity (Coyle-Shapiro & Kessler, 2002; Dabos & Rousseau, 2004). Because perceptions of fairness and justice affect so much of what goes on at the workplace, we believe it is important enough to devote considerable space to the topic.

Justice, Fairness, and Trust

Trust Belief in how a person or an organization will act on some future occasion based upon previous interactions with that person or organization.

The terms "justice," "fairness," and "trust" are often used interchangeably, and although they are closely related, they are still worth differentiating from one another. Justice and fairness are used to characterize an event or an exchange relationship. A worker will describe a pay increase as unfair, a company policy as unjust, or a supervisor as a fair person. **Trust**, on the other hand, is more an expectation than a reality. It is a belief about how a person or an organization *will* act on some future occasion based upon previous interactions with that person or organization (Ferrin, Dirks, & Shah, 2006). One need look no further than the Enron scandal to realize how quickly trust among employees can erode when organizational members discover that leaders have acted irresponsibly. Kramer (1999) characterized trust as a psychological state, a state that becomes increasingly powerful as uncertainty and risk increase. Thus, in a time of low unemployment and a good economy, there is little discussion of the trust that an individual has in an employer. But when unemployment is high or the threat of downsizing, mergers, or acquisitions looms, trust becomes a more potent influence on behavior and emotions.

Kramer (1999) identified several aspects of organizations and institutions that undermine trust. He wrote that trust can be a scarce resource that is difficult to build and easy to lose. Distrust has been defined as a "lack of confidence in the other, a concern that the other may act as to harm one, that he does not care about one's welfare or intends to act harmfully, or is hostile" (Grovier, 1994). As we saw in Chapter 8 on motivation, one compelling view of a person is that of an organism seeking meaning from events, even when these events seem meaningless. In this view, the person is a scientist gathering data or a judge evaluating those data and drawing a conclusion. It seems clear that trust in organizations and institutions—public and private—has eroded over recent decades. In 1964, 75 percent of Americans expressed trust in the government; by 1997, that number had shrunk to 25 percent. During that same period, the trust placed in medical institutions diminished from 73 to 29 percent, in universities from 61 to 30 percent, and in private companies from 55 to 21 percent (Kramer, 1999). Therefore, it is not surprising that employees may not trust their employers. The effect of this distrust is to question the fairness of any action taken by that employer, particularly actions that have an adverse effect on the employee. Such actions would include failure to receive a promotion or satisfactory pay increase, performance evaluations perceived as unfair, and layoffs resulting from downsizing, to mention a few.

As in friendships and romantic relationships, once trust in an organization has been lost, it is extremely hard to rebuild. There are several reasons for this. First, we tend to remember and dwell on negative events as opposed to positive ones (Slovic, 1993). Negative events are simply more visible and memorable. In addition, when making decisions of any kind, most people tend to give greater weight to negative events in the past than positive ones. Finally, it seems that negative gossip in an organization is more likely to be transmitted than positive gossip (Burt & Knez, 1995).

Some research suggests strategies for dealing with loss of trust. One suggestion is that explanations should be given for the event and that these explanations should be in the form of reasons rather than justifications—for example, the manager might acknowledge that he or she *could* have made a different decision, as opposed to characterizing the decision as the one that *should* have been made (Shaw et al., 2003). This research estimates that the likelihood of retaliation (e.g., a lawsuit brought against the company, an act of sabotage) can be reduced by as much as 43 percent with an adequate explanation delivered in a timely manner. Kim, Ferrin, Cooper, and Dirks (2004) suggest that apologies for poor performance (by either a subordinate or a supervisor) can also help repair the damage done by violations of trust.

But it appears that managers are reluctant to follow either of these strategies, instead retreating into silence. As Folger and Skarlicki (2001) observe, managers try to distance themselves from bad news and negative events for any or all of the following reasons: emotional discomfort, fear of being blamed, fear of making a bad situation worse, or even fear of providing a foundation for an eventual lawsuit. As Shaw and colleagues (2003) point out, this "distancing" by the manager actually makes these negative outcomes *more* likely, not *less* so. Bobocel and Zdaniuk (2005) present a detailed description of the role of explanations in restoring or maintaining perceptions of justice.

Colella, Paetzold, and Belliveau (2004) describe a potential dilemma with respect to "explanations." As we saw in Chapter 3, the Americans with Disabilities Act (ADA) provides for accommodations for a disabled worker. These accommodations often involve a change in the nature of the work (e.g., changing the job tasks of the disabled person) or the workplace (e.g., creating special environments for the disabled person). In certain circumstances (e.g., when the disability is not obvious), co-workers may experience feelings of unfairness, but ADA regulations (i.e., privacy stipulations) preclude any explanation to co-workers. These researchers offer some suggestions for maintaining perceptions of fairness even when direct explanations are not possible. These include opportunities for the co-workers to discuss how the changes have affected them, discussions of larger implications of social justice, and so forth. Generally, they suggest that enhancing feelings of procedural justice will mitigate the concerns of co-workers. We will discuss the principles of procedural justice below.

Thus, once an event occurs that damages or destroys trust, that event looms larger in the organizational environment. There is an old saying that captures this dynamic: Fool me once, shame on you; fool me twice, shame on me. People do not like to be fooled and, once they feel they have been fooled, they will take steps to prevent it from happening a second time. People who have lost trust begin to seek out information that will confirm their distrust, and they are less open to information that challenges that distrust. For organizations, the moral is a simple one: If you have the trust of your employees, protect that trust as a scarce resource.

Approaches to Organizational Justice

Organizational justice Type of justice that is composed of organizational procedures, outcomes, and interpersonal interactions.

Although the concept of **organizational justice** has been around for almost 30 years, there is still no generally accepted framework for studying justice in the workplace (Gilliland & Chan, 2001). Most research and theory have concentrated on the various ways in which justice and injustice might arise in organizational settings. A handbook devoted to the topic of organizational justice (Greenberg & Colquitt, 2005) covers both theory and research related to various types of organizational justice. Four types of justice have been suggested: distributive, procedural, interactional, and deontic. We will consider each of them in turn.

Distributive Justice

In most organizational settings, there is either an implicit or an explicit agreement or contract about the exchange relationship between the employer and employee (Schalk & Rousseau, 2001). The employee invests something in the organization (e.g., effort, skill, loyalty), and the organization rewards the employee for that investment. Another way to say this is that an organization distributes rewards to employees based on some scheme or equation. Employees will form an opinion regarding whether or not this distribution scheme is fair. **Distributive justice** concerns the perceived fairness of the allocation of outcomes or rewards to organizational members. You will recall that several of the motivation theories we reviewed in Chapter 8 include the concept of expectations, implying perceptions of fairness in rewards. Others, like equity theory, explicitly include fairness perceptions.

Distributive justice Type of justice in which the allocation of outcomes or rewards to organizational members is perceived as fair.

There are many different definitions of what is "fair" in the distribution of rewards. One definition is based on merit. The people who work hardest or produce the most should get the greatest rewards. This is called the **merit** or **equity norm**. Another definition is based on the notion of equality: Every member gets the same share of rewards, regardless of effort. Finally, the definition of fairness can be based on the **need norm**: People receive rewards in proportion to their needs (Gilliland & Chan, 2001). In the United States, the equity norm is the most common foundation for defining fairness (Greenberg, 1982). Nevertheless, in many countries the **equality norm** is stronger. For example, the Scandinavian countries have a long tradition of distributing rewards based on the equality norm. This is also true of Asian countries such as Japan and China, both of which would be classified as collectivist using the Hofstede (2001) model we presented in Chapter 1. Research has demonstrated that the definition of fairness is influenced not only by individualism–collectivism (Gelfand et al., 2002) but also by another of the Hofstede dimensions: power distance. Individuals from cultures marked by low power distance are much more likely to see violations of trust than their counterparts in cultures marked by high power distance (Lam, Schaubroeck, & Aryee, 2002).

Merit or equity norm Definition of fairness based on the view that those who work hardest or produce the most should get the greatest rewards; most common foundation for defining fairness in the United States.

Need norm Definition of fairness based on the view that people should receive rewards in proportion to their needs.

Equality norm Definition of fairness based on the view that people should receive approximately equal rewards; most common foundation for defining fairness in Scandinavian and Asian countries.

Regardless of how you define distributive justice, there seems to be a mechanism of comparison that leads to justice perceptions. Individuals compare what they get to what they expect to get. There is a subtle difference between what one expects and what one deserves. For example, if your company has a bad year, you might *expect* a modest salary increase, if any, but you may still feel that you *deserve* a substantial increase. It is not completely clear if your feelings of fairness or unfairness spring from expectations or from feelings of deservedness. In addition, it is not clear how strongly the simple favorability or unfavorability of an outcome influences perceptions of fairness. For example, you might not get a reward but grudgingly concede that another person who did get the reward deserved it. You would classify this as unfavorable but fair. Alternatively, you might get a reward that you don't believe you deserve. This would be classified as favorable but unfair. In many cultures (again, primarily collectivist cultures), there is a strong modesty bias that makes individuals reluctant to claim credit for positive outcomes. In these cultures (in contrast to the United States), "fairness" will take on a very different meaning.

As another example, lawsuits have been threatened (and, in some cases, brought) to recover what are considered to be unfair payments or compensation awarded to executives. In Germany, a telecommunications CEO defended a bonus of $27 million as right and fair (*New York Times*, 2005b). He was being tried by the government in an attempt to recover the money, which he called an "appreciation award." Dick Grasso, the former head of the New York Stock Exchange, was pressured to resign when it was discovered that his compensation for a year approached $200 million (McGeehan & Thomas, 2003). A college president (Janofsky, 2005) was pressured to resign when it became public that he was spending university money lavishly on personal needs. In each case, although there was some formal "justification" for the compensation or reimbursement, employees and the public considered these rewards/awards unjust. These are public and high-profile examples of violations of a standard of distributive justice. Many of these examples also highlight the importance of having leaders who are perceived as authentic and trustworthy by employees. The employees, in turn, are likely to work harder toward organizational goals if they feel they are working in a fair and just workplace. We will return to the importance of authentic leaders in Chapter 12.

Since the early 1990s, there has been a major shift in retirement plans in U.S. companies from defined benefit (traditional pension) plans to defined contribution plans such as the popular 401(k). The differences are major. In a defined benefit plan, the employee has (at least in theory) a "contract" with the employer or labor union that provides post-retirement payment for years of service. The plan is a specific bilateral agreement between an employer and an employee. Moreover, it is the employer who typically provides the money and manages it in the company pension fund. A defined contribution plan, in contrast, is portable. If you leave employer A for any reason, you can move or roll over your plan to employer B. In addition, although many employers match employee contributions to some level, it is the employee who provides the bulk of the funding through payroll deductions. The implications are clear. The psychological contract becomes considerably weaker and less stable for employees in a defined contribution plan as compared to those in a defined benefit plan (Westerman & Sundali, 2005). Of course, the psychological contract has already been weakened by downsizings, bankruptcy filings, and the collapse of a number of defined benefits plans (e.g., several major airlines asked the government to guarantee pensions, often at less than 50 percent of what the employees had been promised). Nevertheless, this shift toward defined contribution plans is bound to further weaken the tie between employee and employer.

Procedural Justice

Distributive justice is about outcomes—who gets what. **Procedural justice** is about the process (or procedure) by which rewards are distributed. The U.S. Constitution supports the concept of due process, meaning that individuals have the right to a fair process under the law as well as a fair outcome. An important aspect of fair treatment is the ability to register objections. In labor–management contracts, this is covered by the concept of the grievance, or the right of an individual worker or group of workers to challenge an unfavorable action taken by the organization. In I-O psychology, this ability to challenge a process or outcome has been labeled **voice** (Folger & Cropanzano, 1998). The concept of voice means that the individual has the possibility of influencing a process or outcome. Avery and Quinones (2002) suggested that although voice has many different aspects, the most important is the perception that workers actually have an opportunity to express an objection. Thus, an organization may have many potential channels available for registering objections about policies or events, but unless employees know what these channels are and how to use them, and believe that their objections will actually be considered, these channels are useless in producing feelings of justice and fairness. Schminke, Ambrose, and Cropanzano (2000) suggested that organizations with high degrees of centralization (i.e., procedures that every division or department must follow, centralized HR functions) are more likely to be seen as procedurally unfair than decentralized organizations.

Procedural justice Type of justice in which the process (or procedure) by which ratings are assigned or rewards are distributed is perceived as fair.

Voice Having the possibility of challenging, influencing, or expressing an objection to a process or outcome.

Kernan and Hanges (2002) examined the effect of justice perceptions in a pharmaceutical company following a reorganization. They collected perceived fairness data from the "survivors" of the reorganization—that is, those who were not terminated. Interestingly, they found that survivors' job satisfaction, organizational commitment, intentions to quit, and trust in management were all affected by perceptions of the procedural fairness with which layoffs had been carried out. Further, they found that the single most important determinant of perceptions of procedural justice in this situation was the opportunity for employees to have input into the reorganization procedures (i.e., voice). This is an important finding. The conventional wisdom has been that survivors are happy to have kept their jobs; if they experience any emotion, it is one of relief. In contrast, the results of this study show that the experience of downsizing and reorganization has a negative impact on survivors as well as victims when principles of procedural justice appear to have been violated.

Siegel, Post, Brockner, Fishman, and Garden (2005) examined the relationship between procedural justice and work–life balance. They discovered that when an employee felt that procedures were fairly implemented (regardless of whether the procedures related to an issue of work–life balance!), the stress of work–life conflict was lower and the commitment to the organization remained high, even in the face of the fact that the conflict had not been reduced in any objective way. This finding provides a very strong argument for encouraging procedural fairness. These results suggest that perceptions of procedural fairness can act as an antidote to less-than-perfect working conditions. This is particularly useful information, given the fact that the cost of creating or maintaining perceptions of procedural fairness is so low: High-quality communication and empathy are considerably less expensive than replacing employees or coping with high absenteeism or low productivity.

Schroth and Shah (2000) examined the effect of experiences of procedural fairness on self-esteem. This is an important issue because several theories of work motivation depend on the concept of self-esteem. Thus, it is useful to know which events may enhance or diminish self-esteem. Their study examined the effect of fair and unfair procedures combined with positive and negative outcomes. These researchers discovered that when an interaction was considered procedurally fair and resulted in a positive outcome for the study participant, esteem was enhanced. Conversely, when procedures were considered procedurally fair, but the outcome was negative, esteem was reduced. In the case of negative outcomes, fair procedures led to lower self-esteem than was the case with the unfair condition. Ironically, this result suggests that unfair procedures can insulate an individual from having to consider the possibility that he or she is unqualified or performed poorly. This is similar to the common complaint of sports fans ("We wuz robbed") when their team loses; alternatively, if the outcome is in their favor, they scorn the complaints of the opposing fans. When an applicant fails to obtain a job or promotion, he or she will often seek any opportunity to explain the result as one of unfairness. This is an effective way of protecting self-esteem.

© Andrew Winning/Reuters/©Corbis

For individuals who have lost their jobs, low levels of perceived procedural and distributive justice may be related to a higher probability of filing an employment discrimination claim.

In an intriguing study done with prison inmates, Vermunt, van Knippenberg, van Knippenberg, and Blaauw (2001) examined self-esteem as an antecedent to feelings of unfairness. Inmates with high self-esteem were more likely to see violations of distributive justice, whereas inmates with low self-esteem were more likely to see violations of procedural justice. The researchers proposed that individuals low in self-esteem are more likely to be concerned about social evaluations (e.g., "I was disrespected") than are their counterparts high in self-esteem. The same may hold true for losing a job. Goldman (2001) found evidence demonstrating that low levels of perceived procedural and distributive justice are associated with a higher probability of filing an employment discrimination claim. Unfortunately, due to the design of the study (respondents were asked to recall feelings of fairness after they had been terminated), there is the distinct possibility that feelings of unfairness followed termination rather than preceding it, resulting in a sequence that would be termination → perceptions → lawsuit, rather than perceptions → termination → lawsuit. Nevertheless, it would be interesting to further examine relationships between preexisting levels of self-esteem and both perceptions of fairness and post-termination behaviors. In fact, the larger issue of disposition and personality in the perception of fairness needs a closer examination.

Interactional Justice

A third type of organizational justice is **interactional justice**, the sensitivity with which employees are treated (Bies & Moag, 1986). This concept deals with the extent to which an employee feels respected by the employer. In an organizational layoff, for example, were employees informed as soon as possible, and in a complete and accurate way, about why layoffs were necessary and how they would be accomplished? Were layoff announcements made in a sensitive way (in private, with an opportunity for discussion) or in an insensitive way (through a news release or in an impersonal e-mail memo)? Greenberg (2006) examined insomnia in samples of nurses who had recently had their pay cut due to changes in compensation policies. Nurses reported losing sleep because of these changes and resulting low feelings of organizational justice. However, Greenberg found that insomnia was significantly lower among nurses whose managers had received supervisory training in interactional justice. Colquitt and colleagues (2001) completed a meta-analysis of justice studies and made a compelling argument that interactional justice has two separate facets: interpersonal and informational justice. Figure 11.1 illustrates their proposed typology of justice. In this typology, interpersonal justice deals with the extent to which people are treated with respect, politeness, and dignity. Informational justice addresses the explanations provided to people about procedures and outcomes (Colquitt et al., 2001). Informational justice is defined in terms of the fairness of communication systems and

Interactional justice Type of justice concerned with the sensitivity with which employees are treated and linked to the extent that an employee feels respected by the employer.

BOX 11.1 FINDING A VOICE

An example of the concept of justice occurred in April 2008 when truck drivers held a one-day strike to protest rising fuel prices. Many truckers, who work as independent owner-drivers, found that rising fuel costs reduced or even eliminated their profits: They couldn't make a living when fuel prices doubled, but the delivery rates they were paid remained the same. Although the strike did not include as many truckers as organizers had originally hoped, several organizations noted that a large shutdown of truckers can have a noticeable effect on the nation's transportation network within a few days (Bunkley, 2008). In addition, there have been other one-day strikes (e.g., taxi drivers in New York City in October 2007, fishermen in Japan in July 2008), indicating that people will find a way to have a voice regarding perceived injustice one way or another.

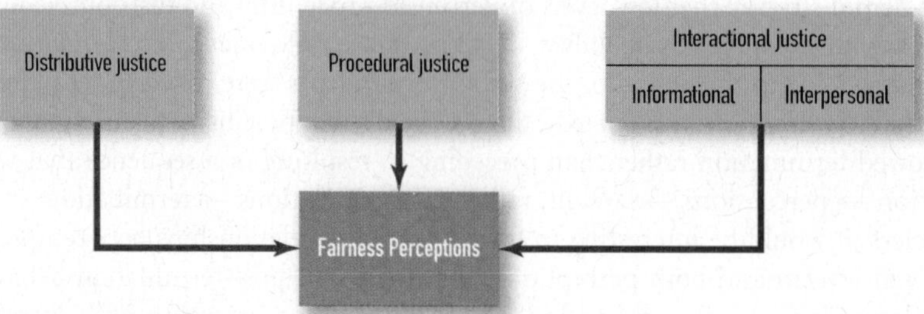

FIGURE 11.1 Types of Justice

channels, particularly with respect to the person charged with communication responsibilities. It is defined by items such as the following:

- Has he or she been candid in communications with you?
- Has he or she explained the procedures thoroughly?
- Has he or she communicated details in a timely manner?

In layoff situations, such as the one we described at the beginning of this chapter, it is precisely the absence of such characteristics that often forms the core of feelings of unfairness (and serves as the foundation for litigation). Skarlicki, Barclay, and Pugh (2008) explored whether employees' perceptions of the employer's integrity affected the relationship between informational justice (providing an adequate explanation for a layoff) and plans for retaliation among those laid off. Results from two studies suggested that providing as much information as possible about a layoff can help limit employee retaliation against the employer, but only when laid-off workers perceived that their employer had high integrity prior to the layoff. In contrast, when those laid off perceived that their employer had low integrity prior to the layoff, explanations for layoffs were not enough (as the saying goes, "Talk is cheap"). Many such workers reported that they considered some form of retaliation (e.g., spreading negative information about the employer or taking legal action).

The differences between interpersonal and informational justice are subtle because providing information can be seen as evidence of respect for the employee (Schminke et al., 2000). Nevertheless, as Colquitt and colleagues (2001) have shown, these do represent two different types of justice. The distinction between procedural justice and interactional justice is also a subtle one. Cropanzano, Byrne, and Prehar (1999) suggested that these two different types of justice are simply distinctions between formal and informal procedures. Procedural justice studies tend to look at company policies, whereas interactional justice studies look at communications between employees and supervisors, including the supervisors' style of communication: cold and impersonal or warm and supportive. Aryee, Budhwar, and Chen (2002) studied various aspects of organizational justice in a public-sector organization in India and found clear evidence that the focus of interactional justice is most often the supervisor. Donovan, Drasgow, and Munson (1998) developed a method to measure feelings of interpersonal justice, which they labeled the PFIT (perceptions of fair interpersonal treatment) scale. The scale concentrates on relationships among employees, co-workers, and supervisors, including items such as the following:

- Supervisors play favorites.
- Employees are treated fairly.
- Employees are trusted.
- Co-workers put one another down.
- Employees' hard work is appreciated.

Roch and Shanock (2006) developed and provided initial validity evidence for a 17-item measure of interactional justice that has promise as well.

Deontic Justice

Cropanzano, Goldman, and Folger (2003; Folger, Cropanzano, & Goldman, 2005) have proposed an additional form of justice: **deontic justice**. The term "deontic" comes from philosophy and refers to moral responsibility or following moral rules. The researchers use this term in connection with the phenomenon in which individuals seeking to correct an injustice will engage in activities that could be seen as working against their own self-interest. A good example is the psychologist David Morris, whom we described in Chapter 1. He remained in Iraq, even though his life was in jeopardy every day, not to promote a personal goal or to improve his standing in some social group. He was there because he felt it was the right thing to do. This is the essence of deontic justice. When we discuss affirmative action in Module 11.2, we will see a clash between the concept of deontic justice (i.e., "This is an appropriate moral action") and distributive justice (i.e., "*I* did not harm *them*, so *they* have no right to a job *I* should have"). Violations of deontic justice might also be perceived in the actions of large corporations (Beugre, 2010). Deontic justice is a very new concept and thus does not have a lot of empirical support. Nevertheless, it appears to hold promise for examining the emotional foundation for conflicts in everyday life—the parties to the conflict are responding to different aspects of fairness.

Deontic justice A form of organizational justice based on what is the correct moral course of action for a company or for an individual.

Justice versus Injustice

Gilliland, Benson, and Schepers (1998) proposed that injustice has a much greater impact than justice on subsequent attitudes, emotions, and behavior. Once an injustice threshold has been exceeded, there is no way to counteract the feelings of injustice. Even when employers try to make up for an injustice with fairer subsequent treatment, they cannot undo the harm caused by the perceived injustice. Gilliland and Chan (2001) suggested that injustice, once experienced, leads to retaliation or reduced effort or motivation, whereas perceptions of justice lead to extra effort and feelings of inclusion and contribution. Currently, justice and injustice are considered two ends of a single continuum, with equal and opposite reactions. But many individuals experience justice quite differently from the way they experience injustice. The experience of injustice has a tendency to linger for a long time, sometimes over decades. Many of us remember for years an instance in which we were "screwed" by an employer, yet we tend to take just treatment for granted. We are also sensitive to incidents in which valued co-workers are treated badly, and we wonder if the same thing could happen to us.

The definition and measurement of justice perceptions is a relatively new area for I-O psychology. As a result, a great deal of basic work must still be done to determine how many different types of justice there are, how each type should be measured, how long-lasting and powerful the emotions created by each type are, and how each type is related to various work behaviors.

Injustice—actual or perceived—often leads to outrage and violence.

Roch and Shanock (2006) have begun some of this important work. This is a very exciting area of research and application and is likely to receive continued attention.

There is also a strong possibility that a great deal of the earlier research on justice will need to be reexamined in light of the research we reviewed in Chapter 9 when we discussed the time course of emotions. You will recall that event or experience sampling is one of the newer approaches for studying emotions and that this research has demonstrated that perceived justice violations occur on almost a daily basis. Research on various forms of justice has not yet embraced this approach, instead looking at long-term associations between justice perceptions and behaviors such as turnover or absenteeism. The value of a shorter-term view of event-related justice, particularly when the measurement of emotions is also involved, has been suggested by several justice scholars (e.g., Gilliland & Paddock, 2005). This is a suggestion worth following.

MODULE 11.1 SUMMARY

- The extent to which workers feel that they are being treated fairly will influence their emotional and behavioral reactions to the work environment. Perceptions of justice have been found to affect organizational citizenship, respect for leaders, thoughts of quitting, tendency to file lawsuits, and job performance.
- The three approaches to justice that have received the most attention are distributive, procedural, and interactional justice. Most research and theory in this area have concentrated on the various ways in which justice and injustice might arise in organizational settings.
- Some researchers have proposed that injustice has a much greater impact than justice on subsequent attitudes, emotions, and behavior. Even when employers try to make up for the injustice with fairer subsequent treatment, they cannot undo the harm caused by the perceived injustice.
- Defining and measuring justice perceptions is a relatively new area for I-O psychology. As a result, there is still much work to be done in determining how many different types of justice there are, how each type should be measured, and how each type relates to various work behaviors.

KEY TERMS

trust
organizational justice
distributive justice
merit or equity norm
need norm
equality norm
procedural justice
voice
interactional justice
deontic justice

MODULE 11.2

The Practical Implications of Justice Perceptions

A substantial body of research suggests clear connections between perceptions of fairness and employee attitudes. For example, McFarlin and Sweeney (1992) discovered that distributive and procedural justice were both important predictors of employee attitudes. Notably, distributive justice was a stronger predictor of pay satisfaction and overall job satisfaction than procedural justice, whereas procedural justice was a stronger predictor of organizational commitment than distributive justice. McFarlin and Sweeney also found some evidence that distributive and procedural justice work jointly to influence behavior and attitudes. If distributive justice was low, procedural justice had a strong influence on the attachment that an individual had to an organization; similarly, if procedural justice was low, distributive justice had a substantial influence on attachment. Skarlicki and Folger (1997) determined that when procedural justice was low, perceptions of distributive injustice resulted in the inappropriate use of sick time, the damaging of equipment, and the spreading of rumors about fellow employees. If this interactive relationship turns out to be true, employers may take some solace in knowing that they can recover from one type of injustice by promoting perceptions of justice in another form.

As you read in Chapter 9, there has been an increasing interest in the emotional experience of work. Much of the research cited above addressed the cognitive aspects of attitudes, not emotions. But remember the last time you were treated unfairly by an employer. Very likely, your reaction was not a cold and impersonal cognitive evaluation but an affective reaction in the form of anger, disgust, or wide-eyed disbelief. Mikula, Scherer, and Athenstaedt (1998) studied the emotional consequences of perceived injustice in participants from 37 countries. They identified the most likely resulting emotions as anger, disgust, and sadness. Weiss, Suckow, and Cropanzano (1999) found that happiness was associated with the experience of distributive justice, and sadness with the experience of distributive injustice. They also found that if an individual did not receive a valued reward and, in addition, had perceptions of procedural unfairness, then the individual experienced anger. This line of research seems to be a promising avenue for understanding violence at work, which we discussed in Chapter 10.

Although virtually any practice of an organization or behavior of a supervisor or co-worker can lead to feelings of unfairness, two particular aspects have received considerable attention: performance evaluation and applicant reactions to selection procedures. We will consider each of these issues next.

Performance Evaluation

In Chapters 4 and 5 we considered the issues of performance and its measurement in some detail. Here we will deal specifically with the perception of fairness or unfairness associated with performance evaluation. When recounting experiences of unfair treatment, employees often include the performance evaluation process—the formal procedure by which a supervisor rates the performance of a subordinate. For example, Landy, Barnes-Farrell, and Cleveland (1980) discovered that an individual's reaction to a performance review was related less to whether the evaluation was positive and more to how the evaluation was carried out. Thus, the issue was a matter of procedural justice more than distributive justice. The conditions that led to the experience of fairness were that (1) the supervisor was familiar with the duties and responsibilities of the subordinate, (2) the supervisor had an adequate opportunity to actually observe the subordinate at the workplace, and (3) the supervisor provided suggestions on how to improve performance. This was a surprise because the conventional wisdom held that people felt fairly treated if their evaluations were good and unfairly treated if their evaluations were poor (i.e., feelings were based on perceptions of distributive justice). It is also instructive to remember that many of these issues arise in litigation that follows layoffs, as we indicated in Chapter 5.

Landy and colleagues (1980) did not tie their results to any considerations of justice, but Greenberg (1986a) did. He suggested that a person would feel justly treated when the following occurred:

1. The supervisor gathered information in a careful manner.
2. The employee had an opportunity to discuss the evaluation with the supervisor after it had been completed.
3. The employee had the opportunity to formally disagree with the evaluation.
4. The supervisor was familiar with the work of the subordinate.
5. The supervisor was consistent in his or her judgment standards across subordinates and across time periods for the same subordinate.

As you can see, conditions 2 and 3 were associated with the concept of voice, which we discussed in the previous module. The concept of voice is common to the experience of fairness in virtually all decisions made about an individual. Employees want to be heard. If a procedure appears arbitrary or unfair, the opportunity to point out that unfairness can reverse the perception of unfairness. In many instances, what *appears* to the employee to be unfair is often simply a misunderstanding of the process or procedure. But if the employee never has the opportunity to object and have the procedure clarified, he or she will always believe that the process was unfair. Folger and Konovsky (1989) found that the feedback process was the most important determinant of feelings of fairness; once again, the concept of voice is key. Cawley, Keeping, and Levy (1998) completed a meta-analysis of 27 studies on the impact of employee participation in the evaluation process on feelings of fairness. They concluded that participation (e.g., discussing the evaluation before it was finalized) had a substantial effect on feelings of fairness by the person being evaluated. Adler and Ambrose (2005) examined whether attributes of performance feedback received by employees in an electronic monitoring system would affect their reactions to monitoring. The results indicated that the constructiveness of the feedback given was significantly related to perceptions of the fairness of electronic monitoring; that is, receiving more constructive feedback increased employees' perceptions that the electronic monitoring system was fair. Additionally, receiving face-to-face feedback from supervisors was associated with higher perceptions of the fairness of electronic monitoring than was computer-mediated feedback.

As we described in Chapter 5, there has been a shift in today's workplace from performance measurement—documenting a given performance level of an employee—to performance management—a dialogue between a supervisor and subordinate about how to maximize performance. This shift clearly increases perceptions of fairness by the employee. Gilliland and Chan (2001) went even further in suggesting that the way managers are treated affects the way they treat their own subordinates. They hypothesized that managers who feel unfairly treated by their bosses might be more sensitive to the issue of fairness when they evaluate their subordinates. They also speculated that an employee who is sensitized to the possibility of unfairness may become oversensitive to the possibility of unfair treatment and will be more likely to feel unfairly treated. As you can see, there are plenty of hypotheses concerning performance evaluation but little conclusive evidence. However, a recent study by Heslin and Vandewalle (2011) found that managers' views about the extent to which employees can change were associated with employees' perceptions of procedural justice regarding their last performance evaluation. Higher perceptions of procedural justice were in turn related to higher organizational citizenship behaviors by the employees. Although much work remains to be done in this area, everyone agrees that performance evaluation will inevitably result in feelings of fairness or unfairness. This makes it a productive area in which to examine the concept of justice.

Applicant Reactions to Selection Procedures

Industrial and organizational psychologists have been involved in research on selection for nearly a hundred years (Landy, 1993), but only in the past 15 years has serious attention been given to understanding the reactions that applicants have to selection devices and selection decisions (Anderson, Born, & Cunningham-Snell, 2001; Ryan & Greguras, 1998). Research on applicant reactions to selection procedures is important for several reasons. First, if applicants are unhappy about the selection process and believe they have been treated unfairly, they may reject the offer of employment. Ployhart and Harold (2004) suggest that rejection often leads to attribution errors on the part of a rejected applicant. To begin with, they attribute the rejection to things other than their own abilities or characteristics, so they are likely to actively seek indicators of unfairness. Second, because applicants talk to other applicants, selection procedures that are considered unfair affect the reputation of the hiring organizations. Finally and increasingly, applicants who believe they have been treated unfairly may end up suing an employer for discrimination. Applicant perceptions of recruiting and selection procedures are closely connected to perceptions of fairness, so this is an excellent opportunity to study the concept of organizational justice.

There are also practical implications for studying applicant perceptions. From an applicant's perspective, understanding and building principles of fairness into the selection process can turn a potentially unpleasant experience into a more pleasant (or at least less *un*pleasant) one. From an organization's perspective, assuring perceived fairness may result in a positive reaction by the applicant to an offer of employment. Even if the applicant is not offered a position or does not accept one that has been offered, that applicant will still have positive or negative feelings about the organization that are likely to be communicated to friends and relatives.

Before reviewing this area of research, we must issue a note of caution. A great deal of this research is based on the use of student participants. The students are asked to role-play an applicant or give a more generalized response about the acceptability and perceived fairness of various selection techniques. In some cases, these students are actually being considered for part-time positions at their schools. The use of student participants in this line of research may be a problem from several perspectives. First, attitudinal and emotional reactions to various devices are likely to develop over time. The first time you take a personality test or complete a biodata form and are rejected for a position, you may be annoyed but convinced that another job will come along. The tenth time you are rejected, you may be enraged and convinced that you are being treated unfairly. In addition, there is a difference between *pretending* you have been rejected and actually being rejected. The first experience is interesting, but the second is punishing. Finally, there is a strong likelihood that college students, on average, have higher intellectual ability than non–college students. This means that they are likely to have more complex reasoning strategies than their nonstudent counterparts. We are not suggesting that the use of students invalidates findings, but our confidence in the research findings will increase as results from nonstudent applicants accumulate. Fortunately, even at this early stage of research, there is some convergence between findings with student and nonstudent populations (e.g., Bauer, Maertz, Dolen, & Campion, 1998; Macan, Avedon, Paese, & Smith, 1994).

Another weakness in a great deal of the research on applicants' reactions to assessment and organizational attractiveness is the cross-sectional nature of the research. It is assumed that fairness reactions enhance organizational attractiveness, but it may be that initial attractiveness of organizations results in perceptions of fairness in selection procedures (Hausknecht, Day, & Thomas, 2004) or that a third variable (e.g., desire to find employment) causes an enhanced view of both the organization and the assessment practices. The best way to examine what causes what is to use longitudinal within-person designs. Chan and Schmitt (2004) have suggested other avenues for tightening up research on applicant reactions to selection procedures.

Anderson, Born, and Cunningham-Snell (2001) have reviewed the available research on applicant reactions. They came to several conclusions, which we have summarized below. Where confirming subsequent research applies, we have added the citation.

- *Recruiting.* Applicants see recruiters as the personification of the organization doing the recruiting; applicants prefer application blanks that state that the firm is an equal opportunity employer.
- *Biographical data.* Applicants have doubts about the validity and fairness of forms that ask for biographical information as part of a selection process; they are less concerned when such forms are used for developmental or training purposes.
- *Cognitive ability tests.* Candidates are more favorable toward cognitive ability tests with concrete items that appear to be related to the job.
- *Computer-based testing.* Candidates are generally favorable toward computer-based testing because it is usually quicker, provides immediate feedback, and results in more timely employment decisions (Richman-Hirsch, Olson-Buchanan, & Drasgow, 2000).
- *Test-taking motivation.* Candidates who are more favorably disposed to a selection procedure have higher test-taking motivation and, consequently, do better on the particular test (Ployhart & Ehrhart, 2002).
- *Assessment centers.* Assessment centers are viewed more favorably than standardized tests because to the candidates they appear to be related more to the job; in addition, applicants also view the face-to-face interaction with assessors favorably.
- *Personality tests.* Applicants react less favorably to personality tests than other types of paper-and-pencil tests; this may be because they are less clearly related to job behavior, because they are longer, or because, unlike ability or knowledge tests, personality tests have no "correct" answers (Rafaeli, 1999).
- *Interviews.* Candidates are more favorable to interviews that appear to be related to the job under consideration (Seijts & Jackson, 2001); they are not greatly influenced by the characteristics of the interviewer; they tend to dislike telephone interviews, particularly those that involve the less personal interactive voice response mode (Bauer,

Truxillo, Paronto, Weekley, & Campion, 2004) compared with face-to-face or teleconference interviews (see also Chapman, Uggerslev, & Webster, 2003); first interviews lead an applicant to form initial impressions of an organization's attractiveness; reactions to subsequent interviews are more likely to be based on unfolding information about job attributes.

- *Work samples.* Applicants express favorable opinions of work samples, which they view as fair and job related (Klingner & Schuler, 2004).
- *Drug testing.* As we saw in Chapter 3 on assessment, applicants who use drugs are less enthusiastic about drug testing; without any controls for applicant drug use, it also appears that favorability toward testing for substance abuse is influenced by how safety-sensitive the job is (Murphy, Thornton, & Prue, 1991; Murphy, Thornton, & Reynolds, 1990).

A meta-analysis reported by Hausknecht and colleagues (2004) confirms many of these conclusions. In another study, Bell, Wiechmann, and Ryan (2006) examined the justice expectations of over 1,800 job applicants for firefighter positions before their participation in a selection system. Previous research indicated that applicants' expectations about the upcoming selection process would influence how they reacted to the selection system. At the time of the initial application, the firefighter applicants took a pretest that assessed expectations of organizational justice and test-taking motivation. A written cognitive ability test was given two weeks after the close of the application process, and applicants completed a posttest survey about their perceptions of organizational justice regarding the selection system immediately after they completed the cognitive ability test. The results indicated that applicants' positive expectations about organizational justice can enhance their perceptions of fairness regarding the selection system, which in turn can lead to higher levels of preassessment motivation and more positive attitudes about accepting a job with the organization. Thus, organizations that earn a reputation for treating applicants well during the selection process can reap benefits from future applicants who are likely to view the selection system positively from the start. Alternatively, organizations that have poor reputations regarding their hiring systems will likely have applicants who begin the process with a skeptical or negative view that may be difficult to alter.

Several studies have compared applicant reactions to selection procedures in the United States (where most initial research was conducted) with those in many other countries, including France, Greece, Spain, Singapore, Italy, Belgium, and the Netherlands (Anderson & Witvliet, 2008; Bertolino & Steiner, 2007; Marcus, 2003; Moscoso & Salgado, 2004; Nikolaou & Judge, 2007; Sylva & Mol, 2009). Across these investigations, respondents were most positive toward interviews, work sample tests, and résumés, and least positive toward graphology, personal contacts, and honesty and integrity tests. This is one area in which an encouraging number of cross-cultural studies have recently been undertaken. Notably, it does not appear that information about the statistical reliability or validity of a particular method or device has much influence on candidates' perceptions of fairness (Lievens, De Corte, & Brysse, 2003). Instead, the strongest predictors of favorability ratings across the different selection procedures were (1) having the opportunity to show what one can do (called "opportunity to perform") in the selection process and (2) the perceived face validity of the selection procedures. This may be one of the reasons why work sample assessment, situational judgment tests, and simulations (discussed in Chapter 3) receive such high reviews from applicants.

A Special Case of Applicant Reactions: Stereotype Threat

In the previous section, we considered the consequences of applicants' fairness perceptions in terms of interpretations and attitudes toward the potential employer, applicants' willingness to file formal complaints, and so forth. This issue has a fairly direct connection between postassessment attitudes and behavior. But there may be another, more subtle, connection between perceptions of fairness and actual assessment procedures. Steele and Aronson (1995) proposed the construct of stereotype threat, which has been defined as "the pressure a person can feel when she is at risk of confirming, or being seen to confirm, a negative stereotype about her group" (Steele & Davies, 2003, p. 312). The most obvious example of such a mechanism (and the paradigm used by Steele and Aronson for their initial research) is an African American job candidate who is told that he or she will be asked to take a test that measures intelligence or general mental ability. There is a common stereotype that African Americans are not as intelligent as whites. African Americans are just as aware of this stereotype as whites, and possibly more so. Thus, the African Americans' awareness of this stereotype results in poorer performance on assessment devices that would be characterized as tests of intelligence (Brown & Day, 2006). The same mechanism has been proposed to account for differences between males and females when being assessed on attributes like mathematical skill, since there is a commonly recognized stereotype that women have less mathematical ability than men (Cadinu, Maass, Rosabianca, & Kiesner, 2005; Johns, Schmader, & Martens, 2005). The critical variable in the operation of this threat is that the individual must believe that the assessment involves an attribute associated with a negative stereotype of his or her demographic group (e.g., intelligence for African Americans, mathematical ability for females).

Most of the work on applicant reactions described above has been done without consideration for race, gender, or other demographic characteristics. In addition, this work on applicant reactions is silent with respect to the actual instructions that accompanied the assessment. As an example, if African Americans or women are told that a test assesses "problem-solving ability" rather than intelligence or mathematical ability, respectively, there is no suppression effect on their scores. This means that reactions of African Americans to a test of "intelligence" may be very different from the reactions of the same individuals if the test were billed as a test of "reasoning." One can also imagine that older applicants might be concerned about tests of "innovativeness" or "flexibility," but not about tests of "problem solving."

This area of research is very new and very contentious. There are debates about whether research done in a laboratory (most of the confirming research has been done with students in controlled environments) will generalize to field settings (Cullen, Hardison, & Sackett, 2004; Sackett, 2003). The actual research results are still quite mixed: Sometimes the effect is found and other times it is not (see a special issue of the journal *Human Performance*, Vol. 16, no. 3, for an extended presentation of the debate; Farr, 2003). Because this research is new, there are insufficient studies to complete a rigorous meta-analysis that might shed some light on the potential importance of the construct (Steele & Aronson, 2004). Nevertheless, this remains a popular area for discussion and policy debate because it presents a possible explanation of the differences in test performance between demographic groups that we discussed in Chapter 3 (Sackett, Hardison, & Cullen, 2004). Because of the policy implications of this research for assessment, there is little doubt that studies of stereotype threat will continue.

An example of stereotype threat: If told she is taking a test of "intelligence," an African American applicant may react differently than if told she is taking a test of "reasoning."

The Special Case of Affirmative Action

Because many, if not most, of the studies on the perceived justice of selection systems have been conducted in the United States, and because U.S. culture tends to reflect the equity or merit principle for decisions about fairness, we don't know much about non-U.S. selection systems (particularly those that do not follow the U.S. model). It may very well be that the clash between a merit-based, equality-based, and need-based definition of distributive justice would be much more potent when justice principles are applied on a multinational level. Even within the U.S. system, the concept of affirmative action generates a great deal of emotion and controversy (Kravitz, 2008). Some individuals, particularly those who might hold racist or sexist views, see affirmative action hiring programs as violating both equality and equity rules (Gilliland, 1993).

As you will recall from the earlier sections on distributive and procedural justice in Module 11.1, these two concepts appear to interact (Brockner & Weisenfeld, 1996). In the context of selection, this means that a negative hiring decision (potentially seen as low on distributive justice) might be perceived as less unfair if procedural justice principles are maintained. It is common for an individual to consider the fairness of procedures when he or she is denied a desired outcome. In contrast, if an outcome is positive (i.e., a job is offered), violations of procedural justice principles will be less salient.

The United States has taken a particularly strong stand on equal employment opportunity. Through laws and policies, American employers promise applicants and employees equal opportunities for employment and job success. That is not to say that individuals are promised equal outcomes—simply equal opportunities. It is assumed that if all individuals have the same opportunity, then success will be dictated by merit—the skills and abilities of the applicant or the performance and motivation of the employee. This philosophy fits in well with the equity definition of distributive justice.

Unlike the equal opportunity philosophy, which stipulates that, here and now, all individuals have an equal opportunity, there is another philosophy that also appears frequently in the American workplace: **affirmative action**. Affirmative action programs (AAPs) acknowledge that particular demographic groups (e.g., women, African Americans, Hispanics, the disabled) may be underrepresented in the work environment, and they provide specific mechanisms for reducing this underrepresentation. This creates a potential problem. In the United States, the equity definition for distributive justice is the most commonly adopted definition. But AAPs provide enhanced opportunities for subgroups based on a principle of equality or need (Crosby, 2004; Crosby, Iyer, Clayton, & Downing, 2003). White men often feel that they are treated unfairly or unjustly because of specific hiring preferences for women or African Americans. Women and African Americans, for their part, often feel that past discrimination has already robbed them of an equal opportunity to succeed, so they believe that they have been treated unfairly under the equity-based definition of distributive justice. Thus, unhappily, both favored (e.g., African American and women beneficiaries of AAPs) and nonfavored (e.g., white men) employees may see themselves as "victims." Under these circumstances, it is easy to understand why AAPs are surrounded by so much emotion.

Affirmative action Program that acknowledges that particular demographic groups may be underrepresented in the work environment; provides specific mechanisms for reducing this underrepresentation.

It is common for people to assume that affirmative action programs are simply hiring quotas, guaranteeing underrepresented employees a percentage of all available jobs. This is incorrect. Quotas are explicitly outlawed by the Civil Rights Act of 1991. Affirmative action programs can take many forms, including the following:

- Specialized recruiting programs intended to reach underrepresented groups in the workforce

- Specialized pre- or post-hire training to develop job-related KSAOs
- Mentoring programs for underrepresented groups
- Planned developmental opportunities such as assignment to particular teams and departments
- Specialized performance feedback programs

If individuals continue to see affirmative action programs as simple mechanical "quota" mechanisms, there will always be negative reactions. Majority applicants and workers will feel unjustly treated, and underrepresented beneficiaries of AAPs will feel unjustly stigmatized and devalued.

AAPs represent one of the clearest examples of organizational actions that permit I-O psychologists to examine the perceptions of workplace justice. In the past 15 years, there has been an increasing interest in studying the reactions of employees and applicants to AAPs. The work of two researchers in particular can be used to describe research in this area. Heilman and her colleagues have concentrated on the issue of gender (Heilman & Alcot, 2001; Heilman & Blader, 2001; Lyness & Heilman, 2006). Kravitz and his colleagues have examined the issue of race (Harrison, Kravitz, Mayer, Leslie, & Lev-Arey, 2006; Kravitz et al., 1997, 2000). As you can imagine, the many studies conducted by these researchers and others on AAPs and their effects on applicants and employees have generated a considerable body of results. Some of the most salient findings are summarized in Table 11.1, which is based on the respective reviews and research of Kravitz and Heilman mentioned above. You are encouraged to refer to these reviews for more detailed information about the specific studies. Once again, we must express a note of caution about samples. Many of the studies use student participants, usually college students. As study participants, students may not be comparable to real-world employees, particularly when asked to imagine an employment setting. To draw any firm conclusions regarding the effects of AAPs on workplace behavior, we will need to develop a broader database with actual applicants and employees of organizations that have implemented AAPs.

Kravitz and colleagues (1997) found that there was slightly more support for AAPs directed toward women and the disabled than toward racial subgroups. However, the

TABLE 11.1 Research Findings on Reactions to Affirmative Action Programs

1. Attitudes toward AAPs are strongly associated with perceptions of fairness.
2. African Americans and women have substantially more positive attitudes toward AAPs than white males.
3. Political conservatives hold more negative attitudes toward AAPs than political liberals.
4. Individuals tend to make assumptions about the AAP that suit their underlying attitudes toward AAPs.
5. Justifications for AAPs that acknowledge the presence of past injustices at the organization are seen more positively than justifications based simply on issues of underrepresentation.
6. AAPs vary in "strength," with the mildest versions simply affirming equal opportunity or providing enhanced training opportunities for target groups and stronger versions explicitly expressing preferences in hiring for target groups, independent of abilities. The stronger the form of the AAP, the stronger the positive and negative attitudes associated with it.
7. Nonbeneficiaries of AAPs (e.g., white males) have a tendency to see beneficiaries (e.g., women and African Americans) as less qualified and poorer performers in the organization.
8. When nonbeneficiaries of an AAP are informed that decisions were based on merit, not group membership, beliefs about the qualifications and performance of the beneficiary or target group member become more positive.
9. Beneficiaries of AAPs often feel stigmatized by being labeled an "AAP" hire, and their performance may be affected by the perceived stigmatization.

BOX 11.2 THE IMPETUS FOR AFFIRMATIVE ACTION PROGRAMS

With respect to governmental agencies and federal contractors, the impetus for affirmative action programs is clear—it is a requirement. For other entities, the reasons can be more complex. Often, they are expressions of what we referred to earlier as deontic justice—the desire to do the right thing.

But occasionally motives can be suspect. The president of Harvard University, Lawrence Summers, came under heavy assault in 2005 for implying that women were not better represented in the sciences because they lacked the requisite reasoning ability and preferred concrete rather than abstract activities. His comments were seen as representing the reason why Harvard had fewer women scientists than one might expect—he was thought to embody the societal and cultural barriers to women succeeding in scientific areas.

Less than one month later, Dr. Summers announced a new, aggressive, and sweeping affirmative action program for women scientists at Harvard. He appointed two task forces to make recommendations about methods of recruiting and support for women scientists on the faculty. He also promised to create a senior recruiting officer (Dillon & Rimer, 2005). It was noted that shortly after a public dispute with a well-known African American faculty member who subsequently left Harvard for Yale, Dr. Summers proposed a similar plan for improving the lot of African Americans at Harvard.

It is impossible to know for sure the motivations for the commitment made by Dr. Summers to female scientists or African Americans at Harvard, but the timing would leave many to believe that the affirmative action initiative was motivated by concerns other than (or at least in addition to) doing the right thing regarding the status of these groups. The moral is that if a leader believes in the value of affirmative action, it might be better to act *before* an incident raising issues about fairness rather than *after* one.

stronger the role that demographic status played in the AAP, the stronger the attitudes and often the active behavioral resistance by employees opposed to the program. James, Brief, Dietz, and Cohen (2001) found similar results. Kravitz and colleagues (1997) suggested that if an AAP is to be successful, at the very least information must be provided that justifies it (other than simple underrepresentation), and the information must stress the importance of merit and qualification as two of the criteria for a decision as well as the past history of the organization in not pursuing workforce diversity. Others have suggested that the positive aspects of workforce diversity be emphasized as a rationale for affirmative action programs (Zuriff, 2004).

Kravitz and Klineberg (2000) presented a basic model that lays out the various influences on attitudes toward AAPs. As Figure 11.2 illustrates, attitudes

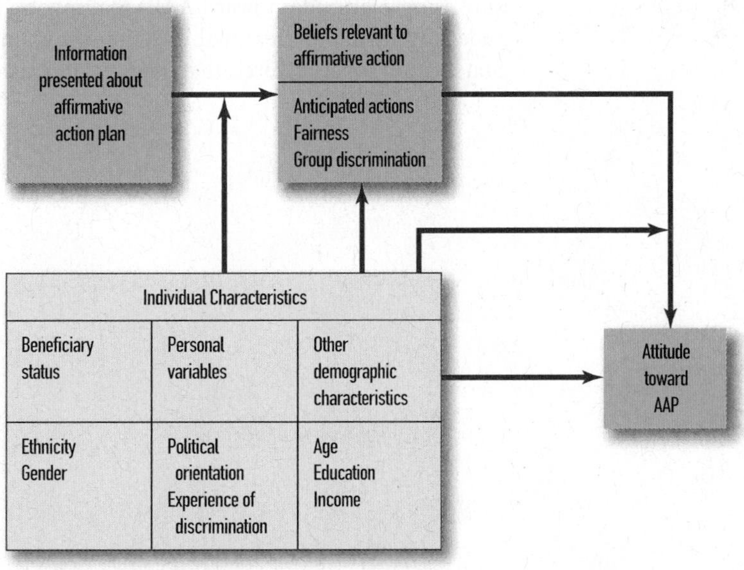

FIGURE 11.2 Conceptual Model of Determinants of Attitudes toward an Affirmative Action Plan

Source: Kravitz, D. A., & Klineberg, S. L. (2000). Reactions to two versions of affirmative action among whites, blacks and Hispanics. *Journal of Applied Psychology, 85*, 597–611. © 2000 by the American Psychological Association. Reprinted by permission of the publisher.

about AAPs will be the result of both individual characteristics and organizational actions. Regardless of the complexities of these attitudes, however, feelings of justice and fairness are at the core of people's reactions. A recent meta-analysis (Harrison et al., 2006) confirmed and strengthened the earlier findings presented above. In particular, the researchers found that AAPs are seen in a negative light when they are positioned as quotas and when organizations merely point out that a target group that receives affirmative action is underrepresented. In contrast, AAPs are seen in a more positive light when they place a lower emphasis on demographic characteristics and when they are framed as enhancing organizational diversity or as remedying previous employment discrimination.

Culture and Affirmative Action Programs

As we indicated earlier, affirmative action programs are peculiarly American. As such, they represent a disparity between an organizational policy and the commonly accepted equity definition of distributive justice. AAPs would likely generate considerably less tension in cultures where need and equality are seen as reasonable foundations for distributive justice. Indeed, people in many countries have a difficult time understanding why AAPs are so controversial in the United States. This provides a cautionary note for the practice of international human resources. American expatriate managers should understand that managers and employees in other countries are not likely to be as concerned about AAPs as are Americans. Further, foreign nationals who come to work in the United States in either a managerial or nonmanagerial role (particularly if they come from collectivist cultures) may have a difficult time understanding American worker resistance to AAPs or the lowered sense of self-esteem in beneficiaries of those programs.

Krings, Tschan, and Bettex (2007) sampled 162 Swiss employees (46 percent female) to assess knowledge of and attitudes toward different types of AAPs for women. They found that knowledge of AAPs was very limited, as about two-thirds of the workers sampled were either not aware of any AAPs or incorrectly named a program that was not actually an AAP. Further, the authors found that AAPs in Switzerland were most frequently associated with programs addressing work–family balance (specifically, child-care measures). Not surprisingly, attitudes toward AAPs that involved child care were more positive than attitudes toward the preferential selection programs that are more common in the United States. Additional research that assesses the links between culture and AAPs is needed.

MODULE 11.2 SUMMARY

- Although almost any practice of an organization or behavior of a supervisor or co-workers can lead to feelings of unfairness, two particular aspects have received considerable attention: performance evaluation and applicant reactions to selection techniques.

- The concept of voice, or worker input, is common to the experience of fairness in most situations. If a procedure appears arbitrary or unfair, the opportunity to point out the unfairness can reverse that perception. In contrast, if employees lack an opportunity to object or have the procedure clarified, they will always believe that the process was unfair.

- I-O psychologists' study of applicant reactions to selection devices and selection decisions began relatively recently. Applicant perceptions of recruiting and selection procedures often lead to perceptions of fairness or unfairness, so this area is important for the study of organizational justice.

- A unique aspect of applicant reactions is the phenomenon of stereotype threat, where an applicant becomes apprehensive, and may perform more poorly on a test, because of stereotypes held about a demographic group to which the applicant belongs.

- The United States has taken a particularly strong stand on equal employment opportunity. Through laws and policies, American employers promise applicants and employees equal opportunities for employment and job success. It is assumed that if all individuals have the same opportunity, then success will be dictated by merit. This philosophy fits in well with the equity definition of distributive justice.

- Affirmative action programs (AAPs) acknowledge that particular demographic groups (e.g., women, African Americans, Hispanics, the disabled) may be underrepresented in the work environment and provide specific mechanisms for reducing this underrepresentation. AAPs represent one of the clearest examples of organizational actions that permit I-O psychologists to examine the perceptions of workplace justice.

KEY TERM

affirmative action

MODULE 11.3

Diversity

What Does Diversity Mean?

Diversity Differences in demographic characteristics; also includes differences in values, abilities, interests, and experiences.

When the word **diversity** is used in the United States, it most often refers to the demographic characteristics of employees. In the popular press, the term "diverse workforce" often means one that is not all white. But to I-O psychologists and, increasingly, forward-looking managers, a diverse workforce is one that includes managers and workers who are both old and young; male and female; white, African-American, Hispanic, and Asian. The term "multinational" also appears frequently to describe a diversity of nationalities (as opposed to skin color, gender, or age). As we will see, diversity is more than demographics. It means diversity in psychological characteristics such as values, abilities, interests, and experiences. Of course, demographic differences often carry those psychological differences with them, but the demographic characteristics are like boxcars, simply transporting the more important variables.

© Sean Justice/©Corbis

Diversity refers to differences in demographic characteristics as well as differences in psychological characteristics including values, abilities, and experiences.

Unfortunately, like affirmative action, the term "diversity" has often taken on sociopolitical meaning. People are asked if they are "for" it or "against" it. As we will see below, it is largely beside the point to be for or against diversity. A diverse workforce is a reality, not a goal or vision. In this module, we will address the issue of diversity not from the sociopolitical but from the organizational perspective.

One final term to keep in mind in our discussion is "multicultural." This is quite different from the terms "diversity" or "multinational." A diverse or multinational workforce is a fact. An employer has or seeks to have a diverse or multinational employee base. A multicultural workforce, on the other hand, is a goal. As Cleveland, Stockdale, and Murphy (2000) explained,

TABLE 11.2 **A Taxonomy for Describing the Content of Diversity**

	ATTRIBUTES MORE LIKELY TO BE TASK-RELATED	*ATTRIBUTES MORE LIKELY TO BE RELATIONSHIP-ORIENTED*
Readily detected attributes	Department/unit membership Organizational tenure Formal credentials and titles Education level Memberships in professional associations	Sex Socioeconomic status Age Race Ethnicity
Underlying attributes	Knowledge and expertise Cognitive skills and abilities Physical skills and abilities	Religion Political memberships Nationality Sexual orientation Gender Class identity Attitudes Values Personality Sexual identity Racial identity Ethnic identity Other social identities

NOTE: The examples shown are illustrative, not exhaustive.

SOURCE: Adapted from Jackson, S. E., May, K. E., & Whitney, K. (1995). Understanding the dynamics of diversity in decision-making teams. In R. Guzzo & E. Salas (Eds.), *Team effectiveness and decision-making in organizations* (pp. 204–261). San Francisco: Jossey-Bass. Copyright © 1995. Reprinted with permission of John Wiley & Sons, Inc.

"Truly multicultural organizations are characterized by full structural and formal integration, minimal prejudice or discrimination, minimal subgroup differences in organizational attachment, and low levels of conflict." R. R. Thomas (1992) described the multicultural environment as "*one* culture reflecting the mixture of diversity in an organization rather than *several* minicultures reflecting the different elements in the mixture."

Jackson, May, and Whitney (1995) proposed that diversity can be considered from several perspectives. First, diversity can be predicated on attributes that are easy to detect (i.e., demographic characteristics) or on attributes that are less detectable (i.e., psychological characteristics). In addition, diversity can be distinguished on the basis of attributes that are related to tasks compared with those that are more relationship oriented. Table 11.2 presents the various ways in which diversity can be considered. Managers and workers tend to define diversity in terms of the readily detected attributes and demographic characteristics listed in the table. For psychologists, however, there is more value in defining diversity in terms of the underlying psychological attributes in that table. You will recognize those attributes from our earlier considerations of individual differences. These are the KSAOs that were described in Chapter 3.

The Dynamics of Diversity

Relational demography The relative makeup of various demographic characteristics in particular work groups.

Pfeffer (1983) coined the term **relational demography** to describe the method by which work groups—and, by extension, organizations—are composed and changed. If an organization attempts to populate itself according to some formal or informal plan (e.g., creative, flexible, or conscientious people), these attempts will influence such things as recruiting, hiring, leadership, motivation, satisfaction, productivity, communication, and turnover (Landy, 2001). For example, Tsui and colleagues found that as work groups increased in racial and gender diversity, absenteeism and turnover increased (Tsui, Egan, & O'Reilly, 1991; Tsui & O'Reilly, 1989). The simplest way to interpret such findings is that as demographic diversity increases, so do variations in values, abilities, and motivations. Because individuals might prefer homogeneity to diversity, they may stay away from work more often (see Hulin's work on withdrawal mechanism that we reviewed in Chapter 9) or even change jobs (Hulin's job withdrawal mechanism) as a way to avoid the conflicting values and interests that characterize a diverse workplace. As we will see in Chapter 14 on organizations, there is a tendency for work groups to seek homogeneity rather than diversity. Individuals generally prefer to associate with others who share their interests and values (Schneider, Goldstein, & Smith, 1995); we might say they view their associations as a matter of in-group and out-group status, which we will cover in Chapters 12 and 13.

Herriot and Pemberton (1995) explained why group members appear to value homogeneity over diversity. They suggested that the following difficulties exist in diverse groups:

1. Others do not agree with your vision or goals.
2. Differences in visions and goals are the result of differences in values. When values are threatened, the result is defensive behavior.
3. When there are differences in vision and goals, there are disagreements about which projects to undertake and how to spend time and money.
4. Different visions are often associated with different analyses of the situation, leading to unproductive communication.
5. Differences in expertise and knowledge lead to disagreement about methods and procedures.

Triandis (2003) identifies additional challenges to diversity anchored in psychological mechanisms. He suggests that since humans are notoriously poor at processing large amounts of information, it is much easier to deal in terms of "us" and "them." Another challenge is that most people are ethnocentric and tend to use their own culture as the standard for

BOX 11.3 THOUGHTS ON FAIRNESS, JUSTICE, AND DIVERSITY

"Nothing is so unequal as the equal treatment of unequal people."—Thomas Jefferson (1743–1826), third president of the United States

"He's fair. He treats us all the same—like dogs."—Defensive tackle Henry Jordan (1935–1977), referring to Vince Lombardi, legendary Green Bay Packers coach

"Fairness, justice, or whatever you call it—it's essential and most companies don't have it. Everybody must be judged on his performance, not his looks or his manners or his personality or who he knows or who he is related to."—Robert Townsend (1920–1998), former president of Avis Rent-A-Car

"Some people think that seeking diversity automatically leads to excellence, but I think focusing on excellence inevitably leads to diversity."—William C. Steere, Jr. (b. 1936), former CEO and director emeritus of the global pharmaceutical firm Pfizer, Inc.

defining "normal," "natural," or "correct." These considerations help to explain why group members may put up resistance to increased workplace diversity.

Group and Multicultural Diversity

The findings described above create a dilemma for organizations. Although some individuals find a diverse work environment stimulating and enjoyable, it appears that workers are generally happier, more committed, and more effective when they work with others who are "like" them. In the past, even if there was some diversity at work, the solitary nature of most work allowed workers to largely ignore the differences in values and interests between themselves and their co-workers. But that is no longer possible, for three reasons. First, work is no longer solitary. One way or another, many if not most workers will be in group or team environments for at least part of the workweek. Second, whether or not an employer finds this desirable, a demographic revolution is occurring at the workplace. Virtually every country has an aging workforce, which is a function of a much greater number of older individuals in the workforce than was the case 20 years ago. Thus, whether an organization seeks to increase age diversity or not, it is happening. In addition, various social, political, and economic shifts—precipitated by agreements like the North American Free Trade Agreement (NAFTA) and European Union laws that guarantee freedom of movement of people among member states—are breaking down national borders and resulting in more culturally diverse work environments. Finally, the very existence of multinational corporations and a global economy suggests that work relationships will become increasingly diverse through events such as international mergers, joint ventures, and acquisitions (Jackson & Schuler, 2003).

Vallaster (2005) conducted three longitudinal studies to understand the social and communication processes in multicultural work groups. She found that the effects of country-of-origin diversity depend on whether employees feel this is a salient issue in a particular context. When employees do perceive important cross-cultural differences, managers need to be proactive in encouraging social interaction, trust, and communication to ensure successful cooperation among culturally diverse group members.

Jackson and Joshi (2001) addressed the issue of multicultural diversity from a training perspective. They reasoned that since multicultural environments will be associated with workforce diversity, the prudent employer will prepare employees to work in these diverse contexts. They noted the need for various types of training, depending on whether only two cultures are involved (e.g., an American–Japanese joint venture) or multiple cultures (e.g., a European Union team assembled from nine member countries). In addition, training for individuals would be different than training for teams. The training architecture they suggested is reproduced in Table 11.3. The issues of cross-cultural training and team training are covered in greater detail in Chapters 7 and 13, respectively.

Although diversity might have been a goal 15 years ago, it is now more of a challenge. As we will see, the problem is not simply one of fostering diversity but one of managing it and fostering adaptation by diverse organizational members (Landy, 2001). Diversity would be an easier strategy to sell if it offered clear bottom-line advantages. Unfortunately, there are simply no convincing data to show that diversity results in enhanced firm, or even work group, performance (Jackson, Joshi, & Erhardt, 2003). But the literature does suggest that diversity is associated with both positive and negative outcomes (van Knippenberg, De Dreu, & Homan, 2004; van Knippenberg & Schippers, 2007). Instead of making the strong business case for diversity (e.g., increased diversity means increased profitability), Kochan and colleagues (2003) suggest a different justification for diversity efforts—a survival case. This case for diversity recognizes that diversity is a reality, not a goal, and that the organizations that manage this reality will be more profitable than those that do not.

TABLE 11.3 Approaches to Training Employees for Work in International Contexts

	DIVERSITY IN ORGANIZATIONS	
	INDIVIDUAL TRAINING	*TEAM TRAINING*
Single culture	Training regarding host country's culture, laws, and language geared for specific overseas assignment	Training modules that involve both parent country and host country nationals in mutual exploration of each other's culture, laws, and language
Multiple cultures	Training programs aimed at developing global manager's generic intercultural competencies (e.g., interpersonal communication skills, ability to tolerate stress, emphasis on personal growth, sense of humor)	Training global, dispersed teams to develop common protocol for communication across distances using e-mail, videoconferencing, and voice messaging facilities
		Team-based training modules designed to facilitate face-to-face interaction among team members
		Socialization of new team members to multicultural context
		Long-term training aimed at developing team identity
		Leadership training designed specifically for multicultural context

SOURCE: Jackson, S. E., & Joshi, A. (2001). Research on domestic and international diversity in organizations: A merger that works? In N. Anderson, D. Ones, H. Sinangil, & C. Viswesvaran (Eds.), *Handbook of industrial, work, and organizational psychology* (Vol. 1, pp. 206–231). London: Sage.

Managing Diversity from the Organizational Perspective

The actual management of diversity will involve virtually all of the tools in the I-O psychologist's toolbag: recruiting, selecting, training, motivating, leading, and so forth. The most effective approach will likely differ for each organization and each situation. Nevertheless, Cleveland and colleagues (2000) have identified the characteristics of organizations most likely to manage diversity successfully. A successful organization will do the following:

1. Exhibit diversity at every level, not just at entry levels.
2. Foster diversity not only in formal levels of the organization but also in less formal social networks.
3. Uncover and root out bias and discriminatory practices.
4. Build commitment and attachment to the organization among all members, not only in-group members.
5. Take steps to reduce interpersonal conflict.
6. Acknowledge and accommodate cultural differences rather than pretend they do not exist.

But just as diversity can be managed effectively, it can also be mismanaged. Herriot and Pemberton (1995) identified two ineffective models for addressing diversity:

1. **Assimilation model**. Recruit, select, train, and motivate employees so that all share the same values and culture. This model assumes there are no advantages to a diverse workforce, an assumption that has been challenged (Jackson et al., 1995).
2. **Protection model**. Identify disadvantaged and underrepresented groups and provide special protections for them. In Module 11.2, we saw that this model often leads to debates about justice and fairness, with resulting increases in dissatisfaction and anger and decreases in commitment and effectiveness.

Assimilation model Model for addressing diversity that recruits, selects, trains, and motivates employees so that they share the same values and culture.

Protection model Model for addressing diversity that identifies disadvantaged and underrepresented groups and provides special protections for them.

The researchers recommended a third model as the ideal for conceptualizing diversity:

3. **Value model**. Value each diverse element of the organization for what it uniquely brings to the organization.

Value model Model for addressing diversity in which each element of an organization is valued for what it uniquely brings to the organization.

The value model captures the concept of multiculturalism as we described it earlier in this module (Cleveland et al., 2000; R. R. Thomas, 1992). Herriot and Pemberton (1995) also identified several HR initiatives that support the value model (multicultural) of diversity:

1. Recruit specifically with diversity in mind.
2. Ensure that career development is available for every member of the organization and hold managers accountable for that universal development.
3. Provide diversity training for all employees and managers.
4. Seek input from diverse group members, not just their managers.
5. Provide support and networks for diverse group members.
6. Develop connections to broader cultural groups in the community.

The recommendations provided for developing and managing a diverse workplace might be distilled into the principles of distributive justice (i.e., fairness in the distribution of outcomes) and procedural justice (particularly in providing an outlet for voice) with which we began this chapter. In other words, diversity will suffer when the environment is closed, exclusive, and unjust. Diversity will thrive if the environment is open, just, and inclusive.

Bernardo Ferdman and colleagues (Holvino, Ferdman, & Merrill-Sands, 2004; Wasserman, Gallegos, & Ferdman, 2008) have written extensively on **inclusion**, which is defined as the degree to which individuals feel safe, valued, and able to be authentic at work both as individuals and as members of various groups (Gale, 2007). In an inclusive multicultural organization, people are sought out because of their unique characteristics and differences, and those differences become part of the fabric of the organization and its operating procedures. This diverse and inclusive climate is fostered by leaders in the highest levels of the organization, and it works best if all HR practices (selection, training, performance evaluation) reinforce such a climate (Nishii & Mayer, 2009; Shore et al., 2011). In Chapter 14, we will discuss different models of fit, and we will see that diversity is compatible with the complementarity model of person–organization fit.

Inclusion The degree to which individuals feel safe, valued, and able to be authentic at work both as individuals and as members of various groups.

One final way of thinking about managing diversity is through the metaphor of organization. As we have seen in Chapters 3, 4, and 5, successful performance arises from the combination of many human attributes in such a way that the *combination* of attributes is optimal for the task at hand. Consider an individual who had only one attribute—intelligence, or conscientiousness, or skill at oral communication. It is unlikely that such an individual could be successful in any 21st-century job you can think of. The same case may be made for diverse work groups. As the tasks and challenges become more complex for a group or an organization, the value of a diverse set of contributors becomes more important.

Diversity Training

During the 1970s, 1980s, and 1990s, many employers instituted diversity training programs as a way of demonstrating their commitment to diversity and proactive compliance with equal employment opportunity regulations. Yet a recent sociological study that analyzed 30 years of data for more than 800 workplaces concluded that "neither diversity training to extinguish stereotypes, nor diversity performance evaluations to provide feedback and oversight to people making hiring and promotion decisions, have accomplished much, if anything" (Dobbin, Kalev, & Kelly, 2007, p. 26). However, the researchers did find that successful diversity programs (1) used mentoring rather than training workshops and (2) had a diversity manager or task force that was responsible for increasing the number of women and minorities in good jobs. Recent studies by I-O psychologists and management researchers provide some insight into the challenges of implementing voluntary diversity training programs (King, Gulik, & Kravitz, 2011). For example, Kulik, Pepper, Roberson, and Parker (2007) examined such programs to see whether trainee demographic characteristics or pre-training competence in understanding diversity would predict which employees would choose to participate. Surprisingly, demographic characteristics (e.g., whether a worker belonged to a protected class in terms of race, ethnicity, age, or gender) did not have an impact on interest in training or on actual training participation. However, pre-training competence levels had a positive effect on both interest in training and actual participation in diversity training. That is, more competent trainees expressed more interest in additional training and were more likely to attend a voluntary training session than were those with low competence who were unaware of their low competence levels and thus were unmotivated to participate in diversity training programs. The authors concluded that this is a case of the "rich getting richer," whereby those who were most aware of diversity issues were the ones who were most interested in participating in diversity programs. If organizations follow Herriot and Pemberton's (1995) recommendation above that diversity training should be mandatory for everyone, then those with low pre-training competence would be receiving just as much training as those with high pre-training competence.

Sanchez and Medkik (2004) examined the effects of diversity awareness training in a field study of 125 managers and supervisors employed by a county government in the southeastern United States. Although initial reactions to the training program were positive, follow-up data and interviews revealed negative reactions that resulted from a lack of clear

BOX 11.4 AN INNOVATIVE DIVERSITY MENTORING PROGRAM

Cargill is a Minneapolis-based company with over 100,000 employees in 59 countries working in over 80 business units. As part of its diversity effort (which is known internally as "Valuing Differences"), the company introduced a program known as "reverse mentoring" in which lower-level female, African American, and gay, lesbian, bisexual, and transgendered employees volunteer to mentor senior managers for a year. The mentors set the agenda for each meeting. The Cargill vice president of corporate diversity reports that the program has been very valuable in broadening the perspective of the senior leaders of the organization (*New York Times*, 2005a). For a company like Cargill, it would be a small step to add mentors from different national cultures to the group.

communication about the initial nomination process for the training program and a lack of post-training coaching and support. The authors concluded that the results of the program suggest that typical one-day diversity training sessions might do more harm than good. Nevertheless, as we discussed in Chapter 7, post-training peer and supervisor support is critical to the success of any training program, and the findings in this study provide an important reminder that the success of any specific training program can be enhanced by following solid principles of effective transfer of training.

Kecia Thomas (2008) has edited a comprehensive book on diversity resistance in organizations. Noted diversity scholars discuss resistance to various types of diversity programs in organizations as well as ways of minimizing such resistance. For example, Chrobot-Mason, Hays-Thomas, and Wishik (2008) provided suggestions for helping diversity programs succeed, including: (1) diagnose pre-training attitudes to identify sources of resistance to diversity training initiatives that can be addressed in advance of training, (2) create organizational support structures and policies to support the intended goals of the diversity training program, and (3) ensure that there is clear support from and participation by upper management in the diversity program. Diversity training can be part of the larger process of organizational socialization, which is the process by which a new employee becomes aware of the values and procedures of the organization. We discuss socialization in greater detail in Chapter 14.

Leadership and Diversity

Organizations need to pay close attention to the dynamics of work groups. Regardless of the values of the upper levels of the organization, work groups may very well strive for the comfort of homogeneity. This will place the major burden for managing diversity on the shoulders of the group or team leader (Lord & Smith, 1999). From the leader's perspective, managing diversity requires understanding any stereotypes that might exist among group members (what Ferdman and Davidson [2004] call interpersonal and intergroup "mush") and challenging them with a view toward breaking them down. Ayoko and Hartel (2003) suggest that in order to do that, the leader must be skilled in conflict resolution as well as open and interested in interacting with people who would be seen as dissimilar to oneself. But managing diversity also requires the leader to bear in mind that each member of the group is an individual, regardless of the attributes (demographic or psychological) he or she might share with other group members.

Each worker, in a sense, has three identities. First, each worker is a member of the organization and should be treated in a manner consistent with the treatment of every other member of the organization. Second, each worker belongs to a cultural group whose members share values. Finally, each worker is an individual with a unique past and future. Managers have always had to deal with the principles of consistency of treatment and the uniqueness of individuals. But the challenge of diversity adds a level of culture that is becoming increasingly important in the workplace. We will return to issues of culture and diversity in the context of leadership in the final module of Chapter 12.

MODULE 11.3 SUMMARY

- Diversity can refer to demographic attributes that are easy to detect or psychological attributes that are more difficult to detect. Although managers and workers tend to define diversity in terms of readily detected attributes such as demographic characteristics, psychologists propose that there is more value in defining diversity in terms of the underlying psychological attributes or KSAOs that were described in Chapter 3.
- Diversity has both costs and benefits. Although initially there will be some tension and lowered effectiveness in demographically and culturally heterogeneous work groups, effectiveness will increase if work groups remain intact. Diversity often enhances the creative efforts of work groups by widening the variety of approaches taken to problem solving.
- Managing diversity involves the I-O psychologist's entire toolbag: recruiting, selecting, training, motivating, and leading. The most effective approach will probably differ for each organization and each situation. However, successful organizations will be more likely to exhibit diversity at every level, foster diversity in formal and informal ways throughout the organization, and uncover and root out bias and discriminatory practices.
- Two ineffective models for addressing diversity are the assimilation model and the protection model. An alternative model for addressing diversity is the value model, in which each diverse element of the organization is valued for what it uniquely brings to the organization. Overall, diversity will thrive if the work environment is open, inclusive, and just.

KEY TERMS

diversity
relational demography
assimilation model
protection model
value model
inclusion

12 Leadership

MODULE 12.1

The Concept of Leadership

Some Conceptual Distinctions

"Pushover." The word stuck in Jenny's mind as she held her head high, walking out after a difficult meeting with the store manager. A recent college graduate, Jenny was assistant manager of a retail department, where she supervised a group of middle-aged employees; they tended to treat her like a daughter, spending much of their workday chatting and taking breaks. How could she get them to take her seriously as their boss? By the next morning, Jenny had decided what needed to happen. She assembled her staff and told them, "I need you to do what you signed on to do. If not, you'll get a new manager who is not going to be as nice as I am" (Ming, 2005, p. 118). Twenty years later, Jenny Ming was president of Old Navy clothing stores and listed in *Fortune* magazine's "50 Most Powerful Women in American Business." Clearly, that first staff meeting was just the beginning of a process of developing leadership attributes and skills that enabled her to succeed in a remarkable way.

Many treatments of leadership concentrate on "high-impact" leaders like Jenny Ming: the corporate CEO, the chairman of the board, the president, the chairman of the Joint Chiefs of Staff. Fascinating as they are, these top-echelon individuals operate in unique environments that most of us will never see. The limitation in deriving our leadership principles from the study of that elite group is that there are not many of them, and each of them is in a dramatically different situation. For these reasons, we will focus less on executives than on middle- and lower-level leaders in organizations—those in positions like the ones Ming held during her first several years out of college. For readers interested in the particular issues related to executive leadership, Silzer's (2002) book will prove useful.

There is another reason to concentrate on lower-level leaders: Virtually every employee in the 21st century will be called upon to display leadership behaviors at some point in time. We might think of this as "episodic" leadership—episodes of work life that require leadership behaviors. As an experienced department member, you might be called upon to fill in for a supervisor who is on vacation, or to lead a project team that has been formed for the purpose of dealing with a specific production problem, or even just to represent your peers in an informal discussion with your manager. It is reasonable to assume that leadership research is relevant for virtually any employee in any organization, regardless of the size or the complexity of the organization.

Leader Emergence versus Leadership Effectiveness

It is important to distinguish between the concepts of **leader emergence** and **leadership effectiveness.** It is tempting to confuse the concepts by assuming that all who emerge as leaders will be effective. While that is sometimes the case, it is not always true. If we are interested in leadership emergence, we might study the characteristics of individuals who *become* leaders. On what basis were they elected, or appointed, or simply accepted? If, on the other hand, we are interested in leadership effectiveness, we might study which behaviors on the part of a designated leader (regardless of how he or she achieved that position) led to an outcome valued by the work group or organization. Even though the concepts are clearly different, Foti and Haunestein (2007) studied leaders who emerged as they went about their leadership duties and found that both leader emergence and leader effectiveness were predicted by high levels of intelligence, dominance, self-efficacy, and self-monitoring.

Leader emergence Study of the characteristics of individuals who become leaders, examining the basis on which they were elected, appointed, or simply accepted.

Leadership effectiveness Study of which behaviors on the part of a designated leader (regardless of how that position was achieved) led to an outcome valued by the work group or organization.

Leader Emergence

Research on the relationship between leader emergence and the Big Five personality factors was examined in a meta-analysis by Judge, Bono, Ilies, and Gerhardt (2002). They found that several of the Big Five factors were associated with leader emergence. Leader emergence was defined as "whether (or to what degree) an individual is viewed as a leader by others" (p. 767). Emotional stability, extraversion, openness to experience, and conscientiousness were all positively associated with individuals who emerged as leaders. Surprisingly, agreeableness was unrelated to leader emergence.

In their meta-analysis, Judge and colleagues (2002) also separated the studies into those conducted in business settings, in military/government settings, and with students. They found that the most consistent correlate of both leader emergence and leadership effectiveness was extraversion. Day, Schleicher, Unckless, and Hiller (2002) found that individuals with a self-monitoring personality (those who are concerned with projecting a positive social appearance) are much more likely to emerge as leaders, particularly in their examination of how promotions are awarded in an organization. In keeping with the distinction we have made above, there are no data to suggest that high self-monitors

BOX 12.1 THE "DYNASTY" EFFECT

Based on an analysis of leader emergence among identical twins, Arvey and colleagues (Arvey, Rotundo, Johnson, Zhang, & McGue, 2006) have proposed a substantial (i.e., 30 percent of the variance) *genetic* component to leadership. A genetic mechanism might be invoked to at least partially explain the "dynasty" effect in U.S. politics that can be cited as far back as the nation's second and sixth presidents (John Adams and his son John Quincy Adams). The effect can also be seen in the 20th century, with President Theodore Roosevelt and his niece Eleanor, who was married to his distant cousin, President Franklin Delano Roosevelt. Perhaps more famous in our time are the Kennedy family (President John F. Kennedy, his brothers Senator Robert F. and Senator Edward M. "Ted" Kennedy, and Ted's son Congressman Patrick Kennedy) and the Bush family (President George H. W. Bush and his sons President George W. Bush and Governor Jeb Bush).

are actually more *effective* as leaders. In fact, Day and colleagues suggest that the opposite may be the case at the highest levels of an organization, where strategic and systems perspectives are more important than human relations skills. This may, in part, explain the oft-cited Peter Principle: People rise to their level of incompetence.

The Problem of Defining Leadership Outcomes

In previous chapters, we have examined various approaches to improving individual performance and, as a result, organizational productivity. In many senses we knew what we were after: decreased absence, increased commitment, more persistence, creativity, and so forth. The situation is not so clear with leadership. Leadership has been variously credited with achieving technological breakthroughs, settling labor problems, bringing an organization back from bankruptcy, increasing share value, increasing consumer confidence, or simply creating a fun place to work. Which of these is the "right" outcome to examine? If we want to develop a theory of leadership impact, which criterion variable should we choose to validate the theory? Day (2001a) pointed out some of the difficulties in assessing leadership outcomes. It is assumed that leaders affect the structure and performance of an organization. But which aspects of structure? Which indicators of performance?

Leaders, particularly those at the top of an organization, are assumed to be visionary, not bound to the here-and-now. In what time frame should we measure or evaluate the outcomes of visionary behavior? A year? Five years? A decade? If we are going to evaluate the outcomes of leadership, when should we start and when should we stop counting? In the late 1970s, the Social Democratic Party, which had ruled Sweden for more than 40 years, was voted out of office. The departing prime minister, Olaf Palme, observed that the new ruling party and prime minister could do little because they came to "a set table." By this, Palme meant that change is slow and, in this case, it would be time for a new election before the new ruling party could accomplish anything of significance. He was right. Within six years, Palme's Social Democratic Party was back in power, the interim government having accomplished very little.

As Day (2001a) pointed out, the effects of a leader's behavior are not always immediately obvious or detectable. Consider the Asian game of Go (known as *wéiqí* in Chinese), an elaborate form of checkers on a much larger board. The object of the game, which may take two to five hours to complete, is to surround all of your opponent's pieces, leaving no escape route. You do this by playing on different parts of the board simultaneously with a "connection plan" in mind that your opponent will not see. Then, at a crucial time, you connect all of your pieces and win the game. There is a lag time between action and result. You may have positioned one of your pieces in a far corner of the board at the beginning of the game, and that piece may be the key to winning the game. It should come as no surprise that Go originated in China, a country with a long-term time orientation. In the same way, a leader may put strategic plans into action, but their effects may not be seen for months or even years. It will be interesting to see if Japanese and Chinese leaders emerge as preeminent in the global business environment because of their characteristically long-term time orientation. Of course, this assumes that the boards of directors share this patience for effects to emerge.

To make matters even more complex, the situations in which leaders find themselves vary, sometimes from day to day (Osborn, Hunt, & Jauch, 2002). On Monday, the CEO of a pharmaceutical firm might discover that the Federal Drug Administration (FDA) has recommended a special warning for certain prescription drugs. On Tuesday, the same CEO might discover that a competitor is about to come out with a new and "better" prescription drug. On Wednesday, the board of directors may ask the CEO to oversee development of a comprehensive plan to introduce new products. Thus, there are many performance indicators to choose from in defining leadership effectiveness.

Negative Leadership Outcomes: The Destructive Leader

So far, we have taken a very positive view of leadership, assuming that a leader is trying to achieve positive outcomes using knowledge, skills, and abilities for the good of the organization. Using a concept we introduced in Chapter 1, we often assume the leader seeks to do "good work." But it is clear that some leaders are not interested in doing good work—or at least not doing work in a good way. These leaders are called destructive leaders, and they are beginning to receive more attention from researchers. A 2007 special issue of the *Leadership Quarterly* focused on the concept of destructive leadership (often referred to as the "dark side" of leadership). Einarsen, Aasland, and Skogstad (2007) define destructive leadership behavior as "the systematic and repeated behavior by a leader, supervisor, or manager that violates legitimate interest of the organization by undermining and/or sabotaging the organization's goals, tasks, resources, and effectiveness and/or the motivation, well-being, or job satisfaction of his/her subordinates" (p. 207). Every organization seems to have one: the manager who verbally abuses subordinates in private with threats and shouts, who has a personal agenda of self-promotion that is different from the stated goals of the group or organization, who drives people out of the department or unit, or who seems immune to any attempt to change his or her style. The destructive leader seems to have particularly toxic effects on workers with little autonomy in their jobs (Schaubroeck, Walumbwa, Ganster, & Kepes, 2007). Einarsen and colleagues (2007) describe the following three types of destructive leaders.

Tyrannical

The tyrannical leader may accept the goals of the organization but seeks to achieve those goals through actively manipulating and humiliating subordinates. The fact that the tyrannical leader often does accomplish organization goals may result in very different evaluations of his or her effectiveness. Upper management views the leader favorably, while subordinates see only a bully. The championship college basketball coach Bobby Knight, nicknamed "The General," could be characterized as a tyrannical leader: Although he was adored by many fans at the schools where he coached, he was also considered a bully by some players (and players' parents) because of his temper and autocratic style.

Derailed

Like the tyrannical leader, the derailed leader behaves abusively—but he or she also engages in anti-organizational behaviors such as laziness, fraud, and theft. Derailed leaders are often characterized as leaders who have hit a substantial pothole on their road to success. Enron's executives Kenneth Lay and Jeffrey Skilling might be examples of the derailed type.

Supportive-Disloyal

Unlike the first two types of destructive leaders, the supportive-disloyal leader actually shows consideration for subordinates but violates the goals of the organization by undermining goal accomplishment. This undermining may result from stealing resources from the organization, granting subordinates excessive benefits, or encouraging loafing or misconduct by subordinates. Einarsen and colleagues (2007) offer the example of a British bakery where many more loaves than would be sold were baked each day to allow bakery workers to steal the bread.

and creative leadership. For that reason, if for no other, research about and application of leadership theories will continue unabated. And, at least for the time being, transformational and charismatic leadership are the versions that are most often craved. They currently attract a great deal of attention, "shine" compared to other, less flashy theories (e.g., leader–member exchange or contingency theory), have committed followers, and result in a substantial addition to the research data on leadership. Nevertheless, a great deal of work needs to be done before we declare that these theories fully explain the effect of leader behavior on followers. It has often been noted that life is a trail, not a campsite. The same might be said of leadership theory: It is about paths, not end states.

MODULE 12.3 SUMMARY

- Leader–member exchange (LMX) theory proposes that leaders adopt different behaviors with individual subordinates. Its advocates argue that subordinates fall into an in-group, in which members have high-quality relationships with their leader, or an out-group, whose members have low-quality relationships with their leader.
- Transformational leadership describes the behavior of inspirational leaders and involves an interaction between leaders and followers in which each raises the other to higher levels of morality and motivation. Transformational leadership is often contrasted with transactional leadership, the process by which leaders simply show followers how to meet goals by adopting certain behaviors.
- Authentic leadership is gaining attention in I-O psychology research. It refers to a leader's sincerity and genuineness, and it includes the ability to share one's true self in a way that inspires and motivates one's followers.
- Charisma is a personal attribute of a leader that compels followers to identify with and attempt to emulate the leader. The followers of charismatic leaders are emotionally attached to the leader, do not question the leader's beliefs or actions, and see themselves as integral to the accomplishment of the leader's goals.

KEY TERMS

leader–member exchange (LMX) theory
in-group members
out-group members
life cycle of a leader–follower relationship
transformational leadership
transactional leadership
idealized influence
inspirational motivation
intellectual stimulation
individualized consideration
laissez-faire leadership
full-range theory of leadership
Multifactor Leadership Questionnaire (MLQ)
authentic leadership
charisma
charismatic leader
charismatic leadership theory

MODULE 12.4

Emerging Topics and Challenges in Leadership Research

Leadership in a Changing Workplace

As we have seen in virtually every chapter, changes in the workplace in the past two decades have been substantial. One consequence of these changes is a very different work environment for leaders. We will review a few of the more salient changes with respect to the challenge of leadership.

Knowledge-Oriented Organizations

Uhl-Bien, Marion, and McKelvey (2007) note that historical models of leadership, particularly those that are top-down and bureaucratic, are best suited for a 20th-century economy, where physical production was essential. By extension, they assert that these older models are ill suited for the 21st-century workplace, which is best characterized as knowledge-oriented. Furthermore, they propose that one of the key characteristics of the 21st-century organization is the need to adapt and learn. Thus, theories of leadership effectiveness must include outcomes such as organizational learning, innovation, and adaptability rather than focusing on bureaucratic and administrative functions of the leader.

Teams/Groups

Groups and teams are increasingly populating today's workplace. There are fewer and fewer single contributors. As we saw earlier in this chapter, many of the traditional leadership models are focused on the relationship between a single leader and a single follower. Things are a bit more complicated now. Certainly, individual interactions between a worker and a manager still take place, but there are also interactions between managers and teams/groups. It is no longer sufficient for a leader to concentrate on influencing individual work group members one by one. The team or group is a separate entity and must be considered independent of its members.

As if teams were not challenging enough, there is also the issue of virtual teams. A **virtual team** consists of geographically or organizationally dispersed members brought together through "a combination of telecommunications and information technologies to accomplish an organizational task" (Townsend, DeMarie, & Hendrickson, 1998, p. 17). As Bell and Kozlowski (2002b) pointed out, virtual teams present novel challenges for a leader, including the socialization of new team members and monitoring of the progress

Virtual team Team that has widely dispersed members working together toward a common goal and linked through computers and other technology.

of the teams as they go about their work. They hypothesized that as the work of a virtual team becomes more complex, the communications will need to be more frequent and intense. By definition, much of this increased communication will not take place in a face-to-face scenario. This will make the monitoring function of the leader increasingly difficult and will also require virtual teams to become more self-managing than leader-directed. These are just a few examples of the challenges that virtual teams will present to leaders.

Telecommuting

The discussion of virtual teams anticipates a related issue. As we have seen in earlier chapters, an increasing number of employees telecommute (i.e., work from home part or all of the workweek). As with virtual teams, telecommuting presents monitoring and communication challenges for a leader. When Lyndon Johnson was majority leader in the Senate and then president, he used his imposing physical presence as a way to influence individuals (Caro, 2002). Johnson would not have been able to use that advantage had the bulk of his communications been by telephone, fax, e-mail, or instant messaging.

Telecommuting comes in many different forms (Adams, 2001). Most common is the home office, but some organizations also have drop-in work centers located close to employees' homes, and others have unassigned work spaces for use by employees who travel a great deal and use regional or branch facilities to do their work. Thus, a manager may be faced with a very basic issue: tracking an employee down on a given day. Adams suggested that effective leaders in a telecommuting environment will need to be much more proactive about communications in both directions. They should not sit and wait for problems to resolve themselves, nor should they allow telecommuting employees to be surprised by an action. With a "sit-and-wait" style, things could easily get out of control before the leader can exert any influence. With a "surprise" style, stress will become a significant obstacle to employee performance. Research indicates that transformational (as opposed to transactional) styles of leadership are more difficult to establish as the physical distance between a leader and followers increases (Howell, Neufeld, & Avolio, 2005). As work evolves in the 21st century, particularly as virtual teams and globalization increase, practicing the principles of transformational leadership will become increasingly difficult.

Temporary Workers

As organizations become "leaner," they are more likely to make use of temporary workers. Often an organization uncertain of long-term business prospects will fill vacant positions with consultants or contract workers. The advantage of hiring temporary workers is that it allows an organization to respond to market changes by quickly increasing or decreasing the workforce. From a leader's perspective, however, temporary workers represent a challenge. As temps are unlikely to have the same commitment or share the same values as full-time employees, they may be more difficult to motivate. In addition, these workers may be expected to support work groups and teams without being a member of any particular team. Some organizations develop an internal pool of "floating" employees and use this pool for dealing with unexpected terminations, illnesses, or resignations (Cascio, 2010). Although these in-house temporary workers may share the same values and have the same level of commitment as full-time employees, they still move rapidly from assignment to assignment and are not likely to be part of a team or to establish a relationship with a manager. There is also the possibility that the temporary workers will affect the behavior of the permanent employees. Harris (2000) suggested that the job satisfaction of permanent employees may decrease owing to feelings of insecurity, including worries about being replaced by temporary or part-time workers.

Fuzzy Job Boundaries

As we have seen, the meaning of a "job" is changing. The concept of a team changes the notion of individual contributions. In addition, rapid changes in technology and work processes also make a job title or job description a moving target. This places increasing pressure on leaders to anticipate how work is evolving and how the work roles of various team members are integrated. There is, however, one stable behavior emerging from the new work environment: organizational citizenship behaviors (OCBs), which we discussed in Chapter 4. Regardless of how rapidly work changes, OCBs performed by individual workers will very likely represent a value added. Thus, one task of the modern leader may be to encourage OCBs among followers.

Male and Female Leaders: Are They Different?

The Demographics of Leadership

In 2012, women were in top leadership positions in some of the largest American corporations, including IBM (Virginia Rometty), Kraft Foods (Irene Rosenfeld), and Pepsico (Indra Nooyi). Females have also been ascending to top positions in government in the United States and abroad. For example, at the time of this writing, three of the last four U.S. secretaries of state have been women (Madeline Albright, Condeleezza Rice, and Hillary Clinton). In 2011, Christine Lagarde, formerly France's finance minister, was named leader of the International Monetary Fund. A greater number of women are running for political office as well. In fact, humorist and *Time* magazine columnist Joel Stein (2012) recently observed, "I was happy about the progress women have made in getting elected to office until I found out who they're replacing: men." Despite Stein's concern, females still make up a fairly small percentage of those in political office and in top leadership positions in corporations. Consider the following statistics regarding women and leadership positions in the early 21st century (Eagly & Karau, 2002). Women make up:

- 46 percent of the U.S. workforce
- 45 percent of executive, administrative, and managerial occupations
- 51 percent of those with bachelor's degrees
- 45 percent of those with advanced degrees
- 4 percent of the five highest-earning officers in each Fortune 500 company
- .4 percent of the CEOs of Fortune 500 companies
- 13 percent of U.S. Senators
- 14 percent of members of the U.S. House of Representatives
- 10 percent of state governors
- 2 percent of high-ranking military officers

What's wrong with this picture? It appears that women are about as highly qualified as men but hold a disproportionately small percentage of leadership positions. The question is why. Is it because they simply do not want leadership positions, or because they lack leadership ability, or because non-job-related forces (e.g., stereotypes held by decision makers) present an obstacle to obtaining leadership positions?

The explosion of lawsuits brought by women seeking managerial and leadership positions would seem to rebut the argument that women simply don't want these positions (Landy, 2005a). Let's examine the other two plausible explanations: Women don't have the necessary skill set and/or temperament for leadership, or women are the victims of stereotyped thinking.

© Sandy Huffaker/The New York Times/Redux Pictures

San Diego Fire Chief Tracy Jarman directs subordinates fighting a wildfire that threatens homes and businesses. If women are as highly qualified as men, why do they hold a disproportionately small percentage of leadership positions?

Hyde (2005) conducted a meta-analysis of research examining gender differences in cognitive variables, communication skills, personality, and physical abilities. The results are sobering. The only substantial difference between males and females appeared in motor performance—particularly in throwing distance and velocity. So unless leadership positions require the CEO to throw the quarterly report the length of the conference table, it would not appear that women have less potential than men to become managers and leaders.

Heilman and Okimoto (2007) argue that women who are successful in male-stereotyped occupations are actually punished for that success, possibly because they are simultaneously seen as *deficient* in skills more commonly associated with women (e.g., communal skills such as behaving in a kind, nurturing, and sympathetic manner). While their success in male-stereotyped positions and occupations is grudgingly acknowledged, such women are still rated lower on things such as likability and desirability as a boss and higher on things such as interpersonal hostility.

In a recent comprehensive meta-analysis, Eagly and her colleagues (Koenig, Eagly, Mitchell, & Ristikari, 2011) examined the extent to which stereotypes of leaders are masculine. They found that leader stereotypes were indeed masculine. However, follow-up analyses indicated that this masculine view of leadership has decreased over time and that masculine stereotypes were less prevalent in certain industries (e.g., education). Indeed, more female leaders are being seen in the educational sector, including the positions of school principal, school district superintendent, and university president.

Eagly and her colleagues (Eagly, Johannesen-Schmidt, & van Engen, 2003; Eagly & Karau, 2002) argue that women have *greater* potential than men for leadership effectiveness as data accumulate linking transformational and transactional styles to effectiveness. They argue that women should have an increasing advantage over men in competing for leadership positions in the 21st century, going so far as to suggest not only that female qualities of egalitarianism, inclusion, and participative styles fit better in the executive suite but that certain male characteristics (e.g., aggressiveness) predict poorer leader effectiveness. As you might imagine, this has led to a debate about the relative advantages of women in leadership positions (Eagly & Carli, 2003a,b; Vecchio, 2002, 2003). As with most debates, the result is a bit more heat than light, particularly since there are very few actual data to examine, in large part because there are so few women leaders.

Nevertheless, Vecchio and Brazil (2007) were able to examine the dynamics of gender and leadership in the behavior of cadets at the U.S. Military Academy at West Point. In order to assess the interactions between leaders and subordinates of the same gender versus leaders and subordinates of the opposite gender, they asked male and female leaders and subordinates to rate the quality of such interactions. The results were interesting. Subordinates reported differences in positivity of the working relationships, with same-gender pairings resulting in more positive rating. But leaders rated the performance of same-gender and different-gender subordinates equally! So it would appear that subordinate differences in rated positivity may not influence a leader's ratings of performance.

Returning to the question of why there are so few women in top leadership positions, Chin, Lott, Rice, and Sanchez-Hucles (2007) point out that one cannot assume that the

BOX 12.3 A SAMPLING OF WOMEN'S THOUGHTS ON LEADERSHIP

"Whatever women must do they must do twice as well as men to be thought half as good. Luckily, this is not difficult."—Charlotte Whitton (1896–1975), first woman in Canada to be mayor of a major city (Ottawa)

"If high heels were so wonderful, men would still be wearing them."—Sue Grafton (b. 1940), novelist

"When women are depressed, they either eat or go shopping. Men invade another country."—Elayne Boosler (b. 1952), actor, writer, director, and blog contributor

"In politics, if you want anything said, ask a man; if you want anything done, ask a woman."—Margaret Thatcher (b. 1925), former British prime minister

"If men can run the world, why can't they stop wearing neckties? How intelligent is it to start the day by tying a noose around your neck?"—Linda Ellerbee (b. 1944), journalist, TV news anchor, author, and cancer survival advocate

challenges to women in leadership roles are homogeneous. They observe that different obstacles appear not only by environment (e.g., business leaders versus political or academic leaders) but also as a function of national culture. In a cross-cultural research study of male and female leaders, Paris, Howell, Dorfman, and Hanges (2009) found that regardless of national culture, female managers were much more likely than male managers to describe the ideal leader as charismatic, team oriented, and participative. So there does seem to be some evidence that men and women hold somewhat different images of the ideal leader. Paris and colleagues also found some evidence that the female ideal leader may have a better fit in, for example, the food and finance industries than in telecommunications.

So, at least for the present, we are left with the question that began this section: Why aren't there more female leaders? In some senses, we need to solve the riddle of leader emergence before we can tackle the question of leader effectiveness. Remember that Day, Schleicher, and colleagues (2002) found differences between men and women in the tendency to self-promote, with men showing greater skill and/or interest in this than women. It may be that men simply take advantage of a flawed system of leader selection to a greater extent than women. This is just one of dozens of explanations for the discrepancy between the "is" and the "expected" that we highlighted above.

The Leadership Styles of Men and Women

Above, we dealt with the issue of who *becomes* a leader. Now let's consider whether leadership is *exercised* differently by women (compared to men) when they assume positions of leadership. In a special issue of the American Psychological Association's *Monitor on Psychology* (Munsey, 2007), the diverse leadership environments of 19 female leaders are described. One of them is Dana Born, an I-O psychologist and Air Force brigadier general. She is the leader of the academic program at the Air Force Academy, as well as the prime liaison between the U.S. Air Force training effort and those of our allies. The stories of these female leaders make it abundantly clear that they face the same challenges as male leaders in similar environments and use the same diversity of leadership strategies as their male counterparts. The difference does not seem to be the nature of the leadership challenges faced by men and women.

© David Zalubowski/AP/Wide World Photos

Air Force Brigadier General Dana Born is the leader of the academic program at the Air Force Academy as well as the prime liaison between the U.S. Air Force training effort and those of our allies.

Eagly and Johnson (1990) conducted a meta-analysis of studies examining leadership style and gender, with interesting results. The stereotypical view is that women lead by emphasizing interpersonal interactions, whereas men lead by emphasizing task completion. No such differences were found in field studies, but they did appear in laboratory studies. This suggests that stereotypes might have been operating in lab studies but not in real organizations. In field studies, however, Eagly and Johnson determined that women tended to prefer democratic and participative styles rather than the autocratic styles favored by men.

Feingold (1994) conducted a meta-analysis of personality differences between men and women in the general psychological literature. Although he did not focus on leadership, some of his findings are relevant to that topic. He found that men tended to be slightly more assertive than women and that women tended to be slightly more extraverted than men. But he also found a large and stable difference between the genders on the attribute of tender-mindedness, which is associated with nurturing behaviors and empathy. Women, not surprisingly, were substantially more tender-minded than men. However, the cross-cultural research of Paris and colleagues (2009) described above found no differences between male and female managers with respect to tender-mindedness (which they called a humane orientation): Neither men nor women considered this characteristic to be important in an ideal leader. When the Feingold results are combined with those of Eagly and Johnson (1990), they suggest a potentially different "style" for male and female leaders, with females tending to favor more participative and democratic interactions with subordinates and to be more aware of interpersonal issues than their male counterparts. Despite the gender-equal finding on the attribute of tender-mindedness, overall, the research of Paris and colleagues (2009) seems to confirm that the ideal female leader and the ideal male leader reflect these stylistic differences.

But the question remains whether these differences matter in terms of the ultimate effectiveness of the leader. Few data are available to answer this question directly. Nevertheless, as described above, there is some theoretical basis for speculating that such differences may have an increasingly important impact on leader effectiveness as transformational styles of leadership become the preferred styles. It is clear that the workplace is being transformed from one characterized by single contributors to one dominated by teams and interacting work groups. This in turn suggests that people skills (e.g., communication, negotiation, conflict resolution) will become increasingly important. As Eagly and her colleagues suggest, this would seem to favor women as leaders.

We hasten to add two qualifiers, however. First, statistical studies such as the meta-analyses described above present us with mean or average differences. But there is also variation within each gender. In all of the studies reviewed, there were male leaders who were nurturant, democratic, empathic, and participatory in style; there were also female leaders who were autocratic, task-oriented, nonempathic, and nonparticipatory. So we should not be misled into assuming that *all* male leaders behave differently from *all* female leaders.

One additional phenomenon to consider when examining gender and leadership has to do with the extent to which the particular industry is a male- or female-dominated industry. Some research suggests that this variable has an effect on the leadership style adopted by female leaders. Gardiner and Tiggemann (1999) studied 60 male and 60 female Australian managers in male-dominated (e.g., automotive, information technology, consulting, timber) and female-dominated (e.g., childhood education, nursing, hairdressing) industries. They found that women in male-dominated industries were less likely to adopt a style that emphasized interpersonal orientations (as opposed to task orientations). Furthermore, they found that while the mental health of female managers in a male-dominated industry was worse if they adopted an interpersonally oriented style, the mental health of male managers in male-dominated industries was better if they adopted an interpersonally oriented style. This intriguing finding suggests the possibility that if women behaved in an expected (interpersonal) way, they encountered resistance. In contrast, when men behaved in an unexpected (interpersonal) way, they encountered no such resistance. Since this last set of findings was peculiar to male-dominated industries, it suggests the potential influence of stereotypes that men hold about women. Thus, a subtle but important issue in considering the issue of men and women as leaders is the extent to which the industry in question is male or female dominated (Koenig et al., 2011).

Personality and Leadership

As you saw in Module 12.2, the trait approach to leadership that characterized the research of early investigators has been largely discredited. In large measure this has happened because the traits investigated were poorly defined and measured—traits like popularity, maturity, and creativity. It was not so much that these traits didn't make any sense; they did. The problem was that they meant something different to and were measured differently by every researcher. They had no scientific credibility.

As we have seen in almost every chapter (but specifically in Chapter 3), the role of personality traits has become more prominent in I-O psychology as a result of the introduction of the Big Five model of personality. I-O psychologists now know what they are measuring and how they are measuring it when they examine personality traits. Using our examples from above, popularity might now be identified as agreeableness and extraversion, maturity might be equated with emotional stability and conscientiousness, and creativity might be considered similar to openness to experience. As we saw in Chapter 3, personality traits are considered "habitual ways of responding"; thus, they involve concrete behaviors. The classical leadership models identified leader traits by having subordinates describe the extent to which a leader behaved in a considerate, structuring, or participative manner. As the Big Five model of personality has emerged, it is now possible to go beyond the work setting and ask how an individual such as a leader behaves in a much wider array of situations.

Virtually every classical and modern leadership theory includes personality traits. Not every model incorporates every one of the Big Five, but in the aggregate, every one of the Big Five factors appears in one or another leadership theory, either directly or indirectly. One interesting aspect of the role of personality in leader effectiveness is that the influence of personality is more apparent to the leader's followers than to his or her managers. Harris and Hogan (1992) found that managers serving under a leader made judgments about the leader's effectiveness based primarily on factors related to technical competence and knowledge. In contrast, the subordinates of the leader made judgments about effectiveness based on personality characteristics, particularly trustworthiness. Van Knippenberg, van Knippenberg, van Kleef, and Damen (2008) suggest that affect or emotion has an explanatory role in leader effectiveness and hypothesize that emotional intelligence might play a role. However, they specify that they are talking about emotional intelligence as an ability, not as a personality characteristic.

Hogan, Curphy, and Hogan (1994) reviewed the research literature on the personality/leader effectiveness relationship and concluded that there is a strong foundation for believing that each of the Big Five factors contributes to leader effectiveness. They also pointed out that the Big Five factors emphasize the "bright side" of leadership: effectiveness. But some leaders fail despite having above-average ability and the "right" personality characteristics. Although some of these failures are the result of situational factors (e.g., the competition, the market, the unavailability of talented subordinates), for others the reasons for failure are more personal. They include arrogance, selfishness, insensitivity, excessive ambition, and compulsivity. We covered these characteristics in some detail in Module 12.1 in the section on destructive leaders. Hogan and colleagues (1994) suggested that the predictors for this type of leader failure are more likely to be found in measures of psychopathology than in measures of the Big Five. Hogan and Hogan (2001) presented data suggesting that leaders fail as a result of one or more of the following four tendencies: a tendency to blow up, show off, or conform when under pressure and an inability to profit from experience. They further suggested that it is unlikely that any of these tendencies would be obvious in traditional assessment scenarios (e.g., interviews, assessment centers) because the pathological manager often has strong social skills and will only reveal his or her dark side to subordinates—and even then, only after an extended period of exposure to them.

Judge, Bono, and colleagues (2002) conducted a meta-analysis on the relationship between personality and leader effectiveness and confirmed what Hogan and colleagues (1994) had hypothesized. They examined leader effectiveness (as measured by ratings of the manager and/or subordinate of the leader) in three different settings: industry, government/military, and students (laboratory experiments in which participants were designated as "leaders" for short-duration projects). In an analysis of 222 correlations from 73 different samples, they demonstrated that emotional stability, extraversion, and openness to experience were positively associated with leader effectiveness in industry settings. In government/military settings, openness was not a predictor of leader effectiveness but conscientiousness was. In industry settings, conscientiousness was not a predictor of leader effectiveness, most likely because of the discretion used in the application of rules in that setting, whereas in the government/military setting importance is attached to following rules and procedures. In student settings, all of the Big Five factors predicted leader effectiveness. Judge and Bono (2000) also looked more specifically at the contribution of Big Five dimensions to transformational leadership behaviors and found that extraversion and agreeableness were somewhat predictive of transformational behaviors on the part of the leader.

In a follow up meta-analysis, Bono and Judge (2004) also found some evidence for a relationship between the personality dimensions of extraversion and agreeableness and transactional effectiveness, but it was very low. They conclude that there is only weak evidence for the hypothesis that personality explains leadership behavior, at least at the level of the Big Five. They suggest that it might be valuable to look at narrower personality traits. It might also be of some value to examine the relationship of core self-evaluations in leader behavior because positive self-regard seems implicated in charismatic and transformational leadership styles. But it is important to distinguish between the healthy concept of core self-evaluations and the pathological concept of narcissism. Judge, LePine, and Rich (2006) found that narcissistic individuals gave themselves high marks on leadership effectiveness and OCB but that others gave the same individuals *low* ratings on both effectiveness and OCB. As we discussed in Chapter 5 on multisource feedback, this can become an increasingly troublesome phenomenon as we deal with leaders higher up on the organizational ladder.

Cross-Cultural Studies of Leadership

> *The Dutch place emphasis on egalitarianism and are skeptical of the value of leadership. Terms like "leader" and "manager" carry a stigma. If a father is employed as a manager, Dutch children will not admit it to their schoolmates.*
>
> *Arabs worship their leaders—*"as long as they are in power!"
>
> *Iranians seek power and strength in their leaders.*
>
> *The Malaysian leader is expected to behave in a manner that is humble, modest, and dignified.*
>
> *Americans appreciate two kinds of leaders. They seek empowerment from leaders who grant autonomy and delegate authority to subordinates. They also respect the bold, forceful, confident, and risk-taking leader as personified by John Wayne. (*House, R. J., Wright, N. S., & Aditya, R. N. (1997). Cross-cultural research on organizational leadership: A critical analysis and proposed theory. In P. C. Early & M. Erez (Eds.), *New perspectives on international industrial and organizational psychology* (pp. 535–625). San Francisco: Jossey-Bass. Reprinted by permission of John Wiley & Sons, Inc.*)*

These quotes came from managers in various countries who were asked to describe accepted leadership styles in their respective countries. They were describing their local leadership *culture.*

You will recall from our discussion of Hofstede's model of culture (see Chapter 1) that we would expect culture to affect the manner in which leadership is expressed, as well as the relative effectiveness of various leadership strategies. For example, the extent to which a culture could be characterized as collectivist or individualist, or high in power distance compared with low in power distance, would be expected to influence the effectiveness of participative versus autocratic or individually directed versus team-directed leadership strategies (Yukl, Fu, & McDonald, 2003).

In 1991, House and his colleagues began planning a massive cross-cultural study of leadership (House, Javidan, & Dorfman, 2001; House et al., 1997). The following are some of the questions they hoped to answer:

1. Are there universally (i.e., across all cultures) endorsed and rejected leader attributes and behaviors?
2. Are there some leader attributes and behaviors that are accepted in some cultures but rejected in others?
3. How does culture influence the acceptance and rejection of leader attributes and behaviors?
4. What is the effect of the presence of a rejected leadership attribute or behavior within a particular culture?

The project was labeled **GLOBE**, an acronym for **global leadership and organizational behavior effectiveness**. The project has now been in place for more than 20 years and involves the efforts of 200 researchers (social scientists and management researchers) in over 60 countries ranging from Albania to Qatar to Zambia. The project is described in great detail in two books that were published by the project's directors (Chhokar, Brodbeck, & House, 2007; House, Hanges, Javidan, Dorfman, & Gupta, 2004). To date, data have been gathered from over 18,000 middle managers in the cooperating countries. The initial stages of the project included the development of the questionnaires that would be used and the collection of data that would permit an analysis of the relationships between culture and leadership practices. Data have been collected and analyzed relative to the culture–leadership questions (questions 1 and 2 above), the results of which we will consider below. In future stages, the relationship between particular leadership styles and subordinate attitudes and performance will be examined within and between cultures. A final phase

Global leadership and organizational behavior effectiveness (GLOBE) Large-scale cross-cultural study of leadership by 170 social scientists and management researchers in over 60 countries.

TABLE 12.7 **Universal and Culture-Specific Aspects of Leadership**

UNIVERSALLY ACCEPTED	UNIVERSALLY REJECTED	CULTURE-SPECIFIC
Integrity—trustworthy, just, honest	Loner Noncooperative	Cunning Sensitive
Charismatic, visionary, inspirational—encouraging, positive, motivational, confidence builder, dynamic	Ruthless Nonexplicit Irritable Dictatorial	Ambitious Status conscious
Team oriented—team building, communicating, coordinating Excellence oriented, decisive, intelligent, win–win problem solver		

SOURCE: Adapted from Brodbeck, F. C., Frese, M., Akerblom, S., Audia, G., Bakacsi, G., Bendova, H., Bodega, D., et al. (2000). Cultural variation of leadership prototypes across 22 European countries. *Journal of Occupational and Organizational Psychology, 73,* 1–29. Copyright © 2000. Reprinted by permission of John Wiley & Sons Ltd.

will involve laboratory and field experiments and studies to test some propositions and hypotheses that emerge from the data collected.

The answers to questions 1 and 2 are both yes. There are accepted leader behaviors that are both universal and culture-specific. In an analysis of the first wave of GLOBE data, Den Hartog et al. (1999) identified a number of leader traits that were universally accepted and rejected as well as certain attributes that were more acceptable in some cultures than in others (see Table 12.7). The list of universally accepted attributes fits neatly with the concepts of transformational and charismatic leadership. In contrast, the universally rejected leadership attributes would never be mistaken for the attributes of a transformational or charismatic leader. The attributes and behaviors that seem to be endorsed or rejected depending on the culture are hard to label, although the traits of ambition and status consciousness might fit into Hofstede's cultural concepts of power distance or individualism/collectivism.

Brodbeck and colleagues (2000) confirmed these findings in a smaller subset of those 60 cooperating nations. They examined GLOBE data from 22 European countries that were members of the European Union (EU) or had applied for membership. As was the case with the larger data set analyzed by Den Hartog, Brodbeck and colleagues found universally accepted and rejected leader attributes and behaviors within the European culture, as well as **culture-specific characteristics** that were more acceptable in some countries than others. As an example of a culture-specific characteristic, autonomous leaders were perceived as more effective in Germany and Russia but less effective in Great Britain and France. Similarly, while leaders who avoid conflict were seen as effective in Sweden and Italy, they were regarded as less effective in the Czech Republic and Poland. It is tempting to explain this difference in terms of the recent political histories of the Czech Republic and Poland; we might not be surprised that these countries value leaders who do not shy away from conflict, considering that they chafed under Soviet domination for decades, agitated for independence, and achieved it with the fall of the Berlin Wall.

Culture-specific characteristics Leader characteristics that are more acceptable in some countries than others.

The implications of these studies seem clear. Transformational and charismatic leader behaviors travel well. This is good news for the multinational company and the global manager (Javidan, Dorfman, Sully de Luque, & House, 2006; Javidan, Stahl, Brodbeck, & Wilderom, 2005). It means that selection and training can emphasize these leader behaviors, which appear relevant regardless of the culture. In essence, these are "core" attributes and behaviors that are not specific to any culture.

It is also cautionary news in the sense that it appears that there are some culture-specific leadership do's and don'ts. Before GLOBE, we knew that these do's and don'ts were bound to exist, but we did not know what they were for a specific culture. We are now beginning to get a roadmap from the GLOBE efforts, and this will also make the leadership process considerably more effective within specific countries and cultures, particularly as the GLOBE results begin to find their way into managerial and leadership training programs.

Finally, the instruments produced as part of the GLOBE project now permit direct comparisons across countries—something that was not possible before GLOBE (Kabasakal & Dastmalchian, 2001). The same is true of the MLQ of Bass and Avolio (Walumbwa, Wang, Lawler, & Shi, 2004). These instruments have permitted researchers to compare and contrast leadership styles in countries as diverse as Turkey, Iran, China, India, Norway, and Taiwan (e.g., Hetland & Sandal, 2003; Spreitzer, Perttula, & Xin, 2005) as well as on specific topics such as leadership characteristics and corporate social responsibility (Waldman, Sully de Luque, Washburn, & House, 2006).

Yukl (2006) has applied Hofstede's theory of national culture to issues related to leadership. As shown in Table 12.8, issues such as participative management, team versus individual work, uncertainty, and conflict are all likely to influence what is considered

TABLE 12.8 **Examples of Cultural Dimensions Related to Leadership**

Power Distance: The extent to which people accept differences in power and status among themselves. In a high power distance culture, leaders have more authority, they are entitled to special rights and privileges, they are less accessible, and they are not expected to share power with subordinates. High: Russia, China, Philippines, Mexico, Venezuela, India Medium: Netherlands, Italy, Pakistan, Japan, Spain, Greece Low: Israel, Austria, Denmark, United Kingdom, New Zealand, United States
Individualism: The extent to which the needs and autonomy of individuals are more important than the collective needs of the work unit or society. In individualistic cultures, people are identified more by their own achievements than by their group memberships or contributions to collective success, and individual rights are more important than social responsibilities. High: United States, Netherlands, United Kingdom, Australia, Canada, Belgium Medium: Russia, Japan, Austria, Israel, Spain, India Low: China, Indonesia, Thailand, Pakistan, Hong Kong, Venezuela
Uncertainty Avoidance: The extent to which people feel comfortable with ambiguous situations and inability to predict future events. In cultures with high avoidance of uncertainty, there is more fear of the unknown, security and stability are more important, conflict is avoided, plans and forecasts are more valued, and there is more emphasis on formal rules and regulations. High: Japan, France, Russia, Argentina, Spain, Belgium Medium: China, Netherlands, Switzerland, Pakistan, Taiwan, Finland Low: Singapore, Hong Kong, Denmark, United Kingdom, Sweden, United States
Gender Egalitarianism: The extent to which men and women receive equal treatment, and both masculine and feminine attributes are considered important and desirable. In cultures with high gender egalitarianism, sex roles are not clearly differentiated, jobs are not segregated by gender, and attributes such as compassion, empathy, and intuition are as important as assertiveness, competitiveness, and objective rationality. High: Denmark, Norway, Finland, Sweden, Netherlands, Chile Medium: Canada, Indonesia, Israel, France, India, China Low: Japan, Austria, Italy, Mexico, Venezuela, Switzerland

SOURCE: Yukl, G. A. (2006). *Leadership in organizations* (6th ed.), Table 14.3, p. 433. © 2006. Reproduced by permission of Pearson Education, Inc., Upper Saddle River, NJ.

"successful" leadership. Moreover, each of these issues has its own cultural context. Note the differences among countries on these issues as presented in the table. Clearly, this table reinforces the notion that a single style of leadership is unlikely to be universally accepted across national boundaries. Reviews have confirmed how important this issue is and how little we know for certain at this point (Dickson, Den Hartog, & Mitchelson, 2003).

Leadership in a Diverse Environment

The U.S. workplace is becoming less white, less native born, less male, and less young. In addition, workers with a variety of disabilities are more likely to be integrated into the mainstream workforce. Each of these changes requires a substantial shift in the thinking and the behavior of a leader. The most substantial challenge might be for the expatriate manager learning the customs and values of a completely different culture. As an example, singling out an individual for praise might be wise in an individualist culture but ill advised in a collectivist culture. Cultural issues are not limited to nationality, however; they also come into play when men and women work together. While managers a generation ago might have assumed that a hunting rifle would make an ideal prize in a monthly sales contest, doing so today with a sales force composed of a significant number of women will likely draw complaints. Another culturally sensitive matter that leaders must face is the commemoration of holidays. How does a leader reconcile Christmas, Hannukah, Kwanza, and Ramadan? What about workers who are Jehovah's Witnesses and celebrate only wedding anniversaries? I-O psychology will need to identify the ways in which the leaders of today and tomorrow solve these dilemmas. Perhaps the answer can be found in cross-cultural research.

The GLOBE project illustrates the complexity of culture for a leader. On the one hand, there are certain universals (both good and bad) and, on the other hand, there are culture-specific issues that present themselves to a leader. The multinational environment can be used both as a model and as a metaphor for any domestic workforce. As we have indicated at various points in this book, domestic workforces are becoming more culturally diverse. A typical U.S. workforce will include Asian, African, Hispanic, eastern European, and Indian workers. As a result of the expansion of the EU, the workforces of many European countries have become similarly diverse in the 21st century. But country of birth is only one level of culture and diversity. Within native-born worker populations, whether in Sweden, Romania, or the United States, there may be subcultures defined by variables other than country of birth. Every country has its disadvantaged work groups. In Sweden, it might be those whose parents emigrated from Middle Eastern countries. In Romania, it might be people with Hungarian surnames. In the United States, it might be African Americans, Asian Americans, Hispanic Americans, or women.

Chrobot-Mason and Ruderman (2003) used the LMX model of leadership, which we discussed in Module 12.3, to suggest a simple heuristic that, in the past, was used to decide who is an in-group and who is an out-group member. It works like this: If you look like the leader (e.g., white male), you may or may not become an in-group member. If you don't look like the leader, it is unlikely that you will become an in-group member. One way to take advantage of all the benefits that a diverse workforce can bring is for leaders to work hard on developing high-quality relationships with members who are not like themselves. This makes perfect sense and is compatible with the latest thinking of those advocating the LMX theory of leadership; that is, leaders should develop high-quality relationships with *all* work group members (Graen & Uhl-Bein, 1995).

An additional implication of the preliminary GLOBE results for domestic diversity issues resides in the universals. It appears that transformational and charismatic leadership is universally valued. Thus, if a leader were to adopt a transformational or charismatic style with a work group, we would expect positive results (in terms of performance) and positive reactions (in terms of the attitudes of group members). This should be true regardless of the diversity of the work group. Transformational leaders are just as likely to enhance the work experience of men and women, African Americans and whites, abled and disabled, young and old.

To be sure, there is a knowledge component involved. Even the transformational leader can stub a toe without specific cultural and subcultural awareness. The studies by Brodbeck and colleagues (2000) and Den Hartog and colleagues (1999) identified attributes and behaviors that were not universal. Domestic transformational leaders need to be aware of the same nonuniversality in leading a work group. Chrobot-Mason and Ruderman (2003) suggested ways that the domestic leader can take these cultural and subcultural differences into account in work group interactions. Thomas (1998) argued that the multicultural leader, domestic or international, needs to understand and appreciate the differences that exist among work group members. The only way to achieve this appreciation is through reflection on one's own culture and the culture of others who populate the workplace.

We would like to end this section on diversity by revisiting Day's (2001b) notion of shared leadership described in Module 12.1. Both Chrobot-Mason and Ruderman (2003) and Thomas (1998) placed substantial emphasis on the behavior of the leader. Since the leader is the lens through which much of organizational culture and climate are viewed, this emphasis is well placed. In addition, however, there is some logic in considering the attitudes and behavior of work group members. If leadership is a shared phenomenon, or a process that belongs to the work group and not solely to the leader, then the entire group must ultimately be involved in the development of "leadership." Of course, at the end of the day, it is the leader's responsibility to develop the environment that helps leadership to emerge as a group concept.

Thus, if there is a formula for advising leaders about how to deal with an increasingly diverse workforce, it would be to embrace transformational leadership styles; devote considerable effort to developing high-quality relationships; and do some thinking, reading, and talking about the cultures and subcultures they are likely to encounter among work group members. Simultaneously, the leader must develop an environment that brings all of the group members into the leadership circle. Mentoring, challenging job assignments, and frequent supportive and individual discussions about organizational and individual member goals and performance are some of ways this environment might be created (Chrobot-Mason & Ruderman, 2003).

Guidelines for Effective Leadership

By now, your head may be swimming with the various challenges to 21st-century leadership—globalization, diversity, telecommuting, teams, and so on—and with a wide variety of leadership models to choose from: transformational, charismatic, transactional, participative, and so forth. Yukl (2006) has been studying and writing about leadership for decades, and although he acknowledges that there is still a great deal to be learned and that many of the findings related to particular approaches are inconsistent, he is willing to accept the role of expert in identifying some guidelines that appear helpful, independent of any particular theory or approach. This is a welcome change from the confusion of dueling theories. We present these practical suggestions to you here:

1. Leaders help followers interpret events. This means identifying threats and opportunities, as well as helping people understand complex problems and environments.
2. Leaders help build and maintain consensus about objectives, priorities, and strategies.
3. Leaders increase efficacy (individual and group) and commitment to tasks and objectives, particularly in the face of obstacles.

4. Leaders foster trust, respect, and cooperation among group members.
5. Leaders foster identification with the group or organization.
6. Leaders help coordinate the activities of group members.
7. Leaders facilitate learning and innovation among group members.
8. Leaders promote and defend their group and organization and obtain necessary resources for their group.
9. Leaders help group members develop skills and prepare them for leadership responsibilities.
10. Leaders promote social justice, as well as ethical and moral behavior.

This is an intimidating list of demands for effective leadership, but given the complexity of being a leader in the 21st century, it is also a realistic one.

MODULE 12.4 SUMMARY

- Changes in the workplace since the 1980s have been substantial, resulting in a very different work environment for leaders. New challenges include leading virtual teams, telecommuters, and temporary workers.
- Some studies suggest that females tend to favor more participative and democratic interactions with subordinates and to be more aware of interpersonal issues than their male counterparts. Research is needed regarding whether these differences actually matter in terms of the ultimate effectiveness of the leader.
- Trait theory is making a comeback in the form of studies examining the relationship of Big Five personality traits and leader effectiveness. This modern approach defines personality traits behaviorally, has a general consensus on the meaning of these personality traits, and considers them in the context of organizational and situational variables. This modern approach is considerably more attractive than traditional trait theory.
- House and his colleagues are conducting a large cross-cultural study of leadership called global leadership and organizational behavior effectiveness (GLOBE). To date, they have found that the list of universally accepted leader attributes fits neatly with the concepts of transformational and charismatic leadership. They have also identified some culture-specific leader characteristics that are more acceptable in some countries than in others.

KEY TERMS

virtual team
global leadership and organizational behavior effectiveness (GLOBE)
culture-specific characteristics

13 Teams in Organizations

© Shelley Dennis/iStockphoto

MODULE 13.1

Types of Teams

Kurt recently completed a graduate program in I-O psychology and was hired by a consulting firm as an entry-level organizational consultant. He has been on the job for one week and has just been assigned to a project team consisting of fellow consultants from different international offices of the consulting firm. The project team's goal is to develop a new software product for a longtime client. Kurt's boss tells him not to worry because these global virtual teams are used all the time, and technology can reduce the geographical boundaries separating team members. Kurt is about to "meet" his teammates by e-mail; tomorrow they will have a videoconference, and, as they work, they will have frequent web-based virtual meetings. Kurt is uneasy about working on this project team because none of his teammates live in the United States and, for many of his teammates, English is not their first language. Kurt is wondering how well this virtual team will work together and whether the geographical, cultural, and language barriers will prevent the team from achieving its objectives. He also has some reservations about the need for using a team for this project instead of simply having individuals provide separate inputs to a project leader.

Kurt's concerns are legitimate, and such concerns are becoming more common as many different kinds of teams are increasingly being used in the workplace. I-O psychology researchers and practitioners have studied a variety of team-related issues (e.g., team composition, selection, training, communication) that we will discuss in this chapter. With the predicted increase in the use of teams in organizations, these issues will continue to be of interest to I-O psychologists, managers, and employees working in teams.

Mohrman, Cohen, and Mohrman (1995) suggested several reasons for the increasing use of teams in organizations:

- Time is saved if work usually performed sequentially by individuals can be performed concurrently by people working in teams.
- Innovation and creativity are promoted because of cross-fertilization of ideas.
- Teams can integrate information in ways that an individual cannot.
- Teams enable organizations to quickly and effectively develop and deliver products and services while retaining high quality.
- Teams enable organizations to learn and retain learning more effectively.

The use of teams in organizations presents both opportunities and challenges to managers and I-O psychologists. For example, the increase in team-based work provides I-O psychologists with opportunities to explore whether personality measures are beneficial for selecting employees who will work well in teams. The increased use of teams presents challenges having to do with team composition, training for teams, the motivation of teams, and the evaluation of team performance. The growing use of virtual teams increases the challenge of team coordination and highlights the need for enhanced communication and trust-building through electronic and social media, including e-mails, texts, and videoconferences (Noe, 2010; Tannenbaum, Mathieu, Salas, & Cohen, 2012). Differences among team members in cultural values can also create difficulties in managing team interactions and processes (Smith, Bond, & Kagitcibasi, 2006). We will discuss each of these topics in this chapter.

Groups and Teams: Definitions

Before describing different types of groups and teams, it is important to consider some definitional issues in this area. Historically, groups have been distinguished from teams. Groups include members who may work together or may just share some resources, but teams always include members whose tasks are interdependent. Moreover, research on groups has traditionally been conducted by social psychologists studying group processes in laboratory settings. In research on groups, for example, undergraduate students are often brought together to complete some group problem-solving or decision-making task. But this research has a major drawback that limits its generalizability to work teams: Groups in laboratory settings do not have a chance to develop their own history, and they often break up after a very brief time. In contrast, research on teams has generally been conducted by organizational psychologists and management researchers in organizational settings that include many variables that make controlled experimentation difficult.

In recent years, I-O psychologists have distinguished between groups and teams less than they previously did (Sundstrom, McIntyre, Halfhill, & Richards, 2000). Guzzo (1995) noted that groups and teams have too much in common to make any grand distinction. Thus, the terms "group" and "team" are increasingly being used interchangeably. In this chapter, we will refer primarily to teams, as they are more relevant to the organizational framework that I-O psychologists use. Except for studies in which previous research has explicitly used groups, we will focus on research on teams, which has greater generalizability and applicability to the work teams that I-O psychologists study.

A **team** is defined as an interdependent collection of individuals who work together toward a common goal and who share responsibility for specific outcomes for their organizations (Sundstrom, DeMeuse, & Futrell, 1990). An additional requirement is that the team be identified as such by those within and outside of the team (West, 2012; West, Borrill, & Unsworth, 1998). No doubt you have been a team member, perhaps in sports or in the cast or crew of a stage production. Other examples of teams include assembly teams, management teams, emergency medical service and rescue teams, firefighter teams, surgery teams, military teams, string quartets, and rock groups.

Team Interdependent collection of individuals who work together toward a common goal and who share responsibility for specific outcomes for their organizations.

Types of Teams

Many different kinds of teams are used in the workplace. Below we discuss the types of teams that have recently received the most attention in organizations. Team types are important to understand because each type of team serves a different purpose or function. In addition, the requirements for team size, structure, and support may differ depending on the team type (Mathieu, Maynard, Rapp, & Gilson, 2008).

Quality Circles

Quality circle Work group arrangement that typically involves 6 to 12 employees who meet regularly to identify work-related problems and generate ideas to increase productivity or product quality.

Quality circles typically involve 6 to 12 employees who meet regularly to identify work-related problems and to generate ideas that can increase productivity or product quality (Guzzo & Dickson, 1996). **Quality circles** are often initiated by management, with meeting times allotted during work hours. Although quality circle membership is often voluntary, a supervisor may suggest that certain employees participate. Quality circles have their origin in participative management techniques that were developed in Japan and exported to the rest of the world (Cordery, 1996). Members of quality circles, however, are not given formal authority. Instead, they seek to have their ideas and solutions adopted and implemented by management.

Research evidence has been mixed for quality circles. Some research indicates that quality circles result in positive outcomes in the short term, but these gains are not sustained over time (Cannon-Bowers, Oser, & Flanagan, 1992; Guzzo & Dickson, 1996). This phenomenon has been called the "honeymoon effect" in quality circles. The honeymoon effect has been attributed to the fact that initial suggestions for improvements are often fairly easy and clear, and they have a favorable impact on the bottom line if they are adopted. Over time, however, it becomes increasingly difficult for quality circle members to make additional suggestions that can increase quality or decrease costs. This lower success rate over time leads to a decrease in the positive attitudes that accompanied initial gains resulting from quality circle suggestions. This honeymoon effect may account for the decreasing popularity of quality circles in many U.S. organizations (Gibson & Tesone, 2001).

Quality circles were most popular in the United States in the 1970s and early 1980s. By the late 1980s, however, many U.S. organizations that had tried quality circles had abandoned them. Nevertheless, the emphasis that many quality circles had on quality and participation has become the foundation for other techniques, including total quality management and self-managing teams, which have remained popular in the United States (Worren, 1996). In addition, Pereira and Osburn (2007) conducted a meta-analysis on the effects of quality circles on employee attitudes and performance. They found that quality circles had a small effect on employee attitudes but a moderate effect on job performance. The authors concluded that "the main emphasis in QCs is in addressing productivity problems and implementing solutions to improve both the quality and quantity of products or services provided. In light of this, it is not surprising to find that QCs have a higher impact on performance" than on employee attitudes (p. 150).

Despite the decline in popularity of quality circles in the United States, they remain popular in Japan, where there is more support for and reinforcement of quality circle principles (Juran, 1992). Indeed, Japanese companies (e.g., Honda, Toyota) that have production plants in the United States developed quality circles in the 1990s and have had unique success with them. For example, Honda Corporation uses a quality circle approach called "The New Honda Circle," which has resulted in improved design and production processes for Honda's cars. As a result, quality circles at Honda have won several nationally recognized awards. Quality circles at Honda include production workers as well as co-workers from engineering, sales, and research and development. In these quality circles, no one is called an employee. Instead, everyone is an associate, and the first-level supervisor is called a team leader. These titles are not just for show; instead, they are indicative of a team culture that encourages participation and reduces the gap between leaders and production workers. In recognition of their suggestions, quality circle members at Honda accumulate points, which may lead to a new car or a vacation. Overall, quality circles and similar participative programs emphasize continuous work improvement, and they serve as an important framework in the achievement of productivity and efficiency at Honda. The contrast between such success stories for Japanese firms in the United States and the overall decline in American quality circles is likely due to the cultural clash between a collectivist activity (quality circle participation) in an individualist (American) culture.

Project Teams

Project team Team that is created to solve a particular problem or set of problems and is disbanded after the project is completed or the problem is solved; also called an ad hoc committee, a task force, or a cross-functional team.

Project teams are created to solve a particular problem or set of problems (Guzzo & Dickson, 1996). Project teams differ from other teams because they are disbanded after the project is completed or the problem is solved. Hackman (1990) noted that project teams have an unusual mix of autonomy and dependence. On the one hand, they are typically free, within broad limits, to proceed with the project work that members determine. On the other hand, they work for some client group and thus are dependent on client preferences. Project teams are also called ad hoc committees, task forces, or cross-functional teams. The term "cross-functional" refers to the different departments or functions from which team members come. For example, a new product development team might include employees from sales, engineering, marketing, production, and research and development units. New product development teams are commonly used to develop innovative products or to identify new solutions to existing problems.

Project teams often have clear deadlines, but members are often uncertain about how to accomplish the task (Gersick & Davis-Sacks, 1990). Thus, team members must work together quickly and creatively to come up with solutions. Haas (2006) found that project teams that were given slack time and decision-making autonomy were able to more effectively gather relevant information and thus were able to complete more high-quality projects.

Line Productions/The Kobal Collection, Ltd./Art Resource

An example of a project team: Making a motion picture involves workers from many different specialties, all coordinated to create the end result.

Project teams raise some organizational challenges because, although team members still belong to their functional units, where they have certain roles to fulfill and their managers decide on rewards and promotions, they must fulfill other roles and expectations on the team. Some employees dislike being assigned to project teams because they feel they are losing out in terms of departmental power, advancement, and rewards. Nevertheless, organizations are increasingly using project teams in matrix organizations, in which individuals work on multiple teams, reporting at the same time to a project manager for a team project and a functional manager in a particular department. Such matrix arrangements help organizations to make the most out of limited human resources.

Production Teams

Production team Team that consists of frontline employees who produce tangible output.

Production teams consist of frontline employees who produce tangible output such as cars, televisions, cell phones, or mined minerals (Guzzo & Dickson, 1996). A common example is a team working on an assembly line in a manufacturing plant that produces automobiles. Other types of production teams include maintenance crews, candy production crews, automotive parts manufacturing teams, coal mining crews, electronic assembly teams, and wood-harvesting teams (Forsyth, 2009; Sundstrom et al., 2000). Many production teams have a meeting each morning to ensure that members are communicating and working interdependently to reach their production goals. In many production teams, members have direct access to other team members, allowing them to bypass supervisors in making and implementing certain decisions. It is often easy to measure the output of production teams in terms of quantity and quality and, therefore, also relatively easy to evaluate the team's performance and to provide feedback (Reilly & McGourty, 1998).

Autonomous work group Specific kind of production team that has control over a variety of functions, including planning shift operations, allocating work, determining work priorities, performing a variety of work tasks, and recommending new hires as work group members.

An **autonomous work group** is a specific kind of production team that has control over a variety of its functions, including planning shift operations, allocating work, determining work priorities, performing a variety of actual work tasks, and making recommendations regarding the hiring of new work group members. Autonomous work groups, which are also known as self-managing or self-directed teams, are used by such industry leaders as AT&T, Coca-Cola, Federal Express, General Electric, Motorola, Texas Instruments, and Xerox (Ivancevich & Matteson, 2002). They were developed in Europe using sociotechnical system approaches to work design that give detailed attention to the social (human) and technical (technological) components of work (Trist & Bamforth, 1951).

The intent of autonomous work groups is to improve the integration of social and technical systems by allowing groups of employees to manage themselves. Management provides the autonomous work groups with the authority, materials, and equipment to perform their jobs (Morgeson, 2005; Pearce & Ravlin, 1987). Work is arranged so that cooperation and communication are encouraged among group members, and autonomous work group members have the opportunity to learn all of the jobs the group is expected to perform. Thus, autonomous work group members often have an enriched work environment because of the opportunity for developing and/or using multiple skills at work.

The senior author of this book observed autonomous work groups in a Saab plant in Trollhatten, Sweden. In this plant, autonomous work groups assembled car bodies, which would come from a central holding area on a large line shaped like a racetrack. Multiple autonomous work groups were located in the center of that racetrack and had the authority to pull a car off the central loop and into their area whenever they saw fit. In the finishing area, their general quota was 11 car bodies a day, but they often worked on as few as 7 or as many as 15 cars a day. In the group area, autonomous work group members had tables and chairs where they could sit and talk and plan. The group would decide when to bring a car body into the work area and which members would work on sanding, reassembling, and other tasks. The autonomous work group would then send the car back to the racetrack when they were finished working on it. This form of redesign worked well in Sweden because it was compatible with the collectivist culture characterized by a low power distance.

Conventional wisdom proposes that autonomous work groups have a favorable impact on the attitudes and behaviors of team members, but research evidence supporting these claims is mixed (Guzzo & Dickson, 1996). Some research has indicated that autonomous work group members are more satisfied with their jobs than members of traditional work groups (Cohen & Ledford, 1994; Cordery, Mueller, & Smith, 1991). However, some studies have found that members of autonomous work groups are more likely to be absent and to leave their jobs than members of traditional work groups (Cordery et al., 1991; Wall, Kemp, Jackson, & Clegg, 1986). The findings of the study by Cordery and colleagues (1991) are particularly difficult to explain because, compared with members of traditional work groups, members of autonomous work groups had higher job satisfaction but also higher absenteeism and turnover. In our experience, one of the common consequences of autonomous work arrangements is that team members decide who will do what, and each member ends up doing what he or she is best at or has always done. Thus, the promised enrichment never occurs, which might explain the lack of positive findings in some autonomous work groups. More recent research suggests that when novel and disruptive events affect the autonomous group's work, an important factor in the group's success will be whether or not an external leader steps in and intervenes with supportive coaching (Morgeson, 2005). In another recent study, Kauffeld (2006) investigated traditional and autonomous work groups across a variety of German organizations and found that independent ratings of team competence in completing various work tasks were higher for autonomous work groups. Nevertheless, given the conflicting findings on the outcomes associated with the use of autonomous work groups, we expect that research will continue on this important type of work group arrangement.

Virtual Teams

On the television show *Star Trek*, being geographically separated by a vast distance was no problem for Captain Kirk and other members of the starship *Enterprise*. They simply said "Beam me up, Scotty" and, with the push of a button, face-to-face encounters were accomplished fairly easily (Robb, 2002). Although conducting meetings in the corporate world with geographically dispersed members has not reached that level of sophistication, much progress has been made in reducing the inconvenience of geographic separation among team members.

Virtual team Team that has widely dispersed members working together toward a common goal and linked through computers and other technology.

A **virtual team** typically has widely dispersed members working together toward a common goal and linked through computers and other technology such as the telephone, videoconferencing, and team support software (Joinson, 2002; Kirkman & Mathieu, 2005). Researchers have suggested that all teams can be evaluated in terms of their "virtualness" (Martins, Gilson, & Maynard, 2004). Some virtual teams may meet in person on a regular basis, but in many virtual teams members rarely, if ever, meet in person. Nevertheless, Cascio (2000b) noted several advantages for organizations that use virtual teams: (1) saving time and travel expenses, (2) providing increased access to experts, (3) expanding labor markets by allowing firms to recruit and retain the best employees regardless of their physical location, and (4) having the opportunity to assign employees to multiple teams at the same time. An additional advantage of a virtual team can be the exchange of different perspectives among team members.

Members of virtual teams may be in different geographic locations within a single country, but given the global economy, the emergence of e-commerce, and the growth in mergers and acquisitions, virtual teams are increasingly likely to include members from various parts of the world (Martins & Schilpzand, 2011). Not surprisingly, the challenges to global virtual teams include time differences, cultural differences, and language barriers. Web-based language training and cross-cultural training are among the tools used to help global virtual team members work together. For example, Royal Dutch Shell Corporation, the oil giant based in the Netherlands, is a large user of virtual team software that provides global project teams with real-time online meeting tools, web-based knowledge management programs, Internet-based team workspaces, and videoconferencing that help to compensate for team members' geographic separation (Robb, 2002).

Rosen, Furst, and Blackburn (2006) surveyed over 400 training and development professionals in investigating the training that is currently used for virtual teams. They found that although the use of virtual teams is expected to increase in many organizations, few organizations have developed meaningful training programs for virtual teams. Respondents who worked in organizations that did have good virtual team training noted that "their organizations saw virtual teamwork as integral to maintaining their competitive advantage with respect to providing customer service and timely new product development. In these organizations, virtual teams enjoyed top management support and operated in a culture where virtual team training was viewed as a high priority and as an investment in the organization" (p. 243).

Trust is also a critical concern in virtual teams. Because of the absence of face-to-face interactions, virtual teams must develop a "gel" or sense of belonging that provides the basis for information exchange and collaborative work (Avolio et al., 2001; Robert, Dennis, & Hung,

BOX 13.1 A SPECIALIZED TEAM: AIRLINE COCKPIT CREW

More than a century after the Wright brothers worked as a team to achieve the first recorded flight (December 17, 1903), teamwork in aviation is still a major concern (Brannick, Prince, & Salas, 2005; Salas, Burke, Bowers, & Wilson, 2001). Airline cockpit crews perform highly interdependent tasks, some that occur routinely in all flights and others that may occur only in rare but well-practiced emergency situations (Ginnett, 1990). Cockpit crews are unique in that they work together for a brief time and must effectively perform critical tasks soon after the crew is formed. Newly formed crews are able to perform effectively soon after they meet because crew members receive extensive training that precedes their work on a particular crew.

Airline cockpit crews rarely run into problems, but the real requirements for effective teamwork occur when they do. A spectacular example is the Hudson River landing of US Airways flight 1549 in January 2009. Moments after take-off, the airplane was crippled by the loss of both engines. By all accounts, the five-member crew (two in the cockpit and three in the cabin) performed complex tasks in an integrated manner that resulted in the safe exit of all 150 passengers and the crew without loss of life or serious injury. Notably, the pilot, Captain Chesley "Sully" Sullenberger, had a master's degree in I-O psychology and was professionally involved in crew resource management research and training.

According to Ginnett (1990), crews benefit from an organizational context that provides the following components:

1. Challenging objectives for safety, on-time performance, and fuel efficiency
2. An educational system that provides training and consultation to supplement members' task expertise
3. An information system that provides the data needed to assess situations and evaluate alternative strategies for handling them

© Steven Day/AP/Wide World Photos

When US Airways flight 1549 had to make an emergency landing in the Hudson River, the crew performed complex tasks in an integrated manner that resulted in the safe exit of all 150 passengers and the crew.

The selection system for airline cockpit crews is also important. Selection focuses on identifying crew members who have task-relevant skills and who can coordinate and communicate well with other team members. The captain of the crew plays a key role. According to Ginnett's case study (1990), key behaviors that a captain displays in leading a cockpit crew include the following:

1. Explicitly discussing tasks that require coordination between the cockpit and the cabin
2. Explicitly setting norms or rules for appropriate crew behavior
3. Appropriately managing the dynamics surrounding the authority inherent in the captain's role

Although some aspects of team performance are unique to airline cockpit crews, these teams also deal with many of the same issues that other teams in organizations must address, including team selection, coordination, communication, setting of norms, and decision making. In addition, much like other teams, airline cockpit crews are strongly influenced by organizational context factors that can enhance or detract from their performance. These team inputs and processes are discussed in detail in the other modules of this chapter.

2009). Cascio (2000b) noted that increased trust and a shared sense of belonging result when virtual team members exhibit virtual-collaboration behaviors, virtual-socialization skills, and virtual-communication skills. **Virtual-collaboration behaviors** include exchanging ideas without criticism, agreeing on responsibilities, and meeting deadlines. **Virtual-socialization skills** include soliciting team members' feedback on the process the team is using to accomplish its goals, expressing appreciation for ideas and completed tasks, and apologizing for mistakes. **Virtual-communication skills** include rephrasing unclear sentences or expressions so that all team members understand what is being said, acknowledging the receipt of messages, and responding within a certain time, such as one business day. Although similar skills are needed to enhance communication in nonvirtual (i.e., traditional) team or work environments, these virtual skills are particularly important because of the increased likelihood of miscommunication when team members are geographically separated and unfamiliar with one another and lack face-to-face interactions.

More generally, an understanding of the problems that are relevant to all teams is helpful in managing virtual teams (Cascio, 2000b). For example, team leaders should provide clear roles and responsibilities, clarify how decisions will be made, and explain the extent to which team members will share responsibility for implementing the team's decisions. Virtual team leadership is also critical in ensuring that team members maintain regular communication and interaction despite the geographic separation (Hambley, O'Neill, & Kline, 2007; Malhotra, Majchrzak, & Rosen, 2007). One study indicated that team goal setting and team-based rewards can increase the effectiveness of virtual teams (Hertel, Konradt, & Orlikowsi, 2004). Thus, it appears that at least some of the individual motivational principles we reviewed in Chapter 8 may also be applicable for team motivation. Because virtual teams are fairly new, research in this area is just beginning. We expect research attention to virtual teams to expand as they become more commonly used in the increasingly technological and global workplace.

Virtual-collaboration behaviors Behaviors that characterize virtual team interactions, including exchanging ideas without criticism, agreeing on responsibilities, and meeting deadlines.

Virtual-socialization skills Skills used in virtual team interactions, including soliciting team members' feedback on the work process used to accomplish team goals, expressing appreciation for ideas and completed tasks, and apologizing for mistakes.

Virtual-communication skills Skills used in virtual team interactions, including rephrasing unclear sentences or expressions so that all team members understand what is being said, acknowledging the receipt of messages, and responding within one business day.

MODULE 13.1 SUMMARY

- A team is an interdependent collection of individuals who work together toward a common goal and who share responsibility for specific outcomes for their organizations. Many different kinds of teams are used in the workplace, including quality circles, project teams, production teams, and virtual teams.
- Quality circles typically involve 6 to 12 employees who meet regularly to identify work-related problems and to generate ideas that can increase productivity or product quality.
- Project teams are created to solve a particular problem or set of problems; they differ from other teams because they are disbanded after the project is completed or the problem is solved.
- Production teams consist of frontline employees who produce tangible output. An autonomous work group is a specific kind of production team that has control over a variety of its functions.
- Autonomous work groups are intended to improve the integration of social and technical systems by allowing groups of employees to manage themselves.
- Organizations that use virtual teams benefit in a variety of ways, including saving time and travel expenses and providing increased access to experts. However, virtual teams, particularly those that rarely meet in person, face a variety of challenges.

KEY TERMS

team
quality circle
project team
production team
autonomous work group
virtual team
virtual-collaboration behaviors
virtual-socialization skills
virtual-communication skills

MODULE 13.2

Input–Process–Output Model of Team Effectiveness

The **input–process–output model of team effectiveness** provides a way to understand how teams perform and how to maximize their performance. Almost every recently developed team effectiveness model uses some form of the input–process–output model (Cohen & Bailey, 1997; Guzzo & Shea, 1992). Inputs include the organizational context, the team task, and team composition. Team processes include norms, communication, coordination, cohesiveness, and decision making (LePine, Piccolo, Jackson, Mathieu, & Saul, 2008). Team outputs include productivity, innovativeness, and team member well-being.

Input–process–output model of team effectiveness A model that provides links among team inputs, processes, and outputs, thereby enabling an understanding of how teams perform and how to maximize their performance.

Figure 13.1 shows this model in which inputs affect team processes, which in turn affect team outputs. This model, which has been supported by a variety of research studies, proposes that inputs affect team outputs *indirectly* through team processes. Research has also indicated that inputs can have a *direct* effect on team outputs (Campion, Medsker, & Higgs, 1993). As you can see in Figure 13.1, there are direct links from team inputs to team outputs as well as indirect links between team inputs and outputs through team processes. In addition, recent research acknowledges important feedback loops in which traditional outputs such as team performance can also serve as inputs to future team processes (Ilgen, Hollenbeck, Johnson, & Jundt, 2005). This feedback loop is represented by the arrow in Figure 13.1 that goes from "Output Variables" to "Input Variables," and it reflects the increasingly dynamic nature of teams, which can adapt and change over time.

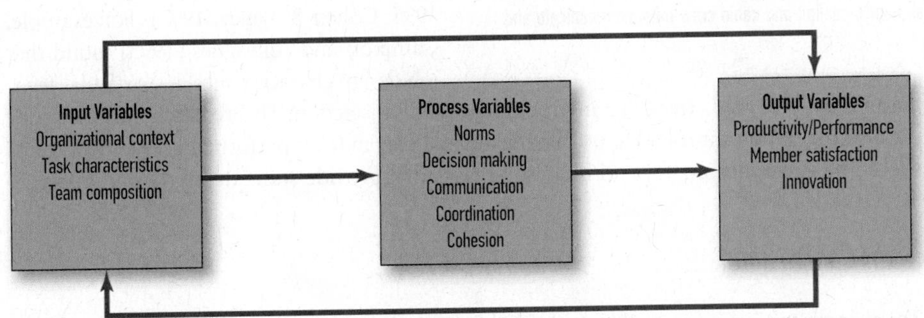

FIGURE 13.1 The Input–Process–Output Model of Team Effectiveness

SOURCE: Adapted from Gladstein, D. L. (1984). Groups in context: A model of task group effectiveness. *Administrative Science Quarterly, 29*, 499–517. © 1984 by Johnson Graduate School of Management, Cornell University. Reproduced by permission of Sage Publications, Inc.

Team Inputs

Organizational Context

The organizational context—which includes the rewards system, the training system, the physical environment, managerial support, and technology—is important to team performance. These contextual influences enhance team interactions and increase team effectiveness by providing resources needed for the performance and continued functioning of the work team. Gladstein (1984) found, for example, that external organizational variables such as market growth were positively related to team sales revenues. Research by Goodman (1986) in coal mines found that technology and other contextual variables directly affect team processes and performance, and they should be included in models of team effectiveness. Furthermore, the organizational reward system is a contextual influence on team performance. For example, teams are more successful if rewards and objectives are focused on team, not individual, behavior (Hackman, 1987). Pritchard's (1995) work on enhancing team motivation with the use of team goals, rewards, and feedback is consistent with this view. We will discuss team appraisal and feedback, as well as Pritchard's work in particular, in Module 13.3.

Team Task

Team performance depends on the task that the team is required to perform. A widely cited way to categorize or classify tasks is the job characteristics approach (Hackman & Oldham, 1980). Job characteristics theory was developed as a way to understand how jobs motivate individuals, but it can be applied to teams as well. Viewed from the team perspective, job characteristics theory suggests that team members are motivated by tasks that require a variety of skills, provide considerable autonomy, are meaningful and important, and provide performance feedback (Fleishman & Zaccaro, 1992; Hackman, 1987). Research has indicated that the job characteristics approach successfully predicts performance in a variety of teams, including management teams, clerical and administrative support teams, and teams of professionals (Campion, Papper, & Medsker, 1996; Cohen & Bailey, 1997). For example, Campion and colleagues (1993) found that job design characteristics, in particular team autonomy, were predictive of team productivity and satisfaction. This research indicated support for the important role that task characteristics play in team performance. As such, teams should be given meaningful and interesting tasks that provide some degree of autonomy.

The importance of teamwork: An airplane's cockpit and cabin crew must communicate and collaborate.

Team composition The attributes of team members, including skills, abilities, experiences, and personality characteristics.

Team Composition

Team composition refers to the attributes of team members, including skills, abilities, experiences, and personality characteristics (Guzzo & Dickson, 1996). As every fan of professional

TABLE 13.1 **Dimensions of the Stevens and Campion Teamwork Test**

- I. **Interpersonal KSAs**
  - A. Conflict Resolution KSAs
    1. The KSA to recognize and encourage desirable but discourage undesirable team conflict
    2. The KSA to recognize the type and source of conflict confronting the team and implement an appropriate resolution strategy
    3. The KSA to implement an integrative (win–win) negotiation strategy rather than the traditional distributive (win–lose) strategy
  - B. Collaborative Problem-Solving KSAs
    4. The KSA to identify situations requiring participative problem solving and to utilize the proper degree and type of participation
    5. The KSA to recognize the obstacles to collaborative group problem solving and implement proper corrective actions
  - C. Communication KSAs
    6. The KSA to understand communication networks and to utilize decentralized networks to enhance communication where possible
    7. The KSA to communicate openly and supportively, that is, to send messages that are
       - a. behavior- or event-oriented
       - b. congruent
       - c. validating
       - d. conjunctive
       - e. owned
    8. The KSA to listen nonevaluatively and to appropriately use active listening techniques
    9. The KSA to maximize the consonance between nonverbal and verbal messages and to recognize and interpret the nonverbal messages of others
    10. The KSA to engage in small talk and ritual greetings as a recognition of their importance
- II. **Self-Management KSAs**
  - D. Goal-Setting and Performance Management KSAs
    11. The KSA to establish specific, challenging, and accepted team goals
    12. The KSA to monitor, evaluate, and provide feedback on both overall team performance and individual team member performance
  - E. Planning and Task Coordination KSAs
    13. The KSA to coordinate and synchronize activities, information, and tasks among team members
    14. The KSA to help establish task and role assignments for individual team members and ensure proper balancing of workload

SOURCE: Stevens, M. J., & Campion, M. A. (1999). Staffing work teams: Development and validation of a selection test for teamwork settings. *Journal of Management, 25,* 207–228.

sports teams can observe from the importance attached to the drafting and trading of players, one important strategy for enhancing team effectiveness is to select the individuals who can make the best contributions to the team. Stevens and Campion (1994) sought to determine the knowledge, skill, and ability (KSA) requirements for teamwork. Their focus was on team KSAs rather than technical KSAs and on selecting individuals who would work well in a team rather than individuals who would complement an existing team. Stevens and Campion identified 14 specific team KSAs (Table 13.1), dividing them into interpersonal KSAs and self-management KSAs.

Stevens and Campion (1993, 1999) also developed and validated a selection test for teamwork. In two samples of production employees, the Teamwork Test was positively correlated with supervisor and peer ratings of teamwork and overall performance. An unexpected finding was that the Teamwork Test had a high correlation with cognitive ability tests. Stevens and Campion suggested that the high correlation may have resulted in part because the Teamwork Test is in a paper-and-pencil format that required some problem solving, reading ability, and verbal skills, all of which overlap with the abilities required in traditional cognitive ability tests. Nevertheless, across the two samples, they found that the Teamwork Test significantly predicted teamwork performance and overall performance even after controlling for the influence of cognitive ability. Thus, the findings in this study indicate that the individual-level KSAs identified by Stevens and Campion can have practical value in the staffing of work teams.

Some studies have indicated that the cognitive abilities and personality traits of team members are important predictors of team performance. First, a meta-analysis by Stewart (2006) indicated that the average cognitive ability of team members has a strong, positive relationship with team performance. Barrick, Stewart, Neubert, and Mount (1998) studied 652 employees comprising 51 work teams and examined whether team composition variables (ability and personality) were related to team performance. They found that teams composed of members higher in cognitive ability, conscientiousness, agreeableness, extraversion, and emotional stability received higher supervisor ratings of team performance. Neuman and Wright (1999) used measures of cognitive ability and personality traits at the team level to predict the performance of 79 four-person teams. After cognitive ability was controlled for, teams composed of members higher in conscientiousness and agreeableness had higher supervisor ratings of work team performance, higher objective measures of work team accuracy, and a greater amount of work completed. Morgeson, Reider, and Campion (2005) found that social skills as measured by a structured interview and scores on four of the Big Five personality dimensions (conscientiousness, extraversion, agreeableness, and emotional stability) significantly predicted contextual performance in employees working in a manufacturing environment with highly interdependent teams. Collectively, these studies indicate that cognitive ability and certain personality traits are beneficial in predicting performance in work teams. Across the studies, there has been relatively less emphasis on openness to experience, which has proven important in the training area and which should receive further consideration in research on team composition.

Cannon-Bowers, Tannenbaum, Salas, and Volpe (1995) identified a shared mental model as a knowledge-based team competency that is critical to team effectiveness. Mental models are organized ways of thinking that allow people to describe, explain, and predict the behavior of others (Smith-Jentsch, Mathieu, & Kraiger, 2005). **Shared mental models** are organized ways for team members to think about how the team will work. Such shared mental models provide team members with a common understanding of task requirements, and they improve coordination processes, which in turn improve team performance (Mohammed, Ferzandi, & Hamilton, 2010).

Shared mental model
Organized way for team members to think about how the team will work; helps team members understand and predict the behavior of their teammates.

Many successful basketball teams have a shared understanding of how the offense will operate under various game situations. Teammates with a shared mental model know when to "run the fast break" or "slow things down" if one of their players gets a rebound from an opponent's missed shot. As another example, emergency medical service (EMS) teams benefit from using shared mental models of the situations they encounter. EMS team members must make quick decisions in unexpected situations, all geared to the survival of the patient. Team members must determine how fast the driver should go and whether or not to use the siren. They also need to determine what the patient needs most urgently and which emergency medical technician is best able to provide it. In both the basketball and EMS examples, when team members have a shared mental model, they are able to predict what their teammates are going to do in different situations, which leads to more effective team performance.

In sum, research indicates that certain KSAs and personality characteristics are positively related to team performance. We expect further research examining individual difference predictors of team performance as organizations continue to use team-based approaches.

Team Diversity

As we discussed in Chapter 11, the issue of diversity in teams and organizations is an interesting and controversial one. Milliken and Martins (1996) noted that although it often provokes intense emotional reactions because of its association with affirmative action and hiring quotas, the term "diversity" simply refers to differences or variety. Such differences among team members come in a variety of forms. Researchers studying diversity in teams often distinguish between demographic diversity and psychological diversity. **Demographic diversity** refers to differences in observable attributes or demographic characteristics such as age, gender, and ethnicity. **Psychological diversity** refers to differences in underlying attributes such as skills, abilities, personality characteristics, attitudes, beliefs, and values. Psychological diversity may also include functional, occupational, and educational backgrounds (van Knippenberg & Schippers, 2007).

Demographic diversity Differences in observable attributes or demographic characteristics such as age, gender, and ethnicity.

Psychological diversity Differences in underlying attributes such as skills, abilities, personality characteristics, attitudes, beliefs, and values; may also include functional, occupational, and educational backgrounds.

Several studies have examined the effects of demographic diversity on individual and team outcomes at work. Research has indicated that individuals who are different from their work team in demographic characteristics (e.g., ethnicity, gender, age) are less psychologically committed to their organizations, less likely to remain with their organizations, and more likely to be absent from work (Tsui, Egan, & O'Reilly, 1991). Jackson and colleagues (1991) suggested that such diversity may lead to discomfort among team members, who may react to this discomfort by withdrawing from the team or organization. However, researchers have also identified some benefits of demographic diversity. Examining gender and ethnic diversity, Watson, Kumar, and Michaelsen (1993) studied groups that were asked to solve complex problems. They found that homogeneous groups initially worked together more effectively and performed better than diverse groups. Over time, however, the demographically diverse groups became more effective than the homogeneous groups at identifying problems and generating alternative solutions to the complex problems they were given. These findings suggest that demographic diversity may be a detriment to newly formed groups but that it can provide advantages if groups are given some time to interact.

Researchers have also investigated the effects of psychological diversity on individual and team outcomes. Psychological diversity among team members increases the pool of knowledge and skills available for completing team tasks. Thus, for idea-generation and decision-making tasks, heterogeneous teams outperform homogeneous teams, which is likely due to the team members bringing a greater variety of perspectives to bear on the tasks (Magjuka & Baldwin, 1991). In essence, diversity helps the team develop more innovative and creative solutions. Not surprisingly, however, teams with diverse functional backgrounds and skills appear to have greater difficulty coordinating their efforts than teams with members who have homogeneous functional backgrounds and skills. In addition, a great deal of heterogeneity in skills and values may make it difficult to establish adequate communication and coordination among team members, particularly when teams are newly formed (Ilgen, 1999). Horwitz and Horwitz (2007) conducted a meta-analysis of the relationship between team diversity and team outcomes. They found that, although demographic diversity was not significantly related to team performance, psychological diversity (which they defined and measured as acquired individual characteristics such as functional expertise, education, and organizational tenure) had a positive impact on team performance, including team problem solving and innovation. The meta-analysis supported the notion that some forms of diversity are more important than others and that psychological diversity can provide organizations with a competitive advantage if it is factored in when selecting and composing teams.

Harrison and his colleagues conducted a series of studies that examined the effects of both demographic and psychological diversity over time. Harrison, Price, and Bell (1998) found that the length of time team members worked together weakened the (negative) effects of demographic diversity on team performance but strengthened the (positive) effects of psychological diversity as team members had opportunities to engage in meaningful interactions. In a follow-up study, Harrison, Price, Gavin, and Florey (2002) found that over time, increasing collaboration among team members weakened the effects of demographic diversity on team outcomes but, once again, strengthened the effects of psychological diversity. In a follow-up to these studies, Bell (2007) conducted a meta-analysis of individual-level predictors of team performance. She found that agreeableness, conscientiousness, openness to experience, collectivism, and preference for teamwork were significant predictors of team performance in organizational settings.

Overall, the research in this area indicates that diversity is a double-edged sword that provides great challenges and great opportunities for teams and organizations (Jackson & Joshi, 2004). The challenges stem partly from the fact that diversity comes in many forms. The opportunities provided by diverse teams stem from their ability to develop more innovative and creative solutions than homogeneous teams. These diversity issues will continue to challenge managers, I-O psychologists, and team members who work in an increasingly multicultural and global workforce.

Team Processes

LePine and colleagues (2008) recently conducted a comprehensive meta-analysis of team processes (e.g., cohesion, communication, coordination, conflict management) and found that they have positive relationships with team performance and team member satisfaction. These results also indicated that relationships among teamwork processes and team performance may vary according to task interdependence and the size of the team. Specifically, the relationship between the teamwork processes and team performance was stronger when team interdependence and team size were larger. In the next few sections, we describe some of these critical team processes.

Norms

Norms Informal and sometimes unspoken rules that teams adopt to regulate members' behavior.

In contrast to organizational policies that specify formal rules and regulations, **norms** are the informal and sometimes unspoken rules that teams adopt to regulate member behavior (Feldman, 1984; Greenberg, 2002). Norms may regulate a variety of behaviors and customs, including unethical behavior, dress code, and the punctuality with which meetings and the workday begin and end. However, the most common norm relates to the productivity of team members. Some work teams have norms for high productivity, whereas other teams provide normative pressure on members to limit their productivity. Violation of productivity norms, which is likely to raise justice and fairness concerns, is often considered more serious than violation of other norms.

Norms are more likely to be enforced if they facilitate team survival, if they simplify the behavior expected of members, and if they clarify what is distinctive about the team's identity (Feldman, 1984). Norms are likely to develop in several different ways: through explicit statements by team members, as carryover behaviors from past situations, or from the first behavior pattern that emerges in the team. A great deal of research has shown that norms have an important impact on conformity, team decision making, and team performance (Forsyth, 2009). In addition, research suggests that norms can have an impact on organizational citizenship behaviors in teams (Ehrhart & Naumann, 2004; Ng & van Dyne, 2005).

Communication and Coordination

Team performance depends heavily on effective communication, including proper information exchange (Swezey & Salas, 1992). Communication involves the transmission of information from one team member to another in a common language. Good communication across team members is important in nearly all teams, but it is particularly necessary with teams whose tasks are highly interdependent and dynamic. For example, flight crew members who are dependent on each other must communicate by providing information, listening actively, and being assertive in making quick decisions if unusual and often time-pressured circumstances arise (Prince, Chidester, Bowers, & Cannon-Bowers, 1992).

Coordination is important in teams because of the interactive work that they conduct. Well-coordinated team members can obtain information from other team members when needed and move easily from one task to another (Swezey & Salas, 1992). Effective groups are able to minimize **coordination losses**, which occur when team members expend their energies in different directions or fail to synchronize their work on time-critical tasks. Coordination or process losses were first observed in rope-pulling exercises in the early days of research on groups. Ringlemann (1913) found that when multiple people were asked to pull simultaneously on a rope, some were pulling while others were resting; thus, the force exerted by the group was always lower than the sum of the force exerted by group members when they pulled individually. Later studies proposed that another phenomenon called **social loafing**, in which team members assume that other members will bear the burden, may have also been a factor in Ringlemann's findings. One or both of these phenomena may be involved in research results showing that team performance declines with the addition of extra members beyond the required minimum (Gladstein, 1984).

Coordination loss Reduced group performance that occurs when team members expend their energies in different directions or fail to synchronize or coordinate their work.

Social loafing Reduced motivation and performance in groups that occurs when there is a reduced feeling of individual accountability or a reduced opportunity for evaluation of individual performance.

Social loafing occurs when reduced feelings of individual accountability result in reduced motivation and performance in groups (Latané, Williams, & Harkins, 1979). Workers are also motivated to engage in social loafing when they believe their behavior is not being monitored, which occurs more frequently in large work groups (Jones, 1984). Considerable research has examined social loafing, which has been documented in groups working on such tasks as creativity problems, brainstorming, and vigilance exercises. Research among intact work groups across two organizations showed that decreases in both task visibility and distributive justice were associated with an increase in social loafing (Liden, Wayne, Jaworski, & Bennett, 2004).

Social loafing is not inevitable when people work together. Shepperd's (1993) review of productivity loss in groups indicated that one way to remedy low productivity is to make individual contributions indispensable in achieving desired group outcomes. Shepperd suggested at least four ways to do this: (1) Increase the difficulty of the task, (2) increase the uniqueness of individual contributions, (3) lead individuals to infer that attaining the collective good depends on their personal contributions, and (4) directly instruct individuals that their contributions are necessary. Based on extensive research on social loafing, these approaches are likely to improve group members' motivation and to increase overall group performance.

Cohesion

As teams mature, they often develop **cohesion**, which is the degree to which team members desire to remain in the team and are committed to the team goal (Forsyth, 2009). Highly cohesive teams are characterized by stability, pride in the team, feelings of unity and satisfaction that hold the team together, strong norms, and pressure for conformity. Cohesive team members are deeply involved in the team's activities, respond positively to one another, and communicate well. Thus, highly cohesive teams have more power over their members than teams with low cohesion (Goodman et al., 1987). A good example of

Cohesion Degree to which team members desire to remain in the team and are committed to team goals.

a cohesive team is a successful hockey team whose members have pride in the team, feelings of unity, and strong norms for hard work during practices and games.

A meta-analysis by Mullen and Cooper (1994) found that cohesion is associated with successful team performance. Their study indicated that the relationship between cohesion and team performance occurs most consistently in project teams, which are truly interdependent; it occurs least consistently in service or sales teams, which are often not very interdependent. A more recent and comprehensive meta-analysis found that cohesion is positively related to both task performance and organizational citizenship behavior (Beal, Cohen, Burke, & McLendon, 2003).

Conflict may result between highly cohesive teams that appear to have tasks or goals that are at odds with one another (K. W. Thomas, 1992). An example is the work performed in clearing the site of the World Trade Center after its destruction by terrorists on September 11, 2001. As described in the book *American Ground: Unbuilding the World Trade Center*, the recovery and cleanup effort gave rise to substantial friction among fire department teams, police teams, and civilian teams (Langewiesche, 2002). The lack of cohesion among civilian volunteers was a factor in their dismissal from the site after the first few weeks. Employees of private organizations, various departments of the city, and other government departments disagreed on responsibilities and priorities. Most notably, firefighters saw their task as bringing out the remains of the approximately 300 fellow firefighters who lost their lives trying to save others; the police were dedicated to finding the bodies of their 35 fallen comrades. The bodies of the police officers were more likely to be found on the periphery of the buildings because these officers were directing the building occupants to safety when the towers collapsed. In contrast, firefighters' remains were more likely to be found in the collapsed stairwells because many of them were still ascending the towers when they collapsed. There was also an image struggle. Firefighters were seen by the press and public as more "heroic" than the police because so many firefighters died inside the buildings. As New York City and Port Authority police forces at the cleanup site watched the image of the firefighters grow, the long-standing jealousies between the two uniformed forces became increasingly strained. At one point firefighters, who were determined to suspend cleanup work until all possible remains of their comrades were found, actually came to blows with police officers, who were equally determined to prevent the firefighters from delaying the cleanup. Civilian workers, in contrast, were chiefly concerned with cleaning up the site and protecting against the further collapse of any buildings. In addition, considering the enormous number of civilians (well over 2,000) who were killed or missing, they felt that nonuniformed remains in the rubble were not being accorded adequate respect. This tragic and traumatic event illustrates the point that as teams become more cohesive, there are increasing conflicts and tensions with other teams that may have different goals.

Robert Mecea/Getty Images, Inc.

Teams occasionally have conflicting goals, as exemplified by the hostility between police and firefighters over how cleanup of the World Trade Center site should proceed.

Research has begun to investigate how cohesive teams might work together to reduce interteam conflicts and to enhance productivity. One study showed that increased contact between teams, including having a boundary-spanning member who works on both teams, can help overcome the problem of strong cohesion within each team (Richter, West, van Dick, & Dawson, 2006). Another study found that collaborative projects across teams were helpful in enhancing innovation in the organization as a whole (West, Hirst, Richter, & Shipton, 2004). These studies offer promise that cohesive teams can work well together, but additional research at the team level of analysis is needed to identify the best solutions to potential interteam conflicts.

Decision Making

Decision making in teams is crucial to their success. Team decision making occurs through defining the problem, gathering information, discussing and evaluating alternatives, and deciding collaboratively on the appropriate course of action. A great deal of research on team decision making has examined the circumstances under which teams make poor decisions. Many faulty group decisions may be attributed to a phenomenon called groupthink, which was first identified by social psychologist Irving Janis. **Groupthink** is a mode of thinking that people engage in when they are deeply involved in a cohesive group and when their desire for agreement overrides their motivation to appraise alternative courses of action realistically (Janis, 1982). Groupthink is a specific example of **group polarization**, which is the tendency for groups to make decisions that are more extreme (i.e., more polarized) than those made by individuals. Researchers originally found that groups tended to make more risky decisions than individuals and called this the **risky-shift phenomenon**. Researchers later discovered that some groups made more cautious decisions than did individuals in the group. Thus, group polarization can involve either more cautious or more risky shifts in judgment following group discussion when compared to the average of individual judgments made prior to discussion (Bettenhausen, 1991). Group polarization occurs because people working in groups tend to shift their opinions in the direction they think is consistent with the values of the group (Forsyth, 2009). Thus, group decisions are often more extreme than the decision that any individual in the group would make.

Groupthink Mode of thinking that group members engage in when they are deeply involved in a cohesive group and when their desire for agreement overrides their motivation to appraise alternative courses of action realistically.

Group polarization Tendency for groups to make more extreme decisions than those made by individuals.

Risky-shift phenomenon Tendency for groups to make more risky decisions than individuals; related to the more general phenomenon of group polarization.

The faulty decision by President John F. Kennedy and his advisors to send commandos into Cuba to capture the area known as the Bay of Pigs has been partly attributed to groupthink (Janis, 1982). In April 1961, President Kennedy and his committee of advisors, which included members of the Central Intelligence Agency, the Joint Chiefs of Staff, and experts on foreign affairs, were contemplating an invasion of Cuba. The plan involved a squad of well-trained commandos who were to capture and defend the Bay of Pigs on the southern coast of Cuba. Once in control there, the commandos were to launch raids against Fidel Castro's army and encourage civilian revolt in the capital, Havana. The Bay of Pigs invasion took place on April 17 and was a disaster. The entire squad of commandos was killed or captured within days, and the U.S. government had to send food and supplies to Cuba as a ransom in return for the release of the surviving commandos (Forsyth, 2009). Janis (1982) described the Bay of Pigs invasion plan as a case of bad group decision making resulting from groupthink and labeled it as one of the "worst fiascos ever perpetrated by a responsible government" (p. 14).

The ill-fated decision by NASA officials to launch the *Challenger* space shuttle in January

"All those in favor say 'Aye.'" "Aye." "Aye." "Aye." "Aye." "Aye."

1986 has also been attributed to groupthink (Morehead, Ference, & Neck, 1991). Despite warnings by some engineers that the cold weather could make the solid rocket boosters on the shuttle too brittle, NASA officials decided to move forward with the launch, which resulted in the explosion of the *Challenger* 73 seconds after liftoff. Similarly, groupthink has been mentioned regarding decisions made during different parts of the construction and flight of the space shuttle *Columbia*, which disintegrated during reentry into the earth's atmosphere in February 2003 (Oberg, 2003).

Janis suggested that groupthink is a disease that infects healthy groups; he identified several symptoms that signal the existence of groupthink, including interpersonal pressure resulting from a highly cohesive group, illusions of invulnerability, and lack of open discussion. Groupthink is also more likely when groups use defective decision-making strategies, such as considering only extreme alternatives, failing to develop contingency plans, and losing sight of overall objectives (Forsyth, 2009). Research suggests that groupthink occurs far more commonly and in a wider range of group settings than Janis originally envisioned (Baron, 2005). In the long run, one important contribution of research on groupthink is the acknowledgment that constructs typically viewed as positive aspects of groups (e.g., cohesiveness) do not necessarily lead to positive outcomes (Kerr & Tindale, 2004; Whyte, 1998). Another contribution is the increased research focus on preventing groupthink.

To prevent groupthink, it is helpful for group members to solicit many different views and to consider a wide diversity of perspectives and alternative courses of action. Group members should also be encouraged to express any doubts they have in a solution that is reached too quickly. Some research has shown that groupthink can be avoided if some individuals are assigned to play devil's advocate role, that is, to criticize proposed courses of action and question the assumptions underlying the popular choice among the group members. In addition, Priem, Harrison, and Muir (1995) found that breaking the group into subgroups is helpful in reducing groupthink. They suggested that one subgroup propose solutions and another subgroup propose solutions opposite to those developed by the first subgroup. The subgroups then interact and devise solutions that are acceptable to both. The researchers found that this approach helped to avoid the premature consensus that often leads to groupthink and led to strong agreement on the final decisions that were made. Because this study was conducted with students who had limited business and managerial experience, the subgroup method of reducing early consensus needs to be tested with more experienced participants in organizational settings before its validity can be fully assessed.

Team Outputs

Team outputs can be divided into several important areas, including team performance, team innovation, and team member well-being (Brodbeck, 1996). Team performance is often reflected in objective measures such as sales revenues, units produced, customers served, and patients treated. In determining what accounts for high team performance, we described team inputs and team processes earlier in this module. Important inputs are the organizational context, the team task, and team composition. For example, we have seen that teams composed of members with high cognitive ability and certain personality characteristics have high team performance. Team processes that are critical for high team performance include communication, coordination, and cohesiveness.

It is important to note that although team performance is often better than individual performance, research has indicated that team outputs are not always superior to individual outputs. Specifically, for some cognitive and decision-making tasks the best individual often outperforms an interacting group (Gigone & Hastie, 1997). So using the output of a team will in some cases result in less optimal outcomes than using the output of the most qualified individual in the team. This cautionary note indicates that although teamwork is indeed appropriate for many situations, managers and I-O psychologists should carefully consider the task or situation before deciding that a team is best suited for a particular project.

A primary reason for implementing teams is to increase innovation in the organization (Axtell, Holman, & Wall, 2006). Several studies have demonstrated that team member diversity leads to more creative team decision making (e.g., Jackson, 1996). In addition, teams and organizations whose goals or objectives relate to innovation are likely to produce more novel and creative ideas and products than teams without clear innovation goals. Miron, Erez, and Naveh (2004) found that the highest levels of innovation result from having team members who are creative as well as an organizational culture (discussed in detail in Chapter 14) that supports innovation. In a comprehensive meta-analysis, Hülsheger, Anderson, and Salgado (2009) found that team processes such as support for innovation and external communication were predictive of innovativeness and creativity in workplace teams.

Fay, Borrill, Amir, Haward, and West (2006) examined two samples of health care employees who worked in teams that were deliberately staffed so that members came from different disciplines and belonged to different professional groups. They proposed that multidisciplinary teams would produce higher team outcomes only if the quality of team processes was high. They found support for this hypothesis when examining the quality of innovations suggested by the health care teams. That is, multidisciplinary teams with positive team processes (shared vision and trust, high frequency of interactions) produced higher-quality innovative ideas than teams that did not have such processes. These research studies suggest that both team inputs and team processes are beneficial in increasing team innovativeness.

Another team output that I-O psychologists have studied is team member well-being and satisfaction. First, some evidence indicates that the implementation of autonomous work groups has a positive effect on group members' job satisfaction. These positive effects are considered to be a result of the increased participation, autonomy, and task variety available in such groups (Cordery, 1996). Similarly, Campion and colleagues (1993) found that three team task characteristics—participation, task variety, and task significance—were positively related to team member job satisfaction in service teams in the insurance industry. Second, working in a team can positively influence an individual's self-esteem (Hackman, 1992). Finally, team process variables (e.g., communication, cohesion) have been shown to positively influence individual member well-being and job satisfaction (West et al., 1998). As we might have expected, research to date indicates that positive interactions in teams contribute to higher team member satisfaction and well-being.

MODULE 13.2 SUMMARY

- The input–process–output model of team effectiveness, which has been supported by a variety of research studies, proposes that inputs affect team outputs indirectly through team processes. Research has also indicated that inputs can have a direct effect on team outputs.
- Inputs include the organizational context, team task, and team composition. The organizational context can enhance team interactions and increase team effectiveness by providing resources needed for performance and continued functioning of the work team.
- Team performance also depends on the task the team is required to perform and the team's composition. Teams should be given meaningful and interesting tasks that provide some degree of autonomy. In addition, research indicates that certain KSAs are positively related to team performance.
- Diversity provides challenges and opportunities for teams and organizations. Challenges may stem from the difficulty that diverse teams often have in coordinating their efforts when they first form. Opportunities stem from their ability to develop more innovative solutions than homogeneous teams.
- Team processes include norms, communication, coordination, cohesiveness, and decision making. Teams that effectively manage these processes have higher performance, make better decisions, and have more satisfactory work experiences.

KEY TERMS

input–process–output model of team effectiveness
team composition
shared mental model
demographic diversity
psychological diversity
norms
coordination loss
social loafing
cohesion
groupthink
group polarization
risky-shift phenomenon

MODULE 13.3

Special Issues in Teams

Team Appraisal and Feedback

As organizational and managerial objectives are increasingly being tied to team goals, managers have become interested in evaluating team performance (Hedge & Borman, 1995). Waldman (1997) found that most employees working in teams tend to favor team-based performance appraisal, the one exception being that individuals with a high need for achievement still prefer individual performance appraisals. Nevertheless, if an organization wants to send a message that team performance is important to organizational success, it is important to appraise team performance (Reilly & McGourty, 1998).

Scott and Einstein (2001) suggested that performance appraisal systems that assess team-level outcomes should provide the team with the information it needs to identify team problems and further develop team capabilities. In the 1990s, Xerox implemented a team performance measurement system that was developed jointly by team members, managers, and customers in order to be aligned with organizational and team goals (Jones & Moffett, 1999). Allstate Insurance and Hewlett-Packard are among several other organizations that have developed strategic team-based performance appraisal systems that increase the likelihood of teams contributing positively to organizational effectiveness. In cases where both individual and team performance are important, team-level feedback helps to emphasize that the interaction among individual team members is what leads to overall success. An example of this type of team-level feedback is a review of a theatrical play; cast members often see reviews as an indicator of team output, even though the critic may comment on the performances of particular actors.

Conducting team performance evaluations and providing feedback to teams, rather than to individuals, presents new challenges to managers in organizations. First, team-level evaluation and feedback are new to most organizations. Second, teams differ in their roles and responsibilities, and developing appraisal systems that assess performance over a wide variety of teams may be difficult. The move to team-based organizations raises old controversies about performance appraisal systems. For example, who should evaluate team performance: the team manager, team members, or customers of the team (Scott & Einstein, 2001)? Discussions of 360-degree feedback in team-based organizations suggest that all of these sources can provide important feedback to the team (Hallam, 2001).

the language from above, the power to make and the responsibility to implement a work-related decision would be vested in the individual subway line and its members—the team that is closest to the actual work process—rather than a central authority that tends to minimize differences between subway lines in pursuit of efficiency through standardization.

Human Relations Theory

As we saw above, classic organizational theory represented a disembodied view of organizational life. It did not consider the interrelationship between an organization's requirements and the characteristics of its members. **Human relations theory** added a personal or human element to the study of organizations.

Human relations theory Theory that adds a personal or human element to the study of organizations; considers the interrelationship between an organization's requirements and the characteristics of its members.

McGregor's Theory X and Theory Y

Just as Weber's classic organizational theory of bureaucracy was a protest against the ills of the earlier organizational model of favoritism, Douglas McGregor's theory was a protest against the impersonal propositions of classic organizational theory. In his influential book *The Human Side of Enterprise*, McGregor (1960) proposed that the beliefs that managers hold about their subordinates influence their behavior toward those subordinates. As a way of making his theory more understandable, McGregor constructed two contrasting beliefs systems, which he labeled Theory X and Theory Y. **Theory X** managers believed that subordinate behavior had to be controlled in order to meet organizational ends—one of the basic propositions of classic organizational theory—and that a lack of focus would lead to apathy and resistance. Theory X managers were likely to use punishments and rewards as mechanisms of control. In contrast, **Theory Y** managers believed that subordinates were active and responsible and would be more motivated to meet organizational goals without unduly constraining organizational or managerial controls. Instead of a rigid use of concrete punishments and rewards, Theory Y managers were more likely to provide expanded responsibilities and challenges to subordinates. Although McGregor proposed these two systems merely as examples of alternative beliefs that managers might hold, many managers saw them as representing an either/or dichotomy, with no other alternatives. Since McGregor's death in 1964, others have proposed alternatives to the Theory X/Y dichotomy (Ouchi, 1981; Schein, 1981).

Theory X Theory developed by McGregor to describe managers who believe subordinates must be controlled to meet organizational ends.

Theory Y Theory developed by McGregor to describe managers who believe subordinates are motivated to meet goals in the absence of organizational controls.

The Growth Perspective of Argyris

Chris Argyris has been an influential organizational theorist for several decades. About the same time that McGregor's propositions were gaining favor among managers and practitioners, Argyris (1972) proposed a natural developmental sequence in humans that could be either enhanced or stunted by the organization. Like Maslow (1943) with his earlier motivational theory, Argyris proposed that growth was a natural and healthy experience for an individual. Furthermore, organizations that acknowledged and aided this growth would be more likely to prosper than those that ignored or actively inhibited this growth. Argyris suggested that individuals developed in the following manner:

1. From passive to active organisms
2. From dependent to independent organisms
3. From organisms requiring immediate gratification to those capable of delaying gratification
4. From organisms able to deal only with concrete operations to those able to deal in abstractions
5. From organisms with few abilities to those with many abilities

If we accept these assumptions (which seem quite reasonable and compatible with what we observe in the world around us), then it follows that certain forms of organization are counterproductive, including highly routine, assembly-line work and organizational structures that emphasize control. Argyris proposed that when individual workers encounter these inhibitions, they will react to them in predictable ways, including absenteeism, turnover, labor actions, and apathy. The organization following the classic model will react to negative worker behavior by exerting even more control, therefore exacerbating the behavior it is attempting to extinguish.

For both McGregor and Argyris, the solution to the organizational puzzle was to integrate the goals of the organization with the goals of the individual. It is interesting to examine current organizational initiatives (e.g., total quality management, Six Sigma, lean manufacturing) in that light. Many of these initiatives emphasize the importance of participation as a member of a team and the critical role of product and process quality. While it is probably true that most workers value the social rewards of teamwork, it is not clear that those same workers value quality to the same extent as do the managers and strategic planners. Nor is it clear that the statistical analyses that form the foundation of many of these systems are as important to workers as the more generalized goal-setting and feedback process. Nevertheless, today's organizations have implemented much of the philosophy and theorizing of both McGregor and Argyris.

Contingency Theories

You will recall from our discussion of leadership in Chapter 12 that some theories were labeled **contingency** (or "it depends") **theories**. The terms "contingency" in the leadership context and "structure/process" in the organizational context imply that behavior must be selected to fit the particular circumstance. Several theorists have departed from the one-best-way approach of the classic theories and suggested that the best way actually depends on the circumstances of the organization.

Contingency theories of organization Theories proposing that the best way to structure an organization depends on the circumstances of the organization.

Woodward

British industrial sociologist Joan Woodward (1958) recognized that the technology employed in a particular company or industry could influence the most effective design for the organization. She contrasted three types of organizations:

- **Small-batch organization**: produces specialty products one at a time
- **Large-batch and mass-production organization**: produces large numbers of discrete units—assembly-line operations
- **Continuous-process organization**: depends on a continuous process for output or product, including organizations such as refineries, chemical plants, and distilleries

Small-batch organization Organization that produces specialty products one at a time.

Large-batch and mass-production organization Organization that produces large numbers of discrete units, often using assembly-line operations.

Continuous-process organization Organization that depends on a continuous process for output or product.

In observing these three types of organizations, Woodward discovered that the span of control varied systematically by type of organization. The largest span of control was observed in mass-production organizations and the smallest in continuous-process environments, with small-batch organizations falling in between. From this observation, she reasoned that different technologies are better served with different structural characteristics.

Woodward's approach was primitive by today's standards, but it did represent a departure from the classic approach. More importantly, she introduced the concept of technology into organizational thinking. This led to the development of more elaborate contingency theories, including the work of Lawrence and Lorsch (1967).

Lawrence and Lorsch

Lawrence and Lorsch (1967) proposed that the stability of the environment dictates the most effective form of organization. Based on their own work as well as the research of Burns and Stalker (1961), Lawrence and Lorsch discovered that organizations in stable environments tended to be more "mechanistic" than those in unstable environments. A **mechanistic organization** depended on formal rules and regulations, made decisions at higher levels of the organization, and had smaller spans of control. In contrast, unstable or rapidly changing environments or industries seemed to spawn "organic" forms of organization. An **organic organization** had larger spans of control, less formalization of procedure, and decision making at middle levels of the organization.

Mechanistic organization Organization that depends on formal rules and regulations, makes decisions at higher levels of the organization, and has small spans of control.

Organic organization Organization with a large span of control, less formalized procedures, and decision making at middle levels.

Lawrence and Lorsch suggested that mechanistic and organic differences exist not only between companies and industries but also within organizations. They proposed that managers in different departments would have very different worldviews based on their environments. Thus, a research and development (R&D) manager would be in an organic environment and therefore less likely to depend on formal rules, would have larger spans of control, and would be more likely to delegate decisions to lower levels of the department. In contrast, a plant or shift manager might be in a mechanistic environment and use more formal rules, retain decision-making authority, and maintain more direct control of activities through smaller spans of control.

The challenge for the organization, then, is to develop an architecture that accommodates both the R&D manager and the plant manager. The former is operating in a rapidly changing environment and the latter in a relatively stable environment. Without intervention, these differences could easily lead to mutual suspicion and disrespect, as well as tension surrounding strategic planning, budgeting, and so forth. Unlike Woodward, who concentrated on differences among industries and companies, Lawrence and Lorsch identified the department as the important level for understanding how organizations operated. They proposed that if departments can adapt and integrate to changing external environments, the organization would prosper. In a broader sense, the same would be true for larger units within the corporation such as multinational locations, regions, or divisions. Now we will consider an even broader contingency theory, one that goes well beyond departmental boundaries.

Mintzberg

Henry Mintzberg is an influential organization theorist who proposed a very sophisticated contingency theory in 1979. The theory has several components to it; in essence, Mintzberg argued that one could describe an organization by looking at several categories of characteristics. These categories include: (1) the key mechanism used by the organization for coordinating its efforts (perhaps *the* largest challenge for any organization), (2) the functions and roles of people in the organization, (3) the extent of centralization or decentralization in decision making in the organization, and (4) the context in which the organization operates.

First, Mintzberg (1989) identified six basic forms of coordination:

1. Mutual adjustments based in informal communication
2. Direct supervision
3. Standardization of work processes
4. Standardization of the KSAOs necessary for production
5. Standardization of outputs
6. Standardization of norms (what we might call "culture")

Mintzberg believed that as work becomes more complex and demanding, coordination shifts from the more informal and dyadic to the more formal through standardization.

Second, in Mintzberg's theory, there are five basic functions or roles (which he called "parts") that characterize people in the organization:

1. *Operating core*: the people responsible for producing the good or service
2. *Strategic apex*: a chief executive, or group of senior leaders, to oversee the entire effort of the organization
3. *Middle line*: the midlevel managers and supervisors who mediate the interactions between the strategic apex and the operating core
4. *Technostructure*: analysts who perform specialized technical support functions, such as engineering or budgeting
5. *Support staff*: employees who perform administrative functions varying from legal to compensation and benefit administration

All of these functions are carried out in an "ideology," which Mintzberg equates with an organization's culture, defined as idiosyncratic traditions and beliefs of the organization. He proposed that it is the inherent tension or interplay between the importance or prominence of these parts that, in turn, creates the diversity of configurations that we see when we look across organizations. Figure 14.2 presents the organizational parts in graphic form. But as we will see shortly, the importance or prominence of a part will change the shape of an organization dramatically.

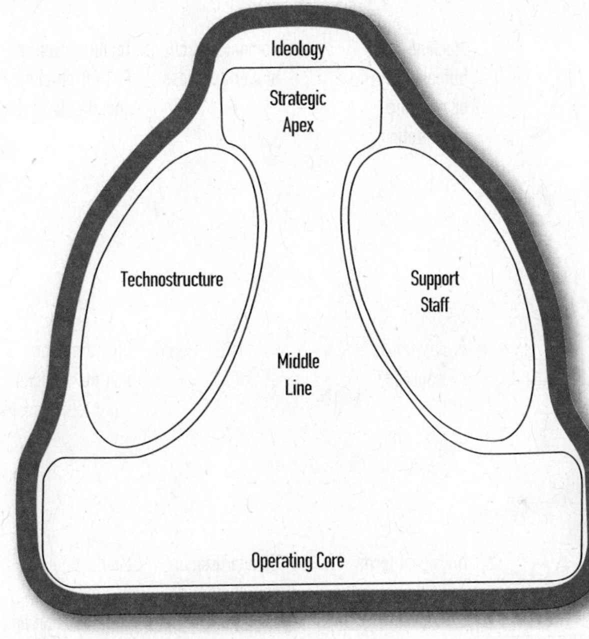

The third defining characteristic of an organization for Mintzberg is its degree and form of centralization. If all decisions were made at the strategic apex, this would be a highly centralized organization. If decisions were spread across the organization based on expertise and knowledge, this would be a decentralized organization. But centralization or decentralization can be horizontal, vertical, or both. Vertical decentralization means delegation of decision-making authority down the managerial chain. Horizontal decentralization is more informal and refers to the willingness of line managers to permit decision making among non–line managers (technostructure and support functions). The final organizational characteristic is the context in which the organization operates. Context includes things such as the age or maturity of the organization, its technical simplicity or complexity, and its size.

Ideology
Strategic Apex
Technostructure
Support Staff
Middle Line
Operating Core

FIGURE 14.2 Mintzberg's Organizational Parts

SOURCE: Mintzberg, H. (1989). *Mintzberg on management: Inside our strange world of organizations*, Figure 6-1, p. 99. New York: Free Press. © 1989 by Henry Mintzberg. Originally published in Mintzberg, H. (1979). *Structuring of organizations: A synthesis of the research* (1st ed.), p. 20. © 1979. Reprinted by permission of Pearson Education, Inc., Upper Saddle River, NJ.

By combining these four components—coordination, roles, centralization, and context—Mintzberg creates some organizational configurations. These configurations are best thought of as variations in the shape of an organization. Consider Table 14.1, which presents five typical (although not exhaustive) shapes. He gives each shape a name (e.g., entrepreneurial, machine bureaucracy) and then describes it with respect to the four components of an organization. This could be seen as a simple descriptive exercise, but it is much more than that. Mintzberg believed that various types (configurations) of organization are best served by the specific forms of coordination, centralization, and role or function influence. As an example, the entrepreneurial shape is both characterized and best served by direct supervision, influence of the strategic apex, and centralization. In contrast, the adhocracy is best described and served by informal coordination, a strong

TABLE 14.1 Mintzberg's Theoretical Models of Organizational Structure

MODEL	*STRUCTURE TYPE*	*PRIMARY COORDINATING MECHANISM*	*PRIMARY COMPONENT OF ORGANIZATION*	*MAIN DESIGN PARAMETERS*	*CONTEXTUAL FACTORS*
	Simple or entrepreneurial organization	Direct supervision	Strategic apex Pull for direction and centralization	Centralization Little specialization Little formalization Organic structure	Young, small Nonsophisticated, simple, nonregulating technical system Simple, dynamic environment Possible extreme hostility or strong power needs of top manager Not fashionable
	Machine bureaucracy or machine organization	Standardization of work process	Technostructure Pull for efficiency and standardization	Behavior formalization Vertical and horizontal job specialization Usually functional grouping Large operating-unit size Vertical centralization and limited horizontal decentralization Action planning	Old, large Regulating, non-automated technical system Simple, stable environment External control Not fashionable
	Professional bureaucracy or professional organization	Standardization of skills	Operating core Pull for proficiency and professionalism	Training Little formalization Horizontal job specialization Vertical and horizontal decentralization	Complex, stable environment Nonregulating, nonsophisticated technical system Fashionable
	Divisional form or diversified organization	Standardization of outputs	Middle line Pull for concentration and balkanization	Market grouping Performance control system Much formalization Limited vertical decentralization	Old, large Diversified markets: technical system divisible, otherwise like Machine Bureaucracy Relatively simple and stable environment Power needs of middle managers Fashionable
	Adhocracy or innovative organization	Mutual adjustment	Support staff (in the administrative adhocracy; together with the operating core in the operating adhocracy) Pull for innovation and collaboration	Liaison devices Little formalization Organic structure Selective decentralization Horizontal job specialization Training Functional and market grouping concurrently	Young (especially operating adhocracy) Complex, dynamic (sometimes disparate) environment Sophisticated and often automated technical system (in administrative adhocracy) Fashionable

SOURCE: Haynes, E. F. (1997). *An application of Mintzberg's configurational theory to community college organizational structure*, Table 2, p. 64. Adapted from Mintzberg, 1981, 1983, 1989. Unpublished dissertation, North Carolina State University. Used by permission of Elizabeth L. Haynes, Ed.D.

support function, and selective decentralization. The last column in Table 14.1 illustrates that the adhocracy and the entrepreneurial organization operate in different contexts.

It is important to note that organizational theories are not simple tools that, if applied, guarantee success. Instead, they are conceptualizations of how the basic task of organizing work gets done. Mintzberg's is the most sophisticated of the contingency theories we have examined. It is also one of the most intuitively appealing of existing theories. Mintzberg's theory makes the point that an organization is embedded in a larger reality. This reality includes history (e.g., context and ideology) and environmental forces (e.g., market challenges, competition). It is the interplay between the internal reality of an organization and the external reality of its environment and history that characterizes the systems theory approach to organizations, which we will consider next.

Systems Theory

Consider the two organizations shown in Figure 14.3. On the left is an organization as it might have been depicted before the introduction of systems theory. On the right is the same organization after the introduction of systems theory. Which figure seems more realistic to you? That's what Daniel Katz and Robert Kahn (1966, 1978) thought as well.

Katz and Kahn

Daniel Katz and Robert Kahn were both social psycholo[illegible] how small groups functioned. In particular, they investigate[illegible] were filled, as well as how the clarity of these roles and the e[illegible] conflict, affected the emotions and behavior of group mem[illegible] liar because we covered the issues of role conflict and amb[illegible] s in Chapter 10 and in our discussion of group and team fu[illegible] and Kahn expanded their interest in groups to cover a mu[illegible] ion. Their text, *The Social Psychology of Organizations*, first [illegible] uch more dynamic view of organizations than had been pr[illegible] anization theory or the more modern approaches. Certainly [illegible] *me-thing* made a difference in how an organization functioned (e.g., the type of industry), and the Lawrence and Lorsch approach that we described earlier in the chapter distinguished between stable and dynamic environments, but systems theory illustrated that many, many forces were in play, both within and outside of an organization, that helped explain what actually went on *in* an organization. This was made clear in Mintzberg's view of the organization. Systems theory is sometimes called open systems theory to emphasize the fact that an organization must be open to its environment if it is to be effective. In recent

FIGURE 14.3 A Systems View of an Organization

years, the FBI and the CIA have been criticized because they were closed to the larger intelligence communities (and to each other). Like Mintzberg, Katz and Kahn were not as much interested in the *best* form of organization. Instead, they sought to *understand* how organizations behaved. In a broad sense, they took as a metaphor the way any living organism interacts with its environment.

The key to understanding systems theory can be seen in Figure 14.4. It is both simple and elegant. The organization takes in (i.e., inputs) resources, transforms those resources, then sends out (i.e., outputs) the results of that transformation. As an example, Apple inputs materials (e.g., plastic, alloys, computer chips), labor (engineers, assemblers, sales and marketing staff), and capital (money from investors, profits from product sales); transforms those inputs into an iPhone; and then outputs (i.e., sells) that iPhone to people like you and me, using the output to create more capital that becomes additional input (see the feedback loop at the bottom of the figure) to keep the system thriving. But the iPhone is not the only output. In the process of producing and selling the iPhone, Apple also outputs prestige, employee morale, investor confidence, and other intangibles. And to make the system even sweeter, Apple connects the device (the iPhone) to another system (various wireless carriers such as AT&T, Verizon, and Sprint), thus enhancing the value of both the service (access to the Internet and a vast array of communication possibilities for the consumer) and the product (a sleek and user-friendly device that signals that the owner has embraced the information age).

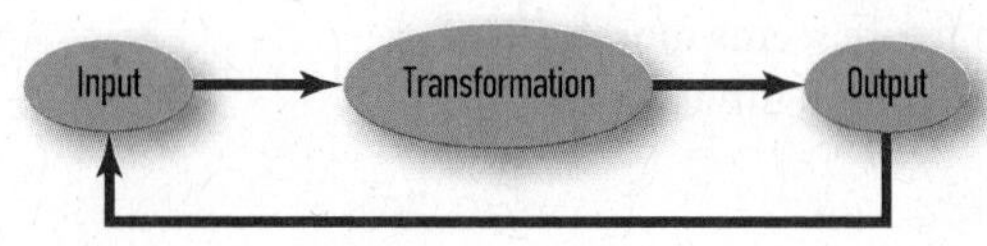

FIGURE 14.4 Systems Theory

By linking these two systems together, Apple further ensures its survival by beating any competitors to the punch and presenting a fully responsive "package" in one device. And Apple accomplishes that transformation within the larger context of external forces such as those that appear on the right side of Figure 14.3. But for the organization to survive in the long term, the transformation process must represent added value to what is represented by the inputs. After factoring in the cost of materials, labor, overhead (heat, light, etc.), Apple must sell the iPhone for a profit.

Systems theory is not really a theory as much as it is a way of thinking. It offers few testable hypotheses or immediate applications. But it does help us understand concepts that seem mysterious when we approach them via classic theories. Take leadership as an example. Systems theory tells us that the type of leadership (and the KSAOs of leaders) needed for effectiveness at different levels of an organization will change as one moves up the organizational ladder. Consider Miner's (2002) adaptation of systems theory to the challenge of leadership. As shown in Figure 14.5, if we contrast first-level supervision with middle-level management and top management, the type of leadership required (as well as cognitive and emotional abilities) changes as we move up the management ladder.

FIGURE 14.5 Leadership and Systems Theory

Source: Miner, J. B. (2002). *Organizational behavior: Foundations, theories, and analyses*, Table 14.2, p. 406. Oxford, U.K.: Oxford University Press. Adapted from Daniel Katz & Robert L. Kahn (1966) *The Social Psychology of Organization* (New York: Wiley), 312. Reproduced with permission of Oxford University Press and John Wiley & Sons, Inc.

Hierarchical level	*First-level supervision*	*Middle management*	*Top management*
Nature of leadership required	Administration – the use of existing structure	Interpolation – supplementing and piecing out the structure	Origination – change creation, and elimination of structure
Required cognitive abilities and skills	Technical knowledge: understanding of rules	Subsystem perspective – two way orientation of leader	Systemic perspective – external and internal
Required emotional abilities and skills	Equity and fairness in applying rules and using sanctions	Integration of the immediate work group with the larger system (good human relations)	Charisma

Conclusions about Theories of Organization

Since organizations are often compared to individuals with respect to personalities, it is tempting to compare the theories of organizations with theories of human motivation. You will recall that we used Weiner's (1992) metaphors to describe motivation theory in Chapter 8. What happens if we apply the same metaphors to organization theory? Starting with the person-as-machine metaphor, the classic organization theories assume that people are machines, responding to the characteristics of an organization in an automatic and reflexive manner. The humanist theories of McGregor and Argyris parallel the more personal and benevolent theories of Maslow, but they are no less mechanical, assuming that people respond to how they are perceived (McGregor's Theories X and Y) or go through stages of development (Argyris).

What is interesting is the discrepancy between many of the theories of organization and the current organizational interventions. Management by objectives (MBO), lean production, Six Sigma, and total quality management systems all use a person-as-scientist model of one form or another, and most assume the unlimited rationality of that scientist. Few of these interventions recognize the elements of the person-as-judge model that have become so prevalent in current theories of individual motivation. Most assume that efficacy will be enhanced and that individuals will seek challenge, but none of them directly recognize the role of efficacy in the judgments or decisions that organizational members make. There is a vigorous debate about whether interventions like Six Sigma or lean production will endure the test of time or will be rejected by cynical employees who do not accept the values or motivational schemes of their leaders. To the extent that these interventions do not recognize the person as judge, but instead assume the person-as-scientist model of motivation, they may very well ultimately fail. What we can say, however, is that there is a gap between organizational theory and motivational theory that will need a bridge if we are to arrive at a complete understanding of the effects of people on organizations and organizations on people.

MODULE 14.1 SUMMARY

- Early theories of organization emphasized relatively static characteristics such as size, chain of command, or the specialization of duties. The best-known early organizational theorist was Max Weber, who proposed the ideal bureaucracy comprising multiple dimensions, principally division of labor, delegation of authority, structure, and span of control.
- McGregor's human relationship approach proposed that the beliefs that managers hold about their subordinates influence their behavior toward those subordinates. He constructed two contrasting belief systems, labeled Theory X and Theory Y, which reflect the degree to which managers believe employees are self-directed or need to be controlled.
- Several theorists have departed from the one-best-way approach of the classic theories, suggesting that the best way depends on the circumstances of the organization. Woodward recognized that the technology employed in a particular company or industry influenced the most effective design for the organization. Lawrence and Lorsch suggested that the stability of the environment dictated the most effective form of organization.
- Mintzberg presented a complex contingency view of the organization that included structural characteristics, role or functions, levels and types of decentralization, and coordination mechanisms. Systems theory represents a more dynamic form of contingency theory.

KEY TERMS

organization
bureaucracy
division of labor
delegation of authority
structure
span of control
organizational chart
classic organizational theory
human relations theory
Theory X
Theory Y
contingency theories of organization
small-batch organization
large-batch and mass-production organization
continuous-process organization
mechanistic organization
organic organization

MODULE 14.2

Some Social Dynamics of Organizations

Organizations by definition are social entities. They represent a collection of individuals who work for a common purpose. As such, they exhibit the characteristics of any social entity, including a climate, a culture, and role expectations. These characteristics can work either to support the goals of the organization or to thwart them. In this module, we will consider the issues of climate and culture, as well as some unique challenges to organizations operating in a multicultural environment. As we saw in Chapter 10, roles, particularly role conflict and ambiguity, are also part of the organizational landscape.

Climate and Culture

You will recall from the opening of this chapter that we asked you to consider a wide variety of organizations: Honda Motor Company, the IRS, and Ben & Jerry's; various emergency response organizations in the New Orleans area; and an organized crime family. Each of these organizations probably evoked a somewhat different feeling in you. The IRS may have evoked a sense of predictability and standardization; Ben & Jerry's, a social and societal feeling; and the organized crime family, fear and fascination. Whether intentionally or unintentionally, organizations bring to mind both feelings and beliefs. Although both the IRS and the organized crime family would claim that a positive feeling of "family" pervades their operations, you may have doubts about the reality of the IRS claim and the tone of the crime family claim. Discussions of culture and climate involve concepts such as beliefs, values, perceptions, and feelings. Culture is often associated with the more cognitive variables such as beliefs and values, and climate is more commonly associated with more affective states such as feelings.

Discussions of and research about organizational climate and culture have been with us for over 50 years and have resulted in many competing definitions and measurement devices (Schneider, 2000). Organizations are of interest to a much broader range of scholars than simply psychologists. Anthropologists, sociologists, and political scientists, to name but a few, are also interested in the way that organizations develop, persist, and change—whether the organization is IBM, the Red Cross, or a village in the Himalayas. Based on this rich research tradition, we can draw at least one general conclusion: There is little agreement about what the concepts mean or how they affect the behavior of organizations or individuals in those organizations. In particular, the terms "climate" and "culture" are often used interchangeably; this has led to conflicting results, interpretations, and recommendations. Nevertheless, it is clear that the psychological center of the consideration of organizations and organizational psychology includes these concepts.

There are many outstanding treatments in the I-O psychology literature of the topic of climate and culture. Ashkanasy and his colleagues (Ashkanasy & Jackson, 2001; Ashkanasy, Wilderom, & Peterson, 2000) have reviewed the history of the concepts as well as the implications for human resource practices domestically and internationally. James and McIntyre (1996) have provided a detailed and compelling description of climate from the perspective of the individual worker. Rentsch (1990) has presented a comprehensive review of the various meanings assigned to culture and climate by organizational researchers. Reichers and Schneider (1990) have presented an excellent chronology of the development of both concepts.

A Brief History of Climate and Culture

Climate A shared perception among employees regarding their work entity: a particular organization, division, department, or work group.

Autocratic climate Organizational climate described by Lewin as highly structured with little opportunity for individual responsibility or risk taking at the lowest levels.

Democratic climate Organizational climate described by Lewin as less structured, with greater opportunity for individual responsibility and risk taking.

In 1939, Lewin, Lippitt, and White described various types of organizations in terms of the "climate" that pervaded them. **Climate** is the shared perception of employees about their work entity: an organization, division, department, or work group. Lewin and colleagues proposed different types of climates, including autocratic and democratic. Lewin's **autocratic climate** in an organization might be expected to be highly structured, with little opportunity for individual responsibility or risk taking at the lowest levels. In contrast, a **democratic climate** in an organization would be characterized as less structured, with greater opportunity for individual responsibility and risk taking. James and McIntyre (1996) conducted statistical analyses of existing climate research and suggested four dimensions, which they labeled as follows:

1. Role stress and lack of harmony
2. Job challenge and autonomy
3. Leadership facilitation and support
4. Work group cooperation, friendliness, and warmth

Table 14.2 presents some examples of typical questionnaire items about organizational climate. As can be seen from these items, the focus is on the perception of an individual in characterizing a climate. But Schulte, Ostroff, and Kinicki (2006) found that in addition to the influence of individual perceptions on individual satisfaction, other influences can be seen from unit-level (i.e., entire branches of a bank) climate measures. Once again, we are confronted with the multilevel nature of behavior. Individual satisfaction comes not only from individual perceptions of work conditions but also from a larger, group-level perception of climate that is independent of the individual's perception.

TABLE 14.2 **Some Typical Questions about Organizational Climate**

Employees are encouraged to develop their skills and abilities.
This is not the type of organization that likes to take risks.
I feel personally close to my co-workers.
If I make a strategic decision related to my work, I feel that my boss will back me up.
I feel that I have a good measure of control in my work.
I am not given much responsibility in my work.

As you can see, the emerging model of climate implies that it can be thought of as a structural concept; it can be applied to any organization (or division, or department, or even work group), and a score or series of scores can be obtained that describes "the" climate of the entity. I-O psychologists have suggested that multiple climates exist within any organization and that these climates are defined less by structural components (e.g., degree of autonomy) than by the goal of the group (Schneider, Bowen, et al., 2000). Thus, Schneider, Salvaggio, and Subarits (2002) identified a "service climate" that relates to customer satisfaction, Kraiger and Smith-Jentsch (2002) identified climates peculiar to air traffic controllers, Baer and Frese (2002) identified climates for initiative and innovation, and Zohar (1980) identified safety climates.

Burke, Borucki, and Kaufman (2002) perceive these identifications of climates as being grounded in the social constructionist perspective and observe that they are related to a specific focus of the researcher (e.g., safety, innovation, learning, team). The Schneider approach would be an example of this perspective. The social constructionist way of identifying climates is contrasted with the generalist perspective (there is one climate in an organization—this is the approach favored by James as described above) and the multiple-stakeholder perspective, which defines climates in terms of object groups (e.g., supervisors, clients, vendors, customers).

Although the quest for the perfect climate measure continues (Patterson et al., 2005), it is not necessary to choose among any of these ways of defining climates. It is unlikely that there is any "best" way to define or measure climate; they all have appeal and potential value. On the one hand, it may be valuable when contrasting organizations or qualitatively different groups within an organization (e.g., R&D versus customer service) to use the generalist dimensions suggested by James and James (1989) to understand those differences. On the other hand, when considering differences between similar departments (e.g., customer service in one geographic region of a company against customer service in a different region) or differences within the same department at different times (e.g., 2008 versus 2011), it might be more useful to examine the "service climate" in some detail (a social constructivist or multiple-stakeholder perspective). Meta-analyses (Carr, Schmidt, Ford, & DeShon, 2003; Parker et al., 2003) have confirmed the assumption that better climate leads to better work outcomes (e.g., performance, attendance, commitment).

By the 1970s there was an increasing awareness that climate was not a large enough concept to capture many of the broader aspects of an organization. It was felt that climate dealt with the constraints on the actions of managers and leaders of the organization but did not address issues of the value and meaning of those actions (Ashkanasy & Jackson, 2001). Therefore, the term **culture** was introduced to refer to the shared beliefs and values created and communicated by the managers and leaders of an organization to employees.

Culture A system in which individuals share meanings and common ways of viewing events and objects.

Because the concept of culture came from the anthropological tradition rather than the psychological tradition, many of the early discussions about the differences between the concepts were confusing. Traditionally, the measurement of climate was accomplished with questionnaires, and the measurement of culture was performed through observation and case study. Despite this inconsistency, culture did seem to be getting at something different from climate. As a result, attempts to use common measurement procedures and questionnaires for measuring culture were developed. One of the best known is the Organizational Culture Inventory (Cooke & Rousseau, 1988; Cooke & Szumal, 2000).

In discussions of the failures of various organizations as evidenced by dissolution, downsizing, and so forth, the organizational culture rather than a climate is often identified as a causal factor (Ashkanasy & Jackson, 2001). One hears talk of a "culture of failure" or a "culture of conformity." Weber (2000) identified the "clash" of cultures as the most likely reason for the failure of mergers and acquisitions, when two different cultures often come face to face. The duration and severity of this clash also appear to be related to the financial performance and stock value of the acquiring company (Ashkanasy & Holmes, 1995).

Organizational Climate and Culture from the Multicultural Perspective

Most discussions of organizational culture and climate assume a single national culture, usually a Western culture like the United States, United Kingdom, or Australia. But in the past decade, organizations have become increasingly multicultural through mergers, acquisitions, and strategic alliances. This means that a new dimension must be added to the discussion of organizational culture and climate. That dimension is the presence of *multiple* national cultures within the same organization. We will consider some of these issues now.

When Cultures Clash

In the early years of the 17th century, Dutch immigrants developed sections of the west coast of Sweden, including the port city of Gothenburg. Unlike a typical Dutch coastal city, Gothenburg had no canals, so to make it look and feel more like "home," the Dutch dug canals throughout the city. When they left many years later, the Swedes filled in the canals.

An American manager moves her family to Tokyo on an assignment from the U.S. company for which she has worked for many years. The U.S. company acquired a much smaller Japanese company and asked some key employees to move to Tokyo to ease the integration of the two companies. The manager reports to an upper-level executive of the acquired Japanese firm. In her first week, she is handed a schedule of weekend retreats that she will be expected to attend with her Japanese colleagues. These retreats are intense off-site events requiring overnight stays. No family members are permitted to accompany her. She is dumbfounded that her new boss would be so inconsiderate as to expect her to abandon her family during non-work hours.

The anecdotes above are examples of a clash of cultures. Since there seems to be no recent effort to unearth the canals dug by the Dutch in Gothenburg, we will focus on the clash of organizational cultures demonstrated in the U.S.-acquired company in Japan. The rise of both the multicultural workplace and the multinational corporation makes these clashes increasingly common. Ashkanasy and Jackson (2001) identified four different models under which multinational companies can operate when confronted with differences in organizational culture:

- *Ethnocentrism.* The values of the parent company predominate; our American expatriate in Japan would simply refuse to take part in the retreats.
- *Polycentrism.* The values of the local company are accepted; our expatriate would agree to attend the retreats.
- *Regiocentrism.* The values of the parent organization and the local company blend together; our American expatriate would suggest that the retreats be held during working hours or that family members be permitted to accompany participants if they would like, although they would be expected to entertain themselves.
- *Geocentrism.* A new corporate-wide policy is developed to handle an issue in a way that would create a global perspective; our expatriate would join a team of individuals from the local and parent company with the goal of developing a workable global policy on retreats.

There is no "correct" choice from the four alternatives presented above. The choice needs to be negotiated by representatives of the two different organizational cultures. The key point is that multinational corporations must acknowledge the existence of different cultures represented in different geographic locations. House and colleagues (1999) have suggested the use of Hofstede's dimensions of the cultures of nations (e.g., power distance, collectivism) to describe the cultures of organizations. These organizational cultures (e.g., of the parent company) can then be compared to the national culture. Thus, the Hofstede dimensions could be used to contrast the culture of the larger U.S. company in our expatriate example with that of the smaller Japanese acquisition. Instead of concentrating on one event at a time (e.g., the off-site retreat), the organizations could deal more directly with larger discrepancies in cultures or shared beliefs.

Aycan and colleagues (2000) collected data that confirm the presence and effect of country-specific cultures on organizational HR practices. They collected data from managers in ten different countries and discovered, for example, that a paternalistic attitude among managers was much more likely to be found in India, Turkey, Pakistan, and China, where paternalism was valued. A paternalistic manager is one who provides "guidance, protection, nurturance, and care to the subordinate, and the role of the subordinate, in return, is to be loyal and deferent to the manager" (p. 197). Positive attitudes toward paternalism were much less likely to be found in Russia, Romania, the United States, Canada, Germany, and Israel. Similarly, Indian, Pakistani, Chinese, Turkish, and Russian managers were much more likely to consider loyalty to their communities as a desired value, and Canadian and U.S. managers were much less likely to endorse it. Finally, they examined the concept of "fatalism" in various cultures. Fatalism was defined as the belief that whatever happens will happen and events are largely out of the control of the individual. Beliefs in fatalism were higher in India and Russia, and lower in most of the other eight countries. These various belief systems in turn affected the extent to which employees were exposed to job enrichment (job redesign), participation in decision making (leadership and motivation), and performance-contingent rewards (motivation and compensation).

The issue of multinational companies and culture is very complex because of the overlap between national cultures and organizational cultures. Nevertheless, we can be fairly certain that the insensitive multinational corporation—and more important, its employees—is more likely to encounter difficulties than one aware of and prepared to negotiate cultural differences. But let's end this section on a positive note. D'Iribarne (2002) presented a case study in which two factories operated successfully by incorporating notions of national culture into their corporate culture. In Morocco, Islamic values and norms were included in a total quality management (TQM) project. In Mexico, family norms and values were merged with an initiative to transform the workplace from an individualist to a collectivist environment. In both instances, the incorporation of the cultural norms of the nation assisted the organizational transformation. Stone-Romero, Stone, and Salas (2003) presented a theory and model that incorporates the cultural background of organizational members into an understanding of employee behavior in a multicultural work environment.

An Application of Culture and Climate: Safety

The traditional approaches to workplace safety (the engineering approach, the personnel approach, the motivational approach) all tend to focus on the individual; collectively they are referred to as the micro-approach. The engineering approach is designed to prevent an individual from performing an unsafe act. The personnel approach assumes that "safe" individuals can be selected or trained. The motivational approach is directed toward changing the choices that an individual worker makes. We would like to discuss safety from a much broader, organizational perspective. To be fair, it is always the individual worker who actually engages in an unsafe act, but it would be incorrect to imply that this act occurs in a social vacuum. There are other, broader forces at work as well. These forces include attitudes and behaviors of supervisors and fellow workers toward safety, management and organizational commitment to safe behavior, and a general climate and culture in the workplace that favors or disfavors safe behavior. The study of these additional forces transforms micro-research into meso-research.

Hofmann, Jacobs, and Landy (1995) have suggested that an organization has three levels and that each level plays a role in safe behavior. The first level is the traditional one: the individual level. It includes employee attitudes, employee behavior, and employee knowledge. The second level, called the micro-organizational level, includes management attitudes, the presence of accountability mechanisms, a willingness on the part of the organization to self-regulate rather than depend on external compliance agencies for regulation, and the presence of joint labor–management groups such as safety committees. The third level, the macro-organizational level, includes communication channels, centralization versus decentralization of decision making, technological complexity, redundancy backup systems, and workforce specialization. For the present discussion, we will concentrate on the second level, micro-organizational issues.

Organizations can be characterized by their respective internal safety cultures—they fall along a continuum from placing strong emphasis on safety to disregarding it. Few would characterize the National Hockey League (NHL) as valuing safety above entertainment or winning. Players are expected to sacrifice their bodies for the sake of victory. In contrast, most of us would agree that regulated industries such as nuclear power, petrochemicals, and commercial aviation should be committed to safety above all else. It is this organizational commitment (or lack thereof) that shapes the attitudes of managers, supervisors, and workers. If the NHL fined owners and coaches for the frequency of injuries among their team members, or awarded championship rings or the Stanley Cup for injury-free seasons, the nature of hockey would change considerably. Certainly, in the wake of increasing evidence about the long-term negative health consequences of concussions, the NHL (along with the National Football League) is now working to find a way to increase the safety of its players while still maintaining the toughness and entertainment in its sport.

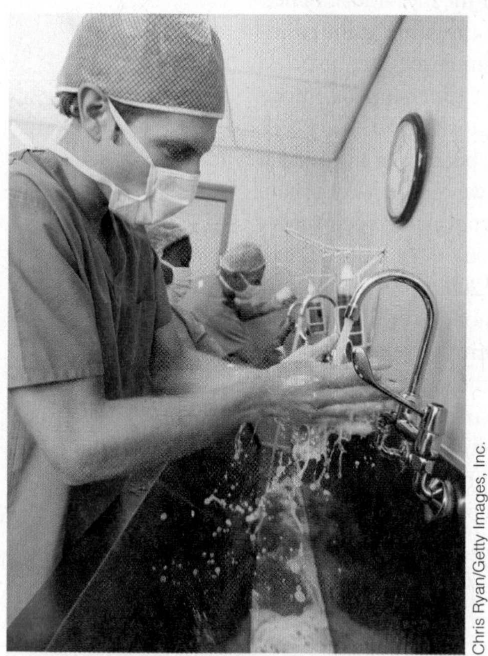

Chris Ryan/Getty Images, Inc.

A culture of safety: By washing their hands frequently, medical personnel reduce the risk of infection for patients as well as for themselves and their fellow workers.

To return to the domain of less spectacular business environments, Gaba, Singer, Sinaiko, Bowen, and Ciavarelli (2003) found dramatic differences between the safety climate among naval aviator squadrons and hospitals. A climate of safety was 12 times more evident among aviators than among hospitals! This is in line with increased concerns by human factors psychologists about patient safety and hospital procedures. For example, Hofmann and Mark (2006) found that a positive safety climate in hospitals was associated with fewer medication errors, fewer back injuries among nurses, fewer urinary tract infections among patients, and greater patient and nurse satisfaction with the quality of nursing care. It is clear that organizations, and even whole industries, vary with respect to their safety climate and culture.

Establishing a safety culture in an organization is not a simple task. It is not enough merely to include safety as one of the stated values of the organization. As the saying goes, "Talk is cheap." It takes hard work to establish and maintain a safety culture. Furthermore, one should not expect to see improved behavior immediately upon establishing a safety climate. Neal and Griffin (2006) show that there is a causal sequence or chain that begins with a safety climate, which in turn affects the motivation to be safe, and finally results in changed behavior. This may take months or even years, but the process clearly begins with a change in safety climate. Additionally, there must be a commitment at every level of the organization. Examples of this cross-level commitment would include the following:

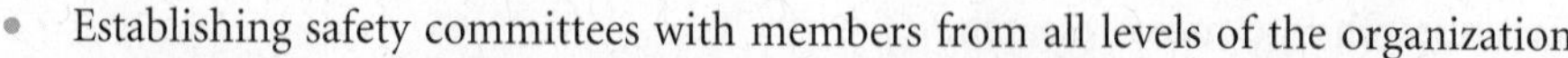

- Establishing safety committees with members from all levels of the organization
- Establishing a budget for safety that does not disappear during periods of economic crisis
- Including safety-related behaviors in the evaluation of employee performance at all levels of the organization

- Establishing high-quality leader–subordinate relationships that foster open discussion of safety-related issues
- Developing a shared attitude toward self-regulation of safety-related behavior at all levels of the organization
- Endorsing the importance of safety training for on-the-job safe behavior (Smith-Crowe, Burke, & Landis, 2003)

Organizational safety is not the responsibility of any single group (e.g., workers *or* supervisors *or* managers *or* executives). The safety climate must pervade all levels of the organization, and all levels of the organization must be involved in a constant dialogue about those issues if the commitment to safety is to be effective (Zacharatos, Barling, & Iverson, 2005). Wallace, Popp, and Mondore (2006) take a larger perspective and demonstrate that this specific safety climate is actually enabled by two broader climates: a positive management–employee relations climate and a positive organizational support climate. In a recent meta-analysis, Beus, Payne, Berman, and Arthur (2010) demonstrated the importance of a safety climate in reducing injuries.

It is tempting to think of a culture as universal within an organization—either a safety culture exists or it doesn't. But that is not necessarily the case. The group leader seems to be central to the process by which a culture is adopted by individual work groups. For example, Clarke (1999) found that even though representatives at various levels of the British Rail Corporation (e.g., drivers, supervisors, and executives) shared a perception that safety was important, they varied in terms of how important they thought that perception was to *other* levels. Drivers did not believe that supervisors or executives understood the influence of working conditions on safety. And supervisors did not believe that executives were aware of the importance of working conditions. Thus, despite the commitment of all parties to safety in the workplace, they tended to doubt each other's level of understanding of the most important factors in creating a safe workplace. If each level of an organization doubts the level of understanding or commitment of the other levels, it is less likely that a truly safe workplace can be established. The belief that others "may not get it" is likely to put a damper on individual safety efforts.

Zohar (2000) studied 53 different work groups in a metal-processing plant. He found that each work group developed its own shared perception of the safety climate of the organization and that substantial differences existed among the work groups on this perception. In essence, there were micro-cultures in the organization. Remember from our discussion in Chapter 1 that a culture is represented by a consensus or shared set of values or perceptions. Zohar found a culture operating at the work group level. More importantly, he found that the group culture predicted accident frequency within that group. He concluded, as did Clarke (1999), that it is insufficient simply to examine an organizational-level climate or culture in the hopes of increasing safety.

More recent work by Zohar and Luria (2005) with production workers confirms not only that a group-level safety climate is important in fostering safe behavior but also that climates vary at the group level, based on the extent to which organizational policies permit discretionary actions by supervisors. If the organization provides considerable leeway in the action of a supervisor (what Mintzberg would refer to as fully decentralized decision making), then a supervisor can have a substantial influence on a group's safety climate. If, on the other hand, the supervisor's behavior is tightly controlled by upper-level managers or by company policy, then there is less room for that supervisor to enhance a safety climate beyond what is suggested by the broader organizational culture. We must consider the interaction of all levels of the organization with respect to safety. It starts with the individual worker but also includes the work group, the leader, and the upper-level managers and executives. Safety does not rest on the shoulders of any one person or level of the organization; instead, it must have the support of all levels. It is truly a multilevel phenomenon. Consider the example in Box 14.1.

BOX 14.1 WHO IS RESPONSIBLE?

It was 2:00 p.m. on a clear summer day in a midwestern city. Traffic was at a standstill in the five westbound lanes of an interstate highway that had been plagued with similar construction-related stoppages for several months. There were no curves or dips in the roadway, just 1.2 miles of straight highway. A commercial trash truck approached the line of stopped cars at 55 miles per hour, braking and swerving a mere seven seconds before plowing into the last cars in the lanes. Each of five cars buckled and plowed into the car in front of it. Four of the cars caught fire but, miraculously, there were no fatalities.

The trash truck driver claimed that he had been distracted by looking in his side-view mirror to make sure no traffic was entering from the right. The explanation was implausible for several reasons. The highway was straight and entering traffic could be easily seen through the windshield; checking a mirror takes less than two seconds, not seven; the driver could have seen the brake lights of the stopped traffic for well over a mile before he arrived at the stoppage. Furthermore, this particular driver navigated that same route every day at the same time and had been doing so for at least three months.

An investigation revealed that the driver had been working 18 hours per day (from 4:00 a.m. until 10:00 p.m.), six days a week, for at least six months prior to the accident. In addition, the driver lived an hour away from the depot where he reported to work. This meant that he arrived home at about 11:00 p.m. and left home the next morning at 3:00 a.m. The simplest explanation was that the driver simply fell asleep on that summer afternoon as he approached the line of cars.

So who was responsible for the accident? The driver who agreed to work these outrageous hours in order to pull in the lucrative overtime? The trash company station manager who decided that overtime hours were cheaper than hiring and training additional employees and incurring the increased overhead represented by additional benefits for these workers? The divisional vice president who bragged about the station manager's ability to control costs? The depot dispatcher who ignored the Department of Transportation rule limiting commercial driving to 60 hours per week? The immediate supervisor of the driver, who knew full well the number of hours that the driver was behind the wheel? The answer, of course, is: all of these people. In fact, in this example, any one of these individuals could have prevented the accident, yet no one acted responsibly or safely. There was a safety failure at multiple levels of the organization, beginning with the driver and ending with the divisional vice president.

Socialization and the Concept of Person–Organization (P–O) and Person–Job (P–J) Fit

Organizational Socialization

Organizational fit is a key concept in organizational change. It is directed at improving the fit between an organization (or an idealized representation of that organization) and its employees by changing the nature of the organization. The premise of organizational change models is that people and organizations can be changed jointly through various interventions. Some of these interventions are aimed directly at changes in organizational structure or process, with little more expected of the individual beyond technical or procedural learning. Other interventions expect considerably more of the employee in terms of changed beliefs, values, and attitudes, as well as increased commitment and motivation.

But the "change" in the match between the individual and the organization can come much earlier, at the point at which a new employee enters the organization. The process by which a new employee becomes aware of the values and procedures of the organization is called **socialization**. It starts at the recruiting stage, when the company provides information to the candidate about its values. It continues as the individual is assessed, with the individual inferring characteristics of the organization based on the assessment procedures it uses. We addressed the issue of the perceived fairness of screening and selection in Chapter 11. An applicant might turn down an offer of employment if he or she perceives the organizational culture implied by the selection process to be an unfair one. Worse, an applicant may accept a job in spite of perceived disagreements with an organization's culture. When a candidate is hired, socialization is present in the interactions between the newcomer and his or her manager as well as in interactions with support departments such as HR or finance.

Socialization Process by which a new employee becomes aware of the values and procedures of an organization.

Recruitment as Socialization

The first stage at which socialization might occur is in recruitment and selection. Researchers have studied the role of attraction and fit in the socialization process in some detail. Among other things, they have found the following:

1. Applicants are attracted to organizations that have cultural characteristics compatible with the applicant's personality (Judge & Cable, 1997). From a cross-cultural perspective, individuals prefer organizations that are compatible with their own national culture (Parkes, Bochner, & Schneider, 2001).
2. Organizations invest considerable effort in attracting and selecting applicants who appear to have values compatible with the culture of the organization (Cable & Parsons, 2001).
3. Organizations often attempt to lure attractive applicants by presenting favorable but inaccurate information about their culture, information intended to signal to the applicant a good fit (Cable, Aiman-Smith, Mulvey, & Edwards, 2000).
4. Interviewers make initial estimates of applicants with respect to the person–organization fit and make recommendations for hiring or further assessment based on those initial estimates (Cable & Judge, 1997).
5. Applicants are more interested in the fit between their own values and the culture of the recruiting organization than they are in the fit between their own demographic characteristics (e.g., age, gender, race) and the characteristics of the representatives of the organization (Cable & Judge, 1996).
6. The positive reputation of a firm (e.g., "top 100" great places to work) increases the attractiveness of the firm and, in turn, both the number and the quality of applicants (Collins & Han, 2004; Turban & Cable, 2003). A firm's positive status also translates into higher-level performance, as one would expect if the quality of the applicant pool, and thus the quality of hires, is improved by the public reputation (Fulmer, Gerhart, & Scott, 2003).
7. Applicants high on conscientiousness prefer to work for larger firms; applicants high on openness to experience prefer to work for multinational companies (Lievens, Decaesteker, Coetsier, & Geirnaert, 2001).

Findings like these are compelling and important. They suggest that long before an individual is involved in an organizational change program or organizational development intervention, steps should be taken to assure a cultural–attitudinal match between that person and the organization.

Orientation as Socialization

Although the recruitment function of an organization can be considered as the start of the socialization process, it is hardly the conclusion. When an individual joins the organization, additional formal and informal steps are taken to further the socialization and fit between the individual and the organization. Socialization can be thought of as institutional and organizational learning on the part of the new employee (Cooper-Thomas & Anderson, 2002). Interestingly, van der Vegt (2002) finds that the greater the attitudinal dissimilarity between the new hire and the assigned work group, the longer this learning or socialization will take. Some formal steps include employee orientation through employee manuals; meetings with HR representatives to discuss benefits and conditions of employment; and meetings with line supervisors and managers to discuss duties, responsibilities, and expectations. Kim, Cable, and Kim (2005) present data that suggest that strong bonds with supervisors can offset the need for more formal institutional socialization processes. Van Mannen and Schein (1979) defined organizational socialization as "the process by which an individual acquires the social knowledge and skills necessary to assume an organizational role" (p. 211). Recall our discussion in Chapter 3 about tacit knowledge. From that perspective, the socialization process is intended to develop that tacit knowledge base, covering both technical and nontechnical aspects of the new organization and position.

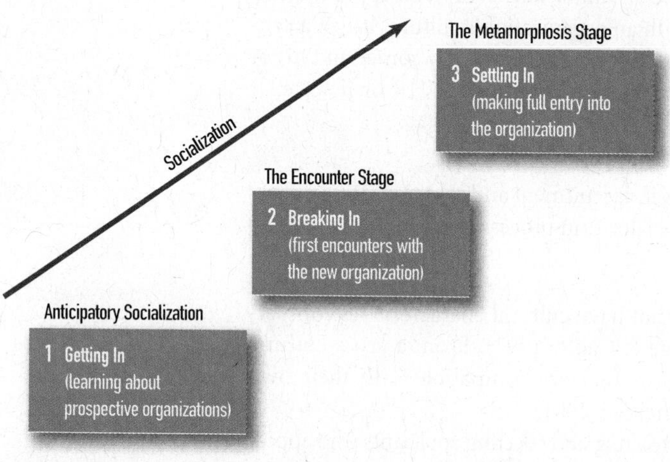

FIGURE 14.6 The Three Stages of Socialization
Organizational socialization generally follows the three stages summarized here: *anticipatory socialization*, which involves getting in; the *encounter stage*, which involves breaking in; and the *metamorphosis stage*, which involves settling in.

SOURCE: Greenberg, J. (2002). *Managing behavior in organizations* (3rd ed.). Fig. 7.1, p. 172. © 2002. Reproduced by permission of Pearson Education, Inc., Upper Saddle River, NJ.

Greenberg (2002) suggested that there are three stages of socialization. The first stage is the recruitment stage that we discussed earlier and Greenberg labeled "anticipatory socialization." But there are at least two subsequent stages: the encounter stage and the metamorphosis stage. These stages are presented graphically in Figure 14.6.

Realistic job preview (RJP) Technique for providing practical information about a job to prospective employees; includes information about the task and context of the work.

A popular technique for providing practical information about a prospective job is called a **realistic job preview (RJP)**, which can include task information as well as information about the context of the work (Phillips, 1998). For the position of bank teller, an RJP would include things like the nature of the training program, the importance of accuracy, the time pressure of the work, the nature of customers (including rude ones), pay and promotion rates, and information on how to move into management. Realistic job previews provide excellent opportunities for anticipatory socialization. Such previews lessen the possibility that the organization has been inaccurately described by a recruiter or inaccurately perceived by an applicant. In the encounter stage, new employees learn work procedures as well as the network of social relations in which the position is embedded. This means that the employee needs to know both the job and the people who populate the work group. Finally, in the metamorphosis stage, the individual is accepted as a fully functioning work group member. Often this metamorphosis is formal, as in the graduation from a training program or the successful completion of a probationary period. Equally often, however, the metamorphosis is more subtle, as is the case when someone is invited to have a drink after work or to join a car pool.

One effective method for guiding the new employee through the socialization process is mentoring. Greenberg (2002) has suggested that like the broader concept of socialization, mentoring also proceeds in stages (see Figure 14.7). Note that mentoring implies a face-to-face social exchange relationship: Even the profiles in Figure 14.7 suggest real people interacting. As you might expect, there is effective and ineffective mentoring. Some tips for effective mentoring are shown in Table 14.3. The "social" part of *social*ization seems to be important. Wesson and Gogus (2005) found that using a computer-based orientation for initial socialization was less effective than interpersonal orientation. The socialization process requires

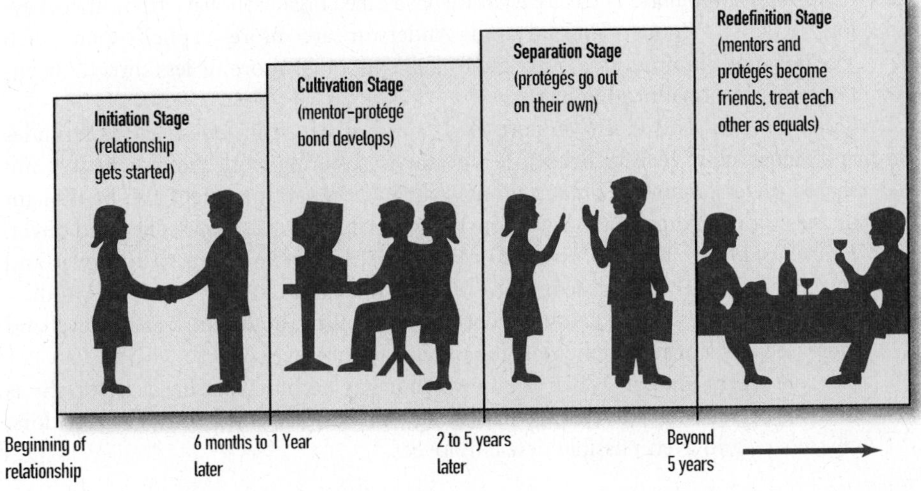

FIGURE 14.7 Mentoring: A Four-Stage Process Relationships between mentors and their protégés tend to develop following the four stages summarized here.

SOURCE: Greenberg, J. (2002). *Managing behavior in organizations* (3rd ed.). Fig. 7.2, p. 176. © 2002. Reproduced by permission of Pearson Education, Inc., Upper Saddle River, NJ.

TABLE 14.3 **Ten Tips for Successful Mentoring**

The long-term success of mentoring can be enhanced by adhering to the suggestions identified here. Both mentors and protégés should familiarize themselves with these guidelines before entering into a relationship.

Mentors should . . .

1. Be responsible to protégés, not for them.
2. Make the mentoring relationship fun and enjoyable.
3. Recognize that their involvement with their protégé extends beyond the workday.
4. Listen carefully to their protégés.
5. Openly acknowledge their failures as well as their successes.
6. Protect their protégés and expect their protégés to protect them.
7. Give their protégés not only directions but also options.
8. Recognize and encourage their protégés' small successes and accomplishments.
9. Encourage independent thinking among their protégés.
10. Focus not only on job skills but also on ethical values.

SOURCE: Greenberg, J. (2002). *Managing behavior in organizations* (3rd ed.). Table 7.2, p. 178. © 2002. Reproduced by permission of Pearson Education, Inc., Upper Saddle River, NJ.

effort, but effective socialization more than pays for itself in employee and work group well-being and stability as well as in organizational productivity, satisfaction, and commitment (Bauer, Bodner, Erdogan, Truxillo, & Tucker, 2007).

Positive Consequences of Socialization

Cooper-Thomas and Anderson (2006) suggest that one must be explicit in identifying anticipated outcomes of newcomer socialization. There is general agreement that successful socialization might result in happier employees, with a greater likelihood of staying in the organization and a greater sense of identification with that organization. But Cooper-Thomas and Anderson identify several discrete indicators or categories to use as indicators of socialization success. Among them are the following:

1. *Role performance.* These are what we have called technical task performance in earlier chapters.

2. *Extra-role performance.* These are what we have called organizational citizenship behaviors (OCBs). Cooper-Thomas and Anderson are more explicit than OCB researchers in limiting this outcome to behaviors that more or less directly facilitate organizational productivity.
3. *Social cohesion.* This is also, in part, OCB, but broader. It includes sharing attitudes and values, coupled with behavior, as a way of fostering work group cohesion and shared understanding of organizational values. Although this might also be thought of as supporting organizational productivity, the impact is less immediate and direct.
4. *Internal stability.* This involves minimizing the disruptive effects of turnover and absenteeism. There are clear implications for this factor in organizational productivity. These would include unmet work responsibilities at the work group level and increased costs of replacement at the organizational level.
5. *External representation.* When the newcomer has become socialized, he or she is likely to present a positive image in dealing with external contacts such as vendors, customers, and even possible new employees.

These organizational outcomes are certainly not novel. We have seen these valued outcomes in many of the earlier chapters when we have dealt with the anticipated positive outcomes associated with selection, or motivation, or leadership. What is unique about the approach of Cooper-Thomas and Anderson is this: They propose that every one of these newcomer behaviors is the direct result of modeling the behavior of peers and supervisors. They are not proposing that this modeling be used *instead of* selection, training, motivation, or leadership but rather that organizational socialization can either enhance or mute the positive effect of these other HR practices.

Imagine joining a work group and watching your new peers hide from the supervisor, refuse to volunteer to help one another, continually direct racist and sexist comments at fellow work group members, look for opportunities to be late or absent, falsify time records, ridicule safety measures, and complain loud and long to anyone outside the organization. If you value the job and want to stay with the organization, the chances are good that you will adopt some, and possibly all, of the behaviors you have seen modeled. The chances are good that if you don't "go along to get along," you will never be permitted to become an "insider" by these peers and supervisors. This would be a grim version of socialization. The bright version introduces you to technically competent peers and supervisors who share their technical knowledge with you, who can be seen lending a hand to one another and you, who embrace and take pride in their group's diversity, who apologize to peers and supervisors on the unusual occasion when they are late or absent, and who internally and externally embrace both the organizational mission statements and the work group responsibility for these organizational objectives as a way of possibly recruiting new work group members. Regardless of whether you look at the grim side or the bright side of the socialization process, it is clear that the process itself—the first weeks or months of employment—can have a substantial effect on both individual and organizational success. Indeed, the effects of the socialization process may be even more important than KSAOs and individually designed motivational programs. This should remind you of our very early discussion of multilevel analysis in Chapter 2. If you were to examine only KSAOs in predicting eventual success, you would miss the importance of the socialization process. If you were to look only at the socialization process, you would miss the importance of individual worker attributes such as cognitive ability or personality. You need to consider multiple levels of influence.

Socialization and National Culture

These five possible outcomes of socialization also strongly suggest that national culture may have an influence on what is modeled and how. It is not hard to imagine that collectivist cultures may emphasize extra-role behaviors and social cohesion as indicators of socialization success, while individualist cultures might emphasize task and technical performance. Bauer, Morrison, and Callister (1998) also suggested that collectivist cultures would be more likely to socialize newcomers as a group rather than as individuals and that newcomers from cultures high in uncertainty avoidance would be more active in seeking socialization information than those from cultures low in uncertainty avoidance. It is also likely that in cultures marked by high power distance, supervisory role modeling would be more important than peer modeling. In cultures marked by low power distance, peer and supervisory modeling might be equally important. Bauer and colleagues (2007) found that successful newcomer socialization reduced uncertainty for these new employees. This suggests that socialization may be more important in cultures high in uncertainty avoidance than those low in uncertainty avoidance. As we mentioned in Chapter 1, Greece is one of the countries highest in uncertainty avoidance; therefore, we would expect successful socialization to be highly valued in Greece. Finally, in cultures with a long-term orientation, internal stability and external representation might appear to be a more important outcome than simply technical or extra-role performance. As you can see, the identification of possible socialization outcomes by Cooper-Thomas and Anderson is a step forward in understanding the dynamics of the eventual fit between a person and an organization, particularly in the cross-cultural context.

As with many other topics covered in this text, socialization research is heavily dominated by American and western European researchers (Bauer & Taylor, 2001). Nevertheless, as both Bauer and her colleagues suggest, it is likely that cultural influences weigh heavily on the socialization process. Schneider (2001) suggested that there may be value in examining the fit between the national culture of an individual and the culture that would describe the organization. Recall the earlier example of the Moroccan and Mexican manufacturing facilities and the efforts to reconcile national and organizational culture (d'Iribarne, 2002). The concept of person–organization fit has been shown to have relevance in China as well (Turban, Lau, Ngo, Chow, & Si, 2001).

These issues are particularly important for expatriate employees who may have become accustomed to one type of socialization process in their home culture and encounter a very different one in the host country. In such circumstances, the expatriate is particularly vulnerable to misinterpretations of the socialization process. For example, an expatriate from a culture characterized by low power distance might interpret the aloofness of a new manager as an indication of disapproval or dislike rather than a simple expression of the national culture. Such a situation places increased emphasis on the need for both the host-country manager and the expatriate employee to understand cultural diversity. For the expatriate experience, the roots of success or failure are closely entwined with the socialization process (Bauer & Taylor, 2001). Regardless of whether the socialization process involves a newcomer to a domestic position or an expatriate, the goal of socialization is to improve the fit between the individual and the organization, the job, or both. We will now examine the notion of fit in greater detail.

Models of Socialization and Person–Organization Fit

I-O psychology has a long history of supporting the notion that **person–job (P–J) fit**—the fit between individuals and the jobs they fill—is important for both the individual and the organization. Vocational counseling was built on that premise, suggesting first that the fit between the intellectual demands of the job and the intelligence of the person would affect the physical and psychological well-being of the person as well as his or her productivity (Viteles, 1932). This was later broadened to include the match of the person's interests and values with the occupation that he or she chose (Holland, 1985; Super, 1973). It was widely accepted that unless there was a fit between the person and the job, as well as the person

Person–job (P–J) fit Extent to which the skills, abilities, and interests of an individual are compatible with the demands of the job.

and the occupation, the result would be an unhappy worker and an unhappy organization. These notions were formalized in the model of work adjustment (Dawis & Lofquist, 1984). A good fit requires a match between not only the abilities of the person and demands of the job (satisfactoriness) but also the rewards desired by the individual and the rewards offered by the organization (satisfaction).

Person–organization (P–O) fit Extent to which the values of an employee are consistent with the values held by most others in the organization.

In the past several decades, the notion of fit has evolved even further to include **person–organization (P–O) fit**, the fit between the person and the organization. In Chapter 10 we discussed how P–O fit and P–J fit are related to the experience of stress, job dissatisfaction, commitment, and turnover. Some research suggests that P–O fit may be at least as important, if not more so, than the fit between the individual and the specific job (P–J fit), particularly for outcomes such as organizational commitment and intentions to leave the organization (Kristof-Brown, Zimmerman, & Johnson, 2005). In a meta-analytic study, Arthur, Bell, Villado, and Doverspike (2006) found that the correlation between P–O fit and performance was approximately .15 (quite modest) compared to the correlation between P–O fit and job satisfaction, which was .31.

P–O fit may have several different meanings. Fit might mean the match between the personality of the applicant and the personality of the organization, between the values of the applicant and the values of the organization, or, more concretely, between what the person needs from an organization and what the specific organization can deliver (Cable & Edwards, 2004). From data they collected in both the United States and Turkey, Erdogan and Bauer (2005) found that a proactive personality (i.e., someone who initiates change rather than simply reacts to a changing environment) appeared to benefit more from a good P–O fit than one that was not proactive. If the P–O fit was good, then a proactive employee would be more satisfied (i.e., would demonstrate higher job and career satisfaction) than one who was not. Erdogan and Bauer speculated that this was because people who adopt organizational values (i.e., a good P–O fit) are more likely to engage in proactive behaviors that are consistent with those values.

In the next section, we give an example of the fit defined as the congruence between the personality of the new hire and the personality of the founder or senior executive of the firm. The work of Cooper-Thomas and Anderson (2006) described above deals with socialization as a very dynamic process, something that happens (or doesn't happen!) to a newcomer in an organization—a form of organizational learning. Thus, fit is something that is to be achieved *after* recruiting and selection. But achieving an eventual fit can be made easier or more difficult by the match or mismatch between organizations and individuals on more stable characteristics. We will consider some of those characteristics below, as well as what happens when the fit is not a good one.

Fit can also be based on similarity or complementarity (Piasentin & Chapman, 2007). Perceived fit based on *similarity* assumes that an individual and an organization share the same values. Perceived fit based on *complementarity* assumes that an individual perceives that his or her departure from a strict match with the values of the organization actually complements rather than cancels out organizational characteristics. As an example, a new IT hire for a start-up venture may be very detail-oriented in his approach, while the organizational culture emphasizes a broader approach. Nevertheless, he will see his appreciation for detail as complementing the tendency toward the broad approaches of others in the organization. He will believe that, unlike marketing, or sales, or production, IT must be detailed in order to support the broader organizational effort. His fit would be based on complementarity rather than similarity.

Schneider's Attraction–Selection–Attrition Model: The Dark Side of Socialization

Schneider (1987) proposed that organizations and individuals go through a process of jointly assessing probable P–O fit based primarily on personality characteristics. His view of organizations was that "people make the place," rather than the organization (i.e., place) molding or shaping the people. He called his model the **attraction–selection–attrition (ASA) model**; simply put, organizations attempt to attract particular types of people. These types have personalities most like those of the founder or highest leaders of the organization. The national columnist and commentator David Brooks has noted a similar phenomenon with respect to where people live and how they arrange their non-work lives (Brooks, 2003). He observed that we live, go to school, and play with people "just like us." In the work version, the attraction phase is accomplished first through recruiting efforts. After a promising candidate has been attracted and assumes the status of an applicant, the selection phase of the model begins. Through various assessment and selection mechanisms (e.g., testing, interviews, recommendations), offers are made to those candidates who still look promising.

Attraction–selection–attrition (ASA) model Model that proposes that organizations and individuals undergo a process of jointly assessing probable fit based primarily on personality characteristics. Through a process of attraction, selection, and attrition, the goal is to make the workforce homogeneous with respect to personality characteristics.

But mistakes can be made, and individuals who have personalities unlike those of the founder or senior executives may still be hired. That is when the attrition phase kicks in. As the poor fit becomes obvious, the new employee, the organization, or both engage in actions that result in the individual leaving. Some of these actions are direct: The employee simply resigns to take another job or the organization terminates the individual. Others are indirect: The employee may be marginalized and given trivial tasks, or left out of important meetings, or excluded from key teams until he or she gets the message and leaves. Or the individual may be given increasingly difficult and conflicting tasks until his or her performance seems below average.

Recall the discussion in Chapter 12 of leader–member exchange (LMX) theory, which posits that leaders inadvertently, or through some unintentional process of which they are unaware, favor one group of employees (the in-group) over another group (the out-group). The attrition phase of Schneider's theory suggests there may be nothing inadvertent or unconscious about the creation of an out-group, in part because the manager of the new hire has been attracted and selected to fit the personality of his or her own manager. Thus, it is a simple matter for this manager to recognize a poor fit between a new employee and the organization's leadership and to take actions to eliminate the individual from the organization. One of these actions is treating the new employee as an out-group member. These are the attraction–selection errors addressed in the attrition phase. The flowchart in Figure 14.8 presents an idealized version of the ASA model. As you can see, the attraction, selection, and attrition process, by virtue of actions taken by the employer and by the applicant or employee, works to make the final workforce homogeneous with respect to personality characteristics. Schneider, Smith, Taylor, and Fleenor (1998) presented preliminary data that support this prediction of homogeneity.

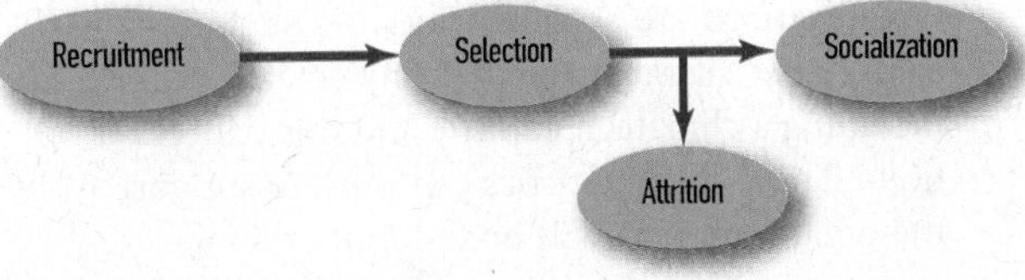

FIGURE 14.8 **Simplified Version of the ASA Model**

SOURCE: Eugene Larson, Advanced Technology Laboratories—Philips Electronics, Bothell, WA. Used by permission.

Schneider's model is intuitively appealing and has attracted a good deal of attention and research (Anderson & Ostroff, 1997). A book by Smith (2007) reviews the current research base for the model. Some evidence suggests that there may be a honeymoon effect in the attraction and selection stages (both the employer and the applicant downplaying differences) but that the differences do appear after employment, making the attrition stage more powerful. Schneider, Goldstein, and Smith (1995) reviewed direct and indirect support for the model. More recently, Giberson, Resick, and Dickson (2005) found clear evidence of a match between CEO personality and employee personality in 32 separate organizations.

There are still many conditions and variables to work out before the model is complete, but it has clear implications even in its incomplete state. The most dramatic of these implications is that attempts to change the culture of an organization are more likely to be accomplished by replacing people rather than by changing the people in the organization. In many turnaround scenarios, a new CEO is brought in with a new vision. The CEO brings many upper-level managers from his or her old company. They introduce the new culture, which is actually the old culture they brought with them from their previous organization. In response, some people leave the organization, whereas others stay and adapt to the new culture. In some settings, the new CEO is explicit about introducing a new culture. For example, Los Angeles chose a new police chief to address a decade of scandal and ineffectiveness. The new chief, William Bratton, announced:

> This is an underperforming department. They know it. If you aren't prepared to embrace it [an agreement between the U.S. Department of Justice and the LAPD], put your retirement papers in, because you won't be part of my command staff driving change in this department. The department needs to clearly understand there's a new sheriff in town. (Cited in Associated Press, 2000)

It might be argued that if Schneider's model correctly describes how organizations change, then the organization should take explicit steps to match the personalities of new hires to the personality of the leader or founder. While this might be effective in the short term, it could be less effective in the long run because the organization would have selected out any diversity in ways of thinking, values, attitudes, and maybe even abilities and skills. What is required is a balanced approach, with diversity in personalities among senior leaders allowing for diversity among followers. In other words, a perfect match between the values and personality of employees and senior leaders may lead to a more cohesive workplace but a less vibrant one. Schneider has not suggested *how* an organization should be staffed. Instead, he has described a process that commonly influences staffing. Schneider's model is exciting and presents an innovation over the traditional way of looking at the concept of organizational change and development as well as socialization.

MODULE 14.2 SUMMARY

- Organizations are social entities. As such, they exhibit the characteristics of any social entity, including a climate, a culture, and role expectations. These characteristics can work to support the organization's goals or to hinder them.
- The emerging model of climate is a structural concept that can be applied to any organization (or division, department, or even work group). Recently, I-O psychologists have suggested that multiple climates, defined by the goals of various work groups, can exist within any organization.
- Culture and climate are two different yet overlapping concepts. Climate is about the context in which action occurs, and culture is about the meaning that is intended by and inferred from those actions.
- The process by which a new employee becomes aware of the values and procedures of the organization is called socialization. It starts at the recruiting stage, when the company informs the candidate about its values. It continues as the individual is evaluated, with the individual inferring characteristics of the organization based on the assessment procedures it uses.
- I-O psychology has long supported the idea that person–job fit is important for both the individual and the organization. In the past several decades, the notion of fit has evolved even further to include the fit between the person and the organization.
- Schneider proposed that organizations and individuals go through a process of jointly assessing fit by means of a model he called attraction–selection–attrition. His view of organizations is that "people make the place" rather than the organization molding or shaping the people.

KEY TERMS

climate
autocratic climate
democratic climate
culture
socialization
realistic job preview (RJP)
person–job (P–J) fit
person–organization (P–O) fit
attraction–selection–attrition (ASA) model

MODULE 14.3

Organizational Development and Change

Organizational development (commonly referred to simply as OD) and organizational change are closely related topics. Organizational change is a process, a goal, or both. OD is a toolbox of various methods for affecting that change. There is a great deal more theory and substance to the concept of organizational change than to the techniques of OD. Indeed, OD might be thought of more as a consulting venue for organizational psychologists than a substantive area. Many texts (e.g., Anderson, 2009) describe OD techniques in detail, so we will discuss the area of organizational change in some detail in this module.

Organizational Change

As recently as 25 years ago, organizational change might have been thought of as a choice. Should we change the structure of the company? Should we introduce a new technology? Should we reconfigure our divisions? The luxury of having a choice about whether to change is now a distant memory. Think of the effect of downsizing. This almost always involves asking fewer employees to do more things. It also almost always involves eliminating middle-level managers, increasing the span of control of those managers left, and increasing the autonomy of the subordinates who remain. This is a massive change in work organization. And virtually every modern organization has downsized or will do so in the near future. Similar massive change can be seen with the increase in mergers, acquisitions, and alliances. Then add the ongoing globalization and technology evolution, and you see a world that is bombarded by change. As we commented in Chapter 11 when considering diversity, change is no longer a choice—it is a reality. And as with our observations regarding diversity, those organizations that can embrace change and thrive on it will survive and prosper, while those that cannot will disappear.

Unfreezing First stage in the process of changing an organization in which individuals become aware of their values and beliefs.

Changing Second stage in the process of changing an organization in which individuals adopt new values, beliefs, and attitudes.

Refreezing Third stage in the process of changing an organization in which the new attitudes and values of individuals are stabilized.

Organizational change theory has used the same anchor for over 60 years. Kurt Lewin (1951) proposed the unfreeze–change–refreeze model, involving three stages in the process of changing an organization:

1. **Unfreezing**, in which individuals become aware of values and beliefs they hold
2. **Changing**, in which individuals adopt new values, beliefs, and attitudes
3. **Refreezing**, which is the stabilization of the new attitudes and values

Various OD techniques are directed at facilitating one or more of those stages. Lewin believed that one could not really understand an organization until one tried to change it (Schein, 1996). In the early decades of the process of organizational change, this belief often led organizations to initiate a change program for the purpose of understanding the nature of their organization. Today, most organizational change initiatives are driven by a problem of some kind rather than by a need for organizational self-examination—for example, a merger or acquisition is not going well, there is a loss of market share or consumer confidence, or a new competitor threatens. As a result, most people now think of organizational change as event-driven, prompted by an external circumstance that requires a revolution or transformation in culture, process, or vision.

Weick and Quinn (1999) acknowledged that some events require immediate attention (and abrupt change), but they are pessimistic about the success of attempts at such episodic change. Instead, they have suggested that the most successful program of change is likely to be one of continuous rather than episodic change. They make a compelling argument, and we will base our discussion of the concept of change on their thoughts.

Episodic Change

Episodic change can be characterized as infrequent, discontinuous, and intentional. We often hear that an organization has embarked on a plan to "reinvent" itself. This would be an intentional plan to replace what it has with something new. Like a military campaign, the change would be launched with fanfare, have a planned end time, and involve clearly articulated pathways to change, with senior leaders disseminating information about the process and desired end state.

Episodic change Organizational change characterized as infrequent, discontinuous, and intentional; often launched with fanfare, with senior leaders clearly articulating pathways to change and disseminating information about the process and desired end state.

Weick and Quinn (1999) described the type of organization that most commonly embraces episodic change as having the following characteristics:

- Tight interconnections between subunits
- Efficiency as a core value
- A concern with adapting to current events in the environment
- Strong organizational cultures and subcultures
- A greater involvement in imitation than innovation as a motivation for change

Episodic change is embraced because it is focused, time-urgent, and minimizes feelings of uncertainty. Organizations that choose the episodic model aspire to a state of equilibrium. When it is reached, they tighten connections between departments even further, establish procedures that will ensure stability, and ignore environmental signals that suggest further change and adaptation. The result is decreased effectiveness, increasing pressures for change, and entry into the next "revolutionary" period.

Beginning in the 1980s, many organizations found themselves struggling to remain profitable in a changing economy. As a result, they tried to increase their quality and quantity of production, diversify their product line, and introduce innovations into their production process—with fewer people. A typical organization announced a one-time layoff that would be expected to solve the problem. The layoff required a transformation (a revolution) of structure and process. Once the transformation was under way, the goal was to get the layoff "over with" and return to a state of equilibrium as quickly as possible. However, most organizations found that increased competition, reduced confidence of consumers and investors, and other challenges made a new revolution necessary in the next fiscal year. So they embarked on another episodic change.

Episodic change is usually slow because it is so large in scope. In addition, it is seldom completed before another revolution is required, which organizations tend to shy away from until things get "bad." Most employees who have been through an episodic change remember it vividly because it was very stressful and disruptive. Such changes tend to be centered on, and driven by, upper levels of the organization because they are strategic and have an end state as a goal. This means that the organization most likely to adopt episodic change is in a state of inertia, sometimes just catching its organizational breath from the last episodic change. For this type of change, Lewin's basic unfreeze–change–refreeze process makes some sense. Ironically, Miller (1993, 1994) suggested that inertia is the unintended consequence of success. Weick and Quinn (1999) summarized Miller's research:

> Successful organizations discard practices, people, and structures regarded as peripheral to success and grow more inattentive to signals that suggest the need for change, more insular and sluggish in adaptation, and more immoderate in their processes, tending toward extremes of risk taking or conservatism. These changes simplify the organization, sacrifice adaptability, and increase inertia. (p. 369)

In spite of the unattractiveness of this picture, many organizations continue to think of change in revolutionary/transformational/episodic ways. They think of "transforming" the old organization into a new one. But the old organization does not *become* the new organization; it is *replaced by* it (Ford & Ford, 1994). However, this replacement goal is seldom successful because it results in either/or thinking (Beer, Eisenstat, & Spector, 1990). As Weick and Quinn (1999) pointed out, the either/or logic maintains that the only way to circumvent "A" (the "bad" form of organization) is to replace it with the opposite, or "not-A." In fact, both A and not-A might be equally problematic. Weick and Quinn acknowledged that episodic change is likely to remain a popular choice among organizations as a model for change. But if episodic change is the model, some modifications of common OD techniques are needed (see Table 14.4).

Continuous Change

Continuous change
Ongoing, evolving, and cumulative organizational change characterized by small, continuous adjustments, created simultaneously across units, that add up to substantial change.

Unlike episodic change, **continuous change** describes a process that is "ongoing, evolving, and cumulative." It is much less likely to be intentional and more likely to be improvised. It is characterized as "small continuous adjustments, created simultaneously across units, [that] cumulate and create substantial change" (Weick & Quinn, 1999, p. 375).

Organizations most likely to be engaged in continuous change attach authority to tasks rather than to positions and shift that authority as tasks change. In such organizations, job descriptions are in a continuous state of flux, and the organization accepts change as a constant (Wheatley, 1992). Another characteristic of the continuous change environment is the short time gap between the identification of a needed change and the execution of that change (Moorman & Miner, 1998).

Because continuous change appears to result in smaller changes than the more revolutionary episodic change, it is tempting to conclude that continuous changes are less

TABLE 14.4 **Suggested Modifications of Common OD Techniques if Episodic Change Is the Model**

LESS EMPHASIS ON	*MORE EMPHASIS ON*
Closely held internal data generation	Data gathered from the environment and shared widely
Slow downward communication	Rapid data analysis to support rapid decision making
Individual unit learning	Learning about the whole organization
Direction from senior management	Shared direction including senior managers and other levels of the organization
Consultant as expert	Client as expert
Leaders who argue well	Leaders who speak differently

SOURCE: Rorty, R. (1989). *Contingency, irony, and solidarity.* New York: Cambridge University Press.

important or have less impact. But the cumulative effect of these changes produces results. As Weick and Quinn (1999) pointed out, successful revolutionary or episodic changes seldom acknowledge the earlier, smaller changes that made the revolution possible. Simply put, this means that lurking behind most successful episodic changes is a supporting cast of earlier and smaller continuous changes.

Lewin's (1951) unfreeze–change–refreeze model does not hold up well for the process of continuous change. Instead, the model needs to be freeze–rebalance–unfreeze, almost the opposite of the episodic sequence. Weick and Quinn (1999) employed the metaphor of Newtonian physics to contrast episodic and continuous change. Bodies in motion tend to remain in motion. Thus, the first step in the continuous change model is freezing in order to stop the motion—to stop changing and examine patterns of change to understand what is happening (Argyris, 1990). The **rebalance** phase reframes what has happened and produces a cognitive framework that gives change deeper meaning. In the unfreezing phase, the organization goes back into the continuous change mode, but now with a revised cognitive architecture with which to make sense of what is going on and thus provide enhanced guidance for additional change. For example, a software company might hold a weekend retreat to review all of the product and process changes that occurred in the past calendar year. As part of this review, it would conduct a "lessons learned" session that distinguishes between changes that added value to the organization and those that did not. As a result, it would formally acknowledge and incorporate certain changes and eliminate others. It would then go back to the workplace with an altered organizational architecture and dive back into the continuous change process.

Rebalance Stage in the freeze–rebalance–unfreeze continuous change process intended to reframe what has happened and produce a cognitive framework that gives change deeper meaning.

A question commonly asked is whether change is managed or led (Kotter, 1995). Using the episodic/continuous distinction, it appears that episodic change is most commonly managed, while continuous change is most commonly led. When we manage change, we tell people what to do. When we lead change, we show people what to do and how to be. Weick and Quinn (1999) concluded that most large bureaucracies are like icebergs; they have rigid structures that change slowly, if ever, on their own. They need to be unfrozen, changed, and refrozen. But embedded within those bureaucracies are pockets of innovation. The challenge for the organization stuck in episodic change is to uncover these pockets and use them as a model to spread a more continuous culture through the organization. One way to do this would simply be to look for the best examples of self-initiated change among the organization's various work groups and departments—groups that are successful at "thinking outside the box"—and put them in the spotlight.

Weick and Quinn (1999) suggested that effective change is not an on-again/off-again phenomenon, nor is it very closely related to planning. They urged researchers and practitioners to concentrate on "changing" rather than "change." Although they did not address the requisite attributes of the people who would engage in this continuous change, it seems clear that certain personality characteristics such as flexibility, willingness to take risks, and a tolerance for ambiguity would be central to the process. Judge, Thoreson, Pucik, and Welbourne (1999), conducting research with six different organizations headquartered on four different continents, discovered that an individual with a personality characterized by a positive self-concept and a willingness to tolerate risk was much better able to cope with organizational change. Although they acknowledged that an organization made up entirely of individuals willing to tolerate risk might be in a dangerous position, the personality with a positive self-concept has also been associated with higher levels of performance.

In addition to the review article by Weick and Quinn (1999), other excellent reviews of organizational change have been written by Hartley (2002), Howard and colleagues (1994), Noer (1999), and Waclawski and Church (2002).

Resistance to Change

The barriers to organizational change are substantial and reside in both individuals and organizations. From the perspective of the individual, these barriers would include the following (Greenberg, 2002):

- *Economic fear.* Change as a threat to job security
- *Fear of the unknown.* The need to make changes in established patterns of organizational and task behavior
- *Fear of altered social relationships.* The possibility of changed co-workers

In addition, van Dam (2005) studied organizational changes in three Dutch hospitals and confirmed the clear link between perceived costs and benefits (e.g., job security, training investment in the current job) for changes and resistance to those changes. This is a person-as-scientist view of resistance to change.

Organizational barriers to change are equally formidable and would include the following:

- *Structural inertia.* Jobs are created with stability in mind; thus it takes considerable effort to change job descriptions, duties, reporting relationships, and so forth.
- *Work group inertia.* Strong norms exist for performing jobs in certain ways. These norms are often codified in written work procedures and labor–management agreements.
- *Threats to power balance.* If the centrality of certain work units changes, power over scarce resources is likely to shift as well.
- *Prior unsuccessful change efforts.* Organizations that have experienced past failures at change will encounter greater caution among organizational members with respect to new initiatives for change.

Many of these barriers can be included under the umbrella of "trust in management." The organization usually emphasizes the positive outcomes of the proposed change. The question is whether they can be believed. Oreg (2005) studied a major organizational change in an Israeli company that was merging two core units. Trust in management turned out to be a significant predictor of resistance to the change and consequent outcomes, such as satisfaction with and commitment to the organization. Recall our discussion of trust in Chapter 11. If the organization has lost the trust of its members, change will be more difficult and resistance, higher.

So, with all of these barriers, is it possible to overcome resistance to change? The answer is yes, but it requires some planning. Nadler (1987) suggested the following steps:

1. Gain the support of the most powerful individuals in the organization.
2. Educate the workforce with an eye toward reducing their individual fears.
3. Get employees meaningfully involved in the change initiative.
4. Provide feedback for change efforts and rewards for successful change at regular intervals.
5. After a successful change, shift the focus from episodic to continual change, thus reducing future barriers to change.

These steps suggest a positive environment for change. Martin, Jones, and Callan (2005) take this a step further by suggesting that in organizations with a generally positive organizational climate, resistance to change will be reduced. In a study of hospital and public-sector employees in Australia who were exposed to a major organizational change, the results confirmed this hypothesis. Employees who perceived the organizational climate to be positive described the change more positively; they reported higher job satisfaction, better psychological well-being, higher commitment, and fewer intentions to quit than their counterparts who perceived the organizational climate to be negative. Herold, Fedor, and Caldwell (2007) find that an employee's sense of self-efficacy also predicts how committed he or she will be to an organizational change. This makes perfect sense, as those with high self-efficacy believe that they can adapt to the change, whatever it may be. Given the barriers to change as well as the steps necessary to reduce those barriers, it is not surprising that most attempts at change fail. This is less a reason to avoid change than a blueprint for how to be one of the organizations successful at it.

Examples of Large-Scale Organizational Change Initiatives

Explicit and implicit theories of organization are the foundation for many attempts at organizational change and development. Although these attempts at change are often viewed as purposefully targeted and directed to only one aspect of the organization, they carry with them some assumptions about "preferred" organizational structure or process. As a result, these interventions may be packaged and presented as motivational interventions. But the underlying assumption is that a change in some aspect of the organization will result in enhanced employee motivation.

Below we will present examples of several different development and change initiatives that have been introduced in the past few decades. These initiatives are intended to replace one form of organization considered ineffective with a more effective one.

Total Quality Management

Total quality management (TQM) A unique way of organizing productive effort by emphasizing team-based behavior directed toward improving quality and meeting customer demands.

W. E. Deming (1986) challenged modern organizations to focus on the customer as an indicator of organizational effectiveness and introduced the concept of total quality management to meet that challenge. **Total quality management** (TQM) is a "cooperative form of doing business that relies on the talents and capabilities of both labor and management to continually improve quality and productivity using work teams" (Jablonski, 1991). Rather than concentrating on the volume of production, TQM focuses on quality and customer demands and expectations. Note the phrase "using work teams" in the definition above. The emphasis is on creating an environment that will "support innovation, creativity, and risk taking to meet customer demands [using] participative problem solving, involving managers, employees, and customers" (Noe, Hollenbeck, Gerhart, & Wright, 2000). The growing acceptance of the centrality of the "quality" concept is recognized by the Malcolm Baldrige National Quality Awards, created in 1987 during the Reagan administration, which are bestowed on organizations that have made substantial improvements in quality.

As was the case with the other organizational initiatives, the TQM approach proposes a unique way to organize productive effort by emphasizing team-based behavior directed toward improving quality. It should come as no surprise that TQM systems are more easily implemented in collectivist rather than individualistic cultures. Cooney and Sohal (2003) conducted a review of the effect of TQM on work design and redesign, with a particular emphasis on the probable consequences—positive and negative—for the workers in such a system. In theory, for example, the heavy emphasis on worker participation should enhance the satisfaction, motivation, and commitment of employees. In practice, however, the "decision" opportunities are often just elaborate opportunities for suggesting improvements, with no real opportunity for making decisions. As a result, employees can become disenchanted with the promise of participation.

Six Sigma Systems

In 1986 the electronics giant Motorola was having quality problems. The CEO at the time formed a project group whose mission was to reduce the defect rate to fewer than 3.4 defects per 1 million opportunities. The statistical symbol for a standard deviation (the statistic we reviewed in Chapter 2) is the Greek letter sigma (Σ). A defect rate of 3.4 per million is equal to more than 6 standard deviations from the number of units or products generated or transactions completed, thus the label Six Sigma. Companies that adopt **Six Sigma systems** train their employees and managers in methods of statistical analysis, project management, and design and problem solving (Barney, 2002). Managers who have mastered the various statistical and procedural aspects of Six Sigma management are known as black belts and are the tutors for less advanced managers who are known as green belts.

Six Sigma systems Approach to quality management that provides training for employees and managers in statistical analysis, project management, and problem-solving methods in order to reduce the defect rate of products.

Although Six Sigma systems were initially developed to monitor quantifiable defect rates, the philosophy has expanded to encompass the use of scientific and statistical methods to develop and test alternative approaches not only for production but also for service and process outcomes. Whatever the unit of effort is—a product, customer invoice, statement in a computer program, response to a customer complaint—the number of defects can be calculated and compared to the total number of units. In addition to demanding near-perfection from employees, Six Sigma requirements are often imposed on suppliers and subcontractors. The Six Sigma philosophy has clear implications for the way that workers and managers interact. Because the workers are closest to the problems and issues of quality, managers are asked to give more authority, power, and responsibility to those workers (Velocci, 1998). Most organizations that have adopted Six Sigma systems claim to see enhanced profitability because of the dual contributions of lower rejection/rework rates and lower production costs that result from "doing it right the first time." Like TQM methods, Six Sigma systems emphasize the value of making changes before defects or errors occur rather than depending on postproduction or process inspections to uncover defects. As is the case with the power transfer from manager to employee, Six Sigma systems also require a substantial shift in power from senior-level executives to lower-level managers. There has been no serious evaluation research on Six Sigma programs; most articles are written like testimonials. Nevertheless, these programs represent dramatic organizational interventions.

Lean Production Manufacturing

In the 1980s Japanese automakers made significant inroads in virtually every Western market. It appeared that the Japanese cars were of higher quality, were priced more competitively, and were more readily available than their American and European counterparts. As a result, Japanese methods of production came under close inspection and were widely imitated. In recent years the "Japanese" method has come to be called **lean production**. Key to this method is the reduction of waste in every form: overproduction, lengthy waiting times for materials, excessive transportation costs, unnecessary stock, and defective product that must be reworked or scrapped. Central to the reduction of this waste is a process known as **just-in-time (JIT) production**, which depends on the detailed tracking of materials and production so that the materials and human resources necessary for production arrive just in time (Ohno, 1998).

Lean production Method that focuses on reducing waste in every form, including overproduction, lengthy waiting times for materials, excessive transportation costs, unnecessary stock, and defective products.

Just-in-time (JIT) production System that depends on the detailed tracking of materials and production so that the materials and human resources necessary for production arrive just in time; central to the reduction of waste in lean production processes.

One of the interesting implications of the lean production system is that for JIT to be successful, both suppliers and customers are drawn into the organizational circle. Customers are expected to provide reliable scheduling information, and suppliers are expected to deliver high-quality materials in a reliable and timely fashion (Delbridge, 2003). In addition, the lean production system depends on a minimum workforce with little or no unexcused absenteeism. For example, the U.S. plants operated by the Honda Motor Company expect no less than 98 percent attendance from every employee (although sick days are counted as excused absences). From a psychological perspective, the lean organization depends on trust—trust that suppliers will provide timely high-quality material, trust that employees will be where they were supposed to be when they are supposed to be there, and trust that customers will communicate in a timely and accurate manner. In 2002, a West Coast dock strike by cargo handlers crippled a great segment of American industry for several weeks. Hardest hit were those companies that had adopted a JIT model and depended on West Coast deliveries. In this instance, that level of trust worked to the short-term disadvantage of companies and customers and demonstrated the Achilles heel of the JIT philosophy.

Spencer Grant/PhotoEdit

Lean production depends on continuous data analysis and behavior change.

Lean manufacturing also depends on the elimination of defects and waste in a manner similar to TQM. This is accomplished by urging (and sometimes requiring) production workers to be actively engaged in procedures to identify process improvements. Because the lean organization has a very narrow safety net, various disruptions (e.g., organized resistance by workers, an unreliable supplier, increased absenteeism or turnover) can place substantial stress on the system and its people. In addition, because priorities may change rapidly based on customer needs and market changes, many, if not all, workers are expected to be multiskilled so that they can switch activities and minimize wasted time (Delbridge, 2003). Without high levels of worker commitment and loyalty, lean organizations are likely to fail. Thurley (1982) suggested that for lean production methods to be successful, the following personnel mechanisms must provide support:

- Performance appraisal
- Motivation
- Self-appraisal and feedback
- Bonuses on the organizational and group/team level
- Job rotation
- Training and self-education
- Organizational redesign

That is a daunting list of supporting mechanisms, and it paints a very demanding picture for the worker. Some observers have criticized lean manufacturing for making "workers feel obliged to contribute to the performance of the organization and to identify with its competitive success" (Delbridge, 2003). Delbridge and Turnbull (1992) went so far as to propose that any success that lean manufacturing enjoys exists because "teamwork represents management by compliance, quality consciousness results in management through blame, and flexibility leads to management by stress" (Delbridge, 2003, p. 39). It is interesting to consider lean manufacturing in light of the concept of OCB that we described in Chapter 4 (Borman & Motowidlo, 1993). You will recall that OCB is distinguished from task performance and is characterized by behaviors such as helping co-workers, devoting extra effort to tasks, and volunteering to carry out tasks not formally assigned. The essence of OCB is that it is *voluntary*; the individual worker goes beyond what is expected. In many new organizational schemes such as TQM, Six Sigma, and lean production manufacturing, OCB is now part of the job description, transforming the voluntary into the expected.

From the perspective of stress, it is easy to see how the demands of these new schemes might easily overwhelm resources, particularly when the employee is at the mercy of suppliers, customers, and even fellow workers. Lean manufacturing, like the initiatives and philosophies described earlier, makes assumptions about the capacities and limitations of the humans who populate the organization. It assumes that, at best, this lean philosophy is compatible with how people construe work. At worst, it assumes that workers can tolerate a high degree of stress and pressure to perform. These assumptions may be overly optimistic. Although there have been few credible evaluations of the effect of lean manufacturing models on workers, a study by Parker (2003) is an exception. She studied workers in a vehicle assembly plant for three years and found that virtually all indicators pointed to a negative effect of the lean manufacturing model on workers, and it appeared to be particularly stressful for assembly-line workers.

In any case, however, lean manufacturing requires a human resource management (HRM) system distinct from one implied by TQM or any of the other initiatives. Organizational initiatives such as lean manufacturing often require a radical redesign of HRM systems in order to be successful.

Emerging Commonalities among Organizational Interventions

Most of the more recent organizational interventions such as TQM, Six Sigma programs, and lean production share some common elements:

1. *They are strategic.* They focus on the mission of the business and place great emphasis on client and customer satisfaction.

2. *They are team centered.* They concentrate on the efforts of individuals working in concert rather than single contributors.
3. *They are statistical.* They make use of sophisticated methods of data collection and analysis and feed those data back to members as a way of guiding behavior.
4. *They are participatory.* They engage members in the process of improving the quality of products.
5. *They are quality focused.* They concentrate on improving the quality of product and process as a way of increasing market share and decreasing costs.

As you can see, organizational interventions are more complex and far-reaching than individual motivational interventions. However, interventions at the organizational level do include many of the components we find at the individual level, including goal setting and feedback, job enrichment and redesign, and participation in decision making. Recall from Chapter 8 the system called ProMES, which was developed by Pritchard (1995). Due to its reliance on multiple processes like statistical analysis, participation in strategic decision making, and goal setting, ProMES appears to be a promising way to bridge the gap between individual and organizational interventions.

MODULE 14.3 SUMMARY

- Organizational development (OD) and organizational change are closely related topics. Organizational change is a process, a goal, or both. OD is a toolbox of various methods for affecting that change.
- The theory of organizational change is strongly influenced by Lewin's three-stage process that characterizes episodic change: unfreezing, changing, and refreezing. A more successful program of change is likely to be one of continuous change, a process that is ongoing and evolving.
- The barriers to organizational change are substantial and reside in both individuals and organizations. Nevertheless, careful advance planning can overcome resistance to change.
- Examples of organizational development and change initiatives introduced in the past few decades include total quality management (TQM), Six Sigma systems, and lean production. These initiatives are intended to replace an ineffective form of organization with a more effective one.

KEY TERMS

unfreezing
changing
refreezing
episodic change
continuous change
rebalance
total quality management (TQM)
Six Sigma systems
lean production
just-in-time (JIT) production

Glossary

360 degree feedback Process of collecting and providing a manager or executive with feedback from many sources, including supervisors, peers, subordinates, customers, and suppliers.

"80 percent" or "4/5ths rule" Guideline for assessing whether there is evidence of adverse impact; if it can be shown that a protected group received less than 80 percent of the desirable outcomes (e.g., job offers, promotions) received by a majority group, the plaintiffs can claim to have met the burden of demonstrating adverse impact.

Absenteeism Type of counterproductive behavior that involves failure of an employee to report for or remain at work as scheduled.

Achievement A facet of conscientiousness consisting of hard work, persistence, and the desire to do good work.

Achievement striving (AS) Subcomponent of the Type A behavior pattern that involves the tendency to be active and to work hard in achieving one's goals.

Action process Process that starts with a goal, proceeds to a consideration of events that may occur in the future, and then progresses to the development of several alternative plans, the selection of a plan, the execution and monitoring of the chosen plan, and the processing of information resulting from the execution of the plan. The last step, feedback, then influences goal development once again.

Action structure Structure that includes the notion that (1) observable action is the result of a number of prior events and plans, hierarchically arranged, and (2) the feedback and resulting regulation of actions occur at different levels.

Action theory (Rubicon theory) Theory that includes broad consideration of the role of intention in motivated behavior as well as the connection between intention and action.

Active practice Involves actively participating in a training or work task rather than passively observing someone else performing the task.

Activity inhibition Psychological term used to describe a person who is not impulsive.

Actual criterion Actual measure of job performance obtained.

Adaptive guidance An instructional approach that provides trainees with information that helps them interpret their past performance and also determine what they should be studying and practicing to improve their future performance.

Adaptive performance Performance component that includes flexibility and the ability to adapt to changing circumstances.

Adverse impact Type of discrimination that acknowledges the employer may not have intended to discriminate against a plaintiff, but an employer practice did have an adverse impact on the group to which the plaintiff belongs.

Adverse impact ratio Obtained by dividing the selection ratio of the protected group by the selection ratio of the majority group; if this ratio is lower than 80 percent, there is evidence of adverse impact.

Adverse (or disparate) treatment Type of discrimination in which the plaintiff attempts to show that the employer actually treated the plaintiff differently than majority applicants or employees; intentional discrimination.

Affect The conscious, subjective aspect of emotion.

Affect circumplex Figure in which opposite emotions appear directly across from each other in the circle.

Affective commitment An emotional attachment to an organization.

Affective outcome Type of learning outcome that includes attitudes or beliefs that predispose a person to behave in a certain way.

Affiliation need Need for approval or connections with others.

Affirmative action Program that acknowledges that particular demographic groups may be underrepresented in the work environment; provides specific mechanisms for reducing this underrepresentation.

Agreeableness Likable, easy to get along with, friendly.

Alarm reaction Stage of the general adaptation syndrome in which the body mobilizes resources to cope with added stress.

Altruism Helpful behaviors directed toward individuals or groups within the organization, such as offering to help a co-worker who is up against a deadline.

American Psychological Association (APA) The major professional organization for psychologists of all kinds in the United States.

Americans with Disabilities Act Federal legislation enacted in 1990 requiring employers to give applicants and employees with disabilities the same consideration as other applicants and employees, and to make certain adaptations in the work environment to accommodate disabilities.

Apprenticeship Formal program used to teach a skilled trade.

Assessment center Collection of procedures for evaluation that is administered to groups of individuals; assessments are typically performed by multiple assessors.

Assimilation model Model for addressing diversity that recruits, selects, trains, and motivates employees so that they share the same values and culture.

Attempted leadership A situation that occurs when a leader accepts the goal of changing a follower and can be observed attempting to do so.

Attitudes Relatively stable feelings or beliefs that are directed toward specific persons, groups, ideas, jobs, or other objects.

Attraction–selection–attrition (ASA) model Model that proposes that organizations and individuals undergo a process of jointly assessing probable fit based primarily on personality characteristics. Through a process of attraction, selection, and attrition, the goal is to make the workforce homogeneous with respect to personality characteristics.

Authentic leadership A style of leadership that emphasizes the genuineness and integrity of the leader, usually accompanied by a life story.

Autocratic climate Organizational climate described by Lewin as highly structured with little opportunity for individual responsibility or risk taking at the lowest levels.

Automaticity Occurs when tasks can be performed with limited attention; likely to develop when learners are given extra learning opportunities after they have demonstrated mastery of a task.

Autonomous work group Specific kind of production team that has control over a variety of functions, including planning shift operations, allocating work, determining work priorities, performing a variety of work tasks, and recommending new hires as work group members.

Autonomy Extent to which employees can control how and when they perform the tasks of their job.

Base rate Percentage of the current workforce that is performing successfully.

Behavioral approach Begun by researchers at Ohio State University, leadership theory that focused on the kinds of behavior engaged in by people in leadership roles and identified two major types: consideration and initiating structure.

Behavioral criteria Measures of how well the behaviors learned in training transfer to the job.

Behavioral modeling Learning approach that consists of observing actual job incumbents (or videos of job incumbents) who demonstrate positive modeling behaviors, rehearsing the behavior using a role-playing technique, receiving feedback on the rehearsal, and trying out the behavior on the job.

Behavioral observation scale (BOS) Asks the rater to consider how frequently an employee has been seen to act in a particular way.

Behaviorally anchored rating scales (BARS) Rating format that includes behavioral anchors describing what a worker has done, or might be expected to do, in a particular duty area.

Behaviorist approach Approach developed by B. F. Skinner that placed the emphasis for behavior and directed activity directly on the environment rather than on any internal needs or instincts.

Bias Technical and statistical term that deals exclusively with a situation where a given test results in errors of prediction for a subgroup.

Big 5 A taxonomy of five personality factors; the Five Factor Model (FFM).

Biodata Information collected on an application blank or in a standardized test that includes questions about previous jobs, education, specialized training, and personal history; also known as biographical data.

Biofeedback Stress management technique that teaches individuals to control certain body functions, such as heart rate, blood pressure, and even skin temperature, by responding to feedback from an electronic instrument.

Blended learning An instructional approach that uses distance learning in combination with face-to-face learning.

Branching programming Type of programmed instruction that provides a customized approach enabling each learner to practice material he or she had difficulty with when it was first presented.

Buffer or **moderator hypothesis** Hypothesis that social support moderates or reduces health problems by protecting individuals from the negative effects of work stressors.

Bullying Harassing, offending, socially excluding, or assigning humiliating tasks to a person of subordinate status repeatedly and over a long period of time.

Bureaucracy Structure proposed by sociologist Max Weber (1864–1920) to be the ideal form of organization; included a formal hierarchy, division of labor, and a clear set of operating procedures.

Burnout Extreme state of psychological strain resulting from a prolonged response to chronic job stressors that exceed an individual's resources to cope with them.

Central tendency error Error in which raters choose a middle point on the scale to describe performance, even though a more extreme point might better describe the employee.

Challenge-related stressors Work demands or circumstances that, although potentially stressful, have potential gains for individuals.

Changing Second stage in the process of changing an organization in which individuals adopt new values, beliefs, and attitudes.

Charisma A personal attribute of a leader that hypnotizes followers and compels them to identify with and attempt to emulate the leader.

Charismatic leader Followers are emotionally attached to this leader, never question the leader's beliefs or actions, and see themselves as integral to the accomplishment of the leader's goals.

Charismatic leadership theory Approach to leadership theory with many different versions of the notion that charisma is related to leadership; in one version, in a crisis situation, followers perceive charismatic characteristics in an individual and accept that person as a leader; in another version, certain leader behaviors (use of innovative strategies) contribute to a charismatic aura.

Checklist List of behaviors presented to a rater who places a check next to each of the items that best (or least) describe the ratee.

Circadian cycle The 24-hour physiological cycle in which humans tend to be active during hours of light and inactive during hours of darkness.

Class certification Judge's decision based on several criteria that determine whether individual plaintiffs can file together under a class action suit.

Classic organizational theory Theory that assumes there is one best configuration for an organization, regardless of its circumstances; places a premium on control of individual behavior by the organization.

Classroom lecture Training method in which the trainer communicates through spoken words and audiovisual materials what trainees are supposed to learn; also commonly used to efficiently present a large amount of information to a large number of trainees.

Climate A shared perception among employees regarding their work entity: a particular organization, division, department, or work group.

Clinical decision making Uses judgment to combine information and to make a decision about the relative value of different candidates or applicants.

Coaching A practical, goal-focused form of personal, one-on-one learning for busy employees that may be used to improve performance, enhance a career, or work through organizational issues or change initiatives.

Cognitive ability Capacity to reason, plan, and solve problems; mental ability.

Cognitive ability test A test that allows individuals to demonstrate what they know, perceive, remember, understand, or can work with mentally; includes problem identification, problem-solving tasks, perceptual skills, the development or evaluation of ideas, and remembering what one has learned through general experience or specific training.

Cognitive outcome Type of learning outcome that includes declarative knowledge, or knowledge of rules, facts, and principles.

Cognitive restructuring Type of stress intervention that focuses on changing perceptions and thought processes that lead to stress; reduces stress by changing the individual's perception of, or capacity to meet the demands of, the work environment.

Cognitive task analysis Consists of methods for decomposing job and task performance into discrete, measurable units, with special emphasis on eliciting mental processes and knowledge content.

Cognitive test battery Collection of tests that assess a variety of cognitive aptitudes or abilities; often called Multiple Aptitude Test Batteries.

Cohesion Degree to which team members desire to remain in the team and are committed to team goals.

Collectivist culture A culture that values the group more than the individual.

Commitment Psychological and emotional attachment an individual feels to a relationship, an organization, a goal, or an occupation.

Comparable worth Notion that people who are performing jobs of comparable worth to the organization should receive comparable pay.

Comparison other A co-worker or idealized other person to which the individual compares himself or herself in determining perceived equity.

Compensable factors Factors in a job evaluation system that are given points that are later linked to compensation for various jobs within the organization; factors usually include skills, responsibility, effort, and working conditions.

Compensatory system Model in which a good score on one test can compensate for a lower score on another test.

Competencies Sets of behaviors, usually learned by experience, that are instrumental in the accomplishment of desired organizational results or outcomes.

Competency modeling Process that identifies the characteristics desired across all individuals and jobs within an organization; these characteristics should predict behavior across a wide variety of tasks and settings, and provide the organization with a set of core characteristics that distinguish it from other organizations.

Comprehensive staffing model Model that gathers enough high-quality information about candidates to predict the likelihood of their success on the varied demands of the job.

Compressed workweek Schedule that permits an employee to work for longer than eight hours a day and fewer than five days a week.

Computer adaptive testing (CAT) Presents a test taker with a few items that cover the range of difficulty of the test, identifies a test taker's approximate level of ability, and then asks only questions to further refine the test taker's position within that ability level.

Computer-based training Includes text, graphics, and/or animation presented via computer for the express purpose of teaching job-relevant knowledge and skills.

Concurrent validity design Criterion-related validity design in which there is no time lag between gathering the test scores and the performance data.

Conscientiousness Quality of having positive intentions and carrying them out with care.

Consideration Type of behavior identified in the Ohio State studies; included behavior indicating mutual trust, respect, and a certain warmth and rapport between the supervisor and group.

Construct Psychological concept or characteristic that a predictor is intended to measure; examples are intelligence, personality, and leadership.

Construct validity Validity approach in which investigators gather evidence to support decisions or inferences about psychological constructs; often begins with investigators demonstrating that a test designed to measure a particular construct correlates with other tests in the predicted manner.

Constructive work dissatisfaction A type of dissatisfaction that energizes individuals and is beneficial for motivating them to join attempts at organizational change.

Content-related validation design Demonstrates that the content of the selection procedure represents an adequate sample of important work behaviors and activities and/or worker KSAOs defined by the job analysis.

Contingency approach Leadership theory proposed to take into account the role of the situation in the exercise of leadership.

Contingency theories of organization Theories proposing that the best way to structure an organization depends on the circumstances of the organization.

Contingent reward A reward that depends on or is contingent on a particular response.

Continuance commitment Perceived cost of leaving an organization.

Continuous change Ongoing, evolving, and cumulative organizational change characterized by small, continuous adjustments, created simultaneously across units, that add up to substantial change.

Continuous-process organization Organization that depends on a continuous process for output or product.

Continuous reward A reward that is presented every time a correct response occurs.

Control theory Theory based on the principle of a feedback loop that assumes that an individual compares a standard to actual outcome and adjusts behavior to bring the outcome into agreement with the standard.

Coordination loss Reduced group performance that occurs when team members expend their energies in different directions or fail to synchronize or coordinate their work.

Core self-evaluations Assessments that individuals make of their circumstances; elements of core evaluations include self-esteem, self-efficacy, locus of control, and the absence of neuroticism.

Coronary-prone personality Alternative name given to Type A behavior pattern (TABP) because of its links to coronary heart disease and heart attacks.

Correlation coefficient Statistic assessing the bivariate, linear association between two variables. Provides information about both the magnitude (numerical value) and the direction (+ or −) of the relationship between two variables.

Counterproductive work behavior (CWB) Voluntary behavior that violates significant organizational norms and threatens the well-being of the organization, its members, or both.

Criterion An outcome variable that describes important aspects or demands of the job; the variable that we predict when evaluating the validity of a predictor.

Criterion contamination Occurs when an actual criterion includes information unrelated to the behavior one is trying to measure.

Criterion deficiency Occurs when an actual criterion is missing information that is part of the behavior one is trying to measure.

Criterion-referenced cut score Established by considering the desired level of performance for a new hire and finding the test score that corresponds to the desired level of performance; sometimes called "domain-referenced" cut score.

Criterion-related validity Validity approach that is demonstrated by correlating a test score with a performance measure; improves researcher's confidence in the inference that people with higher test scores have higher performance.

Critical incident technique Approach in which subject matter experts are asked to identify critical aspects of behavior or performance in a particular job that led to success or failure.

Critical incidents Examples of behavior that appear "critical" in determining whether performance would be good, average, or poor in specific performance areas.

Critical thinking skills Require active involvement in applying the principles under discussion.

Cross-cultural training Designed to prepare individuals from one culture to interact more effectively with individuals from different cultures; the goal is to develop understanding of basic differences in values and communication styles.

Cross-training Training that involves rotating team members through different positions on the team so that they can acquire an understanding of the duties of their teammates and an overview of the team's task.

Cross-validation Process used with multiple regression techniques in which a regression equation developed on a first sample is tested on a second sample to determine if it still fits well; usually carried out with an incumbent sample, and the cross-validated results are used to weight the predictor scores of an applicant sample.

Cultural assimilator Written or computer-based tool for individual use which presents a collection of scenarios describing challenging, cross-cultural critical incidents.

Culture A system in which individuals share meanings and common ways of viewing events and objects.

Culture shock Condition typically experienced four to six months after expatriates arrive in a foreign country; symptoms include homesickness, irritability, hostility toward host nationals, and inability to work effectively.

Culture-general assimilator Used to sensitize people to cross-cultural differences they may encounter across a wide variety of cultures.

Culture-specific assimilator Assimilator developed for a particular culture.

Culture-specific characteristics Leader characteristics that are more acceptable in some countries than others.

Cut score Specified point in a distribution of scores below which candidates are rejected; also known as a "cutoff score."

Declarative knowledge (DK) Understanding what is required to perform a task; knowing information about a job or job task.

Deep acting Emotional labor that consists of managing one's feelings, including emotions required by the job.

Delegation of authority A concept that describes which lower-level employees report to employees above them in an organization.

Demand–control model A model suggesting that two factors are prominent in producing job stress: job demands and individual control; developed by Karasek.

Democratic climate Organizational climate described by Lewin as less structured, with greater opportunity for individual responsibility and risk taking.

Demographic diversity Differences in observable attributes or demographic characteristics such as age, gender, and ethnicity.

Deontic justice A form of organizational justice based on what is the correct moral course of action for a company or for an individual.

Dependability A facet of conscientiousness, consisting of being disciplined, well organized, respectful of laws and regulations, honest, trustworthy, and accepting of authority.

Depersonalization Burnout that occurs when individuals become hardened by their job and tend to treat clients or patients like objects.

Deposition Interview under oath taken by an opposing attorney in a lawsuit.

Descriptive statistics Summarize, organize, and describe a sample of data.

Destructive criticism Negative feedback that is cruel, sarcastic, and offensive; usually general rather than specific and often directed toward personal characteristics of the employee rather than job-relevant behaviors.

Determinants of performance Basic building blocks or causes of performance, which are declarative knowledge, procedural knowledge, and motivation.

Development Formal education, job experiences, mentoring relationships, and assessments of personality and abilities that help employees prepare for the future.

Dictionary of Occupational Titles (D.O.T.) Document that includes job analysis and occupational information used to match applicants with job openings; a major purpose of the *D.O.T.* was, and still is, for use in occupational counseling.

Differential psychology Scientific study of differences between or among two or more people.

Discovery Process in which lawyers are given access to potential witnesses who will be called by the other side, as well as any documents relevant to the complaints.

Dishonesty Employee theft of goods and theft of time (arriving late, leaving early, taking unnecessary sick days) or dishonest communications with customers, co-workers, or management.

Disinterestedness Characteristic of scientists who should be objective and uninfluenced by biases or prejudices when conducting research.

Dissonance theory Theory suggested by Festinger that observed that tension exists when individuals hold "dissonant cognitions" (incompatible thoughts). This approach assumes that individuals always seek some sense of "balance" (i.e., absence of tension) and that they will direct their behavior toward reducing the tension resulting from dissonant cognitions.

Distance learning Approach that allows trainees to interact and communicate with an instructor by using audio and video (television, computer, or radio) links that allow for learning from a distant location.

Distress Type of stress resulting from chronically demanding situations that produces negative health outcomes.

Distributed practice Provides individuals with rest intervals between practice sessions, which are spaced over a longer period of time.

Distributive justice Type of justice in which the allocation of outcomes or rewards to organizational members is perceived as fair.

Diversity Differences in demographic characteristics; also includes differences in values, abilities, interests, and experiences.

Division of labor The division of tasks performed in an organization into specialized jobs and departmental functions.

Drive Nonhuman equivalent of "motives" and "needs."

Duties Groups of similar tasks; each duty involves a segment of work directed at one of the general goals of a job.

Ecology model Underlying model for life history biodata instruments. Proposes that the events that make up a person's history represent choices made by the individual to interact with his or her environment. These choices can signal abilities, interests, and personality characteristics.

Effective leadership A situation that occurs when a leader changes a follower's behavior, resulting in both leader and follower feeling satisfied and effective.

Effectiveness Evaluation of the results of performance; often controlled by factors beyond the actions of an individual.

Electronic performance monitoring Monitoring work processes with electronic devices; can be very cost effective and has the potential for providing detailed and accurate work logs.

Emotion An effect or feeling, often experienced and displayed in reaction to an event or thought and accompanied by physiological changes in various systems of the body.

Emotion-focused coping Type of coping directed at reducing the emotional response to a problem by avoiding, minimizing, or distancing oneself from the problem.

Emotional exhaustion Burnout that occurs when individuals feel emotionally drained by work.

Emotional intelligence (EI) A proposed kind of intelligence focused on people's awareness of their own and others' emotions.

Emotional intelligence quotient (EQ) Parallels the notion of intelligence quotient (IQ); a score on a test of emotional intelligence.

Emotional labor Regulation of one's emotions to meet job or organizational demands; can be achieved through surface acting and deep acting.

Emotional stability Displaying little emotion; showing the same emotional response in various situations.

Employee assistance program (EAP) Counseling provided by an organization to deal with workplace stress, alcohol or drug difficulties, and problems stemming from outside the job.

Employee comparison methods Form of evaluation that involves the direct comparison of one person with another.

Employee engagement A positive work-related state of mind that includes high levels of energy, enthusiasm, and identification with one's work.

Episodic change Organizational change characterized as infrequent, discontinuous, and intentional; often launched with fanfare, with senior leaders clearly articulating pathways to change and disseminating information about the process and desired end state.

Equal Pay Act of 1963 Prohibits discrimination on the basis of sex in the payment of wages or benefits, where men and women perform work of similar skill, effort, and responsibility for the same employer under similar working conditions.

Equality norm Definition of fairness based on the view that people should receive approximately equal rewards; most common foundation for defining fairness in Scandinavian and Asian countries.

Equity theory Motivational theory developed by Adams (1965) that suggested that individuals look at their world in terms of comparative inputs and outcomes. Individuals compare their inputs and outcomes with others (e.g., peers, co-workers) by developing an input/outcome ratio.

Equivalent forms reliability Calculated by correlating measurements from a sample of individuals who complete two different forms of the same test.

Eustress Type of stress that provides challenges that motivate individuals to work hard and meet their goals.

Exhaustion Stage of the general adaptation syndrome in which overall resistance drops and adverse consequences (e.g., burnout, severe illness, and even death) can result unless stress is reduced.

Expatriate Manager or professional assigned to work in a location outside of his or her home country.

Expectancy An individual's belief that a particular behavior (e.g., effort, hard work) will lead to higher performance.

Expectancy framework Approach in which employees' expectations about the relationship between how much effort they expend and how well they perform are important to their motivation and learning.

Experimental control Characteristic of research in which possible confounding influences that might make results less reliable or harder to interpret are eliminated; often easier to establish in laboratory studies than in field studies.

Experimental design Participants are randomly assigned to different conditions.

Expert performance Performance exhibited by those who have been practicing for at least 10 years and have spent an average of 4 hours per day in deliberate practice.

Expert witness Witness in a lawsuit who is permitted to voice opinions about organizational practices.

External criteria Assess whether changes as a result of training occur when trainees are back on the job.

Extrinsic satisfaction Satisfaction that derives from aspects extrinsic, or external, to job tasks, such as pay or benefits.

Facet satisfaction Information related to specific facets or elements of job satisfaction.

Fairness Value judgment about actions or decisions based on test scores.

False negative Decision in which an applicant was rejected but would have performed adequately or successfully; decision is false because of the incorrect prediction that the applicant would not perform successfully and negative because the applicant was not hired.

False positive Decision in which an applicant was accepted but performed poorly; decision is false because of the incorrect prediction that the applicant would perform successfully and positive because the applicant was hired.

Feedback Knowledge of the results of one's actions; enhances learning and performance in training and on the job.

Feedback loop Connection between knowledge of results and the intermediate states that occur between goal commitment and performance.

Fidelity Extent to which the task trained is similar to the task required on the job.

Field theory Approach developed by Kurt Lewin, who proposed that various forces in the psychological environment interacted and combined to yield a final course of action.

Fight-or-flight reaction Adaptive response to stressful situations exhibited by animals and humans in which they choose to either fight or attempt to escape.

Five Factor Model (FFM) A taxonomy of five personality factors, composed of conscientiousness, extraversion, agreeableness, emotional stability, and openness to experience.

Fixed shift A particular shift that is permanently assigned to a worker.

Flextime Schedule in which individual workers are given discretion over the time they report to work and the time they leave work on a given day.

Flynn effect Phenomenon in which new generations appear to be smarter than their parents by a gain of 15 points in average intelligence test score per generation; named after the political scientist who did extensive research on the topic.

Forced-choice format Requires the rater to choose two statements out of four that could describe the ratee.

Forced distribution rating system Requires evaluators to place employees into performance categories based on a predetermined percentage of employees in different categories (low, moderate, high).

Frame-of-reference (FOR) training Training based on the assumption that a rater needs a context or "frame" for providing a rating; includes (1) providing information on the multidimensional nature of performance, (2) ensuring that raters understand the meaning of anchors on the scale, (3) engaging in practice rating exercises, and (4) providing feedback on practice exercises.

Frustration–aggression hypothesis Hypothesis that frustration leads to aggression; ultimately found to be too broad—aggression is only one possible response to frustration and not everyone responds to frustration with aggression.

Full-range theory of leadership Hierarchical model that ranges from laissez-faire leadership through transactional leadership to transformational leadership.

Functional personality at work The way that an individual behaves, handles emotions, and accomplishes tasks in a work setting; a combination of Big Five factors.

"g" Abbreviation for general mental ability.

g-ocentric model Tendency to understand and predict the behavior of workers simply by examining "g."

General adaptation syndrome (GAS) A nearly identical response sequence to almost any disease or trauma (poisoning, injury, psychological stress); identified by Hans Selye.

General mental ability The nonspecific capacity to reason, learn, and solve problems in any of a wide variety of ways and circumstances.

Generalizability theory A sophisticated approach to the question of reliability that simultaneously considers all types of error in reliability estimates (e.g., test–retest, equivalent forms, and internal consistency).

Generalize To apply the results from one study or sample to other participants or situations.

Generalized compliance Behavior that is helpful to the broader organization, such as upholding company rules.

Global leadership and organizational behavior effectiveness (GLOBE) Large-scale cross-cultural study of leadership by 170 social scientists and management researchers in over 60 countries.

Job demand Component of demand–control model that refers to the workload or intellectual requirements of the job.

Job Descriptive Index (JDI) One of the most extensively researched and documented job satisfaction instruments; assesses satisfaction with five distinct areas: the work itself, supervision, people, pay, and promotion.

Job embeddedness The many and varied types of commitment that individuals feel toward co-workers, teams, organizations, and careers.

Job enrichment A motivational approach that involves increasing the responsibility and interest level of jobs in order to increase the motivation and job satisfaction of employees performing those jobs.

Job evaluation Method for making internal pay decisions by comparing job titles to one another and determining their relative merit by way of these comparisons.

Job ladder or job family Cluster of positions that are similar in terms of the human attributes needed to be successful in those positions or in terms of the tasks that are carried out.

Job maturity A subordinate's job-related ability, skills, and knowledge.

Job rotation Approach that involves moving employees to various departments or areas of a company, or to various jobs within a single department.

Job satisfaction Positive attitude or emotional state resulting from the appraisal of one's job or job experience.

Job withdrawal Action that represents an individual's willingness to sever ties to an organization and the work role; includes intentions to quit or retire.

Judgmental measure Evaluation made of the effectiveness of an individual's work behavior; judgment most often made by supervisors in the context of a performance evaluation.

Judgmental performance measure Evaluation made of the effectiveness of an individual's work behavior, most often by supervisors in the context of a yearly performance evaluation.

Justice hypothesis of workplace violence Hypothesis that some violent acts can be understood as reactions by an employee to perceived injustice.

Just-in-time (JIT) production System that depends on the detailed tracking of materials and production so that the materials and human resources necessary for production arrive just in time; central to the reduction of waste in lean production processes.

Knowledge A collection of specific and interrelated facts and information about a particular topical area.

Knowledge test Assesses the extent to which individuals understand course or training materials; also administered for licensing and certification purposes.

KSAOs Individual attributes of knowledge, skills, abilities, and other characteristics that are required to successfully perform job tasks.

Laissez-faire leadership Leaders provide little guidance to their followers; lowest level of leadership identified by Bass (1997), who contrasted it with transactional leadership and transformational leadership.

Large-batch and mass-production organization Organization that produces large numbers of discrete units, often using assembly-line operations.

Layoff Job loss due to employer downsizing or reductions in force; often comes without warning or with a generic warning that the workforce will be reduced.

Leader The individual in a group given the task of directing task-relevant group activities or, in the absence of a designated leader, carrying the primary responsibility for performing these functions in the group.

Leader development A process that concentrates on developing, maintaining, or enhancing individual leader attributes such as knowledge, skills, and abilities.

Leader emergence Study of the characteristics of individuals who become leaders, examining the basis on which they were elected, appointed, or simply accepted.

Leader–member exchange (LMX) theory Leadership theory proposing that leaders adopt different behaviors with individual subordinates; the particular behavior pattern of the leader develops over time and depends to a large extent on the quality of the leader–subordinate relationship.

Leadership development A process that concentrates on the leader–follower relationship and on developing an environment in which the leader can build relationships that enhance cooperation and resource exchange.

Leadership effectiveness Study of which behaviors on the part of a designated leader (regardless of how that position was achieved) led to an outcome valued by the work group or organization.

Lean production Method that focuses on reducing waste in every form, including overproduction, lengthy waiting times for materials, excessive transportation costs, unnecessary stock, and defective products.

Learning A relatively permanent change in behavior and human capabilities produced by experience and practice.

Learning criteria Measures that assess how much was learned in the training program.

Learning organization Company that emphasizes continuous learning, knowledge sharing, and personal mastery.

Leniency error Occurs with raters who are unusually easy in their ratings.

Life cycle of a leader–follower relationship A description of more recent versions of leader–member exchange (LMX) theory, which includes a dynamic process in which the task of the leader is to drive the relationship from a tentative first-stage relationship to a deeper, more meaningful one.

Limited rationality The inability of humans to reason and make decisions in perfectly rational ways.

Linear Relationship between two variables that can be depicted by a straight line.

Linear programming Type of programmed instruction in which all trainees proceed through the same material.

Locus of control The extent to which an individual views events as resulting from his or her own actions (an internal LOC) or from outside causes (an external LOC).

Locus of control (LOC) Construct that refers to the belief of individuals that what happens to them is under their control (internal LOC) or beyond their control (external LOC).

Lordstown Syndrome Act of sabotage named after a General Motors plant plagued with acts of sabotage.

Low personal accomplishment Burnout in which individuals feel they cannot deal with problems effectively and understand or identify with others' problems.

Macro-research The study of collective behavior.

Maslow's need theory Theory that proposed that all humans have a basic set of needs and that these needs express themselves over the life span of the individual as internal "pushes" or drives. Identified five basic needs sets: physiological, security, love or social, esteem, and self-actualization.

Massed practice Conditions in which individuals practice a task continuously and without rest.

Mastery orientation Orientation in which individuals are concerned with increasing their competence for the task at hand; they view errors and mistakes as part of the learning process.

Mean The arithmetic average of the scores in a distribution; obtained by summing all of the scores in a distribution and dividing by the sample size.

Measure of central tendency Statistic that indicates where the center of a distribution is located. Mean, median, and mode are measures of central tendency.

Measurement Assigning numbers to characteristics of individuals or objects according to rules.

Mechanistic organization Organization that depends on formal rules and regulations, makes decisions at higher levels of the organization, and has small spans of control.

Median The middle score in a distribution.

Mental ability Capacity to reason, plan, and solve problems; cognitive ability.

Mental Measurements Yearbook Widely used source that includes an extensive listing of tests as well as reviews of those tests.

Mental test Instrument designed to measure a subject's ability to reason, plan, and solve problems; an intelligence test.

Merit or equity norm Definition of fairness based on the view that those who work hardest or produce the most should get the greatest rewards; most common foundation for defining fairness in the United States.

Meso-research The study of the interaction of individual and collective behavior.

Meta-analysis Statistical method for combining and analyzing the results from many studies to draw a general conclusion about relationships among variables.

Metric Standard of measurement; a scale.

Micro-research The study of individual behavior.

Minnesota Satisfaction Questionnaire (MSQ) A commonly used job satisfaction instrument that assesses particular aspects of work (e.g., achievement, ability utilization) as well as scores for extrinsic satisfaction and intrinsic satisfaction.

Mobbing Situation in which a target is selected and bullied by a group of people rather than an individual.

Mode The most common or frequently occurring score in a distribution.

Mood Generalized state of feeling not identified with a particular stimulus and not sufficiently intense to interrupt ongoing thought processes.

Motivation (M) Concerns the conditions responsible for variations in intensity, persistence, quality, and direction of ongoing behavior.

Motivational Trait Questionnaire (MTQ) A 48-item questionnaire that provides a standardized method of assessing six distinct aspects of general performance motivation.

Motivator needs Higher-level needs described in Herzberg's two-factor theory. Herzberg proposed that meeting such needs resulted in the expenditure of effort as well as satisfaction.

Multifactor Leadership Questionnaire (MLQ) Self-report instrument used in the development and validation of the theory of transformational leadership.

Multinational staffing Procedures that involve staffing for organizations in more than one country.

Multiple correlation coefficient Statistic that represents the overall linear association between several variables (e.g., cognitive ability, personality, experience) on the one hand, and a single variable (e.g., job performance) on the other hand.

Multiple hurdle system Constructed from multiple hurdles so that candidates who do not exceed each of the minimum dimension scores are excluded from further consideration.

Multiple regression analysis Results in an equation for combining test scores into a composite based on the correlations among the test scores and the correlations of each test score with the performance score.

Muscular endurance Physical ability to continue to use a single muscle or muscle group repeatedly over a period of time.

Muscular power Physical ability to lift, pull, push, or otherwise move an object; unlike endurance, this is a one-time maximum effort.

Muscular tension Physical quality of muscular strength.

Need Internal motivation that is thought to be inborn and universally present in humans.

Need norm Definition of fairness based on the view that people should receive rewards in proportion to their needs.

Negative affectivity (NA) Disposition wherein individuals are prone to experience a diverse array of negative mood states (e.g., anxiety, depression, hostility, and guilt).

Nonexperimental design Does not include any "treatment" or assignment to different conditions.

Nonlinear Relationship between two variables that cannot be depicted by a straight line; sometimes called "curvilinear" and most easily identified by examining a scatterplot.

Norm group Group whose test scores are used to compare and understand an individual's test score.

Normative commitment An obligation to remain in an organization.

Norming Comparing a test score to other relevant test scores.

Norms Informal and sometimes unspoken rules that teams adopt to regulate members' behavior.

Norm-referenced cut score Based on some index of the test takers' scores rather than any notion of job performance.

Objective performance measure Usually a quantitative count of the results of work such as sales volume, complaint letters, and output.

Observational design The researcher observes employee behavior and systematically records what is observed.

Occupational commitment Commitment to a particular occupational field; includes affective, continuance, and normative commitment.

Occupational health psychology Area of psychology that involves the application of psychology to improving the quality of work life and to protecting and promoting the safety, health, and well-being of workers.

Occupational Information Network (O*NET) Collection of electronic databases, based on well-developed taxonomies, that has updated and replaced the *Dictionary of Occupational Titles* (*D.O.T.*).

On-the-job training Involves assigning trainees to jobs and encouraging them to observe and learn from more experienced employees.

Organic organization Organization with a large span of control, less formalized procedures, and decision making at middle levels.

Organization A group of people who have common goals and who follow a set of operating procedures to develop products and services.

Organizational analysis Component of training needs analysis that examines organizational goals, available resources, and the organizational environment; helps to determine where training should be directed.

Organizational chart Diagram of an organization's structure.

Organizational citizenship behavior (OCB) Behavior that goes beyond what is expected.

Organizational identification (OID) The process whereby individuals derive a feeling of pride and esteem from their association with an organization. Individuals may also take pains to distance themselves from the organization for which they work—this would be called organizational disidentification.

Organizational justice Type of justice that is composed of organizational procedures, outcomes, and interpersonal interactions.

Organizational psychology Field of psychology that combines research from social psychology and organizational behavior and addresses the emotional and motivational side of work.

Outcome/input ratio Ratio that results when employees compare their inputs and outcomes to those of others (e.g., peers, co-workers) to determine if they are being treated equitably.

Outcomes The compensation, satisfaction, and other benefits employees derive from their work.

Out-group members People who have low-quality relationships with their leader and little latitude for negotiating their work roles.

Overall satisfaction Overall assessment of job satisfaction that results either from mathematically combining scores based on satisfaction with specific important aspects of work or a single overall evaluative rating of the job.

Overt integrity test Asks questions directly about past honesty behavior (stealing, etc.) as well as attitudes toward various behaviors such as employee theft.

Paired comparison Technique in which each employee in a work group or a collection of individuals with the same job title is compared with every other individual in the group on the various dimensions being considered.

Paper and pencil test One of the most common forms of industrial testing that requires no manipulation of any objects other than the instrument used to respond.

Part learning Training approach in which subtasks are practiced separately and later combined.

Participative behavior Type of behavior identified in the Michigan studies; allows subordinates more participation in decision making and encourages more two-way communication.

Path–goal theory of motivation First formal work motivation theory to suggest that people weighed options before choosing among them. Reasoned that if a worker saw high productivity as a path to the goal of desired rewards or personal goals (e.g., a pay increase or promotion, or increased power, prestige, or responsibility), he or she would likely be a high producer.

People skills A nontechnical term that includes negotiating skills, communication skills, and conflict resolution skills.

Perceptual-motor abilities Physical attributes that combine the senses (e.g., seeing, hearing, smell) and motion (e.g., coordination, dexterity).

Performance Actions or behaviors relevant to the organization's goals; measured in terms of each individual's proficiency.

Performance components May appear in different jobs and result from the determinants of performance; John Campbell and colleagues identified eight performance components, some or all of which can be found in every job.

Performance management System that emphasizes the link between individual behavior and organizational strategies and goals by defining performance in the context of those goals; jointly developed by managers and the people who report to them.

Performance orientation Orientation in which individuals are concerned about doing well in training and being evaluated positively.

Performance test Requires the individual to make a response by manipulating a particular physical object or piece of equipment.

Person analysis Component of training needs analysis that identifies which individuals within an organization should receive training and what kind of instruction they need.

Person-as-intentional approach Motivational approach that assumes that individuals are intentional in their behavior.

Person as judge Metaphor in which an individual seeks information about the extent to which the person and others are perceived as responsible for positive and negative events. The person looks for evidence of intention in the actions of others and considers those intentions in choosing a personal course of action.

Person as machine Metaphor that suggests that people's behaviors/actions are reflexive and involuntary and are performed without conscious awareness.

Person as scientist Metaphor that suggests that people are active information gatherers and analysts who seek knowledge and understanding as a way of mastering their environment.

Person–job (P–J) fit Extent to which the skills, abilities, and interests of an individual are compatible with the demands of the job.

Person–organization (P–O) fit Extent to which the values of an employee are consistent with the values held by most others in the organization.

Personality An individual's behavioral and emotional characteristics, generally found to be stable over time and in a variety of circumstances; an individual's habitual way of responding.

Personality-based integrity test Test that infers honesty and integrity from questions dealing with broad constructs such as conscientiousness, reliability, and social responsibility and awareness.

Personality-Related Position Requirements Form (PPRF) Job analysis instrument devoted to identifying personality predictors of job performance.

Personnel measure Measure typically kept in a personnel file including absences, accidents, tardiness, rate of advancement, disciplinary actions, and commendations of meritorious behavior.

Personnel psychology Field of psychology that addresses issues such as recruitment, selection, training, performance appraisal, promotion, transfer, and termination.

Physical abilities Bodily powers such as muscular strength, flexibility, and stamina.

Physical fidelity Extent to which the training task mirrors the physical features of the task performed on the job.

Policy capturing Technique that allows researchers to code various characteristics and determine which weighed most heavily in raters' decision making.

Positive affectivity (PA) Disposition in which individuals are prone to describe themselves as cheerful, enthusiastic, confident, active, and energetic.

Positive reinforcement Occurs when desired behavior is followed by a reward, which increases the probability that the behavior will be repeated.

Power approach Leadership theory that examines the types of power wielded by leaders.

Power motive The desire to attain control or power that results from people learning that the exercise of control over others or the environment is pleasing.

Power test Has no rigid time limits; enough time is given for a majority of the test takers to complete all of the test items.

Predictive validity design Criterion-related validity design in which there is a time lag between collection of the test data and the criterion data.

Predictor The test chosen or developed to assess attributes (e.g., abilities) identified as important for successful job performance.

Pretest posttest control group design Generally includes random assignment of participants to conditions, a control group, and measures obtained both before and after training has occurred.

Primary prevention strategy Stress prevention strategy concerned with modifying or eliminating stressors in the work environment.

Problem-focused coping Type of coping directed at managing or altering a problem causing the stress.

Procedural justice Type of justice in which the process (or procedure) by which ratings are assigned or rewards are distributed is perceived as fair.

Procedural knowledge Familiarity with a procedure or process; knowing "how."

Procedural knowledge and skill (PKS) Knowing how to perform a job or task; often developed through practice and experience.

Process emotion Reaction that results from consideration of the tasks one is currently doing.

Production team Team that consists of frontline employees who produce tangible output.

Productivity Ratio of effectiveness (output) to the cost of achieving that level of effectiveness (input).

Programmed instruction Approach in which trainees are given instructional materials in written or computer-based forms that positively reinforce them as they move through the material at their own pace.

Progression hypothesis A progression of withdrawal behaviors that start with tardiness, increase to absenteeism, and eventually result in a decision to quit or retire.

Progressive muscle relaxation Stress management technique to relax the muscles, thereby helping to progressively relax the entire body.

Project team Team that is created to solve a particular problem or set of problems and is disbanded after the project is completed or the problem is solved; also called an ad hoc committee, a task force, or a cross-functional team.

ProMES The Productivity Measurement and Enhancement System; a motivational approach that utilizes goal setting, rewards, and feedback to increase motivation and performance.

Prospective emotion Reaction that results from a consideration of the tasks one anticipates doing.

Protection model Model for addressing diversity that identifies disadvantaged and underrepresented groups and provides special protections for them.

Psychological contracts Beliefs that people hold regarding terms of an exchange agreement between themselves and the organization.

Psychological diversity Differences in underlying attributes such as skills, abilities, personality characteristics, attitudes, beliefs, and values; may also include functional, occupational, and educational backgrounds.

Psychological fidelity Extent to which the training task helps trainees to develop the knowledge, skills, abilities, and other characteristics (KSAOs) necessary to perform the job.

Psychological maturity The self-confidence and self-respect of the subordinate.

Psychometric training Training that makes raters aware of common rating errors (central tendency, leniency/severity, and halo) in the hope that this will reduce the likelihood of errors.

Psychometrician Psychologist trained in measuring characteristics such as mental ability.

Psychometrics Practice of measuring a characteristic such as mental ability, placing it on a scale or metric.

Psychomotor abilities Physical functions of movement, associated with coordination, dexterity, and reaction time; also called motor or sensorimotor abilities.

Qualitative methods Rely on observation, interview, case study, and analysis of diaries or written documents and produce flow diagrams and narrative descriptions of events or processes.

Quality circle Work group arrangement that typically involves 6 to 12 employees who meet regularly to identify work-related problems and generate ideas to increase productivity or product quality.

Quantitative methods Rely on tests, rating scales, questionnaires, and physiological measures, and yield numerical results.

Quasi-experimental design Participants are assigned to different conditions, but random assignment to conditions is not possible.

Quid pro quo sexual harassment Involves direct requests for sexual favors, for example, when sexual compliance is mandatory for promotions or retaining one's job.

Rating errors Inaccuracies in ratings that may be actual errors or intentional or systematic distortions.

Reaction criteria Measures of trainee impressions of the training program.

Realistic job preview (RJP) Technique for providing practical information about a job to prospective employees; includes information about the task and context of the work.

Rebalance Stage in the freeze–rebalance–unfreeze continuous change process intended to reframe what has happened and produce a cognitive framework that gives change deeper meaning.

Refreezing Third stage in the process of changing an organization in which the new attitudes and values of individuals are stabilized.

Regression line Straight line that best "fits" the scatterplot and describes the relationship between the variables in the graph; can also be presented as an equation that specifies where the line intersects the vertical axis and what the angle or slope of the line is.

Reinforcement theory Theory that proposes that behavior depends on three simple elements: stimulus, response, and reward. Proposed that if a response in the presence of a particular stimulus is rewarded (i.e., reinforced), that response is likely to occur again in the presence of that stimulus.

Relational demography The relative makeup of various demographic characteristics in particular work groups.

Relations-oriented behavior Type of behavior identified by University of Michigan researchers as an important part of a leader's activities; similar to consideration in the Ohio State model.

Reliability Consistency or stability of a measure.

Research design Provides the overall structure or architecture for the research study; allows investigators to conduct scientific research on a phenomenon of interest.

Resigned work satisfaction A type of satisfaction associated with reduced work effort and a reduced willingness to change or adapt.

Resistance Stage of the general adaptation syndrome in which the body copes with the original source of stress, but resistance to other stressors is lowered.

Results criteria Measures of how well training can be related to organizational outcomes such as productivity gains, cost savings, error reductions, or increased customer satisfaction.

Retrospective emotion Reaction that results from a consideration of the tasks one has already completed.

Revery obsession Australian psychologist Elton Mayo proposed that this mental state resulted from the mind-numbing, repetitive, and difficult work that characterized U.S. factories in the early 20th century, causing factory workers to be unhappy, prone to resist management attempts to increase productivity, and sympathetic to labor unions.

Risky-shift phenomenon Tendency for groups to make more risky decisions than individuals; related to the more general phenomenon of group polarization.

Role The expectations regarding the responsibilities and requirements of a particular job.

Role ambiguity Stressor that occurs when employees lack clear knowledge of what behavior is expected in their job.

Role conflict Stressor that occurs when demands from different sources are incompatible.

Role overload Stressor that occurs when an individual is expected to fulfill too many roles at the same time.

Role stressors Collective term for stressors resulting from the multiple task requirements or roles of employees.

Rotating shift A shift that changes over a certain period of time.

Routing test Preliminary test used in computer adaptive testing that identifies a test taker's approximate level of ability before providing additional questions to refine the test taker's position within that ability level.

Sabotage Acts that damage, disrupt, or subvert the organization's operations for personal purposes of the saboteur by creating unfavorable publicity, damage to property, destruction of working relationships, or harming of employees or customers.

Scatterplot Graph used to plot the scatter of scores on two variables; used to display the correlational relationship between two variables.

Science Approach that involves the understanding, prediction, and control of some phenomenon of interest.

Scientific management A movement based on principles developed by Frederick W. Taylor who suggested that there was one best and most efficient way to perform various jobs.

Scientist-practitioner model A model that uses scientific tools and research in the practice of I-O psychology.

Score banding Approach in which individuals with similar test scores are grouped together in a category or score band, and selection within the band is then made based on other considerations.

Screen in test Used to add information about the positive attributes of a candidate that might predict outstanding performance; tests of normal personality are examples of screen in tests in the employment setting.

Screen out test Used to eliminate candidates who are clearly unsuitable for employment; tests of psychopathology are examples of screen out tests in the employment setting.

Secondary prevention strategy Stress prevention strategy that involves modifying responses to inevitable demands or stressors.

Selection ratio (SR) Index ranging from 0 to 1 that reflects the ratio of positions to applicants; calculated by dividing the number of positions available by the number of applicants.

Self-efficacy The belief in one's capability to perform a specific task or reach a specific goal.

Self-esteem A sense of positive self-worth that is considered to be an important resource for coping.

Self-presentation A person's public face or "game face."

Self-regulation Process by which individuals take in information about behavior and make adjustments or changes based on that information. These changes, in turn, affect subsequent behavior (e.g., strategies, goal commitment).

Sensory abilities Physical functions of vision, hearing, touch, taste, smell, and kinesthetic feedback (e.g., noticing changes in body position).

Settlement discussions Conducted by the parties in a lawsuit in an attempt to reach a mutually satisfying resolution of the complaint before proceeding with all of the other steps that lead to a trial.

Severity error Occurs with raters who are unusually harsh in their ratings.

Sexual harassment Unwelcome sexual advances, requests for sexual favors, and other conduct of a sexual nature constitute sexual harassment when submission to or rejection of this conduct explicitly or implicitly affects an individual's employment, unreasonably interferes with an individual's work performance, or creates a hostile work environment.

Shared mental model Organized way for team members to think about how the team will work; helps team members understand and predict the behavior of their teammates.

Shift work Scheduling of work into temporal shifts; common in particular occupational groups such as nurses, blue-collar workers, and public safety personnel.

Simple ranking Employees are ranked from top to bottom according to their assessed proficiency on some dimension, duty area, or standard.

Simulator Teaching tool designed to reproduce the critical characteristics of the real world in a training setting that produces learning and transfer to the job.

Situational interview Asks the interviewee to describe in specific and behavioral detail how he or she would respond to a hypothetical situation.

Situational judgment test Commonly a paper and pencil test that presents the candidate with a written scenario and asks the candidate to choose the best response from a series of alternatives.

Six Sigma systems Approach to quality management that provides training for employees and managers in statistical analysis, project management, and problem-solving methods in order to reduce the defect rate of products.

Skew The extent to which scores in a distribution are lopsided or tend to fall on the left or right side of the distribution.

Skill-based outcome Type of learning outcome that concerns the development of motor or technical skills.

Skills Practiced acts, such as shooting a basketball, using a computer keyboard, or persuading someone to buy something.

Small-batch organization Organization that produces specialty products one at a time.

Social desirability Desire to be appealing to others.

Social learning theory Cognitive theory that proposes that there are many ways to learn, including observational learning, which occurs when people watch someone perform a task and then rehearse those activities mentally until they have an opportunity to try them out.

Social loafing Reduced motivation and performance in groups that occurs when there is a reduced feeling of individual accountability or a reduced opportunity for evaluation of individual performance.

Social support The comfort, assistance, or information an individual receives through formal or informal contacts with individuals or groups.

Socialization Process by which a new employee becomes aware of the values and procedures of an organization.

Society for Industrial and Organizational Psychology (SIOP) An association to which many I-O psychologists, both practitioners and researchers, belong. Designated as Division 14 of the American Psychological Association (APA).

Span of control A concept that describes the number of positions or people reporting to a single individual—the width—in an organization.

Speed test Has rigid and demanding time limits so most test takers will be unable to finish the test in the allotted time.

Staffing decisions Associated with recruiting, selecting, promoting, and separating employees.

Stamina Physical ability to supply muscles with oxygenated blood through the cardiovascular system; also known as cardiovascular strength or aerobic strength or endurance.

Standard deviation Measure of the extent of spread in a set of scores.

Standard error of measurement (SEM) Statistic that provides a measure of the amount of error in a test score distribution; function of the reliability of the test and the variability in test scores.

Stanford–Binet test A well-known intelligence test designed for testing one individual at a time. Originally developed by Alfred Binet and Theodore Simon in 1905, the Binet–Simon test was updated starting in 1916 by Lewis Terman and colleagues at Stanford University, which led to the test's current name.

Statistical artifacts Characteristics (e.g., small sample size, unreliable measures) of a particular study that distort the observed results. Researchers can correct for artifacts to arrive at a statistic that represents the "true" relationship between the variables of interest.

Statistical control Using statistical techniques to control for the influence of certain variables. Such control allows researchers to concentrate exclusively on the primary relationships of interest.

Statistical decision making Combines information according to a mathematical formula.

Statistical power The likelihood of finding a statistically significant difference when a true difference exists.

Statistical significance Indicates that the probability of the observed statistic is less than the stated significance level adopted by the researcher (commonly $p \leq .05$). A statistically significant finding indicates that, if the null hypothesis were true, the results found are unlikely to occur by chance, and the null hypothesis is rejected.

Strains Reaction or response to stressors.

Stress hormone Chemical (e.g., adrenaline, noradrenaline, epinephrine, or cortisol) released in the body when a person encounters stressful or demanding situations.

Stress inoculation Common type of stress management training that usually combines primary prevention and secondary prevention strategies.

Stress management training A program useful for helping employees deal with workplace stressors that are difficult to remove or change.

Stressors Physical or psychological demands to which an individual responds.

Structure The formal way that an organization is designed in terms of division of labor, delegation of authority, and span of control; represented by the number of levels—or height—in an organization.

Structured interview Consists of very specific questions asked of each candidate; includes tightly crafted scoring schemes with detailed outlines for the interviewer with respect to assigning ratings or scores based on interview performance.

Subgroup norming Approach that develops separate lists for individuals within different demographic groups, then ranks the candidates within their respective demographic group.

Subject matter expert (SME) Employee (incumbent) who provides information about a job in a job analysis interview or survey.

Successful leadership A situation that occurs when a follower changes his or her behavior as a function of the leader's effort.

Surface acting Emotional labor that consists of managing or faking one's expressions or emotions.

Survey design Research strategy in which participants are asked to complete a questionnaire or survey.

Tacit knowledge Action-oriented, goal-directed knowledge, acquired without direct help from others; colloquially called "street smarts."

Task analysis Component of training needs analysis that examines what employees must do to perform the job properly.

Task performance Proficiency with which job incumbents perform activities that are formally recognized as a part of their job.

Task-oriented behavior Type of behavior identified by University of Michigan researchers as an important part of a leader's activities; similar to initiating structure from the Ohio State studies.

Task-oriented job analysis Approach that begins with a statement of the actual tasks as well as what is accomplished by those tasks.

Taxonomy An orderly, scientific system of classification.

Team Interdependent collection of individuals who work together toward a common goal and who share responsibility for specific outcomes for their organizations.

Team composition The attributes of team members, including skills, abilities, experiences, and personality characteristics.

Team coordination training Training that involves teaching team members about sharing information, managing conflict, solving problems, clarifying roles, and making decisions; used to help team members learn to employ the resources of the entire team effectively.

Team leader training Training of the team's leader in conflict resolution and team coordination.

Team-role theory Theory proposed by Belbin that effective teams contain a combination of individuals capable of working in nine team roles; used by organizations and management consultants in Europe and Australia to assess and develop teams.

Telecommuting Accomplishing work tasks from a distant location using electronic communication media.

Termination for cause An individual is fired from an organization for a particular reason; the individual has usually been warned one or more times about a problem, and either cannot or will not correct it.

Tertiary prevention strategy Stress prevention strategy focused on healing the negative effects of stressors.

Test An objective and standardized procedure for measuring a psychological construct using a sample of behavior.

Test battery Collection of tests that usually assess a variety of different attributes.

Test–retest reliability Calculated by correlating measurements taken at time one with measurements taken at time two.

Theory Y Theory developed by McGregor to describe managers who believe subordinates are motivated to meet goals in the absence of organizational controls.

Think-aloud protocol Approach used by cognitive psychologists to investigate the thought processes of experts who achieve high levels of performance; an expert performer describes in words the thought process that he or she uses to accomplish a task.

Time and motion studies Studies that broke every action down into its constituent parts, timed those movements with a stopwatch, and developed new and more efficient movements that would reduce fatigue and increase productivity.

Time horizon Cultural dimension that affects whether managers and employees focus on short-term or long-term goals.

Time urgency Subcomponent of the Type A behavior pattern that refers to the feeling of being pressured by inadequate time.

TIP (The Industrial-Organizational Psychologist) Quarterly newsletter published by the Society for Industrial and Organizational Psychology; provides I-O psychologists and those interested in I-O psychology with the latest relevant information about the field.

Title VII of the Civil Rights Act of 1964 Federal legislation that prohibits employment discrimination on the basis of race, color, religion, sex, or national origin, which define what are known as protected groups. Prohibits not only intentional discrimination, but also practices that have the unintentional effect of discriminating against individuals because of their race, color, national origin, religion, or sex.

Total quality management (TQM) A unique way of organizing productive effort by emphasizing team-based behavior directed toward improving quality and meeting customer demands.

Trainee motivation Extent to which trainees are interested in attending training, learning from training, and transferring the skills and knowledge acquired in training back to the job.

Trainee readiness Refers to whether employees have the personal characteristics necessary to acquire knowledge from a training program and apply it to the job.

Training Systematic acquisition of skills, concepts, or attitudes that results in improved performance in another environment.

Training evaluation Involves the systematic collection of descriptive and judgmental information that can be used to make effective training decisions.

Training needs analysis A three-step process of organizational, task, and person analysis; required to develop a systematic understanding of where training is needed, what needs to be taught or trained, and who will be trained.

Trait approach Leadership theory that attempted to show that leaders possessed certain characteristics that nonleaders did not.

Transactional leadership Leaders show followers how they can meet their personal goals by adopting a particular behavior pattern; the leader develops social contracts with followers in which certain behaviors will be rewarded.

Transfer of training Degree to which trainees apply the knowledge, skills, and attitudes gained in training to their jobs.

Transfer of training climate Workplace characteristics that either inhibit or facilitate the transfer to the job of what has been learned in training.

Transformational leadership Leadership theory that describes the behavior of inspirational political leaders who transform their followers by appealing to nobler motives such as justice, morality, and peace.

Triangulation Approach in which researchers seek converging information from different sources.

True negative Decision in which an applicant was rejected and would have performed poorly if he or she were hired; decision is true because of the correct prediction that the applicant would not be a good performer and negative because the applicant was not hired.

True positive Decision in which an applicant was accepted and performed successfully; decision is true because of the correct prediction that the applicant would be a good performer and positive because the applicant was hired.

Trust Belief in how a person or an organization will act on some future occasion based upon previous interactions with that person or organization.

Two-factor theory Theory proposed by Herzberg that suggested that there were really two basic needs, not five as suggested by Maslow, and that they were not so much hierarchically arranged as independent of each other.

Type A behavior pattern (TABP) Set of characteristics exhibited by individuals who are engaged in a chronic struggle to obtain an unlimited number of poorly defined things from their environment in the shortest period of time; subcomponents include hostility, achievement strivings, impatience/irritability, and time urgency.

Ultimate criterion Ideal measure of all of the relevant aspects of job performance.

Unfreezing First stage in the process of changing an organization in which individuals become aware of their values and beliefs.

Uniform Guidelines on Employee Selection Procedures Official government guidelines designed to assist employers, labor organizations, employment agencies, and licensing and certification boards to comply with federal requirements.

Unstructured interview Includes questions that may vary by candidate and that allow the candidate to answer in any form he or she may prefer.

Utility analysis Technique that assesses the economic return on investment of human resource interventions such as staffing and training.

Valence The strength of a person's preference for a particular outcome.

Validity The accurateness of inferences made based on test or performance data; also addresses whether a measure accurately and completely represents what was intended to be measured.

Validity coefficient Correlation coefficient between a test score (predictor) and a performance measure (criterion).

Value model Model for addressing diversity in which each element of an organization is valued for what it uniquely brings to the organization.

Variability The extent to which scores in a distribution vary.

Vertical culture A culture that accepts and depends upon distances between individuals.

Vertical transfer Transfer across different levels of the organization; concerned with the link between individual training outcomes and outcomes at higher levels of the organization such as teams.

VIE theory Motivation theory that assumed that individuals rationally estimate the relative attractiveness and unattractiveness of different rewards or outcomes (valence), the probability that performance will lead to particular outcomes or rewards (instrumentality), and the probability that effort will lead to performance (expectancy).

Virtual-collaboration behaviors Behaviors that characterize virtual team interactions, including exchanging ideas without criticism, agreeing on responsibilities, and meeting deadlines.

Virtual-communication skills Skills used in virtual team interactions, including rephrasing unclear sentences or expressions so that all team members understand what is being said, acknowledging the receipt of messages, and responding within one business day.

Virtual-socialization skills Skills used in virtual team interactions, including soliciting team members' feedback on the work process used to accomplish team goals, expressing appreciation for ideas and completed tasks, and apologizing for mistakes.

Virtual team Team that has widely dispersed members working together toward a common goal and linked through computers and other technology.

Voice Having the possibility of challenging, influencing, or expressing an objection to a process or outcome.

Walk-through testing Requires an employee to describe to an interviewer in detail how to complete a task or job-related behavior; employee may literally walk through the facility (e.g., a nuclear power plant), answering questions as he or she actually sees the displays or controls in question.

Weighted checklist Includes items that have values or weights assigned to them that are derived from the expert judgments of incumbents and supervisors of the position in question.

Welfare-to-work program Program that requires individuals to work in return for government subsidies.

"West versus the Rest" mentality Tendency for researchers to develop theories relevant to U.S. situations, with less concern given to their applicability in other countries.

Whole learning Training approach in which the entire task is practiced at once.

Withdrawal behaviors Absenteeism, turnover, tardiness, and retirement may be different manifestations of a larger construct called withdrawal.

Work diary Job analysis approach that requires workers and/or supervisors to keep a log of their activities over a prescribed period of time.

Work–family balance Area of research that investigates whether the satisfaction that one experiences at work is in part affected by the satisfaction that one experiences in non-work, and vice versa.

Work–family conflict Situation that occurs when workers experience conflict between the roles they fulfill at work and in their personal lives.

Work–life balance Area of research that investigates whether the satisfaction that one experiences at work is in part affected by the satisfaction that one experiences in non-work and vice versa, particularly to the extent that one environment has demands that conflict with the other.

Work sample test Assessment procedure that measures job skills by taking samples of behavior under realistic job-like conditions.

Worker-oriented job analysis Approach that focuses on the attributes of the worker necessary to accomplish the tasks.

Work withdrawal Action that represents an attempt by the individual to withdraw from work but maintain ties to the organization and the work role; includes lateness and absenteeism.

References

Academy of Management (1990). *The Academy of Management code of conduct.* Ada, OH: Author.

Ackerman, P. L., & Cianciolo, A. T. (1999). Psychomotor abilities via touch-panel testing: Measurement innovations, construct and criterion validity. *Human Performance, 12,* 231–273.

Ackerman, P. L., & Cianciolo, A. T. (2002). Ability and task constraint determinants of complex task performance. *Journal of Experimental Psychology: Applied, 8*(3), 194–208.

Ackerman, P. L., Beier, M. E., & Boyle, M. O. (2002). Individual differences in working memory within a nomological network of cognitive and perceptual speed abilities. *Journal of Experimental Psychology: General, 131,* 567–589.

Ackerman, P. L., Beier, M. E., & Boyle, M. O. (2005). Working memory and intelligence: The same or different constructs? *Psychological Bulletin, 131,* 30–60.

Adams, J. D. (2001). Managing dispersed work effectively. *OD Practitioner, 33*(1), 381–391.

Adams, J. S. (1965). Inequity in social exchange. In K. Berkowitz (Ed.), *Advances in experimental social psychology* (Vol. 2, pp. 267–299). New York: Academic Press.

Adams, S. (1996). *Dogbert's top secret management handbook.* New York: HarperCollins.

Adelmann, P. K. (1995). Emotional labor as a potential source of job stress. In S. L. Sauter & L. R. Murphy (Eds.), *Organizational risk factors for job stress* (pp. 371–381). Washington, DC: American Psychological Association.

Adler, G. S., & Ambrose, M. L. (2005). An examination of the effect of computerized performance monitoring feedback on monitoring fairness, performance, and satisfaction. *Organizational Behavior and Human Decision Processes, 97,* 161–177.

Aguinis, H. (2009). *Performance management* (2nd ed.). Boston: Pearson Education.

Aguinis, H. (2011). Organizational responsibility: Doing good and doing well. In S. Zedeck (Ed.), *APA handbook of industrial and organizational psychology* (Vol. 3, pp. 855–879). Washington, DC: American Psychological Association.

Aguinis, H., & Henle, C. A. (2002). The search for universals in cross-cultural organizational behavior. In J. Greenberg (Ed.), *Organizational behavior: The state of the science* (2nd ed., pp. 373–411). Mahwah, NJ: Erlbaum.

Aguinis, H., Henle, C. A., & Beaty, J. C. (2001). Virtual reality technology: A new tool for personnel selection. *International Journal of Selection and Assessment, 9,* 70–83.

Aguinis, H., & Kraiger, K. (2009). Benefits of training and development for individuals and teams, organizations, and society. *Annual Review of Psychology, 60,* 451–474.

Aguinis, H., & Roth, H. (2002). *Teaching in China: Culture-based challenges.* Unpublished manuscript, University of Colorado at Denver.

Alboher, M. (2008, May 29). Hot ticket in B-school: Bringing life values to corporate ethics. *New York Times,* p. C5.

Alge, B. J. (2001). Effects of computer surveillance on perceptions of privacy and procedural justice. *Journal of Applied Psychology, 86,* 797–804.

Alge, B. J., Ballinger, G. A., & Green, S. (2004). Remote control: Predictors of electronic monitoring intensity and secrecy. *Personnel Psychology, 57,* 377–410.

Allen, T. D., & Armstrong, J. (2006). Further examination of the link between work–family conflict and physical health: The role of health-related behaviors. *American Behavioral Scientist, 49,* 1204–1221.

Allen, T. D., Herst, D. E., Bruck, C. S., & Sutton, M. (2000). Consequences associated with work-to-family conflict: A review and agenda for future research. *Journal of Occupational Health Psychology, 5,* 278–308.

Allen, T. D., McManus, S. E., & Russell, J. E. (1999). Newcomer socialization and stress: Formal peer relationships as a source of support. *Journal of Vocational Behavior, 54,* 453–470.

Alliger, G. M., Tannenbaum, S. I., Bennett, W., Traver, H., & Shotland, A. (1997). A meta-analysis of the relations among training criteria. *Personnel Psychology, 50,* 341–358.

Amalfe, C. A., & Adelman, H. A. (2001, August 13). Forced rankings: Latest plaintiffs' target. *The New Jersey Lawyer,* pp. 1–10.

American Educational Research Association, American Psychological Association, and National Council on Measurement in Education. (1999). *Standards for educational and psychological testing.* Washington, DC: American Educational Research Association.

American Heart Association. (2002). *American Heart Association statistical facts.* Dallas, TX: Author.

American Heart Association. (2006). Heart disease and stroke statistics—2006 update: A report from the American Heart Association Statistics Committee and Stroke Statistics Subcommittee. *Circulation, 113,* 85–151.

American Management Association. (2001). *Workplace monitoring and surveillance.* New York: Author.

American Psychological Association (APA). (2002). Ethical principles of psychologists and code of conduct. *American Psychologist, 47,* 1597–1611.

American Society for Personnel Administration & American Compensation Association. (1981). *Elements of sound base pay administration.* Scottsdale, AZ: American Compensation Association and Berea, OH: American Society for Personnel Administration.

American Society for Training and Development. (2010). *The 2010 State of the Industry Report.* Alexandria, VA: Author.

Americans with Disabilities Act (1990). PL 101–336, 104 Statute 327, July 26.

Anastasi, A., & Urbina, S. (1997). *Psychological testing* (7th ed.). Upper Saddle River, NJ: Prentice Hall.

Anderson, D. L. (2009). *Organizational development: The process of leading organizational change.* Thousand Oaks, CA: Sage.

Anderson, N., Born, M., & Cunningham-Snell, N. (2001). Recruitment and selection: Applicant perspectives and outcomes. In N. Anderson, D. Ones, H. Sinangil, & C. Viswesvaran (Eds.), *Handbook of industrial, work, and organizational psychology* (Vol. 1, pp. 200–218). London: Sage.

Anderson, N., Herriot, P., & Hodgkinson, G. P. (2001). The practitioner–researcher divide in industrial, work, and organizational (IWO) psychology: Where are we now, and where do we go from here? *Journal of Occupational and Organizational Psychology, 74,* 391–411.

Anderson, N., & Ostroff, C. (1997). Selection as socialization. In N. Anderson & P. Herriott (Eds.), *Handbook of selection and appraisal* (2nd ed., pp. 413–440). London: Wiley.

Anderson, N., & Sleap, S. (2004). An evaluation of gender differences on the Belbin Team Role Self-Perception Inventory. *Journal of Occupational and Organizational Psychology, 77,* 429–437.

Anderson, N., & Witvliet, C. (2008). Fairness reactions to personnel selection methods: An international comparison between the Netherlands, the United States, France, Spain, Portugal, and Singapore. *International Journal of Selection and Assessment, 16*, 1–13.

Antonakis, J., & Avolio, B. J. (2003). Context and leadership: An examination of the nine-factor full-range leadership theory using the Multifactor Leadership Questionnaire. *Leadership Quarterly, 14*, 261–295.

Antonioni, D., & Park, H. (2001). The effects of personality similarity on peer ratings of contextual work behaviors. *Personnel Psychology, 54*, 331–360.

Aratani, L. (2008, August 23). Flextime has green appeal and lures young workers. *Washington Post*, p. A01.

Argyris, C. (1965). *Organization and innovation*. Homewood, IL: Irwin.

Argyris, C. (1972). *The applicability of organizational sociology*. Cambridge, UK: Cambridge University Press.

Argyris, C. (1990). *Overcoming organizational defenses: Facilitating organizational learning*. Boston: Allyn & Bacon.

Arthur, W., Bell, S. T., Villado, A. J., & Doverspike, D. (2006). The use of person–organization fit in employment decision making: An assessment of its criterion-related validity. *Journal of Applied Psychology, 91*, 786–801.

Arthur, W., Bennett, W., Edens, P. S., & Bell, S. T. (2003). Effectiveness of training in organizations: A meta-analysis of design and evaluation features. *Journal of Applied Psychology, 88*, 234–245.

Arthur, W., Day, E. A., McNelly, T. L., & Edens, P. A. (2003). A meta-analysis of the criterion-related validity of assessment center dimensions. *Personnel Psychology, 56*, 125–154.

Arvey, R. D. (1986). Sex bias in job evaluation procedures. *Personnel Psychology, 39*, 315–335.

Arvey, R. D. (1992). Constructs and construct validation: Definitions and issues. *Human Performance, 5*, 59–69.

Arvey, R. D., Bouchard, T. J., Carroll, J. B., Cattell, R. B., Cohen, D. B., Dawis, R. U., et al. (1995). Mainstream science on intelligence. *The Industrial-Organizational Psychologist, 32*(4), 67–72.

Arvey, R. D., Bouchard, T. J., Segal, N. L., & Abraham, L. M. (1989). Job satisfaction: Environmental and genetic components. *Journal of Applied Psychology, 74*, 187–192.

Arvey, R. D., Landon, T. E., Nutting, S. M., & Maxwell, S. E. (1992). Development of physical ability tests for police officers: A construct validation approach. *Journal of Applied Psychology, 77*, 996–1009.

Arvey, R. D., Rotundo, M., Johnson, W., Zhang, Z., & McGue, M. (2006). The determinants of leadership role occupancy: Genetic and personality factors. *Leadership Quarterly, 17*, 1–20.

Aryee, S., Budhwar, P. S., & Chen, Z. X. (2002). Trust as a mediator of the relationship between organizational justice and work outcomes: Test of a social exchange model. *Journal of Organizational Behavior, 23*, 267–285.

Ash, P. (1976). The assessment of honesty in employment. *South African Journal of Psychology, 6*, 68–79.

Ashforth, B. E., Harrison, S. H., & Corley, K. G. (2008). Identification in organizations: An examination of four fundamental questions. *Journal of Management, 34*, 325–374.

Ashkanasy, N. M. (2004). Emotion and performance. *Human Performance, 17*, 137–144.

Ashkanasy, N. M., & Daus, C. S. (2005). Rumors of the death of emotional intelligence in organizational behavior are vastly exaggerated. *Journal of Organizational Behavior, 26*, 441–452.

Ashkanasy, N. M., & Holmes, S. (1995). Perceptions of organizational ideology following merger: A longitudinal study of merging accounting firms. *Accounting, Organizations and Society, 20*, 19–34.

Ashkanasy, N. M., & Jackson, C. R. A. (2001). Organizational climate and culture. In N. Anderson, D. Ones, H. Sinangil, & C. Viswesvaran (Eds.), *Handbook of industrial, work, and organizational psychology* (pp. 332–345). London: Sage.

Ashkanasy, N. M., Wilderom, C. P. M., & Peterson, M. F. (Eds.). (2000). *Handbook of organizational climate and culture*. Thousand Oaks, CA: Sage.

Associated Press. (2000, October 4). New chief vows to change LAPD. *Denver Post*, p. 7a.

Associated Press. (2004, June 4). Study: Women must enter male bastions for pay parity. *Denver Post*, p. 7A.

Associated Press. (2005, October 28). Lawsuit dismissed in "wrong beer" case. Retrieved March 24, 2009, from www.cbsnews.com/stories/2005/10/28/ap/national/mainD8DGO4884.shtml

Associated Press. (2007, May 28). Tests and licenses sought for guides in Philadelphia. *New York Times*, p. A13.

Atkins, P. W. B., Wood, R. E., & Rutgers, P. J. (2002). The effects of feedback format on dynamic decision making. *Organizational Behavior and Human Decision Processes, 88*, 587–604.

Atwater, L. E. (1998). The advantages and pitfalls of self-assessment in organizations. In J. W. Smither (Ed.), *Performance appraisal: State of the art in practice* (pp. 331–369). San Francisco: Jossey-Bass.

Atwater, L., & Brett, J. (2006). Feedback format: Does it influence manager's reactions to feedback? *Journal of Occupational and Organizational Psychology, 79*, 517–532.

Atwater, L., Waldman, D., Ostroff, C., Robie, C., & Johnson, K. M. (2005). Self–other agreement: Comparing its relationship with performance in U.S. and Europe. *International Journal of Selection and Assessment, 13*, 25–40.

Austin, J. T., & Vancouver, J. B. (1996). Goal constructs in psychology: Structure, process and content. *Psychological Bulletin, 120*, 338–375.

Avery, D. R., & Quinones, M. A. (2002). Disentangling the effects of voice: The incremental roles of opportunity, behavior, and instrumentality in predicting procedural fairness. *Journal of Applied Psychology, 87*, 81–86.

Avolio, B. J., & Bass, B. M. (1991). *The full range leadership development program: Basic and advanced manuals*. Binghamton, NY: Bass, Avolio, and Associates.

Avolio, B. J., Bass, B. M., & Jung, D. I. (1999). Re-examining the components of transformational and transactional leadership using the Multifactor Leadership Questionnaire. *Journal of Occupational and Organizational Psychology, 72*, 441–462.

Avolio, B. J., & Gardner, W. L. (2005). Authentic leadership development: Getting to the root of positive forms of leadership. *Leadership Quarterly, 16*, 315–338.

Avolio, B. J., Kahai, S., Dumdum, R., & Sivasubramaniam, N. (2001). Virtual teams: Implications for e-leadership and team development. In M. London (Ed.), *How people evaluate others in organizations* (pp. 337–358). Mahwah, NJ: Erlbaum.

Avolio, B. J., & Sivasubramaniam, N. (2002). *Re-examining the components of the multifactor leadership theory: When too few is probably not enough.* Unpublished manuscript, Binghamton University, Binghamton, NY.

Axtell, C. M., Holman, D. J., & Wall, T. D. (2006). Promoting innovation: A change study. *Journal of Occupational and Organizational Psychology, 79*, 509–516.

Aycan, Z., Kanungo, R. N., Mendonca, M., Yu, K., Deller, J., Stahl, G., & Kurshid, A. (2000). Impact of culture on human resource management practices: A 10-country comparison. *Applied Psychology: An International Review, 49*(1), 192–221.

Ayoko, O. B., & Hartel, C. E. J. (2003). The role of space as both a conflict trigger and a conflict control mechanism in culturally heterogeneous workgroups. *Applied Psychology: An International Review, 52*, 383–412.

Bachiochi, P. D., & Weiner, S. P. (2002). Qualitative data collection and analysis. In S. G. Rogelberg (Ed.), *Handbook of research methods in industrial and organizational psychology* (pp. 161–183). Cambridge, MA: Blackwell.

Bachrach, D. G., Powell, B. C., Bendoly, E., & Richey, R. G. (2006). Organizational citizenship behavior and performance evaluations: Exploring the impact of task interdependence. *Journal of Applied Psychology, 91*, 193–201.

Baer, M., & Frese, M. (2002). Innovation is not enough: Climate for initiative and psychological safety, process innovation, and firm performance. *Journal of Organizational Behavior, 24*, 45–68.

Bagozzi, R. P., Verbeke, W., & Gavino, J. C. (2003). Culture moderates the self-regulation of shame and its effects on performance: The case of salespersons in the Netherlands and the Philippines. *Journal of Applied Psychology, 88*, 219–233.

Bakker, A. B., & Leiter, M. P. (Eds.). (2010). *Work engagement: A handbook of essential theory and research.* New York: Psychology Press.

Baldwin, T. T., & Ford, J. K. (1988). Transfer of training: A review and directions for future research. *Personnel Psychology, 41*, 63–105.

Baltes, B. B., Briggs, T. E., Huff, J. W., Wright, J. A., & Neuman, G. A. (1999). Flexible and compressed workweek schedules: A meta-analysis of their effects on work-related criteria. *Journal of Applied Psychology, 84*, 496–513.

Balzer, W. K., Smith, P. C., Kravitz, D. A., Lovell, S. E., Paul, K. B., Reilly, B. A., & Reilly, C. E. (1990). *User's manual for the Job Descriptive Index (JDI) and the Job in General (JIG) scales.* Bowling Green, OH: Bowling Green State University.

Bandura, A. (1986). *Social foundation of thought and action: A social cognitive theory.* Englewood Cliffs, NJ: Prentice Hall.

Bandura, A. (1997). *Self-efficacy: The exercise of control.* New York: W. H. Freeman.

Bandura, A. (2002). Social cognitive theory in cultural context. *Applied Psychology: An International Review, 51*, 269–290.

Banks, C. G., & Cohen, L. (2005). Wage and hour litigation: I-O psychology's new frontier. In F. J. Landy (Ed.), *Employment discrimination litigation: Behavioral, quantitative, and legal perspectives* (pp. 336–370). San Francisco: Jossey-Bass.

Banks, C. G., & May, K. E. (1999). Performance management: The real glue in organizations. In A. I. Kraut & A. K. Korman (Eds.), *Evolving practices in human resource management* (pp. 118–145). San Francisco: Jossey-Bass.

Banks, C. G., & Murphy, K. R. (1985). Toward narrowing the research–practice gap in performance appraisal. *Personnel Psychology, 38*, 335–345.

Barbian, J. (2002). A little help from your friends. *Training, 39*, 38–41.

Barboza, D. (2007, August 23). Scandal and suicide in China: A dark side of toys. *New York Times.*

Baritz, L. (1960). *Servants of power.* Middletown, CT: Wesleyan University Press.

Barling, J. (1996). The prediction, experience, and consequences of workplace violence. In G. R. Vandenbos & E. Q. Bulatao (Eds.), *Violence on the job: Identifying risks and developing solutions* (pp. 29–50). Washington, DC: American Psychological Association.

Barling, J., & Boswell, R. (1995). Work performance and the achievement strivings and impatience–irritability dimensions of Type A behavior. *Applied Psychology: An International Review, 44*, 143–153.

Barling, J., Kelloway, E. K., & Iverson, R. D. (2003). High-quality work, job satisfaction, and occupational injuries. *Journal of Applied Psychology, 88*, 276–283.

Barnes, G. M., & Morgeson, F. P. (2007). Typical performance, maximal performance, and performance variability: Expanding our understanding of how organizations value performance. *Human Performance, 20*, 259–274.

Barney, M. (2002). Six Sigma. *The Industrial-Organizational Psychologist, 39*(4), 104–107.

Baron, H., & Chaudry, A. (1997). A multi-media approach to assessing customer service potential. *SHL Research Division: Research Note.*

Baron, R. A. (1988). Negative effects of destructive criticism: Impact on conflict, self-efficacy, and task performance. *Journal of Applied Psychology, 73*, 199–207.

Baron, R. A. (1990). Countering the effects of destructive criticism: The relative efficacy of four interventions. *Journal of Applied Psychology, 75*, 235–245.

Baron, R. A. (2000a). Counterfactual thinking and venture formation: The potential effects of thinking about "what might have been." *Journal of Business Venturing, 15*, 79–92.

Baron, R. A. (2000b). Psychological perspectives on entrepreneurship: Cognitive and social factors in entrepreneurs' success. *Current Directions in Psychological Science, 9*, 15–18.

Baron, R. A. (2002). OB and entrepreneurship: The reciprocal benefits of closer conceptual links. *Research in Organizational Behavior, 24*, 225–269.

Baron, R. A. (2003). Human resource management and entrepreneurship: Some reciprocal benefits of closer links. *Human Resource Management Review, 13*, 253–256.

Baron, R. A. (2004). Workplace aggression and violence: Insights from basic research. In R. W. Griffin & V. O'LearyKelly (Eds.), *The dark side of organizational behavior* (pp. 23–61). San Francisco: Jossey-Bass.

Baron, R. A., & Ensley, M. D. (2006). Opportunity recognition as the detection of meaningful patterns: Evidence from comparisons of novice and experienced entrepreneurs. *Management Science, 52*, 1331–1344.

Baron, R. A., & Markman, G. D. (2000). Beyond social capital: How social skills can enhance entrepreneurial success. *Academy of Management Executive, 14*, 106–116.

Baron, R. A., & Tang, J. (2009). Entrepreneurs' social skills and new venture performance: Mediating mechanisms and cultural generality. *Journal of Management, 35*, 282–306.

Baron, R. S. (2005). So right it's wrong: Groupthink and the ubiquitous nature of polarized group decision making. In M. P. Zanna (Ed.), *Advances in experimental social psychology* (Vol. 37, pp. 219–253). San Diego, CA: Elsevier Academic Press.

Barrett, G. V. (2001). *Emotional intelligence: The Madison Avenue approach to professional practice.* Paper presented at the 16th annual conference of the Society for Industrial and Organizational Psychology, San Diego, CA.

Barrett, G. V., & Kernan, M. C. (1987). Performance appraisal and termination: A review of court decisions since *Brito* v. *Zia* with implications for personnel practices. *Personnel Psychology, 40*, 489–503.

Barrick, M. R., & Mount, M. K. (1991). The Big Five personality dimensions and job performance. A meta-analysis. *Personnel Psychology, 44*, 1–26.

Barrick, M. R., & Mount, M. K. (1993). Autonomy as a moderator between the Big Five personality dimensions and job performance. *Journal of Applied Psychology, 78*, 111–118.

Barrick, M. R., & Mount, M. K. (2005). Yes, personality matters: Moving on to more important matters. *Human Performance, 18*, 359–372.

Barrick, M. R., Mount, M. K., & Judge, T. A. (2001). Personality and performance at the beginning of the new millennium: What do we know and where do we go next? *International Journal of Selection and Assessment, 9*, 9–30.

Barrick, M. R., Stewart, G. L., Neubert, M. J., & Mount, M. K. (1998). Relating member ability and personality to work-team processes and team effectiveness. *Journal of Applied Psychology, 83*, 377–391.

Barry, B., & Stewart, G. L. (1997). Composition, process, and performance in self-managed groups: The role of personality. *Journal of Applied Psychology, 82*, 62–78.

Barsade, S. G., & Gibson, D. E. (2007). Why does affect matter in organizations? *Academy of Management Perspectives, 21*, 36–59.

Bartol, K. M., Durham, C. C., & Poon, J. M. (2001). Influence of performance evaluation rating segmentation on motivation and fairness perceptions. *Journal of Applied Psychology, 86*, 1106–1119.

Barton, J. (1994). Choosing to work at night: A moderating influence on individual tolerance to shift work. *Journal of Applied Psychology, 79*, 449–454.

Bartone, P. T., Roland, R. R., Picano, J. J., & Williams, T. J. (2008). Psychological hardiness predicts success in U.S. Army Special Forces candidates. *International Journal of Selection and Assessment, 16*, 78–90.

Bartram, D. (2002). Assessment center validity: Has it dropped? *SHL Research Division*, Research Note, March.

Bartram, D. (2005). The Great Eight competencies: A criterion-centric approach to validation. *Journal of Applied Psychology, 90*, 1185–1203.

Bartram, D. (2007). Increasing validity with forced-choice criterion measurement formats. *International Journal of Selection and Assessment, 15*, 263–272.

Bass, B. M. (1960). *Leadership, psychology, and organizational behavior.* New York: Harper & Row.

Bass, B. M., & Avolio, B. J. (1997). *Full range leadership development: Manual for the Multifactor Leadership Questionnaire.* Palo Alto, CA: Mindgarden.

Bass, B. M., & Steidlmeier, P. (1999). Ethics, character, and authentic transformational leadership behavior. *Leadership Quarterly, 10*, 181–217.

Bauer, T. N., Bodner, T., Erdogan, B., Truxillo, D. M., & Tucker, J. S. (2007). Newcomer adjustment during organizational socialization: A meta-analytic review of antecedents, outcomes, and methods. *Journal of Applied Psychology, 92*, 707–721.

Bauer, T. N., Erdogan, B., Liden, R. C., & Wayne, S. J. (2006). A longitudinal study of the moderating role of extraversion: Leader–member exchange, performance, and turnover during new executive development. *Journal of Applied Psychology, 91*, 298–310.

Bauer, T. N., Morrison, E. W., & Callister, R. R. (1998). Organizational solutions. *Research in Personnel and Human Resources Management, 16*, 178–214.

Bauer, T. N., & Taylor, S. (2001). Toward a globalized conceptualization of organizational socializations. In N. Anderson, D. Ones, & C. Viswesvaran (Eds.), *Handbook of industrial, work, and organizational psychology* (Vol. 1, pp. 409–423). London: Sage.

Bauer, T. N., Truxillo, D. M., Paronto, M. E., Weekley, J. A., & Campion, M. A. (2004). Applicant reactions to different selection technology: Face-to-face, interactive voice response, and computer-assisted telephone screening interviews. *International Journal of Selection and Assessment, 12*, 135–148.

Baum, J. R., & Locke, E. A. (2004). The relationship of entrepreneurial traits, skills, and motivation to subsequent venture growth. *Journal of Applied Psychology, 89*, 587–598.

Baumeister, R. F., Smart, L., & Boden, J. M. (1996). Relation of threatened egotism to violence and aggression: The dark side of self-esteem. *Psychological Review, 103*, 5–33.

Beal, D. J., Cohen, R. R., Burke, M. J., & McLendon, C. L. (2003). Cohesion and performance in groups: A meta-analytic clarification of construct relations. *Journal of Applied Psychology, 88*, 989–1004.

Beal, D. J., Weiss, H. M., Barros, E., & MacDermid. (2005). An episodic process model of affective influences on performance. *Journal of Applied Psychology, 90*, 1054–1068.

Beaty, J. C., Jr., Cleveland, J. C., & Murphy, K. R. (2001). The relation between personality and contextual performance in "strong" versus "weak" situations. *Human Performance, 14*, 125–148.

Becker, T. E., & Kernan, M. C. (2003). Matching commitments to supervisors and organizations to in-role and extra-role performance. *Human Performance, 16*, 327–348.

Beer, M., Eisenstat, R. A., & Spector, B. (1990). *The critical path to corporate renewal.* Boston: Harvard Business School.

Belbin, R. M. (1981). *Management teams: Why they succeed or fail.* London: Heinemann.

Belbin, R. M. (1993). *Team roles at work.* London: Butterworth-Heinemann.

Belkin, M. (2008, June 12). Why Dad's résumé lists car pool. *New York Times*, pp. C1–C2.

Bell, B. S., & Kozlowski, S. W. J. (2002). Adaptive guidance: Enhancing self-regulation, knowledge and performance in technology-based training. *Personnel Psychology, 55*, 267–306.

Bell, B. S., & Kozlowski, S. J. (2008). Active learning: Effects of core training design elements on self-regulatory processes, learning, and adaptability. *Journal of Applied Psychology, 93*, 296–316.

Bell, B. S., Wiechmann, D., & Ryan, A. M. (2006). Consequences of organizational justice expectations in a selection system. *Journal of Applied Psychology, 91*, 455–466.

Bell, S. T. (2007). Deep-level composition variables as predictors of team performance: A meta-analysis. *Journal of Applied Psychology, 92*, 595–615.

Bellavia, G., & Frone, M. R. (2005). Work–family conflict. In J. Barling, E. K. Kelloway, & M. R. Frone (Eds.), *Handbook of work stress.* Thousand Oaks, CA: Sage.

Ben-Shakhar, G., Bar-Hillel, M., Bilu, Y., Ben-Abba, E., & Flug, A. (1986). Can graphology predict occupational success? Two empirical studies and some methodological ruminations. *Journal of Applied Psychology, 71*, 645–653.

Benjamin, L. T. (1997). A history of Division 14 (The Society for Industrial and Organizational Psychology). In D. A. Dewsbury (Ed.), *Unification through division: Histories of the divisions of the American Psychological Association* (Vol. 2, pp. 459–466). Washington, DC: American Psychological Association.

Benjamin, L. T., Jr. (2003). Harry Hollingworth and the shame of applied psychology. In D. B. Baker (Ed.), *Thick description and fine texture* (pp. 38–56). Akron, OH: University of Akron Press.

Benjamin, L. T., Jr. (2006). Hugo Munsterberg's attack on the application of scientific psychology. *Journal of Applied Psychology, 91*, 414–425.

Bennett, J. B., & Lehman, W. E. (2001). Workplace substance abuse prevention and help seeking: Comparing team-oriented and informational training. *Journal of Occupational Health Psychology, 6*, 243–254.

Bentein, K., Stinglhamber, F., & Vandenberghe, C. (2002). Organization-, supervisor-, and workgroup-directed commitments and citizenship behaviors: A comparison of models. *European Journal of Work and Organizational Psychology, 11*, 341–362.

Bentein, K., Vandenberg, R., Vandenberghe, C., & Stinglhamber, F. (2005). The role of change in the relationship between commitment and turnover: A latent growth modeling approach. *Journal of Applied Psychology, 90*, 468–482.

Bernardin, H. J., Dahmus, S. A., & Redmon, G. (1993). Attitudes of first-line supervisors toward subordinate appraisals. *Human Resource Management Journal, 32*, 315–324.

Bernardin, H. J., Hennessey, H. W., & Peyfritte, J. (1995). Age, racial, and gender bias as a function of criterion specificity: A test of expert testimony. *Human Resource Management Review, 5*, 63–77.

Bernardin, H. J., & Pence, E. C. (1980). Effects of rater training: Creating new response sets and decreasing accuracy. *Journal of Applied Psychology, 65,* 60–66.

Bernerth, J. B., Armenakis, A. A., Field, H. S., Giles, W. F., & Walker, H. J. (2007). Leader–member social exchange (LMSX): Development and validation of a scale. *Journal of Organizational Behavior, 28,* 979–1003.

Berry, C. M., Gruys, M. L., & Sackett, P. R. (2006). Educational attainment as a proxy for cognitive ability in selection: Effects on levels of cognitive ability and adverse impact. *Journal of Applied Psychology, 91,* 696–705.

Berry, C. M., Ones, D. S., & Sackett, P. R. (2007). Interpersonal deviance, organizational deviance, and their common correlates: A review and meta-analysis. *Journal of Applied Psychology, 92,* 410–424.

Berry, C. M., Sackett, P. R., & Tobares, V. (2010). A meta-analysis of conditional reasoning tests of aggression. *Personnel Psychology, 63,* 361–384.

Bertolino, M., & Steiner, D. D. (2007). Fairness reactions to selection methods: An Italian study. *International Journal of Selection and Assessment, 15,* 197–205.

Bertua, C., Anderson, N., & Salgado, J. F. (2005). The predictive validity of cognitive ability tests: A UK meta-analysis. *Journal of Occupational and Organizational Psychology, 78,* 387–409.

Bettenhausen, K. L. (1991). Five years of groups research: What we have learned and what needs to be addressed. *Journal of Management, 17,* 345–381.

Beugre, C. D. (2010). Resistance to socialization into organizational corruption: A model of deontic justice. *Journal of Business and Psychology, 25,* 533–541.

Beus, J. M., Payne, S. C., Bergman, M. E., & Arthur, W. A. (2010). Safety climate and injuries: An examination of theoretical and empirical relationships. *Journal of Applied Psychology, 95,* 713–727.

Bhawuk, D. P. S. (1998). The role of culture theory in cross-cultural training: A multimethod study of culture-specific, culture-general, and culture theory-based assimilators. *Journal of Cross-Cultural Psychology, 29,* 630–655.

Bhawuk, D. P. S., & Brislin, R. W. (2000). Cross-cultural training: A review. *Applied Psychology: An International Review, 49,* 162–191.

Bies, R. J., & Moag, J. S. (1986). Interaction justice: Communication criteria for fairness. *Research on Negotiation in Organization, 1,* 43–55.

Bies, R. J., & Tripp, T. M. (2005). The study of revenge in the workplace: Conceptual, ideological, and empirical issues. In S. Fox & P. E. Spector (Eds.), *Counterproductive work behavior: Investigations of actors and targets* (pp. 65–81). Washington, DC: American Psychological Association.

Bing, M. N., Stewart, S. M., Davison, H. K., Green, P. D., McIntyre, M. D., & James, L. R. (2007). An integrative typology of personality assessment for aggression: Implications for predicting counterproductive workplace behavior. *Journal of Applied Psychology, 92,* 722–744.

Bing, M. N., Whanger, J. C., Davison, H. K., & VanHook, J. B. (2004). Incremental validity of the frame-of-reference effect in personality scale scores: A replication and extension. *Journal of Applied Psychology, 89,* 150–157.

Bingham, W. V., & Moore, B. V. (1931). *How to interview.* New York: Harper Brothers.

Binning, J. F., & Barrett, G. V. (1989). Validity of personnel decisions: A conceptual analysis of the inferential and evidential bases. *Journal of Applied Psychology, 74,* 478–494.

Birkeland, S. A., Manson, T. M., Kisamore, J. L., Brannick, M. T., & Smith, M. A. (2006). A meta-analytic investigation of job applicant faking on personality measures. *International Journal of Selection and Assessment, 14,* 317–335.

Blakely, G. L., Blakely, E. H., & Moorman, R. H. (1998). The effects of training on perceptions of sexual harassment allegations. *Journal of Applied Social Psychology, 28,* 71–83.

Blau, G. (1994). Developing and testing a taxonomy of lateness behavior. *Journal of Applied Psychology, 79,* 959–970.

Blau, G. (2003). Testing a four-dimensional structure of occupational commitment. *Journal of Occupational and Organizational Psychology, 76,* 469–480.

Bligh, M. C., Kohles, J. C., Pearce, C. L., Justin, J. E., & Stovall, J. F. (2007). When the romance is over: Follower perspectives of aversive leadership. *Applied Psychology: An International Review, 56,* 528–557.

Bluedorn, A. C. (2002). *The human organization of time: Temporal realities and experience.* Stanford, CA: Stanford University Press.

Bluen, S. D., Barling, J., & Burns, W. (1990). Predicting sales performance, job satisfaction, and depression by using the achievement strivings and impatience–irritability dimensions of Type A behavior. *Journal of Applied Psychology, 75,* 212–216.

Bluestone, B., & Rose, S. (1997). Overworked and underemployed: Unraveling an economic engine. *The American Prospect On-line, 31.* Retrieved March 6, 2003, from www.prospect.org/archives/31/31bluefs.html

Bobko, P., Roth, P. L., & Potosky, D. (1999). Derivation and implications of meta-analytic matrix incorporating cognitive abilities, alternative predictors, and job performance. *Personnel Psychology, 52,* 561–589.

Bobocel, D. R., & Zdaniuk, A. (2005). How can explanations be used to foster organizational justice? In J. Greenberg & J. A. Colquitt (Eds.), *Handbook of organizational justice* (pp. 469–498). Mahwah, NJ: Erlbaum.

Bohle, P., & Tilley, A. J. (1998). Early experience on shiftwork: Influences on attitudes. *Journal of Occupational and Organizational Psychology, 71,* 61–79.

Bolino, M. C., & Turnley, W. H. (2008). Old faces, new places: Equity theory in cross-cultural contexts. *Journal of Organizational Behavior, 29,* 29–50.

Bommer, W. H., Johnson, J. L., Rich, G. A., Podsakoff, P. M., & McKenzie, S. B. (1995). On the interchangeability of objective and subjective measures of employee performance: A meta-analysis. *Personnel Psychology, 48,* 587–605.

Bommer, W. H., Rich, G. A., & Rubin, R. S. (2005). Changing attitudes about change: Longitudinal effects of transformational leader behavior on employee cynicism about organizational change. *Journal of Organizational Behavior, 26,* 733–753.

Bonett, D. G., & Wright, T. A. (2007). Comments and recommendations regarding the hypothesis testing controversy. *Journal of Organizational Behavior, 28,* 647–659.

Bono, J. E., & Anderson, M. H. (2005) Advice and influence networks of transformational leaders. *Journal of Applied Psychology, 90,* 1306–1314.

Bono, J. E., Foldes, H. J., Vinson, G., & Muros, J. P. (2007). Workplace emotions: The role of supervision and leadership. *Journal of Applied Psychology, 92,* 1357–1367.

Bono, J. E., & Judge, T. A. (2004). Personality and transformational and transactional leadership: A meta-analysis. *Journal of Applied Psychology, 89,* 901–910.

Bordia, P., & Blau, G. (2003). Moderating effect of allocentrism on the pay referent comparison–pay level satisfaction relationship. *Applied Psychology: An International Review, 52,* 499–514.

Borman, W. C. (2004a). Introduction to the special issue. Personality and the prediction of job performance: More than the Big Five. *Human Performance, 17,* 267–269.

Borman, W. C. (2004b). The concept of organizational citizenship. *Current Directions in Psychological Science, 13,* 238–241.

Borman, W. C., & Brush, D. H. (1993). More progress toward a taxonomy of managerial performance requirements. *Human Performance, 6,* 1–21.

Borman, W. C., Buck, D. E., Hanson, M. A., Motowidlo, S. J., Stark, S., & Drasgow, F. (2001). An examination of the comparative reliability, validity, and accuracy of performance ratings made using computerized adaptive rating scales. *Journal of Applied Psychology, 86,* 965–973.

Borman, W. C., Houston, J. S., Schneider, R. J., & Ferstl, K. L. (2008). *Adaptive personality scales: The concept and initial validation results.* Presentation at Personnel Decisions Research Institute, Tampa, FL.

Borman, W. C., & Motowidlo, S. J. (1993). Expanding the criterion domain to include elements of contextual performance. In N. Schmitt & W. C. Borman (Eds.), *Personnel selection in organizations* (pp. 71–98). San Francisco: Jossey-Bass.

Borman, W. C., Penner, L. A., Allen, T. D., & Motowidlo, S. J. (2001). Personality predictors of citizenship performance. *International Journal of Selection and Assessment, 9,* 52–69.

Boselie, P., Dietz, G., & Boon, C. (2005). Commonalities and contradictions in HRM and performance research. *Human Resource Management Journal, 15*(3), 67–94.

Boswell, W. R., Olson-Buchanan, J. B., & LePine, M. A. (2004). Relations between stress and work outcomes: The role of felt challenge, job control, and psychological strain. *Journal of Vocational Behavior, 64,* 165–181.

Botan, C. (1996). Communication work and electronic surveillance. *Communication Monographs, 63,* 293–313.

Bouchard, T. J., Jr. (2004). Genetic influence on human psychological traits. *Current Directions in Psychological Science, 13*(4), 148–151.

Bowe, J., Bowe, M., & Streeter, S. (2000). *Gig: Americans talk about their jobs at the turn of the millennium.* New York: Three Rivers Press.

Bowers, B. (2008, June 12). Six months later, start-ups find their goals are elusive. *New York Times,* p. C10.

Bowler, M. C., & Woehr, D. J. (2006). A meta-analytic evaluation of the impact of dimension and exercise factors on assessment center ratings. *Journal of Applied Psychology, 91,* 1114–1124.

Bowling, N. A., & Beehr, T. A. (2006). Workplace harassment from the victim's perspective: A theoretical model and meta-analysis. *Journal of Applied Psychology, 91,* 998–1012.

Bowling, N. A., Hendricks, E. A., & Wagner, S. H. (2008). Positive and negative affectivity and facet satisfaction: A meta-analysis. *Journal of Business and Psychology, 23,* 115–125.

Boyd, C. (2002). Customer violence and employee health and safety. *Work, Employment and Society, 16*(1), 151–169.

Brannick, M. T., Levine, E. L., & Morgeson, F. P. (2007). *Job and work analysis: Methods, research and applications for human resource management* (2nd ed.). Thousand Oaks, CA: Sage.

Brannick, M. T., Prince, C., & Salas, E. (2005). Can PC-based systems enhance teamwork in the cockpit? *International Journal of Aviation Psychology, 15,* 173–187.

Bray, D. W., Campbell, R. J., & Grant, D. L. (1974). *Formative years in business: A long-term AT&T study of managerial lives.* New York: Wiley.

Brayfield, A. H., & Crockett, W. H. (1955). Employee attitudes and employee performance. *Psychological Bulletin, 52,* 396–424.

Brett, J. M., Tinsley, C. H., Janssens, M., Barsness, Z. I., & Lytle, A. L. (1997). New approaches to the study of culture in industrial/organizational psychology. In P. C. Earley & M. Erez (Eds.), *New perspectives on international industrial/organizational psychology* (pp. 75–129). San Francisco: Jossey-Bass.

Brief, A. P., & Weiss, H. M. (2002). Organizational behavior: Affect in the workplace. *Annual Review of Psychology, 53,* 279–307.

Briner, R. B., & Reynolds, S. (1999). The costs, benefits, and limitations of organizational level stress interventions. *Journal of Organizational Behavior, 20,* 647–664.

Briner, R. B., & Rousseau, D. M. (2011). Evidence-based I-O psychology: Not there yet. *Industrial and Organizational Psychology: Perspectives on Science and Practice, 4,* 3–22.

Brislin, R. W., & Kim, E. S. (2003). Cultural diversity in people's understanding and uses of time. *Applied Psychology: An International Review, 52,* 363–382.

Brockner, J., & Weisenfeld, B. M. (1996). An integrative framework for explaining reactions to decisions: Interactive effects of outcomes and procedures. *Psychological Bulletin, 120,* 189–208.

Brodbeck, F. (1996). Work group performance and effectiveness: Conceptual and measurement issues. In M. A. West (Ed.), *Handbook of work group psychology.* Chichester, UK: Wiley.

Brodbeck, F. C., Frese, M., Akerblom, S., Audia, G., Bakacsi, G., Bendova, H., Bodega, D., et al. (2000). Cultural variation of leadership prototypes across 22 European countries. *Journal of Occupational and Organizational Psychology, 73,* 1–29.

Brooks, D. (2003, September). People like us. *The Atlantic Monthly,* pp. 29–32.

Brown, K. G. (2001). Using computers to deliver training: Which employees learn and why? *Personnel Psychology, 54,* 271–296.

Brown, K. G., & Ford, J. K. (2002). Using computer technology in training: Building an infrastructure for active learning. In K. Kraiger (Ed.), *Creating, implementing, and managing effective training and development* (pp. 192–233). San Francisco: Jossey-Bass.

Brown, K. G., & Gerhardt, M. W. (2002). Formative evaluation: An integrative practice model and case study. *Personnel Psychology, 55,* 951–983.

Brown, K. G., Le, H., & Schmidt, F. L. (2006). Specific aptitude theory revisited: Is there incremental validity for training performance? *International Journal of Selection and Assessment, 14,* 87–100.

Brown, R. P., & Day, E. A. (2006). The difference isn't black and white: Stereotype threat and the race gap on Raven's Advanced Progressive Matrices. *Journal of Applied Psychology, 91,* 979–985.

Brown, V. R., & Vaughn, E. D. (2011). The writing on the (Facebook) wall: The use of social networking sites in hiring decisions. *Journal of Business and Psychology, 26,* 219–225.

Bruggemann, A., Groskurth, P., & Ulich, E. (1975). *Arbeitszufriedenheit.* Bern, Switzerland: Huber.

Bruk-Lee, V., & Spector, P. E. (2006). The social stressors–counterproductive work behaviors link: Are conflicts with supervisors and coworkers the same? *Journal of Occupational Health Psychology, 11,* 145–156.

Brunet v. City of Columbus. (1995). 6th Circuit 58 F.2d 251.

Buckley, C., & Rashbaum, W. K. (2006, November 27). A day after a fatal shooting, questions, mourning and protest. *New York Times.* Retrieved July 31, 2008, from www.nytimes.com/2006/11/27/nyregion/27shot.html?_r=1&oref=slogin

Buckley, M. R., Riaz Hamdani, M., Klotz, A. C., & Valcea, S. (2011). Into the great wide open: Bridging the micro-macro divide in the organizational sciences. In D. D. Bergh & D. J. Ketchen (Eds.), *Building methodological bridges: Vol. 6. Research methodology in strategy and management* (pp. 31–68). Bingley, UK: Emerald Group Publishing.

Bulatao, E. Q., & Vandenbos, G. R. (1996). Workplace violence: Its scope and issues. In G. R. Vandenbos & E. Q. Bulatao (Eds.), *Violence on the job: Identifying risks and developing solutions* (pp. 1–23). Washington, DC: American Psychological Association.

Bunkley, N. (2008, March 30). To protest fuel prices, truckers plan strike. *New York Times*, p. A05.

Burke, M. J., Borucki, C. C., & Kaufman, J. D. (2002). Contemporary perspectives on the study of psychological climate: A commentary. *European Journal of Work and Organizational Psychology, 11*(3), 325–340.

Burlington Industries v. Ellerth (1998). 118 S. Ct. 2257.

Burns, J. M. (1978). *Leadership*. New York: Harper & Row.

Burns, T., & Stalker, G. M. (1961). *The management of innovation.* London: Tavistock.

Burt, R., & Knez, M. (1995). Kinds of third party effects on trust. *Journal of Rational Sociology, 7*, 255–292.

Business and Legal Reports. (2005a). Judge says Dial must pay $3m in bias suit over strength test. HR.BLR.com, October 3. Retrieved October 10, 2005, from hr.blr.com/display.cfm?id=16737

Business and Legal Reports. (2005b). What is the definition of "job applicant"? HR.BLR.com, October 7. Retrieved October 10, 2005, from hr.blr.com/display.cfm?id=16758

Büssing, A. (1992). A dynamic view of job satisfaction. *Work and Stress, 6*, 239–259.

Büssing, A. (2002). Motivation and satisfaction. In A. Sorge (Ed.), *Organization* (pp. 371–387). London: Thomson Learning.

Büssing, A., & Bissels, T. (1998). Different forms of work satisfaction: Concept and qualitative research. *European Psychologist, 3*, 209–218.

Buster, M. A., Roth, P. L., & Bobko, P. (2005). A process for content validation of education and experience-based minimum qualifications: An approach resulting in federal court approval. *Personnel Psychology, 58*, 771–799.

Butler, A. B. (2007). Job characteristics and college performance and attitudes: A model of work–school conflict and facilitation. *Journal of Applied Psychology, 92*, 500–510.

Cable, D. M., Aiman-Smith, L., Mulvey, P. W., & Edwards, J. R. (2000). The sources and accuracy of job applicants' beliefs about organizational culture. *Academy of Management Journal, 43*, 1076–1085.

Cable, D. M., & Edwards, J. R. (2004). Complementary and supplementary fit: A theoretical and empirical integration. *Journal of Applied Psychology, 89*, 822–834.

Cable, D. M., & Judge, T. A. (1996). Person–organization fit, job choice decisions, and organizational entry. *Organizational Behavior and Human Decision Processes, 67*, 294–311.

Cable, D. M., & Judge, T. A. (1997). Interviewers' perceptions of person–organization fit and organizational selection decisions. *Journal of Applied Psychology, 82*, 562–577.

Cable, D. M., & Parsons, C. K. (2001). Socialization tactics and person–organization fit. *Personnel Psychology, 54*, 1–23.

Cadinu, M., Maass, A., Rosabianca, A., & Kiesner, J. (2005). Why do women underperform under stereotype threat? Evidence for the role of negative thinking. *Psychological Science, 16*, 572–578.

Caher, J. (2003, July 14). NY rejects Fla. telecommuter's bid. *The National Law Journal*, p. 15.

Caligiuri, P. M., Hyland, M. M., Bross, A. S., & Joshi, A. (1998). Testing a theoretical model for examining the relationship between family adjustment and expatriate's work adjustment. *Journal of Applied Psychology, 83*, 598–614.

Caliguri, P. M., Tarique, I., & Jacobs, R. R. (2009). Selection for international assignments. *Human Resource Management Review, 19*(3), 251–262.

Campbell, J. P. (1990). The role of theory in industrial and organizational psychology. In M. D. Dunnette & L. M. Hough (Eds.), *Handbook of industrial and organizational psychology* (pp. 39–74). Palo Alto, CA: Consulting Psychologists Press.

Campbell, J. P. (1999). The definition and measurement of performance in the new age. In D. R. Ilgen & E. D. Pulakos (Eds.), *The changing nature of performance* (pp. 399–430). San Francisco: Jossey-Bass.

Campbell, J. P., & Campbell, R. J. (1988). *Productivity in organizations: New perspectives from industrial and organizational psychology.* San Francisco: Jossey-Bass.

Campbell, J. P., Gasser, M. B., & Oswald, F. L. (1996). The substantive nature of job performance variability. In K. R. Murphy (Ed.), *Individual differences and behavior in organizations* (pp. 258–299). San Francisco: Jossey-Bass.

Campbell, J. P., McCloy, R. A., Oppler, S. H., & Sager, C. E. (1993). A theory of performance. In N. Schmitt & W. C. Borman (Eds.), *Personnel selection in organizations* (pp. 35–70). San Francisco: Jossey-Bass.

Campbell, J. P., McHenry, J. J., & Wise, L. L. (1990). Modeling job performance in a population of jobs. *Personnel Psychology, 43*, 313–333.

Campion, M. A., Cheraskin, L., & Stevens, M. J. (1994). Career-related antecedents and outcomes of job rotation. *Academy of Management Journal, 37*, 1518–1542.

Campion, M. A., Fink, A. A., Ruggeberg, B. J., Carr, L., Phillips, G. M., & Odman, R. B. (2011). Doing competencies well: Best practices in competency modeling. *Personnel Psychology, 64*, 225–262.

Campion, M. A., Medsker, G. J., & Higgs, A. C. (1993). Relations between work group characteristics and effectiveness: Implications for designing effective work groups. *Personnel Psychology, 46*, 823–850.

Campion, M. A., Papper, E. M., & Medsker, G. J. (1996). Relations between work team characteristics and effectiveness: A replication and extension. *Personnel Psychology, 49*, 429–452.

Cannon, W. B. (1929). *Bodily changes in pain, hunger, fear, and rage.* New York: Appleton-Century.

Cannon-Bowers, J. A., Oser, R., & Flanagan, D. L. (1992). Work teams in industry: A selected review and a proposed framework. In R. W. Swezey & E. Salas (Eds.), *Teams: Their training and performance* (pp. 355–378). Stamford, CT: Ablex.

Cannon-Bowers, J. A., Tannenbaum, S. I., Salas, E., & Volpe, C. E. (1995). Defining competencies and establishing team training requirements. In R. A. Guzzo & E. Salas (Eds.), *Team effectiveness and decision making in organizations* (pp. 333–380). San Francisco: Jossey-Bass.

Caponecchia, C., & Wyatt, A. (2011). *Preventing workplace bullying: An evidence-based guide for managers and employees.* New York: Routledge/Taylor & Francis.

Caprara, G. V., Steca, P., Zelli, A., & Capanna, C. (2005). A new scale for measuring adults' prosocialness. *European Journal of Psychological Assessment, 20*, 77–89.

Carless, S. A., Fewings-Hall, S., Hall, M., Hay, M., Hemsworth, P. H., & Coleman, G. J. (2007). Selecting unskilled and semi-skilled blue-collar workers: The criterion-related validity of the PDI-employment inventory. *International Journal of Selection and Assessment, 15*, 337–342.

Caro, R. A. (2002). *Master of the Senate: The years of Lyndon Johnson.* New York: Knopf.

Carr, J. Z., Schmidt, A. M., Ford, J. K., & DeShon, R. P. (2003). Climate perceptions matter: A meta-analytic path analysis relating molar climate, cognitive and affective states, and individual level work outcomes. *Journal of Applied Psychology, 88*, 605–619.

Carr, S. (2012). Pro-social I-O: Project Organizational Gini Coefficient. *The Industrial-Organizational Psychologist, 49*(3), 102–104.

Carr, S. C. (2005, September 1–4). *I/O psychology and poverty reduction: Back to making a difference?* Paper presented at the New Zealand Psychological Society annual conference, Dunedin.

Carr, S. C. (2007). I-O psychology and poverty reduction: Past, present, and future. *The Industrial-Organizational Psychologist, 44*(3), 49–55.

Carroll, J. B. (1993). *Human cognitive abilities: A survey of factor-analytic studies.* Cambridge, UK: Cambridge University Press.

Carroll, W. R. (2008). The effects of electronic performance monitoring on performance outcomes: A review and meta-analysis. *Employee Rights and Employment Policy Journal, 12*(1), 29–48.

Carter, G. W., Dorsey, D. W., & Niehaus, W. J. (2004, April). The use of transactional data in occupational analysis: Textmining of on-line job listings. In J. M. Ford (Chair), *Automated text analysis in I/O psychology: Research to practice.* Symposium conducted at the 19th annual conference of the Society for Industrial and Organizational Psychology, Chicago.

Cartwright, S., & Cooper, C. L. (2005). Individually targeted interventions. In J. Barling, E. K. Kelloway, & M. R. Frone (Eds.), *Handbook of work stress* (pp. 607–622). Thousand Oaks, CA: Sage.

Cascio, W. F. (1998a). *Applied psychology in human resource management* (5th ed.). Englewood Cliffs, NJ: Prentice Hall.

Cascio, W. F. (1998b). *Managing human resources* (5th ed.). New York: McGraw-Hill.

Cascio, W. F. (1998c). The virtual workplace: A reality now. *The Industrial-Organizational Psychologist, 35*(4), 32–36.

Cascio, W. F. (2000a). *Costing human resources: The financial impact of behavior in organizations* (4th ed.). Cincinnati, OH: Southwestern.

Cascio, W. F. (2000b). Managing a virtual workplace. *Academy of Management Executive, 14,* 81–90.

Cascio, W. F. (2006). *Managing human resources: Productivity, quality of work life, profits* (7th ed.). Burr Ridge, IL: Irwin/McGraw-Hill.

Cascio, W. F. (2010). *Managing human resources: Productivity, quality of work life, profits* (8th ed.). Burr Ridge, IL: Irwin/McGraw-Hill.

Cascio, W. F., & Aguinis, H. (2008). Staffing 21st-century organizations. In J. P. Walsh & A. P. Brief (Eds.), *Academy of Management Annals* (Vol. 2). Retrieved from carbon.cudenver.edu/~haguinis/AOMAnnals.pdf

Cascio, W. F., & Aguinis, H. (2011). *Applied psychology in human resource management* (7th ed.). Englewood Cliffs, NJ: Prentice Hall.

Casimir, G. (2001). Combinative aspects of leadership style: The ordering and temporal spacing of leadership behaviors. *Leadership Quarterly, 12,* 245–278.

Catalano, R., Novaco, R., & McConnell, W. (1997). A model of the net effect of job loss on violence. *Journal of Personality and Social Psychology, 72,* 1440–1447.

Cawley, B. D., Keeping, L. M., & Levy, P. E. (1998). Participation in the performance appraisal process and employee reactions: A metaanalytic review of field investigations. *Journal of Applied Psychology, 83,* 615–633.

Centers for Disease Control and Prevention (2011). *Heart disease and stroke prevention. Addressing the nation's leading killers: At a glance 2011.* Retrieved 12/26/2011 from http://www.cdc.gov/chronicdisease/resources/publications/AAG/dhdsp.htm

Centra, J. A. (1993). *Reflective faculty evaluation.* San Francisco: Jossey-Bass.

Cervone, D., Shadel, W. G., Smith, R. E., & Fiori, M. (2006). Self-regulation: Reminders and suggestions from personality science. *Applied Psychology: An International Review, 55,* 333–385.

Chadwick-Jones, J. K., Nicholson, N., & Brown, C. (1982). *The social psychology of absenteeism.* New York: Praeger.

Chan, D. (2004). Individual differences in tolerance for contradiction. *Human Performance, 17,* 297–324.

Chan, D., & Schmitt, N. (1997). Video based versus paper and pencil method of assessment in situational judgment tests: Subgroup differences in test performance and face validity perceptions. *Journal of Applied Psychology, 82,* 143–159.

Chan, D., & Schmitt, N. (2002). Situational judgment and job performance. *Human Performance, 15,* 233–254.

Chan, D., & Schmitt, N. (2004). An agenda for future research on applicant reactions to selection procedures: A construct-oriented approach. *International Journal of Selection and Assessment, 12,* 9–23.

Chan, D., & Schmitt, N. (2005). Situational judgment tests. In N. Anderson, A. Evers, & O. Voskuijil (Eds.), *Blackwell handbook of personnel selection* (pp. 292–342). Oxford, UK: Blackwell.

Chan, K., & Drasgow, F. (2001). Toward a theory of individual differences and leadership: Understanding the motivation to lead. *Journal of Applied Psychology, 86,* 481–498.

Chao, G. T., & Moon, H. (2005). The cultural mosaic: A metatheory for understanding the complexity of culture. *Journal of Applied Psychology, 90,* 1128–1140.

Chapman, D. S., Uggerslev, K. L., & Webster, J. (2003). Applicant reactions to face-to-face and technology-mediated interviews: A field investigation. *Journal of Applied Psychology, 88,* 944–953.

Chapman, D. S., & Zwieg, D. I. (2005). Development of a nomological network for interview structure: Antecedents and consequences of the structured selection interview. *Personnel Psychology, 58,* 673–702.

Charness, N. (Ed.). (1985). *Aging and human performance.* New York: Wiley.

Chee, L. S. (1994). Singapore Airlines: Strategic human resource initiatives. In D. Torrington (Ed.), *International human resource management: Think globally, act locally* (pp. 143–159). Upper Saddle River, NJ: Prentice Hall.

Chen, G., Gully, S. M., & Eden, D. (2004). General self-efficacy and self-esteem: Toward theoretical and empirical distinction between correlated self-evaluations. *Journal of Organizational Behavior, 25,* 375–395.

Chen, P. Y., & Spector, P. E. (1992). Relationships of work stressors with aggression, withdrawal, theft, and substance abuse: An exploratory study. *Journal of Occupational and Organizational Psychology, 65,* 177–184.

Chen, Z., Lam, W., & Zhong, J. A. (2007). Leader–member exchange and member performance: A new look at individual-level negative feedback-seeking behavior and team-level empowerment climate. *Journal of Applied Social Psychology, 37,* 202–212.

Cheng, B.-S., Jiang, D. Y., & Riley, J. H. (2003). Organizational commitment, supervisory commitment, and employee outcomes in the Chinese context: Proximal hypothesis or global hypothesis? *Journal of Organizational Behavior, 24,* 313–334.

Cherniss, C. (2010). Emotional intelligence: Toward clarification of a concept. *Industrial and Organizational Psychology, 3*(2), 110–126.

Cherrington, D. J. (1980). *The work ethic: Working values and values that work.* New York: Amacom.

Cheung, F. M. (2004). Use of Western and indigenously developed personality tests in Asia. *Applied Psychology: An International Review, 53,* 173–191.

Cheung, F. M., Leung, K., Zhang, J. X., Sun, H. F., Gan, Y. Q., Song, W. Z., & Xie, D. (2001). Indigenous Chinese personality constructs: Is the five-factor model complete? *Journal of Cross-Cultural Psychology, 32,* 407–433.

Chhokar, J. S., Brodbeck, F. C., & House, R. J. (Eds.). (2007). *Culture and leadership across the world: The GLOBE book of in-depth studies of 25 societies.* New York: Taylor & Francis/Erlbaum.

Chi, N., Grandey, A. A., Diamond, J. A., & Krimmel, K. R. (2011). Want a tip? Service performance as a function of emotion regulation and extraversion. *Journal of Applied Psychology, 96,* 1337–1346.

Chin, J. L., Lott, B., Rice, J. K., & Sanchez-Hucles, J. (2007). *Women and leadership: Transforming visions and diverse voices.* Malden, MA: Blackwell.

Chmiel, N. (2000). History and context for work and organizational psychology. In N. Chmiel (Ed.), *Introduction to work and organizational psychology: A European perspective* (pp. 3–19). Malden, MA: Blackwell.

Christian, M. S., Garza, A. S., & Slaughter, J. E. (2011). Work engagement: A quantitative review and test of its relations with task and contextual performance. *Personnel Psychology, 64,* 89–136.

Chrobot-Mason, D., Hays-Thomas, R., & Wishik, H. (2008). Understanding and defusing resistance to diversity training and learning. In K. M. Thomas (Ed.), *Diversity resistance in organizations: Manifestations and solutions* (pp. 23–54). New York: Erlbaum.

Chrobot-Mason, D., & Ruderman, M. N. (2003). Leadership in a diverse workplace. In M. S. Stockdale & F. J. Crosby (Eds.), *The psychology and management of workplace diversity* (pp. 100–121). Oxford, UK: Blackwell.

Church, A. (2001). Is there a method to our madness? The impact of data collection methodology on organizational survey results. *Personnel Psychology, 54,* 937–969.

Clarke, S. (1999). Perceptions of organizational safety: Implications for the development of safety culture. *Journal of Organizational Behavior, 20,* 185–198.

Clarke, S., & Robertson, I. T. (2005). A meta-analytic review of the Big Five personality factors and accident involvement in occupational and non-occupational settings. *Journal of Occupational and Organizational Psychology, 78,* 355–376.

Cleveland, J. N. (2005). What is success? Who defines it? Perspectives on the criterion problem as it relates to work and family. In E. E. Kossek & S. J. Lambert (Eds.), *Work and life integration: Organizational, cultural and individual perspectives* (pp. 319–346). Mahwah, NJ: Erlbaum.

Cleveland, J. N., & Murphy, K. R. (1992). Analyzing performance appraisal as goal-directed behavior. In G. Ferris & K. Rowland (Eds.), *Research in personnel and human resources management* (Vol. 10, pp. 121–185). Greenwich, CT: JAI Press.

Cleveland, J. N., Stockdale, M., & Murphy, K. R. (2000). *Women and men in organizations.* Mahwah, NJ: Erlbaum.

Clevenger, J., Pereira, G. M., Weichmann, D., Schmitt, N., & Harvey, V. S. (2001). Incremental validity of situational judgment tests. *Journal of Applied Psychology, 86,* 410–417.

Cohen, A., & Thomas, C. B. (2001, April 16). An up-close look at how one company handles the delicate task of downsizing. *Time,* pp. 38–40.

Cohen, J. (1988). *Statistical power analysis for the behavioral sciences* (2nd ed.). Hillsdale, NJ: Erlbaum.

Cohen, J. (1994). The earth is round ($p < .05$). *American Psychologist, 49,* 997–1003.

Cohen, M. S., Freeman, J. T., & Thompson, B. (1998). Critical thinking skills in tactical decision making: A model and a training strategy. In J. A. Cannon-Bowers & E. Salas (Eds.), *Making decisions under stress: Implications for individual and team training* (pp. 155–189). Washington, DC: American Psychological Association.

Cohen, R. J., & Swerdlik, M. E. (2010). *Psychological testing and assessment: An introduction to tests and measurement* (7th ed.). New York: McGraw-Hill.

Cohen, S., & Edwards, J. R. (1989). Personality characteristics as moderators of the relationship between stress and disorder. In R. W. Neufeld (Ed.), *Advances in the investigation of psychological stress* (pp. 235–283). New York: Wiley.

Cohen, S., & Hebert, T. B. (1996). Psychological factors and physical disease from the perspective of psychoimmunology. *Annual Review of Psychology, 47,* 113–142.

Cohen, S., & Wills, T. A. (1985). Stress, social support, and the buffering hypothesis. *Psychological Bulletin, 98,* 310–357.

Cohen, S. G., & Bailey, G. E. (1997). What makes teams work? Group effectiveness from the shop floor to the executive suite. *Journal of Management, 23,* 239–290.

Cohen, S. G., & Ledford, G. E. (1994). The effectiveness of self-managing teams: A quasi-experiment. *Human Relations, 47,* 13–43.

Colbert, A. E., Mount, M. K., Harter, J. K., Witt, L. A., & Barrick, M. R. (2004). Interactive effects of personality and perceptions of the work situation on workplace deviance. *Journal of Applied Psychology, 89,* 599–609.

Colella, A., Paetzold, R. L., & Belliveau, M. A. (2004). Factors affecting coworkers' procedural justice inferences of the workplace accommodations of employees with disabilities. *Personnel Psychology, 57,* 1–23.

Collins, C. J., & Han, J. (2004). Exploring applicant pool quantity and quality: The effects of early recruitment practice strategies. And firm reputation. *Personnel Psychology, 57,* 685–717.

Collins, C. J., Hanges, P. J., & Locke, E. A. (2004). The relationship of achievement motivation to entrepreneurial behavior: A meta-analysis. *Human Performance, 17,* 95–117.

Collins, D. B., & Holton, E. F. (2004). The effectiveness of managerial leadership development programs: A metaanalysis of studies from 1982 to 2001. *Human Resource Development Quarterly, 15,* 217–248.

Collins, J. M., Schmidt, F. L., Sanchez-Ku, M., Thomas, L., McDaniel, M. A., & Le, H. (2003). Can basic individual differences shed light on the construct meaning of assessment center evaluations? *International Journal of Selection and Assessment, 11,* 17–29.

Colquitt, J. A., Conlon, D. E., Wesson, M. J., Porter, C. O., & Ng, K. Y. (2001). Justice at the millennium: A meta-analytic review of 25 years of organizational justice research. *Journal of Applied Psychology, 86,* 425–445.

Colquitt, J. A., LePine, J. A., & Noe, R. A. (2000). Toward an integrative theory of training motivation: A metaanalytic path analysis of 20 years of research. *Journal of Applied Psychology, 85,* 678–707.

Combs, J., Liu, Y., Hall, A., & Ketchen, D. (2007). How much do high-performance work practices matter? A meta-analysis of their effects on organizational performance. *Personnel Psychology, 59,* 501–528.

Confessore, S. J., & Kops, W. J. (1998). Self-directed learning and the learning organization: Examining the connection between the individual and the learning environment. *Human Resource Development Quarterly, 9,* 365–375.

Conger, J. A., & Kanungo, R. (1987). Toward a behavioral theory of charismatic leadership in organizational settings. *Academy of Management Review, 12,* 637–647.

Conner, D. S. (2003). Social comparison in virtual work environments: An examination of contemporary referent selection. *Journal of Occupational and Organizational Psychology, 76,* 133–147.

Conte, J. M. (2005). Review and critique of emotional intelligence measures. *Journal of Organizational Behavior, 26,* 433–440.

Conte, J. M., Dean, M. A., Ringenbach, K. L., Moran, S. K., & Landy, F. J. (2005). The relationship between work attitudes and job analysis ratings: Do rating scale type and task discretion matter? *Human Performance, 18,* 1–21.

Conte, J. M., Landy, F. J., & Mathieu, J. E. (1995). Time urgency: Conceptual and construct development. *Journal of Applied Psychology, 80,* 178–185.

Conte, J. M., Mathieu, J. E., & Landy, F. J. (1998). The nomological and predictive validity of time urgency. *Journal of Organizational Behavior, 18,* 1–13.

Conte, J. M., Schwenneker, H. H., Dew, A. F., & Romano, D. M. (2001). The incremental validity of time urgency and other Type A subcomponents in predicting behavioral and health criteria. *Journal of Applied Social Psychology, 31,* 1727–1748.

Conway, J. M., Lombardo, K., & Sanders, K. C. (2001). A metaanalysis of incremental validity and nomological networks for subordinate and peer ratings. *Human Performance, 14,* 267–303.

Conway, N., & Briner, R. B. (2005). *Understanding psychological contracts at work: A critical evaluation of theory and research.* Oxford, UK: Oxford University Press.

Cooke, R. A., & Rousseau, D. M. (1988). Behavioral norms and expectations: A quantitative approach to the assessment of organizational culture. *Group and Organizational Studies, 13*, 245–273.

Cooke, R. A., & Szumal, J. L. (2000). Using the organizational culture inventory to understand the operating cultures of organizations. In N. M. Ashkenasy, C. P. M. Wilderom, & M. F. Peterson (Eds.), *Handbook of organizational climate and culture* (pp. 147–162). Thousand Oaks, CA: Sage.

Cooney, R., & Sohal, A. (2003). The human impact of total quality management. In D. Holman, T. Wall, C. Clegg, P. Sparrow, & A. Howard (Eds.), *The new workplace: A guide to the human impact of modern working practices* (pp. 37–53). Chichester, UK: Wiley.

Cooper, C. L., & Cartwright, S. (1994). Healthy mind, healthy organization: A proactive approach to occupational stress. *Human Relations, 47*, 455–471.

Cooper, C. L., & Cartwright, S. (2001). A strategic approach to organizational stress management. In P. A. Hancock & P. A. Desmond (Eds.), *Stress, workload, and fatigue. Human factors in transportation* (pp. 235–248). Mahwah, NJ: Erlbaum.

Cooper, C. L., Dewe, P. J., & O'Driscoll, M. P. (2001). *Organizational stress: A review and critique of theory, research, and applications.* Thousand Oaks, CA: Sage.

Cooper, C. L., & Sadri, G. (1991). The impact of stress counseling at work. *Journal of Social Behavior and Personality, 6*, 411–423.

Cooper, M. (1999, February 5). Officers in Bronx fire 41 shots, and an unarmed man is killed. *New York Times.* Retrieved July 31, 2008, from query.nytimes.com/gst/fullpage.html?res=9B06E2DE163BF936A35751C0A96F958260&scp=5&sq=Amadou+Diallo&st=nyt

Cooper-Hakim, A., & Viswesvaran, C. (2005). The construct of work commitment: Testing an integrative framework. *Journal of Applied Psychology, 131*, 241–259.

Cooper-Thomas, H., & Anderson, N. (2002). Newcomer adjustment: The relationship between organizational socialization tactics, information acquisition and attitudes. *Journal of Occupational and Organizational Psychology, 75*, 423–437.

Cooper-Thomas, H. D., & Anderson, N. (2006). Organizational socialization: A new theoretical model and recommendations for future research and HRM practices in organizations. *Journal of Managerial Psychology, 21*, 492–516.

Coovert, M. D., Thompson, L. F., & Craiger, J. P. (2005). Technology. In J. Barling, E. K. Kelloway, & M. R. Frone (Eds.), *Handbook of work stress* (pp. 299–324). Thousand Oaks, CA: Sage.

Cordery, J. L. (1996). Autonomous work groups and quality circles. In M. A. West (Ed.), *Handbook of work group psychology* (pp. 225–246). Chichester, UK: Wiley.

Cordery, J. L., Mueller, W. S., & Smith, L. M. (1991). Attitudinal and behavioral effects of autonomous group working: A longitudinal field study. *Academy of Management Journal, 34*, 464–476.

Costa, P. T., & McCrae, R. R. (1997). Longitudinal stability of personality. In R. Hogan, J. Johnson, & S. Briggs (Eds.), *Handbook of personality psychology* (pp. 123–139). San Diego, CA: Academic Press.

Coyle-Shapiro, J. A.-M., & Kessler, I. (2002). Exploring reciprocity through the lens of the psychological contract: Employee and employer perspectives. *European Journal of Work and Organizational Psychology, 11*, 69–86.

Coyne, T. (2002, March 23). Employee kills four colleagues in Indiana. *Rocky Mountain News*, p. 11A.

Crino, M. D. (1994). Employee sabotage: A random or preventable phenomenon? *Journal of Managerial Issues, 6*(3), 311–330.

Crocker, J., & Park, L. E. (2004). The costly pursuit of self-esteem. *Psychological Bulletin, 130*(3), 392–414.

Cronbach, L. J., & Meehl, P. E. (1955). Construct validity in psychological tests. *Psychological Bulletin, 52*, 281–302.

Cropanzano, R. (2001). *Justice in the workplace: From theory to practice* (Vol. 2). Mahwah, NJ: Erlbaum.

Cropanzano, R., Byrne, Z. S., & Prehar, C. A. (1999). *How workers manage relationships in a complex social world: A multi-foci approach to procedural and interactional justice.* Paper presented at the First International Round Table: Innovations in organizational justice, Nice, France.

Cropanzano, R., Goldman, B., & Folger, R. (2005). Self-interest: Defining and understanding a human motive. *Journal of Organizational Behavior, 26*, 985–991.

Crosby, F. J. (2004). *Affirmative action is dead: Long live affirmative action.* New Haven, CT: Yale University Press.

Crosby, F. J., Iyer, A., Clayton, S., & Downing, R. A. (2003). Affirmative action: Psychological data and the policy debates. *American Psychologist, 58*, 93–115.

Crosby, F. J., Stockdale, M. S., & Ropp, S. A. (2007). *Sex discrimination in the workplace.* Malden, MA: Blackwell.

Cullen, M. J., Hardison, C. M., & Sackett, P. R. (2004). Using SAT–grade and ability–job performance relationships to test predictions derived from stereotype threat theory. *Journal of Applied Psychology, 89*, 220–230.

Cunningham, J. W., Boese, R. R., Neeb, R. W., & Pass, J. J. (1983). Systematically derived work dimensions: Factor analysis of the Occupational Analysis Inventory. *Journal of Applied Psychology, 68*, 232–252.

Cushner, K., & Brislin, R. W. (1996). *Intercultural relations: A practical guide* (2nd ed.). Thousand Oaks, CA: Sage.

Cynkar, A. (2007). Reducing subgroup differences in testing. *Monitor on Psychology, 38*(9), 69.

Dabos, G. E., & Rousseau, D. M. (2004). Mutuality and reciprocity in psychological contracts of employees and employers. *Journal of Applied Psychology, 89*, 52–72.

Dalal, R. S. (2005). A meta-analysis of the relationship between organizational citizenship behavior and counter-productive work behavior. *Journal of Applied Psychology, 90*, 1241–1255.

Dalessio, A. T., & Silverhart, T. A. (1994). Combining biodata test and interview information: Predicting decisions and performance criteria. *Personnel Psychology, 47*, 303–315.

Daley, T., Whaley, S. E., Sigman, M. D., Espinosa, M. P., & Neumann, C. (2003). IQ on the rise: The Flynn effect in rural Kenyan children. *Psychological Science, 14*(3), 215–219.

Dansereau, F., Graen, G., & Haga, W. J. (1975). A vertical dyad linkage approach to leadership within formal organizations: A longitudinal investigation of the role-making process. *Organizational Behavior and Human Performance, 13*, 46–78.

Darley, J. M., Messick, D. M., & Tyler, T. R. (Eds.). (2001). *Social influences on ethical behavior in organizations.* Mahwah, NJ: Erlbaum.

Daus, K. S., & Ashkanasy, N. M. (2005). The case for the ability-based model of emotional intelligence in organizational behavior. *Journal of Organizational Behavior, 26*, 453–466.

Davies, M., Stankov, L., & Roberts, R. D. (1998). Emotional intelligence: In search of an elusive construct. *Journal of Personality and Social Psychology, 75*, 989–1015.

Davis, D. D. (1998). International performance measurement and management. In J. W. Smither (Ed.), *Performance appraisal: State of the art in practice* (pp. 95–131). San Francisco: Jossey-Bass.

Davis-Blake, A., & Pfeffer, J. (1989). Just a mirage: The search for dispositional effects in organizational research. *Academy of Management Review, 14*, 385–400.

Dawes, R. M. (1988). *Rational choice in an uncertain world.* San Diego, CA: Harcourt Brace Jovanovich.

Dawis, R. V., & Lofquist, L. H. (1984). *A psychological theory of work adjustment: An individual differences model and its applications.* Minneapolis: University of Minnesota Press.

Day, A. L., & Carroll, S. A. (2003). Situation and patterned behavior description interviews. *Human Performance, 16,* 25–47.

Day, A. L., & Livingstone, H. A. (2001). Chronic and acute stressors among military personnel: Do coping styles buffer their negative impact on health? *Journal of Occupational Health Psychology, 6,* 348–360.

Day, D. V. (2001a). Assessment of leadership outcomes. In S. Zaccaro & R. Klimoski (Eds.), *The nature of organizational leadership: Understanding the performance imperatives confronting today's leaders* (pp. 384–412). San Francisco: Jossey-Bass.

Day, D. V. (2001b). Leadership development: A review in context. *Leadership Quarterly, 11*(4), 581–613.

Day, D. V., Schleicher, D. J., Unckless, A. L., & Hiller, N. J. (2002). Self-monitoring personality at work: A metaanalytic investigation of construct validity. *Journal of Applied Psychology, 87,* 390–401.

Dean, M. A., Roth, P. L., & Bobko, P. (2008). Ethnic and gender group differences in assessment center ratings: A meta-analysis. *Journal of Applied Psychology, 93,* 685–691.

Dean, M. A., & Russell, C. J. (2005). An examination of biodata theory-based constructs in a field context. *International Journal of Selection and Assessment, 13,* 139–149.

De Cremer D. (2002). Charismatic leadership and cooperation in social dilemmas: A matter of transforming motives? *Journal of Applied Psychology, 32,* 997–1016.

Deery, S. J., Iverson, R. D., & Walsh, J. T. (2006). Toward a better understanding of psychological contract breach: A study of customer service employees. *Journal of Applied Psychology, 91,* 166–175.

DeFrank, R. S., & Ivancevich, J. M. (1998). Stress on the job: An executive update. *Academy of Management Executive, 12,* 55–66.

De Fruyt, F., Aluja, A., Garcia, L. F., Rolland, J., & Jung S. C. (2006). Positive presentation management and intelligence and the personality differentiation by intelligence hypothesis in job applicants. *International Journal of Selection and Assessment, 14,* 101–112.

De Hoogh, A. A. B., Den Hartog, D. N., Koopman, P. L., Thierry, H., Van den Berg, P. T., Van der Weide, J. G., & Wilderom, C. P. M. (2005). Leader motives, charismatic leadership, and subordinates' work attitude in the profit and voluntary sector. *Leadership Quarterly, 16,* 17–38.

De Jonge, J., & Dormann, C. (2006). Stressors, resources and strain at work: A longitudinal test of the triple match principle. *Journal of Applied Psychology, 91,* 1359–1374.

Delbridge, R. (2003). Workers under lean manufacturing. In D. Holman, T. Wall, C. Clegg, P. Sparrow, & A. Howard (Eds.), *The new workplace: A guide to the human impact of modern working practices* (pp. 19–36). Chichester, UK: Wiley.

Delbridge, R., & Turnbull, P. (1992). Human resource maximization: The management of labour under a JIT system. In P. Blyton & P. Turnbull (Eds.), *Reassessing human resource management* (pp. 56–73). London: Sage.

Deming, W. E. (1986). *Out of crisis.* Cambridge, MA: MIT, Center for Advanced Engineering Study.

Den Hartog, D. N., De Hoogh, A. H. B., & Keegan, A. E. (2007). The interactive effects of belongingness and charisma on helping and compliance. *Journal of Applied Psychology, 92,* 1131–1139.

Den Hartog, D. N., House, R. J., Hanges, P. J., Ruiz-Quintanilla, S. A., Dorfman, P. W., & GLOBE Associates. (1999). Culture-specific and cross-culturally generalizable implicit leadership theories: Are attributes of charismatic/transformational leadership universally endorsed? *Leadership Quarterly, 10*(2), 219–256.

Den Hartog, D. N., & Koopman, P. L. (2001). Leadership in organizations. In N. Anderson, D. S. Ones, H. K. Sinangil, & C. Viswesvaran (Eds.), *Handbook of industrial, work, and organizational psychology* (Vol. 2, pp. 166–187). London: Sage.

Deshpande, S. P., & Viswesvaran, C. (1992). Is cross-cultural training of expatriate managers effective? A metaanalysis. *International Journal of Intercultural Relations, 16,* 295–310.

Detert, J. R., Trevino, L. K., Burris, E. R., & Andiappan, M. (2007). Managerial modes of influence and counterproductivity in organizations: A longitudinal business-unit-level investigation. *Journal of Applied Psychology, 92,* 993–1005.

Deutsch, C. (2004, September 9). If at first you don't succeed, believe harder. *New York Times,* p. BU7.

Dickson, M. W., Den Hartog, D. N., & Mitchelson, J. K. (2003). Research on leadership in a cross-cultural context: Making progress and raising new questions. *Leadership Quarterly, 14,* 729–768.

Diener, E. (2000). Subjective well-being: The science of happiness and a proposal for a national index. *American Psychologist, 55,* 34–43.

Diener, E., & Biswas-Diener, R. (2008). *Rethinking happiness: The science of psychological wealth.* Malden, MA: Blackwell.

Dierdorff, E. C., & Surface, E. A. (2008). Assessing training needs: Do work experience and capability matter? *Human Performance, 21,* 28–48.

Digman, J. M. (1990). Personality structure: Emergence of the five factor model. *Annual Review of Psychology, 41,* 417–440.

Dillon, S., & Rimer, S. (2005, February 4). Harvard seeks to advance opportunities for women. *New York Times,* p. A13.

Dingfelder, S. F. (2005, March). Psychology in Iraq's "red zone." *Monitor on Psychology,* pp. 34–35.

d'Iribarne, P. (2002). Motivating workers in emerging countries: Universal tools and local adaptations. *Journal of Organizational Behavior, 23,* 243–256.

Dobbin, F., Kalev, A., & Kelly, B. (2007). Diversity management in corporate America. *Contexts, 6*(4), 21–28.

Doerr, K. H., Mitchell, T. R., Freed, T., Schriesheim, C. A., & Zhou, X. (2004). Work flow policy and within-worker and between-workers variability in performance. *Journal of Applied Psychology, 89,* 911–921.

Dolezalek, H. (2004). Building better learners. *Training, 1,* 30–34.

Dollard, J., Doob, L., Miller, N., Mowrer, D., & Sears, R. (1939). *Frustration and aggression.* New Haven, CT: Yale University Press.

Donovan, J., & Radosevich, D. (1999). A meta-analytic review of the distribution of practice effect: Now you see it, now you don't. *Journal of Applied Psychology, 84,* 795–805.

Donovan, M. A., Drasgow, F., & Munson, L. J. (1998). The perceptions of fair interpersonal treatment scale: Development and validation of a measure of interpersonal treatment in the workplace. *Journal of Applied Psychology, 83,* 683–692.

Donovan, M. A., Drasgow, F., & Probst, T. M. (2000). Does computerizing paper and pencil attitude scales make a difference? New IRT analyses offer insight. *Journal of Applied Psychology, 85,* 305–313.

Dorman, L. (2008, August 27). Golf tour's rule: Speak English to stay in play. *New York Times,* p. A1.

Douglas, S. C., & Martinko, M. J. (2001). Exploring the role of individual differences in the prediction of workplace aggression. *Journal of Applied Psychology, 86,* 547–559.

Douthitt, E. A., & Aiello, J. R. (2001). The role of participation and control in effects of computer monitoring on fairness perceptions, task satisfaction, and performance. *Journal of Applied Psychology, 86,* 867–874.

Drasgow, F. (2004). Innovative computerized test items. In K. Kempf-Leonard (Ed.), *Encyclopedia of social measurements* (Vol. 2, pp. 283–290). San Diego, CA: Academic Press.

Drenth, P. J., & Heller, F. (2004). The dangers of research myopia in work and organizational psychology: A plea for broadening and integration. *Applied Psychology: An International Review, 53,* 599–613.

Driskell, J. E., Willis, R. P., & Copper, C. (1992). Effect of overlearning on retention. *Journal of Applied Psychology, 77,* 615–622.

DuBois, C. L., & DuBois, D. A. (October, 2010). A call for I-O leadership in "going green." *The Industrial-Organizational Psychologist, 48*(2), 12–19.

Dubois, D. A., Shalin, V. L., Levi, K. R., & Borman, W. C. (1998). A cognitively-oriented approach to task analysis. *Training Research Journal, 3,* 103–142.

DuBois, D. D. (1999). Competency modeling. In D. G. Landon, K. S. Whiteside, & M. M. McKenna (Eds.), *Intervention resource guide: 50 performance improvement tools* (pp. 106–111). San Francisco: Jossey-Bass.

DuBois, D. L., & Flay, B. R. (2004). The healthy pursuit of self-esteem: Comment on the alternative to the Crocker and Park (2004) formulation. *Psychological Bulletin, 130,* 415–420.

DuBois, R. L., Sackett, P. R., Zedeck, S., & Fogli, L. (1993). Further exploration of typical and maximum job performance criteria: Definitional issues, prediction, and black–white differences. *Journal of Applied Psychology, 78,* 205–211.

Dudley, N. M., Orvis, K. A., Lebeicki, J. E., & Cortina, J. M. (2006). A meta-analytic investigation of conscientiousness in the prediction of job performance: Examining the intercorrelations and the incremental validity of narrow traits. *Journal of Applied Psychology, 91,* 40–57.

Duncan, T. S. (1995, April). Death in the office: Workplace homicides. *The FBI Law Enforcement Bulletin.* Retrieved June 6, 2003, from www.nsi.org/tips/workdeth.txt

Dunleavy, E. M., Aamodt, M. G., Cohen, D. B., & Schaeffer, P. (2008). A consideration of international differences in the legal context of selection. *Industrial and Organizational Psychology: Perspectives on Science and Practice, 1,* 247–254.

Dunn, W. L. S. (1993). *Managers' perceptions of the validity of personality and general mental ability.* Unpublished doctoral dissertation, University of Iowa.

Dunnette, M. D. (1966). Fads, fashions, and folderol. *American Psychologist, 21,* 343–352.

Dunnette, M. D. (1999). Introduction. In N. G. Peterson, M. D. Mumford, W. C. Borman, P. R. Jeanneret, & E. A. Fleishman (Eds.), *An occupational information system for the 21st century* (pp. 3–8). Washington, DC: American Psychological Association.

Dwight, S. A., & Donovan, J. J. (2003). Do warnings not to fake reduce faking? *Human Performance, 16,* 1–23.

Dye, D., & Silver, M. (1999). The origins of O*NET. In N. G. Peterson, M. D. Mumford, W. C. Borman, P. R. Jeanneret, & E. A. Fleishman (Eds.), *An occupational information system for the 21st century* (pp. 9–20). Washington, DC: American Psychological Association.

Eagly, A. H. (2005). Achieving relational authenticity in leadership: Does gender matter? *Leadership Quarterly, 16,* 459–474.

Eagly, A. H., & Carli, L. L. (2003a). The female leadership advantage: An evaluation of the evidence. *Leadership Quarterly, 14,* 807–834.

Eagly, A. H., & Carli, L. L. (2003b). Finding gender advantage and disadvantage: Systematic research integration is the solution. *Leadership Quarterly, 14,* 851–859.

Eagly, A. H., Johannesen-Schmidt, M. C., & van Engen, M. L. (2003). Transformational, transactional, and laissez-faire leadership styles: A meta-analysis comparing men and women. *Psychological Bulletin, 129,* 569–591.

Eagly, A. H., & Johnson, B. T. (1990). Gender and leadership style: A meta-analysis. *Psychological Bulletin, 108,* 233–256.

Eagly, A. H., & Karau, S. J. (2002). Role congruity theory of prejudice toward female leaders. *Psychological Bulletin, 109,* 807–834.

Earley, P. C., & Erez, M. (1997). Introduction. In P. C. Earley & M. Erez (Eds.), *New perspectives on international industrial/organizational psychology* (pp. 1–10). San Francisco: Jossey-Bass.

Edwards, J. R. (1996). An examination of competing versions of the person–environment fit approach to stress. *Academy of Management Journal, 39,* 292–339.

Edwards, J. R., Baglioni, A. J., & Cooper, C. L. (1990). Examining relationships among self-report measures of Type A behavior pattern: The effects of dimensionality, measurement error and differences in underlying constructs. *Journal of Applied Psychology, 75,* 440–454.

Edwards, J. R., & Rothbard, N. P. (1999). Work and family stress and well-being: An examination of person–environment fit in the work and family domains. *Organizational Behavior and Human Decision Processes, 77,* 85–129.

Ehigie, B. O., & Otukoya, O. W. (2005). Antecedents of organizational citizenship behavior in a government-owned enterprise in Nigeria. *European Journal of Work and Organizational Psychology, 14,* 389–399.

Ehrhart, M. G., & Naumann, S. E. (2004). Organizational citizenship behavior in work groups: A group norms approach. *Journal of Applied Psychology, 89,* 960–974.

Einarsen, S. (2000). Harassment and bullying at work: A review of the Scandanavian approach. *Aggression and Violent Behavior: A Review Journal, 4,* 371–401.

Einarsen, S., Aasland, M. S., & Skogstad, A. (2007). Destructive leadership behavior: A definition and conceptual model. *Leadership Quarterly, 18,* 207–216.

Einarsen, S., Hoel, H., Zapf, D., & Cooper, C. (Eds.). (2002). *Bullying and emotional abuse in the workplace.* London: Taylor & Francis.

Eliot, R. S., & Buell, J. C. (1983). The role of the central nervous system in sudden cardiac death. In T. M. Dembroski, T. Schmidt, & G. Blunchen (Eds.), *Biobehavioral bases of coronary-prone behavior.* New York: Karger.

Ellemers, N., de Gilder, D., & van den Heuvel, H. (1998). Career-oriented vs. team-oriented commitment and behavior at work. *Journal of Applied Psychology, 83,* 717–730.

Ellin, A. (2000, March 29). Training programs often miss the point on the job. *New York Times,* p. C12.

Ellingston, J. E., Sackett, P. R., & Connelly, B. S. (2007). Personality assessment across selection and development contexts: Insights into response distortion. *Journal of Applied Psychology, 92,* 386–395.

Elliott, R. H., & Jarrett, D. T. (1994). Violence in the workplace: The role of human resource management. *Public Personnel Management, 23,* 287–299.

Ellis, S., & Davidi, I. (2005). After-event reviews: Drawing lessons from successful and failed experience. *Journal of Applied Psychology, 90,* 857–871.

Englebrecht, A. S., & Fischer, A. H. (1995). The managerial performance implications of a developmental assessment center process. *Human Relations, 48,* 387–404.

Ensher, E. A., Grant-Vallone, E. J., & Donaldson, S. I. (2001). The effects of perceived discrimination on job satisfaction, organizational commitment, citizenship behavior, and grievances. *Human Resource Development Quarterly, 12,* 53–72.

EnterpriseOne (2006–7). Thinking big from day one. Copyright 2006–2007, Government of Singapore. Retrieved August 25, 2008, from www.business.gov.sg/EN/CaseStories/case_startbiz_daysolutions.htm

Epitropaki, O., & Martin, R. (2005). The moderating role of individual differences in the relation between transformational/transactional leadership perceptions and organizational identification. *Leadership Quarterly, 16,* 569–589.

Erdogan, B., & Bauer, T, N. (2005). Enhancing career benefits of employee proactive personality: The role of fit with jobs and organizations. *Personnel Psychology, 58*, 859–891.

Erez, A., & Isen, A. M. (2002). The influence of positive affect on the components of expectancy motivation. *Journal of Applied Psychology, 87*, 1055–1067.

Erez, A., & Judge, T. A. (2001). Relationship of core self-evaluations to goal setting, motivation and performance. *Journal of Applied Psychology, 86*, 1270–1279.

Erez, M. A. (1997). Culture-based model of work motivation. In P. C. Earley & M. Erez (Eds.), *New perspectives on international industrial and organizational psychology* (pp. 193–242). San Francisco: New Lexington Press.

Erez, M. A., & Eden, D. (2001). Introduction: Trends reflected in work motivation. In M. Erez, U. Kleinbeck, & H. Thierry (Eds.), *Work motivation in the context of a globalizing economy* (pp. 1–12). Mahwah, NJ: Erlbaum.

Erez, M. A., & Gati, E. (2004). A dynamic, multi-level model of culture: From the micro level of the individual to the macro level of a global culture. *Applied Psychology: An International Review, 53*, 583–598.

Ericsson, K. A., & Charness, N. (1994). Expert performance: Its structure and acquisition. *American Psychologist, 49*, 725–747.

Ericsson, K. A., & Simon, H. A. (1993). *Protocol analysis: Verbal reports as data.* Cambridge, MA: MIT Press.

Eriksen, W., & Einarsen, S. (2004). Gender minority as a risk factor of exposure to bullying at work: The case of male assistant nurses. *European Journal of Work and Organizational Psychology, 13*, 473–492.

Ethics Resource Center. (2005). *National business ethics survey: How employees view ethics in their organizations 1994–2005.* Washington, DC: Author.

Evans, G. W., & Johnson, D. (2000). Stress and open-office noise. *Journal of Applied Psychology, 85*, 779–783.

Everton, W., Mastrangelo, P., & Jolton, J. (2003). Surfin' USA: Using your work computer for personal reasons. *The Industrial-Organizational Psychologist, 40*(4), 90–93.

Ewen, R. B., Smith, P. C., Hulin, C. L., & Locke, E. A. (1966). An empirical test of the Herzberg two-factor theory. *Journal of Applied Psychology, 50*, 544–550.

Faragher v. City of Boca Raton (1998). 118 S. Ct. 2275.

Farr, J. L. (2003). Introduction to the special issue: Stereotype threat effects in employment settings. *Human Performance, 16*, 179–180.

Farr, J. L., Hofmann, D. A., & Ringenbach, K. L. (1993). Goal orientation and action control theory: Implications for industrial and organizational psychology. In C. L. Cooper & I. T. Robertson (Eds.), *International review of industrial and organizational psychology* (pp. 193–232). New York: Wiley.

Farr, J. L., & Ringseis, E. L. (2002). The older worker in organizational context: Beyond the individual. In C. Cooper & I. Robertson (Eds.), *International review of industrial and organizational psychology* (Vol. 17, pp. 31–76). Chichester, UK: Wiley.

Fay, D., Borrill, C., Amir, Z., Haward, R., & West, M. A. (2006). Getting the most out of multidisciplinary teams: A multi-sample study of team innovation in health care. *Journal of Occupational and Organizational Psychology, 79*, 553–567.

Fay, D., & Frese, M. (2001). The concept of personal initiative: An overview of validity studies. *Human Performance, 14*(1), 97–124.

Feather, N. T., & Rauter, K. A. (2004). Organizational citizenship behaviours in relation to job status, job insecurity, organizational commitment and identification, job satisfaction and work values. *Journal of Occupational and Organizational Psychology, 77*, 81–94.

Feild, H. S., & Holley, W. H. (1982). The relationship of performance appraisal system characteristics to verdicts in selected employment discrimination cases. *Academy of Management Journal, 25*, 392–406.

Feingold, A. (1994). Gender differences in personality: A metaanalysis. *Psychological Bulletin, 116*, 429–456.

Feldman, D. C. (1984). The development and enforcement of group norms. *Academy of Management Review, 9*, 47–53.

Feldman, D. C., & Lankau, M. J. (2005). Executive coaching: A review and agenda for future research. *Journal of Management, 31*, 829–848.

Feldman, J. M. (1981). Beyond attribution theory: Cognitive processes in performance appraisal. *Journal of Applied Psychology, 66*, 127–148.

Feldman, T. B., & Johnson, P. W. (1994, August). *Violence in the workplace: A preliminary investigation.* Paper presented at the annual meeting of the American Bar Association, New Orleans, LA.

Ferdman, B. M., & Davidson, M. N. (2004). Some learning about inclusion: Continuing the dialogue. *The Industrial-Organizational Psychologist, 41*(4), 31–37.

Ferrin, D. L., Dirks, K. T., & Shah, P. P. (2006). Direct and indirect effects of third-party relationships on interpersonal trust. *Journal of Applied Psychology, 91*, 870–883.

Ferster, C. B., & Skinner, B. F. (1957). *Schedules of reinforcement.* New York: Appleton-Century-Crofts.

Festinger, L. (1957). *A theory of cognitive dissonance.* Evanston, IL: Row Peterson.

Fiedler, F. E. (1967). *A theory of leadership effectiveness.* New York: McGraw-Hill.

Fields, D., Dingman, M. E., Roman, P. M., & Blum, T. C. (2005). Exploring predictors of alternative job changes. *Journal of Occupational and Organizational Psychology, 78*, 63–82.

Finder, A. (2006, June 11). When a risque online persona undermines the chance for a job. *New York Times*, p. 1.

Fine, S. A. (1988). Functional job analysis. In S. Gael (Ed.), *Job analysis for business, industry, and government* (Vol. 2, pp. 1019–1035). New York: Wiley.

Finkle, R. B. (1976). Managerial assessment centers. In M. D. Dunnette (Ed.), *Handbook of industrial and organizational psychology* (pp. 861–888). Chicago: Rand McNally.

Finn, F. A., Mason, C. M., & Bradley, L. M. (2007). Doing well with executive coaching: Psychological and behavioral impacts. In G. Solomon (Ed.), *Academy of Management 2007 annual meeting proceedings: Doing well by doing good* (pp. 1–34). Philadelphia: Academy of Management.

Finnigan, A. (2001). The 100 best companies for working women: The inside story. *Working Woman.* Retrieved March 6, 2003, from www.workingwoman.com/oct_2001/inside_01.shtml

Fisher, C. D. (2003). Why do lay people believe that satisfaction and performance are correlated? Possible sources of a commonsense theory. *Journal of Organizational Behavior, 24*, 753–777.

Fisher, C. D., & Ashkanasy, N. M. (2000). The emerging role of emotions in work life: An introduction. *Journal of Organizational Behavior, 21*, 123–129.

Fisher, C. D., & Noble, C. S. (2004). A within-person examination of correlations of performance and emotions while working. *Human Performance, 17*, 145–168.

Fisher, S. G., Hunter, T. A., & Macrosson, W. D. (2001). A validation study of Belbin's team roles. *European Journal of Work and Organizational Psychology, 10*, 121–144.

Flanagan, J. C. (1954). The critical incidents technique. *Psychological Bulletin, 51*, 327–358.

Fleishman, E. A. (1967). Performance assessment based on an empirically derived task taxonomy. *Human Factors, 9*, 349–366.

Fleishman, E. A., & Harris, E. F. (1962). Patterns of leadership behavior related to employee grievances and turnover. *Personnel Psychology, 15*, 43–56.

Fleishman, E. A., & Mumford, M. D. (1989). Individual attributes and training performance. In I. L. Goldstein (Ed.), *Training and development in organizations* (pp. 183–255). San Francisco: Jossey-Bass.

Fleishman, E. A., Quaintance, M. K., & Broedling, L. A. (1984). *Taxonomies of human performance: The description of human tasks.* San Diego, CA: Academic Press.

Fleishman, E. A., & Reilly, M. E. (1992). *Handbook of human abilities: Definitions, measurements, and job task requirements.* Palo Alto, CA: Consulting Psychologists Press.

Fleishman, E. A., & Zaccaro, S. J. (1992). Toward a taxonomy of team performance functions. In R. W. Swezey & E. Salas (Eds.), *Teams: Their training and performance* (pp. 31–56). Stamford, CT: Ablex.

Fletcher, C. (2001). Performance appraisal and management: The developing research agenda. *Journal of Occupational and Organizational Psychology, 74,* 473–487.

Flynn, J. R. (1999). Searching for justice. *American Psychologist, 54,* 5–20.

Folger, R., & Baron, R. A. (1996). Violence and hostility at work: A model of reactions to perceived injustice. In G. R. Vandenbos & E. Q. Bulatao (Eds.), *Violence on the job: Identifying risks and developing solutions* (pp. 51–86). Washington, DC: American Psychological Association.

Folger, R., & Cropanzano, R. (1998). *Organizational justice and human resource management.* Thousand Oaks, CA: Sage.

Folger, R., Cropanzano, R., & Goldman, B. (2005). What is the relationship between justice and morality? In J. Greenberg & J. A. Colquitt (Eds.), *Handbook of organizational justice* (pp. 215–246). Mahwah, NJ: Erlbaum.

Folger, R., & Konovsky, M. A. (1989). Effects of procedural and distributive justice on reactions to pay raise decisions. *Academy of Management Journal, 32,* 115–130.

Folger, R., & Skarlicki, D. P. (2001). Fairness as a dependent variable: Why toughness can sometimes lead to bad management. In R. Cropanzano (Ed.), *Justice in the workplace: From theory to practice* (pp. 97–118). Mahwah, NJ: Erlbaum.

Ford, D. L. (1985). Job-related stress of the minority professional. In T. A. Beehr & R. S. Bhagat (Eds.), *Human stress and cognition in organizations* (pp. 287–323). New York: Wiley.

Ford, J. D., & Ford, L. W. (1994). Logics of identity, contradiction, and attraction in change. *Academy of Management Review, 19,* 756–785.

Ford, J. K., Smith, E. M., Weissbein, D. A., Gully, S. M., & Salas, E. (1998). Relationships of goal orientation, metacognitive activity, and practice strategies with learning outcomes and transfer. *Journal of Applied Psychology, 83,* 218–233.

Forsyth, D. R. (2006). *Group dynamics* (4th ed.). Belmont, CA: Wadsworth.

Forsyth, D. R. (2009). *Group dynamics* (5th ed.). Belmont, CA: Wadsworth.

Foti, R. J., & Haunestein, N. M. A. (2007). Pattern and variable approaches in leadership emergence and effectiveness. *Journal of Applied Psychology, 92,* 347–355.

Fowers, B. J., & Richardson, F. C. (1996). Why is multiculturalism good? *American Psychologist, 51,* 609–621.

Fox, M. L., Dwyer, D. J., & Ganster, D. C. (1993). Effects of stressful job demand and control on physiological and attitudinal outcomes in a hospital setting. *Academy of Management Journal, 36,* 289–318.

Fox, S., & Spector, P. E. (1999). A model of work frustration–aggression. *Journal of Organizational Behavior, 20,* 915–931.

Fox, S., & Spector, P. E. (Eds.). (2005). *Counterproductive workplace behavior: Investigations of actors and targets.* Washington, DC: American Psychological Association.

Fox, S., & Stallworth, L. E. (2005). Racial/ethnic bullying: Exploring links between bullying and racism in the U.S. workplace. *Journal of Vocational Behavior, 66,* 438–456.

Francis-Smythe, J. A., & Robertson, I. T. (2003). The importance of time congruity in the organization. *Applied Psychology: An International Review, 52,* 298–321.

Freedman, J. L., & Edwards, D. R. (1988). Time pressure, task performance, and enjoyment. In J. E. McGrath (Ed.), *The social psychology of time* (pp. 113–133). Newbury Park, CA: Sage.

French, J. R. P., Caplan, R. D., & Harrison, R. V. (1982). *Mechanisms of job stress and strain.* New York: Wiley.

French, J. R. P., & Raven, B. H. (1959). The bases of social power. In D. Cartwright (Ed.), *Studies of social power* (pp. 150–157). Ann Arbor, MI: Institute for Social Research.

Frese, M. (1999). Social support as a moderator of the relationship between work stressors and psychological dysfunctioning: A longitudinal study with objective measures. *Journal of Occupational Health Psychology, 3,* 179–192.

Frese, M., & Fay, D. (2001). Personal initiative: An active performance concept for work in the 21st century. In B. M. Staw & R. M. Sutton (Eds.), *Research in Organizational Behavior* (Vol. 23, 133–187). Greenwich, CT: JAI Press.

Frese, M., Krauss, S. I., Keith, N., Escher, S., Grabarkiewicz, R., Luneng, S. V., Heers, C., Unger, J., & Friedrich, C. (2007). Business owners' action planning and its relationship to business success in three African countries. *Journal of Applied Psychology, 92,* 1481–1498.

Frese, M., & Zapf, D. (1994). Action as core of work psychology: A German approach. In M. Dunnette, L. Hough, & H. C. Triandis (Eds.), *Handbook of industrial and organizational psychology* (2nd ed., Vol. 4, pp. 271–340). Palo Alto, CA: Consulting Psychologists Press.

Fried, Y., Tiegs, R. B., & Bellamy, A. R. (1992). Personal and interpersonal predictors of supervisors' avoidance of evaluating subordinates. *Journal of Applied Psychology, 77,* 462–468.

Friedman, M., & Rosenman, R. (1959). Association of specific overt behavior pattern with blood and cardiovascular findings. *Journal of the American Medical Association, 169,* 1286–1296.

Friedman, M., & Rosenman, R. (1974). *Type A behavior and your heart.* New York: Knopf.

Friedman, S. D., & Greenhaus, J. H. (2000). *Work and family—Allies or enemies? What happens when business professionals confront life choices?* Oxford, UK: Oxford University Press.

Frone, M. R. (2000a). Interpersonal conflict at work and psychological outcomes: Testing a model among young workers. *Journal of Occupational Health Psychology, 5,* 246–255.

Frone, M. R. (2000b). Work–family conflict and employee psychiatric disorders: The National Comorbidity Survey. *Journal of Applied Psychology, 85,* 888–895.

Frone, M. R. (2006). Prevalence and distribution of illicit drug use in the workforce and in the workplace: Findings and implications from a U.S. national survey. *Journal of Applied Psychology, 91,* 856–869.

Frost, B. C., Ko, C. E., & James, L. R. (2007). Implicit and explicit personality: A test of a channeling hypothesis for aggressive behavior. *Journal of Applied Psychology, 92,* 1299–1319.

Fulkerson, J. R., & Tucker, M. F. (1999). Diversity: Lessons from global human resource practices. In A. I. Kraut & A. K. Korman (Eds.), *Evolving practices in human resource management* (pp. 249–274). San Francisco: Jossey-Bass.

Fulmer, I. S., Gerhart, B., & Scott, K. S. (2003). Are the 100 best better? An empirical investigation of the relationship between being a "great place to work" and firm performance. *Personnel Psychology, 56,* 965–993.

Gaba, D. M., Singer, S. J., Sinaiko, A. D., Bowen, J. D., & Ciavarelli, A. P. (2003). Differences in safety climate between hospital personnel and naval aviators. *Human Factors, 45,* 173–185.

Gael, S. (1988). *The job analysis handbook for business, industry, and government.* New York: Wiley.

Gajendran, R. S., & Harrison, D. A. (2007). The good, the bad, and the unknown about telecommuting: Meta-analysis of psychological mediators and individual consequences. *Journal of Applied Psychology, 92,* 1524–1541.

Galaif, E. R., Newcomb, M. D., & Carmona, J. V. (2001). Prospective relationships between drug problems and work adjustment in a community sample of adults. *Journal of Applied Psychology, 86,* 337–350.

Gale, J. (2007). Interview with Bernardo M. Ferdman. *San Diego Psychologist, 22*(2), 14–15.

Galinsky, E., Bond, J. T., & Hill, E. J. (2004, April). When work works: A status report on work flexibility. *Families and Work Institute.* Retrieved September 4, 2008, from familiesandwork.org/3w/research/downloads/status.pdf

Gallagher, J. (2002, March 13). Judge likely to OK Ford payouts. *Detroit Free Press,* p. D8.

Ganster, D. C., Fox, M. L., & Dwyer, D. J. (2001). Explaining employees' health care costs: A prospective examination of stressful job demands, personal control, and physiological reactivity. *Journal of Applied Psychology, 86,* 954–964.

Ganster, D. C., & Murphy, L. R. (2000). Workplace interventions to prevent stress-related illness: Lessons from research and practice. In C. L. Cooper & E. A. Locke (Eds.), *Industrial and organizational psychology: Linking theory with practice* (pp. 34–51). Malden, MA: Blackwell.

Ganster, D. C., & Schaubroeck, J. (1995). The moderating effects of self-esteem on the work stress–employee health relationship. In R. Crandall & P. L. Perrewe (Eds.), *Occupational stress: A handbook* (pp. 167–177). London: Taylor & Francis.

Ganzach, Y. (1995). Negativity (and positivity) in performance evaluation: Three field studies. *Journal of Applied Psychology, 80,* 491–499.

Gardiner, M., & Tiggemann, M. (1999). Gender differences in leadership style, job stress, and mental health in male- and female-dominated industries. *Journal of Occupational and Organizational Psychology, 72,* 301–315.

Gardner, H. (1983). *Frames of mind: The theory of multiple intelligences.* New York: Basic Books.

Gardner, H. (1993). *Multiple intelligences: The theory in practice.* New York: Basic Books.

Gardner, H. (2002, February 22). Good work, well done: A psychological study. *The Chronicle of Higher Education,* p. B7(3).

Gardner, H., Csikszentmihalyi, M., & Damon, W. (2001). *Good work: When excellence and ethics meet.* New York: Basic Books.

Garonzik, R., Brockner, J., & Siegel, P. A. (2000). Identifying international assignees at risk for premature departure: The interactive effect of outcome favorability and procedural fairness. *Journal of Applied Psychology, 85,* 13–20.

Garson, B. (1972, June). Luddites in Lordstown. *Harpers Magazine,* pp. 67–73.

Garson, B. (1994). *All the livelong day* (2nd ed.). New York: Penguin Books.

Gatewood, R. D., & Feild, H. S. (2001). *Human resource selection* (5th ed.). New York: Harcourt.

Geisinger, K. F., Spies, R. A., Carlson, J. F., & Plake, B. S. (2007). *The seventeenth mental measurements yearbook.* Lincoln, NE: Buros Institute of Mental Measurements.

Gelade, G. A., & Ivery, M. (2003). The impact of human resource management and work climate on organizational performance. *Personnel Psychology, 56,* 383–404.

Gelfand, M. J., Erez, M., & Aycan, Z. (2007). Cross-cultural organizational behavior. *Annual Review of Psychology, 58,* 479–515.

Gelfand, M. J., Higgins, M., Nishii, L. H., Raver, J. L., Dominguez, A., Murakami, F., Yamaguchi, S., & Toyama, M. (2002). Culture and egocentric perceptions of fairness in conflict and negotiation. *Journal of Applied Psychology, 87,* 833–845.

Gelfand, M. J., Nishii, L. H., Holcombe, K. M., Dyer, N., Ohbuchi, K., & Fukono, M. (2001). Cultural influences on cognitive representations of conflict: Interpretations of conflict episodes in the United States and Japan. *Journal of Applied Psychology, 86,* 1059–1074.

Gellatly, I. R., & Irving, P. G. (2001). Personality, autonomy, and contextual performance of managers. *Human Performance, 14,* 231–245.

Georgopoulos, B. S., Mahoney, G. M., & Jones, N. W. (1957). A path–goal approach to productivity. *Journal of Applied Psychology, 41,* 345–353.

Gerhart, B. (2005). The (affective) dispositional approach to job satisfaction: Sorting out the policy implications. *Journal of Organizational Behavior, 26,* 59–78.

Gersick, C. J. (1988). Time and transition in work teams: Toward a new model of group development. *Academy of Management Journal, 31,* 9–41.

Gersick, C. J. (1989). Marking time: Predictable transition in task groups. *Academy of Management Journal, 32,* 274–309.

Gersick, C. J., & Davis-Sacks, M. L. (1990). Summary: Task forces. In J. R. Hackman (Ed.), *Groups that work (and those that don't)* (pp. 146–153). San Francisco: Jossey-Bass.

Gerstner, C., & Day, D. V. (1997). Meta-analytic review of leader–member exchange theory: Correlates and construct issues. *Journal of Applied Psychology, 82,* 827–844.

Gibby, R. E., & Zickar, M. J. (2008). A history of the early days of personality testing in American industry: An obsession with adjustment. *History of Psychology, 11,* 164–184.

Giberson, T. R., Resick, C. J., & Dickson, M. W. (2005). Embedding leaders' characteristics: An examination of homogeneity of personality and values in organizations. *Journal of Applied Psychology, 90,* 1002–1010.

Gibson, C. B., Porath, C. L., Benson, G. S., & Lawler, E. E. (2007). What results when firms implement practices: The differential relationship between specific practices, firm financial performance, customer service, and quality. *Journal of Applied Psychology, 92,* 1467–1480.

Gibson, C. B., Waller, M. J., Carpenter, M., & Conte, J. M. (2007). Antecedents, consequences, and moderators of time perspective heterogeneity for knowledge management in MNO teams. *Journal of Organizational Behavior, 28,* 1005–1034.

Gibson, J. W., & Tesone, D. V. (2001). Management fads: Emergence, evolution, and implications for managers. *Academy of Management Executive, 15,* 122–133.

Giessner, S. R., & van Knippenberg, D. (2008). "License to fail": Goal definition, leader group prototypicality, and perceptions of leadership effectiveness after leader failure. *Organizational Behavior and Human Decision Processes, 105,* 14–35.

Gigone, D., & Hastie, R. (1997). Proper analysis of the accuracy of group judgments. *Psychological Bulletin, 121,* 149–167.

Gilboa, S., Shirom, A., Fried, Y., & Cooper, C. (2008). A meta-analysis of work demand stressors and job performance: Examining main and moderating effects. *Personnel Psychology, 61,* 227–271.

Gill, C. M., & Hodgkinson, G. P. (2007). Development and validation of the Five-Factor Model Questionnaire (FFMQ): An adjectival-based personality inventory for use in occupational settings. *Personnel Psychology, 60,* 731–766.

Gilliland, S. W. (1993). The perceived fairness of selection systems: An organizational justice perspective. *Academy of Management Review, 18,* 694–734.

Gilliland, S. W., Benson, L., III, & Schepers, D. H. (1998). A rejection threshold in justice evaluations: Effects on judgment and decision making. *Organizational Behavior and Human Decision Processes, 76,* 113–131.

Gilliland, S. W., & Chan, D. (2001). Justice in organizations. In N. Anderson, D. Ones, H. K. Sinangil, & C. Viswesvaran (Eds.), *Handbook of industrial, work, and organizational psychology* (Vol. 2, pp. 143–165). London: Sage.

Gilliland, S. W., & Cherry, B. (2000). Managing "customers" of selection processes. In J. Kehoe (Ed.), *Managing selection in changing organizations* (pp. 158–195). San Francisco: Jossey-Bass.

Gilliland, S. W., & Paddock, L. (2005). Images of justice: Development of justice integration theory. In S. W. Gilliland, D. D. Steiner, & D. P. Skarlicki (Eds.), *What motivates fairness in organizations?* (pp. 49–78). Greenwich, CT: Information Age Publishing.

Gilmore, J. H., & Pine, B. J. (2007). *Authenticity: What consumers really want.* Cambridge, MA: Harvard Business School Press.

Ginnett, R. C. (1990). Airline cockpit crew. In J. R. Hackman (Ed.), *Groups that work (and those that don't).* San Francisco: Jossey Bass.

Gist, M. E., & McDonald-Mann, D. (2000). Advances in leadership training and development. In C. L. Cooper & E. A. Locke (Eds.), *Industrial and organizational psychology: Linking theory with practice* (pp. 52–71). Malden, MA: Blackwell.

Gist, M. E., Schwoerer, C., & Rosen, B. (1989). Effects of alternative training methods on self-efficacy and performance in computer software training. *Journal of Applied Psychology, 74,* 884–891.

Gladstein, D. L. (1984). Groups in context: A model of task group effectiveness. *Administrative Science Quarterly, 29,* 499–517.

Glaister, K. W. (2005). Virgin Atlantic Airways—The dirty tricks episode. Retrieved October 18, 2005, from www.olredlion.here2stay.org.uk/ethics/virgin%case.htm

Glazer, S., & Beehr, T. A. (2005). Consistency of implications of three role stressors across four countries. *Journal of Organizational Behavior, 26,* 467–487.

Gleick, J. (1999). *Faster: The acceleration of just about everything.* New York: Pantheon.

Gneezy, U., Niederle, M., & Rustichini, A. (2003). Performance in competitive environments: Gender differences. *Quarterly Journal of Economics, 128,* 1049–1074.

Goff, S. J., Mount, M. K., & Jamison, R. L. (1990). Employer-supported child care, work/family conflict, and absenteeism: A field study. *Personnel Psychology, 43,* 793–809.

Goffin, R. D., Rothstein, M. G., & Johnston, N. G. (1996). Personality testing and the assessment center: Incremental validity for managerial selection. *Journal of Applied Psychology, 81,* 746–756.

Goffin, R. D., Rothstein, M. G., Reider, M. J., Poole, A., Krajewski, H. T., Powell, D. M., Jelley, R. B., Boyd, A. C., & Mestdagh, T. (2011). Choosing job-related personality traits: Developing valid personality-oriented job analysis. *Personality and Individual Differences, 51,* 646–651.

Goldberg, C. B. (2007). The impact of training and conflict avoidance on responses to sexual harassment. *Psychology of Women Quarterly, 31*(1), 62–72.

Golden, T. D. (2006). The role of relationships in understanding telecommuter satisfaction. *Journal of Organizational Behavior, 27,* 319–340.

Golden, T. D., Veiga, J. F., & Simsek, Z. (2006). Telecommuting's differential impact on work–family conflict: Is there no place like home? *Journal of Applied Psychology, 91,* 1340–1350.

Goldman, B. M. (2001). Toward an understanding of employment discrimination claiming: An integration of organizational justice and social information processing theories. *Personnel Psychology, 54,* 361–386.

Goldstein, I. L., & Ford, J. K. (2002). *Training in organizations: Needs assessment, development, and evaluation* (4th ed.). Belmont, CA: Wadsworth.

Goldstein, I. L., Zedeck, S., & Schneider, B. (1993). An exploration of the job analysis–content validity process. In N. Schmitt & W. C. Borman (Eds.), *Personnel selection in organizations* (pp. 3–34). San Francisco: Jossey-Bass.

Goleman, D. (1995). *Emotional intelligence.* New York: Bantam Books.

Gollwitzer, P. M. (1993). Goal achievement: The role of intentions. In W. Strobe & M. Hewstone (Eds.), *European review of social psychology* (Vol. 4, pp. 141–185). London: Wiley.

Gollwitzer, P. M. (1999). Implementation intentions: Strong effects of simple plans. *American Psychologist, 54,* 493–503.

Gollwitzer, P. M., Heckhausen, H., & Ratajczak, H. (1990). From weighing to willing: Approaching a change decision through pre- or post-decisional mentation. *Organizational Behavior and Human Decision Processes, 45,* 41–65.

Goodman, P. S. (1986). The impact of task and technology on group performance. In P. S. Goodman (Ed.), *Designing effective work groups* (pp. 120–167). San Francisco: Jossey-Bass.

Goodman, P. S., Ravlin, E., & Schminke, M. (1987). Understanding groups in organizations. *Research in Organizational Behavior, 9,* 121–173.

Gorman, C. A., & Rentsch, J. R. (2009). Evaluating frame-of-reference rater training effectiveness using performance schema accuracy. *Journal of Applied Psychology, 94,* 1336–1344.

Gosling, S. D., Vazire, S., Srivastava, S., & John, O. P. (2004). Should we trust web-based studies? A comparative analysis of six preconceptions about Internet questionnaires. *American Psychologist, 59*(2), 93–104.

Goulet, L. R., & Frank, M. L. (2002). Organizational commitment across three sectors: Public, non-profit, and for profit. *Public Personnel Management, 31,* 201–210.

Graen, G. B. (1969). Instrumentality theory of work motivation. *Journal of Applied Psychology, 52,* 261–280.

Graen, G. B., Liden, R. C., & Hoel, W. (1982). Role of leadership in the employee withdrawal process. *Journal of Applied Psychology, 67,* 868–872.

Graen, G. B., & Uhl-Bein, M. (1995). Relationship-based approach to leadership: Development of the leader–member (LMX) exchange theory over 25 years. Applying a multi-level domain approach. *Leadership Quarterly, 6,* 219–247.

Grandey, A. A. (2000). Emotional regulation in the workplace: A new way to conceptualize emotional labor. *Journal of Occupational Health Psychology, 5,* 95–110.

Grandey, A. A. (2003). When the show must go on: Surface and deep acting as determinants of emotional exhaustion and peer-rated service delivery. *Academy of Management Journal, 46,* 86–96.

Grandey, A. A., Dickter, D. N., & Sin, H. P. (2004). The customer is not always right: Customer aggression and emotion regulation of service employees. *Journal of Organizational Behavior, 25,* 397–418.

Grandey, A. A., Fisk, G. M., & Steiner, D. D. (2005). Must "service with a smile" be stressful? The moderating role of personal control for American and French employees. *Journal of Applied Psychology, 90,* 893–904.

Grandey, A. A., Kern, J., & Frone, M. (2007). Verbal abuse from outsiders versus insiders: Comparing frequency, impact on emotional exhaustion, and the role of emotional labor. *Journal of Occupational Health Psychology, 12,* 63–79.

Grant, A. M., & Cavanagh, M. J. (2007). Evidence-based coaching: Flourishing or languishing? *Australian Psychologist, 42,* 239–254.

Grant-Vallone, E. J., & Donaldson, S. I. (2001). Consequences of work–family conflict on employee well-being over time. *Work and Stress, 15,* 214–226.

Green, B., Kingsbury, G., Lloyd, B., Mills, C., Plake, B., Skaggs, et al. (1995). *Guidelines for computerized adaptive-test (CAT) development and use in education* (credit by examination program). Washington, DC: American Council on Education.

Green, F., & Montgomery, S. M. (1998). The quality of skill acquisition in young workers' first job. *Labour, 12*(3), 473–487.

Greenberg, J. (1982). Approaching equity and avoiding inequity in groups and organizations. In J. Greenberg & R. L. Cohen (Eds.), *Equity and justice in social behavior* (pp. 389–345). New York: Academic Press.

Greenberg, J. (1986a). Determinants of perceived fairness of performance evaluations. *Journal of Applied Psychology, 71*, 340–342.

Greenberg, J. (1986b). The distributive justice of organizational performance evaluations. In H. W. Bierhof, R. L. Cohen, & J. Greenberg (Eds.), *Justice in social relations* (pp. 337-351). New York: Plenum.

Greenberg, J. (1994). Using socially fair treatment to promote acceptance of a work site smoking ban. *Journal of Applied Psychology, 79*, 288–297.

Greenberg, J. (2002). *Managing behavior in organizations* (3rd ed.). Upper Saddle River, NJ: Prentice Hall.

Greenberg, J. (2006). Losing sleep over organizational justice: Attenuating insomniac reactions to underpayment inequity with supervisory training in interactional justice. *Journal of Applied Psychology, 91*, 58–69.

Greenberg, J. (2008). Understand the vital human quest for self-esteem. *Perspectives on Psychological Science, 3*, 48–55.

Greenberg, L., & Barling, J. (1999). Predicting employee aggression against co-workers, subordinates, and supervisors: The roles of person behaviors and perceived workplace factors. *Journal of Organizational Behavior, 20*, 897–913.

Greenfield, P. M. (1997). You can't take it with you: Why ability assessments don't cross cultures. *American Psychologist, 52*, 115–124.

Greenhaus, J. H., & Powell, G. N. (2006). When work and family are allies: A theory of work–family enrichment. *Academy of Management Review, 31*, 72–92.

Greenwald, A. J., & Gillmore, G. M. (1997). Grading leniency is a removable contaminant of student ratings. *American Psychologist, 52*, 1209–1217.

Griffin, M. A., Landy, F. J., & Mayocchi, L. (2002). Australian influences on Elton Mayo: The construct of revery in industrial society. *History of Psychology, 5*(4), 356–375.

Grönlund, A. (2007). More control, less conflict? Job demand–control, gender and work–family conflict. *Gender, Work and Organization, 14*(5), 476–497.

Gross, M. L. (1962). *The brain watchers*. New York: Random House.

Grovier, T. (1994). An epistemology of trust. *International Journal of Moral Social Studies, 8*, 155–174.

Grzywacz, J. G., Arcury, T. A., Marin, A., Carrillo, L., Burke, B., Coates, M. L., & Quandt, S. A. (2007). Work–family conflict: Experiences and health implications among immigrant Latinos. *Journal of Applied Psychology, 92*, 1119–1130.

Grzywacz, J. G., & Butler, A. B. (2008). Work–family conflict. In J. Barling & C. Cooper (Eds.), *Handbook of organizational behavior* (pp. 451–468). Thousand Oaks, CA: Sage.

Guernsey, L. (2000, March 2). Bookbag of the future. *New York Times*, pp. D1, D7.

Guion, R. M. (1965). *Personnel testing*. New York: McGraw-Hill.

Guion, R. M. (1980). On trinitarian doctrines of validity. *Professional Psychology, 11*, 385–398.

Guion, R. M. (1998). *Assessment, measurement and prediction for personnel decisions*. Mahwah, NJ: Erlbaum.

Guion, R. M. (2011). *Assessment, measurement and prediction for personnel decisions* (2nd ed.). Mahwah, NJ: Erlbaum.

Gulino et al. v. Board of Education of the New York City School District of the City of New York and the New York State Education Department. (2002). New York, NY, 86 Civ. 8414 (CBM).

Gully, S. M., Payne, S. C., Koles, K. L., & Whiteman, J. K. (2002). The impact of error training and individual differences on training outcomes: An attribute–treatment interaction perspective. *Journal of Applied Psychology, 87*, 143–155.

Gunasegaran, A., & Losefsky, P. (2008, July/August). Self-starter: Bart Knaggs. *The Alcalde*, p. 104.

Gutierres, S. E., Saenz, D. S., & Green, B. L. (1994). Job stress and health outcomes among white and Hispanic employees: A test of the person–environment fit model. In G. P. Keita & J. J. Hurrell (Eds.), *Job stress in a changing workforce: Investigating gender, diversity, and family issues* (pp. 107–125). Washington, DC: American Psychological Association.

Gutman, A. (2001). On the legal front—so what's new at the EEOC? *The Industrial-Organizational Psychologist, 39*, 78–84.

Gutman, A. (2008). Legal environment for selection in the United States. *Industrial and Organizational Psychology: Perspectives on Science and Practice, 1*, 255–257.

Gutman, A., & Dunleavy, E. M. (2011a, July). On the legal front: Supreme Court hears oral arguments in Wal-Mart v. Dukes. *The Industrial-Organizational Psychologist, 49*(1), 49–54.

Gutman, A., & Dunleavy, E. M. (2011b, October). On the legal front: A review of the Supreme Court ruling Wal-Mart v. Dukes: Too big to succeed? *The Industrial-Organizational Psychologist, 49*(2), 75–80.

Gutman, A., Koppes, L., & Vadonovich, S. (2010). *EEO law and personnel practices* (3rd ed.). New York: Routledge/Taylor & Francis Group.

Guzzo, R. A. (1995). Introduction: At the intersection of team effectiveness and decision making. In R. A. Guzzo & E. Salas (Eds.), *Team effectiveness and decision making in organizations* (pp. 1–8). San Francisco: Jossey-Bass.

Guzzo, R. A., & Dickson, M. W. (1996). Teams in organizations: Recent research on performance and effectiveness. *Annual Review of Psychology, 46*, 307–338.

Guzzo, R. A., & Shea, G. P. (1992). Group performance and intergroup relations in organizations. In M. D. Dunnette & L. M. Hough (Eds.), *Handbook of industrial and organizational psychology* (2nd ed., Vol. 3, pp. 269–313). Palo Alto, CA: Consulting Psychologists Press.

Haas, M. R. (2006). Knowledge gathering, team capabilities, and project performance in challenging work environments. *Management Science, 52*, 1170–1184.

Haccoun, R. R., & Hamtiaux, T. (1994). Optimizing knowledge tests for inferring learning acquisition levels in single group training evaluation designs: The internal referencing strategy. *Personnel Psychology, 47*, 593–604.

Hacker, W. (1992). *Expertkönnen: Erkönnen und vermitteln*. Göttingen, Germany: Hogrefe Verlag für Angewandte Psychologie.

Hackman, J. R. (1987). The design of work teams. In J. W. Lorsch (Ed.), *Handbook of organizational behavior* (pp. 315–342). Englewood Cliffs, NJ: Prentice Hall.

Hackman, J. R. (1990). *Groups that work (and those that don't)*. San Francisco: Jossey-Bass.

Hackman, J. R. (2003). Learning more by crossing levels: Evidence from airplanes, hospitals, and orchestras. *Journal of Organizational Behavior, 24*, 905–922.

Hackman, J. R., & Oldham, G. R. (1975). Development of the job diagnostic survey. *Journal of Applied Psychology, 60*, 159–170.

Hackman, J. R., & Oldham, G. R. (1976). Motivation through the design of work: Test of a theory. *Organizational Behavior and Human Performance, 16*, 250–279.

Hackman, J. R., & Oldham, G. R. (1980). *Work redesign*. Reading, MA: Addison-Wesley.

Hall, D. T. (2002). *Careers in and out of organizations*. Thousand Oaks, CA: Sage.

Hall, D. T., Otazo, K. L., & Hollenbeck, G. P. (1999). Behind closed doors: What really happens in executive coaching. *Organizational Dynamics, 27*, 39–53.

Hallam, G. (2001). Multisource feedback for teams. In D. W. Bracken, C. W. Timmreck, & A. H. Church (Eds.), *The handbook of multisource feedback* (pp. 289–300). San Francisco: Jossey-Bass.

Halpern, D. F. (1998). Teaching critical thinking for transfer across domains. *American Psychologist, 53*, 449–455.

Hambley, L. A., O'Neill, T. A., & Kline, T. J. (2007). Virtual team leadership: The effects of leadership style and communication medium on team interaction styles and outcomes. *Organizational Behavior and Human Decision Processes, 103*, 1–20.

Hanisch, K. A., & Hulin, C. L. (1990). Job attitudes and organizational withdrawal: An examination of retirement and other voluntary withdrawal behaviors. *Journal of Vocational Behavior, 37*, 60–78.

Hannafin, K. M., & Hannafin, M. J. (1995). The ecology of distance learning environments. *Training Research Journal, 1*, 49–69.

Hannum, K. M. (2007). Measurement equivalence of 360 degree assessment data: Are different raters rating the same constructs? *International Journal of Selection and Assessment, 15*, 293–301.

Harold, C. M., McFarland, L. A., & Weekley, J. A. (2006). The validity of verifiable and non-verifiable biodata items: An examination across applicants and incumbents. *International Journal of Selection and Assessment, 14*, 336–346.

Harper, K. M. (2005). *The psychology of poker for women.* Unpublished manuscript.

Harris, C., Daniels, K., & Briner, R. B. (2003). A daily diary study of goals and affective well-being at work. *Journal of Occupational and Organizational Psychology, 76*, 401–410.

Harris, G., & Hogan, J. (1992). *Perceptions and personality correlates of managerial effectiveness.* Paper presented at the 13th annual Psychology in the Department of Defense Symposium, Colorado Springs, CO.

Harris, M. M. (1998). Competency modeling: Viagraized job analysis or impotent imposter. *The Industrial-Organizational Psychologist, 36*(2), 37–42.

Harris, M. M. (2000). *Human resource management: A practical approach* (2nd ed.). New York: Dryden Press.

Harris, M. M. (2008). *Handbook of research in international human resource management.* Mahwah, NJ: Erlbaum.

Harrison, D. A., Kravitz, D. A., Mayer, D. M., Leslie, L. M., & Lev-Arey, D. (2006). Understanding attitudes toward affirmative action programs in employment: Summary and meta-analysis of 35 years of research. *Journal of Applied Psychology, 91*, 1013–1036.

Harrison, D. A., Price, K. H., & Bell, M. P. (1998). Beyond relational demography: Time and the effects of surface- and deep-level diversity on work group cohesion. *Academy of Management Journal, 41*, 96–107.

Harrison, D. A., Price, K. H., Gavin, J. H., & Florey, A. T. (2002). Time, teams, and task performance: Changing effects of surface- and deep-level diversity on group functioning. *Academy of Management Journal, 45*, 1029–1045.

Harrison, J. K. (1992). Individual and combined effects of behavior modeling and the cultural assimilator in cross-cultural management training. *Journal of Applied Psychology, 77*, 952–962.

Harter, J. K., Schmidt, F. L., & Hayes, T. L. (2002). Business-unit-level relationship between employee satisfaction, employee engagement, and business outcomes: A meta-analysis. *Journal of Applied Psychology, 87*, 268–279.

Hartig, T., Kylin, C., & Johansonn, G. (2007). The telework tradeoff: Stress mitigation vs. constrained restoration. *Applied Psychology: An International Review, 56*, 231–253.

Hartigan, J., & Wigdor, A. K. (1989). *Fairness in employment testing: Validity generalization, minority issues, and the general aptitude test battery.* Washington, DC: National Academies Press.

Hartley, D., & West, K. (2007). Taking it personally: Tailoring training for more relevance. *Training and Development, 61*(11), 21–23.

Hartley, J. (2002). Organizational change and development. In P. B. Warr (Ed.), *Psychology at work* (5th ed., pp. 399–425). London: Penguin.

Harvey, R. J. (1991). Job analysis. In M. D. Dunnette & L. M. Hough (Eds.), *Handbook of industrial and organizational psychology* (2nd ed., Vol. 1, pp. 71–163). Palo Alto, CA: Consulting Psychologists Press.

Harvey, R. J. (1993, May). The common-metric questionnaire: Applications and current research. In S. Fine (Chair), *Multipurpose job analysis: New approaches supporting integrated human resource management.* Symposium presented at the annual conference of the Society for Industrial and Organizational Psychology, San Francisco.

Haslam, S. A. (2004). *Psychology in organizations: The social identity approach* (2nd ed.). London: Sage.

Hattrup, K., Mueller, K., & Aguirre, P. (2008). An evaluation of the cross-national generalizability of organizational commitment. *Journal of Occupational and Organizational Psychology, 81*, 219–240.

Hauenstein, N. M. A. (1998). Training raters to increase the accuracy of appraisals and the usefulness of feedback. In J. W. Smither (Ed.), *Performance appraisal: State of the art in practice* (pp. 404–443). San Francisco: Jossey-Bass.

Hausknecht, J. P., Day, D. V., & Thomas, S. C. (2004). Applicant reactions to selection procedures: An updated model and meta-analysis. *Personnel Psychology, 57*, 639–683.

Hawkridge, D. (1999). Distance learning: International comparisons. *Performance Improvement Quarterly, 12*, 9–20.

Haynes, E. F. (1997). *An application of Mintzberg's configurational theory to community college organizational structure.* Unpublished dissertation.

Hayward, M. L., Shepherd, D. A., & Griffin, D. (2006). A hubris theory of entrepreneurship. *Management Science, 52*, 160–172.

Heckhausen, H., Gollwitzer, P. M., & Weinert, F. E. (Eds.). (1987). *Jenseits des Rubikon: Der Wille in den Humanwissenschaften.* Berlin: Springer Verlag.

Hedge, J. W., & Borman, W. C. (1995). Changing conceptions and practices in performance appraisal. In A. Howard (Ed.), *The changing nature of work* (pp. 451–481). San Francisco: Jossey-Bass.

Hedge, J. W., & Borman, W. C. (2008). *The I-O consultant: Advice and insights for building a successful career.* Washington, DC: American Psychological Association.

Hedge, J. W., & Teachout, M. S. (1992). An interview approach to work sample criterion measurement. *Journal of Applied Psychology, 77*, 453–461.

Heggestad, E. D., & Kanfer, R. (2001). Individual differences in trait motivation: Development of the Motivational Trait Questionnaire. *International Journal of Educational Research, 33*, 751–776.

Heggestad, E. D., Morrison, M., Reeve, C. L., & McCloy, R. A. (2006). Forced-choice assessments of personality for selection: Evaluating issues of normative assessment and faking resistance. *Journal of Applied Psychology, 91*, 9–24.

Heilman, M. E., & Alcot, V. B. (2001). What I think you think of me: Women's reactions to being viewed as beneficiaries of preferential selection. *Journal of Applied Psychology, 86*, 574–582.

Heilman, M. E., & Blader, S. L. (2001). Assuming preferential selection when admissions policy is unknown: The effects of gender rarity. *Journal of Applied Psychology, 86*, 188–193.

Heilman, M. E., & Chen, J. J. (2005). Same behavior, different consequences: Reactions to men's and women's altruistic citizenship behavior. *Journal of Applied Psychology, 90*, 431–441.

Heilman, M. E., & Okimoto, T. G. (2007). Why are women penalized for success at male tasks? The implied communality deficit. *Journal of Applied Psychology, 92*, 81–92.

Hemingway, M. (2001). Qualitative research in I-O psychology. *The Industrial-Organizational Psychologist, 38*(3), 45–51.

Hemingway, M. A., & Conte, J. M. (2003). The perceived fairness of layoff practices. *Journal of Applied Social Psychology, 33*, 1588–1617.

Hendricks, J. W., & Payne, S. C. (2007). Beyond the Big Five: Leader goal orientation as a predictor of leadership effectiveness. *Human Performance, 20,* 317–343.

Heneman, R. L. (1986). The relationship between supervisory ratings and results-oriented measures of performance: A meta-analysis. *Personnel Psychology, 39,* 811–826.

Heneman, R. L., Ledford, G. E., Jr., & Gresham, M. T. (2000). The changing nature of work and its effects on compensation design and delivery. In S. L. Rynes & B. Gerhart (Eds.), *Compensation in organizations* (pp. 195–240). San Francisco: Jossey-Bass.

Hermans, H. J. M., & Kempen, H. J. G. (1998). Moving cultures: The perilous problems of cultural dichotomies in a globalizing society. *American Psychologist, 53,* 1111–1120.

Hermelin, E., Lievens, F., & Robertson, I. T. (2007). The validity of assessment centres for the predication of supervisory performance ratings: A meta-analysis. *International Journal of Selection and Assessment, 15,* 405–411.

Herold, D. M., Fedor, D. B., & Caldwell, S. D. (2007). Beyond change management: A multilevel investigation of contextual and personal influences on employees' commitment to change. *Journal of Applied Psychology, 92,* 942–951.

Herriot, P., & Pemberton, C. (1995). *Competitive advantage through diversity.* London: Sage.

Hersey, P., & Blanchard, K. H. (1977). *The management of organizational behavior* (3rd ed.). Englewood Cliffs, NJ: Prentice Hall.

Hersey, R. B. (1932). *Worker's emotions in shop and home: A study of individual workers from the psychological and physiological standpoint.* Philadelphia: University of Pennsylvania Press.

Hersey, R. B. (1955). *Zest for work: Industry rediscovers the individual.* New York: Harper.

Hertel, G., Konradt, U., & Orlikowsi, B. (2004). Managing distance by interdependence: Goal setting, task interdependence, and team-based rewards in virtual teams. *European Journal of Work and Organizational Psychology, 13,* 1–28.

Herzberg, F. (1966). *Work and the nature of man.* Cleveland: World Publishing.

Herzberg, F., Mausner, B., Peterson, R. O., & Capwell, D. F. (1957). *Job attitudes: Review of research and opinion.* Pittsburgh, PA: Psychological Service of Pittsburgh.

Herzberg, F., Mausner, B., & Snyderman, B. (1959). *The motivation to work.* New York: Wiley.

Heslin, P. A., & Vandewalle, D. (2011). Performance appraisal procedural justice: The role of manager's implicit person theory. *Journal of Management, 37,* 1694–1718.

Hetland, H., & Sandal, G. M. (2003). Transformational leadership in Norway: Outcomes and personality correlates. *European Journal of Work and Organizational Psychology, 12*(2), 147–170.

Hiemstra, A. M., van der Kooy, K. G., & Frese, M. (2006). Entrepreneurship in the street food sector of Vietnam: Assessment of psychological success and failure factors. *Journal of Small Business Management, 44,* 474–481.

Highhouse, S. (1999). The brief history of personnel counseling in industrial-organizational psychology. *Journal of Vocational Behavior, 55,* 318–336.

Highhouse, S. (2002). Assessing the candidate as a whole: A historical and critical analysis of individual psychological assessment for personnel decision making. *Personnel Psychology, 55,* 363–396.

Hmieleski, K., & Baron, R. A. (2008). When does entrepreneurial self-efficacy enhance versus reduce firm performance? *Strategic Entrepreneurship Journal, 2*(1), 57–72.

Hochschild, A. R. (1983). *The managed heart: Commercialization of human feeling.* Berkeley: University of California Press.

Hoeft, S., & Schuler, H. (2001). The conceptual basis of assessment centre ratings. *International Journal of Selection and Assessment, 9,* 114–123.

Hoel, H., Cooper, C. L., & Faragher (2001). The experience of bullying in Great Britain: The impact of organizational status. *European Journal of Work and Organizational Psychology, 10,* 485–496.

Hoffman, B. J., Blair, C. A., Meriac, J. P., & Woehr, D. J. (2007). Expanding the criterion domain? A quantitative review of the OCB literature. *Journal of Applied Psychology, 92,* 555–566.

Hoffmann, C. C. (1999). Generalizing physical ability test validity: A case study using test transportability, validity generalization, and construct-related validation evidence. *Personnel Psychology, 52,* 1019–1041.

Hofmann, D. A., Jacobs, R. R., & Landy, F. J. (1995). High reliability process industries: Individual, micro, and macro organizational influences on safety performance. *Journal of Safety Research, 26,* 131–149.

Hofmann, D. A., & Mark, B. (2006). An investigation of the relationship between safety climate and medication errors as well as other nurse and patient outcomes. *Personnel Psychology, 59,* 847–869.

Hofstede, G. (1980). *Culture's consequences: International differences in work-related values.* Beverly Hills, CA: Sage.

Hofstede, G. (1984). *Culture's consequences: International differences in work-related values.* Newbury Park, CA: Sage.

Hofstede, G. (1993). Cultural constraints in management theories. *Academy of Management Executive, 7,* 91.

Hofstede, G. (2001). *Culture's consequences: Comparing values, behaviors, institutions, and organizations across nations.* Thousand Oaks, CA: Sage.

Hogan, J. (1991a). Physical abilities. In M. D. Dunnette & L. M. Hough (Eds.), *Handbook of industrial and organizational psychology* (2nd ed., Vol. 2, pp. 753–831). Palo Alto, CA: Consulting Psychologists Press.

Hogan, J. (1991b). Structure of physical performance in occupational tasks. *Journal of Applied Psychology, 76,* 495–507.

Hogan, J., Davies, S., & Hogan, R. (2007). Generalizing personality-based validity evidence. In S. Morton McPhail (Ed.), *Alternative validation strategies: Developing new and leveraging existing validity evidence* (pp. 180–229). San Francisco: Jossey-Bass.

Hogan, J., & Roberts, B. W. (1996). Issues and non-issues in the fidelity-bandwidth trade-off. *Journal of Organizational Behavior, 17,* 627–637.

Hogan, R. (2005). Comments. *Human Performance, 18,* 405–407.

Hogan, R., Curphy, G. J., & Hogan, J. (1994). What we know about leadership: Effectiveness and personality. *American Psychologist, 49,* 493–504.

Hogan, R., & Hogan, J. (2001). Assessing leadership: A view from the dark side. *International Journal of Selection and Assessment, 9*(1/2), 40–51.

Hogan, R., Hogan, J., & Roberts, B. W. (1996). Personality measurement and employment decisions. *American Psychologist, 51,* 469–477.

Holland, B., & Hogan, R. (1998). Remodeling the electronic cottage. *The Industrial-Organizational Psychologist, 36*(2), 21–22.

Holland, J. L. (1985). *Making vocational choices: A theory of careers* (2nd ed.). Englewood Cliffs, NJ: Prentice Hall.

Hollander, E. P., & Julian, J. W. (1969). Contemporary trends in the analysis of the leadership process. *Psychological Bulletin, 71,* 387–397.

Hollenbeck, G. P. (2001). Coaching executives: Individual leader development. In R. F. Silzer (Ed.), *The 21st century executive: Innovative practices for building leadership at the top.* San Francisco: Jossey-Bass.

Hollenbeck, G. P., & McCall, M. W. (1999). Leadership development: Contemporary practices. In A. I. Kraut & A. K. Korman (Eds.), *Evolving practice in human resource management* (pp. 172–200). San Francisco: Jossey-Bass.

Hollingworth, H. L., & Poffenberger, A. T. (1923). *Applied psychology.* New York: D. Appleton and Company.

Holvino, E., Ferdman, B. M., & Merrill-Sands, D. (2004). Creating and sustaining diversity and inclusion in organizations: Strategies and approaches. In M. S. Stockdale & F. J. Crosby (Eds.), *The psychology and management of workplace diversity* (pp. 245–276). Malden, MA: Blackwell.

Hom, P. W., & Griffeth, R. W. (1995). *Employee turnover.* Cincinnati, OH: Southwestern.

Hoppock, R. (1935). *Job satisfaction.* New York: Harper & Row.

Horner, K. L. (1996). Locus of control, neuroticism, and stressors: Combined influences on reported physical illness. *Personality and Individual Differences, 21,* 195–204.

Horwitz, S. K., & Horwitz, I. B. (2007). The effects of team diversity on team outcomes: A meta-analytic review of team demography. *Journal of Management, 33,* 987–1015.

Hosking, D. M. (1988). Chairperson's address: Organizing through skillful leadership. *British Psychological Society: The Occupational Psychologist, 4,* 4–11.

Hough, L. M. (1992). The "Big Five" personality variables—construct confusion: Description vs. prediction. *Human Performance, 5,* 139–155.

Hough, L. M., Eaton, N. K., Dunnette, M. D., Kamp, J. D., & McCloy, R. A. (1990). Criterion-related validities of personality constructs and the effect of response distortions on those validities. *Journal of Applied Psychology, 75* [Monograph], 581–595.

Hough, L. M., & Ones, D. S. (2001). The structure, measurement, validity and use of personality variables in industrial, work, and organizational psychology. In N. Anderson, D. S. Ones, H. K. Siningal, & C. Viswesvaran (Eds.), *Handbook of industrial, work, and organizational psychology* (pp. 233–277). London: Sage.

House, J. S. (1981). *Work stress and social support.* Reading, MA: Addison-Wesley.

House, R. J. (1971). A path–goal theory of leader effectiveness. *Administrative Science Quarterly, 16,* 321–339.

House, R. J. (1977). A 1976 theory of charismatic leadership. In J. G. Hunt & L. L. Larson (Eds.), *Leadership: The cutting edge* (pp. 189–207). Carbondale: Southern Illinois University Press.

House, R. J., Hanges, P. J., Javidan, M., Dorfman, P. W., & Gupta, V. (2004). *Culture, leadership, and organizations.* Thousand Oaks, CA: Sage.

House, R. J., Hanges, P. J., Ruiz-Quintanilla, S. A., Dorfman, P. W., Javidan, M., Dickson, M., et al. (1999). Cultural influences on leadership and organization: Project GLOBE. In W. Mobley, J. Gessner, & V. Arnold (Eds.), *Advances in global leadership* (Vol. 1, pp. 171–234). Stamford, CT: JAI Press.

House, R. J., Javidan, M., & Dorfman, P. (2001). Project GLOBE: An introduction. *Applied Psychology: An International Review, 50*(4), 489–505.

House, R. J., & Mitchell, T. R. (1974). Path–goal theory of leadership. *Contemporary Business, 3*(Fall), 81–98.

House, R. J., & Singh, J. V. (1987). Organizational behavior: Some new directions for I-O psychology. *Annual Review of Psychology, 38,* 669–718.

House, R. J., Wright, N. S., & Aditya, R. N. (1997). Cross-cultural research on organizational leadership: A critical analysis and proposed theory. In P. C. Early & M. Erez (Eds.), *New perspectives on international industrial and organizational psychology* (pp. 535–625). San Francisco: Jossey-Bass.

Houser, J. D. (1927). *What the employer thinks.* Cambridge, MA: Harvard University Press.

Hovorka-Mead, A. D., Ross, W. H., Jr., Whipple, T., & Renchin, M. B. (2002). Watching the detectives: Seasonal student employees' reactions to electronic monitoring with and without advance notification. *Personnel Psychology, 55,* 329–362.

Howard, A. (2001). Identifying, assessing, and selecting senior leaders. In S. J. Zaccaro & R. J. Klimoski (Eds.), *The nature of organizational leadership: Understanding the performance imperatives confronting today's leaders* (pp. 305–346). San Francisco: Jossey-Bass.

Howard, A., & Associates (1994). *Diagnosis for organizational change: Methods and models.* New York: Guilford.

Howell, J. M., Neufeld, D. J., & Avolio, B. J. (2005). Examining the relationship of leadership and physical distance with business unit performance. *Leadership Quarterly, 16,* 273–285.

Hubbard, A. (2002). Successful ethics training. *Mortgage Banking, 62*(June), 104–108.

Hubert, A. B., & Veldhoven, M. (2001). Risk sectors for undesirable behavior and mobbing. *European Journal of Work and Organizational Psychology, 10,* 415–424.

Huffcutt, A. I., Conway, J. M., Roth, P. L., & Stone, N. J. (2001). Identification and meta-analytic assessment of psychological constructs measured in employment interviews. *Journal of Applied Psychology, 86,* 897–913.

Huffcutt, A. I., & Roth, P. L. (1998). Racial group differences in employment interview evaluations. *Journal of Applied Psychology, 83,* 179–189.

Huffcutt, A. I., Weekley, J. A., Wiesner, W. H., DeGroot, T. G., & Jones, C. (2001). Comparison of situational and behavior description interview questions for higher-level positions. *Personnel Psychology, 54,* 619–644.

Huffcutt, A. I., & Woehr, D. J. (1999). Further analysis of the employment interview validity: A quantitative evaluation of interviewer-related structuring methods. *Journal of Organizational Behavior, 20,* 549–560.

Huffman, A. H., Watrous-Rodriguez, K. M., Henning, J. B., & Berry, J. (2009). Working through environmental issues: The role of the I/O psychologist. *The Industrial-Organizational Psychologist, 47*(2), 27–35.

Hui, C., Lee, C., & Rousseau, D. M. (2004). Psychological contract and organizational citizenship behavior in China: Investigating generalizability and instrumentality. *Journal of Applied Psychology, 89,* 311–321.

Hui, C. H., & Yee, C. (1999). The impact of psychological collectivism and workgroup atmosphere on Chinese employees' job satisfaction. *Applied Psychology: An International Review, 48,* 175–185.

Hulin, C. L. (1991). Adaptation, persistence, and commitment in organizations. In M. D. Dunnette & L. M. Hough (Eds.), *Handbook of industrial and organizational psychology* (2nd ed., Vol. 2, pp. 445–505). Palo Alto, CA: Consulting Psychologists Press.

Hulin, C. L., & Mayer, L. J. (1986). Psychometric equivalence of a translation of the Job Descriptive Index into Hebrew. *Journal of Applied Psychology, 71,* 83–94.

Hull, C. L. (1928). *Aptitude testing.* Yonkers, NY: World Book.

Hülsheger, U. R., Anderson, N., & Salgado, J. F. (2009). Team-level predictors of innovation at work: A comprehensive meta-analysis spanning three decades of research. *Journal of Applied Psychology, 94,* 1128–1145.

Hülsheger, U. R., Maier, G. W., & Stumpp, T. (2007). Validity of general mental ability for the prediction of job performance and training success in Germany: A meta-analysis. *International Journal of Selection and Assessment, 15*(1), 3–18.

Hunt, S. T. (2002). On the virtues of staying "inside of the box": Does organizational citizenship behavior detract from performance in Taylorist jobs? *International Journal of Selection and Assessment, 10,* 152–159.

Hunthausen, J. M., Truxillo, D. M., Bauer, T. N., & Hammer, L. B. (2003). A field study of frame-of-reference effects on personality test validity. *Journal of Applied Psychology, 88,* 545–551.

Hurtz, G. M., & Donovan, J. J. (2000). Personality and job performance: The Big Five revisited. *Journal of Applied Psychology, 85*, 869–879.

Huselid, M. A. (1995). The impact of human resource management practices on turnover, productivity, and corporate financial performance. *Academy of Management Journal, 38*, 635–672.

Hyde, J. S. (2005). The gender similarities hypothesis. *American Psychologist, 60*, 581–592.

Iacono, W. G., & Lykken, D. T. (1997). The validity of the lie detector: Two surveys of scientific opinion. *Journal of Applied Psychology, 82*, 426–433.

Ibison, D. (2006, April 24). Japanese version of "The Apprentice" gets fired. *Los Angeles Times.* Retrieved July 28, 2008, from articles.latimes.com/2006/apr/24/business/ft-japan24

Ilgen, D. R. (1999). Teams embedded in organizations: Some implications. *American Psychologist, 54*, 129–139.

Ilgen, D. R., Hollenbeck, J., Johnson, M., & Jundt, D. (2005). Teams in organizations: From input–process–output models to IMOI models. *Annual Review of Psychology, 56*, 517–543.

Ilgen, D. R., & Pulakos, E. D. (1999). Employee performance in today's organizations. In D. R. Ilgen & E. D. Pulakos (Eds.), *The changing nature of performance: Implications for staffing, motivation, and development.* San Francisco: Jossey-Bass.

Ilies, R., Dimotakis, N., & De Pater, I. E. (2010). Psychological and physiological reactions to high workloads: Implications for well-being. *Personnel Psychology, 63*(2), 407–436.

Ilies, R., & Judge, T. A. (2003). On the heritability of job satisfaction: The mediating role of personality. *Journal of Applied Psychology, 88*, 750–759.

Ilies, R., Morgeson, F. P., & Nahrgang, J. D. (2005). Authentic leadership and eudemonic well-being: Understanding leader–follower outcomes. *Leadership Quarterly, 16*, 373–394.

Ilies, R., Nahrgang, J. D., & Morgeson, F. P. (2007). Leader–member exchange and citizenship behaviors: A meta-analysis. *Journal of Applied Psychology, 92*, 269–277.

International Test Commission (2000). *International guidelines for test use.* Louvain-la-Neuve, Belgium: Author.

Isen, A. M., Clark, M., & Schwartz, M. F. (1976). Duration of the effect of good mood on helping: "Footsteps on the sands of time." *Journal of Personality and Social Psychology, 34*, 385–393.

Ivancevich, J. M., & Matteson, M. T. (2002). *Organizational behavior and management* (6th ed.). New York: McGraw-Hill.

Jablonski, J. R. (1991). *Implementing total quality management: An overview.* San Francisco: Pfeiffer.

Jackson, M. (2002, September 8). Can a test gauge the value of an MBA? *New York Times*, p. B6.

Jackson, S. E. (1996). The consequences of diversity in multidisciplinary work teams. In M. A. West (Ed.), *Handbook of work group psychology* (pp. 53–76). Chichester, UK: Wiley.

Jackson, S. E., Brett, J. F., Sessa, V. I., Cooper, D. M., Julin, J. A., & Peyronnin, K. (1991). Some differences make a difference: Individual dissimilarity and group heterogeneity as correlates of recruitment, promotions, and turnover. *Journal of Applied Psychology, 76*, 675–689.

Jackson, S. E., & Joshi, A. (2001). Research on domestic and international diversity in organizations: A merger that works? In N. Anderson, D. Ones, H. Sinangil, & C. Viswesvaran (Eds.), *Handbook of industrial, work, and organizational psychology* (Vol. 1, pp. 206–231). London: Sage.

Jackson, S. E., & Joshi, A. (2004). Diversity in social context: A multi-attribute, multi-level analysis of team diversity and performance in a sales organization. *Journal of Organizational Behavior, 25*, 801–830.

Jackson, S. E., Joshi, A., & Erhardt, N. L. (2003). Recent research on team and organizational diversity: SWOT analysis and implications. *Journal of Management, 29*, 801–830.

Jackson, S. E., May, K. E., & Whitney, K. (1995). Understanding the dynamics of diversity in decision-making teams. In R. Guzzo & E. Salas (Eds.), *Team effectiveness and decision-making in organizations* (pp. 204–261). San Francisco: Jossey-Bass.

Jackson, S. E., & Seo, J. (2010). The greening of strategic HRM scholarship. *Organizational Management Journal, 7*, 278–290.

Jackson, S. E., & Schuler, R. S. (1985). A meta-analysis and conceptual critique of research on role ambiguity and role conflict in work settings. *Organizational Behavior and Human Decision Processes, 36*, 16–78.

Jackson, S. E., & Schuler, R. S. (2003). Cultural diversity in crossborder alliances. In D. Tjosvold & K. Leung (Eds.), *Cross-cultural management: Foundations and future* (pp. 123–154). Aldershot, UK: Ashgate.

Jackson, S. E., & Schuler, R. S. (2006). *Managing human resources through strategic partnerships* (9th ed.). Mason, OH: Thomson.

Jackson, S. E., Schuler, R. S., & Werner, S. (2011). *Managing human resources* (11th ed.). Mason, OH: Southwestern/Cengage Learning.

Jahoda, M. (1981). Work, employment and unemployment: Values, theories and approaches in social research. *American Psychologist, 36*, 184–191.

Jamal, M. (2007). Type A behavior in a multinational organization: A study of two countries. *Stress and Health, 23*, 101–109.

James, E. H., Brief, A. P., Dietz, J., & Cohen, R. R. (2001). Prejudice matters: Understanding the reactions of whites to affirmative action programs targeted to benefit blacks. *Journal of Applied Psychology, 86*, 1120–1128.

James, L. A., & James, L. R. (1989). Integrating work environment perceptions: Explorations in the measurement of meaning. *Journal of Applied Psychology, 69*, 85–98.

James, L. R. (1998). Measurement of personality via conditional reasoning. *Organizational Research Methods, 1*, 131–163.

James, L. R., Ko, C. E., & McIntyre, M. D. (2008, April). *Dealing with arbitrary metrics in conditional reasoning.* Paper presented at the Annual SIOP Conference, San Francisco.

James, L. R., & McIntyre, M. D. (1996). Perceptions of organizational climate. In K. R. Murphy (Ed.), *Individual differences and behavior in organizations* (pp. 416–450). San Francisco: Jossey-Bass.

Janis, I. L. (1982). *Groupthink: A study of foreign policy decisions and fiascos* (2nd ed.). Boston: Houghton Mifflin.

Janofsky, M. J. (2005, October 26). College chief at American agrees to quit for millions. *New York Times*, p. A20.

Javidan, M., Dorfman, P. W., Sully de Luque, M., & House, R. J. (2006). In the eye of the beholder: Cross-cultural lessons in leadership from project GLOBE. *Academy of Management Perspectives, 20*, 67–90.

Javidan, M., Stahl, G. K., Brodbeck, F., & Wilderom, C. P. M. (2005). Cross-border transfer of knowledge: Cultural lessons from project GLOBE. *Academy of Management Executive, 19*(2), 59–76.

Jeanneret, P. R. (1992). Applications of job component/synthetic validity to construct validity. *Human Performance, 5*, 81–96.

Jeanneret, P. R., & Strong, M. H. (2003). Linking O*NET job analysis information to job requirement predictors: An O*NET application. *Personnel Psychology, 56*, 465–492.

Jentsch, F., & Bowers, C. A. (1998). Evidence for the validity of PC-based simulations in studying aircrew coordination. *International Journal of Aviation Psychology, 8*, 243–260.

Jeppensen, J. C. (2002). Creating and maintaining the learning organization. In K. Kraiger (Ed.), *Creating, implementing, and managing effective training and development* (pp. 302–330). San Francisco: Jossey-Bass.

Jex, S. M. (1998). *Stress and job performance: Theory, research, and implications for managerial practice.* Thousand Oaks, CA: Sage.

Johns, G. (1997). Contemporary research on absence from work: Correlates, causes and consequences. *International Review of Industrial and Organizational Psychology, 12*, 115–173.

Johns, G. (2001). In praise of context. *Journal of Organizational Behavior, 22*, 31–42.

Johns, M., Schmader, T., & Martens, A. (2005). Knowing is half the battle: Teaching stereotype threat as a means of improving women's math performance. *Psychological Science, 16*, 175–179.

Johnson, J. L., & O'Leary-Kelly, A. (2003). The effects of psychological contract breach and organizational cynicism: Not all social exchange violations are created equal. *Journal of Organizational Behavior, 24*, 627–647.

Johnson, J. W. (2001). The relative importance of task and contextual performance dimensions to supervisor judgments of overall performance. *Journal of Applied Psychology, 86*, 984–996.

Johnson, J. W., Carter, G. W., & Dorsey, D. W. (2003, April). *Linking O*NET descriptors to occupational aptitudes using job component validation.* Poster presented at the 18th Annual Conference of the Society for Industrial and Organizational Psychology, Orlando, FL.

Johnson, M. (1999). Use anti-harassment training to shelter yourself from suits. *HR Magazine, 44*(October), 76–81.

Joinson, C. (2002, June). Managing virtual teams. *HR Magazine, 47*, 68–73.

Joireman, J., Kamdar, D., Daniels, D., & Duell, B. (2006). Good citizens to the end? It depends: Empathy and concern with future consequences moderate the impact of a short-term time horizon on organizational citizenship behaviors. *Journal of Applied Psychology, 91*, 1307–1320.

Jones, G. R. (1984). Task visibility, free riding, and shirking: Explaining the effect of structure and technology on employee behavior. *Academy of Management Review, 9*, 684–695.

Jones, J. M. (1988). Cultural differences in temporal perspectives: Instrumental and expressive behaviors in time. In J. E. McGrath (Ed.), *The social psychology of time: New perspectives* (pp. 21–38). Thousand Oaks, CA: Sage.

Jones, J. W., Barge, B. N., Steffy, B. D., Fay, L. M., Kunz, L. K., & Wuebker, L. J. (1988). Stress and medical malpractice: Organizational risk assessment and intervention. *Journal of Applied Psychology, 73*, 727–735.

Jones, R. G. (2011). *Nepotism in organizations.* New York: Routledge.

Jones, R. G., & Whitmore, M. D. (1995). Evaluating developmental assessment centers as interventions. *Personnel Psychology, 48*, 377–388.

Jones, S., & Moffett, R. G. (1999). Measurement and feedback for teams. In E. Sundstrom (Ed.), *Supporting team effectiveness: Best management practices for fostering high performance.* San Francisco: Jossey-Bass.

Judge, T. A., & Bono, J. E. (2000). Five factor model of personality and transformational leadership. *Journal of Applied Psychology, 85*, 751–765.

Judge, T. A., & Bono, J. E. (2001). Relationship of core self-evaluation traits—self-esteem, generalized self-efficacy, locus of control, and emotional stability—with job satisfaction and job performance: A meta-analysis. *Journal of Applied Psychology, 86*, 80–92.

Judge, T. A., Bono, J. E., Erez, A., & Locke, E. A. (2005). Core self-evaluations and job and life satisfaction: The role of self-concordance and goal attainment. *Journal of Applied Psychology, 90*, 257–268.

Judge, T. A., Bono, J. E., Ilies, R., & Gerhardt, M. W. (2002). Personality and leadership: A qualitative and quantitative review. *Journal of Applied Psychology, 87*, 765–780.

Judge, T. A., Bono, J. E., & Locke, E. A. (2000). Personality and job satisfaction: The mediating role of job characteristics. *Journal of Applied Psychology, 85*, 237–249.

Judge, T. A., & Cable, D. M. (1997). Applicant personality, organizational culture, and organization attraction. *Personnel Psychology, 50*, 359–394.

Judge, T. A., Colbert, A. E., & Ilies, R. (2004). Intelligence and leadership: A quantitative review and test of theoretical propositions. *Journal of Applied Psychology, 89*, 542–552.

Judge, T. A., & Erez, A. (2007). Interaction and intersection: The constellation of emotional stability and extraversion in predicting performance. *Personnel Psychology, 60*, 573–596.

Judge, T. A., Erez, A., Bono, J. E., & Thoreson, C. J. (2003). The core self-evaluations scale: Development of a measure. *Personnel Psychology, 56*, 303–331.

Judge, T. A., Fluegge, E., Hurst, C., & Livingston, B. A. (2006). Leadership. In C. L. Cooper & J. Barling (Eds.), *Handbook of organizational behavior.* Thousand Oaks, CA: Sage.

Judge, T. A., & Hulin, C. L. (1993). Job satisfaction as a reflection of disposition: A multiple source causal analysis. *Organizational Behavior and Human Decision Processes, 56*, 388–421.

Judge, T. A., & Hurst, C. (2007). Capitalizing on one's advantages: Role of core self-evaluations. *Journal of Applied Psychology, 92*, 1212–1227.

Judge, T. A., & Ilies, R. (2002). Relationship of personality to performance motivation: A meta-analytic review. *Journal of Applied Psychology, 87*, 797–807.

Judge, T. A., & Ilies, R. (2004). Affect and job satisfaction: A study of their relationship at work and at home. *Journal of Applied Psychology, 89*, 661–673.

Judge, T. A., LePine, J. A., & Rich, B. L. (2006). Loving yourself abundantly: Relationship of the narcissistic personality to self and other perceptions of workplace deviance, leadership, task, and contextual performance. *Journal of Applied Psychology, 91*, 762–776.

Judge, T. A., Locke, E. A., & Durham, C. C. (1997). The dispositional causes of job satisfaction: A core evaluations approach. *Research in Organizational Behavior, 19*, 151–188.

Judge, T. A., Locke, E. A., Durham, C. C., & Kluger, A. N. (1998). Dispositional effects on job and life satisfaction: The role of core evaluations. *Journal of Applied Psychology, 83*, 17–34.

Judge, T. A., Parker, S., Colbert, A. E., Heller, D., & Ilies, R. (2001). Job satisfaction: A cross-cultural review. In N. Anderson, D. Ones, H. Sinangil, & C. Viswesvaran (Eds.), *Handbook of industrial, work, and organizational psychology* (Vol. 2, pp. 25–52). London: Sage.

Judge, T. A., & Piccolo, R. F. (2004). Transformational and transactional leadership: A meta-analytic study of their relative validity. *Journal of Applied Psychology, 89*, 755–768.

Judge, T. A., Piccolo, R. F., & Ilies, R. (2004). The forgotten ones? The validity of consideration and initiating structure in leadership research. *Journal of Applied Psychology, 89*, 36–51.

Judge, T. A., Scott, B. A., & Ilies, R. (2006). Hostility, job attitudes, and workplace deviance: Test of a multi-level model. *Journal of Applied Psychology, 91*, 126–138.

Judge, T. A., Thoreson, C. J., Bono, J. E., & Patton, G. K. (2001). The job satisfaction–job performance relationship: A qualitative and quantitative review. *Psychological Bulletin, 127*, 376–407.

Judge, T. A., Thoreson, C. J., Pucik, V., & Welbourne, T. M. (1999). Managerial coping with organizational change: A dispositional perspective. *Journal of Applied Psychology, 84*, 107–122.

Judge, T. A., van Vianen, A. E. M., & De Pater, I. E. (2004). Emotional stability, core self-evaluations and job outcomes: A review of the evidence and an agenda for future research. *Human Performance, 17*, 325–346.

Judge, T. A., Woolf, E. F., Hurst, C., & Livingston, B. (2006). Charismatic and transformational leadership: A review and an agenda for future research. *Zeitschrift fur Arbeits- u. Organisationspsychologie, 50*, 203–214.

Juran, J. M. (1992). *Juran on quality by design: The new steps for planning quality into goods and services.* New York: Free Press.

Kaat, J. (2004, May 11). Technology in the dugout. Popular Mechanics.com. Retrieved September 25, 2005, from www.popularmechanics.com/science/sports/1283276.html?page=2&c=y

Kabanoff, B. (1991). Equity, equality, power, and conflict. *Academy of Management Review, 16*, 416–441.

Kabasakal, H., & Dastmalchian, A. (2001). Introduction to the special issue on leadership and culture in the Middle East. *Applied Psychology: An International Review, 50*, 479–488.

Kaeter, M. (1993). Cross-training: The tactical view. *Training, 30*(3), 35–36.

Kahn, R. L., & Byosiere, P. (1992). Theoretical framework for the study of stress in organizations. In M. D. Dunnette & L. M. Hough (Eds.), *Handbook of industrial and organizational psychology* (2nd ed., Vol. 3, pp. 571–650). Palo Alto, CA: Consulting Psychologists Press.

Kahneman, D., Slovic, P., & Tversky, A. (Eds.). (1982). *Judgment under uncertainty: Heuristics and biases*. New York: Cambridge University Press.

Kanfer, R., & Ackerman, P. L. (2000). Individual differences in work motivation: Further explorations of a trait framework. *Applied Psychology: An International Review, 49*, 470–482.

Kanfer, R., & Ackerman, P. L. (2004). Aging, adult development, and work motivation. *Academy of Management Review, 29*, 440–458.

Kanfer, R., & Kantrowitz, T. M. (2002). Ability and nonability predictors of job performance. In S. Sonnentag (Ed.), *Psychological management of individual performance* (pp. 27–50). New York: Wiley.

Karasek, R. A. (1979). Job demands, job decision latitude, and mental strain: Implications for job redesign. *Administrative Sciences Quarterly, 24*, 285–308.

Karasek, R. A., & Theorell, T. (1990). *Healthy work*. New York: Basic Books.

Katz, D., & Kahn, R. L. (1966). *The social psychology of organizations*. New York: Wiley.

Katz, D., & Kahn, R. L. (1978). *The social psychology of organizations* (2nd ed.). New York: Wiley.

Katzell, R. A., & Austin, J. T. (1992). From then to now: The development of industrial-organizational psychology in the United States. *Journal of Applied Psychology, 77*, 803–835.

Kauffeld, S. (2006). Self-directed work groups and team competence. *Journal of Occupational and Organizational Psychology, 79*, 1–21.

Kauffeld, S., Jonas, E., & Frey, D. (2004). Effects of a flexible work-time design on employee and company-related aims. *European Journal of Work and Organizational Psychology, 13*, 79–100.

Kay, E., Meyer, H., & French, J. (1965). Effects of threat in a performance interview. *Journal of Applied Psychology, 49*, 311–317.

Kehoe, J. F., & Olson, A. (2005). Cut scores and employment discrimination litigation. In F. J. Landy (Ed.), *Employment discrimination litigation: Behavioral, quantitative and legal perspectives* (pp. 410–449). San Francisco: Jossey-Bass.

Keita, G. P., & Hurrell, J. J. (1994). *Job stress in a changing workforce: Investigating gender, diversity, and family issues*. Washington, DC: American Psychological Association.

Keith, N., & Frese, M. (2008). Effectiveness of error management training: A meta-analysis. *Journal of Applied Psychology, 93*, 59–69.

Keller, F. J., & Viteles, M. S. (1937). *Vocational guidance throughout the world*. New York: Norton.

Kelley, H. (1967). Attribution theory in social psychology. In D. Levine (Ed.), *Nebraska symposium on motivation* (pp. 192–238). Lincoln: University of Nebraska Press.

Kelloway, E. K., Loughlin, C., Barling, J., & Nault, A. (2002). Self-reported counterproductive behaviors and organizational citizenship behaviors: Separate but related constructs. *International Journal of Selection and Assessment, 10*, 143–151.

Kenny, D. A., & DePaulo, B. M. (1993). Do people know how others view them? An empirical and theoretical account. *Psychological Bulletin, 114*, 145–161.

Kernan, M. C., & Hanges, P. J. (2002). Survivor reactions to reorganization: Antecedents and consequences of procedural, interpersonal, and informational justice. *Journal of Applied Psychology, 87*, 916–928.

Kerr, N. L., & Tindale, R. S. (2004). Group performance and decision making. *Annual Review of Psychology, 55*, 623–655.

Khanna, C., & Medsker, G. J. (2010). 2009 income and employment survey results for the Society for Industrial and Organizational Psychology. *The Industrial-Organizational Psychologist, 48*(1), 23–38.

Kidder, D. L., & Parks, J. M. (2001). The good soldier: Who is (s)he? *Journal of Organizational Behavior, 22*, 939–959.

Kim, J., & Wilemon, D. (2007). The learning organization as facilitator of complex NPD projects. *Creativity and Innovation Management, 16*, 176–191.

Kim, P. H., Ferrin, D. L., Cooper, C. D., & Dirks, K. T. (2004). Removing the shadow of suspicion: The effects of apology versus denial for repairing competence- versus integrity-based trust violations. *Journal of Applied Psychology, 89*, 104–118.

Kim, T.-Y., Cable, D. M., & Kim, S.-P. (2005). Socialization tactics, employee proactivity, and person–organization fit. *Journal of Applied Psychology, 90*, 232–241.

King, E., Gulick, L., & Kravitz, D. (2011). Emerging evidence on diversity training programs. In M. Paludi (Ed.), *Praeger handbook on understanding and preventing workplace discrimination* (Vols. 1 and 2, pp. 61–67). Westport, CT: Praeger.

King, M. L., Jr. (1956, August 11). Speech to Alpha Phi Alpha fraternity, Chicago.

King, N. (1970). Clarification and evaluation of the two-factor theory of job satisfaction. *Psychological Bulletin, 74*, 18–31.

Kinicki, A. J., McKee-Ryan, F. M., Schriesheim, C. A., & Carson, K. P. (2002). Assessing the construct validity of the Job Descriptive Index: A review and meta-analysis. *Journal of Applied Psychology, 87*, 14–32.

Kinicki, A. J., Prussia, G. E., Wu, B. J., & McKee-Ryan, F. M. (2004). A covariance structure analysis of employees' response to performance feedback. *Journal of Applied Psychology, 89*, 1057–1069.

Kinney, J. A. (1995a). *Essentials of managing workplace violence*. Charlotte, NC: Pinkerton Services.

Kinney, J. A. (1995b). *Violence at work: How to make your company safer for employees and customers*. Englewood Cliffs, NJ: Prentice Hall.

Kirkman, B. L., & Mathieu, J. E. (2005). The dimensions and antecedents of team virtuality. *Journal of Management, 31*, 700–718.

Kirkpatrick, D. L. (1959). Techniques for evaluating training programs. *Journal of the American Society of Training Directors, 13*, 3–9.

Kirkpatrick, D. L. (1998). *Evaluating training programs: The four levels* (2nd ed.). San Francisco: Berrett-Koehler.

Klehe, U.-C. (2004). Choosing to choose: Institutional pressures affecting the adoption of personnel selection procedures. *International Journal of Selection and Assessment, 12*(4), 327–342.

Klehe, U.-C., & Anderson, N. (2007a). The moderating influence of personality and culture on social loafing in typical versus maximal performance situations. *International Journal of Selection and Assessment, 15*, 250–262.

Klehe, U.-C., & Anderson, N. (2007b). Working hard and working smart: Motivation and ability during typical and maximum performance. *Journal of Applied Psychology, 92*, 978–992.

Klehe, U.-C., Anderson, N., & Hoefnagels, E. A. (2007). Social facilitation and inhibition during maximum versus typical performance situations. *Human Performance, 20*, 223–239.

Klein, C., Diaz-Granados, D., Salas, E., Le, H., Burke, S. C., Lyons, R., & Goodwin, G. F. (2009). Does team building work? *Small Group Research, 40*(2), 181–222.

Klein, H. J., Noe, R. A., & Wang, C. (2006). Motivation to learn and course outcomes: The impact of delivery mode, learning goal orientation, and perceived barriers and enablers. *Personnel Psychology, 59,* 665–702.

Klein, H. J., & Weaver, N. A. (2000). The effectiveness of an organizational-level orientation training program in the socialization of new hires. *Personnel Psychology, 53,* 47–66.

Klein, K., & Kozlowski, S. (2000). *Multilevel theory, research, and methods in organizations: Foundations, extensions, and new directions.* San Francisco: Jossey-Bass.

Klein, K. J., & Zedeck, S. (2004). Theory in applied psychology. *Journal of Applied Psychology, 89,* 931–933.

Klein, S., Sanders, A. M., & Huffman, A. H. (2011, April). Green outcomes: Partnering with organizations to demonstrate unintended eco-benefits. *The Industrial-Organizational Psychologist, 48*(4), 39–46.

Klingner, Y., & Schuler, H. (2004). Involving participants' evaluations while maintaining validity by a work-sample intelligence test hybrid. *International Journal of Selection and Assessment, 12,* 120–134.

Klis, M. (2003, August 21). Home video: Controversial strike-zone monitoring evaluates and upsets umpires; pitchers are angry too. *Denver Post,* p. D1.

Kluemper, D., & Rosen, P. (2009). Future employment selection methods: Evaluating social networking websites. *Journal of Managerial Psychology, 24,* 567–580.

Kluemper, D., Rosen, P., & Mossholder, K. (2012). Social networking websites, personality ratings, and the organizational context: More than meets the eye? *Journal of Applied Social Psychology, 42*(5), 1143–1172.

Kluger, A. N., & DeNisi, A. (1996). Effects of feedback intervention on performance: A historical review, a meta-analysis, and a preliminary feedback intervention theory. *Psychological Bulletin, 119,* 254–284.

Knorz, C., & Zapf, D. (1996). Mobbing: An extreme form of social stressors at the workplace. *Zeitschrift für Personalforschung, 12,* 352–362.

Ko, J., Price, J. L., & Mueller, C. W. (1997). Assessment of Meyer and Allen's three-component model of organizational commitment in South Korea. *Journal of Applied Psychology, 82,* 961–973.

Kobasa, S. C. (1979). Stressful life events, personality, and health: An inquiry into hardiness. *Journal of Personality and Social Psychology, 37,* 1–11.

Kobasa, S. C., Maddi, S. R., & Kahn, S. (1982). Hardiness and health: A prospective study. *Journal of Personality and Social Psychology, 42,* 168–177.

Kochan, T., Bezrukova, K., et al. (2003). The effects of diversity on business performance: Report of the diversity research network. *Human Resource Management, 42,* 3–21.

Koenig, A. M., Eagly, A. H., Mitchell, A. A., & Ristikari, T. (2011). Are leader stereotypes masculine? A meta-analysis of three research paradigms. *Psychological Bulletin, 137*(4), 616–642.

Koeppel, D. (2004, March 7). The new cost of keeping workers happy. *New York Times,* p. BU11.

Kolb, A. Y., & Kolb, D. A. (2005). Learning styles and learning spaces: Enhancing experiential learning in higher education. *Academy of Management Learning and Education, 4,* 193–212.

Kolb, D. A. (2005). *Learning style inventory, version 3.1.* Boston: Hay/McBer Training Resources Group.

Kolmstetter, E. (2003). I-O's making an impact: TSA transportation security screener skill standards, selection system, and hiring process. *The Industrial-Organizational Psychologist, 40*(4), 39–46.

König, C. J., Bühner, M., & Mürling, G. (2005). Working memory, fluid intelligence and attention are predictors of multitasking performance but polychronicity and extraversion are not. *Human Performance, 18,* 243–266.

Konrad, A. M., Ritchie, J. E., Lieb, P., & Corrigal, E. (2000). Sex differences and similarities in job attribute preferences: A meta-analysis. *Psychological Bulletin, 112,* 593–641.

Koppes, L. L. (Ed.). (2007). *Historical perspectives in industrial and organizational psychology.* Mahwah, NJ: Lawrence Erlbaum Associates.

Korabik, K., & McDonald, L. M. (1991). Sources of stress and ways of coping among male and female managers. *Journal of Social Behavior and Personality, 6,* 1–14.

Kornhauser, A. W. (1929). Industrial psychology in England, Germany and the United States. *Personnel Journal, 8,* 421–434.

Kotter, J. P. (1995). Leading change: Why transformation efforts fail. *Harvard Business Review, 73*(March/April), 59–67.

Kozlowski, S. J. W., & Bell, B. S. (2008). Team learning, development and adaptation. In V. I. Sessa & M. London (Eds.), *Group learning* (pp. 15–44). Mahwah, NJ: Erlbaum.

Kozlowski, S. W. J., Brown, K. G., Weissbein, D., Salas, E., & Cannon-Bowers, J. A. (2000). A multilevel approach to training effectiveness: Enhancing horizontal and vertical transfer. In K. J. Klein & S. W. J. Kozlowski (Eds.), *Multilevel theory, research and methods in organizations: Foundations, extensions, and new directions* (pp. 157–210). San Francisco, CA: Jossey-Bass.

Kozlowski, S. W. J., Chao, G. T., & Morrison, R. F. (1998). Games raters play: Politics, strategies, and impression management in performance appraisal. In J. W. Smither (Ed.), *Performance appraisal: State of the art in practice* (pp. 163–208). San Francisco: Jossey-Bass.

Kozlowsky, M., Sagie, A., Krausz, M., & Singer, A. (1997). Correlates of employee lateness: Some theoretical considerations. *Journal of Applied Psychology, 82,* 79–88.

Kraiger, K. (2003). Perspectives on training and development. In W. C. Borman, D. R. Ilgen, & R. J. Klimoski (Eds.), *Handbook of psychology, Vol. 12: Industrial and organizational psychology* (pp. 171–92). Hoboken, NJ: Wiley.

Kraiger, K., & Ford, J. K. (2006). The expanding role of workplace training: Themes and trends influencing training research and practice. In L. L. Koppes (Ed.), *Historical perspectives in industrial and organizational psychology* (pp. 281–309). Mahwah, NJ: Erlbaum.

Kraiger, K., Ford, J. K., & Salas, E. (1993). Application of cognitive, skill-based, and affective theories of learning outcomes to new methods of training evaluation. *Journal of Applied Psychology, 78,* 311–328.

Kraiger, K., & Jerden, E. (2007). A new look at learner control: Meta-analytic results and directions for future research. In S. M. Fiore & E. Salas (Eds.), *Where is the learning in distance learning? Toward a science of distributed learning and training* (pp. 65–90). Washington, DC: American Psychological Association.

Kraiger, K., & Smith-Jentsch, K. (2002). *Evidence of the reliability and validity of collective climates in work teams.* Unpublished manuscript.

Krajewski, H. T., Goffin, R. D., McCarthy, M. M., Rothstein, M. G., & Johnston, N. (2006). Comparing the validity of structured interviews from managerial-level employees: Should we look to the past or focus on the future? *Journal of Occupational and Organizational Psychology, 79,* 411–432.

Kramer, R. M. (1999). Trust and distrust in organizations: Emerging perspectives, enduring questions. *Annual Review of Psychology, 50,* 569–598.

Krantz, D. S., & McCeney, M. K. (2002). Effects of psychological and social factors on organic disease: A critical reassessment of research on coronary heart disease. *Annual Review of Psychology, 53,* 341–369.

Krause, D. E., & Thornton, G. C. (2008). International perspectives on current assessment center practices and future challenges. In S. Schlebusch & G. Roodt (Eds.), *Assessment centers: Unlocking potential for growth* (pp. 285–301). Randburg, SA: Knowres Publishing.

Krause, S. I., Frese, M., Friedrich, C., & Unger, J. M. (2005). Entrepreneurial orientation: A psychological model of success among southern African small business owners. *European Journal of Work and Organizational Psychology, 14*, 314–344.

Kraut, A. I., & Korman, A. K. (1999). The DELTA forces causing change in human resource management. In A. I. Kraut & A. K. Korman (Eds.), *Evolving practices in human resource management* (pp. 3–22). San Francisco: Jossey-Bass.

Kravitz, D. A. (2008). The diversity–validity dilemma: Beyond selection—the role of affirmative action. *Personnel Psychology, 61*, 173–193.

Kravitz, D. A., Harrison, D. A., Turner, M. E., Levine, E. L., Chaves, W., Brannick, M., et al. (1997). *Affirmative action: A review of psychological and behavioral research.* Bowling Green, OH: Society for Industrial and Organizational Psychology.

Kravitz, D. A., & Klineberg, S. L. (2000). Reactions to two versions of affirmative action among whites, blacks and Hispanics. *Journal of Applied Psychology, 85*, 597–611.

Kravitz, D. A., Klineberg, S. L., Avery, D. R., Nguyen, A. K., Lund, C., & Fu, E. J. (2000). Attitudes toward affirmative action: Correlations with demographic variables and with beliefs about targets, actions and economic effects. *Journal of Applied Social Psychology, 30*, 1109–1136.

Kreiner, G. E., & Ashforth, B. E. (2004). Evidence toward an expanded model of organizational identification. *Journal of Organizational Behavior, 25*, 1–27.

Krings, F., Tschan, F., & Bettex, S. (2007). Determinants of attitudes toward affirmative action in a Swiss sample. *Journal of Business and Psychology, 21*, 585–611.

Kristof-Brown, A. L., Zimmerman, R. D., & Johnson, E. C. (2005). Consequences of individuals' fit at work: A meta-analysis of person–job, person–organization, person–group, and person–supervisor fit. *Personnel Psychology, 58*, 281–342.

Kudish, J. D., Rotolo, C. T., Avis, J. M., Fallon, J. D., Roberts, F. E., Rollier, T. J., & Thibodeaux, H. F. (1998). *A preliminary look at assessment center practices worldwide: What's hot and what's not.* Paper presented at the 26th annual meeting of the International Congress on Assessment Center Methods, Pittsburgh, PA.

Kulik, C. T., Pepper, M. B., Roberson, L., & Parker, S. K. (2007). The rich get richer: Predicting participation in voluntary diversity training. *Journal of Organizational Behavior, 28*, 753–769.

Kunin, T. (1955). The construction of a new type of attitude measure. *Personnel Psychology, 8*, 70–71.

Kunin, T. (1998). The construction of a new type of attitude measure. *Personnel Psychology, 51*, 823–824 (reprinted from 1955).

Kupperschmidt, B. R. (2000). Multigenerational employees: Strategies for effective management. *Health Care Manager, 19*, 65–76.

Kurz, R., & Bartram, D. (2002). Competency and individual performance: Modeling the world of work. In I. T. Robertson, M. Callinan, & D. Bartram (Eds.), *Organizational effectiveness: The role of psychology* (pp. 227–255). New York: Wiley.

Kwiatkowski, R., Duncan, D. C., & Shimmin, S. (2006). What have we forgotten—and why? *Journal of Occupational and Organizational Psychology, 79*, 183–201.

Laabs, J. J. (1992) Surveillance: Tool or trap? *Personnel Journal, 71*, 96–104.

Lacey, M. (2005, February 2). Accents of Africa: A new outsourcing frontier. *New York Times*, pp. C1, C6.

Lam, S. S., Schaubroeck, J., & Aryee, S. (2002). Relationship between organizational justice and employee work outcomes: A cross-national study. *Journal of Organizational Behavior, 23*, 1–18.

Lance, C. E. (2008). Why assessment centers do not work the way they are supposed to. *Industrial and Organizational Psychology, 1*, 84–98.

Landsberger, H. A. (1958). *Hawthorne revisited: Management and the worker, its critics and developments in human relations in industry.* Ithaca: New York State School of Industrial and Labor Relations.

Landy, F. J. (1986). Stamp collecting versus science: Validation as hypothesis testing. *American Psychologist, 41*, 1183–1192.

Landy, F. J. (1987). *Psychology: The science of people* (2nd ed.). Englewood Cliffs, NJ: Prentice Hall.

Landy, F. J. (1989). *Psychology of work behavior* (4th ed.). Pacific Grove, CA: Brooks/Cole.

Landy, F. J. (1992). Hugo Munsterberg: Victim or visionary? *Journal of Applied Psychology, 77*, 787–802.

Landy, F. J. (1993). Early influences on the development of industrial and organizational psychology. In American Psychological Association, *Exploring applied psychology* (pp. 81–118). Washington, DC: American Psychological Association.

Landy, F. J. (1997). Early influences on the development of industrial and organizational psychology. *Journal of Applied Psychology, 82*, 467–477.

Landy, F. J. (2001). Age, race and gender in organizations. In N. J. Smelser & P. B. Baltes (Eds.), *International encyclopedia of social and behavioral sciences* (pp. 271–275). Oxford, UK: Pergamon.

Landy, F. J. (2002a, April 12–14). *Legal implications of web-based applicant screening.* Paper presented at the annual meeting of the Society for Industrial and Organizational Psychology, Toronto, Canada.

Landy, F. J. (2002b, April 12–14). *Does classical measurement theory apply to I-O psychology? The reliability of job performance ratings.* Paper presented at the annual meeting of the Society for Industrial and Organizational Psychology, Toronto, Canada.

Landy, F. J. (2005a). *Employment discrimination litigation: Behavioral, quantitative, and legal perspectives.* San Francisco: Jossey-Bass.

Landy, F. J. (2005b). Some historical and scientific issues related to research on emotional intelligence. *Journal of Organizational Behavior, 26*, 411–424.

Landy, F. J. (2006). The long, frustrating, and fruitless search for social intelligence. In K. R. Murphy (Ed.), *A critique of emotional intelligence: What are the problems and how can they be fixed?* Mahwah, NJ: Erlbaum.

Landy, F. J. (2007). The validation of personnel decisions in the twenty-first century: Back to the future. In S. M. McPhail (Ed.), *Alternative validation strategies* (pp. 409–426). San Francisco: Jossey-Bass.

Landy, F. J. (2008a). Stereotypes, bias, and personnel decisions: Strange and stranger. *Industrial and Organizational Psychology: Perspectives on Science and Practice, 1*, 379–392.

Landy, F. J. (2008b). Stereotypes, implicit association theory, and personnel decisions: I guess we will have to agree to disagree. *Industrial and Organizational Psychology: Perspectives on Science and Practice, 1*, 444–453.

Landy, F. J. (2009). Revisiting Landy & Farr. In J. L. Outtz (Ed.), *Adverse impact in organizations* (pp. 227–248). San Francisco, CA: Jossey-Bass.

Landy, F. J., Barnes-Farrell, J., & Cleveland, J. N. (1980). Perceived fairness and accuracy of performance evaluation: A follow-up. *Journal of Applied Psychology, 65*, 355–356.

Landy, F. J., Bland, R. E., Buskirk, E. R., Daly, R. E., Debusk, R. F., Donavan, E. J., et al. (1992). *Alternatives to chronological age in determining standards of suitability for public safety jobs.* University Park, PA: Center for Applied Behavioral Sciences.

Landy, F. J., & Farr, J. L. (1980) Performance rating. *Psychological Bulletin, 87*, 72–107.

Landy, F. J., & Farr, J. L. (1983). *The measurement of work performance: Methods, theory, and applications.* New York: Academic Press.

Landy, F. J., Zedeck, S., & Cleveland, J. N. (1983). *Performance measurement and theory.* Hillsdale, NJ: Erlbaum.

Langewiesche, W. (2002). *American ground: Unbuilding the World Trade Center*. New York: North Point Press.

Lanning v. *SEPTA* (1998). U.S. Dist. LEXIS, 9388.

Lanning v. *SEPTA*, 181, F.3d 478 (3rd Cir. 1999); *cert. denied*, 120 S. Ct. 970 (2000).

Lanning v. *SEPTA*, U.S. Dist. LEXIS, 17612 (2000).

LaPolice, C. C., Carter, G. W., & Johnson, J. J. (2005, April). *Linking O*NET descriptors to occupational literacy requirements using job component validation*. Poster presented at the 20th Annual Conference of the Society for Industrial and Organizational Psychology, Los Angeles.

Laris, M., & Brulliard, K. (2005, September 3). Bad communications hinders area's aid efforts. *Washington Post*, p. A23.

Latané, B., Williams, K., & Harkins S. (1979). Many hands make light the work: The causes and consequences of social loafing. *Journal of Personality and Social Psychology, 37*, 822–832.

Latham, G. P. (1986). Job performance and appraisal. In C. Cooper & I. Robertson (Eds.), *International review of industrial and organizational psychology* (pp. 117–155). Chichester, UK: Wiley.

Latham, G. P. (2007). Theory and research on coaching practices. *Australian Psychologist, 42*, 268–270.

Latham, G. P., & Budworth, M.-H. (2007). The study of work motivation in the 20th century. In L. Koppes (Ed.), *The history of industrial and organizational psychology* (pp. 353–382). Mahwah, NJ: Erlbaum.

Latham, G. P., & Pinder, C. (2005). Work motivation theory and research at the dawn of the twenty-first century. *Annual Review of Psychology, 56*, 485–516.

Latham, G. P., & Wexley, K. N. (1981). *Increasing productivity through performance appraisal*. Reading, MA: Addison-Wesley.

Lauver, K. J., & Kristof-Brown, A. (2001). Distinguishing between employees' perceptions of person–job and person–organization fit. *Journal of Vocational Behavior, 59*, 454–470.

Lawler, E. E. (1973). *Motivation in work organizations*. Monterey, CA: Brooks/Cole.

Lawrence, P. R., & Lorsch, J. (1967). *Organization and environment*. Cambridge, MA: Harvard University Press.

Lazarus, R. S. (1991). Progress on a cognitive-motivational-relational theory of emotion. *American Psychologist, 46*, 819–834.

Lazarus, R. S. (2000). Toward better research on stress and coping. *American Psychologist, 55*, 665–673.

Lazarus, R. S., & Folkman, S. (1984). *Stress, appraisal, and coping*. New York: Springer.

LeBlanc, P. M., Hox, J. J., Schaufeli, W. B., Taris, T. W., & Peeters, M. C. W. (2007). Take care! The evaluation of a team-based burnout intervention program for oncology care providers. *Journal of Applied Psychology, 92*, 213–227.

LeBreton, J. M., Barksdale, C. D., Robin, J., & James, L. R. (2007). Measurement issues associated with conditional reasoning tests: Indirect measurement and test faking. *Journal of Applied Psychology, 92*, 1–16.

Lee, K., Ashton, M. C., & de Vries, E. E. (2005). Predicting workplace delinquency and integrity with the HEXACO and five-factor models of personality structure. *Human Performance, 18*, 179–197.

Lee, K., Ashton, M. C., & Shin, K-H. (2005). Personality correlates of workplace anti-social behavior. *Applied Psychology: An International Review, 54*, 81–98.

Lee, K., Carswell, J. J., & Allen, N. J. (2000). A meta-analytic review of occupational commitment: Relations with person- and work-related variables. *Journal of Applied Psychology, 85*, 799–811.

Lee, R. T., & Ashforth, B. E. (1996). A meta-analytic examination of the correlates of the three dimensions of job burnout. *Journal of Applied Psychology, 81*, 123–133.

Lefkowitz, J. (2003). *Ethics and values in industrial-organizational psychology*. Mahwah, NJ: Erlbaum.

Lefkowitz, J. (2004). Contemporary cases of corporate corruption: Any relevance for I-O psychology? *The Industrial-Organizational Psychologist, 42*(2), 21–26.

Lefkowitz, J. (2006). The constancy of ethics amidst the changing world of work. *Human Resource Management Review, 16*, 245–268.

Lefkowitz, J. (2008). To prosper, organizational psychology should . . . expand the values of organizational psychology to match the quality of its ethics. *Journal of Organizational Behavior, 29*, 439–453.

Lefkowitz, J. (2012). Ethics in industrial-organizational psychology. In S. J. Knapp et al. (Eds.), *APA handbook of ethics in psychology: Vol. 2. Practice, teaching, and research* (pp. 149–167). Washington, DC: American Psychological Association.

LePine, J. A., Erez, A., & Johnson, D. (2002). The nature and dimensionality of organizational citizenship behavior: A critical review and meta-analysis. *Journal of Applied Psychology, 87*, 52–65.

LePine, J., Piccolo, R. F., Jackson, C., Mathieu, J., & Saul, J. (2008). A meta-analysis of teamwork process: Towards a better understanding of the dimensional structure and relationships with team effectiveness. *Personnel Psychology, 61*, 273–307.

Lester, S. W., Turnley, W. H., Bloodgood, J. M., & Bolino, M. C. (2002). Not seeing eye to eye: Differences in supervisor and subordinate perceptions of and attributions for psychological contract breach. *Journal of Organizational Behavior, 23*, 39–56.

Levine, E. L., Maye, D. M., Ulm, R. A., & Gordon, T. R. (2006). A methodology for developing and validating minimum qualifications (MQs). *Personnel Psychology, 50*, 1009–1023.

Levine, E. L., & Sanchez, J. I. (2007). Evaluating work analysis in the 21st century. *Ergometrika, 4*, 1–11.

Levine, R. V. (1997). *A geography of time: The temporal misadventures of a social psychologist, or how every culture keeps time just a little bit differently*. New York: HarperCollins.

Levitt, S. D., & Dubner, S. J. (2005). *Freakonomics*. New York: HarperCollins.

Lewin, K. (1935). *A dynamic theory of personality*. New York: McGraw-Hill.

Lewin, K. (1938). *The conceptual representation and the measurement of psychological forces*. Durham, NC: Duke University Press.

Lewin, K. (1951). *Field theory in social psychology*. New York: Harper.

Lewin, K., Lippitt, R., & White, R. K. (1939). Patterns of aggressive behavior in experimentally created "social climates." *Journal of Social Psychology, 10*, 271–299.

Lewis, S., & Cooper, C. L. (1999). The work–family research agenda in changing contexts. *Journal of Occupational Health Psychology, 4*, 382–393.

Leymann, H. (1990). Mobbing and psychological terror at workplaces. *Violence and Victims, 5*, 119–126.

Leymann, H. (1996). The content and development of mobbing at work. *European Journal of Work and Organizational Psychology, 5*, 165–184.

Liden, R. C., Wayne, S. J., Jaworski, R. A., & Bennett, N. (2004). Social loafing: A field investigation. *Journal of Management, 30*, 285–304.

Lievens, F., & Anseel, F. (2004). Confirmatory factor analysis and invariance of an organizational citizenship behaviour measure across samples in a Dutch-speaking context. *Journal of Occupational and Organizational Psychology, 77*, 299–306.

Lievens, F., Anseel, F., Harris, M. M., & Eisenberg, J. (2007). Measurement invariance of the pay satisfaction questionnaire across three countries. *Educational and Psychological Measurement, 67*, 1042–1051.

Lievens, F., Buyse, T., & Sackett, P. R. (2005). The operational validity of a video-based situational judgment test for medical college admissions: Illustrating the importance of matching predictor and criterion construct domains. *Journal of Applied Psychology, 90*, 442–452.

Lievens, F., Conway, J. M., & De Corte, W. (2008). The relative importance of task, citizenship and counter-productive performance to job performance ratings: Do rater source and team-based culture matter? *Journal of Occupational and Organizational Psychology, 81*(1), 1–18.

Lievens, F., Decaesteker, C., Coetsier, P., & Geirnaert, J. (2001). Organizational attractiveness for prospective applicants: A person–organization fit perspective. *Applied Psychology: An International Review, 50*, 30–51.

Lievens, F., De Corte, W., & Brysse, K. (2003). Applicant perceptions of selection procedures: The role of selection information, belief in tests, and comparative anxiety. *International Journal of Selection and Assessment, 11*, 67–77.

Lievens, F., De Corte, W., & Schollaert, E. (2008). A closer look at the frame-of-reference effect in personality scale scores and validity. *Journal of Applied Psychology, 93*, 268–279.

Lievens, F., De Fruyt, F., & van Dam, K. (2001). Assessors' use of personality traits in descriptions of assessment center candidates: A five-factor model perspective. *Journal of Occupational and Organizational Psychology, 74*, 623–636.

Lievens, F., & De Paepe, A. (2004). An empirical investigation of interviewer-related factors that discourage the use of high structure interviews. *Journal of Organizational Behavior, 25*, 29–46.

Lievens, F., Harris, M. M., van Keer, E., & Bisqueret, C. (2003). Predicting cross-cultural training performance: The validity of personality, cognitive ability, and dimensions measured by an assessment center and a behavior description interview. *Journal of Applied Psychology, 88*, 476–489.

Lievens, F., & Sackett, R. R. (2006). Video-based versus written situational judgment tests: A comparison in terms of predictive validity. *Journal of Applied Psychology, 91*, 1181–1188.

Lievens, F., Sanchez, J. I., & De Corte, W. (2004). Easing the inferential leap in competency modeling: The effects of task-related information and subject matter expertise. *Personnel Psychology, 57*, 881–904.

Likert, R. (1967). *The human organization: Its management and value.* New York: McGraw-Hill.

Lim, D. H., & Morris, M. L. (2006). Influence of trainee characteristics, instructional satisfaction, and organizational climate on perceived learning and training transfer. *Human Resource Development Quarterly, 17*(1), 85–115.

Littrell, L. N., Salas, E., Hess, K. P., Paley, M., & Riedel, S. (2006). Expatriate preparation: A critical analysis of 25 years of cross-cultural training research. *Human Resource Development Review, 5*, 355–388.

Liu, C., Spector, P. E., & Shi, L. (2007). Cross-national job stress: A quantitative and qualitative study. *Journal of Organizational Behavior, 28*, 209–239.

Liu, X., & Batt, R. (2007). The economic pay offs to informal training: Evidence from routine service work. *Industrial and Labor Relations Review, 61*, 75–89.

Locke, E. A. (1968). Toward a theory of task motivation and incentives. *Organizational Behavior and Human Performance, 3*, 157–189.

Locke, E. A. (1976). The nature and causes of job satisfaction. In M. D. Dunnette (Ed.), *Handbook of industrial and organizational psychology* (pp. 1297–1343). Chicago: Rand McNally.

Locke, E. A. (1980). Latham vs. Komaki: A tale of two paradigms. *Journal of Applied Psychology, 65*, 16–23.

Locke, E. A. (2001). Self-set goals and self-efficacy as mediators of incentives and personality. In M. Erez, U. Kleinbeck, & H. Thierry (Eds.), *Work motivation in the context of a globalizing economy* (pp. 13–26). Mahwah, NJ: Erlbaum.

Locke, E. A. (2005). Why emotional intelligence is an invalid concept. *Journal of Organizational Behavior, 26*, 425–431.

Locke, E. A., & Henne, D. (1986). Work motivation theories. In C. L. Cooper & I. T. Robertson (Eds.), *International review of industrial and organizational psychology* (pp. 1–35). Chichester, UK: Wiley.

Locke, E. A., & Latham, G. P. (1990). *A theory of goal setting and task performance.* Englewood Cliffs, NJ: Prentice Hall.

Locke, E. A., & Latham, G. P. (1996). Goal setting theory: An introduction. In R. M. Steers, L. W. Porter, & G. A. Bigley (Eds.), *Motivation and leadership at work* (pp. 95–122). New York: McGraw-Hill.

Locke, E. A., & Latham, G. P. (2002). Building a practically useful theory of goal setting and task motivation: A 35-year odyssey. *American Psychologist, 57*, 705–717.

Locke, E. A., Shaw, K. N., Saari, L. M., & Latham, G. P. (1981). Goal setting and task performance. *Psychological Bulletin, 90*, 125–152.

Locke, K., & Golden-Biddle, K. (2002). An introduction to qualitative research. In S. Rogelberg (Ed.), *Handbook of research methods in industrial and organizational psychology* (pp. 99–118). Cambridge, MA: Blackwell.

Logan, M. S., & Ganster, D. C. (2005). An experimental evaluation of a control intervention to alleviate job-related stress. *Journal of Management, 31*, 90–107.

Loher, B. T., Hazer, J. T., Tsai, A., Tilton, K., & James, J. (1997). Letters of reference: A process approach. *Journal of Business and Psychology, 11*, 339–355.

London, M. (2002). *Leadership development: Paths to self-insight and professional growth.* Mahwah, NJ: Erlbaum.

London, M., & Mone, E. M. (1999). Continuous learning. In D. R. Ilgen & E. D. Pulakos (Eds.), *The changing nature of performance: Implications for staffing, motivation, and development.* San Francisco: Jossey-Bass.

Longnecker, C. O., Sims, H. P., & Gioia, D. A. (1987). Behind the mask: The politics of performance appraisal. *Academy of Management Executive, 1*, 183–193.

Lord, R. G., Klimoski, R. J., & Kanfer, R. (Eds.). (2002). *Emotions in the workplace: Understanding the structure and role of emotions in organizational behavior.* San Francisco: Jossey-Bass.

Lord, R. G., & Smith, W. G. L. (1999). Leadership and the changing nature of performance. In D. R. Ilgen & E. D. Pulakos (Eds.), *The changing nature of performance: Implications for staffing, motivation, and development* (pp. 192–239). Santa Barbara, CA: New Lexington Press.

Loughlin, C., & Barling, J. (2001). Young workers' work values, attitudes and behaviors. *Journal of Occupational and Organizational Psychology, 74*, 543–558.

Love, K. G., Bishop, R. C., Heinisch, D. A., & Montei, M. S. (1994). Selection across two cultures: Adapting the selection of American assemblers to meet Japanese job performance demands. *Personnel Psychology, 47*, 837–846.

Lovelace, K., & Rosen, B. (1996). Differences in achieving person–organization fit among diverse groups of managers. *Journal of Management, 22*, 703–722.

Lovell, J. (2007, December 9). Left-hand turn elimination. *New York Times*, p. 80.

Lowman, R.L. (Ed.) (2006). *The ethical practice of psychology in organizations* (2nd ed.). Washington, DC: American Psychological Association & Society for Industrial and Organizational Psychology.

Lubinski, D. (2000). Scientific and social significance of assessing individual differences: Sinking shafts at a few critical points. *Annual Review of Psychology, 51*, 405–444.

Lubinski, D. (2004). Introduction to the special section on cognitive abilities: 100 years after Spearman's (1904) "General intelligence, objectively determined and measured." *Journal of Personality and Social Psychology, 86*, 96–111.

Lubinski, D., Benbow, C. P., Webb, R. M., & Bleske-Recheck, A. (2006). Tracking exceptional human capital over two decades. *Psychological Sciences, 17*, 194–199.

Lucas, R. E., Clark, A. E., Georgellis, Y., & Diener, E. (2004). Unemployment alters the set point for life satisfaction. *Psychological Science, 15*(1), 8–13.

Luchak, A. A., & Gellatly, I. R. (2007). A comparison of linear and non-linear relations between organizational commitment and work outcomes. *Journal of Applied Psychology, 92*, 783–793.

Lundberg, U., & Frankenhauser, M. (1999). Stress and workload of men and women in high-ranking positions. *Journal of Occupational Health Psychology, 4*, 142–151.

Lutgen-Sandvik, P., Tracy, S. J., & Alberts, J. K. (2007). Burned by bullying in the American workplace: Prevalence, perception, degree and impact. *Journal of Management Studies, 44*, 835–860.

Luthans, F. (2002). The need for and meaning of positive organizational behavior. *Journal of Organizational Behavior, 23*, 695–706.

Luthans, F., Paul, R., & Baker, D. (1981). An experimental analysis of the impact of contingent reinforcement on salespersons' performance behavior. *Journal of Applied Psychology, 66*, 314–323.

Lykken, D. T., McGue, M., Tellegen, A., & Bouchard, T. J., Jr. (1992). Emergenesis: Genetic traits that may not run in families. *American Psychologist, 47*, 1565–1577.

Lyness, K. S., & Heilman, M. E. (2006). When fit is fundamental: Performance evaluations and promotions of upper-level female and male managers. *Journal of Applied Psychology, 91*, 777–785.

Lyubomirsky, S., King, L., & Diener, E. (2005). The benefits of frequent positive affect: Does happiness lead to success? *Psychological Bulletin, 131*, 803–855.

Macan, T. H., Avedon, M. J., Paese, M., & Smith, D. E. (1994). The effects of applicants' reactions to cognitive ability tests and an assessment center. *Personnel Psychology, 47*, 715–738.

MacCoun, R. J. (1998). Biases in interpretation and use of test results. *Annual Review of Psychology, 49*, 259–287.

Macey, W. H. (2002, April). *Perspectives on September 11th: What the data says.* Paper presented at the annual conference of the Society for Industrial and Organizational Psychology, Toronto, Ontario, Canada.

Macey, W. H., & Schneider, B. (2008). The meaning of employee engagement. *Industrial and Organizational Psychology, 1*, 3–30.

Machin, M. A. (2002). Planning, managing, and optimizing transfer of training. In K. Kraiger (Ed.), *Creating, implementing, and managing effective training and development* (pp. 263–301). San Francisco: Jossey-Bass.

Mack, D. A., Shannon, C., Quick, J. D., & Quick, J. C. (1998). Stress and the preventative management of workplace violence. In R. W. Griffin, A. O'Leary-Kelly, & J. Collins (Eds.), *Dysfunctional behavior in organizations: Violent and deviant behavior* (pp. 119–141). Stamford, CT: JAI Press.

Maddi, S. R. (2005). On hardiness and other pathways to resilience. *American Psychologist, 60*, 261–262.

Maddi, S. R., & Kobasa, S. C. (1984). *The hardy executive: Health under stress.* Homewood, IL: Dow Jones-Irwin.

Magjuka, R. J., & Baldwin, T. T. (1991). Team-based employee involvement programs: Effects of design and administration. *Personnel Psychology, 44*, 793–812.

Mahoney, K. T., & Baker, D. B. (2002). Elton Mayo and Carl Rogers: A tale of two techniques. *Journal of Vocational Behavior, 60*, 437–450.

Mahoney, T. A. (1988). Productivity defined: The relativity of efficiency, effectiveness, and change. In J. P. Campbell & R. J. Campbell (Eds.), *Productivity in organizations* (pp. 13–39). San Francisco: Jossey-Bass.

Malhotra, A., Majchrzak, A., & Rosen, B. (2007). Leading virtual teams. *Academy of Management Perspectives, 21*(1), 60–70.

Malos, S. B. (1998). Currrent legal issues in performance appraisal. In J. W. Smither (Ed.), *Performance appraisal: State of the art in practice* (pp. 49–94). San Francisco: Jossey-Bass.

Malos, S. (2005). The importance of valid selection and performance appraisal: Do management practices figure in case law? In F. J. Landy (Ed.), *Employment discrimination litigation: Behavioral, quantitative, and legal perspectives* (pp. 373–409). San Francisco: Jossey-Bass.

Man, D. C., & Lam, S. S. K. (2003). The effects of job complexity and autonomy on cohesiveness in collectivistic and individualistic work groups: A cross-cultural analysis. *Journal of Organizational Behavior, 24*, 979–1001.

Mangos, P. M., Steele-Johnson, D., LaHuis, D., & White, E. D. (2007). A multiple-task measurement framework for assessing maximum–typical performance. *Human Performance, 20*, 241–258.

Marchel, C., & Owens, S. (2007). Qualitative research in psychology: Could William James get a job? *History of Psychology, 10*, 301–324.

Marcus, B. (2003). Attitudes toward personnel selection methods: A partial replication and extension in a German sample. *Applied Psychology: An International Review, 52*, 515–532.

Marcus, B., Goffin, R. D., Johnston, N. G., & Rothstein, M. G. (2007). Personality and cognitive ability as predictors of typical and maximum managerial performance. *Human Performance, 20*, 275–285.

Marcus, B., Lee, K., & Ashton, M. C. (2007). Personality dimensions explaining relationships between integrity tests and counterproductive behavior: Big Five, or one in addition. *Personnel Psychology, 60*, 1–34.

Marcus, B., & Schuler, H. (2004). Antecedents of counterproductive behavior at work: A general perspective. *Journal of Applied Psychology, 89*, 647–660.

Markham, S. E., Scott, K. D., & McKee, G. H. (2002). Recognizing good attendance: A longitudinal, quasi-experimental filed study. *Personnel Psychology, 55*, 639–660.

Markman, G. D., Baron, R. A., & Balkin, D. B. (2005). Are perseverance and self-efficacy costless? Assessing entrepreneurs' regretful thinking. *Journal of Organizational Behavior, 26*, 1–19.

Markovits, Y., Davis, A. J., & van Dick, R. (2007). Organizational commitment profiles and job satisfaction among Greek private and public sector employees. *International Journal of Cross-Cultural Management, 7*(1), 77–99.

Marks, M. A., Sabella, M. J., Burke, C. S., & Zaccaro, S. J. (2002). The impact of cross-training on team effectiveness. *Journal of Applied Psychology, 87*, 3–13.

Marsh, H. W., & Roche, L. A. (1997). Making students' evaluations of teaching effectiveness effective. *American Psychologist, 52*, 1187–1197.

Marshall, A. E. (1985). Employment qualifications of college graduates: How important are they? *Employment Counseling, 22*(4), 136–143.

Martin, A. J., Jones, E. S., & Callan, V. J. (2005). The role of psychological climate in facilitating employee adjustment during organizational change. *European Journal of Work and Organizational Psychology, 14*, 263–289.

Martin, R., Thomas, G., Charles, K., Epitropaki, O., & Manamara, R. (2005). The role of leader–member exchange in mediating the relationship between locus of control and work reactions. *Journal of Occupational and Organizational Psychology, 78*, 141–147.

Martinko, M. J., & Zellars, K. L. (1998). Toward a theory of workplace violence and aggression: A cognitive appraisal perspective. In R. W. Griffin, A. O'Leary-Kelly, & J. Collins (Eds.), *Dysfunctional behavior in organizations: Violent and deviant behavior.* Stamford, CT: JAI Press.

Martins, L. L., Gilson, L. L., & Maynard, M. T. (2004). Virtual teams: What do we know and where do we go from here? *Journal of Management, 30*, 805–835.

Martins, L. L., & Schilpzand, M. C. (2011). Global virtual teams: Key developments, research gaps, and future directions. In A. Joshi, H. Liao, & J. J. Martocchio (Eds.), *Research in personnel and human resources management* (Vol. 30, pp. 1–72). Greenwich, CT: JAI Press.

Maslach, C., Jackson, S. E., & Leiter, M. P. (1996). *Maslach Burnout Inventory manual* (3rd ed.). Palo Alto, CA: Consulting Psychologists Press.

Maslach, C., & Leiter, M. P. (2008). Early predictors of job burnout and engagement. *Journal of Applied Psychology, 93*, 498–512.

Maslach, C., Schaufeli, W. B., & Leiter, M. P. (2001). Job burnout. *Annual Review of Psychology, 52,* 397–422.

Maslow, A. H. (1943). A theory of motivation. *Psychological Review, 50,* 370–396.

Maslow, A. H. (1971). *The farthest reaches of human nature.* New York: Viking.

Masuda, T., Ellsworth, P. C., Mesquita, B., Leu, J., Tanida, S., & van de Veerdonk, E. (2008). Placing the face in context: Cultural differences in the perception of facial emotion. *Journal of Personality and Social Psychology, 94*(3), 365–381.

Mathieu, J. E., & Leonard, R. L. (1987). Applying utility concepts to a training program in supervisory skills: A time-based approach. *Academy of Management Journal, 30,* 828–847.

Mathieu, J. E., & Martineau, J. W. (1997). Individual and situational influences in training motivation. In J. K. Ford, S. W. J. Kozlowski, K. Kraiger, E. Salas, & M. S. Teachout (Eds.), *Improving training effectiveness in work organizations* (pp. 199–222). Mahwah, NJ: Erlbaum.

Mathieu, J. E., Maynard, M. T., Rapp, T. L., & Gilson, L. L. (2008). Team effectiveness 1997–2007: A review of recent advancements and a glimpse into the future. *Journal of Management, 34,* 410–476.

Maurer, T. J., & Rafuse, N. E. (2001). Learning, not litigating: Managing employee development and avoiding claims of age discrimination. *Academy of Management Executive, 15,* 110–121.

Maurer, T. J., & Solamon, J. M. (2006). The science and practice of a structured employment interview coaching program. *Personnel Psychology, 59,* 433–456.

May, G. L., & Kahnwieler, W. M. (2000). The effect of mastery practice design on learning and transfer behavior in behavior modeling training. *Personnel Psychology, 53,* 353–374.

May, K. (1998). Work in the 21st century: The role of I-O in work-life programs. *The Industrial-Organizational Psychologist, 36*(2), 79–82.

Mayer, J. D., Roberts, R. D., & Barsade, S. G. (2008). Human abilities: Emotional intelligence. *Annual Review of Psychology, 59,* 507–536.

Mayo, E. (1923a). The irrational factor in society. *Journal of Personnel Research, 1,* 419–426.

Mayo, E. (1923b). Irrationality and revery. *Journal of Personnel Research, 1,* 477–483.

Mayo, E. (1923c). The irrational factor in human behavior. *Annals of the American Academy of Political and Social Science, 110,* 117–130.

McArdle, W. D., Katch, F. I., & Katch, V. L. (2001). *Exercise physiology: Energy, nutrition, and human performance* (5th ed.). Philadelphia: Lippincott, Williams, and Wilkins.

McCall, M. W. (2010). Recasting leadership development. *Industrial and Organizational Psychology: Perspectives on Science and Practice, 3,* 3–19.

McCall, M. W., Lombardo, M. M., & Morrison, A. M. (1988). *The lessons of experience: How successful executives develop on the job.* Lexington, MA: Lexington Books.

McCarthy, J., & Goffin, R. (2004). Measuring job interview anxiety: Beyond weak knees and sweaty palms. *Personnel Psychology, 57,* 607–637.

McCauley, C. D. (2001). Leader training and development. In S. J. Zaccaro & R. J. Klimoski (Eds.), *The nature of organizational leadership: Understanding the performance imperatives confronting today's leaders* (pp. 347–383). San Francisco: Jossey-Bass.

McCauley, C. D., Ruderman, M. N., Ohlott, P. J., & Morrow, J. E. (1994). Assessing the developmental components of managerial jobs. *Journal of Applied Psychology, 79,* 544–560.

McClelland, D. C. (1985). *Human motivation.* Glenview, IL: Scott Foresman.

McCloy, R. A., Campbell, J. P., & Cudek, R. (1994). A confirmatory test of a model of performance determinants. *Journal of Applied Psychology, 79,* 493–503.

McCormick, E. J., Jeanneret, P. R., & Mecham, R. C. (1972). A study of job characteristics and job dimensions as based on the Position Analysis Questionnaire. *Journal of Applied Psychology, 56* [Monograph], 347–368.

McCrae, R. R., & Costa, P. T., Jr. (1985). Updating Norman's "adequate taxonomy": Intelligence and personality dimensions in natural language and in questionnaire. *Journal of Personality and Social Psychology, 49,* 710–721.

McCrae, R. R., & Costa, P. T., Jr. (1987). Validation of the five factor model of personality across instruments and observers. *Journal of Personality and Social Psychology, 52,* 81–90.

McCrae R. R., & Terracciano A., & 79 Member of the Personality Profiles of Cultures Project (2005). Personality profiles of cultures: Aggregate personality traits. *Journal of Personality and Social Psychology, 89,* 407–425.

McDaniel, M. A., Hartman, N. S., Whetzel, D. L., & Grubb, W. L. (2007). Situational judgment tests, responses instructions, and validity: A meta-analysis. *Personnel Psychology, 60,* 63–91.

McDaniel, M. A., Kepes, S., & Banks, G. C. (2011). The Uniform Guidelines are a detriment to the field of personnel selection. *Industrial and Organizational Psychology: Perspectives on Science and Practice, 4,* 419–514.

McDaniel, M. A., Morgeson, F. P., Finnegan, E. B., Campion, M. A., & Braverman, E. P. (2001). Use of situational judgment tests to predict job performance: A clarification of the literature. *Journal of Applied Psychology, 86,* 730–740.

McDaniel, M. A., & Nguyen, N. T. (2001). Situational judgment tests: A review of practice and constructs assessed. *International Journal of Selection and Assessment, 9,* 103–113.

McDaniel, M. A., Whetzel, D. L., Schmidt, F. L., & Maurer, S. D. (1994). The validity of employment interviews: A comprehensive review and meta-analysis. *Journal of Applied Psychology, 79,* 599–616.

McElroy, J. C., Morrow, P. C., & Rude, S. N. (2001). Turnover and organizational performance: A comparative analysis of the effects of voluntary, involuntary, and reduction-in-force turnover. *Journal of Applied Psychology, 86,* 1294–1299.

McFarlin, D. B., & Sweeney, P. D. (1992). Distributive and procedural justice as predictors of satisfaction with personal and organizational outcomes. *Academy of Management Journal, 35,* 626–637.

McGeehan, P., & Thomas, L., Jr. (2003, September 14). Market chief stands firm in storm over pay. *New York Times,* pp. 1, 14.

McGrath, J. E., & O'Connor, K. M. (1996). Temporal issues in work groups. In M. A. West (Ed.), *Handbook of work group psychology* (pp. 25–52). Chichester, UK: Wiley.

McGregor, D. (1960). *The human side of enterprise.* New York: McGraw-Hill.

McKeachie, W. J. (1997). Student ratings: The validity of use. *American Psychologist, 52,* 1218–1225.

McKean, E. (Ed.). (2005). *The New Oxford American Dictionary* (2nd ed.). New York: Oxford University Press.

McKee-Ryan, F. M., Song, Z., Wanberg, C. R., & Kinicki, A. J. (2005). Psychological and physical well-being during unemployment: A meta-analytic study. *Journal of Applied Psychology, 90,* 53–76.

McManus, M. A., & Kelly, M. L. (1999). Personality measures and biodata: Evidence regarding their incremental predictive value in the life insurance industry. *Personnel Psychology, 52,* 137–148.

McMurrer, D. P., van Buren, M., & Woodwell, W. (2000). *The 2000 ASTD state of the industry report.* Washington, DC: American Society for Training and Development.

Mead, A. D., & Drasgow, F. (1993). Equivalence of computerized and paper-and-pencil cognitive ability tests: A meta-analysis. *Psychological Bulletin, 114,* 449–458.

Medsker, G. J., Katkowski, D. A., & Furr, D. (2005). *2003 employment survey results for the Society for Industrial and Organizational Psychology.* Unpublished manuscript available from SIOP (www.siop.org).

Meehl, P. E. (1954). *Clinical vs. statistical prediction.* Minneapolis: University of Minnesota Press.

Meindl, J. R. (1990). On leadership: An alternative to conventional wisdom. In B. M. Staw & L. L. Cummings (Eds.), *Research in organizational behavior* (Vol. 12, pp. 159–203). Greenwich, CT: JAI Press.

Meister, J. C. (1994). *Corporate quality universities: Lessons in building a world class workforce.* New York: McGraw-Hill.

Melchers, K. G., Lienhardt, N., Aarburg, M. V., & Kleinmann, M. (2011). Is more structure really better? A comparison of frame-of-reference training and descriptively anchored rating scales to improve interviewers rating quality. *Personnel Psychology, 64,* 53–87.

Merton, R. K. (1973). *The sociology of science.* Chicago: University of Chicago Press.

Mesmer-Magnus, J. R., & Viswesvaran, C. (2007). Inducing maximal versus typical learning through the provision of a pretraining goal orientation. *Human Performance, 20,* 205–222.

Messick, D. N., & Tenbrussel, A. (1996). *Codes of conduct: Behavioral research into business ethics.* New York: Russell Sage Foundation.

Messick, S. (1995). Validity of psychological assessment: Validation of inferences from person's responses and performances as scientific inquiry into score meaning. *American Psychologist, 50,* 741–749.

Meyer, J., & Allen, N. (1997). *Commitment in the workplace: Theory, research, and application.* Thousand Oaks, CA: Sage.

Meyer, J. P., Allen, N. J., & Smith, C. A. (1993). Commitments to organization and occupations: Extension and test of a three-component conceptualization. *Journal of Applied Psychology, 78,* 538–551.

Mikkelsen, E. G., & Einarson, S. (2001). *The role of victim personality in workplace bullying.* Unpublished manuscript, Psykologisk Institut, Risskov, Denmark.

Mikula, G., Scherer, K. R., & Athenstaedt, U. (1998). The role of injustice in the elicitation of differential emotional reactions. *Personality and Social Psychology Bulletin, 24,* 769–783.

Miles, D. E., Borman, W. C., Spector, P. E., & Fox, S. (2002). Building an integrative model of extra role work behaviors: A comparison of counterproductive work behavior with organizational citizenship behavior. *International Journal of Selection and Assessment, 10,* 51–57.

Miller, D. (1993). The architecture of simplicity. *Academy of Management Review, 18,* 116–138.

Miller, D. (1994). What happens after success: The perils of excellence. *Journal of Management Studies, 31,* 325–358.

Miller, D. T. (2001). Disrespect and the experience of injustice. *Annual Review of Psychology, 52,* 527–553.

Milne, S. H., Blum, T. C., & Roman, P. M. (1994). Factors influencing employees' propensity to use an employee assistance program. *Personnel Psychology, 47,* 123–145.

Miner, A. G., Glomb, T. M., & Hulin, C. (2005). Experience sampling mood and its correlates at work. *Journal of Occupational and Organizational Psychology, 78,* 171–193.

Miner, J. B. (2002). *Organizational behavior: Foundations, theories, and analyses.* Oxford, UK: Oxford University Press.

Miner-Rubino, K., & Cortina, L. M. (2007). Beyond targets: Consequences of vicarious exposure to misogyny at work. *Journal of Applied Psychology, 92,* 1254–1269.

Ming, K. (2005, March). Shop to the top! If your mom were the president of Old Navy (like mine is!) you'd want her advice on more than just performance fleece and flip-flops! *CosmoGirl!,* p. 118.

Mintzberg, H. (1979). *The structuring of organizations: A synthesis of the research.* Englewood Cliffs, NJ: Prentice Hall.

Mintzberg, H. (1981). Organizational Design: Fashion or Fit? *Harvard Business Review, 59*(1), 108–116.

Mintzberg, H. (1983). *Structure in Fives: Designing Effective Organizations.* Englewood Cliffs, NJ: Prentice Hall.

Mintzberg, H. (1989). *Mintzberg on management: Inside our strange world of organizations.* New York: Free Press.

Mio, J. S., Riggio, R. E., Levin, S., & Reese, R. (2005). Presidential leadership and charisma: The effects of metaphor. *Leadership Quarterly, 16,* 287–294.

Miron, E., Erez, M., & Naveh, E. (2004). Do personal characteristics and cultural values that promote innovation, quality, and efficiency compete or complement each other? *Journal of Organizational Behavior, 25,* 175–199.

Mitchell, T. R., Holtom, B. C., Lee, T. W., Sablynski, C. J., & Erez, M. (2001). Why people stay: Using job embeddedness to predict voluntary turnover. *Academy of Management Journal, 44,* 1102–1121.

Mitchell, T. R., Thompson, K. R., & George-Falvy, J. (2000). Goal setting: Theory and practice. In C. L. Cooper & E. A. Locke (Eds.), *Industrial and organizational psychology* (pp. 216–243). Malden, MA: Blackwell.

Mitchell, T. W. (1994). The utility of biodata. In G. S. Stokes & M. D. Mumford (Eds.), *Biodata handbook: Theory, research, and the use of biographical information in selection and performance prediction* (pp. 485–516). Palo Alto, CA: Consulting Psychologists Press.

Mohammed, S., Ferzandi, L., & Hamilton, K. (2010). Metaphor no more: A 15-year review of the team mental model. *Journal of Management, 36,* 876–910.

Mohrman, S. A., Cohen, S. G., & Mohrman, A. M. (1995). *Designing team-based organizations.* San Francisco: Jossey-Bass.

Monk, T. H., Folkard, S., & Wedderburn, A. I. (1996). Maintaining safety and high performance on shiftwork. *Applied Ergonomics, 27,* 17–23.

Monk, T. H., & Wagner, J. A. (1989). Social factors can outweigh biological ones in determining night shift safety. *Human Factors, 31,* 721–724.

Montes, S. D., & Zweig, D. (2009). Do promises matter? An exploration of the role of promises in psychological contract breach. *Journal of Applied Psychology, 94*(5), 1243–1260.

Moon, H. (2001). The two faces of conscientiousness: Duty and achievement striving in escalation of commitment dilemmas. *Journal of Applied Psychology, 86,* 533–540.

Moorman, C., & Miner, A. S. (1998). Organizational improvisation and organizational memory. *Academy of Management Review, 23,* 698–723.

Moran, S. K., Wolff, S. C., & Green, J. E. (1995). Workers' compensation and occupational stress: Gaining control. In L. R. Murphy & J. J. Hurrell (Eds.), *Job stress interventions* (pp. 355–368). Washington, DC: American Psychological Association.

Morehead, G., Ference, R., & Neck, C. P. (1991). Group decision fiascos continue: Space shuttle *Challenger* and a revised groupthink framework. *Human Relations, 44,* 539–550.

Morgeson, F. P. (2005). The external leadership of self-managing teams: Intervening in the context of novel and disruptive events. *Journal of Applied Psychology, 90,* 497–508.

Morgeson, F. P., Campion, M. A., Dipboye, R. L., Hollenbeck, J. R., Murphy, K., & Schmitt, N. (2007). Reconsidering the use of personality tests in personnel selection contexts. *Personnel Psychology, 60,* 683–729.

Morgeson, F. P., Mumford, T. V., & Campion, M. A. (2005). Coming full circle: Using research to address 27 questions about 360-degree feedback programs. *Consulting Psychology Journal: Practice and Research, 57,* 196–209.

Morgeson, F. P., Reider, M. H., & Campion, M. A. (2005). Selecting individuals in team settings: The importance of social skills, personality characteristics, and teamwork knowledge. *Personnel Psychology, 58,* 583–611.

Morris, J. A., & Feldman, D. C. (1996). The dimensions, antecedents, and consequences of emotional labor. *Academy of Management Review, 21,* 986–1010.

Morris, M. A., & Robie, C. (2001). A meta-analysis of the effects of cross-cultural training on expatriate performance and adjustment. *International Journal of Training and Development, 5,* 112–125.

Morrison, D., Cordery, J., Girardi, A., & Payne, R. (2005). Job design, opportunities for skill utilization, and intrinsic job satisfaction. *European Journal of Work and Organizational Psychology, 14*(1), 59–79.

Morrison, E. W., Chen, Y., & Salgado, S. R. (2004). Cultural differences in newcomer feedback seeking: A comparison of the United States and Hong Kong. *Applied Psychology: An International Review, 53*, 1–22.

Morrison, J. L., & Meister, J. C. (2000, July/August). Corporate universities: An interview with Jeanne Meister. *The Technology Source.* Retrieved from ts.mivu.org/default.asp?show=article&id=1034

Morrissey, J. (2007, November 14). AT&T to sell equipment to monitor workplaces. *New York Times*, p. C5.

Morrow, C. C., Jarrett, M. Q., & Rupinski, M. T. (1997). An investigation of the effect and economic utility of corporate-wide training. *Personnel Psychology, 50*, 91–119.

Mortimer, J. T., Pimental, E. E., Ryu, S., Nash, K., & Lee, C. (1996). Part-time work and occupational value formation in adolescence. *Social Forces, 74*(4), 1405–1423.

Moscoso, S., & Salgado, J. F. (2004). Fairness reactions to personnel selection techniques in Spain and Portugal. *International Journal of Selection and Assessment, 12*, 187–196.

Moser, K., & Galais, N. (2007). Self-monitoring and job performance: The moderating role of tenure. *International Journal of Selection and Assessment, 15*, 83–93.

Motowidlo, S. J., Borman, W. C., & Schmit, M. J. (1997). A theory of individual differences in task and contextual performance. *Human Performance, 10*, 71–83.

Motowidlo, S. J., Packard, J. S., & Manning, M. R. (1986). Occupational stress: Its causes and consequences for job performance. *Journal of Applied Psychology, 71*, 618–629.

Motowidlo, S. J., & Tippins, N. (1993). Further studies of the low fidelity simulation in the form of a situational inventory. *Journal of Occupational and Organizational Psychology, 66*, 337–344.

Motowidlo, S. J., & van Scotter, J. R. (1994). Evidence that task performance should be distinguished from contextual performance. *Journal of Applied Psychology, 79*, 475–480.

Mount, M. K., & Barrick, M. R. (1995). The Big Five personality dimensions: Implications for research and practice in human resources management. In G. R. Ferris (Ed.), *Research in personnel and human resources management* (Vol. 13, pp. 153–200). Greenwich, CT: JAI Press.

Mount, M. K., & Barrick, M. R. (2002). *The personal characteristics inventory.* Libertyville, IL: The Wonderlic Corporation.

Mount, M. K., Witt, L. A., & Barrick, M. R. (2000). Incremental validity of empirically keyed bio-data scales over GMA and the five factor personality constructs. *Personnel Psychology, 53*, 299–323.

Moyer, R. S., & Nath, A. (1998). Some effects of brief training interventions on perceptions of sexual harassment. *Journal of Applied Social Psychology, 28*, 333–356.

Muchinsky, P. (2004). When the psychometrics of test development meets organizational realities: A conceptual framework for organizational change, examples, and recommendations. *Personnel Psychology, 57*, 175–209.

Mueller, K., Liebig, C., & Hattrup, K. (2007). Computerizing organizational attitude surveys: An investigation of the measurement equivalence of a multifaceted job satisfaction measure. *Educational and Psychological Measurement, 67*, 658–678.

Mueller-Hanson, R., Heggestad, E. D., & Thornton, G. C. (2003). Faking and selection: Considering the use of personality from select-in and select-out perspectives. *Journal of Applied Psychology, 88*, 348–355.

Mueller-Hanson, R. A., & Phillips, G. M. (2005). Everything you need to know about I-O internships: Follow-up responses for undergraduate and high school level internships. *The Industrial-Organizational Psychologist, 42*(3), 117–119.

Mullen, B., & Cooper, C. (1994). The relation between group cohesiveness and performance: An integration. *Psychological Bulletin, 115*, 210–227.

Mumford, M. D., Baughman, W. A., Supinski, E. P., & Anderson, L. E. (1998). A construct approach to skill assessment: Procedures for assessing complex cognitive skills. In M. D. Hakel (Ed.), *Beyond multiple choice: Evaluating alternatives to traditional testing for selection* (pp. 75–112). Mahwah, NJ: Erlbaum.

Mumford, M. D., & Owens, W. A. (1982). Life history and vocational interests. *Journal of Vocational Behavior, 21*, 330–348.

Mumford, M. D., & Peterson, N. G. (1999). The O*NET content model: Structural considerations in describing jobs. In N. G. Peterson, M. D. Mumford, W. C. Borman, P. R. Jeanneret, & E. A. Fleishman (Eds.), *An occupational information system for the 21st century* (pp. 21–30). Washington, DC: American Psychological Association.

Mumford, M. D., Snell, A. F., & Reiter-Palmon, R. (1994). Personality and background data: Life history and self concepts in an ecological system. In G. S. Stokes, M. D. Mumford, & W. A. Owens (Eds.), *Handbook of background data research: Theories, measures, and applications* (pp. 122–147). Palo Alto, CA: Consulting Psychologists Press.

Mumford, M. D., & Stokes, G. S. (1991). Developmental determinants of individual action: Theory and practice in applying background measures. In M. D. Dunnette & L. M. Hough (Eds.), *Handbook on industrial and organizational psychology* (2nd ed., Vol. 3, pp. 61–138). Palo Alto, CA: Consulting Psychologists Press.

Mumford, M. R., Uhlman, C. E., & Kilcullen, R. N. (1992). The structure of life history: Implications for the construct validity of background data scales. *Human Performance, 5*, 109–137.

Mumford, T. V., Campion, A. A., & Morgeson, F. P. (2007). The leadership skills strataplex: Leadership skill requirements across organizational levels. *Leadership Quarterly, 18*, 154–166.

Mumford, T. V., Van Iddekinge, C. H., Morgeson, F. P., & Campion, M. A. (2008). The team role test: Development and validation of a team role knowledge situational judgment test. *Journal of Applied Psychology, 93*, 250–267.

Munsey, C. (2007). Women leaders. *APA Monitor, 38*(7), 64–80.

Munsterberg, H. (1913). *Psychology and industrial efficiency.* Boston: Houghton Mifflin.

Murphy, K. R. (1996). Individual differences and behavior: Much more than "g." In K. R. Murphy (Ed.), *Individual differences and behavior in organizations* (pp. 3–30). San Francisco: Jossey-Bass.

Murphy, K. R. (1997). Editorial. *Journal of Applied Psychology, 82*, 1–3.

Murphy, K. R. (2002). *Validity generalization: A critical review.* Mahwah, NJ: Erlbaum.

Murphy, K. R. (2006). *A critique of emotional intelligence: What are the problems and how can they be fixed?* Mahwah, NJ: Erlbaum.

Murphy, K. R. (2008). Explaining the weak relationship between job performance and ratings of job performance. *Industrial and Organizational Psychology, 1*, 148–160.

Murphy, K. R., & Cleveland, J. N. (1995). *Understanding performance appraisal: Social, organizational, and goal-based perspectives.* Thousand Oaks, CA: Sage.

Murphy, K. R., Cleveland, J. N., Skattebo, A. L., & Kinney, T. B. (2004). Raters who pursue different goals give different ratings. *Journal of Applied Psychology, 89*, 158–164.

Murphy, K. R., & Davidshofer, C. O. (2005). *Psychological testing: Principles and applications* (6th ed.). Upper Saddle River, NJ: Prentice Hall.

Murphy, K. R., & DeShon, R. (2000a). Interrater correlations do not estimate the reliability of job performance ratings. *Personnel Psychology, 53*, 873–900.

Murphy, K. R., & DeShon, R. (2000b). Progress in psychometrics: Can industrial and organizational psychology catch up? *Personnel Psychology, 53*, 913–924.

Murphy, K. R., & Dzieweczynski, J. L. (2005). Why don't measures of broad dimensions of personality perform better as predictors of job performance? *Human Performance, 18*, 343–357.

Murphy, K. R., & Myors, B. (2004). *Statistical power analysis: A simple and general model for traditional and modern hypothesis tests.* Mahwah, NJ: Erlbaum.

Murphy, K. R., Thornton, G. C., & Prue, K. (1991). Influence of job characteristics on the acceptability of employee drug testing. *Journal of Applied Psychology, 76,* 447–453.

Murphy, K. R., Thornton, G. C., & Reynolds, D. H. (1990). College students' attitudes toward employee drug testing programs. *Personnel Psychology, 43,* 615–631.

Murphy, L. R. (1996). Stress management in work settings: A critical review of the health effects. *American Journal of Health Promotion, 11,* 112–135.

Myors, B. et al. (2008). International perspectives on the legal environment for selection. *Industrial and Organizational Psychology: Perspectives on Science and Practice, 1,* 206–246.

Nadler, D. A. (1987). The effective management of organizational change. In J. W. Lorsch (Ed.), *Handbook of organizational behavior* (pp. 358–369). Upper Saddle River, NJ: Prentice Hall.

Naglieri, J. A., Drasgow, F., Schmit, M., Handler, L., Prifitera, A., Marglis, A., & Velasquez, R. (2004). Psychological testing on the Internet. *American Psychologist, 59,* 150–162.

Nagy, M. S. (2002). Using a single-item approach to measure facet job satisfaction. *Journal of Occupational and Organizational Psychology, 75,* 77–86.

National Evaluation Systems, Inc. (2002). *The Liberal Arts and Sciences Test (LAST).* Amherst, MA: Author.

National Research Council (NRC). (1999). *The changing nature of work.* Washington, DC: National Academies Press.

National Research Council (NRC). (2010). *A database for a changing economy: Review of the occupational information network (O*NET).* Washington, DC: National Academies Press.

National Safe Workplace Institute. (1989). *Workplace violence prevention manual.* Newark, NJ: Author.

Neal, A., & Griffin, M. A. (2006). A study of the lagged relationships among safety climate, safety motivation, safety behavior, and accidents at the individual and group levels. *Journal of Applied Psychology, 91,* 946–953.

Neisser, U., Boodoo, G., Bouchard, T. J., Boykin, A. W., Brody, N., Ceci, S. J., et al. (1996). Intelligence: Knowns and unknowns. *American Psychologist, 51,* 77–101.

Nemanich, L. A., & Keller, R. T. (2007). Transformational leadership in an acquisition: A field study of employees. *Leadership Quarterly, 18,* 49–68.

Neubert, M. I., & Cady, S. H. (2001). Program commitment: A multistudy of its impact and antecedents. *Personnel Psychology, 54,* 421–448.

Neuman, G. A., & Wright, J. (1999). Team effectiveness: Beyond skills and cognitive ability. *Journal of Applied Psychology, 84,* 376–389.

Neuman, J. H., & Baron, R. A. (2005). Aggression in the workplace: A social-psychological perspective. In S. Fox & P. E. Spector (Eds.), *Counterproductive workplace behavior: Investigations of actors and targets* (pp. 13–40). Washington, DC: American Psychological Association.

Neuman, W. (2007, August 3). Subway deaths raise questions on the selection of supervisors. *New York Times,* p. B1.

Newman, D. A., & Harrison, D. A. (2008). Been there, bottled that: Are state and behavioral work engagement new and useful construct wines? *Industrial and Organizational Psychology, 1,* 31–35.

New York Times. (2005a, April 3). Leadership in diversity: Cargill. *New York Times Magazine,* Section 6.

New York Times. (2005b, January 29). German trial hears defense of a bonus, p. W7.

New York Times. (2005c, September 17). California: Power failure tied to mix-up. National Briefing (AP), West, p. A12.

Ng, K. Y., & van Dyne, L. (2005). Antecedents and performance consequences of helping behavior in work groups. *Group and Organization Management, 30,* 514–540.

Ng, T. W. H., Sorenson, D. L., & Eby, L. T. (2006). Locus of control at work: A meta-analysis. *Journal of Organizational Behavior, 27,* 1057–1087.

Nicholson, N., Brown, C. A., & Chadwick-Jones, J. K. (1976). Absence from work and job satisfaction. *Journal of Applied Psychology, 61,* 728–737.

Nicholson, N., & Johns, G. (1985). The absence culture and the psychological contract—Who's in control of absence? *Academy of Management Review, 10,* 397–407.

Niederle, M., & Vesterlund, L. (2005). *Do women shy away from competition? Do men compete too much?* NBER Working Paper w11474, July. Stanford University, Department of Economics.

Nikolaou, I., & Judge, T. (2007). Fairness reactions to personnel selection techniques in Greece: The role of core-self evaluations. *International Journal of Selection and Assessment, 15,* 206–219.

Nishii, L. H., & Mayer, D. M. (2009). Do inclusive leaders help to reduce turnover in diverse groups? The moderating role of leader–member exchange in the diversity to turnover relationship. *Journal of Applied Psychology, 94,* 1412–1426.

Noe, R. A. (2010). *Employee training and development* (5th ed.). New York: McGraw-Hill.

Noe, R. A., Hollenbeck, J. R., Gerhart, B., & Wright, P. M. (2000). *Human resource management* (3rd ed.). New York: McGraw-Hill.

Noe, R. A., Hollenbeck, J. R., Gerhart, B., & Wright, P. M. (2010). *Human resource management* (4th ed.). New York: McGraw-Hill.

Noer, D. M. (1999). Helping organizations change: Coping with downsizing, mergers, reengineering, and reorganizations. In A. I. Kraut & A. K. Korman (Eds.), *Evolving practices in human resource management* (pp. 275–301). San Francisco: Jossey-Bass.

Normand, J., Salyards, S. D., & Mahoney, J. J. (1990). An evaluation of pre-employment drug testing. *Journal of Applied Psychology, 75,* 629–639.

Northrup, L. C. (1989). *The psychometric history of selected ability constructs.* Washington, DC: Office of Personnel Management.

Nyfield, G., & Baron, H. (2000). Cultural context in adapting selection practices across borders. In J. Kehoe (Ed.), *Managing selection in changing organizations: Human resource strategies* (pp. 242–268). San Francisco: Jossey-Bass.

Nyhus, E. K., & Pons, E. (2004). The effects of personality on earnings. *Journal of Economic Psychology, 26,* 363–384.

Oakland, T. (2004). Use of educational and psychological tests internationally. *Applied Psychology: An International Review, 53,* 157–172.

Oberg, J. (2003, August 20). NASA requires overhaul at top. *USA Today.*

O'Boyle, E. H., Humphrey, R. H., Pollack, J. M., Hawver, T. H., & Story, P.A. (2011). The relation between emotional intelligence and job performance: A meta-analysis. *Journal of Organizational Behavior, 32,* 788–818.

Oh, I., & Berry, C.M. (2009). The five-factor model of personality and managerial performance: Validity gains through the use of 360 degree performance ratings. *Journal of Applied Psychology, 94,* 1498–1513.

Ohno, T. (1998). *Just-in-time: For today and tomorrow.* Cambridge, UK: Productivity Press.

Oldham, G. R., Cummings, A., Mischel, L. J., Schmidtke, J. M., & Jhou, J. (1995). Listen while you work? Quasi-experimental relations between personal stereo-headset use and employee work responses. *Journal of Applied Psychology, 80,* 547–564.

O'Leary-Kelly, A. M., Tiedt, P., & Bowes-Sperry, L. (2004). Answering accountability questions in sexual harassment: Insights regarding harassers, targets, and observers. *Human Resource Management Review, 14,* 85–1006.

Olson, R., Verley, J., Santos, L., & Salas, C. (2004). What we teach students about the Hawthorne studies: A review of content within a sample of introductory I-O and OB textbooks. *The Industrial-Organizational Psychologist, 41*(3), 23–39.

Olson-Buchanan, J. B. (2001). Computer-based advances in assessment. In F. Drasgow & N. Schmitt (Eds.), *Measuring and analyzing behavior in organizations* (pp. 44–87). San Francisco: Jossey-Bass.

Olson-Buchanan, J. B., Drasgow, F., Moberg, P. J., Mead, A. D., Kennan, P. A., & Donovan (1998). Conflict resolution skills assessment: A model-based, multi-media approach. *Personnel Psychology, 51*, 1–24.

Ones, D. S., & Viswesvaran, C. (1996). Bandwidth-fidelity dilemma in personality measurement for personnel selection. *Journal of Organizational Behavior, 17*, 609–626.

Ones, D. S., & Viswesvaran, C. (1999). Relative importance of personality dimensions for expatriate selection: A policy capturing study. *Human Performance, 12*(3/4), 275–294.

Ones, D. S., & Viswesvaran, C. (2001). Integrity tests and other criterion-focused occupational personality scales (COPS) used in personnel selection. *International Journal of Selection and Assessment, 9*, 31–39.

Ones, D. S., & Viswesvaran, C. (2002). Introduction to the special issue: Role of general mental ability in industrial, work, and organizational psychology. *Human Performance, 15*, 1–3.

Ones, D. S., Viswesvaran, C., & Schmidt, F. L. (1993). Comprehensive meta-analysis of integrity test validities: Findings and implications for personnel selection and theories of job performance. *Journal of Applied Psychology, 78* [Monograph], 679–703.

Ones, D. S., Viswesvaran, C., & Schmidt, F. L. (2003). Personality and absenteeism: A meta-analysis of integrity tests. *European Journal of Personality, 17*, Supplement 1 (March), 19–38.

Onishi, N. (2005, May 1). A jolt to team Japan: Bonus demands. *New York Times*, p. 8.

Oreg, S. (2005). Personality, context, and resistance to organizational change. *European Journal of Work and Organizational Psychology, 15*, 73–101.

Organ, D. W., & Ryan, K. (1995). A meta-analytic review of attitudinal and dispositional predictors of organizational citizenship behavior. *Personnel Psychology, 48*, 775–802.

Osborn, R. N., Hunt, J. G., & Jauch, L. R. (2002). Toward a contextual theory of leadership. *Leadership Quarterly, 13*, 797–837.

Oser, R. L., Salas, E., Merket, D. C., & Bowers, C. A. (2001). Applying resource management training in naval aviation: A methodology and lessons learned. In E. Salas, C. A. Bowers, & E. Edens (Eds.), *Improving teamwork in organizations: Applications of resource management training* (pp. 283–301). Mahwah, NJ: Erlbaum.

Ouchi, W. (1981). *Theory Z: How American business can meet the Japanese challenge.* Reading, MA: Addison-Wesley.

Padilla, A., Hogan, R., & Kaiser, R. B. (2007). The toxic triangle: Destructive leaders, susceptible followers, and conducive environments. *Leadership Quarterly, 18*, 176–194.

Panasonic. (2011, January 5). *Panasonic pledges major new eco-sustainability goals.* Retrieved from http://www.prnewswire.com/news-releases/panasonic-pledges-major-new-eco-sustainability-goals—three-year-plan-to-double-sale-of-energy-efficient-products-and-grow-environmental-school-programs-112971899.html

Paquin, A. R., Roch, S. G., & Sanchez-Ku, M. L. (2007). An investigation of cross-cultural differences on the impact of productivity interventions: The example of ProMES. *Journal of Applied Behavior Science, 43*, 427–448.

Paris, L. D., Howell, J. P., Dorfman, P. W., & Hanges, P. J. (2009). Preferred leadership prototypes of male and female leaders in 27 countries. *Journal of International Business Studies, 40*(8), 1396–1405.

Park, G., Lubinski, D., & Benbow, C. P. (2007). Contrasting intellectual patterns predict creativity in the arts and sciences: Tracking intellectually precocious youth over 25 years. *Psychological Science, 18*, 948–952.

Parker, C. P., Baltes, B. B., Young, S. A., Huff, J. W., Altmann, R. A., Lacost, H. A., & Roberts, J. E. (2003). Relationships between psychological climate and work outcomes: A meta-analytic review. *Journal of Organizational Behavior, 24*, 389–416.

Parker, S. (2003). Longitudinal effects of lean production on employee outcomes and the mediating role of work characteristics. *Journal of Applied Psychology, 88*, 620–634.

Parker, S. K., Chmiel, N., & Wall, T. D. (1997). Work characteristics and employee well being within a context of strategic downsizing. *Journal of Occupational Health Psychology, 2*, 289–303.

Parker-Pope, T. (2008, March 25). When the bully sits in the next cubicle. *New York Times*, p. D5.

Parkes, K. R. (1999). Shiftwork, job type, and the work environment as joint predictors of health-related outcomes. *Journal of Occupational Health Psychology, 4*, 256–268.

Parkes, L. P., Bochner, S., & Schneider, S. K. (2001). People–organization fit across cultures: An empirical investigation of individualism and collectivism. *Applied Psychology: An International Review, 50*, 81–108.

Paronto, M. E., Truxillo, D. M., Bauer, T. N., & Leo, M. C. (2002). Drug testing, drug treatment, and marijuana use: A fairness perspective. *Journal of Applied Psychology, 87*, 1159–1166.

Paterson, D. G. (1923). Methods of rating human qualities. *Annual Proceedings of the American Academy of Political and Social Scientists, 110*, 81–93.

Patterson, M. G., West, M. A., Shackelton, V. J., Dawson, J. F., Lawthom, R., Maitlis, S., Robinson, D. L., & Wallace, A. M. (2005). Validating the organizational climate measure: Links to managerial practices, productivity and innovation. *Journal of Organizational Behavior, 26*, 379–408.

Paul, R. J., & Townsend, J. B. (1998). Violence in the workplace: A review with recommendations. *Employee Responsibilities and Rights Journal, 11*, 1–14.

Payne, S. C., Youngcourt, S. S., & Beaubien, J. M. (2007). A metaanalytic examination of the goal orientation nomological net. *Journal of Applied Psychology, 92*, 128–150.

Pearce, J. A., & Ravlin, E. C. (1987). The design and activation of self-regulating work groups. *Human Relations, 40*, 751–782.

Pearlman, K., & Sanchez, J. (2010). Work analysis. In J. L. Farr & N. Tippens (Eds.), *Handbook of employee selection* (pp. 73–98). Mahwah, NJ: Erlbaum.

Peatling, S., & Malkin, B. (2004, March 13). Employers face ban on e-mail spying. *The Sydney Morning Herald*, p. 3.

Pedulla, T. (2005, February 25). Dangerous game, in the wrong hands. *USA Today*, p. 3C.

Peeters, H., & Lievens, F. (2005). Situational judgment tests and their predictiveness of college students' success: The influence of faking. *Educational and Psychological Measurement, 65*, 70–89.

Pekrun, R., & Frese, M. (1992). Emotions in work and achievement. *International Review of Industrial and Organizational Psychology, 7*, 153–200.

Penney, L. M., & Spector, P. E. (2002). Narcissism and counterproductive work behavior: Do bigger egos mean bigger problems? *International Journal of Selection and Assessment, 10*(1/2), 126–134.

Penney, L. M., & Spector, P. E. (2005). Job stress, incivility, and counterproductive work behavior (CWB): The moderating role of negativity. *Journal of Organizational Behavior, 26*, 777–796.

Pereira, G. M., & Osburn, H. G. (2007). Effects of participation in decision making on performance and employee attitudes: A quality circles meta-analysis. *Journal of Business and Psychology, 22*, 145–153.

Perlow, L., & Weeks, J. (2002). Who's helping whom? Layers of culture and workplace behavior. *Journal of Organizational Behavior, 23,* 345–361.

Perry, E. L., Kulik, C. T., & Schmidtke, J. M. (1998). Individual differences in the effectiveness of sexual harassment awareness training. *Journal of Applied Social Psychology, 28,* 698–723.

Peterson, D. B. (2002). Management development: Coaching and mentoring programs. In K. Kraiger (Ed.), *Creating, implementing, and managing effective training and development* (pp. 160–191). San Francisco: Jossey-Bass.

Peterson, M. F., Smith, P. B., Akande, A., Ayestaran, S., Bochner, S., Callan, V., et al. (1995). Role conflict, ambiguity, and overload: A 21-nation study. *Academy of Management Journal, 38,* 429–452.

Peterson, N. G., Borman, W. C., Hanson, M. A., & Kubisiak, U. C. (1999). Summary of results, implications for O*NET applications and future directions. In N. G. Peterson, M. D. Mumford, W. C. Borman, P. R. Jeanneret, & E. A. Fleishman (Eds.), *An occupational information system for the 21st century* (pp. 289–296). Washington, DC: American Psychological Association.

Peterson, N. G., Hough, L. M., Dunnette, M. D., Rosse, R. L., Houston, J. S., Toquam, J. S., et al. (1990). Project A: Specification of the predictor domain and development of new selection/classification tests. *Personnel Psychology, 43,* 247–276.

Peterson, N. G., Mumford, M. D., Borman, W. C., Jeanneret, P. R., & Fleishman, E. A. (Eds.) (1999). *An occupational information system for the 21st century.* Washington, DC: American Psychological Association.

Peterson, N. G., Mumford, M. D., Borman, W. C., Jeanneret, P. R., Fleishman, E. A., Levin, K. Y., et al. (2001). Understanding work using the occupational information network (O*NET): Implications for practice and research. *Personnel Psychology, 54,* 451–492.

Pfeffer, J. (1981). *Power in organizations.* Marshfield, MA: Pitman.

Pfeffer, J. (1983). Organizational demography. In L.L. Cummings and B.M. Staw (Eds.). *Research in Organizational Behavior* (Vol. 5, pp. 299–357). Greenwich, CT: JAI Press.

Pfeffer, J., & Salancik, G. R. (1978). *The external control of organizations: A resource dependence perspective.* New York: Harper & Row.

Phillips, J. M. (1998). Effects of realistic job previews on multiple organizational outcomes: A meta-analysis. *Academy of Management Journal, 41,* 673–690.

Phillips, J. M., & Gully, S. A. (1997). Role of goal orientation, ability, need for achievement, and locus of control in the self-efficacy and goal-setting process. *Journal of Applied Psychology, 82,* 792–802.

Piasentin, K. A., & Chapman, E. S. (2007). Perceived similarity and complementarity as predictors of subjective person–organization fit. *Journal of Occupational and Organizational Psychology, 80,* 341–354.

Piccolo, R. F., Judge, T. A., Takahashi, K., Watanabe, N., & Locke, E. A. (2005). Core self-evaluations in Japan: Relative effects on job satisfaction, life satisfaction and happiness. *Journal of Organizational Behavior, 26,* 965–984.

Piller, C. (1993). Bosses with X-ray eyes. *MacWorld, 10*(7), 118–123.

Pitariu, H. D. (1992). I/O psychology in Romania: Past, present and intentions. *The Industrial-Organizational Psychologist, 29*(4), 29–33.

Plass, S. (2008, September 2). Wage gaps for women frustrating Germany. *New York Times, p. C1.*

Plomin, R., & Spinath, F. M. (2004). Intelligence, genetics, genes, and genomics. *Journal of Personality and Social Psychology, 86,* 112–129.

Ployhart, R., & Ehrhart, M. G. (2002). Modeling the practical effects of applicant reactions: Subgroup differences in test-taking motivation, test performance, and selection rates. *International Journal of Selection and Assessment, 10,* 258–270.

Ployhart, R. E., & Harold, C. M. (2004). The applicant attribution-reaction theory (AART): An integrative theory of applicant attributional processing. *International Journal of Selection and Assessment, 12,* 84–98.

Ployhart, R. E., Weekley, J. A., Holtz, B. C., & Kemp, C. (2003). Web-based and paper-and-pencil testing of applicants in a proctored setting: Are personality, biodata, and situational judgment tests comparable? *Personnel Psychology, 56,* 733–752.

Ployhart, R. E., Wiechmann, D., Schmitt, N., Sacco, J. M., & Rogg, K. (2003). The cross-cultural equivalence of job performance ratings. *Human Performance, 16,* 49–79.

Podsakoff, N. P., LePine, J. A., & LePine, M. A. (2007). Differential challenge stressor–hindrance stressor relationships with job attitudes, turnover intentions, turnover, and withdrawal behavior: A metaanalysis. *Journal of Applied Psychology, 92,* 438–454.

Podsakoff, P. M., MacKenzie, J. B., Paine, P., & Bachrach, D. G. (2000). Organizational citizenship behaviors: A critical review of the theoretical and empirical literature and suggestions for future research. *Journal of Management, 26,* 513–563.

Popper, M., & Mayseless, O. (2003). Back to basics: Applying a parenting perspective to transformational leadership. *Leadership Quarterly, 14,* 41–65.

Porath, C. L., & Bateman, T. S. (2006). Self-regulation: From goal orientation to job performance. *Journal of Applied Psychology, 91,* 185–192.

Porter, L. W., & Lawler, E. E. (1968). *Managerial attitudes and performance.* Homewood, IL: Irwin.

Porter, L. W., Steers, R. M., Mowday, R. T., & Boulian, P. V. (1974). Organizational commitment, job satisfaction, and turnover among psychiatric technicians. *Journal of Applied Psychology, 59,* 603–609.

Posthuma, R. A., Morgeson, F. P., & Campion, M. A. (2002). Beyond employment interview validity: A comprehensive narrative review of recent research and trends over time. *Personnel Psychology, 55,* 1–82.

Posthuma, R. A., Roehling, M. V., & Campion, M. A. (2006). Applying U.S. employment discrimination laws to international employers: Advice for scientists and practitioners. *Personnel Psychology, 59,* 705–739.

Potosky, D., & Bobko, P. (2004). Selection testing via the Internet: Practical considerations and exploratory empirical findings. *Personnel Psychology, 57,* 1003–1034.

Powell, G. N., & Butterfield, D. A. (2002). Exploring the influence of decision makers' race and gender on actual promotions to top management. *Personnel Psychology, 55,* 397–428.

Praslova, L. (2008). The legal environment for selection in Russia. *Industrial and Organizational Psychology, 1,* 264–265.

Prichard, J. S., & Stanton, N. A. (1999). Testing Belbin's team role theory of effective groups. *Journal of Management Development, 18,* 652–665.

Priem, R. L., Harrison, D. A., & Muir, N. K. (1995). Structured conflict and consensus outcomes in group decision making. *Journal of Management, 21,* 691–710.

Prince, C., Chidester, T. R., Bowers, C., & Cannon-Bowers, J. A. (1992). Aircrew coordination: Achieving teamwork in the cockpit. In R. W. Swezey & E. Salas (Eds.), *Teams: Their training and performance* (pp. 355–378). Stamford, CT: Ablex.

Pritchard, R. D. (1992). Organizational productivity. In M. Dunnette & L. Hough (Eds.), *Handbook of industrial and organizational psychology* (2nd ed., Vol. 3, pp. 443–471). Palo Alto, CA: Consulting Psychologists Press.

Pritchard, R. D. (1995). *Productivity measurement and improvement: Organizational case studies.* New York: Praeger.

Pritchard, R. D., Harrell, M. M., DiazGranados, D., & Guzman, M. J. (2008). The Productivity Measurement and Enhancement System: A meta-analysis. *Journal of Applied Psychology, 93*(3), 540–567.

Pritchard, R. D., Paquin, A. R., DeCuir, A. D., McCormick, M. J., & Bly, P. R. (2001). The measurement and improvement of organizational productivity: An overview of ProMES, the productivity measurement and enhancement system. In R. D. Pritchard, H. Holling, F. Lammers, & B. D. Clark (Eds.), *Improving organizational performance with the Productivity Measurement and Enhancement System: An international collaboration* (pp. 3–50). Huntington, NY: Nova Science.

Pritchard, R. D., Weaver, S. J., & Ashwood, E. (2011). *Evidence-based productivity improvement: A practical guide to the Productivity Measurement and Enhancement System (ProMES)*. New York: Routledge/Taylor & Francis.

Probst, T. M. (2000). Wedded to the job: Moderating effects of job involvement on the consequences of job insecurity. *Journal of Occupational and Health Psychology, 5*, 63–73.

Probst, T. M. (2003). Development and validation of the job security index and the job security satisfaction scale: A classical test theory and IRT approach. *Journal of Occupational and Organizational Psychology, 76*, 451–467.

Probst, T. M., & Lawler, J. (2006). Cultural values as moderators of employee reaction to job insecurity: The role of individualism and collectivism. *Applied Psychology: An International Review, 55*, 234–254.

Pugh, S. D. (2001). Service with a smile: Emotional contagion in the service encounter. *Academy of Management Journal, 44*, 1018–1027.

Pugh, D. S., Groth, M., & Hennig-Thurau, T. (2011). Willing and able to fake emotions: A closer examination of the link between emotional dissonance and employee well-being. *Journal of Applied Psychology, 96*, 377–390.

Pulakos, E. D., Arad, S., Donovan, M. A., & Plamondon, K. E. (2000). Adaptability in the workplace: Development of a taxonomy of adaptive performance. *Journal of Applied Psychology, 85*, 612–624.

Pulakos, E. D., Dorsey, D. W., & Mueller-Hanson, R. (2005). PDRI's adaptability research program. *The Industrial-Organizational Psychologist, 43*(1), 25–32.

Purvanova, R. K., Bono, J. E., & Dzieweczynski, J. (2006). Transformational leadership, job characteristics, and organizational citizenship performance. *Human Performance, 19*, 1–22.

Putka, D. J., & Sackett, P. R. (2010). Reliability and validity. In J. L. Farr & N. Tippens (Eds.), *Handbook of employee selection* (pp. 9–49). London: Taylor & Francis.

Pyszczynski, T., Greenberg, J., Solomon, S., Arndt, J., & Schimel, J. (2004). Why do people need self-esteem? A theoretical and empirical review. *Psychological Bulletin, 130*(3), 435–468.

Quick, J. C., Quick, J. D., Nelson, D. L., & Hurrell, J. J. (1997). *Preventative stress management in organizations*. Washington, DC: American Psychological Association.

Quick, J. C., & Tetrick, L. E. (Eds.). (2010). *Handbook of occupational health psychology* (2nd ed.). Washington, DC: American Psychological Association.

Raabe, B., Frese, M., & Beehr, T. A. (2007). Action regulation theory and career self-management. *Journal of Vocational Behavior, 70*, 297–311.

Rafaeli, A. (1999). Pre-employment screening and applicants' attitudes toward an employment opportunity. *Journal of Social Psychology, 139*(6), 700–712.

Rafferty, A. E., & Griffin, M. A. (2004). Dimensions of transformational leadership: Conceptual and empirical extensions. *Leadership Quarterly, 15*, 329–354.

Rafferty, A. E., & Griffin, M. A. (2006). Perceptions of organizational change: A stress and coping perspective. *Journal of Applied Psychology, 91*, 1154–1162.

Rapp, A., Ahearne, M., Mathieu, J., & Schillewart, N. (2006). The impact of knowledge and empowerment on working smart and working hard: The moderating role of experience. *International Journal of Research in Marketing, 23*, 279–293.

Rastegary, H., & Landy, F. J. (1993). The interactions among time urgency, uncertainty, and time pressure. In O. Svenson & A. J. Maule (Eds.), *Time pressure and stress in human judgment and decision making* (pp. 217–239). New York: Plenum.

Rauch, A., & Frese, M. (2007a). Let's put the person back into entrepreneurship research: A meta-analysis on the relationship between business owners' personality traits, business creation, and success. *European Journal of Work and Organizational Psychology, 16*, 353–385.

Rauch, A., & Frese, M. (2007b). Born to be an entrepreneur? Revisiting the personality approach to entrepreneurship. In J. R. Baum, M. Frese, & R. A. Baron (Eds.), *The psychology of entrepreneurship* (pp. 41–66). Mahwah, NJ: Erlbaum.

Raymark, P. H., Schmit, M. J., & Guion, R. M. (1997). Identifying potentially useful personality constructs for employee selection. *Personnel Psychology, 50*, 723–736.

Rayner, C., & Keashly, L. (2005). Bullying at work: A perspective from Britain and North America. In S. Fox & P. E. Spector (Eds.), *Counterproductive work behavior: Investigations of actors and targets* (pp. 271–296). Washington, DC: American Psychological Association.

Ree, M. J., & Carretta, T. R. (2002). g2K. *Human Performance, 15*, 3–23.

Ree, M. J., Earles, J. A., & Teachout, M. S. (1994). Predicting job performance: Not much more than "g." *Journal of Applied Psychology, 79*, 518–524.

Reichers, A. E., & Schneider, B. (1990). Climate and culture: An evolution of constructs. In B. Schneider (Ed.), *Organizational climate and culture* (pp. 5–39). San Francisco: Jossey-Bass.

Reilly, R. R., & McGourty, J. (1998). Performance appraisal in team settings. In J. W. Smither (Ed.), *Performance appraisal: State of the art in practice* (pp. 245–277). San Francisco: Jossey-Bass.

Rentsch, J. R. (1990). Climate and culture: Interaction and qualitative differences in organizational meanings. *Journal of Applied Psychology, 75*, 668–681.

Restubog, S. D., Bordia, P., & Tang, R. L. (2007). Behavioral outcomes of psychological contract breach in a non-Western culture: The moderating role of equity sensitivity. *British Journal of Management, 18*, 376–386.

Reuters. (2012, January 12). Wage rises, reforms keep China inflation entrenched. Reuters news article.

Reynolds, D. (2004). EEOC and OFCCP guidance on defining a job applicant in the Internet age: SIOP's response. *The Industrial-Organizational Psychologist, 42*(2), 127–138.

Reynolds, D. H., & Rupp, D. E. (2010). Advances in technology-facilitated assessment. In J. C. Scott & D. H. Reynolds (Eds.), *Handbook of workplace assessment: Evidence-based practices for selecting and developing organizational talent* (pp. 609–641). San Fransisco: Jossey-Bass.

Rhoades, L., & Eisenberger, R. (2002). Perceived organizational support: A review of the literature. *Journal of Applied Psychology, 87*, 698–714.

Rice, R. W., Gentile, D. A., & McFarlin, D. B. (1991). Facet importance and job satisfaction. *Journal of Applied Psychology, 76*, 31–39.

Rich, M. (2008, July 27). Literacy debate: Online, R U really reading? *New York Times*, p. A1.

Richardson, K. M., & Rothstein, H. R. (2008). Effects of occupational stress management intervention programs: A meta-analysis. *Journal of Occupational Health Psychology, 13*, 69–93.

Richman-Hirsch, W. L., Olson-Buchanan, J. B., & Drasgow, F. (2000). Examining the impact of administration medium on examinee perceptions and attitudes. *Journal of Applied Psychology, 85*, 880–887.

Richtel, M. (2008, June 14). Lost in e-mail, tech firms face self-made beast. *New York Times, p. A1, A14.*

Richter, A. W., West, M. A., van Dick, R., & Dawson, J. F. (2006). Boundary spanners' identification, intergroup contact, and effective intergroup relations. *Academy of Management Journal, 49*, 1252–1269.

Riketta, M., & van Dick, R. (2005). Foci of attachment in organizations: A meta-analytic comparison of the strength and correlates of workgroup versus organizational identification and commitment. *Journal of Vocational Behavior, 67*, 490–510.

Ringlemann, M. (1913). Research on animate sources of power: The work of man. *Annales de l'Institut National Agronomique*, 2nd series, Vol. 12, pp. 1–40.

Ripley, A., Tumulty, K., Thompson, M., & Carney, J. (2005, September 19). 4 places where the system broke down. *Time*, pp. 36, 38.

Rizzo, J. R., House, R. J., & Lirtzman, S. I. (1970). Role conflict and ambiguity in complex organizations. *Administrative Science Quarterly, 15*, 150–163.

Robb, D. (2002). Virtual workplace. *HR Magazine, 47*, 105–114.

Robert, C., Probst, T. M., Martocchio, J. J., Drasgow, F., & Lawler, J. L. (2000). Empowerment and continuous improvement in the United States, Mexico, Poland, and India: Predicting fit on the basis of the dimensions of power distance and individualism. *Journal of Applied Psychology, 85*, 643–658.

Robert, L. P., Dennis, A. R., & Hung, Y. T. C. (2009). Individual swift trust and knowledge-based trust in face-to-face and virtual team members. *Journal of Management Information Systems, 26*, 241–279.

Roberts, B. W., Chernyshenko, O. S., Stark, S., & Goldberg, L. R. (2005). The structure of conscientiousness: An empirical investigation based on seven major personality questionnaires. *Personnel Psychology, 58*, 103–139.

Roberts, B. W., Harms, P. D., Caspi, A., & Moffit, T. E. (2007). Predicting the counterproductive employee in a child-to-adult prospective study. *Journal of Applied Psychology, 92*, 1427–1436.

Roberts, B. W., & Mroczek, D. K. (2008). Personality trait stability and change. *Current Directions in Psychological Science, 17*, 31–35.

Roberts, R. D., Zeidner, M., & Matthews, G. (2001). Does emotional intelligence meet traditional standards for an intelligence? Some new data and conclusions. *Emotion, 1*(3), 196–231.

Robinson, M. (1999, September 8). Ford agrees to pay $7.75 million to settle sexual harassment case. *The Oregonian*, p. D2.

Robinson, S. L. (2006). Trust and breach of the psychological contract. In R. M. Kramer (Ed.), *Organizational trust: A reader*. Oxford, UK: Oxford University Press.

Robinson, S. L., & Bennett, R. J. (1995). A typology of deviant workplace behaviors: A multidimensional scaling study. *Academy of Management Journal, 38*, 555–572.

Roch, S. G., & Shanock, L. R. (2006). Organizational justice in an exchange framework: Clarifying organizational justice distinctions. *Journal of Management, 32*, 299–322.

Roch, S. G., Sternburgh, A. M., & Caputo, P. M. (2007). Absolute vs. relative performance rating formats: Implications for fairness and organizational justice. *International Journal of Selection and Assessment, 15*, 302–316.

Rode, J. C., Mooney, C. H., Arthaud-Day, M. L., Near, J. P., Baldwin, T. T., Rubin, R. S., & Bommer, W. H. (2007). Emotional intelligence and individual performance: Evidence of direct and moderated effects. *Journal of Organizational Behavior, 28*, 399–421.

Roe, R. A., & van den Berg, P. T. (2003). Selection in Europe: Context, developments, and research agenda. *European Journal of Work and Organizational Psychology, 12*(3), 257–287.

Roethlisberger, F. J., & Dickson, W. J. (1939). *Management and the worker*. Cambridge, MA: Harvard University Press.

Rogelberg, S. G. (2002). *Handbook of research methods in industrial and organizational psychology*. Cambridge, MA: Blackwell.

Rogelberg, S. G., & Brooks-Laber, M. E. (2002). Securing our collective future: Challenges facing those designing and doing research in industrial and organizational psychology. In S. G. Rogelberg (Ed.), *Handbook of research methods in industrial and organizational psychology* (pp. 479–485). Cambridge, MA: Blackwell.

Rogelberg, S. G., & Gill, P. M. (2004). The growth of industrial and organizational psychology: Quick facts. *The Industrial-Organizational Psychologist, 42*(1), 25–27.

Rogers, W., Maurer, T., Salas, E., & Fisk, A. (1997). Task analysis and cognitive theory: Controlled and automatic processing. Task analytic methodology. In J. K. Ford, S. W. J. Kozlowski, K. Kraiger, E. Salas, & M. S. Teachout (Eds.), *Improving training effectiveness in work organizations* (pp. 19–46). Mahwah, NJ: Erlbaum.

Rohrer, D., & Pashler, H. (2007). Increasing retention without increasing study time. *Current Directions in Psychological Science, 16*(4), 183–186.

Romanov, K., Appelberg, K., Honkasalo, M., & Koskenvuo, M. (1996). Recent interpersonal conflict at work and psychiatric morbidity: A prospective study of 15,530 employees aged 24–64. *Journal of Psychosomatic Research, 40*, 169–176.

Ronen, S. (1981). Arrival and departure patterns of public sector employees before and after implementation of flexitime. *Personnel Psychology, 34*, 817–822.

Ronen, S. (1997). Personal reflections and projections: International industrial/organizational psychology at a crossroads. In P. C. Earley & M. Erez (Eds.), *New perspectives on industrial/organizational psychology* (pp. 715–731). San Francisco: Jossey-Bass.

Rorty, R. (1989). *Contingency, irony, and solidarity*. New York: Cambridge University Press.

Rosca, A., & Voicu, C. (1982). *A concise history of psychology in Romania*. Bucharest: Editura Stiintifica Psychologica si Enciclopedica.

Rosen, B., Furst, S., & Blackburn, R. (2006). Training for virtual teams: An investigation of current practices and future needs. *Human Resource Management, 45*, 229–247.

Rosse, J. G. (1988). Relations among lateness, absence, and turnover: Is there a progression of withdrawal? *Human Relations, 41*(7), 517–531.

Roth, P. L., BeVier, C. A., Switzer, F. S., & Schippmann, J. S. (1996). Meta-analyzing the relationship between grades and job performance. *Journal of Applied Psychology, 81*, 548–556.

Roth, P. L., & Bobko, P. (2000). College grade point average as a personnel selection device: Ethnic group differences and potential adverse impact. *Journal of Applied Psychology, 85*(3), 399–406.

Roth, P. L., Bobko, P., & McFarland, L. A. (2005). A meta-analysis of work sample test validity: Updating and integrating some classic literature. *Personnel Psychology, 58*, 1009–1037.

Roth, P. L., Huffcutt, A. I., & Bobko, P. (2003). Ethnic group differences in measures of job performance: A new meta-analysis. *Journal of Applied Psychology, 88*, 694–706.

Rothstein, H. R. (1990). Interrater reliability of job performance ratings: Growth to asymptote level with increasing opportunity to observe. *Journal of Applied Psychology, 75*, 322–327.

Rotter, J. B. (1966). Generalized expectancies for internal versus external control of reinforcement. *Psychological Monographs, 80* (1, Whole No. 609).

Rotundo, M., & Sackett, P. R. (2002). The relative importance of task, citizenship, and counterproductive performance to global ratings of job performance: A policy capturing approach. *Journal of Applied Psychology, 87*, 66–80.

Rousseau, D. M. (1995). *Psychological contracts in organizations: Understanding written and unwritten agreements*. Newbury Park, CA: Sage.

Rousseau, D. M., & Barends, E. G. (2011). Becoming an evidence-based HR practitioner. *Human Resource Management Journal, 21*(4), 221–235.

Rousseau, D., & House, R. J. (1994). MESO organizational behavior: Avoiding three fundamental biases. In C. L. Cooper & D. Rousseau (Eds.), *Trends in organizational behavior* (Vol. 1, pp. 13–30). London: Wiley.

Ruderman, M. N., Ohlott, P. J., Panzer, K., & King, S. N. (2002). Benefits of multiple roles for managerial women. *Academy of Management Journal, 45*, 369–386.

Rudolph, C. W., & Baltes, B. B. (2008). Main effects do not discrimination make. *Industrial and Organizational Psychology: Perspectives on Research and Practice, 1*, 415–416.

Rupp, D., & Spencer, C. (2006). When customers lash out: The effects of customer interactional injustice on emotional labor and the mediating role of discrete emotions. *Journal of Applied Psychology, 91*, 971–978.

Russell, J. A. (1991). Culture and categorization of emotions. *Psychological Bulletin, 110*, 426–450.

Russell, S. S., Spitzmuller, C., Lin, L. F., Stanton, J. M., Smith, P. C., & Ironson, G. H. (2004). Shorter can also be better: The abridged Job in General scale. *Educational and Psychological Measurement, 64*, 878–893.

Ryan, A. M., Chan, D., Ployhart, R. E., & Slade, L. A. (1999). Employee attitude surveys in a multinational organization: Considering language and culture in assessing measurement equivalence. *Personnel Psychology, 52*, 37–58.

Ryan, A. M., & Greguras, G. J. (1998). Life is not multiple choices. In M. Hakel (Ed.), *Alternatives to traditional assessment* (pp. 183–202). Mahwah, NJ: Erlbaum.

Ryan, A. M., West, B. J., & Carr, J. Z. (2003). Effects of the terrorist attacks of 9/11/01 on employee attitudes. *Journal of Applied Psychology, 88*, 647–659.

Ryan, T. A. (1970). *Intentional behavior*. New York: Ronald Press.

Rynes, S. L., & Gerhart, B. (2001). *Compensation in organizations*. San Francisco: Jossey-Bass.

Rynes, S. L., Gerhart, B., & Parks, L. (2005). Personnel psychology: Performance evaluation and pay for performance. *Annual Review of Psychology, 55*, 571–600.

Sacco, J. M., Scheu, C. R., Ryan, A. M., & Schmitt, N. (2003). An investigation of race and sex similarity effects in interviews: A multilevel approach to relational demography. *Journal of Applied Psychology, 88*, 852–865.

Sackett, P. R. (2002). The structure of counterproductive work behaviors: Dimensionality and relationships with facets of job performance. *International Journal of Selection and Assessment, 10*, 5–11.

Sackett, P. R. (2003). Stereotype threat in applied selection settings: A commentary. *Human Performance, 16*, 295–309.

Sackett, P. R. (2007). Revisiting the origins of the typical–maximum performance distinction. *Human Performance, 20*, 179–185.

Sackett, P. R., & Arvey, R. D. (1993). Selection in small *N* settings. In N. Schmitt & W. C. Borman (Eds.), *Personnel selection in organizations* (pp. 418–447). San Francisco: Jossey-Bass.

Sackett, P. R., Berry, C. M., Weinaman, S. A., & Laczo, R. M. (2006). Citizenship and counterproductive behavior: Clarifying relations between the two domains. *Human Performance, 19*, 441–464.

Sackett, P. R., & DeVore, C. J. (2001). Counterproductive behaviors at work. In N. Anderson, D. S. Ones, H. K. Sinangil, & C. Viswesvaran (Eds.), *Handbook of industrial, work, and organizational psychology* (Vol. 1, pp. 145–164). London: Sage.

Sackett, P. R., Hardison, C. M., & Cullen, M. J. (2004). On interpreting stereotype threat as accounting for African American–white differences on cognitive tests. *American Psychologist, 59*, 7–13.

Sackett, P. R., & Lievens, F. (2008). Personnel selection. *Annual Review of Psychology, 59*, 419–450.

Sackett, P. R., & Mullen, E. J. (1993). Beyond formal experimental design: Towards an expanded view of the training evaluation process. *Personnel Psychology, 46*, 613–627.

Sackett, P. R., & Tuzinski, K. A. (2001). The role of dimensions and exercises in assessment center judgments. In M. London (Ed.), *How people evaluate others in organizations* (pp. 111–134). Mahwah, NJ: Erlbaum.

Sackett, P. R., & Wanek, J. E. (1996). New developments in the use of measures of honesty, integrity, conscientiousness, dependability, trustworthiness, and reliability for personnel selection. *Personnel Psychology, 49*, 787–829.

Sackett, P. R., & Wilk, S. L. (1994). Within group norming and other forms of score adjustment in pre-employment testing. *American Psychologist, 49*, 929–954.

Sackett, P. R., Zedeck, S., & Fogli, L. (1988). Relations between typical and maximum measures of job performance. *Journal of Applied Psychology, 73*, 482–486.

Sagie, A., Birati, A., & Tziner, A. (2002). Assessing the costs of behavioral and psychological withdrawal: A new model and an empirical demonstration. *Applied Psychology: An International Review, 51*, 67–89.

Saks, A. M., & Ashforth, B. E. (1997). A longitudinal investigation of the relationships between job information sources, applicant perceptions of fit, and work outcomes. *Personnel Psychology, 50*, 395–426.

Saks, A. M., & Belcourt, M. (2006). An investigation of training activities and transfer of training in organizations. *Human Resource Management, 45*, 629–648.

Salamon, S., & Deutsch, Y. (2006). OCB as a handicap: An evolutionary psychological perspective. *Journal of Organizational Behavior, 27*, 185–199.

Salas, E., Burke, S. C., Bowers, C. A., & Wilson, K. A. (2001). Team training in the skies: Does crew resource management (CRM) training work? *Human Factors, 43*, 641–674.

Salas, E., Burke, S. C., & Cannon-Bowers, J. A. (2002). What we know about designing and delivering team training: Tips and guidelines. In K. Kraiger (Ed.), *Creating, implementing, and managing effective training and development* (pp. 234–259). San Francisco: Jossey-Bass.

Salas, E., & Cannon-Bowers, J. A. (1997). Methods, tools, and strategies for team training. In M. Quinones & A. Dutta (Eds.), *Training for 21st century technology: Applications for psychology research* (pp. 249–280). Washington, DC: American Psychological Association.

Salas, E., & Cannon-Bowers, J. A. (2001). The science of training: A decade of progress. *Annual Review of Psychology, 52*, 471–499.

Salas, E., Nichols, D. R., & Driskell, J. E. (2007). Testing three team training strategies in intact teams: A meta-analysis. *Small Group Research, 38*, 471–488.

Salgado, J. F. (1997). The five factor model of personality and job performance in the European Community. *Journal of Applied Psychology, 82*, 30–43.

Salgado, J. F. (1998). Big Five personality dimensions and job performance in army and civil occupations: A European perspective. *Human Performance, 11*, 271–288.

Salgado, J. F. (2001). Some landmarks of 100 years of scientific personnel selection at the beginning of the new century. *International Journal of Selection and Assessment, 9*(1/2), 3–8.

Salgado, J. F. (2002). The Big Five personality dimensions and counterproductive behavior. *International Journal of Selection and Assessment, 10*, 117–125.

Salgado, J. F., & Anderson, N. (2002). Cognitive and GMA testing in the European Community: Issues and evidence. *Human Performance, 15*, 75–96.

Salgado, J. F., Anderson, N., Moscoso, S., Bertua, C., & de Fruyt, F. (2003). International validity generalization of GMA and cognitive abilities: A European Community meta-analysis. *Personnel Psychology, 56*, 573–605.

Salgado, J. F., & Moscoso, S. (2002). Comprehensive meta-analysis of the construct validity of the employment interview. *European Journal of Work and Organizational Psychology, 11*, 299–324.

Salgado, J. F., & Moscoso, S. (2003). Internet-based personality testing: Equivalence of measures and assessees' perceptions and reactions. *International Journal of Selection and Assessment, 11*, 194–205.

Salgado, J. F., Viswesvaran, C., & Ones, D. S. (2001). Predictors used for personnel selection: An overview of constructs, methods and techniques. In N. Anderson, D. S. Ones, H. K. Sinangil, & C. Viswesvaran (Eds.), *Handbook of industrial, work, and organizational psychology* (pp. 165–199). Thousand Oaks, CA: Sage.

Salin, D. (2001). Prevalence and forms of bullying among professionals: A comparison of two different strategies for measuring bullying. *European Journal of Work and Organizational Psychology, 10*, 425–442.

Salvendy, G. (2006). *Handbook of human factors and ergonomics* (3rd ed.). New York: Wiley.

Sanchez, J. I., & Levine, E. L. (1999). Is job analysis dead, misunderstood, or both? New forms of work analysis and design. In A. I. Kraut & A. K. Korman (Eds.), *Evolving practices in human resource management* (pp. 43–68). San Francisco: Jossey-Bass.

Sanchez, J. I., & Levine, E. (2001). The analysis of work in the 20th and 21st centuries. In N. Anderson, D. Ones, H. K. Sinangil, & C. Viswesvaran (Eds.), *Handbook of industrial, work, and organizational psychology* (Vol. 1, pp. 71–89). London: Sage.

Sanchez, J. I., & Levine, E. (2012). The rise and fall of job analysis and the future of work analysis. *Annual Review of Psychology, 63,* 397–425.

Sanchez, J. I., & Medkik, N. (2004). The effects of diversity awareness training on differential treatment. *Group and Organization Management, 29,* 517–536.

Sandal, G. M., & Endresen, I. M. (2002). The sensitivity of the CPI good impression scale for detecting "faking good" among Norwegian students and job applicants. *International Journal of Selection and Assessment, 10,* 304–311.

Santayana, G. (1905). *Life of reason.* New York: Scribners.

Sapolsky, R. M. (1998). *Why zebras don't get ulcers: An updated guide to stress, stress-related diseases, and coping.* New York: Freeman.

Sauter, S., Murphy, L. R., & Hurrell, J. J. (1990). A national strategy for the prevention of work-related psychological disorders. *American Psychologist, 45,* 1146–1158.

Schaffer, R. H. (1953). Job satisfaction as related to need satisfaction in work. *Psychological Monographs, 67* (No. 304).

Schalk, R., & Rousseau, D. M. (2001). Psychological contracts in employment. In N. Anderson, D. Ones, H. Sinangil, & C. Viswesvaran (Eds.), *Handbook of industrial, work, and organizational psychology* (Vol. 2, pp. 133–142). London: Sage.

Schaubroeck, J., & Kuehn, K. (1992). Research design in industrial and organizational psychology. In C. L. Cooper & I. T. Robertson (Eds.), *International review of industrial and organizational psychology* (Vol. 7, pp. 99–121). Chichester, UK: Wiley.

Schaubroeck, J., Walumbwa, F. O., Ganster, D. C., & Kepes, S. (2007). Destructive leader traits and the neutralizing influence of an "enriched" job. *Leadership Quarterly, 18,* 236–251.

Schaufeli, W. B., & Bakker, A. B. (2004). Job demands, job resources, and their relationship with burnout and engagement: A multisample study. *Journal of Organizational Behavior, 25,* 293–315.

Schaufeli, W. B., & Enzmann, D. (1998). *The burnout companion to study and practice: A critical analysis.* London: Taylor & Francis.

Schaufeli, W. B., Leiter, M. P., Maslach, C., & Jackson, S. E. (1996). *Maslach Burnout Inventory: General survey.* Palo Alto, CA: Consulting Psychologists Press.

Schaufeli, W. B., & Salanova, M. (2007). Work engagement: An emerging psychological concept and its implications for organizations. In S. W. Gilliland, D. D. Steiner, & D. P. Skarlicki (Eds.), *Managing social and ethical issues in organizations: Vol. 5* (pp. 135–177). *Research in social issues in management.* Greenwich, CT: Information Age Publishers.

Schaufeli, W. B., Taris, T. W., & Van Rhenen, W. (2008). Workaholism, burnout, and engagement: Three of a kind or three different kinds of employee well-being? *Applied Psychology: An International Review, 57,* 173–203.

Scheiber, N. (2004, May 9). As a center for outsourcing, India could be losing its edge. *New York Times,* p. BU3.

Schein, E. (1981). Does Japanese management style have a message for managers? *Sloan Management Review, 23,* 55–68.

Schein, E. (1996). Kurt Lewin's change theory in the field and in the classroom: Notes toward a model of managed learning. *Systems Practice, 9,* 27–47.

Schein, V. E. (2008). *Poor women and work in developing countries: Research opportunities for I-O psychologists.* Paper presented at the 2008 Annual Conference of SIOP, San Francisco.

Schmidt, F. L. (1996). Statistical significance testing and cumulative knowledge in psychology: Implications for training of researchers. *Psychological Methods, 1,* 115–129.

Schmidt, F. L., & Hunter, J. E. (1992). Development of causal models of processes determining job performance. *Current Directions in Psychological Sciences, 1,* 89–92.

Schmidt, F. L., & Hunter, J. E. (1998). The validity and utility of selection methods in personnel psychology: Practical and theoretical implications of 85 years of research findings. *Psychological Bulletin, 124,* 262–274.

Schmidt, F. L., & Hunter, J. E. (2002a). History, development, and impact of validity generalization and meta-analysis methods, 1975–2001. In K. R. Murphy (Ed.), *Validity generalization: A critical review* (pp. 31–66). Mahwah, NJ: Erlbaum.

Schmidt, F. L., & Hunter, J. E. (2002b). Are there benefits from NHST? *American Psychologist, 57,* 65–66.

Schmidt, F. L., & Hunter, J. E. (2004). General mental ability in the world of work: Occupational attainment and job performance. *Journal of Personality and Social Psychology, 86,* 162–173.

Schmidt, F. L., Viswesvaran, C., & Ones, D. S. (2000). Reliability is not validity is not reliability. *Personnel Psychology, 53,* 901–911.

Schmidt, F. L., & Zimmerman, R. D. (2004). A counter-intuitive hypothesis about employment interview validity and some supporting evidence. *Journal of Applied Psychology, 89,* 553–561.

Schminke, M., Ambrose, M. L., & Cropanzano, R. (2000). The effect of organizational structure on perceptions of procedural fairness. *Journal of Applied Psychology, 85,* 294–304.

Schmit, M. J., & Ryan, A. M. (1993). The Big Five in personnel selection: Factor structure in applicant and non-applicant populations. *Journal of Applied Psychology, 78,* 966–974.

Schmit, M. J., Ryan, A. M., Stierwalt, S. L., & Powell, A. B. (1995). Frame-of-reference effects on personality scale scores and criterion-related validity. *Journal of Applied Psychology, 80,* 607–620.

Schmitt, N. (2004). Beyond the Big Five: Increases in understanding and practical utility. *Human Performance, 17,* 347–357.

Schmitt, N., Gilliland, S. W., Landis, R. S., & Devine, D. (1993). Computer-based testing applied to selection of secretarial applicants. *Personnel Psychology, 46,* 149–165.

Schmitt, N., Gooding, R. Z., Noe, R. A., & Kirsch, M. (1984). Meta-analysis of validity studies published between 1964 and 1982 and the investigation of study characteristics. *Personnel Psychology, 37,* 407–422.

Schmitt, N., & Kunce, C. (2002). The effects of required elaboration of answers to biodata questions. *Personnel Psychology, 55,* 569–587.

Schneider, B. (1987). The people make the place. *Personnel Psychology, 40,* 437–454.

Schneider, B. (2000). Organizational culture and climate: The psychological life of organizations. In N. Ashkenasy, C. Wilderom, & M. Peterson (Eds.), *Handbook of organizational culture and climate* (pp. xvii–xxi). London: Sage.

Schneider, B. (2001). Fits about fit. *Applied Psychology: An International Review, 50,* 141–152.

Schneider, B., Bowen, D. E., Ehrhart, M. G., & Holcombe, K. M. (2000). The climate for service: Evolution of a construct. In N. Ashkenasy, C. Wilderom, & M. Peterson (Eds.), *Handbook of organizational culture and climate* (pp. 21–36). London: Sage.

Schneider, B., Goldstein, H. W., & Smith, D. B. (1995). The ASA framework: An update. *Personnel Psychology, 48,* 747–773.

Schneider, B., Hanges, P. J., Smith, D. B., & Salvaggio, A. N. (2003). Which comes first: Employee attitudes or organizational financial and market performance? *Journal of Applied Psychology, 88,* 836–851.

Schneider, B., Salvaggio, A. N., & Subarits, M. (2002). Climate strength: A new direction for climate research. *Journal of Applied Psychology, 87,* 220–229.

Schneider, B., & Schmitt, N. (1986). *Staffing organizations.* Glenview, IL: Scott Foresman.

Schneider, B., Smith, D. B., Taylor, S., & Fleenor, J. (1998). Personality and organizations: A test of the homogeneity of personality hypothesis. *Journal of Applied Psychology, 83,* 462–470.

Schneider, R. J., Goff, M., Anderson, S., & Borman, W. C. (2003). Computerized adaptive rating scales for measuring managerial performance. *International Journal of Selection and Assessment, 11,* 237–246.

Schneider, R. J., Hough, L. M., & Dunnette, M. D. (1996). Broadsided by broad traits: How to sink science into five dimensions or less. *Journal of Organizational Behavior, 17,* 639–655.

Schriesheim, C. A., Castro, S. L., Zhou, A., & DeChurch, L. A. (2006). An investigation of path-goal and transformational leadership theory predictions at the individual level of analysis. *Leadership Quarterly, 17,* 21–38.

Schroth, H. A., & Shah, P. P. (2000). Procedures: Do we really want to know them? An examination of the effects of procedural justice on self-esteem. *Journal of Applied Psychology, 85,* 462–471.

Schuler, R. S., & Jackson, S. E. (Eds.). (2007). *Strategic human resource management.* Malden, MA: Blackwell.

Schulte, M., Ostroff, C., & Kinicki, A. J. (2006). Organizational climate systems and psychological climate perceptions: A cross-level study of climate-satisfaction relationships. *Journal of Occupational and Organizational Psychology, 79,* 645–671.

Schwartz, S. H. (1999). A theory of cultural values and some implications for work. *Applied Psychology: An International Review, 48,* 23–47.

Schweyer, A. (2006). Managing the virtual global workforce. *Human Resources* (Australia). Retrieved April 12, 2007 from www.humanresourcemagazine.com.au/

Schyns, B., Felfe, J., & Blank, H. (2007). Is charisma hyper-romanticism? Empirical evidence from new data and a meta-analysis. *Applied Psychology: An International Review, 56,* 505–527.

Schyns, B., Kroon, B., & Moors, G. (2008). Follower characteristics and the perception of leader–member exchange. *Journal of Managerial Psychology, 23*(7), 772–788.

Schyns, B., Paul, T., Mohr, G., & Blank, H. (2005). Comparing antecedents and consequences of leader–member exchange in a German working context to findings in the U.S. *European Journal of Work and Organizational Psychology, 14,* 1–22.

Scott, B. A., & Judge, T. A. (2006). Insomnia, emotions, and job satisfaction: A multilevel study. *Journal of Management, 32,* 622–645.

Scott, J. C. (2011). SIOP granted NGO consultative status with the United Nations. *The Industrial-Organizational Psychologist, 49(2),* 111–113.

Scott, J. C., & Reynolds, D. H. (Eds.). (2010). *Handbook of workplace assessment: Evidence-based practices for selecting and developing organizational talent.* San Fransisco, CA: Jossey-Bass.

Scott, S. G., & Einstein, W. O. (2001). Strategic performance appraisal in team-based organizations. *Academy of Management Executive, 15,* 107–116.

Scullen, S. E., Bergey, P. K., & Aiman-Smith, L. (2005). Forced distribution rating systems and improvement of workforce potential: A baseline simulation. *Personnel Psychology, 58,* 1–32.

Seijts, G. H., & Jackson, S. E. (2001). Reactions to employment equity programs and situational interviews: A laboratory study. *Human Performance, 14,* 247–265.

Seligman, M. E., & Csikszentmihalyi, M. (2000). Positive psychology. *American Psychologist, 55,* 5–14.

Selye, H. (1976). *The stress of life.* New York: McGraw-Hill.

Selye, H. (1956). *The stress of life.* New York: McGraw-Hill.

Semmer, N. (2002, January 8). *Job satisfaction: A central but underestimated concept in the psychology of work.* Paper presented at the University of Giessen, Germany.

Senge, P. M. (1990). *The fifth discipline: The art and practice of learning organizations.* New York: Doubleday.

Senior, B. (1997). Team roles and team performance: Is there "really" a link? *Journal of Occupational and Organizational Psychology, 70,* 241–258.

Shaffer, M. A., & Harrison, D. A. (2001). Forgotten partners of international assignments: Development and test of a model of spouse adjustment. *Journal of Applied Psychology, 86,* 238–254.

Shamir, B., & Eilam, G. (2005). "What's your story?" A life-stories approach to authentic leadership development. *Leadership Quarterly, 16,* 395–417.

Shamir, B., House, R. J., & Arthur, M. B. (1993). The motivational effects of charismatic leadership: A self-concept-based theory. *Organizational Science, 4,* 1–17.

Shamir, B., & Kark, R. (2004). A single-item graphic scale of organizational commitment. *Journal of Occupational and Organizational Psychology, 17,* 115–123.

Shane, S., Nicolaou, N., Cherkas, L., & Spector, T. D. (2010). Genetics, the Big Five, and the tendency to be self-employed. *Journal of Applied Psychology, 95,* 1154–1162.

Sharf, J. C., & Jones, D. P. (2000). Employment risk management. In J. Kehoe (Ed.), *Managing selection in changing environments: Human resource strategies* (pp. 271–318). San Francisco: Jossey -Bass.

Shaw, J. C., Wild, E., & Colquitt, J. A. (2003). To justify or excuse? A meta-analysis review of the effects of explanations. *Journal of Applied Psychology, 88,* 444–458.

Shaw, J. D., & Gupta, N. (2004). Job complexity, performance, and well-being: When does supplies–values fit matter? *Personnel Psychology, 57,* 847–879.

Sheldon, K. M. (2004). The benefits of "sidelong" approach to self-esteem need satisfaction: Comment on Crocker and Park (2004). *Psychological Bulletin, 130*(3), 421–424.

Shelter, B. (2008, June 23). ABC and writers skirmish over after-hours e-mail. *New York Times,* p. C4.

Shenon, P. (2004, February 6). Report faults lax controls on screeners at airports. *New York Times,* p. A22.

Shepperd, J. (1993). Productivity loss in performance groups: A motivation analysis. *Psychological Bulletin, 113,* 67–81.

Shippmann, J. S., Ash, R. A., Battista, M., Carr, L., Eyde, L. D., Hesketh, B., et al. (2000). The practice of competency modeling. *Personnel Psychology, 53,* 703–740.

Shore, L. M., Randel, A. E., Chung, B. G., Dean, M. A., Ehrnart, K. H., & Singh, G. (2011). Inclusion and diversity in work groups: A review and model for future research. *Journal of Management, 37,* 1262–1289.

Siegel, P. A., Post, C., Brockner, J., Fishman, A. Y., & Garden, C. (2005). The moderating influence of procedural fairness on the relationship between work–life conflict and organizational commitment. *Journal of Applied Psychology, 90,* 13–24.

Silzer, R. (2002). *The 21st century executive: Innovative practices for building leadership at the top.* San Francisco: Jossey-Bass.

Silzer, R., & Jeanneret, P. R. (1998). *Individual psychological assessment: Predicting behavior in organizational settings.* San Francisco: Jossey-Bass.

Simon, H. A. (1960). *The new science of management decision.* New York: Harper & Row.

Simon, S. J., & Werner, J. M. (1996). Computer training through behavior modeling, self-paced, and instructional approaches: A field experiment. *Journal of Applied Psychology, 81,* 648–659.

Siskin, B R., & Trippi, J. (2005). Statistical issues in litigation. In F. J. Landy (Ed.), *Employment discrimination litigation: Behavioral, quantitative, and legal perspectives* (pp. 132–166). San Francisco: Jossey-Bass.

Sitzmann, T., Brown, K. G., & Casper, W. J. (2008). A review and meta-analysis of the nomological network of trainee reactions. *Journal of Applied Psychology, 93*, 280–295.

Skarlicki, D. P., Barclay, L. J., & Pugh, S. D. (2008). When explanations for layoffs are not enough: Employer's integrity as a moderator of the relationship between informational justice and retaliation. *Journal of Occupational and Organizational Psychology, 81*, 123–146.

Skarlicki, D. P., & Folger, R. (1997). Retaliation in the workplace: The role of procedural, distributive and interactional justice. *Journal of Applied Psychology, 82*, 434–443.

Skinner, B. F. (1938). *The behavior of organisms.* Englewood Cliffs, NJ: Prentice Hall.

Skinner, B. F. (1954). Science of learning and the art of teaching. *Harvard Educational Review, 24*, 86–97.

Slaughter, J. E., Zickar, M. J., Highhouse, S., & Mohr, D. C. (2004). Personality trait inferences about organizations: Development of a measure and assessment of construct validity. *Journal of Applied Psychology, 89*, 85–103.

Slovic, P. (1993). Perceived risk, trust, and democracy. *Risk Analysis, 13*, 675–682.

Smith, A. (1990). Stress and information processing. In M. Johnston & L. Wallace (Eds.), *Stress and medical procedures: Oxford medical publications* (pp. 58–79). Oxford, UK: Oxford University Press.

Smith, B. (Ed.). (2007). *The people make the place: Exploring dynamic linkages between individuals and organizations.* Mahwah, NJ: Erlbaum.

Smith, C. A., Organ, D. W., & Near, J. P. (1983). Organizational citizenship behavior: Its nature and antecedents. *Journal of Applied Psychology, 68*, 653–663.

Smith, C. S., Robie, C., Folkard, S., Barton, J., MacDonald, I., Smith, I., et al. (1999). A process model of shiftwork and health. *Journal of Occupational and Health Psychology, 4*, 207–218.

Smith, D. B., Schneider, B., & Dickson, M. W. (2005). Meso-organizational behavior: Comments on a third paradigm. In W. Nord (Ed.), *Handbook of organizational studies* (2nd ed., pp. 149–164). London: Sage.

Smith, P. B., Bond, M. H., & Kagitcibasi, C. (2006). Defining the way forward: Theories and frameworks. In P. B. Smith, M. H. Bond, & C. Kagitcibasi (Eds.), *Understanding social psychology across cultures: Living and working with others in a changing world* (pp. 30–55). London: Sage.

Smith, P. B., & Noakes, J. (1996). Cultural differences in group processes. In M. A. West (Ed.), *Handbook of work group psychology* (pp. 477–501). Chichester, UK: Wiley.

Smith, P. C., Kendall, L. M., & Hulin, C. L. (1969). *Job satisfaction in work and retirement: A strategy for the study of attitudes.* Chicago: Rand McNally.

Smith-Crowe, K., Burke, M. J., & Landis, R. S. (2003). Organizational climate as a moderator of safety knowledge–safety performance relationships. *Journal of Organizational Behavior, 24*, 861–876.

Smither, J.W., & London, M. (2009). *Performance management: Putting research into action.* San Francisco: Jossey-Bass.

Smither, J. W., London, M., Flautt, R., Vargas, Y., & Kucine, I. (2003). Can working with an executive coach improve multisource feedback ratings over time? A quasiexperimental study. *Personnel Psychology, 56*, 23–44.

Smither, J. W., London, M., & Reilly, R. R. (2005). Does performance improve following multisource feedback? A theoretical model, meta-analysis, and review of empirical findings. *Personnel Psychology, 58*, 33–66.

Smithikrai, C. (2007). Personality traits and job success: An investigation in a Thai sample. *International Journal of Selection and Assessment, 15*, 134–138.

Smith-Jentsch, K. A., Cannon-Bowers, J., Tannenbaum S., & Salas, E. (2008). Guided team self-correction. *Small Group Research, 39*, 303–327.

Smith-Jentsch, K. A., Jentsch, F. G., Payne, S. C., & Salas, E. (1996). Can pretraining influences explain individual differences in learning? *Journal of Applied Psychology, 81*, 110–116.

Smith-Jentsch, K. A., Mathieu, J. E., & Kraiger, K. (2005). Investigating linear and interactive effects of shared mental models on safety and efficiency in a field setting. *Journal of Applied Psychology, 90*, 523–535.

Smith-Jentsch, K. A., Salas, E., & Brannick, M. T. (2001). To transfer or not to transfer? Investigating the combined effects of trainee characteristics, team leader support, and team climate. *Journal of Applied Psychology, 86*, 279–292.

Smola, K. W., & Sutton, C. D. (2002). Generational differences: Revisiting generational work values for the new millennium. *Journal of Organizational Behavior, 23*, 363–382.

Society for Human Resources Management (SHRM). (1990). *Code of ethics.* Alexandria, VA: Author.

Society for Human Resource Management (SHRM). (2009). *SHRM poll assistance organizations offer to help employees deal with high gas prices.* Retrieved October 27, 2011, from http://www.shrm.org/Research/SurveyFindings/Articles/Pages/AssistanceOrganizationsOffertoHelpEmployeesDealWithHighGasPrices-SHRMPoll.aspx

Society for Industrial and Organizational Psychology (SIOP). (2011). Personal Communication, Larry Nader, August 24, 2011.

Society for Industrial and Organizational Psychology (SIOP). (2003). *Principles for the validation and use of personnel selection techniques* (4th ed.). Bowling Green, OH: Author.

Sokal, M. M. (1982). James McKeen Cattell and the failure of anthropometric mental testing: 1890–1901. In W. R. Woodward & M. G. Ash (Eds.), *The problematic science: Psychology in nineteenth century thought* (pp. 322–345). New York: Praeger.

Sonnentag, S., Binnewies, C., & Mojza, E. J. (2008). "Did you have a nice evening?" A day-level study on recovery experiences, sleep, and affect. *Journal of Applied Psychology, 93*, 674–684.

Sosik, J. J. (2005). The role of personal values in the charismatic leadership of corporate managers: A model and preliminary field study. *Leadership Quarterly, 16*, 221–244.

Sothmann, M., Saupe, K., Jesenof, D., Blaney, J., Fuhrman, S., Woulfe, T., et al. (1990). Advancing age and cardio-respiratory stress of fire suppression: Determining a minimum standard for aerobic fitness. *Human Performance, 3*, 217–236.

Sparks, K., Cooper, C., Fried, Y., & Shirom, A. (1997). The effects of hours of work on health: A meta-analytic review. *Journal of Occupational and Organizational Psychology, 70*, 391–408.

Spearman, C. (1927). *The abilities of man.* New York: Macmillan.

Spector, P. E. (2000). *Industrial and organizational psychology: Research and practice* (2nd ed.). New York: Wiley.

Spector, P. E. (2001). Research methods in industrial and organizational psychology: Data collection and data analysis with special consideration to international issues. In N. Anderson, D. S. Ones, H. K. Sinangil, & C. Viswesvaran (Eds.), *Handbook on industrial, work, and organizational psychology* (pp. 10–26). London: Sage.

Spector, P. E. (2005). Introduction: The dispositional approach to job satisfaction. *Journal of Organizational Behavior, 26*, 57–58.

Spector, P. E., & Fox, S. (2002). An emotion-centered model of voluntary work behavior: Some parallels between counterproductive work behavior and organizational citizenship behavior. *Human Resource Management Review, 12*, 269–292.

Spector, P. E., & Fox, S. (2005). A model of counterproductive work behavior. In S. Fox & P. E. Spector (Eds.), *Counterproductive workplace behavior: Investigations of actors and targets* (pp. 151–174). Washington, DC: American Psychological Association.

Spence, J. T., Helmreich, R. L., & Pred, R. S. (1987). Impatience versus achievement strivings on the Type A pattern: Differential effects on students' health and academic achievement. *Journal of Applied Psychology, 72*, 522–528.

Spitzmüller, C., & Stanton, J. M. (2006). Examining employee compliance with organizational surveillance and monitoring. *Journal of Occupational and Organizational Psychology, 79*, 245–272.

Spreitzer, G. M., Pertulla, K. H., & Xin, K. (2005). Traditionality matters: An examination of the effectiveness of transformational leadership in the United States and Taiwan. *Journal of Organizational Behavior, 26*, 205–227.

Sprigg, C. A., Stride, C. B., Wall, T. D., Holman, D. J., & Smith, P. R. (2007). Work characteristics, musculoskeletal disorders, and the mediating role of psychological strain: A study of call center employees. *Journal of Applied Psychology, 92*, 1456–1466.

Stahl, G. K., & Caligiuri, P. (2005). The effectiveness of expatriate coping strategies: The moderating role of cultural distance, position level, and time on the international assignment. *Journal of Applied Psychology, 90*, 603–615.

Stajkovic, A. D., & Luthans, F. (2003). Behavioral management and task performance in organizations: Conceptual background, metaanalysis, and test of alternative models. *Personnel Psychology, 56*, 155–194.

Stanley, A. (2004, December 18). No rookie now, "Apprentice" feeds on office tension. *New York Times*, pp. 18, 28.

Staw, B. M., Bell, N. E., & Clausen, J. A. (1986). The dispositional approach to job satisfaction: A lifetime longitudinal test. *Administrative Science Quarterly, 31*, 56–77.

Staw, B. M., & Cohen-Charash, Y. (2005). The dispositional approach to job satisfaction: More than a mirage, but not yet an oasis. *Journal of Organizational Behavior, 26*, 59–78.

Steele, C. M., & Aronson, J. (1995). Stereotype threat and the intellectual test performance of African-Americans. *Journal of Personality and Social Psychology, 69*, 797–811.

Steele, C. M., & Aronson, J. A. (2004). Stereotype threat does not live by Steele and Aronson (1995) alone. *American Psychologist, 59*, 47–48.

Steele, C. M., & Davies, P. G. (2003). Stereotype threat and employment testing: A commentary. *Human Performance, 16*, 311–326.

Steele, P., Schmidt, J., & Shultz, J. (2008). Refining the relationship between personality and subjective well-being. *Psychological Bulletin, 134*, 138–161.

Steers, R. M., Porter, L. W., & Bigley, G. A. (1996). *Motivation and leadership at work*. New York: McGraw-Hill.

Stein, J. (2012, March 26). Running like a girl. *Time*, p. 60.

Stern, D., Stone, J. R., Hopkins, C., & McMillan, M. (1990). Quality of student's work experience and orientation toward work. *Youth and Society, 22*, 263–282.

Sternberg, R. J. (2004). Culture and intelligence. *American Psychologist, 59*, 325–338.

Sternberg, R. J., & Kaufmann, J. C. (1998). Human abilities. *Annual Review of Psychology, 49*, 479–502.

Sternberg, R. J., & Wagner, R. K. (1993). The g-ocentric view of intelligence and job performance is wrong. *Current Directions in Psychological Science, 2*, 1–5.

Sternberg, R. J., Wagner, R. K., & Okagaki, L. (1993). Practical intelligence: The nature and role of tacit knowledge in work and at school. In H. Reese & J. Puckett (Eds.), *Advances in lifespan development* (pp. 205–227). Hillsdale, NJ: Erlbaum.

Sternberg, R. J., Wagner, R. K., Williams, W. M., & Horvath, J. A. (1995). Testing common sense. *American Psychologist, 50*, 912–927.

Stevens, M. J., & Campion, M. A. (1993). *The Teamwork-KSA Test*. Chicago: NCS-London House.

Stevens, M. J., & Campion, M. A. (1994). The knowledge, skill, and ability requirements for teamwork: Implications for human resource management. *Journal of Management, 20*, 503–530.

Stevens, M. J., & Campion, M. A. (1999). Staffing work teams: Development and validation of a selection test for teamwork settings. *Journal of Management, 25*, 207–228.

Stewart, G. (2002, April 3). Golfers' children handled with care. *Los Angeles Times*, p. D3.

Stewart, G. L. (1999). Trait bandwidth and stages of job performance: Assessing individual effects for conscientiousness and its subtraits. *Journal of Applied Psychology, 84*, 959–968.

Stewart, G. L. (2006). A meta-analytic review of relationships between team design features and team performance. *Journal of Management, 32*, 29–54.

Stewart, W. H., & Roth, P. L. (2001). Risk propensity differences between entrepreneurs and managers: A meta-analytic review. *Journal of Applied Psychology, 86*, 145–153.

Stinglhamber, F., & Vandenberghe, C. (2003). Organizations and supervisors as sources of support and targets of commitment: A longitudinal study. *Journal of Organizational Behavior, 24*, 252–270.

Stone-Romero, E. F. (2002). The relative validity and usefulness of various empirical research designs. In S. G. Rogelberg (Ed.), *Handbook of research methods in industrial and organizational psychology* (pp. 77–98). Cambridge, MA: Blackwell.

Stone-Romero, E. F., Stone, D. L., & Salas, E. (2003). The influence of culture on role conceptions and role behaviour in organizations. *Applied Psychology: An International Review, 52*(3), 328–362.

Strauss, J. P., Barrick, M. R., & Connerley, M. L. (2001). An investigation of personality similarity effects (relational and perceived) on peer and supervisor ratings and the role of familiarity and liking. *Journal of Occupational and Organizational Psychology, 74*, 637–657.

Strober, M. H. (1994). Gender and occupational segregation. In *The International Encyclopedia of Education*. London: Pergamon.

Stumpp, T., Muck, P. M., Hulsheger, U. R., Judge, T. A., & Maier, G. W. (2010). Core self-evaluations in Germany: Validation of a German measure and its relationships with career success. *Applied Psychology: An International Review, 59*, 674–700.

Sugrue, B., & Rivera, R. (2005). *2005 ASTD state of the industry report*. Alexandria, VA: American Society for Training and Development.

Sundstrom, E., DeMeuse, K. P., & Futrell, D. (1990). Work teams: Applications and effectiveness. *American Psychologist, 45*, 120–133.

Sundstrom, E., McIntyre, M., Halfhill, T., & Richards, H. (2000). Work groups: From the Hawthorne studies to work teams of the 1990s and beyond. *Group Dynamics: Theory, Research, and Practice, 1*, 44–67.

Super, D. E. (1973). The work values inventory. In D. Zytowski (Ed.), *Contemporary approaches to interest measurement* (pp. 189–205). Minneapolis: University of Minnesota Press.

Sutton, R. I. (1991). Maintaining norms about expressed emotions: The case of bill collectors. *Administrative Science Quarterly, 36*, 245–268.

Sutton, R. I. (2007). *The no asshole rule: Building a civilized workplace and surviving one that isn't*. New York: Warner Business Books.

Sutton, R. I., & Rafaeli, A. (1988). Untangling the relationship between displayed emotions and organizational sales: The case of convenience stores. *Academy of Management Journal, 31*, 461–487.

Svenson, O., & Maule, J. A. (1993). *Time pressure and stress in human judgment and decision-making*. New York: Plenum.

Sweeney, P. D., & McFarlin, D. B. (2005). Wage comparisons with similar and dissimilar others. *Journal of Occupational and Organizational Psychology, 78*, 113–131.

Swezey, R. W., & Salas, E. (1992). Guidelines for use in team-training development. In R. W. Swezey & E. Salas (Eds.), *Teams: Their training and performance* (pp. 219–245). Stamford, CT: Ablex.

Sylva, H., & Mol, S. T. (2009). E-Recruitment: A study into applicant perceptions of an online application system. *International Journal of Selection and Assessment, 17*(3), 311–323.

Symon, G., Cassell, C., & Dickson, R. (2000). Expanding our research and practice through innovative research methods. *European Journal of Work and Organizational Psychology, 9*(4), 457–462.

Szalma, J. L., & Hancock, P. A. (2011). Noise effects on human performance: A meta-analytic synthesis. *Psychological Bulletin, 137*(4), 682–707.

Tajfel, H., & Turner, J. C. (1986). The social identity theory of intergroup behaviour. In S. Worchel & W. Austin (Eds.), *Psychology of intergroup relations* (pp. 7–24). Chicago: Nelson.

Takeuchi, R. (2010). A critical review of expatriate adjustment research: Progress, emerging trends, and prospects. *Journal of Management, 36*, 1040–1064.

Takeuchi, R., Lepak, D. P., Wang, H., & Takeuchi, K. (2007). An empirical examination of the mechanisms mediating between high-performance work systems and the performance of Japanese organizations. *Journal of Applied Psychology, 4*, 1069–1083.

Tang, C. Y., & MacDermid-Wadsworth, S. (2008). *2008 National study of the changing workplace (NSCW). Time and workplace flexibility.* Families and Work Institute. Retrieved October 27, 2011, from http://www.familiesandwork.org/site/research/reports/time_work_flex.pdf

Tang, T. L., & Ibrahim, A. H. (1998). Antecedents of organizational citizenship behavior revisited: Public personnel in the United States and in the Middle East. *Public Personnel Management, 46*, 259–293.

Tannenbaum, S. I., Mathieu, J. E., Salas, E., & Cohen, D. (2012). Teams are changing: Are research and practice evolving fast enough? *Industrial and Organizational Psychology: Perspectives on Science and Practice, 5*, 2–24.

Task Force on Assessment Center Guidelines. (1989). *Guidelines and ethical considerations for assessment center operations.* Pittsburgh, PA: Author.

Taylor, M. S., Fisher, C. D., & Ilgen, D. R. (1984). Individuals' reactions to performance feedback in organizations: A control theory perspective. In K. M. Rowland & G. R. Ferris (Eds.), *Research in personnel and human resources management* (Vol. 2, pp. 161–187). Greenwich, CT: JAI Press.

Taylor, P. J., Russ-Eft, D. F., & Chan, D. W. (2005). A meta-analytic review of behavior modeling training. *Journal of Applied Psychology, 90*, 692–709.

Taylor, P. J., & Small, B. (2002). Asking applicants what they *would* do versus what they *did* do: A meta-analytic comparison of situational and past behavior employment interview questions. *Journal of Occupational and Organizational Psychology, 75*, 277–294.

Telegraph.co.uk. (2007, August 18). Chinese boss of toy firm involved in Mattel recall commits suicide. *Daily Telegraph.*

Tellegen, A., & Waller, N. G. (2000). Exploring personality through test construction: Development of the Multidimensional Personality Questionnaire. In S. R. Briggs & J. M. Cheek (Eds.), *Personality measures: Development and evaluation* (pp. 261–292). Greenwich, CT: JAI Press.

Tepas, D. I., Paley, M. J., & Popkin, S. M. (1997). Work schedules and sustained performance. In G. Salvendy (Ed.), *Handbook of human factors and ergonomics* (2nd ed., pp. 1021–1058). New York: Wiley.

Tesluk, P. E., & Jacobs, R. R. (1998). Toward an integrated model of work experience. *Personnel Psychology, 51*, 321–355.

Tett, R. P., & Burnett, D. D. (2003). A personality trait-based interactionist model of job performance. *Journal of Applied Psychology, 88*, 500–517.

Tett, R. P., & Christiansen, N. D. (2007). Personality tests at the crossroads: A response to Morgeson, Campion, Dipboye, Hollenbeck, Murphy, and Schmitt (2007). *Personnel Psychology, 60*, 967–993.

Tett, R. P., Guterman, H. A., Bleir, A., & Murphy, P. J. (2000). Development and content validation of a "hyperdimensional" taxonomy of managerial competence. *Human Performance, 13*, 205–251.

Tett, R. P., Steele, J. R., & Beauregard, R. S. (2003). Broad and narrow measures on both sides of the personality–job performance relationship. *Journal of Organizational Behavior, 24*, 335–356.

Thomas, K. M. (1998). Psychological readiness for multicultural leadership. *Management Development Forum, 1*(2), 99–112.

Thomas, K. M. (2008). *Diversity resistance in organizations: Manifestations and solutions.* New York: Erlbaum.

Thomas, K. W. (1992). Conflict and negotiation processes in organizations. In M. D. Dunnette & L. M. Hough (Eds.), *Handbook of industrial and organizational psychology* (2nd ed., Vol. 3, pp. 651–717). Palo Alto, CA: Consulting Psychologists Press.

Thomas, R. R., Jr. (1992). Managing diversity: A conceptual framework. In S. E. Jackson & Associates (Eds.), *Diversity in the workplace: Human resource initiatives* (pp. 306–317). New York: Guilford.

Thompson, L. F., Surface, E. A., Martin, D. L., & Sanders, M. G. (2003). From paper to pixels: Moving personnel surveys to the web. *Personnel Psychology, 56*, 197–227.

Threlkeld, R., & Brozoska, K. (1994). Research in distance education. In B. Willis (Ed.), *Distance education: Tools and strategies* (pp. 44–66). Englewood Cliffs, NJ: Educational Technology Publications.

Thurley, K. (1982, February). The Japanese model: Practical reservations and surprising opportunities. *Personnel Management*, pp. 36–39.

Thurstone, L. L. (1938). Primary mental abilities. *Psychometric Monographs, 1.*

Tierney, P., Bauer, T. N., & Potter, R. E. (2002). Extra-role behavior among Mexican employees: The impact of LMX, group acceptance, and job attitudes. *International Journal of Selection and Assessment, 10*, 292–303.

Tierney, P., Farmer, F. M., & Graen, G. B. (1999). An examination of leadership and employee creativity: The relevance of traits and relationships. *Personnel Psychology, 52*, 591–620.

Tippins, N. T., Beaty, J., Drasgow, F., Gibson, W. M., Pearlman, K., Segall, D. O., & Shepherd, W. (2006). Unproctored Internet testing in employment settings. *Personnel Psychology, 59*, 189–225.

Tolbert, A. S., & McLean, G. N. (1995). Venezuelan culture assimilator for training United States professionals conducting business in Venezuela. *International Journal of Intercultural Relations, 19*, 111–125.

Tolbert, A. S., McLean, G. N., & Myers, R. C. (2002). Creating the global learning organization. *International Journal of Intercultural Relations, 26*, 463–472.

Tosi, H. L., Misangyi, V. F., Fanelli, A., Waldman, D. A., & Yammarino, F. J. (2004). CEO charisma, compensation, and firm performance. *Leadership Quarterly, 15*, 405–420.

Totterdell, P. (2005). Work schedules. In J. Barling, E. K. Kelloway, & M. R. Frone (Eds.), *Handbook of work stress* (pp. 35–62). Thousand Oaks, CA: Sage.

Townsend, A. M., DeMarie, S. M., & Hendrickson, A. R. (1998). Virtual teams: Technology and the workplace of the future. *Academy of Management Executive, 12*, 17–29.

Tracey, J. B., Tannenbaum, S. I., & Kavanagh, M. J. (1995). Applying trained skills on the job: The importance of the work environment. *Journal of Applied Psychology, 80*, 239–252.

Trahair, R. C. S. (1984). *The humanist temper: The life and work of Elton Mayo.* New Brunswick, NJ: Transaction.

Triandis, H. C. (1995a). Culture specific assimilators. In S. M. Fowler (Ed.), *Intercultural sourcebook: Cross-cultural training methods* (Vol. 1, pp. 179–186). Yarmouth, ME: Intercultural Press.

Triandis, H. C. (1995b). *Individualism and collectivism.* Boulder, CO: Westview.

Triandis, H. C. (2003). The future of workforce diversity in international organizations: A commentary. *Applied Psychology: An International Review, 52*, 486–495.

Triandis, H. C., & Bhawuk, D. P. S. (1997). Culture theory and the meaning of relatedness. In P. C. Earley & M. Erez (Eds.), *New perspectives on international industrial/organizational psychology* (pp. 13–51). San Francisco: Jossey-Bass.

Triandis, H. C., & Brislin, R. (1984). Cross-cultural psychology. *American Psychologist, 39,* 1006–1016.

Trieman, D. J., & Hartmann, H. I. (1981). *Women, work, and wages: Equal pay for jobs of equal value.* Washington, DC: National Academy Press.

Trist, E. L., & Bamforth, K. W. (1951). Some social and psychological consequences of the longwall method of coal-getting. *Human Relations, 4,* 3–38.

Trompenaars, F., & Hampden-Turner, C. (1998). *Riding the waves of culture: Understanding cultural diversity in global business* (2nd ed.). New York: McGraw-Hill.

Tschan, F., Rochat, S., & Zapf, D. (2005). It's not only clients: Studying emotion work with clients and co-workers with an event-sampling approach. *Journal of Occupational and Organizational Psychology, 78,* 195–220.

Tsui, A. S., Egan, T. D., & O'Reilly, C. A. (1991). Being different: Relational demography and organizational attachment. *Academy of Management Best Paper Proceedings, 37,* 183–187.

Tsui, A. S., & O'Reilly, C. A. (1989). Beyond simple demographics: The importance of relational demography in superior–subordinate dyads. *Academy of Management Journal, 32,* 402–423.

Tubre, T. C., & Collins, J. M. (2000). Jackson and Schuler (1985) revisited: A meta-analysis of the relationships between role ambiguity, role conflict, and job performance. *Journal of Management, 26,* 155–169.

Tuckey, M., Brewer, N., & Williamson, P. (2002). The influence of motives and goal orientation on feedback seeking. *Journal of Occupational and Organizational Psychology, 75,* 195–216.

Tuckman, B. W., & Jensen, M. A. (1977). Stages of small-group development revisited. *Group and Organization Studies, 2,* 419–427.

Turban, D. C., & Cable, D. M. (2003). Firm reputation and applicant pool characteristics. *Journal of Organizational Behavior, 24,* 733–751.

Turban, D. C., Lau, C.-M., Ngo, H.-Y., Chow, I. H. S., & Si, S. X. (2001). Organizational attractiveness of forms in the People's Republic of China: A person–organization fit perspective. *Journal of Applied Psychology, 86,* 194–206.

Turner, N., Barling, J., Epitropaki, O., Butcher, V., & Milner, C. (2002). Transformational leadership and moral reasoning. *Journal of Applied Psychology, 87,* 304–311.

Turner, S. M., DeMers, S. T., Fox, H. R., & Reed, G. M. (2001). APA's guidelines for test user qualifications. *American Psychologist, 56,* 1099–1113.

Tyler, G. P., & Newcombe, P. A. (2006). Relationship between work performance and personality traits in Hong Kong organizational settings. *International Journal of Selection and Assessment, 14*(1), 37–50.

Tziner, A., Fisher, M., Senior, T., & Weisberg, J. (2007). Effects of trainee characteristics on training effectiveness. *International Journal of Selection and Assessment, 15,* 167–175.

Tziner, A., & Kopelman, R. E. (2002). Is there a preferred performance rating format? A non-psychometric approach. *Applied Psychology: An International Review, 51,* 479–503.

Tziner, A., Murphy, K. R., & Cleveland, J. N. (2001). Relationships between attitudes toward organizations and performance appraisal systems and rating behavior. *International Journal of Selection and Assessment, 9,* 226–239.

Tziner, A., Murphy, K. R., & Cleveland, J. N. (2002). Does conscientiousness moderate the relationship between attitudes and beliefs regarding performance appraisal and rating behavior? *International Journal of Selection and Assessment, 10,* 218–224.

Uhl-Bien, M., Marion, R., & McKelvey, B. (2007). Complexity leadership theory: Shifting leadership from the industrial age to the modern era. *Leadership Quarterly, 18,* 298–318.

Ulewicz, M. (2005). Evaluating the U.S. naturalization test redesign. APA Online: Psychological Science Agenda, Vol. 19(2). Retrieved February 15, 2005, from www.apa.org/science/psa/feb5natural.html

Ulmer, D. K., & Schwartzburd, L. (1996). Treatment of time pathologies. In R. Allan & S. Scheidt (Eds.), *Heart and mind: The practice of cardiac psychology.* Washington, DC: American Psychological Association.

Uniform Guidelines on Employee Selection Procedures. (1978). *Federal Register, 43,* 38290–38315.

Unsworth, K. L., & West, M. A. (2000). Teams: The challenges of cooperative work. In N. Chmiel (Ed.), *Introduction to work and organizational psychology* (pp. 137–146). Oxford, UK: Blackwell.

Utsch, A., Rauch, A., Rothfuss, R., & Frese, M. (1999). Who becomes a small-scale entrepreneur in a post-socialist environment: On the differences between entrepreneurs and managers in East Germany. *Journal of Small Business Management,* 37(3), 31–42.

Valentine, S., & Fleischman, G. (2004). Ethics training and businesspersons' perceptions of ethics. *Journal of Business Ethics, 52,* 381–390.

Vallaster, C. (2005). Cultural diversity and its impact on social interactive processes: Implications from an empirical study. *International Journal of Cross-Cultural Management, 5,* 139–163.

Vancouver, J. (2005). The depth of history and explanation as benefit and bane for psychological control theories. *Journal of Applied Psychology, 90,* 38–52.

van Dam, K. (2005). Employee attitudes toward job changes: An application and extension of Rusbult and Farrell's investment model. *Journal of Occupational and Organizational Psychology, 78,* 253–272.

Vandenbos, G. R., & Bulatao, E. Q. (Eds.). (1996). *Violence on the job: Identifying risks and developing solutions.* Washington, DC: American Psychological Association.

van der Klink, J. J., Blonk, R. W., Schene, A. H., & van Dijk, F. J. (2001). The benefits of interventions for work-related stress. *American Journal of Public Health, 91,* 270–276.

van der Vegt, G. S. (2002). Effects of attitude dissimilarity and time on social integration: A longitudinal panel study. *Journal of Occupational and Organizational Psychology, 75,* 439–452.

van der Zee, K. I., Bakker, A. B., & Bakker, P. (2002). Why are structured interviews used so rarely in personnel selection? *Journal of Applied Psychology, 87,* 176–184.

van Dick, R. (2004). My job is my castle: Identification in organizational contexts. In C. L. Cooper & I. T. Robertson (Eds.), *International review of industrial and organizational psychology* (Vol. 19, pp. 171–203). London: Wiley.

van Dick, R., Hirst, G., Grojean, M. W., & Wieseke, J. (2007). Relationships between leader and follower organizational identification and implications for follower attitudes and behaviour. *Journal of Occupational and Organizational Psychology, 80,* 133–150.

van Dierendonck, D., Schaufeli, W. B., & Buunk, B. P. (2001). Burnout and inequity among human service professionals. *Journal of Occupational Health Psychology, 6,* 43–52.

van Drunen, P., & van Strien, P. J. (1999). Psychology in the Netherlands: Recent trends and current situation. *European Psychologist, 4,* 263–271.

van Eerde, W., & Thierry, H. (1996). Vroom's expectancy models and work-related criteria: A meta-analysis. *Journal of Applied Psychology, 81,* 575–586.

van Emmerick, I. H., Euwema, M. C., & Bakker, A. B. (2007). Threats of workplace violence and the buffering effect of social support. *Group and Organization Management, 32,* 152–175.

van Knippenberg, D., De Dreu, C., & Homan, A. C. (2004). Work group diversity and work performance: An integrative model and research agenda. *Journal of Applied Psychology, 89,* 1008–1022.

van Knippenberg, D., & Schippers, M. C. (2007). Work group diversity. *Annual Review of Psychology, 58,* 515–541.

van Knippenberg, D., & Sleebos, E. (2006). Organizational identification versus organizational commitment: Self-definition, social exchange, and job attitudes. *Journal of Organizational Behavior, 27*, 571–584.

van Knippenberg, B., & van Knippenberg, D. (2005). Leader self-sacrifice and leadership effectiveness: The moderating role of leader prototypicality. *Journal of Applied Psychology, 90*, 25–37.

van Knippenberg, D., van Knippenberg, B., van Kleef, G. A., & Damen, F. (2008). Leadership, affect and emotions. In N. M. Ashkanasy & C. L. Cooper (Eds.), *Research companion to emotion in organizations* (pp. 465–475). London: Edward Elgar.

van Mannen, J., & Schein, E. H. (1979). Toward a theory of organizational commitment. In B. M. Staw (Ed.), *Research in organizational behavior* (Vol. 1, pp. 197–216). Greenwich, CT: JAI Press.

van Rooy, D. L., Viswesvaran, C., & Pluta, P. (2005). An evaluation of construct validity: What is this thing called emotional intelligence? *Human Performance, 18*, 445–462.

van Scotter, J. R., Motowidlo, S. J., & Cross, T. C. (2000). Effects of task performance and contextual performance on systemic rewards. *Journal of Applied Psychology, 85*, 526–535.

Vardi, Y., & Weiner, Y. (1996). Misbehavior in organizations: A motivational framework. *Organizational Science, 7*, 151–165.

Vardi, Y., & Weitz, E. (2004). *Misbehavior in organizations: Theory, research, and management.* Mahwah, NJ: Erlbaum.

Vecchio, R. P. (1981). An individual differences interpretation of the conflicting interpretations generated by equity theory and expectancy theory. *Journal of Applied Psychology, 66*, 470–481.

Vecchio, R. P. (2002). Leadership and gender advantage. *Leadership Quarterly, 13*, 835–850.

Vecchio, R. P. (2003). In search of gender advantage. *Leadership Quarterly, 14*, 643–671.

Vecchio, R. P., & Brazil, D. M. (2007). Leadership and sex-similarity: A comparison in a military setting. *Personnel Psychology, 60*, 303–335.

Velocci, A. L., Jr. (1998). Pursuit of Six Sigma emerges as an industry trend. *Aviation Week and Space Technology, 149*(20), 52–58.

Vermunt, R., van Knippenberg, D., van Knippenberg, B., & Blaauw, E. (2001). Self-esteem and outcome fairness: Differential importance of procedural and outcome considerations. *Journal of Applied Psychology, 86*, 621–628.

Vey, M. A., & Campbell, J. P. (2004). In-role or extra-role organizational citizenship behavior: Which are we measuring? *Human Performance, 17*, 119–135.

Vinacke, E. (1962). Motivation as a complex problem. *Nebraska Symposium on Motivation, 10*, 1–45.

Vinchur, A. J. (2005). Charles Samuel Myers and Otto Lipmann: Early contributors to industrial psychology. *The Industrial-Organizational Psychologist, 43*(2), 31–35.

Viswesvaran, C., Ones, D. S., & Hough, L. M. (2001). Do impression management scales in personality inventories predict managerial job performance ratings? *International Journal of Selection and Assessment, 9*, 277–289.

Viswesvaran, C., Schmidt, F. L., & Ones, D. S. (2005). Is there a general factor in ratings of job performance? A meta-analytic framework for disentangling substantive and error influences. *Journal of Applied Psychology, 90*, 108–131.

Viteles, M. S. (1932). *Industrial psychology.* New York: Norton.

Viteles, M. S. (1953). *Motivation and morale in industry.* New York: Norton.

Vroom, V. H. (1964). *Work and motivation.* New York: Wiley.

Vroom, V. H., & Jago, A. G. (1988). *The new leadership: Managing participation in organizations.* Englewood Cliffs, NJ: Prentice Hall.

Vroom, V. H., & Yetton, P. W. (1973). *Leadership and decisionmaking.* Pittsburgh, PA: University of Pittsburgh Press.

Waclawski, J. (1999). The real world: Generation X or generation gap? *The Industrial-Organizational Psychologist, 37*(1), 79–90.

Waclawski, J., & Church, A. H. (2002). *Organizational development: A data-driven approach to organizational change.* San Francisco: Jossey-Bass.

Wade-Benzoni, K., Okumura, T., Brett, J., Moore, D., Tenbrunsel, A. E., & Bazerman, M. (2002). Cognitions and behavior in asymmetric social dilemmas: A comparison of two cultures. *Journal of Applied Psychology, 87*, 87–95.

Wai, J., Lubinski, D., & Benbow, C. P. (2005). Creativity and occupational accomplishments among intellectually precocious youth: An age 13 to age 33 longitudinal study. *Journal of Educational Psychology, 97*, 484–492.

Waldman, D. A. (1997). Predictors of employee preferences for multirater and group-based performance appraisal. *Group and Organization Management, 22*, 264–287.

Waldman, D. A., Sully de Luque, M., Washburn, N., & House, R. J. (2006). Cultural and leadership predictors of corporate social responsibly values of top management: A GLOBE study of 15 countries. *Journal of International Business Studies, 37*, 823–837.

Walker, A. (1999). Combating age discrimination at the workplace. *Experimental Aging Research, 25*, 367–377.

Wall, T. D., Kemp, N. J., Jackson, P. R., & Clegg, C. W. (1986). Outcomes of autonomous work groups: A field experiment. *Academy of Management Journal, 29*, 280–304.

Wallace, C., & Chen, G. (2006). A multilevel integration of personality, climate, self-regulation, and performance. *Personnel Psychology, 59*, 529–557.

Wallace, J. C., Popp, E., & Mondore, S. (2006). Safety climate as a mediator between foundation climates and occupational accidents: A group-level investigation. *Journal of Applied Psychology, 91*, 681–688.

Waller, M. J., Conte, J. M., Gibson, C., & Carpenter, M. (2001). The impact of individual time perception on team performance under deadline conditions. *Academy of Management Review, 26*, 586–600.

Walumbwa, F. O., Avolio, B. J., Gardner, W. L., Wernsing, T. S., & Peterson, S. J. (2008). Authentic leadership: Development and validation of a theory-based measure. *Journal of Management, 34*, 89–126.

Walumbwa, F. O., Luthans, F., Avey, J. B., & Oke, A. (2011). Authentically leading groups: The mediating role of collective psychological capital and trust. *Journal of Organizational Behavior, 32*, 4–24.

Walumbwa, F. O., Wang, P., Lawler, J. J., & Shi, K. (2004). The role of collective efficacy in the relations between transformational leadership and work outcomes. *Journal of Occupational and Organizational Psychology, 77*, 515–530.

Walumbwa, F. O., Wang, P., Wang, H., Schaubroeck, J., & Avolio, B. J. (2010). Psychological processes linking authentic leadership to follower behaviors. *Leadership Quarterly, 21*, 901–914.

Wanberg, C. R., Glomb, T. M., Song, Z., & Sorenson, S. (2005). Job search and persistence during unemployment: A 10-wave longitudinal study. *Journal of Applied Psychology, 90*, 411–430.

Wanek, J. E., Sackett, P. R., & Ones, D. S. (2003). Toward an understanding of integrity test similarities and differences: An item level analysis of seven tests. *Personnel Psychology, 56*, 873–894.

Wang, M., & Russell, S. S. (2005). Measurement equivalence of the Job Descriptive Index across Chinese and American workers: Results from confirmatory factor analysis and item response theory. *Educational and Psychological Measurement, 65*, 709–732.

Wanous, J. P., Reichers, A. E., & Hundy, M. J. (1997). Overall job satisfaction: How good are single-item measures? *Journal of Applied Psychology, 82*, 247–252.

Warr, P. B. (1999). Well-being in the workplace. In D. Kahneman, E. Diener, & N. Schwarz (Eds.), *Well-being: The foundations of hedonic psychology* (pp. 392–412). New York: Russell Sage Foundation.

Warr, P. B. (2006). Some historical developments in I-O psychology outside the USA. In L. Koppes (Ed.), *Historical perspectives in industrial and organizational psychology* (pp. 81–107). Mahwah, NJ: Erlbaum.

Warr, P. B. (2007). *Work, happiness, and unhappiness*. Mahwah, NJ: Erlbaum.

Wasserman, I. C., Gallegos, P. V., & Ferdman, B. M. (2008). Dancing with resistance: Leadership challenges in fostering a culture of inclusion. In K. M. Thomas (Ed.), *Diversity resistance in organizations: Manifestations and solutions* (pp. 175–200). New York: Taylor & Francis.

Wasti, S. A. (2003a). The influence of cultural values on antecedents of organizational commitment: An individual-level analysis. *Applied Psychology: An International Review, 52*, 533–554.

Wasti, S. S. (2003b). Organizational commitment, turnover intentions and the influence of cultural values. *Journal of Occupational and Organizational Psychology, 76*, 303–321.

Wasylyshyn, K. M. (2003). Executive coaching: An outcome study. *Consulting Psychology Journal: Practice and Research, 55*, 94–106.

Watson, W. E., Kumar, K., & Michaelsen, L. K. (1993). Cultural diversity's impact on interaction process and performance: Comparing homogenous and diverse task groups. *Academy of Management Journal, 36*, 590–602.

Webb, R. M., Lubinski, D., & Benbow, C. P. (2007). Spatial ability: A neglected dimension in talent searches for intellectually precocious youth. *Journal of Educational Psychology, 99*, 397–420.

Weber, M. (1947). *The theory of social and economic organization* (A. R. Henderson & T. Parsons, Trans. and Eds.) New York: Oxford University Press.

Weber, Y. (2000). Measuring cultural fit in mergers and acquisitions. In N. Ashkenasy, C. Wilderom, & M. Peterson (Eds.), *Handbook of organizational culture and climate* (pp. 309–320). London: Sage.

Webster, E. C. (1982). *The employment interview: A social judgment process*. Schomberg, Ontario, Canada: SIP Publications.

Webster, J., & Hackley, P. (1997). Teaching effectiveness in technology-mediated distance learning. *Academy of Management Journal, 40*, 1282–1309.

Weekley, J. A., & Jones, C. (1997). Video based situational testing. *Personnel Psychology, 50*, 25–49.

Weekley, J. A., & Ployhart, R. E. (2005). Situational judgment: Antecedents and relationships with performance. *Human Performance, 18*, 81–104.

Weekley, J. A., & Ployhart, R. E. (2006). An introduction to situational judgment testing. In J. A. Weekley & R. E. Ployhart (Eds.), *Situational judgment tests: Theory, measurement, and application* (pp. 1–9). Mahwah, NJ: Erlbaum.

Weekley, J. A., Ployhart, R. E., & Harold, C. M. (2004). Personality and situational judgment tests across applicant and incumbent settings: An examination of validity, measurement, and subgroup differences. *Human Performance, 17*, 433–461.

Weick, K., & Quinn, R. (1999). Organizational change and development. *Annual Review of Psychology, 50*, 361–386.

Weiner, B. (1991). Metaphors in motivation and attribution. *American Psychologist, 46*, 921–930.

Weiner, B. (1992). *Human motivation: Metaphors, theories, and research*. London: Sage.

Weinstein, M. (2008). Getting McSmart: A day in the life at Hamburger University. *Training Magazine, 45*(4), 44–47.

Weiss, D. J., Dawis, R. V., England, G. W., & Lofquist, L. H. (1967). *Manual for the Minnesota Satisfaction Questionnaire*. Minneapolis: Industrial Relations Center, University of Minnesota.

Weiss, H. M. (2002a). Conceptual and empirical foundations for the study of affect at work. In R. G. Lord, R. L. Klimoski, & R. Kanfer (Eds.), *Emotions in the workplace: Understanding the structure and role of emotions in organizational behavior* (pp. 20–63). San Francisco: Jossey-Bass.

Weiss, H. M. (2002b). Deconstructing job satisfaction: Separating evaluations, beliefs, and affective experiences. *Human Resource Management Review, 12*, 173–194.

Weiss, H. M., & Cropanzano, R. (1996). Affective events theory: A theoretical discussion of the structure, causes, and consequences of affective experiences at work. *Research in Organizational Behavior, 18*, 1–74.

Weiss, H. M., Suckow, K., & Cropanzano, R. (1999). Effects of justice conditions on discrete emotions. *Journal of Applied Psychology, 84*, 786–794.

Welch, J. (2004, October 28). Five questions to ask . . . *Wall Street Journal*, p. A14.

Wells, D., & Schminke, M. (2001). Ethical development and human resource training. *Human Resource Management Review, 11*, 135–158.

Welsh, L. T., Wanberg, C. R., Brown, K. G., & Simmering, M. J. (2003). E-learning: Emerging uses, best practices, and future directions. *International Journal of Training and Development, 7*, 245–258.

Wentworth, D. K. (2002). The schizophrenic organization. *The Industrial-Organizational Psychologist, 39*(4), 39–41.

Werner, J. M., & Bolino, M. C. (1997). Explaining U.S. courts of appeals decisions involving performance appraisal: Accuracy, fairness, and validation. *Personnel Psychology, 50*, 1–23.

Wessel, J. L., & Ryan, A. M. (2008). Past the first encounter: The role of stereotypes. *Industrial and Organizational Psychology: Perspectives on Research and Practice, 1*, 409–411.

Wesson, M. J., & Gogus, C. I. (2005). Shaking hands with a computer: An examination of two methods of organizational newcomer orientation. *Journal of Applied Psychology, 90*, 1018–1026.

West, M. A. (2012). *Effective teamwork: Practical lessons from organizational research* (3rd ed.). Oxford, UK: Blackwell/British Psychological Society.

West, M. A., Borrill, C. S., & Unsworth, K. L. (1998). Team effectiveness in organizations. In C. L. Cooper & I. T. Robertson (Eds.), *International Review of Industrial and Organizational Psychology* (Vol. 13, pp. 1–48). Chichester, UK: Wiley.

West, M. A., Hirst, G., Richter, A., & Shipton, H. (2004). Twelve steps to heaven: Successfully managing change through developing innovative teams. *European Journal of Work and Organizational Psychology, 13*, 269–299.

Westerman, J. W., & Sundali, J. (2005). The transformation of employee pensions in the United States: Through the looking glass of organizational behavior. *Journal of Organizational Behavior, 26*, 99–103.

Wexley, K. N., & Latham, G. P. (2002). *Developing and training human resources in organizations* (3rd ed.). Upper Saddle River, NJ: Prentice Hall.

Wheatley, M. J. (1992). *Leadership and the new science*. San Francisco: Berrett-Koehler.

White, R. E., Thornhil, S., & Hampson, E. (2007). A biosocial model of entrepreneurship: The combined effects of nurture and nature. *Journal of Organizational Behavior, 28*, 451–466.

Whitney, D. J., & Schmitt, N. (1997). Relationship between culture and response to biodata items. *Journal of Applied Psychology, 82*, 113–129.

Whyte, G. (1998). Recasting Janis's groupthink model: The key role of collective efficacy in decision fiascoes. *Organizational Behavior and Human Decision Processes, 73*, 185–209.

Whyte, W. H. (1956). *The organization man*. New York: Simon & Schuster.

Wickens, C. D., & Hollands, J. G. (2000). *Engineering psychology and human performance* (3rd ed.). Upper Saddle River, NJ: Prentice Hall.

Wickens, C. D., Lee, J., Gordon, S. E., & Liu, Y. (2004). *Introduction to human factors engineering* (2nd ed.). New York: Prentice Hall.

Wickramasinghe, V., & Jayabandu, S. (2007). Towards workplace flexibility: Flexitime arrangements in Sri Lanka. *Employee Relations, 29*, 554–575.

Wiese, B. S., & Freund, A. M. (2005). Goal progress makes one happy, or does it? Longitudinal findings from the work domain. *Journal of Occupational and Organizational Psychology, 78*, 287–304.

Wigdor, A. K., & Green, B. F. (1991). *Performance assessment in the workplace*. Washington, DC: National Academy Press.

Wilber, D. Q. (2007, January 12). A crash's improbable impact: '82 Air Florida tragedy led to broad safety reforms. *Washington Post*, p. A01.

Wilkerson, J. M. (1999). The impact of job level and prior training on sexual harassment labeling and remedy choice. *Journal of Applied Social Psychology, 29*, 1605–1623.

Williams, K. J., Suls, J., Alliger, G. M., Learner, S. M., & Wan, C. K. (1991). Multiple role juggling and daily mood states in working mothers: An experience sampling study. *Journal of Applied Psychology, 76*, 664–674.

Williams, M. L., McDaniel, M. A., & Nguyen, N. T. (2006). A meta-analysis of the antecedents and consequences of pay-level satisfaction. *Journal of Applied Psychology, 91*, 392–413.

Willness, C. R., Steel, P., & Lee, K. (2007). A meta-analysis of the antecedents and consequences of workplace sexual harassment. *Personnel Psychology, 60*, 127–162.

Winefield, A. H., & Tiggemann, M. (1990). Employment status and psychological well-being: A longitudinal study. *Journal of Applied Psychology, 75*, 455–459.

Winefield, A. H., Winefield, H. R., Tiggemann, M., & Godney, R. D. (1991). A longitudinal study of the psychological effects of unemployment and unsatisfactory employment on young adults. *Journal of Applied Psychology, 76*, 424–431.

Witt, L. A., Kacmar, M., Carlson, D. S., & Zivnuska, S. (2002). Interactive effects of personality and organizational politics on contextual performance. *Journal of Organizational Behavior, 23*, 911–926.

Witt, L. A., & Spitzmüller, C. (2007). Person–situation predictors of maximum and typical performance. *Human Performance, 20*, 305–315.

Woehr, D. J., & Feldman, J. (1993). Processing objective and question order effects on the causal relationship between memory and judgment in performance appraisal: The tip of the iceberg. *Journal of Applied Psychology, 78*, 232–241.

Woehr, D. J., & Huffcutt, A. I. (1994). Rater training for performance appraisal: A quantitative review. *Journal of Occupational and Organizational Psychology, 67*, 189–205.

Woehr, D. J., Sheehan, M. K., & Bennett, W. (2005). Assessing measurement equivalence across rating sources: A multi-trait multi-rater approach. *Journal of Applied Psychology, 90*, 592–600.

Wood, R. E., & Bandura, A. (1989). Social-cognitive theory of organizational management. *Academy of Management Review, 14*, 361–384.

Wood, R. E., George-Falvy, J., & Debowsky, S. (2001). Motivation and information search on complex tasks. In M. Erez, U. Kleinbeck, & H. Thierry (Eds.), *Work motivation in the context of a globalizing economy* (pp. 33–57). Hillsdale, NJ: Erlbaum.

Woodward, J. (1958). *Management and technology*. London: Her Majesty's Stationery Office.

Worren, N. (1996). Management fashion. *Academy of Management Review, 21*, 613–614.

Wright, L. (1988). The Type A behavior pattern and coronary artery disease. *American Psychologist, 43*, 2–14.

Wright, P. M., Gardner, T. M., Moynihan, L. M., & Allen, M. R. (2005). The relationship between HR practices and firm performance: Examining causal order. *Personnel Psychology, 58*, 409–446.

Wright, P. M., Gardner, T. M., Moynihan, L. M., Park, H. J., Gerhart, B., & Delery, J. E. (2001). Measurement error in research on human resources and firm performance: Additional data and suggestions for future research. *Personnel Psychology, 54*, 875–901.

Wright, T. A., & Bonett, D. G. (2002). The moderating effects of employee tenure on the relation between organizational commitment and job performance: A meta-analysis. *Journal of Applied Psychology, 87*, 1183–1190.

Wright, T. A., & Cropanzano, R. (2000). Psychological well-being and job satisfaction as predictors of job performance. *Journal of Occupational Health Psychology, 5*, 84–94.

Wu, C. H., & Griffin, M. A. (2011). Longitudinal relationships between core self-evaluations and job satisfaction. *Journal of Applied Psychology, 97*, 331–342.

Xenikou, A. (2005). The interactive effect of positive and negative occupational attributional styles on job motivation. *European Journal of Work and Organizational Psychology, 14*, 43–58.

Xie, J. L. (1996). Karasek's model in the People's Republic of China: Effects of job demands, control, and individual differences. *Academy of Management Journal, 39*, 1594–1618.

Yen, H. (2005, October 21). Death in streets took a back seat to dinner. *Seattle Times*, p. 12A. Retrieved November 28, 2005, from seattletimes.nwsource.com/html/nationworld/2002574244_fema21.html

Yerkes, R. M., & Dodson, J. D. (1908). The relation of strength of stimulus to rapidity of habit-formation. *Journal of Comparative Neurology and Psychology, 18*, 459–482.

Young, M. C., White, L. A., & Heggestad, E. D. (2001). *Faking resistance of the army's new non-cognitive selection measure*. AIM paper presented at the 109th Annual Convention of the American Psychological Association, San Francisco.

Yukl, G. (1981). *Leadership in organizations*. Englewood Cliffs, NJ: Prentice Hall.

Yukl, G. (1998). *Leadership in organizations* (4th ed.). Upper Saddle River, NJ: Prentice Hall.

Yukl, G. (2006). *Leadership in organizations* (6th ed.). Upper Saddle River, NJ: Pearson Prentice Hall.

Yukl, G., Fu, P. P., & McDonald, R. (2003). Cross-cultural differences in perceived effectiveness of influence tactics for initiating or resisting change. *Applied Psychology: An International Review, 52*, 68–82.

Yun, G. J., Donahue, L. M., Dudley, N. M., & McFarland, L. A. (2005). Rater personality, rating format, and social context: Implications for performance appraisal ratings. *International Journal of Selection and Assessment, 13*, 97–107.

Zacharatos, A., Barling, J., & Iverson, R. D. (2005). High performance work systems and occupational safety. *Journal of Applied Psychology, 90*, 77–93.

Zapf, D. (1999). Organizational, work group-related, and personal causes of mobbing/bullying at work. *International Journal of Manpower, 20*, 70–85.

Zapf, D., & Einarsen, S. (2005). Mobbing at work: Escalated conflicts in organizations. In S. Fox & P. E. Spector (Eds.), *Counterproductive work behavior: Investigations of actors and targets* (pp. 237–270). Washington, DC: American Psychological Association.

Zapf, D., & Gross, C. (2001). Conflict escalation and coping with workplace bullying: A replication and extension. *European Journal of Work and Organizational Psychology, 10*(4), 497–522.

Zedeck, S. (1992). Introduction: Exploring the domain of work and family concerns. In S. Zedeck (Ed.), *Work, families and organizations* (pp. 1–32). San Francisco: Jossey-Bass.

Zellars, K. J., Tepper, B. J., & Duffy, M. K. (2002). Abusive supervision and subordinates' organizational citizenship behaviors. *Journal of Applied Psychology, 87*, 1068–1078.

Zemke, R., Raines, C., & Filipczak, B. (2000). *Generations at work: Managing the clash of veterans, boomers, Xers, and Nexters in your workplace*. Washington, DC: American Management Association.

Zhang, S., & Fulford, C. (1994). Are time and psychological interactivity the same thing in distance learning television classroom? *Educational Technology, 34*, 58–64.

Zhao, H., Seibert, S.E., & Lumpkin, G.T. (2010). The relationship of personality to entrepreneurial intentions and performance: A meta-analytic review. *Journal of Management, 36*(2), 381–404.

Zhao, H., Wayne, S. J., & Glibkowski, B. C. (2007). The impact of psychological contract breach on work-related outcomes: A meta-analysis. *Personnel Psychology, 60*, 647–680.

Zhou, J., & Martocchio, J. J. (2001). Chinese and American managers' compensation award decisions: A comparative policy capturing study. *Personnel Psychology, 54*, 115–145.

Zhu, W., Chew, R. K. H., & Spangler, W. D. (2005). CEO transformational leadership and organizational outcomes: The mediating role of human-capital-enhancing human resource management. *Leadership Quarterly, 16*, 39–52.

Zickar, M. (2003). Remembering Arthur Kornhauser: Industrial psychology's advocate for worker well-being. *Journal of Applied Psychology, 88*, 363–369.

Zimmerman, A. (2004, May 26). Big retailers face overtime suits as bosses do more "hourly" work. *Wall Street Journal*, pp. 1, 2.

Zimmerman, R. D., Mount, M. K., & Goff, M. (2008). Multi-source feedback and leaders' goal performance: Moderating effects of rating purpose, rater perspective, and performance dimension. *International Journal of Selection and Assessment, 16*, 121–134.

Zipkin, A. (2004, May 6). Hard to trust anyone these days. *New York Times*, p. C6.

Zogby International (2007, September). U.S. workplace bullying survey. Conducted in conjunction with the Workplace Bullying Institute. Retrieved October 10, 2008, from bullyinginstitute.org/wbi-zogby2007.html

Zohar, D. (1980). Safety climate in industrial organizations: Theoretical and applied Implications. *Journal of Applied Psychology, 65*, 96–102.

Zohar, D. (2000). A group-level model of safety climate: Testing the effect of group climate on microaccidents in manufacturing jobs. *Journal of Applied Psychology, 85*, 587–596.

Zohar, D. (2002). Modifying supervisory practices to improve subunit safety: A leadership-based intervention model. *Journal of Applied Psychology, 87*, 156–163.

Zohar, D., & Luria, G. (2005). A multilevel model of safety climate: Cross-level relationships between organization and group-level climates. *Journal of Applied Psychology, 90*, 616–628.

Zohar, D., Tzischinski, O., & Epstein, R. (2003). Effects of energy availability on immediate and delayed emotional reactions to work events. *Journal of Applied Psychology, 88*, 1082–1093.

Zuriff, G. E. (2004). Is affirmative action fair? *American Psychologist, 58*, 124–125.

Zweig, D., & Webster, J. (2002). Where is the line between benign and invasive? An examination of psychological barriers to the acceptance of awareness monitoring systems. *Journal of Organizational Behavior, 23*, 605–633.

Name Index

Subject Index

SOCIAL AND PSYCHOLOGICAL ENVIRONMENT

Pre-1900

- Psychology emerges as a science distinct from philosophy and physiology; dominated by research on the senses and consciousness
- The American Psychological Association (APA) is founded in 1892
- Clinical psychology emerges as one of the few applications of psychology to real-world problems
- F. Galton develops the science of fingerprinting as a way of demonstrating the principles of Darwin's theory of evolution
- Typical Americans and Europeans are fascinated with phrenology (assessing personality from bumps on the skull) and hypnotism

1900–1920

- Scientific Management captivates the United States, Europe, and Japan
- Time and motion studies become popular in industry
- World War I begins and ends
- Elton Mayo asserts that unions are examples of psychopathology in Australia
- The Eugenics movement (the improvement of races through breeding) attracts many psychologists, including J. McK. Cattell
- The success of the psychological testing of army recruits is used to promote employment testing in industry, and eventually, to justify immigration quotas for many central and southern European ethnic groups
- University-based and private I-O consulting firms begin to appear

1920–1940

- Social psychology, child psychology, and behaviorism attract great attention
- A major economic depression affects employment
- America prepares for a new war in Europe
- Manufacturing processes become more technically sophisticated
- Scientific techniques for attitude measurement are introduced
- Race discrimination in housing, immigration, and employment become important national topics

1940–1960

- Social psychologists begin to emphasize groups, teams and attitudes
- World War II begins and ends; the Korean war begins
- Industry experiences frequent and disruptive strikes
- Behaviorism wanes and cognitive psychology emerges
- APA forms a committee to establish technical and scientific standards for tests
- The United States Employment Service publishes the *Dictionary of Occupational Titles*, a comprehensive description of thousands of jobs
- The assessment center is introduced by the U.S. Office of Strategic Services as a method for selecting spies and sabotage agents

1960–1980

- Personality theory and research migrate from clinical to social psychology
- John and Robert Kennedy, Martin Luther King, Jr., and Malcolm X are assassinated
- The Vietnam war begins and ends
- The transistor replaces the vacuum tube, which is then replaced by the computer chip
- Racially based riots occur in most large cities
- Title VII of the Civil Rights Act of 1964 addresses discrimination in employment
- The Federal government issues administrative guidelines defining adverse impact and employment discrimination
- Three Mile Island nuclear accident raises questions about safety cultures

1980–Present

- Class action lawsuits brought by ethnic minority and female workers become common
- Laws protecting older workers (ADEA) and disabled workers (ADA) are passed
- The U.S. Civil Rights Act of 1964 is amended by the Civil Rights Act of 1991 to prohibit quota hiring
- Downsizings, acquisitions, and mergers become commonplace
- The workplace becomes more diverse and multinational
- The *Challenger* and *Columbia* disasters raise questions about safety cultures
- The communist bloc in Europe dissolves; NAFTA is passed; European Union (EU) formed and expanded
- Terrorists destroy the World Trade Center in New York in 2001
- Draft of Human Genome completed, highlighting importance of biological perspectives on many different fields of scientific study
- Terrorists destroy the World Trade Center in New York in 2001
- Increasingly unstable economy
- In 2008, Barack Obama becomes the first African American to be elected President of the United States
- In 2010, the rescue of 33 Chilean miners after 69 days of being trapped 700 meters (2,300 feet) underground shows the importance of teamwork and organization across multiple agencies and groups